READINGS IN RESOURCE MANAGEMENT AND CONSERVATION

READINGS IN RESOURCE MANAGEMENT AND CONSERVATION

Edited and with Introductions by IAN BURTON
and ROBERT W. KATES
with the assistance of Lydia Burton

THE UNIVERSITY OF CHICAGO PRESS
CHICAGO AND LONDON

International Standard Book Number: 0-226-08237-7
Library of Congress Catalog Card Number: 65-14427

THE UNIVERSITY OF CHICAGO PRESS, CHICAGO 60637
The University of Chicago Press, Ltd., London

Published 1965. Third Impression 1970
Printed in the United States of America

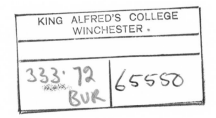

WARNING TO CHILDREN

Children, if you dare to think
Of the greatness, rareness, muchness,
Fewness of this precious only
Endless world in which you say
You live, you think of things like this:
Blocks of slate enclosing dappled
Red and green, enclosing tawny
Yellow nets, enclosing white
And black acres of dominoes,
Where a neat brown paper parcel
Tempts you to untie the string.
In the parcel a small island,
On the island a large tree,
On the tree a husky fruit.
Strip the husk and pare the rind off:
In the kernel you will see
Blocks of slate enclosed by dappled
Red and green, enclosed by tawny
Yellow nets, enclosed by white
And black acres of dominoes,
Where the same brown paper parcel—
Children, leave the string untied!
For who dares undo the parcel
Finds himself at once inside it,
On the island, in the fruit,
Blocks of slate about his head,
Finds himself enclosed by dappled
Green and red, enclosed by yellow
Tawny nets, enclosed by black
And white acres of dominoes,
With the same brown paper parcel
Still untied upon his knee.
And, if he then should dare to think
Of the fewness, muchness, rareness,
Greatness of this endless only
Precious world in which he says
He lives—he then unties the string.

Robert Graves

PREFACE

Our point of departure for this volume is a recognition of the need to acquaint students in courses in conservation and resource management with some of the wide variety of material to be found outside the standard texts. This might have been attempted in the form of a new text with considerable deviations from conventional approaches. We have rejected this alternative, partly because it appeared to be premature and overambitious and partly because we know of at least one such text that is in preparation.

An anthology can perform several functions that a textbook can do less easily. It can be rich and varied in flavor by including a range of readings in the original. It can incorporate polemical statements which are difficult to present in the traditional textbook format. By the inclusion of papers on topics of current concern, the reader can be given an opportunity to feel some of the excitement of a research frontier. It is also possible to include some less readily accessible or fugitive materials of high quality that would not otherwise be available to large groups of readers.

Exploitation of these advantages can make an anthology more like a monograph or treatise than a text, but a weak point is often the failure to provide an orderly framework or organization of the field in the way that may be expected from a monograph. We have attempted to mitigate this weakness by our selections and in our inclusion of short bridge-passages as introductions to each chapter. We would be the first to acknowledge that we have not built an adequate conceptual framework for resource management and conservation, but the field is wide, varied, and amorphous. With due deference, we suggest that the authors of texts on this subject have not themselves been notably successful in this endeavor.

We have attempted to give this volume cohesion by limiting our selections to the social and behavioral science aspects of resource management, and by deliberately omitting the biological and physical science aspects. Although we have introduced technology as a significant variable, we have only dealt with its broader implications, and not with problems of engineering. There is also a considerable literature on the public administration of resources which is largely unrepresented.

Nevertheless, our aim has been to provide more than a potpourri of social science readings that appeal to us in some personal way. We believe that we have taken a small step toward a conceptualization of a field which lacks structure and form as it also lacks theory. However, our selections in the main reflect and do not remove these defects.

We have had in mind as our principal objective the provision of a volume which will help to facilitate an improvement in the teaching and content of undergraduate courses in conservation and resource management. The book is also designed to provide general background material for graduate work. It contains a selection from the literature with which graduate students should be familiar before proceeding to specialization and research on a particular topic or problem area. We hope that professionals in the field will use the author and subject index as a tool in their work.

No anthology such as this can avoid offending more by its omissions than pleasing by its inclusions, since the overwhelming majority of the relevant literature has to be rejected. The principal basis for inclusion of papers has been their suitability in terms of the purpose and framework of the volume. This has involved some assessment of the quality of papers and their compatibility or relation to other papers, particularly in the avoidance of repetition. We have also been influenced by such negative factors as the length of papers and the cost of permission to reprint copyrighted items.

The advice and support of many colleagues has encouraged us in our difficult task of selection. Among those who have been particularly helpful are Edward Ackerman, Harold J. Barnett, Wesley Calef, S. V. Ciriacy-Wantrup, Joseph L. Fisher, Norton Ginsburg, Clarence Glacken, Maynard Hufschmidt, Henry Jarrett, John Krutilla, David Lowenthal, Robert Lucas, Arthur Maass, Marion Marts, A. J. W. Scheffey, Anthony Scott, Derrick Sewell, John F. Timmons, Norman Wengert, and M. Gordon Wolman.

We are grateful to the authors and publishers who readily gave permission to reproduce their material. Appropriate acknowledgements are made in the body of the book.

We owe a special debt to Lydia Burton who has secured more permissions from publishers than we have been able to use, and has assumed major responsibility for the technical editing, the preparation of the author and subject indexes, as well as the final proofreading. Without her many hours of labor and her constant urging of the editors to live up to their responsibilities, it is doubtful if the book would ever have been produced.

While we must accept final responsibility for the contents and organization of the book, it owes much to the continued stimulation of our students, to the enlightened criticism of our professional colleagues, and to the inspiration of our teachers, especially Gilbert F. White.

IAN BURTON
ROBERT W. KATES

UNIVERSITY OF TORONTO
CLARK UNIVERSITY

CONTENTS

PART III. The Management of an Expanding Resource Base

GENERAL INTRODUCTION

UNTYING THE STRING

In the period since World War II, the United States has probably used more non-renewable resources than all the rest of the world's population has used during the history of man on earth prior to that time. The voracious appetite of the United States and other highly developed countries for natural resources contrasts sharply with the near subsistence-level economy of the majority of the world's population. A purpose of this book is to explore some of the dimensions of this topic, particularly with reference to the problems of resource management and conservation in the United States and other technologically advanced nations. There are also worldwide implications in many of the papers and some of these implications have been made explicit.

One dimension of the topic is the theoretical question of man's relationship to his natural environment.[1] This is a classical and complex problem which each generation ponders anew and attempts to answer in its own fashion, for its own time.[2] Conclusions about the nature of the relationship depend largely on the view that is taken of man and environment.

In the papers selected for this volume, man is seen variously as a biological population, an exploiter, a conserver, and a manager of resources; as an economic optimizer, a nature lover, and in many other guises—all of them involving some implicit or explicit assumptions about his inherent rationality.

Nature is also variously regarded—now as an impersonal force that molds the destinies of man, now as a complex web of life arranged in a delicate balance that we disturb at our peril, now as a malleable set of resources that may be used at will.

Our selections aim at presenting a diversity of views. No two are identical and they range between two poles. In its extreme form, one pole is determinist in its view of nature,[3] Malthusian in its concern with the adequacy of re-

[1] A recent synthesis of the literature is found in Philip L. Wagner's book, *The Human Use of the Earth* (Glencoe: The Free Press, 1960).

[2] An example of a new theoretical approach is the one developed by Walter Firey in *Man, Mind, and Land: A Theory of Resource Use* (Glencoe: The Free Press, 1960).

[3] The history of environmentalist thought in geography is described in G. Tatham, "Environmentalism and Possibilism," *Geography in the Twentieth Century*, ed. T. G. Taylor (London: Methuen & Co., 1951), pp. 128–62. See also A. F. Martin, "The Necessity for Determinism, A Metaphysical Problem Confronting Geographers," *Transactions and Papers of the Institute of British Geographers*, No. 17 (1951), 1–11; O. H. K. Spate, "Toynbee and Huntington: A Study in Determinism," *Geographical*

sources,[4] and conservationist in its prescription for policy.[5] The opposite pole is possibilist in its attitude toward nature,[6] optimistic in its view of technological advance and the sufficiency of resources,[7] and generally concerned with technical and managerial problems of development.[8]

Sufficient material has been included to give a taste of the range of thought on the subject, including some of the more extreme positions. The selection is not intended to confuse, but to portray a state of confusion in which contending, sometimes contradictory, views compete for the support of the public and the politicians and all those who in some way have a share in the process of decision-making about natural resources. The aim of the editors will be achieved if the reader leaves this volume with a more profound sense of the complexities of resource problems and a greater knowledge of the varied ways of approaching them.

The two poles are brought into sharp contrast in Part I of the book. Here we raise the Malthusian problem of population growth and the finite earth. The land-man equation is considered in terms of its components. In the first chap-

---

Journal, CXVIII (1952), 406–28; A. C. Montefiore and W. M. Williams, "Determinism and Possibilism," *Geographical Studies,* II, No. 1 (1955), 1–11; Emrys Jones, "Cause and Effect in Human Geography," *Annals of the Association of American Geographers,* XLVI (1956), 367–77.

Classical works include Ellen C. Semple, *Influences of Geographic Environment on the Basis of Ratzel's System of Anthropo-geography* (New York: Henry Holt & Co., 1911); Ellsworth Huntington, *Civilization and Climate* (New Haven: Yale University Press, 1915); Thomas Griffith Taylor, *Environment and Race, A Study of the Evolution, Migration, Settlement, and Status of the Races of Man* (Oxford: Oxford University Press, 1927).

For a discussion of neo-determinism and present trends in geography, see Ian Burton, "The Quantitative Revolution and Theoretical Geography," *The Canadian Geographer,* VII, No. 4 (1963), 151–62. The role of environmentalism in sociology is described in Franklin Thomas, *The Environmental Basis of Society: A Study in the History of Sociological Theory* (London: Century, 1925). For a more philosophical treatment, see Émile Callot, *La Société et son environnement. Essai sur les principes des sciences sociales* (Paris: Marcel Rivière, 1952).

4 Some of the best known "neo-Malthusian" works on the scarcity of resources and growing populations, written in polemical style are Harrison Brown, *The Challenge of Man's Future* (New York: Viking Press, 1954); Fairfield Osborn, *The Limits of the Earth* (Boston: Little Brown & Co., 1953); *idem, Our Plundered Planet, ibid.,* 1948; William Vogt, *The Road to Survival* (New York: William Sloane & Assoc., 1948); *idem, People: Challenge to Survival, ibid.,* 1960.

5 See especially the publications of the Izaak Walton League, Conservation Foundation, National Audubon Society, National Wildlife Federation, Sierra Club, Soil Conservation Society of America, Wilderness Society.

6 See for example, Lucien Febvre, *La terre et l'evaluation humaine: Introduction géographique à l'histoire* (Paris: Albin Michel, 1922); and also Robert S. Platt, "Environmentalism versus Geography," *American Journal of Sociology,* LIII (1948), 351–58; *idem,* "Determinism in Geography," *Annals of the Association of American Geographers,* XXXVIII (1948), 126–32.

7 For a review of some recent findings see Ian Burton and Robert W. Kates, "Slaying the Malthusian Dragon: A Review," *Economic Geography,* XL, No. 1 (1964), 82–89.

8 A "management view" can be found in many of the papers in the *Natural Resources Journal.* See for example Gilbert F. White, "The Choice of Use in Resource Management," *ibid.,* I, No. 1 (1961), 23–40.

ter the focus is on the *human denominator*. An attempt is made to show how the population of the world has grown, and what can be said about future growth and the future need for food supplies. Then the capacity of the earth to support the expanding denominator is examined closely. What is the nature of the *limits of the earth* that Malthus could see so clearly?

The remainder of the book follows the implications of each of the two poles. The issues generated are considered separately in Parts II and III. The second part turns to the *conservation of limited resources*. Conservation is not so much a subject to be studied as a point of view. While it is difficult to generalize about the conservationist view, it is often characterized by a concern for the negative and destructive consequences of man's use of the earth. Emphasis is placed on man's numerical increase and the seemingly insatiable demands he places on the finite, limited earth, so that there is progressively less and less of the natural order of things that does not show the disturbing influence of his touch. It is also held that if man continues in his present fashion, it will mean not only the destruction of nature, but ultimately his own downfall as well.

Chapter 3 describes *the growth of a movement* in the United States which stems from such a view of the world. The conservationist view has been and is now especially influential in the formulation of resource policies. Our selection includes statements from the writings of the founders of the movement as well as more recent supporters. Chapter 4 shows that the Conservation Movement stands upon a number of value judgments and involves a variety of ethical and aesthetic assumptions described as *the conservation ethic*. A characteristic element in the conservation ethic is a concern for the quality of life, both now and in the future.

The third part of the book is concerned principally with aspects of resource management. The distinction between conservation and management is at best tenuous. The management approach, however, is often concerned with the development of resources in order to meet specific and clearly stated goals. It is in a sense more scientific in that tests, measures, and criteria are explicitly sought, and off-the-cuff value judgments are viewed with suspicion.

Primarily this is an approach that has emerged under conditions of rapidly changing technology and focuses upon the *management of an expanding resource base*.

A long chapter (Chapter 5) is devoted to a number of case studies designed to provide some substantive material and to relate in a critical fashion some of the *managerial experience* gained, most of it in very recent years. We are aware that this will not look like management to many in the field of resource management. Our aim is not to provide material on how to manage specific resources—there is an abundance of such material in the varied professional fields[9]—but to illustrate some of the perplexing problems in resource management, many of which have not yet been satisfactorily resolved. Hence Chapter 5 has a somewhat negative bias. This should not be interpreted to mean that we are unsympathetic to resource management, but rather that we are anxious to see continued improvement in the field. From a pedagogic point of view, descriptions of partial success are often more stimulating than the much trumpeted accounts of unmitigated success that characterize so much of the popular writing in this field.

The remainder of the book is devoted to three special aspects of resource management. The first is the question of resources in economic development. This problem has been the subject of so much research and writing in the post-World War II period that it seems churlish to attempt to deal with it in four selections. We are only concerned with the role of resources, however, and feel that some discussion, however brief, of economic development is necessary in the changing world perspective of resource use and development, and in view of the increasing role played by the United States in resource development overseas.

Close to the heart of the field of conservation and resource management lie the variables of *scientific and technological change*. These are treated at some length in Chapter 7. One of the most important aspects of this change is that the range of possibilities facing resource managers is constantly being widened. This in turn creates the need for new systems, methods, and approaches to the *choice of alternatives*. The final chapter takes up this problem and proceeds from a discussion of some of the technical and more objective criteria for choice that have been and are being developed, down to a point where once again the question of the quality of life is raised. This question which stands at the root of the Conservation Movement thus emerges again at the end of all the efforts in the direction of a management approach. The journey has not been fruitless, however, for the points raised by Barnett and Morse are posed rather differently from those raised by the Conservationists, and we are in a position to begin exploring for new and better answers.

[9] See for example, H. H. Bennett, *Soil Conservation* (New York: McGraw-Hill, 1939); E. A. Colman, *Vegetation and Watershed Management* (New York: Ronald Press, 1953); K. P. Davis, *American Forest Management* (New York: McGraw-Hill, 1954); L. A. Stoddard and A. D. Smith, *Range Management* (New York: McGraw-Hill, 1955), first pub. 1943; R. K. Linsley, Jr. and J. B. Franzini, *Elements of Hydraulic Engineering* (New York: McGraw-Hill, 1955); R. K. Frevert *et al.*, *Soil and Water Conservation Engineering* (New York: John Wiley, 1955); R. D. Forbes and A. B. Meyer (eds.), *Forestry Handbook* (New York: Ronald Press, 1955); Gordon M. Fair and John C. Geyer, *Elements of Water Supply and Waste-Water Disposal* (New York: John Wiley, 1958); O. W. Israelsen and V. E. Hansen, *Irrigation Principles and Practices* (New York: John Wiley, 1962).

PART I

THE MALTHUSIAN EQUATION

CHAPTER 1

THE HUMAN DENOMINATOR

In 1798 Thomas Malthus, an English clergyman and teacher of political economy, published his *Essay on the Principle of Population.*[1] Malthus' main thesis was that population always tends to increase up to the limits of the means of subsistence, which is controlled ultimately by the finite limits of the earth. After noting the capacity of human beings to reproduce themselves, and the tendency for populations to double every 25 years, Malthus concluded that:

> Whether we refer to particular countries or the whole earth, the supposition of a future capacity in the soil to increase the necessaries of life every 25 years by a quantity equal to that which is at present produced must be decidedly beyond the truth.[2]

The Malthusian view of the truth is that:

> By the laws of nature man cannot live without food. Whatever may be the rate at which population would increase if unchecked, it never can actually increase in any country beyond the food necessary to support it. But by the laws of nature in respect to the powers of a limited territory, the additions which can be made in equal periods to the food which it produces must, after a short time, either be constantly decreasing, which is what would really take place, or, at the very most, must remain stationary so as to increase the means of subsistence only in arithmetic progression. Consequently, it follows necessarily that the average rate of the *actual* increase of population over the greatest part of the globe, obeying the same laws as the increase of food, must be totally of a different character from the rate at which it would increase if unchecked.[3]

The checks that Malthus could see operating in the England of his day were disease, war, and famine, associated with considerable misery and vice, especially among the poorer classes. The only escape that Malthus could see was in "moral restraint" or a voluntarily imposed check on population growth by late marriage and strict sexual continence. The prospects for this alternative did not seem great, and hence Malthus' name is widely associated with gloomy predictions of the inevitability of war, disease, and famine, as least in the long run, for the overwhelming majority of mankind.

[1] T. R. Malthus, *An Essay on the Principle of Population* (London: J. Johnson, 1798). For a broader perspective on Malthus and the England of his day, see D. V. Glass, *Introduction to Malthus* (New York: John Wiley & Sons, 1953).

[2] Quoted from Malthus, "A Summary View of the Principle of Population," *On Population* (New York: New American Library of World Literature, Inc., 1960), p. 30. First published 1830. This is a readily accessible source of Malthus' own writing.

[3] *Ibid.*, p. 31.

Was Malthus right? Does population increase in geometric progression up to the limits of the means of subsistence? There are many who think so.[4] Neo-Malthusian views are common among the upholders of conservation,[5] and are usually strong among advocates of birth control and family planning.[6]

Our concern in this chapter is not to illustrate the views of those who are alarmed at the current population explosion. Such views are given wide currency in popular journals and the press.[7] Nor is our concern to present the latest population estimates.[8] It is commonly asserted that the world population is growing by 150,000 persons daily, or an annual increase of over 50 million. Under these circumstances, any estimate we give would be out-of-date by the time this book is available to readers.

Instead of these approaches, our aim is to illustrate some other dimensions of the problem. The article by Deevey shows the growth of human population in long-term perspective, with a series of population estimates back to the dawn of man on earth.[9] This paper also raises questions about the relationship of surges in population growth to periods of rapid technological advance.

The dangers of simple extrapolation of the exponential curves of present population growth are underscored both by Deevey's suggestion of three distinct population surges followed by a leveling off and a period of stability, and by Dorn's caveats on the pitfalls of population projection,[10] well illustrated by some recent experience.

The Malthusian equation is not concerned solely with total numbers of population. If it is to be meaningfully translated into the problems of everyday living, population must be expressed in terms of its requirements. Hence to evaluate the Malthusian hypothesis, we must convert population units into

4 See for example, Robert C. Cook, "Malthus' Main Thesis Still Holds," *Perspectives on Conservation,* ed. H. Jarrett (Baltimore: Johns Hopkins Press for Resources for the Future, Inc., 1958), pp. 72–78.

5 See the volume of essays sponsored by the Conservation Foundation, *Our Crowded Planet, Essays on the Pressure of Population,* ed. Fairfield Osborn (New York: Doubleday, 1962).

6 See for example the publications of organizations concerned with population control, including the Planned Parenthood Federation of America and the Population Reference Bureau, publishers of *Population Bulletin.*

7 Many such statements may be found in a popular treatment in *Does Overpopulation Mean Poverty?* ed. Joseph M. Jones (Washington: Center for International Economic Growth, 1962).

8 The *Demographic Yearbook* issued by the United Nations is the best source of estimates of world population. An informative note on the availability of national population census data and methods of evaluating their reliability can be found in a recent issue, U.N., Dept. of Economic and Social Affairs, *Demographic Yearbook 1962* (New York: U.N., 1963), pp. 1–11.

9 Many estimates of population back to 1650 are based on A. M. Carr-Saunders, *World Population: Past Growth and Present Trends* (London: Oxford University Press, 1936), pp. 1–45; or W. F. Willcox, *Studies in American Demography* (Ithaca: Cornell University Press, 1940), pp. 22–51. M. K. Bennett carries these estimates back to the year 1,000 A.D. in *The World's Food* (New York: Harper & Bros., 1954), pp. 3–22.

10 See also John Hajnal, "The Prospects for Population Forecasts," *Journal of the American Statistical Association,* L, No. 270 (1955), 309–22.

their equivalents in food requirements. Sukhatme, in presenting a set of estimates of food needs and adequacy for the whole world, demonstrates the inordinate difficulty involved in developing such standards.[11] The inadequacy of our data is paradoxically severe precisely in those countries that might come closest to providing stringent tests of the Malthusian thesis.

The exponential growth in world population is well documented, and concern over its explosive qualities is found in the literature.[12] This chapter provides additional depth through historical perspective and certain insights into the complex methodological problems in evaluating the numbers and requirements of the human denominator.[13]

11 For a detailed statement of the physiological basis of food requirements see R. Passmore, "Estimation of Food Requirements," *Journal of the Royal Statistical Society,* ser. A, CXXV (1962), 387–96. Other aspects of food requirements are explored from other stances by Bennett, *op. cit.*, and J. de Castro, *The Geography of Hunger* (Boston: Little Brown & Co., 1952). Examples of recent projections of food production and consumption may be found in the U.S., Dept. of Agric., Economic Research Service, *The World Food Budget, 1962 and 1966* (Washington: Government Printing Office, 1961); and Food and Agriculture Organization of the United Nations, *Commodity Review 1962, Special Supplement: Agricultural Commodities-Projections for 1970* (Rome: Food and Agriculture Organization of the United Nations, 1962).

12 A thorough discussion is found in the U.N., Dept. of Social Affairs, *The Determinants and Consequences of Population Trends* (New York: U.N., 1953). A recent review of the latest trends is in the article by Dorn, "World Population Growth," *The Population Dilemma,* ed. P. M. Hauser (Englewood Cliffs: Prentice-Hall, Inc., 1963), pp. 7–28.

13 Several basic readers are available for students of population problems. *Demographic Analysis,* ed. J. J. Spengler and O. D. Duncan (Glencoe: The Free Press, 1956); *idem, Population Theory and Policy* (Glencoe: The Free Press, 1956); *The Study of Population: An Inventory and Appraisal,* ed. P. M. Hauser and O. D. Duncan (Chicago: University of Chicago Press, 1959).

EDWARD S. DEEVEY, JR.

THE HUMAN POPULATION

Almost until the present turn in human affairs an expanding population has been equated with progress. "Increase and multiply" is the Scriptural injunction. The number of surviving offspring is the measure of fitness in natural selection. If number is the criterion, the human species is making great progress. The population, now passing 2.7 billion, is doubling itself every 50 years or so. To some horrified observers, however, the population increase has become a "population explosion." The present rate of increase, they point out, is itself increasing. At 1 per cent per year it is double that of the past few centuries. By A.D. 2000, even according to the "medium" estimate of the careful demographers of the United Nations, the rate of increase will have accelerated to 3 per cent per year, and the total population will have reached 6.267 billion. If Thomas Malthus' assumption of a uniform rate of doubling is naïve, because it so quickly leads to impossible numbers, how long can an accelerating annual increase, say from 1 to 3 per cent in 40 years, be maintained? The demographers confronted with this question lower their eyes: "It would be absurd," they say, "to carry detailed calculations forward into a more remote future. It is most debatable whether the trends in mortality and fertility can continue much longer. Other factors may eventually bring population growth to a halt."

• Edward S. Deevey, Jr., is Professor of Biology, Yale University.

Reprinted from *Scientific American,* CCIII (September, 1960), 195–204, with permission of the author and the editor.

So they may, and must. It comes to this: explosions are not made by force alone, but by force that exceeds restraint. Before accepting the implications of the population explosion, it is well to set the present in the context of the record of earlier human populations. As will be seen, the population curve has moved upward stepwise in response to the three major revolutions that have marked the evolution of culture [*see* Fig. 1*b*]. The tool-using and toolmaking revolution that started the growth of the human stem from the primate line gave the food-gatherer and hunter access to the widest range of environments. Nowhere was the population large, but over the earth as a whole it reached the not insignificant total of 5 million, an average of .04 person per square kilometer (.1 person per square mile) of land. With the agricultural revolution the population moved up two orders of magnitude to a new plateau, multiplying 100 times in the short span of 8,000 years, to an average of 1 person per square kilometer. The increase over the last 300 years, a multiplication by 5, plainly reflects the first repercussions of the scientific-industrial revolution. There are now 16.4 persons per square kilometer of the earth's land area. It is thus the release of restraint that the curve portrays at three epochal points in cultural history.

But the evolution of the population size also indicates the approach to equilibrium in the two interrevolutionary periods of the past. At what level will the present surge of numbers reach equilibrium? That is again a question of restraint, whether it is to be imposed by the limitations of man's new command over his environment or by his command over his own nature.

The human generative force is neither new nor metabiological, nor is it especially strong in man as compared with other animals. Under conditions of maximal increase in a suitable environment empty of competitors, with births at maximum and deaths negligible, rats can multiply their numbers 25 times in an average generation time of 31 weeks. For the water flea *Daphnia,* beloved by ecologists for the speedy answers it gives, the figures are 221 times in a generation of 6.8 days. Mankind's best efforts seem puny by contrast: muliplication by about 1.4 times in a generation of 28 years. Yet neither in human nor in experimental populations do such rates continue unchecked. Sooner or later the births slow down and the deaths increase, until—in experiments, at any rate—the growth tapers off, and the population effectively saturates its space. Ecologists define this state (of zero rate of change) as equilibrium, without denying the possibility of oscillations that average out to zero, and without forgetting the continuous input of energy (food, for instance) that is needed to maintain the system.

Two kinds of check, then, operate to limit the size of a population, or of any living thing that grows. Obviously the environment (amount of space, food, or other needed resources) sets the upper limit; sometimes this is manipulatable, even by the population itself, as when it exploits a new kind of food in the same old space, and reaches a new, higher limit. More subtly, populations can be said to limit their own rates of increase. As the numbers rise, female fruit flies, for example, lay fewer eggs when jostled by their sisters; some microorganisms battle each other with antibiotics; flour beetles accidentally eat their own defenseless eggs and pupae; infectious diseases spread faster, or become more virulent, as their hosts become more numerous. For human populations pestilence and warfare, Malthus' "natural restraints," belong among these devices for self-limitation. So, too, does his "moral restraint," or voluntary birth control. Nowadays a good deal of attention is being given, not only to voluntary methods, but also to a fascinating new possibility: mental stress.

Population control by means of personality derangement is probably a vertebrate patent; at least it seems a luxury beyond the reach of a water flea. The general idea, as current among students of small mammals, is that of hormonal imbalance (or stress, as defined by Hans Selye of the University of Montreal); psychic tension, resulting from overcrowding, disturbs the pituitary-adrenal system and diverts or suppresses the hormones governing sexuality and parental care. Most of the evidence comes from somewhat artificial experiments with caged rodents. It is possible, though the case is far from proved, that the lemming's famous mechanism for restoring equilibrium is the product of stress; in experimental populations of rats and mice, at least, anxiety has been observed to increase the death rate through fighting or merely from shock.

From this viewpoint there emerges an interesting distinction between crowding and overcrowding among vertebrates: overcrowding is what is perceived as such by members of the population. Since the human rate of increase is holding its own and even accelerating, however, it is plain that the mass of men, although increasingly afflicted with mental discomfort, do not yet see themselves as overcrowded. What will happen in the future brings other questions. For the present it may be noted that some kind of check has always operated, up to now, to prevent populations from exceeding the space that contains them. Of course space may be non-Euclidean, and man may be exempt from this law.

The commonly accepted picture of the growth of the population out of the long past takes the form of the graph in Figure

1*a*. Two things are wrong with this picture. In the first place the basis of estimates, back of about A.D. 1650, is rarely stated. One suspects that writers have been copying each other's guesses. The second defect is that the scales of the graph have been chosen so as to make the first defect seem unimportant. The missile has left the pad and is heading out of sight—so it is said; who cares whether there were a million or a 100 million people around when Babylon was founded? The difference is nearly lost in the thickness of the draftsman's line.

These calculations exaggerate the truth in a different way: by condensing into single sums the enormous length of prehistoric time. To arrive at the total of 36 billion Paleolithic hunters and gatherers I have assumed mean standing populations of half a million for the Lower Paleolithic, and two million for the Middle and Upper Paleolithic to 25,000 years ago. For Paleolithic times there are no archeological records worth considering in such calculations. I have used some figures for modern hunting tribes, quoted by Robert J. Braidwood and Charles A. Reed, though they are not guilty of my extrapolations. The assumed densities per square kilometer range from a tenth to a third of those estimated for eastern North America before Columbus came, when an observer would hardly have described the woods as full of Indians. (Of course I have excluded any New World population from my estimates prior to the Mesolithic climax of the food-gathering and hunting phase of cultural evolution.) It is only because average generations of 25 years succeeded each other 39,000 times that the total looms so large.

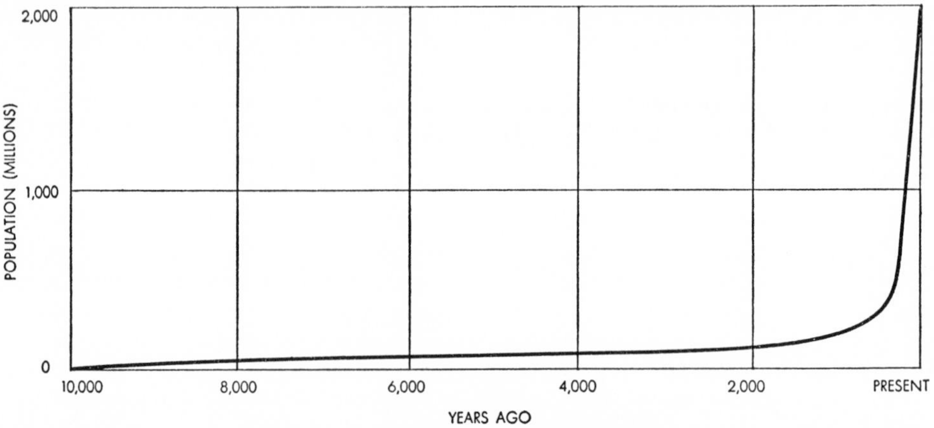

FIG. 1*a*.—Arithmetic population curve plots the growth of human population from 10,000 years ago to the present. Such a curve suggests that the population figure remained close to the base line for an indefinite period from the remote past to about 500 years ago, and that it has surged abruptly during the last 500 years as a result of the scientific-industrial revolution.

I cannot think it unimportant that (as I calculate) there were 36 billion Paleolithic hunters and gatherers, including the first tool-using hominids. One begins to see why stone tools are among the commonest Pleistocene fossils. Another 30 billion may have walked the earth before the invention of agriculture. A cumulative total of about 110 billion individuals seem to have passed their days, and left their bones, if not their marks, on this crowded planet. Neither for our understanding of culture nor in terms of man's impact upon the land is it a negligible consideration that the patch of ground allotted to every person now alive may have been the lifetime habitat of 40 predecessors.

For my estimates as of the opening of the agricultural revolution, I have also depended upon Braidwood and Reed. In their work in Mesopotamia they have counted the number of rooms in buried houses, allowing for the areas of town sites and of cultivated land, and have compared the populations so computed with modern counterparts. For early village-farmers, like those at Jarmo, and for the urban citizens of Sumer, about 2500 B.C., their estimates (9.7 and 15.4 persons per square kilometer) are probably fairly close. They are intended to apply to large tracts of inhabited country, not to pavement-bound clusters of artisans and priests. Nevertheless, in extending these estimates to continent-wide areas, I have divided the lower figure by 10, making it one per square kilometer. So much of Asia is unirrigated and non-urban even today that the figure may still be too high. But the Maya, at about the same level of culture (3,000 or 4,000 years later), provide a useful standard of comparison. The present population of their classic homeland averages .6 per square kilometer, but the land can support a population about a hundred times as large, and probably did at the time of the classic climax. The rest of the New World, outside Middle America, was (and is) more thinly settled, but a world-wide average of one per square kilometer seems reasonable for agricultural, pre-industrial society.

For modern populations, from A.D. 1650 on, I have taken the estimates of economic historians, given in such books as the treatise *World Population and Production,* by Wladimir S. and Emma S. Woytinsky. All these estimates are included in Figure 1*b*. Logarithmic scales are used in order to compress so many people and millennia onto a single page. Foreshortening time in this way is convenient, if not particularly logical, and back of 50,000 years ago the time scale is pretty arbitrary anyway. No attempt is made to show the oscillations that probably occurred, in glacial and interglacial ages, for example.

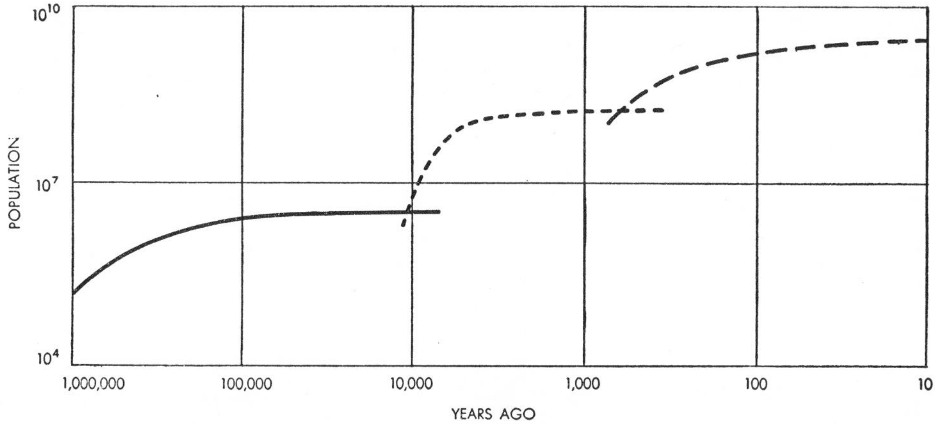

FIG. 1*b*.—Logarithmic population curve makes it possible to plot, in a small space, the growth of population over a longer period of time and over a wider range (from 10^4, or 10,000, to 10^{10}, or 10 billion, persons). Curve, based on assumptions concerning relationship of technology and population as shown in Figure 2, reveals three population surges reflecting tool-making or cultural revolution (*solid line*), agricultural revolution (*short dash*) and scientific-industrial revolution (*long dash*).

The stepwise evolution of population size, entirely concealed in graphs with arithmetic scales, is the most noticeable feature of this diagram. For most of the million-year period the number of hominids, including man, was about what would be expected of any large Pleistocene mammal—scarcer than horses, say, but commoner than elephants. Intellectual superiority was simply a successful adaptation, like longer legs; essential to stay in the run-

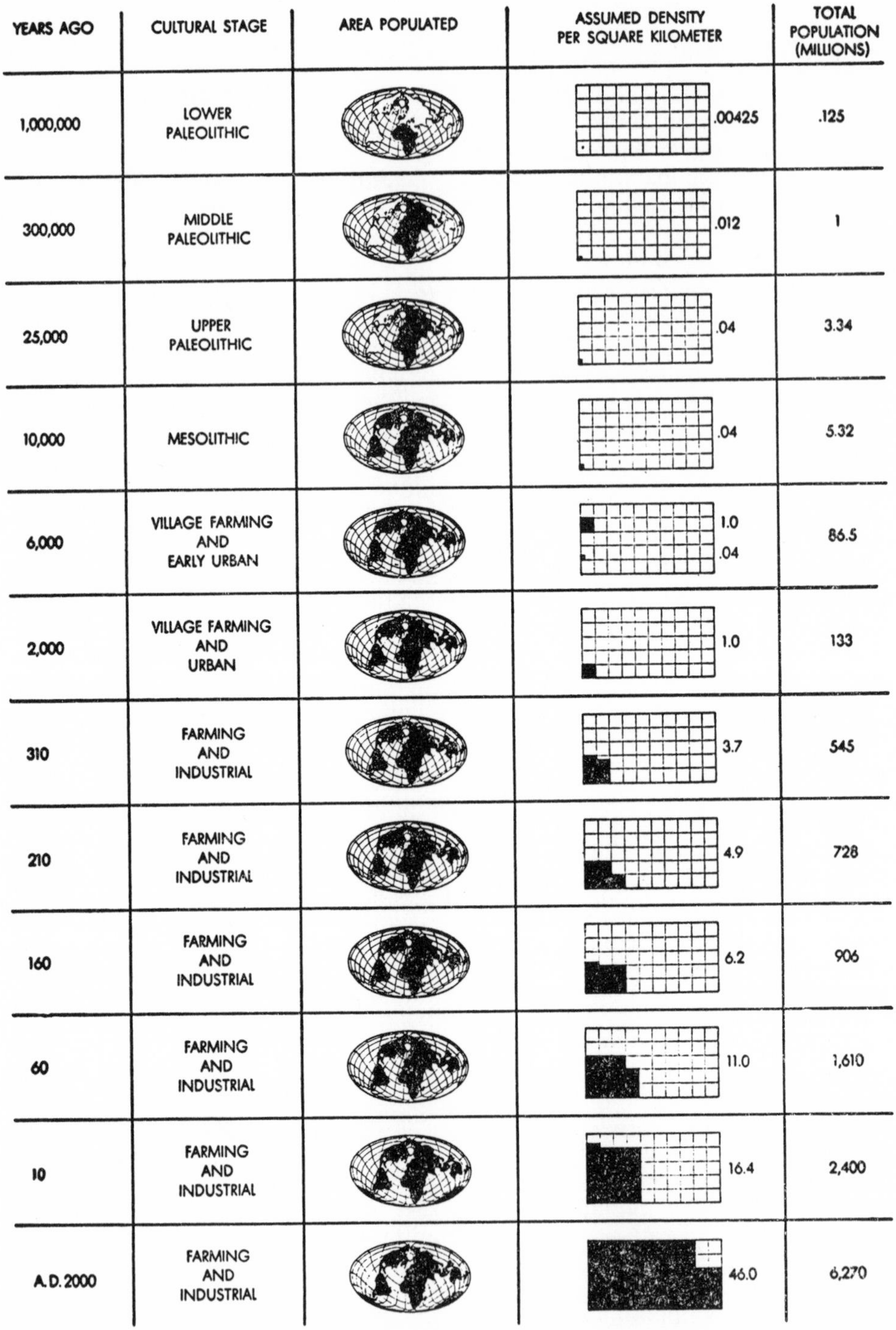

YEARS AGO	CULTURAL STAGE	AREA POPULATED	ASSUMED DENSITY PER SQUARE KILOMETER	TOTAL POPULATION (MILLIONS)
1,000,000	LOWER PALEOLITHIC		.00425	.125
300,000	MIDDLE PALEOLITHIC		.012	1
25,000	UPPER PALEOLITHIC		.04	3.34
10,000	MESOLITHIC		.04	5.32
6,000	VILLAGE FARMING AND EARLY URBAN		1.0 .04	86.5
2,000	VILLAGE FARMING AND URBAN		1.0	133
310	FARMING AND INDUSTRIAL		3.7	545
210	FARMING AND INDUSTRIAL		4.9	728
160	FARMING AND INDUSTRIAL		6.2	906
60	FARMING AND INDUSTRIAL		11.0	1,610
10	FARMING AND INDUSTRIAL		16.4	2,400
A.D. 2000	FARMING AND INDUSTRIAL		46.0	6,270

FIG. 2.—Population growth, from inception of the hominid line 1 million years ago through the different stages of cultural evolution to A.D. 2000 is shown in the chart. In Lower Paleolithic stage, population was restricted to Africa (*shaded area on world map in third column*), with a density of only 0.00425 persons per square kilometer (*fourth column*) and a total population of only 125,000 (*column at right*). By the Mesolithic stage, 10,000 years ago, hunting and food-gathering techniques had spread the population over most of the earth and brought the total to 5,320,000. In the village farming and early urban stage, population increased to a total of 86,500,000 and a density of 1 person per square kilometer in the Old World and 0.04 per square kilometer in the New World. Today the population density exceeds 16 persons per square kilometer, and pioneering of the antarctic continent has begun.

ning, of course, but making man at best the first among equals. Then the food-gatherers and hunters became plowmen and herdsmen, and the population was boosted by about sixteen times, between 10,000 and 6,000 years ago. The scientific-industrial revolution, beginning some 300 years ago, has spread its effects much faster, but it has not yet taken the number as far above the earlier base line.

The long-term population equilibrium implied by such base lines suggests something else. Some kind of restraint kept the number fairly stable. "Food supply" offers a quick answer, but not, I think, the correct one. At any rate, a forest is full of game for an expert mouse-hunter, and a Paleolithic man who stuck to business should have found enough food on 2 square kilometers, instead of 20 or 200. Social forces were probably more powerful than mere starvation in causing men to huddle in small bands. Besides, the number was presumably adjusted to conditions in the poorest years, and not to average environments.

The main point is that there were adjustments. They can only have come about because the average female bore two children who survived to reproduce. If the average life span is 25 years, the "number of children ever born" is about four (because about 50 per cent die before breeding), whereas a population that is really trying can average close to eight. Looking back on former times, then, from our modern point of view, we might say that about two births out of four were surplus, though they were needed to counterbalance the juvenile death toll. But what about the other four, which evidently did not occur? Unless the life expectancy was very much less than I have assumed (and will presently justify), some degree of voluntary birth control has always prevailed.

Our 40 predecessors on earth make an impressive total, but somehow it sounds different to say that nearly 3 per cent of the people who have ever lived are still around. When we realize that they are living twice as long as their parents did, we are less inclined to discount the revolution in which we are living. One of its effects has just begun to be felt: the mean age of the population is increasing all over the world. Among the more forgivable results of Western culture, when introduced into simpler societies, is a steep drop in the death rate. Public health authorities are fond of citing Ceylon in this connection. In a period of a year during 1946 and 1947 a campaign against malaria reduced the death rate there from 20 to 14 per 1,000. Eventually the birth rate falls too, but not so fast, nor has it yet fallen so far as a bare replacement value. The natural outcome of this imbalance is that acceleration of annual increase which so bemuses demographers. In the long run it must prove to be temporary, unless the birth rate accelerates, for the deaths that are being systematically prevented are premature ones. That is, the infants who now survive diphtheria and measles are certain to die of something else later on, and while the mean life-span is approaching the maximum, for the first time in history, there is no reason to think that the maximum itself has been stretched. Meanwhile the expectation of life at birth is rising daily in most countries, so that it has already surpassed 70 years in some, including the United States, and probably averages between 40 and 50.

It is hard to be certain of any such world-wide figure. The countries where mortality is heaviest are those with the least accurate records. In principle, however, mean age at death is easier to find out than the number of children born, the frequency or mean age at marriage, or any other component of a birth rate. The dead bones, the court and parish records and the tombstones that archeology deals with have something to say about death, of populations as well as of people. Their testimony confirms the impression that threescore years and ten, if taken as an average and not as a maximum lifetime, is something

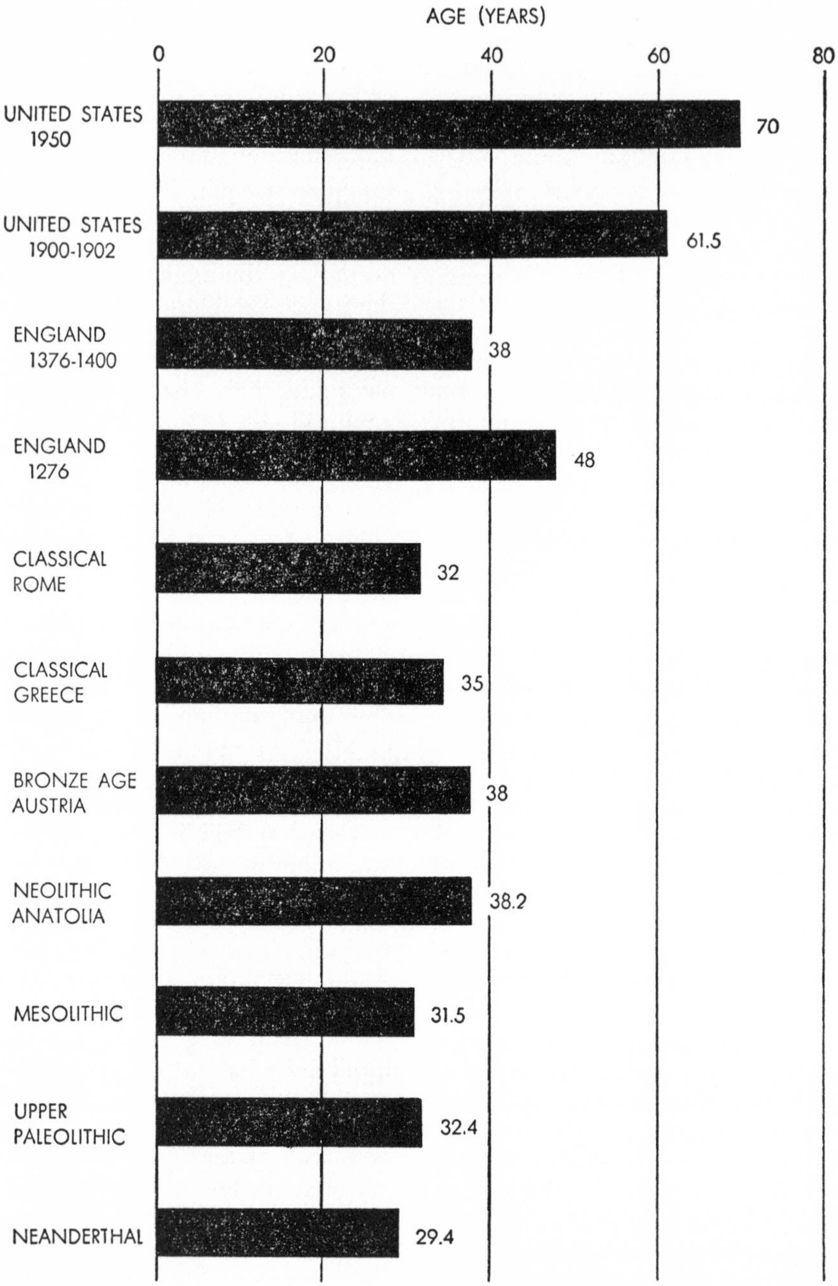

FIG. 3.—Longevity in ancient and modern times is charted. From time of Neanderthal man to the fourteenth century A.D., life span appears to have hovered around 35 years. An exception is thirteenth-century England. Increase in longevity partly responsible for current population increase has come in modern era. In U.S., longevity increased about 10 years in the last half-century.

decidedly new. Of course the possibilities of bias in such evidence are almost endless. For instance, military cemeteries tend to be full of young adult males. The hardest bias to allow for is the deficiency of infants and children; juvenile bones are less durable than those of adults and are often treated less respectfully. Probably we shall never know the true expectation of life at birth for any ancient people. Bypassing this difficulty, we can look at the mean age at death among the fraction surviving to adolescence.

The "nasty, brutish, and short" lives of Neanderthal people have been rather elaborately guessed at 29.4 years. The record, beyond them, is not one of steady improvement. For example, Neolithic farmers in Anatolia and Bronze Age Austrians averaged 38 years, and even the Mesolithic savages managed more than 30. But in the golden ages of Greece and Rome the life span was 35 years or less. During the Middle Ages the chances of long life were probably no better. The important thing about these averages is not the differences among them, but their similarity. Remembering the crudeness of the estimates, and the fact that juvenile mortality is omitted, it is fair to guess that human life-expectancy at birth has never been far from 25 years—25 plus or minus 5, say—from Neanderthal times up to the present century. It follows, as I have said, that about half the children ever born have lived to become sexually mature. It is not hard to see why an average family size of four or more, or twice the minimum replacement rate, has come to seem part of a God-given scheme of things.

The 25-fold upsurge in the number of men between 10,000 and 2,000 years ago was sparked by a genuine increase in the means of subsistence. A shift from animal to plant food, even without agricultural labor and ingenuity, would practically guarantee a 10-fold increase, for a given area can usually produce about 10 times as much plant as animal substance. The scientific-industrial revolution has increased the efficiency of growing these foods, but hardly, as yet, beyond the point needed to support another 10 times as many people, fewer of whom are farmers. At the present rate of multiplication, without acceleration, another 10-fold rise is due within 230 years. Disregarding the fact that developed societies spend 30 to 60 times as much energy for other purposes as they need for food, one is made a little nervous by the thought of so many hungry mouths. Can the increase of efficiency keep pace? Can some of the apparently ample energy be converted to food as needed, perhaps at the cost of reducing the size of Sunday newspapers? Or is man now pressing so hard on his food supply that another 10-fold increase of numbers is impossible?

The answers to these questions are not easy to find, and students with different viewpoints disagree about them. Richard L. Meier of the University of Michigan estimates that a total of 50 billion people (a 20-fold increase, that is) can be supported on earth, and the geochemist Harrison Brown of the California Institute of Technology will allow (reluctantly) twice or four times as many. Some economists are even more optimistic; Arnold C. Harberger of the University of Chicago presents the interesting notion that a larger crop of people will contain more geniuses, whose intellects will find a solution to the problem of feeding *still* more people. And the British economist Colin Clark points out that competition for resources will sharpen everyone's wits, as it always has, even if the level of innate intelligence is not raised.

An ecologist's answer is bound to be cast in terms of solar energy, chlorophyll, and the amount of land on which the two can interact to produce organic carbon. Sources of energy other than the sun are either too expensive or non-renewable or both. Land areas will contine for a very long time to be the places where food is grown, for the sea is not so productive as the land, on the average. One reason, some-

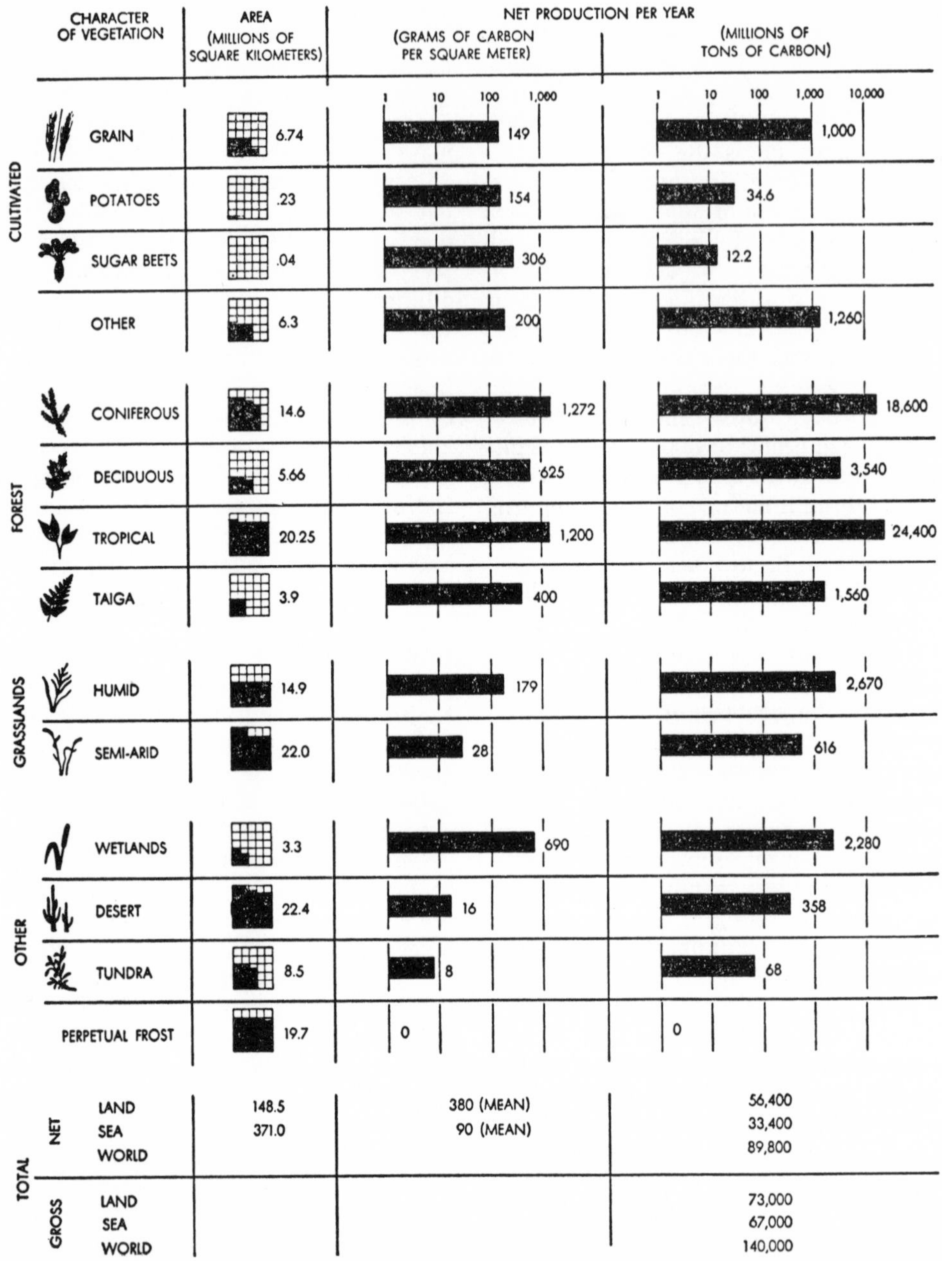

CHARACTER OF VEGETATION
AREA (MILLIONS OF SQUARE KILOMETERS)
NET PRODUCTION PER YEAR
(GRAMS OF CARBON PER SQUARE METER)
(MILLIONS OF TONS OF CARBON)
1
10
100
1,000
10,000
CULTIVATED
GRAIN 6.74 149 1,000
POTATOES .23 154 34.6
SUGAR BEETS .04 306 12.2
OTHER 6.3 200 1,260
FOREST
CONIFEROUS 14.6 1,272 18,600
DECIDUOUS 5.66 625 3,540
TROPICAL 20.25 1,200 24,400
TAIGA 3.9 400 1,560
GRASSLANDS
HUMID 14.9 179 2,670
SEMI-ARID 22.0 28 616
OTHER
WETLANDS 3.3 690 2,280
DESERT 22.4 16 358
TUNDRA 8.5 8 68
PERPETUAL FROST 19.7 0 0
TOTAL
NET
LAND 148.5 380 (MEAN) 56,400
SEA 371.0 90 (MEAN) 33,400
WORLD 89,800
GROSS
LAND 73,000
SEA 67,000
WORLD 140,000

FIG. 4.—Production of organic matter per year by the land vegetation of the world—and thus its ultimate food-producing capacity—is charted in terms of the amount of carbon incorporated in organic compounds. Cultivated vegetation (*top left*) is less efficient than forest and wetlands vegetation, as indicated by the uptake of carbon per square meter (*third column*), and it yields a smaller over-all output than forest, humid grasslands, and wetlands vegetation (*fourth column*). The scales at top of third and fourth columns are logarithmic. Land vegetation leads sea vegetation in efficiency and in net and gross tonnage (*bottom*). The difference between the net production and gross production is accounted for by the consumption of carbon in plant respiration.

times forgotten, is that the plants of the sea are microscopic algae, which, being smaller than land plants, respire away a larger fraction of the carbon they fix. The culture of the fresh-water alga *Chlorella* has undeniable promise as a source of human food. But the high efficiencies quoted for its photosynthesis, as compared with agricultural plants, are not sustained outdoors under field conditions. Even if *Chlorella* (or another exceptionally efficient producer, such as the water hyacinth) is the food plant of the future, flat areas exposed to sunlight will be needed. The 148.5 million square kilometers of land will have to be used with thoughtful care if the human population is to increase 20-fold. With a population of 400 per square kilometer (50 billion total) it would seem that men's bodies, if not their artifacts, will stand in the way of vital sunshine.

Plants capture the solar energy impinging on a given area with an efficiency of about .1 per cent. (Higher values often quoted are based on some fraction of the total radiation, such as visible light.) Herbivores capture about a one-tenth of the plants' energy, and carnivores convert about 10 per cent of the energy captured by herbivores (or other carnivores). This means, of course, that carnivores, feeding on plants at second hand, can scarcely do so with better than 1 per cent efficiency ($1/10 \times 1/10$ equals $1/100$). Eugene I. Rabinowitch of the University of Illinois has calculated that the current crop of men represents an ultimate conversion of about 1 per cent of the energy trapped by land vegetation. Recently, however, I have reexamined the base figure—the efficiency of the land-plant production—and believe it should be raised by a factor of three or four. The old value came from estimates made in 1919 and in 1937. A good deal has been learned since those days. The biggest surprise is the high productivity of forests, especially the forests of the Temperate Zone.

If my new figures are correct, the population could theoretically increase by 30 or 40 times. But man would have to displace all other herbivores and utilize all the vegetation with the 10 per cent efficiency established by the ecological rule of tithes. No land that now supports greenery could be spared for non-agricultural purposes; the populace would have to reside in the polar regions, or on artificial "green isles in the sea, love"—scummed over, of course, by 10 inches of *Chlorella* culture.

The picture is doubtless overdrawn. There is plenty of room for improvement in present farming practice. More land could be brought under cultivation if a better distribution of water could be arranged. More efficient basic crops can be grown and used less wastefully. Other sources of energy, notably atomic energy, can be fed back into food production to supplement the sun's rays. None of these measures is more than palliative, however; none promises so much as a 10-fold increase in efficiency; worse, none is likely to be achieved at a pace equivalent to the present rate of doubling of the world's population. A 10-fold, even a 20-fold, increase can be tolerated, perhaps, but the standard of living seems certain to be lower than today's. What happens then, when men perceive themselves to be overcrowded?

The idea of population equilibrium will take some getting used to. A population that is kept stable by emigration, like that of the Western Islands of Scotland, is widely regarded as sick—a shining example of a self-fulfilling diagnosis. Since the fall of the death rate is temporary, it is those two or more extra births per female that demand attention. The experiments with crowded rodents point to one way they might be corrected, through the effect of anxiety in suppressing ovulation and spermatogenesis and inducing fetal resorption. Some of the most dramatic results are delayed until after birth: litters are carelessly nursed, deserted, or even eaten. Since fetuses, too, have endocrine glands, the specter of maternal transmission of anxiety now looms: W. R. Thompson of Wesleyan University has shown that the offspring of frustrated mother mice are more "emotional" throughout their own lives, and my student Kim Keeley has confirmed this.

Considered abstractly, these devices for self-regulation compel admiration for their elegance. But there is a neater device that men can use: rational, voluntary control over numbers. In mentioning the dire effects of psychic stress I am not implying that the population explosion will be contained by cannibalism or fetal resorption, or any power so naked. I simply suggest that vertebrates have that power, whether they want it or not, as part of the benefit—and the price—of being vertebrates. And if the human method of adjusting numbers to resources fails to work in the next 1,000 years as it has in the last million, subhuman methods are ready to take over.

SELECTED BIBLIOGRAPHY

BROWN, HARRISON, BONNER, JAMES, AND WEIR, JOHN. *The Next Hundred Years: Man's Natural and Technical Resources.* New York: Viking Press, Inc., 1957.

FRANCIS, ROY GUSTAF. *Population Ahead.* Minneapolis: University of Minnesota Press, 1958.

MEIER, RICHARD L. *Science and Economic Development: New Patterns of Living.* New York: John Wiley & Sons, Inc., 1956.

WOYTINSKY, W. S., AND WOYTINSKY, E. S. *World Population and Production: Trends and Outlook.* New York: Twentieth Century Fund, 1953.

One hundred persons multiplying at 1 per cent per year . . . for the 5000 years of human history, would have produced a contemporary population of 2.7 billion persons per square foot of land surface of the earth! Such an exercise in arithmetic, although admittedly dramatic and propagandistic, is also a conclusive way of demonstrating that a 1 per cent per year increase in world population could not have taken place for very long in the past; nor can it continue for very long into the future.

PHILIP M. HAUSER, *Science* (June 3, 1960), CXXXI, No. 3414, 1641–47.

HAROLD F. DORN

PITFALLS IN POPULATION FORECASTS AND PROJECTIONS

"Experts on population have projected their curves into the future and the outlook is startling. Manufacturers who try to estimate future markets have been expecting a population of 140 million by 1940, but the calculations of our contributors . . . show . . . that hardly more than 132 or 133 million are to be expected by 1940. . . .

"As our statisticians look further into the future, they see possibilities of still greater declines in growth with the probability of a stationary population. They show that we shall probably attain a population between 145 and 190 million during the present century with the probability that the actual population will be nearer the lower figure than the higher. Such a prospect is radically different from that predicted a generation or even a decade ago."[1]

These words written by President Hoover's Research Committee on Social Trends in 1933 marked the beginning of a new era in the development of demography. Population forecasts were not new in the United States. Since the earliest days of the nation, geologists, business men, writers, economists, statesmen, and even presidents had published predictions concerning the growth of the population of the United States. But no single group of these forecasters ever had been generally recognized as having special competence to prognosticate demographic changes. As a result, persons from all walks of life felt free to peer into the crystal ball of the future and to chart the growth of the nation's population.

The words of President Hoover's Research Committee on Social Trends recognized a particular group, called demographers, and gave endorsement to their special ability to forecast population changes. This endorsement was widely accepted by the public, by business men, by governmental agencies, and by fellow scholars and scientists.

It was an auspicious beginning. Seven years later the Director of the Bureau of the Census announced that the population of the United States on April 1, 1940 numbered 131,669,275 persons. Allowing for underenumeration, officially recognized by the Bureau of the Census, demographers nearly a decade prior to this date had predicted the total population more accurately than the Bureau of the Census had been able to count the actual population! In the words of Irene Taeuber in an article reprinted with approval by the editors of *Population Index,* "With improved data, new techniques, and the precise measurement of the demographic transition that was occurring, demography tended to become science rather than literature."[2]

• Harold F. Dorn (1906–63) was a statistician, well known for his work on population projections and vital statistics.

Revision of a paper presented before a joint meeting of the American Statistical Association and the Population Association of America in New York City, December 30, 1949. Reprinted from *Journal of the American Statistical Association,* XLV (September, 1950), 311–34, with permission of the editor.

[1] *Recent Social Trends in the United States,* Report of the President's Research Committee on Social Trends, (New York and London: McGraw-Hill, 1933), I, xx.

[2] Irene Taeuber, "Population Studies in the United States," *Population Index,* XII (1946), 254.

Confidence in the reliability of estimates of future population became widespread. O. E. Baker undoubtedly expressed the opinion held by many demographers and non-demographers alike when he said, "The population of the United States ten, twenty, even fifty years hence, can be predicted with a greater degree of assurance than any other economic or social fact, provided the immigration laws are unchanged."[3]

This belief gained wide acceptance in spite of the fact that estimates frequently were prefaced with disavowals of predictive accuracy. The following statement by Thompson and Whelpton is typical:

Some care must be exercised in the use and interpretation of these estimates. It is to be emphasized that they are not predictions of future population size, nor are they to be assumed to indicate the probable sex and age structure. They are, strictly speaking, merely statements of what the size and the sex, age, color, and nativity composition of the population would be at specified future times if birth rates, death rates, and immigration were to follow certain specified trends.

While it is true that the fertility and mortality assumptions have been chosen with regard to the indicated trends of vital rates, the purpose of the estimates is to show the approximate range within which future populations would fall under the influence of current trends, rather than to arrive at a single most probable figure.[4]

But most readers obviously assumed that these sentences were merely a polite bow to scientific caution and did not take them very seriously. Nor can they hardly be blamed. For why should demographers be continually revising population forecasts with ever increasingly elaborate assumptions if they themselves did not believe that the forecasts had some validity? And were not demographers writing papers and making speeches which either implicitly or explicitly accepted the validity of the forecasts? It seemed incredible that demographers were merely doing sums in arithmetic for self-entertainment; they must be serious and really believe that the projected population estimates were in fact reasonable forecasts or predictions of the future.

So overwhelming was this belief that economists, governmental officials and business men accepted the projections as being substantially correct. This acceptance was buttressed by the developments of population change during the decade of the 1930's.

On January 31, 1941, the Bureau of the Census reported, "If the 1930 birth and death rates had continued, the population of the country would more than reproduce its numbers by about 11 per cent per generation. . . . In 1940, however, as a result of changes in fertility and mortality during the decade, the population was no longer maintaining its numbers. As a matter of fact, if the 1940 birth and death rates continue, the population would in the long run fail to reproduce itself by about 4 per cent per generation."[5]

But, as a matter of historical fact, the 1940 birth and death rates did not continue unchanged. The men and women who bear children refused to have their personal relationships regulated by governmental press releases. By 1942 the birth rate had increased 20 per cent since 1939. Concerning this increase, the Metropolitan Life Insurance Company stated, "the conditions of 1942, continued unchanged into the future, would lead us to a population eventually increasing at the rate of 18 per cent per generation."[6] Did this really mean that the hypothetical John Q. Public, who in January 1941 was doomed to become an ancestor without progeny, now could look

[3] O. E. Baker, "Population Trends in Relation to Land Utilization," *Proceedings of the Second International Conference of Agricultural Economists* (1930), p. 284.

[4] Warren S. Thompson and P. K. Whelpton, *Estimates of Future Population of the United States 1940–2000* (Washington: National Resources Planning Board, 1943), pp. 3–4.

[5] U.S., Bureau of the Census, ser. P-5, No. 2 (January 31, 1941).

[6] Metropolitan Life Insurance Company, *Statistical Bulletin* (August, 1943).

forward to a long, if not numerous, line of descendants?

In my analysis of this change in the birth rate in September 1942 I pointed out that the increase had resulted principally from a larger number of first and second births and concluded:

> It is not possible to permanently maintain a population by an increase in the number of first and second births alone, especially when the number of births of the fourth order and higher is decreasing. For this reason the computation of net reproduction rates based on the number of births registered during one year not only is unwise but may also be misleading. . . .
>
> The apparent increase in the birth rate since 1933 is the result of an increase in the number of first and second births and, consequently, does not represent an increase in the lifetime fertility of the women of childbearing ages. It is doubtful that this increase will continue beyond 1942. After that date a decline seems inevitable, at least for the duration of the war. If such is the case, the potential decrease of the population, somewhat prematurely announced by the Bureau of the Census in 1941, will become a reality.[7]

After increasing slightly during 1943, the birth rate started declining but by the end of 1945 still was about 13 per cent higher than in 1939. Beginning in 1946 the trend was abruptly reversed; the 1947 birth rate exceeded the 1939 rate by nearly 50 per cent. This was the highest birth rate since possibly 1920. Concerning this, Whelpton said in a report of the National Office of Vital Statistics dated October 7, 1948, "It is just as improbable that the high rate of 1947 will remain in effect as it was that the low rates of 1933 would do so. Both were the results of unusual conditions—the great depression of the early 1930's and the demobilization and high prosperity following World War II."[8]

During 1948 the birth rate declined about 4 per cent. By now some demographers were becoming uneasy. The April 1949 issue of *Population Index* stated, "Until recently the course of population development in Western nations was generally believed to be well charted and understood. This is now a matter of some doubt."[9]

The disquietude of consumers of population forecasts was vigorously expressed by Joseph S. Davis of the Food Research Institute at Stanford University before the American and Western Farm Economics Association in Laramie, Wyoming on August 20, 1949. With all the righteous indignation of a trusting wife who has just discovered the activity of a philandering husband, Professor Davis charged:

> I am ashamed that, like most of my fellow social scientists, I have so long accepted the conclusions of the population specialists with naïve faith . . . it is disheartening to have to assert that the best population forecasts deserve little credence even for 5 years ahead, and none at all for 20–50 years ahead. . . . Population forecasting is *not* a simple matter. Available techniques do *not* permit reliable prediction to be made for 5, 10, 20, or 50 years ahead. The best may be *far* wrong. Our net reproduction rate is *not* near unity, but has been well above it ever since 1940. It is *not* reliable as a basis for prediction. There is *no* assurance of any peak population at any future date. The age structure of the population does *not* "inherently" point to cessation of growth and eventual population decline. Our major population problems are not prevention of such decline. There is no adequate basis for expecting the fertility rate, or the crude birth rate, to drop to or below the level of the early 1930's and to remain at that low level . . . planning for food, agriculture, industry, schools, etc., can *not* be safely done on the basis of supposedly expert population forecasts. . . . If we continue to build on the crumbling foundations I have described, we shall have no excuse for consequent errors in our own work.[10]

[7] Harold F. Dorn, "The Potential Rate of Increase of the Population of the United States," *American Journal of Sociology,* LVIII (1942), 185–87.

[8] P. K. Whelpton, "The Meaning of the 1947 Baby Boom," *Vital Statistics, Special Reports,* XXXIII (National Office of Vital Statistics, 1948), 7.

[9] *Population Index,* XV (1949), 123.

[10] Joseph S. Davis, "Our Amazing Population Upsurge," *Journal of Farm Economics,* Proceedings Number (November, 1949).

With this devastating indictment Professor Davis arraigned demographers before the bar of judgment not only of fellow social scientists but of the entire nation. Are they guilty or not guilty? Before rendering final judgment let us first look at the development of demography, and more especially population forecasting, in historical perspective and then examine briefly the current demographic situation.

Early Forecasts

As I pointed out previously, forecasting the future population of the United States is not a recent development. Benjamin Franklin, as early as 1751, estimated that the population of the colonies was doubling about every 20 years due to natural increase alone.[11] The early forecasters had almost no basic demographic data beyond the total size of the population available as a guide, and even these meager data covered only a very few years. It is not surprising then that forecasts prepared during the early years of the nineteenth century assumed an indefinite increase in population at a geometric rate. Several presidents, including Thomas Jefferson and Abraham Lincoln, in the days when presidents undoubtedly prepared their own papers, advised Congress that the population of the nation would continue to increase at a rapid rate. In his second message to Congress, Lincoln thought that the total population very likely might be as large as 102 million in 1900 and 217 million around 1925.[12]

By the middle of the nineteenth century the belief that population could continue to increase according to the Malthusian Law, $P = Ce^{rt}$,* was being questioned. The Compendium of the United States Census for 1850 summarized the projections of various forecasters and presented a number of new estimates based on a decrease in the rate of growth.

Several of these early predictions proved to be surprisingly accurate for relatively long periods of time. The estimates of Bonynge published in 1852 did not deviate from subsequent census enumerations by as much as 3 per cent until 60 years later in 1910 when his estimate exceeded the census enumeration by 5 per cent.[13] His estimates for later dates, however, have considerably exceeded census enumerations, and the estimate of 703 million for 2000, seems likely to be at least 3 to 4 times the possible population on that date.

Another remarkably accurate series of predictions were those prepared by Gannett for the National Conservation Commission in 1909.[14] These deviated by not more than 3 per cent from the census enumerations from 1910 through 1940; his estimate for 1950, 150 million, will miss the census count probably by less than 1 per cent. The estimate of 249 million for 2000 undoubtedly is considered by most demographers as at least 25 per cent too high. But as will be pointed out later it is viewed as being exceedingly probable or even somewhat too low by some economists. It should be remembered though that the year, 2000, is nearly a century after the preparation of the original estimate.

But as Gannett so aptly remarked, "Several predictions of our population have been made at various times by different and more or less complicated and elaborate methods. One or two of these predictions have by accident hit very near the truth, as made known by later censuses, but all have been finally wide of the mark."[15] Moreover these estimates were all wide of the mark because they assumed a

11 Joseph J. Spengler, "Population Predictions in Nineteenth Century America," *American Sociological Review,* I (1936), 905–21.

12 *Ibid.*, p. 911.

* Ed. note: P = population at the end of a period of years (t); C = a constant; e = mathematical constant 2.71818; r = average annual rate of change.

13 Francis Bonynge, *The Future Wealth of America* (New York: Author, 1852).

14 Henry Gannett, "Estimates of Future Population," *Report of the National Conservation Commission,* II (1909), 7–9.

15 *Ibid.*, p. 8.

much larger increase in population than actually took place. Evidence is abundant to demonstrate that the slower than expected increase of population did not result from population increase outrunning means of subsistence. Something had happened to the Malthusian Law.

By the end of the nineteenth century, some persons trained in the more rigorous disciplines of mathematics and the natural sciences began to question the value of qualitative wisdom or the mechanical extrapolation of trend curves such as the Malthusian Law as methods of prediction. One of the first of these was Pritchett writing in the *Quarterly Publications of the American Statistical Association* in 1891 and again in the *Popular Science Monthly* in 1900.[16] He observed that the Malthusian Law could not accurately describe the growth of population in the United States and that, in general, the Law was irrational since with indefinite increase in time population also would increase without limit, which is manifestly impossible.

Pritchett restated the general law of population growth as follows:

> When not disturbed by war, famine, immigration, etc., population increase goes on at a constantly decreasing rate. It should be possible to express this law by means of some rational mathematical function.
>
> And it does not in the least diminish the value of such a mathematical formula, for the purpose of prediction, that it is based upon no knowledge of the real causes of the phenomena which it connects together.[17]

Examining the growth of population from 1790 to 1880 Pritchett observed that it could be reproduced very closely by a third degree power series, $P = A + Bt + Ct^2 + Dt^3$.* The fact that this function had no upper asymptote and that it extrapolated backward in time P would become zero or even negative apparently did not seriously disturb Pritchett. So firm was his faith in the ability of rational mathematical functions to describe demographic phenomena that he prepared estimates for ten centuries in advance.

His faith brought little credit to the American Statistical Association which published his forecasts nor did it positively advance knowledge of how to forecast population growth. The estimate for 1910 was only 3 per cent too high but the error increased rapidly thereafter. The estimate for 1950, 191 million, will be about 27 per cent in excess of the census enumeration. The estimates of 386 million for 2000 and of 41 billion for 2900 do not appear realistic at this time.

LOGISTIC CURVE†

Attempts to predict population growth by means of some rational mathematical function involving population and time reached their zenith in 1920 in the publication by Pearl and Reed of a paper in which they derived an empirical curve which conformed to certain reasonable postulates concerning the growth of populations.[18] This was an independent discovery of a function which much earlier in 1838 had been suggested by the Belgian mathematician, Verhulst, but which had remained unnoticed undoubtedly due to the absence of sufficient reliable demographic data by which its validity could

[16] H. S. Pritchett, "A Formula for Predicting the Population of the United States," *Quarterly Publication of the American Statistical Association,* II (1891), 278–86; "The Population of the United States during the Next Ten Decades," *Popular Science Monthly,* LVIII (1900), 49–53.

[17] "The Population of the United States during the Next Ten Decades," *ibid.*

* Ed. note: P = population at the end of a period of years (t); A, B, C, D are constants.

† Ed. note: Further information on the use of logistic growth curves in population projections may be found in W. Isard, *Methods of Regional Analysis* (New York: Jointly by Technology Press of the Mass. Inst. of Technology and John Wiley & Sons, 1960).

[18] Raymond Pearl and Lowell J. Reed, "On the Rate of Growth of the Population of the United States since 1790 and Its Mathematical Representation," *Proceedings of the National Academy of Science,* VI (1920), 275–88.

be tested.[19] This curve, $P = K(1 + e^{a+bt})^{-1}$*, now known as the logistic, was placed on a firm rational basis by Lotka shortly after the publication of the paper by Pearl and Reed.[20]

I do not believe it essential for the purposes of this discussion to develop the rational basis of the logistic. It will be sufficient to state that it is in harmony with our rational ideas about population growth. Moreover, there can be no doubt concerning the theoretical validity of the logistic as a description of many diverse types of growth phenomena. But the question confronting us is, does the logistic represent the past growth of the population of the United States with such reliability that it can, with confidence, be used to predict the future?

Pearl and Reed fitted their first logistic to the population of the United States from 1790 to 1910 before the results of the 1920 census were available. They forecast the 1920 and 1930 populations with an error of less than 1 per cent. The forecast overestimated the 1940 population by 3.5 per cent and it will underestimate the 1950 population by about 1 per cent. (These forecasts, together with others discussed below, are presented in Table 1.) The projections are accurate enough to satisfy all except the most captious critics and set an example of forecasting ability which might well be the envy of other social scientists.

But was this accuracy really due to the discovery of the natural law of population growth and the superior ability of demographers to foresee the future or was it merely a fortuitous historical event such as the earlier forecasts prepared during the nineteenth century which were mentioned above?

As soon as a preliminary count of the 1940 census enumeration was announced Pearl and Reed published a comparison of this count with the estimate by Logistic I.[21] Even though the estimate exceeded the census count only by about 3.5 per cent Pearl and Reed did not have the courage of their convictions. Apparently they agreed in part at least with Thompson and Whelpton who earlier had written, "An S-shaped curve has been fitted to the past population of the United States by Pearl and Reed and prolonged to indicate the future population. To the authors, it seems probable that these estimates will prove too high due to restricted immigration and lowered birth rates."[22]

Pearl and Reed were prepared for this contingency. Their earlier investigations of the ability of the logistic to describe the growth of a great variety of populations had led to the enunciation of the principle that any population can be expected to continue to follow, in its later growth, the same logistic curve it has followed in its earlier growth only if no serious changes have occurred in conditions governing previous growth. If changes do occur, a new logistic should be computed.

In spite of the fact that the 1940 forecast met rigid mathematical tests for a good forecast in that it deviated from the census enumeration by less than twice the standard error of forecast, Pearl and Reed decided to compute Logistic II from census data for the entire period 1790–1940. The fit to past growth was remarkably close and resulted in an estimated 1940 population less than 1 per cent greater than the census count. Pearl and Reed did not express a clear choice for either Logistic I or Logistic

19 P. F. Verhulst, "Notice sur la loi que la Population suit dans son accroisissement," *Correspondance Mathématique et physique publiée par A. Quetelet,* X (1838), 113–21.

* Ed. note: P = population; K = upper limit of population; e = mathematical constant 2.71818; a and b are constants; t = time period in years.

20 Alfred J. Lotka, *Elements of Physical Biology* (Baltimore: Williams and Wilkins, 1925).

21 Raymond Pearl, Lowell J. Reed, and Joseph F. Kish, "The Logistic Curve and the Census Count of 1940," *Science,* XCII (1940), 486–88.

22 Thompson and Whelpton, "The Population of the Nation," *Recent Social Trends in the United States, op. cit.,* p. 46.

TABLE 1

ENUMERATED AND ESTIMATED POPULATION OF THE UNITED STATES

(in millions)

YEAR	CENSUS[a]	PEARL[b]-REED[b]		DUBLIN[c] 1931		SCRIPPS[d] 1928	SCRIPPS[e] 1931	SCRIPPS 1933[f]		SCRIPPS 1935[g]			SCRIPPS 1943[h]			SCRIPPS 1947[i]			CENSUS[j] 1949
		I	II	High	Low			High	Low	High	Medium	Low	High	Medium	Low	High	Medium	Low	
						(Jan. 1)	(Jan. 1)				(April 1)						(July 1)		(July)
1900...	76.0																		
1910...	92.0		91.4																
1920...	105.7	107.4	106.1																
1930...	122.8	122.4	120.1			123.6													
1940 ..	131.7	136.3	132.8	131.0	131.0	138.3	132.5	134.5	132.5	132.6	132.0	131.2							
1941...	133.2																		
1942...	134.7																		
1943...	136.5																		
1944...	138.1																		
1945...	139.6									139.2	137.0	134.1	138.7	138.5	138.3				
1946...	141.2																140.8		
1947...	144.0																142.2		144.0
1948...	146.6																143.3		146.2
1949...	149.2																144.5		148.2
1950...		148.7	143.8	139.0	139.0	151.6	139.8	148.5	140.5	146.1	141.6	136.2	145.0	144.4	143.0	148.0	146.0	144.9	149.9
1960...		159.2	153.0	147.0	146.0	162.7	143.9			159.5	149.4	137.1	156.5	153.4	147.7	162.0	155.1	149.8	160.0
1970...		167.9	160.4	151.0	148.0	171.5	144.6		146.0	172.8	155.0	134.0	167.9	160.5	148.7	177.1	162.0	151.6	
1980...		174.9	166.3	154.0	148.0		142.9	190.0	145.0	185.8	158.3	127.6	179.4	165.4	145.8	increases	increases	declines	
1990...		180.4	170.8	154.0	145.0		declines		declines		declines	declines	189.4	167.1	138.9	there-	until	there-	
2000...		184.7	174.3	152.0	140.0	186.0	there-		there-		there-	there-	198.7	166.6	129.1	after	about	after	
		ulti-	ulti-				after		after		after	after		declines	declines		2000		
		mate	mate														then		
		197.3	184.0														declines		

[a] Enumerated population, 1900–40; calculated as of July 1, 1941–49.

[b] *Science*, XCII (1940), 486–88.

[c] *Problems of Population* (1932), pp. 115–25.

[d] *American Journal of Sociology*, XXXIV (1928), 253–70.

[e] *Problems of Population* (1932), pp. 77–86.

[f] *Recent Social Trends*, p. 48.

[g] *J. Amer. Stat. Assn.*, XXI (1936), 457–73. (High is based on high fertility, low mortality, 200,000 net immigrants annually beginning 1940; medium is based on medium fertility and mortality with 100,000 net immigrants annually beginning 1940; low is based on low fertility, high mortality, no net immigration.)

[h] National Resources Planning Board (1943), p. 29. (High is based on high fertility, low mortality, no net immigration; medium is based on medium fertility and mortality, 100,000 net immigrants annually beginning 1945; low is based on low fertility, high mortality, no net immigration.)

[i] Bureau of the Census (1947). (High is based on high fertility, low mortality, 200,000 net immigrants per year beginning 1945; medium is based on medium fertility and mortality, 100,000 net immigrants annually beginning 1950; low is based on low fertility, high mortality, no net immigration.)

[j] Bureau of the Census, ser. P-25, No. 18 (1949).

II* but suggested that the relative merits should be decided by future events. However, they seemed to have a slight preference for the fledgling Logistic II over the time tested Logistic I which had remained tried and true for 30 years.

Alas, their faith was ill rewarded. In 1950, Logistic I will underestimate the census count by about 1 per cent but the newer Logistic II will fail in its first test since it will underestimate the census count by about 4 per cent. This may not appear large when compared with predictive errors of many other social, economic, and biological phenomena but it fails to meet the mathematical requirements for a good forecast since it will deviate by about twice the standard error of forecast from the census count and what is worse this error will become progressively greater in the future. No, here was not a mathematical law which could mysteriously, within its parameters, contain the forces governing past population growth in such a manner that, following the demographer's touch, the future would be accurately portrayed. Just as for the Malthusian Law, something had happened to the logistic law.

Use of Net Reproductive Rates

A method of analysis of population growth, different in conception from those discussed so far in this paper, had gained widespread acceptance by the early 1930's. In 1911, Sharpe and Lotka had shown that a population continuously subject to a fixed set of fertility rates for women of each age and a fixed set of mortality rates for each age, in the absence of migration, ultimately would assume a stable age distribution.[23] The ultimate birth rate, death rate, and rate of natural increase, therefore, could be computed and compared with those prevailing at any time prior to stabilization. These ultimate rates were called true birth and death rates and their difference, the true rate of natural increase.

These concepts were extended by Lotka in subsequent papers, but were first brought forceably to the attention of demographers by the publication of a paper by Dublin and Lotka in the *Journal of the American Statistical Association* in 1925 in which these concepts were applied to the analysis of population growth in the United States.[24] They pointed out that as a result of high fertility and mortality rates in the past, the current age distribution of the population was unusually favorable to a high crude rate of natural increase. However, if the existing fertility and mortality rates should continue unaltered in the absence of migration, the age distribution of the population would change in such a manner that the annual rate of natural increase would be reduced about 50 per cent, from 11.1 to 5.5 per 1,000.

Lotka also showed how to compute the ratio of total births in two generations. This had been first shown by Böckh in 1884, but had been subsequently overlooked.[25] This ratio, now known as the net reproduction rate, was given wide publicity by the publications of Kuczynski beginning in 1928.[26]

Net reproduction rates for all possible segments of the population were computed and published. When the requisite birth and death statistics were lacking, demographers invented ingenious substitutes for the net reproduction rate. Never before had the procreative effort of a population been so closely studied.

As demographers kept a sensitive finger

* Ed. note: Logistic I and Logistic II refer to sucsive attempts by Pearl and Reed to find a curve to predict future population.

[23] F. R. Sharpe and A. J. Lotka, "A Problem in Age-Distribution," *Philosophical Magazine,* XXI (1911), 435–38.

[24] Louis I. Dublin and Alfred J. Lotka, "On the True Rate of Natural Increase," *Journal of the American Statistical Association,* XX (1925), 305–99.

[25] R. Böckh, *Statistisches Jahrbuch der Stadt Berlin* (Berlin: Stat. Amt der Stadt Berlin, 1884), p. 30.

[26] Robert R. Kuczynski, *The Balance of Births and Deaths* (New York: Macmillan, 1928).

on the fluttering demographic pulse of the population, their regular bulletins pointed more and more to the possibility that the population of the United States was but a withering branch of a decaying ancestral tree. Not only was the true or potential rate of population growth rapidly declining to a level which would eventually result in a decrease in the size of the total population but also the actual excess of births over deaths was becoming smaller and smaller. In 1939 I pointed out that during 1935 and 1936, the first two years for which vital statistics then were available on a residence basis, 5 of the 93 cities of 100,000 or more population and 14 cities of 50,000–99,999 population actually had more registered deaths than births.[27]

It is not surprising that population forecasts based on the true rate of natural increase reflected the pessimism of the time. In 1931, Dublin presented two projections of the population of the United States before the General Assembly of the International Union for the Scientific Investigation of Population Problems in London.[28]

The most optimistic forecast assumed that the birth rate would continue to fall until it reached a level which would support a stationary population under the best mortality conditions foreseeable. An expectation of life at birth of 70 years by 1970 seemed the maximum possible. Accordingly, Dublin assumed that the true birth rate and death rate would be equal and stabilized at 14.3 by 1970 and that they would continue at that level until 2100.

With these assumptions the population of the United States faced a dismal future. In the absence of migration, it would reach a maximum of 154 million between 1980 and 1990 and then decline to 140 million by 2100. Even so Dublin reported, "the supposition on which this first estimate is based seems altogether too optimistic."

His second "more reasonable" estimate assumed that the true birth rate would fall to a level of 13 per 1,000 by 1970 and then gradually decline until it reached a level of 10 per 1,000 by 2100. With the same mortality assumption as before and in the absence of migration, a maximum population of 148 million would be reached by 1970 followed by a decline to 140 million by 2000 and to 76 million by 2100.

These predictions are remarkable not so much for their specific numerical values as for the fact that a prominent American demographer had stated publicly that the population of the United States almost certainly would decline in the very near future. The most pessimistic of previous forecasters had assumed merely that the rate of increase would approach zero at some distant time. Moreover, Dublin expressed the opinion that "my extreme prediction for 2100 may turn out to be conservative after all."

It is hardly necessary to ask, how have these forecasts stood the test of time? The census enumeration in April 1950 will report a population larger than the maximum resulting from Dublin's second forecast and within 3 or 4 million of the maximum forecast by his first optimistic projection. No, the true rate of natural increase and the net reproduction rate, in spite of their theoretical importance, did not hold the key to the future. In fact they seemed to obscure the future. Just as with the Malthusian Law and the logistic curve, something was wrong with the net production rate.

Estimates of Scripps' Foundation

The most authoritative and widely accepted series of population estimates have been those flowing from the tireless industry of Whelpton of the Scripps Foundation. His procedure which he terms the analytical method, "consists of (1) analyzing mortality, fertility, and migration trends in different population segments, (2)

27 Harold F. Dorn, "The Natural Decrease of Population in Certain American Communities," *Journal of the American Statistical Association,* XXXIV (1939), 106–9.

28 Louis I. Dublin, "The Outlook for the American Birth Rate," *Problems of Population,* ed. G. H. L. F. Pitt-Rivers (London: G. Allen, 1932), pp. 115–25.

framing hypotheses regarding the future trends of these factors by observing their previous behaviour and appraising the influence of changing industrial, social, and legal conditions, and (3) building up successive hypothetical populations, beginning with the last actual population, by applying hypothetical factors to different population segments. The results thus show the composition as well as the size of the indicated future population."[29]

The first of these predictions was published in 1928.[30] I shall call the numerical results of Whelpton's computations, predictions or forecasts for convenience in discussion. However, he had steadfastly maintained that he was not predicting the size of the population at some future date. "No claim is made that the Scripps Foundation estimates represent a law of population growth. They are simply the results of an empirical process. . . . These estimates represent simply what will happen under certain conditions of immigration, birth rates, and death rates, conditions that are believed to be reasonable, based on the experience of recent years."[31]

I shall not digress to discuss whether a rose is a rose. Regardless of Whelpton's protestation, the results of his computations have been widely regarded and used as forecasts of future population change not only by fellow demographers but by other social scientists and by governmental officials and businessmen.

The 1928 projection missed the 1930 enumerated population by less than 1 per cent but overestimated the 1940 census enumeration by about 7 million or somewhat more than 5 per cent. In 1950 though, it will again be within 1 per cent of the census population. The population would continue to increase at a decreasing rate, reaching 186 million by 2000. Although prepared by an entirely different method, these estimates were closely similar both in trend and absolute size to those resulting from Logistic I prepared by Pearl and Reed.

Concerning these estimates Whelpton said, "It is true that striking medical discoveries may cause the population to vary upward from these predictions. More likely, however, wars or a greater practice of birth control may cause a variation downward."[32]

Additional study apparently convinced Whelpton that the last sentence was true, for 3 years later before the same sessions of the International Population Union at which Dublin presented the estimates mentioned above, he read a paper which made the pessimistic Dublin appear relatively optimistic.[33] The population of the United States now was scheduled to reach a maximum of 144.6 million by 1970 and to decline rapidly thereafter.

Whelpton explained this radical change in point of view as follows:

> The fact that the present estimates indicate a population for 1975, which is about 31,000,000 below that indicated by the estimates prepared four years ago, serves to illustrate the cumulative effect during a 45 year period of the acceleration in the decline in the birth rate from 1927 to 1931, since the same method of estimating was followed in both cases and little change was made in the trends of death rates and immigration. Perhaps the actual course of population growth will lie between the two extremes, although at present it appears as though the lower estimates are the more probable, and that the maximum during the century will not exceed 150,000,000, even though surpassing the 142,600,000 mark resulting from our present calculations.[34]

The population projections of the Scripps Foundation were given an aura of

29 P. K. Whelpton, *Needed Population Research* (Lancaster Pa.: The Science Press Printing Co., 1938), pp. 6–7.

30 P. K. Whelpton, "Population of the United States, 1925 to 1975," *American Journal of Sociology,* XXXIV (1928), 253–70.

31 *Ibid.*, pp. 267, 270.

32 *Ibid.*, p. 270.

33 P. K. Whelpton, "The Future Growth of the Population of the United States," *Problems of Population, op. cit.*, pp. 77–86.

34 *Ibid.*

authority with their acceptance by President Hoover's Research Committee on Social Trends. Here was the stamp of approval of fellow social scientists who presumably would be expected to be most critical. Moreover, the Committee had at least quasi-official standing.

The report of the Committee published in 1933 contained two alternative forecasts of population prepared by the Scripps Foundation.[35] The low estimate did not differ materially from the forecast presented by Whelpton before the International Population Union in 1931. The high estimate was somewhat less than Whelpton's 1928 forecast up until 1950 but after that date it assumed a less rapid decline in the rate of growth so that the population would number 190 million by 1980.

The authors placed very little confidence in the high estimate. Concerning it, Thompson and Whelpton said, "It is believed by the authors, however, that the actual population will be considerably nearer the minimum than the maximum figure, especially by 1980."[36] They preferred a forecast obtained as a weighted average of the two estimates but giving increasingly greater weight to the lower up to 75 per cent for 1980. On this basis the future population would be about 143 million in 1950, increasing slowly thereafter to about 157 million by 1980. The future still looked dark.

The interest and concern of various governmental agencies about the effects of the gloomy population outlook upon the nation found expression in a report, *The Problems of a Changing Population,* published by the National Resources Committee in 1938.[37] Revised estimates of future population changes, prepared by the Scripps Foundation, were included in this report and strongly influenced the Committee's recommendations.

The estimates prepared for this report represented a full-blown shotgun approach to population forecasting. All possible combinations of the various assumptions concerning the trend of fertility, mortality, and migration gave eighteen series of possible future population change. This wide variety of projections emphasized the position Whelpton always had maintained but which few people really believed, namely that his projections were not forecasts of actual populations but were intended to show the inevitable consequences of the continuation of certain assumed trends in fertility, mortality, and migration. Only three series will be mentioned, here, those selected by Whelpton to represent high, medium, and low estimates.

The low series was more pessimistic than any previously published. The population would reach a maximum of about 137 million between 1955 and 1960 and thereafter decline rapidly.[38] The high series resulted in forecasts slightly lower than the high estimates prepared for the President's Research Committee on Social Trends. The total population would continue to increase, though at a decreasing rate, and by 1980 would number about 186 million. Whelpton did not consider either of these very probable for he said, "At the present time it seems to us that the medium series will be closer to what happens than the high or low, though probably somewhat too high. According to this series, the population will reach its maximum of about 160,000,000 soon after 1980, and then begin to dwindle numerically."[39]

This opinion was shared even more strongly by the Committee on Population Problems for it did not even include the high estimate in the body of its report. The highest estimate shown in detail by the Committee was Whelpton's medium series

35 *Recent Social Trends in the United States, op. cit.*, pp. 48–49.

36 *Ibid.*, p. 48.

37 *The Problems of a Changing Population* (Washington: National Resources Committee, 1938).

38 P. K. Whelpton, "An Empirical Method of Calculating Future Population," *Journal of the American Statistical Association,* XXXI (1936), 457–73.

39 *Ibid.*, pp. 470–71.

which assumed medium fertility, medium mortality, and net immigration of 100,000 annually after 1940. As pointed out above these assumptions would result in a declining population before the end of the century. The possibility that the population of the United States, before the end of the century, would reach a maximum from which it would decline was becoming almost a truism. Even a governmental agency could endorse this belief without criticism. A slight modification of the medium estimate (assuming no net immigration) was republished, with apparent approval, by the Bureau of the Census in 1941.[40]

The onset of the war, a somewhat more rapid decline in mortality than had been anticipated, and the continuation of the upward turn in the birth rate which had started in the middle 1930's led the National Resources Planning Board to request the Scripps Foundation to revise the 1937 forecast. The revised estimates published in 1943 were higher than the 1937 figures but under most combinations of assumptions concerning the trend of fertility and mortality, a gradual slowing down and an eventual cessation of population growth was projected.[41] As Thompson and Whelpton said, "the outlook for the population of the United States remained much the same."

In spite of war casualties, the population continued to increase so rapidly that by 1945 it exceeded the highest estimate made only 3 years previously. Although the Scripps Foundation saw no reason for materially altering its long-range projections of fertility and mortality trends, it was apparent that the "baby boom" had made obsolete the base population on which future projections rested. Accordingly, a set of revised estimates were prepared and published in 1947 under the sponsorship of the Bureau of the Census.[42]

Whelpton summarized these by saying, "The outlook after 1950 is for a continuation of the long time decline in population growth, both in absolute number and rate. Moreover, there is a strong possibility that within a few decades the population will reach its maximum size and will begin to decrease unless heavy immigration is resumed."[43] This view also must have been shared by the Bureau of the Census for it had selected the forecasts based on medium fertility and mortality and no net immigration for publication in advance of the complete report.[44] According to this set of assumptions, a maximum population of some 165 million would be reached about 1990 after which a decline would occur.

Because of the interest in such figures, the report contained a series of annual forecasts for 1946–49. By the time the report was published in the latter half of 1947, the actual population at that time, as subsequently calculated by the Bureau of the Census, exceeded the number forecast in the report by nearly 2 million.

With population increase outstripping the speed of governmental printing presses, heroic action clearly was called for. On February 14, 1949 the Bureau of the Census issued revised forecasts of population for July 1, 1948 to 1955.[45] The forecast for July 1, 1950 was nearly 2 million greater than the highest and 5 million greater than the lowest 1947 forecast for that date. As of December, 1949, it is likely that this "revised" estimate may be nearly 2 million too low.

Reasons for Past Failures

Demography, is it science or literature? It is no answer to the record I have just

[40] U.S., Bureau of the Census, ser. P-3, No. 15 (July 23, 1941).

[41] *Estimates of Future Population of the United States 1940–2000, op. cit.*

[42] *Forecasts of the Population of the United States, 1945–75* (Washington: Bureau of the Census, 1947).

[43] *Ibid.*, p. 39.

[44] U.S., Bureau of the Census, ser. P-46, No. 7 (September 15, 1946).

[45] U.S., Bureau of the Census, ser. P-25, No. 18 (February, 1949).

sketched to say as did the editors of *Population Index* in their review of the 1947 forecasts prepared by the Scripps Foundation and the Bureau of the Census, "the revised estimates are not predictions. They are projections. . . ."[46] Predictions, estimates, projections, forecasts; the fine academic distinction among these terms is lost upon the user of demographic statistics. So long as numbers which purport to be possible future populations are published they will be regarded as forecasts or predictions irrespective of what they are called by the demographers who prepare them.

What is wrong with the methods of forecasting population I have just described? Must they be discarded as unsound and should demographers, as Professor Davis suggests, return to qualitative wisdom as a forecasting method?[47]

It is hardly necessary to mention why the Malthusian Law failed. It is inherently irrational since it assumes that population will increase indefinitely with indefinite increase in time. But what of the logistic curve, popularly known as the law of population growth?

So far as I have been able to judge neither Pearl nor Reed, at least as soon as the first flushes of parental pride had subsided, maintained that the logistic was anything more than empirical curve which described exceptionally well the past growth of the population of the United States. Its standing as a law of population growth was critically examined by Wilson and Puffer in 1933 in a publication apparently little known to demographers with the conclusion, "If . . . the statement that the logistic . . . affords a rational law to such an extent as to permit the extrapolation of the curve for forecasting purposes and the interpretation of the constants as constants of nature, we are forced to take serious exception to it. . . ."[48]

The use of the logistic as an empirical curve to describe population growth implies that the parameters average the factors which produced the observations. When the curve is extrapolated for predictive purposes, this implication is absurd unless the growth of population actually has an inherent stability. At first thought, it may seem preposterous to assume that there can be any inherent stability in population growth. But observations on many human populations in the past reveal that there has been amazing stability in population growth over long periods of time.

Furthermore in forecasting we are interested, from the statistical point of view, primarily in the trend line. For any given year in the future, the observed point may fall above or below the projected trend line; except in unusual instances, it will not fall exactly on the curve. But granting all this, it seems unlikely that the logistic will be used extensively for forecasting population growth in the United States.

I have already pointed out that Logistic I projected from 1910 has predicted the subsequent population with remarkable accuracy. However, Logistic II projected from 1940 probably will run well below the growth of population for at least 20 to 30 years and possibly longer. In other words, it will depart systematically from the probable growth of population. Even though the general trend may be roughly correct, the projected curve is biased. But by what criteria shall we determine that the logistic should be projected from 1900, 1910, 1920, or some other date?

The logistic does not explicitly reveal the relative influence of the elementary demographic factors, births, deaths, and migration upon population change. Instead it conceals their separate effects within its parameters. For the analysis of current demographic changes, this is a serious defect. On the other hand, the work of

[46] *Population Index,* XIV (1948), 195.

[47] Joseph S. Davis, *The Population Upsurge in the United States,* War and Peace Pamphlets No. 12 (Stanford: Food Research Inst., Stanford University, 1949).

[48] Edwin B. Wilson and Ruth R. Puffer, "Least Squares and Laws of Population Growth," *Proceedings of the American Academy of Arts and Sciences,* LXVIII (1933), 287–382.

Lotka has demonstrated that the use of mathematical functions, of which the logistic is one, illuminates many fundamental theoretical problems in demography.[49] Interestingly enough, however, this virtue, as will be pointed out below, is one of the reasons for the failure of certain population forecasts in the past.

There are many statistical difficulties with the logistic such as the fact that a population must be past the point of inflection of the curve before future growth can be described with even rough accuracy and the fact that the curve is not linear in its parameters so that projections of components of the total population present knotty theoretical and practical problems, but these were exhaustively discussed by Wilson and Puffer so that I shall not mention them further here.

There is another, perhaps more important, reason for the failure of the logistic as a predictive curve in the present stage of demographic development of the population of the United States, even though the logistic may be the method of choice for forecasting the future of populations in a different stage of demographic development. This reason I wish to discuss in connection with the explanation for the failure of the true rate of natural increase and the net reproduction rate as methods of forecasting population.

By 1920 some, if not all demographers, realized that the change in the total size of the population was not a reliable guide to the future growth of the population of the United States. As annual statistics of births and deaths became more generally available, population change was analyzed in terms of the crude rate of natural increase and migration.

By 1925, due largely to the work of Lotka, the crude rate of natural increase as a measure of the inherent capacity of a population to replace itself was abandoned in favor of the true rate of natural increase and its correlative, the net reproduction rate. This resulted from the realization that the crude rate of natural increase was affected so strongly by the existing age composition that it was a misleading index of the inherent capacity of the population to replace itself. The net reproduction rate, being independent of the existing age structure, became the measure par excellence, of the inherent replacement power of the population.

A series of annual net reproduction rates were computed. Strangely enough, it did not appear inconsistent to demographers that the inherent replacement capacity of the population should fluctuate from one year to another just as the crude rate of natural increase. No one seriously questioned the practice of using the fertility and mortality rates of a single year as a measure of long time prospects of population growth; whatever doubts may have arisen were quieted by using the average for several years.

Demographers acted as if hypnotized by the logical power of the theoretical analysis of demographic changes in a stable population and ignored a fact which they knew full well, that the population of the United States was not stable. Actually, except for the temporary age structure of the population, the age-specific fertility rates which are the basis of the net reproduction rate are affected by all the other factors which produce annual fluctuations in the crude birth rate, a rate which had been abandoned as a measure of the inherent capacity for replacement. The sex ratio, variations in the marriage rate both currently and in the past, changes in child spacing, the number of children previously born to a family, response to changes in economic conditions, these and many other factors determine the net reproduction rate of a given year.

As Hajnal so aptly remarked, "The question, 'To what extent is the population replacing itself according to the rates of *this* year?' is a futile question. In however refined a way we analyze the fertility rates

[49] Alfred J. Lotka, *Analyse demographique avec application particuliere l'espèce humaine* (Paris: Hermann et Cie, 1939).

of a given year they will still reflect temporary fluctuations."[50] Whelpton graphically illustrated this fact when he calculated that if the first birth rates derived from the fertility experience of 1942 were to continue unchanged, 1,000 women living through the childbearing ages would produce 1,084 first births, a feat of demographic prowess which undoubtedly would have aroused the envy even of the goddess Diana.[51]

Until it was forcefully impressed upon them by the changes in fertility before, during, and after World War II, demographers did not appreciate the full implications of a fact which they had been pointing out for several years, the extent to which the number of births during a given interval of time is the result of planned control of fertility. The failure to evaluate correctly the role of voluntary control of fertility operating either through the postponement of marriage or through the deliberate spacing of children after marriage is a major factor in the failure of demographers to foresee with precision the trend of future population growth. The measurement of this factor requires different methods of analysis than those hitherto available or used.

This explanation of the failure of the net reproduction rate to project reliably the future trend of fertility applies equally well to the extrapolation of age-specific fertility rates, for these are but the basic elements of the reproduction rate.

With the widespread adoption of methods of controlling fertility the decision of a couple to have or not to have a child in a given year is strongly influenced by the number of children already in the family and by prevailing economic conditions. This means that not only the number of births but also the average size of existing incompleted families may fluctuate irregularly from year to year. Moreover, family limitation may be exercised before the desired size of family is reached. Thus even though the ultimate number of children is fixed, the spacing of births over the reproductive period may vary widely from time to time.

The only way to form a correct judgment of long time population growth is to analyze carefully the trend in the marriage rate and the number of children per marriage. Except for changes in migration and in mortality, which at the present time exert a relatively minor influence compared with fertility, the principal factor in the long time trend of population growth is the trend in the size of completed families.

Fortunately recent studies indicate that the size of completed families, although declining for at least a century, has showed remarkable stability compared with indexes of current fertility.[52] It may be a matter of doubt as to whether this size ever has dropped below the level necessary to permanently replace the population but if it has, it certainly is not as far below as indicated by the net reproduction rates.

Recapitulation

You have heard the charge; I have reviewed the evidence. What is the verdict? I find demographers guilty of

1. Giving the impression that projected populations were relatively inevitable and certain.

2. Underestimating the effects of scientific developments on lowering mortality rates.

3. Believing that the demographic development of a theoretical stable population must inherently characterize current

[50] J. Hajnal, "The Analysis of Birth Statistics in the Light of the Recent International Recovery of the Birth-Rate," *Population Studies,* I (1947), 137–64.

[51] P. K. Whelpton, "Reproduction Rates Adjusted for Age, Parity, Fecundity, and Marriage," *Journal of the American Statistical Association,* XLI (1946), 501–16.

[52] T. J. Woofter, "Completed Generation Reproduction Rates," *Human Biology,* XIX (September, 1947); P. K. Whelpton, "Cohort Analysis of Fertility," *American Sociological Review,* XIV (December, 1949).

demographic developments in an actual unstable population.

4. Assuming that the observed fertility and mortality of a single year or short period of years is a reliable guide to future trends.

5. Giving undue weight to recent downward cyclical fluctuations in fertility while making long range population projections.

6. Assuming that because birth rates have declined for several generations they must inevitably continue to decline.

7. Forgetting that the voluntary control of fertility can cause the birth rate to rise as well as to fall.

8. Consistently overestimating the rate of decrease in the growth of the population of the United States.

9. Being too uncritical of the work of fellow demographers.

How does this analysis affect the outlook for future population growth? Does it imply that most of the assumptions of demographers concerning the trend of population should be discarded? Does it mean that we should reject, as Professor Davis believes, the view "that growth of the United States population, so rapid as to double in 50–100 years is certainly over?"

Professor Davis' answer to these questions is an unequivocal, categorical yes.

> There is now strong reason *not* to expect, within this century, *any* peak followed by leveling off and decline. . . . Barring extreme catastrophes, my own guess is that the population in 2000 will be between 200 and 300 million. But this is only a guess. The range between these projections for the year 2000 is extremely wide; and I believe that no one can yet appraise the factors that will be at work with sufficient accuracy to make a dependable forecast within a range of 50 million. It is often important to realize what we cannot know.
>
> Furthermore, I make bold to challenge the view—held by almost all demographers of all schools—that our population must, later if not sooner, reach a peak of any size, at any time, from which a decline is probable if not inevitable.[53]

[53] Davis, *op. cit.*

The principal explanation of the fluctuations in the birth rate since 1930 may be found in fluctuations in the marriage rate and in the spacing of children during the reproductive period of family life. As yet there is no conclusive evidence that the size of completed families has increased permanently. However, it is too early to tell whether the high birth rate of the present decade represents merely a "catching up" of postponed births together with some drawing on the future or a real increase in the eventual size of families formed during this period. As of now, the former conclusion appears more likely, although it would not be surprising, if economic conditions remain favorable, for the size of families completed during 1960 to 1965 to be somewhat greater than the size of families being completed at the present time. Any large increase though would represent a major demographic revolution.

In summary, the belief that the rate of population growth in the United States is slowing down remains substantially correct. However, the rate at which it is slowing down and the date on which the total size of the population may become essentially stationary now appear quite different than before the war. The possibility of a decline in total numbers before the end of the century seems unlikely, although we should not forget that the birth rate can decline just as rapidly as it can rise.

A preliminary assessment of the possibility of a continuation of the large numerical natural increase of the 1940's through the decade 1950 to 1960 should be possible within the next 2 years. The total number of registered births during the first 10 months of 1949 was about 1 per cent larger than the number registered during the corresponding period of 1948. However, the provisional marriage rate based on marriage licenses issued during the first 9 months of 1949 is about 14 per cent below the figure for 1948. The number of marriage licenses issued in cities of 100,000 or more, January–October, 1949, is lower than the number issued for the same period during any year since 1941 with the exception of 1944. Normally, a drop of this magnitude should be reflected in a drop in the number of births during 1950 and 1951. Whether or not this will be true, only time will tell.

The estimation of population for periods as short as even 5 years in the future probably will become increasingly difficult unless economic conditions remain stabilized. If the present analysis is correct, the widespread adoption of voluntary methods of birth control make probable a sharp response of fertility to marked fluctuations in economic conditions. This may be true even though the long time trend in population change continues to be well charted. It remains to be seen, however, whether a continuation of the present or even a rising standard of living will result in a permanent rise in the average size of completed families. If it does, it will be a new experience in the demographic history of the United States. At present the odds seem to be against such an event happening. It is well to remember, though, that past experience shows future events have little respect for the opinions of demographers and economists alike.

It is easy to make predictions with a minimum of information. The easiest horrible example is to assume that what is happening now will *continue* to happen. All that we need is a population figure, a growth rate, and a slide rule—no common sense, no discretion, no background.

Let me give [an example]: California's population is 16 million, its growth rate 3.8 per cent per year; the United States has 180 million people and a growth rate of 1.6 per cent per year. California's population extrapolates to 72 million at the end of the century, to 100 million in the year 2010, and in about 115 years—that would be 2075—it overtakes the national population. That is, all Americans then would be living in California!

D. B. LUTEN, "Parks and People," *Landscape,* XII, No. 2 (1962–63), 4.

P. V. SUKHATME

THE WORLD'S HUNGER AND FUTURE NEEDS IN FOOD SUPPLIES

INTRODUCTION

Part of the world's population is inadequately nourished, quantitatively as well as qualitatively. Opinions regarding the estimate vary over a very wide range—from two-thirds to a negligible proportion. Estimates of the future needs in food supplies to insure an adequate level of nutrition to the world's population also correspondingly vary. The Freedom-from-Hunger Campaign launched by the Food and Agriculture Organization of the United Nations,[1] the "Food for Peace" program announced by the United States, and the growing concern over the "population explosion" call for a reappraisal of the situation. The task is, however, not easy since the available statistics of food consumption, nutrient intake and requirement are meager, and those that exist vary in concepts, coverage, and reliability. In fact, much of the statistical information for appraising hunger and future needs necessarily originates from surveys not sufficiently investigated as to their quality, or from old data, intelligent guesswork, and even projections and speculation in fields not yet covered by regular statistical activities. Part I of this paper assesses in broad numerical terms the extent and magnitude of hunger in the world, and Part II attempts to provide an understanding of the amount of food supplies needed for the world's growing population to meet the deficiency within a foreseeable future.

PART I. APPRAISAL OF HUNGER

EARLIER ATTEMPTS

The first comprehensive statistical appraisal of hunger in the world was made in the *World Food Survey*.[2] The analysis referred to the prewar situation and covered 70 countries whose peoples made up about 90 per cent of the world's population. The *Survey* attempted to disclose the main gaps between actual consumption and nutritional targets and called attention to the possibilities existing for closing these gaps. It stressed that many of the prewar figures for food supplies and even population were only rough estimates and stated that "total calorie estimates . . . are probably accurate within 5 per cent in most instances for countries with an average intake of 3,000 calories per person per day, and within 10 per cent for those with an average of around 2,000." The results on calorie levels were summarized in the following words:

> Calculations based on the prewar populations of the individual countries show that in the years before the war—in areas containing over half the world's population, food supplies at the

• P. V. Sukhatme is Director, Statistics Division, Food and Agriculture Organization of the United Nations, Rome.

Read before the Royal Statistical Society, May 17, 1961. Reprinted from *The Journal of the Royal Statistical Society,* CXXIV, Part IV (1961), 463–525, with permission of the author and the editor.

[1] B. R. Sen, *The Basic Freedom—Freedom from Hunger* (Rome: Food and Agriculture Organization of the United Nations, 1960).

[2] U.N., Food and Agriculture Organization, *World Food Survey* (Washington: FAO, 1946).

retail level (not actual intake) were sufficient to furnish an average of less than 2,250 calories *per caput* daily. Food supplies furnishing an average of more than 2,750 calories *per caput* daily were available in areas containing somewhat less than a third of the world's population. The remaining areas, containing about one-sixth of the world's population, had food supplies that were between these high and low levels.

As regards the adequacy of the calorie levels, it was suggested that "a *per caput* calorie intake of 2,550–2,650 should be taken as the minimum level to which intake should be raised in the low-calorie countries." Setting the findings on calorie intake levels against this requirement, Boyd Orr concluded that "a lifetime of malnutrition and actual hunger is the lot of at least two-thirds of mankind."[3]

Several others expressed similar views. For example, Cépède and Lengellé wrote: "L'enquête mondiale sur l'alimentation a montré que pratiquement les 2/3 de la population du globe avaient un niveau alimentaire dangereusement inférieur au 'minimum vital.' " They continued: "Malheureusement les études ultérieures n'ont fait que confirmer les résultats de l'enquête mondiale sur l'alimentation et ont même prouvé que le *désastre* était encore plus étendu qu'on ne s'y attendait de prime abord."[4]

A second appraisal of the world's hunger was made in the *Second World Food Survey*.[5] It was essentially concerned with the same basic questions as the first, viewed in the light of changes that had occurred in the postwar period and the greater knowledge available. The most important improvement in this survey, as compared with the first, was the incorporation of tentative estimates of national calorie requirements taking into account age, sex, body weight, and environmental temperature. The results of this survey showed that the postwar average food supply per person over large areas of the world remained below the prewar level even until 1950. It was found that in areas covering 59 per cent of the world's population, food supplies at the retail level were sufficient to furnish an average of less than 2,200 calories daily. Food supplies furnishing an average of over 2,700 calories *per caput* daily were available in areas containing 28 per cent of the world's population. The remaining areas, containing 13 per cent of the world's population, had food supplies that were between these high and low levels, the corresponding prewar figures being 39, 30, and 31 per cent.

This postwar picture was obviously worse than the prewar situation, but it appeared to be less serious at the time than the prewar situation evaluated in 1946. Whereas in 1946 the prewar situation was compared against a minimum requirement of 2,600 calories, in 1952 the postwar situation was compared against a much lower figure of requirement based on the new FAO scale.[6] The gap between the desired and the actual thus appeared much less in 1952 than in the prewar situation evaluated in 1946, not because of any intrinsic improvement in the food situation but because nutritionists changed their ideas of what is needed between 1946 and 1952. As Bennett puts it, "In all instances of suggested shortages or hunger, the gap between the actual and the desirable appears less, often much less, than what Lord Boyd Orr indicated. In short, further study has made the picture of world hunger look less somber than it did before."[7] Bennett goes even further. He doubts that the data available are sufficient to allow far-reaching conclusions concerning hunger in the

[3] J. Boyd Orr, "The Food Problem," *Scientific American,* CLXXXIII (1950), 11–15.

[4] M. Cépède and M. Lengellé, *Economie alimentaire du globe—essai d'interprétation* (Paris: Librairie de Médicis, 1953).

[5] U.N., FAO, *Second World Food Survey* (Rome, 1952).

[6] U.N., FAO, *Calorie Requirements,* Nutritional Studies, No. 3 (Washington, 1950).

[7] M. K. Bennett, *The World's Food* (New York: Harper & Bros., 1954).

world. He suspects that requirements are somewhat overestimated and consumption underestimated, at any rate for underdeveloped countries.

Bennett's views are shared by other authors. Thus Farnsworth, going even further, writes:

> The available evidence, critically examined, does *not* support the presumption that there are hundreds of millions or *even* tens of millions of seriously undernourished people in the world whose health and labor productivity would be markedly improved by the consumption of additional grain. The most trustworthy evidence rather suggests that the percentage of people seriously undernourished is extremely small.[8]

Many others have written on the magnitude of the hunger problem. These will not be referred to here. The object in mentioning a few of these studies is to show that opinion varies on the subject and that there are enormous difficulties in interpreting the available data on intake and requirements in assessing hunger.

DEFINITION OF HUNGER

Following common usage, we shall distinguish between the two terms "undernutrition" and "malnutrition." By "undernutrition" we shall mean an inadequacy in calorie intake, such that if allowed to continue for a long enough time there is either loss of normal body weight for the same physical activity or reduction in physical activity for the same body weight or both. This definition is strictly appropriate to adults, not to children. For children the inadequacy in calorie intake is determined in relation to satisfactory growth and physical development and a high degree of activity characteristic of healthy children. Undernutrition clearly refers to the inadequacy in the quantity of the diet. We shall use the term "hunger" in the sense of "undernutrition." By "malnutrition" we shall mean the lack or inadequacy of particular (or several) essential nutrients, such that if made good, the clinical signs of specific deficiency diseases are eliminated and, further, with appropriate increase in the intake of nutrients the subclinical signs associated with poor health are also removed. It refers to the inadequacy in the quality of the diet which if made good enables a person to lead a healthy active life. The two terms are naturally not mutually exclusive, because it is likely that a person who is undernourished is also malnourished, though the reverse may not hold.

It follows that the method of demonstrating that undernutrition or malnutrition exists is to set estimates of intake of energy or nutrient against the corresponding requirement. For example, if for a long enough period of time the actual intake of calories is found to be lower than the respective requirements, we may conclude that during this period food supplies were inadequate to meet the needs of the people and that the people were hungry. This was the method used by FAO on a country basis in its *Second World Food Survey* to demonstrate the existence of hunger. The method provides an estimate of the total calorie deficiency for a country, region or the world, but does not allow any conclusions as to the number of people who have actually been hungry. Calorie needs vary with age, sex, weight, physical activity, and environmental conditions. Consequently, more information in the form of a bivariate frequency distribution $f(x, y)$ for intake, x, and requirement, y, has to be available in order to estimate the proportion of the population which is hungry. Given such a distribution referring to a long enough period of time, we can express the proportion u formally as

$$u = \iint_{x<y} f(x, y)\, dx\, dy. \qquad (1)$$

[8] H. Farnsworth, "The Role of Wheat in Improving Nutritional Status and Labor Productivity in Lesser Developed Countries," *Proceedings of the International Wheat Surplus Utilization Conference* (Brooklings, South Dakota, 1959), pp. 52–65.

In a later section we shall indicate the method of evaluating this expression in order to estimate the proportion of people who are hungry.

Considerations similar to those for calories hold for other essential nutrients in order to measure malnutrition. The difficulty, however, is that no acceptable standards have yet been evolved for the various nutrients. Some progress has been made in defining protein requirements but not enough to measure the extent of inadequacy in protein intake in the different countries. Protein, moreover, is only one of the many essential nutrients. Vitamins and minerals must also be taken into account. In the absence of standards for the individual nutrients we shall use an indirect approach to measure the extent of malnutrition. We shall describe this in a later section.

SOURCES AND LIMITATIONS OF AVAILABLE STATISTICS FOR APPRAISING HUNGER

Food balance sheets.—There are two ways of assessing food consumption levels —food balance sheets and household surveys. A food balance sheet shows the food supply in a country at retail level[9] as measured by the total production of individual commodities,[10] adjusted for in-and-out movements of trade, for changes in stocks, and for any quantities used for animal feed, seed, and manufacturing and the amounts wasted during distribution up to retail level. It also shows the contents of food supplies expressed in terms of calories and nutrients on a *per caput* basis at retail level.

As can be seen, this approach to the measurement of the average national calorie and nutrient supplies per head is only indirect, the food supplies available for human consumption commodity by commodity being for the most part estimated as residuals. Thus, the estimate of *per caput* calorie supply per day at retail level may be written as

$$C = \Sigma(P + I + J_1 - E - J_2 - S - F - W - M)RN \frac{1}{(\text{Pop.})\,365}, \qquad (2)$$

where the summation is over commodities. For any commodity J_1 and J_2 represent the stocks at the beginning and at the end of the consumption year; I and E represent the imports and exports, respectively, during the consumption year; P stands for the production during the year; S for seeds; F for feeds; W for waste; and M for amounts used in manufacture for purposes other than food; R represents the extraction factor to fit with the form in which the commodity is measured at the retail level and N the corresponding content of calories (or nutrients). Clearly, the accuracy of the calorie and nutrient supply estimates depends not only on the accuracy with which the statistic of P, J, I, E, S, F, W, and M are available but also on the accuracy of R, N, and the population figure as at mid-year.

Of these, the statistics of I and E are known to be fairly reliable for most commodities. The basis for adjustment of stocks is lacking in most countries, but if a food balance sheet is constructed as an average over a period of years, this factor may not materially affect the accuracy of the final figure. The statistics of M are known fairly accurately for the economically developed countries but not for others. The statistics of S, F, and W are little more than intelligent guesses in most countries. However, for most of the underdeveloped countries the magnitude of S, F, and W relative to P is also small. This is particularly true in the case of cereals which make by far the largest contribution to the calorie and nutrient supplies of the people in most of the underdeveloped areas. In other words, whereas an error in

9 I.e., "as purchased" or as brought into the kitchen.

10 Alchoholic beverages are excluded.

the estimates of *S, F, M,* and *W* may make a difference to the end total, a similar error with regard to *P* could completely falsify the picture.

The quantity within brackets in (2) is called the gross food supply. For determining the net food supply we need to know the extraction rate *R* for different commodities, as for example, rice from paddy, oil from oilseeds, flour from wheat, etc. An accurate estimate of *R* is difficult to make since the extraction practices very considerably from one country or part of a country to another. Thus, rice may be consumed as brown, home-pounded, parboiled, unmilled, or white milled rice, with extraction rates varying from some 80 to 65 per cent and even less. Besides, estimates of the proportion of rice consumed in different forms are lacking in most of the rice-eating countries. Hence, *R* has necessarily to be determined on the basis of limited information which may not be representative of the total supplies in a country. The same holds for *N*. To continue with the example of rice, the protein content is known to vary from 7.5 to 6.7 per cent and the fat content from 1.8 to 0.7 per cent, depending on the form in which rice is consumed. To give another example, the calorie content of pork meat (carcass) is known to vary from 290 to 480 per 100 grams, depending on whether the carcass is thin, medium, or fat, and other characteristics. The fat content likewise varies over a wide range. Accurate statistics of meat of the requisite description and of the corresponding nutrient content are not available. Consequently, the use of extraction rates and of nutrient conversion factors based on limited local information or tables designed for use in a wide geographical area, such as the FAO *Food Composition Tables,*[11] can at best provide a rough approximation to the true values. Finally, the estimates of calorie and nutrient supplies depend on the accuracy of the population statistics as at the middle of the consumption year. Reasonably accurate statistics of population are available for most countries, but there still exist large areas in Africa and parts of Asia where population censuses have not been taken and for which the population estimates can be little more than intelligent guesses. Even in countries where population censuses have been taken an appreciable error may enter in extrapolating a population figure for a postcensus year. Indeed, the results of the 1960 population censuses now coming in show that the population during the last decennium in many countries of the Far East has increased at a considerably faster rate than has been taken into consideration in constructing food balance sheets in FAO publications. As an example, a preliminary count of the population in the census just concluded in the Philippines shows that the population during the last decennium increased at a rate of 3 per cent per annum, whereas the food balance sheet for 1958 used in this study has been prepared using a population figure based on the rate of increase of only 2 per cent since the previous census. Consequently a revision of the population estimate alone can introduce a difference of some 150 calories in the estimate of calorie supply for 1958.

Such are the errors to which the food balance sheet estimates of calorie and nutrient supplies are subject. It is difficult to see how these errors in the different components of the expression (2) accumulate to influence the accuracy of the final calorie and nutrient supply estimates. Clearly, some of these errors would cancel each other while others may accumulate as a result of successive transformations. A considerable amount of statistical study of these errors is needed before precise conclusions can be formulated regarding the relative contributions of the different errors to the final estimates of calorie and nutrient supplies. What appears undisputed, however, is that the principal error in the estimation of gross supplies, and hence of the final figure for the calorie and nutrient supplies, is contributed by the

[11] U.N., FAO, *Food Composition Tables,* Nutritional Studies, No. 11 (Rome, 1954).

estimate of total production of the individual commodities.

The status of production statistics varies a great deal from one country to another. Reports on area and yield rate from farmers and crop reporters usually form the basis for determining production in a country. Where land is cadastrally surveyed and the reporting agency is numerically adequate and properly trained, acreage statistics are known to be fairly reliable. On the other hand, yield rate statistics are often determined by the impressions of the reporters. A number of experimental studies have been conducted in different parts of the world to test the accuracy of the yield rate statistics reported by the crop reporters. Work carried out in India during the early 1940's shows that the yield rate was usually underestimated in good years, overestimated in bad years and on the average underestimated by varying degrees up to 10 per cent, depending upon the crop and the season.[12] India for this reason took the far-reaching step of introducing objective methods of crop sampling for estimating on a nationwide basis the annual statistics of yield rate for major commodities like wheat and rice. Similar experiences have been reported from Ceylon, Burma, the U.A.R., and other countries where FAO's technical assistance statisticians have helped to put the systems of official statistics of agricultural production on an objective basis.[13] Food

[12] Indian Council of Agricultural Research, *Sample Surveys for the Estimation of Yield of Food Crops,* Bull. Series, No. 1 (New Delhi: ICAR, 1950); P. V. Sukhatme and V. G. Panse, "Crop Surveys in India—II," *Journal of Indian Society of Agricultural Statistics,* III, No. 2 (1951), 97–168.

[13] R. S. Koshal, *Report to the Government of Ceylon on the Development of Sample Surveys for the Estimation of Agricultural Production,* FAO Report No. 276 (Rome, 1954); Koshal, *Report to the Government of the Union of Burma on the Development of Sample Surveys for the Estimation of Agricultural Production and for Evolving Plans of Increasing Production,* FAO Report No. 392 (Rome, 1955); Koshal, *Progress Reports to the Government of UAR* (Egypt) (1956–58), unpublished.

balance sheets prepared in FAO are based on improved and revised estimates of food production made available by the technical assistance experts.

It is a fortunate circumstance for statistics, though not for men, that the major contribution to the calorie supplies in most of the underdeveloped countries is made by cereals and pulses. With the increasing importance attached by the countries to the improvement of the statistics of production of these commodities, we may expect the food balance sheets to provide a fairly good indicator of the gross supplies and hence of the consumption levels in these countries. In the economically developed countries several food groups contribute to the calorie and nutrient supplies. Fortunately, however, many of the food items contributing appreciably to the calorie and nutrient supplies in these countries, like sugar, fats, milk, and meat, are manufactured and processed through industrial establishments, and their production can be relatively easily determined, so that for all practical purposes the food balance sheet estimates of consumption levels for the developed countries can be regarded as fairly satisfactory. Cépède and Lengellé attempted to determine the margin of error in the food balance sheet estimates from an examination of the internal consistency of the data and concluded that food balance sheets for underdeveloped countries can be trusted to give a picture of the food supply within ±10 per cent and those for the developed countries within ±5 per cent. Such checks have limited value, since specialists constructing food balance sheets will almost always insure internal consistency of data. A proper check is the field check on the various components which go to make up a food balance sheet. It will be a long time before such checks are developed. In the meantime, such evidence as is available suggests that while the accuracy of food balance sheet estimates for a number of individual countries leaves much to be desired, especially for the underdeveloped countries, they are in general a good enough indicator of the consumption levels for a broad numerical assessment of hunger on a regional and world-wide basis.

Food balance sheet data published by FAO,[14] Organization for European Economic Cooperation,[15] and Economic Commission for Europe[16] form the principal sources used in this paper for appraising hunger. These include some 50 countries covering about half the world's population. Food balance sheets have also been prepared in FAO for some 15 other countries including mainland China and U.S.S.R., but they are provisional in character and not yet published. Very few food balance sheets for countries in Africa are available in FAO. For other countries in this region we have drawn upon the food balance sheets published by the Foreign Agricultural Service[17] of the United States (1960–61), keeping fully in mind, however, the limitations to which FAS itself has drawn attention in this publication. Of the 83 food balance sheets used in this study, covering some 95 per cent of the world's population, 70 refer to the period 1956–58, while others refer to varying years or periods between 1951 and 1956.

Household food consumption surveys.—Food balance sheet data relate to total food supplies in a country, and as such represent only the average consumption levels for the population as a whole. They do not provide information on the distribution of food consumption among the population. Only well-conducted household surveys can provide information of this sort.

There are three basic methods of collecting data on food consumption in household surveys. The first consists in distributing account books and asking housewives to enter therein in chronological order details regarding the type and quantity of foodstuffs bought or otherwise obtained for household consumption. The second method consists in interviewing the selected households on the quantities of various food items consumed in a specified period of time. In the third method the quantities of each of the several foodstuffs (whether purchased or otherwise obtained) used during the survey period are weighed. Foodstuffs may be weighed daily or oftener, before they are used for preparing meals, or else they may be weighed at the beginning and at the end of the survey period. In the latter case, records have to be kept of the foods brought into or leaving the home during the survey period, including records of losses and wastage.

There are several difficulties in conducting food consumption surveys which are common to all these techniques. The first concerns the selection of the sample households. If a statistically valid procedure of estimation is to be used, the sample households should be randomly selected. However, experience shows that many of the households included in the sample do not like to take the trouble of either recording or weighing systematically the quantities of foods consumed in the households. The sample is thus reduced to those households which are willing to cooperate. This difficulty can be lessened to some extent with the interview method, but other biases enter in the application of this method. Firstly, households do not know precisely the quantities of the various food items consumed by them in their respective households. The difficulty is particularly great in the rural areas of underdeveloped countries where farmers largely use the foods grown by them on their farms. More-

[14] U.N., FAO, *Production Yearbook* (Rome, 1960).

[15] Organization for European Economic Cooperation, *Food Consumption in the OEEC Countries, Part I: Food Balance Sheets* (Paris: OEEC, 1960).

[16] Economic Commission for Europe, *Economic Survey for Europe in 1958* (Geneva: ECE, 1959).

[17] U.S., Dept. of Agriculture, Foreign Agricultural Service, *Food Balances in Foreign Countries. Part I: Estimates for 16 Countries of Western Europe. Part II: Estimates for 12 Countries in the Far East. Part III: Estimates for 20 Republics of Latin America. Part IV: Estimate for 28 Countries of Africa and Western Asia* (Washington: FAS, 1960–61).

over, it is common experience in these countries that people have little idea of the units used in expressing quantities for statistical purposes. The method of weighing foodstuffs used for preparing meals with the help of trained investigators helps to provide accurate information, but even in this method biases may enter. Thus, what is known as the prestige bias may come into play, and households may either use food in quantities which are considerably in excess of the normal or change the pattern of their consumption in favor of the more expensive foods. This may particularly apply in the first few days. In any case, the normal course of life in the households is likely to be disturbed, with its consequential effect on the representability of the data, though the effect of this disturbance is somewhat mitigated as the investigators come to know the households better through the extension of the period of observation to a week or longer, as necessary. Information about expenditure on different food items is perhaps somewhat easier to collect than information on quantities, but the method is applicable to purchased items only and further information of this kind is of limited use for assessing the food consumption level.

The length of time for which information on food consumption should be recorded for each selected household presents a further difficulty in conducting household food consumption surveys. In view of the seasonal variation in the availability of foods, the consumption of at least some food items is subject to considerable changes in the course of a year. Households do not, however, like to keep records of food consumption for a long period of time. If they are interviewed for long periods they will not recall all the details. In such cases the respondents are invariably pressed into giving estimates of food consumption which are considered as plausible by the enumerator himself. Interviewing for short periods, such as a week or ten days, with a new selection or partial replacement of households periodically, may provide more accurate information on the average food consumption levels but may at the same time lead to increased costs and the so-called end effects which consist of including in (or excluding from) the period of observation events actually outside it. While this variation in the method may in theory provide an unbiased estimate of the average consumption levels, it may not necessarily yield a satisfactory picture of the distribution of food consumption by calorie and nutrient supplies among households. The method of weighing foodstuffs may help to eliminate this difficulty, but will lead to even greater costs. Because of their increased costs, such household surveys based on the method of weighing of foodstuffs, also known as household dietary surveys, are usually conducted on small samples mostly confined to poor segments of the population residing in small areas. Over a period of years, however, such surveys may provide a valuable record of information.

Altogether, it seems to be exceedingly difficult to collect accurate data on food consumption through household surveys. This is one explanation for the very limited number of nationwide surveys on food consumption conducted in different countries of the world. The *Review of Food Consumption Surveys* published by FAO[18] shows that of the 57 surveys reported from all over the world, only 17 provided any information on the quantities of food consumed by the surveyed households, and of these only 8 were nationwide surveys based on interviews. Even among these 8 surveys, 4 were based on too small a sample of households to permit any valid estimation of the consumption levels applicable to the country as a whole, while the others differed considerably in concepts and methodology. A comparison of the calorie and nutrient supplies, as estimated from these nationwide food consumption surveys, with the corresponding food balance sheet figures, shows that the two dif-

[18] U.N., FAO, *Review of Food Consumption Surveys* (Rome, 1958).

fer by varying amounts up to 40 per cent. Part of the difference can be explained in terms of differential coverage, definitions, meals taken outside the households, etc. For the greater part, however, the difficulty in reconciling estimates from the two sources would seem to lie mostly in the unknown nature and magnitude of errors in the data collected by the interview method. The most that food consumption surveys based on this method can provide, at any rate for underdeveloped countries, are estimates of the ratios between the consumption of certain foodstuffs and of their distribution in the population. As an example, food consumption surveys may provide a reasonably reliable guide to the distribution of the proportion of calories derived from cereals, starchy foods, and sugar which, as we shall show in a later section, is a significant indicator of the nutritional quality of a diet. Food consumption survey data may equally be used with advantage to bring out relationships between food consumption levels and the factors influencing them. Except for such uses, however, we believe that the available data are too inadequate and insufficiently known to provide a reliable picture of the absolute levels of consumption and the distributions of food consumption in the population. Accordingly, we prefer to base our appraisal of the world's hunger mainly on the data from food balance sheets, supplemented where available by data from household dietary surveys based on objective methods of weighing.

Calorie requirements.—The second type of data needed for the appraisal of hunger is that on the calorie requirements of the population. We need to know not only the average *per caput* calorie requirement but also the variation around it in the population. The former is needed to test the adequacy of the national consumption levels, the latter to provide the basis for estimating the proportion of the people who are hungry. The FAO scale of calorie requirements provides the means of deriving this information.

The FAO scale is based on an approach involving the use of a defined "reference" man and woman aged between 20 and 30 years, living in a climate with mean annual temperature of 10° C., with a weight of 65 kg for the "reference" man and 55 for the "reference" woman. Both man and woman are presumed to live a healthy, active life. The man is assumed to require on the average 3,200 calories a day and the woman 2,300 calories a day, generally corresponding to the observed values of the food consumed by men and women of these types. The scale gives adjustment factors for age, weight, and environmental temperature but not for physical activity. For children the requirements are based on the criterion of satisfactory growth and physical development and a high degree of activity characteristic of healthy children. Special allowances are suggested for adolescents and for pregnant and lactating women.

Table 1 gives the FAO reference requirement scale, and also by way of example the actual requirement scale derived from it, for the population of India with environmental temperature of 20° C. and with reference weight of 55 kg for men and 45 kg for women. The average *per caput* requirement applicable to the country is obtained from the table by multiplying the actual requirement of each age and sex group by the proportion of the people in different groups. A broad idea of the distribution of the actual requirements can likewise be obtained by classifying the population by actual requirements. As can be seen, the variance of this distribution includes the variance between sexes and that between age groups within sexes but does not include the component due to variation within age groups due mainly to physical activity. The FAO report on calorie requirements,[19] however, gives information on the range of variation among healthy active adults of the reference age group.

[19] U.N., FAO, *Calorie Requirements,* Nutritional Studies, No. 15 (Rome, 1957).

It can be seen that the accuracy with which the actual requirement scale can be derived from the reference requirement scale and the applicability of the derived scale to any given population clearly depend upon the accuracy of the reference scale itself and the accuracy with which the different variable factors are known for the population. As regards the former, the reference scale, though known to be tentative, is based on the best knowledge at present available. Among the determining factors the age and sex composition of calories in the average *per caput* calorie requirement. Physical activity is most difficult to assess and precisely for this reason it has been assumed in the FAO scale that the average level of activity for the country remains the same as that ascribed to the reference man and woman. On the other hand, although correlated with age, its influence on the level of requirement is likely to be even greater than that of other factors. As an example, direct observation by physiological methods shows that energy expenditure rates vary from 2.5 calories

TABLE 1

REFERENCE REQUIREMENT SCALE AND ACTUAL REQUIREMENT SCALE FOR INDIA

Age Group	Reference Requirement Scale Male	Reference Requirement Scale Female	Age Group	Population of India Male	Population of India Female	Actual Requirement Scale Male	Actual Requirement Scale Female
	(Calories *per caput* per day)			(%)		(Calories *per caput* per day)	
Under 1	1,120		Under 1	3.3		1,288	
1– 3	1,300		1– 4	10.1		1,288	
4– 6	1,700		5– 9	12.8		1,843	
7– 9	2,100						
10–12	2,500	2,400	10–14	11.4		2,603	
13–15	3,100	2,600	15–19	5.2	4.9	3,012	2,064
16–19	3,600	2,400					
20–29	3,200	2,300	20–29	8.7	8.4	2,691	1,888
30–39	3,104	2,231	30–39	7.1	6.4	2,611	1,831
40–49	3,008	2,162	40–49	5.2	4.6	2,530	1,775
50–59	2,768	1,990	50–59	3.3	3.1	2,328	1,633
60–69	2,528	1,817	60–69	1.7	1.7	2,126	1,492
70+	2,208	1,587	70+	1.1	1.1	1,857	1,302

the population is known reasonably accurately for many countries. No appreciable error can therefore arise from this source. But the same cannot be said of the other factors, namely, the reference weight, the environmental temperature, and the physical activity. As an example, if the weight of healthy, active adults of 20 to 30 years in the country were to differ from the true value by, say, 5 kg, it would account for a difference of over 100 calories in the estimated *per caput* calorie requirement. It is likewise difficult to assess accurately the average environmental temperature for the country. If it were only to differ by 5° C. it would introduce a difference of some 50 per minute for very light work to over 10 calories per minute for heavy work.[20] Allowing for the rest pauses involved in any muscular work, physiologists estimate that these rates would lead to energy expenditure of 2,400 calories for an 8-hour work shift for heavy work as compared to 768 calories for a sedentary worker doing a similar shift. These probably represent extreme limits, but they show how even a small deviation from the basic assumption that the average physical activity of the

[20] E. H. Christensen, "Physiological Valuation of Work in the Nykroppa Iron Works," *Ergonomics Society Symposium on Fatigue,* ed. W. R. Floyd and A. T. Welford (London: Lewis, 1953).

population is the same as that for the "reference" may lead to considerable variation in the average levels of requirements for the different countries.

In fact, based on considerations such as those given above, it has been argued[21] that the FAO scale possibly overestimates actual requirements for the underdeveloped countries compared with those for the developed countries. The argument is that the physical activity of the average individual in underdeveloped countries is less than that of a person in the more developed countries owing to the prevalence of large-scale underemployment and low labor productivity in these areas. It is difficult to refute such arguments in the absence of proper means of assessing the level of physical activity for the entire population. On the other hand, one is hardly impressed with the argument, for while there is widespread underemployment in underdeveloped countries, it is also true that the people are required to do manual work unaided by modern tools and implements. Conditions vary a lot from one country to another: while in certain parts mechanization is rapidly changing the character of many occupations and the general trend is probably in the direction of lower human energy expenditure, and hence lower calorie requirements, it would be some time before this trend is in evidence in the underdeveloped countries.

Finally, we would refer to one more source of error. Calorie requirements based on the FAO scale refer to the physiological level, that is to calories from foods actually consumed. In practice, on the other hand, they are often needed at the retail level. Allowances must therefore be made for loss in the homes of edible foods through spoilage during storage, losses through cooking, wastage on plates, and by being fed to pets. The FAO Committee on Calorie Requirements concluded from the limited data available that in most countries these losses do not exceed 10 per cent of the calories at the retail level. Accordingly, it has been common practice to adjust requirements at the physiological level by the addition of 10 per cent to bring them up to the retail level. The allowance for losses of edible foods will obviously vary with the type of foods and the climate, storage facilities, and social customs. Thus, losses during storage due to poor and humid conditions in homes of rural people in underdeveloped countries are undoubtedly much larger than those incurred in the more developed countries. On the other hand, plate wastage is reported to be very high, often amounting to 10 per cent or even more, in developed countries as compared with that in the underdeveloped countries where it can be assumed to be almost negligible. There may be other cases where plate wastage and spoilage in storage in homes together may be lower than 10 per cent, as, for example, we believe is the case in Japan. The error arising from uniformly adopting a 10 per cent allowance for losses of edible foods needs to be kept in mind in evaluating the adequacy of the consumption levels in different countries.

To sum up, the calorie requirements based on the FAO scale are subject to several sources of error. The reference scale itself is no more than tentative, while its application in practice is necessarily limited by the insufficiency of information on the different determining factors. On the other hand, the scale is based on the best knowledge at present available and has received wide approval from the national authorities, and the limitations imposed on its application in practice are perhaps no greater than those arising from insufficiency of information in estimating actual consumption levels. We have stressed and illustrated the effects of the various sources of error on the intake and requirement statistics because it is necessary in our view to appreciate the nature of the approximations involved before attempting to evaluate the expression for the proportion of people who are hungry.

[21] Bennett, *op. cit.*

CONSUMPTION LEVELS AND THEIR TRENDS BY REGIONS

Want of space precludes us from giving the basic data on consumption levels country by country. Instead, we shall present the data in summary form. Table 2 shows the average *per caput* food supplies by major food groups and by regions and groups of regions. Group I comprises the low-calorie areas and includes the Far East, Near East, Africa, and Latin America, excluding the River Plate countries (Argentina, Uruguay, and Paraguay); Group II comprises the remainder. The table brings out the principal features of the diet in the different regions. It will be seen that the diet in Group I countries consists chiefly of cereals and starchy roots. These together amount to an average consumption of about 580 grams *per caput* per day. Group II countries, on the other hand, while consuming slightly more cereals and starchy roots than Group I countries, consume six times as large a quantity of animal products. This contrast is brought out in Table 3, which shows the calories derived from the different foods in the average diets of the different regions. The table shows that Group I countries consume around 2,150 calories *per caput* per day, with 78 per cent of the calories derived from cereals, starchy roots, and sugar. The food consumed by Group II countries provides about 3,050 calories *per caput* per day, the share of cereals, starchy roots, and sugar being 57 per cent. The contrast between the Group I and Group II countries is seen to be even more striking when a comparison is made of the levels of protein supplies by their sources. Thus, Group I countries consume about 9 grams of animal protein *per caput* per day, which is only one-fifth the consumption per head in Group II countries. The disparity in the fats supply levels is also large with a little

TABLE 2

CONSUMPTION LEVELS BY REGION

Item	Far East	Near East	Africa	Latin America	Europe	North America	Oceania	Group I[a]	Group II[b]	World
	(grams *per caput* per day at the retail level)									
Food groups:										
Cereals[1]	404	446	330	281	375	185	243	389	328	370
Starchy roots[2]	156	44	473	247	377	136	144	189	316	227
Sugar[3]	22	37	29	85	79	113	135	29	88	47
Pulses and nuts[4]	56	47	37	46	15	19	11	53	16	42
Vegetables and fruits[5]	128	398	215	313	316	516	386	169	362	227
Meat[6]	24	35	40	102	111	248	312	30	152	67
Eggs[7]	3	5	4	11	23	55	31	4	30	12
Fish[8]	27	12	16	18	38	26	22	24	34	27
Milk[9]	51	214	96	240	494	850	574	79	573	228
Fats and oils[10]	9	20	19	24	44	56	45	12	47	22
Calories[11]	2,070	2,470	2,360	2,470	3,040	3,120	3,250	2,150	3,060	2,420
Total proteins (grams)	56	76	61	67	88	93	94	58	90	68
Animal proteins (grams)	8	14	11	25	36	66	62	9	44	20
Fats (grams)	28	45	56	61	94	142	137	34	106	56

[a] Group I comprises the Far East, Near East, Africa, and Latin America, excluding River Plate countries.

[b] Group II comprises Europe, North America, Oceania, and the River Plate countries.

[1] In terms of flour and milled rice. [2] Includes sweet potatoes, cassava, and other edible roots. [3] Includes raw sugar; excludes syrups and honey. [4] Includes cocoabeans. [5] In terms of fresh equivalent. [6] Includes offal, poultry, and game expressed in terms of carcass weight, excluding slaughter fats. [7] Fresh egg equivalent. [8] Landed weight. [9] Excludes butter; includes milk products as fresh milk equivalent. [10] Pure fat content. [11] Rounded to the nearest ten.

over 30 grams *per caput* per day in Group I countries and over 100 grams *per caput* per day in Group II countries. It is probable that the disparity in the actual consumption of fats between the two regions is somewhat smaller than the supply figures indicate, owing to larger discards of animal fats during cooking and plate-wastage stages in Group II countries. But even so, the disparity must be considered very large.

Table 4 shows the composition of diets in terms of calories derived from carbohydrates, proteins, and fats. The share of calories that comes from proteins is seen to be remarkably steady between regions. That from fats is seen to increase from 12 per cent in the Far East to 25 per cent in Europe and 40 per cent in North America, while that from carbohydrates is seen to be the highest in the Far East, amounting to about 78 per cent, as compared with 65 per cent in Europe and 51 per cent in North America. The larger share of calories from fats in Europe and more particularly in North America and Oceania is due to the large consumption of animal products in these countries compared with that in the low-calorie countries.

Table 5 shows the trends in calorie and protein supplies for the prewar, the early postwar, and the recent periods covered in this study. It appears that the current level of calorie supplies has reached, and even

TABLE 3

COMPOSITION OF AVERAGE REGIONAL DIETS: CALORIES DERIVED FROM MAJOR FOOD GROUPS

(*Per caput* per day at the retail level)

Food Groups	Far East		Near East		Africa		Latin America		Europe	
	Calories	%	Calories	%	Calories	%	Calories	%	Calories	%
Cereals	1,428	69.2	1,574	63.7	1,185	50.2	995	40.2	1,335	43.9
Starchy roots	156	7.5	33	1.3	445	18.9	252	10.2	268	8.8
Sugar	78	3.8	157	6.4	112	4.8	323	13.0	300	9.9
Pulses and nuts	167	8.1	157	6.4	155	6.6	162	6.6	60	2.0
Vegetables and fruits	40	1.9	183	7.4	123	5.2	125	5.1	98	3.2
Meat	50	2.4	61	2.5	85	3.6	217	8.8	222	7.3
Eggs	5	0.2	7	0.3	6	0.3	16	0.6	33	1.1
Fish	20	1.0	8	0.3	8	0.3	12	0.5	28	0.9
Milk	43	2.1	120	4.9	70	3.0	161	6.5	321	10.6
Fats and oils	79	3.8	169	6.8	167	7.1	211	8.5	373	12.3
Total	2,070	100	2,470	100	2,360	100	2,470	100	3,040	100

Food Groups	North America		Oceania		Group I		Group II		World	
	Calories	%	Calories	%	Calories	%	Calories	%	Calories	%
Cereals	668	21.4	881	27.1	1,376	64.1	1,168	38.2	1,317	54.3
Starchy roots	97	3.1	105	3.2	186	8.7	227	7.4	198	8.2
Sugar	495	15.9	563	17.3	106	4.9	349	11.4	179	7.4
Pulses and nuts	75	2.4	51	1.6	167	7.8	62	2.0	135	5.6
Vegetables and fruits	181	5.8	130	4.0	65	3.0	118	3.9	81	3.3
Meat	570	18.2	690	21.2	62	2.9	322	10.5	140	5.8
Eggs	79	2.5	45	1.4	6	0.3	43	1.4	17	0.7
Fish	20	0.7	13	0.4	17	0.8	26	0.9	20	0.8
Milk	434	13.9	369	11.4	58	2.7	345	11.3	144	6.0
Fats and oils	497	16.0	402	12.4	103	4.8	399	13.0	192	7.9
Total	3,120	100	3,250	100	2,150	100	3,060	100	2,420	100

exceeded, the prewar level in all regions except the Far East where it is still somewhat lower than the prewar level. For the world as a whole the level of calorie supplies would appear to have just reached the prewar level. Total protein supplies for the world as a whole *per caput* per day have gone up since the early postwar period but have still not reached the prewar level. The gap remains particularly large in the Far East. Animal protein supplies for the world as a whole have exceeded the early postwar as well as the prewar level. This, however, is due to considerable increase in consumption in Europe and North America. On the other hand, the animal protein supplies for the underdeveloped regions have barely reached or are still below the prewar level.

UNDERNUTRITION

Table 6 compares region by region the existing levels of calorie supplies with the corresponding requirements, shown to the nearest 50. It shows that the calorie supplies for the Near East, Africa, and Latin America are about equal to their requirements, those for the Far East fall short of the requirements by about 10 per cent,

TABLE 4

PERCENTAGE OF CALORIE SUPPLIES FROM CARBOHYDRATES, PROTEIN, AND FAT IN AVERAGE REGIONAL DIETS

Region	Percentage of Calories from			
	Carbohydrates	Proteins	Fats	Total
Far East	78	10	12	100
Near East	74	11	15	100
Africa	71	9	20	100
Latin America	69	10	21	100
Europe	65	10	25	100
North America	51	10	39	100
Oceania	54	10	36	100
World	71	10	19	100

TABLE 5

AVERAGE SUPPLIES OF CALORIES, TOTAL PROTEINS, AND ANIMAL PROTEINS BY REGION

(*Per caput* per day at the retail level for prewar, early postwar, and recent periods)

Region	Calories			Total Proteins (Grams)			Animal Proteins (Grams)		
	Prewar	Early Postwar	Recent	Prewar	Early Postwar	Recent	Prewar	Early Postwar	Recent
Far East	2,170	1,910	2,070	63	54	56	8	6	8
Near East	2,320	2,190	2,470	76	70	76	15	14	14
Africa	2,180	2,100	2,360	61	61	61	15	15	11
Latin America	2,140	2,380	2,470	66	67	67	30	29	25
Europe	2,850	2,870	3,040	85	91	88	27	31	36
North America	3,140	3,120	3,120	89	90	93	50	60	66
Oceania	3,270	3,180	3,250	97	95	94	65	65	62
World	2,410	2,260	2,420	72	66	68	18	18	20

while those for Europe, North America, and Oceania are not only sufficient to meet their average needs but in fact exceed them by about 20 per cent.

Evidence of hunger.—These gaps between the supply and requirement levels need, however, to be interpreted with care, since within regions the calorie intake as well as the requirement varies considerably. For example, the apparent self-sufficiency of calorie supplies in the Near East is due to the high level of supplies in Turkey, Egypt, and Israel which account for about one-half the population in the region. The other countries in the region, which include Iran, Iraq, Saudi Arabia, and Jordan, and form a relatively poor stretch of area, have calorie supplies of only between 2,100 and 2,200 *per caput* per day. The same observation applies to the Far East where, for example, Japan and Taiwan are relatively much better fed than other countries in the region. Within-country variations are even larger. It is, however, beyond the scope of this paper to lay out the details of these variations within regions. Our main object in giving this table is to bring out the large variation in calorie supply between regions against the relatively small variation in calorie requirements. Thus, while admittedly the calorie needs of the people in the Group I countries are smaller than those of the people in Europe and North America, as wide a difference as 900–1,000 calories between the consumption levels of the two can hardly be justified on grounds of differences in age distribution, stature and climate. To accept such a low level on consumption for the underdeveloped countries is, in the words of Wright, to "condemn the underdeveloped countries to a permanent and possibly an increasingly serious state of undernutrition."[22]

TABLE 6

CURRENT LEVELS OF CALORIE SUPPLIES AND CALORIE REQUIREMENTS BY REGIONS

(*Per caput* per day at the retail level)

Region	Calorie Supplies[a]	Calorie Requirement	Calorie Supplies as % of Calorie Requirement
Far East	2,050	2,300	89
Near East	2,450	2,400	102
Africa	2,350	2,400	98
Latin America	2,450	2,400	102
Europe	3,000	2,600	115
North America	3,100	2,600	119
Oceania	3,250	2,600	125
Group I	2,150	2,300	93
Group II	3,050	2,600	117
World	2,400	2,400	100

[a] Rounded to the nearest 50.

In particular, the foregoing observation holds for the Far East, where we find a gap of 11 per cent between the average calorie supply and the requirement. We cannot overstress the significance of this gap. Considered in terms of total supplies the gap is seen to be large enough to feed the entire population of the Near East. The gap may either persist all through the year or be particularly felt in periods pre-

[22] N. C. Wright, "The Current Food Supply Situation in Present Trends," paper read at the 122d Annual Meeting of the British Association for the Advancement of Science (Cardiff, 1960).

ceding the harvests. Again, it may be shared by the majority of the population or fall heavily on the poorer sections. In actual fact, the privileged and well-to-do everywhere will eat all they need and perhaps more. The poor will take only what they can afford, which may not always fully meet their needs. This is well brought out in Table 7, which shows the level of calorie supply by level of expenditure for Maharashtra State, India. The survey was conducted in 1958 and covered the entire State with a population of about 40 million. The table gives the average total calorie supply and also the calorie supply derived from cereals which forms the cheapest source of energy for the low-income people and which, as such, as particularly relevant here. In the absence of data on requirements of the several expenditure groups, any such data need to be interpreted with caution as regards the proportion of people with inadequate food supplies, since the different expenditure (income) groups are not wholly comparable. As an example, a part of the increase in calorie supply with the increase in the level of expenditure may be due to a higher proportion of adults in the higher expenditure groups and/or to the additional activity which higher wage-earning groups may be required to undertake in a developing economy. The table shows that the calorie supply increases rather steeply with the increased level of expenditure in the lower expenditure classes, but the rate of increase diminishes in the higher expenditure groups until the calorie supply purchased more or less stabilizes itself. The point is further illustrated by similar data from the All-India surveys of agricultural labor.[23] These surveys showed that in practically every part of the country the consumption of food grains by families with lower consumer expenditure was considerably below the consumption by families with a somewhat higher consumer expenditure living side by side and doing similar work. It was clear that there are a large number of agricultural labor families in India who for want of income live on quantitatively inadequate diets and who thus remain underfed even in staple food grains.

TABLE 7

CALORIE SUPPLY BY EXPENDITURE LEVEL—MAHARASHTRA STATE, INDIA, 1958[a]

ITEM	MONTHLY PER CAPITA EXPENDITURE IN RS.							AVERAGE
	0–8	8–11	11–13	13–18	18–24	24–34	>34	
Total calories	1,120	1,560	1,850	2,190	2,440	2,530	3,340[b]	2,100
Calories derived from cereals	940	1,300	1,510	1,740	1,860	1,800	2,150	1,590

[a] I am indebted to Mr. M. A. Telang, Director of Statistics, Maharashtra, for these unpublished data collected in the course of the fourteenth round of the NSS India.

[b] This value appears unduly high. It is stated that this is partly due to the exclusion from the household size of guests and laborers taking meals.

By contrast, we find that in the developed countries like the U.K. and U.S.A. there is no insufficiency of food even in the poorest classes. Relevant data from nationwide consumer surveys for the U.K. and U.S.A. in 1955, shown in Table 8, support this statement. The tables show that calorie supply, while increasing with income, is not appreciably influenced by rising income on anything like the scale noticed in India. Further, the level of calorie supply even for the lowest-income

[23] India, Ministry of Labour, *Report on Intensive Survey of Agricultural Labour, Vol. I: All-India, 1950–51* (New Delhi, 1954); India, Ministry of Labour and Employment, *Agricultural Labour in India: Report on the Second Agricultural Labour Enquiry, Vol. I: All-India, 1956–57* (New Delhi, 1960).

groups in these countries is seen to be higher than the average requirement.

Incidence of hunger.—The foregoing analysis suggests that an appreciable part of the population in the low-calorie countries goes hungry at least part of their lives. It does not, however, make possible an estimate of this proportion for which we must turn to expression (1) above. The evaluation of this expression, however, presents a serious difficulty owing to lack of information on the frequency function $f(x, y)$. What are generally available are the calorie intake distributions of households on a consumer unit[24] ("reference" man) basis and information on the range of variation to be expected in calorie requirements of healthy adults of 20–30 years in the population typical of the reference man. In what follows we shall give an approximate expression for evaluating (1) using the above types of information and illustrate its use on the data from different countries.

The distribution of calorie intake among households on a consumer unit basis is of the form

$$g\left(\frac{CX}{R}\right),$$

where C is a constant representing the requirement of the reference man in the population; X is the total calorie intake per day of a household; and R is the corresponding total requirement based on age and sex for the activity level of the reference man. It can also be written as

$$g(\bar{X}),$$

where $\bar{X}$ is the intake per consumer unit of a household and R/C is the number of consumer units therein. This distribution corresponds to

$$f\left(C\frac{x}{y}\right),$$

TABLE 8

CALORIE SUPPLY BY INCOME LEVEL

	UNITED KINGDOM, 1955 — Weekly Income of Head of Household (£)				
	0–6	6–9	9–15	15–24	24 and Over
Calories *per caput* per day	2,627	2,676	2,635	2,657	2,675

	UNITED STATES, SPRING, 1955 — Household Disposable Income (Dollars/Year)								
	0–1,000	1,000–1,999	2,000–2,999	3,000–3,999	4,000–4,999	5,000–5,999	6,000–7,999	8,000–9,999	10,000 and Over
Calories *per caput* per day									
Urban	2,870	2,760	2,900	3,010	3,030	3,110	3,200	3,080	3,260
Rural non-farm	3,110	3,160	3,330	3,260	3,330	3,270	3,250	3,490	3,360
Rural farm	3,570	3,770	3,740	3,640	3,650	3,630	3,530	3,620	3,650

24 The term "consumer unit" in this paper is used to connote nutrition unit for calories. The calorie requirement of a consumer unit is that of a "reference" man, namely, a healthy active adult male of 20–30, adjusted for average national weight and environmental temperature.

derivable from (1), but differs from it in that it relates to households instead of individuals and, further, that R does not completely specify the total requirement Y for the household owing to the omission from it of the contribution due to physical activity. In fact, the calorie requirement of a household on a consumer unit basis can be written as

$$\bar{Y} = \frac{Y}{R/C} = C + P + E,$$

where P and E represent respectively the contributions of physical activity and of residual variables. If $\bar{Y}$ were known then the proportion of the households in which undernourishment exists would be given by

$$u = \int_{\bar{X}/\bar{Y}<1} g\left(\frac{C\bar{X}}{\bar{Y}}\right) d\left(\frac{C\bar{X}}{\bar{Y}}\right). \quad (3)$$

$\bar{Y}$ is, however, not known, but the range of variation in $\bar{Y}$ on a consumer unit basis is known. Further, the expected value of $\bar{Y}$ is equal to C. We may, therefore, assuming independence between $\bar{X}$ and $\bar{Y}$ for practical evaluation, replace (3) by

$$u' = \int g(\bar{X})\, d(\bar{X}), \quad (4)$$

the integral being evaluated over the range $\bar{X} < C - 3\sigma_{\bar{Y}}$, where $\sigma_{\bar{Y}}$ is the standard deviation of $\bar{Y}$ on a consumer unit basis and reflects the variation due to the component $P + E$ in Y. Ordinarily, in a healthy active population with no one underfed, one would expect, assuming normal distribution, no more than 1 per cent of the households to have calorie intake on a consumer unit basis below $C - 3\sigma_{\bar{Y}}$. Consequently, in any observed intake distribution the proportion of households with calorie intake per consumer unit falling below $C - 3\sigma_{\bar{Y}}$ can be considered to provide an estimate of the underfed in the population. In actual fact, the proportion of persons underfed may be larger than is obtained from (4), since one would a priori expect a positive correlation between intake and requirement. However, the degree of underestimation is likely to be small for all practical purposes since in (4) we are concerned with the correlation between $\bar{X}$ and $\bar{Y}$ after eliminating the effects on intake of age, sex, and weight. Although in a healthy active population of reference age, sex, and weight the intake is expected to be equal on the average to the energy expenditure, the available evidence indicates that the correlation between the two is small.[25]

An estimate of the standard deviation of energy expenditure among consumer units is needed for evaluating (4). We have no data from which to provide it since studies on the variation in energy expenditure in healthy adults of 20–30 years relate only to certain specified groups of the population. There are, however, the opinions of nutrition experts on the normal range of variation in energy expenditure based on these and related studies among people. Thus, according to the National Academy of Sciences[26] the usual upper level of energy expenditure for a man and woman at heavy work is about 20–25 per cent higher than the reference requirement, that is about 3,800–4,000 calories for a man and 2,800–2,900 calories for a woman. For sedentary people the respective figures are 2,500 and 1,800. FAO[27] likewise states that in most countries "the number of persons engaged in work calling for a calorie intake in excess of 4,000 daily (for example, groups of persons who are engaged in logging or digging coal) will be relative-

[25] O. G. Edholm, J. G. Fletcher, E. M. Widdowson, and R. A. McCance, "The Energy Expenditure and Food Intake of Individual Men," *British Journal of Nutrition,* IX, No. 3 (1955), 286–300; R. C. Garry, R. Passmore, G. M. Warnock, and J. V. G. A. Durnin, *Studies on Expenditure of Energy and Consumption of Food by Miners and Clerks, Fife, Scotland, 1952,* Special Report Series 289 (London: Medical Research Council, 1955).

[26] National Academy of Sciences, National Research Council, *Recommended Dietary Allowances,* Publication No. 302 (Washington: NAS-NRC, 1953).

[27] U.N., FAO, *Calorie Requirements, op. cit.*

ly small. At the other extreme, the number of truly sedentary people is not large. A range of daily expenditure requiring between 2,400–4,000 calories would appear to include most men. Many occupations which involve heavy work are brought within these ranges by virtue of seasonal fluctuations, as in agriculture, or because of the intermittent nature of the daily work as in numerous industrial operations in which voluntary and involuntary pauses for rest are frequent. Again, while recreation is a significant item in energy expenditure, there are few active sports or recreations which are pursued uniformly throughout the year." Assuming "most people" to mean 95 per cent and that the variation of energy expenditure among consumer units is normal, we may conclude that the standard deviation of the distribution of consumer units will be approximately 400 calories.

TABLE 9

DISTRIBUTION OF HOUSEHOLDS SURVEYED IN BURMA BY CALORIE SUPPLIES PER CONSUMER UNIT

Calories	% Frequency
Under 1,300	0.3
1,300	5.2
1,700	20.3
2,100	29.4
2,500	23.9
2,900	10.4
3,300	5.7
3,700	3.3
4,100	1.0
4,500	0.5
	100.0

We shall illustrate the method on data of a nationwide nutritional survey for Ceylon.[28] The survey was conducted during the period March 1948 to October 1949 and included 1,307 families distributed between the urban, rural, and estate populations more or less in proportion to the census figures for these populations. The sample, which was drawn by the Director of Census and Statistics, was an area sample, the areas chosen being representative of the different districts of the country.

The survey in each area covered 7 consecutive days. Homes were visited three times a day, and all foodstuffs consumed by the households were weighed on portable balances to the nearest quarter ounce. The foods were weighed before preparation and cooking and only the portions to be eaten were weighed. The sex and ages of all members of the household consuming food were noted, and in calculating the consumption units of the family, notice was taken of any absence from meals or the presence of any guests.

The survey gave an over-all average consumption of approximately 2,500 calories per consumer unit with a standard deviation of 1,200. The calorie requirement per consumer unit for Ceylon, on the other hand, assuming negligible waste of edible foods comes to 2,700 approximately. The standard deviation of the requirement of a reference man, as we saw in the preceding paragraphs, is 400 calories, so that its value for a household of 4 consumer units on consumer unit basis can be placed at 200. Consequently, assuming a normal distribution, we obtain for the proportion of households with calorie level below 2,100 (i.e., 2,700—[3 $\times$ 200]) per consumer unit a value of 0.37. In other words, we estimate the proportion of families undernourished in Ceylon during 1948–49 at a little over one-third.

Based on the results of this survey, Cullumbine estimates that the number of families with inadequate calorie intake was 45 per cent. The higher estimate of Cullumbine, apart from the difference in method, is due to the difference in calorie requirement, which he assumes at 2,200 calories per adult man and 2,500 for laborers.

We shall next illustrate the method on the data for Burma given in Table 9, based on diet surveys carried out in 369

[28] H. Cullumbine, "A National Sample Survey in Ceylon," *Ceylon Journal of Medical Science*, VIII, No. 1 (1951), 17–50.

households.[29] The survey was carried out in representative areas of the different districts, and within each selected area 20–30 households representing the population preponderant in the area were studied. The method was similar to that in Ceylon. The data were collected by trained volunteers of the locality who were well known to the families to be visited. The records of the quantity and kind of foodstuffs consumed were obtained by two daily visits at the time of preparation for cooking of the principal meals. Due allowance was made for meals taken by guests and for members absent from the household.

It can be seen from the table that in two-thirds of the surveyed households the calorie intake falls short of the requirement per consumer unit, which for Burma is approximately 2,700. This does not, however, mean that the population covered by two out of every three households is underfed, any more than the population covered *by* one out of every four households found to fall short of the corresponding requirement in the U.S.A.[30] can be considered as underfed: clearly some people will need less than the stipulated requirement, while others may need more, depending upon the extent to which the different individual factors. including physical activity, deviate from those of the reference man for Burma. Even if the distribution of intake were to have an average equal to the requirement, hunger might exist among large sections of the population if the variance of intake per consumer unit were larger than the variance of requirement of the reference man in the population. We have, therefore, to turn to expression (4) in order to estimate the proportion of people who go hungry.

As for Ceylon, the calorie requirement per consumer unit for Burma is 2,700 and σ_{P+E} can be placed at 200. The distribution in Table 9 shows that the proportion of households with intake below 2,100 calories is approximately 25 per cent so that, assuming the sample to be representative, we may conclude that the proportion of the population underfed in Burma during the year of the survey was roughly 0.25.

Our third illustration refers to pre-partition India. Table 10 gives the calorie intake distribution for 843 groups of households surveyed in pre-partition India over a 14-year period from 1935 to 1948 covering some 12,500 households.[31] The average number of households per group was 15. The data were collected by the actual weighing of foodstuffs during house-to-

TABLE 10

DISTRIBUTION OF 843 GROUPS OF HOUSEHOLDS SURVEYED IN PRE-PARTITION INDIA BY CALORIE SUPPLIES PER CONSUMER UNIT

Calories	% Frequency
Under 1,001	1.3
1,001	3.0
1,251	4.6
1,501	10.0
1,751	14.0
2,001	13.6
2,251	14.2
2,501	13.4
2,751	11.0
3,001	7.2
3,251	3.4
Over 3,500	4.3
	100.0

[29] U. M. Gale, *Reports on the Dietary and Nutritional Surveys Conducted in Certain Areas of Burma* (Rangoon: Supt. Govt. Printing & Stationery, 1948).

[30] U.S., Dept. of Agriculture, *Dietary Levels of Households in the United States,* Household Food Consumption Survey 1955, Report No. 6 (Washington: GPO, 1957).

[31] W. R. Aykroyd, *Note on the Results of Diet Surveys in India, Burma, and Ceylon* (Coonoor: Indian Research Fund Assn., 1948); Indian Council of Medical Research, *Results of Diet Surveys in India, 1935–48,* Special Report Series, No. 20 (New Delhi: ICMR, 1951); K. Mitra, *A Supplement to the Results of Diet Surveys in India, 1935–48,* Special Report Series, No. 20 (New Delhi: ICMR, 1953).

house visits by investigators over a continuous period varying from 7 to 21 days. The households selected for the surveys were drawn mostly from the low-income stratum of the population. The surveys were spread out fairly evenly through the different seasons of the individual years. For each household included in the survey the number of consumer units was determined. These surveys, which constitute a unique record of the dietary studies conducted in the country, have been extensively drawn upon by a number of authors and are believed to provide a reasonably reliable picture of the consumption levels of the low-income households. The average of the distribution works out to approximately 2,350 calories per consumer unit compared with the requirement, as seen from Table 1, of approximately 2,700 calories. Allowing for the size of the group and the intraclass correlation among consumer units of a group, it may be inferred that the distribution of requirement appropriate for interpreting Table 10 will have a standard deviation of approximately 100 calories. It would, therefore, appear that most groups of households in Table 10 will require to take more than 2,400 calories per consumer unit per day in order to meet their needs. In actual fact we find that about 55 per cent of the groups of households took less than 2,400 calories per consumer unit. One cannot but consider this to be real evidence of widespread hunger in the surveyed households. The latter, however, mainly included households from a low-income stratum of India, estimated at about two-fifths of India's population. There will undoubtedly be some households with inadequate calorie supplies in the middle-income groups of the country, but no estimates of the proportion of such households is available. It would appear, however, generalizing from the evidence furnished by Table 10, that about a quarter of India's households were underfed during 1935–48. This estimate is necessarily very rough owing to lack of information on the representative character of the households. It is interesting to note that the estimate is not appreciably different from one made by the Famine Enquiry Commission,[32] which concluded that even in normal times about 30 per cent of India's people go hungry.

It may be argued that the data on which this conclusion is based refer to the period 1935–48 and that the consumption levels have since probably improved. This, however, does not appear to be the case. Table 11 shows the average daily intake of foodstuffs per consumer unit as revealed by surveys conducted by the Indian Council of Medical Research (ICMR) during 1935–48 and those carried out during

TABLE 11

AVERAGE DAILY INTAKE OF FOODSTUFFS IN OUNCES PER CONSUMER UNIT AS REVEALED BY SURVEYS IN INDIA

Food Groups	1935–48	1955–58
Cereals	16.62	16.59
Pulses	2.26	2.39
Leafy vegetables	0.85	0.71
Other vegetables	4.10	3.20
Ghee and oils	0.92	0.52
Milk	3.31	2.81
Meat, fish, and eggs	0.94	0.47
Fruits (and nuts)	0.58	0.21
Sugar and jaggery	0.67	0.71

32 Famine Enquiry Commission, *Report on Bengal* (New Delhi, 1945).

1955–58. Although the families surveyed during 1955–58 were not the same as those surveyed in the earlier period, the two groups are stated to be broadly comparable and, further, each included a large number of families from different parts of the country.[33] The table shows that there has been no appreciable quantitative change in the diet of the people during the last 15 years. The estimate which we made in the previous paragraph regarding the proportion of the people who are hungry would thus seem to hold good even today.

There is a distinct paucity of data on calorie distributions for other underdeveloped countries. Such data as are available relate to limited sections of the population and are based on small samples. But their analysis leads to much the same conclusions as those for Ceylon, Burma, and India. It would obviously be rather bold to generalize on the basis of such limited evidence for pre-partition India (India and Pakistan), Burma, Ceylon, and other countries. We believe, however, that the conclusion which holds for the subregion comprising India, Pakistan, Ceylon, and Burma (which together account for one-third of the population in the Far East) will probably also hold with small differences for other countries in the region since, except for Japan and Taiwan, the calorie supply *per caput* in these other countries is of the same order as that for this subregion, and further, it falls short of the respective requirements.

However, the factor which is likely to make the biggest difference to the estimate of the proportion of the world's people who are hungry is the estimate for Mainland China. The food balance sheet for Mainland China for 1957–58 prepared in FAO shows that the calorie consumption level for this country is around 2,100 as against the consumption level of 1,950 for India and Pakistan. On the other hand, the requirement for Mainland China is also likely to be higher compared with that of India and Pakistan, in view of the more intensive use of labor in that country and lower environmental temperature. Even granting that conditions in Mainland China have improved substantially in the last 10 years, the obviously inflated estimates of agricultural production, presented in the *Ten Great Years*,[34] and the recent famine in the country suggesting a lack of reserves from the exceptionally good crops reported for the previous years, indicate that consumption in Mainland China has not yet reached a level where the existence of hunger on an appreciable scale even in normal times can be ruled out. Granted that the proportion of hungry in Mainland China is somewhat smaller than in the subregion comprising India, Pakistan, Burma, and Ceylon, it is nevertheless likely to be appreciable and possibly, in our view, to approach 20 per cent. Putting together this evidence, it would seem that about one-fifth of the population in the Far East and possibly more is undernourished. We have already seen that, though the over-all average calorie supply in other underdeveloped regions is about equal to the respective over-all requirements, there are a number of countries in these regions for which the average calorie supply falls considerably short of the corresponding requirement, indicating the existence of hunger. For the world as a whole the proportion of hungry would thus seem to be between 10 per cent and 15 per cent. In other words, we estimate that between 300 and 500 million people in the world are underfed.

It is interesting to use the foregoing approach to analyse the situation in the developed countries. Table 12 presents two calorie distributions on a consumer unit basis, one for rural families of the North Central region of the U.S.A., from the food

[33] C. G. Pandit and K. S. Rao, *Nutrition in India, 1946–58* (New Delhi: ICMR, 1960).

[34] People's Republic of China, State Statistical Bureau, *Ten Great Years* (Peking: Foreign Language Press, 1960).

consumption survey conducted in 1952,[35] and the other from a nationwide survey conducted in 1955; both were based on a recall method, using the week preceding the interview as the reference period. In a well-developed country one would expect most households to have sufficient calorie supplies. The calorie requirement per consumer unit for the United States at the retail level is approximately 3,500, and the standard error per household on the basis of its average size of 2.5 consumer units can be placed at approximately 300 calories per consumer unit. One would therefore expect most households to have calorie supplies exceeding 2,600 per consumer unit. The data shown in Table 12 accord with these expectations and show that the proportion of underfed or hungry in the United States is negligible. In a well-fed country, however, one would expect that not only would there be no one hungry but that the average intake would equal the average requirement and, further, that the variance of intake would also be equal to the variance of requirement. The data for the U.S.A. show that the calorie supply purchased per consumer unit exceeds the requirement at the retail level by 500, and, further, that the number of households exceeding the requirement plus three times the standard error per household on a consumer unit basis approximates to 30 per cent for the North Central region and indeed approaches 50 per cent for the nation as a whole. This would indicate that a large proportion of people in the States is overeating. It is of course possible that the requirement is underestimated. Some evidence in support of this hypothesis has been reported by Harries and Hollingsworth.[36] Alternatively, the intake may have been overestimated. Possibly all three situations exist.

TABLE 12

DISTRIBUTION OF HOUSEHOLDS BY CALORIE SUPPLIES PER CONSUMER UNIT PER DAY, UNITED STATES

CALORIES	NORTH CENTRAL REGION U.S. 1952[a]		U.S. 1955[b]			
	Rural Farm %	Rural Non-farm %	Rural Farm %	Rural Non-farm %	Urban %	Total %
Under 2,000	2	3				
2,000–2,499	3	6	5	10	14	12
2,500–2,999	12	14				
3,000–3,499	19	22	9	10	14	12
3,500–3,999	22	19	11	17	17	16
4,000–4,999	27	25	27	28	28	28
5,000–5,999	15	11	20	17	15	16
6,000 and over			27	17	13	16

Sources of data: [a] Orshansky *et al.* (1957).
[b] U.S. Department of Agriculture (1957).

EVIDENCE AGAINST HUNGER EXAMINED

In an earlier section we referred to the views of Farnsworth and Bennett. They suspect that calorie requirements for un-

[35] M. Orshansky, C. Lebovit, E. Blake, and M. Moss, *Food Consumption and Dietary Levels of Rural Families in the North Central Region, 1952,* Agric. Information Bull. No. 157 (Washington: USDA, 1957).

[36] J. M. Harries and D. F. Hollingsworth, "Food Supply, Body Weight, and Activity in Great Britain, 1943–49," *British Medical Journal,* I (1953), 75–78.

derdeveloped countries according to the FAO international scale are overestimated and the actual consumption levels seriously underestimated. We have already dealt with the former criticism. The evidence that consumption in underdeveloped countries is underestimated is mainly based on the results of the National Sample Survey (NSS) of India conducted in 1949–50.[37] Farnsworth states that "the official sample survey of Indian food grain consumption in 1949–50, supported by supplementary evidence, suggested that the population actually consumed during that period 20 to 27 per cent more domestic food grain than the official crop estimates indicated was available for consumption. Although similar survey information was not collected for other Indian foods, the probability (based on common experience elsewhere) is that the production of such subsidiary crops was underestimated by a still larger percentage."[38] On the basis of this reasoning, Farnsworth increases the Indian calorie level for 1953–55 from 1,850, which means serious undernourishment, to some 2,200 calories, thus demonstrating that there was no significant undernourishment during this period in India. This result is then generalized for other countries.

We have examined the NSS data on food consumption referred to by Farnsworth, and found that neither the supplementary evidence put forward in the NSS report nor the internal consistency of the reported data nor their method of collection was such as to inspire confidence in the accuracy of the report. The principal external evidence put forward in support of the NSS estimates of food consumption is the recomputed results of some selected diet surveys conducted during 1935–48 referred to by Aykroyd and Mitra. When, however, the estimates from the two sources are examined region by region, they bring out such serious divergencies between the two that comparison of the combined estimates in order to establish agreement seems wholly unjustified.[39] Other external evidence consists in comparing the National Income Committee (NIC) estimate of *per caput* consumer expenditure, namely, Rs. 265, with the NSS estimate of Rs. 220, which is stated to be not inconsistent with the former! In actual fact, the NIC estimate has been worked out on the basis of the *available* official statistics for 1948–49 which the NSS seeks to prove are too low for agricultural production. The only worthwhile evidence which the NSS report mentions in support of the accuracy of the data is that of the crop survey estimate in Bengal, but even here the gross production as estimated from the direct crop survey has been confused with the net production available for consumption.

Turning to the internal evidence for consistency of data, we wish to recall that the NSS sought to estimate not only consumption but also production of food crops. The NSS estimate of the latter was 39 million tons, while the estimate of production of food grains derived from its consumption estimates came to 60 million tons. The NSS report dismisses the former as being a gross underestimate without giving any reasons as to why there should be such grossly inconsistent estimates of the same entities based on the same survey. In actual fact, the divergence between the estimate of production and that of production derived from consumption would be larger since the NSS estimate of production derived from consumption suffers by the omission from it of the allowances for seed and feed requirements and normal postharvest losses. If one were to allow for these at the customary rate of 12.5 per cent used in India, the NSS estimate of production derived from consumption would be of the order of some 69 million tons, against the official estimate of only

[37] India, Ministry of Finance, *The National Sample Survey, General Report No. I on the First Round, Oct. 1950–Mar. 1951* (Calcutta, 1952).

[38] Farnsworth, *op. cit.*

[39] V. M. Dandekar, "On the National Sample Survey Estimates of Consumption of Food Grains in India," *Indian Economic Journal,* I, No. 2 (1953), 153–65.

49 million tons and the NSS's own estimate of production of only 39 million tons. In other words, the level of calorie supplies per person per day in India would be of the order of some 2,400 calories. It is hard to believe that India is the best-fed country in the Far East, which it would be if one were to accept the NSS estimate of consumption.

In view of some of the techniques used, it is perhaps not surprising that the NSS should have overestimated consumption. Not only was the period of reference too long, namely a year, but in most cases it was far removed from the time of the enquiry. The questions for such a long period of enquiry were also worded in such a way that the respondent could not proceed to answer them by recalling all the factual items and adding them together; the answer was more probably some plausible whole figure, sometimes perhaps suggested by the investigator. Possibly, the investigator himself sought a plausible weekly or monthly figure which by suitable multiplication was converted into an annual figure. Moreover, there was a circumstance, namely the compulsory procurement of surplus food grains from the cultivators, which in all probability induced them to overstate their requirements of food grains. To quote Dandekar, "it seems therefore altogether inappropriate to check the production estimates of food grains against such consumption estimates."[40]

As for incomplete coverage and methodology, it should be recalled that Indian estimates have been adjusted for growing coverage and based on objective methods of crop sampling since the war. Farnsworth refers to the use of a low value of R for the extraction rate from paddy to rice. We are inclined to agree with Farnsworth that the extraction rate used in India, namely 0.67, is perhaps a little on the low side. However, there are other counterbalancing losses which also merit consideration, such as losses in storage under humid and poor conditions in mills and warehouses, which are estimated at a much higher figure than is allowed for in the food balance sheet for India. To conclude: while there certainly exists considerable scope for further improvement in the estimate of calorie supplies for India and other underdeveloped countries, we cannot agree that the calorie supplies are grossly underestimated, as Farnsworth believes, on the basis of NSS data on food consumption for 1949–50.

There have been a number of food consumption surveys conducted by the NSS since 1949–50, but their results have been reported in terms of expenditures and not quantities.[41] The only NSS data for which quantities are reported are those for the State of Maharashtra for the year 1958 shown in Table 7. These data, as we saw, give an average calorie supply at retail level of 2,100. One can only hope that these data from other rounds of the NSS will be made available soon. In the meantime, it is encouraging to note that the methodology used by NSS in its surveys since 1949–50 has undergone a considerable change for the better. Thus, whereas the reference period in 1949–50 was twelve months, it is now one month and even less in some of the enquiries. This in itself may not suffice to eliminate the bias to which we have referred above, because consumption of food grains, especially in the rural areas, comprises largely the consumption of home-grown food grains and this is not an accountable operation such as, for example, the purchase of food grains. It is for this reason that any enquiry into consumption of food grains in the rural areas needs to be supplemented by a sample enquiry which provides for the measurement of the quantities used for consumption by the investigator entering the kitchen, as was done in the case of the numerous dietary surveys conducted by ICMR during 1935–48.

[40] *Ibid.*

[41] K. N. Raj, "Some Features of the Economic Growth of the Last Decade in India," *Economic Weekly Annual* (Bombay, 1961), pp. 253–71.

MALNUTRITION

Malnutrition refers to inadequacy in the quality of the diet. Unlike the quantitative aspect of diet, however, quality cannot be measured in terms of a single nutrient, as proteins, vitamins, and minerals must all be taken into account. But while a single nutrient cannot properly reflect nutritional quality, the protein content deserves special attention not only because protein is one of the most important nutrients but also because most foods rich in protein are also very good sources of many other essential nutrients. This is particularly true of proteins of animal origin which more closely resemble those constituting the human tissues and are therefore readily assimilable. The value of milk proteins to children in the post-weaning years is especially great in this context. Therefore, the animal protein content is probably an even more significant indicator of nutritional quality than the total protein content.

We have already drawn attention to the wide gap between the quality of diets in the low-calorie countries and in the developed countries as indicated by the animal protein content of the respective diets. As an example, Table 2 shows that the average animal protein content of the diet in the Far East is only 8 grams *per caput* per day, against a figure of 36 grams for Europe and 66 for North America. Whether so high an intake as 66 grams *per caput* per day is nutritionally desirable is a matter of some difference of opinion among the experts. We have, however, a considerable body of indirect evidence which suggests that the existing low levels of animal proteins in the diets of the low-calorie countries are seriously inadequate. One example of this evidence would be to show, side by side, the composition of diets, say 50 or 100 years back, for countries which have made substantial progress and compare it with the composition of diets in countries of the Far East today. Table 13 presents such data for France, U.K., and India.

TABLE 13

TREND IN THE COMPOSITION OF DIETS IN SELECTED COUNTRIES

(kg/*per caput* per year)

	France[a] 1840	U.K.[b] 1880	France 1954/55—1956/57	U.K. 1954/55—1956/57	India 1954/55—1956/57
Cereals	271	137[c]	111	88	130
Starchy roots	234	134	129	98	11[d]
Meat	20	41	69	68	2 (Meat and Eggs)
Eggs	....	5	10	12	
Liquid milk	....	97	89	149	40

Sources of data:

[a] Cépède and Lengellé (1953).

[b] Drummond and Wilbraham (1958).

[c] Estimated from the known figures for wheat flour in 1880 (127) and the ratio o other cereals to wheat flour in other years.

[d] Including cassava and sweet potatoes.

The data for France for 1840 are obviously suspect, since the three items in the table would alone provide a calorie supply of over 3,000 per person. The source mentioned for these statistics would indicate that they probably refer to production per person rather than consumption. Even so, the data are indicative of the tremendous shift which has taken place in the dietary habits of France, with heavy emphasis on meat and possibly other animal products, compared with that on cereals in 1840. The same is true of the U.K. By contrast, the intake of animal products including milk, in India, even today is much below the level in 1880 in the U.K. and, as far as is comparable, also the level in 1840 in

France. While admittedly there are climatic and other differences between France, the U.K., and India, these differences in diet are significant in the light of the improvements in health which have taken place in these countries during the last 50 years or so; for example, expectation of life in France has increased from 47 years in 1900 to 66 years in 1950, in the U.K. it has increased from 54 in 1910 to 70 in 1956, while the corresponding improvement in India, though impressive, still does not bring expectation of life there to more than 38 years. Infant mortality in India is 100 against 33 in France and 23 in England and Wales. We have no comparable statistics of morbidity, but unquestionably an Indian has much less resistance to diseases than the average person in France or the U.K., owing largely to the very low intake of protective foods. What is true of India vis-à-vis France and the U.K. is true of the Far East, Africa and the Near East vis-à-vis Europe and North America. Although part of this improvement is undoubtedly due to general advances in medicine and sanitary control, there is general agreement that the improvement in the composition of diet in more developed countries over the last few decades has contributed materially to the decrease in mortality rates, increase in longevity, and greater resistance to diseases. The striking improvement in the physical condition of the people of Japan since the war and the simultaneous improvement in the quality of their diet through larger intake of protective foods provide another example of such evidence.

TABLE 14

INFLUENCE OF DIET ON THE WORKING EFFICIENCY IN COSTA RICA

Year	Cubic Meters of Stone Moved per Worker
1943	240
1944	338
1945	1,025
1946	1,157

An excellent example of the influence of diet on the work output of man is reported from Costa Rica.[42] While an average Costa Rican has apparently sufficient calories to eat, it was found that the Costa Rican worker lacked the stamina and working efficiency as measured by his capacity to carry stones for building the highway. The figures in Table 14 show a great increase in carrying capacity between 1943 and 1946. Although part of the increase was due to training, the principal share was stated to be due to the change in workers' diets which provided for a large intake of protective foods based on the experience in the United States.

Evidence of malnutrition due to deficiencies of nutrients is furnished by numerous dietary and clinical studies reported from different parts of the world. As an example, *kwashiorkor* is widely prevalent in Africa, especially among children, and there are a host of other diseases, such as beriberi, A-vitaminosis, and anemia directly ascribed to or aggravated by the shortage of protective foods. Claims have been made that almost all children in the areas surveyed in Africa suffered for a period of from 1 to 5 years from serious protein malnutrition, which retarded their growth and adversely influenced their body build, activity and duration of life. We shall not, however, list here the evidence of these reports as they are too numerous, limited in scope and coverage, and somewhat technical for numerical appraisal in this paper.

It will be clear from the foregoing that there exists a large mass of evidence suggestive of serious and widespread malnutrition in the low-calorie countries. In the absence of agreed standards of nutritional quality, however, the incidence of malnutrition in the population cannot be esti-

42 N. Stearns, "The Road That Food Built," *Harper's Magazine* (1950), pp. 9–16.

mated. The most that can be done is to estimate its incidence by reference to the nutritional quality of diets in the developed countries using appropriate indicators for the purpose.

The indicator we propose is the one used in the *Second World Food Survey,* namely, the proportion of total calories derived from cereals, starchy roots, and sugar. It is by no means a fully satisfactory indicator of the quality of diet. For example, in countries where starchy roots are preponderant in the diet the incidence of malnutrition is likely to be larger than where cereals make a major contribution to the calories in the diet. Nevertheless, it is one of the best available indicators of the quality of diet and has been so recommended by the ECOSOC Committee on Levels of Living. A ratio exceeding two-thirds for this indicator was taken as clear evidence of serious malnutrition, but no attempt was made to estimate the proportion of people suffering from malnutrition.

Table 15 shows that this indicator, like the animal protein content, varies over a wide range between countries and regions. Household surveys further indicate that the standard deviation of this indicator per household, in countries with a moderate value, such as the U.K. and France, is of the order of 0.10. This means that at most 10 per cent of the households in the U.K. would exceed 0.80. Food consumption survey data for Maharashtra, collected in the fourteenth round of the NSS, India, show that 60 per cent of the households exceed this value. If one were to accept the U.K. as providing a standard of nutritional quality of diet to which less-developed countries would seek to raise the level of the quality of their diets, then by reference to the U.K. one might say that over 60 per cent of the people in Maharashtra are malnourished. We must stress again that any estimate of this nature suffers from two limitations: first, the estimate will depend on the indicator chosen to describe the nutritional quality of the diet, and second, it will vary with the standard chosen.

TABLE 15

Percentage of Calories Derived from Cereals, Starch Roots, and Sugar in Selected Countries and by Region

Far East Country	%	Near East Country	%	Africa Country	%	Latin America Country	%
China Mainland	83	Egypt	77	Morocco	75	Argentina	51
India	76	Turkey	75	Nigeria	74	Mexico	72
Region	80	Region	72	Region	74	Region	64

Europe Country	%	North America Country	%	Oceania Country	%
Germany, W.	50	Canada	43	Australia	49
United Kingdom	48	U.S.A.	40	New Zealand	43
Region	63	Region	40	Region	48

To sum up, we have seen that 10 per cent to 15 per cent of the world's population are undernourished. We cannot give a corresponding figure to describe the incidence of malnutrition, but the available evidence such as we have presented indicates that the incidence of malnutrition is far higher. If conditions in India are any indication of the extent of malnutrition in other low-calorie countries, which we believe they are—insofar as this can be judged by the values of the indicator shown in Table 15, and by the evidence of numerous small-scale experiments on social feeding with better diets reported from different parts of the world, showing increased working efficiency and improved health and vigor—the incidence of malnutrition in the low-calorie countries relative to the U.K. and France can be placed at well over 50 per cent. Experience shows that the majority of the undernourished are also malnourished. We believe, therefore, that we shall not be far from the truth if we say that relative to the nutritional standards enjoyed by the people of the U.K. and France and relative to the actual calorie requirements of the countries based on the FAO international scale, between one-third to one-half of the world's people suffer from undernutrition or malnutrition.[43]

Part II. The World's Future Needs in Food Supplies

THE OBJECT

In this part we shall attempt to estimate the amount of foods needed for the world's growing population so as to make good within a foreseeable future the deficiencies in the quantity and quality of diets brought out in Part I of the paper. Our objective, therefore, will be to estimate what ought to be achieved to insure reasonably adequate nutrition rather than to work out projections of future demands for foods based on present income elasticities and trends in population and income. In doing so, however, we shall take care to insure that the suggested increases in food supplies are realistic from the economic and production points of view, although we are aware that any such program will necessarily call for appropriate planning and policy measures to implement it.

Estimates of the world's future needs in food supplies have been made previously.[44] These, however, differ widely from each other because of differences in nutritional concepts and methodology. As they have no direct bearing on the approach we propose to follow here, we shall not refer to them any further.

NUTRITIONAL TARGETS

The formulation of quantitative nutritional goals to which the existing consumption levels are sought to be raised constitutes the first step in computing future needs in food supplies. The guiding principles in formulating these goals are clearly:

1. To insure quantitative adequacy.
2. To improve the quality of the diet by increasing the intake of protective foods, especially of animal origin.

The first requires that we should so formulate the calorie target as to make good the calorie shortage in the low-calorie countries. In reality, it implies that we ought to aim at calorie supply levels which are at least as high as the national requirements and preferably higher, so as to allow for unequal distribution of calories among the population and for additional needs in a developing economy. Further, calorie requirements must be looked at from a dynamic rather than a static aspect; otherwise, as Wright observed, "man will find himself in a vicious circle of poverty leading to low food intake; low food intake leading to reduced body weight and low levels of activity; low levels of activity leading to decreased productivity; and decreased productivity leading to still greater poverty."[45] While the national average calorie requirements based on the existing values of the determining factors would thus form the lower limit for the calorie target in any immediate or medium-term approach to improve the level of nutrition in the low-calorie countries, we visualize a higher level for the calorie target as a long-term objective, as specified in Table 16.

[43] Sen, *op. cit.*

[44] U.N., FAO (1946, 1952), *op. cit.*

[45] Wright, *op. cit.*

As for quality, we shall aim at targets approaching the level enjoyed by the developed countries insofar as this is feasible and advisable under the conditions of the low calorie countries. If animal protein is taken to indicate the quality of diet, then raising it by even a moderate amount would imply increasing several-fold the *per caput* availability of animal products in the low-calorie countries. Furthermore, animal products are much more costly compared with products of vegetable origin so that, even if it were possible to produce the needed supplies, most people in the low-calorie countries might not be able to afford them, at any rate in the near future.

For these reasons, and also because the value of animal proteins at the high-intake level in the developed countries has been somewhat underemphasized in recent years, we shall aim at only a moderate level of animal proteins as our long-term objective and approach it in gradual steps consistent with the capacity of the people to absorb the additional supplies. Accordingly, we have proposed targets for animal proteins at three levels: low, medium, and high. The low or immediate target is one in which we seek only a modest increase of an order of some 3 grams of animal proteins *per caput* per day and which one may expect to achieve over, say, a 10-year period. The medium or intermediate target is one which seeks to raise the existing level of animal proteins by some 7 to 8 grams a day and which can be achieved over a period of some 20 years from now. The high or long-term target is one which aims at raising the animal protein content by some 12 grams *per caput* per day and which we may view as a long-term plan for the countries to aim at by the turn of the century. We should add that, although we call it a high target, it aims at raising the existing level of 9 grams of animal protein in low-calorie countries to a level of only 20 grams a day, against a level of 44 now enjoyed by the developed countries. The precise year by which one might expect to achieve the different targets would clearly depend upon the planned rate of growth of economic development and the increase made possible as a result in the purchasing power of the people.

TABLE 16

TARGETS FOR CALORIES AND ANIMAL PROTEINS BY REGIONS

	Calories (*per caput* per day)	Animal Proteins (grams *per caput* per day)
Far East:		
Low target	2,300	10
Medium target	2,300	15
High target	2,400	20
Near East	2,470	20
Africa:		
Low target	2,400	15
High target	2,450	20
Latin America (excluding River Plate countries)	2,400	20

Ordinarily, one would aim at achieving quantitative adequacy first and only then at an improvement in the quality of diet. When, however, the quantitative inadequacy is small, however widespread, and the major deficiency in the diet is the lack of nutritional balance, as we saw to be the case with the population of the low-calorie countries, nutritional targets, even of short-term type, should in our view be so formulated as to aim at an improvement, however small, in the quality of the diet, simultaneously with an increase in calorie supplies. If this were not done, the diets would be even more unbalanced than they are now. Accordingly, we shall aim in the short-term target at achieving not only a calorie supply level equal to the national average calorie requirement but also a modest improvement in quality. In the medium or intermediate target we shall mainly emphasize improvement in the quality of diet, while in the long-term target we shall provide for further increases in calorie supply as well as in animal protein levels.

Targets, to be realistic, ought to be defined in relation to the existing levels for each country or socioeconomic group within it. We feel, however, that such targets are best drawn by the countries themselves in the light of first-hand knowledge of the patterns of consumption and the resources available in the countries. Our purpose in this paper is only to give a broad idea of the order of change in food supplies needed to raise the world's level of nutrition. This will be amply served by specifying targets for regions as a whole. It does not mean that we are aiming at a uniform degree of nutritional adequacy in all countries within a region. Indeed, we are aware that in using regional targets we shall be concealing the differences between and within countries and that, in consequence, we shall be considerably underestimating the world's future needs.

The different targets for calories and animal proteins region by region which we propose are given in Table 16. We have not proposed any explicit targets for vegetable proteins. Instead, we shall postulate that the total proteins are to be in no case less than the existing supplies. For the well-fed countries, no changes are proposed in the existing levels of supplies of calories and proteins.

METHOD OF TRANSLATING NUTRITIONAL TARGETS IN TERMS OF FOOD

There exists no unique solution in terms of quantities of different foods (or groups thereof) to satisfy the nutritional targets, since there are ten different food groups for which we seek a solution while the nutrients for which the targets are drawn up number only three. Certain additional conditions need therefore to be imposed. The condition which seems to us reasonable in the context of the close relationship between hunger and poverty is that, while meeting the nutritional targets, the total foods should cost the least to the consumer. This condition reduces the problem of computing quantities to one of linear programming and hence provides a unique solution.

Let

- x_j denote the quantity *per caput* of food j (net) to be computed ($j = 1, 2, \ldots, 10$);
- c_j denote the relative cost to the consumer of the jth food ($j = 1, 2, \ldots, 10$);
- b_1, b_2, b_3 denote the targets for calories, animal proteins, and total proteins, respectively; and
- a_{1j}, a_{2j}, a_{3j} denote the number of calories, and the number of grams of animal proteins, and vegetable proteins, respectively, in the unit quantity of the jth food (net), ($j = 1, 2, \ldots, 10$).

We then have

$$\sum_j a_{1j} x_j \geq b_1 ,$$

$$\sum_j a_{2j} x_j \geq b_2 ,$$

$$\sum_j (a_{2j} + a_{3j}) x_j \geq b_3 ,$$

subject to the condition that

$$\sum_j c_j x_j$$

is minimum.

Table 16 gives relevant data for b_1 and b_2, while those for b_3 can be found in Table 1. As regards the values for a_{1j}, a_{2j}, and a_{3j} we have drawn upon the FAO Food

Composition Tables. Data on relative costs to the consumer of the different food groups are not readily available, but the related data on regional producer prices for the period 1952–56 expressed in the form of wheat price relatives are known.[46] We have used these data for the purposes of this paper. It is a well-known fact that the solution of the problem as formulated above can yield positive values for at most three food groups, which is unrealistic both from the nutritional and production points of view. One of the basic points to be taken into account in computing the quantities of food groups is clearly to insure that no large changes are introduced into the existing dietary pattern of the people, at any rate not in the immediate future. Likewise, the computed changes should be feasible of achievement and within economic reach of the people within a reasonable period of time. A starting point for any solution must therefore be the existing levels of supplies for the different food groups, modified where necessary, so as to satisfy these basic criteria. These modifications in fact constitute the additional restraints necessary to obtain a realistic solution. As an example, it is conceivable that the target for animal proteins for the Far East could be met by an increase in the supplies of fish alone, which in this region is the cheapest source of animal proteins. An upper limit on the quantity target for fish consistent with the production feasibility and dietary pattern is therefore clearly called for. Likewise, the calorie target and the vegetable proteins target could be met by increases in the supplies of cereals and pulses alone, entirely to the exclusion of fruits and vegetables and other food groups of vegetable origin. Any such solution, while achieving the nutritional targets at the cheapest cost to the consumer, will normally be unacceptable to people since the consumption *per caput* of cereals in the low-calorie countries is already as large as, or even larger than, in the well-fed countries, and to increase it further when the calorie shortage is marginal in character would only add to the lack of balance in diet. For this reason it is necessary to put appropriate upper limits on the *per caput* supplies in cereals which may vary with the level of the target. Furthermore, within the groups of plant and animal products it is necessary to place lower limits which are above the existing levels on some of the relatively costly products. Fruits and vegetables, for example, are the most costly source of calories and proteins among the plant products, but they alone can provide many of the vitamins and minerals essential for good nutrition. Or, again, eggs are by far the most costly source of calories and animal proteins among animal products. Unless appropriate lower limits, higher than the existing supplies but consistent with what the consumer can afford and with what is agriculturally feasible, are placed on those food groups, we cannot provide for the desirable share thereof in the diets of the people. Much the same reasoning applies to the food supplies in fats, which are one of the costliest items in the diet but which nevertheless are needed to improve the palatability and acceptability of diets.

Such are the considerations which have led us to formulate additional restraints in the form of lower limits for certain food groups and upper limits for others in order to make the solutions realistic from the nutritional, economic and production points of view. These solutions for the quantity targets on a *per caput* basis for the different food groups are shown in Table 17. The existing levels of supplies are also shown. The table also gives the resulting total values for vegetable proteins and animal proteins. In the last row of the table we give the index of *per caput* food required, based on the price weights as specified above.

IMPLICATIONS OF POPULATION GROWTH

The calculations given in Table 17 show only the changes needed to improve

[46] U.N., FAO, *Manual of Index Numbers of Agricultural Production* (Rome, 1960).

the present diet to higher levels of nutrition. They do not reflect the increases required to meet the needs of the growing population. In calculating the total food supplies for future years we shall use population projections based on the "medium" assumption as prepared by the UN[47] which in its study has taken into account the relevant factors influencing population growth. These population projections for the different regions and the world as a whole are shown in Table 18 for the successive decades up to the year 2000. They show that for areas covered by the Group II countries, which are already enjoying adequate levels of nutrition, the population is expected to increase moderately, reaching one and a half times its present size by the turn of the century. For the undernourished Group I countries, however, the population is expected to grow faster. Thus, the population is expected to be doubled in Africa, trebled in Latin America, and to grow to two and a half times its present size in the Far East and the Near East by the turn of the century. For the world as a whole, the population is expected to have more than doubled by the year 2000. These expectations imply that even at the present level of diet the food supplies would have to be increased by 100 per cent for Africa, 200 per cent for Latin America excluding the River Plate coun-

[47] U.N., *The Future Growth of Population,* Population Studies No. 28 (New York, 1958).

TABLE 17

"PER CAPUT" QUANTITIES OF MAJOR FOOD GROUPS REQUIRED TO MEET NUTRITIONAL TARGETS AS COMPARED WITH EXISTING LEVELS OF SUPPLIES, WITH THE CALORIE AND PROTEIN LEVEL

Item	Food Supplies (grams per day)										
	Far East				Near East		Latin America (Excluding River Plate Countries)		Africa		
	Available	Required: Short-term Target	Required: Intermediate Target	Required: Long-term Target	Available	Required	Available	Required	Available	Required: Short-term Target	Required: Long-term Target
Cereals	404	429	384	368	446	401	281	281	330	330	330
Starchy roots	156	156	156	156	44	44	241	241	473	426	355
Sugar	22	25	29	33	37	44	84	84	29	32	35
Pulses and nuts	56	73	82	92	47	47	52	52	37	37	37
Vegetables and fruits	128	192	256	307	398	398	313	313	214	214	214
Meat	24	30	42	60	35	53	67	74	40	56	72
Eggs	3	4	6	8	5	10	9	10	4	6	8
Fish	27	38	54	74	12	15	20	21	16	20	24
Milk	51	73	119	137	214	307	204	216	96	143	203
Fats and oils	9	12	15	18	20	25	21	23	19	22	23
Total calories	2,070	2,300	2,300	2,400	2,470	2,470	2,370	2,410	2,360	2,420	2,460
Vegetable proteins (grams per day)	48	55	54	55	62	57	42	42	50	49	48
Animal proteins (grams per day)	8	10	15	20	14	20	19	20	11	15	20
Over-all index of food required	100	120	141	167	100	117	100	105	100	114	128

tries, and 150 per cent for the Far East and the Near East by the year 2000. In other words, the food supplies would have to be increased by about 150 per cent in the low-calorie countries and by some 120 per cent in the world as a whole, in order to cover the increases in population alone without improvement in the present level of nutrition. Clearly, much larger food supplies would be needed if, in addition to providing for the increases in population, allowance is to be made for improving the present level of nutrition. Estimates of the index of the needs in total food supplies are obtained by multiplying the index for the population growth shown in Table 18 by the index of the *per caput* quantities needed to achieve the different nutritional targets given in Table 17. The results are shown in Table 19 for the different regions. Estimates so obtained do not take into account changes due to shifts in the age and sex composition of the population. In actual fact, with the improvement in diet and better control of health and sanitary conditions, mortality rates are likely to decline. In addition, fertility rates may also undergo changes. We have analysed the effects, on the average *per caput* requirement of the population, of the shifts in the sex and age composition due to changes in these factors as projected by UN for Burma and South Viet Nam for 1980.[48] The results are shown in Table 20. It will be seen that the effect of the shift in the age and sex composition of the population on calorie requirements is a small decrease. However, this might be offset by gain in weight and higher protein requirements should the diet be improved in the meantime.

DISCUSSION OF RESULTS

Far East.—Table 17 shows that the increases in food supplies *per caput* needed to meet the low target for the Far East are some 5 per cent in cereals, 30 per cent in pulses, 50 per cent in fruits and vegetables, 30 per cent in meat, eggs, and fish, and 40 per cent in milk. Although the changes needed in cereals and pulses together are small relative to those in animal products, they account for the major share in meeting the calorie shortage. This is in line with the basic aim of minimizing the additional cost to the consumer. Even so, as the table shows, the change needed in animal products is substantial, amounting to a little over 40 per cent in keeping with their importance in improving the quality of diet. The large increase in fruits and vegetables also enriches the diet by providing an increased supply of minerals and vitamins.

Interpreted in terms of future needs, the low target implies that for every 100 million increase in population, the Far East will need to provide a total of some 16 million tons of additional cereals, 3 million tons of additional pulses, 7 million tons of additional fruits and vegetables, 3 million tons of additional meat, eggs, and fish, and 3 million tons of additional milk. Assuming that the period needed for the realization of the low target is 10 years, Tables 17 and 18 together show that the total food supplies in the Far East would have to be increased by some 30 per cent in cereals, 60 per cent in pulses, 90 per cent in fruits and vegetables, and over 70 per cent in animal products. This works out roughly to an annual over-all[49] increase over the 10 years at a simple rate of 5 per cent in total food supplies and 2 per cent in *per caput* food supplies.

The trend of *per caput* over-all supplies over the last 10 years for countries in the Far East is known to be of the order of 1 per cent.[50] It is evident, therefore, that the

48 U.N., *Future Population Estimates by Sex and Age: Population Report III. The Population of SE Asia (Including Ceylon and China: Taiwan), 1950–80,* Population Studies No. 30 (New York, 1958).

49 Here, and in what follows, the over-all changes are measured by the index of food supplies with quantities weighted by relative producer prices (1952–56).

50 U.N., FAO, *State of Food and Agriculture* (Rome, 1960).

present rate is wholly inadequate to meet the minimum nutritional needs of the population in the Far East by 1970 and that much bigger efforts would be needed over the next 10 years to achieve them. On the other hand, any attempt to push up the rate of increase in *per caput* availability of food supplies must be accompanied by a proportionate effort to increase the purchasing power of the people so that they may absorb the additional *per caput* availability of foods. If, therefore, one were to aim at attaining the minimum nutritional needs by 1970, the economic development plans would have to provide for an adequate increase in *per caput* income which, with the known income elasticity for foods, would approach the rate of increase in *per caput* food availability of 2 per cent. The Third Five-Year Plan of India provides for a planned increase of this order and shows that the growth rate suggested by us is not unreasonable to aim at under the conditions prevailing in underdeveloped countries. To the extent that such a growth rate cannot be achieved, the attainment of the nutritional target would necessarily be delayed.

The medium or intermediate target calls for larger changes in *per caput* food supplies. They range from a decrease over the present *per caput* level of some 5 per cent in cereals to an increase of some 50 per cent in pulses, 100 per cent in fruits and vegetables, 90 per cent in meat, eggs, and fish, and 135 per cent in milk. When the quantity targets for the medium level are compared with those for the low level, the changes are found to range from some 4 per cent increase in plant products (excluding vegetable fats) to 50 per cent increase in animal products. These changes clearly bring out the emphasis placed on the improvement in the quality of diet as we pass from the low to the medium target. Interpreted in terms of future needs the medium target implies a provision of some 33 million tons of plant products, in place of 28 million now available, and some 8 million tons of animal products, in place of 4 million now available, for every 100 million population of the future.

The medium level represents what may be called a reasonably good level of nutrition to which people in the region can rightfully aspire in the course of the next

TABLE 18

PROJECTED GROWTH OF THE WORLD'S POPULATION BY REGIONS

(Medium assumption: 1958 population = 100 millions)

REGION	YEAR									
	1958		1970		1980		1990		2000	
Europe	626	100	711	114	792	127	871	139	947	152
North America	192	100	225	117	254	132	283	147	312	163
Oceania	15	100	19	129	22	150	26	171	29	195
Latin America										
River Plate countries	25	100	30	120	35	140	39	156	44	176
Excluding River Plate countries	170	100	235	138	314	185	416	245	548	322
Far East	1,498	100	1,863	124	2,317	155	2,904	194	3,639	243
Near East	125	100	165	132	203	162	256	205	327	262
Africa	208	100	232	112	283	136	345	166	421	202
Group I	2,001	100	2,495	125	3,117	156	3,921	196	4,935	247
Group II	858	100	985	115	1,103	128	1,219	142	1,332	155
World total	2,859	100	3,480	122	4,220	148	5,140	180	6,267	219

20 years or so. Its achievement by 1980 implies an annual increase of 2 per cent in *per caput* availability of food supplies, thus calling for a continuation of the efforts needed to attain the low target by 1970. On the other hand, the rate of over-all increase in total food supplies would have to be a little higher than called for to reach the low target by 1970, owing to the accelerated growth in population between 1970 and 1980 as compared with that in the preceding decade.

The implications of the long-term target, which aims at a supply of 20 grams of animal proteins *per caput* in place of the existing level of 8 grams and at a calorie level about 100 higher than the requirement calculated according to the FAO scale, can be similarly studied from the figures given in the last columns of Tables 17 and 19. Assuming that a period of 30 years is needed to reach the high target, we shall need an over-all increase of 7.5 per cent in total food supplies and 2 per cent in *per caput* food supplies per annum as in the previous decades. If the long-term target is not reached by, say, the turn of the century the *per caput* rate of increase will be proportionately smaller. But even so, the over-all growth in total food supplies will have to be accomplished at an accelerated rate from one decade to another, in order that the present level of nutrition can be brought to the level implied in the long-term target.

To conclude, it would seem that we must aim at an over-all increase in *per caput* food supplies of some 2 per cent per annum to achieve for the Far East the low target by 1970, the medium target by 1980, and the high target before the turn of the present century. In terms of total needs, this means that the over-all supplies would have to be increased by 50 per cent to achieve the low target by 1970, by some 120 per cent to achieve the medium target by 1980 and by 220 per cent and 300 per cent to achieve the high target by 1990 and 2000, respectively. In other words, the present over-all total supplies would have to be more than quadrupled by the turn of the century in order to raise the level of nutrition of peoples in the region to that implied in the long-term target. The increase needed will be even larger if we are to aim at a more ambitious target from the nutritional point of view and/or if the population is to grow faster than under the "medium" assumption.

TABLE 19

OVER-ALL INDEX OF NEEDS IN TOTAL FOOD SUPPLIES, 1970–2000

(Available = 100)

	1970	1980	1990	2000
Far East				
Low target	148	186	233	292
Medium target	175	219	274	343
High target	207	259	324	406
Near East	154	190	240	307
Africa				
Low target	128	155	189	230
High target	143	174	212	259
Latin America (excluding River Plate countries)	145	194	257	338

Near East.—Coming to the Near East, Table 17 shows that the *per caput* per day changes in food supplies needed to achieve the nutritional target range from a decrease of 45 in cereals to an increase of 120 in animal products: These changes correspond to a *per caput* decrease of 10 per cent in cereals and a *per caput* increase of some 45 per cent in animal products. The over-all change *per caput* needed to achieve the target, as shown by the index of *per caput* food required based on producer price weights, is 17 per cent and is seen to be only one-quarter as large as the change needed to bring the Far East to the same level of nutrition. However, as in the Far East, the Near East population is also expected to grow at an accelerated rate to 2.5 times its present size by the turn of the century. The over-all changes in total food supplies needed to cover this population growth as well as the suggested improvement in the level of nutrition are given in Table 19, and show that the total food supplies would have to be increased by some 90 per cent by 1980 and over 200 per cent by the year 2000. These figures compare with an estimated increase of over 160 per cent in total food supplies for the Far East by 1980 and 300 per cent by the year 2000 in order to bring both regions to the same improved level of nutrition.

Africa.—Table 17 shows that changes for Africa are similar to those for the Near East, except that whereas the change in food supplies in the Near East calls for a decrease in *per caput* supplies of cereals, the change for Africa calls for a decrease in starchy roots. The over-all change in *per caput* supplies needed to achieve the short-term target is seen to be 14 per cent and that needed for the long-term target 28 per cent. The population of Africa according to the UN forecast is, however, expected to grow at a lower rate than that of the Near East. The over-all increases in the total food supplies needed to cover the population increase, as well as the suggested long-term improvement in the level of nutrition, are consequently of the same order as for the Near East, being some 75 per cent by 1980 and 160 per cent by the turn of the century.

Latin America (excluding River Plate countries).—Table 17 shows that the *per caput* changes needed for this region are much smaller than those for the Far East, Near East, and Africa, namely no change in plant products as a whole and some 7 per cent in animal products. The over-all change in food supplies *per caput* needed in order to achieve the suggested level of nutrition in this region is only 5 per cent. This small increase needed to realize the nutritional target is due to the fact that the region is enjoying a relatively high level of nutrition as compared with

TABLE 20

PRESENT AND FUTURE CALORIE REQUIREMENTS "PER CAPUT" DAY AT RETAIL LEVEL FOR BURMA AND SOUTH VIET NAM

Country	Year	Projection	Calorie Requirement	Requirement in 1980 as % of 1950
Burma	1950	Actual	2,270	100
	1980	Conservative[a]	2,250	99
		Normal mortality decline and moderate fertility decline	2,260	99
South Viet Nam	1950	Actual	2,290	100
	1980	Conservative[a]	2,260	99
		Normal mortality decline and high fertility	2,260	99
		Low mortality and high fertility	2,240	98

[a] This assumption implies:
1. Constant fertility.
2. Mortality decline at a rate which from average observations for the world as a whole appears normal. In particular, it is assumed that expectation of life at birth, for high and moderate levels of mortality, increases by 2.5 years every 5 years.

other low-calorie regions. As against this, however, the population in Latin America is expected to grow faster, according to the UN forecast, than in the other regions. As a consequence the region will need an over-all increase in total food supplies nearly the same as or even higher than that for the Near East, namely some 90 per cent by 1980 and some 240 per cent by the year 2000.

WORLD'S FUTURE NEEDS

Tables 21 and 22 summarize the results regarding the future needs in food supplies for the low-calorie countries and for the world as a whole. For want of space the results are presented for selected food groups and for the medium and high targets only.

It can be seen from Table 21 that the food supplies *per caput* available to the

TABLE 21

"PER CAPUT" FOOD SUPPLIES AVAILABLE AND NEEDED BY SOME MAJOR FOOD GROUPS WITH CALORIE AND PROTEIN LEVELS

(Per day at retail level)

Item	Medium Target (grams)						High Target (grams)			
	Available		Required		Per Cent Required Available		Required		Per Cent Required Available	
	Group I	World	Group I	World	Group I	World	Group I	World	Group I	World
Cereals	389	370	371	358	95	97	359	350	92	95
Pulses and nuts	53	42	73	56	138	133	76	58	143	138
Vegetables and fruits	169	227	265	294	157	130	304	321	180	141
Animal foods	136	333	249	412	183	124	292	442	215	133
Over-all index	100	100	133	114	133	114	150	122	150	122
Total calories	2,150	2,420	2,340	2,560	109	105	2,410	2,610	112	108
Vegetable proteins (grams)	49	48	53	51	108	106	53	51	102	106
Animal proteins (grams)	9	20	16	24	178	120	20	27	222	135
Total proteins (grams)	58	68	69	75	119	110	73	78	126	115

TABLE 22

INDEX OF NEEDS IN TOTAL FOOD SUPPLIES BY SELECTED MAJOR FOOD GROUPS: GROUP I COUNTRIES AND WORLD

(Available = 100)

Commodity Group	Group I Countries						World					
	Medium Target			High Target			Medium Target			High Target		
	1980	1990	2000	1980	1990	2000	1980	1990	2000	1980	1990	2000
Cereals	148	186	234	144	180	227	144	175	212	141	171	208
Pulses and nuts	215	270	341	223	280	353	197	239	291	204	248	302
Vegetables and fruits	245	308	388	281	353	445	192	234	285	209	254	309
Animal products	285	359	452	335	421	531	184	223	272	197	239	292
Over-all index	207	261	329	234	294	371	169	206	251	181	220	268

low-calorie countries would have to be increased by one-third to achieve the medium target and by one-half to achieve the long-term target. The increases needed *per caput* for the world as a whole are naturally smaller, being 14 per cent and 22 per cent, respectively.

The needs in total food supplies are given in Table 22. Aiming at the achievement of the medium target by 1980 and the long-term target by the year 2000, we find that the total supplies in cereals in the low-calorie countries would have to be increased by some 50 per cent by 1980 and 125 per cent by the year 2000, the corresponding increases for pulses and animal products being 115 per cent and 185 per cent for 1980, and 250 per cent and 430 per cent for the year 2000, respectively. The over-all increase in total food supplies needed by the low-calorie countries by 1980 and 2000 are seen to be some 110 per cent and 270 per cent, respectively.

For the world as a whole the table shows that the total supplies needed by 1980 would have to be higher by some 45 per cent in cereals, 95 per cent in pulses, and 85 per cent in animal products, while those needed by the year 2000 would have to be higher by some 110 per cent in cereals, 200 per cent in pulses, and 190 per cent in animal products. The over-all change in the world's total food supplies needed to achieve the medium target by 1980 and the high target by the year 2000 are seen to be 70 per cent and 170 per cent, respectively. In actual fact, the supplies needed would be much larger, since people who are already enjoying adequate diets in quality, quantity, or both, would continue to enjoy them and possibly even improve further upon them. *The broad conclusion thus is that should population grow according to the UN medium forecast, the world's total food supplies would have to be doubled by 1980 and trebled by the turn of the century in order to provide a reasonably adequate level of nutrition to the peoples of the world.*

Discussion on Dr. Sukhatme's Paper

Mr. R. F. George (in proposing the vote of thanks):

It seems curious that the frequency with which statisticians have put [this] subject before us has been so uneven. It is 7 years since the question was discussed in world-wide terms by Mr. Colin Clark, who dealt with the supply and requirements of farm products. Since then we have had occasional papers on family income and expenditure but not until the last Ordinary Meeting, a month ago, did the question of nutrition come before us, and then we had two papers on nutrition and diets. This evening we have contemplated the possible condition of 6,267 million persons in 40 years' time: last month by way of contrast, we considered the diets of 118 bank clerks aged 40–55 in Brighton and Southend.

In a paper of this length, containing such a mass of figures, it would be surprising if every statement satisfied all statisticians or those other scientists engaged in the social aspects of nutrition. I shall deal with only broad questions of principle and leave to others criticism or appreciation of particular points of substance and detail.

First of all, I am by no means clear about the use of the word "hunger." It figures prominently in the title and is defined where it is used in the sense of undernutrition. Surely hunger is essentially a subjective experience—that uneasy feeling arising from lack of food. Undernutrition I take it is an objective judgement based essentially on a comparison with laboratory standards. It may be argued that hunger for the purpose of studies such as this is a technical term, but it has been used for centuries in the more general sense and I question the wisdom of accepting the term as a measure of the extent to which the intake of food falls short of what is considered scientifically desirable—that I would continue to call undernutrition. Could it be accepted that one can be hungry and by nutritional standards adequately nourished, while, on the other hand, one can be undernourished and yet not hungry?

Dr. Sukhatme has put before us an exercise touching on the past, the present, and the future. The past is represented by the generally accepted standards of man's requirements—these are now the results of several decades' work in the physiological laboratory and are presumably in the constant process of being put to the test and improved as necessary. Man's requirements are therefore fairly firmly known and accepted. It is stated in the paper that the apparent improvement between 1946 and 1952 could have been mainly the result of changed standards rather than any intrinsic increases in food availability. Dr. Sukhatme reminds us of the difficulty of establishing a firm nutrition standard and applying it throughout the world. In particular, calorie requirements vary from person to person acording to several factors, e.g., weight, sex, expenditure of effort, climate. If, therefore, a conclusive and definitive standard were devised for each type of person, it would still be open to question whether the several results could be amalgamated to give an appropriate single standard for the so-called average man, even by sectors of the globe. Similar difficulties are likely in determining man's requirements of protein, fat, and other nutrients. These difficulties would not matter greatly in developing Dr. Sukhatme's argument if there were some means of assessing the approximate margin of error. If this were indeed possible, the result might qualify any conclusion on the subject of the world's nutritional needs and, therefore, on the degree of under (or over) nutrition intake.

The present is represented in the paper by the existing estimates of consumption levels. The *per capita* consumption levels in grams for a number of specified food groups should not, I imagine, be accepted with the degree of accuracy implied in the figures given in Table 2. This is implicitly acknowledged by Dr. Sukhatme when he compares the relative merits of measuring food consumption by means of food balance sheets and food consumption surveys. The inadvisability of depending on the latter for a world assessment of consumption needs no emphasis, and it is clearly preferable to depend on estimates of national availability as indicated by the balance sheet technique. But does Dr. Sukhatme go rather too far in saying, "we may expect the food balance sheets to provide a fairly good indicator of the gross food supplies and hence of the consumption levels in the underdeveloped countries . . . ?" He recognizes that checks should be applied, but there are so few checks available that in the light of present knowledge such advice can hardly be more than a pious hope. There are surely aspects of food consumption which, particularly in underdeveloped societies, are extremely difficult to measure. What is known, for example, of fish consumption in the communities bordering on the thousands of coastline miles in Asia? When the economic organization of agriculture is essentially primitive and domestic in structure, what is known of the output and even the number of family small-holdings? It is relevant in this connection to mention that in the Group I countries, mainly the underdeveloped regions of the world, there are no less than 70 per cent of the world's population—rising to almost 80 per cent in the projected population for the year 2000. Any deficiency in our knowledge of their food habits must have a large effect on such conclusions as may be drawn on the world's food supplies and therefore on the adequacy or inadequacy of availability.

The future is clearly represented in the population estimates of the United Nations. Many of us will remember the time spent 25 years ago on forecasts of the population of the U.K. for the end of the century—one, if I remember rightly, gave only a few million persons as a result. The most favorable indicated a startling decline, and voices were raised in despair. Within 10 years the whole picture completely changed. I hesitate to say whether an estimate of the population of the U.K. 60 years ahead is more hazardous than one for the world only 40 years ahead, but it would surely be unwise to accept the figure of 6,267 million as authoritative.

May I here introduce a note of warning about the increasing habit of confusing projections and forecasts. A statistical projection, to my way of thinking, is a forward estimate of what will be the figure at a given time according to present trends or on the basis of stated variations from present trends. A statistical forecast is that particular projection that seems most likely to happen. Thus we may have several projections but, I suggest, only one forecast—and if this view be accepted, should not Table 18, giving the UN estimates at 10-year intervals to the year 2000, be entitled "Forecast Growth of the World's Population by Regions"?

I hope I have not given the impression of being thoroughly destructive. My intention is essentially to underline and emphasize the qualifications which Dr. Sukhatme himself has expressed. These are important and can hardly be overemphasized. This is an emotional subject with a strong humanitarian content. It is therefore doubly important that we should not be easily moved by any conclusion without freely realizing the nature of the evidence. This is not in any way a criticism of Dr. Sukhatme's work—every one of us will admire the ingenuity and courage he has brought to bear in developing the argument, and indeed the way he has so fully exposed the nature of the evidence on which he builds his case. I therefore suggest that his conclusion that 10 to 15 per cent of the world's population are undernourished is rather more categorically stated than is justified. My own view is that this may not be far from the mark but it is a possibility rather than an incontrovertible fact.

Dr. Sukhatme's final conclusion about the rate at which world food supplies would have to be developed during the next 40 years in order to meet world needs is still startling enough to be arresting even if the figures were substantially discounted. Those with the power to influence the development of agriculture in backward countries and to improve productivity in more advanced countries have a deep responsibility to discharge. The Society is indeed grateful to Dr. Sukhatme for presenting the arguments leading to this firm exposure of responsibility.

It is with much pleasure that I propose a warm vote of thanks to him for this paper which cannot fail to take a prominent place in the international literature on the subject.

Dr. I. Leitch (in seconding the vote of thanks): Mr. George has struck such a note of extreme caution that I should like to make one or two points which will perhaps blunt the impact of this astonishing paper. Those of us who have followed the estimates of world food supplies and requirements since FAO started are not surprised by this picture of the position, and none of us is liable to underestimate the dangers of mis-estimation, but I think one or two points can be made to alter the shape of the picture.

We all know the difficulties of estimating production and food supplies, and we know that not enough stress is laid on the difficulty of estimating the losses between production and consumption. During the war I was asked repeatedly for information on the question of waste, and I went into the matter, with some assistance, as thoroughly as was possible at that time. I got quite extensive information on wastage of cereals. Canada officially estimated that the total waste of cereals in that country from production to Lake Winnipeg, where grain is shipped abroad, was only a fraction of 1 per cent, probably about 0.3 per cent, as a result of having elevators right from the farm to shipboard. On the other hand, in the southern United States where maize is largely stored in open slatted crates the wastage was anything up to 30 per cent.

In the underdeveloped or emergent countries where facilities for storage are extremely poor a possible 30 per cent wastage of cereals would make a crippling difference to available food supplies, and one of the first tasks of any international organization, or of any of the better-provided countries, ought to be to do something about minimizing the loss of food when it has been produced.

There is also the difficulty of estimating what is going to happen to population, and I like to think that, if population grows at anything like the forecast rate, we will be able to reckon on a complete change in the ratio of producers to consumers, or alternatively, earners to dependants. In this country there has been a great change in that respect in the last 100 years. A hundred years ago, when the first dietary surveys in this country were made, the standard was interpreted by a medical man and a chemist, in terms of grains of carbon and nitrogen, and at that time, because of the American cotton famine, the population in the Midlands was starving and suffering from all the diseases we should now call deficiency diseases, except beriberi. If the present forecast includes an extension of expectation of life and not merely a multiplication of numbers, we can look forward to there being many more earners in the world in relation to the number of dependants. Then the question arises, how are these people going to earn?

Just before the war we were engaged in the Carnegie Dietary Survey, a combined dietary and clinical survey which covered sections of this country, with special reference to families with children, not a random sample. At that time, 1938–39, there were between 2 and 3 million unemployed. In the Carnegie Dietary Survey many of the families of the unemployed had, by the B.M.A. standard, 60 per cent of their calorie requirements.

On a rough comparison the FAO standard is a little higher than the B.M.A., so that these families probably had a little less than 60 per cent on FAO standards of the moment.

Mr. George was worried about the definition of "hunger." Let me explain what hunger meant in terms of the unemployed in 1938 and 1939. The children were undergrown; they were light for their height. At the Rowett Research Institute in Aberdeen we had batches of them from a slum school in order to do some vitamin deficiency tests on them, and we gave them a proper meal. Most of them could not eat it; they were unable to eat what a normal child of their age would have eaten, and those who did eat it had stomach cramp. I am quite sure these children, when they arrived at the Institute in the morning, were not conscious of being hungry, nor of being hungry when they sat down to lunch. It is possible to have a calorie hunger without feeling hungry, and it is possible to make a clear objective definition that does not involve the subjective.

One must remember the extraordinary progress that can be made in a very short time if people have to do it and if the means are there. Look how this country increased food supplies during the war. I hold no brief for the accuracy of present-day nutrition standards. They are no more than tentative and just as subject to modification or complete revision as estimates of supplies. Some are much too high and subject to revision as we succeed in demonstrating that they do not apply in practice, but it is much more difficult to pull down an estimate of requirements than it is to put it up. People are more willing to believe we need more than that we need less, and we should not be too pessimistic about this picture.

If the population comes, provided employment can be found for the adults—and I hope their expectation of life may go up so that they have not 15 years of productive life but, as in this country, 50—I think we may take it for granted that by the year 2000 we shall be in sight of a solution to all these problems,. and we ought to congratulate Dr. Sukhatme on the courage with which he puts forward this estimate.

Mr. Colin Clark: One's first observation is that physiology must be an even more inexact science than economics. I used to work with Lord Boyd Orr in the 1930's. In those days it was shown that we needed 35 grams of animal protein and 100 grams of fat per day. On subsequent experience, however, these figures have been progressively modified, and physiologists now say that while these substances are convenient and agreeable to have in the diet we can, if required, do without them altogether. Many physiologists now regard fat as not only unnecessary, but indeed harmful. Dr. Sukhatme stated that previous ideas about requirements of fat and animal protein were now being "de-emphasized"—which shows that the English art of polite understatement has become an Indian art as well.

FAO, like other organisms, makes its own survival its first objective, and when that happens Public Relations take precedence over statistics. You start a world campaign against hunger first and supply evidence for it afterwards. FAO's statements on "hunger" have been chaotic. Lord Boyd Orr's statement that two-thirds of the world's population was hungry came about through his confusing two columns in a statistical table—of highly inaccurate statistics in any case—which FAO had prepared for him. Last September, at the British Association meeting at Cardiff, we had a statement quite solemnly made by Dr. Norman Wright that it was now half the world which was hungry. Dr. Wright ignored the FAO calorie requirement tables and proclaimed a new and much higher standard of his own. When I criticized him, however, he seemed quite pleased, which seems to indicate that there are wheels within wheels even in FAO itself. We had a similar statement put into the mouth of the Duke of Edinburgh when he visited Rome last month. Now we have a statement with which I think we can agree, that the true order of magnitude of the figure is about one-tenth of the world's population.

I think that there is probably more hunger in China, and less in the rest of Asia, than the speaker has indicated. FAO of course cannot say this, but—in my view—one of the principal causes of hunger is Communism. It is extraordinarily difficult to obtain accurate information on this matter from Communist countries—witness the very widely conflicting reports received at the time about events in Soviet Russia in the early 1930's, which nevertheless appear to have led to a large number of deaths, as demonstrated by subsequent Census results. Much the same can probably be said of China now, though on a much larger scale. The situation in pre-Communist China was not at all good either. The speaker did not mention Buck's figures for 1931, which showed that, in the colder wheat-growing regions, 30 villages out of 89 were below calorie requirement standard, while some, however, were far above. In the warmer rice-growing regions the number of villages below requirements was 5 out of 47. The high inter-village variance of the figures suggests that they are due to chance fluctuations of harvests, in a country with few facilities for commerce or transport, and that in any given village therefore hunger will be intermittent rather than continuous.

It seems to me that the speaker treated the distribution of people's diets around the mean as a more or less chance distribution, whereas in fact, as we all know, it is a function of income. He quoted the figures for Maharashtra, which appear plausible in the light of other information. At the Oxford Agricultural Economics Institute we are trying to collect information on incomes in primitive peasant agriculture. The FAO calorie standard, converted into grain units, and making some allowance for requirements of textile fibres and of non-cereal foods, is about a quarter-ton of grain-equivalent per person per year.

Any agricultural family so primitive, or so poor, as to have an income at or near this level will devote most of any additional income to the provision of more food. But our studies show that once income has reached the level of 0.3–0.4 tons of grain-equivalent per person per year, the desire for additional food becomes less urgent, and increments of income will be spent on other objects. If we are not careful we may come to a point where we are trying to make people eat more, and they do not want to.

Applying the FAO calorie requirements table to Ceylon, allowing for temperature and for the body weight of the people, one would agree with Cullumbine's rather than with the speaker's figure.

The speaker pointed out serious errors in the National Sample Survey in India. Here the main error lay in understatements of production, because at that time rationing was in force. In Ceylon, on the other hand, people had some grounds for concealing their consumption. At prices prevailing in Ceylon at that time, incomes at the lower quoted level would represent the equivalent of three-quarters of a ton of grain per person a year. I cannot believe that there was serious undernourishment at that income level. I admit that my evidence is still very scanty but, judging by Ceylon, I think that the speaker has overstated the problem for the rest of Asia, but has underestimated the seriousness of the position in China.

May I congratulate him on his use here of linear programming. I am always critically on the watch for attempts to use such new techniques where they are not applicable; but linear programming has been successfully used for choosing economic diets for pigs, and I see no reason why it should not be used for choosing diets for humans.

The last sentences of the paper may at first sight look like a formidable proposition. The proposals appear much less difficult, however, if we restate the requirement only as a continued upward trend of 3 per cent per annum in world agricultural production. On recent experience, there should be no difficulty in maintaining this.

Dr. Aykroyd: Dr. Sukhatme's study of the amount of undernutrition and malnutrition in the world, followed by estimates of future needs resulting from population growth, is interesting and important. Hunger is an emotional word with many "overtones." The nutrition worker generally avoids it and prefers the term "undernutrition."

Dr. Sukhatme has brought together in one paper a great deal of the relevant data available on this particular subject and has drawn from them cautious and tentative conclusions. His paper is of particular interest to me since I was concerned with the two FAO *World Food Surveys* and also with the program of dietary surveys in India to which he referred. It is interesting to recall that when we started that program, about 1935, we were rather more interested in *what* people ate in India than in the quantity of food they ate; Dr. Sukhatme has, however, been able to use these figures with reference to the calorie yield of Indian diets rather than their composition.

He reached an estimate that one-fourth of the population of India does not obtain enough food to satisfy its calorie needs. This figure is quite close to the one reached by the Famine Enquiry Commission (1945), of which I was a member; the Commission, using the dietary survey data then available, put forward an estimate of 30 per cent.

I think that Dr. Sukhatme makes out a good case for his conclusion that 10 to 15 per cent of the world's population is underfed, i.e., between 300 and 500 million people. That is plenty to be going on with. This percentage is rather different from Boyd Orr's figure in 1950. He said that a lifetime of malnutrition and hunger is the lot of two-thirds of mankind. This statement, which has caused some trouble, was made by Orr personally, and not in his capacity as first Director General of FAO.

I must, however, quarrel to some extent with Dr. Sukhatme's statement on malnutrition. There is plenty of evidence that malnutrition is widespread in most of the developing countries, particularly among children, but very little of this evidence is capable of quantitative expression. Food supply and food consumption data do indeed bring out large differences in the composition of diets, particularly with respect to animal protein, in different regions of the world. I would agree that the incidence of malnutrition is higher than the incidence of undernutrition, but I do not think it is justifiable to assess the incidence of malnutrition in the underdeveloped countries at something like 50 per cent, with consumption levels of France and England as the basis of comparison. Admittedly, Dr. Sukhatme approached this question with considerable caution.

The statement of the present Director General of FAO that between one-third and one-half of the world's population suffers from some form of hunger and malnutrition has a rather dubious ring, quite apart from the fact that there is only one form of hunger. When people hear this statement they are likely to be impressed by the higher and more dramatic figure. That may, of course, be a good thing in many ways. It excites public interest and draws attention to the urgent need to increase food supplies which has been referred to by various speakers. In my view, however, such a figure is not justified on scientific grounds. It may be correct, but the data to support it are not available.

Apart from such estimates, there is abundant ammunition to persuade the world that an enormous effort is needed to expand food production. We have evidence of the wide extent of malnutrition, particularly in children, with effects ranging from retardation in growth to serious disease and death. Even more striking are the future projections, and here I think FAO and Dr. Sukhatme are on completely firm ground. Food supplies in the underdeveloped countries generally will have to be increased by 100 to 150 per cent by the year 2000 to feed the greater population of that year, as calculated by one of the UN projections, even at present consumption levels. Any raising of these levels will call for substantially larger increases in supply. Even if we take the year 1980, the increases needed on the same basis are enormous, and indeed rather horrifying.

The FAO Freedom from Hunger Campaign is surely fully justified on this basis alone. We can argue about projections and so on, but surely common sense tells us that very large increases in world population are likely to occur within the next 20 to 40 years. FAO might be well advised to place its main emphasis on future needs rather than to rely too much on difficult and somewhat dubious estimates of the extent of malnutrition throughout the world.

Mr. W. F. Searle: The more I think about Dr. Sukhatme's paper the more I am impressed by the boldness of his approach. When we have digested his estimates we shall have to decide whether, for any specific purpose, we think they are sufficiently reliable. If one stresses the margins of error, as any scientist would want to do, the ministers and senior civil servants responsible for meeting the problem will not be impressed by them. If the estimates are exaggerated, they will fail to impress. I admire Dr. Sukhatme's way of handling the delicate balance between these two extremes.

I wish I could speak about the Far East —that seems to be the exciting part of the world from the point of view of this paper —but, thinking in terms of regions, the one I know something about is Africa. The figures for Africa are probably the most tentative of all the figures in this paper. The situation is improving and each year, to my own knowledge, more data become available.

If there are adequate resources, a full production survey with reasonably small sampling errors is possible, but if, as is so common, the resources are far smaller than are needed, a choice has to be made. In countrywide estimates the sampling errors for some crops are uncomfortably large and the figures for the less-important crops probably not worth the paper they are written on. On the other hand, if you concentrate on one part of the country or on some form of agricultural problem, although you probably give much more help to the people responsible for agricultural policy, you are not in a position to provide the kind of countrywide estimates that FAO would like from every country.

Nevertheless, for countries like those in Africa food balance sheets can be produced, and I believe quite a number have been produced since Dr. Sukhatme wrote his paper. They are made up from partial surveys, from countrywide surveys with large sampling errors and from a variety of other data and estimates. If I were producing a balance sheet, when I had put together all the available data, would I be influenced by what I felt was a reasonable calorie requirement? Could I take all these partial and sometimes scrappy data and produce figures that were independent of my own concept of a reasonable calorie requirement? I suspect I could not and cannot help feeling that some food balance sheet data are not independent in this sense.

Few people can know Africa well; the area is too wide and the countries too diverse. But had I been asked what figure I would have expected to find for Africa in the last column in Table 6 I should have said about 100 per cent. I have checked this impression with a colleague who is very knowledgeable on African agriculture, and his impression confirms my own.

I am not trying to make this point strongly. All I want to say is that, in Table 6, one of the more difficult estimates, that for Africa, is in my view completely credible. On the other hand, I do not think any useful statements can be made about the number of people in Africa who are undernourished, and I sympathize completely with Dr. Sukhatme's approach. He has used what is known about Africa and other regions in order to reduce the percentage for undernourishment estimated for the Far East, with the aim of arriving at a broad estimate for the world as a whole.

My present feelings are that Dr. Sukhatme has not given an exaggerated account of undernourishment in the world. I think it is a very fair assessment. I doubt whether the same can be said for his figure of malnutrition, but this is an extremely difficult problem and not susceptible to the form of analysis he has applied to undernourishment.

Dr. Yates: I should like to add my congratulations and thanks to those of the other speakers to Dr. Sukhatme for presenting such a stimulating paper, and one that I think has put before us in very careful terms the evidence on what is one of the major problems facing the world today. I have myself worked for short periods in India over the last decade in connection with agricultural research with a view to increasing food production, and although I cannot claim to know India at all well, all my visits there have impressed me with the extreme seriousness of the problem in that part of the world.

The reasons are obvious. Although science and technology in food production are making very rapid strides, the application of that science in the emergent countries has yet a long way to go. Quite apart from that, medical science has been advancing certainly as fast, and has been applied very much faster, particularly in its public health aspects, to the control of infectious diseases, transmissible diseases, and so on, so that we have in consequence what is described as the population explosion. It is clear that spread of medical knowledge cannot be stopped. People and administrations are not going to allow bad medical conditions to persist merely so as not to get into difficulties in other directions.

I would certainly support the thesis that Dr. Sukhatme's figures give a sound general picture of the situation. There is no need to quibble about details of small percentages. We are faced with the very rapidly growing population in many parts of the world and will have to produce a lot more food. If that thesis is accepted and the causes of the present situation are seen in their true light, namely population growth, one of the morals of this paper and the whole study of the subject is that not only must we increase the quantity of food and improve its quality—and I may say I regard malnutrition as the more serious problem—we must also expend as much effort on putting across to the populations —and this is something the countries themselves must do—that population growth must be controlled. In other words, communities which have adjusted their birth rates to meet very high death rates due to bad health conditions, malnutrition, and undernutrition in the past must now get these birth rates down to fit with the new conditions. Famines have largely been controlled by better transport, and health conditions have improved. If populations are to reap the benefit of better health conditions and improved food supply, they must control the birth rates.

Looking at the history of human populations, it seems that in the long run the birth rate broadly adjusts itself to the requirements. In fact it can happen quite quickly. It has happened quite quickly in Western Europe and the situation has been changing quite rapidly in both directions. It is salutary to look at predictions about population trends made at the turn of the century and indeed later, and compare them with what has actually happened; some of the causes of the discrepancies are fairly obvious, others are not so clear. But although adjustments can take place quite rapidly, they take time to produce an effect. Even if the birth rate were very substantially lowered in, say, the Far East we should still be faced with a large increase in population because of the children already born and to be born in the next 10 to 20 years, and the longer expectation of life due to the spread of medical science. Whatever the desirable population for different countries, progress toward an improved standard of living would be very much more rapid if countries were not faced with a population explosion. At present one gets the impression, both from this paper and from actual experience in India, that one is running very fast to stay where one is, like the Red Queen in *Alice Through the Looking Glass,* and unless there is a major breakthrough in the techniques of food production—and that there may be on the scientific side—the food problem will continue.

On the question of malnutrition, I am perfectly prepared to accept an estimate of one-third, and this is so serious that we must certainly do something about it. Animal products require a great many more acres per calorie to produce than do cereals, and even if it is possible to achieve a rapid increase in the production per acre of cereals and similar foods, some of those acres at present devoted to such crops will have to be diverted to animal products if we are to tackle malnutrition.

In hot, and particularly in hot humid countries, calorie requirements are lower than in temperate climates, because people avoid all unnecessary exertion in order not to get too hot. This is important in assessing whether a country such as India is undernourished. But such considerations should not be used to minimize the importance of the subject or the seriousness of the situation and the vital need for all of us to do quite a lot about it.

Dr. Sukhatme (in reply): I am grateful for the numerous comments I have received. I was aware of the many limitations to the methods and data in the paper and had anticipated that these would provoke discussion, argument, and thought.

Replying first to a point raised by Dr. Leitch, the losses on grains usually allowed for in the food balance sheets for underdeveloped areas are of the order of some 3 per cent, and these were too low according to most experts. Likewise the losses within homes were likely to be larger than have been allowed for in the paper. I would therefore agree with her on the need to estimate losses accurately since this may well change the shape of the picture.

Dr. Leitch also referred to the need to apply science in underdeveloped areas in increasing food production. Experience however shows, as Dr. Yates said, that emergent countries have a long way to go in applying science successfully. Many difficulties must be overcome in applying science—social, economic, and technological. For example, water is a limiting factor; the possibilities of increasing irrigation are limited, the rainfall is concentrated in a period of a few weeks, soil erosion is difficult to prevent and soil moisture even more difficult to retain. When in addition one takes into account the social structure, with the associated ignorance and poverty of the masses, the difficulties become only too apparent.

Mr. Clark referred to the discrepancy between my figure of 2,700 calories and Cullumbine's estimate of 2,200 for an average adult and of 2,500 for an average laborer in Ceylon and thought the latter would be the more correct figure allowing for temperature and body weight in accordance with the FAO calorie scale. I do not agree with this and would refer Mr. Clark to Table 1 in my paper, which relates to India but is equally applicable to Ceylon. Furthermore Cullumbine's figures refer to the average adult man, while mine refer to the "reference" man. However, notwithstanding the lower requirement figure, Cullumbine puts his estimate of the underfed at a higher figure than mine. Surely Mr. Clark cannot accept Dr. Cullumbine's lower requirement figure and yet not accept his estimate of the proportion which is underfed. Cullumbine's estimate of requirement is not based on the FAO scale nor does he allow for the variation in calorie needs among "reference" units due to physical activity and other factors.

Dr. Aykroyd agrees that I have a good case for my conclusion that the underfed in the world amount to some 10 to 15 per cent but is less happy with my estimate of malnutrition. Dr. Yates, on the other hand, from his knowledge of conditions in India and elsewhere accepts my estimate of malnutrition as perfectly reasonable. Dr. Aykroyd was associated with the write-up of the first and second world food surveys of FAO, where a figure of two-thirds for the proportion of calories derived from cereals, starchy roots, and sugar was somewhat arbitrarily assumed in order to demonstrate the widespread incidence of malnutrition in underdeveloped countries. All I have done is to go a step further by replacing the figure of two-thirds by information on the actual variation of the indicator in reasonably well-fed countries and relating it to the distribution of the same indicator in underdeveloped areas. I am glad Dr. Aykroyd agrees that I am on firm ground in estimating the future needs in food supplies. By referring to the need to increase the food supplies by 100 to 150 per cent by the year 2000 to maintain the present consumption levels and stating that any raising of the present levels will mean substantial further increases, Dr. Aykroyd in effect accepts my estimates of the extent of hunger and malnutrition in the world, though he would have liked to see more data to substantiate the estimate of malnutrition. As he told us, his original intention in starting the program of dietary surveys in India was to ascertain what people ate rather than how much they ate. Unfortunately, the original data are not available in sufficient detail and, while the data on calorie intake have been summarized in a form suitable for broad statistical analysis, those on the quality of diet were not so summarized and that explains why I was not able to substantiate my estimate of malnutrition with more data from his surveys.

The following written contributions were received after the meeting:

Dr. D. J. Finney: Dr. Sukhatme's paper must surely be one of the most important that any of us have heard presented to our Society. Even if our consciences will let us treat hunger and malnutrition in Asia and Africa as matters outside our responsibility, we cannot afford to neglect their close connection with world peace and the very existence of our own children. I would like to believe that Dr. Sukhatme chose to offer us this paper neither for his own satisfaction nor as an honor to us, but in the belief that for our Society to be informed on this subject would contribute greatly to the proper understanding and discussion of one of man's major problems.

Viewed in this light, some of what has been said by speakers in comment on the paper must be regarded as irresponsible. Attention has been directed not to the significance of Dr. Sukhatme's findings but to criticism of methodological and textual detail. Certainly the statisticians of a later generation will have an easier task in explaining why the population *changed* as it did than we have today in predicting how it *will change,* but can anyone doubt that Dr. Sukhatme and his colleagues are right to do the best they can with information now available? Several speakers have contrasted with scholarly care the meaning of "hunger" and "malnutrition." No one has suggested that we refrain from argument over differences of a few per cent that must depend upon personal opinion, or that we join in recognition of the gravity of the situation and consider what responsible statistical opinion should be doing to impress on our own Government and on others the nature of a task that urgently demands far more attention.

Mr. Clark has expressed Dr. Sukhatme's final sentence as a requirement that world supplies increase by 3 per cent per annum for the remainder of this century and has implied that this reduces the conclusion to its proper proportions. Do we know whether this is within the bounds of possibility? Are world fertilizer deposits and resources of irrigation water sufficient to make an adequate contribution to this increase? How is the rest to be attained—by varietal improvement, changes in cultivations, and the bringing of new land into production? Even if all other potentialities exist, can the habits of the cultivator and systems of marketing and distribution be modified to a sufficient extent? Whether we speak of a doubling or of a 3 per cent annual increase, it is imperative that Dr. Sukhatme's essential first stage be followed quickly by a study of these further questions. And 2000 is only an arbitrary mark on a long road: how much longer can a 3 per cent increase be maintained, and is this long enough for man to surmount the religious, social and scientific problems of population stability?

Dr. Sukhatme would be the first to admit that both his data and his analysis have imperfections and controversial aspects, though I suspect that he could have documented and defended his treatment fairly successfully at the expense of lengthening an already long paper. If we can assist him by providing new information or improved statistical methods for his problem, I think he would be grateful. "Analysis of so vast a problem must rest upon inadequate information and intelligent guesswork, and not only upon firm numerical facts, and the respectable statistician should have no part in this": is that to be our attitude? This view is neither helpful nor responsible; if it were to prevail, we should insure either that the analysis is undertaken by those less competent to handle a complex numerical problem and less well informed than are the statisticians or that nothing at all is done.

On such an issue, it is easy to obscure objective statistical thought by emotions, but I do not think that the founders of our Society would have shared our apparent reluctance to permit entry of human values into our discussions. I fear that Dr. Sukhatme's paper is followed by some pages that bring little credit to the Society. We shall not redeem ourselves unless we refuse to regard the paper as merely an exercise in statistical methodology, a character properly possessed by most of the papers we receive. If we are satisfied that the broad trends suggested by Dr. Sukhatme are the best prediction of truth that the statistician can make today, we should seek ways in which corporate action by our Society can insure that those responsible for agricultural, nutritional, and population policy in Britain and the world are informed on these views.

Mr. Moss: Although Dr. Sukhatme has himself drawn attention to the limitations of his data, there are very practical reasons why such a problem should have been tackled by somebody. In the first place, it leads to conclusions which, however provisional, are necessary for many practical and at times critical decisions which have to be made, frequently under conditions of great stress. If the general conclusions of this paper are anywhere near the truth then such decisions may have to be made on food policy on an international scale in the years ahead. It is better that the results of systematic and critical use of available data are ready when such decisions have to be made than that policy should be decided on the basis of guesswork.

Secondly, if we consider the early history of National Income and Expenditure statistics, it seems clear that unless a start had been made with what would now be regarded as limited data such work would not now be considered of fundamental importance to efficient government policy making.

Most of the differences in the opinions expressed during the discussion relate to doubts about the data available. Any international exercise of this sort depends on national data and the limitations of the data reflect shortcomings at the national level.

Dr. Sukhatme deals with two main sources of data:

Food balance sheets give consumption as residuals and depend for their utility on many components which in Dr. Sukhatme's words are "little more than intelligent guesses." The whole can be no better than the parts which make it up and much improvement based on direct measurement of the component parts is necessary before food balance sheets can be accepted as giving a wholly satisfactory picture. We need better information about the effects of different methods of preparation; the part played by food hoarders and speculators in diverting production from some areas to others and the size of the stocks which are diverted in this way; and the nutritional composition of foodstuffs such as meat. I agree with Mr. Searle that sampling methods properly applied could help to improve the data which are used to build up food balance sheets.

Household food surveys, on the other hand, provide a direct measure of consumption. Many different techniques are available. Dr. Sukhatme has drawn attention both in this paper and elsewhere to criticisms of some of the results drawn from the National Sample Survey in India. This survey relies on interviewing rather than record books. Clearly the early results relying on one year's memory for consumption could not have been very satisfactory and the recent reduction to a shorter memory period should help, although even one month's memory of food consumption seems rather long. In work for which I was responsible in Ceylon a year or two ago we used a combination of interview and record book methods. Interviewers visited selected households each day for a month in order to obtain daily records of food consumption and other expenditure. In this way a monthly record of consumption was obtained which in my view suffers from very few of the deficiencies of long memory periods or the defects of the record book method. In a recent paper published in the Indian Government Journal, *Agricultural Situation in India*, C. Mathia has made some detailed suggestions for different forms of questioning to be addressed to different sections of the population. This could be fruitful because the same methods of collecting food consumption are not necessarily valid for all sections of the population. Methods used for collecting data from old people, for example, may have to be very different from those used with the more active sections of the population. The National Sample Survey is a multi-purpose survey in which periodic rounds of enquiry using a standardized sampling procedure are used to collect information on many different kinds of topics. This means that in any quota of interviewing, field workers may have to cover quite a wide range of topics. There are other reasons, organizational and financial, for using multi-purpose surveys and in Indian conditions these may be weighty. Since food consumption, even in fairly simple economies, is made up of different items for which conditions of acquisition vary, if information is to be adequate it must be detailed. Multi-purpose surveys then may not be the best vehicle for such a complex problem. Dr. Sukhatme's reference to the National Sample Survey results in India are not necessarily applicable, therefore, to other kinds of sample survey techniques which are available in the food consumption field.

Since sample surveys are based on direct contact and can be made on a small scale with control over the operating staff, experimental variations can be attempted so as to discover which methods produce data which agree most closely with accepted data from other sources. Very often we find that other data about domestic consumption clear of retail stocks and export and import variations are not available for comparison. This is why food balance sheets can be produced only after considerable manipulation of the available data. In such cases it may well be that the food survey data have as much face utility and validity as information emerging from the various administrative processes which is not collected precisely for the purpose of estimating food consumption.

The conclusion I would draw from all this is that at present neither one method nor the other is conclusive. If we use them together we probably get a better picture than any one method by itself can give us. Both, therefore, have a part to play, and I have already referred to the use of sampling methods for improving some of the component parts of food balance sheets.

There is, I think, an important point arising out of the discussion concerning the relationships between international statistical activities and national work. Future exercises on the problem Dr. Sukhatme has attempted will give us better conclusions only if the data on which they are based can be improved. These improved data will have to be produced at the national level, and governments will probably only make the funds available if it can be shown that there are policy or operational decisions which can be helped. These are the kind of practical considerations on the national level which will decide whether or not better national statistics become available for use in further attempts to solve the problem Dr. Sukhatme has dealt with today. That is to say, the more national statisticians and researchers can develop work which can be applied to national problems of public importance the more likely is it that material will become available which will permit the international statistician to produce improved and developed versions of today's paper. But somebody had to start the process and our thanks are due to Dr. Sukhatme for having given a strong stimulus by bringing before us today and making full use of what is now available.

Miss Schulz: Dr. Sukhatme has presented a survey over the largest possible field—the whole world—and his many qualifications have already warned us not to place excessive importance on specific figures, many of which cannot be more than broad approximations; for they are derived from estimated food supplies divided by estimated numbers that are adjusted for estimated age and sex distributions. I am more than suspicious of figures in the *World Food Surveys* and Food Balance Sheets that show calories down to the last unit and food intake not only to the last gram but sometimes with one and even two decimals. Dr. Sukhame accepts as correct the production figures of the Food Balance Sheets for Ceylon, which—according to the Food Balance Sheets—represent rough estimates of the total quantities as reported by village headmen. Dr. Sukhatme concludes from these figures that one-third of all the families in Ceylon were undernourished. The difficulty of obtaining reliable figures of food consumption is in fact enormous. In his foreword to *The Biology of Human Starvation,* Sir Jack Drummond wrote, "Time and again it was claimed that people were unable to obtain significant quantities of food over and above the official rations" (in France, Belgium, and afterward Germany) "providing about 1,000 to 1,400 calories per day. . . . Body weight and facial appearance and the psychological picture represented by these people often revealed the truth that they were getting not a little extra food by hook or by crook. . . ." Dr. Sukhatme referred to the *Burma Survey* for which consumption figures were collected by trained volunteers of the locality. From these figures he concludes that two-thirds of the surveyed households had less than the required standard supply of 2,700 calories per day. It seems to me at least uncertain that the total food intake was registered correctly. The trained volunteers of the locality are unlikely to have been more efficient than the skilled U.S. workers who in 1936 collected data on the nutritional intake of white and Negro adults. According to the data obtained by them the calorific intake of the Negroes, both men and women, was very much below that of the whites, and these figures were frequently quoted as proof of the degree of poverty among the Negroes. But if we consider the figures obtained of calorific intake against the average body weights, standard and actual, of this sample group, the picture is considerably less gloomy:

	Intake of Calories (per day)	Actual Body Weight (lb.)	Standard Weight Based on Height (lb.)
Males:			
White......	2,522	157	170
Negro......	2,005	152	163
Females:			
White......	1,736	139	138
Negro......	1,315	142	138

If figures of calorific supplies, requirements, and intake are difficult to establish, this is even more so with respect to protein. Sherman established his figure of 0.5 grams of protein requirement per kilogram of body weight by means of careful—though necessarily restricted—studies of nitrogen intake and output. For infants and growing children he considered 10 per cent of the calorific intake in the form of protein sufficient, provided it was the right form of protein. The best protein for children is no doubt that supplied by milk. But certain vegetarian foods—certain legumes, especially soya beans, nuts, and even whole wheat—can supply all essential proteins, if eaten in sufficient quantities. Moreover, certain diets are protein sparers: a constant nitrogen balance is attained at a lower level of protein intake from a diet rich in carbohydrates than from a diet rich in fat. The fact is that we still know very little indeed of man's essential needs for protein. Darling and others reported in the *Journal of Nutrition* on an experiment regarding the effects of variations in dietary protein on the physical well-being of men doing manual work. Three groups of eight subjects were each tested for 2 months on diets which contained, for the first group, from 39 to 57 grams of protein per day; for the second group, from 95 to 115 grams; for the third group, from 157 to 192 grams. No beneficial or harmful effects were shown by any of these men. They all were given endurance tests and regular tests for nitrogen balance and blood constituents.

What we have to guard against is, I think, the confusing of undernutrition with a low standard of living. When Mary Kingsley, the niece of Charles Kingsley, traveled in Africa, she shared the food of her African guides and bearers, amongst it snake and crocodile. "Crocodile," she wrote, "tastes musty." What is the calorific value, what is the protein content, of the flesh of the crocodile? What amounts of nutriment are gathered or caught wild? There is at present undoubtedly much undernutrition in the world; some areas suffer from it always, others in years when crops fail for specific reasons. To discover these areas, and, when necessary, send to them promptly what is required to combat starvation, is an essential task. But even in these areas, the long-term help, which goes to the root of the evil, must consist in the education of the people, the advancement of their agricultural methods, the introduction of industries, and the development of the means of communication, so as to supply them with the purchasing power that will enable them not only to buy the essential foods which they may be unable to produce themselves but also to raise their standard of living in general. The indiscriminate supply of foods to areas that have a low standard of living but where medical surveys show that people on the whole enjoy a fair health can, I think, be dangerous, because it may induce the people not to supplement the coarse indigenous food by the more refined foods supplied to them but to replace it in part by these foods. By doing this they may dangerously upset the nutritional balance which they had established instinctively with their local diet.

Dr. P. W. R. Morpurgo: I want to ask one question and make one comment on Dr. Sukhatme's greatly appreciated paper. How are his estimates of hunger and malnutrition affected by the use of household rather than individual consumption data? It is, for example, possible for a household to show average consumption figures equal to requirements for calories and protein, with the man overeating, the woman/women undereating, and the child(ren)—with rather greater need for protein per kilogram body weight—having a low (and possibly unbalanced) protein intake. Unless such situations are considered within Dr. Sukhatme's set of equations, it would appear helpful to know more about the division of food within households and individual food consumption.

The comment is to stress the need for intensive and preferably multi-disciplinary team research to help elucidate why food production frequently falls below technically feasible yields. Illuminating comments upon this gap were recently made by Dr. Aykroyd.[51] Many partial explanations have been advanced; the full answers are clearly not yet known and await very substantial research efforts.

Professor John Yudkin: After these many points of detail, and detailed criticism, I want, as a nutritionist, to stress the importance of the general aspects of Dr. Sukhatme's paper. For what is noteworthy about it is not the extent to which it is correct or incorrect in this or that particular, but that he has made by far the most detailed attempt to answer this incredibly difficult problem of food needs. It may well be that the answer he suggests will in time prove only an approximation to the truth. A full answer would require much more knowledge than we now have, not only of variety of food intakes, but of the exact distribution about the average. This distribution will undoubtedly be different for different foods, in different groups within the populations, and in different populations. We must remember, too, that the assessment of undernutrition and malnu-

51 W. R. Aykroyd, "Food Supplies and Food Needs," *Annales Nestlé* (Vevey, 1961), pp. 202–12.

trition implies a knowledge of requirements for nutrients and calories as well as a knowledge of intakes. Just as there is a variation in intakes, so there is also variation in requirements, which differ not only with different individuals but for the same individual at different times. It would be possible also to argue that there is an interrelationship between these two, insofar as those with higher caloric requirements are likely to eat more food. An indication of some of the enormous difficulties raised is given when one thinks that this possible meeting of increased caloric need will be accompanied by increased intake of nutrients, the needs for which are not necessarily increased in proportion.

The fact that the problem is so huge and so difficult has meant that most of us have often despaired of finding the answer. All the more then do we admire Dr. Sukhatme for his careful and laborious work. Since he has given us all the assumptions upon which his own calculations have been made, I have no doubt that future and perhaps better estimates will have to be based on this courageous and pioneer attempt. Only those who would rather have no answer than an imperfect and tentative answer will quibble at Dr. Sukhatme's remarkable and fascinating paper.

Dr. Sukhatme subsequently replied in writing as follows:

Several speakers have referred to the need for caution in accepting the UN population forecasts and by implication those of future food needs. As Dr. Finney puts it, "The statisticians of a later generation will have an easier task in explaining why the population changed as it did than we have today in predicting how it will change." One can only do one's best with the information available to predict the future so that our concern and responsibility can be brought home in good time for us to act.

It may well be that the population may not grow at the rate of 2 to 3 per cent per annum now reported from some of the underdeveloped countries. Such an increase cannot continue long without adversely affecting the standard of living of the masses. On the other hand, we must face the facts. Death rates have come down sharply in the last decade or so without material changes in illiteracy, transport, communications, and market economy, which characterize modern economic development. Birth rates show no signs of diminishing, although with the increase in the population they will eventually adjust to the death rates. This will, however, as Dr. Yates says, take time, and I see no reason for my estimate of the increase in food supplies needed by 1980 being appreciably altered unless countries in the Far East take immediate measures to stabilize population. In fact I foresee that in the next decade or two we shall have more dependants to each earner and *ceteris paribus* more consumption than savings for the investments needed for economic growth. However, I believe the tide will turn after a decade or two, though perhaps gradually, and we may well witness a reduction in birth rate and a steady growth in population. Frankly, the problem of what is going to happen to population, especially at such a distant date as the year 2000, is too complex to answer, since it depends on many social and economic factors, and this was why I put my conclusions in a way which depended for their validity on the fulfilment or otherwise of the UN population projections. Nothing, however, would please me more than for the UN projections and in consequence my estimates of future needs in food supplies to turn out to be exaggerated. Mr. George is worried about my use of the word "hunger." I used it in the title to cover both undernutrition and malnutrition and in the paper have dealt separately with the two. The major preoccupation for over a quarter of the people in the Far East is to get enough food to satisfy their calorie needs irrespective of the composition of their diets. A bottle of milk or an egg a day is a long way off for most of them. Because of this I used the word "hunger" to denote undernutrition also (or calorie deficiency) although I realize that I would have done better to avoid it. I did not believe this could cause any confusion since I have defined the terms clearly in the paper.

Mr. Clark refers to Lord Boyd Orr's confusing two columns in a statistical table when he stated that "a lifetime of malnutrition and hunger was the lot of at least two-thirds of mankind." I do not know to which table this referred, but on this occasion Mr. Clark himself has confused hunger (calorie deficiency) with malnutrition and put into the mouths of Lord Boyd Orr and Dr. Wright what they did not say. I am pleasantly surprised that he agrees with my statement in the paper, but may I remind him that when I say that between 10 to 15 per cent of the world's population is hungry I refer to underfed (or calorie deficient) people. If I add my estimate of the malnourished, I come to a figure of between one-third to one-half. This latter figure was also in Dr. Wright's mind at the British Association Meeting at Cardiff where he said that "while the extent of malnutrition cannot . . . be measured in quantitative terms and while the figures used for assessing the degree of undernutrition are open to criticism, the statement that at least half the world's population is either undernourished or malnourished does appear to be broadly justified."

While I agree with Mr. Clark that the distribution of the people's diet is a function of income; the fact that the income level of Ceylon is higher than in neighboring countries owing mainly to estates of tea and rubber does not prove that the proportion of underfed in Ceylon is smaller than in the adjoining countries. So far as one knows, the distribution is exceedingly unequal and explains in fact the presence of an appreciable proportion of underfed among the population.

I have taken note of his comments on Communist China and can only hope that in due course more information will be available on what is happening in that unknown subcontinent.

Mr. Searle asked whether food balance sheets could be considered independent in the sense that they are uninfluenced by the level of calorie requirements one has in mind when preparing the food balance sheets. I agree that they are not. On the other hand, I have recently compared *per caput* calorie supplies derived from food balance sheets for a few countries in Africa prepared by two different agencies, one set by the Foreign Agricultural Service of the United States and the other by an FAO consultant who has worked in Africa for over 20 years as a statistical adviser. Examining the two sets commodity by commodity showed that the differences largely arise from the estimates of production of the principal food crops, cassava in particular and coarse grains to some extent. I therefore agree with him regarding the use of objective methods of measurement and sampling for improving the reliability of the production estimates and in consequence of the food balance sheet data. The need is particularly great in Africa since, as Mr. Searle observes, the figures for Africa are the most tentative in the paper. In addition, since cassava does not necessarily imply consumption—because of its use as reserve food crop—food consumption surveys are called for.

I very much agree with Dr. Yates in stressing the importance of the substantive findings of my paper instead of quibbling about details of small percentages one way or the other. His view was that the picture presented was sound and that much more effort and energy would be needed "if we are to produce more and better food to meet the challenge of the growing population and to improve the world's level of consumption." He reminded us that animal products required many more acres per calorie to produce than cereals and that in many countries it was hard to find the necessary spare land. He added that the food problem would remain unless drastic measures to apply science and to awaken the masses were taken in the underdeveloped areas.

Dr. Finney wondered whether the possibilities of raising the world's food production were great enough to meet the estimated needs and suggested a detailed study of the problem. He asked whether, even if the necessary potential for increasing production did exist, the cultivator would change his methods and whether the annual rate of increase of 3 per cent compound needed to meet the future needs could be maintained for long.

We have a study of this type in hand at FAO. It seems clear that economic development will be retarded so long as population continues to grow at its present rate of over 2 per cent. If fertility is eventually to adjust to the low death rate, as it probably will, the sooner this happens in the Far East the better, on account of the obvious economic advantages this will offer.

Mr. Moss effectively answers those who doubt the wisdom of making statistical exercises which become outmoded by time and cites a useful analogy from the world of national account statistics. His other important point concerns the need to improve national statistics so that in time food balance sheet and household survey data may not only complement each other but prove an effective tool for providing a reliable picture of the food situation within countries. His work in Ceylon points the way.

Miss Schulz seems suspicious of all the figures except perhaps those published in the United States and the developed countries. While I have not minimized the difficulties of collecting data on food consumption and the limitations of such data as are available, I would not argue if, using the same or other evidence, she reached a somewhat different figure of the extent of hunger and malnutrition. When, however, she compares the NSS data of household surveys in India with the Ceylon food balance sheet she is obviously in error. Perhaps she intended to compare the NSS data of 1949–50, collected by interviews and with a reference period of a year, with the data of dietary surveys in Ceylon and Burma collected by the weighing method, but surely she cannot regard them as equally accurate. That would amount to ignoring the role of objective methods of reducing non-sampling errors stressed by Mr. Moss and Mr. Searle. In any case, I should like to make clear that my estimate of the proportion underfed in Ceylon is not based on the food balance sheet data for that country. Miss Schulz's main point appears to be that one is likely to confuse calorie hunger with low standard of living and that, notwithstanding the former, if medical surveys show that people on the whole enjoy fair health, there is little point in advocating increased and better-quality food intake. In fact there is abundant evidence that ill-health and disease due to lack of good-quality protein are widely prevalent in the underdeveloped areas, especially among children between 1 and 5, and pregnant and lactating mothers. Moreover, there is much evidence from experiments on social feeding pointing to the need for more protective foods in the diets of children and other vulnerable groups.

Miss Schultz rightly observes that the best protein for growing children is supplied by milk. This is available, though hardly in adequate quantities, when infants are breast-fed. The difficulty begins after weaning, when it is neither possible to put the infants on protein-rich solid foods nor for the families to afford milk in sufficient quantities. Thus, the *per caput* supply of milk available in India hardly provides more than 3 to 4 grams of protein per day and even this quantity is rarely available to children who need it most. Certain vegetables, especially soya beans, and other leaves, of course, contain essential proteins, but we have not yet reached the stage where such proteins can be provided in palatable and digestible form within reach of the poor in these countries. In the circumstances, to argue against a small increase in animal proteins to cover the needs of children and other vulnerable groups of the population, or against undue importance being attached to the stature by those who have an abundance to eat, can hardly appeal to anyone, nor have I suggested an indiscriminate supply of milk and other animal products without ensuring measures to increase the purchasing power of the people. I am afraid Miss Schulz is only distorting the picture I have presented when she says: "The indiscriminate supply of foods to areas that have a low standard of living . . . can . . . be dangerous."

Dr. Morpurgo asked how the estimates of hunger and malnutrition are affected by the use of household rather than individual consumption data. What little evidence there is shows that the distribution of food supplies within households in underdeveloped areas is not equitable and that the earners often consume proportionately more at the expense of children and the aged. One may find the same even in households where the total intake is sufficient for the total requirements. For lack of adequate data on the intake of individuals I have not gone into this question but it is hoped that more data will be collected to throw light on this.

Professor Yudkin has drawn attention to the interrelationship between calorie requirement and food intake and its possible effect on the assessment of undernutrition, malnutrition, and future needs in food supplies. I had in fact referred to this point in my original text. *A priori* one would expect a positive correlation between intake and requirement, and in consequence expression (4) in Part I will underestimate the extent of undernutrition. On the other hand, as Professor Yudkin points out, several factors may influence the assessment. As an example, we have no adequate knowledge of the energy variation among the healthy active adults of reference age and weight. We do not know the errors in converting *per caput* requirements in terms of the calorie distribution of consumer units. Even with regard to the correlation between intake and energy expenditure we have no precise information. Available data indicate that, although on average intake equals energy expenditure in healthy active adults, the correlation between the two—when they refer to the same day—is small. There is some evidence that energy expenditure is made up by increased intake after a lag of a day or two, which suggests time-lag correlation between the two. There is no doubt that the combined effects of these various factors must influence my assessment of the problem. The aim of my paper was to assess, in broad terms, the extent of hunger and malnutrition and its probable trends should population grow at its present rate. I would therefore agree with Professor Yudkin that my answer may turn out to be only a rough approximation to the truth, but I believe it is sufficiently accurate to show the magnitude of the problem and the effort needed if we are to play our part in improving the standard of living of the people in the underdeveloped areas.

Marie Antoinette earned a niche in history's hall of fame by proposing to feed the starving people of France on cake since they had no bread. At the present moment in history, we, the incredibly fortunate 6 per cent, having pre-empted much of the earth's industrial bread . . . seem to be able to offer our less fortunate neighbors little more than a pious hope that they will be able to eat granite some fine day a century or so hence. This offer of stone for bread out-Antoinettes Marie with a vengeance. If this is the best we can offer the earth's people in this time of crisis, surely we will have nobody but ourselves to blame when the deluge engulfs us.

ROBERT C. COOK, "Malthus' Main Thesis Still Holds," in H. JARRETT (ed.), *Perspectives on Conservation* (Baltimore: Johns Hopkins Press for Resources for the Future, Inc., 1958), pp. 77–78.

CHAPTER 2

THE LIMITS OF THE EARTH

A basic characteristic of the Malthusian equation is that the numerator (land or resources) remains relatively fixed while the denominator (population) continues to expand at a rate that some observers find alarming. Hence the ratio of land to man becomes ever smaller, and it becomes possible to write persuasive descriptions of impending catastrophe. Descriptions may be found in accounts by Osborn, Vogt, and others, cited in the Introduction to this volume. In the selection from his work included in this chapter, Osborn phrases the need for decision largely in terms of population growth, but the reason for his concern is that "now as we look, we can see the limits of the earth."

What is the nature of these limits that Malthus assumed and that Osborn can see so clearly? Stamp addressed himself to this question and found that even with present levels of technology, much potentially cultivable land is not yet in use. The earth may be limited, but it is not as full as it appears to be at first glance.

Nevertheless, catastrophe is still possible, even probable. Although natural hazards continue to plague humanity, famine, disease, and violent events in nature can no longer threaten the human race.[1] The major threats are now of human origin. The closest, perhaps, is the danger of nuclear war. A longer run danger may stem from the failure to control the growth of human populations. A clearly defined problem will be the process of converting to dependence on water power, atomic energy, and solar energy as the fossil fuels become completely exhausted. Apart from the ever-present threat of nuclear war, there is yet time to evade dangers and to solve problems. However, as Harrison Brown points out, "We are quickly approaching the point where, if machine civilization should, because of some catastrophe, stop functioning, it will probably never again come into existence."[2]

The reasons for this are in a sense Ricardian. As the higher quality and more accessible resources are used up, we become increasingly dependent upon our technology to provide and develop resources. Given the collapse of that

1 For a classification of natural hazards and a discussion of their role in resource management, see Ian Burton and Robert W. Kates, "The Perception of Natural Hazards in Resource Management," *Natural Resources Journal,* III, No. 3 (1964), 412–41.

2 Harrison Brown, *The Challenge of Man's Future* (New York: The Viking Press, 1960), p. 222. First published, 1954.

technology, no high-quality resources will be accessible to enable a more primitive level of technology to begin the long climb back to the present stage of development. The higher one climbs, the farther the distance to fall. And next time, the fall may well be in Ciriacy-Wantrup's term, "irreversible."[3]

In this context, it becomes pertinent to ask about the nature of our technology and of the culture that supports it.

As Carl Sauer has pointed out,[4] natural resources are not an absolute or objectively definable reality. Natural resources are cultural appraisals, that is, they are a function of culture, and can only be defined in terms that are meaningful and significant to that culture. Firey has elaborated these appraisals, suggesting that for any given people and habitat, persistent resource use must be physically possible, culturally adoptable, and economically gainful.[5] Zimmerman has illustrated an extreme form of this position by showing that what to one cultural group may be natural resistances or "neutral stuff," is a valued resource to another.[6] Spoehr takes up this point in the paper included here and argues that the whole view implicit in the concept of resources is peculiar to some societies and not others. To many peoples, there is no clear distinction between man and nature. If resources do not exist for some non-western societies in the western sense, then it becomes pointless to talk about limits. The concept does not apply.

The cautious optimism expressed by Fisher and the complex systems of population and resource relationships described by Ackerman do not support the view that man is being hard pressed by the limits of the earth.[7] Nevertheless, the difficulties of projecting technological change or of knowing the future course of population growth do give reason for caution.[8] There is need for the adoption of conservation policies as Fisher suggests, as a form of insurance policy against the unknowns of the future, including the unknown rate of advance of our technology.[9]

3 See chap. 8 in this volume.

4 Carl O. Sauer, *Agricultural Origins and Dispersals* (New York: American Geographical Society, 1952), pp. 2–3.

5 W. Firey, *Man, Mind, and Land: A Theory of Resource Use* (Glencoe: The Free Press, 1960), pp. 14–38.

6 E. W. Zimmermann, *World Resources and Industries* (New York: Harper & Bros., 1933); see esp. pp. 3–20. Revised, 1951.

7 See also Joseph L. Fisher and Neal Potter, "Resources in the United States and the World," *The Population Dilemma,* ed. P. M. Hauser (Englewood Cliffs: Prentice-Hall, Inc., 1963), pp. 94–124.

8 Harrison Brown, James Bonner, and John Weir, *The Next Hundred Years* (New York: Viking Press, 1957).

9 Paul W. McGann, "Technological Progress in Minerals," *Natural Resources and Economic Growth,* ed. J. J. Spengler (Washington: Resources for the Future, Inc., 1961), pp. 74–97; Thomas B. Nolan, "The Inexhaustible Resource of Technology," *Perspectives on Conservation,* ed. H. Jarrett (Baltimore: Johns Hopkins Press for Resources for the Future, Inc., 1958), pp. 49–66.

L. DUDLEY STAMP

WORLD RESOURCES AND TECHNOLOGY

The Basic World Problem

The fundamental problem that faces the world today is the rapidly increasing pressure of population on physical resources, particularly on resources of land.[1]

In contrast to the position at the end of the eighteenth century, when Thomas Robert Malthus published the first edition of *An Essay on the Principle of Population as It Affects the Future Improvement of Society,* there are no new lands to be discovered. At that time, the existence of Antarctica was unknown, neither Australia nor New Zealand had even been roughly charted, the whole heart of Africa was unexplored by Europeans, and the great fertile plains of the American West lay an unbroken stretch of grassland. Today, exploration has come to mean the more detailed study of what is already known to exist. The area of the earth's land surface is fixed and, broadly speaking, inextensible. Although the reclamation of the former Zuyder Zee and the alluvial banks at the mouth of the Rhine represent a gigantic national effort of the Dutch, in terms of the world's land area, such additions are infinitesimal. The world's land area has been calculated at 57,168,000 square miles—36,586,000,000 acres or 14,812,000,000 hectares. This includes 4,410,000 square miles for Antarctica; and even if it is proved that the "land" is in two parts separated by an ice-filled oceanic trench, at the temperatures prevailing, permanent ice is a rock and may be regarded as constituting part of the earth's land surface.

Against the background of a fixed, inextensible land area is the phenomenon of the human race expanded at a rate never before reached in world history. The knowledge and practice of death control have spread much more rapidly than the knowledge and practice of birth control. Within the last 50 years, the old "killers" such as malaria, yellow fever, cholera, plague, typhoid, smallpox, and diphtheria, even tuberculosis and venereal diseases, have so far been brought under control that the knowledge and skill exist to eliminate them. Maternal mortality has become almost a thing of the past in the more advanced countries, and infantile mortality has been reduced to a third or a quarter of old figures. Expectation of life has been doubled; at the other end of the scale, in countries such as Britain and France, one person in eight is now in the old-age pension class over sixty-five. As sanitary conditions are improved and health services expanded in the less-developed countries, the net rate of population increase is bound to rise, unless there is an unexpectedly sudden swing toward universal family planning.

The present position may be summarized by referring first to total world population.

• L. Dudley Stamp (deceased 1966) was Professor Emeritus of Geography, University of London.

Reprinted from a symposium, "Population Control," published in *Law and Contemporary Problems,* XXV, No. 3 (Summer, 1960), 389–96, with permission of the author and the editor. (Published by the Duke University School of Law, Durham, N.C.

[1] The ideas in this article are extended and full references to sources are contained in L. Dudley Stamp, *Our Developing World* (London: Faber and Faber, 1960).

The last of the great "unknowns" was eliminated when China carried out its modern-style census of 1953; not more than half a dozen significant countries have now no modern census, and every year figures collected by United Nations assume a greater accuracy as regards both total population and rate of increase. On January 1, 1960, the total of 2,900,000,000 is almost certainly within 5 per cent of the truth—probably within 2 per cent. In the last few years, the net annual increase has been given first as 1.3 per cent, then as 1.5 per cent, in 1958 as 1.6 per cent, and in 1959 as 48,000,000, or nearly 1.7 per cent. Thus, the world is adding unto itself a net population increase equivalent to the whole population of Australia in less than 3 months, of Canada in about 5 months, and of even crowded Britain in only a year. In 24 hours, the equivalent of a town of 130,000 is added to the total. In terms of birth rate—more than three every second—the position is still more alarming.

Land and People

The immediate problem of population pressure on land can be studied on at least four levels. The first is the world or global level. Although it may be of interest to attempt to calculate how many people could be supported, with existing knowledge and techniques, on the earth's land surface, this is, in fact, of rather theoretical interest, because the world is far from being one united whole.

The second, or national level, is far more realistic. There are some nations rich in land resources, some rich in total area rather than usable land, and others rich from any point of view. It is difficult for an American, for example, from a country where labor rather than land is in short supply, to realize that for another country, where land is desperately short, it is output per unit area that matters and output per man-hour can almost be disregarded.

In the third place, most of the larger countries exhibit contrasts within their own boundaries. In some cases—Brazil and Australia are examples that spring to mind—the contrasts are extreme, and so regional planning becomes of national importance.

In the fourth place, there are the intimate land-people relationships that affect the siting of towns, and even of individual farms and homesteads. It should be the prime objective of physical planning to secure for the people the maximum advantages possible from an intelligent use of land. They need space for living, but their livelihood and the economic well-being of the community depend upon the right location for industry and commerce. Indeed, planned industrial location is often—even usually—the keystone for intelligent use of land. The people also need space for recreation, but if possible without sacrificing those scarce areas with soil and microclimate best suited for production of fruit and vegetables, milk, and other foods that are best when fresh-produced near home.

To take first the global situation, if the 2,900,000,000 people living today were each given an equal share of the earth's land surface, each would have some 12.5 acres. But this would include appropriate proportions of the ice-covered polar lands, the arid deserts, and the great mountains. In general terms, about a fifth of the earth's land surface is too cold to support permanent settlement based on the cultivation of the land and the production of food, although there will be pockets of settlement based on the exploitation of minerals; another fifth is too arid and has no known water resources; another fifth is too elevated or mountainous; and another tenth lacks soil and consists of almost bare rock. This leaves about 30 per cent with adequate moisture, temperature, and soil to be potentially cultivable, and it has become usual to refer to this as the oecumene, or habitable earth's surface. The 12.5 acres that is the share of each world citizen is thus reduced to 4 acres of potentially usable land.

How much is actually used at the present day? Taking the average of all the varied techniques of cultivation—the digging stick, the hoe, the ox-plow, and the huge mechanical cultivators, as well as the varied foodstuffs—it is about 1.1 acre per head. In other words, on a world average, it takes the produce of rather over one acre to support one human being. The parts of the cultivated lands used for non-food crops—cotton, jute, oilseeds, rubber, and the many others—are counterbalanced by food contributed from the great grazing or range lands of the world. Even then, if the existing techniques were applied and all the "potentially cultivable land" were actually used, it would seem possible for the world to support four times its present population.

Against this world yardstick, it is interesting to compare individual countries. Some contrasted ones have been set out in Table 1.

When one is concerned with the basic land resources of any given country, it is worthwhile to see how it compares with the world as a whole or with one of the countries given above. Clearly a country with an abundance of land can enjoy certain advantages—wide roads, cloverleaf junctions, national and state parks, nature reserves—that can scarcely be contemplated in a country where pressure on land is already desperate as it is in so many of the crowded states of Europe.

TABLE 1

ACRES OF LAND PER HEAD OF POPULATION

Area	Total Land	Potentially Cultivable	Actually Cultivated
World	12.5	4.0	1.1
United States	14.0	6.0(?)	3.5+
Canada	140.0	20.5	4.0+
Brazil	41.0	30.0	1.0−
United Kingdom	1.1	0.6	0.55−
England and Wales	0.8	0.6	0.55−
Netherlands	0.8	0.6	0.55−
India	2.1	1.0	0.95
Pakistan	3.0	1.0	0.7
Burma	9.0	4.0	1.15+
Japan	1.1	0.2(?)	0.15
Uganda	10.0	9.0	1.0

+ indicates a normal surplus available for export.
— indicates a permanent deficiency in home supplies requiring supplement by import.

THE MEASUREMENT OF LAND RESOURCES

The measurement of land resources, actual and potential, is an extraordinarily complex subject. If the purpose is to ascertain the maximum population that can be supported by the production of the world as a whole, or any given country, there can probably be no final answer, even assuming present technological levels. Necessity is ever the mother of invention: 3,000,000 people are now crowded into parts of the very hilly lands of Hong Kong and the New Territories covering in all only 391 square miles; yet, the Chinese market gardeners feeding almost pure sands with human, animal, and artificial manures can very nearly satisfy the needs for the vegetables that make up a major part of the people's diet. It takes the produce of over 3 acres of improved farm land to provide food adequate for a present day American diet; yet, the Japanese relying on high-calorie, high-yielding rice, deriving much of their needed protein from beans and much of the remainder from fish, manage to feed perhaps six or seven people from each cultivated acre. From this one point of view, Japanese agriculture is twenty times as "efficient" as American. Thus, the whole question of land resources and their measurement bristles with difficulties —the meaning of efficiency, the concept of carrying capacity, and the aim of dietary planning are but examples.

Taking first food production on a world basis, it would seem that at present, increase in output is rather more than keeping pace with population. Using Food and Agriculture Organization statistics, the position would seem to be that shown in Table 2. If, however, this world position appears satisfactory, it is far from being so in many countries. In contrast to the vast stock piles of foodstuffs that embarrass the United States and Canada, the people of India are getting less food per head today than they had 30 years ago.

TABLE 2

ESTIMATED WORLD PRODUCTION OF MAJOR FOODSTUFFS

(Million Metric Tons)

Foodstuffs	1934–38	1948–52	1957–58
Wheat	95.0	113.5	122.4
Barley	28.5	36.0	49.7
Corn	94.1	119.6	137.6
Rice	70.2	74.8	88.2
Sugar	21.0	26.4	35.6
Meat	26.9	30.5	39.2
Farm products index	85	100	117
Population index	90	100	112

In studying the question of the feeding of mankind, one of our objects must be to discover where diets are adequate, where they are inadequate. But diets vary enormously, and it is always difficult to make comparisons between rice-eaters and bread-eaters, or between those relying largely on meat-milk-eggs and the vast numbers of almost pure vegetarians. In his presidential address to the International Geographical Congress at Rio de Janeiro in 1956, the writer introduced a measure that he called the Standard Nutrition Unit (SNU).

Even when seasons allow double or treble-cropping, the world's farmers think primarily in terms of an annual harvest, and so the unit chosen was one of annual farm output. Provided a diet is sufficiently varied, the intake of the minor but important elements well known to the nutritionist is likely to be adequate or can be easily supplemented if the basic quantity supplying calories for the daily working of the human machine is adequate. Although many nutritionists lay down a rule that half a daily minimum intake of protein of 80 grams should be *animal* protein—i.e., meat—the fact remains that for more than half the world, the intake of animal protein is less than 10 grams (one-third of an ounce) per day, and for the vegetarian quarter of mankind, it is negligible. We are on surer ground with caloric requirements, and so the writer chose a farm production of 1,000,000 calories per annum as the Standard Nutrition Unit. It does not matter whether the farmer is producing rice, wheat, corn, meat, milk, or other staples, his output can be converted into calories.

After farm output, there follows a deduction for seed and loss in milling and other forms of preparation and cooking. The average loss was calculated in several ways and approximated to 10 per cent, so that the farm output of 1,000,000 calories per annum becomes 900,000 available for consumption. This is 2,460 calories per day, which may be accepted as a reasonable world standard for an "average" human being. A lower figure is adequate where people are lighter in weight than world standard and in hot countries and with diminution in physical effort. Detailed studies in Indian villages show 2,000 calories per day just adequate for maintenance of health; on the other hand, figures of 3,000 calories per day in North America and certain European countries include wastage of food after preparation that can be very high but cannot be calculated.

The Standard Nutrition Unit can be used in a variety of ways. First, by converting national total production of food into these units, one gets a measure of the adequacy or inadequacy of a country's total production. Second, it is a measure of efficiency in farming output between one country and another. It is here that we realize that some diets are much more extravagant of land than others. The multiple-cropped lands of Japan, with a dietic reliance on rice, yield 6, 7, or even 8 Units per acre. An intensively farmed acre of wheat in Northwest Europe yields 4 Units, but with the varied meat-milk-bread-vegetable-fruit diet of Britain, it takes rather more than 1 acre to produce 1 Unit—i.e., to feed one person. Most extravagant of land is the meat diet and an extensive form of mechanized farming, with an output under North American conditions of about 0.3 Unit per improved acre. Some countries such as Spain and Australia have low outputs because of the vagaries of climate; others, such as India, because of the primitive level of farming techniques.

The New Agricultural Revolution

This leads us to consider the developments taking place in farming all over the world—along many lines simultaneously and with such remarkable rapidity that the expression "new agricultural revolution" is not inappropriate.

Mechanization of agriculture is an obvious and world-wide phenomenon. The farm horse, and incidentally his demand on land for his feed, is disappearing with incredible rapidity all over the world. Soon the horse will become, as it was in the Roman Empire 2,000 years ago, just a symbol of pomp and power for police and politicians. The fact that Britain can claim to be the most highly mechanized farming country in the world in terms of number of implements per farmed acre raises an interesting issue. Is the farming there, and elsewhere, already overmechanized? The world over, the farmer tends to be an individualist; an incorporated farming company is a rarity in the free world, and large-scale farming has its problems in other countries. The average British full-time farm is 100 acres—it would seem slightly larger than the American average —and every British farmer seems to be aiming to possess a full range of mechanical equipment, despite the fact that some machines may be used only for a few days in the year. Is this efficiency, or is it overmechanization? It would also seem that mechanization with machines at present available is not necessarily the answer in the tropics, where land management presents problems quite different from those in mid-latitudes. But there is no doubt that mechanization—and with it, marriage of town and country, farm and factory, farmer and mechanic—is playing and will play a major role in the agricultural revolution. With it goes road haulage and the improvement of access.

More recent than mechanization, but just as important, is the chemicalization of agriculture. So-called artificial fertilizers are applied to land in quantities undreamed of a few years ago. Minute quantities of certain trace elements have rendered fertile lands long regarded as sterile. Chemicalization is altering the whole relationship between the farmer and the land. The application of chemical manures may destroy the natural structure of a soil and the minute inhabitants of the soil—its flora and fauna—but at the same time, soil conditioners may break up a heavy clay soil and render it workable. In many cases, we are moving toward hydroponics, where a sterile mixture of mineral grains replaces a soil and nutrients are supplied as required by the crop concerned. In another field, fungicides and insecticides—indeed, sprays of all kinds—are very powerful weapons against many of the farmer's old enemies. The growing use of "weed killers" —selective herbicides—has opened up many difficult questions of the balance of plant and animal life, the danger of poisoning crops in neighboring fields, and of poisoning animals.

Chemicalization is linked in many ways with a third line of development—the work of the plant and animal geneticist, the breeding of strains that emphasize such desirable trends as a higher yield by exploiting hybrid vigor in corn, an early vegetative growth in grass, or a higher yield of milk from cows or eggs from hens. Artificial insemination, the preservation of semen over long periods in cold storage, and the manipulation of heat and light to vary the reproductive cycle are but some of the other current lines of research.

The actual reclamation of land by irrigation and drainage is extending the cultivable area, but there are still vast fields unconquered. It was primarily in the 1930's that the coincidence of an economic depression with a succession of bad seasons focused attention in the United States on the evils of soil erosion and all that stemmed from "dust bowl" conditions. The concept of soil conservation was put over with a bang—soil erosion must be stopped or the world would starve. It is true that much soil erosion, owing to the foolish haste of man in plowing up the grasslands or leveling the forests, is bad, but erosion as a whole is an inexorable process of nature. There would be no fertile valley-delta in Egypt to support 20,000,000 people if it were not for erosion in the mountains of Ethiopia; the Netherlands would scarcely exist were it not for past erosion in the Alps. It is high time that attention were focused on trapping and retaining the valuable material swept down by every muddy river in the world.

How Many People Can the World Support?

Although the proud boast in President Truman's Point IV declaration—"for the first time in history, humanity possesses the knowledge and the skill to relieve the suffering" of the half of the world living in misery, hunger, and disease—is not easily substantiated to the full, there is no doubt that the world can support many times its present population. We have scarcely begun to cultivate the seas systematically; but taking only the land areas, three times the land cultivated at present remains to be conquered. Difficult though that task may be, these are the lands with adequate water, heat, and soil. Where necessity demands, as many as 4,000 persons are being supported by the produce of a square mile of farm land against a world average of about 600 persons.

But this introduces quite a different idea. We can talk about the carrying capacity of land and say that with highly intensive subsistence farming as many as 4,000 persons per square mile may be supported. Farming, however, is rapidly becoming a highly scientific and specialized business. The farm must be adequately supplied with capital; the farmer must have the intelligence to use the knowledge and advice of experts, to know how to manage land, crops, livestock, and the tax collector; and his hired man must be a good mechanic and, if animals are involved, at least halfway to being a veterinarian. If this is true, the business of food production will gradually pass into the hands of experts. This has already happened in the more advanced countries, where the farming population has dropped to under 10 per cent of the employed population, as contrasted with 50 to 80 per cent or more in many of the underdeveloped countries.

According to the admittedly imperfect figures published by FAO in 1950, agriculture still occupied 59 per cent of the total population of the world, as compared with 62 per cent in 1937. Undoubtedly, the drop in recent years has been very rapid. Although Indian economists are worried by the slow improvement of agriculture, it is estimated from another point of view that changes in rural life have already sent 60,000,000 landless peasants drifting to the towns. A square mile of really intensively farmed land may support, as noted previously, a population of subsistence farmers and their families totaling 4,000, but the maximum *output* from that square mile under efficient commercial farming could probably be obtained by a total population of less than a tenth of that number.

There is certainly no doubt that efficiency in farming and the output of land involves a reduction in the labor force. This has been seen in operation over the past few decades in many countries, including Britain. We may hazard a guess that the present 59 per cent of mankind engaged in or directly dependent upon farming could be reduced to 10 per cent at the most. In a great primary producer like Canada, growing vast quantities of food for export, it was already down to 16 per cent in 1956; in the United States, to 13 per cent in 1955; in Belgium, to 13 per cent in 1950; in the Netherlands, to 14 per cent, in 1950; and in Britain, producing half the food consumed, to 5 per cent in 1951.

The world's greatest problem may soon be not the difficulty of feeding the increasing population, but what to do with the hundreds of millions displaced by an efficient agriculture.

JOSEPH L. FISHER

PERSPECTIVES ON POPULATION AND RESOURCES

If the population of the world were to go on increasing at the present rate of nearly 2 per cent a year, today's 3 billion persons would double by the year 2000 and would double again every thirty-seven years thereafter. By A.D. 2500 the globe would be one vast anthill with an average density over all the land areas equal to that now to be found on Manhattan Island below Central Park during the daytime. If population were to increase at 1 per cent a year, the same result would inevitably follow; it would just take longer.

On the other hand, if the 3 billion men, women, and children now living on earth were packed into a box the shape of a cube, allowing a space 6 feet by 2 feet by 1 foot for each one, the box would be about five-eighths of a mile on an edge. If this box were pushed off the edge of the Grand Canyon of the Colorado and tumbled to the bottom, it would appear to be about the size of a child's play block to an observer looking down from the rim. On this basis of "standing room only," the anthill of people that would exist if all the world were as crowded as Manhattan could fit in the Grand Canyon and hardly be noticed.

But who wants to be wedged into a box? Such examples are good for amusing or frightening readers of the Sunday supplements and pseudo-science fiction, but for little else. They do, perhaps, point to the importance of the way one looks at population and resources: one's perspective at the corner of Fifth Avenue and 42nd Street at noon is quite different from that on the Grand Canyon's rim. Otherwise they are fantasies, statistically impeccable though they may be. They are of no help to persons seeking to understand and mitigate the many large problems that grow out of the resources-population relationship.

Despite the pace of change of the modern world and the chance of unforeseen events, history remains our most reliable guide to the unfolding future. Few of the great innovations fail to cast some shadow before them. The remarkable advances in atomic energy—some of which, like the use of radioactive isotopes, have already found widespread application, and others of which, like the production of electric power, are now on the verge of widespread development—were foretold at least several decades ago in the findings of the scientists. As long ago as 1905, Einstein put forth his hypothesis that energy varied directly with mass times the velocity of light squared. Not long afterward Goddard began experimenting with rockets, building upon scientific discoveries going back at least as far as Newton and designs hinted at by Leonardo da Vinci.

In speculating about the future of population and resources we are influenced not only by the dismal analyses of Malthus and Ricardo 150 years ago and by the subsequent more optimistic speculations of scientists and engineers, but we may also be guided by an examination of ever-im-

• Joseph L. Fisher is President, Resources for the Future, Inc.

Reprinted from the *Annual Report* (Washington: Resources for the Future, Inc., 1963), pp. 1–7, with permission of the editor.

proving statistical knowledge about population and resources.

Central to our recent book, *Resources in America's Future,* were a number of studies in which, based largely on past and current trends, we undertook to look ahead as far as 1980 and 2000 in terms of systematic and disciplined projections of population, demand for natural resources, and resource supply problems. These studies have elaborated for the United States a picture in which anticipated population growth can be accommodated so far as supplies of food products, most construction materials, energy sources, water, and other raw materials are concerned—but not without numerous problems such as having enough good quality fresh water in a particular place, or enough high-grade sawtimber at a particular time, or enough open space and recreation land near large cities. But the over-all view is one of adequacy to support many more people at rising levels of living.

The analyses accompanying these projections specify clearly that the favorable trends will not continue unless technologic advances and economic adaptations of them continue, unless foreign sources of raw materials remain open, and unless government resource policies and private management of resource enterprises improve in farsightedness, flexibility, and consistency. But each of these provisos is judged to present difficulties and opportunities well within the capacity of research, policy, and action to deal with successfully.

These rather comforting conclusions are developed for the United States; the findings should not be transferred to other parts of the world, certainly the more densely populated and less developed areas, without looking carefully into demographic, resource, and other trends in these places. In a study now under way Neal Potter and I have made a preliminary attempt to examine these trends for other world areas on the basis of rather sketchy and unreliable statistical trends. For what they are worth, the trends indicate that the very rapid population increase in most of the less developed countries will continue to be accompanied by even more rapid increases in demand for food products, energy supplies, fresh water, and metal products. There will be a combination, that is, of more people with larger requirements per person. In the last few decades most of these countries have been able to meet increases in such demands and to register small but encouraging gains in levels of living. To continue these gains and boost them to higher levels is by no means impossible, but it will require the strenuous effort of the labor force plus vigorous enterprise in both government and private sectors of the countries' economies. Further assistance from more advanced countries undoubtedly will be of critical importance, as will the maintenance and improvement of a general world system in which all countries may pursue their objectives in peace and in cooperation with one another.

We venture the very tentative view that for the world as a whole effective demand for resources by the year 2000 might require increases in supply of the following magnitudes:

1. A tripling of aggregate food output just to provide adequate calories, and considerably more to provide adequate proteins and vitamins.
2. A fivefold increase in energy output.
3. Perhaps a fivefold increase in output of iron ore and ferroalloys, and somewhat less in copper, but a much larger increase in bauxite-aluminum.
4. A possible tripling or more of lumber output.

These estimates were reached after considering population and economic trends in various areas of the world during the past decade or more and after considering per capita resource demands that might arise if less developed areas reached levels now found in the more developed places.

The population projections used—nearly 7 billion by 2000—were those most recently published by the United Nations as "high" figures. Recent evidence indicates that the high estimates may prove to be nearer the mark than lower estimates; furthermore, high estimates have the advantage of testing more severely the adequacy of resource supplies. If a country can meet a high demand, it should have less trouble meeting any lower level.

No uniform picture of resource adequacy is presented by the various major world regions. The outlook can be optimistic, at least to the end of this century, for the United States, Canada, Western Europe, the Soviet Union, Eastern Europe, Australia, New Zealand, and a few other places. In the densely populated, less developed areas the outlook is precarious, especially for food supplies. The prospects for fairly rapidly increasing per capita energy consumption appear much more favorable. Fortunately, more abundant and reasonably cheap energy, plus related capital investments and knowledge, can lift food output through the production of more fertilizers, the pumping of irrigation water, greater use of mechanized farm equipment, and through rural electrification. But the problem of sufficient food, in quantity and quality, will remain a severe one.

Such an effort to look ahead at the world population-resource picture serves to highlight the kind of information we need to answer more definitely the question: Are resources becoming more or less scarce in various parts of the world? Only after reliable information becomes available on trends of resource production, consumption, price, sources, and the like, shall we be able to make projections that are meaningful and examine in specific terms the position of the less developed countries in relation to sustained increases in their levels of living. For the time being, the matter will have to remain largely speculative with the answer hinging on many *if's* regarding technological innovation, efforts to reduce the birth rate, the transfer of investment funds, technical aid from more developed countries, and so on.

The question inevitably arises: Would the world, or the heavily populated poorer countries, be better off with fewer people or with slower rates of population increase? The search for the optimum population or optimum rate of population increase is a difficult one, whatever the term "optimum" may mean. Economists usually mean by "optimum population increase" (or decrease) that rate which maximizes per capita income over time. The optimum population, therefore, depends not only on the rate of population increase, the discovery and availability of raw materials, and the rate of technological development, but also on the capacity of social organizations and institutions to embrace change. Much depends also on how hard and long people want to work; the trade-off point between more leisure time and more work is significant. People and cultures take different views on this question.

It is quite likely that the material level of living in the less developed countries would increase more rapidly if there were fewer people and if population increase were less, although simply to assert this does not prove it. Babies eventually grow up and become producers as well as consumers. By stimulating demand, a growing population casts a favorable influence over the amount of investment that developers are willing to make. On the other hand, a very large population can make it difficult for a country to produce a margin over and above what is needed simply to keep the population alive. New capital formation is hard to come by, children have to go to work before they are sufficiently educated and trained for more productive jobs, health standards will be low with insufficient amounts and qualities of food, and horizons of ambitions will tend to be limited to scraping enough together to meet immediate needs.

The upshot of our preliminary world

studies and projections seems to be that in the perspective of three or four decades ahead the population-resources outlook is not without elements of hope. The trend in living levels in most places has been upward, though in many instances painfully slow. It is an open question whether material aspirations will run so far in advance of what can be achieved that mass frustration will set in. This in turn would be destructive of peaceful and reasonably democratic social orders. Modest material gains may not be enough. All the resource economist can say is that foreseeable population increases over the next thirty or so years will not inevitably outstrip resource supplies. The opposite seems more likely: that improved technology applied more widely, harder work, and better management will make possible continued gains in levels of living. Furthermore, a number of less developed countries appear to be on the threshold of takeoff into rapid economic development following the recent path of such countries as Japan and the Soviet Union and the earlier path of the countries of Western Europe and North America.

In certain of the less material aspects of life, many observers foresee dire consequences in continued rapid population increase. Open spaces will diminish; natural areas will be spoiled; soil, air, and water will be increasingly polluted; and traditional ways of life will fall victims of the increased density of people and economic activity. These conclusions follow from a particular view of the world and its future, to which demonstrations of material adequacy are beside the point. Inevitably, for such persons, the answer in large measure lies in reducing the rate of increase in population; for some it means reducing the actual number of people. This point of view, especially in its extreme form, fails to recognize current trends: almost certainly there are going to be more people for some years ahead regardless of the problems they may cause or what efforts may be undertaken to slow the rate of growth. A more moderate approach would entail efforts to check population increase combined with more emphasis on careful planning to retain numerous natural areas and to abate environmental pollution.

In this regard recent trends are not entirely disappointing. In the United States, for example, a century ago we had no system of national forests and national parks, whereas now more than 200 million acres are in these categories. A number of wilderness areas have already been designated and Congress for several years has seemed to be on the verge of giving official status as protected areas to large additional areas. Stream pollution has become a more vexing problem in many respects as cities have grown and industries have spread; on the other hand, the more extreme consequences of pollution, such as epidemics of typhoid, seem to be a thing of the past. Furthermore, water pollution abatement techniques are improving; public bodies and private corporations seem to be willing to devote more money to these activities, and we are beginning to undertake water quality control for whole river basins on the basis of systematic analysis of interrelated hydrologic, biochemical, economic, and other data that bear on the problem.

So far as the bulk of the world's population in Asia, Africa, and Latin America is concerned, demographic, technologic, and economic evidence is not conclusive on the question of population versus resources. The coin could come down on either side. History permits a cautious optimism, as do the most disciplined projections that we have been able to muster.

Where does this leave us with regard to programs for the conservation of natural resources? Will these programs be necessary to survival, to rising levels of living? Or will they prove to be more or less useless, victims of the onrush of science and technology and the cleverness of social adaptation?

Several reasons for vigorous efforts

toward conservation will remain important, but fear of running out of things is not one of the better ones. Conservation, or wise and careful use with an eye to the future as well as the present, will be desirable as a matter of prudence. "Waste not, want not" is still a serviceable maxim. It can, in fact, be said that conservation is society's insurance policy against the risk that the rate of technological development will slow down, or that the rate of population increase will not slow down, or that projections of resource demands and supplies will be far off the mark, as they have been frequently in the past. A large share of conservation activity makes good sense by economic calculations, but society would be well advised to carry out even more. The general welfare for future years can justify fairly large premiums in the form of programs for soil and water conservation and for the preservation of scenery and wildlife, although, here too, it is important to do things as economically as possible.

Much of the enthusiasm and dedication of the conservation movement can usefully be directed toward combating tendencies toward resource deterioration. Efforts in planning, investment, and education will be necessary if quality standards are to be maintained and improved. Pollution of water, soil, and air, and disfigurement of the general environment are formidable antagonists today. In many ways the resource and environmental quality has improved during past decades. Typhoid and malaria have been all but eliminated in this country and are being brought rapidly under control in many less developed regions of the world. More and more houses are being constructed to meet acceptable standards. Soil conservation and rural electrification are spreading in most countries. But in terms of technical, economic, and aesthetic possibilities, quality performance in handling resources is far below what it could be.

Looking beyond the year 2000, continued rapid population increase unmatched by continued technological innovation and social and policy adaptation would lead to disaster, as many have prophesied. However, the capacity of human beings to adjust their behavior and institutions to emerging problems should not be underrated. Birth control and family planning, so full of difficulties today, could undergo substantial change during several decades while population continued to increase at 2 per cent a year. On this matter, research in the biological and social sciences is progressing and may well open new avenues to the solution of age-old problems. The rapid spread of urbanization in virtually all parts of the world, including the less developed countries, will also be a factor working in the direction of smaller families, as will gains in family income, if the experience of the more developed countries is any criterion. To the extent that the technical aid programs of the advanced countries can include research, information, and education about family planning for voluntary use in the less developed, high-birthrate countries, the more opportunities there will be for bringing population increase within the ambit of individual choice and action. Limitation of population may be desirable not so much because of the possible effect of smaller numbers on living levels, but as a way of asserting some degree of rational influence over one more factor in man's relationship with his environment.

In view of the uncertainties that lie in the more distant future—technological developments impossible to foresee, resource discoveries not now dreamed of, and unthought-of measures of individual and social control in response to obvious needs—it seems unwise to try to look in any systematic and disciplined way much beyond the end of the century. Prophets of course will want to look much farther into the future, but social scientists and technical people had better not try to look farther ahead than they can see, at least dimly. And even the prophets should consider the possibilities of discovery and technological advance as well as the trends of birth and death. More significant but more difficult, they should not overlook the extraordinary capacity of human beings and institutions to react to emerging problems in new and constructive ways. In any case the significant trends and forces bearing on population and resources should be monitored carefully and frequently so that changes in direction may be seen promptly and opportunities for helpful action may be seized.

World War II was not a Malthusian check; in spite of the horrendous numbers of soldiers and civilians killed, in spite of the massive genocide perpetrated by the Nazis, food production was decreased much more than population; by 1945 intake per capita was 16 per cent lower than the 1934–38 average.

JEAN MAYER, "Food and Population: The Wrong Problem?" *Daedalus, Journal of the American Academy of Arts and Sciences,* XCIII, No. 3 (Summer, 1964), 837.

ALEXANDER SPOEHR

CULTURAL DIFFERENCES IN THE INTERPRETATION OF NATURAL RESOURCES

An examination of the interpretation that different peoples have placed on the natural resources on which they depend falls in the more general field of human ecology. The relation of any human population to its natural resources is only part of a more inclusive set of relationships between such a population and its total natural environment. "Human ecology," though variously and often vaguely defined as a field of specific subject matter, emphasizes relationships with the environment and, as Bates[1] has said, achieves its greatest usefulness as a point of view. The subject of this paper, therefore, is a part of human ecology, and the following remarks will stress a point of view rather than attempt a synthesis of a body of scientific literature.

I am indebted to Carl Sauer for pointing out that the concept "natural resources" is largely derived from our own society's ceaseless attempt at finding new and more intensive uses for the raw materials of nature. It is doubtful that many other societies, most of which are less involved with technological development, think about natural resources in the same way as we do. It is probable that the term itself, with the feeling tones that it carries, is primarily a product of our own industrial civilization. For this reason it is not possible to take the body of ethnographic accounts of different peoples and obtain a clear-cut view as to exactly what interpretation has been placed on their natural resources by non-Western societies in different places and at different times. In ethnographic accounts chapters dealing with such peoples are seldom written quite that way.

In the following review it has been necessary to tie a cross-cultural comparison of the interpretation of natural resources to several rather arbitrarily selected reference points. Three have been chosen, and will be examined in turn: (1) natural resources in relation to technology; (2) natural resources in relation to social structure; and (3) natural resources and the interpretation of habitat. Of these three reference points, the first is most restricted in scope. The remaining two involve a progressively wider range of subject matter.

Natural Resources and Technology

It is a truism that every society must adapt itself to its environment to survive. This adaptation is largely effected through the particular technology that a given society has developed and maintains. Viewed in world perspective and from the vantage point of man's history on earth, the variety of technical systems is very great, ranging from the simple technology of food-collectors such as the Australian aborigines or the Great Basin Indians of North America to the highly complex technology of Western industrial civilization. Various classifications of technologies have been devised, and no attempt will be made here to extend

Reprinted from William L. Thomas, Jr. (ed.), *Man's Role in Changing the Face of the Earth* (Chicago: University of Chicago Press, 1956), pp. 93–102, with permission of the author. (© 1956 by The University of Chicago.)

[1] Marston Bates, *The Nature of Natural History* (New York: Charles Scribner's Sons, 1950).

them.[2] The point is rather that, regardless of the degree of complexity of a given technology, every technology is necessarily based on a thorough knowledge of the natural resources which are utilized through the working of the technology. A food-collecting technology may be of a very simple order, but the men who practice it must of necessity have a sound empirical knowledge of that sector of the natural environment that provides the food they seek.

This point is made merely to emphasize that so-called primitive peoples do not exist in a state of ignorance of the natural world about them. It is true that the knowledge they possess is essentially empirical and that the over-all characteristics of a people's technology tend to direct their interest to those particular resources of nature on which they depend. Thus the population densities of some of the Micronesian atolls are so high in relation to their few square miles of dry-land area that these communities could not possibly survive without the fish resources of the atoll lagoons. A large sector of the technology of these atoll dwellers is comprised of skills and techniques associated with fishing, the building of canoes, and seamanship, which in turn is related to an intimate knowledge of fish species, the habits and relative abundance of various species, whether or not they are poisonous, and similar matters. A given technology, by making possible a particular kind of adaptations, tends to crystallize interest and knowledge around that segment of natural resources on which the technology depends.

Anthropological literature abounds also in examples of different peoples inhabiting the same or very similar habitats but who have made use of different sectors of the resources of their habitat. There may be a high degree of selectivity of particular resources around which the technology is centered. An interesting example can be given from Hawaii. In the days when the Hawaiians had their islands to themselves, they were fishermen and farmers. Their agricultural economy was built particularly on the cultivation of taro, which was grown chiefly in irrigated plots in the bottom-land areas of coastal valleys, usually with very high rainfall. Such a valley, famous in local history, is that of Waipio on the island of Hawaii. It is estimated that at one time from 3,000 to 4,000 people lived in Waipio. During the nineteenth and twentieth centuries the economy of Hawaii completely changed. With the influx of immigrants from America, Europe, and Asia, the economy of the island of Hawaii changed to large-scale agriculture, centered on sugar cane, coffee, and cattle-raising, for none of which Waipio is suitable. The valley's population today has dwindled to 26 persons, and a great part of it has been abandoned. Its soil resources are neglected, for present-day large-scale agricultural technology in use on the island is not suited to them, and they have been bypassed.

The example from Hawaii again illustrates the point that interest in specific natural resources and the uses to which they are put is greatly conditioned by the nature of the technology imposed upon such resources. Technology is in itself a part of man's culture, and the interpretation of specific resources cannot be understood except as a facet of human culture.

To a considerable degree, the interest of our own society in the availability, renewability, and exploitability of natural resources springs from our singular bent toward technological invention. It is true that technological invention has been a potent force throughout man's long history on earth. Yet, viewed against the background of human history, our industrial civilization of the twentieth century has developed in a very short time. One of its characteristics, related, of course, to the growth of science, is its concern with invention. This concern the anthropologist does not find to be shared with all societies.

[2] C. D. Forde, *Habitat, Economy and Society: A Geographical Introduction to Ethnology* (London: Methuen; New York: Harcourt, Brace & Co., 1934).

Among many, once an adaptation to a given environment has been made through the medium of a particular technology, the manner of thought imbedded in the culture of these societies may actually militate against the inventive process. One of the best examples is given by Raymond Firth in his outstanding study of the economy of Tikopia, a very isolated small island in the southwestern Pacific. Firth[3] notes that the material culture and the technology of Tikopia are very closely adjusted to the resources of the island environment. He notes further that the Tikopians are in no way loath to accept trade goods in the form of useful tools. However, the Polynesian people of this small island "have formulated no particular doctrine of technical invention."[4] Their interest is centered on legendary origins of how they themselves came to be rather than on technological origins and on the technical processes of invention and change.

Although the variety of cultures possessed by non-literate, non-Western societies is so great that the appellation "primitive" is usually a misnomer, it is true that such societies are generally small and tied to a local habitat. Every local habitat imposes certain limitations on a purely local technology. The people of a Pacific atoll must of necessity exist within the limitations of an atoll environment. It is true that as taro raisers the Marshall Islanders have challenged the natural limitations of their atoll environment by excavating large pits in the coral lime sands of the atoll islets and, by creating humus, through filling these pits with decaying vegetable matter, are able to raise taro. This is a small-scale example of how one society has successfully challenged environmental restrictions. Yet the contrast is great when compared with the manner in which contemporary Western industrial civilization has freed itself from local environmental bonds and through its technology is world-wide in scope. Chapple and Coon have pointed out that technologically less complex societies tend to exploit single landscapes, whereas "we . . . live in all environments, not by exploiting single landscapes, separately, but by pooling and redistributing the products of all types of environment."[5] A marked difference in the cultural interpretation of natural resources among different peoples follows from this fact. In small-scale preliterate societies concern with natural resources tends to be local; ours is world-wide.

Natural Resources and Social Structure

So far we have touched on the relation of resources to technology, which in the last analysis comprises the characteristics of a society's tool system for converting raw materials into finished products. The techniques available to a society, however, are but one facet of its total economy. The latter comprehends also a body of generally accepted concepts regarding the control and use of resources, goods, and productive processes—such as those concepts embodied in the terms "income," "capital," and "rent"—and, in addition, the particular manner in which human beings are organized to carry out activities generally labeled as economic. In this latter category are the particular ways in which the individuals working in a factory or on a farm are organized, or the manner in which the market of a Mexican town is organized. In each case, interpersonal relations tend to fall in definable patterns, into a system of relationships that tends to persist so long as the common end—such as the exchange of goods—is being pursued. This organization of human beings in economic activity is but part of the total social structure of a society. Economic organization is related at many points to

[3] Raymond Firth, *Primitive Polynesian Economy* (London: G. Routledge & Sons, 1939).

[4] *Ibid.*, p. 86.

[5] E. D. Chapple and C. S. Coon, *Principles of Anthropology* (New York: Henry Holt & Co., 1942).

other segments of social structure. Thus, the organization of a craft industry carried out in individual households is closely related to the prevailing characteristics of the system of relations among the kinfolk of the various households. A people's kinship system is only in part an aspect of their economy.

This point is made because the use of natural resources is controlled by the nature of social structure in addition to a body of productive techniques alone. One cannot consider the link between natural resources and man merely as a matter of converting raw materials into goods through a given technology in order to house, feed, and clothe so-and-so many people, essential as these facts are.

For purposes of illustration and contrast, the following example from a technologically less complex society may be useful.

To the atoll dwellers of the Marshall Islands the coconut palm, as well as the fish resources of the sea, is a mainstay of life. A relatively simple body of techniques employing hand labor makes possible the use of the coconut for food, for export as copra, and for a variety of other products. However, the control of the coconut palm as a natural resource, the organization of production whereby it is converted into usable goods, and the distribution of income derived from its production are all linked to Marshallese social structure. The Marshall Islanders retain a feudal-like class system of nobility and commoners. Title to all the land of the atoll nominally rests with the paramount chief. Usufruct rights are apportioned among the lesser chiefs and, in turn, among the commoners. Land is not sold, and our own concepts of ownership of real property are foreign to the system. The commoners cultivate the land, and the nobility receive tribute in the form of produce. Today, a share of cash receipts from the sale of copra is also remitted to the paramount chief as tribute. In addition, land rights are, for the most part, held by lineages of kinfolk who trace descent in the matrilineal line. Each lineage has a head who represents the lineage, and the headship as an office is also passed down the matrilineal line. Lineages, the class organization, and land tenure are all interrelated elements of a single system. As a result, to the Marshallese, the control and use of land resources are mediated through the particular characteristics of their social structure.

The significance of cultural factors in relation to resources is perhaps most clearly discerned during periods of rapid change. Cultural change is a complex, but not a haphazard, phenomenon. At times it may follow a rigidly defined course that from a biologist's point of view is nonadaptive, insofar as the conservation and use of resources are concerned. An oft-quoted example is found in the cattle-raising peoples of East Africa, among whom cattle are so highly regarded and are so fundamental a basis of status within the community that the greatest resistance to a reduction of herds has been encountered among these people, despite serious depletion of resources.[6] A somewhat similar case is provided by the resistance of the Navaho to reduction of sheep on their overgrazed ranges.

The purpose of these examples is simply to emphasize that any group "interprets" its natural resources within the framework of its own social structure. The point at which this probably is most apparent is in the organization of production, for it is in production that the manner of control and the use of natural resources are most evident. The initial point in the productive process is the conversion of raw materials into goods. The raw materials are derived from resources in their natural state. If the resources are especially limited, restrictive rights to their use may exist. Our own concepts of "ownership" may be viewed as the conjunction of our own particular social

[6] Margaret Read, "Native Standards of Living and African Culture Change," Supplement to *Africa,* XI, No. 3 (1938).

system and limited resources. Yet Western ideas of ownership are by no means universal and are but one example of how an exclusive right may be culturally defined. The Pacific islands provide examples of differently conceived rights to resources, where Western concepts of ownership are not applicable. Yet, among these peoples, rights controlling how resources, particularly land, are to be used and who is entitled to exercise control can also be viewed as the conjunction of social structure and habitat. The case of the Marshallese has been noted. For more extensive analyses of other island societies the reader is referred to Firth,[7] to Hogbin,[8] and to Herskovits' general review of the problem of ownership and land tenure.[9]

Natural Resources and Habitat

Natural resources are physically a part of habitat, and habitat is but one aspect of that complex of physical, chemical, and biological processes, with their resultant products, which we call "nature." Modern man has conceptually isolated natural resources as that segment of the physical world that has a present or potential use for the survival and physical well-being of man, to be developed as far as possible through the application of scientific knowledge. Yet natural resources are still a part of nature.

The title of this paper, with its emphasis on the "interpretation" of natural resources, implies a comparison of attitudes held by different peoples toward natural resources. But, to return to a point made earlier, concern for the development of "natural resources" seems largely a facet of modern civilization. What is necessary is an examination, not merely of culturally conditioned attitudes toward natural resources, but of how various peoples have come to regard their relationship with their respective habitats (of which resources are but a part) and indeed with the entire physical universe in which they exist. It is at this point that the most fundamental contrast can be discerned between the Western industrial world and small-scale, often preliterate, societies.

This subject has been explored and presented, in a much more expert fashion than that of which I am capable, by Robert Redfield in his book, *The Primitive World and Its Transformations*.[10] It is a subject that anthropologists have long pondered, though few with the breadth of interest displayed by Redfield. His presentation is the point of departure for the following paragraphs.

For the purpose of this essay there are two questions that are particularly relevant: (1) How have men, in different times and places, regarded nature, and hence the habitats in which they dwell? (2) How have these attitudes affected what men feel they should do about conserving and developing their habitats for human use?

In regard to the first question, the initial point to be made is taken from Redfield and the writers that he in turn draws upon. It is that virtually every people regards the universe in some sort of structured cosmology. The degree to which this cosmology is systematized varies enormously. The points of emphasis vary enormously. But everywhere, and since ancient times, man has pondered his relation to the physical facts of the universe and has attempted to see man, nature, and the supernatural in some sort of understandable relation. In this, my feeling from reading the accounts of ethnologists is the same as Redfield's[11]—that

[7] Raymond Firth, *Primitive Economics of the New Zealand Maori* (London: Routledge; New York: E. P. Dutton & Co., 1929); *Primitive Polynesian Economy, op. cit.*

[8] H. I. Hogbin, *Experiments in Civilization: The Effects of European Culture on a Native Community of the Solomon Islands* (London: G. Routledge & Sons, 1939).

[9] M. J. Herskovits, *Economic Anthropology* (New York: Alfred A. Knopf, 1952).

[10] Robert Redfield, *The Primitive World and Its Transformations* (Ithaca: Cornell University Press, 1953).

[11] *Ibid.*, pp. 105–6.

preliterate peoples, in regarding the universe, "think of an orderly system originally set running by divine will and thereafter exhibiting its immanent order." Whether the gods do or can interfere in the machine they have set running is either not thought about or perhaps not reported sufficiently by ethnologists. It seems more probable that preliterate peoples tend to regard the universe as operating under irreversible laws, once these are set in motion.

And how is man's place regarded in this scheme? To what degree is he subject also to an order established under supernatural sanction? Here at least most preliterate societies offer a contrast with our own. The contrast is well exemplified in the opening paragraph of Elsdon Best's monograph, *Forest Lore of the Maori.* The contrast is shown both in Best's point of view and in that of the Maori of whom he was writing:

> The outlook of the Maori, as in connection with natural phenomena and nature generally, often differed widely from our own; thus he looked upon the far spread forests of his island home as being necessary to his welfare, and also as being of allied origin. This peculiar outlook was based on the strange belief that man, birds, and trees are descended from a common source; their ultimate origin lay with the primal pair, Rangi the Sky Parent and Papa the Earth Mother, though they were actually brought into being by Tane the Fertilizer, one of the seventy offspring of the above-mentioned prmial parents.[12]

Man, to many peoples, is not set apart from nature but is part of a single order, combining man, nature, and the gods. When man utilizes the resources of nature, it is within the framework of this system of ideas. Thus, in writing of the lack of interest in technological invention displayed by the island people of Tikopia, Firth notes[13] that the Tikopia are governed by their theory of natural resources, which "may be described briefly as a theory of the human utilization of resources under supernatural control, which governs not only their fertility, but also the social and economic relationships of those who handle them."

Within this essentially stable system, man and nature are not conceptually opposed but are considered as parts of the same thing. The totemic rites of the Australian Karadjeri, whereby the economically and socially important species of plants and animals were believed to be assured of normal increase, reflected a similar manner of thought.[14] When Gayton, writing of the integration of culture and environment effected through economic activity, ceremony, and myth among the Yokuts Indians, states that "men and animals were peers,"[15] much the same idea is expressed.

In his consideration of the involvement of man and nature in the thought of preliterate and ancient societies, Redfield notes[16] that the men of these societies did not "confront" nature. For them, "being already in nature, man cannot exactly confront it." Rather, Redfield suggests, the relation is one of mutuality, existing under a moral order that binds man, nature, and the gods in one.

The modern Western world has undergone a major transformation from this orientation. Man has been conceptually separated from nature, and God from both. Speaking of the development of Western thought since classical times, Redfield states:

> The subsequent development of a world view in which God and man are both separated from nature, and in which the exploitation of mate-

[12] Elsdon Best, *Forest Lore of the Maori,* Bull. No. 14 (Wellington, N.Z.: Dominion Museum, 1942).

[13] Firth, *Primitive Polynesian Economy, op. cit.,* p. 88.

[14] A. P. Elkin, *Studies in Australian Totemism,* Oceania Monograph, No. 2 (Sydney, 1933).

[15] A. H. Gayton, "Culture-Environment Integration: External References in Yokuts Life," *Southwestern Journal of Anthropology,* II (1946), 262.

[16] Redfield, *op. cit.,* p. 104.

rial nature comes to be a prime attitude, may be attributable to our Western world almost entirely and so might be regarded, as Sol Tax has suggested . . . as a particular "cultural invention." By the seventeenth century in European philosophy God was outside the system as its mere clockmaker. To the early American, nature was God's provision for man's exploitation. . . . The contemporary Western world, now imitated by the Orient, tends to regard the relation of man to nature as a relation of man to physical matter in which application of physical science to man's material comfort is man's paramount assignment on earth.[17]

These observations may appear overdrawn to some, but they illustrate what I believe is a fundamental contrast in the thinking of the Western world, as contrasted to preliterate and ancient peoples. It is a contrast that in itself is at least a partial answer to our second question posed earlier—namely, how has this contrasting attitude affected what men feel they should do about developing their habitats for human use? Certainly the tenor of contemporary American thought holds that habitat is something apart from man and is to be manipulated to his advantage. In the world of today, with the ever growing millions of human beings to clothe, feed, and house, this attitude has a very immediate and practical import.

On the other hand, despite the long history of the growth of technology, throughout which some men as far back as the earliest periods of human history must have been concerned with improving tools to develop resources for human use, preliterate societies lack the pervading instrumental attitude toward nature generally characteristic of ourselves. The difference probably accounts for the significance of magic associated with technology, which Malinowski long ago reported for the Trobriand Island. Among these people, although their full technological skill is called upon in an enterprise, such as gardening, fishing, or voyaging, recourse to magic is had to fill the inevitable gap between the application of human skill and the certainty of success.

The contrasting attitudes of Western and preliterate thought lead to another question. For several decades anthropologists have been attempting to observe the changes that take place in small scale, for the most part preliterate, societies, when they come in contact with Western industrial civilization. Insofar as the interpretation of natural resources is concerned, is not the contrast just discussed at the root of the change that takes place? I suspect it is. To review all the evidence is beyond the scope of this paper, but I quote an anthropological colleague, John Gillin, comparing the Indian and the Ladino cultures (crystallized out of contact with Spain) of Guatemala:

The principal and fundamental goal of Indian cultures is to effect a peaceful adjustment or adaptation to the universe. In contrast, the main goal of Ladino culture is to effect control of the universe by man. The Indian wishes to come to terms with the universe, the Ladino wishes to dominate it. . . . The Indian attitude is not one of abject submission to natural and supernatural forces. The basic assumptions in Indian cultures, however, do hold that man is in a world which operates according to certain laws or rules ultimately controlled by that part of the universe which we would call the supernatural or unseen, that this general plan of things is ongoing or immutable, that man must learn certain patterns of action and attitude to bring himself into conformity with this scheme of things, and that if he does so he will receive the minimum amount of punishment or misfortune and the maximum rewards of which such a scheme is capable. . . . The Ladino, on the other hand, assumes that the universe, including its supernatural department, can be manipulated by man. . . .[18]

The gradual adoption of this attitude could, I believe, be documented from other societies in contact with the West. It seems to have been, for instance, a concomitant of the extension of the copra industry to

[17] *Ibid.*, pp. 109–10.

[18] John Gillin, "Ethos and Cultural Aspects of Personality," *Heritage of Conquest*, ed. Sol Tax (Glencoe: The Fress Press, 1952), p. 196.

various islands of the Pacific during the nineteenth and twentieth centuries. The development of the copra industry in the Marshall Islands was almost certainly accompanied by a marked change in attitude toward land, whereby it came to be regarded as a resource to be controlled and manipulated by man to his best advantage, in a fashion comparable to the Ladino point of view described by Gillin. To what degree the extension of this attitude follows the penetration of a money economy into societies such as the Marshallese, together with the growth of trade and a widening in the range of wants, is not clear.

If these contrasting attitudes toward nature, and in consequence toward natural resources, have been correctly described in these paragraphs, I should like to turn to some ramifications in regard to the interpretation of nature by our own society.

To the degree that the Western world is composed of almost completely urbanized individuals, it not merely regards habitat, and consequently natural resources, as an entity that is to be dominated and manipulated by man but tends to relegate the whole matter to a handful of specialists and, in effect, to place nature outside its immediate sphere of concern. Urban man has become so far removed from his biological moorings and so immersed in the immediate problems of urban living that he stands as an "egocentric man in a homocentric world." Despite the millions of Americans who annually visit our national parks each year, it is to be doubted that much change is thereby effected in the basic urban attitude. The aesthetic principles underlying American conservation movements can perhaps best be viewed as a minority reaction to the prevailing urban point of view. Conservation, in the sense of the attempt by the Save-the-Redwoods League to preserve stands of California giant sequoias from extinction, is an effort to protect modern man from himself. Such efforts are not, to my knowledge, found among preliterate peoples living in small communities in close and personal relation to nature. Among most of them, though it is largely unrecorded in the reports of the ethnologists, I suspect that the aesthetic appreciation of nature is a common feature of daily life. Yet I should add that most of my own field experience has been in the congenial islands of the Pacific.

If the prevailing mode of thought tends to regard nature as a physical entity apart from man, with the corollary that man's duty is to develop and dominate to the best of his ability the resources of his habitat, there are nevertheless certain countercurrents in contemporary scientific thought that cannot be ignored. These countercurrents are well exemplified by Darwin and Faraday.

Darwin opened our eyes to the functioning of organic nature, and his mode of thought led to discovery of new facts and relationships in the living world. Darwin dealt with man's place in nature and with man as a part of a huge, dynamic biocoenose, of which man was only a small part, actually not very different from the other parts, and subject to the same processes and regularities. In his point of view as to man's integration with the natural world, Darwin might be considered as close to the way in which preliterate peoples regard nature, except for the fundamental difference that the former developed his point of view on the basis of observed reality: the latter, on recourse to the sanction of man-created legend and myth. Darwin left to his successors the concept of man as a part of nature, whatever qualities man may possess that distinguish him from other forms of life.

Faraday, on the other hand, introduced us to inanimate forces which could be made to serve man's needs and wants. He stimulated the invention of new devices and the formation of a great new technology based on the use of natural forces. He also stimulated the creation of a homocentric world, a modern, mechanized, exploiting world of men whose contemplating largely centers about themselves and who attempt to plan, arrange, and administer in their own name. Whereas the heritage of Darwin has provided the fascination of biological revelation, that of Faraday has brought the excitement attending the accomplishment and application of the physical sciences.

In a modern world where men are dedicated to exploiting to the utmost the natural resources of this planet—a dedication that is stimulated by the very numbers of men on earth—the point of view exemplified by Faraday is necessarily uppermost. It could hardly be otherwise. Yet one cannot forget the bearded figure of Darwin watching quietly from the shadows.

Additional References

Bates, Marston. "Human Ecology," *Anthropology Today: Selections,* ed. Sol Tax. Chicago: University of Chicago Press, 1953.

Bews, J. W. *Human Ecology.* London: H. Milford, 1935.

Darwin, Sir Francis (ed.). *Charles Darwin's Autobiography.* New York: Henry Schuman, 1950.

Evans-Pritchard, E. E. *The Nuer: A Description of the Modes of Livelihood and Political Institutions of a Nilotic People.* Oxford: Clarendon Press, 1940.

Firth, Raymond. *Malay Fishermen: Their Peasant Economy.* London: Kegan Paul, Trench, Trubner & Co., 1946.

Herskovits, M. J. *Man and His Works.* New York: Alfred A. Knopf, 1948.

Kluckhohn, Clyde, and Leighton, Dorothea. *The Navaho.* Cambridge: Harvard University Press, 1946.

Malinowski, Bronislaw. *Coral Gardens and Their Magic.* 2 vols. London: Allen & Unwin, 1935.

Mead, Margaret. *Mountain Arapesh. II. Supernaturalism,* "Anthropological Papers," Vol. XXXIV, Part III. New York: American Museum of Natural History, 1940.

Sears, P. B. *Charles Darwin: The Naturalist as a Cultural Force.* New York: Charles Scribner's Sons, 1950.

Spoehr, Alexander. *Majuro: A Village in the Marshall Islands.* "Fieldiana: Anthropology," Vol. XXXIX. Chicago: Chicago Natural History Museum, 1949.

Tax, Sol. "World View and Social Relations in Guatemala," in *American Anthropologist,* XLIII (1941).

———. *Penny Capitalism: Guatemalan Indian Economy,* Smithsonian Institution Pub. No. 10. Washington: GPO, 1953.

———. (ed.). *Heritage of Conquest: The Ethnology of Middle America.* Glencoe: Free Press, 1952.

Thurnwald, R. *Economics in Primitive Communities.* London: Oxford University Press, 1932.

FAIRFIELD OSBORN

THE HOUR OF DECISION

Someone, sometime, somewhere ended a book with a "Conclusion." This idea had its drawbacks, but it became a custom and, as Plutarch remarked, "We are more sensible of what is done against custom than against nature."

There can be no such thing as a *conclusion* in any book that treats of human affairs and problems, because we strange beings, we people, do the most unexpected things and are capable of adapting ourselves in unforeseeable ways to new circumstances. Beyond that, no book, or innumerable series of books, could anticipate all the factors that may have a bearing upon the future of human life upon this earth. More than once, in writing these pages, there has been great enticement to deal less with material or physical matters and more with the many exciting elements, intellectual and moral, that make human life what it is—and what it may be. We must have faith that humanity will triumph in the end in reaching its incomparable destiny. But always in speculating regarding the ultimate, one is drawn inexorably to consideration of the immediate, of the first need of all needs, of the means toward the barest living, of the question of minimal survival—adequacy of food and of other essential natural resources.

We are under the power of a timeless principle, exerting its influence relentlessly on a global scale. This principle is closely related to the law of supply and demand. It finds expression in a simple ratio wherein the numerator can be defined as "resources of the earth" and the denominator as "numbers of people." The numerator is *relatively* fixed and only partially subject to control by man. The denominator is subject to substantial change and is largely, if not entirely, subject to control by man. If we are blind to this law, or delude ourselves into minimizing its power, of one thing we can be assured—the human race will enter into days of increasing trouble, conflict, and darkness.

How is one justified in giving as categorical an opinion as this regarding the future, even though it concerns a trend and not a finality? Presumably the best response is to sum up the reasons that appear to justify it and in doing so search for courses of action that would ward off a future so unnecessary and so dismal.

In view of the fact that the denominator of this timeless principle, namely, numbers of people, is to the greater degree subject to control by man, let's commence with a review of the general facts of population growth, making sure to consider them through the perspective of recent history.

Three hundred years ago, or in the middle of the seventeenth century, the earth's population is estimated to have been approximately 470,000,000 people, or about one-fifth of today's number. There are various valid reasons for assuming that it had not previously much exceeded that number. However, the eighteenth century proved to be a period of major change. It witnessed the beginnings of better means

• Fairfield Osborn is Chairman of the Conservation Foundation, New York.

Reprinted from Fairfield Osborn, *The Limits of the Earth* (Boston: Little, Brown & Co., 1953), pp. 206–26, with permission of the author and the publisher.

of communication and transport, the introduction of the steam engine and an incipient improvement in medical care. It was a time of stirring, of new impulses, of breaking away from the prolonged era of medievalism. The revelation of new land and wealth in the Western Hemisphere had a profound psychological effect upon the minds of men. The earth was a vast place, after all. The fascination of new horizons galvanized the thoughts of European peoples. In a material sense this New World soon began to contribute to the welfare of Europe. At the same time the Far East shared in some degree these new influences. In effect the eighteenth century was a growing period—the dawn of the Industrial Revolution. As a consequence of these various encouraging influences, the population of the world increased by about 400,000,000 people in a century and a half, and at the opening of the nineteenth century had risen to about 870,000,000 people.

Then there came, at a steadily accelerating rate, the explosive increase in human numbers. The new forces of industrial production, the extension of commerce, of rapid transport of food and other materials and, above all, the revolutionary advances in the medical sciences spread their influences throughout the world. From the point of view of population growth the most important factor was the widespread adoption of better sanitation, the control of pestilence and plagues, and the consequent lowering of the death rate, including the reduction of infant mortality. These advances, in greater or less degree, affected every country, whether in Europe, the New World, or the Orient. In the short span of four generations, or a hundred years, the world's population almost doubled and as the twentieth century opened stood at approximately 1,600,000,000.

Since the year 1900 this extraordinary upward surge in the numbers of people has continued. Another 800,000,000, in round numbers, have been added to the world population within the last 50 years, bringing us up to a present population of about 2,400,000,000. By the end of the present century, if the same rates of increase continue, and barring the cataclysm of atomic war, the total world population will stand at 3,600,000,000.

There are various ways by which one can attempt to visualize the significance of this almost incredible population growth. For instance, the present rate of increase results, each year, in approximately 30 million additional people—a number equal to the population of almost four cities the size of London or New York, or to put it another way, of six cities the size of Paris or Tokyo. Perhaps a more vivid comparison is that the net increase since the year 1900, namely, some 800 million people, exceeds the sum total of the populations of Europe, North and South America, and Africa in that year. No wonder we are witness to a succession of violent and mounting pressures upon the social and political institutions of our times.

A few general observations should be made here regarding the distribution of population as well as regarding population increase. It is well to bear in mind that throughout historical times, as is the case today, at least half of all the world's people have lived in Asia. Consequently, the greatest pressures of people appear to be there. Further, in view of the fact that a number of Asiatic countries contain the largest populations of any of the world's regions, they have produced the largest numerical increase. This fact has given rise to the misconception that the rate of increase in Far Eastern countries is greater than in countries in other parts of the world. This is not true. For example, the rate of increase in Europe since the year 1800 is considerably greater than that in India during the same period. This surprising circumstance is principally due to the steady decline in the death rate in Europe during this period. Further, there are a number of instances of countries or regions—in the Americas, in Africa, or even a few in Europe—where the present rate of increase is either as great as, or in some cases greater than, that of India or other countries in the Far East.

On the other hand, there is a distinct tendency, which must not go unrecognized, for the rate of population growth to diminish in countries whose people have attained the advantages, both material and cultural, provided by modern civilization. A majority of the people in the world today, however, are living without these advantages. Consequently, it is not really sufficiently accurate to speak of a world population problem if, in doing so, one disregards the fact that the elements involved in the problem vary greatly in different countries or areas. Attempts are made from time to time to classify the people of the world into different categories designed to indicate differences in population patterns and food supply. For example, one authority has recently published a study that divides the countries of the world into the following three groups or areas.

The first consists of most of Western Europe, of North America, and of Australia and New Zealand. This group contains about one-fifth of the world's population and is characterized as having low birth rates, low death rates, high average food supply (estimated 3,000 calories per day) and a relatively stable population.

The second group, containing another one-fifth of the world's population, consists of Eastern and Southeastern Europe, Spain, a few South American countries like Brazil and Argentina, and finally Japan. This group is described as having a moderate and rising industrial activity, a high but falling birth rate and a medium but falling death rate. These areas have the highest rates of natural increase largely because their birth rate has not been falling as fast as their death rate. They have a food level of between 2,300 to 2,800 calories per day—and so are living in a marginal state where countless individuals are underfed or suffering actual privation.

The third group is described as the truly critical one—and rightly so. It contains three-fifths of the world's population and takes in most of Asia and some of its adjacent islands, most of Africa as well as major portions of South and Central America. Its population of almost 1.5 billion people lives at or near a starvation level, with an estimated 2,000 calories or less per day for each individual. It has a high and constant birth rate, a high but widely fluctuating death rate, which drops when harvests are good and there are no epidemics, and soars under opposite conditions. It represents a majority of the human race, innumerable people, living in a crisis whose monotone is interrupted only by catastrophe.

A grouping of the world's peoples, such as the above, which highlights the differences in population and food conditions, is certainly invaluable in providing a clearer comprehension of the situation which faces humanity. However, as in all summaries that contain generalized statements, there is great risk of misunderstanding. For instance, the first group, which includes the countries in Western Europe and North America, is characterized as having "low birth rates . . . and a relatively stable population." Although this is generally true, two startling exceptions come to mind at once—and there are others. For instance, at this very time, the rates of net annual increase in the populations of both Holland and the United States are greater than the rate of India! As a matter of fact the birth rate in the United States in the year 1952 was unexpectedly high—climbing to 25 per thousand of population from a low of 16.6 per thousand in 1933. Both presumably represent temporary conditions, but the rise is illustrative of the fluctuations that may occur.

Considerable differences exist between both the birth and death rates of countries within any of the groups that have been described above. As we all know, almost every people or country possesses at least some individual characteristic, whether political, social, religious, or economic. In the main, therefore, each country must find its own way through the dilemma created by population growth and resource inadequacy. And yet cooperative study and action can lead to practices that can prove invaluable to all.

A theory that the birth rate is highest among the ill-fed, and more particularly among those who lack protein in their diet, is not supportable as a uniform biological principle for mankind. There exists an overwhelming mass of evidence which confirms the self-evident fact that well-nourished people have the highest fertility potential and which also endorses the all-important truth that birth rate is primarily a consequence of economic and cultural influences.

It is sometimes said that one method of checking population increase is to provide an adequate diet and raise standards of living. There are scarcely any grounds for the belief that such a plan, even if it were possible to put it generally into effect, would produce the results that are constantly becoming more imperative. We have just seen that some high-living-standard countries, including even such countries as Holland and the United States, are capable of having a rapid rate of population increase. Further than that, even if it were possible to provide far more adequate diets to the hundreds of millions of presently undernourished people, the great likelihood is that the consequence would solely be more and more people. The infinitely tragic fact is that starvation is at present the only controlling factor to constantly increasing human numbers in a vast portion of our world. There are those who believe that this must always be so. They discredit the intelligence of mankind and disavow the possibilties that exist for the future of civilization. We do not live to extenuate the miseries of the past or to accept as incurable those of the present.

There are stirrings within the minds of men—awakenings to what can and to what must be done. Already one great country in the Far East, India, is initiating a program to control population growth. Other peoples and countries are becoming more and more conscious of the nature of the dilemma. Sweden has adopted a program, unique of its kind, aimed at attaining a population improved as to quality and not diminishing in quantity. A world meeting on the subject of population, under the auspices of the United Nations, is now in prospect. Even though it is planned that this conference shall be statistical and technical in character, and free of what might be called social or political programming, it should prove yet one more step forward to understanding. The foundation of hope for the future lies in such understanding, all in good time transmitted through the processes of enlightenment and education to peoples of all countries. Such forward steps represent an attainable alternate to the creed of the pessimist, who holds that our civilization is incapable of delivering itself from a problem of this character and magnitude.

The rapid and continuing growth in world population is not necessarily due to increase in the birth rate. In the main it is due to the decline in the death rate. This decline is, of course, a direct consequence of advances in medical science, of widespread adoption of better sanitation and other public health measures. The successes that have been gained so far in the conquest of epidemics and disease and in the alleviation of bodily pain and suffering represent, probably, the most beneficent accomplishment of modern times. The continuance and further development of public health measures, as an essential part of humanitarianism, is infinitely desirable. At the same time it would be a gross delusion if it were not clearly recognized that such measures represent a potent, man-made control over natural forces that keep population in check.

This latter fact lies at the heart of a rational consideration concerning the desirability of using direct and effective means to control population growth. It lies at the crux of the argument as to whether birth control is good or undesirable. The situation is simply this. Modern man has gained the immeasurable benefits that have resulted from the advancement of medical science, whose techniques have largely removed the control of human numbers resulting from epidemics, plagues, and disease. It must not be supposed that epidemics or pathological conditions are abnormal in nature. Wild animal populations are subject to them, and epidemics are one controlling factor upon population growth, although it seems that a principal one is lack of food supply. In effect, then, medical science through "unnatural methods" has at one and the same time ameliorated suffering and vastly increased human numbers. It is an irony of life that this great good should also bring this great problem in its train. The question remains. If we are to accept, as of course we must, the continuing and ever-greater boon that public health measures afford humanity, must we not take adequate steps to abolish the disastrous consequences of overpopulation, to which medical science is an unintentional contributor?

One of the principal impediments to an objective approach to birth control stems from religious dogma. This has been true during much of the past just as it is today. Beliefs concerning the inviolability of the human soul and ethical conceptions of the rights and wrongs of human action have greatly affected human thinking as to whether man is justified in interfering with natural procreation. Gandhi, India's great spiritual leader and ascetic, held that abstinence from intercourse was the desirable and indeed the only method that should be used to keep population in check. It is noteworthy that many of his followers, now become leaders in India, have grown to realize that relief from their country's population crisis cannot be gained if reliance is placed upon abstinence alone and, consequently, that the adoption of other and more realistic approaches is imperative.

In the Western world the attitude of the Catholic church is, at the present time, a strong influence in discouraging open discussion and preventing a completely detached approach to a problem which is of such overriding importance to the future welfare and happiness of mankind. Speaking as a Protestant, I think it unjustified, indeed wrong, that those of other faiths should attack the Catholic attitude with a violence that is all too frequent. The answer to the present common emergency will be too long delayed if the search for it is clouded by bitterness or misunderstanding.

It can never be amiss to recall that the Catholic church is one of the foremost defenders of the free world against the evils of communism and at the same time a bulwark in modern society against the dissolution of the family as a social unit. Both of these significant accomplishments, however, create a paradox. Communism flourishes best amidst conditions of need or want, and such conditions are unquestionably fostered by the pressures of ever-increasing numbers of people upon limited resources. In contrast, the welfare of the family is diminished when standards of living inevitably decline in the face of overpopulation. This is the hour when different faiths and creeds can well join together in the attempt to resolve a paradox that is common to all.

Time presses on. Every 24 hours there are 75,000 or more additional people on the earth.

How will the ever-increasing needs of our world's constantly larger population be met? It is clear from the considerations in earlier pages that the returns being gained from agriculture in the cultivated regions of the earth are barely able to meet existing demands—and in many instances failing to. It is also evident that the potentialities of such regions as the Amazon or parts of Africa offer no early or even assured solution. Further, it is apparent . . . that present knowledge of practical means to draw upon the life resources of the oceans of the world, or to create artificial subsistence, or to convert salt water to fresh for important extensions of agricultural lands is in each and every case in an incipient stage. Perhaps one day these new resources, or new methods of providing essential resources, may be of importance, but that day, at best, is a long way off.

It is said quite often—particularly by specialists who are themselves responsible for the invaluable advances being made in agricultural techniques—that if existing knowledge could be universally applied the problem would be resolved. There is no way of disputing such a statement, and, therefore, no purpose can be gained in trying to deny it. However, the statement bears resemblance to one that might be made to the effect that if everyone would act just as he should there would be no need for law courts, police officers, or even standing armies.

The effort toward a far more extensive adoption of sound and competent agricultural methods is indeed essential—nor, as it happens, is such an effort unrelated to the realization of higher ethical standards. As a case in point, the land-tenure systems that still prevail in many countries are not only inefficient but inequitable. Recent land revolutions in India, the Near East, Italy, and elsewhere are a sign of the times, and, it must be recognized, they have occurred frequently before in history. The Russians are committed to seeking the solution through the establishment of collective farms, where all lands belong to the state. The aim of the free world is the encouragement of individual ownership and responsibility—a system that not only answers the desire for freedom of action but, competitively, holds greater promise of results. It is questionable whether, regardless of the "urge" from the state, any collective Soviet farm could match the extraordinary and long-sustained results produced, for example, by the land-holding farmers of northern Europe, or by farming communities such as those of the Amish and the Mennonites in the United States, where land and individual welfare, present and future, are one.

More equitable land-tenure systems are obviously an important requirement in the development of world agriculture. Even with all the faith one must hold in the future, these changes for the better can, at best, be accomplished only gradually. Better land use, not unlike better morals, is hard to attain.

The prospects for a substantial increase in agricultural production must be measured, in large part, in the light of past accomplishments as well as of existing conditions. As to the former, the recent report of the United Nations Food and Agriculture Organization is so significant that it cannot be disregarded. It will be recalled that this survey states that the increase in world food supply, during somewhat more than the last decade, has failed to keep pace with population growth—food supply having increased by 9 per cent and population by 12 per cent. This failure has occurred despite all the current efforts to close the gap. As to existing conditions, one need only recall the present situation in Europe, the weakening of the position of the food-surplus countries, the impediments that lie ahead in the undeveloped regions, such as Africa or the Amazon, to realize the magnitude of the task in the face of known realities.

It is to be expected that there can be no general agreement as to the prospective rate of increase in world food production—any more than there can be a commonly shared opinion concerning any future event. Some maintain that the blight of soil erosion, so prevalent, and even accelerating, in many countries, will offset the advances that are being made in technical knowledge and that consequently we shall be fortunate if the present rates of production are maintained. Others—and especially those who, as professionals, are intimately aware of the recently discovered values of better crop species, such as hybrid corn, or are themselves making discoveries in the science of soil chemistry—

envisage immeasurable results if these new knowledges could be generally applied. Still others suggest that there must be extensive regions on the earth that are not now being used, though failing to define where these regions may be or to analyze their presumed potentialities. Finally, others claim that we can fill our needs from the oceans, or create synthetic substitutes, or that the genii of technology, when they really put their minds to the task, will find the answers to the question for which humanity is now waiting. It is profoundly hoped that this book will throw the light of realism on these urgent questions and, among other things, will dispel illusions regarding imaginary new horizons.

A settlement of existing differences of opinion is obviously most difficult. All must be tempered by two overriding considerations. The first is the condition of man himself, or, specifically, the cultural, economic, and even political circumstances which govern his actions. The second is the natural environment or, specifically, the conditions of climate, land form, soil, vegetation, and water supply which are favorable or otherwise to human existence.

Out of the welter of conflicting opinions and bold, if not careless, forecasts, only one valid or practical observation can be made. It will be time to conjecture how many people the earth is capable of supporting when the increase in the production of vital resources from agriculture, or through other means, is demonstrably keeping pace with population growth. This it is not now doing.

It is a rather curious contemporary circumstance, when well-founded opinions are of the essence, that some scientists are playing the role of prophets of abundance. In entering the realm of conjecture, they are abandoning the so-called scientific method, which demands conclusions based on known facts and conditions. Theirs is a heavy and unenviable responsibility if, as time runs on, their anticipations are proved groundless and public opinion has been grossly misled. A recent headline in a newspaper with an international circulation ran, WORLD HELD ABLE TO FEED 4 BILLION. Within the last few years there have been a number of similar widely quoted statements from "authoritative sources." One's first reaction might well be that the world is not now successful in feeding half that number. In justice to the authors of such statements, they almost invariably cover their positions with the proviso which runs, "If present knowledges could be efficiently applied throughout the world." This, of course, is the crux of the matter. The barrier is not so much lack of knowledge as that imposed by conditions, cultural, and economic, that govern men's actions. These conditions are the existing verities that no one, scientist or otherwise, is justified in disregarding.

Quite apart from food supply, there is the other question as to the adequacy of the earth's stores of minerals, chemicals, and petroleum, as well as other energy producers, to meet the expanding demands of our industrial civilization. These other natural resources, spoken of as "non-renewable," are finite, so that one day many of them will be exhausted. The mounting tempo in the use of the non-renewable resources . . . is exemplified by the statement that the quantity of most metals and mineral fuels used in the United States in the last 40 years exceeds the total used throughout the entire world in all preceding history. A consideration of the implication of facts such as these is not within the purpose of this book. Nevertheless, it is evident that, year by year, the entire problem of adequacy of natural resources for the maintenance and development of our civilization is becoming more acute. There is no doubt that science and technology face their greatest opportunities in the discovery of new inorganic resources or in the replacement of one diminishing raw material by another of which there are larger reserves. Presumably, there are within the earth large quantities of non-renewable resources that have not as yet been discovered and put to use. These and similar technological expectancies will not, however, answer the primal question of food supply and other organic resources needed to support life as well as a substantial part of the world's industry.

The discovery of nuclear energy marks an epoch in the history of man. On the other hand, it becomes a meaningless incident if we do not intelligently conserve, use, and develop the life-supporting elements of the earth—its soils, forests, and water resources—and at the same time measure the numbers of people who can be supported by the productivity of the earth. Impressive beyond comprehension are the technological advances of this era. The stark fact remains—nuclear energy means nothing to the man whose body is starving.

Some people who are wedded to the magical idea of limitless technological development may say, "Give us time. The day may come when even nuclear energy, in some manner, can be employed as an agent to provide for the needs of innumerable people." Even if we care to envision such a fantasy becoming a reality, we still must ask ourselves, "Is the purpose of our civilization really to see how much the earth and the human spirit can sustain?" The decision is still ours to make, assuming we recognize that the goal of humanitarianism is not the quantity but the quality of living.

If we evade the choice, the inevitable looms ahead of us—even sterner forces will make the decision for us. We cannot delay or evade. For now, as we look, we can see the limits of the earth.

[We] either deny that the earth has limits or speculate in great detail on what the limit is. How many people can the earth support, we ask. Then we make estimates ranging from the six billion we must expect by the end of this century to many more, to easily as many as 80 billion.

The estimate depends on what we demand in the way of living standards and what we assume in the way of technological capability. Most debate of this sort is pointless. The earth can support the number of people it does, and these days it can be made to support 2 per cent more each year, with perhaps slightly better or slightly worse living conditions than last year. If this growth continues, however, inevitably the time will come when steadily and remorselessly the entire earth will support each day a few less than the day before. This has already happened in some regions.

If we continue to insist that there is no population problem, it is still unlikely that our fate will be universal starvation. More likely we will see collapse of our administrative machinery, social chaos, failure of the extraction and processing and fabrication industries, and destruction of the network of supply and communication upon which urban beings are so dependent. None of us appreciates fully the intricacy of this web.

DANIEL B. LUTEN, "How Dense Can People Be?" *Sierra Club Bulletin* (December, 1963).

EDWARD A. ACKERMAN

POPULATION AND NATURAL RESOURCES

The relation between population and resources may be one of the social equations first understood by man. From the earliest tribal life, the relation between the productivity of the hunting ground and the numbers and welfare of the tribe must have been very clear. It therefore is not surprising that we find mention of population-resource relations early in the recorded history of more complex societies. The administrators and intellectuals of early China, the Greek city-states, and Rome gave thought to population-resource problems. (See United Nations, Population Division, 1953, pp. 21 ff., for a résumé and useful list of references on the history of population study.)

Beginning with the records we have of the observations of Confucius, Plato, Aristotle, and lesser men among ancient civilizations, it is possible to trace remarkably continuous attention to this subject down to our time. Malthus was only one of a long series of analytical students of society who have found definite correlations between human groups and the attributes of those parts of the earth which support them. The dominant subject of interest has always been the relation of amount of resources to numbers of people, adequately sustained. This is still the point of departure for any general treatment of population-resource relations.

• Edward A. Ackerman is Executive Officer of the Carnegie Institution of Washington, D.C.

Reprinted from Philip M. Hauser and Otis Dudley Duncan (eds.), *The Study of Population* (Chicago: University of Chicago Press, 1959), pp. 621–48, with permission of the author.

However, this simply described correlation, while most important, is only a beginning for the description of the relation of human social groups to the resources which support them. First, resources must be identified not only in their amount but also in their quality (productivity) and stability and by their relation to other "conditioning" features of the natural environment. Second, resources become productive to men now mainly through the medium of culture. The technical attributes of the many cultures in the world differ widely and have vastly different meaning for the resources which are put to use through these cultures. In addition, cultures differ in the standard of living of the society, in the territorial extent of political jurisdiction, in institutional inheritances, in trading relations, in frugality, and in other respects. Finally, social groups differ not only in number and density of settlement on the earth's surface but also in health, age classes, mortality and natality, rates of natural increase, migration, and nature of employment. All these demographic features theoretically warrant examination for their correlation with the attributes of natural resources.

The relation of population and natural resources therefore concerns a relatively large number of variables. If all the attributes of culture, human demography, and resources are taken into account, a very large number of permutations occurs. Obviously, therefore, an understanding becomes possible only with some attempt to isolate or group the variables, analyzing the place of each major grouping in turn.

If one were to consider the relation of population and resources as species of equation, the equation might be described roughly in terms of a demand side and a supply side. On the demand side are population numbers and standard of living; on the supply side, all the attributes of resources and all the attributes of culture except for standard of living. The equation might be written:

$$PS = RQ(TAS_t) + E_s + T_r \pm F - W ,$$

or

$$P = \frac{RQ(TAS_t) + E_s + T_r \pm F - W}{S} ,$$

where the symbols have these meanings:

- P numbers of people
- S standard of living
- R amount of resources
- Q factor for natural quality of resources
- T physical technology factor
- A administrative techniques factor
- S_t resource stability factor
- W frugality element (wastage, or intensity of use)
- F institutional advantage and "friction" loss element consequent upon institutional characteristics of the society
- E_s scale economies element (size of territory, etc.)
- T_r resources added in trade

To most of the elements in this equation one cannot presently attach specific, accurate values in any population study. Nonetheless, the general composition of the relation involved in the resource-adequacy question would seem to be described in the equation.

In the succeeding discussion the component parts of this generalized equation will be analyzed briefly. Six steps will be taken in this analysis: (1) presentation of some observed general relations between numbers of people and the physicial environment, including amount of resources; (2) mention of the effect of standard of living as it affects the demand side of the equation; (3) introduction of certain features of culture which affect the supply side of the equation; (4) consideration of certain dynamic or "feedback" elements, wherein density of population in itself affects the productivity of resources—i.e., intensity of demand can and does affect the amount of supply; (5) consideration of all resource and pertinent culture attributes as they correlate with demographic attributes other than number; and (6) application of the above type of analysis to study of the world's population.

Observed Correlation between Numbers of People and the Physical Environment

The first step in understanding present-day resource-population relations is very easily taken with the aid of a few atlas maps of the world.[1] An examination of them readily reveals the following correlations:

1. Concentration of the greater part of the world's population in a few regions (Far East, Indian peninsula, parts of southeast Asia, Mediterranean basin, western, central, and eastern Europe, and eastern United States). These densely populated regions generally are the sites of the past most productive agricultural lands. They usually have at least a one-hundred-day growing season, a favorable precipitation-evaporation ratio, and relatively extensive lands of low relief, suitable for unrestricted cultivation.

2. Further concentration within the heavily settled regions in two types of environment, depending upon the prevalent culture: for the dominantly agrarian cultures of the Middle and Far East, concentration within the alluvial valleys of the great rivers, where irrigation agriculture has the best opportunity for development (the valleys of the Ganges and the Yangtze

[1] Such as those in the *Encyclopaedia Britannica World Atlas* (Chicago: Encyclopaedia Britannica); *Goode's School Atlas* (Chicago: Rand McNally Co.); or the *Oxford Advanced Atlas* (New York: Oxford University Press).

are examples); for the industrialized Western cultures, concentration in those areas where access to mineral resources in combination encourages the growth of modern manufacturing and the cities which are based on manufacturing, directly or indirectly. Coal and iron have been the most important resource determinants of this type of population concentration in the past, but petroleum and natural gas also are now commencing to serve industrial concentrations which influence population growth. The belt of dense settlement which extends from French Flanders through the Low Countries and Germany into Bohemia and Polish Galicia is an example of the former; the Gulf Coast region of Texas and Louisiana in the United States is an example of the latter. Within the United States, California's growing concentration of population has been considered to depend mainly on the "amenities" afforded by an attractive physical environment.[2]

3. Excepting some islands of development which have parallel environmental conditions with those of the large regions of heavy population concentration, the remainder of the world is made up of sparsely settled lands. These lands are of three main types: (*a*) The high latitude and high altitude environments, which have basic similarities. Agriculture in them generally must cope with infertile soils and short, undependable growing seasons; forest growth is slow or nonexistent; and natural livestock ranges are of very low capacity. Northern Canada, Iceland, and the larger part of the Scandinavian peninsula offer examples of this environment. (*b*) Arid and semiarid environments, generally characterized by evaporation potentials greater than the precipitation which they receive (deficit water budgets). The Great Basin of the United States, the Sahara, and Arabia, as examples, all contain fertile soils and other resources, but thus far they have been able to support only sparse populations because their water resources are so limited. (*c*) The tropical savannas and rain forests. Here a combination of infertile soils, insect annoyance and destruction, bacterial disease, stubbornly persistent and commercially unusable vegetation, and fungus decay have discouraged widespread dense settlement. The southern part of the Indian peninsula may be considered an exception in this environment, with central Africa and the Brazilian Amazon country more typical.

4. The sparsely settled parts of the world are dotted with cases of denser settlement, depending almost entirely on local resources. Where water is available in arid regions, as in an exotic stream like the Nile or the Indus, a strip or a spot of dense settlement is certain. Where commercially exploitable industrial minerals exist, particularly petroleum (Arabia) or the metals (Great Basin of the United States), cases of denser senttlements also may be found in all of these natural environments.

From these broad observations one can draw a few conclusions as to the correlation between resources and density of settlement: men are to be found in numbers only where there is a supply of fresh water usable through the techniques with which their culture has armed them; in mature agrarian civilizations numbers are a function of the amount of level land in combination with the amount of water available; for the industrial cultures numbers of people probably have a calculable direct relation to the amount and quality of industrially usable minerals available to an area, particularly iron and coal—however, this relationship is obscured and probably overshadowed by the technological attributes of the prevailing cultural differences among industrialized nations today. Taken the world over, the "conditioning" features of the natural environment, which include the thermal energy received in the atmosphere[3] and topography, share with resources the natural influences on density

[2] See E. L. Ullman, "A New Force in Regional Growth," *Proceedings, Western Area Development Conference* (1954), pp. 68–71.

[3] From insolation or through transfer by the air-mass movement system of the atmosphere.

of settlement. A glance at any world map of temperature and surface configuration regions readily shows the direct correlation between present sparse populations and mountain lands and lands without a dependable growing season.

Standard of Living and Resource-Population Relations

The simple relation of resources to numbers of people is altered by the quality of life which characterizes a social group. Most commonly this is referred to as the standard of living. It is the first of a series of cultural attributes which alter the basic relation of P (numbers of people) $= R$ (amount of resources). It is the only cultural attribute to be entered in the "demand" side of the balance. For purposes of resource-population relations, habits of material consumption are convenient measurements of the standard of living. A group which has a habitual 3,500-calorie daily diet composed of 40 per cent animal proteins obviously will have lesser numbers in relation to a given food-producing resource than a cereal-eating population with a 1,600-calorie diet dependent on the same resource. The disparity in consumption habits may be much greater in demands for fuel, clothing, shelter, and material consumption for aesthetic or recreational ends. Modern industrial nations show ranges in residential electricity consumption from 150 kilowatt hours to 8,000 kilowatt hours annually. Yearly paper consumption may range from 25 pounds for one group to 300 or more for another. The range is equally great for a long list of materials which enter daily life—high-strength textile fibers, metals, building materials of all kinds, and many other items. If a comparison is made between the underdeveloped non-industrial nations and the industrialized, the range of consumption averages is even greater.

While summary comparative measurements of the standard of living among different nations and different social groups are not easily compiled, data on average income do give some crude measure of the capacity of a social group to consume and of its habits of consumption. According to the Statistical Office of the United Nations (1950),[4] the known range in average annual income among the nations of the world in 1949 was from $1,453 (United States) to $27 (China) and $25 (Indonesia). These figures, and the known differences in consumption rates of both food and materials, suggest that one inhabitant of the United States may equal twenty or more inhabitants of China or Indonesia when resource-population relations are considered. Standard of living thus adds another dimension to resource-population relations. It is not possible to consider population-support problems in terms of numbers of people alone; instead, numbers at a given or assumed standard of materials and food consumption must enter the calculation.

Cultural Alterations of Resource-Population Correlations

There are four additional attributes of culture which may alter the simplified resource-population relation, $P = R$. They are technology (including transportation techniques), territorial extent of political jurisdiction, trading relations, and the "friction losses" caused by institutional inheritance. All of these must be entered on the "supply" side of the balance.

TECHNOLOGY

The history of most technological change has been a broadening of the supply base of resources, both geographically and in kind. Thus, little-known minerals of yesterday, like germanium, are vital to the technology of today. The petroleum resources of Arabia are essential to the economic health of Europe and Japan, while the United States draws uranium, copper, chrome, manganese, and other minerals from the corners of the earth. It is impor-

[4] U.N., Statistical Office, *National and Per Capita Income in 70 Countries, 1949* (New York: U.N., 1950).

tant to understand that nineteenth- and twentieth-century technological history does not constitute a story of liberation from dependence on resources; it is only a liberation from extreme dependence on *local* resources.

The centers of dense population today are dependent on resources, just as always before, but their resource base may be in hundreds of localities, separated by many thousands of miles. The technology of advanced industrial cultures like the United States has permitted them to command resources from wide areas, while less advanced groups are forced to continue dependence on a much more limited area of resource supply. A superior culture, like a vigorous vegetative growth, can obtain nourishment from a wide area which contributes to its size. We can say that a positive correlation of resources and size of population still obtains for technologically advanced cultures, even though some independence from adjacent resources becomes clear. Thus technology does not supplant resources but extends the geographical reach of the population group for resources and accordingly its capacity to grow.

Technology also gives values to local materials. The much-used example of Chinese peasant families burning grass for cooking fuel as they sat above great underground coal beds illustrates the meaning of technology-resource relations. Materials are given value as resources only insofar as technology can turn them to the use of people. In a sense, the true objective of technology is to make the most common materials serve as many of man's needs as possible. The atmosphere was made a chemical resource when commercial nitrogen extraction became possible. Through technology, sea water has become a source of metal (magnesium); coal and silicon have become fiber resources; and granite may be a future source of energy. Thus technology can provide depth, as well as geographical breadth, to the resource base of a culture group. The ultimate in depth will be dependence on common materials for all major needs, no matter how complex the industrial structure of the social group. The more advanced the technical equipment of a social or political group, the larger the number of people which can be supported from a given set of resources.

TERRITORIAL EXTENT

Territorial extent of political jurisdiction also may alter simple population-resource relations. Its effects are noted mainly in economies of scale and in the diversity of resources employed. A group large enough in numbers to permit a very complex division of labor, and possesing a geographically extended territory, is likely to possess, employ, and exploit a greater diversity of natural resources than a geographically more restricted group. A diversity of resources, in fact, may lead to a variety of skills and encourage a complex division of labor. This is certainly true of the United States, and it is becoming true of the Soviet Union. The same population group can take advantage of economies of scale which a geographically more restricted group finds it difficult to organize. For instance, there appears to be an optimum size on the order of tens of thousands of square miles for an electric power generating and transmission system depending wholly or partly on hydroelectrical facilities. Efficient management of natural water supplies for irrigating land appears to require extended territory for the most productive combination. This is seen especially in arid, semiarid, and subhumid climates. The profitable exploitation of some low-grade ores also may have a scale attribute. Given a large enough domestic market, large-scale extraction facilities become possible, permitting the processing of low-grade materials. Other things being equal, a large territory like that of the United States or the Soviet Union can give added value to resources; one political jurisdiction permits economies of scale which are difficult to achieve under several political jurisdictions of lesser extent. A large group with geographically extended territory can produce more in relation to effort applied to natural resources than a smaller, geographically limited group.

TRADING RELATIONS

Trading relations, by extending the resource base of a group of people, afford a substitute for size of political jurisdiction. These relations usually have gone hand in hand with technological differences in the past, but they have favored the development of local specializations and therefore of certain scale economies. Trading relations explain the concentrations of people in Japan, Great Britain, Germany, Belgium, the Netherlands, Switzerland, and to a lesser extent France and Italy—concentrations far beyond the capacity of indigenous resources. Since they extend a population's geographical reach for resources, foreign-trading relations must always be considered an important alteration of domestic population-resource ratios.

A simple illustration of the effect of this cultural factor occurs in Iceland. Although that country depends mainly on one modest resource, a marine fishery, trade relations have permitted the development of a social group of number and economic quality unachievable under isolation. The situation of the Icelandic people today can be compared with that of Eskimo or other fishing-hunting peoples under similar environmental conditions.

One can conclude that these cultural factors alter natural resource-population relations by creating resources from physical materials, by extending the geographical "reach" of the social group, and by permitting economies of scale. One must look to technology, territorial size of political jurisdiction, and trading relations, no less than to indigenous resources, for explanation of population concentrations.

GEOGRAPHICAL INCIDENCE OF THREE MAJOR CULTURE FACTORS

The major areas in which resource-population relations thus far have been affected by the territorial extent of political jurisdiction have been the United States and the Soviet Union, although the full effects of this circumstance are only now coming into force in the Soviet Union. By the geographical extent of their territory alone, the peoples of both countries have opportunities for efficiency which smaller nations can acquire only through the more difficult route of trading relations. To a lesser extent, the same characteristic has operated in the British Commonwealth and in Brazil. In these countries, and in any other, this factor becomes influential only to the extent that a cohesive transportation system exists and operates. Because of transport deficiencies, economies of scale have never meant much to mainland China. Finally, the factor operates only in the presence of a moderate density of population. Transportation networks arise and economies of scale become possible only when there are numbers of people to be served. Thus Canada and Australia have large and diverse territories which predispose them to economies of scale in resource use, but they have profited little from their territories thus far because of sparsity of settlement.

Technology and trade relations have operated to a degree all over the earth, but their effects have been most pronounced on resource-population relations in the British Isles, in the European peninsula, and in Japan. The numbers of people in these parts of the earth are now far beyond the capacity of local resources to support without extensive trading relations, and therefore without extending the natural resource base. Particularly for the western European countries, technology has brought out the latent values of the indigenous resource base of the peninsula in a manner paralleled few other places in the world. The German chemical industry is a good case in point, in the way it has made use of coal, salt, potash, and a few other minerals. Perhaps more than for any other nation, the size of Germany during the twentieth century has been closely related to its technical proficiency.

Japan likewise is an interesting case of the effect of technology and trading relations on numbers. In a sense, its history offers very nearly a control situation to judge the broad effects of technology and trade relations. Until the Meiji Restoration in the late nineteenth century, Japan existed with very little trade and with a centuries-old technology which had changed very slowly. The story of the nation's overnight conversion to modern manufacturing and trading is well known. With this conversion the numbers of people in Japan also changed. From a nation which had remained at a relatively stable level somewhere between 25 and 30 millions for about 250 years, Japan commenced to grow at a striking rate. It now is three times the size of pre-Meiji Japan, and it is likely to grow to at least 100 million in the near future. The "inflationary" effect of technology and trade relations on numbers of people possessing a given domestic resource base is here clearly told.

GAINS AND LOSSES ASSOCIATED WITH INSTITUTIONAL INHERITANCE

Institutional inheritance alone causes social groups throughout the world to function with varying effectiveness in transforming physical materials into resources and resources into consumers' goods. Economic institutions can favor or discourage savings and capital formation, the appearance of competent entrepreneurs, the provision of flexible and adequate training in skills, co-ordinated resource development planning, and other mechanisms which determine the progress of resource exploitation and the production of goods usable by men.[5] These institutions, which in part may be correlated with cultural advancement, are most effective within the advanced industrialized nations. Within countries like the United States, Canada, most western European nations, Australia, Japan, and the Soviet Union, the positive operation of these institutional factors is most clearly seen. To a lesser degree, their positive operation also characterizes countries like Mexico, Brazil, Venezuela, and India, which are in the process of industrialization and co-ordinating use of their resources. These factors are perhaps least favorable in some of the "underdeveloped" lands of low population density, like Madagascar, Angola, Borneo, and Paraguay.

These institutions are one of the most influential cultural attributes determining the effectiveness of resource exploitation. In a sense, the application of technology and the extension of trade depend on the vigor of these institutions, although the institutions themselves may differ greatly in form. Not all institutional inheritance represents gain in resource use. Nearly all, if not all, societies in the world have some institutional and ideological inheritances which cause losses in the supporting capacity of resources, as compared to the optimum obtainable under a given technological stage. The incidence of these losses has relatively little relation to cultural advancement. The industrially advanced nations suffer from them as well as the underdeveloped. Furthermore, there are collective losses from the point of view of the world as a whole, as well as from the point of view of the individual societies.

For the world as a whole, the most important of these inheritances are political boundaries and territorial restrictions, which in many instances prevent the achievement of scale economies which are known to be possible in large geographical units; prevent the movement of people from the densely settled, resource-deficient parts of the world to the lands which have low ratios of population to potential resources; permit artificial restrictions of production (like the United States "soil bank") which are of apparent national advantage; and deny to groups possessing both labor force and requisite techniques timely access to undeveloped resources.

[5] For a concise description of the institutional factor in its association with energy resource development and use, see E. S. Mason, *Energy Requirements and Economic Growth* (Washington: National Planning Assn., 1955).

In the same class we must place economic institutions which *in the balance* depress domestic economic benefits to social groups as a whole because they favor special interests within those groups. "Friction" of this kind may come in the form of pre-empting facilities, like storage sites for water, for use at levels below full productivity; maintenance of technically obsolete processes or procedures; needless "fashion" obsolescence of durable consumers' goods; depressing initiative toward efficient management (e.g., the tenant farmer problem); and in other ways.

In other words, there exists considerable "friction" in the process of matching people's needs against the resources upon which the world can draw. To the political inheritances should be added certain social inheritances which contribute to "friction" —like some customs following from religion or other social tradition. A good example is the Hindu attitude toward the existence of cattle, which in effect allows cattle to compete with human beings for the product of some land and water resources in India.

The "Feedback" Elements—Effects of Density of Population upon Resources and upon Certain Related Cultural Attributes

Thus far we have considered a static correlation of resources and numbers of people. That is, density of settlement on the earth's surface varies according to observable attributes of the physical environment. Several facets of culture add different and larger dimensions to resources, but our interest still has centered on the numbers supportable at a specific standard of living by a given type and quantity of resource endowment. This is the effect of resources, in whatever dimensions several qualities of culture give them, upon numbers of people in specific geographical locations on the surface of the earth. At this point our "equation" is $PS = RT + E_s + T_r$, in which P equals number of people, S equals standard of living, R equals amount of resources, T equals physical technology factor, E_s equals scale economies element, and T_r equals resources added in trade.

The next step in understanding population-resource relations is the introduction of some dynamic elements or factors. Density of population in itself has some effect on resources and on some attributes of culture which in turn influence the productivity of resources. In other words, population density per se may alter both the physical resources and pertinent culture attributes in a manner which changes the resources' capacity to support people. While we have few statistical data to measure these features, historical information, methodical field observation, and cartographic analysis give us grounds for some qualitative comments.

The relation of density of settlement to resources may be examined in several particulars. The resource itself may be affected in its stability, productive life, and quality; the affected culture attributes are intensity or completeness of resource use (the wastage element) and administrative techniques, or the type of management. All of these appear to be correlatable with density or sparsity of settlement, and they all affect the "supply" side of the balance.

The density of settlement here considered is not that of numbers of people per unit of area. Instead, it is that of population as related to the *employed* resources upon which the social group depends. This relation may or may not coincide with geographical or areal density of settlement. A high population-resource ratio may be found in many regions with geographically sparse population, and employed and potential resources differ. (Potential resources are those natural resources which may be considered employable with the use of the most advanced, economically proven technology of the world, although not actually employed at the time in question.) China in the past has had a high ratio of population to employed resources. On the other hand, the ratio of population to potential resources was and presumably still is somewhat lower. Population-resource relations are here limited to those which concern resources employed under the culture existing in the area during the period treated.

STABILITY, PRODUCTIVE LIFE, AND QUALITY OF THE RESOURCE

Resource stability is a consideration particularly applicable to those resources which can endure near-permanent exploitation under proper management. Soil, water, forests, range lands, fisheries, and other animal life are the principal resources of this type, commonly referred to as the "renewable" resources. These also are the resources which have been used longest by men, and about which there is abundant historical evidence. The ideal management for these resources is "sustained-yield" production, whereby the resource is so maintained that it will continue in production at an optimum level indefinitely. Such management is particularly difficult for the renewable resources because their natural productivity varies, sometimes within a wide range. Most renewable resources respond to the vagaries of climate, particularly of precipitation, and to a certain degree also of temperature. At the same time, the human needs for production from the resources are at best a constant, and more likely an ascending, curve. Here we have the basis of one of the most frequently recurring resource-population problems: a capricious physical environment, but unchanging or increasing human needs. Most societies have attempted to meet the problem by coping with the environment rather than by adjusting human needs. In this process of adjustment, density of settlement has played an important role, although not always a consistent one.

Paradoxically, the most stable resources have been observed not under the conditions of dense or sparse settlement but where (and at times when) moderate to high densities prevail. The instability of the soil and forest resources of the United States during the last part of the nineteenth and the first part of the twentieth centuries exhibited the tendency of a social group with abundant resources to regard all of them as expendable. During this period the known abundance of unoccupied land containing a measure of naturally stored plant nutrients encouraged the "mining" of soils in many parts of the United States. While other factors certainly contributed, relatively sparse settlement made the development of new territory and farms on virgin land more tempting than the development of new management techniques for erosion-susceptible lands. The story of forest exploitation in the United States during the same period is even more striking. Because of the great abundance of forested land, the productivity of millions of acres was seriously impaired by poor cutting practices, burning, and other wasteful events. For a long period future needs seemed so distant to a relatively small population that sustained yield for the renewables had little attraction. In a land weighted with the problems of communication and transportation imposed by distance, the need for rapid development seemed much more important.

In different ways, parts of this story have been mirrored in Australia, Africa, South America, and the Soviet Union. Sparse settlement has been accompanied by exploitation which impaired the productivity of the renewable resources, in some cases making them locally barren.

We do not know at exactly what stage of settlement density resource management practices tend to favor the maintenance of more stable renewable resources. It is apparent that the United States entered into this stage in the 1930's and is still adjusting its management in the direction of more stable resources. Notable progress has been made since that time in both agriculture and forestry, although the transition is not yet complete, as shown in the unstable dry-farming of some semiarid lands.

This stage also is exhibited in western European countries and in Japan, where the adjustment toward stable renewable resources has become much more complete than in the United States. In this stage soil erosion is rare, dependence on fertilizers for agricultural production exceeds dependence on naturally provided plant nutrients, sustained yield is applied widely to biotic resources used in the economy, and waters are carefully controlled in settled areas. As long as population density does not increase in relation to resources—because of migration, absence of natural increase, improved techniques of exploiting resources, extension of trading areas, or for other reasons—stable resources are the normal expectation for a social group having a moderately high density of population.[6] This appears to be illustrated in the histories of several western European countries, including Germany, France, the Netherlands, Belgium, the Scandinavian countries, Great Britain, and Switzerland. Japan also is a case in point.

However, if population densities move very high without the relief of demographic, technical, or trading outlets, the stability of renewable resources again appears to be affected adversely. Such undoubtedly was the case for mainland China for many decades. The same tendency has been shown in the past in India, Iran, Greece, Italy, and other Mediterranean lands. It is difficult to separate the effects of political instability upon the deterioration of resources from those of population pressure. An example may suggest the correlation between density and resource stability at this stage.

There can be little doubt that population pressure in China forced agriculture into topographic situations and climatic environments which were not suited to continued intensive cultivation. Eroding lands on a grand scale resulted during droughts. Population pressure also forced the collection of forest products in a manner which progressively shortened the wood-growing cycle, greatly reduced forest land productivity, and contributed further to erosion. These conditions contributed to the sediment loading of streams; in turn, aggrading lower channels increased the flood hazards and reduced the productivity of the normally stable alluvial lands of the lower valleys—the centuries-old heart of the Chinese economy. Permanent or lasting loss of productive sections of the renewable resources and sharply fluctuating production from the remaining resources characterized that very densely settled country. Excessively high population-resource ratios in this instance resulted in resource instability.

To a degree, productive life and quality of resources are implied in comment upon resource stability. However, a few additional comments are specifically appropriate to these characteristics of resource use.

For any "funded" resource (those not renewed by life or weathering processes), it is obvious that greater numbers of people decrease the life of an employed resource, other things being equal. It is also clear that as the intensity of use increases under population pressure, the actual service of the resource is greater, considering salvage, working of small mines or other small production units, etc. The conditions prevailing in Japanese coal mining are a good example. Thin, deep-lying, faulted, and otherwise broken seams, sometimes of low quality, are parts of working mines in Japan. Their counterparts in the United States are scarcely touched. Thus intensity of use does help to extend the useful life of the funded resources, but the employment of such marginal production is only a temporary alleviation to the accelerated use of a funded resource which accompanies increasing densities of population.

Water illustrates best the effect of numbers of people upon productive life and quality of a resource. Under given conditions of supply, the highest quality is gen-

6 Statement of the numerical meaning of the generalized terms applied to population density here has been avoided because no satisfactory summary means exists to integrate varied resources into a total which can be compared with population numbers.

erally that of the unused resource or the resource of the sparsely settled area. Because water is a convenient waste carrier, because micro-organisms survive and grow in it, and because it is a solvent for a number of minerals, water quality almost always has deteriorated as density of population increased in an area. While modern technology occasionally has effected a reversal of water conditions, the world as a whole shows a remarkably high positive correlation between density of settlement and decline of water quality, whether by bacterial pollution from residential waste, addition of organic or inorganic foreign materials by industry, mineralization through irrigation use, or sediment addition from eroding lands.

Under those conditions of population pressure (or sparsity) which have affected the stability of the land and biotic resources, the life of water resources at a given level of use has also been affected. This has been most commonly illustrated in the shortened life of storage sites where heavy sedimentation became part of the altered regimen of a stream. Conservation storage for consumptive use or energy production becomes ineffective as accumulated sediment leaves less space for water. While a certain amount of water continues to be available from runoff, the useful life of part of the water resource is shortened by population conditions which favor eroding land.

INTENSITY OF RESOURCE USE AND CONSUMPTION HABITS

Two attributes of culture which affect the capacity of resources show some correlation with density of population: the intensity of use and the type of administrative technique or management. Some statistical data (where they are available) give indications of the intensity of resource use. Per capita amounts of agricultural land, forest land, and data on unit area production in agriculture suggest the intensity of land use. The fact that Japan had about one-fifteenth as much cultivated land per capita as the United States in the 1950's (about 0.16 and 2.5 acres per capita) suggests that Japan uses its agricultural land more completely than the United States, which is the case. The same indication is given by data on the unit area productivity of Japanese farms (which hold world record yields for some crops, e.g., rice), by the ratio of irrigated area to total cultivated area, and by the percentage of multiple-cropped land. However, conclusions on the intensity of resource use may be safely derived only by supplementing the statistical data normally gathered with competent special field observation. The manner in which a social group uses the materials it has in everyday family life is a good indicator. Few statistics are to be found on such matters.

It is obvious that the denser the settlement, the more complete the use of resources, assuming a given stage of technology and a given standard of living. While the imprint of population will show on all resource use, the best illustrations come from the food-producing resources. These resources, and particularly the agricultural lands, have been significant in all societies of any size in nearly all ages. Differences in the use of cultivable lands which distinguish the lands of high-density settlement from the lands of lesser density are here used to illustrate the correlation between numbers of people and intensity of resource use.

The best illustrations occur in Japan and China, where aggressive and vital peoples have been faced with the problems of high population density for centuries. The cultivation of these lands, by comparison to that of the Western Hemisphere or even some European countries, has the following characteristics: (1) Wherever engineering knowledge has permitted and water supply was available, lands have been irrigated. Discovery of the vastly superior yields under irrigation, even in humid climates, was made long ago in the densely settled sections of the Far East. (2) Wherever possible, cultivable land is multiple-cropped, making full use of the actual growing season. (3) To the full extent that materials are available, fertilizers are placed on the land. The Far Eastern habit of collecting night soil and applying it to crops is nothing more than a search for all the potential fertilizing materials. (4) Land is used sparingly for the support of livestock. Production of human food through livestock conversions (i.e., meat or dairy products) is avoided in favor of direct consumption of crops by human beings. (5) Crops with high calorie yields per unit area are favored. This is one reason for the popularity of rice in the Far East and for the production of maize, sweet potatoes, millets, and sorghums on sites not suited to rice. Production of sufficient calories is the usual problem of a people living close to the margin of its food resource productivity. The popularity of high-calorie crops therefore has been a natural evolution. (6) Cultivation generally extends onto lands considered poorly suited to agriculture under sparser settlement. Examples in Japan are the tilling of steep hillsides (usually through terrace preparation), planting of beach sands, and cropping of floodways. Few places naturally flat enough for cultivation (or suited to artificial leveling) are ignored. Land-use management is sparing in the use of cultivable lands for purposes other than agriculture. Roads and housing, wherever possible, are kept on the land of poorest agricultural quality in a locality, like the hill borders of a flood plain in Japan. Farm management also is efficient in use of the land. There are few idle field borders; even the dikes between irrigated fields customarily are planted during the growing season, and roadsides as well.

The impression given by these attributes of land use in the densely settled countries has been vividly summarized by Archibald MacLeish:

> In other countries a farm is meadows and a wood lot and a corner that the plow leaves: room to turn about and to turn about in. In Japan a farm is as rigid and tight a thing as a city lot—a patch here and a triangle here and a square or so somewhere else; every road corner of land diked and leveled off even though the growing surface is less than a man's shirt; every field soaked with manure and worked and reworked as carefully and as continuously as a European farmer works a seedbed . . . nothing thrown away, nothing let go wild, nothing wasted.[7]

All these characteristics of farming contrast with practices prevailing in lands of sparser population. For the United States in the past one might very well take the opposite of each of the land use attributes which were set down for Japan and China. There has been a tendency to depend on natural fertility of the soil; irrigation until recently was considered appropriate only to arid environments; animal conversion is favored by comparison to direct use of high-calorie crops; multiple-cropping generally is not economic; and so on. Parallels to United States practice could be found in Canada, Argentina, and Australia.

The description of how agricultural resources are used carries some implications about the characteristics of consumption under conditions of dense population. Minimal animal conversion of crops and concentration upon high-calorie crops could not be undertaken without corresponding adjustments, or willingness to adjust, by consumers. This is typical of the densely settled lands. Diets generally have been designed with a mineral protein, minimal animal protein, and low (but sometimes adequate) protective food content. The diets are relatively high in calorie-producing foods by comparison to the protein and protective food intake. At the same time, they are low-calorie diets by comparison to those of countries or societies with higher ratios of resources to people. The daily diets of the people of Japan, for instance, have probably been within the 2,200–2,500-calorie range per person for many years.

[7] A. MacLeish, "Of Many Men on Little Land," *Fortune* (1936).

In the United States, on the other hand, a 3,300-calorie average prevails.[8]

Diet indicates one characteristic of consumption in the densely settled lands. Consumption of food and materials is adjusted (on the average) close to the minimal needs of the individual under the physical circumstances which prevail. For instance, both fuel consumption and housing space are low in the densely settled country. The average Japanese, for instance, has one-third the housing space of the average American.

There are other characteristics. Only low initial wastage is tolerated. When a tree is cut in a country like Japan, China, India, or Italy, the bark, limbs, and even the roots and needles are put to use as a matter of habit. Salvage is very carefully and consistently practiced by the people. Again Japan may serve as an example.

Most Japanese become conscious of conservation in their childhood. Even families in relatively comfortable circumstances teach their children at meals to clean every grain of rice from the bowls. No person with good manners would think of doing otherwise. Children from the more humble families, who constitute a large proportion of Japan's population, are drilled in conservation even more unceasingly. It is they who are sent to glean animal dung from the streets for the home garden . . . to clean up the carpenter's shavings and sawdust, or to pick the unburned bits of coal out of the railroad or factory cinder piles. They gather the few papers and tins which may have been left at the roadside, and they are taught how carefully all inedible kitchen materials must be saved to be placed on the squash or eggplants of the back yard. Every child learns that nothing is wasted in a Japanese house or on the Japanese street.[9]

POPULATION DENSITY AND RESOURCE MANAGEMENT

Administrative techniques and concepts of management vary greatly with culture. Any attempt to suggest correlation between numbers of people and resource management therefore must isolate clearly the assumptions and specific situations under which it applies. Management in itself is a cultural reaction to the situation of the social group, since the group appraises the physical environment in which it lives and the technological assets at its command.

Management of resources may have a variety of objectives, including maximum short-term output, maximum long-term output, stabilization of output, improvement of resource quality, territorial development, creation of employment opportunities, or still other objectives. Even from the point of view of groups, any one of these objectives may be present, or prevail.

The attributes of resource management which would seem to have some correlation with different densities of population are degree of public or private control over management, the application of planning or collective foresight, and the centralization or decentralization of administration over resource development and production.

Such correlations at present are imperfectly understood, but they obviously exist. Generally speaking, the land of sparse settlement has favored a high degree of control for private management and is apt to be concerned about short-term maximum output rather than long-term output; application of collective foresight has little stimulus, while territorial development and

[8] The 1951–52 daily average food supply per person entering the American home was estimated to be 3,225 calories, excepting alcoholic beverages. About 90 calories per person should be added from alcohol, making the total food available at the place of consumption 3,315 calories per day. Wastage is included in these totals and should be deducted if net actual consumption is sought (J. F. Dewhurst *et al.*, *America's Needs and Resources: A New Survey* [New York: Twentieth Century Fund, 1955], p. 156).

[9] E. A. Ackerman, *Japan's Natural Resources and Their Relation to Japan's Economic Future* (Chicago: University of Chicago Press, 1953), p. 490.

the creation of employment opportunities[10] are favored objectives in resource management. Management in a situation of sparse settlement tends to be decentralized. This description certainly fitted the United States of almost the entire period from the time of first settlement to 1930. It fits Canada; it may be applied to Brazil and other South American countries, and to parts of Africa. The public-land policy of the United States and its prevailing forestry practices during the period mentioned were perfect illustrations of management within a society which had a high ratio of resources to population. The ideal was maximum short-term output and the most rapid possible territorial development with a minimum of public management responsibility.

On the other hand, dense settlement tends to be accompanied by the application of collective foresight, a higher degree of public (i.e., governmental) control over management, greater centralization of administration, and more concern for long-term maximum output. Almost every western European country illustrates this tendency, and the United States of the mid-twentieth century has been unable to escape it. Indeed, the United States of 1933–50 moved rapidly in the direction of this management pattern. Japan is an excellent example of the emergence of management characteristics of this kind.

An illustration of the meaning of these differences of management may be taken from forestry. Under the concepts of forest land use which prevailed in the United States for many decades, ownership of the forest land brought with it the right to use the land and trees in any way suited to the owner's taste or habit, including the destruction of the property if he so wished. In Japan, on the other hand, no forest landowner has had such control over his property, at least since 1907. Under national laws a Japanese prefectural government administration may take over management of a private forest property considered to be managed poorly by the private owner.[11] While an owner does not lose title to net proceeds from his property, he does not have the choice of doing whatever he wishes with his land.

Correlations of population density and type of resource management must cover some apparent exceptions. China, for instance, has been a densely settled country for centuries. Yet within the twentieth century many of its resources were managed with little planning or foresight, and little public control over management appeared anywhere in the country. However, this could not be considered a contradiction of the tendencies here described, for China had few of the management characteristics of a sparsely settled land except the extreme decentralization of management. With a confused and somewhat anarchical governmental structure (in practice), the development of a strong public hand in resource management could hardly be expected nationally, even though the incentive for such action was very great. But there were within China some regional examples of careful public control, as on the famous Min River delta irrigation system in Szechwan. In a sense, these fitted the pattern of management for a densely settled country. Under a tightly organized national government, the national aspects of resource management are known to be changing already within China.

The case of the Soviet Union also may seem an exception, since it appears (at least popularly) to be a country with a relatively sparse settlement. Actually, the Soviet Union has had three lands, a densely settled west and sparsely settled Arctic and middle-latitude Asiatic sections. The resource-management pattern which has evolved for Soviet resources since 1918 is one which might be expected for the dense-

10 Provision of land for farmers desiring property ownership is here considered one form of creating employment opportunities.

11 Japan, Forest Law No. 43, amended in 1911, 1939, 1943, 1946, 1947, 1948, and 1950. Also the Afforestation Temporary Measures Law (No. 150), 1950.

ly settled European and Caucasian parts of the Union in the presence of a well-organized national administration. The superposition of this type of management on relatively empty Soviet Asia is the same phenomenon as the reflection of United States resource-management trends in Alaska. Management, therefore, is not to be correlated with density of population within a given area but *with density of population within the dominant section of the political unit to which the area belongs.* With this in mind, the resource-management pattern of the Soviet Union does not appear to be an exception to the tendencies described above.

The management associated with population densities of the higher order generally tends to minimize or eliminate practices which tolerate wastage from a public point of view. This management tends also to institute the gains and economies which can be obtained from integrated planning and management of resources; it encourages long-term stability; and it tends to lengthen the productive life and long-term production. However, it may reduce the immediate, or short-term, productivity. Other things being equal, the dense settlement tends to introduce management directed toward a higher long-term productivity for the resources of a social group.

Further Dynamic Relations: Correlation of Resources and Pertinent Culture Attributes with Demographic Attributes Other than Number

In the foregoing discussion the only demographic attributes used in analyzing the relation among resources, culture, and population have been numbers of people and standard of living. As other demographic attributes are examined, further correlations may be observed. Where available resources and their productivity per capita differ, one may expect covariance to be shown between resources and health features, age classes, mortality and birth rates, rates of natural increase, migration, and employment, separately or severally.

Past analysis has not supported a direct correlation between employed resources and each of these demographic attributes, and it may be difficult and pointless at any time. There appears to be little doubt that per capita productivity of resources is a component in the variation of each of these attributes among different social groups in the world. However, covariance is most directly shown when the functioning economy of the group is examined as a whole, including the component of natural resource availability and productivity. In particular, the extension of the resource base through participation in the international trade community and the stage of technology characterizing a group must be considered in combination with resources for the supplement or multiplier which must be reckoned for the local resource base.

To illustrate such analysis and correlation, one may divide the major settled sections of the world into four types of area. The main distinctions are those of technology and population-resource ratios. Since the more important geographical expressions of culture correspond with political units rather than with features of the natural environment, the units of these four types are the countries of the world. On the one hand are the industrially organized technology-source areas, like western Europe and Anglo-America; on the other are the technology-deficient areas, like India, China, and most of Africa. (The technology-source areas are those where a general advance of technology is taking place under the stimulus of indigenous invention; the technology-deficient areas are those which are advancing—if at all—by borrowing or adapting technology from the source areas.) Each of these may be divided into two subtypes, those having a low ratio of population to resources and those having a high ratio of population to resources. Thus there are technology-source areas with a relatively high ratio of population to employed and potential resources (western Europe, Japan), technology-source areas with a low ratio of population to resources (Canada, United States, Australia), technology-deficient areas with a high ratio of population to potential and employed resources (India, China, French North Africa), and technology-deficient areas with a low ratio of population to potential resources (central and east Africa, Latin America, southeast Asia).

Where the employed-resource base is meager (and unrelieved by trade or technical advancement), the classical pattern in the past has been the one described for non-industrialized countries of dense population: high birth and mortality, low rates of natural increase, a predominance of the younger age classes, and lessened individual vigor because of the level of nutrition. There is strong incentive toward emigration, given an opportunity to emigrate, because underemployment is a chronic characteristic of the society. Actual mobility, considering the mass, however, is low. This is the pattern today for the technology-deficient areas having a high ratio of population to potential and employed resources.

The technology-deficient areas with a low ratio of population to potential local resources may exhibit some of the same characteristics as the dense population countries, reflecting their technical inability to make use of the resources which are at hand. This is well illustrated in Africa. On the other hand, the social groups within countries of this type would seem to have a somewhat different demographic pattern, considered over broad areas. They have shown high birth rates, moderate to high death rates, and moderate to high rates of natural increase. Health problems exist in major proportions, although health deficiencies resulting from poor nutrition on the whole are less prominent than in the technology-deficient dense population areas. Incentives to migration still exist, in response to local conditions, and mobility on the whole would seem to be rather high. These areas have some attraction for emigrants from the dense population areas, but because of capital scarcity and technology deficiencies their capacity for absorbing numbers of immigrants is relatively low.

The more advanced industrial areas or countries, here labeled "technology-source areas," show a still different pattern of these demographic characteristics. Low death rates appear to be the outstanding characteristic of their demographic past, but they also exhibit low to middle-range birth rates, low to moderate rates of natural increase, high ratios of adults to children, and a relatively healthy population. The chief difference between the lands having abundant resources and those having a high ratio of population but advanced technology would appear to be in the recently higher birth rates of the former, with corresponding higher rates of natural increase. A difference in migration characteristics also appears. The resource-abundant areas have a high degree of internal mobility, while the high population areas (mainly western Europe and Japan) show more tendency to migration to other countries or continents.

Even such general observations on the correlation of resources and natality, mortality, migration, natural increase, and health give some basis for later important conclusions. We are concerned here with the basic elements in the dynamics of population history. While the presentation of detailed statistical evidence is needed to give a full pattern, superficially it appears that the correlations between these demographic attributes and technology are closer than the correlation with resource conditions.

The ready correlation between population dynamics and technology, which obscures the correlation with resource conditions, may be more apparent than real. Technical advancement has given a social group not only the power to convert potential resources into employed resources but also the power to extend the group's reach to resources beyond the group's own immediate territory. Thus the technologically advanced but domestically resource-poor countries are not actually resource-poor when their ability to command food and materials in trade is considered. Technical proficiency has given a group the capacity to extend its resources both in depth within its own territory and extraterritorially, as previously observed. Considering the world trade community in peacetime operation, there has been no resource-poor but technically advanced country.

Application of Resource Analysis to Population Questions

The attributes of resources and culture discussed above give at least a partial checklist for evaluating two important demographic questions: methods of making population projections and methods of estimating resource adequacy. The validity of Malthusianism or other deterministic concepts of resource-population relations is a specialized part of the latter question.

resources, culture, and projections

Viewed both from a theoretical point of view and from the experience of history, the most direct response by numbers of people to resource conditions is under conditions of trade isolation, minimal standards of living (near the subsistence level), and little flexibility in technology. Under these conditions fluctuations in the natural productivity of resources have had immediate and sometimes violent effects on the numbers of people dependent on a given set of resources. These conditions and effects have been most pronounced among the agrarian societies of Asia (and Africa, to a lesser extent) as productivity of the land fluctuated from drought, flood, pests, permanent erosion or sedimentation injury, or other changes in the physical and biotic environment. In periods of low productivity the immediate effects on numbers of people come through starvation and migration, as classically illustrated in China and on the Indian peninsula many times.

The opposite situation is equally clear. As there are departures from these elemental conditions for social groups, there are intervening "cushions" which soften the impact of resource changes upon numbers of people dependent upon these resources. Where resources for a period have permitted high standards of consumption, where extensive trading connections have become normal, or where the society has an alert technical component, fluctuations in natural productivity have a lessened effect on numbers of people. Fluctuations (or a downward trend) in natural productivity of resources may be reflected in a lower standard of living; they may elicit technological efforts or increased efforts toward trade. Where one or all of these factors afford a cultural "cushion," resource changes may be reflected only in an upward trend of the population curve during productivity improvements. Declines in resource conditions tend to be absorbed by the cushions, with little visible effect on numbers.

A good illustration of the effect of a resource change under these conditions occurred in the 1933–38 "dust bowl" conditions on the Great Plains of the United States. Severe declines in the natural productivity of the cultivable and grazing lands of the plains were followed by declines in standard of living for those most directly affected and by the application of technology to problems created by prevailing methods of occupancy. Severe as the dust bowl damages were physically, their net effect on numbers of people *in the United States* was probably very slight, both immediately and for the long term. Standard of living and technology effectively cushioned the impact of a natural event which would have had famine results in the China of the same day.

The meaning of these relations for population projections is easily outlined. As social and economic organization develops for any particular region or group of people, the isolation of resource-population ratios becomes increasingly difficult, and with it demographic projections which depend partly upon resource estimates. The uncertainty which attends estimates of resource effectiveness for modern nations is emphasized by (1) an imperfect understanding of the impact and even the direction of change which eventually will result from the overlap of many extraterritorial spheres of interest in resources; (2) our present inability to predict the exact temporal progress or the type of technical change in a society, even though we now can ascertain the direction of change and something of the general rate; and (3) our inability to appraise the meaning or limits of increasing appetites for material consumption on the part of social groups throughout the world. We can reasonably say that the culture variables at this time appear of dominant importance in the projection of relations between resources and numbers of people.

All three of the major culture attributes affecting resource supply show traits of rapid change. Trade relations may be subject to very rapid change, responding to intranational or international political events. Perhaps the most constant feature is the direction of change in technology, which during this century has been constantly in the direction of more efficient use of resources and materials. However, "break-throughs" like those on nuclear fission and fusion may accelerate the rate of technical change unpredictably.

Standards of consumption also have a certain stability, considered on a group basis. While individual rates of consumption may vary considerably (as in wartime), the habits of group consumption, all products taken into account, generally have a consistent per capita trend in one direction or another. The sharpest fluctuations appear to be the temporary upward departures of wartime economies. Taken over a long period, the consumption rates for industrial nations in this century generally have had an upward trend. The non-industrial "Malthusian" populations have undoubtedly shown a downward tendency in per capita materials consumption.

In sum, resource data are of value in judging the accuracy of projections for non-industrialized societies; in them the relation of resources and numbers of people is at its simplest. For the more advanced cultures and social groups who participate in world trade, resource data are meaningful only in proportion to the accuracy of knowledge about the direction of change in technology, standards of living, trade relations, and other pertinent cultural features. Such knowledge is not accurate at the present time. For advanced cultures, therefore, the resource-adequacy check on population projections has very limited usefulness.

ANALYSIS OF WORLD RESOURCE ADEQUACY AND VALIDITY OF DETERMINISTIC THEORIES

Consideration of resource-population relations inevitably ends in a summation of curves representing the dynamics of world population, the advance of technical skills, and the deteriorating earth. Since the days of Malthus the resultant of these curves has been interpreted in two principal ways: an open-ended view of the future, which stresses the capacity of technical advance to overtake both population increase and deteriorating earth resources[12] and the Malthusian, or neo-Malthusian view.[13] These views necessarily become distilled into generally optimistic or pessimis-

[12] K. F. Mather, *Enough and To Spare* (New York: Harper & Bros., 1944); C. E. Kellogg, "The Earth Can Feed Her People," *Farm Policy Forum,* II (1949), 1–5; H. T. Eldridge, "Population Growth and Economic Development," *Land Economics,* XXVIII (1952), 1–9.

[13] F. Osborn, *Our Plundered Planet* (Boston: Little, Brown & Co., 1948); R. C. Cook, *Human Fertility: The Modern Dilemma* (New York: William Sloane Assoc., 1951); W. Vogt, *Road to Survival* (New York: William Sloane Assoc., 1948); J. Huxley, "World Population," *Scientific American,* CXCIV (1956), 64–76; "Political and Economic Planning," *World Population and Resources* (London, 1955).

tic outlooks on the future of human society when they are translated into public consciousness.

Actually, the neo-Malthusian view or statements of the opposing position often are misleading in their simplification. It should be obvious from knowledge of biology that there are theoretical size limits to the total population which might be fed and settled on the face of the earth.[14] It should be equally obvious that the present-day population has not approached those theoretical limits, whatever they may be.[15]

On the other hand, there are very important existing regional population problems for which application of the neo-Malthusian view would appear to be fully justified. Examination of world data on diets (a good indicator of resource adequacy) gives convincing evidence of the influence which resource availability must have upon numbers of people and other demographic attributes in the technology-deficient areas with a high ratio of population to resources. All these areas have a diet close to the minimum needed for subsistence. (China, Korea, India, Egypt, Java, Pakistan, and a number of smaller countries all have a daily average per capita intake of less than 2,400 calories.)[16] Where diets of 2,500 calories or less exist in technology-deficient countries with high population-potential resource ratios, it is probably safe to assume that some Malthusian "controls" exist or may become effective at any time. The most ominous thing about the world resource-population position is that about half the people of the world are to be found in countries which may be described in these terms. For them there is a present resource adequacy problem, and there is likely to be continued difficulty in matching resources to population.

Data on diets, furthermore, show that there is an additional large segment of the world's population which lives adjacent to potential resources of some size but which still exists close to the subsistence level of the technology-deficient densely settled lands. Most of the technology-deficient countries of low population-potential resource ratios fall into this group. They are exemplified by much of Africa and Latin-America. These people, who comprise about a sixth of the world's population, have a problem in the immediate adequacy of their employed resources, a position which they suffer because of technical deficiencies.

Third, an additional sixth of the world's people live in lands where industrial organization and technology have permitted them to extend their resource base through world trade, supplementing the low per capita productivity of their domestic resources. These are the western European countries and Japan. Their position is relatively secure, as far as resources are concerned, for the time being. Over the long run, however, these countries are vulnerable to competing demands from other lands for the resources which they now draw upon outside their own territory.

Finally, about a sixth of the world's people live in technically advancing societies and possess territory affording relatively low ratios of population to potential resources. These are the people of the United States, the Soviet Union, Canada, Australia, and possibly Argentina and New Zealand. Presumably these peoples have

[14] E. S. Deevey, "The Human Crop," *Scientific American,* CXCIV (1956), 105–12 offers an interesting fresh approach to the means of calculating the theoretical limits.

[15] A number of estimates of the theoretical carrying capacity of the earth have been made in the past. They range from twice to about six times the earth's present population of 2.5 billion. See W. E. Boerman, "De Voedelscapaciteit der Aarde en de toekomstige Wereldbevolking," *Tijdschrift voor Economische Geographie,* XXXI (1940), 121–32; A. Penck, "Die Trägfahigkeit der Erde," *Lebensraumfragen Europäischer Völker,* ed. K. H. Dietzel, *et al.,* (Leipzig: Quelle & Meyer, 1941); R. M. Salter, "World Soil and Fertilizer Resources in Relation to Food Needs," *Chronica Botanica,* XI (*Freedom from Want,* 1948), 226–35; R. Mukerjee, *Races, Lands, and Food* (New York: Dryden Press, 1946).

[16] See U.N., Population Division, *Determinants and Consequences of Population Trends* (New York: UN, 1953), p. 402.

room for future accommodation of increasing population.

In this general classification of the countries of the world there are the basic facts for considering the adequacy of world resources. Essentially, it is a question of the size of future population which the resources of the world can support. Considered ecologically, we know that the population of the world cannot go on increasing indefinitely, but is the day of final reckoning far off? How clear is our view of the limitations imposed by resources? How much can technical progress in the future inflate the present capacity of resources to support people?

Assuming a degree of international political stability and no catastrophic world conflicts, the emergence of a few changes in resource-population relations over the world appears likely within the next few decades.

a) Resource deterioration within the technology-deficient densely settled countries can be arrested and resources given substantial added carrying power by now feasible technical advances within their economies. Thus, either larger numbers of people in these countries at the present level of life or an improved standard of living for numbers equal to the present is possible. There is at least promise of some economic margin within which conditions may be more favorable to stabilization of population than at present.

b) Technical advances within the technology-deficient sparsely populated areas can add substantial carrying capacity to these lands. This capacity may be used for the support of a continuing natural increase within these countries, for the support of immigrants from densely settled lands, for an increased standard of living, or for all three. The economic margin for future population within lands like Brazil appears to be fairly large, although the practical obstacles to emigration may make it of relatively small importance to the densely settled lands. There must be reservations also about the *rate* of development because of serious biotic obstacles in the natural environment.

c) Nearly all the world's peoples have ambitions toward higher standards of living, to an extent never experienced before. Within at least some of the technology-source areas of low population-resource ratios like the United States and Canada, higher standards of living are being realized. Increased pressure for resource production is therefore generated even though the numbers of people remain the same. However, population is increasing in all these countries, thus hastening the time when the abundant potentials of these lands may be completely used by descendants of the present societies in them.

d) To a lesser but still significant extent, standards of living in other technology-source areas appear to have an upward tendency.

e) The dynamic technical centers of the world, like the United States, have recently had a rapidly increasing capacity to absorb materials and capital, not only from within their own boundaries, but from abroad as well. The development of Caribbean and Middle Eastern oil, South American copper and tin, African copper and uranium, and a variety of other minerals throughout the world illustrates the reach that even the nations with abundant resources can generate as technology moves ahead. The appetite of the technically advanced countries for the provision of materials from the world at large may very well increase.[17] This may be expected to continue at the same time that technically retarded countries develop needs for foreign materials to support industrial economies.

[17] The appetite of the advanced industrial nations for raw materials from abroad may be illustrated by the minerals situation of the United States in recent years. It was almost wholly dependent on foreign countries for a supply of tin, nickel, asbestos, graphite, antimony, manganese, chromite, columbium, beryl, cobalt, diamonds, and quartz. More than half of the bauxite, lead, and mercury came from abroad, along with substantial quantities of tungsten, fluorspar, copper, zinc, iron ore, potash, and petroleum (Dewhurst, *op. cit.*, p. 939).

f) Energy supplies are likely to be more mobile than at any time in previous world history. Energy is the key resource in technical advancement, not only in introducing industrial fabrication but also converting potential resources into employed ones. Furthermore, energy use enables the demand for materials to shift from scarce to abundant resources.[18] Many of the technology-deficient areas of the world have continued in that state because of the cost of obtaining adequate energy supplies within them. When the transportation of very small amounts of material can provide large supplies of energy, a distinctly new geographical relation of resources will prevail.[19] This situation seems destined eventually to convert many of the now "potential" resources of the technology-deficient areas into employed resources.

g) International organization which gives new economies of scale in resource use will be experimented with and probably developed on a much more permanent basis than previously. The regional economic co-operation now being attempted in Europe may have other and later counterparts elsewhere in the world.[20]

h) Public health measures seem likely to influence death rates in an unprecedented manner in all the technology-deficient areas of the world. Assuming no corresponding immediate decrease in birth rates, demographic conditions in all the technology-deficient countries may present sharply increased demands for production within a relatively short period.

i) Taken the world over, there can be little doubt that substantial increases in food production are within technical reach. Furthermore, the capacity of applied biology to add still further to the potential food resources of the earth must be considered promising. Even if it is food at higher costs than those prevailing, it will be demographically significant food.

These new elements in judging the future balance of population and resources give both debits and credits. They all seem significant enough to warrant a summation of their meaning for the future capacity of resources to meet the needs of men. The practical objective of an analysis of resource adequacy is that of sensing the timing and location of social crisis before it occurs. What should be of interest is not the crude estimate of numbers of people possible on earth but the equilibrium between numbers of people as existing social groups and the resources they must draw upon for their life.[21]

Social crisis in this instance may be defined as deteriorating conditions of individual nutrition and material welfare, or the political crisis which arises in anticipation of such conditions. Crises of this kind have arisen countless times the world over during the period of recorded history. They have been met in four general ways: social disorder and reorganization, emigration (military conquest is one means of achieving emigration), technical advance,

18 The manufacture of aluminum, which derives from an abundant natural resource, is a good example; aluminum has taken over many functions for which copper, a naturally more scarce material, formerly was essential. The substitution of plastics for many other metals also illustrates the place of energy in shifting economic demand away from scarce materials.

19 J. Moch provides an interesting examination of this point ("Technology and the Future," *Bulletin of the Atomic Scientists,* XII [1956], 112–18).

20 Generation and distribution of electric energy hitherto has been much cramped by national boundaries. This appears to be no longer necessary in Western Europe (Bardon, Fleischer, and van Rhijn, "La coordination de la production et du transport de l'électricité en Europe occidentale," *Proceedings, Fifth World Power Conference,* Sec. N [1956]; G. W. Hoffman, "Toward Greater Integration in Europe: Transfer of Electric Power across International Boundaries," *Journal of Geography,* LV [1956], 165–76). Other experiments of importance to resource use include the European Coal and Steel Community and the Organization for European Economic Co-operation.

21 This view is somewhat different from, although related to, a suggestion made by A. Sauvy ("Le 'faux problèm' de la population mondiale," *Population,* IV [1949], 447–62). He has maintained that the real population problem is not the earth's carrying capacity but how world and regional population trends may affect human welfare.

and the extension of resource base through trade.

The future of emigration, considering the friction of national boundaries, appears to be a very limited one, unlikely to make the world more of a unit in considering resource adequacy than it now is. Accordingly, world estimates of resource totals have only limited meaning in appraising this question. Total agricultural and food-production potentials certainly are far beyond the production of the present, and mineral exploration still has many opportunities facing it. However, these potentialities mean very different things to people of the four principal types of countries which have been described here.

The basic ingredients for judgment of impending population-resource crises for the type countries are the standard of living (or consumption) trend, the extent and condition of employed and potential resources, the technological advancement trend, trends in international economic organization, degree of group consciousness of impending crises, and the trend in numbers of people. Weighting one side of the balance at the present time are the general upward trend of both numbers and standard of living and the deteriorating productivity of employed resources. The three conspire to place increasing pressure upon resources. Other things remaining equal, the result would be certain and even sharp decline in per capita availability of resources, with eventual depressing effects first on standard of living and finally on numbers of people.

On the other side of the balance, tending to lift the level of resource availability or to lessen pressure upon resources, are technological advancement, group consciousness of crisis, and international economic organization. Technological advancement lifts the level of resource availability by exploring and discovering resources, by shifting demands from scarce to abundant resources, by adding production capacity to employed resources, and by converting potential to employed resources. Group consciousness of crisis can result in conscious stabilization of group numbers, as now appears to be the possibility in Japan. (This element is entering the national scene in India, in Indonesia, and possibly also in China. While its influence to date has been most profound in Japan, it would appear to be a factor which must be taken account of in the future of all the technology-deficient densely populated lands.) International economic organization, in turn, can raise the level of employed resource productivity through contributing scale economies, providing timely access to undeveloped resources, and removing artificial restrictions on production from employed resources.

A projected balance made up of these factors is not simply struck. In fact, it is doubtful that we have the data to arrive at an accurate understanding of the balance for any single social group, much less the balance for the world as a whole at any specific time in the future. To assess the effects of these forces, data on their present significance are needed. We also need the capacity to predict the rate and direction of the forces' change. We have little of such data or capacity at this time. Our view of technology especially may be thus characterized, and that on international economic organization is similar, but to a lesser degree.

Recognizing the great need for additional data and the disturbing influence of technical "mutations" upon resource-use projections of any kind, identification of a few problem areas of future resource adequacy still seems possible. It seems reasonably clear that technical advance is likely to occur over almost the entire world. For all countries experiencing it. such advance certainly means a shift from land as a limiting resource in production to minerals as the limiting resources. Technological advances also generally have meant standard of living advances. Future population-resource crises therefore will be traceable as much to the standard-of-living pressure as to the number of people. In a sense, this means a double pressure on the limiting resources as compared to former times. Because the limiting resources for an industrial society are mainly mineral—and even the largest nation does not have mineral self-sufficiency—the resource pressures of the future are almost certain to be international as well as national. Until the present, limitations have been those of energy sources needed to commence industrial and technical advance. With the already forecast increased mobility and abundance of energy supplies, the pressure for production of metals and other industrial raw materials is likely to be increased greatly by the entry of new nations among the international buyers of industrial raw materials.

These likely events appear to have different meanings for five different types of country.[22] To the four types already described a fifth may be added to cover the sparsely populated lands of the world which have few potential land resources and probably little capacity to support a permanent population of any large size. The five types of country then are: (1) the technology-source areas of low population-potential resource ratio, or the United States type; (2) the technology-source areas of high population-resource ratios, or the European type; (3) the technology-deficient areas of low population-resource ratio, or the Brazil type; (4) the technology-deficient areas of high population-resource ratio, or the China type; and (5) the arctic-desert type, technology-deficient and possessing few food-producing resources.

Considering substantial limitations of data, the forces which can affect the resource-population balance may be summarized for these five types of country about as follows (see also Table 1): The United States type has abundant resources and strong upward trends in the application of technology which are likely to en-

TABLE 1

TRENDS AFFECTING RESOURCE ADEQUACY IN FIVE TYPE AREAS OF THE WORLD

Type	Application of Technology	Land Productivity	Mineral Productivity	Standard of Living	Numbers of People	Pressure for Use of Foreign Resources	Summary Characteristics
1. United States..	U+	U+	U	U+	U	U	Little resource limitation on numbers, some on standard of living; economically strong competition for product of foreign resources
2. European.....	U+	U−	D	U−	U−	U+	Strong pressure for attachment to foreign resources; where frustrated, crisis possible
3. Brazil.........	U	U+	U+	U	U+	N	Little resource limitation on numbers; domestic orientation
4. China.........	U	U	U	U−	U	U	Continued consciousness of impending crisis; increasing pressure for attachment to foreign resources
5. Arctic-desert...	U	N	U+	U	N	N	Development by type 1, 2, 4 countries inevitable; strong competition for resources; however, few people

U+ strong upward trend
U, U− } upward trend
D downward trend
N very little or very few

[22] Here used to mean a social group or groups and the territory recognized to be under the group's or groups' joint jurisdiction.

courage growth in numbers and rise in standard of living. The voracious capacity for mineral consumption already revealed by these economies may continue to make them strong competitors for the product of some resources beyond their borders. Resource-population crises within these lands would seem unlikely for at least a century. These lands are likely to be disturbing in the world resource situation only as they draw minerals to support a high standard of living for their numbers, or the wartime equivalent, modern military machines.

The European type, in spite of a certain strong technology, has limited domestic resources which place strong pressure for attachment of some sort to foreign resources. If their trade position does not permit them to continue and expand such attachments, crises are probable.

The China type, in spite of improving application of technology and the conversion of potential into employed resources, is likely to have continued consciousness of impending crisis; in this lies a principal hope for maintaining the population-resource balance in the face of ambitions for a rising standard of living. Increasing pressure for attachment to foreign mineral resources is certain as industrialization proceeds, a pressure likely to be felt internationally because of the great size of these social groups.

The Brazil type is characterized by limitations on numbers and standard of living likely to be in the rate of application of technology rather than potential resources. These countries are likely to have a domestic orientation and may continue to provide minerals for the three preceeding types. They are more likely to contribute to an alleviation of crises elsewhere than to experience them. However, development is confronted with the unusual biotic obstacles of the tropical environments and may not be rapid for this reason.

The arctic-desert type has water deficiencies, low energy receipt from the atmosphere, or other lacks which make these lands poor prospects for the support of many people. However, they are certain to provide mineral resources badly needed in other parts of the world. Countries of the United States, European, and China types are certain to support their development, as already has been the case with Middle Eastern petroleum. These lands, above all, are likely to contribute to the alleviation of crises elsewhere, while adding little to the world's total population. Should a technical "breakthrough" be reached in the economical conversion of salt water into fresh, the arid lands in this classification may be able to make substantial additions to the world's food-producing capacity, and they may be the site of some additional dense settlement.

DEMOGRAPHIC SCIENCE AND THE EVALUATION OF RESOURCE ADEQUACY

Considering these general observations and the paucity of firm data on forces which actually will determine resource adequacy in the several lands of the world, the immediate value of the neo-Malthusian and anti-Malthusian views must be qualified. A sense of impending *general* crisis is not factually supported; on the other hand, a sense of security in the future is no more firmly founded. Instead of analyzing the absolute supporting capacity of the entire earth, or parts of it, it may be most useful to identify conditions favoring crisis over a reasonably short future period. (A period on the order of fifty to seventy-five years is suggested.) This can be done if recognition of the diversity of the earth and its social groups is preserved. This approach will make the best use of the misty window from which we now view the forces in operation and will set up a framework within which a constant revision of view becomes essential. Because of the great uncertainty of the direction taken by social application of technical advances, this appears realistic.

Within these limitations, two important questions of resource adequacy appear for the next decades. The first concerns the countries of the China type. Will crisis in these countries be averted by the application of technology, by improved access to resources through trade, and by social action following consciousness of impending crisis? The second concerns countries of the European type. Will the continuing advance of technology and the needed further extension of trade for resources avert crisis in these countries? The certain increasing competition for the product of foreign mineral resources from almost all quarters of the earth makes the position of this type of country a particularly vulnerable one. It will be vulnerable until the time when technology has eliminated scarce mineral resources from the essential supplies of modern industrial plants. That is not yet in sight. A supplemental question changes the importance of these two questions only in degree. Will international economic organization be improved so as to lessen the risk of crisis arising in the above two areas, which contain two-thirds of the world's population?

Demography and the related sciences which treat resource adequacy have taken some important steps toward an understanding of these problems. Perfected systems for investigating and recording vital statistics are gradually being put into operation. Some knowledge of the feasibility of conscious population stabilization is being obtained. Better knowledge of the resource content of the earth's crust is being gained each year. It is now understood that the simple classification of the world's lands into industrialized and underdeveloped countries must give way to a more complex but also more meaningful classification when resource adequacy is analyzed.

The next steps will be the organization of more carefully co-ordinated population-resource-technology studies than have been possible in the past. Such studies might be applied to the problems of the two classes of countries within which the continuance of or first appearance of crises within the next few decades seems likely. Among other things, the studies might comprise (*a*) an appraisal of the limits of resource development in the problem lands, according to the existing technology available there or elsewhere in the world; (*b*) estimate of the demands of those populations for food and materials from other parts of the world commuuity, assuming that adequate standards of consumption are to be established or preserved; (*c*) appraisal of the likelihood of competition for materials needed from the world community by these countries, and the intensity of that competition; (*d*) identification of fruitful subjects for the application of technical effort and social experiment; (*e*) identification of regional affinities among countries which have resource deficiencies and potential complementary resource relations; (*f*) identification of the responsibility and capacity of international trade organization for reducing the risk of crisis within the problem classes of countries.

It is over this route that we are likely to arrive at some temporary understanding of what the limits of the earth amount to in the immediate future. It may be a long time before we understand the *permanent* limits of the earth—if, indeed, we ever discover them.

Additional References

Bates, M. *The Prevalence of People.* New York: Scribner, 1955.

Bennett, M. K. *The World's Food: A Study of the Interrelations of World Populations, National Diets, and Food Potentials.* New York: Harper & Bros., 1954.

Blake, J., Davis, K., and Stycos, J. M. *"Economic Status and Fertility Control in Jamaica."* New York: Conservation Foundation, 1955.

Bonné, A. "Land Resource and the Growth of World Population," in Research Council of Israel, Special Publication No. 2, 1953.

Brown, H. *The Challenge of Man's Future.* New York: Viking, 1954.

———. "Raw Materials, Energy, Population, and the Spread of Industrialization," *Resources of the World: A Speculative Projection.* Pasadena: California Institute of Technology, 1956.

Clark, C. "Population Growth and Living

Standards," *International Labour Review,* LXVIII (1953), 99–117.

COALE, A. J., AND HOOVER, E. M. "Population Growth and Economic Development in India, 1956–1986." Princeton: Office of Population Research, Princeton University, 1956.

GREBENIK, E. "World Population and Resources," *Political Quarterly,* XXVI (1955), 371–79.

HERTZLER, J. O. *The Crisis in World Population: A Sociological Examination, with Special Reference to the Underdeveloped Areas.* Lincoln: University of Nebraska Press, 1955.

LEWIS, W. A. *The Theory of Economic Growth.* London: Allen & Unwin, 1955. (Esp. chap. 6, "Population and Resources," pp. 304–75.)

MEIER, R. L. *Modern Society and the Human Fertility Problem.* New York: Wiley, 1959.

Milbank Memorial Fund. *The Interrelations of Demographic, Economic, and Social Problems in Selected Underdeveloped Areas.* New York: Author, 1954.

OSER, J. *Must Men Starve? The Malthusian Controversy.* New York: Abelard-Schuman, 1956.

RUSSELL, SIR E. J. *World Population and World Food Supplies.* London: Allen & Unwin, 1954.

SAX, K. *Standing Room Only: The Challenge of Overpopulation.* Boston: Beacon Press, 1955.

STAMP, L. D. *Natural Resources, Food, and Population in Intertropical Africa: A Report on a Geographical Symposium Held at Makerere College.* Kampala, Uganda: University of East Africa, 1955.

. . . all this debate on how many men can live on earth evades the issue, which really is the quantity of beings versus the quality of living. If we neglect to choose, the choice, perhaps an unpleasant one, will be forced upon us.

The ultimate question is moral and ethical, not technological at all. In terms of my purposes, the world is already supporting too many people and it should, for some time to come, support progressively fewer and fewer in almost all of its regions, including the United States.

But, you may counter, surely in this economy of surpluses we would not be better off with fewer people. True, ours is an economy of surpluses, but still a society of deteriorating education, of inadequate public facilities. An economy of *private* surpluses, yes, but how about the one-third still ill-housed, ill-fed? How about the complaints that we cannot afford parklands, or decent medical care; that we cannot afford to support our aged, or care for our delinquents, or dispose of our wastes properly? What is the state of our resources when our major oil, mining, and lumber companies say that if we set aside a mere one-hundredth of our land so that it can remain wild, it will jeopardize our resource base? What you see here is a society that won't admit that it exists to serve its economy but that has no way of evaluating social qualities except to price them. Such a market-place mandate is madness and can lead only to disaster.

DANIEL B. LUTEN, "How Dense Can People Be?" *Sierra Club Bulletin* (December, 1963).

PART II

THE CONSERVATION OF LIMITED RESOURCES

CHAPTER 3

THE GROWTH OF A MOVEMENT

The concept of a limited, finite earth has long been one of the firm supports of the conservationist view. It was strongly reinforced in the United States by the closing of the frontier[1] marked by the report of the census of 1890.[2] This helped to bring Americans to a new realization of the limits of their domain. The three decades that followed, 1890–1920, were to see the greatest flowering of the Conservation Movement—its classical period.

Today, the Conservation Movement is a varied collection of organizations and individuals. A recent issue of the *Conservation Directory* lists over 350 private and governmental agencies concerned with aspects of conservation.[3] Yet we may question, with Grant McConnell, whether this profusion of organizations, characterized by diversity of purpose and diffusion of action, can now accurately be called a movement.

In the early years of the present century, interest in conservation was at its peak and formed the nucleus for a powerful surge of liberal views. One of the basic manifestos of that movement, the "Declaration of Governors for Conservation of Natural Resources," is included in this chapter. This declaration was presented at the White House Conference on Conservation in 1908. It may be symptomatic of a changed federal-state relationship that no "Governors' Declaration" is to be found in the record of the White House Conference on Conservation initiated by President John F. Kennedy.[4]

The idea of conservation is much older than such manifestos, and incorporates ideas, according to Glacken, whose origins were to be found in the writings of the ancient world.[5]

1 Frederick J. Turner, "The Significance of the Frontier in American History," *Annual Report of the American Historical Association for 1893* (Washington, 1894), pp. 199–227.

2 U.S., Census Office, *Eleventh Census, 1890,* I (Washington: Government Printing Office, 1895), xxxiv.

3 National Wildlife Federation, *Conservation Directory, 1963: A Listing of Organizations and Officials Concerned with Natural Resources* (Washington, 1963).

4 The White House Conference on Conservation, *Official Proceedings,* May 24th and 25th, 1962 (Washington: Government Printing Office, 1963).

5 For more detailed discussion and an excellent bibliography on early views of man and nature see Clarence J. Glacken, "Changing Ideas of the Habitable World," *Man's Role in Changing the Face of the Earth,* ed. W. L. Thomas (Chicago: University of Chicago Press, 1956), pp. 70–92. A discus-

A necessary, if not sufficient, condition for the idea of conservation is the realization of the power that man possesses to change his relationship with a finite, natural world. Men intimately involved with nature at a primitive level of technology have little or no conscious concept of conservation.[6] For the idea of conservation to take hold, flourish, and grow into a movement, a consciousness of man's destructive control over nature is required. Such consciousness was given its early and profound expression by George Perkins Marsh in *Man and Nature, or Physical Geography as Modified by Human Action.*[7] This book, a chapter of which follows, is the spiritual godfather of the Conservation Movement whose flowering it preceded by forty years. The flowering of the Movement is described by one of the Movement's early participants, Charles Van Hise.

Under Theodore Roosevelt, Gifford Pinchot, Francis G. Newlands, and others, the Movement became both a crusade and ideology. But if today conservation appears to be many things to many men, even in that period, its motivation and purpose seemed obscure. Two views that seek to explain the early character and motivation of the Conservation Movement are presented, and they are somewhat in conflict. McConnell expresses the more widely held view that the Conservation Movement was influenced by two major themes: a deep spiritual belief in natural order, and a Progressivism that fought for wise development of resources for the many, rather than for the avaricious few.[8] Hays has another view. For him the Conservation Movement was a reflection of the spirit of applied scientific rationality that was abroad in the land.[9]

Cold light of reason or white heat of indignation—the net effect was the same—to illuminate paths of resource development in a way new to an America that had just grown aware of the possible limits to its earth. A major achievement was to apply the brake to over-zealous resource exploitation and destruction. A less welcome result, as Barnett shows in this chapter, was to but-

---

sion of nineteenth- and twentieth-century views is found in J. R. Whitaker, "World View of Destruction and Conservation of Natural Resources," *Annals of the Association of American Geographers,* XXX (September, 1940), 143–62.

[6] See Alexander Spoehr's article "Cultural Differences in the Interpretation of Natural Resources," included in chap. 2 of this volume, reprinted from *Man's Role in Changing the Face of the Earth, op. cit.*, pp. 93–102.

[7] The circumstances surrounding its authorship and an assessment of its impact on the thought of its time can be found in chap. 13 entitled "Man and Nature" in David Lowenthal, *George Perkins Marsh: Versatile Vermonter* (New York: Columbia University Press, 1958), pp. 246–76.

[8] A clear exposition of the latter theme can be found in J. Leonard Bates, "Fulfilling American Democracy: The Conservation Movement, 1907–21," *Mississippi Valley Historical Review,* XLIV (June, 1957), 29–57. See also the excerpt from Pinchot's *Breaking New Ground* in chap. 4 of this volume.

[9] Hays bases much of his argument on original documents and early writings of the principals involved in the Movement. See for example the opening paragraph of W J McGee, "Water as a Resource," *Annals, American Academy of Political and Social Science,* XXXIII (May, 1909), 521.

tress and make respectable the Malthusian and Ricardian doctrines of increasing resource scarcity, which still wield a powerful influence today. A beneficial legacy is that there remains a group of aware citizens and vocal politicians who are alive to the destructive powers of a complex urban and industrial society, and who rise *en masse* to the defense of nature whenever the call is given, as in the concern over extensive use of chemical pesticides.[10]

[10] Rachel L. Carson, *Silent Spring* (Boston: Houghton Mifflin, 1962); President's Science Advisory Committee, *Use of Pesticides* (Washington: Government Printing Office, 1963).

CLARENCE J. GLACKEN

THE ORIGINS OF THE CONSERVATION PHILOSOPHY

One of the most powerful and deep-seated ideas in Western thought is that the earth and the arrangements of living nature observable on it are the products of divine effort and design. This idea was widely but by no means universally held by the classical thinkers, the whole argument with statements for and against being lucidly summarized in the second book of Cicero's *On the Nature of the Gods*. It is also a basic idea of the Old and the New Testaments, both of which, moreover, reveal a strong feeling for the beauties of nature, the Psalms perhaps being the outstanding example.

Historically, the view of the earth as a planet designed and made habitable for all forms of life has involved two attitudes toward living nature: it is beautiful and it is useful. In Christian thought there has been nothing accidental in the combining of these attributes, for the earth was beautiful because it was an expression of the perfection of the Creator, and it was useful to man because he could get from it physical sustenance and the religious inspiration to worship his Creator. This conception of the earth was a dominant one through the Middle Ages and early modern times and was still important in the nineteenth century, as shown by the number of natural theologies written by scientific men, such as the geologists John MacCulloch and Hugh Miller,[1] although it had come under increasing criticism beginning in the eighteenth century because of the teleology which was assumed in the argument from design. As a consequence of this belief, the Western idea of man as part of nature has never been quite forgotten despite opposing tendencies such as the divorecement of humanistic and scientific inquiry and specialization within disciplines.

There was one significant assumption in this religious conception of nature: in the natural order of things, men would use their environment, changing it for their own ends and improving on its natural state; in descriptions of nature which appear in works with this theme, both pristine and domesticated nature are described, the descriptions often intermingling: the forests of the mountains are set off from the tilled fields of the lowlands; the olive or the fruit trees form neat rows on the borders of wild-growing low-lying shrubs; the peasant huts are built along the stream; the domestic animals tended by their herders graze in the forest.

In the writings from the seventeenth to the nineteenth century which were devoted to the design argument, whether in natural theology, philosophy, natural history, geography, biology, or other disciplines, nature was conceived of as a usufruct and man, as the highest being in the creation

• Clarence J. Glacken is Associate Professor of Geography, University of California, Berkeley.

Reprinted from the *Journal of Soil and Water Conservation,* XI, No. 2 (1956), 63–66, with the permission of the author and editor. (Published by the Soil Society of America.)

[1] John MacCulloch, *Proofs and Illustrations of the Attributes of God, from the Facts and Laws of the Physical Universe: Being the Foundation of Natural and Revealed Religion* (3 vols; London: J. Duncan, 1837); Hugh Miller, *The Testimony of the Rocks: or, Geology in Its Bearings on the Two Theologies, Natural and Revealed* (Edinburgh: T. Constable & Co., 1857).

had responsibilities as well as privileges in using it. His role with regard to the rest of creation was often looked upon as that of a steward or a caretaker of God. In the works of such physico-theologists as John Ray and William Derham, man has the role of a partner of God in improving primeval nature, in conversions of natural landscapes for his own purposes, in agriculture, in the clearing of forests, in the drainage of swamps: his improvements in soil fertility through the use of manuring and marling were other instances of the partnership of man and his Creator not only in maintaining but in improving the earth, through his inventiveness, for his enjoyment and use and for the greater glory of God.[2]

In addition to these ideas, there were others of a more humble and practical origin which in their cumulative effects had a great influence on the development of conservation, ideas based on observations that human activities brought about undesirable changes in nature. These observations accumulated not in philosophies and in natural theologies but in learned and technical works; one sees them in increasing number in the eighteenth century. It is these two trends, one, aesthetic, philosophical, and religious, the other, practical and technical, that have characterized ideas of conservation throughout its history.

These notices, mostly descriptive of local conditions, began to accumulate in the late Middle Ages. For the most part they concerned the use of the forests. Concern about them was not a new phenomenon; one has glimpses of it in classical and postclassical times, in the legislation of Roman, Byzantine, Merovingian, and Carolingian times. The forests of Europe were related intimately both to the economics and the amenities of life, and there were conflicts of interest in using them. The most obvious—and the one that has been emphasized in modern times—was the indirect conservation of the forests because they were royal or noble hunting reserves. They were also the source of wood fuel to keep kilns and smelters going, and of wood for building purposes. Forests were often centers of the beekeeping industry which was important before sugar was known, and there was a lively trade in beeswax for making candles used by monasteries in the forest wilderness. Forests were grazing lands and the early attitudes toward them, and the legislation enacted regarding them, cannot be understood without realizing that their importance as grazing lands for sheep, cattle, goats, and especially for swine often was equal to or greater than their significance as wood producers. It was the complex role of the forest in the economy which brought about laws and regulations governing the uses of forests in every European country.[3]

The practice of transhumance often meant clearance of forest lands to increase mountain pastures at the expense of trees. There were conflicts too between farmer and herder in the width and use of sheep runs through agricultural land. It was, however, the extensions of agriculture and industry at the expense of the forests that were most conspicuous: Agriculture meant cutting and burning of trees, the *assarts,* the *Brandwirtschaft* that continued in some parts of northwestern Europe, in Finland for example, until the latter part of the nineteenth century. Furthermore, wood and water were the great sources of energy before the age of coal. Another explanation for the growth of the conservation idea thus is to be sought in conflicts of interest with regard to use. There are two famous

[2] John Ray, *The Wisdom of God Manifested in the Works of the Creation* (12th ed. corrected; London: J. Rivington, 1759); William Derham, *Physico-theology: or, a Demonstration of the Being and Attributes of God from His Works of Creation* (new ed., 2 vols.; Vol. II; London: A. Strahan, 1798).

[3] For an introduction to this literature, see Alfred Louis Ferdinand Maury, *Les forêts de la France dans l'antiquité et au moyen âge, nouveaux essais sur leur topographie, leur histoire et la législation qui les régissait* (Paris: Académie des Inscriptions et Belles Lettres, 1856); Adam Schwappach, *Handbuch der Forst- und Jagdgeschichte Deutschlands,* (2 vols.; Vol. I; Berlin: Springer, 1886–88).

illustrations of these conflicts, John Evelyn's *Silva,* which was first published in 1664, and the celebrated forest ordinance of Colbert of 1669.

In his *Silva,* a landmark in the history of silviculture, Evelyn describes the encroachments of agriculture, the dangers of grazing and of metallurgy; the competition in land use can plainly be seen. Agriculture, Evelyn said, was extending itself at the expense of the forests, and the iron mills were destroying them because of their demands for charcoal to reduce the ore and in the working of iron. Evelyn's remarks reveal the existence of problems posed by the innovator and the conserver: the distribution of minerals which a culture finds useful, even indispensable, conflicts with the preservation of the forest whose existence is governed by entirely different physical circumstances. Early modern conservation ideas are really a recognition of the fact that the distribution of mineral deposits with relation to forests, even with the industrial development existing before the Industrial Revolution, meant the slow, relentless destruction of nature.[4]

One of the merits in studying the history of legislation is that laws are excellent indications of the abuses which provoked their enactment; they are less trustworthy guides regarding accomplishments because of the gap between intent and enforcement. Colbert's famous declaration that France would perish for lack of wood was not a sudden outcry against forest destruction; it was a condemnation of practices which had been commonplace in France for centuries, for the ordinance, approved by Louis XIV, was the latest and most complete of a series of decrees dating back to the thirteenth century. One general provision of this long law sums up rather well the problems it was trying to solve:

> We forbid them [the Grand Masters of the Forests] to permit or suffer any kilns, furnaces, charcoal-making, grubbing and up-rooting, lifting or removal of beacons, acorns, and other produce from our forests, contrary to the provisions of these presents, on pain of arbitrary fine, and reparation of all our damage and interests.[5]

From the late eighteenth to the mid-nineteenth century, the literature relating to conservation increased both in scope and in depth; there has been no break in the continuity since those times. French, Italian, German, Austrian foresters, engineers, and hydrologists studied the problem of deforestation as the cause of Alpine torrents, among whom the names of Fabre and Surell are perhaps the best known. In this period the long discussions concerning the deforestation and climatic change were pursued with vigor, including among the scientists such famous names as von Humboldt, Boussingault, and Becquerel.[6] New works on land reclamation and the making of polders—the Dutch with their long experience had already created an extensive literature—were part of an effort to extend these techniques throughout Europe to reclaim land. Studies on the fixation of sand dunes, important because the encroaching sands inundated villages, were made from the dune areas of the Atlantic and North Sea shores to those of Pomerania and East Prussia. Fixation through the planting of maritime pines had already been undertaken in the Landes region of France in 1795. Scientists began investigating soil erosion of the Mediterranean basin and of Asia Minor; Carl Fraas, for example, made an extensive study of the

[4] John Evelyn, *Silva: or, a Discourse of Forest Trees, and the Propagation of Timber in His Majesty's Dominions* (new ed.; Vol. II; London: J. Dodsley, 1776), pp. 256–69 (Book III, chap. 6).

[5] John C. Brown (trans.), *French Forest Ordinance of 1669: with Historical Sketch of Previous Treatment of Forests in France* (Edinburgh: Oliver and Boyd, 1883), p. 73 (chap. 1, art. 18).

[6] For an introduction to this literature, see George P. Marsh, *Man and Nature: or, Physical Geography as Modified by Human Action* (New York: Scribners, 1864); John C. Brown, *Reboisment in France . . .* (London: C. K. Paul & Co., 1880). On Fabre and Surell, see pp. 15–59. Antoine César Becquerel, "Forests and Their Climatic Influence," *Annual Report . . . of the Smithsonian Institution . . . for the Year 1869* (Washington, 1871), pp. 394–416.

deterioration of the lands of Asia Minor and the eastern Mediterranean, ascribing it to the loss of vegetative cover.[7]

Despite its volume and scope, there was no real synthesis of this literature until George P. Marsh published in 1864 *Man and Nature; or Physical Geography as Modified by Human Action.* Marsh had an impressive command of his subject, the result of travel, observation, and exhaustive reading of the contemporary literature; he documented his work in modern fashion, and, in addition to its other merits, it is a valuable reference work on the history of conservation. Marsh's main examples were the countries of northwest Europe and the Mediterranean. In making a study of lands which had a long history of human settlement, Marsh warned his countrymen—by comparing environments of old with those of newly settled regions—of the dangers of disturbing the balance of nature. The lands of the New World would require careful husbanding if they were to remain habitable for future generations. He wrote his work to show the immense power exerted by man throughout history in modifying the natural environment, discussing his role in plant and animal domestication and in the activities of domesticated animals like sheep, goats, and camels, really extensions of human activity; the consequences of deforestation, Marsh's chief concern, for it was the preoccupation of many scientists of that period; man's effects upon the waters and upon the sands.

The importance of Marsh's work from a conservation point of view is that it clearly demonstrated that conservation was an historical, cultural, and philosophical problem. Throughout history the earth had been changed by peoples who neglected or ignored the effects of their destruction of the natural environment. It is noteworthy that virtually all of his examples refer to the period prior to the Industrial Revolution.

In the work of Marsh, the idea of an organized and harmonious nature designed by the Creator for the use of all organic life and with man at the apex of the scale is merged with this vast technical literature. From it came a philosophy of nature and of man's responsibility in maintaining it as a usufruct. Man should be faithful to his stewardship, for the earth was beautiful and useful because the Creator had intended it to be so.

Long before Marsh's time, however, American agricultural writers, naturalists, and farmers had already observed and written about deforestation, soil exhaustion, and soil erosion. Some of this literature was inspired by English writings, but much of it came from the observation of local conditions. Among the most well-known of these early conservationists were Jared Eliot, Thomas Jefferson, John Taylor, and Edmund Ruffin.[8]

Another American, Nathaniel S. Shaler, was an outstanding figure in the last quarter of the nineteenth century because, like Marsh, he looked at conservation from a world point of view and because he was interested in so many phases of the subject. Shaler, a geologist, expressed a conservationist philosophy similar to that of Marsh, but he emphasized more than Marsh had the importance of understanding soils and the seriousness of soil erosion. In an article which appeared in the *National Geographic Magazine,* Shaler, who was no pessimist, warned his countrymen in vigorous language of the danger that their soils would wash away if they neglected to care for them. His monograph on soils was prepared to assist anyone desiring an un-

[7] C. Fraas, *Klima und Pflanzenwelt in der Zeit, ein Beitrag zur Geschichte Beider* (Landshut: J. G. Wölfe, 1847).

[8] For an introduction to this literature, see Angus McDonald, *Early American Soil Conservationists,* U.S. Dept. of Agric. Misc. Pub. No. 449 (Washington: USDA, 1941); Hugh Hammond Bennett, *Thomas Jefferson, Soil Conservationist,* U.S. Dept. of Agric. Misc. Pub. No. 548 (Washington: USDA, 1944); Gilbert Chinard, "The American Philosophical Society and the Early History of Forestry in America," *Proceedings of the Amer. Philosophical Society,* LXXXIX (1945), 444–488.

derstanding of soils, an essential study he thought for settlers in a new country whose traditions concerning the soil of a district were comparatively meager. Shaler was a man of very broad interests; in his later writings, he presented one of the earliest and most interesting analyses of mineral consumption by modern civilization, and he advanced ideas concerning the resources of the seas, future energy sources, and the changes which man, with his growing numbers, would continue to make on inorganic matter and organic life on earth. Shaler represents a shift from the old emphasis on deforestation, characteristic of Marsh and his predecessors, to a new one, concerned with the contemporary and future uses of the forests, soils, and minerals.[9]

The expanding economies of the latter part of the nineteenth century produced a correspondingly expanding literature on the need for conservation. A German economic geographer, Ernst Friedrich, popularized the word *Raubwirtschaft* (plunder economy), attempting at the same time to find a rationale in man's exploitation of the world and finding it in the formula that unwise destructive exploitation led to poverty and distress which in turn would lead to rational exploitation.[10] The British parliament investigated the causes of deforestation in India. Studies of the tropical plantation, of shifting agriculture and grazing in the tropics were beginning to appear. There was a growing literature of protest against the wholesale killing of the plume birds, the bison, the big game of Africa, seals, and whales; one writer referred to the times as an "age of extermination."

In the United States, the rapid extension of settlement had brought about an awareness, among men interested in conservation, of the changes which were transforming the country. It was different from old Europe where the contrast between virgin land and settled land was deep in the past. In America the contrast was real to a single generation. In the sixties Marsh was warning of possibilities which were realities in the nineties. There is a vigor, a comprehensiveness, a sense of urgency in this late nineteenth and early twentieth century American literature; the tone is unmistakable in the early report of Frederick Hough, in the Report of the National Conservation Commission which followed the White House Conference of 1908, in the proceedings of the first Conservation Congress in Seattle, and in the pages of Van Hise's famous textbook.[11] There is an emphasis on the need of maintaining the balance of nature, on developing resources without waste, on the intimate association between a nation and its resources (perhaps nowhere more eloquently expressed than in this literature), and the need of safeguarding and of restoring the natural beauties of the country. Although these investigations had their origin, as Gifford Pinchot has said,[12] in the movement for forest conservation which is so closely associated with his name, it should be remembered that forestry was a broad term. These men were interested in the forests, in the streams, in the grazing lands, and

9 See Nathaniel S. Shaler, "The Origin and Nature of Soil," *Twelfth Annual Report of the United States Geological Survey, 1890–91. Part I—Geology* (Washington: USGS, 1891), pp. 213–345; "The Economic Aspects of Soil Erosion," *National Geographical Magazine,* VII (1896), 328–38, 368–77; *idem, Man and the Earth* (New York: Fox, Duffield, & Co., 1906).

10 Ernst Friedrich, "Wesen und Geographische Verbreigtung der 'Raubwirtschaft,'" *Petermanns Mitteilungen,* L (1904), 68–79, 92–95.

11 Franklin B. Hough, *Report upon Forestry. Prepared under the Direction of the Commissioner of Agriculture, in Pursuance of an Act of Congress Approved August 15, 1876* (Washington: GPO, 1878). See also, *Report of the National Conservation Commission* (3 vols.; February, 1909), Senate Doc. No. 676, 60th Cong., 2d Sess.; *Addresses and Proceedings of the First National Conservation Congress Held at Seattle, Washington, August 26–28, 1909.* Published by the Executive Comm. of the National Conservation Congress, 1910. Charles R. Van Hise, *The Conservation of Natural Resources in the United States* (New York: Macmillan, 1910).

12 Gifford Pinchot, "How Conservation Began in the United States," *Agricultural History,* XI (1936), 255.

in the soils; the idea of conservation had expanded to include the material resources and values. There was a great deal of optimism in America during this period, but a few men also took advantage of the unparalleled opportunity to soberly study the immense power which modern societies had acquired to change their physical environments.

Although it would be rash to attempt in this brief space a summary of contemporary conservation ideas, a few general observations may be helpful in understanding the literature of today and how it differs from that of the nineteenth and the early part of the twentieth century.

In the first place, much more is known about the nature and distribution of the world's soils. Speaking generally, from classical antiquity to the time of Liebig in the middle of the nineteenth century, the main preoccupation of students of soils was with the maintenance of the fertility of arable lands; soil science, closely identified with agricultural chemistry, was practical in its goals and in its research. In the late nineteenth century, the work of Hilgard in America and of Dokuchaiev and his school in Russia called attention to the need of studying soils in their own right and independently of the practical considerations of agriculture. From these investigations of little-worked or virgin soils of the United States and Russia our modern concepts of the nature of soils have been derived, and soil science today is much more closely related to conservation than it was in the last century.

In the second place, the ecological point of view is much more in evidence today than it was in the past. The idea of a close and interlocking relationship in nature is an old one; its origin can be traced to the idea that nature was a divinely arranged harmony. The concept of the unity of nature, however, was given more specific meaning by von Humboldt's studies of plant geography, by Darwin's concept of the web of life, and by many of the late nineteenth century ecologists. Modern studies of the populations of biotic communities, of the history of vegetational change, and of the effects of cultural changes in biotic communities have done much to broaden the theoretical bases of conservation, even though there has been criticism of some ecological theory such as succession and the climax concepts.

In the third place, the American dust storms of the thirties have had a great influence on conservation ideas because they occurred in combination with the depression and the widespread migration from the Dust Bowl. Their effect was to revive an old but neglected point of view that conservation was deeply involved in history and in the cultural values of a society. The surveys of Bennett and of Jacks and Whyte which followed called attention to the world-wide nature of these problems.[13]

Since the end of World War II, a new combination of old ideas has resulted in a greater emphasis on the power of human cultures in changing the environment, on the relation of custom and law to conservation, and on the increased growth of the world's population. There have also been renewed attempts to create a conservation ethic and philosophy, a moral and aesthetic attitude toward nature which, I cannot help but feel, is the modern substitute for the earlier scientific and religious belief that the world of nature with all its beauty was a harmonious whole designed by the Creator.

[13] Bennett, *Soil Conservation* (New York and London: McGraw-Hill, 1939); G. V. Jacks and R. O. Whyte, *Vanishing Lands: A World Survey of Soil Erosion* (New York: Doubleday, Doran, & Co., 1939).

GEORGE P. MARSH

THE EARTH AS MODIFIED BY HUMAN ACTION

Reaction of Man on Nature

The revolutions of the seasons, with their alternations of temperature and of length of day and night, the climates of different zones, and the general conditions and movements of the atmosphere and the seas, depend upon causes for the most part cosmical, and, of course, wholly beyond our control. The elevation, configuration, and composition of the great masses of terrestrial surface, and the relative extent and distribution of land and water, are determined by geological influences equally remote from our jurisdiction. It would hence seem that the physical adaptation of different portions of the earth to the use and enjoyment of man is a matter so strictly belonging to mightier than human powers, that we can only accept geographical nature as we find her and be content with such soils and such skies as she spontaneously offers.

But it is certain that man has reacted upon organized and inorganic nature, and thereby modified, if not determined, the material structure of his earthly home. The measure of that reaction manifestly constitutes a very important element in the appreciation of the relations between mind and matter, as well as in the discussion of many purely physical problems. But though the subject has been incidentally touched upon by many geographers, and treated with much fulness of detail in regard to certain limited fields of human effort and to certain specific effects of human action, it has not, as a whole, so far as I know, been made matter of special observation or of historical research by any scientific inquirer. Indeed, until the influence of geographical conditions upon human life was recognized as a distinct branch of philosophical investigation, there was no motive for the pursuit of such speculations; and it was desirable to inquire how far we have, or can, become the architects of our own abiding place only when it was known how the mode of our physical, moral, and intellectual being is affected by the character of the home which Providence has appointed, and we have fashioned, for our material habitation.

It is still too early to attempt scientific method in discussing this problem, nor is our present store of the necessary facts by any means complete enough to warrant me in promising any approach to fulness of statement respecting them. Systematic observation in relation to this subject has hardly yet begun, and the scattered data which have chanced to be recorded have never been collected. It has now no place in the general scheme of physical science, and is matter of suggestion and speculation only, not of established and positive conclusion. At present, then, all that I can hope is to excite an interest in a topic of much economical importance by pointing out the directions and illustrating the modes in which human action has been, or may be, most injurious or most beneficial in its influence upon the physical conditions of the earth we inhabit.

• George P. Marsh (1801–82) is best known for his pioneering work in conservation.

Abridged from George P. Marsh, *The Earth as Modified by Human Action* (Charles Scribner's Sons, 1882), pp. 8–55.

We cannot always distinguish between the results of man's action and the effects of purely geological or cosmical causes. The destruction of the forests, the drainage of lakes and marshes, and the operations of rural husbandry and industrial art have unquestionably tended to produce great changes in the hygrometric, thermometric, electric, and chemical condition of the atmosphere, though we are not yet able to measure the force of the different elements of disturbance, or to say how far they have been neutralized by each other, or by still obscurer influences; and it is equally certain that the myriad forms of animal and vegetable life, which covered the earth when man first entered upon the theater of a nature whose harmonies he was destined to derange, have been, through his interference, greatly changed in numerical proportion, sometimes much modified in form and product, and sometimes entirely extirpated.

The physical revolutions thus wrought by man have not indeed all been destructive to human interests, and the heaviest blows he has inflicted upon nature have not been wholly without their compensations. Soils to which no nutritious vegetable was indigenous, countries which once brought forth but the fewest products suited for the sustenance and comfort of man—while the severity of their climates created and stimulated the greatest number and the most imperious urgency of physical wants—surfaces the most rugged and intractable, and least blessed with natural facilities of communication, have been brought in modern times to yield and distribute all that supplies the material necessities, all that contributes to the sensuous enjoyments and conveniences of civilized life. The Scythia, the Thule, the Britain, the Germany, and the Gaul which the Roman writers describe in such forbidding terms, have been brought almost to rival the native luxuriance and easily won plenty of Southern Italy; and, while the fountains of oil and wine that refreshed old Greece and Syria and Northern Africa have almost ceased to flow, and the soils of those fair lands are turned to thirsty and inhospitable deserts, the hyperborean regions of Europe have learned to conquer, or rather compensate, the rigors of climate, and have attained to a material wealth and variety of product that, with all their natural advantages, the granaries of the ancient world can hardly be said to have enjoyed.

Observation of Nature

In these pages it is my aim to stimulate, not to satisfy, curiosity, and it is no part of my object to save my readers the labor of observation or of thought. For labor is life. Self is the schoolmaster whose lessons are best worth his wages; and since the subject I am considering has not yet become a branch of formal instruction, those whom it may interest can, fortunately, have no pedagogue but themselves. To the natural philosopher, the descriptive poet, the painter, the sculptor, and indeed every earnest observer, the power most important to cultivate, and, at the same time, hardest to acquire, is that of seeing what is before him. Sight is a faculty; seeing, an art. The eye is a physical but not a self-acting apparatus, and in general it sees only what it seeks. Like a mirror, it reflects objects presented to it; but it may be as insensible as a mirror, and not consciously perceive what it reflects.

It has been maintained by high authority, that the natural acuteness of our sensuous faculties cannot be heightened by use, and hence, that the minutest details of the image formed on the retina are as perfect in the most untrained as in the most thoroughly disciplined organ. This may be questioned, and it is agreed on all hands that the power of multifarious perception and rapid discrimination may be immensely increased by well-directed practice. This exercise of the eye I desire to promote, and, next to moral and religious doctrine, I know no more important practical lessons in this earthly life of ours—which, to the wise man, is a school from the cradle to the grave—than those relating to the employment of the sense of vision in the study of nature.

The pursuit of physical geography, embracing actual observation of terrestrial surface, affords to the eye the best general training that is accessible to all. The majority of even cultivated men have not the time and means of acquiring anything beyond a very superficial acquaintance with any branch of physical knowledge. Natural science has become so vastly extended, its recorded facts and its unanswered questions so immensely multiplied, that every strictly scientific man must be a specialist and confine the researches of a whole life within a comparatively narrow circle. The study I am recommending, in the view I propose to take of it, is yet in that imperfectly developed state which allows its votaries to occupy themselves with broad and general views attainable by every person of culture, and it does not now require a knowledge of special details which only years of application can master. It may be profitably pursued by all; and every traveler, every lover of rural scenery, every agriculturist, who will wisely use the gift of sight, may add valuable contributions to the common stock of knowledge on a subject which, as I hope to convince my readers, though long neglected, and now inartificially presented, is not only a very important but a very interesting field of inquiry.

Measurement of Man's Influence

The exact measurement of the geographical and climatic changes hitherto effected by man is impracticable, and we possess, in relation to them, the means of only qualitative, not quantitative analysis. The fact of such revolutions is established partly by historical evidence, partly by analogical deduction from effects produced, in our own time, by operations similar in character to those which must have taken place in more or less remote ages of human action. Both sources of information are alike defective in precision; the latter, for general reasons too obvious to require specification; the former, because the facts to which it bears testimony occurred before the habit or the means of rigorously scientific observation upon any branch of physical research, and especially upon climatic changes, existed.

Uncertainty of Our Historical Conclusions on Ancient Climates

The invention of measures of heat and of atmospheric moisture, pressure, and precipitation, is extremely recent. Hence, ancient physicists have left us no thermometric or barometric records, no tables of the fall, evaporation, and flow of waters, and even no accurate maps of coast lines and the course of rivers. Their notices of these phenomena are almost wholly confined to excessive and exceptional instances of high or of low temperatures, extraordinary falls of rain and snow, and unusual floods or droughts. Our knowledge of the meteorological condition of the earth, at any period more than two centuries before our own time, is derived from these imperfect details, from the vague statements of ancient historians and geographers in regard to the volume of rivers and the relative extent of forest and cultivated land, from the indications furnished by the history of the agriculture and rural economy of past generations, and from other almost purely casual sources of information.

Among these latter we must rank certain newly laid open fields of investigation, from which facts bearing on the point now under consideration have been gathered. I allude to the discovery of artificial objects in geological formations older than any hitherto recognized as exhibiting traces of the existence of man; to the ancient lacustrine habitations of Switzerland and of the *terremare* of Italy, containing the implements of the occupants, remains of their food, and other relics of human life; to the curious revelations of the Kjökkenmöddinger, or heaps of kitchen refuse, in Denmark and elsewhere, and of the peat mosses in the same and other northern countries; to the dwellings and other evidences of the industry of man in remote ages sometimes laid bare by the movement of sand dunes on the coasts of France and of the North Sea; and to the facts disclosed on the tide-washed flats of the latter shores by excavations in Halligs or inhabited mounds which were probably raised before the era of the Roman Empire. These remains are memorials of races which have left no written records—races which perished at a period beyond the reach of even historical tradition. The plants and animals that furnished the relics found in the deposits were certainly contemporaneous with man; for they are associated with his works, and have evidently served his uses. In some cases, the animals belonged to species well ascertained to be now altogether extinct; in some others, both the animals and the vegetables, though extant elsewhere, have ceased to inhabit the regions where their remains are discovered. From the character of the artificial objects, as compared with others belonging to known dates, or at least to known periods of civilization, ingenious inferences have been drawn as to their age; and from the vegetable remains which accompany them, as to the climates of Central and Northern Europe at the time of their production.

There are, however, sources of error which have not always been sufficiently guarded against in making these estimates. When a boat, composed of several pieces of wood fastened together by pins of the same material, is dug out of a bog, it is inferred that the vessel, and the skeletons and implements found with it, belong to an age when the use of iron was not known to the builders. But this conclusion is not warranted by the simple fact that metals were not employed in its construction; for the Nubians at this day build boats large enough to carry a half dozen persons across the Nile, out of small pieces of acacia wood pinned together entirely with wooden bolts, and large vessels of similar construction are used by the islanders of the Malay archipelago. Nor is the occurrence of flint arrow heads and knives, in conjunction with other evidences of human life, conclusive proof as to the antiquity of the latter. . . . some Oriental tribes still continue to use the same stone implements as their ancestors . . . and the North American Indians now manufacture weapons of stone, and even of glass, chipping them in the latter case out of the bottoms or thick bottles, with great facility.

We may also be misled by our ignorance of the commercial relations existing between savage tribes. Extremely rude nations, in spite of their jealousies and their perpetual wars, sometimes contrive to exchange the products of provinces very widely separated from each other. The mounds of Ohio contain pearls, thought to be marine, which must have come from the Gulf of Mexico, or perhaps even from California, and the knives and pipes found in the same graves are often formed of far-fetched material, that was naturally paid for by some home product exported to the locality whence the material was derived. The art of preserving fish, flesh, and fowl by drying and smoking is widely diffused, and of great antiquity. The Indians of Long Island Sound are said to have carried on a trade in dried shell fish with tribes residing very far inland. From the earliest ages, the inhabitants of the Faroe and Orkney Islands, and of the opposite mainland coasts, have smoked wild fowl and other flesh. Hence it is possible that the animal and the vegetable food, the remains of which are found in the ancient deposits I am speaking of, may sometimes have been brought from climates remote from that where it was consumed.

The most important, as well as the most trustworthy conclusions with respect to the climate of ancient Europe and Asia, are those drawn from the accounts given by the classical writers of the growth of cultivated plants; but these are by no means free from uncertainty, because we can seldom be sure of an identity of species, almost never of an identity of race or variety, between vegetables known to the agriculturists of Greece and Rome and those of modern times which are thought most nearly to resemble them. Besides this, there is always room for doubt whether the habits of plants long grown in different countries may not have been so changed by domestication or by natural selection, that the conditions of temperature and humidity which they required twenty centuries ago were different from those at present demanded for their advantageous cultivation.

Even if we suppose an identity of species, of race, and of habit to be established between a given ancient and modern plant, the negative fact that the latter will not grow now where it flourished two thousand years ago does not in all cases prove a change of climate. The same result might follow from the exhaustion of the soil, or from a change in the quantity of moisture it habitually contains. After a district of country has been completely or even partially cleared of its forest growth, and brought under cultivation, the drying of the soil, under favorable circumstances, goes on for generations, perhaps for ages. In other cases, from injudicious husbandry, or the diversion or choking up of natural watercourses, it may become more highly charged with humidity. An increase or diminution of the moisture of a soil almost necessarily supposes an elevation or a depression of its winter or its summer heat, and of its extreme if not of its mean annual temperature, though such elevation or depression may be so slight as not sensibly to raise or lower the mercury in a thermometer exposed to the open air. Any of these causes, more or less humidity, or more or less warmth of soil, would affect the growth both of wild and of cultivated vegetation, and consequently, without any appreciable change in atmospheric temperature, precipitation, or evaporation, plants of a particular species might cease to be advantageously cultivated where they had once been easily reared.

Uncertainty of Modern Meteorology

We are very imperfectly acquainted with the present mean and extreme temperature, or the precipitation and the evaporation of any extensive region, even in countries most densely peopled and best supplied with instruments and observers. The progress of science is constantly detecting errors of method in older observations, and many laboriously constructed tables of meteorological phenomena are now thrown aside as fallacious, and therefore worse than useless, because some condition necessary to secure accuracy of result was neglected, in obtaining and recording the data on which they were founded.

To take a familiar instance: it is but recently that attention has been drawn to the great influence of slight differences in station upon the results of observations of temperature and precipitation. Two thermometers hung but a few hundred yards from each other differ not unfrequently five, sometimes even ten degrees in their readings, and when we are told that the annual fall of rain on the roof of the observatory at Paris is two inches less than on the ground by the side of it, we may see that the height of the rain-gauge above the earth is a point of much consequence in making estimates from its measurements. The data from which results have been deduced with respect to the hygrometrical and thermometrical conditions, to the climate in short, of different countries, have very often been derived from observations at single points in cities or districts separated by considerable distances. The tendency of errors and accidents to balance each other authorizes us, indeed, to entertain greater confidence than we could otherwise feel in the conclusions drawn from such tables; but it is in the highest degree probable that they would be much modified by more numerous series of observations, at different stations within narrow limits.

There is one branch of research which is of the utmost importance in reference to these questions, but which, from the great difficulty of direct observation upon it, has been less successfully studied than almost any other problem of physical science. I refer to the proportions between precipitation, superficial drainage, absorption, and evaporation. Precise actual measurement of these quantities upon even a single acre of ground is impossible; and in all cabinet experiments on the subject, the conditions of the surface observed are so different from those which occur in nature, that we cannot safely reason from one case to the other. In nature, the inclination and exposure of the ground, the degree of freedom or obstruction of the flow of water over the surface, the composition and density of the soil, its temperature, the presence or absence of perforations by worms and small burrowing quadrupeds—upon which the permeability of the ground by water and its power of absorbing and retaining or transmitting moisture depend—the dryness or saturation of the subsoil, vary at comparatively short distances; and though the precipitation upon very small geographical basins and the superficial flow from them may be estimated with an approach to precision, yet even here we have no present means of knowing how much of the water absorbed by the earth is restored to the atmosphere by evaporation, and how much carried off by infiltration or other modes of underground discharge. When, therefore, we attempt to use the phenomena observed on a few square or cubic yards of earth, as a basis of reasoning upon the meteorology of a province, it is evident that our data must be insufficient to warrant positive general conclusions. In discussing the climatology of whole countries, or even of comparatively small local divisions, we may safely say that none can tell what percentage of the water they receive from the atmosphere is evaporated; what absorbed by the ground and conveyed off by subterranean conduits; what carried down to the sea by superficial channels; what drawn from the earth or the air by a given extent of forest, of short pasture vegetation, or of tall meadow-grass; what given out again by surfaces so covered, or by bare ground of various textures and composition, under different conditions of atmospheric temperature, pressure, and humidity; or what is the amount of evaporation from water, ice, or snow, under the varying exposures to which, in actual nature, they are constantly subjected. If, then, we are so ignorant of all these climatic phenomena in the best-known regions inhabited by man, it is evident that we can rely little upon theoretical deductions applied to the former more natural state of the same regions—less still to such as are adopted with respect to distant, strange, and primitive countries.

Stability of Nature

Nature, left undisturbed, so fashions her territory as to give it almost unchanging permanence of form, outline, and proportion, except when shattered by geologic convulsions; and in these comparatively rare cases of derangement, she sets herself at once to repair the superficial damage, and to restore, as nearly as practicable, the former aspect of her dominion. In new countries, the natural inclination of the ground, the self-formed slopes and levels, are generally such as best secure the stability of the soil. They have been graded and lowered or elevated by frost and chemical forces and gravitation and the flow of water and vegetable deposit and the action of the winds, until, by a general compensation of conflicting forces, a condition of equilibrium has been reached which, without the action of man, would remain, with little fluctuation, for countless ages.

We need not go far back to reach a period when, in all that portion of the North American continent which has been occupied by British colonization, the geographical elements very nearly balanced and compensated each other. At the commencement of the seventeenth century, the soil, with insignificant exceptions, was covered with forests; and whenever the Indian, in consequence of war or the exhaustion of the beasts of the chase, abandoned the narrow fields he had planted and the woods he had burned over, they speedily returned, by a succession of herbaceous, arborescent, and arboreal growths, to their original state. Even a single generation sufficed to restore them almost to their primitive luxuriance of forest vegetation. The unbroken forests had attained to their maximum density and strength of growth, and, as the older trees decayed and fell, they were succeeded by new shoots or seedlings, so that from century to century no perceptible change seems to have occurred in the wood, except the slow, spontaneous succession of crops. This succession involved no interruption of growth, and but little break in the "boundless contiguity of shade"; for, in the husbandry of nature, there are no fallows. Trees fall singly, not by square roods, and the tall pine is hardly prostrate, before the light and heat, admitted to the ground by the removal of the dense crown of foliage which had shut them out, stimulate the germination of the seeds of broad-leaved trees that had lain, waiting this kindly influence, perhaps for centuries.

Formation of Bogs

Two natural causes, destructive in character, were, indeed, in operation in the primitive American forests, though, in the Northern colonies, at least, there were sufficient compensations; for we do not discover that any considerable permanent change was produced by them. I refer to the action of beavers and of fallen trees in producing bogs, and of smaller animals, insects, and birds, in destroying the woods.

Bogs generally originate in the checking of watercourses by the falling of timber or of earth and rocks, or by artificial obstructions across their channels. If the impediment is sufficient to retain a permanent accumulation of water behind it, the trees whose roots are overflowed soon perish, and then by their fall increase the obstruction, and, of course, occasion a still wider spread of the stagnating stream. This process goes on until the water finds a new outlet, at a higher level, not liable to similar interruption. The fallen trees not completely covered by water are soon overgrown with mosses; aquatic and semi-aquatic plants propagate themselves, and spread until they more or less completely fill up the space occupied by the water, and the surface is gradually converted from a pond to a quaking morass. The morass is slowly solidified by vegetable production and deposit, then very often restored to the forest condition by the growth of black ashes, cedars, or, in southern latitudes, cypresses, and other trees suited to such a soil, and thus the interrupted harmony of nature is at last re-established.

In countries somewhat further advanced in civilization than those occupied by the North American Indians, as in medieval Ireland, the formation of bogs may be commenced by the neglect of man to remove, from the natural channels of superficial drainage, the tops and branches of trees felled for the various purposes to which wood is applicable in his rude industry; and, when the flow of the water is thus checked, nature goes on with the processes I have already described. In such half-civilized regions, too, windfalls are more frequent than in those where the forest is unbroken, because, when openings have been made in it for agricultural or other purposes, the entrance thus afforded to the wind occasions the sudden overthrow of hundreds of trees which might otherwise have stood for generations and have fallen to the ground, only one by one, as natural decay brought them down. Besides this, the flocks bred by man in the pastoral state keep down the incipient growth of trees on the half-dried bogs, and prevent them from recovering their primitive condition.

Young trees in the native forest are sometimes girdled and killed by the smaller rodent quadrupeds, and their growth is checked by birds which feed on the terminal bud; but these animals, as we shall see, are generally found on the skirts of the wood only, not in its deeper recesses, and hence the mischief they do is not extensive.

In fine, in countries untrodden by man, the proportions and relative positions of land and water, the atmospheric precipitation and evaporation, the thermometric mean, and the distribution of vegetable and animal life, are maintained by natural compensations, in a state of approximate equilibrium, and are subject to appreciable change only from geological influences so slow in their operation that the geographical conditions may be regarded as substantially constant and immutable.

Natural Conditions Favorable to Geographical Change

There are, nevertheless, certain climatic conditions and certain forms and formations of terrestrial surface, which tend respectively to impede and to facilitate the physical degradation both of new countries and of old. If the precipitation, whether great or small in amount, be equally distributed through the seasons, so that there are neither torrential rains nor parching droughts, and if, further, the general inclination of grounds be moderate, so that the superficial waters are carried off without destructive rapidity of flow, and without sudden accumulation in the channels of natural drainage, there is little danger of the degradation of the soil in consequence of the removal of forest or other vegetable covering, and the natural face of the earth may be considered as virtually permanent. These conditions are well exemplified in Ireland, in a great part of England, in extensive districts in Germany and France, and, fortunately, in an immense proportion of the valley of the Mississippi and the basin of the great American lakes, as well as in many parts of the continents of South America and of Africa, and it is partly, though by no means entirely, owing to topographical and climatic causes that the blight, which has smitten the fairest and most fertile provinces of Imperial Rome, has spared Britannia, Germania, Pannonia, and Moesia, the comparatively inhospitable homes of barbarous races, who, in the days of the Caesars, were too little advanced in civilized life to possess either the power or the will to wage that war against the order of nature which seems, hitherto, an almost inseparable condition precedent of high social culture, and of great progress in fine and mechanical art.

Destructive changes are most frequent in countries of irregular and mountainous surface, and in climates where the precipitation is confined chiefly to a single season, and where, of course, the year is divided into a wet and a dry period, as is the case throughout a great part of the Ottoman Empire, and, indeed, in a large proportion of the whole Mediterranean Basin.

In mountainous countries various causes combine to expose the soil to constant dangers. The rain and snow usually fall in greater quantity, and with much inequality of distribution; the snow on the summits accumulates for many months in succession, and then is not unfrequently almost wholly dissolved in a single thaw, so that the entire precipitation of months is in a few hours hurried down the flanks of the mountains, and through the ravines that furrow them; the natural inclination of the surface promotes the swiftness of the gathering currents of diluvial rain and of melting snow, which soon acquire an almost irresistible force and power of removal and transportation; the soil itself is less compact and tenacious than that of the plains, and if the sheltering forest has been destroyed, it is confined by few of the threads and ligaments by which nature had bound it together, and attached it to the rocky groundwork. Hence every considerable shower lays bare its roods of rock, and the torrents sent down by the thaws of spring, and by occasional heavy discharges of the summer and autumnal rains, are seas of mud and rolling stones that sometimes lay waste and bury beneath them acres, and even miles, of pasture and field and vineyard.

Destructiveness of Man

Man has too long forgotten that the earth was given to him for usufruct alone, not for consumption, still less for profligate waste. Nature has provided against the absolute destruction of any of her elementary matter, the raw material of her works; the thunderbolt and the tornado, the most convulsive throes of even the volcano and the earthquake, being only phenomena of decomposition and recomposition. But she has left it within the power of man irreparably to derange the combinations of inorganic matter and of organic life, which through the night of aeons she had been proportioning and balancing, to prepare the earth for his habitation, when in the fulness of time his Creator should call him forth to enter into its possession.

Apart from the hostile influence of man, the organic and the inorganic world are, as I have remarked, bound together by such mutual relations and adaptations as secure, if not the absolute permanence and equilibrium of both, a long continuance of the established conditions of each at any given time and place, or at least, a very slow and gradual succession of changes in those conditions. But man is everywhere a disturbing agent. Wherever he plants his foot, the harmonies of nature are turned to discords. The proportions and accommodations which insured the stability of existing arrangements are overthrown. Indigenous vegetable and animal species are extirpated, and supplanted by others of foreign origin, spontaneous production is forbidden or restricted, and the face of the earth is either laid bare or covered with a new and reluctant growth of vegetable forms, and with alien tribes of animal life. These intentional changes and substitutions constitute, indeed, great revolutions; but vast as is their magnitude and importance, they are, as we shall see, insignificant in comparison with the contingent and unsought results which have flowed from them.

The fact that, of all organic beings, man alone is to be regarded as essentially a destructive power, and that he wields energies to resist which Nature—that nature whom all material life and all inorganic substance obey—is wholly impotent, tends to prove that, though living in physical nature, he is not of her, that he is of more exalted parentage, and belongs to a higher order of existences, than those which are born of her womb and live in blind submission to her dictates.

There are, indeed, brute destroyers, beasts and birds and insects of prey—all animal life feeds upon, and, of course, destroys other life—but this destruction is balanced by compensations. It is, in fact, the very means by which the existence of one tribe of animals or of vegetables is secured against being smothered by the encroachments of another; and the reproductive powers of species, which serve as the food of others, are always proportioned to the demand they are destined to supply. Man pursues his victims with reckless destructiveness; and, while the sacrifice of life by the lower animals is limited by the cravings of appetite, he unsparingly persecutes, even to extirpation, thousands of organic forms which he cannot consume.

The earth was not, in its natural condition, completely adapted to the use of man, but only to the sustenance of wild animals and wild vegetation. These live, multiply their kind in just proportion, and attain their perfect measure of strength and beauty, without producing or requiring any important change in the natural arrangements of surface, or in each other's spontaneous tendencies, except such mutual repression of excessive increase as may prevent the extirpation of one species by the encroachments of another. In short, without man, lower animal and spontaneous vegetative life would have been practically constant in type, distribution, and proportion, and the physical geography of the earth would have remained undisturbed for indefinite periods, and been subject to revolution only from slow development, from possible, unknown cosmical causes, or from geological action.

But man, the domestic animals that serve him, the field and garden plants the products of which supply him with food and clothing, cannot subsist and rise to the full development of their higher properties, unless brute and unconscious nature be effectually combated, and, in a great degree, vanquished by human art. Hence, a certain measure of transformation of terrestrial surface, of suppression of natural, and stimulation of artificially modified productivity becomes necessary. This measure man has unfortunately exceeded. He has felled the forests whose networks of fibrous roots bound the mould to the rocky skeleton of the earth; but had he allowed here and there a belt of woodland to reproduce itself by spontaneous propagation, most of the mischiefs which his reckless destruction of the natural protection of the soil has occasioned would have been averted. He has broken up the mountain reservoirs, the percolation of whose waters through unseen channels supplied the fountains that refreshed his cattle and fertilized his fields; but he has neglected to maintain the cisterns and the canals of irrigation which a wise antiquity had constructed to neutralize the consequences of its own imprudence. While he has torn the thin glebe which confined the light earth of extensive plains, and has destroyed the fringe of semi-aquatic plants which skirted the coast and checked the drifting of the sea sand, he has failed to prevent the spreading of the dunes by clothing them with artificially propagated vegetation. He has ruthlessly warred on all the tribes of animated nature whose spoil he could convert to his own uses, and he has not protected the birds which prey on the insects most destructive to his own harvests.

Purely untutored humanity, it is true, interferes comparatively little with the arrangements of nature, and the destructive agency of man becomes more and more energetic and unsparing as he advances in civilization, until the impoverishment, with which his exhaustion of the natural resources of the soil is threatening him, at last awakens him to the necessity of preserving what is left, if not of restoring what has been wantonly wasted. The wandering savage grows no cultivated vegetable, fells no forest, and extirpates no useful plant, no noxious weed. If his skill in the chase enables him to entrap numbers of animals on which he feeds, he compensates this loss by destroying also the lion, the tiger, the wolf, the otter, the seal, and the eagle, thus indirectly protecting the feebler quadrupeds and fish and fowls, which would otherwise become the booty of beasts and birds of prey. But with stationary life, or at latest with the pastoral state, man at once commences an almost indiscriminate warfare upon all the forms of animal and vegetable existence around him, and as he advances in civilization, he gradually eradicates or transforms every spontaneous product of the soil he occupies.

Human and Brute Action Compared

It is maintained by authorities as high as any known to modern science, that the action of man upon nature, though greater in *degree*, does not differ in *kind* from that of wild animals. It is perhaps impossible to establish a radical distinction *in genere* between the two classes of effects, but there is an essential difference between the motive of action which calls out the energies of civilized man and the mere appetite which controls the life of the beast. The action of man, indeed, is frequently followed by unforeseen and undesired results, yet it is nevertheless guided by a self-conscious will aiming as often at secondary and remote as at immediate objects. The wild animal, on the other hand, acts instinctively, and, so far as we are able to perceive, always with a view to single and direct purposes. The backwoodsman and the beaver alike fell trees; the man that he may convert the forest into an olive grove that will mature its fruit only for a succeeding generation, the beaver that he may feed upon the bark of the trees or use them in the construction of his habitation. The action of brutes upon the material world is slow and gradual, and usually limited, in any given case, to a narrow extent of territory. Nature is allowed time and opportunity to set her restorative powers at work, and the destructive animal has hardly retired from the field of his ravages before nature has repaired the damages occasioned by his operations. In fact, he is expelled from the scene by the very efforts which she makes for the restoration of her dominion. Man, on the contrary, extends his action over vast spaces, his revolutions are swift and radical, and his devastations are, for an almost incalculable time after he has withdrawn the arm that gave the blow, irreparable.

The form of geographical surface, and very probably the climate of a given country, depend much on the character of the vegetable life belonging to it. Man has, by domestication, greatly changed the habits and properties of the plants he rears; he has, by voluntary selection, immensely modified the forms and qualities of the animated creatures that serve him; and he has, at the same time, completely rooted out many forms of animal if not of vegetable being. What is there, in the influence of brute life, that corresponds to this? We have no reason to believe that, in that portion of the American continent which, though peopled by many tribes of quadruped and fowl, remained uninhabited by man or only thinly occupied by purely savage tribes, any sensible geographical change had occurred within twenty centuries before the epoch of discovery and colonization, while, during the same period, man had changed millions of square miles, in the fairest and most fertile regions of the Old World, into the barrenest deserts.

The ravages committed by man subvert the relations and destroy the balance which nature had established between her organized and her inorganic creations, and she avenges herself upon the intruder, by letting loose upon her defaced provinces destructive energies hitherto kept in check by organic forces destined to be his best auxiliaries, but which he has unwisely dispersed and driven from the field of action. When the forest is gone, the great reservoir of moisture stored up in its vegetable mould is evaporated, and returns only in deluges of rain to wash away the parched dust into which that mould has been converted. The well-wooded and humid hills are turned to ridges of dry rock, which encumbers the low grounds and chokes the watercourses with its debris, and—except in countries favored with an equable distribution of rain through the seasons, and a moderate and regular inclination of surface—the whole earth, unless rescued by human art from the physical degradation to which it tends, becomes an assemblage of bald mountains, of barren, turfless hills, and of swampy and malarious plains. There are parts of Asia Minor, of Northern Africa, of Greece, and even of Alpine Europe, where the operation of causes set in action by man has brought the face of the earth to a desolation almost as complete as that of the moon; and though, within that brief space of time which we call "the historical period," they are known to have been covered with luxuriant woods, verdant pastures, and fertile meadows, they are now too far deteriorated to be reclaimable by man, nor can they become again fitted for human use, except through great geological changes, or other mysterious influences or agencies of which we have no present knowledge, and over which we have no prospective control. The earth is fast becoming an unfit home for its noblest inhabitant, and another era of equal human crime and human improvidence, and of like duration with that through which traces of that crime and that improvidence extend, would reduce it to such a condition of impoverished productiveness, of shattered surface, of climatic excess, as to threaten the depravation, barbarism, and perhaps even extinction of the species.

Physical Improvement

True, there is a partial reverse to this picture. On narrow theaters, new forests have been planted; inundations of flowing streams restrained by heavy walls of masonry and other constructions; torrents compelled to aid, by depositing the slime with which they are charged, in filling up lowlands, and raising the level of morasses which their own overflows had created;

ground submerged by the encroachments of the ocean, or exposed to be covered by its tides, has been rescued from its dominion by diking; swamps and even lakes have been drained, and their beds brought within the domain of agricultural industry; drifting coast dunes have been checked and made productive by plantation; seas and inland waters have been repeopled with fish, and even the sands of the Sahara have been fertilized by artesian fountains. These achievements are more glorious than the proudest trimphs of war, but, thus far, they give but faint hope that we shall yet make full atonement for our spendthrift waste of the bounties of nature.

Limits of Human Power

It is, on the one hand, rash and unphilosophical to attempt to set limits to the ultimate power of man over inorganic nature, and it is unprofitable, on the other, to speculate on what may be accomplished by the discovery of now unknown and unimagined natural forces, or even by the invention of new arts and new processes. But since we have seen aerostation, the motive power of elastic vapors, the wonders of modern telegraphy, the destructive explosiveness of gunpowder, of nitroglycerine, and even of a substance so harmless, unresisting, and inert as cotton, there is little in the way of mechanical achievement which seems hopelessly impossible, and it is hard to restrain the imagination from wandering forward a couple of generations to an epoch when our descendants shall have advanced as far beyond us in physical conquest, as we have marched beyond the trophies erected by our grandfathers. There are, nevertheless, in actual practice, limits to the efficiency of the forces which we are now able to bring into the field, and we must admit that, for the present, the agencies known to man and controlled by him are inadequate to the reducing of great Alpine precipices to such slopes as would enable them to support a vegetable clothing, or to the covering of large extents of denuded rock with earth, and planting upon them a forest growth. Yet among the mysteries which science is hereafter to reveal, there may be still undiscovered methods of acomplishing even grander wonders than these. Mechanical philosophers have suggested the possibility of accumulating and treasuring up for human use some of the greater natural forces, which the action of the elements puts forth with such astonishing energy. Could we gather, and bind, and make subservient to our control, the power which a West Indian hurricane exerts through a small area in one continuous blast, or the momentum expended by the waves, in a tempestuous winter, upon the breakwater at Cherbourg, or the lifting power of the tide, for a month, at the head of the Bay of Fundy, or the pressure of a square mile of sea water at the depth of five thousand fathoms, or a moment of the might of an earthquake or a volcano, our age—which moves no mountains and casts them into the sea by faith alone—might hope to scarp the rugged walls of the Alps and Pyrenees and Mount Taurus, robe them once more in a vegetation as rich as that of their pristine woods, and turn their wasting torrents into refreshing streams.

Could this old world, which man has overthrown, be rebuilded, could human cunning rescue its wasted hillsides and its deserted plains from solitude or mere nomad occupation, from barrenness, from nakedness, and from insalubrity, and restore the ancient fertility and healthfulness of the Etruscan sea coast, the Campagna and the Pontine marshes, of Calabria, of Sicily, of the Peloponnesus and insular and continental Greece, of Asia Minor, of the slopes of Lebanon and Hermon, of Palestine, of the Syrian desert, of Mesopotamia and the delta of the Euphrates, of the Cyrenaica, of Africa proper, Numidia, and Mauritania, the thronging millions of Europe might still find room on the Eastern continent, and the main current of emigration be turned toward the rising instead of the setting sun.

But changes like these must await not only great political and moral revolutions in the governments and peoples by whom those regions are now possessed, but, especially, a command of pecuniary and of mechanical means not at present enjoyed by those nations, and a more advanced and generally diffused knowledge of the processes by which the amelioration of soil and climate is possible than now anywhere exists. Until such circumstances shall conspire to favor the work of geographical regeneration, the countries I have mentioned, with here and there a local exception, will continue to sink into yet deeper desolation, and in the meantime the American continent, Southern Africa, Australia, New Zealand, and the smaller oceanic islands, will be almost the only theaters where man is engaged, on a great scale, in transforming the face of nature.

Importance of Physical Conservation and Restoration

Comparatively short as is the period through which the colonization of foreign lands by European emigrants extends, great and, it is to be feared, sometimes irreparable injury has already been done in the various processes by which man seeks to subjugate the virgin earth; and many provinces, first trodden by the *Homo sapiens* Europae within the last two centuries, begin to show signs of that melancholy dilapidation which is now driving so many of the peasantry of Europe from their native hearths. It is evidently a matter of great moment, not only to the population of the states where these symptoms are manifesting themselves, but to the general interests of humanity, that this decay should be arrested, and that the future operations of rural husbandry and of forest industry, in districts yet remaining substantially in their native condition, should be so conducted as to prevent the widespread mischiefs which have been elsewhere produced by thoughtless or wanton destruction of the natural safeguards of the soil. This can be done only by the diffusion of knowledge on this subject among the classes that, in earlier days, subdued and tilled ground in which they had no vested rights, but who, in our time, own their woods, their pastures, and their ploughlands as a perpetual possession for them and theirs, and have, therefore, a strong interest in the protection of their domain against deterioration.

Physical Restoration

Many circumstances conspire to invest with great present interest the questions: how far man can permanently modify and ameliorate those physical conditions of terrestrial surface and climate on which his material welfare depends; how far he can compensate, arrest, or retard the deterioration which many of his agricultural and industrial processes tend to produce; and how far he can restore fertility and salubrity to soils which his follies or his crimes have made barren or pestilential. Among these circumstances, the most prominent, perhaps, is the necessity of providing new homes for a European population which is increasing more rapidly than its means of subsistence, new physical comforts for classes of the people that have now become too much enlightened and have imbibed too much culture to submit to a longer deprivation of a share in the material enjoyments which the privileged ranks have hitherto monopolized.

To supply new hives for the emigrant swarms, there are, first, the vast unoccupied prairies and forests of America, of Australia, and of many other great oceanic islands, the sparsely inhabited and still unexhausted soils of Southern and even Central Africa, and, finally, the impoverished and half-depopulated shores of the Mediterranean, and the interior of Asia Minor and the farther East. To furnish to those who shall remain after emigration shall have conveniently reduced the too dense population of many European states, those means of sensuous and of intellectual wellbeing which are styled "artificial wants" when demanded by the humble and the poor, but are admitted to be "necessaries" when claimed by the noble and the rich, the soil must be stimulated to its highest powers of production, and man's utmost ingenuity and energy must be tasked to renovate a nature drained, by his improvidence, of fountains which a wise economy would have made plenteous and perennial sources of beauty, health, and wealth.

In those yet virgin lands which the progress of modern discovery in both hemispheres has brought and is still bringing to the knowledge and control of civilized man, not much improvement of great physical conditions is to be looked for. The proportion of forest is indeed to be considerably reduced, superfluous waters to be drawn off, and routes of internal communication to be constructed; but the primitive geographical and climatic features of these countries ought to be, as far as possible, retained.

In reclaiming and reoccupying lands laid waste by human improvidence or malice, and abandoned by man, or occupied only by a nomad or thinly scattered population, the task of the pioneer settler is of a very different character. He is to become a coworker with nature in the reconstruction of the damaged fabric which the negligence or the wantonness of former lodgers has rendered untenantable. He must aid her in reclothing the mountain slopes with forests and vegetable mould, thereby restoring the fountains which she provided to water them; in checking the devastating fury of torrents, and bringing back the surface drainage to its primitive narrow channels; and in drying deadly morasses by opening the natural sluices which have been choked up, and cutting new canals for drawing off their stagnant waters. He must thus, on the one hand, create new reservoirs, and, on the other, remove mischievous accumulations of moisture, thereby equalizing and regulating the sources of atmospheric humidity and of flowing water, both which are so essential to all vegetable growth, and, of course, to human and lower animal life.

I have remarked that the effects of human action on the forms of the earth's surface could not always be distinguished from those resulting from geological causes, and there is also much uncertainty in respect to the precise influence of the clearing and cultivating of the ground, and of other rural operations, upon climate. It is disputed whether either the means or the extremes of temperature, the periods of the seasons, or the amount or distribution of precipitation and of evaporation, in any country whose annals are known, have undergone any change during the historical period. It is, indeed, as has been already observed, impossible to doubt that many of the operations of the pioneer settler *tend* to produce great modifications in atmospheric humidity, temperature, and electricity; but we are at present unable to determine how far one set of effects is neutralized by another, or compensated by unknown agencies. This question scientific research is inadequate to solve, for want of the necessary data; but well-conducted observation, in regions now first brought under the occupation of man, combined with such historical evidence as still exists, may be expected at no distant period to throw much light on this subject.

Australia and New Zealand are, perhaps, the countries from which we have a right to expect the fullest elucidation of these difficult and disputable problems. Their colonization did not commence until the physical sciences had become matter of almost universal attention, and is, indeed, so recent that the memory of living men embraces the principal epochs of their history; the peculiarities of their fauna, their flora, and their geology are such as to have excited for them the liveliest interest of the votaries of natural science; their mines have given their people the necessary wealth for procuring the means of instrumental observation, and the leisure required for the pursuit of scientific research; and large tracts of virgin forest and natural meadow are rapidly passing under the control of civilized man. Here, then, exist greater facilities and stronger motives for the careful study of the topics in question than have ever been found combined in any other theater of European colonization.

In North America, the change from the natural to the artificial condition of terrestrial surface began about the period when the most important instruments of meteorological observation were invented. The first settlers in the territory now constituting the United States and the British American provinces had other things to do than to tabulate barometrical and thermometrical readings, but there remain some interesting physical records from the early days of the colonies, and there is still an immense extent of North American soil where the industry and the folly of man have as yet produced little appreciable changes. Here, too, with the present increased facilities for scientific observation, the future effects, direct and contingent, of man's labors, can be measured, and such precautions taken in those rural processes which we call improvements, as to mitigate evils, perhaps, in some degree, inseparable from every attempt to control the action of natural laws.

In order to arrive at safe conclusions, we must first obtain a more exact knowledge of the topography, and of the present superficial and climatic condition of countries where the natural surface is as yet more or less unbroken. This can only be acomplished by accurate surveys, and by a great multiplication of the points of meteorological registry, already so numerous; and as, moreover, considerable changes in the proportion of forest and of cultivated land, or of dry and wholly or partially submerged surface, will often take place within brief periods, it is highly desirable that the attention of observers, in whose neighborhood the clearing of the soil, or the drainage of lakes and swamps, or other great works of rural improvement, are going on or mediated, should be especially drawn not only to revolutions in atmospheric temperature and precipitation, but to the more easily ascertained and perhaps more important local changes produced by these operations in the temperature and the hygrometric state of the superficial strata of the earth, and in its spontaneous vegetable and animal products.

The rapid extension of railroads, which now everywhere keep pace with, and sometimes even precede, the occupation of new soil for agricultural purposes, furnishes great facilities for enlarging our knowledge of the topography of the territory they traverse, because their cuttings reveal the composition and general structure of surface, and the inclination and elevation of their lines constitute known hypsometrical sections, which give numerous points of departure for the measurement of higher and lower stations, and of course for determining the relief and depression of surface, the slope of the beds of watercourses, and many other not less important questions.

The geological, hydrographical, and topographical surveys, which almost every general and even local government of the civilized world is carrying on, are making yet more important contributions to our stock of geographical and general physical knowledge, and, within a comparatively short space, there will be an accumulation of well established constant and historical facts, from which we can safely reason upon all the relations of action and reaction between man and external nature.

But we are, even now, breaking up the floor and wainscoting and doors and window frames of our dwelling, for fuel to warm our bodies and to seethe our pottage, and the world cannot afford to wait till the slow and sure progress of exact science has taught it a better economy. Many practical lessons have been learned by the common observation of unschooled men; and the teachings of simple experience, on topics where natural philosophy has scarcely yet spoken, are not to be despised.

CHARLES R. VAN HISE

HISTORY OF THE CONSERVATION MOVEMENT

Until late in the nineteenth century the resources of this country were commonly regarded as inexhaustible. Some of them were considered an obstruction to the country's development. Over very large areas of the country the forests were regarded as an enemy to be destroyed and burned. Indeed at the present time this is locally true. Our lands were supposed to be illimitable. Any man might have a farm for the asking. It was held, and indeed is held by many at this time, that our mineral resources will last through the indefinite future, and therefore that they may be drawn upon advantageously as rapidly as possible.

It is under the prevalence of these ideas that our laws and customs have grown up. The laws and customs have been adapted to the ideas of the people. If the ideas are incorrect, it may be that our laws in reference to the natural resources are defective.

That these ideas in reference to the illimitable supply of our natural resources are incorrect has been appreciated by the scientist for many years. The foresters, the physiographers, the geologists, have shown the severe limitations of many of them. These views have been emphasized by the situation in other countries. The mountains of France, of Spain, of China, have been denuded of their forests in large measure, so that the supply of wood is inadequate to meet the needs of the people. In consequence of the removal of the forests from the mountains, the soil and disintegrated rock have been carried away by the running water and the bare rocks left protruding where once was thick vegetation resting upon abundant soil. The debris carried down from the mountains to the lowlands has destroyed extensive areas of once rich land.

It has long been known that in Spain and Italy, warm countries, because of insufficient fuel, the people suffer more from the cold than here in America. In the absence of forests and coal, fuel is so expensive as practically to be unavailable to the average citizen of those countries; and hence they shiver through the winter.

Many intelligent men have appreciated that in India and China a large proportion of the people are insufficiently nourished. It is probably true that more than half of the people of the world tonight will go to bed hungry; at least they will not have received sufficient nourishment during the day to be the most efficient tomorrow. You, who have read history, know how, during the years of abundant rains, the people of India and China multiply, and how in dry years famine and scourge come and reduce them again to the number that can be supplied by the fruits of the land. In scripture we read that the seven fat years were eaten up by the seven lean years; and this has been the history of eastern countries for thousands of years.

The modern conservation movement is the direct result of the work of scientific

• Charles R. Van Hise (1857–1918) was a geologist active in the conservation movement, and was President of the University of Wisconsin from 1903 to 1918.

Reprinted from *The Conservation of Natural Resources in the United States* (New York: The Macmillan Co., 1921), pp. 2–14.

men. The great question of conservation has been more forwarded by the rapid reduction of our forests than by any other cause. The forests are the one natural resource which has been so rapidly destroyed that in the early seventies it began to be appreciated that, if existing practice were continued, the end was not in the far distant future.

As the result of a memorial presented by the American Association for the Advancement of Science in 1873, re-enforced by another memorial of the association in 1890, the movement was inaugurated which resulted in a forestry bureau in the department of agriculture, and in laws which led to the first national reserve in 1891. The national forest movement was further advanced later as the result of an elaborate consideration of the question by the National Academy of Sciences in 1897. The principle of the national forest once established, these forests were enlarged from time to time, but the great withdrawals of the forests from private entry have been during the past 10 years.

Another line of forces which resulted in the modern conservation movement came directly from the work of Major J. W. Powell, and especially the publication of his "Lands of the Arid Region." Mainly as a result of this volume and the influence of Major Powell, in 1888 an irrigation division of the United States Geological Survey was established; and authority was given to the Secretary of the Interior to withdraw from private entry reservoir sites and other areas which in the future would be necessary for irrigation purposes.

For the past quarter of a century many of the scientific men of the country have been raising a warning voice in reference to the other natural resources of the country. The limitations of our supplies of gas, oil, and coal have been pointed out. Many have described the denudation of the land and the widespread destruction of the soil; but notwithstanding the above facts, it cannot be said that there was any national movement for conservation. Indeed, it is probable that such a movement could not have been inaugurated until the situation had become grave, until the menace to the future had become serious.

Among the men who have promoted the modern conservation movement, Mr. Gifford Pinchot has first place. While his work was primarily directed to the conservation of the forest, his vision, with enlarging horizon, saw the connection of the forests to the other resources of the country; and he therefore extended his campaign of education to include with the conservation of the forest the conservation of all natural resources which are limited in amount.

It was seen by Mr. Pinchot and other scientists, notably McGee, that there is a close connection between the forests and waters. There was a strong public demand that our rivers maintain a uniform flow for water powers and for navigation. Therefore those primarily interested in forests and those interested in waters became associated in the conservation movement. In consequence of the public sentiment in reference to waterways and forests, President Roosevelt, on March 14, 1907, appointed the Inland Waterways Commission. This commission included a number of representative congressmen, an engineer, a statistician, a forester, an irrigation chief, and a geologist.[1] This Inland Waterways Commission in its first report to the President emphasized the interlocking character of the problem of natural resources and pointed out how the control and use of water would conserve coal and iron and the soil and at the same time also make necessary the preservation of the forests.

The White House Conference grew out of the Inland Waterways Commission. On a trip of that commission in May, 1907, it was suggested that there be a conference at Washington the ensuing year to con-

[1] The Inland Waterways Commission consisted of the following: Theodore E. Burton, Chairman; Francis G. Newlands, Vice-Chairman; W J McGee, Secretary; William Warner, John H. Bankhead, Alexander MacKenzie, F. H. Newell, Gifford Pinchot, Herbert Knox Smith.

sider the conservation of the natural resources.

Chairman Theodore E. Burton and Commissioner Gifford Pinchot were authorized to convey to the President the ideas of the commission in reference to this matter. Later it was suggested that since the question of conservation concerned not only the nation, but every state, such conference should include the governors. On October 3, 1907, the Inland Waterways Commission, through its chairman and secretary, Mr. Burton, and Mr. W J McGee, sent to President Roosevelt a letter, requesting that he call a conference which should primarily be a congress of governors.

The President approved the plan and in November of that year called a conference of the governors, each governor being invited to be accompanied by three assistants or advisers. But as the time approached for the meeting, the idea grew and there were finally included in the invitation of the President, the Vice-President, members of the Cabinet, both branches of Congress, heads of the scientific bureaus of Washington, representatives of the great national societies, both scientific and industrial, representatives of journals, and notable citizens.

Thus there assembled May 13, 1908, at the East Room of the White House, the President, Vice-President, seven members of the Cabinet, nine justices of the Supreme Court, many members of Congress, the governors of thirty-four states, and representatives of the other twelve, the governors of all the territories, including Alaska, Hawaii, and Puerto Rico, the President of the Board of Commissioners of the District of Columbia, representatives of sixty-eight national societies, four special guests, forty-eight general guests, and the members of the Inland Waterways Commission.

Never before in the history of the nation had so representative an audience gathered together. For the first time in the history of the country the governors were assembled to consider a great national question. Even during the extreme stress of the Civil War the governors had not been asked to consult with the President and with one another upon the state of the nation. Apparently President Roosevelt must have thought that the question of conservation was one of fundamental importance before he took so far-reaching a step. Never before in the history of the nation had the scientific men of the country met upon equal footing with those engaged in politics. This in itself was sufficient to mark the White House Conference as a meeting of the first importance in reference to the future of the nation.

The audience of May 13 was indeed an impressive one. Upon the right of the President sat the Vice-President and the members of his Cabinet. Upon his left were the justices of the Supreme Court. Before him were assembled the governors, the members of Congress, many of the leading scientific men of the country, and numerous other delegates.

The conference was opened by a notable address by President Roosevelt. And he, I think, above any other public man of the country has shown a wonderful capacity to quickly and broadly comprehend the salient points of a great new movement.

Hence he was able, although not a man of science, to present most effectively and in wonderful proportion the views which the scientific men had been developing through the past 25 years with reference to conservation.

Following President Roosevelt's address there were a series of addresses by scientific men, by governors, by eminent citizens. The scope of these papers extended to the minerals, the forests, the soils, and the waters of the country.[2] The facts presented in reference to our important resources were so startling, that the governors drew up strong series of resolutions[3] covering the entire subject of conservation,

2 Proceedings of a Conference of Governors in the White House, Washington, D.C., May 13–15, 1908 (Washington: GPO, 1909).

3 [Editor's note.—See the following selection in this volume.]

pointing out the extravagance and reckless waste of the past, and making it clear that upon the conservation of our natural resources depends the foundation of our prosperity. The governors unanimously requested the President from time to time as occasion demanded to again call them together to consider with him and with Congress the great question of conservation. Also they recommended the states to establish conservation commissions to cooperate with one another and with a similar national commission. Several of the governors announced that their very first acts upon reaching their respective states would be to appoint such commissions.

Shortly after the White House Conference the President appointed the National Conservation Commission, consisting of forty-nine well-known men, about one-third of whom are engaged in politics, one-third in the industries, and one-third in scientific work. This commission was divided into four sections, assigned respectively to the minerals, the waters, the forests, and the soils. Gifford Pinchot, generally recognized as the most potent force underlying the conservation movement, was appropriately named chairman of the Conservation Commission.[4] Since the White House Conference of December, 1909, forty-one state conservation commissions and fifty-one conservation commissions, representing national organizations, have been created.

At the first meeting of the executive committee of the National Conservation Commission, held in Chicago, June 19, 1908, it was agreed that the initial step was to have made an inventory of our natural resources. It was there pointed out that to the present time, we, as a nation, are in the position of a man who, bequeathed a fortune, has gone on spending it recklessly, never taking the trouble to ask the amount of his inheritance or how long it is likely to last.

This executive committee therefore determined so far as practicable to have made an estimate of the existing available resources what proportion of these resources have already been utilized or exhausted, the rate of increase in their consumption, and if this rate continues how long these resources will last. The commission had no funds at its disposal, and therefore was obliged to depend upon existing organizations for this work. Fortunately the President gave an order directing that the heads of the scientific bureaus at Washington utilize their forces in making investigations requested by the commission, so far as such investigations lay in their respective fields. As a result of requests by the National Conservation Commission, the heads of several bureaus placed a considerable number of experts upon conservation work during the summer and autumn of 1908.

The full national commission assembled December 1 of that year to hear the reports of the experts and the secretaries of the four sections. Based upon these reports the commission drew up a report which they presented to the governors again assembled December 8, 1908, and by the governors this report was, with their indorsement, transmitted to the President, January 11, 1909. The report of this commission, the statements of the secretaries, and the reports of the experts have since been published in three volumes.[5] These volumes give the first available inventory of the natural resources of the nation. This inventory is of course but an approximation to the truth, but it is an immense advance over guesses as to the natural wealth of the nation. It does furnish a basis for quantitative and therefore scientific discussion of the future of our resources. In advance of the appearance of the report it would not have been possible to give this set of lectures. Indeed, they are based upon the material contained in these volumes to

[4] The full personnel and organization of the National Conservation Commission are found in the *Report of the National Conservation Commission,* I, Sen. Doc. No. 676, 60th Cong., 2d Sess., 1909, 115–17.

[5] *Ibid.*

a greater extent than upon all other sources of information.

The next step of President Roosevelt, after appointing the national commission, was to invite the governors of Canada and Newfoundland, and the President of Mexico, to appoint commissioners to consider with the commissioners of the United States the question of conservation. In consequence of these invitations the first North American Conservation Conference was held in Washington, February 18, 1909. As at the White House Conference, a broad statement was adopted embodying the principles of conservation applicable to the North American continent, which the commissioners were expected to urge upon their respective countries.

To crown the brilliant series of administrative acts to bring the question of conservation to the foreground of human consciousness, President Roosevelt on February 16, 1909, requested the powers of the world to meet at The Hague for the purpose of considering the conservation of the natural resources of the entire globe.

During President Roosevelt's administration, the Secretary of the Interior, James R. Garfield, withdrew from private entry a large area of the public domain, either permanently or for a time, until the lands withdrawn could be studied with reference to their wisest utilization. The larger portion of the great forests which still remained the property of the nation when Roosevelt became President—more than 148,000,000 acres—was made a part of the national forests during his administration. Also the coal lands of the West, both in the United States and Alaska, were withdrawn from private entry until they could be studied by the geological survey and a report made upon them as to their value and as to methods of disposal. More than 80,000,000 acres altogether were withdrawn by him for this purpose. About 1,500,000 acres in several states along twenty-nine streams were withdrawn with reference to withholding from private entry the water power sites. Finally, 4,700,000 acres of phosphate lands in Idaho, Wyoming, and Montana were withdrawn from private entry until they could be studied by the geological survey and appropriate laws made in reference to their exploitation.

Thus, during President Roosevelt's administration, more than 234,000,000 acres of land were withdrawn from private entry, the greater portion of which is to be permanently retained as the property of the nation.

President Roosevelt also recommended that the fee of all of the coal, oil, and gas lands still remaining in the possession of the government be retained permanently, and that the same be leased under proper regulations.

Concerning President Roosevelt, there has been much difference of opinion in political matters. He has been severely criticized by many, warmly commended by others, but his aggressive action for the conservation of our resources has been commended by all parties alike. In the future I believe that what he did to forward this movement and to bring it into the foreground of the consciousness of the people will place him not only as one of the greatest statesmen of this nation but one of the greatest statesmen of any nation of any time.

In marked contrast to the position of President Roosevelt in reference to conservation was the attitude of the Sixtieth Congress. President Roosevelt asked an appropriation for the National Conservation Commission; and Senator Knute Nelson, of Minnesota, introduced an amendment to the sundry civil bill asking for an appropriation of $25,000 for the necessary rent, assistance, and traveling expenses of the commission. This amendment went to the Senate committee on appropriations, of which Senator Eugene Hale was and is chairman, but the amendment was lost, having failed of favorable action in the committee. Thus an appropriation for the Conservation Commission asked by President Roosevelt failed in the Senate, and the commission was left without any funds.

This was unfortunate enough, but it would not have been fatal had the commission still retained the authority to ask the heads of the scientific bureaus to have their forces do work desired by the commission, which was appropriate and proper for their respective bureaus to undertake; but in the House of Representatives there was attached a clause to the sundry civil bill, which after the passage of that act prevented all bureaus from doing any work for any commission, council, board, or similar body, appointed by the President, without reference to whether or not such work was appropriate for such bureaus to undertake. Thus, so far as lay in its power, Congress made without avail the appointment by the President of the National Conservation Commission.

This clause of the sundry civil bill was introduced by James A. Tawney, of Minnesota, and its adoption was advocated by him. This congressman should be held responsible to the people of the nation for so far as lay in his power rendering without avail the appointment of the National Conservation Commission.

As has already been pointed out, the first report of the National Conservation Commission contains the only authentic statement as to the amounts of our natural resources, the amounts which have been exhausted, and their probable future life. The report was published as a Senate document in a small edition. The popular edition of this volume, recommended by the commission, was refused approval by the then committee on printing of the house, consisting of Charles P. Landis, of Indiana, James Breck Perkins, of New York, and D. E. Finley, of South Carolina. For thus preventing the people from gaining the advantage of the results of the great work of the Conservation Commission they should be held primarily responsible.

As yet the attitude of the Sixty-first Congress is undetermined. To the present time (June 1, 1910) none of the conservation measures recommended by President Taft have been passed.

After the adoption of the Tawney clause and before the organization of the Association next to be mentioned, the organization of the conservation movement was carried forward by the Joint Committee on Conservation, an unofficial body established at the second conference of the governors.

In the autumn of 1909 there was organized the National Conservation Association.[6] This association is to be the center of a great propaganda for conservation. It is hoped that all organizations interested in special phases of the conservation movement will become affiliated with it. The association is to have a board of managers, consisting of one representative of each state and territory; and each state is to have a committee. It is the duty of any state committee and its member of the board to develop the conservation movement in the state which they represent, and to be the channel of communication between the local and national organizations.

The foregoing sketch of the rise of the conservation movement shows that it grew out of the work of scientific men. Until recently the movement was not organized, and it was partial, that is, mainly confined to the forests and arid land; it only became national when President Roosevelt called the White House Conference in 1908.

With the foundation of the National Conservation Association, the great movement for the conservation of the natural resources of the United States may be said to have been fairly launched. Already a large number of the more intelligent people of the country are beginning to grasp its importance, beginning to understand that upon conservation rests the possibility of

[6] Honorary President, Charles W. Eliot, Cambridge, Mass.; President, Gifford Pinchot, Washington, D.C.; Vice-President, Walter L. Fisher, Chicago, Ill.; Treasurer, Overton Price, Washington, D.C.; Secretary, Thomas R. Shipp. Executive Committee: Pinchot, Chairman; James R. Garfield, Cleveland, Ohio; John F. Bass, Chicago, Ill.; Bernard N. Baker, Baltimore, Md.; Charles L. Pack, Lakewood, N.J.; John N. Teal, Portland, Ore.

a numerous and well-nourished population in this country. But as yet the great majority of the people have almost no knowledge of the movement. It is comparatively easy to get a subject into the consciousness of the cultivated group. It is enormously difficult to accomplish this work with the millions. And the conservation of our resources can only be accomplished by the cooperation of the nation, the states, and the individuals. Therefore there is before us a profound and wide campaign of education which must begin at the universities, in national and state organizations, and must extend from them through the secondary and primary schools to the whole people. There is no other question before the nation of such fundamental importance to the distant future of the country. . . . it seems to me that the universities should take part in the leadership in this movement for the advancement of the nation as they have in others. . . .

Bringing an appreciation of the importance of conservation to the foreground of human consciousness is a work which cannot be done by one man or one organization in one year, or by many men and many organizations in many years. It is a campaign of education which will extend through generations. But losses have already been so great that the movement should be carried forward as rapidly as possible, especially in preventing further wanton waste. This must be done if our descendants are to have transmitted to them their heritage not too greatly depleted. . . .

DECLARATION OF GOVERNORS FOR CONSERVATION OF NATURAL RESOURCES

Introduction

The Declaration of Governors contained in this bulletin was adopted by the conference of governors of the states and territories called by the President to consider the conservation of our natural resources, and which met at the White House May 13, 14, and 15, 1908. Besides the governors there were invited to the conference the members of the Cabinet, the justices of the Supreme Court, the members of both Houses of Congress, representatives of the great national organizations, the Inland Waterways Commission, and, as special guests, Hon. William Jennings Bryan, Mr. James J. Hill, Mr. Andrew Carnegie, and Mr. John Mitchell. The late ex-President Grover Cleveland was also invited as a special guest, but illness prevented him from attending. At the request of the President each governor brought with him to the conference three citizens from his state or territory to act as assistants or advisers.

The object of the conference was stated by the President in his letter of invitation to the governors in which he said:

> It seems to me time for the country to take account of its natural resources, and to inquire how long they are likely to last. We are prosperous now; we should not forget that it will be just as important to our descendants to be prosperous in their time.

Papers which discussed the present state of our various natural resources were read by experts and specialists in each respective line, and these were followed by an open discussion among the governors of the points brought out.

The conference then appointed a committee to draft a declaration, consisting of the following: Governor Newton C. Blanchard, of Louisiana; Governor John Franklin Fort, of New Jersey; Governor J. O. Davidson, of Wisconsin; Governor John C. Cutler, of Utah; and Governor Martin F. Ansel, of South Carolina.

This committee prepared and submitted the declaration which follows, and it was unanimously adopted by the conference of governors as embodying their conclusions on the question of conservation.

Declaration of Principles

We, the governors of the States and Territories of the United States of America, in conference assembled, do hereby declare the conviction that the great prosperity of our country rests upon the abundant resources of the land chosen by our forefathers for their homes, and where they laid the foundation of this great nation.

We look upon these resources as heritage to be made use of in establishing and promoting the comfort, prosperity, and happiness of the American people, but not to be wasted, deteriorated, or needlessly destroyed.

We agree that our country's future is involved in this; that the great natural resources supply the material basis upon which our civilization must continue to depend, and upon which the perpetuity of the nation itself rests.

We agree, in the light of the facts brought to our knowledge and from information received from sources which we cannot doubt, that this material basis is

Reprinted from Charles R. Van Hise, *The Conservation of Natural Resources in the United States* (New York: The Macmillan Co., 1921), Appendix I, 381–84, with the permission of the publisher.

threatened with exhaustion. Even as each succeeding generation from the birth of the nation has performed its part in promoting the progress and development of the Republic, so do we in this generation recognize it as a high duty to perform our part; and this duty in large degree lies in the adoption of measures for the conservation of the natural wealth of the country.

We declare our firm conviction that this conservation of our natural resources is a subject of transcendent importance, which should engage unremittingly the attention of the Nation, the States, and the people in earnest cooperation. These natural resources include the land on which we live and which yields our food; the living waters which fertilize the soil, supply power, and form great avenues of commerce; the forests which yield the materials for our homes, prevent erosion of the soil, and conserve the navigation and other uses of the streams; and the minerals which form the basis of our industrial life, and supply us with heat, light, and power.

We agree that the land should be so used that erosion and soil wash shall cease; and that there should be reclamation of arid and semiarid regions by means of irrigation, and of swamp and overflowed regions by means of drainage; that the waters should be so conserved and used as to promote navigation, to enable the arid regions to be reclaimed by irrigation, and to develop power in the interests of the people; that the forests which regulate our rivers, support our industries, and promote the fertility and productiveness of the soil should be preserved and perpetuated; that the minerals found so abundantly beneath the surface should be so used as to prolong their utility; that the beauty, healthfulness, and habitability of our country should be preserved and increased; that sources of national wealth exist for the benefit of the people, and that monopoly thereof should not be tolerated.

We commend the wise forethought of the President in sounding the note of warning as to the waste and exhaustion of the natural resources of the country, and signify our high appreciation of his action in calling this conference to consider the same and to seek remedies therefor through cooperation of the Nation and the States.

We agree that this cooperation should find expression in suitable action by the Congress within the limits of and coextensive with the national jurisdiction of the subject, and, complementary thereto, by the legislatures of the several States within the limits of and coextensive with their jurisdiction.

We declare the conviction that in the use of the national resources our independent States are interdependent and bound together by ties of mutual benefits, responsibilities, and duties.

We agree in the wisdom of future conferences between the President, Members of Congress, and the governors of States on the conservation of our natural resources with a view of continued cooperation and action on the lines suggested; and to this end we advise that from time to time, as in his judgment may seem wise, the President call the governors of States and Members of Congress and others into conference.

We agree that further action is advisable to ascertain the present condition of our natural resources and to promote the conservation of the same; and to that end we recommend the appointment by each State of a commission on the conservation of natural resources, to cooperate with each other and with any similar commission of the Federal Government.

We urge the continuation and extension of forest policies adapted to secure the husbanding and renewal of our diminishing timber supply, the prevention of soil erosion, the protection of headwaters, and the maintenance of the purity and navigability of our streams. We recognize that the private ownership of forest lands entails responsibilities in the interests of all the people, and we favor the enactment of laws looking to the protection and replacement of privately owned forests.

We recognize in our waters a most valuable asset of the people of the United States, and we recommend the enactment of laws looking to the conservation of water resources for irrigation, water supply, power, and navigation, to the end that navigable and source streams may be brought under complete control and fully utilized for every purpose. We especially urge on the Federal Congress the immediate adoption, of a wise, active, and thorough waterway policy, providing for the prompt improvement of our streams and the conservation of their watersheds required for the uses of commerce and the protection of the interests of our people.

We recommend the enactment of laws looking to the prevention of waste in the mining and extraction of coal, oil, gas, and other minerals with a view to their wise conservation for the use of the people, and to the protection of human life in the mines.

Let us conserve the foundations of our prosperity.

Adopted May 15, 1908, at the White House, Washington, D.C.

GRANT McCONNELL

THE CONSERVATION MOVEMENT—PAST AND PRESENT

The conservation movement by most accounts is now half a century old. If one were to judge from the almost universal deference paid to conservation as an idea or by the number of organized groups and public agencies reiterating its importance, he might well decide that the movement remains strong and vital today. The judgment would not be entirely wrong. Books and articles on problems of conservation appear in numbers, governmental reports having to do with it are frequent, and meetings on its problems occur with regularity.

Yet it is true that in the years which have passed since the century's first decade the fires of the earlier movement have subsided and still burn only in scattered groups, many of which were never part of the original movement. The generation of leaders who first fanned those fires now is largely retired. Veneration is given to their names and to the cause they made the nation's. In their day, conservation could be hailed with some justice as the most democratic movement the country had seen in years. For a time it was the most conspicuous cause on the American political scene. Today, however, the movement is small, divided, and frequently uncertain. Measures are taken to protect this part of the natural heritage or that, but these are defensive and little more. Those against whom the defenses are made respond persuasively with the charge that the defenders themselves are but the representatives of particular interest groups and are hence no better than those whom they accuse.

The conservation movement of the first decade was a phenomenon the like of which we shall not see again. Around the cause of conservation it was possible in that simple time to gather men of good will from nearly all stations, all skills and types of education. Perhaps most striking then was the number of natural scientists who lent their names and energies. They included geographers, geologists, botanists, biologists, and others of even more retiring professions.

The louder voices, however, belonged to men whose calling was political. It was from these that the movement of the early part of the century took both character and vitality. In one sense the very movement was their invention. If we are to credit the leading player in the scene, here is how it happened:

> I was riding my old horse Jim in Rock Creek Park one day . . . I think it was in February, 1907 . . . when suddenly the idea that put the stone on the end of the club occurred to me, The idea was that all these natural resources which we had been dealing with as though they were in watertight compartments actually constituted one united problem. That problem was the use of the earth for the permanent good of man. . . . The idea was so new that it did not even have a name. Of course, it had to have a name. Our little inside group discussed it a great deal. Finally Overton Price suggested that we should call it "conservation" and the President said "O.K." So we called it the conservation movement.[1]

• Grant McConnell is Associate Professor of Political Science, University of Chicago.

Reprinted from the *Western Political Quarterly*, VII (1954), 463–78, with the permission of the author and the editor. (Published by the Institute of Government, University of Utah.)

[1] Gifford Pinchot, "How Conservation Began in the United States," *Agricultural History*, XI (Oc-

The rider was Gifford Pinchot, "The Forester," and one of Theodore Roosevelt's chief lieutenants. A man of character and a gifted politician, he left a mark upon our history that is still to be assessed. With a succession of conferences, congresses, societies, articles, and books, he made conservation the hallmark of his chief's administration. This resulted in the reversal of a land policy older than the nation itself. In the end he even helped tip the electoral scales so that in 1912 an incumbent president was rejected at the polls.

It was a tremendous individual performance. Yet the movement was more than the man, and the claims which have been made by and for Pinchot are larger than the merit. The movement in truth was older than the ride through Rock Creek Park or the introduction of scientific forestry into the United States. It comprehended more than the many groups which Pinchot and his coterie sponsored. A more accurate statement regarding the accomplishment of the Pinchot group would be that it made conservation a political movement in the period between 1900 and 1910. In this time conservation was made to carry the burden of a particular set of political ideals and objectives. These were deeply imbued with the doctrines of Progressivism. Both the early successes and the later dilemmas of the movement derive from the overly simple dogmas of that time. To understand the difficulties of conservation today it is necessary to look back to two quite separate sources of the movement.

The first of these sources was in the ways of thinking to which natural science was committed in the nineteenth century. These rested on the supposition of a natural order in which all things moved according to natural law, in which the most delicate and perfect balance was maintained up to the point at which man entered with all his ignorance and presumption. From that point onward, there was a succession of "disturbed harmonies" in the natural order, with implications of destruction extending ultimately to man himself. There has been no better statement of this than that in a remarkable book published during the Civil War:

> Man has too long forgotten that the earth was given to him for usufruct alone, not for consumption, still less for profligate waste. Nature has provided against the absolute destruction of any of her elementary matter, the raw material of her works; the thunderbolt and the tornado, the most convulsive throes of even the volcano and the earthquake being only phenomena of decomposition and recomposition. But she has left it within the power of man irreparably to derange the combinations of inorganic matter and of organic life, which through the night of aeons she had been proportioning and balancing, to prepare the earth for his habitation, when in the fulness of time, his Creator should call him forth to enter into its possession.[2]

Mingled throughout with the careful ecological studies of soil, plant and animal life was the sense of awe before the works of God, before the orderly mysteries established by His benevolence.

It would be difficult in tracing the religious roots of this view of the internal harmony of the natural order to say just which emanated from a purely deistic conception of things and which from deeper springs of mysticism. Deeper springs there were; it is not impossible that in the long run they will be seen to have been the more important in conservation's history. If the words of one man were to be taken as representative of all of those who have felt the influence of these springs, they would be words of John Muir. Scientist and mystic in one, he spoke precisely and yet out of a Scottish Hebraism that sought respect

---

tober, 1937), 255–56. The story is also told in Pinchot's autobiography, *Breaking New Ground* (New York: Harcourt Brace & Co., 1947), p. 322.

[2] George Perkins Marsh, *Man and Nature* (New York: Charles Scribner & Co., 1864), p. 35. In many ways this book remains the most impressive work on the problems of conservation. The debt which later writers owe it is frequently unacknowledged. The phrase "disturbed harmonies" recurs often in it.

for divinity in all the wild things of Creation. Let one passage stand for many in his writings. Here he was speaking of his favorite area, the Sierra Nevada:

> Benevolent, solemn, fateful, pervaded with divine light, every landscape glows like a countenance hallowed in eternal repose; and every one of its living creatures, clad in flesh and leaves, and every crystal of its rocks, whether on the surface shining in the sun or buried miles deep in what we call darkness, is throbbing and pulsing with the heartbeats of God.[3]

In a conception such as this, to preserve, protect, and defend the heritage is an act and obligation of worship. If man himself in the process of worship is renewed, reborn, recreated, this is not the end but the miraculous by-product of the fulfillment.

By comparison with this attitude of worship, the passion which came from the political leadership was arrogant and materialistic. There was first the assumption of invention which we have already noted.[4] More important, however, was the body of political doctrine imparted to the movement by the new leadership. The point which now stood first was that all the goods, all the benefits of nature, were there for the use of man. The restraints were to be imposed upon recklessness and waste. As the principles of the movement were stated by Gifford Pinchot, they were three. "The first principle of conservation is development, the use of the natural resources now existing on this continent for the benefit of the people who live here now."[5] This was in part a reply to those critics who claimed to believe that the goal of conservationists was the mere "withholding of resources for future generations," a form of hoarding. Yet, granting the necessity of answering this criticism, it remained true that this first principle was one to which the part of the movement under Pinchot's guidance was deeply committed.

The second principle was that "conservation stands for the prevention of waste. . . . The first duty of the human race is to control the earth it lives upon."[6] Here indeed was the foundation of the crusade launched in 1907. This was the appeal with the most universal attraction and the one which reached back to those who had already spoken. There could be no opposition to this as a principle.

The third principle, however, was the one from which the real force of the movement derived. As Pinchot stated it, "The natural resources must be developed and preserved for the benefit of the many, and not merely the profit of the few."[7] In this assertion, Pinchot claimed for the cause of conservation all the zeal and political fervor that had been left without leadership by the collapse of the Populist movement, and that had variously focused on the rapacity of the railroads, high finance and monopoly. The assertion of this third principle was a call sure to focus the resentments of "the common man" against the high-handedness of the powerful and wealthy few. Given the temper of the era, there was no other principle which could have infused an equal force into the cause of conservation. It was a principle that was being invoked in various ways against the exercise of monopoly in all areas. Although the antimonopoly as a principle was not an unqualified policy of the official Progressive leadership either then or later, Pinchot did succeed—and this was his essential achievement—in directing the energies and the enthusiasm of the Progressive movement in its early stages to conservation. Ultimately the failure of the conservation movement ever to regain the strength it had in the century's first decade derives

[3] John Muir, *Our National Parks* (Boston and New York: Houghton Mifflin Co., 1901), p. 76.

[4] The partisans of the school of Muir have not failed to note that the original impulse to conservation came well before the day of Pinchot and his followers; e.g., Muir's biographer observes that "conservation as a Government policy stemmed from the Harrison administration and the work of John W. Noble." Linnie Marsh Wolfe, *Son of the Wilderness, The Life of John Muir* (New York: Alfred A. Knopf, 1945), p. 314.

[5] Gifford Pinchot, *The Fight for Conservation* (New York: Doubleday Page & Co., 1910), p. 46.

[6] *Ibid.*

[7] *Ibid.*

from the impossibility to sustain or repeat Pinchot's advocacy of the principle. Since the end of Progressivism the force of this appeal has gone instead to many causes other than those dealing with natural resources, to the labor movement and an array of efforts of social and economic reform.

It was really remarkable to what a degree conservation became identified with Progressivism. As the Pinchot-led conferences went on, conservation grew and expanded. It came to include the conservation of man himself. The list of topics that were discussed at the Conservation Congresses is illuminating. Included with the familiar subjects of forests, soil, and water were the following: the conservation of child life and of manhood, the public control of railroads, the regulation of speculation and gambling in foodstuffs, the establishment of parcel post, agricultural extension, the coordination of governmental agencies, the development of river and lake navigation, improved sanitation in Cuba and the Philippines, better rural schools, a rural credit system, and the treatment of river drainage systems as units.[8] Conservation crept into discussions and studies of topics which today we would regard as quite distinct from the saving of natural resources. For example, when President Theodore Roosevelt appointed his landmark Commission on Country Life in 1908, Gifford Pinchot was one of the members. A chapter on forest conservation appeared in the Commission's broad discussion of the human problems of farming.[9] When the treatise of the time on conservation was written, inevitably it had a section entitled, "The Conservation of Man Himself."[10]

To an important degree, then, the conservation movement of the first part of the century was Progressivism itself. Within a few years it was made to comprehend very nearly all of the specific aims of the Progressive cause. And just here lay the explanation for the remarkable success of conservation in that era. In one sense the conservation movement consisted of an alliance of specific groups with inherently divergent interests. In another sense it was the realization in political form of a delusively simple idea, that of equality.

The conservation movement of today bears the marks of its dual origins. The most conspicuous of these marks is the disagreement among the various groups which speak for conservation. On the one hand, it is apparent that some of the groups seek different goals. They appear at times to represent particular interests, some as selfish as the special interests which were so denounced in the Progressive era. On the other hand, there is a fundamental cleavage in the ideas which are asserted as the true meaning of conservation. In one sense this cleavage is that between progressivism and conservatism. In another sense it is that between humanism and something more mystical.

The Progressive element in conservation, as we have seen, was that which gave the movement force and momentum. It seemed to have the merits of simplicity and directness. If there was opposition, this could

[8] Resolutions on these topics were passed at the National Conservation Congresses of 1911 and 1912. See *Proceedings,* Third National Conservation Congress (Kansas City, Mo., 1912), pp. xxii ff.; *Proceedings,* Fourth National Conservation Congress (Indianapolis, 1912), pp. 18–23.

[9] *Report* of Commission on Country Life (Chapel Hill: University of North Carolina Press, 1944). This was originally printed as Senate Document 705, 60th Cong., 2d Sess., 1909. It was also reprinted by the Spokane Chamber of Commerce in 1911.

[10] Charles Richard Van Hise, *The Conservation of Natural Resources* (New York: The Macmillan Co., 1910), pp. 364 ff. This book written by a president of the University of Wisconsin went through many printings and has served as a model for later works. For example, *Our Natural Resources and Their Conservation,* ed. A. E. Parkins and J. R. Whitaker (New York: John Wiley & Sons, 1939), specially acknowledges the debt to the Van Hise work. It includes a chapter by Ellsworth Huntington, "The Conservation of Man" (chap. 19).

come only from selfishness. Nevertheless, as the years have passed, the Progressive element is the one which has declined in strength. The clarity of the vision seen and proclaimed by Gifford Pinchot has diminished to the point at which it is difficult to say whether conservation still carries any of the meaning which he gave it.

The most frequent comment on the present conservation movement is that the many groups speaking in its name do not agree. In truth, the groups which take an interest in the broad field of natural resources are numerous. When the President's Water Resources Policy Commission came to study its problem, one much more narrow than the large field of resources, more than two hundred organizations offered their views.[11] This situation was probably characteristic of the widespread concern in different sectors of the population about resources problems. Some of the groups were local bodies which had immediate and obvious concern with the problems before the Commission; others were national organizations with less tangible interests in the matter. The disagreement was often direct and strong. Nevertheless, "conservation" was a goal accorded almost universal respect. In the face of this situation, what does "conservation" mean today? Where lies the unity among those who present it as their own goal?

The answers are less easy to give now than in the time of Gifford Pinchot. In his day one simple formula seemed to solve all such problems, "the greatest good of the greatest number for the longest time."[12] The policy was that of seeking "the common good." In the face of this amended utilitarianism, any opposition was necessarily selfish and evil. And, indeed, there was abundant justification in the particular battles which Pinchot had to fight for believing that the cause of conservation was that of good against evil.[13] It was the cause of the public interest against the special interests, the defense of the common heritage against predatory selfishness. Yet, looking back on the struggles of that day, it is worth observing that even the worst offenders of that time have had their latter-day defenders.[14]

The utilitarian formula was adequate for deriving an answer to the questions of the day of the first Roosevelt. If the question was posed, should the remaining virgin forests of the West be given to the lumbermen to be cut as fast as had been those of Wisconsin and Minnesota or should they be set aside for intelligent management in the interest of all the people? the answer was clear. There was no ambiguity before such an alternative. Whatever the inherent difficulties of Jeremy Bentham's calculus, they were not apparent when the principle was applied to problems as elementary as these.

Nevertheless, it is interesting that Pinchot and his followers felt the need of some amendment to the utilitarian principle. This lay in the element of time. "For the longest time," "in the long run," these phrases are still used in connection with the tradition of Progressive conservation. In some way this seemed to be implicit in the name which had been chosen for the movement. Beyond this, however, a vague feeling persisted that the simple "greatest good" formula was not entirely adequate for solving the problems before the nation. Natural resources must not be used up in any one generation, however widely their

[11] President's Water Resources Policy Commission, *A Water Policy for the American People,* Report of the Commission, I (Washington, 1950), 318–19. This was exclusive of governmental bodies.

[12] Pinchot, *The Fight for Conservation, op. cit.*, p. 47.

[13] Numerous incidents might be cited. The most notorious, of course, was that involving Secretary of Interior Ballinger and the Alaska coal lands. See A. T. Mason, *Bureaucracy Convicts Itself* (New York: Viking Press, 1941). Also Pinchot, *Breaking New Ground, op. cit.*, pp. 395–458.

[14] Here the most conspicuous example is Secretary Ickes' defense of his predecessor, Ballinger, in the controversy with Pinchot. See the article by Ickes, "Not Guilty!" *Saturday Evening Post,* CCXII (May 25, 1940).

benefits might be distributed in that period. Yet this refinement of the principle brought its own difficulties. Was this a principle of hoarding that was being asserted? Over how long a period must our stock of resources be spread? The matter was not pressing when the issue related to renewable resources, such as forests (which were the outstanding object of concern in the early part of the century). This aspect of the problem has become more important, however. Recent years have brought an astronomical increase in our consumption of our materials. The Second World War and the ensuing prosperity have given the problem an urgency it has never had before. This was basically the problem set before the recent President's Materials Policy Commission: "Has the United States of America the material means to sustain its civilization?"[15] Immediately the time element was most important. The answer given by the Commission was in effect a rejection of the more stringent injunctions to save which might seem to derive from the principles of conservation:

> The Nation faces a very real and growing conservation problem, but many of our difficulties in agreeing on what to do about it arise from a failure to recognize the economic dimensions of the problem. One popular fallacy is to regard our resource base as a fixed inventory which, when used up, will leave society with no means of survival. A related fallacy is that physical waste equals economic waste: the feeling that it is wasteful to use materials in ways that make them disappear. This attitude can lead to devoting a dollar's worth of work "saving" a few cents' worth of waste paper and old string.

In the eyes of the Commission these fallacies make "a hairshirt conception of conservation," whereas conservation must mean "something very different from simply leaving oil in the ground or trees in the forest."[16] It is apparent, then, that the relatively simple problem of conserving for the future is itself complex and offers no simple solution to the proper use of resources.[17]

What has followed from the other part of the utilitarian formula laid down by Pinchot? He stated the problem in perhaps as simple a form as possible: "For whose benefit shall they (our natural resources) be conserved—for the benefit of the many, or for the use and profit of the few?"[18] The question so stated carried its own answer. Yet, even as the principle has been echoed by writers on conservation, there has been a nagging and growing sense that its meaning is far from clear.[19] While the answer

[15] This is the question with which chap. 1 of the Commission's report begins. President's Materials Policy Commission, *Resources for Freedom,* Report of the Commission (Washington, 1952), p. 1.

[16] *Ibid.*, p. 21. If such an answer could be given in the context of high level prosperity and open warfare, it is evident that during depression it had even more force. Compare the following statement: "In approaching the subject of conservation, in the past, our entire thinking has been clouded by a tacit assumption that we were living under an economy of scarcity. The major objectives, therefore, have been to restrict, to limit, and even to withhold and hoard. At times and under certain circumstances, all these are desirable and even necessary, but as a concept, conservation designed merely to save can have no more than academic interest to a society which at times threatens to suffocate in over-abundance." "National Planning in Resource Use," *Our Natural Resources and Their Conservation,* ed. Parkins and Whitaker, *op. cit.*, p. 592.

[17] The time element is regarded as the central problem of conservation by S. V. Ciriacy-Wantrup, *Resources Conservation, Economics and Policies* (Berkeley and Los Angeles: University of California Press, 1952). This work is directed to the task of giving precise economic meaning to the term "conservation." Necessarily, it uses the term in a manner foreign to those within the movement. Although this approach rejects the utilitarian formulas, it shares the materialist and egalitarian bias of the Pinchot school.

[18] Pinchot, *The Fight for Conservation, op. cit.*, p. 109.

[19] For example, E. G. Cheyney and T. Schantz-Hansen quote the National Resources Committee to the effect that our resources should be conserved and used "for the benefit of all of our people" and go on to state, "Just how our natural wealth is to be distributed to give the greatest good to the greatest number of people is a puzzling problem." *This Is Our Land, The Story of Conservation in the United States* (St. Paul: Webb Book Pub. Co., 1940), p. 18.

to the question posed by Pinchot might be clear, the actual problems of conservation as they have been put since his time have not been so easy to solve. One recent example will suffice. This involved a proposed synthetic shale-oil plant in the upper Colorado River Basin. To be competitive, it would have to be large. If it were large it would use up almost all of the water in the area for its operations. The actual question raised here was, which is worth more—more irrigated land or more and cheaper oil?[20] Nothing in the utilitarian formula, with or without the element of time, gives a clue to the proper answer.

In some sense the difficulties here were appreciated by the leaders of the conservation movement from the very beginning. Accordingly, a supplementary principle was laid down. This was that of multiple use of resources. Primarily this applied to the forests, but to some extent it has characterized the whole of the Progressive element in conservation. This was the meaning which has repeatedly been assigned to "the greatest good of the greatest number." Perhaps more than any other principle this is the one which has most clearly characterized the policy of the U.S. Forest Service. As it is usually stated, it has the aura of an infallible device for automatically calculating the proper assignment of uses and values of resources under the management of the Service. Here is a characteristic statement:

> The central thought in the management and use of the resources of the national forests is to so adjust one use to the other that the greatest net public benefit will result—to obtain the greatest total of crops, uses and services. Where necessary the attainable maximum of any one of these can be relinquished if the grand total of public values is thereby increased. Where one use must be exclusive, the highest use in the public interest is given the right of way. Where two or more uses can occupy a given area wtih some concession by each, a suitable compromise is effected. Thus, in the first case, where recreational use would incur risk of pollution of a city water supply, it is excluded from the watershed; where public use would create an unacceptable risk on an area of unusual fire hazard on which a new tree crop is being fostered, the public is excluded during the fire season; where a water-power development would destroy or seriously impair the recreational or aesthetic value of a lake, it is excluded if the latter values are held to be paramount in the public interest. In the second case, timber cutting is usually permitted on watersheds, but so regulated as to avoid impairment of the watershed value. . . . Almost every national forest furnishes an example of a large variety of overlapping uses so harmonized as to avoid any measurable conflict. . . .[21]

To analyze this statement would require an extended discussion. However, it may be briefly observed that there is, first, an underlying assumption of some single correct balance of uses which "is in the public interest"; second, there is a bias toward *measurable* benefits. Obviously, the most practical unit of measurement is the dollar. Third, there are repeated points in the making of decisions at which the exercise of discretion is essential to the reaching of any decision, no matter how rigidly the principle of multiple use is adhered to. To "give the right of way" to "the highest use of the public interest" may require little more than honesty and public spirit on the part of the administrator *if* the "highest use" is known. To say this, however, is to beg the real question. Actually there is nothing in the principle of multiple use which will make the highest use known. Any decision that will in fact be made will be in terms of the particular set of values held by the administrator or, perhaps, by the particular set of pressures that are brought to bear on him. It may have been true in 1933, when the statement was written, that there was little measurable conflict in the uses of the forests. However, in the near future conflict will inevitably in-

[20] This question was raised by Oscar Chapman, Under-Secretary of the Interior, in the U.S., Senate, Comm. on Interior and Insular Affairs, *Hearings on Natural Resources Policy,* 81st Cong., 1st Sess., 1950.

[21] C. M. Granger of the U.S. Forest Service, in *A National Plan for American Forestry,* published as Sen. Doc. No. 12, 73d Cong., 1st Sess., 1933.

crease and the decisions of administrators become less easy to make. The West, in which most of the forests are located, has a rapidly growing population, and the pressures on the use of public lands are increasing. It is altogether probable that the ease with which solutions to problems of conflicts of uses of public lands have been reached in the past is no more than a reflection of the relative abundance of these land resources in the past.[22]

A number of problems inevitably flow from the ambiguities in the Progressive stream of conservation. The first of these is planning. The first stage in the program of conservation was the deliberate withdrawal of resources from private exploitation. Although the implication of planning was not apparent at the time at which the action was taken, the obligation to decide on the proper uses and rates of use followed necessarily from that action. Since the portion of resources withdrawn constituted only a part of the whole, the obligation to make rational decisions on these matters from the standpoint of public policy could be deferred. However, as the time for greater use of the withdrawn resources has approached, all the problems inherent in planning have come to the fore. Specifically, the basic issue here is this: what criteria are there for deciding on either the rate of uses or the distribution of uses? How are these criteria to be derived? As we have seen, neither the utilitarian calculus nor the principle of multiple use is of great help in reaching answers. What is there to save an administrator in the field of natural resources from making his decisions purely in terms of his own personal values? Where are the limits upon his discretion? Appeal either to the utilitarian calculus or the principle of multiple use can only disguise the element of irresponsibility. This has probably been the basic dilemma of the Progressive stream in conservation: its program necessarily led to planning but created no definite criteria for making the decisions involved in planning.[23]

The second problem involved is that of interest representation. Here again there is a dilemma. On the one hand, the "greatest good" formula and the multiple use principle imply an extensive distribution of the benefits of natural resources among different groups. On the other hand, these principles have in practice been taken to imply the existence of some discoverable correct balance or mixture of uses and users. While it might be held that the "greatest good" formula is but a device for securing compromise and adjustment among the various contending interest groups, this does not in fact seem to have been the position of any of the conservation leaders. A plan for the adequate representation of the many groups interested might be derived from the utilitarian calculus. Conservation would thereby come to have a procedural meaning of some merit. Nevertheless, this implication has never been fully developed within the conservation movement.

The part of the utilitarian formula which has the greater definiteness is the phrase "the greatest number." From this, however, there has developed an additional

[22] It is worth observing that the sharpest controversies over the multiple-use concept so far have arisen with regard to the assignment of costs in multiple-purpose dams. Attempts have been made to establish a formula in the cost/benefit ratio to solve the administrative problem. This formula, however, cannot be regarded as a value-free device for answering such questions. The particular decisions here will in fact continue to be made as before, in terms of the value systems of the deciding administrators and the particular sets of pressures brought to bear.

[23] Ciriacy-Wantrup emphasizes planning in conservation, *op. cit.*, pp. 347 ff. While there is here some suggestion of criteria for solving the time problem of resource use, it is apparent from his suggestion of the use of "administrative valuation" for extra market values (pp. 238–40) that the administrator's problem is necessarily thrown back on the administrator's own personal value system. It is noteworthy that much of the controversy over conservation has revolved around the issue of public ownership of resources. See for example, issues of *Natural Resources Notes,* issued by the Chamber of Commerce of the United States, Washington.

complexity. Inevitably, this fundamentally egalitarian principle has involved the conservation movement in the crosscurrents of localism and nationalism. The issue caused one of the sharpest controversies in the early days of the movement.[24] In recent years this has become more and more the crux of arguments over conservation. Despite some uncertainty on the principle involved,[25] many who are in the conservation movement today feel that their cause is better served by the federal government than by those of the states. This has been apparent in recent controversies involving off-shore oil, the release of virgin timber from the Olympic National Park and the regulation of grazing lands. Necessarily, state ownership or regulation would favor the oil industry, the lumbermen and the stockmen respectively. The point of view opposing the conservation forces has probably never been more clearly put than by Congressman Barrett of Wyoming in arguing against continuation of the Jackson Hole National Monument: "I do not know why 2900 people in New York should have more to say than one man in Wyoming."[26]

Here, it would seem, is the explanation for the general disappearance of the Progressive stream in the conservation movement. It cannot be said in any sense that the movement which had such astonishing vigor during the years preceding the First World War is still alive today. Its doctrines remain in the official policies of the Forest Service and other agencies dealing with natural resources; there are scattered small groups which still work for its objectives. Nevertheless, there is neither any regular congress of conservation, nor any widespread agreement on the meaning of the word. Various reasons have been assigned for this change,[27] but the most important is that Gifford Pinchot's revelation of a basic unity among the problems of natural resources was either mistaken or unclear. His doctrine was inadequate to hold together all the many groups having an interest in natural resources. Although it was sufficient to bring together people who were concerned with such relatively simple problems as stopping the rapid destruction of the forests, it could not yield solutions to the more complex questions of conflict in use which came thereafter. The decline of Progressive conservation was due ultimately to a failure of ideas.

The conservation movement as it exists today consists almost wholly of groups that lie outside of the Progressive tradition. Their interests and their objectives differ profoundly from those which motivated Pinchot and his followers. Perhaps the best characterization of the movement today in contrast to the movement of the early part of the century is that it is politically an alliance of particular interest groups that have little in common among their objectives. There is a core of ideas, it is true, but this is less important than

[24] At the Second National Conservation Congress a group of western state governors spoke out vigorously against the tendencies of the conservation movement to "lock up" resources and to restrict the economic development of their states. Their argument was a strong assertion of states rights and of the superior efficiency of state managements. See *Proceedings,* Second National Conservation Congress (Washington, 1911), speeches by the Governors of Montana, Washington, and Wyoming especially, pp. 52–75. Sen. Albert J. Beveridge gave the strongest reply to the localist view. His speech began: "Mr. Chairman, Ladies, and Gentlemen: The United States IS (applause), the American people are a Nation (applause), —not forty-six Nations," pp. 146–52.

[25] For a discussion of this principle see my article, "Big Government Bogy," *The Nation,* CLXXVII (November 14, 1953), 386–87.

[26] Mr. Barrett was challenging the right of the members of the New York Zoological Society to be represented on the question of the Monument. U.S., Congress, House, Comm. on Public Lands, *Hearings on a Bill To Abolish the Jackson Hole National Monument,* 80th Cong., 1st Sess., 1948, p. 62.

[27] Stephen Raushenbush has given a list of five reasons, some of which are the complicating problems mentioned here. Although all are relevant, it seems that the inherent confusions in Progressive doctrine are more important. See Stephen Raushenbush, "Conservation in 1952," *Annals of the American Academy of Political and Social Science,* CCLXXXI (May, 1952), 1–3.

the necessity for common action to achieve the varied individual goals.

It is not easy to define the group of organizations which may be taken as properly belonging to the contemporary conservation movement. In fact, the difficulty of formulating a coherent list of conservation organizations is one of the major problems of the movement.[28] Many groups speak in the name of conservation, but which of them are compatible, which are to be included in the common federation? For example, can a conservation federation include both the Congress of Industrial Organizations and the Chamber of Commerce of the United States? Should organizations with such diverse interests within themselves properly be regarded as conservation organizations?[29]

The most definite description of the present conservation movement that can be given is the list of organizations that belong to the Natural Resources Council of America. This is a service organization formed in 1946, whose objective is "to advance the attainment of sound management of natural resources in the public interest." Hopes have been held for it that it would become a means of gaining cooperation among the various member organizations. However, the difficulties have been so great that as yet the Council is no more than an agency for providing information on congressional and governmental activities related to natural resources to its members. In 1952 an attempt was made to formulate a general policy on which all its members could agree. The policy, which can be stated only in very general terms, cannot be regarded as the basis for any meaningful program.[30] In the meantime, the Council adheres to its original principle that it "shall not undertake to control the policies or actions of member organizations." At the present time there are just under forty clubs and societies in the Council. The list is diverse. It includes outdoor clubs, professional societies, sportsmen's organizations and others less easy to categorize: The Mountaineers, the American Society of Mammalogists, the National Association of Biology Teachers, the Sport Fishing Institute, the Friends of the Land, and The Wilderness Society, to take but a few names. Most of the groups are small. A few, however, boast large membership and resources. The National Wildlife Federation has access to approximately $900,000 from its sale of stamps and other materials relating to wildlife. The Izaak Walton League has a large membership (approximately 60,000) but is afflicted with a large annual turnover.

The Natural Resources Council is in itself of little importance except insofar as its existence indicates that a number of groups with diverse interests have found some purpose in common. If the different groups are examined they will be found to have certain fairly definite individual interests. The largest group is that concerned with hunting and fishing.[31] After these there are groups interested in bird preservation, wildflowers, soil conservation, national parks, and wilderness preservation, and the various scientific societies. The reasons for the difficulty of formulating a common program are fairly clear.

Nevertheless, this group of organizations does have a nucleus of ideas that is more tangible than that which once bound the Progressive conservation movement togeth-

[28] This point was made to the writer by Richard M. Leonard, President of the Sierra Club, one of the most determined and effective conservation organizations in existence.

[29] The CIO has been very active in supporting conservation causes. Its spokesman in these matters, Anthony Wayne Smith, is highly respected in conservation circles. The Chamber of Commerce also has repeatedly taken positions supporting conservation causes. One of its leaders here is Horace M. Albright, a pioneer administrator of the National Park Service.

[30] Natural Resources Council of America, *A Conservation Policy for the United States* (Washington, October 12, 1952).

[31] Tabulations of hunters and fishermen throughout the country range up to 17,000,000. Obviously, however, to regard all these as belonging to the conservation movement would be an error.

er. Each society mentioned above *asserts some superior value*. This follows from the fact that most of the groups here have particular fields of interest—fish, game, soil, wilderness, and so on. The unity among them rests on the fact that the values asserted are not incompatible. To a lesser degree it also rests on the fact that the particular values cherished by these groups are noncommercial. In this latter sense the groups are united by their opposition to the common foe of exploitation for economic benefit. Here that foe is in some instances the drive for developments which are measurable in commercial or financial terms. The best examples of this are to be seen in the opposition of most of the Natural Resources Council groups to projects such as the Echo Park Dam in the Dinosaur National Monument or the Panther Mountain Dam in the Adirondacks. A similar issue has been the persistent conflict over the boundaries of the Olympic National Park and the right to use timber contained within its present boundaries.[32]

Looking beyond the particular values asserted and the need of their various sponsors for common action, however, what outlook is shared by these conservationists?[33] In very broad terms it can be said that the advocates of the various causes just listed do have a common point of view. Its components may be stated somewhat as follows: First, certain uses of resources are intrinsically more important than others and should be favored—no matter how few the people who choose to make such uses. Thus, there is a value in wilderness as such for the sake of which, considering the few wilderness areas left in the nation, they should receive protection against uses which would necessarily destroy them.[34]

The other component is more general and more difficult to phrase. It is the sense of obligation which man has toward his natural environment. This is essentially the point made by George Perkins Marsh in the nineteenth century. In part this derives from a concern for preserving the biotic balance from which man has emerged. Here, perhaps, the best example is the attitude of some of the stronger proponents of soil conservation. Thus, during the recent controversy over reorganization of the Soil Conservation Service, it was apparent that much of the opposition to retrenchment came from a profound and almost religious belief that there is some *right* way of treating the land, the fundamental resource on which all life depends.[35] Many of those engaged in soil conservation have a genuine-

32 The dispute over the Echo Park Dam is one of the most bitter disputes related to conservation in many years. The argument for the dam is perhaps best presented in . . . files of the *Salt Lake Tribune;* the case against it in the *Sierra Club Bulletin,* Vol. XXXIX (February, 1954). The dispute over Panther Mountain Dam is discussed at some length in the *New York Times* (November 1, 1953). The controversy over the boundaries of the Olympic National Park may be sampled in the hearings of the House Comm. on Public Lands at Lake Crescent, Washington, 80th Cong., 1st Sess., 1948.

33 It is an interesting fact that the term "conservationists," is applied almost exclusively today to members of the groups considered in this section.

34 At times, it is true, attempts are made to justify wilderness preservation in terms of an appeal to large numbers of people. Thus, the Izaak Walton League considers such areas as a "part of our natural heritage that should not be sacrificed to the greed of the few." See Kenneth A. Reid, Exec. Director, "Program of the Izaak Walton League," *American Planning and Civic Annual, 1946–1947.* A more forthright statement is that of the Wilderness Society, which begins: "The wilderness (the environment of solitude) is a natural mental resource having the same basic relation to man's ultimate thought and culture as coal, timber, and other physical resources, have to his material needs." *Memorandum for the Legislative Reference Service,* (Washington: Library of Congress, 1949), p. 3.

35 Here the text may be taken from Hugh Hammond Bennett: "Stated in simplest terms, conservation of the soil is a matter of using land as it should be used." *Soil Conservation* (New York: McGraw-Hill, 1939), p. 313. The heat generated in the controversy over the SCS reorganization may be sensed in recent numbers of the *Tuesday Letters* issued by the National Assoc. of Soil Conservation Districts, League City, Texas.

ly dedicated attitude toward their work. At the same time, it is interesting to note, many of them are politically very conservative.

In larger terms it may be said that this attitude toward conservation places man in an almost secondary position in relation to the natural environment. The most eloquent general statement of this is to be found in the writings of the late Aldo Leopold. His argument may be summarized cursorily as follows: Man is "only a member of a biotic team" and exists as part of a larger community between land and man. The land in turn is "one organism." Accordingly there is an obligation resting on man to respect the land (by which is meant "all of the things on, over, or in the earth") and to conserve it. Conservation thus means "a state of harmony between men and land." "The last word in ignorance is the man who says of an animal or plant: 'What good is it?' If the land mechanism as a whole is good, then every part is good, whether we understand it or not." Recognition of this obligation to the land and the things of the land constitutes a "land ethic" which must be observed lest man perish materially and spiritually.[36]

It is apparent, then, that the differences between the two streams of the conservation movement are profound. The one tends to emphasize an accommodation of uses, each of which may be presumed to stand on more or less even footing, except as one or another use appeals to greater or smaller numbers of people. Given the character of American society, this amounts to an emphasis on material values. The other elevates certain values to a preferred position, no matter how few the people to whom these appeal. It elevates nonmaterial above material values as a matter of principle. The one is inherently liberal; the other has highly conservative implications.

These differences have been expressed in various ways in the years since the birth of the conservation movement. At times they amount merely to an indifference of one side to the concerns of the other.[37] At other times they result in direct opposition and antagonism. The present controversy over the Echo Park Dam is an almost classic example. Both sides to this dispute consider themselves to be arguing for the cause of conservation.[38] Sometimes, indeed, it has been possible for these very different groups to cooperate on particular issues.[39] It remains true, however, that the two types of conservation follow generally divergent paths.

If today we see a conservation movement that is both different in content and weaker than that which was for a time the most conspicuous political movement alive, the reasons are comprehensible. The conservation movement of that earlier day was essentially the policy of Progressivism in the field of natural resources. The underlying idea of that policy was equality. It was

[36] These quotations have been taken from Aldo Leopold, *A Sand County Almanac* (New York: Oxford University Press, 1949), pp. 202–7, and *Round River, from the Journals of Aldo Leopold,* ed. Luna B. Leopold (New York: Oxford University Press, 1953), pp. 145–46.

[37] An excellent example: "We hold little anxiety that the strictly utilitarian controls on forests, oil, mines, and fisheries will be seriously relaxed under our present concept of government. These related to our basic material security; every phase of our national life depends directly or indirectly upon these administrative controls. But the national parks represent those intangible values which cannot be turned directly to profit or material advantage," Ansel Adams, "The Meaning of the National Parks," *The Living Wilderness* (Autumn, 1950), p. 4.

[38] Probably the prototype of this conflict was the battle over building the Hetch Hetchy Dam in a Yosemite-like canyon of the Sierra Nevada. The dam was fought bitterly by John Muir and his followers. Pinchot supported the dam. The result was an intense personal dislike between the two. See Wolfe, *op. cit.*, pp. 311–14.

[39] Such co-operation may be seen in the various groups appearing to oppose a transfer of land from the Forest Service to the Bureau of Land Management as desired by livestock interests. See, for example, hearings of the House Comm. on Public Lands at Ely, Nevada, 80th Cong., 1st Sess., 1948.

perhaps inevitable that the alliance of interest groups that supported Progressivism in this area could not continue to cohere for long. It was certain that the ideal of equality could not remain indefinitely in harness to the narrower conception of conservation. Without a more cohesive set of ideas than the vision of "the use of the earth for the permanent good of man," this movement was bound to dissolve. On the other hand, the almost religious ideas that were stated by George Perkins Marsh, John Muir, and Aldo Leopold have continued to carry great force with a continuing group of believers. The result has been the return of the conservation movement to this smaller and perhaps more dedicated group. The ideas of Progressivism are not dead; they continue in the policies of different agencies dealing with natural resources. Despite their ambiguities, these ideas are not without validity. Neither are those of the older tradition that is prominent today. The political result, however, is confusion and uncertainty as to the meaning of conservation.

Henry Thoreau would scoff at the notion that the Gross National Product should be the chief index to the state of the nation, or that automobile sales figures on consumer consumption reveal anything significant about the authentic art of living. He would surely assert that a clean landscape is as important as a freeway, he would deplore every planless conquest of the countryside, and he would remind his countrymen that a glimpse of grouse can be more inspiring than a Hollywood spectacular or color television. To those who complain of the complexity of modern life, he might reply, "If you want inner peace find it in solitude, not speed, and if you would find yourself, look to the land from which you came and to which you go."

STEWART UDALL, *The Quiet Crisis* (New York: Holt, Rinehart & Winston, 1963), p. 190.

SAMUEL P. HAYS

CONSERVATION AND THE GOSPEL OF EFFICIENCY

The conservation movement has contributed more than its share to the political drama of the twentieth century. A succession of colorful episodes—from the Pinchot-Ballinger controversy, through Teapot Dome, to the Dixon-Yates affair—have embellished the literature of the movement, and called forth fond memories for its later leaders. Cast in the framework of a moral struggle between the virtuous "people," and the evil "interests," these events have provided issues tailor-made to arouse the public to a fighting pitch, and they continue to inspire the historian to recount a tale of noble and stirring enterprise. This crusading quality of the conservation movement has given it an enviable reputation as a defender of spiritual values and national character. He who would battle for conservation fights in a worthy and patriotic cause, and foolhardy, indeed, is he who would sully his reputation by opposition!

Such is the ideological tenor of the present-day conservation movement and of its history as well. But, however much an asset in promoting conservation, this dramatic fervor has constituted a major liability in its careful analysis. For the moral language of conservation battles differed markedly from the course of conservation events. Examining the record, one is forced to distinguish sharply between rhetoric and reality, between the literal meaning of the terminology of the popular struggle and the specific issues of conservation policy at stake. Conservation neither arose from a broad popular outcry, nor centered its fire primarily upon the private corporation. Moreover, corporations often supported conservation policies, while the "people" just as frequently opposed them. In fact, it becomes clear that one must discard completely the struggle against corporations as the setting in which to understand conservation history and permit an entirely new frame of reference to arise from the evidence itself.

Conservation, above all, was a scientific movement, and its role in history arises from the implications of science and technology in modern society. Conservation leaders sprang from such fields as hydrology, forestry, agrostology, geology, and anthropology. Vigorously active in professional circles in the national capital, these leaders brought the ideals and practices of their crafts into federal resource policy. Loyalty to these professional ideals, not close association with the grass-roots public, set the tone of the Theodore Roosevelt conservation movement. Its essence was rational planning to promote efficient development and use of all natural resources. The idea of efficiency drew these federal scientists from one resource task to another, from specific programs to comprehensive concepts. It molded the policies which they proposed, their administrative techniques, and their relations with Con-

• Samuel P. Hays is Professor of History, State University of Iowa.

Reprinted from Samuel P. Hays, *Conservation and the Gospel of Efficiency* (Cambridge: Harvard University Press, 1959), pp. 1–4, with the permission of the author and the publisher.

gress and the public. It is from the vantage point of applied science, rather than of democratic protest, that one must understand the historic role of the conservation movement.[1]

The new realms of science and technology, appearing to open up unlimited opportunities for human achievement, filled conservation leaders with intense optimism. They emphasized expansion, not retrenchment; possibilities, not limitations. True, they expressed some fear that diminishing resources would create critical shortages in the future. But they were not Malthusian prophets of despair and gloom. The popular view that in a fit of pessimism they withdrew vast areas of the public lands from present use for future development does not stand examination. In fact, they bitterly opposed those who sought to withdraw resources from commercial development. They displayed that deep sense of hope which pervaded all those at the turn of the century for whom science and technology were revealing visions of an abundant future.

The political implications of conservation, it is particularly important to observe, grew out of the political implications of applied science rather than from conflict over the distribution of wealth. Who should decide the course of resource development? Who should determine the goals and methods of federal resource programs? The correct answer to these questions lay at the heart of the conservation idea. Since resource matters were basically technical in nature, conservationists argued, technicians, rather than legislators, should deal with them. Foresters should determine the desirable annual timber cut; hydraulic engineers should establish the feasible extent of multiple-purpose river development and the specific location of reservoirs; agronomists should decide which forage areas could remain open for grazing without undue damage to water supplies. Conflicts between competing resource users, especially, should not be dealt with through the normal processes of politics. Pressure group action, logrolling in Congress, or partisan debate could not guarantee rational and scientific decisions. Amid such jockeying for advantage with the resulting compromise, concern for efficiency would disappear. Conservationists envisaged, even though they did not realize their aims, a political system guided by the ideal of efficiency and dominated by the technicians who could best determine how to achieve it.

This phase of conservation requires special examination because of its long neglect by historians. Instead of probing the political implications of the technological spirit, they have repeated the political mythology of the "people versus the interests" as the setting for the struggle over resource policy. This myopia has stemmed in part from the disinterestedness of the historian and the social scientist. Often accepting implicitly the political assumptions of eliteism, rarely having an axe of personal interest to grind, and invariably sympathetic with the movement, conservation historians have considered their view to be in the public interest. Yet, analysis from outside such a limited perspective reveals the difficulty of equating the particular views of a few scientific leaders with an objective "public interest." Those views did not receive wide acceptance; they did not arise out of widely held assumptions and values. They came from a limited group of people, with a particular set of goals, who played a special role in society. Their definition of the "public interest" might well, and did, clash with other competing definitions. The historian, therefore, cannot understand conservation leaders simply as defenders of the "people." Instead, he must examine the experiences and goals peculiar to them; he must describe their role within a specific sociological context.

[1] A statement of a contrary point of view is given in J. Leonard Bates, "Fulfilling American Democracy: The Conservation Movement, 1907–21," *Mississippi Valley Historical Review,* XLIV (June, 1957), 29–57.

HAROLD J. BARNETT

MALTHUSIANISM AND CONSERVATION: THEIR ROLE AS ORIGINS OF THE DOCTRINE OF INCREASING ECONOMIC SCARCITY OF NATURAL RESOURCES

Social Importance

The belief is held in contemporary society that there is an imbalance of some kind between economic availability of natural resources and population growth. More specifically, the view is that natural resources are economically scarce, and that this impairs economic growth. The view is not confined to any one group. In varied forms it is voiced by numerous professions and intellectual disciplines. In significant degree it may be said that "public opinion" subscribes to one form or another of a doctrine of economic scarcity of resources.

Two of America's leading physicians, for example, have expressed themselves forcefully on the economic scarcity of natural resources relative to human numbers and goods consumption. The late Dr. Allen Gregg, Director of the Rockefeller Foundation medical division, has queried, "Is Man a Biological Cancer?"

> There is an alarming parallel between the growth of a cancer in the body of an organism and the growth of human population in the earth's ecological economy. If this idea is valid, and if man is indeed hurrying off to such a macabre "summit," humanity should now face the question of an optimum population, not only in terms of politics and economics, but in terms of a more healthy relationship between the human species and other forms of life on the planet Earth.[1]

Dr. A. J. Carlson posed the same dilemma in earthier simile:

> The number one problem facing man today and tomorrow is overpopulation and starvation. Two-thirds of the people in our world are poorly nourished. Almost half of mankind—a billion people—are actually starving. Despite this tragic situation, the world population is increasing by about 75,000 per day, that is, we have that many births above deaths. If we breed like rabbits, in the long run we have to live and die like rabbits.[2]

Other leading life scientists have also spoken out about resource economic scarcity and its adverse consequences for economic welfare and growth. Sir Charles Galton Darwin[3] is quite pessimistic. He believes that society as a whole will tend to breed without limit. And, further, it is precisely the poorest intellectual stock, he believes, which will breed at high rates. Given scarce natural resources, the result is

• Harold J. Barnett is Chairman of the Department of Economics, Washington University.

Reprinted from *Demographic and Economic Change in Developed Countries*, Universities-National Bureau Committee for Economic Research, Special Conference Series No. 11 (Princeton: Princeton University Press, 1960), pp. 423–56, with the permission of the author and the publisher.

1 Gregg, "Hidden Hunger at the Summit," *Population Bulletin*, XI, No. 5 (1955), 74. Summary of a speech to the American Association for the Advancement of Science.

2 Carlson, "Science Versus Life," *Journal of the American Medical Association*, CLVII (April 16, 1955), 1437–41.

3 Darwin, *The Next Million Years* (London: R. Hart Davies, 1952).

a tendency of civilization relatively to proliferate its lesser quality specimens and to shrink the numbers of its abler ones. The "weak" shall inherit the earth. In America, Paul Sears, Fairfield Osborn, and William Vogt have been influential expositors of the natural resource scarcity–population growth dilemma. Mr. Osborn closes one of his books with:

> We are under the power of a timeless principle, exerting its influence relentlessly on a global scale. This principle . . . finds expression in a simple ratio wherein the numerator can be defined as "resources of the earth" and the denominator as "numbers of people.' The numerator is *relatively* fixed and only partially subject to control by man. The denominator is subject . . . to control by man. If we are blind to this law, or delude ourself into minimizing its power, of one thing we can be assured—the human race will enter into days of increasing trouble, conflict, and darkness.[4]

Professor Sears is more moderate and philosophical in his statements. But Mr. Vogt, on the other hand, is even stronger in his views:

> . . . unless population control and conservation are included, other means [to save the world] are certain to fail. . . .[5]
>
> We must adjust our demand to the supply, either by accepting less per capita (lowering our living standards) or by maintaining less people. Since our civilization cannot survive a drastic lowering of standards, we cannot escape the need for population *cuts*.[6]
>
> Population "experts" say that, given time, populations will level off and stabilize themselves. To this the obvious answer is, *there is not time*.[7]

Outstanding people from the other physical sciences have also hewn to the view of a population-natural resources conflict. For example, Harrison Brown has . . . written:

> A substantial fraction of humanity today is behaving . . . as if it were engaged in a contest to test nature's willingness to support humanity, and if it had its way, it would not rest content until the earth is covered completely and to a considerable depth with a writhing mass of human beings, much as a dead cow is covered with a pulsating mass of maggots.[8]

Similar views are widespread among social scientists, although perhaps less so than among the physical ones. We find (ignoring for the moment, economists and demographers) expressions from political scientists, sociologists, the legal profession, and other social disciplines. Occasionally, the expressions are of alarm or urgency; and occasionally they are as simple and straightforward as some of the physical scientists' expressions in flatly asserting a contradiction between a limited earth and a burgeoning population and standard of living. For example, lawyer Samuel Ordway, in his recent book,[9] is not less forceful than the above quotations. Usually, however, the social scientists' expressions are rather more hedged or complicated on the conflict between natural resource scarcity and economic growth. Examples are recent writings of Lyle Craine, Luther Gulick, Ernest Griffith, and J. O. Hertzler, among others.[10]

I therefore conclude that the social importance of the doctrine of natural resource scarcity is demonstrated in the simple fact of widespread belief in one form or another of the proposition. The views represent a substantial segment of public opinion. As

[4] Osborn, *Limits of the Earth* (Boston: Little Brown & Co., 1953), pp. 206–7; italics in original.

[5] Vogt, *Road to Survival* (New York: Wm. Sloane, Inc., 1948), p. 264.

[6] *Ibid.*, p. 265; italics added.

[7] *Ibid.*, p. 282; italics in the original.

[8] Brown, *Challenge of Man's Future* (New York: Viking Press, 1954), p. 221.

[9] Ordway, *Resources and the American Dream* (New York: The Ronald Press, 1953).

[10] Craine, "Natural Resources and Government," *Public Administration Review,* XVI (Summer, 1956), 212–22; Gulick, "The City's Challenge in Resource Use," *Perspectives on Conservation,* ed. H. Jarrett (Baltimore: Johns Hopkins Press for Resources for the Future, Inc., 1958); Griffith, "Main Lines of Conservation Thought and Action," *ibid.*; Hertzler, *The Crisis in World Population* (Lincoln: University of Nebraska Press, 1956).

accepted intellectual views, they are taught in the public schools.[11]

But the social importance of the doctrine of natural resource scarcity goes beyond the fact of wide public belief. In many countries, the public beliefs have, rather naturally, found expression in laws, creation of agencies, and modes of governmental (and private) behavior. In this country major parts of the platforms of both political parties concern policies for scarce natural resources. Public policies based upon the doctrine of natural resource scarcity are, in part, responsible for federal or state land reclamation programs, resource reservation practices, and controls on rates of use of some natural resources. Prominent examples are forest reservations, limitations on the use of oil and gas, and preferential tax treatment in certain natural resources industries. Foreign countries also have public policies resulting from natural resource scarcity views. Among recent developments, the situation of the oil-rich countries is particularly interesting. The problem here is sometimes visualized as that of managing petroleum reserves so as to assure economic transformation of the underdeveloped countries before the reserves run out.[12]

Thus, it would appear that the doctrine of natural resource scarcity relative to population growth and economic development is an important social question for two reasons: because thoughtful public opinion views it as such; and because public policies are being formed, in part with these public views as their origin.

11 See, for example, American Association of School Administrators, *Conservation Education in American Schools* (Washington: National Education Assn., 1958).

12 C. Kindleberger, "Exhaustible Resources, Foreign Trade and Foreign Investment," mimeographed; S. V. Ciriacy-Wantrup, *Resource Conservation—Economics and Policies* (Berkeley and Los Angeles: University of California Press, 1952); A. Scott, *Natural Resources: The Economics of Conservation* (Toronto: University of Toronto Press, 1955).

Contemporary Economist and Demographer Writings

In general, so far as I have been able to tell, economists and demographers are not in the vanguard of alarmed writers on the natural resources-growth dilemma. In this sense their views are similar to those already characterized for other social scientists. Here, also, there are exceptions, such as demographer Robert Cook, editor of the *Population Bulletin,* and there are probably others known to the professional demographers. . . . Among economists, it is possible to interpret some . . . pieces by Joseph Spengler and Henry Villard as exceptions; my own view, however, is that these articles are not, in fact, calls for urgent action, but, rather, forceful presentations of natural resources–population dilemma.[13]

Although probably not alarmed concerning natural resource scarcity, economists (and, so far as I know, demographers) also generally see natural resource economic scarcity as a drag on economic advance. The advance in output per capita from technological improvement and other reasons is subject to a degree of offset from this scarcity. In economic writings exceptions to the idea of limited natural resources as an obstacle to growth are very few. So far as I know, the strongest appear in Erich Zimmermann's monumental work.[14] Other exceptions take the form primarily of denying major importance to this negative influence, rather than quarrelling with its presence. For example, George Stigler . . . states:

> A larger economy should be more efficient than a small economy; this has been the standard view of economists since the one important disadvantage of the large economy, di-

13 J. Spengler, "Population Threatens Prosperity," *Harvard Business Review* (January–February, 1956); H. Villard, "Some Notes on Population and Living Levels," *The Review of Business and Economic Statistics* (May, 1955).

14 Zimmermann, *World Resources and Industries* (New York: Harper & Bros., 1950), particularly chap. 50.

minishing returns to natural resources, has proved to be unimportant.[15]

Similar derogations of the significance of an adverse natural resources influence in modern industrial societies, although less flatly stated, appear in writings of E. S. Mason and Harold Moulton.[16] In general, however, the major body of literature takes seriously the retarding force of natural resources scarcity, as an important obstacle in economic growth—for example, the thoughtful book by Horace Belshaw.[17]

In view of wide belief that economic scarcity of resources in fact impairs economic growth in modern societies, it might be thought that it has been theoretically and empirically proved. But this is not the case. Rather, the proposition is assumed to be a factual statement. Either it is considered sufficiently obvious to need no proof, or else there is simple reference to "Conservation" or the "Malthusian dilemma." Elsewhere, Chandler Morse and I have examined the economic theory of natural resource scarcity as an impediment to growth.[18] And, elsewhere, I have argued it is an hypothesis, not a fact, and made a preliminary and exploratory empirical analysis of whether it is possible to observe any development of resource scarcity in the United States economy between 1870 and 1956.[19] The results of these efforts, so far, have not removed my uncertainty as to whether there is necessarily, in a growing modern economy, a development of natural resource scarcity which operates to retard economic growth and threaten future economic welfare.

Stimulated by this finding for modern industrial societies, I have set myself the task of trying to chase down and examine the origins of the natural resource scarcity doctrine. Perhaps by examination of the doctrine *in situ,* I can find elaboration which will show, as modern writing does not, under what circumstances the widespread belief is justified, or which will at least explain why the belief is widespread.

In economic literature, the principal lead for such historical investigation is what has been termed the "first American conservation movement." So closely has natural resource scarcity doctrine been identified with this movement that the terms "conservation problem" and "natural resource scarcity" are frequently used as synonyms, the former being the more common. For example, two of the major professional books on the economics of natural resources are titled *Resource Conservation—Economics and Policies* (S. V. Ciriacy-Wantrup) and *Natural Resources: The Economics of Conservation* (A. Scott). Professor A. C. Pigou, in his statement that the natural resource scarcity problem generates a danger which justifies public policy concern, also points to the conservation movement for authority:

> But there is wide agreement that the State should protect the interests of the future *in some degree* against the effects of our irrational discounting and of our preference for ourselves over our descendants. The whole movement for "conservation" in the United States is based on this conviction. It is the clear duty of Government, which is the trustee for unborn generations, as well as for its present citizens, to watch over, and, if need be, by legislative enactment, to defend, the exhaustible natural resources of the country from rash and reckless spoilation.[20]

15 Stigler in a paper presented at the Conference on Income and Wealth, National Bureau of Economic Research, October 17–18, 1958.

16 Mason, "An American View of Raw Materials Problems," *Journal of Industrial Economics,* I, No. 1 (1952); Moulton, *Controlling Factors in Economic Development* (Washington: The Brookings Institution, 1959).

17 Belshaw, *Population Growth and Levels of Consumption* (London: George Allen & Unwin, 1956).

18 Morse and Barnett, *Scarcity and Growth* (Baltimore: Johns Hopkins Press for Resources for the Future, Inc., 1963).

19 Barnett, "Measurement of Natural Resource Scarcity and Its Economic Effects," paper presented to Conference on Research in Income and Wealth, October 17–18, 1958.

20 Pigou, *Economics of Welfare* (London: Macmillan & Co., 1946), pp. 29–30; italics in the original.

In general, I think most American economists believe that conservation is concerned with the problem of economic scarcity of natural resources relative to economic welfare and growth.

Among non-economists, the signal pointing to the conservation movement as a means of understanding the problem of natural resource scarcity and economic growth is even stronger. Leading expositors of the resource scarcity view today, in fact, frequently see themselves as descendants of the first conservation movement and inheritors of its reform mission.

Contemporary demographic and economic literature also suggests going back a hundred years earlier and examining Malthus, for inquiry into the origins of the resource scarcity-growth doctrine. Such indication comes up particularly in connection with analyses of economic development in the so-called backward nations.

Malthus

An elementary statement of the Malthusian view of economic scarcity of natural resources and the retardation of growth therefrom is about as follows. The doctrine of natural resource scarcity and its economic effect reflect natural law. By the laws of nature, natural resources are limited and population multiplies. In the absence of social preventive checks, population increases to the limits of subsistence. The limits of nature constitute scarcity, and the dynamic economic tendency toward subsistence levels of living is economic scarcity effect. The dynamics of economic growth are thus dominated by scarcity of natural resources and the law of population growth.

With respect to natural resource scarcity, Malthus believed,

> Man is necessarily confined in room. When acre has been added to acre till all the fertile land is occupied, the yearly increase of food must depend upon the melioration of the land already in possession. This is a fund, which, from the nature of all soils, instead of increasing, must be gradually diminishing.[21]

With respect to the law of population growth, Malthus believed that there is

> the constant tendency in all animated life to increase beyond the nourishment prepared for it[22] . . . population invariably increases where the means of subsistence increase.[23]

The theory was, thus, that man's propensity for breeding was in conflict with the world's limited natural resource availability, and his ability to extract economic goods therefrom.

Is Malthus the originator of the doctrine? It appears clear from the *Essay* that his generalization of the problem of population pressure on scarce natural resources derived more from the contemporary policy problem of the Poor Laws, and from social observation and empirical analysis, than from purely abstract thought. In part, the social conditions of the time generated his ideas, and the ideas were thereby unlikely to be wholly new.[24]

Keynes in his sympathetic biography of Malthus states that, "his leading idea had been largely anticipated in a clumsier way by other eighteenth-century writers."[25] In Malthus, then, we do not find the origin of the doctrine that resource scarcity restrains economic growth, but rather a clear and forceful statement on an attractive generalized level.

It is also possible to quarrel with the characterization of Malthusianism as the origin of subsequent doctrine on natural resource scarcity and effect on three other grounds. First, it may be charged that the *Essay* is far more an analysis of population

21 Malthus, *An Essay on the Principles of Population* (London: Ward, Lock & Co., 1890), p. 4.

22 *Ibid.*, p. 2.

23 *Ibid.*, p. 14.

24 I have also examined other historical writings as possible keys to the resource scarcity gospel. Some of these—particularly works of Ricardo, Mill, G. P. Marsh, and W. S. Jevons—I have found to be of equal or greater importance as origins of the doctrine.

25 J. M. Keynes, *Essays in Biography* (Chester Springs, Pa.: Dufour, 1950), p. 100.

than of natural resources, and that natural resource scarcity and effect are more asserted than demonstrated. Second, it may be stated that while the Malthusian doctrine describes a natural resource scarcity effect upon economic *growth,* it does not entail an economic scarcity effect in a stationary society. And, third, Malthus apparently did not raise the problem of depletion at all. All of these points are valid. Their implications, however, do not deny to the Malthus *Essay* the role of intellectual parent of the family of subsequent views on natural resource scarcity and its economic effect. But they do suggest that resource scarcity doctrine has developed since Malthus.

Although for its subject matter the Malthusian theory far surpassed its contemporaries in logic, precision, and clarity, it is not a complete statement, in the modern economic model sense, of the relation of natural resources to economic growth. It is useful to attempt the construction of such a model, by using his text as a basis for filling in gaps and providing a modern formulation.

STATIC MODEL

First, there is posited a social production function consistent with Malthus' view:

$$O = F\ (R, L, C)$$

where O is physical national output, R is physical quantity of natural resources employed, L is physical quantity of labor employed, and C is physical quantity of capital employed. The functional relationship is a description of all possible efficient combinations of the inputs to product output with given techniques and social parameters. Each of the variables—the three inputs and the output—is either homogeneous in quality, or is characterized by an invariant frequency distribution of quality. This difficult assumption is necessary if the function is to be a meaningful, precise mathematical statement.

In order to yield a specific output figure under these conditions, the availability of natural resources, labor, and capital and the extent of their employments must be specified. Under Malthusian assumptions, as they are simplified and imputed to him for exposition here, the following may be specified as the availability and employment rules. The quantity of available natural resource is fixed; natural resources are indestructible. The available quantities of each of labor and capital are variable. If fully employed, labor's marginal productivity equals subsistence, and capital's marginal productivity will be positive. If natural resources are free and not yet fully employed, their marginal productivity will be zero. Once they are fully employed, marginal productivity will become positive. Reservation policies in supply of any factor from existing stock may be adopted for institutional, psychological, or other reasons. Since these would affect marginal productivities, let it be assumed that each individual reservation policy, if adopted, is persistent and independent of the other reservation policies.

The form of the Malthusian static social production function is required to be such that the marginal productivities of labor and capital individually and together are monotonically declining. And, therefore, the second partial derivatives of output with respect to labor, capital, or both, are negative.

GROWTH MODEL

The final conditions are those needed to convert the above Malthusian static model into a Malthusian growth one. That is, we need rules for changes in factor quantities and in technological and institutional parameters. For simplicity, the labor force, may be assumed to be a fixed proportion of population. The population level, in turn, increases exponentially as a function of time, subject to two biological constraints. Its rate of increase may not exceed that permited by a maximum biological rate of reproduction characteristic of human females (increase from improved longevity is thus ignored); and the level of population may not exceed that set by the biological minimum of food and other subsistence goods required to sustain life. Capital availability increases no faster than population. Natural resource availability is invariant. And technology and institutional conditions are invariant. Finally, we need a time horizon, and for this we assume a very long term. This completes the Malthusian long-term growth model.

In summary, the Malthusian growth model constructed here has five conditions:

a) A very long term.
b) An exponential population increase function; and appropriate limits on capital increase.
c) Given natural resources.
d) Unchanging technology and institutional conditions.
e) Homogeneous or constant-composition input and output variables; a law of variable proportions (eventually diminishing marginal productivity) for labor and capital applicable to this static *social production function,* as stated above under "Static Model."

This model is illustrated in Charts 1 and 2. If resource stock is fixed at r_1 and the whole stock is employed, then output increases less than in proportion to increases in labor plus capital. The output expansion path is *EHM*. As labor and capital increase from a_1, their marginal productivity $[\Delta O/\Delta (L+C)]$ declines steadily, reaching zero when labor + capital are equal to a_2. The decline in output per capita from o_1/a_1 to o_2/a_2 may never be reached, since the latter figure may be below the level of subsistence. Or, if o_2/a_2 is above subsistence, population will continue to grow

CHART 1

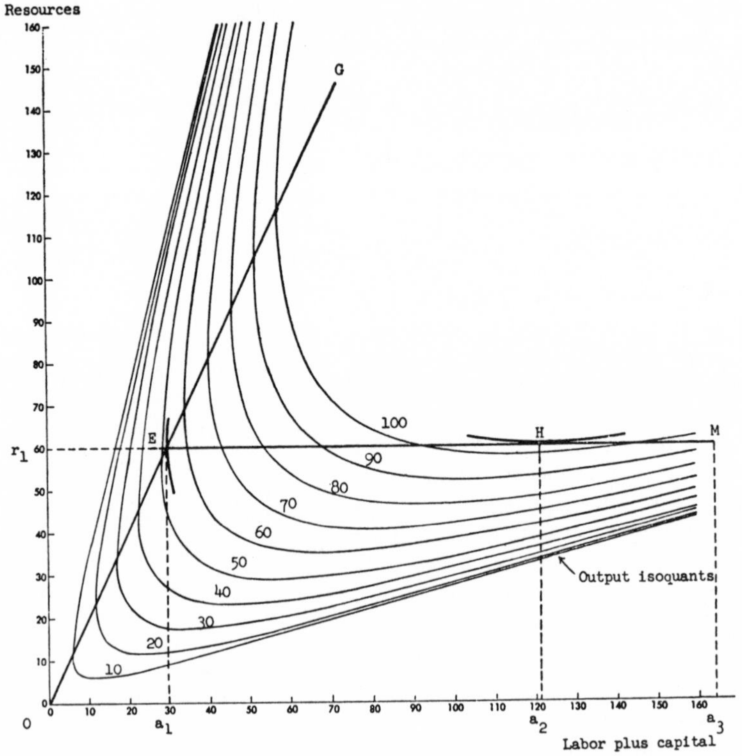

CHART 2

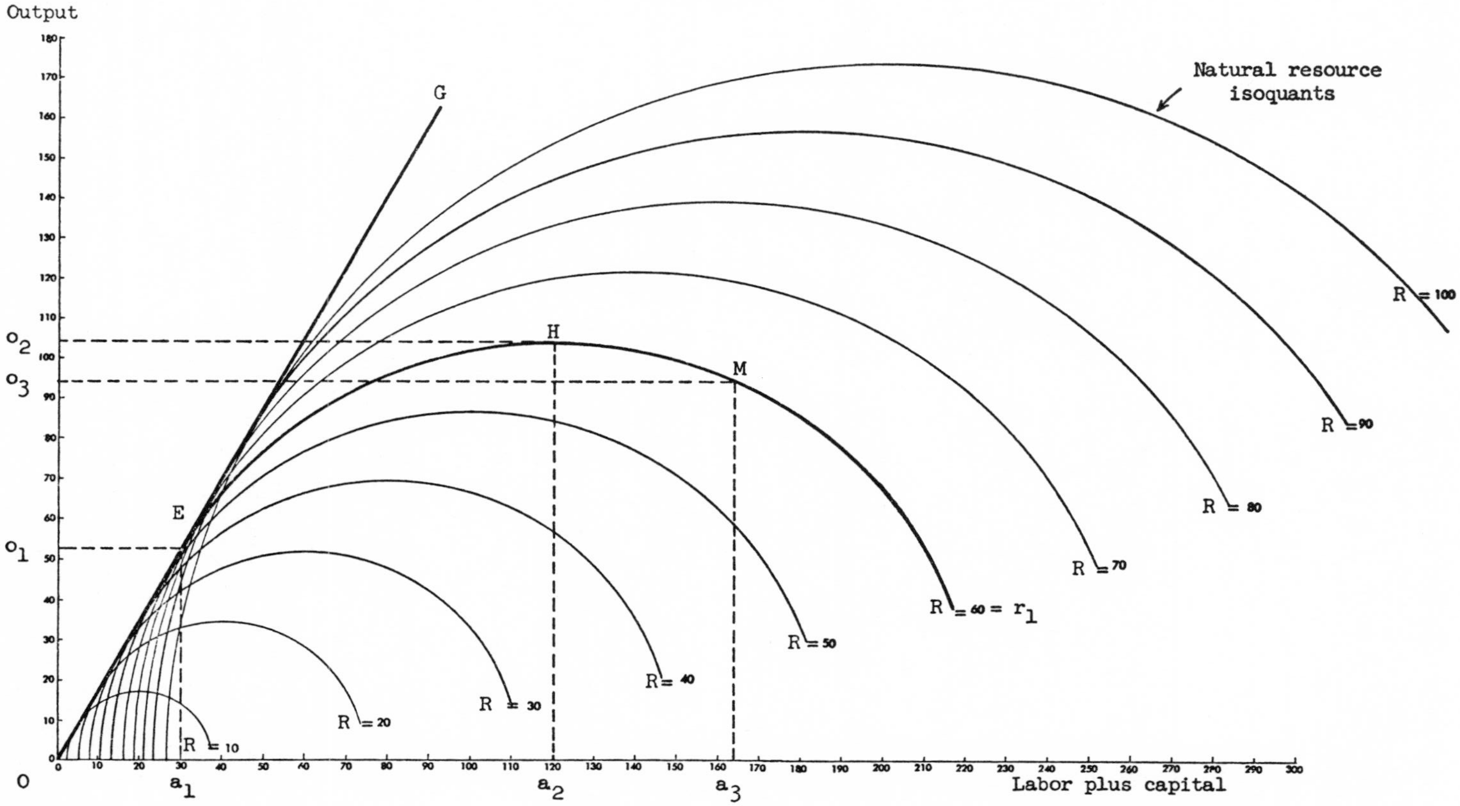

Output
Natural resource
isoquants
G
H
M
E
o_2
o_3
o_1
O
a_1
a_2
a_3
Labor plus capital
R = 10
R = 20
R = 30
R = 40
R = 50
R = 60 = r_1
R = 70
R = 80
R = 90
R = 100

even though output declines, so that eventual stable output might be o_3; then output per capita will be at subsistence, at o_3/a_3, a level below o_2/a_2. Thus while we are sure that output growth will cease someplace on the path *EHM*, we don't know at which point unless we can define subsistence. Note that alternative social definitions of subsistence are possible.

The charts show that the assumed conditions inevitably produce resource scarcity *eventually*. But they also show that the mere definition of a fixed physical world is not, in itself, economic scarcity of resources. To be economically scarce, the fixed natural resources must be of *small* amount relative to $L+C$ and the sociotechnical parameters. In the charts "small" is defined as an amount less than r_1/a_1. From this it follows that while a fixed world (or universe) always contains a *threat* of resource economic scarcity, nevertheless onset of scarcity depends on the other conditions as well. So long as resources are large enough to permit output expansion along the path *OEG*, resource economic scarcity is not yet experienced.[26]

If economic growth is defined as increasing output, then Malthusianism is a simple, extreme case of a general hypothesis of inhibition of economic growth from limited natural resources. The beginning state of the model is irrelevant to the eventual outcome of population being limited by food subsistence. Timing of the outcome, however, is influenced by the beginning state. Any outside disturbance in effect creates a new beginning state. If the closed model is disturbed by, for example, improved technology, the Malthusian limitation will at that point be avoided. But provided the impulse is a "one-shot" affair, the economy will absorb the impact of the disturbance and immediately thereafter again trend toward a new Malthusian equilibrium combination of total output, population and subsistence levels of living.

As indicated, the conditions described are *sufficient* for an eventual Malthusian outcome of subsistence living and cessation of economic growth, namely stable population and no increase in output per capita. The following five classes of conditions are also *necessary:*

a) It is only in the very long term that the model necessarily operates to its equilibrium solution. In a short term, there can be economic growth, since resources do *not* become scarce until the ratio of population to resources rises beyond a critical level (a_1/r_1 in the charts).

b) Except for persistent population increase and appropriate limits on rate of capital increase, there is not necessarily sufficient labor to drive to the limit of subsistence average returns. The critical population/resources level has to be reached via population growth. And of course Malthus' "exponential rate" of population increase and my assumption of capital increase at the same rate yield one case of such growth.

c) Except for limited natural resources, output could rise as fast as, or faster than, population. And, of course, Malthus' "fixed land" is one case which satisfies "limited natural resources."

d) Only when the rate of technological and organizational advance is too slow to offset the declining marginal returns to population increase would output per capita be forced down to the subsistence level. And, of course, "fixed technology and institutions" satisfies this condition.

e) Except for diminishing marginal returns to labor and capital in the social production function, social output could increase as fast as, or faster than, labor and capital additions.

26 The charts are drawn to follow R. G. D. Allen's "more general normal type" of production function, *Mathematical Analysis for Economists* (London: Macmillan & Co., 1947), p. 288. In my charts, $O = [2H\ (L + C)\ R = A\ (L + C)^2 = B(R)^2]^{1/2}$, where $H = 2$ and $A = B = 1$.

It is also apparent, however, that while each of these classes of conditions is necessary, the particular conditions are not. The specifications of *particular* conditions I have given (exponential population growth, fixed land, etc.) are more stringent than absolutely necessary for Malthus' conclusions. Some insight into this question is developed below.

STRATEGIC VARIABLES AND SENSITIVITY

That the five types of conditions are necessary for the Malthusian scarcity model is an important truth, frequently overlooked. The dynamic forces which tend to coerce economic evolution toward Malthus' conclusion are sometimes viewed as a population problem; or a natural resource problem; or a race between technology and population; or in still other simplified ways. Such simplifications do not, of course, deny the existence of the other relations characterized here as necessary; but frequently these relations are admitted only implicitly or not recognized at all. Further, incomplete specification of the entire model permits implicit introduction of other assumptions and views. These latter are sometimes dangerous to sensible analysis, and are partly responsible for a fraction of nonsense in resources literature.

The conditions required for the Malthusian scarcity effect, which is known as the Malthusian dilemma, constitute a multivariable, dynamic model, containing the variables and kinds of relations described. Every one of them, as we have seen, is potentially important. Yet it is true that if one makes certain assumptions, certain of the variables and conditions become unimportant, while others become dominant or strategic.

TIME HORIZON

The assumption concerning time horizon (*a* above) is extremely prejudicial to the question of which variables are strategic. Let an extremely "long-term" be assumed as the setting for the analysis. Then the entire outcome of the Malthus model hangs on whether or not the annual rate of population increase *exceeds zero*—depends, that is, on whether or not population more than reproduces itself, however minutely. Population is the strategic variable, and given a finite world the population equation is virtually the only important relation. Assume, for example, a net reproduction rate of 0.016, very roughly the present world rate, a considerable part of which is due to improved longevity. This involves a birth rate less than half of the rate to which Malthus' empirical work led him. Then the world population would increase *one hundred-fold* in 290 years, and *one thousand-fold* in 435 years. Let the annual net reproducing rate be still lower—set it at 0.001, about 1/30 of Malthus' finding. Then the long-term doom from scarcity is only deferred. The 2.5 billion living bodies of 1950 generate

25 billion in A.D. 4,300, a ten-fold increase,
250 billion in A.D. 6,600, a hundred-fold increase, and
2,500 billion in A.D. 8,900, a thousand-fold increase.

And this numbers game may be played without end, *with an unspecified long-term horizon.* We observe, therefore, that if implicitly the time horizon is a very long or endless one, then given only that we live in a finite universe, the crucial question is whether net rate of reproduction is positive, for this makes ultimate population boundless. No other question is very relevant: technological change, capital formation, utilization of the depths of the earth or its atmosphere and solar energy, etc., are submerged in people and endless time. If time is infinite, so is population; and if time is extremely long, then population is extremely large.

Now let the time horizon be a closer one—25, 50, even 100 years. If the present annual net reproduction rate of about 0.016 is continued, the following world populations result at decade intervals:

Year	World Population (in Billions)
1950.	2.5
1960.	2.9
1970.	3.4
1980.	4.0
1990.	4.7
2000.	5.5
2010.	6.5
2020.	7.6
2030.	8.9
2040.	10.4
2050.	12.2

For these shorter periods the population variable no longer nullifies the other terms in the model. For the earlier part of the 100 years, population level may be less significant than availability of advanced technology and capital for the lower income areas of the world; employment of new lands, intensity of land use, and availability of chemical fertilizers; institutional arrangements for domestic and international trade and exchange; and other conditions. Even for the latter 50 years, population level would not appear to be obviously dominant. It is no longer enough to define scarcity as a finite world, as Malthus did. It becomes necessary to ask how great or how little a volume of resources constitutes economic scarcity.

RATE OF POPULATION INCREASE

We now discuss the second necessary condition of the Malthus model—annual rate of population increase (r). The annual rate of net population reproduction is important for economic growth over moderately distant time periods. This is demonstrated in the following table:

WORLD POPULATION (IN BILLIONS)

	$r=0.03$ (Malthus)	$r=0.016$ (Present)	$r=0.001$
1950.	2.5	2.5	2.50
1975.	5.2	3.7	2.57
2000.	11.0	5.5	2.63
2025.	22.9	8.2	2.69
2050.	48.0	12.2	2.77

If explicitly or implicitly one uses the Malthus rate, then Malthus was surely right. Population *is* the strategic variable for periods longer than 50 years or so. On the other hand, one might be inclined to project the present rate of world population increase, a far lower rate than Malthus', and partly reflecting increased life-span. Then population must be considered, but other elements may not be neglected, as they were by Malthus. If one posits $r=0.001$, then population is not a significant variable, and may be neglected.

For Malthus the population function is independent of level of consumption (or output), except that consumption per capita may not be less than subsistence levels. This was central and explicit to Malthus' analysis and conclusion, and is necessary to them. For if, in consequence of increase in income per capita, the birth rate should fall, scarcity and scarcity effect can conceivably be avoided. Natural resource scarcity and only some of the other conditions are not sufficient for the Malthus model; it is required that population *not* vary inversely with income.

It may now be seen why Malthus emphasized the population level. For unchecked $r=0.03$ is a monstrous force. Population multiplies by almost 20 in the first century, by about 2.5 million in the fifth, and by the year A.D. 3,000 the population mass would exceed the earth's, and if closely packed would be five times as bulky.[27] If Malthus did believe $r=0.03$, then the relative neglect of other variables is understandable. For in this case and given a finite world, none of the other variables is important.

NATURAL RESOURCE AVAILABILITY

The third condition for Malthus formulation is limited economic availability of

[27] It is noted that *any* positive rate of population increase will do these things if one's time horizon is distant enough. Villard, *op. cit.*, observed that the *present* world net reproduction rate would yield a population size equal to the weight of the earth in only a couple thousand years or so.

natural resources. So far as I can tell, this assumption derived directly from the fact that the world's agricultural lands were of limited physical extent.

Several questions may be asked. Was Malthus unaware that agricultural land varied in economic quality? Malthus *was* aware that agricultural land was not homogeneous. But this was not important to his theory and practical concern over conflict between the "natural" birth rate and the global limits of all agricultural land. His thesis was the basic and ultimate inconsistency between a natural birth rate tending to double population each 25 years and the food availability from the limited agricultural territory, the earth. For him there was no question but that the unhomogeneity of land could be ignored. The fixed agricultural land of the globe meant natural resource scarcity. In his own words, "what is true . . . in reference to a single farm, must necessarily be true of the whole earth, from which the necessities of life for the actual population are derived."[28]

Was Malthus unaware that there were natural resources other than land? His *Essay* hardly mentions them, but we may be sure he was aware of them. But, again, they could be ignored, for the reason given above, and also because his society was primarily an agricultural one, whose major problem was food for subsistence.

These oversimplifications do not disturb me. The mark of good theory is not that it describes reality completely, in all respects faithfully, but that it captures only the essence of only that part of reality which is under consideration. Good theory, like art, simplifies, abstracts, and highlights. The proper question is whether Malthus believed his theory and conditions to be essentially accurate. And to this, the answer is certainly that he did.

TECHNOLOGY AND INSTITUTIONS

Malthus assumed that technology and economic organization were, if not fixed, at least not subject to radical change. But the beginnings of the industrial revolution were observable about Malthus even when he wrote the first *Essay,* and there was significant industrial advance as he went through successive editions. In the *Essay* he comments, for example, on the remarkable advances in productivity in textiles. Was it solely because his estimate of r that technological change was given so little attention? There is no way of knowing for certain, of course. An $r = 0.03$ is sufficient reason for ignoring technological change. But, in addition, it would have required prophetic genius, rather than analytical brilliance, for Malthus to appreciate the significance of such phenomena as technological change. The phenomena which entirely transform the equations of the Malthus model are advances which did not take place until after the study was completed and his conclusions had congealed. The important ones are the increase in biological and chemical knowledge, development of the earth sciences, the industrial applications of such knowledge, and the recent atomic energy advances. Such events as Wohler's synthesis of urea, the discovery of cell composition of living things, Liebig's advances in organic chemistry, Mendeleev's periodic table, Mendel's laws, Pasteur's bacteriological discoveries, and the great biological, chemical, and nuclear advances which followed did not take place until much later. Without these advances there was no reason for Malthus to doubt man's dependence upon naturally fertile soil; to doubt applicability of a principle of diminishing returns to increments of population; or to place much confidence in man's ability to limit procreation, since in Malthus' view this required sexual continence. It is only with access to the above and other technological changes that, concurrent with striking increases in ouput per capita and food availability, r begins to decline, land perhaps ceases to be economically fixed, dependence on natural agricultural fertility diminishes sharply, and the single industry principle of diminishing

[28] D. V. Glass (ed.), *Introduction to Malthus* (New York: John Wiley & Sons, 1953), p. 145.

returns, while a truism in a static model, may become anachronistic with respect to changing social output and economic growth.

LAW OF DIMINISHING RETURNS

The last of the five conditions that concerns us here is "the law of diminishing returns"; the condition as defined earlier is a necessary one for Malthusian results. The degree of importance and the sensitivity of the results are empirical questions which are left for separate study. What is necessary at this point is that some of the confusion in what the "law" is be cleared away. It must be realized that the diminishing returns principle which is required by the Malthusian formulation is *not* the one which *modern* economists view as a natural (although abstract) law; i.e., the Malthusian condition is not our familiar, well-accepted, necessarily true "law" at all. There are a considerable number of quite different propositions of diminishing returns extant.[29] I discuss here four which are seemingly or actually embodied in the Malthusian dynamic model.

One of the diminishing returns propositions is the *end result* of the Malthusian economic growth model. Any simple statement of output behavior in the Malthusian theory seems to be itself a statement of the diminishing returns principle. For example, thus: during economic growth, output increases less than in proportion to the increase of population. But despite historical sanction, it is really inappropriate to use the diminishing returns term so. As already described, the Malthusian economic growth model in the most sparse form we could state it is a complex of five quite separate types of conditions, all necessary, so that it is misleading to imply that it is a singular principle, and to cloak it with the validity today credited to the "law of diminishing returns." I labor the point not for professional economists, who are no longer much given to the practice, but for noneconomists.

A second "diminishing returns" proposition, which is *not* required in my Malthusian formulation, is *static model diminishing returns to social scale*. This proposition, according to modern usage, is that if all factor input quantities are increased proportionately, output will increase by lesser degree. Thus, the social production function is such that if factor inputs are doubled, output will less than double. This is unnecessary to the Malthus model I have constructed. He did not need this condition because in his *dynamic* model he built in the severe limitation of no increase of the factor land. With this model, one cannot ask whether outputs will double if all inputs are doubled, since his land input is fixed.

A third principle of diminishing returns, the true "law" of economics, is the static law of variable proportions applied to a homogeneous (or invariant composition) output and individually homogeneous (or invariant composition) inputs. This states, for the production of individual commodities, under invariant socio-technical conditions, that after some point additions of a single factor will yield diminishing marginal returns. Formulated rigorously, this is a provable proposition; it is law.

However, the Malthusian model doesn't use *this* universally acceptable assumption, but rather a fourth proposition which is a dubious modification of it. Malthus requires that the principle be applicable to a whole economy, i.e., to a *social* production function. The condition for the Malthus model is that in a static *social* production function the marginal productivity of each factor is monotonically declining, and the second partial derivatives are negative. The point, briefly, is that the *social* production function, as distinct from a commodity one, involves unhomogeneous outputs, technologies, and inputs. Recourse to the homely case of limits of ability to raise wheat with men and horses on an acre

[29] See, for example, T. Schultz, "Diminishing Returns in View of Progress in Agricultural Production," *Journal of Farm Economics* (October, 1932), pp. 640–49.

must be viewed as an analogy, not proof, unless the social production function produces only wheat with acres, men, and horses. This is not the place to elaborate on the difference between a commodity production function and a social one. But its importance is illustrated by the fact that the difference is major in accounting for so-called external economies.

My interest in this diminishing returns discussion has been in establishing that: (*a*) there are a good many views of diminishing returns; (*b*) only one of them (the third, above) is the accepted law of diminishing returns; (*c*) this one is not the Malthusian condition; (*d*) the Malthusian condition is of uncertain validity.

The First Conservation Movement

"Conservation," a coined term, was a part of the "Progressive" political reform platform of the Theodore Roosevelt presidential period. It was also a social movement underlying that political reform effort. Conservation doctrine, it is true, began with a focus on natural resources. But with the success of the political activity in which it was embedded, the doctrine was quickly broadened to include other social welfare ideas of the Progressive political program. In terms of ideas, conservation was a wide-ranging assemblage of views concerning all the individual natural sciences, economics, political science, public administration, sociology, engineering, art, and public health.

To see it as a political program and a successful and practical political power makes clear features of conservation which are otherwise difficult to understand. It has contradictions, just as the later Roosevelt's New Deal had an NRA "big business" program in the midst of its policies of benefit for the "little man." How does it happen that the conservation movement moved from natural resources to doctrine and policies on immigration, anti-industrialization, trustbusting, pure food laws, child labor, Anglo-Saxon supremacy, etc.? One clue here is that it was a successful political movement; these and their architects are rarely consistent in thought or action. Was the conservation movement dominated by its leaders and flavored by their personalities, rather than intellectually led and constructed with scholarly rigor? To ask is to answer: was there ever a successful political movement which was not? Were there manipulation, power alliances, scare propaganda, and other behavior different from the high personal-life ethics of conservation leaders? Again, of course there were—this was American politics. For example, Theodore Roosevelt blanketed in 75 million acres of forests to the control of Pinchot's Forest Service by outmaneuvering Congress: between the time that Congress passed a bill to revoke the President's authority to create new forest reserves and the time of Roosevelt's signature, he created new national forests of this volume.[30] As a successful political movement, conservation was opportunistic, expedient, and compromising in high degree.

Conservation was thus the banner of a crusading political march led by one of the most able, vigorous, and successful Presidents of our time, during the tenure of his office and his peak of power. Much of conservation's history and contributions can be understood in this light, and much will not be understood otherwise. If it was a political and social movement, then, as a corollary, it was not simply a set of consistent ideas. We need this insight to understand its unhomogeneous support and membership; its dynamism of subject matter, approach, and goals; and its metamorphosis, senescence, and relative decline after its incandescent years.

As it was a successful political and social movement in American national life, so conservation could not be revolutionary in

[30] S. Hays, "The First American Conservation Movement, 1890–1920," pp. 84–85. This unpublished Harvard doctoral dissertation (1952) is an outstanding ***political history*** of the movement. [Ed. note: Later published as ***Conservation and the Gospel of Efficiency;*** see Part II, chap. 3, in this volume.]

its *immediate* impact. However, conservation could be, and was, revolutionary in part of its *doctrine,* and in its *eventual* influence upon American society. The doctrine of "conservation of nature" was an American part of a major revolution in thought in the Western world against the then dominant social philosophy of the self-regulating market economy. Marxism was one European part of that revolution in ideas. The same period saw the beginning of the now successful revolution against the social idea that labor is merely a factor input to the production function in a purely competitive market, and that wages are, according to natural law, merely a factor return from a laissez-faire distribution system. And as with labor, so with the "land" factor of classical economics. Conservation views rejected the idea of nature as purely the classical market place phenomenon "land."

With the vantage of hindsight, Karl Polanyi, writing 50 years later, describing the larger revolution of Western society against the self-regulating economy, never even mentioning conservation or any of its adherents, has phrased the essence of the conservationists' revolutionary rejection of land laissez faire with wonderful succinctness and accuracy:

> What we call Land is an element of nature inextricably interwoven with man's institutions. To isolate it and form a market out of it was perhaps the weirdest of all undertakings of our ancestors.
>
> Traditionally, land and labor are not separated; labor forms part of life, land remains part of nature, life and nature form an articulate whole. Land is thus tied up with organizations of kinship, neighborhood, craft, and creed —with tribe and temple, village, guild, and church. . . .
>
> . . . The economic function is but one of the many vital functions of land. It invests man's life with stability; it is the site of his habitation; it is a condition of his physical safety; it is the landscape and the seasons. We might as well imagine his being born without hands and feet as carrying on his life without land. And yet to separate land from man and organize society in such a way as to satisfy the requirements of a real estate market was a vital part of the utopian concept of a market economy."[31]

It would be interesting, if I could, definitively to summarize the intellectual and idea origins of the conservation movement. There is clearly a debt to Spinoza's naturalism and ethics; to Darwin's biological naturalism; to Spencer's further development to evolutionistic doctrine; to Mill's apostasy regarding a self-regulating land market; and to Henry George's trumpeting on land monopolists and unearned increment. In this extremely difficult order of social analysis. unfortunately, social and political historians of ideas have not (so far as I have been able to learn) performed the difficult research task of definitively identifying conservation ideas and tracing them to their sources. And such a task is, in any case, beyond the needs of this study. My endeavor is merely to identify and understand that major part of conservation doctrine which was concerned with the economics of natural resource scarcity.

LIMITS

The conservation literature of the period 1890–1920 abounds with quantitative estimates and descriptions of physical natural resource endowments, and exhortation to amplify these estimates. One of the most important practical contributions of the conservation movement, according to its leaders, was the inception of a program to inventory the nation's natural resource wealth. The historic Governor's Conference and Inland Waterways Conference were responsible for literally thousands of estimates of the physical quantities and characteristics of natural resources within the nation's boundaries. And the non-quantitative discussions continually emphasized that these estimates, and the ones proposed to be made, represented the nation's natural resource wealth. It is quite clear from the record that *economic* natural resource

[31] Polanyi, *The Great Transformation: The Political and Economic Origins of Our Time* (Boston: Beacon Press, 1957), p. 178. First published, 1944.

scarcity was equated with these estimates of finite physical resources within the nation. As with Malthus, finite natural resource physical limits constitute economic scarcity. But the definition of resources differs:

> We have a limited supply of coal, and only a limited supply. Whether it is to last for a hundred or a hundred and fifty or a thousand years, the coal is limited in amount, unless through geological changes which we shall not live to see, there will never be any more of it than there is now. But coal is in a sense the vital essence of our civilization. If it can be preserved, if the life of the mines can be extended, if by preventing waste there can be more coal left in this country after we of this generation have made every needed use of this source of power, then we shall have deserved well of our descendants.[32]
>
> We have timber for less than thirty years at the present rate of cutting. The figures indicate that our demands upon the forest have increased twice as fast as our population.
>
> Our supplies of iron ore, mineral oil, and natural gas are being rapidly depleted, and many of the great fields are already exhausted. Mineral resources such as these when once gone are gone forever.[33]

The conservationist concepts of limits and thereby economic scarcity are, unlike Malthus', multidimensional. Natural resources are specific in type, location, qualities, and relationships, one to another; and economic scarcity (limit) characterizes all the dimensions. Thus one type of natural resource may be more scarce than another, one quality more scarce than another, etc. The aggregate of all resources is clearly capable of being characterized by multidimensional scarcity magnitudes by (say) a vector description. It is also possible that this total of resources is susceptible to a more aggregative type of measurement and description, of fewer dimensions than the arraying of all types, locations, qualities, etc.

[32] Gifford Pinchot, *The Fight for Conservation* (New York: Doubleday Page & Co., 1910), p. 43.

[33] *Ibid.*, pp. 123–24.

ECOLOGICAL BALANCE

As we have learned in the past few generations (in considerable degree from the stimulus of the conservation movement and its educational efforts), there are small and large systems of interdependency among nature's biological organisms and its geological and atmospheric features. Forest watersheds, for example, play an important role in moderating and equalizing water flow from uneven rainfall, by initial retention and slow release. In the absence of forest (or other plant) cover, soil is washed into the rivers, rivers flood and cave their banks, etc. The conception of ecological balance has been widely presented in scholarly and popular literature.[34]

Additional meaning is thereby given to the doctrine of economic scarcity by the conservation view of nature as a system in ecological balance. The analogy of a chain as strong as its weakest link is relevant. Quantities and qualities of individual natural resources are dependent one upon another. In a dynamic world, constraints additional to the over-all limits described above are imposed by the requirement of "balance." This "scarcity" in no way depends upon man. It derives from interdependencies. It would be true in a dynamic world even if man did not in a substantial way modify nature.

ECOLOGICAL DAMAGE AND DESTRUCTIVE UTILIZATION BY MAN

In conservationist view, stated in an extreme way, nature *sans* man was a world optimally balanced ecologically. It follows then that modern man's activities, *however prudent,* are necessarily damaging to natural ecological balance, and the ecological system is a weakened one. This constitutes an additional component of economic scarcity doctrine. The scarcity of limits (above) is tighter because of the constraint

[34] E. P. Odum, *Fundamentals of Ecology* (Philadelphia: W. B. Saunders Co., 1954); J. H. Storer, *The Web of Life* (New York: Signet Books, 1956). I am indebted to the late Arthur Kraft for the latter reference.

of balance (above), and is aggravated by upset of ecological balance from civilized man's presence.

A few examples will be helpful. Civilized man appropriates land for his cities and highways. Land is thus removed from the natural ecological system; at the very minimum, natural resource capacity is reduced. He eliminates forests and puts the Great Plains under the plow, and thereby changes nature's balance. Buffalo and other wildlife disappear, soil is lost, and rivers silt. The point here is *not* poor management. It is that nature's ecological system once contained only several million inhabitants in the United States area, who were more or less nomadic, and today it has almost 170 million.

The economic scarcities arising from the limits of nature and the constraint of ecological balance are further inevitably subject to aggravation by modern man's destructive utilization of mineral resources. Fuel mineral resources once burned are forever lost. Metallic minerals can furnish repeated use by secondary metal recovery, but, even under the best of circumstances, metals are eventually dissipated by corrosion, wear, and other loss. This generation of additional economic scarcity is thus a necessary consequence in a society which utilizes non-renewable mineral resources. The rate of such deterioration in resource availability can be moderated only as society chooses to consume less of these natural resources.

WASTE AND WISE USE

All of the foregoing economic scarcities occur even under conditions of wise use of resources. In conservation doctrine, the above scarcities are in practice inescapable. The limits of the nation are physical bounds. The facts of ecological interdependencies are physical. Man's weakening of the natural ecological system occurs because of the physical drains by his large numbers and industrialized society.

But these scarcity forces are greatly aggravated by *waste*. In conservation literature, waste is given much attention as a source of economic scarcity of natural resources. This is not to say that there is attributed to waste more importance than "limits" or "ecological balance" or "upset of balance" as the origins of scarcity. Rather, waste is emphasized because the other origins of scarcity tend to be of a non-active, constraining type, whereas waste is an active input to generation of scarcity. In this sense, waste is similar to the pressure of large modern societies in weakening ecological balance and exploiting irreplaceable mineral resources. Like these scarcity forces, waste depends upon man's activities. But unlike them, waste is easily avoidable by "wise use." Waste is man's foolishness in aggravating an already existing and ineluctable situation of natural resource scarcity.

What constitutes waste? The conservationist slogan answer of "unwise" or "inefficient" use does not carry us very far. I have therefore distilled four types of "waste vs. wise use" from the enormous conservation literature of the period as my own interpretive summary of the meaning of waste in conservation doctrine.

1. One type of waste is destructive utilization of a natural resource where it would be possible to procure approximately the same kind of product or service by nondestructive use of that resource, of a renewable resource, or of another, more plentiful resource. If arid grazing land is turned to crop production, with subsequent erosion, this is waste. If hydropower dams are permitted to silt with eventual reduction or total loss of their output, this is waste. If coal, oil, or gas, irreplaceable in nature, are used to generate electric power while undeveloped water power sites remain unexploited, this is waste.

The list of examples can be greatly multiplied, by means of the following simple rules I have concocted of what conservationists meant by "waste avoidance" and "wise use":

a) renewable resources, such as forests, grazing land, crop land, water, should not be physically damaged or destroyed;

b) renewable resources should be used in place of non-renewable ones, insofar as physically possible;

c) plentiful mineral resources should be used before less plentiful ones, insofar as physically possible.

These rules are not the ones of a laissez-faire economy. Such an economy is guided by revenue maximization and cost minimization in the producing sphere, and utility maximization and freedom of choice in the consumer one. In conservation doctrines, such a society is wasteful and generates natural resource scarcity.

2. The second type of waste is failure to procure the maximum of sustained physical yield of useful extractive products from nature's *renewable* resources. Whereas the first type of waste includes *over*-exploitation of renewable resources to the point where their capacities are reduced, this type of waste is *under*-exploitation. Production of crops, fish, livestock, timber, and hydropower should be maximized to the limits of sustained physical yield from the respective resources. In two ways, it is wasteful to partake less than fully from nature's ecological bounty. If nature's perennial yield is not used, then this is viewed as waste in an elemental sense, as leaving fruit to rot on the tree or vine is waste. And if the renewable resources are not used to the maximum of their sustained physical yield potential, then non-renewable resources will tend to be drawn upon. Thus failure to maximize sustained physical yield of useful extractive product generates natural resource scarcity too.

3. As the second type of waste characterized mismanagement of renewable resources, so the third type of waste which generates resource scarcity relates to *mismanagement of non-renewable ones*. Waste occurs with respect to mineral resources from failure to maximize the yield of extractive product from the physical resources which are destroyed. As noted earlier, there is serious doubt that the pools of oil in the earth should be tapped so rapidly. But to the extent that a pool is tapped and drawn upon, then it is wasteful, and productive of scarcity, not to maximize the volume of petroleum eventually withdrawn from the pool. Again, this is quite a simple and straightforward notion. If a resource is to be used, then let it be used, not spoiled. To conduct oil production in such a way as to make only 20 per cent of the pool recoverable, or coal mining so as to leave 50 per cent of the deposit underground and unrecoverable—these are waste and generate scarcity.

4. The fourth type of waste in conservation doctrine, no less productive of scarcity than the others, results from unwise use *not* of the natural resource itself, but of the *extractive products yielded* by it. Gas must be withdrawn for use, and not flared. Mineral fuels were withdrawn from nature to furnish useful heat; to burn them in furnaces of low thermal efficiency is wasteful. Metals were mined and timber cut to provide useful services; since they are physically recoverable as secondary materials and scrap, they must be so recovered or there is waste. This is further extension to the utilization sphere of the principle of maximizing physical yield and minimizing physical destruction of natural resources.

Unlike the other scarcity forces enumerated earlier, waste is remediable. Waste results from ignorance or apathy of man in his individual behavior; from physical inefficiency in use of natural resources because of improper criteria built into the laissez-faire system; from inefficient government activity and inadequate government intervention in the economic sphere; and other causes.

SOCIAL EFFECTS OF SCARCITY

What, according to conservation doctrine, are the consequences of natural resource scarcity, from the facts: that nature is limited; that nature is an ecological balance; that modern society is damaging to that ecology and necessarily destructive of mineral resources; and that wasteful behavior aggravates scarcity?

As the result of scarcity, major portions

of the population are unnecessarily separated from livelihood on the land and association with the land, with resultant evil social consequences. There is reduction in the relative numbers of the most valuable group of citizenry, the independent farmer, and a weakening of agrarianism as the core of national life. There is damage to the ethical system. Values are perverted by crass materialism and urban pleasures. There is increased industrialism and urbanism, an undesirable development and a poor trade for the former agricultural society. The beauty and wonder of Nature are increasingly lost, to ourselves and our descendants. There is psychic damage, to the individual, the family, the community, and the nation.

The man on the farm is valuable to the Nation, like any other citizen, just in proportion to his intelligence, character, ability, and patriotism; but, unlike other citizens, also in proportion to his attachment to the soil. That is the principal spring of his steadiness, his sanity, his simplicity and directness, and many of his other desirable qualities. He is the first of home makers.

The nation that will lead the world will be a Nation of Homes.[35]

True moral inspiration came not only from contact with nature in parks but also from the physical vigor of honest outdoor toil. Rural life was a religious and moral life, containing "'that fine sense of soul that brings the individual into touch with Universal Purpose."[36]

Urban life, on the other hand, was stultifying.[37]

EFFECTS OF SCARCITY ON ECONOMIC STRUCTURE

The economic effects of scarcity, in conservation literature, may be differentiated in two groups: (*a*) those involving economic structure and organization of the nation; and (*b*) those involving productivity, cost, and price.

The conservationists found that, except as remedial steps were taken by government and by improved behavior of the citizenry, the forces of natural resource scarcity coupled with the high efficiency of the trust form of industrial organizations would produce monopoly, resulting in maldistributions of income among the populace so severe as to be inconsistent with a democratic society.

From scarcity and monopoly control there would increasingly develop larger and larger profits—unearned increment—as the land and urban monopolies exerted their powers. The monopolist tentacles would creep outward, to entrap and stifle the sectors of the economy immediately adjacent to the land sector and the further reaches. The eventual outcome would be severe maldistribution of land and property ownership, and of income.

The Roosevelt resource administrators interpreted the "Trust" problem largely in terms of how corporations had interfered with their work. Business organizations which approved administration policies and which cooperated in them were "good" trusts, but those which opposed them were "bad." "Bad" trusts were the speculators, private irrigation companies, livestock companies which cut down fences on the public domain, and others which interfered with the administration's attempt to rationalize the use and development of resources. Private corporations or individuals who were able to prevent the fullest development of a river by controlling some strategic site were "bad" trusts. At the same time, the administration believed that any monopoly which, because of its control of production, the market, or patents, was able to prevent the most efficient and cheapest production and sale of goods was also a "bad" trust.[38]

COST AND PRODUCTIVITY EFFECTS OF SCARCITY

Conservation literature viewed scarcity as a powerful force working to reduce labor productivity and to increase real cost of all products. The growing economy would increasingly press upon already scarce resources. Destructive utilization of minerals would make them more scarce. Encroach-

[35] Pinchot, *op. cit.*, pp. 22–23.

[36] Thomas F. Walsh in "Humanitarian Aspect of National Irrigation," *Forestry and Irrigation* (December, 1902), pp. 8, 505–9.

[37] Hays, *op. cit.*, pp. 245–46.

[38] *Ibid.*, pp. 240–41.

ment of cities and highways would further reduce available resources. And waste would be the final turn of the screw to grind the American society to poverty and misery. Output per worker would decline steadily. The real cost of commodities would rise steadily. Real income per capita would steadily fall, to subsistence levels.

. . . it (is) certain that the United States has already crossed the verge of a timber famine so severe that its blighting effects will be felt in every household in the land. The rise in the price of lumber which marked the opening of the present century is the beginning of a vastly greater and more rapid rise which is to come. We must necessarily begin to suffer from the scarcity of timber long before our supplies are completely exhausted. . . .

What will happen when the forests fail? In the first place, the business of lumbering will disappear. It is now the fourth greatest industry in the United States. All forms of building industries will suffer with it, and the occupants of houses, offices, and stores must pay the added cost. Mining will become vastly more expensive; and with the rise in the cost of mining there must follow a corresponding rise in the price of coal, iron, and other minerals. The railways . . . will be profoundly affected, and the cost of transportation will suffer a corresponding increase. Water power for lighting, manufacturing, and transportation, and the movement of freight and passengers by inland waterways, will be affected still more directly than the steam railways. The cultivation of the soil, with or without irrigation, will be hampered by the increased cost of agricultural tools, fencing, and the wood needed for other purposes about the farm.[39]

INTERPRETING CONSERVATION ECONOMIC DOCTRINE

My purpose in probing into the first conservation movement was to improve understanding of this important source of the doctrine of natural resource scarcity, both because the movement was an important development in the nation's history and because much contemporary view derives from that movement. I wanted to unearth the assumptions of this doctrine and observe the logic of the analysis. I wanted to ascertain the extent to which quantitative economic evidence was drawn upon. I was interested in the elements and details from which the crucial scarcity generalizations were compounded. And I was interested in the conservation movement's own antecedents and major sources of ideas. The quest, I think, has been at least partly successful. I have dug out premises, ascertained the structure of the analysis, and detailed the conservation theses in various ways. I have learned the important fact that quantitative economic analysis of antecedent nineteenth century economic evidence did not in any rigorous way enter the analysis of economic scarcity and economic effect.

But a word of warning is appropriate. For a variety of reasons, it is extremely difficult to ascertain and interpret the economic doctrine of scarcity of the first conservation movement. The leading figures of the movement were not economists, and there is no evidence in their writings that they had any substantial training in economic analysis. This means that there is little or no recourse to rigorous economic formulation and statement, and thereby that the meanings of terms are sometimes uncertain to an economist-reviewer of the literature.

The difficulty is aggravated by the fact, observed earlier, that early conservation writings were instruments of a political and social reform movement. Such writings were several stages removed from scholarly standards, economic or other. The writings were replete with slogans, exhortation, half-truths, catch phrases, etc.; and at a distance of 50 years, it is not easy to discern core from these frills. Nor may contemporary conservationists be appealed to for interpretation, for theirs is comprised of several different movements.

Despite the difficulties and uncertainties, I believe that I have accurately characterized the essential elements in the conservation doctrine of natural resource scarcity. The movement was enormously successful in its own time. And its influence reaches to the present. As in Presi-

[39] Pinchot, *op. cit.*, pp. 15–17.

dent Taft's time, so today, "A great many people are in favor of conservation, no matter what it means."[40] To the extent I have been successful, then the discussion is not only a useful contribution in its own terms, but also speaks to conservation beliefs which most of us hold as received doctrine, in some degree.

The views of most other economists on the conservation movement differ from the interpretive summary I have presented above. So far as I know, most professional economists who have made important contributions in the economics of natural resources tend to consider the conservation movement as concerned with the economic problem of time rate of use of natural resources. This is true of S. V. Ciriacy-Wantrup, A. Scott, E. Heady, H. Hotelling, and J. Ise, among others. I find this interpretation of the conservation movement to be incomplete, and possibly misleading.

Part of conservation doctrine was indeed this familiar proposition: it can be constructed from the Malthusian case by simply assuming that some resources can be, and others necessarily are, destroyed by use. In Chart I, for example, let it merely be assumed that the resource axis gradually is "eaten away"; or in Chart 2, that resources are used up, and the economy is forced onto lower level resource isoquants. In both cases the expansion paths fall to lower levels. This, essentially, is the time rate of use problem—that there is a fixed stock whose exhaustion and changing availability depend on the time distribution of use.

But part of conservation doctrine, and the *gestalt* in which time rate of use appeared, go quite far beyond the time rate problem. To characterize conservation in this way, to refer to conservation as (for example) Pigou does in the quotation given earlier, has two defects. It credits conservation with contributions made earlier and more systematically by Malthus, Ricardo, and Jevons, among others. And it fails to credit conservation with an important and partly successful revolution of social ideas and applied political economy.

The concept of "ecological balance" is importantly different from time rate of use of a stock, and moreover is not even a very familiar idea in academic work on economics of natural resources. The additional idea of "ecological damage" was also a novel, or at least an undeveloped one, for economic thought. The conservationists even modified the classical notion of "limits": the resource "limits" conceived by the conservation movement as relevant were those within national boundaries, and the economic objective was national self-sufficiency—hardly consistent with the trade assumptions of classical economics. Of the hundreds of papers in the *Proceedings* of the 1908 Conference of Governors in the White House and the three-volume 1909 Report of the National Conservation Commission to the President, only four (by count of titles) looked outside the United States, and these did so primarily from the standpoint of U. S. interest.

With respect to "waste" and "wise use," the characteristic economist view is that this conservation doctrine has little meaning and is of no value for economic analysis. With respect to meaning, I continue to differ. The codification I have given to waste (above) has meaning—government administrators could follow these rules (and some do, with results that in my view are frequently unfortunate). Of course, the rules are at variance with economic common sense and understanding based on laissez-faire premises. But this is the essence of the matter—conservation doctrine did, in significant degree, reject laissez-faire principles; it questions the quality, even more than the mechanics, of modern civilization. This is why the intelligent men among them could plead for their view of "wise use" and avoidance of waste, to the mystification of later economists.[41]

[40] W. H. Taft, *Outlook,* May 14, 1910, p. 57, quoted in J. Ise, *The U.S. Forest Policy* (New Haven: Yale University Press, 1920), p. 373.

[41] Where the economist defines the term "conservation" narrowly, with explicit warning of its

Two Concluding Observations

I hope I will be forgiven if, in closing, I indulge in some subjective speculation and express some personal prejudices.

CHANGED MEANING OF RESOURCES

In Malthus' time, and to a lesser extent (but still true) during the period of the conservation furor, a considerable part of "final" or virtually final output was agricultural goods—foodstuffs, natural fibers, timber, game, etc. To this extent, increase in these outputs could be, and was, viewed as identical with economic growth. Now as to how these goods would be further processed again there was a simple answer. They would be *mechanically* shaped from the gifts of nature—the wheat grain would be taken out; the hide separated from the meat; the timber sawed to size; the fibers combed twisted, and woven, etc. Turning to the derivation of the basic substances from nature, man's role here also was a *mechanical* one. Thus, if a man stood on a square mile of land, or a nation on 3 million, the natural resources relevant for economic activity could be easily identified and measured. They were acres of crop land or pasture, board feet of standing timber, etc.

delimitation, there can be no confusion. I agree, for example, with E. S. Mason, who has recently written, "If . . . conservation is defined as 'a shift in the time distribution of use of a resource in the direction of the future,' we have a set of issues that can be analyzed, but one which represents only a small part of the traditional concern of conservationists." But note that the subject thus defined omits the principal concerns which have rallied the major groups in the historical and contemporary conservation movements, and which have made conservation a major public policy issue. I am arguing that the larger questions can also be defined and merit analysis by economists. I thus think Prof. Mason is too strong in his comment that, "If conservation is defined as a 'wise use of resources' nothing escapes its ken, but the invitation to subjective value judgments is so sweeping as to leave little room for rational analysis."

What has happened in advanced Western nations since these times to the meaning of final goods, the methods by which they are produced, and the definition of natural resources is so profound that we find the novelty difficult and seek simplification in possibly archaic analogies. With respect to the meaning of goods, more than 90 per cent of the increase in real gross national products in the United States since 1870 has been of non-agricultural origin. With respect to the method of transforming materials into final goods, this has become far less a purely mechanical one, and to a considerable degree a controlled heat or electrochemical process. Finally, the natural resource building blocks have changed radically—they are atoms and molecules. That is, the natural resource input is to a far less degree acres, and to far greater degree particular atmospheric and other molecules.

This has changed the meaning of "natural resources" for societies which indeed have modern technologies and access to capital. We now look more at contained molecules of iron, magnesium, aluminum, coal, nitrogen, etc., and at their naturally existing chemical combinations, than at acres or board feet. While in a sense, the same ultimate world limits still exist, in a more significant sense they do not. How many taconite iron atoms or sea water magnesium atoms and bromine molecules constitute plenitude, and how many scarcity? In significant degree, further, even the ultimate limits are different from Malthus'. His natural resources were conceived for a two-dimensional world nourished by acreage. Ours is a three-dimensional one, sustained by subsurface resources. His society could reach natural resources to only insignificant distances above and below his acres. We have multiplied our "reach" by many thousands.

"NEW" RESOURCE SCARCITY

I am greatly impressed by a new form of resource scarcity—the problem of space, privacy, and nature preservation. Actually it is not new, as a quotation from Mill indicates:

There is room in the world, no doubt, and even in old countries, for a great increase of population, supposing the arts of life to go on improving, and capital to increase. But even if innocuous, I confess I see very little reason for desiring it. . . . A population may be too crowded, though all be amply supplied with food and raiment. It is not good for man to be kept perforce at all times in the presence of his species. A world from which solitude is extirpated, is a very poor ideal. Solitude, in the sense of being often alone, is essential to any depth of meditation or of character; and solitude in the presence of natural beauty and grandeur, is the cradle of thoughts and aspirations which are not only good for the individual, but which society could ill do without. Nor is there much satisfaction in contemplating the world with nothing left to the spontaneous activity of nature; with every rood of land brought into cultivation, which is capable of growing food for human beings; every flowery waste or natural pasture ploughed up, all quadrupeds or birds which are not domesticated for man's use exterminated as his rivals for food, every hedgerow or superfluous tree rooted out, and scarcely a place left where a wild shrub or flower could grow without being eradicated as a weed in the name of improved agriculture.[42]

It may surprise this audience to learn that by far the largest fraction of *contemporary* conservationists are concerned with this form of resource scarcity, and not with minerals or agricultural land shortages.

This category of doctrine already includes a "quality scarcity" concern over fouling streams, disfiguring land, and air pollution. And I guess it should also include concern over atmospheric and land contamination by radioactivity.

As to whether this is a proper area for economic analysis, this is obviously a decision for the individual economist. It has been sanctioned as a problem in political economy from Mill to Pigou at least. It is part of the problem of social investment and communal resource use which is increasingly concerning economists. Finally, it is a problem of sizeable economic dimensions.

[42] J. S. Mill, *Principles of Political Economy* (London: Longmans, Green, Reader & Dyer, 1871), Bk. IV, chap. 7, p. 454.

I believe the basic issue in resources today to be not quantity but quality. The great concern in the management of resources should be the maximization of quality of output. It is not the quality of the resource itself that we are concerned with, but with its capacity to enhance the quality of life. This is a sticky problem, and it becomes involved in many subjective evaluations, but it seems to me that we can no longer avoid the fact that the management of our natural environment should be geared toward an apparatus which will maximize the quality of life within that landscape.

This may mean lower quantities of certain goods . . . utilizing greater quantities of certain goods in order to get higher qualities of other goods which are more important. This becomes a very important and exceedingly difficult conceptual problem. It means devising systems of analysis in which the alternatives, in terms of the resulting quality of life, are fully conceived and presented so that society can understand what these alternatives really are. The ultimate purpose should be to consider the alternatives in terms of the quality of life that will result, rather than thinking in terms of enhancing the quality of the resources themselves.

Ayers Brinser, "Comments on University Resource Programs," *Resources, the Metropolis and the Land-Grant University*, Pub. No. 410 (Amherst: University of Massachusetts Cooperative Extension Service, 1963), p. 44.

CHAPTER 4

THE CONSERVATION ETHIC

This chapter highlights the value judgments that underlie much conservationist thought. Our point of departure is Herfindahl's query, "What is conservation?" We are here concerned less with a movement and more with the basic idea of conservation. As Herfindahl suggests, there is no one central idea of conservation. It is rather an ambiguous, vaguely conceived notion which reflects great disparities in the views of its proponents. There is a famous statement, ascribed to William H. Taft, that sums up this position. "There are a great many people in favor of conservation," Taft said, "no matter what it means."[1]

There is, nevertheless, a persistent thread common to most supporters of conservation. This is a preoccupation with questions of values. Such a preoccupation is itself a source of the ambiguity of conservation. There is no universally accepted system of values, for conservation or for anything else. So, as Weaver replies to the opening question, conservation is more ethics than economics.

There are some value judgments which figure strongly in the conservation ethic. At last three of these stand out. The first is a belief in the inherent virtue or goodness of the natural order of things, which is frequently conceived as being a beautiful teleological harmony. This view is exemplified in Paul Sears's substitution of a thermodynamic steady state of nature for natural harmony. A second judgment is seen in zealous efforts to preserve nature as an end in itself. This is often accompanied by a belief that preserved nature should be for the use of the people and not for a privileged few. This view is forcefully restated in the excerpt from Gifford Pinchot's *Breaking New Ground.*

A third judgment is that the present generation has a moral responsibility toward future generations. The "countless millions yet unborn" are always on the side of conservation. Price explores this question and asks how we should weight the dimly perceived needs of future generations against our own vivid and pressing requirements. To many conservationists, the weighting commonly accepted or assumed by the decision-makers in our society has not been satisfactory. They would like to see a shift toward a more favorable disposition to the future.

[1] Quoted in J. W. Milliman, "Can People Be Trusted with Natural Resources?" *Land Economics,* XXXVIII, No. 3 (1962), 199–218.

In his paper, Galbraith issues a challenge of a different nature. He is not concerned with the discounting process that favors the present so heavily, but with our conventional wisdom as to what constitutes our present needs. The urgent needs or demands shown in resource projections are already notorious for not allowing for changes in price that might reflect realistic or increasing costs. Galbraith goes one better and suggests that even realistic costing may lead to unwise consumption patterns in a world where wants are managed in favor of consumer hardware and against public needs with their low material requirements.

In an environment marked by the increasing complexity of the relations between man and nature, Hauser's value problems may become even more crucial. For while the increase in complexity calls forth new skills and techniques, it also confuses the direction in which those skills should be applied. More than ever there is need for informed discourse concerning the world around us.

It is in this dialogue that the aesthetics of natural harmony, the ethic of living community, and the values of future orientation and less rapid development are as relevant today as at any time. But a debate presupposes other points of view at least worthy of respectful attention. These are to be found in great variety. To some the cruel mechanisms of natural selection are repugnant. The valuation of human beings over all other forms of life is an ethic, deserving thoughtful appraisal. Concern with present development for the benefit of those living may paradoxically prove best for future generations as well.[2] There is a conflict of moral judgments concerning alternatives of natural resource development. By calling attention to this conflict, the conservation ethic plays an important role in our resource policy, constantly bringing us back to the value judgments on which our choices ultimately rest.

[2] In the North American context, we have argued that "if Canada would do well by future generations, this end can best be served by developing resources now, both for domestic consumption and for export," Ian Burton and Robert W. Kates, "Canadian Resources and American Requirements," *The Canadian Journal of Economics and Political Science,* XXX, No. 2 (1964), 265–69. See esp. p. 268.

ORRIS C. HERFINDAHL

WHAT IS CONSERVATION?

A discussion between two conservationists who are interested in conserving different things often degenerates into polite name calling or worse. Smith will tell Jones that he doesn't know what *true* conservation is. And Jones will reply acidly that what Smith proposes—far from being conservation—is profligate waste. Finally the discussion ends from boredom or exhaustion, with each conservationist walking away shaking his head and saying to himself that he doesn't see how anyone could hold such inane views. The outsider viewing this fruitless exchange is puzzled. If both parties are for conservation, which everybody seems to think is a good thing, what are they quarreling about?

One of the difficulties is that the word conservation is used with varying meanings, often without telling the other party to the discussion what one's own definition is. But the confusion is not simply a matter of failing to let the other fellow in on one's private definition, for many users of this term seem to have no clear definition of their own and seem to prefer the ambiguity that results.

The imprecision surrounding use of the word "conservation" has been associated with widespread attempts to appropriate its persuasive sound for special interests. If a certain proposal is labeled a conservation proposal, or to go even further, if the proposal is said to represent *true* conservation—implying that there is a subtle but compelling case for its adoption—there is probably a tendency for more favorable reaction than if a less emotive term is used. After all, if a person is asked whether it is better to conserve or not conserve, he no doubt will vote for conservation. Of course it would be unthinking of him to vote at all since he didn't ask the questioner what meaning was to be given to conservation, but the point is that the mere mention of the word tends to stimulate favorable response rather than a search for meaning.

The confusion surrounding use of the term conservation and the attempt to appropriate favorable reaction to it for special interest proposals and programs is readily apparent to even the most cursory examination. It is an interesting exercise to go over speeches or writings on conservation matters and to ask what definition of conservation the person might have had in mind. Quite often it turns out that he believes his policy should be adopted *because* it will conserve (that is, save for future use or preserve for use) a *particular* resource product, for example, water for irrigation. But confusion arises when the city dweller insists that the water should go to the city for drinking, cooling, etc., because *that* is really conservation.

Sometimes general definitions are given. A widely favored one is the following: "Conservation is the use of natural resources for the greatest good of the greatest number for the longest time." This is the definition that Gifford Pinchot, the founder of what historians are wont to call the Conservation Movement, was fond of

• Orris C. Herfindahl is Senior Research Associate, Resources for the Future, Inc., Washington.

Reprinted from *Three Studies in Minerals Economics* (Washington: Resources for the Future, Inc., 1961), pp. 1–12, with permission of the author and the publisher.

using. Pinchot credits the definition to W J McGee (who insisted on no periods after the initials), a freewheeling intellect of very wide interests and great ability who worked with John Wesley Powell and later with Pinchot.[1]

When this definition is read off rapidly —conservation is the use of natural resources for the greatest good of the greatest number for the longest time—the three superlatives have a delightful ring. If this is conservation, how could anyone be opposed to it? No one could be, of course, unless he stops to ask himself how three variables can be maximized at the same time. Imagine a father trying to distribute a bag of candy to his children so as to maximize the amount of candy received by each child who gets candy *and* the number of children receiving candy *and* the length of time the candy will be visible.

Still another general formulation has enjoyed great popularity with politicians for over half a century, and with others whose audiences are of opposing minds. Again let us take Pinchot's formulation, which may have been fathered by him: "Conservation implies both the development and the protection of resources, the one as much as the other. . . ."[2] On the surface, this should command general assent, for who among us is opposed to development? Who is opposed to the protection of resources? The trouble comes when the blanks are filled in. Suppose that development means covering a canyon with a lake for purposes of power and irrigation while preservation means leaving the canyon alone so that its beauty can be seen. An excellent example is provided by the Echo Park controversy. It was indeed impossible both to develop the dam site and at the same time preserve one of the products of this natural resource, namely, the beauty of Echo Park and the nearby canyons. Unfortunately, a verbal incantation that reconciles the irreconcilable does not in fact resolve the very real conflict between development and preservation. There is no inconsistency between development and preservation, however, if one's objective is the "conservation" of only one of the uses of the resource.

In the case of mineral resources, the stock of which is used up in the act of consumption—perhaps with some recirculation—the injunction to develop and preserve simultaneously is even more mystifying than it was in the preceding case. Development in the case of minerals means production, but preservation presumably means postponement of consumption. How can both be done simultaneously except by accumulating an ever larger inventory of metal above the ground?

Pinchot's casual approach to the problem of definition is even further illustrated on the same page where we are admonished both to develop and to preserve. For example, "The essence of conservation is the application of common sense to the common problems for the common good." Or, "Conservation is simple, obvious, and right." Comment would be superfluous.

Slackness and confusion in definition, so clearly exemplified in the writings of Pinchot and his contemporaries, have continued down to the present. It is only the exceptional writer on conservation whose use of the word is not self-contradictory or a mere camouflage, whether deliberate or not, for the promotion of some special interest such as special wilderness areas, irrigation, power, and so on. The definitions of Pinchot's time, perhaps better called slogans, have been repeated ever since. "The greatest good for the greatest number for the longest time" will be with us for a long time to come. And almost any speech on natural resources coming out of the Department of the Interior contains the contradictory admonitions to develop and to preserve within the same sentence.

What is the origin of this confusion in definition? Why has it continued for so long? In my view this indifference to clar-

[1] Gifford Pinchot, *Breaking New Ground* (New York: Harcourt, Brace & Co., 1947), p. 326.

[2] *Proceedings of the Joint Conservation Conference,* X, Sen. Doc. No. 676, 60th Cong., 2d Sess., 1909, 123.

ity of definition rests in considerable part on the existence of deep underlying conflicts among various interest groups in the area of conservation policy, by which I mean the policy problems involved in determining how natural resources are used. Proponents of special conservation interests, in their zeal to alter governmental policy, have made clarity and consistency of definition a secondary consideration. Indeed, clear definition might lose all the advantage to be gained from using so fine sounding a word as "conservation" or the related "develop and preserve." Clarity about real intentions might unnecessarily antagonize those who otherwise would not press home to the real meaning behind generalities.

Certainly one of the dominant conflicts in the field of conservation was and is the conflict between development and what I shall call nature preservation. By development is meant the use of natural resources in such a way as to involve the construction of auxiliary capital goods such as dams, roads, processing plants, hotels, etc. "Nature preservation" is a term which embraces the whole spectrum of groups interested in preserving various aspects of nature as she is (or is it with some "development"?) for the direct enjoyment of individuals. Such diverse things are involved as birds (to be preserved for eye, ear, and palate), solitude, scenery, trees, flowing water, naturally still water (that is, natural lakes), etc. This is sometimes said to constitute the birds and bees school of conservation, a phrase that can be uttered with a tone of either affection or derision, depending on whether one is in or out of the group.

The antagonism between development and nature preservation has always been present in the field of conservation. Even the founder of the movement in the United States, Gifford Pinchot, was not disposed to ride both these horses at the same time. It is quite clear on reading his writings that he was a developmentalist first and a preservationist only secondarily, if at all. For example, in 1903 Pinchot made the following statement in an address to the Society of American Foresters:

> The object of our forest policy is not to preserve the forests because they are beautiful . . . or because they are refuges for the wild creatures of the wilderness . . . but . . . the making of prosperous homes. . . . Every other consideration comes as secondary.[3]

It is not surprising that the nature preservationist groups became increasingly dissatisfied with Pinchot's views on what conservationists should be doing, and that they came to feel he was using the Conservation Movement to promote policies to which they were strongly opposed. This divergence in points of view was an important factor in bringing about the disintegration of the Conservation Movement.[4]

The conflict between development and nature preservation has erupted from time to time in pitched battles. For example, New York's constitutional provision requiring the Adirondack State Park lands to be kept "forever wild"—that is, with no lumbering—was the subject of intense controversy in the constitutional revisions of 1895 and 1915, and there are always attempts to nibble away at it. Most recently the nature preservationists tilted with developmentalists who wanted a thruway constructed to pass through the eastern part of the Park. This controversy is especially interesting for our purposes because it also provided an example of the conflict between development and preservation *within* the ranks of the preservationists. That is to say, the preservationists were divided, with one group, whose *bona fides* is not open to question, supporting the thruway partly on the ground that it would not prevent the preservation of anything worth preserving. The constitutional amendment required to allow construction of the thruway (called the Northway) was passed, and construction is in progress.

[3] Quoted in Samuel P. Hays, *Conservation and the Gospel of Efficiency* (Cambridge: Harvard University Press, 1959), p. 41.

[4] *Ibid., passim.*

The Hetch-Hetchy controversy, involving construction of a dam across a beautiful valley to supply water for San Francisco, is still remembered by many. The establishment and the regulations governing the uses of wildlife refuges, national parks, and national forests have been and continue to be the source of controversy between the two groups. Recently an intense struggle has been going on over a bill that would establish wilderness areas on certain parts of Federal land holdings.

These few brief references give only a hint of the depth and pervasiveness of the perennial conflict between development and nature preservation. It should be emphasized again, however, that this is not the only controversy within the groups who call themselves conservationists. Various types of development often turn out to be incompatible with each other: irrigation versus urban water supply, for example. And within the nature preservation group there are latent conflicts that come into the open every now and then. The split over construction of the Northway has been mentioned, but there are many more. For example, the National Park Service—certainly a nature preservationist organization—frequently comes under fire because it concedes too much to development in the form of roads, accommodations, and so on. Struggles within the preservationist group frequently involve a difference of view in the amount and type of development in the form of facilities that should accompany "preservation."

It is these conflicts, then, which are an important source of uncritical or intentional usage according to which the statement that a certain action or policy is conservative in nature (in the everyday meaning of conserve) is meant to imply the desirability of that action or policy. "Build the dam, because that will *conserve* water and prevent its waste in spring floods." Or, "It is only by not building the dam that the natural beauties of the valley can be *conserved*." Each side has tried to wrap itself in the favorable reaction surrounding the word conservation.

Broadly speaking, there are two ways by which usage can be brought to heel so that it will aid rather than hinder understanding. One way is to say that the goal of conservation policy is to adjust outputs through time in such a way as to maximize the return from *all* resources at the disposal of society. In the process of doing this, some resources will be used up, perhaps "completely," and there may be a gradual transformation of "natural" resources into man-made capital "goods" of many different types. To put it differently, this view of conservation policy equates it with "wise use of resources."

This is a view that enjoys considerable currency. If carefully adhered to, it avoids what we have called the main difficulty in usage, for on this view you cannot say that a certain policy represents "true conservation" until a *complete* economic analysis of its effects has been attempted, and no reasonable person can ask for more than that. But to equate conservation with "wise use" is to attain a defensible usage only by assimilating the problem of conservation completely into the general economic problem of maximizing output and by departing radically from the everyday meaning of the word "conserve."

It is preferable, in my opinion, to preserve common usage and to agree that a conservative act is one which saves something for future use instead of present use or which saves something for use instead of nonuse. This usage leaves open the possibility that the conservation of one resource may entail the sacrifice of another resource which others may want to conserve. Thus there is *no* justification for concluding that a certain policy should be adopted simply because it conserves some resource, for it may involve so much cost either in the form of current productive services required (e.g., to build a dam) and/or in the destruction of *other* resources that it is not justified. A proper usage, if the everyday meaning of "conserve" is retained, should *not* involve the implicit view that conservation is always desirable. Sometimes it is, but sometimes it is not. The question always is whether the gains outweigh the costs.

If this obvious but important point is neglected, the way is open to advocate policies that make no economic sense at all. An extreme example is provided by those who have been able to conclude—without examining costs—that government policy should be directed to the *full* regulation of nearly all the nation's streams over the long run. (Full regulation means the complete or nearly complete evening out of flow on a stream. The usual means for doing this is to build storage capacity behind dams.) Other cases of error resulting from neglect of costs may be more subtle. For example, no satisfactory argument can be constructed for an indiscriminate policy of maximum sustained yield from "forest lands." Nor can a satisfactory argument be made for a policy to conserve coal by requiring coal operators to mine 100 per cent or any other percentage of the coal in a deposit. Such questions cannot be discussed usefully without reference to costs.

Conflicts within the conservation area will not be eliminated even if the term conservation is used in a proper way; that is, without pretense that a particular conservation policy is desirable, *ipso facto,* without reference to costs. But clear usage is a tool which at least will not hinder—and probably will aid—the resolution of conflicts over the use of resources. It is likely that a clear usage, always with the realization that conservative action is desirable only if benefits exceed costs, will be of increasing importance, for the intensity of conflicts over the use of certain resources probably will increase as time goes on.

In the future as in the past, however, many conservation problems will continue to be settled for us by the working of the private market system. This is especially true of the minerals industries. By and large, we accept the price system as the arbiter between the present and the future, and there is little prospect that this practice will be abandoned. We do not, for example, impose a tax on the production of copper in order to save copper for use by future generations. The problem of the level of recovery is left to the mining company, the smelter, and the refiner. The reason why the price system can be trusted to yield a suitable solution to many of the conservation problems involving minerals is that costs and benefits involved in mining and related activities effectively enter into the calculations of private firms to a greater extent than is true for the exploitation of other natural resources.

The petroleum industry in the United States constitutes a notable exception, of course. The fact that single ownership was not coextensive with oil pools required some sort of action to prevent the needless multiplication of oil wells and to prevent economically wasteful loss of oil underground. Our attempts to cope with these problems seem to be running into increasing difficulty, however, not because the problem of rational exploitation of an oil pool has suddenly become more difficult from a technical point of view, but because the particular method of control in vogue is yielding some undesired results.

The elements of our control system are, first, control (actually only partial) of total production of the industry. The objectives are mixed, of course, being both conservation and control of price. If control of price were not involved there would be no restriction of production of individual wells below "efficient capacity" or perhaps MER (maximum efficient rate). The second element of the system is spacing regulation. A third element is limitation of imports. An additional point, so important it must be called a fourth element of the system, is that there is essentially no restriction on the development of new producing capacity other than the test of profitability. The combined effect of these factors is the development of capacity to produce far in excess of current production, as could easily have been predicted.

The difficult conservation problems—and this includes U.S. petroleum production—arise in those cases where relevant costs and benefits are not united in the calculations of a single economic unit. In some cases, the benefits from a certain action cannot be appropriated by the business that would have to pay for the action. Elimination of stream pollution is a case in point. Or the benefits from a certain action may be worth the cost to a firm, but perhaps this action imposes costs on others for which the firm does not have to pay. Logging and grazing may increase the rapidity of runoff, for example, an effect that may be of no concern to the logger or grazer but which may be of prime importance to downstream users of the water. Sometimes a governmental decision-making unit may neglect certain costs or benefits because it is engaged in stimulating one type of resource use. This may even be viewed—in practice if not legally—as its official mission. Sometimes certain costs or benefits are not brought to bear on a decision because they cannot be quantified in money terms or can be described only in vague nonquantitative terms.

It is likely that in the natural resource area this type of problem will become more pressing as time goes on, both because demands for each of the possible uses of some resources are growing relative to supply, and because new rival demands are rising rapidly whereas before they may have been inconsequential.

Consider, for example, just a few of the various parties with at least partially conflicting interests in the way land and streams are used. There is irrigation vs. power, irrigation vs. domestic and industrial water use, uses requiring dams vs. the scenery, fishing, etc., associated with flowing streams, in particular the whole complex of benefits associated with flowing streams vs. domestic and industrial water use. There is the sand and gravel pit or the clay pit with its ugliness and sometimes dangerous pools of water vs. the residential area with its small children, logging vs. scenery, highways bringing a greater density of people to remote areas vs. solitude, logging and grazing vs. the people downstream who want a slower runoff, and so on.

There are two factors that will tend to intensify these conflicts as time goes on. One is the increase in population, with its obvious effects on the demands for the many different uses of water and on the supply of open space. The other factor is what appears to be an increasing per capita demand for many particular forms of outdoor recreation and for outdoor recreation in general. A number of these forms of recreation do require extensive space and a low density of people. The changing structure of demands for services of resources arising from these two factors suffices to insure no easing of problems in the conservation area.

Exploitation of minerals may be less affected than will be the use of other natural resources, but even here the increased density of population will have its effect—by zoning or otherwise—especially on the ubiquitous minerals. And even in areas where population density remains low, mineral operations will experience more frequent collisions with the various forms of outdoor recreation activity. This will not be a new problem, but it will arise more frequently.

How are the conflicts to be resolved? A first step has already been suggested; namely, to stop pretending that a policy is desirable just because it entails the conservation of something.

Some conflicts can be solved easily since they involve situations in which all the potential users of a resource can *effectively* voice their demands in monetary form. In such cases the presumption in our society (but perhaps rebuttable in some instances!) is that the highest bidders should win, whether the resource is in public or private ownership. It is highly desirable that an effort be made to develop new forms of organization and procedure to permit more extensive use of the market to resolve questions of resource use.

But in many cases there are serious difficulties standing in the way of a thoroughgoing market solution of the problem of rival demands. While interference with and modification of the market's solution will not necessarily yield a better result, the possibility is open. Regulation of the way a resource is used may be desirable where the private user does not take account of significant costs or benefits that his action imposes or gives to others. Some decisions have long-lasting consequences requiring an estimate of demands and costs far into the future, with some cases involving social penalties for underestimate (or overestimate) that may not effectively enter into the private decision. Some benefits and costs do not yield easily, if at all, to valuation in terms of money even for current flows of benefits and costs, let alone those of the future. Here we must analyze and calculate as best we can, trying to search out *all* benefits and costs, some of which may have to be measured and described in nonmonetary terms. It should be recognized that there *are* benefits flowing from natural resources for which individuals cannot express their preferences in money terms simply because there is no feasible way for this to be done. In particular, it will not do to argue that society "needs" lumber or minerals but that scenery, etc., can always be dispensed with. This is an unreal choice, for the problem always involves a specific location. If consumers could express their preferences in economic terms, they might well indicate that they want a particular slope to be forested rather than bare.

A consequence of the fact that some flows of benefits and costs do not receive effective expression in monetary terms is that some of the decisions about the use of natural resources inevitably involve substantial redistributions of real income. The losers from the destruction of the beauties of nature are rarely compensated. The point is not that they should be compensated or that "nature" must always be preserved. The point is that, at a minimum, those whose responsibility it is to make decisions on the use of certain resources should be aware that attention to total costs and benefits may not be enough, for the effects on the real incomes of particular individuals may be substantial.

Unfortunately there is no magic formula that will resolve these problems. The "multiple use" solution, for example, is certainly applicable in many cases, but in some cases it turns out to be just a slogan serving to camouflage the complete sacrifice of one use to others. For example, a reservoir may yield multiple uses including certain forms of recreation, but it is also true that construction of a reservoir entails the complete sacrifice of all uses that depend on the presence of a flowing stream. Once again the lesson is that no slogan, not even one so appealing as multiple use, can resolve all the conflicts present in resource use. Some uses are simply inconsistent with some other uses.

In any particular decision involving incompatible uses, one or the other must be sacrificed, of course. But for a group of decisions involving different projects, uses need not be inconsistent for all projects in an area taken together. It is only by paying close attention to the evolving pattern of use decisions that it is possible to give recognition and at least partial satisfaction to incompatible demands. An indiscriminate application of a multiple-use slogan runs the danger that certain uses which are inconsistent with "multiple use" will get neglected in decision after decision, thus securing no recognition in the final picture that emerges.

In many cases the instrument for resolution of conflict will have to be the political process. The participants include not only those ordinarily thought of as politicians, but the varied types of participants in any significant political problem such as interested voters, government employees, lobbyists, journalists, and so on. Obviously *some* sort of resolution comes out of the process, but the question is how to make the results better. Certainly information and understanding of effects are necessary. Apart from this we need ingenuity and imagination in the formulation of new or variant solutions—new compromises, if you like. And in this area, as in many others, the majority ought to take very seriously its obligation not to trample unheedingly over the minority. In the case of nature preservation issues, especially, certain segments of the population may receive an important part of their real income—measured in satisfaction—from publicly or privately owned resources in which they have no legal interest.

If this advice is taken to heart by the participants in these conservation problems, a change in posture will be required in some cases. While it may seem tactically wise—and may even be pleasant—to oppose all dam construction or to damn the wilderness enthusiasts as a minute nonworking portion of the population with perverted tastes, any progress toward a more suitable resolution of conflicts as they arise is going to be made by those who are less inflexible. An abandonment of fixed positions would be helpful.

The main burden of this discussion perhaps will not be attractive to those who believe that greater conservation of some one thing is always desirable, whether that be songbirds, irrigation water, trees, or grass for sheep, for we have downgraded the term. As often used, it is taken to imply sufficiency for action. The view suggested here, on the other hand, is that a conservative act may or may not be desirable, depending on all the associated benefits and costs and perhaps on the redistribution of real incomes involved. But this downgrading of the term, if it should be called that, does not carry with it any implication that conservation issues are unimportant. Rather, insistence that acts of conservation should not be undertaken simply because something is conserved reflects a view that conservation problems are so important that it is unwise to deal with them on the basis of slogans.

> Beyond all plans and programs, true conservation is ultimately something of the mind—an ideal of men who cherish their past and believe in their future. Our civilization will be measured by its fidelity to this ideal as surely as by its art and poetry and system of justice. In our perpetual search for abundance, beauty, and order we manifest both our love for the land and our sense of responsibility toward future generations.
>
> Stewart Udall, *The Quiet Crisis* (New York: Holt, Rinehart & Winston, 1963), p. 188.

EDWARD T. PRICE

VALUES AND CONCEPTS IN CONSERVATION

Geographers in the United States seem to have committed their profession to a shepherding of natural resources. It is fitting that students of the earth's surface should keep tab on its riches, take part in planning its management, and apprise the coming generation of its potentialities. Depletion has so shockingly marked the history of American resources that its opposite—conservation—has been adopted as the keynote, if not the definition, of both public and private[1] programs for using our resources *wisely*.[2] Wisdom here involves effective judgment as to satisfaction of total wants. It seems proper to inquire into these wants as they affect our decisions and into bases of our judgment in determining whether it is depletion or conservation we really wish.

This paper will be limited to a consideration of the ideological foundations of natural resource conservation as a means to future material welfare. The social and spiritual values that may depend on material welfare are beyond its scope.

• Edward T. Price is Head of the Department of Geography, University of Oregon.

Reprinted from *Annals of the Association of American Geographers,* XLV, No. 1 (March, 1955), 65–84, with permission of the author and the editor.

1 The anomaly of big business in the thick of the fight on the side of conservation is discussed by Erich W. Zimmermann, *World Resources and Industries* (New York: Harper & Bros., 1951), pp. 801, 804.

2 Harold Innis ("The Economics of Conservation," *Geographical Review,* XXVIII [1938], 137) has questioned the lack of philosophy in American conservation literature. Specifically, "the whole question of conservation is begged by its definition as 'wise use.' "

Any plan for the future requires construction of some idea of future conditions and an appraisal of alternative programs in the currency of a social or individual value system. Basic to the appraisal of a future plan is the establishment of a rate of exchange whereby a future value may be measured in present terms. Questions involving the conservation of natural resources hinge on the concepts and values of the future. Both are elements of culture; the values always, and the concepts often, lack objective foundations which are free from the thought patterns of a particular society. Like other phases of resource utilization, optimum time distribution of use varies from one society to another.

Basic Values and Ideas

LIMITATIONS ON THE FUTURE OF PRIMITIVE MAN

Distant future may be nonexistent to primitive man, whose thought begins with the tangible and finds trouble enough in what can be seen but not understood. Even his past enjoys an existence that the future cannot. [An] analyst of man's changing outlook[3] suggests that the fixity and stability of primitive society lead to an emphasis on the past; this emphasis in turn reinforces the stability. With a more conscious mode of existence, man's intellect (replacing instinct) begins to comprehend the future by extrapolating the process by which the present has been steadily transformed into the past. A working concept of

3 Roderick Seidenberg, *Posthistoric Man* (Chapel Hill: University of North Carolina Press, 1950), pp. 75–76.

the future is developed. Seidenberg suggests that only the dead had a future in Ancient Egypt and Medieval Christianity, whereas later generations show an "increasing concern with the yet unborn" and a growing curiosity about the collective future.

A people without a future has no reason to conserve. Such a society might survive either through inability to destroy its resources or through instinctual practices which actually effect the necessary protection. When change is not conceived, it may not occur; witness the introduction to the Americans' time scale of the Rio Grande Valley Indians who felt it foolhardy to move people into an irrigated area which would last only a few hundred years before its reservoir silted up. It is doubted that *Homo sapiens* has ever been totally without a future. The storage of food for tomorrow's meal is probably characteristic of the most primitive man. The preservation of fire or the materials for making it must have involved specific planning, and any tool or weapon fashioned for specialized use is predicated on a future. Consciousness of the more distant future may have been slow to emerge. Even so retrospective a pattern as ancestor worship, however, may have strong implications for the future in that it assumes descendants to carry on the proper reverence for the past.

EXPANDING FUTURE OF INDUSTRIAL MAN

At the other end of human time, is man's interest in the future yet increasing? The greater predictability envisioned by Darwin[4] might help to satisfy man's curiosity and to solidify his concept. As the future and the effect of conserving action become more certain, any purpose of conservation becomes the clearer. The planting of a fruit tree and the building of a factory are acts which are often explainable only on the basis of the interest of a later generation. The increase of life expectancy itself has definite implications for conservation, but the main concern here will be the more distant future of subsequent generations.

Predictability has actually been high in ages when progress was nonexistent and in totalitarian states that exerted an actual control. The predictability we enjoy through increased understanding may be more than offset by the pace of change now occurring. Man's very ability to comprehend has contributed to change no less than to his ability to foresee the change. An assurance of ultimate predictability seems to rest on the assumption of a finiteness of nature for man to circumscribe.[5] Seidenberg's[6] assumption of predictability involves increasing *ex ante* control. Man's interest in the future may yet increase while his knowledge of the intermediate future (the predictability of his own state at a given time before the hypothetical perimeters are approached) does not increase.

Margaret Mead suggests that the "emerging American character"[7] is oriented more to the present than was the American character of a decade ago. She attributes this short-term change to the uncertainty of the future in a world in which America is threatened by outside dangers. The quickening of economic pace not merely to meet these dangers, but also to raise the present level of living (largely through increased employment), results in a more rapid use of resources. Concern for the future may underlie the change, but, with a high uncertainty, economic provision for the future is relatively futile.

SELF-IDENTIFICATION WITH PEOPLE OF THE FUTURE

Given an image of the future in which men like ourselves will inhabit the earth indefinitely, what is our relation to them? The influence that governs any deliberate

[4] Charles Galton Darwin, *The Next Million Years* (Garden City: Doubleday, 1953), p. 55.

[5] Seidenberg, *op. cit.*, p. 68, "perimeters of the future." Darwin, *op. cit.*, pp. 27–38.

[6] Seidenberg, *op. cit.*, pp. 89–90.

[7] Wm. Snyder lecture, Los Angeles City College, April 20, 1953.

action we may take with respect to them[8] is the degree of our sympathy toward them or identification of ourselves with them as fellow human beings. A maximization of our present satisfaction demands assurance of their satisfaction also. A long discussion of the nature of our identification with people of the future is beyond the scope of this paper. It may involve the whole concept of immortality whether one conceives himself as living in the future through his natural or cultural descendants or as a surviving consciousness. Socrates' rule that one should behave as if his soul was eternal might even be extended to treatment of material things.

Sympathy for others varies among individuals, but must be a well-nigh universal trait, essential as it is for the survival of a social animal such as man. It is translated into resource utilization plans by individuals and by groups with the aid of such institutions as governments and religion.

If we assume responsibility for resources, toward what future people are we to direct our sympathies? And what is the material expression of sympathy for a person of the future? Is every mortal soul an act of God and therefore entitled to our attention? If so, sympathy may demand equality of wealth or of opportunity for all peoples. This idea is embodied in religions and in political philosophies professed by millions of people. It is logically extended into the future in the same terms. The obligation to others may call only for some minimum standard conceived as the necessities of life or of living; this specification could likewise be extended to future populations. Or should we now assume that people are brought into the world at Man's discretion and that each is responsible only for his own line?

An individual identifies himself with different organized and unorganized groups. Within a group, relevant to a particular purpose, mutual responsibility is recognized; outside the group it may be denied. The aspirations for the future may involve only one's own group; indeed the individual's hope may sometimes embrace an institution rather than the people who form it. Concern for another group decreases with increase of its remoteness and of the ignorance regarding it, with increasing difference in habit and lack of common interest.

A rough parallel is suggested between spatial or social remoteness and temporal remoteness. The remote group has an unreality which is similar to that of the future. Much of the aid to remote parts of the world today, however, involves an element of material self-interest which the remote future cannot offer us. A material evaluation of the future must be fashioned entirely on a non-material level.

The tenets of some religious sects may lead man to abandon responsibility for his resources to God, but such neglect is likely to occur where end results of particular actions are not evident. The future may qualify here. The philosophy that God will take care of men as He wishes logically leads to no conscious conservation at all. The conditions under which He made manna available to the children of Israel suggest that conservation is no business of men, that it may be a social form of miserliness.

THE POPULATION OF THE FUTURE

Questions of resources and of population are plainly inseparable; each is a function of the other. The values with regard to population become even more involved than those with regard to resources. It is my intent to examine primarily the resources, considering solutions for differing population conditions, but with little evaluation of population itself.

The populations of the future may be controlled collectively or individually; they may grow or shrink in a manner beyond

[8] So long as we assume that the future itself cannot affect us. If our spirits can be disturbed by action of our descendants or if an avenging deity can act in their interest, selfish motives may induce us to consider them. Prospect of reincarnation provides material interest in the future.

human control. The prevailing ideas of the population of the future, among whom the resources must somehow be divided, fall into three groups: (1) the Malthusian population, living at a meager subsistence level, always saturating the available food resources; (2) a population controlled by the will of man, maintained at a comfortable level; and (3) a freely growing population, comfortable because outstripped by a growing availability of resources. As between the first and second, if the two coexist in different societies, the first tends to win out in the long run as the greater numbers of the more fertile group surpass and ultimately displace the others. Expansion of the French at the expense of the English in portions of modern Canada has occurred through the action of many individuals; encouragement of population increase by dictatorial governments has aimed partly at gaining a similar advantage. Hope that the third condition will be fulfilled obviates any problem that growing populations might entail.

If quantity of future population is important, material resources are also important under all three assumptions. If, however, size of population is entirely subordinate to material living standards, material resources may be worthy of consideration under none of the assumptions. If a future society is deemed optimum only if it surpasses minimum standards of resource-man ratio *and* number of people, it is only under the second assumption that material resources, and therefore their conservation, are worthy of concern.

CONVENTIONAL CONCEPTS OF RESOURCES

Resources are commonly defined in terms of usefulness in fulfilling human wants. The concept is highly dynamic in involving all the changing patterns of want and technology in relation to all nature.[9] Wise use of resources is no more than fulfillment of this definition.

The resources of primitive peoples are relatively fixed and unchanging, especially if territorial boundaries are established. Opportunities for expansion are rare. Totemism and taboo may place some irrational limits on use of raw materials, but general concepts of resources probably depend on tangible experience. The resource base must seem painfully finite unless faith is placed in Providence. Many gathering tribes are reported to collect from different portions of their territories in systematic rotation[10]; some shifting cultivators rotate their crop land on a short-term basis.[11] These practices suggest a recognized pinch of resources. (Some primitive peoples have deliberately undertaken to prevent population increase, while others have refused to be concerned with it. Efforts at control of population and resources would be futile for groups who could not keep others from moving into their territories.)

A pattern of resource expansion, either technical or territorial, may stimulate the imagination to theories of indefinite increase. Concepts of either expansion or of ultimate perimeters depend more and more on abstract ideas. Since the future presents many unknowns on both sides of the man-nature complex, current concepts of the future shape of resources are highly divergent.

Natural resources should be viewed as a whole and in terms of their total effect. Some resources are interchangeable in use; others stimulate one another in use. The fertility of a certain cotton field may be maintained by the use and depletion of phosphate mineral deposits. Its soil may be preserved from erosion by consuming petroleum in tractors used to build diversion terraces. When the petroleum is gone, liquid fuels may be prepared from the more plentiful coal. The coal may also be used as a raw material in the production of a

9 See Zimmermann, *op. cit.*, pp. 3–17.

10 E.g., the Paiutes in C. Darryl Forde, *Habitat, Economy, and Society* (New York: Dutton, 1949), pp. 35–39.

11 O. H. K. Spate, "Changing Native Agriculture in New Guinea," *Geographical Review,* XLIII (1953), 170.

fiber that competes with cotton. An alternative use for the cotton field may involve food production on a completely self-sustaining basis. Neither phosphate nor petroleum nor coal nor soil may be isolated as a separate problem. Even if certain important functions are dependent on single resources, we must nevertheless choose among all resources in allocating the limited effort which is available for exploiting them.[12]

Most resources are now conceived as either renewable or non-renewable. These concepts are relative to human time; both break down on a geologic or astronomic time scale. Renewable resources can be managed to provide an annual production or *flow* for an indefinitely long period. Non-renewable resources are the finite *stocks* of minerals which, once used and dispersed, are henceforth unavailable. Under certain conditions of use of certain resources the human and geologic time scales overlap, producing borderline cases between flow and stock resources. Certain ground water deposits can be quickly consumed by rapid pumping for irrigation, but would be flow resources if pumped for household and livestock. The standing timber in a forest represents a stock which can be consumed, but the rate of growth ultimately limits the production.

The organic resources which alone provide man's basic necessity—food—are inherently flow resources. The mineral resources include our chief present sources of energy and a major portion of our structural materials. The use of mineral resources has been expanded particularly rapidly in the industrial age. A great portion of their uses might be classed as nonessential. Except for such resources as water, water power, and air, the minerals are exhaustible. It seems fortunate that our vital needs are met by flow resources. Nevertheless many flow resources can be destroyed, and attention to their protection seems necessary. Some important stock resources may be replaceable by flow resources in the future, others by extremely plentiful stock resources. The possible use of direct solar energy in large quantities illustrates the former; an example of the latter is possible production of the abundant element aluminum from a much greater variety of rock and regolith than the scarce bauxite used now. In a complex society, however, the stock resources may become needed tools in the exploitation of flow resources. Thus food may depend on stock resources too.

WHAT LIMITS RESOURCES?

It is patently impossible in our present state of knowledge to fathom the ultimate availability of energy, structural materials, and foods. Conflicting ideas stem from emphasizing differing portions of our experience and from differing applications of logic to develop concepts of the ultimate. The concept of stock resources suggests that certain materials will soon be exhausted. The extrapolation of the events of the last two or three centuries suggests the happy solution that technology will develop new uses and new materials faster than we consume the stocks. Recovery of certain minerals from the sea, use of lower grade deposits, continued increase of proven petroleum reserves even in the United States, development of common materials to replace scarcer ones, and the hope of solar energy to replace stored energy—all these suggest the trend. Led on by such promises, we can well consider our resources as infinite,[13] superior even to the bounty of an ever-providing God. Faith is placed in human ingenuity and to man belongs the responsibility of discovering, but not of saving. Is such a faith a new human instinct in an age of intelligence, a promise of a *deus ex machina* for every impasse, eagerly accepted by an

[12] C. H. Hammar, "Society and Conservation," *Journal of Farm Economics,* XXIV (1942), 109–10.

[13] Eugene Holman, "Our Inexhaustible Resources," *Atlantic Monthly,* CLXXXIX, No. 6 (June, 1952), 29–32.

audience carried away by its own enjoyment of plenty?

The rationale of this idea of infinite resources rests on the assumption that the utilization of resources under certain conditions stimulates techniques which make more resources available in the future. In other words present and future resource use are complementary.[14] Certainly such a relation has not existed for all societies nor indefinitely for individual resources. Britain's shortage of most raw materials during most of the last hundred years and the increasing dependence of the United States on imports of raw materials are evidences that even these clever peoples find their resources finite. If the resources of any one country are finite, it seems safe to believe that the resources of the world are finite. Though technological expansion may, among other things, be a function of size of population and size of the earth, it is doubted that any combination of both surpasses a critical point beyond which everything is possible. The idea of indefinitely continuing progress may, however, have validity within certain broad limits.

One may accept the concept of expanding resources in its theoretical state based on current patterns of technological advance and economic utility yet wonder whether society can sustain the march into greater complexity. Faced with diminishing returns from our investments, we may find the incentives inadequate. Faced with more capital outlay per unit of output, we may find that the risk mounts too rapidly. Faced with ever more intricate social organization, we may be unable to keep it running smoothly. Physical materials are not resources if societies cannot organize themselves to exploit them.

Another concept of infinitude of resources is based on the laws of conservation of matter and energy.[15] Both are indestructible and hence may theoretically be used any number of times, though it is recognized that they may become unavailable. Thermodynamics indicates, however, that unavailability (chaos) is an ultimate tendency. Energy, once used, passes to a lower state; the leveling of all energy would leave none available for any organized purpose. The utilization of specialized materials results in their dispersal, whereas we have been able to exploit materials only when they are relatively concentrated. The ultimate of unavailability is a perfectly uniform mixture of all substances in a uniform energy state. No material would be concentrated, nor would energy be available to concentrate it.

Perhaps it is this last condition that suggested the equivalence of energy to all other resources[16] (as it is now known to be equivalent to matter itself). Given the energy and a machine to do the job, any material could be separated from all other materials even in the most chaotic state. Chemical reactions among the elements or compounds isolated could produce any recombination desired. Doubtful assumptions appear even in the theoretical state of this concept. When man acquires the ultimate knowledge of which he is capable, does it follow that he can prepare mechanisms for all conceivable transformations and transmutations on the additional condition that he can make up the energy deficits involved?

And what of the organic resources? Whatever special order organic resources

[14] Complementarity between two quantities requires that, if one is an independent variable and the other is dependent, the dependent variable will increase or decrease when the independent variable increases or decreases respectively. The opposite of complementarity is competitiveness, which requires that the change in one should be opposite to the change in the other. In the long run a true stock resource must illustrate competitiveness between present and future use; each pound can be used at any time, but only once. Holman's concept, relative to resources as a whole, involves a perpetually expanding economy, each period built on the preceding.

[15] Hammar, *op. cit.*, p. 112.

[16] *Ibid.*, p. 120.

represent is destroyed in their consumption. Organic evolution seems to represent a specialized reversal of the greater tendency toward chaos.[17] Within our experience organisms have sprung only from other organisms. What assumptions may lead us to believe that energy is the necessary and sufficient condition for their duplication?

Objectives of Conservation Policy

CONDITIONS FOR CONSIDERING CONSERVATION

The faiths and beliefs of the population will determine what goals societies attempt to achieve through conservation. Even though we conceive the dimensions and basic values of the future to be those of the present, and even though the population of the future be within man's control, we encounter unknowns in trying to predict resource discoveries and developments. We must either recognize uncertainty or build some arbitrary concept. As already demonstrated, certain premises lead to the conclusion that conservation is not necessary. If present and future use are complementary, the resources problem is, of course, how to use them faster. Conservation may be a matter of interest only if present use sometimes competes with future use. The acceptance of one or the other of these basic principles—competitiveness or complementarity—for the long run is a matter of faith. My considerations of conservation are necessarily based on the assumption that present use competes with future use. This is not to deny that each condition does exist for particular resources.[18]

EVEN USE OVER ALL TIME

A philosophy of equality of opportunity for all generations regardless of time demands that resources be kept in a state not below their natural level. If we assume an indefinite time span for *Homo sapiens,* stock resources could be used only at their geologic rate of accretion or destruction—in other words, practically not at all. More rapid use is impossible in the long run anyway. It might, however, be possible to use some metals in non-expendable tools and machines. Flow resources could never be allowed to fall below the level of maximum net productivity. The even more exacting condition that all individuals are entitled to equal portions of the earth's material goods could never be attempted unless all the future were known. Consumption of goods would have to be greatest in periods of greatest population. Such a plan might be impossible in the case of perishables in any event.

PREFERENCE FOR PRESENT

Few people today accept the idea of leaving great blocks of our resources untouched.[19] These resources are recognized only in terms of use, and conservation programs are tools to facilitate maximization of some function of this use.

A resource plan must be made in the present. Most individuals and societies give some preference to the present, if for no other reason, because they do not have to bargain with the people of future generations. For that matter many individuals also give preference to the present within their own lives in spending their money

[17] Seidenberg, *op. cit.*, pp. 148–50.

[18] Hammar, *op. cit.*, pp. 115–16, 119, recognizes both relationships and suggests differing "restrictive" and "expansive" policies for handling the respective resources.

[19] The idea is usually dismissed merely on the basis that it is ridiculous. Ridiculous it is in terms of the very fact of our present usage of resources. The idea is nevertheless the result of logical application of assumptions that may be as likely as their opposites and of values that many people maintain. The refusal of the Old Order Amish to use mechanical power on their farms may be partly supported by fear of destroying resources; in contrast their use of soil is considered excellent. Correlative with dismissing the idea of leaving resources untouched is the sense of having to maintain the cultural capital we have accumulated in the process of using them.

or borrowing when they do not have it (though we must realize that a person who borrows when he is young to repay when he is older is not expressing a pure time preference; as repayer he does not plan to be in the same circumstances as he was when borrower).

Preference for the present may be justified as an uncertainty allowance even though we hold the basic philosophy that the future and its people are precisely as important as the present. The uncertainties of the future include the possibilities that new resources may replace those we save (obsolescence), that populations may be smaller, and that catastrophe or evolution may bring an end to *Homo sapiens*. These unknowns are the more likely the longer the time. The possibility that future generations would not need resources as we do can be introduced through a time discount which would allow each successive generation a smaller share of what appears to be available. If the time discount equals the rate of increase of per capita productivity, we might hope to balance depletion with technological advance. The time discount rate could, of course, be negative to allow for the possibility of greater need in the future. Since the one certainty is present usefulness of resources, such rationally determined time discounts would normally favor the present. Once the time discount rate is established, the share of each generation in known stock resources may be apportioned according to a formula described below. Some shifts of flow resource use toward the present may also be indicated.

PREVENTION OF WASTE

In opposition to the Puritan view of saving for the virtue of saving,[20] a significant philosophy in the United States today holds that we should enjoy our resources as intensely as we can. The limit on rate of use set by this philosophy is simply the rate at which we can use. A condition often attached is the limitation of conservation effort to prevention of waste. Waste presumably means some form of exhaustion without use. The concept waste must be defined economically since many forms of waste do not involve wanton carelessness. In the case of petroleum it seems an obvious waste to blow by-product natural gas to the air. The abandonment of recoverable oil in the formation because of overly rapid production is less obvious, but may be equally costly. Is the production of carbon black from natural gas waste? Or the burning of oil or gas under a steam boiler when the more plentiful coal would be only slightly more expensive? Does each stock resource have a highest value, use for other purpose than which constitutes waste? If so, who is the waster, the boiler operator or the union responsible for the high cost of coal? Is it waste to spill a little overflow gasoline on the ground to save valuable time in filling an automobile's tank? Visitors in this country are amazed at the frequency of such occurrences. Waste must be defined in relation to the aim of the particular system of values. A philosophy of prevention of waste must be identical with some philosophy of use.

PROTECTION OF POTENTIAL RESOURCES

Another important end of conservation depends on unrecognized values of known substances. Many of our present resources were not considered valuable in times past. So long as the present trend continues, new resources will continue to be created out of today's *neutral stuff*.[21] The extinction of unused plant and animal species and varieties may show disregard for the future.[22] The purposive preservation of this diversity of biota against the possibility of new demands and new techniques is necessarily

[20] J. K. Galbraith, "The Unseemly Economics of Opulence," *Harper's Magazine*, CCIV, No. 1220 (January, 1952), 58.

[21] This term has been applied to resource theory by Zimmermann, *op. cit.*, p. 8.

[22] Carl O. Sauer, "Theme of Plant and Animal Destruction in Economic History," *Journal of Farm Economics*, XX (1938), 770.

a social matter. It is impossible to set other than arbitrary standards for determining expenditures to this end and for guessing at the benefits to be derived in the future. Any physically irreversible process involves potential loss even though no presently usable value is involved.

TRIUMPH OF DEPLETION

The diversity of peoples and societies embraces a wide range of attitudes and abilities in regard to the utilization of resources. The crucial decisions with regard to resource utilization are likely to be made by those who favor depletion. The conservatives necessarily lose out for several reasons. Those who favor depletion are more aggressive in obtaining control of resources, for depletion yields higher immediate profits than conservation. Depletion is often irreversible, whereas conservation is *sua natura* reversible. The nations depleting resources (their own and others') have used them partly to build military power which further insures their control. Economic emulation and military competition have forced other individuals and nations, respectively, to develop their own resources in similar fashion. Certain fugitive resources[23] especially promote competition for their capture.

The depleters then control the earth; it was previously suggested that the prolific will control the earth. We can hardly know whether we are now in transition from the first condition to the second. That the two groups are largely different at the present, however, may be only coincidental.

HOPE FOR CONSERVATION

Conservation, however, may be a process which tends toward self-justification and self-acceleration. If a conservation measure should make some future condition more certain, then other conservation measures would be safer and more plausible. The reduction of uncertainty increases future values for either public or private planners. It not only reduces the risk involved in the investment, but also increases the likelihood that the benefits can be enjoyed to the utmost.

The most valuable resource is probably worthless without other resources with which it is used. The simultaneous planning of all resources in a great integrated scheme may justify measures which alone would not be worth the effort. A measure which assures the future of one resource may enable a private concern to carry out another measure which will increase future availability of another resource. The process may build up, step by step, with plan after plan falling into place in a generally more certain future.

Conservation always increases some future availability at the expense of current investment, though it need not curtail present use of the same material.[24] Even conservation by curtailment of present use, however, may start a chain reaction if the shortage of one material reduces the demand for others.

GROUP EFFECT ON RESOURCES

History shows that some societies have been particularly effective in conserving their resources, while others have been as notable for their failures. It would be of interest to know which successes and which failures were incidental by-products of some general cultural conditions and which were direct results of conscious values and ideas of the group or its individuals. A small hunting and gathering tribe carefully working its territory seems to require a group spirit or control if the resources are to be preserved; such resources, fugitive with respect to individual interest, might easily succumb to the pressure of people working on a narrow margin. Soil destruction in the Mediterranean region and the

[23] Resources which are not effectively owned until exploited: e.g., petroleum when the pool underlies several properties; fish in oceans, lakes, and rivers; uncontrolled public grazing lands.

[24] For a technical definition of conservation, see S. V. Ciriacy-Wantrup, *Resource Conservation* (Berkeley: University of California Press, 1952), pp. 51–53, 379–80.

European overseas settlements[25] has been effected by peoples who, at least temporarily, could expand their resources. Protection of European soils during one of these expansions has been effected by rooted individuals who did not identify their own opportunities with the expansion. Yet inability to expand resources to keep pace wth population growth must lead to depletion. The unstable combination of a growing population and fading resources can result only in tragedy.[26] The impact of European entry on natives of other continents has often upset the behavior patterns which kept their resources in equilibrium; the appearance of traders in Africa resulted in sad depletion of the particular resources which the natives gathered in exchange for trinkets.[27]

PRESENT AIMS

We may reasonably state Occidental society's present conservation philosophy in the following approximate terms. Resources should be enjoyed to the utmost; we should often protect flow resources from irreversible reduction in flow; we should make a reasonable effort to keep stock resources from becoming unavailable in the future, but not at the expense of depriving large numbers of people of their use; we are hopeful that technology will so broaden our resource base that we will not have to worry about depletion of our present resources; generally we prefer enjoying our luxuries while they last to sharing them with our descendants.

As has always been the case, man does not know what lies ahead of him. Can such ignorance justify a failure to plan on the basis of what is known, while relying on what is unknown?

25 Sauer, *op. cit.*, pp. 766–67.

26 This specter particularly was developed by William Vogt in *Road to Survival* (New York: William Sloane Assoc., Inc., 1948).

27 Jean Brunhes, *Human Geography* (Chicago and New York: Rand McNally, & Co., 1920), pp. 338–39.

LIMITS OF PRESENT VISION

In this state of ignorance how far ahead is man interested in looking? Few can worry seriously about matters that will run beyond their children's lives. We have a few thousand years of recorded history, but this period has been characterized by complementarity of the past and present in resource use. Hitler thought to excite his subjects by referring to events that would assure Germany's future for a thousand years. Certainly a hundred thousand would have seemed a ridiculous figure. Were Germans really concerned about a time so remote as a thousand years? (It is hard to believe that Americans could be.) Perhaps man, in his dreamier moments, may actually be motivated by such prospect.

Conservation and Present Economic Systems

LAISSEZ FAIRE AND CONSERVATION

Although natural resources are material and hence quite properly handled by the standards of the economic system, it is doubtful that our laissez faire structure based on money and credit was designed to meet society's need for conservation. Means of exchange are based largely on present needs, and systems of credit usually involve times no longer than the human life span. Long-lived institutions such as governments and corporations may prolong this period in come cases, but none have life expectancies comparable with mankind's. Our most familiar capital goods such as buildings, roads, and machinery wear out and are renewed with surprising rapidity. Are our accountants instructed to write off our natural resources in the same business-like fashion? To the extent that men accept the system and use it, we must agree that our conservation values are expressed in its terms. However, it probably acts at times in a manner counter to society's direct conservation goals, and group action is taken accordingly. Fortunately the system does provide means whereby the future can often assert its own values. It is also good public policy to try to make the desired type of resource use economic; this condition effected, the program requires little administration.

THE IMPORTANCE OF THE INTEREST RATE

The economic link in any plan that involves a span of time is the interest rate. It must be used in computing cost of investment and in discounting deferred income. It is the means of comparing a value at one time with a value at another. Many rigidities and variations in risk keep interest rates from equalizing at any time. Generally, in a free economy, the interest rate is a function of the supply of and demand for money, measuring the (marginal) return to the investor of money or goods; it largely controls the rate of penalty for assets now rather than in the future.[28] Government manipulation may make money available at considerably different rates, thus upsetting the function of the rate as a yardstick whereby society tends to use scarce savings to best advantage.[29] (Any investment that returns more than the input, however, can be conceived as a benefit to society; accumulation of even very poor investments can account for vast material progress.)

Any value to be gained in the future can be reduced to a present equivalent by discounting at the interest rate a number of times equal to the time units separating the future from the present. Investment of the present value now in any of a selection of enterprises would be estimated to be equivalent to the future value at the future time. Thus any properly priced investment is estimated to be equivalent to any other in its growth in value at the going interest rate. The value of any enterprise may be calculated on the basis of the profit it will yield in the future, each return being discounted to the present. In theory the owner-operator of a productive enterprise may operate it to the end of his career and then sell it or may sell it at any earlier date, investing the money in another enterprise; his net return and worth will be the same.

The interest rate is not in itself an expression of time preference. It serves to guide the decision of a person in choosing whether to save or spend. Some would choose to save even if the interest rate were negative (and inflation may make it effectively so); others choose to spend even if the interest rate is very high.

The interest rate is an expression of confidence in the future. The money received from mining a resource (which a high interest rate favors by the rapid reduction of the value of deferred production) can be invested only in something that depends on other resources. If resources as a whole seemed to be near exhaustion, the interest rate as well as the prices would be expected to rise markedly.[30] An entire economy cannot expand indefinitely while its resources are shrinking. The recent rise in prices of products of the United States petroleum industry, in which present and future are part of a quasi-self-contained system, is an example. The justification for the present price rises, and therefore higher return on investment is not higher cost of petroleum on the market but higher cost of exploration for (scarcer) oil for the future.

On the basis of uncertainties and other criteria society might establish a rational rate of time preference for future planning. It would be coincidental if such time preference equaled the going interest rate. In the short run, society's best time preference is probably the going interest rate, encouraging, as it does, the expansion of the economy, but nothing assures the indefinite continuance of this going rate. In the long run, society's interest may demand a different time preference for allocation of

28 Frank H. Knight, "Professor Fisher's Interest Theory: A Case in Point," *Journal of Political Economy,* XXXIX (1931), 176–212.

29 Ciriacy-Wantrup, "Economic Aspects of Land Conservation," *Journal of Farm Economics,* XX (1938), 469–71.

30 Harold Hotelling, "The Economics of Exhaustible Resources," *Journal of Political Economy,* XXXIX (1931), 145.

scarce resources. Within a generation, time preference can be determined by current economic conditions, but a plan for allocation between generations involves unknowns. The long-run time preference for society is probably lower than present interest rates. What avails it, however, when going rates tend virtually to wipe out values much more than 50 years distant?[31] Current interest rates are such that important long-range objectives may be masked. Can our future be so uncertain that we are not justified in planning a lifetime ahead? The interest rate itself may have some relation to the human life span.[32] Favoring of certain projects such as conservation, which might otherwise be uneconomical, may be a goal of government-determined low interest rates (which may also favor resource-depleting investments). In some cases the greater certainty of benefit from a public project in the interest of all society may justify the lower interest rate which in turn is needed to justify the project. The social time preference rate equals the interest rate only to the extent that we can assume a perpetually expanding total resource base. If we cannot, "The nation's future may not properly be discounted to present worth and private gain."[33]

SOCIETY'S INTEREST AGAINST THE INDIVIDUAL'S

Society is necessarily conceived as a permanent entity, while the individual is ephemeral and less likely to take so long a viewpoint when he has to compete with his fellows in the short run. Society's lower time preference leads to a higher state of conservation as its optimum. In certain emergencies, on the other hand, society's time preference may be much higher.

Society's interest may differ from the free play of capitalism in other ways than the time preference rate. A private operator's costs and gains may represent only a part of the costs and gains of society as a whole. Many social costs, such as rehabilitation of the workers of exhausted mines, are not borne by the private producer. Society's benefits are normally greater than those of the producer, since society shares in the consumer's benefits also.[34] A given commodity may be used in several ways, some of which are easily replaceable and some of which are not important; other uses may be keys to the use of other recources which would justify very high scarcity values. Yet under free competition the utilization of the resource would proceed just as if these higher values did not exist. Exhaustion of a resource for lower uses today may preclude higher uses in the future. The limitation of resources to higher uses under free competition is effected by rising prices. Higher values far in the future, however, are worth little today. Prices do not rise unless scarcity or exhaustion is imminent, perhaps within 50 years, and only slowly for much of that period.

The sum of the actions of a number of identical, but independent, individual consumers is often different from the action which would result from a collective agreement among the individuals; if the latter may be said to represent a rational social end for the group involved (the social end must ultimately be measured by the consumers rather than by the producers), the former must not be identical with the social end. In our society, unit action is usually a resort in emergencies or in cases when the independent individuals obviously hurt themselves in the short run. As an

[31] Ciriacy-Wantrup, *Resource Conservation, op. cit.*, p. 79; certain public agencies are using up to 60 years for their planning periods, figuring interest as low as 3 per cent.

[32] Ciriacy-Wantrup, "Economic Aspects of Land Conservation," *op. cit.*, pp. 469–70.

[33] Ralph H. Hess, "Conservation and Economic Evolution," in Richard T. Ely *et al.*, *The Foundations of National Prosperity* (New York: Macmillan, 1917), p. 184.

[34] Hotelling, *op. cit.*, p. 144; L. C. Gray and Mark Regan, "Needed Points of Development and Reorientation in Land Economic Theory," *Journal of Farm Economics,* XXII (1940), 44.

example suppose that a certain perishable (when captured) fugitive flow resource that goes into a consumer good is cheaply available to the point of its own extinction. It is clearly to the interest of any consumer to limit use to the extent of maintaining the flow at an optimum rate. The consumers enjoy using the resource at a greater rate. Few consumers will refrain from use at the greater rate for the individual's abstention will gain little in that he only makes the limited supply available to someone else. If the resource is exploited by a number of producers, only extinction will result unless collective action is taken. (The voluntary unitization of oil pools is a good example in the area of stock resources.) In this situation, as in some others, monopoly makes for conservation, though usually not at the socially most desirable level. A consumer monopoly would also make for conservation with a different distribution of surplus values between producer and consumer.

Optimum rate of present flow for a private operator under competitive conditions is also optimum rate of flow for society[35] (though, of course, a reorganization of the economy which changed the distribution of consumer spending power would change the demand for particular resources and lead to new optimum use rates). This ideal equality of individually and socially determined action is upset by imperfect markets for assets, uncertainty and conditions that lead to uncertainty, taxes, ignorance, monopoly, interruption of operations, and many other conditions. Ciriacy-Wantrup[36] implies that a major part of society's conservation effort could be spent efficiently in averting the wasteful effects of these conditions.

[35] Ciriacy-Wantrup, *Resource Conservation, op. cit.*, p. 234. Hotelling, *op. cit.*, p. 143, demonstrates the equality of the private and social optima over a period of time in exploiting exhaustible resources, assuming free competition and the use of the private interest rate as the social time preference.

[36] *Resource Conservation, op. cit.*, Part III, pp. 97–219.

CONSERVATION AND PRICES

One simple collective action affecting conservation is to raise the price to the consumer. This conservation occurs automatically when a material approaches exhaustion or otherwise becomes scarce. It is very effective if the end is only to conserve; if applied to consumer goods the effect is to eliminate the poor as consumers; the poor of today make way for the rich of the future. Few modern nations would choose to carry out action with this net result. If society raised the price of a stock resource to what it would be worth if very scarce, it would, in effect, anticipate the approaching exhaustion of the resource by limiting it to its highest uses.

FLOW RESOURCES AND FREE ENTERPRISE

A flow resource normally has some natural rate of availability in its original state. The net return (output minus input) is likely to be a steady optimum at some different level of the standing reserve of the resource. It is characteristic of flow resources that production and return can nearly always be temporarily increased by reducing (mining) the standing reserve. The long run result may be a decline in production which, within certain limits, can be restored at some cost. In other cases the decline may be irreversible or total and final.

Consider a riverine fish population which saturates its food resources in the natural state. Moderate reduction of the population by fishing may allow a more rapid rate of growth of food for human use as pressure on the fish feed is relieved. The maximum sustained catch will be obtained if the population is below its natural state. In any season the catch can be increased by expenditure of more effort; the continued reduction of the population may reduce the reproduction rate and likewise the catch in subsequent years. The stock can be built up only by reducing the catch for a few seasons or by establishment of hatcheries. Complete reduction of the stock in any stream can probably be overcome by the expense of artificial restocking. Complete extinction in all streams is final; the same species can never be renewed.

The first aim of the owner-operator of a property producing a flow resource is to provide for his own needs during his lifetime. If he were entirely dependent on the property and on getting the most out of it, he would presumably reap an annual harvest averaging somewhat above the long-run optimum, ending with a badly depleted or irreversibly ruined resource. Suppose, however, the owner-operator had a son to whom he wished to pass on the property; he would have to make a direct evaluation involving another generation, planning to turn the property over to his son in a state that would represent his idea of the proper division between the two generations in this intimate case. Most owners would hope to maintain the property in its optimum producing state; no time preference would be expressed; the property would be managed for equal production in all years. This process could be extended through all time, though allocation of capital costs needed to meet changing conditions and short-run problems would be varied. The European peasant family is likely to identify itself with the productive land on which it is dependent. Preservation of the land has an object quite apart from any market values involved. The more mobile American is less likely to take such an attitude. But even some of the least mobile and neediest American farmers have not succeeded in preserving the soil on their hillside farms in the Appalachians.

In a specialized society interest in one's own children demands interest in the society too. The preservation of a property, however, does not normally require direct interest of the owner in the next generation. The owner can sell his property for its value under normal conditions. His maximum return from the property includes the sale price (which might be borrowed ahead of time) when he finally disposes of it. This sale price is really an assertion of the interest of the next generation in continued production and an expression of its confidence that it can be sold again to another generation. (However, the ability of coming generations to buy depends partly on inheritance. In some primitive societies the coming generation takes over more forcibly.) Through this process a continuity is assured, which tends to preserve flow resources indefinitely. Even a short-run interest in maintaining production from season to season often serves to preserve a flow resource indefinitely. The Nootka transported salmon spawn from other streams when one stream began to run low;[37] their interest probably covered only a few coming seasons, but continuance of the practice would maintain the fishing forever.

WHEN IS DEPLETION PROFITABLE?

The depletion of a flow resource is theoretically profitable when and only when the ratio of the reduction in flow to the year's extra harvest is less than the going interest rate. The mining of such a resource would yield a sum of money which, if invested at the going rate, would give a better return than the resource. Socially, irreversible action is of extremely questionable wisdom. In destroying a flow of present value, it is the present, perhaps, rather than the future, that must be discounted. In the recent past private enterprise has often found sustained-yield operation of forests unprofitable. The annual growth is such a small fraction of the stand that the greater present value of the stand outweighs the prospect of a continuing annual return (the unit cost of production, tax structure, and other matters must be considered here too). The fact that the forest may come back after a long period of time is of value to society, but is not considered by the company that abandons the cutover land. Abandonment of milpa farms that will not be touched again for genera-

[37] Forde, *op. cit.*, p. 78.

tions may be equally final as far as the individuals involved are concerned.

COLLECTIVE ACTION IN FLOW RESOURCES

A society often takes action with regard to resources which is not justified under going time preference rates. The government of the Netherlands has reclaimed land from the sea at great expense; the government is repaid by the user at an interest rate below that demanded for other investments. Yet society in this crowded land considers the addition of permanently productive land a good investment. Sweden's policy of operating its slow-growing forests on a sustained-yield basis may not maximize present gains, but it satisfies the Swedes that the operation will continue smoothly and that the future of Sweden will therefore be safer. Similarly any centralized economy may act directly on its idea of the public good and bring into use resources other nations would leave idle or readjust the time distribution of resource use in a manner out of line with that produced by the free play of individuals. A paternalistic government in crowded China might find it expedient to use for food production land which lay idle under the former free economy. Even if it would not feed the families that cultivated it, the total food available could be increased.

PROTECTION OF FLOW RESOURCES

The aims of society and of the individuals who operate most flow resources are not highly divergent. The maintenance of an optimum flow is a common aim, and substantial agreement on what constitutes an optimum flow is usual. Particularly undesirable in most cases is an irreversible reduction or cessation of flow. Against this we have several lines of defense. The last is government action, which may be applied when other methods fail. It may take the form of fiat, tax policy, subsidy, penalty, government operation, or some indirect action. Next is collective action by the producers; it is difficult under anti-trust laws in the United States, whereas collective action at the consumer level must nearly always be carried out by pressure on the government. Ahead of this is the interest of the operator, who will protect his property if the yield is high enough in spite of an irresponsible consumer demand for supercritical production. Even if the resource is fugitive in nature so that no individual operator can have an effective vested interest in its perpetuation, the excessive cost of capture in the depleted state may prevent the reduction in flow from becoming total. When a game animal becomes scarce, it may no longer be worth the effort to hunt; a small population may survive which, if later protected, is capable of rebuilding the population. Finally the flow of some resources such as rainfall may not be seriously affected by human action.

DEPLETION IN EMERGENCIES

The institutional and cyclical imperfections in the ideal economy may at times produce a critical period which will be particularly serious when the health or life of the planning agent (human or corporate) is threatened. If such crises can be weathered only by irreversible depletion of the resource, the decision is evident. Averting such crises may be a major goal of social action.[38] On a larger scale the life of the society itself may require irreversible depletion of resources, as during a war or famine; a decision in favor of conserving the resource would destroy, wholly or partially, the end to which the resource was to be put. The proper balance between impairment of resource and impairment of population must be struck in terms of the relative values of the future and the present. Overpopulated areas are chronically in such a state of emergency. Subsistence farmers of the Appalachians and at times com-

[38] Ciriacy-Wantrup, *Resource Conservation, op. cit.*, pp. 251–67.

mercial wheat growers of the Great Plains must sacrifice their resources in order to live.

CHECKS ON EXHAUSTION OF STOCK RESOURCES

The optimum use of stock resources may be more widely divergent, as between individual evaluation and social evaluation.

If the exploitation and consumption of a stock resource entailed no inertia, the product might be used up in an infinitesimally short time. In actuality the utilization of these resources requires effort (in discovery, in mining, in development of uses and of equipment in which they are utilized). The cumulative annihilation of these resources can increase only as total effort involved accumulates, and this last process requires time. The rate of use of minerals has grown at a rate proportional to itself (complementarity); while the deposits last, mineral use grows like a rolling snowball. Extrapolation of the present curve suggests no satiation point to man's appetite for these materials.

A secondary brake on the rate of use of stock resources lies in the fact that the capital needed for their exploitation will be available only in such quantities as can be justified by the deposits. Assuming a constant demand for the product, a constant cost of production, and a going interest rate, the proper rate of exploitation of a particular deposit can be determined, and its life will be finite; a maximum difference is obtained between initial capital investment (determining rate of production) and present total net operating return (which decreases the longer the production period).[39] The long-run social value of this brake on rate of production cannot be very great. While our economic system usually provides for an indefinite use of flow resources, it helps very little in providing for a long-term distribution of use of stock resources.

LONG-RANGE OUTLOOK FOR STOCK RESOURCES

The early build-up period in the development of a new stock resource is one of temporal complementarity in resource use. If it ultimately leads to depletion, a temporarily competitive condition will ensue. Use of uranium and similar fissionable materials for atomic energy and warfare may increase rapidly as new methods of using them develop. They could be used in almost unlimited quantities. Since the supply is limited, however, such a process must sow the seeds of its own end. For some resources we may assume that the relationship of present and future use is complementary in the short run (in which our economic forces operate) but competitive in the long run. This year's use increases next year's, but may decrease that of a hundred or a thousand years hence. The complementary condition hastens the time of competitiveness.

How can rational societies allocate in time their use of stock resources if they do not subscribe to the theory of indefinite increase of resource use? As already suggested they can use some time discount for uncertainty. The fraction of the estimated recoverable stock resource to be made available in any one interval is equal to the rate by which each successive interval is discounted.[40] Both discount rate and estimated resource would be subject to revision at any time. If neither changes after such a plan is instituted, stock resource use will taper off along the same sort of curve

[39] This has been more generally stated by L. C. Gray, "Economic Possibilities of Conservation," *Quarterly Journal of Economics,* XXVII (1913), 505–6; the proper rate of mining has been developed mathematically by Hotelling, *op. cit.*, pp. 140–42.

[40] If the time preference or discount rate is r, the use in the nth future interval will be a fraction of the present use equal to $(1-r)^n$. Since the geometric series $\sum_{0}^{\infty} n\ (1-r)^n$, which sums these successive use rates over all time, converges (i.e., has a finite value), finite amounts can be assigned each interval even though the plan cover an infinite length of time.

by which it has grown. If this plan lengthens the period of resource use, the time discount rate is equivalent to a lowered interest rate. Sweden's control on the rate of mining her iron ore is a good example of the assertion of a socially, but not economically, determined rate. Sweden's resources appear distinctly limited to a society that identifies itself with that part of the earth. As already demonstrated, if our knowledge becomes total, and the world thereby becomes measured, society should theoretically have no time preference as such; a proper allocation of people and resource use could be made over all time.

Many acts of man make stock resources which would otherwise be available for use in the future either unavailable or much more difficult to recover. The mining of one coal seam may make an overlying seam unavailable as the caving breaks it up into small pockets. These acts are similar to irreversible reduction in flow of certain resources. They bear the same set of relations to private exploiters and to public goals.

Conclusion

If nations are independent societies, it may develop that survival is dependent on keeping pace with other nations. Then utilization of stock resources is necessary. This sort of competition between nations would lead to a pattern of resource depletion (or expansion?) similar to that which characterizes utilization within a capitalistic nation even though all nations involved were communistic. The merging of the world into a single totalitarian nation on the other hand could conceivably reduce the exploitation of stock resources.

High taxes, socialization, and communization are said to destroy incentives, leading to lowered standards of living. We may say that taxation, which is essentially involved in all these, is, to the extent of the taxation, an identification of individual interest with that of society. If this incentive theory is correct and if it is indeed society's wish to conserve by deferment of use, then value, means, and end are all accordant in a totalitarian society whose resources are exhaustible. They are likewise accordant in an aggressive capitalistic society whose present and future resources are complementary. The predictability effected by totalitarian control will tend to justify any plan which is made. Economic stagnation too might have the effect of making the most abundant resources exhaustible. Free societies tend to socialize resources whose use shows markedly competitive relations with future use. Laissez-faire capitalism, when most of the economy is expanding, is not suited to the management of particular resources which are shrinking.

In contrast to simpler primitive societies and totalitarian societies, our society is recognized as one whose values do not "add up." Values in regard to conservation are not exceptional. The soil conservationist and the petroleum conservationist alike exert the same consumer pressures on the exhaustion of both soil and petroleum as do other citizens. It is one thing to look at the land and worry about what is happening to it, another to shop in a competitive market and keep up with the neighbors.

The conflicts that lie behind the perennial arguments about conservation are not merely the result of individual differences and points of view. Even if we ignore residuals from other days, they trace from conflicting threads in the social fabric. Conservation ideas involve abstract values, while the object of the ideas is strictly material. Can ideas really apply? Current experience tells us that material use increases itself, while reason tells us that the world is finite. Many of our personal conflicts span the ideologies of the free and totalitarian worlds. Most of us have a basic totalitarian view of the need for a rational social action combined with a capitalist's enjoyment of material goods. Most of us hold idealistic views of the unity of mankind in all space and time, but are accustomed to acting in our short-run interest and for ourselves or small groups. Prevailing uncertainties thwart man's desire to reason precisely. They even shake the idea of society's eternity. Is it any wonder if at some point in his chain of reason man gives up the attempt and abandons pure rationality for pragmatism? The state of conservation is determined by the interaction of faith, reason, and immediate and ultimate values. The balance of the various conflicts shifts with these variables.

We can, I think, classify under three headings the conservationist objections to leaving decisions about resource use to the individual.

In the first place, the conservationist believes that the maximum social benefit is not achieved by each individual's maximizing his private benefit because there are certain social benefits to be derived from conservation which are not appreciable to the individual business. . . .

Secondly, the conservationist argues that the laissez-faire theory of resource use is inapplicable. The conservationist may accept the assertion that the maximum benefit for the greatest number will emerge from the profit-maximizing efforts of entrepreneurs *in perfect competition* but argues that it should not be carried over to a real world in which there are ubiquitous elements of ignorance, risk, and monopoly. Even if it could be proved that perfect competition leads to ideal utilization of resources, would not these "imperfections" demand government intervention?

The third motive for state intervention is perhaps unique to the conservation question: the individual business will manage natural resources in the light of the going rate of interest. The final conservationist objection to individual management is that the going rate of interest, as determined by the market, is "myopic," or shortsighted, and is not the best rate of interest from a "social" point of view. The correct social rate of interest would be lower than the market rate at present determined and would induce more owners to conserve their resources than is now the case.

ANTHONY SCOTT, *Natural Resources: The Economics of Conservation*, Canadian Studies in Economics No. 3 (Toronto: University of Toronto Press, 1955), p. 57.

GIFFORD PINCHOT

WHAT IT ALL MEANS

The conservation of natural resources, and of human resources as well, began to spread from America to all the world as the firm basis of permanent prosperity among men and of lasting peace among nations. But what does it all mean?

I believe, and I have made no secret of my belief, that a good forester must also be a good citizen. I have tried to be both, with what success it is not for me to say. But at least I am not without experience.

What I have learned in more than half a century of active life, whatever else it may be, is not mere book theory. The conclusions I have reached are based on what I myself have lived, and seen, and known, and had to fight. They are the direct results of responsible work in forestry and conservation; in public administration, national and state; in politics, national, state, and local; in city, farm, and frontier; in college and church; in many other phases of American life; and on personal acquaintance with every state in the Union.

Through all my working days, a part of my job, in office and out, and a most essential part, has been to estimate and understand public opinion, and to arouse, create, guide, and apply it.

What then, as I see it, is the conclusion of the whole matter?

• Gifford Pinchot (1865–1946), a leading conservationist, was at one time Head, U.S. Forest Service, and later Governor of the Commonwealth of Pennsylvania.

Reprinted from Gifford Pinchot, *Breaking New Ground* (New York: Harcourt, Brace & World, 1947), pp. 504–10, with permission of the publisher.

This: The earth and its resources belong of right to its people. Without natural resources life itself is impossible. From birth to death, natural resources, transformed for human use, feed, clothe, shelter, and transport us. Upon them we depend for every material necessity, comfort, convenience, and protection in our lives. Without abundant resources prosperity is out of reach.

Therefore the conservation of natural resources is the fundamental material problem. It is the open door to economic and political progress. That was never so true as now.

The first duty of the human race on the material side is to control the use of the earth and all that therein is. Conservation means the wise use of the earth and its resources for the lasting good of men. Conservation is the foresighted utilization, preservation, and/or renewal of forests, waters, lands, and minerals for the greatest good of the greatest number for the longest time.

Since conservation has become a household word, it has come to mean many things to many men. To me it means, everywhere and always, that the public good comes first.

To the use of the natural resources, renewable or non-renewable, each generation has the first right. Nevertheless no generation can be allowed needlessly to damage or reduce the future general wealth and welfare by the way it uses or misuses any natural resource.

Nationally, the outgrowth and result of conservation is efficiency. In the old world that is passing; in the new world that is coming, national efficiency has been and will be a controlling factor in national safety and welfare.

Internationally, the central purpose of conservation is permanent peace. No nation, not even the United States, is self-sufficient in all the resources it requires. Throughout human history one of the commonest causes of war has been the demand for land. Land (agricultural land, forest land, coal, iron, oil, uranium, and other mineral-producing land) means natural resources.

Therefore, worldwide practice of conservation and fair and continued access by all nations to the resources they need are the two indispensable foundations of continuous plenty and of permanent peace.

Conservation is the application of common sense to the common problems for the common good. Since its objective is the ownership, control, development, processing, distribution, and use of the natural resources for the benefit of the people, it is by its very nature the antithesis of monopoly. So long as people are oppressed by the lack of such ownership and control, so long will they continue to be cheated of their right to life, liberty, and the pursuit of happiness, cheated out of their enjoyment of the earth and all that it contains. It is obvious, therefore, that the principles of conservation must apply to human beings as well as to natural resources.

The conservation policy then has three great purposes.

1. Wisely to use, protect, preserve, and renew the natural resources of the earth.
2. To control the use of the natural resources and their products in the common interest and to secure their distribution to the people at fair and reasonable charges for goods and services.
3. To see to it that the rights of the people to govern themselves shall not be controlled by great monopolies through their power over natural resources.

Two of the principal ways in which lack of conservation works out in damage to the general welfare are (*a*) by destruction of forests, erosion of soils, injury of waterways, and waste of non-renewable mineral resources. Here is strong reason for government control. (*b*) By monopoly of natural and human resources, their products and application, and of the instruments by which these are made available.

Monopoly means power—power not only over the supply of natural resources, but also power to fix prices and to exact unfair profits which lead to higher living costs for the people. It is the very essence of democracy that the greatest advantage of each of us is best reached through common prosperity of all of us. Monopoly is the denial of that great truth.

Monopoly of resources which prevents, limits, or destroys equality of opportunity is one of the most effective of all ways to control and limit human rights, especially the right of self-government.

Monopoly on the loose is a source of many of the economic, political, and social evils which afflict the sons of men. Its abolition or regulation is an inseparable part of the conservation policy.

And that is far from the whole story. What the people are forced to pay for Concentrated Wealth and its monopolies is by no means confined to an unjustly high cost of living. A moral and intellectual price, a price in knowledge and understanding, in education, in degradation of standards, and in limited freedom of thought and action, must be paid also. Here may well be the heaviest cost of all.

Said Louis D. Brandeis in an opinion from the Supreme Court bench:

> Those who won our independence believed that the final end of the State was to make men free to develop their faculties. They valued liberty both as an end and as a means. They believed liberty to be the secret of happiness, and courage to be the secret of liberty. They believed that freedom to think as you will and to speak as you think are means indispensable to the discovery and spread of political truth; that the greatest menace to

freedom is an inert people; that public discussion is a political duty; and that this should be a fundamental principle of the American government.

How far Concentrated Wealth is willing to go in pursuit of profit has been clearly shown in this war and the last. In both wars profit was put before patriotism by certain great concentrations of capital which traded, through international cartels, with similar concentrations in the enemy's country, even to the extent of furnishing military supplies for hostile armies. To them profit justified anything.

(When I speak of Concentrated Wealth I refer to the many forms of concentration of economic power by which greedy men have sought domination. I mean the monopoly power of great corporations, of banks and insurance companies, of utilities and power companies, as well as individual fortunes. The devices by which Concentrated Wealth controls men and resources are many, complicated and devious. The financial manipulations, control of prices, interlocking directorates, monopolization of patents and materials, and last but not least, the concentration of ownership of newspapers and radio broadcasting networks, are all part of the far-reaching web of Concentrated Wealth.)

Concentrated Wealth attributes the prosperity and progress of the United States to what it calls free enterprise. To it free enterprise means freedom to take, keep, and control all the resources, services, and opportunities it can, and charge for them the last possible cent. It overlooks the three main factors in our progress: first, our incomparable natural resources, some of them still in the hands of the people; second, government by the people, so far as we have actually had it; and third, the drive and stimulus of mixed races adventuring in a new land.

Concentrated Wealth can only maintain its strangle hold over the general welfare if it can get the people to accept its exactions, and especially the methods by which it gets its power, as normal and natural. For the people can destroy monopoly at any time they choose to exert themselves.

The monopolists must accustom people to their tyranny by a constant stream of praise for great corporations and of free enterprise according to their own interpretations, as well as discrediting of liberal movements and leaders—all of which is facilitated by their ever increasing control of the press, the radio, and other news outlets.

They are infinitely resourceful in their campaigns. On the highly controversial issue of state or national regulation of natural resources and public utilities, the Economic Royalists, as F. D. R. called them, are for whichever is the least effective. Thus, when certain of the states began to enforce effective regulation, they were all out against state control. But when T. R. used the power of the Federal government to limit exploitation, Concentrated Wealth made an about-face and became the foremost advocate and defender of states' rights. It is so still today.

In many states huge sums are poured out for the upkeep of political machines and the financing of primary and general elections, for the purpose of controlling legislation and also executive action and judicial decisions. It is far more prevalent than the general public has any idea of. This is not mere theory. It is based on evidence secured by personal experience over many years and in many parts of the country.

Because so much of my work has been done in public office, I have had the need and the opportunity to understand what makes politics tick. For many years I have known and had to fight the political servants of the great special interests, who were never more dangerous than they are today.

But in the hearts of the American people democracy has not been denied. The Four Freedoms of Franklin Roosevelt—Freedom of Speech, Freedom of Worship,

Freedom from Want, and Freedom from Fear—have, I am confident, been accepted by those whom Abraham Lincoln called the plain people, accepted as their right, and no more than their right. If that is true, we have come to a turning point.

At each turning point in human history two great human forces have fought for control. One demanded a greater share of prosperity and freedom for the many. The other strove for the concentration of power, privilege, and wealth in the hands of the few. One wanted to go forward to better things. The other strove to go back to what it call "the good old days."

Just as feudalism, with its tyranny, finally made itself intolerable, so too plutocracy, with its rule over the man by the dollar, with its hardships for the many and its luxury for the few, with its greed and its injustice, must be made to travel the same road. It is time for America and the world to move on from a social order in which unregulated profit is the driving force. It is time to move up to a social order in which equality of opportunity will cease to be a dream and actually come to pass.

I do not pretend to foretell just what that order will be or by what steps it will be reached. When it comes, I want it to come by development and not by revolution.

When it comes, I hope and believe the new order will be based on cooperation instead of monopoly, on sharing instead of grasping, and that mutual helpfulness will replace the law of the jungle. When it comes, I hope and believe that great unregulated concentrations of wealth, with their enormous power for evil, will no longer be allowed to exist.

I believe in free enterprise—freedom for the common man to think and work and rise to the limit of his ability, with due regard to the rights of others. But in what Concentrated Wealth means by free enterprise—freedom to use and abuse the common man—I do not believe. I object to the law of the jungle.

The earth, I repeat, belongs of right to all its people, and not to a minority, insignificant in numbers but tremendous in wealth and power. The public good must come first.

The rightful use and purpose of our natural resources is to make all the people strong and well, able and wise, well-taught, well-fed, well-clothed, well-housed, full of knowledge and initiative, with equal opportunity for all and special privilege for none.

Whatsoever ye would that men should do to you, do ye even so to them.

That is the answer.

JOHN C. WEAVER

CONSERVATION: MORE ETHICS THAN ECONOMICS

I have often wondered heretically if conservation could, as such, be considered a field of knowledge. Indeed I have long speculated as to whether conservation could in itself be defended as a clearly definable subject for a formal course in the school or college curriculum. That conservation is, however, a way of life, a state of mind, which should pervade every educational process of man, I think there can be no doubt.

In a cogent phrase, the late Aldo Leopold of the University of Wisconsin defined conservation as the attainment and maintenance of "a state of harmony between men and land." This is the conservation idea. This is the goal that in the interests of ultimate survival, man must not fail to attain. This is a destiny that society can achieve only through the rising crescendo of voices of individual men and women whose common convictions cannot in the aggregate be denied.

The most profoundly persuasive case for the conservation idea with which I am familiar is carried in the central threads of the collection of Aldo Leopold's essays published under the title *A Sand County Almanac* (Oxford University Press, New York, 1949). Anyone who has not lived its pages has an inspiring and poetic intellectual experience before him. Let me either remind you of, or draw your attention to, some of the more sober conclusions expressed in the pages of this little book.

To Leopold, the conservational concept was imbedded in the realm of moral and ethical behavior, of religion itself. He said:

> All ethics so far evolved rest upon a single premise: that the individual is a member of a community of interdependent parts. His *instincts* prompt him to compete for his place in that community, but his *ethics* prompt him also to cooperate, perhaps in order that there may be a place to compete for.

Professor Leopold went on to observe that "conservation is getting nowhere because it is incompatible with our Abrahamic concept of land. We abuse land because we regard it as a commodity belonging to us. When we see land as a community to which we belong, we may begin to use it with love and respect. There is no other way for land to survive the impact of mechanized man. . . ."

Let me in conclusion throw Leopold's gauntlet of challenge down before you:

> Despite nearly a century of propaganda, conservation still proceeds at a snail's pace. . . . The usual answer to this dilemma is "more conservation education." No one will debate this, but is it certain that only the *volume* of education needs stepping up? Is something lacking in the *content* as well?
>
> It is difficult to give a fair summary of its content in brief form, but, as I understand it, the content is substantially this: obey the law, vote right, join some organizations, and practice what conservation is profitable on your own land; the government will do the rest.

• John C. Weaver is Vice-President for Instruction and Dean of the Faculties, Ohio State University.

Reprinted from *Economic Geography,* XXXV, No. 4 (October, 1959), Guest Editorial, with permission of the author and the editor.

Is not this formula too easy to accomplish anything worthwhile? It defines no right or wrong, assigns no obligations, calls for no sacrifice, implies no change in the current philosophy of values. In respect of land-use, it urges only enlightened self-interest. Just how far will such education take us?

Many a conservation project represents a beautiful piece of social machinery, but all too often it is coughing along on two cylinders because we have been too timid, and too anxious for quick success, to tell the people involved the true magnitude of their obligations. Obligations have no meaning without conscience, and the problem we face is the extension of the social conscience from people to land.

No important change in ethics was ever accomplished without an internal change in our intellectual emphases, loyalties, affections, and convictions. . . . Conservation has not yet touched these foundations of conduct. . . . In our attempt to make conservation easy, we have made it trivial.

In a word, and in the final analysis, conservation is ethics, not economics.

Four million students were enrolled in U.S. colleges and graduate schools in 1960. The Bureau of the Census estimates that 6 million will seek admission or continued enrollment in 1965, 8 in 1970, 10 in 1975, 12 in 1980. No one questions our ability to feed these youngsters. But are we as a nation at all prepared for a tripling of the size of our colleges and universities in 15 years? We need a population policy and we need it soon, for the United States as well as for the world at large, not because we cannot step up food production, but because we believe, like Plato and Aristotle, in trying for excellence rather than in rejoicing in numbers. Excellent human subjects will not be produced without abundance of cultural as well as material resources. We are likely to run out of copper before we run out of food, of paper before we run out of copper. We are short even in this country now of housing, of hospitals, and of educational institutions. Needs are, of course, infinitely more acute in most other areas of the world.

JEAN MAYER, "Food and Population: The Wrong Problem?" *Daedalus, Journal of the American Academy of Arts and Sciences,* XCIII, No. 3 (Summer, 1964), 844.

JOHN KENNETH GALBRAITH

HOW MUCH SHOULD A COUNTRY CONSUME?

Conservationists are unquestionably useful people. And among the many useful services that they have recently rendered has been that of dramatizing the vast appetite which the United States has developed for materials of all kinds. This increase in requirements we now recognize to be exponential. It is the product of a rapidly increasing population and a high and (normally) a rapidly increasing living standard. The one multiplied by the other gives the huge totals with which our minds must contend. The President's Materials Policy Commission[1] emphasized the point by observing that our consumption of raw materials comes to about half that of the non-Communist lands, although we have but 10 per cent of the population, and that since World War I our consumption of most materials has exceeded that of all mankind through all history before that conflict.

This gargantuan and growing appetite has become the point of departure for all discussions of the resource problem. In the face of this vast use what is happening to our domestic reserves of ores, to our energy sources, to the renewable resources? Are we being made excessively dependent on foreign supplies? How can we insure that they will continue to flow in the necessary volume and with the necessary increases to our shores? How is our security affected?

The high rate of use has catalyzed conservationist activity on many other fronts. Because of it we have been busily assessing reserves of various resources and measuring the rate of depletion against the rate of discovery. We have become concerned with the efficiency of methods of recovery. As a result, for example, of the meteoric increase in natural gas consumption, the prospect for further increase, and the limited supplies at least within the borders of continental United States, we have had an increasing concern over what was flared or otherwise lost. The large requirements and the related exhaustion of domestic reserves support the concern for having ready stocks of materials in the event of national emergency. (Support for this also comes from the not inconsiderable number of people who, in this instance, find prudence a matter of some profit.) Our large fuel requirements have deeply affected our foreign policy even though it remains a canon of modern diplomacy that any preoccupation with oil should be concealed by calling on our still ample reserves of sanctimony.

Finally, and perhaps most important, the high rate of resource use has stirred interest in the technology of resource use and substitution. Scores of products would already have become scarce and expensive had it not been for the appearance of substitute sources of materials or substitute

• John Kenneth Galbraith is Professor of Economics, Harvard University.

Reprinted from Henry Jarrett (ed.), *Perspectives on Conservation* (Baltimore: The Johns Hopkins Press for Resources for the Future, Inc., 1958), pp. 89–99, with permission of the author and the publisher.

[1] References here are to *Resources for Freedom* (Washington: Government Printing Office, 1952). Summary of Volume I, hereinafter cited as PMPC, Summary.

materials. We still think of innovation in terms of the unpredictable and fortuitous genius which was encouraged by the patent office. In fact, input/output relationships for investment in innovation, not in the particular case but in general, are probably about as stable as any other. And investment in such innovation may well substitute, at more or less constant rates, for investment in orthodox discovery and recovery. This means, in less formidable language, that if a country puts enough of its resources into researching new materials or new sources of materials, it may never be short of the old ones. We cannot necessarily rely on the market for this investment—market incentives did not get us synthetic nitrogen, synthetic rubber, or atomic energy—to mention perhaps the three most important new materials substitutes or sources of this century. We shall have to initiate publicly much of the needed innovation, and much of it will have to be carried to the point of commercial feasibility by public funds. We shall have to be watchful to anticipate needed investment in innovation. We will be making another of our comfortable and now nearly classic errors if we assume that it will all be taken care of automatically by the free enterprise system.

But the role of research and innovation is not part of this story. I cite it only because one must do so to keep the resource problem in focus. In the future, as in the past, substitution nurtured by science will be the major hope of the conservationist. I am not unimpressed with the importance of what I have now to say. But I would not wish it thought that I identify all resource salvation therewith.

In my opening sentences I spoke agreeably about the conservationist as a citizen. May I now trade on those graceful words and be a trifle rude? Any observer of the species must agree that he is also frequently capable of marked illogicality combined with what may be termed selective myopia. There are many manifestations of this. Nothing, for example, is more impressive than the way the modern conservationist rises in awesome anger—particularly, I think, along the Eastern Seaboard—at a proposal to dam and thus to desecrate some unknown stream in some obscure corner of some remote national park, and at the same time manages to remain unperturbed by the desecration of our highways by the outdoor advertising industry. Were the Governor of New York, in some moment of political aberration to propose a minor modification of the state's "forever wild" proviso as it applies to the state parks, he would be jeopardizing his future. When he seeks to make the highways of his state less hideous, he can hope, at most, for the applause of Robert Moses, the *New York Times*, the most determined garden clubs, and a few eccentrics. One may formulate a law on this: the conservationist is a man who concerns himself with the beauties of nature in roughly inverse proportion to the number of people who can enjoy them.

There is, I sense, a similar selectivity in the conservationist's approach to materials consumption. If we are concerned about our great appetite for materials, it is plausible to seek to increase the supply, to decrease waste, to make better use of the stocks that are available, and to develop substitutes. But what of the appetite itself? Surely this is the ultimate source of the problem. If it continues its geometric course, will it not one day have to be restrained? Yet in the literature of the resource problem this is the forbidden question. Over it hangs a nearly total silence. It is as though, in the discussion of the chance for avoiding automobile accidents, we agree not to make any mention of speed!

I do not wish to overstate my case. A few people have indeed adverted to the possibility of excess resource consumption —and common prudence requires me to allow for discussions which I have not encountered. Samuel H. Ordway in his *Re-*

sources and the American Dream[2] has perhaps gone farthest in inquiring whether, in the interests of resource conservation, some limits might be placed on consumption. He has wondered if our happiness would be greatly impaired by smaller and less expensive automobiles, less advertising, even less elaborate attire. And he argues, without being very specific about it, that the Congress should face the question of use now as against use by later generations.

By contrast, The Twentieth Century Fund, in its effort to match materials and other resource requirements to use, takes present levels of consumption and prospective increases as wholly given. It then adds to prospective needs enough to bring families at the lower end of the income distribution up to a defined minimum. While the authors are, on the whole, sanguine about our ability to meet requirements, they foresee difficulties with petroleum, copper, lead, zinc, and the additive alloys for steel.[3] I would say on the whole that The Twentieth Century Fund's approach represents a kind of norm in such studies.

The President's Materials Policy Commission took a similar although slightly more ambiguous position which is worth examining in some slight detail. It began by stating its conviction that economic growth was important and, in degree, sacrosanct. "First, we share the belief of the American people in the principle of Growth."[4] (It is instructive to note the commission's use of a capital G. A certain divinity is associated with the word.) *Growth* in this context means an increasing output of consumers' goods and an increase in the plant by which they are supplied. Having started with this renunciation, the commission was scarcely in a position to look critically at consumption in relation to the resource problem, and it did not.

Yet the PMPC could not entirely exclude the problem of consumption from consideration. In the course of its formal recommendations it asked that the armed services in "designing military products, and in drawing up specifications, focus on using abundant rather than scarce materials, and on using less of any material per unit of product where this can be done without significantly affecting quality or performance." And it asked for "greater emphasis on care and maintenance of military equipment and conservation in use and increase[d] scrap recovery of all kinds."[5] But it almost certainly occurred to the able members of the commission that this was straining furiously at the gnat. Why should we be worried about the excess steel in a tank but not in an automobile? What is gained from smaller radar screens if the materials go into larger TV screens? Why should the general be denied his brass and his wife allowed her plumage? There is an obvious inconsistency here.

As a result the PMPC did venture on. Although it did not support the observation with any concrete recommendation, it did comment with some vigor on present tendencies in consumption. "The United States," it observed, "has been lavish in the use of its materials. . . . Vast quantities of materials have been wasted by over-designing and over-specification. We have frequently designed products with little concern for getting maximum service from their materials and labor. We drive heavier automobiles than is necessary for mere transportation, and we adorn them with chromium. . . . We blow thousands of tons of unrecoverable lead into the atmosphere each year from high-octane gasoline because we like a quick pickup. We must become aware that many of our production and consumption habits are extremely ex-

2 (New York: The Ronald Press, 1954).

3 J. Frederic Dewhurst & Assoc., *America's Needs and Resources: A New Survey* (New York: The Twentieth Century Fund, 1955).

4 PMPC, Summary, p. 5.

5 *Ibid.*, p. 10.

pensive of scarce materials and that a trivial change of taste or slight reduction in personal satisfaction can often bring about tremendous savings."[6]

The captious will want to inquire, if the losses in satisfaction here are trivial and the savings are tremendous, why the commission did not seize the opportunity to urge savings. Why did it make no recommendations? But given its position on growth and the meaning of growth, it could in fact go no further. At first glance it does not seem impossible to pick out kinds of consumption which seem especially wasteful—things which reflect not use but wasteful use. Surely the utility of an automobile is not diminished if it is lighter or if its gasoline contains less lead. But this is a distinction that cannot be made. Consumption, it quickly develops, is a seamless web. If we ask about the chromium we must ask about the cars. The questions that are asked about one part can be asked about all parts. The automobiles are too heavy and they use irreplaceable lead? One can ask with equal cogency if we need to make all the automobiles that we now turn out. This question gains point when we reflect that the demand for automobiles depends on that remarkable institution called planned obsolescence, is nurtured by advertising campaigns of incredible strategic complexity, and on occasion requires financial underwriting that would have seemed rather extravagant to Charles Ponzi.

As with automobiles so with everything else. In an opulent society the marginal urgency of all kinds of goods is low. It is easy to bring our doubts and questions to bear on the automobiles. But the case is not different for (say) that part of our food production which contributes not to nutrition but to obesity, that part of our tobacco which contributes not to comfort but to carcinoma, and that part of our clothing which is designed not to cover nakedness but to suggest it. We cannot single out waste in a product without questioning the product. We cannot single out any one product without calling into question all products. Thus having specifically endorsed ever more luxurious standards of consumption—for this is what is meant by growth—the PMPC obviously could not pursue the notion of wasteful consumption without involving itself in a major contradiction. It made its gesture against the automobiles and then, wisely, it stopped.

There are several reasons why our consumption standards have not been called in question in the course of the conservation discussion over the last fifty years. There is also some divergence between those that are given, or which come first to mind, and those that are ultimately operative. Thus, to recur once more to the PMPC, it simply stated its belief that economic stagnation is the alternative to growth, meaning uninhibited increases in consumption. No one, obviously, wants stagnation. But does this argument really hold? Clearly we can have different rates of growth of consumption. In other contexts we are not nearly so committed to the notion of all-out increase in consumption. In 1957 economic output was virtually constant. This leveling off of output—stagnation if I may use the pejorative term—was more or less, a goal of public policy. The purpose of the tight money policy was to reduce the rate of investment spending and thus of economic expansion in order hopefully to win a measure of price stability. In this context we weren't so appalled by the idea of a lower rate of growth—something approaching what the PMPC would have had to call stagnation. As I write, in the first quarter of 1958, we have had something more than a leveling off; we have experienced a rather sharp reduction in output. But even this, at least in some quarters, has not been regarded with great alarm. We are being told that breathing spells are inevitable in the free enterprise system.

6 *Ibid.*, p. 16.

Also, as I shall suggest in a moment, we can have patterns of growth which make heavy drafts on materials and other patterns which are much more lenient in their requirements.

In any case, if our levels of consumption are dangerously high in relation to the resource base, or are becoming so—and the PMPC at least expressed its concern—it would obviously be better to risk stagnation now than to use up our reserves and have not stagnation but absolute contraction later on. Those who sanctify growth but also say that the resource position is serious are, in effect, arguing that we have no alternative to having our fling now even though, more or less literally, there is hell to pay later on. This is an odd posture for the conservationist.

It is also suggested that uninhibited consumption has something to do with individual liberty. If we begin interfering with consumption, we shall be abridging a basic freedom.

I shan't dwell long on this. That we make such points is part of the desolate modern tendency to turn the discussion of all questions, however simple and forthright, into a search for violation of some arcane principle, or to evade and suffocate common sense by verbose, incoherent, and irrelevant moralizing. Freedom is not much concerned with tail fins or even with automobiles. Those who argue that it is identified with the greatest possible range of choice of consumers' goods are only confessing their exceedingly simple-minded and mechanical view of man and his liberties.

In any case, one must ask the same question as concerns growth. If the resource problem is serious, then the price of a wide choice now is a sharply constricted choice later on. Surely even those who adhere to the biggest supermarket theory of liberty would agree that their concept has a time dimension.

Finally it will be said that there is nothing that can be done about consumption. This of course is nonsense. There is a wide range of instruments of social control. Taxation; specific prohibitions on wasteful products, uses, or practices; educational and other hortatory efforts; subsidies to encourage consumption of cheaper and more plentiful substitutes are all available. Most have been used in past periods of urgency.

And here, indeed, is the first reason we do not care to contemplate such measures. The latter forties and the fifties in the United States were marked by what we must now recognize as a massive conservative reaction to the idea of enlarged social guidance and control of economic activity. This was partly, no doubt, based on a desire to have done with the wartime apparatus of control. In part, it was a successful conservative reaction to the social intervention of the New Deal. In part, it was the resurgence of a notably oversimplified view of economic life which seized on this moment to ascribe a magical automatism to the price system (including the rate of interest) which, as we are again gradually learning, it does not have. Euphemisms have played a prominent part in this revolt. Many have found it more agreeable to be in favor of liberty than against social responsibility. But the result has been to rule out of discussion, or at least to discriminate heavily against, measures which by their nature could be accomplished only by according increased responsibilities to the state.

Since consumption could not be discussed without raising the question of an increased role for the state, it was not discussed.

However, tradition also abetted this exclusion of consumption levels from consideration. Economics is a subject in which old questions are lovingly debated but new ones are regarded with misgiving. On the whole it is a mark of stability and sound scholarship to concern oneself with questions that were relevant in the world of Ricardo. In the Ricardian world, to be literal about it, goods were indeed scarce. One might talk, although without courting great popularity, about redistributing wealth and income and thus curbing the luxurious consumption of the classes. But the notion that people as a whole might have more than a minimum—that there might be a restraint on the consumption of the community as a whole—was unthinkable. In modern times this has, of course, become thinkable. Goods are plentiful. Demand for them must be elaborately contrived. Those who create wants rank among our most talented and highly paid citizens. Want creation—advertising—is a $10 billion industry. But tradition remains strongly against questioning or even thinking about wants.

Finally, we are committed to a high level of consumption because, whether we need the goods or not, we very much need the employment their production provides. I need not dwell on this. The point is decidedly obvious at this writing in early 1958. We are not missing the cars that Detroit is currently not producing. Nor are we missing the steel that Pittsburgh and Gary are currently not making. The absence of these products is not causing any detectable suffering. But there is much suffering and discomfort as the result of the failure of these industries to employ as many men as in the recent past. We are chained to a high level of production and consumption not by the pressure of want but by the urgencies of economic security.

What should be our policy toward consumption?

First, of course, we should begin to talk about it—and in the context of all its implications. It is silly for grown men to concern themselves mightily with supplying an appetite and close their eyes to the obvious and obtrusive question of whether the appetite is excessive.

If the appetite presents no problems—if resource discovery and the technology of use and substitution promise automatically to remain abreast of consumption and at moderate cost—then we need press matters no further. At least on conservation grounds there is no need to curb our appetite.

But to say this, and assuming that it applies comprehensively to both renewable and non-renewable resources, is to say that there is no materials problem. It is to say that, except for some activities that by definition are non-critical, the conservationists are not much needed.

But if conservation is an issue, then we have no honest and logical course but to measure the means for restraining use against the means for insuring a continuing sufficiency of supply and taking the appropriate action. There is no justification for ruling consumption levels out of the calculation.

What would be the practical consequences of this calculation—taken honestly and without the frequent contemporary preoccupation not with solution but with plausible escape—I do not pretend to say. As I suggested at the outset, I am impressed by the opportunities for resource substitution and by the contribution of technology in facilitating it. But the problem here is less one of theory than of technical calculation and projection. As such it is beyond the scope both of this paper and my competence. It has been my task to show that at any time that the calculation is unsanguine, restraint on consumption can no longer be excluded as a remedy.

However, let me conclude with one suggestion. There may be occasions, in the future, when in the interest of conservation we will wish to address ourselves to the consumption of particular products. (This, as noted, can only be in the context of a critical view of all consumption.) The modern automobile may be a case in point. I share the view that this is currently afflicted by a kind of competitive elephantiasis. As a result, it is making a large and possibly excessive claim on iron, petroleum, lead, and other materials; but much more seriously it is making excessive inroads on urban and rural driving and standing space and on the public funds that supply this space.

But in the main it would seem to me that any concern for materials use should be general. It should have as its aim the shifting of consumption patterns from those which have a high materials requirement to those which have a much lower requirement. The opportunities are considerable. Education, health services, sanitary services, good parks and playgrounds, orchestras, effective local government, a clean countryside, all have rather small materials requirements. I have elsewhere argued that the present tendency of our economy is to discriminate sharply against such production.[7] A variety of forces, among them the massed pressures of modern merchandising, have forced an inordinate concentration of our consumption on what may loosely be termed consumer hardware. This distortion has been underwritten by economic attitudes which have made but slight accommodation to the transition of our world from one of privation to one of opulence. A rationalization of our present consumption patterns —a rationalization which would more accurately reflect free and unmanaged consumer choice—might also be an important step in materials conservation.

[7] *The Affluent Society* (Boston: Houghton Mifflin, 1958).

PHILIP M. HAUSER

THE CRUCIAL VALUE PROBLEMS

As a demographer and statistician, I should, I suppose, be expected to comment on Professor Galbraith's paper by evaluating whatever population projections and possibly consumption functions he might have used to quantify the magnitude of, and the rate—to some the alarming rate—of increase in, consumption in the United States and especially in respect of relatively scarce and non-renewable materials.

But although Galbraith alludes to the great and increasing rate of consumption, he has seen fit not to quantify anything. He thus has left me in something of a fix: have slide rule with no place to travel. This situation calls for the criticism of a philosopher concerned with the normative rather than of a demographer or statistician. But having been trained also as a sociologist, I find it is not too difficult a matter to switch to philosophy in treating what Galbraith feels are the really basic problems in consumption and conservation, insofar at least as the philosophical heights can be scaled by an economist.

Before dealing with Galbraith in kind, however, I should like to point to a few fundamental statistics with which he obviously is familiar and that he uses as a point of departure in his discussion. I refer first of all to the fact that the postwar boom in marriages and babies has drastically altered both short-run and long-run population growth in the United States. With the relatively conservative projections of the United States Bureau of the Census, it is likely that our population may increase over 1950 by some 55 million at the lower limit and by over 75 million at the upper limit, to reach a level of from 207 to 228 million by 1975. Broader limits are possible which could, as Whelpton has shown, result in a possible population of 193 million to 243 million by 1975.

The Census projections indicate in the brief span of 25 years an addition to the population of the United States equivalent to all of Western Germany at the lower limit and all of Indonesia or Pakistan at the upper limit. The Whelpton projection allows for an addition to the size of the nation within a quarter of a century of a population the equivalent of all of Japan.

Increments of this magnitude, of a population consuming at United States levels of living, obviously point to appreciable acceleration in the rate of utilization of many resources and to depletion or threatened depletion of a number of critical things including oil, copper, lead, zinc, additive alloys for steel, and, on a local basis, water.

The worriments of conservationists, if warranted before World War II, were justifiedly exacerbated by the prodigious consumption of the war, together with the course of demographic events in the postwar world. If one wishes to use what is perhaps the ultimate weapon in the cause of conservation in the United States, it is necessary only to point to the Social Secu-

• Philip M. Hauser is Chairman of the Department of Sociology, University of Chicago.

Reprinted from Henry Jarrett (ed.), *Perspectives on Conservation* (Baltimore: The Johns Hopkins Press for Resources for the Future, Inc., 1958), pp. 100–105, with permission of the author and the publisher.

rity Administration's (T. N. E. Greville's) projections of future population, which demonstrate that the continuation of present fertility levels along with reasonable mortality gains would, within a century, by the year 2050, produce a population in the United States of about 1 billion people. If one were to use present consumption functions, let alone taking into account their secular trends, and apply them to a population of 1 billion persons, I am sure the cost of not conserving our natural resources could easily be made to match hostile ICBM's in potential horror and human misery. On the other hand, it is possible, as Harrison Brown has indicated, that the control of solar and nuclear energy could, with cheap enough power, provide us with an almost limitless supply of "things" from the air, the sea, and the earth.

One can, therefore, depending on one's temperament, be so impressed with rates of resource consumption and the prospect of a population of a billion as to make these items the significant facts for policy and action. In this position, vigorous conservation policies seem indicated. Contrariwise, if one's faith in science is predominant, especially now that the Army has equipped us with an Explorer to compete with Sputnik, one might conclude that innovation, recovery, and cheap energy will indefinitely, or as far as it is necessary to foresee the future, provide us with all the things we need. In this position, conservation programs may be regarded as palliatives for the more excitable members of our society.

This choice of alternative and conflicting postures in respect of the need for conservation is presented and skillfully exploited by Galbraith. He appropriately points to the uncertainties in respect to the need for conservation. What is more important, he justifiably depicts the vulnerability of those who accept the premise that there is such a need; he then proceeds to explore the problem of what to do about it in a highly segmental and selective, rather than in a holistic manner. In doing so he reduces the problem of conservation to specific problems of values. His discussion is, therefore, concerned largely with policy decisions or value judgments. Hence my labeling of Galbraith's paper as essentially philosophical and normative in character.

Before considering the value questions involved, an observation or two on the question of the need for conservation which may reveal my own bias is appropriate. In my judgment there is adequate justification for conservation measures for both internal and external reasons. In the former category, I would place the desirability of not unduly risking the levels of living of future generations of Americans. Even though it must be admitted that technological advance, innovation, recovery and, above all, the possibility of cheap energy may obviate the need for conservation of many if not all things, it is by far the lesser risk to future generations to proceed on the assumption that needed non-renewable materials may be exhausted. Especially is this the case when the current sacrifices involved are nominal.

In the category of external reasons I would place the requirements, and for the time being increasing ones, of national security. To the extent that our free enterprise system results in greater exploitation of scarce and strategic resources than does the competitive Communist system, we may be jeopardizing our and the free world's way of life and our national future by risking their exhaustion.

If these and other considerations dictate a policy of conservation then, and only then, are we confronted with the value questions Galbraith raises. His major contribution lies, I believe, in his making explicit and answering in the affirmative the question usually avoided, when the need to conserve is accepted as a premise, namely: is it desirable to curb the United States appetite to consume? Galbraith is quite aware that the affirmative answer requires increased government interventionism. For he feels, and it is difficult to disagree, that the free private enterprise system will not find a way, via the market mechanism, to place itself on, and hold itself to, a national resources diet.

Thus, accepting the need for conservation provides the first value dilemma and leads Galbraith to the unpopular position that the United States appetite for consumption needs curbing. This conclusion inexorably leads to perhaps an even more unpopular position—namely, that the federal government must do the curbing. The second major value question, then, is that centering on the desirability of further extension of federal government powers that would enable it, like the stern and relentless wife, to force the United States economy on a diet that would be "good" for it—for national security in even the short run, or for levels of living of future generations of Americans in the long run.

As an aspect of arguing the need for increased federal controls, Galbraith treats the restriction of "freedom" counter argument with some impatience. But then this impatience is understandable if one accepts the premises from which he starts—namely, that the general welfare is to be given priority over individual freedom, and that the individual freedom which would be infringed would indeed be far from basic and could, like the restrictions of liberty represented by traffic signals, even increase welfare and perhaps life itself. The choice of values offered here, "freedom" vs. "control," offers an endless platform for debate but not in this context if you are a converted conservationist. Galbraith argues that you cannot be both a conservationist and have the freedom of unrestrained appetite.

In pursuing the matter of social control, Professor Galbraith does not hesitate to deal with another major value question, or more accurately a whole series of value questions, in respect of the instruments of social control of consumption. His references to "taxation," "prohibitions," "education and other hortatory methods," "subsidies," and the like make it apparent that control, if agreed upon, is possible, even if unpalatable. He is probably correct in linking the avoidance of the question of control of appetite to consume with the fear of government interventionism. I believe it desirable to emphasize that his brief reference to the fact that today "the masses of the people might have more than a minimum" is a major reason for the difference between the need for conservation in contemporary life as compared with that in earlier periods and a basic factor in the need for government intervention.

Not content with forcing these issues, Galbraith proceeds to push the question of control into specific areas, thereby inviting specific as well as general opposition. His observations about automobiles at least show his courage if not audacity; and his references to food, tobacco, and clothing show his insistence on dealing with the big issues first and the little ones later, if necessary.

A fourth major question is made explicit in Galbraith's consideration of "growth," another of the sacred values on the American economic and political scene. This is in a sense the most difficult of all of his questions to face. For we have never as a nation seriously considered the alternatives to growth, even though I suspect there is no one who would not be forced to admit that on a finite globe (or in a finite solar system shall we say now in the post-Sputnik era) there must be some limit to "growth." Galbraith's insistence that there are alternatives to growth other than "stagnation" and consideration of the implications of alternative patterns of growth must necessarily, I believe, become elements in the armory of any logical, that is, consistent conservationist.

It is now apparent that I have little to say in my critique beyond restating, not necessarily with improvement, Galbraith's presentation. Accepting, as I do, the premise that it is necessary and desirable to conserve our resources, I find that Galbraith has put the proper questions and provided the rational answers. That the questions will be embarrassing to many, and that the answers will be provocative, and considered even dangerous by some, does not make them less apposite. I rather suspect that Galbraith has enjoyed this opportunity to force conservationists to face the implications of their position. In doing so he has performed a service, in my judgment, not only for conservationists but, also, for the nation at large. For with increased maturity we cannot for very much longer play the role of the fun-loving heir who avoids facing the hard reality of the finite limits of the heritage he has dissipated and the need to go to work.

For his part, Galbraith once again has demonstrated his willingness and ability to rise above principles when confronted with conflicting facts. More specifically, Galbraith has, in putting his questions and suggesting the answers, pointed to additional places in our economic and political order where departure from neo-classical economic postures may be indicated. In suggesting additional areas of federal interventionism, Professor Galbraith is, even in this present post–Senator McCarthy climate, indulging in possibly dangerous forms of economic and political heresy. He may, therefore, be endowed with a combination of prescience and courage, or of intellectual myopia and foolhardiness. Which of these designations turns out to be correct will require, of course, the 20–20 vision which will come with hindsight.

PAUL B. SEARS

ETHICS, AESTHETICS, AND THE BALANCE OF NATURE

Professor Galbraith's thoughtful, salty, and good-humored paper boldly opens up one of the least popular aspects of the resource problem—namely, the importance of a reasonable frugality. Another basic but unpopular aspect is, of course, our increasing population pressure. This, too, has recently been discussed from the standpoint of economics. Joseph Spengler of Duke University and Earle Rauber of the Federal Reserve Bank of Atlanta have both, independently, given solid arguments against the popular doctrine, "the more the merrier" or "each mouth a new customer."

I feel no particular mission to defend conservationists, so-called, against his gentle strictures, yet perhaps I am expected to make some comment on them. It would take a bolder student of life and environment than I am to enter the lists on behalf of all who assume, or have imposed on them, the title of conservationist.

The problem of man and resources is an exceedingly complicated one. The whole history of the conservation movement has been an evolution from concern with single resources to realization of their interdependence and of the need for viewing the problem in its entirety. I am inclined to be patient with those who are on the way but have not yet arrived, despite the difficulties they sometimes cause.

• Paul B. Sears is Professor Emeritus of Conservation, Yale University.

Reprinted from Henry Jarrett (ed.), *Perspectives on Conservation* (Baltimore: The Johns Hopkins Press for Resources for the Future, Inc., 1958), pp. 106–11, with permission of the author and the publisher.

There are also several philosophical approaches to the problem. One of them, for instance, is by way of the concepts of accounting that identify assets, liabilities, income, expense, and depreciation. One of the common difficulties in dealing with resources is the failure to allow for depreciation (or depletion) in figuring income. On the other hand, it is well known that the outcome of any accounting system varies with its initial assumptions. Plenty of assumptions are involved in dealing with natural resources.

The estimation of capital resource assets is a thorny job to begin with. Space, which is basic, can of course be measured, and we know that the surface area of the earth is finite. Water supply in terms of average rainfall can be computed, but until Thornthwaite's studies of evapotranspiration we were uncertain as to the net amount available for storage and direct use. We know now that for the North Central states this is not more than one-third of the total.

Estimates of oil, minerals, and forest resources involve not only distribution and extent, but quality as well. For each of these resources the standard practice has been one of high-grading, exploiting the richest first. Modern technology makes it possible to utilize directly, or to improve, resources of lower grade, but only by increasing capital expenditures, as Harrison Brown and others have pointed out. In the case of forest resources such improvement has been rendered especially difficult by the destruction of the best seed stock, as in New England. Soil depletion, for example, in Central America, has often gone so far as to expose parent material beyond any present technical means of restoration.

The aesthetic approach also has its merits although, as Dr. Galbraith points out, it is often pressed so hard as to defeat its own purpose. Certainly, sound and satisfying design is integral to good conservation, and it has been true in my experience that Sir Francis Younghusband, the British explorer, was quite right in his belief that there are only two kinds of landscape that are tolerable—one where man has never been; the other where he has achieved harmony.

While I do not doubt that human aesthetics has profound roots in biological evolution, I am equally certain that it can be modified, even perverted, by cultural experience during the development of the individual. Now that a large majority of people live divorced from primary natural landscapes, any intuitive preference for them is no longer effective, convincing, or even safe unless sustained by some more rational argument. The likes and dislikes of a minority, even a highly vocal one, can scarcely be expected to prevail on their merits, however sound these may be. This is especially true when, as Dr. Galbraith says, this minority seems to insist on retaining beauty in inverse ratio to the number who can enjoy it.

A third approach is the ethical whose basic importance is revealed in the title of Dr. Galbraith's paper by its inclusion of the word "should." This word implies an imperative choice of ends and such a choice must be a moral decision. That he has a choice is revealed in his call for a greater measure of self-restraint and discipline in the use of resources. Yet any austerity is tempered by his reminder, following Samuel Ordway, of the rich satisfactions that are possible under a less wildly consumptive economy.

He also refers to "resource salvation" and reminds us quietly that "if the resource problem is serious, then the price of a wide choice now is a much constricted choice later on." This latter proposition has had impressive analytical treatment by Harrison Brown in *The Challenge of Man's Future,*[1] and by Deevey in an important but neglected review that includes a discussion of dietary pressures, published a few years ago in *Ecology*.[2]

There have been some excellent statements of the ethical approach to conservation, notably by Aldo Leopold, Fraser Darling, and Albert Schweitzer. The common element in all is an insistence on ends greater than the immediate satisfaction of the individual. Even the doctrine of laissez faire gets its day in court by claiming that in allowing each individual to seek his own welfare, a greater good—i.e., the ultimate welfare of all—will be secured. The men I have named include in their concern a respect for all living things, and for the order of nature in general.

My own rather pragmatic assumption is that the human adventure is worth maintaining for as long and at as high a quality as possible. It happens that this, in my judgment, does no violence to a respect for the order of nature—indeed, requires it. It is clear that Dr. Galbraith is similarly concerned with the continuity of human culture even though he does not say so in so many words. There are times when ethical assumptions gain more by being taken for granted beyond question than by being paraded, and this seems to be one.

Speaking then of practical means, he suggests a doctrine so old and out of fashion that it has all the merit of novelty. He has suggested that we work on the denominator of the supply/demand ratio, by beginning to face realistically the possibility of lessening our present dizzy rate of consumption. If ever I heard a subversive idea, this is it. And if ever I welcomed one, this is the occasion.

Our technological culture, with the notable exception of the medical arts (which themselves are not free from a growing tinge of commercialism) is geared to the

1 (New York: Viking Press, 1954).

2 E. S. Deevey, Jr., "Recent Textbooks of Human Ecology," *Ecology,* XXXII (1951), 345–51.

speedy elaboration of consumer goods from natural resources. By comparison, the attention given to insuring an adequate future supply of such resources is meager and more often intuitive than analytical. Yet realistic analysis is essential, not only to reinforce intuition, however sound, but to lay the foundation for effective action.

Such analysis may be cultural, biological, or physical, as I see it. The economic accounting approach mentioned in the beginning of my comments is, I believe, subsumed in the cultural, since I happen to agree with the late George Wehrwein that economics is fundamentally a matter of human behavior. I have long since found it convenient to view the conservation problem as a resultant of the interplay of resources, population, and culture.

As a rough approximation, we can identify a sequence of four phases in our cultural analysis,

Sources → Elaboration →
Distribution → Consumption,

each dependent upon that which precedes it. When sources of material or energy are lacking, the process stops. If the raw products cannot be converted into usable form, there is nothing to distribute and consume. Should distribution break down, no matter how ample the supply the consumer is in want. I saw precisely this happen in the early 1930's when there were heaps of unmarketed wheat in western Kansas and bread lines a few hundred miles east of them.

At the present time, to a degree never before known in history, the fabrication of goods has been developed out of all proportion to other phases of the sequence. The dynamic no longer comes solely from the consumer and his urgent needs. Instead of this pull from those who want, we now have a push from those who produce and whose chief problem is disposal of what they have produced with such facility.

Man, whatever else he may be, is a biological organism. The sequence I have just mentioned reveals some interesting features in terms of biological analysis. The process in nature from which it derives is as follows

Materials and Energy (Sources) →
Organic Synthesis (Elaboration) →
Food Chain (Distribution) → Utilization
(Consumption).

In nature, however, the process does not end there but is cyclic. It is geared to the re-use of materials following utilization at a fairly stable rate, so that, as Darwin long ago pointed out, species populations remain fairly constant.

What technological man has done is to introduce a vast change into the tempo rather than the character of this cycle. He has, as we have said, vastly speeded it up in the intermediate stages, while at the same time through his dissipation of reserves, enormously slowed it down at the phase of return for reuse. It is this inevitable trend of human activity, rather than any transient inventory of resources or any promise of new sources or technological expedients, that concerns the ecologist so profoundly.

But since physical analysis seems to be at present more convincing than biological, how does it apply to the sequence sketched above? So far as we can tell, during the billion and a half years that life has existed on earth the dynamic system approximated that known as a steady state. Activated by the income of solar energy, a pattern of highly integrated use of that energy, to sustain life and maintain the system in working order, was developed. The interval between energy fixation and its final dissipation to increase the entropy of our solar system was prolonged by the way in which life and environment were organized. Residual effects, such as soil, topography, and productive plant and animal communities, were the expression of this relatively efficient process. The appropriate analogy is an industrial plant which utilizes a suitable fraction of current income to maintain its productive efficiency instead of expending it all in dividends.

Here, in the thermodynamic steady state we observe in nature, we have a model which should be taken very seriously in the shaping of human culture. Speaking purely as a scientist and ignoring so far as I can my own ethical and aesthetic preferences, few things disturb me more than our general neglect of what I regard as the physical basis of our whole enterprise.

Our choice lies between that of an expanding economy (a concept without physical warrant so far as I know) and that of a steady state such as prevailed during all of prehuman biological time. It is most gratifying to note that Professor Galbraith, in his comment on the report of the President's Materials Policy Commission and that of The Twentieth Century Fund, has sensed the gravity of this fundamental decision. He might well have added the report of the President's Water Policy Commission, with its initial assumption of an expanding economy, as well as numerous other more ebullient pronouncements.

And finally, while he has left the thorny population problem to the demographers, it is supremely encouraging to see how squarely he has faced the issue of unnecessary and artificially stimulated consumption.

The notions of "restoring the balance of nature" and "coming to terms with nature" are . . . in danger of becoming shibboleths. I have collected a number of such phrases, the stock-in-trade of conservation literature: our growing mastery over the environment brings "the revenge of an outraged nature on man"; unless we return to 'harmony,' "nature will ultimately take the matter in hand and restore equilibrium in her own drastic and remorseless way"; countries that disregarded the warnings have suffered the revenue of nature, for "nature always has the last word"; "you cannot cheat nature out of her rights and in the long run get away with it."

The disasters envisaged in these warnings are far from chimerical; to avert them we need a better understanding of our remote as well as our proximate impact on the environment. But unless some such catastrophe is inevitable—in which case no effort would matter—one must conclude that man is free to remake nature, as he is to destroy it. In fact, the balance of nature which serves as a point of departure for many of the admonitions cited does not exist. Unless one assumes that whatever is, is right, nature is full [of] imperfections. Many forms of life are clumsy, ineffectual, and maladapted. There are more extinct than living species, and relatively few members of any species reach maturity. Man is the only exception, because man interferes with nature enough to insure the survival of most infants and children. . . . Indeed, man has been upsetting the natural order continually. . . . The process is bound to continue. If man's interference with the rest of nature has sometimes been catastrophic, the lesson is not that he should—or can—stop meddling; he must create new patterns. . . .

David Lowenthal, "The American Creed of Nature as Virtue," *Landscape,* IX (Winter, 1959–60), 24–25.

PART III

THE MANAGEMENT OF AN EXPANDING RESOURCE BASE

CHAPTER 5

THE MANAGERIAL EXPERIENCE

Our viewpoint has now shifted closer to the ground. This chapter moves us from the lofty concerns with the population explosion and the quality of life, down to a more pragmatic consideration of the year-to-year management of individual resource complexes.[1] The emphasis is more empirical, less theoretical.

This change is accompanied by a different view of resources. There is less concentration upon the implications of a finite world. The concern of the resource managers described here is more with the manipulation of a flexible or (for some) expanding resource base. The studies selected have been chosen to record, analyze, and place in historical perspective a variety of management activity.

The first selection comes from the *Geological Survey Report of 1888*. Despite its age, it has a remarkably contemporary ring in its concern to appraise forest reserves accurately and in its implied criticisms both of excessive preoccupation with the natural science aspect of resources and of the fervent penchant for preservation.

The series of case studies which follows is both descriptive and analytical. They range in tone from relatively bland endorsement to caustic criticism. Milliman summarizes briefly a much larger work on water supply problems and concludes that despite recurrent reports of water shortage in urban supply, over-investment in facilities has occurred in several important areas. Macinko is also interested in water problems, primarily with irrigation development. He compares the intentions and accomplishments of the Columbia Basin Project and studies the effects of external technological change, time lag in construction, and changing values both in public and private goals on the record of project accomplishment. A third review of water-resource development is the assessment of the TVA by one of its early protagonists.

Two traditional goals of resource management receive thoughtful appraisal. Gould's study of the 50 years of experience of the Harvard Forest is a review of the success of the sustained-yield concept applied to a small area. The expressions of serious doubt about the viability of sustained yield are supported by the careful observations of the Forest staff. Another common man-

[1] The term "resource complex" was suggested by J. R. Whitaker in "Sequence and Equilibrium in Destruction and Conservation of Natural Resources," *Annals of the Association of American Geographers,* XXXI (1941), 129–44.

agerial goal is that of multiple use, but the problem of irreconcilable resource use has been little explored. Marts and Sewell carefully present the implications of management under mixed motivation arising from multiple goals.

Managerial goals of sustained yield or multiple use are administrative-technical goals.[2] Much too little attention has been paid to the divergence of these goals from the aspirations of individual resource managers or to the differences in objectives and methods among managers themselves.[3] Blase and Timmons, Fonaroff, and Lucas investigate these differences in three studies in widely scattered areas: soil resources of Western Iowa, range resources on the Navajo Indian Reservation, and the wilderness resources of the Quetico-Superior area on the Minnesota-Ontario border. White's paper on river-basin analysis highlights some of the major problems confronting students of the social science aspects of development. The description of the kinds of problems tackled by geographers is illustrative of the difficulties involved in attempting to straddle the gap between physical science and behavioral science aspects of resource management.

The studies in this chapter differ in subject, type of resource, and regional setting, in objective, and in research technique. Taken together, they suggest a picture of managerial activity marked by less success than is normally assumed. This picture may be somewhat distorted both by hindsight, with its focus on past error, and by selectivity, for there are few reviews of managerial experience[4] and fewer still that meet standards of scholarship. Discounting

2 These goals may have their quantitative expression as well. One such early expression is Morris L. Cooke's, "On Total Conservation," in University of Pennsylvania Bicentennial Conference, *Conservation of Renewable Resources, Some Fundamental Aspects of the Problem* (Philadelphia: University of Pennsylvania Press, 1949), pp. 149–59. More recently such goals are often expressed as "needs"; see, for example, U.S., Dept. of Agric., *Basic Statistics of the National Inventory of Soil and Water Conservation Needs,* Statistical Bull. 317 (Washington: Government Printing Office, 1962). On water needs, see the reports of the U.S., Senate Select Committee on National Water Resources, 86th Cong., 2d Sess., 1960. See especially Committee Prints Nos. 7 (*Future Water Requirements for Municipal Use*), 8 (*Future Water Requirements for Principal Water-Using Industries*), 11 (*Future Needs for Navigation*), 12 (*Land and Water Potentials and Future Requirements for Water*), 13 (*Estimated Water Requirements for Agricultural Purposes and Their Effects on Water Supplies*), 14 (*Future Needs for Reclamation in the Western States*), 17 (*Water Recreation Needs in the United States, 1960–2000*), 29 (*Water Requirements for Pollution Abatement*), 32 (*Water Supply and Demand*).

3 There may also be considerable variation within the scientific-technical communities as well. Such variation is described and explained in one example by Ashley L. Schiff, *Fire and Water: Scientific Heresy in the Forest Service* (Cambridge: Harvard University Press, 1962) as a function of conflict with predetermined administrative goals, and in another example by Robert Kates, *Hazard and Choice Perception in Flood-Plain Management,* Dept. of Geog. Research Paper No. 78 (Chicago: Dept. of Geography, University of Chicago, 1962) as a function of the uncertainty of natural events.

4 Other case studies include the following: Arthur Maass, *Muddy Waters: The Army Engineers and the Nation's Rivers* (Cambridge: Harvard University Press, 1951); Arthur E. Morgan, *The Miami Conservancy District* (New York: McGraw-Hill, 1951); William E. Leuchtenberg, *Flood Control Politics: The Connecticut River Valley Problem, 1927–50* (Cambridge: Harvard University Press, 1953); Evan Vogt, *Modern Homesteaders: The Life of a Twentieth-Century Frontier Community* (Cambridge: Belknap Press, 1955); Jacquelyn Beyer, *Integration of Grazing and Crop Agriculture: Resources Management Problems in the Uncompahgre Valley Irrigation Project,* Dept.

these biases, the studies speak of failure to anticipate change or to accommodate differences in values, and in so doing they underscore two intractable managerial problems.[5]

---

of Geog. Research Paper No. 52 (Chicago: Dept. of Geography, University of Chicago, 1957); Lyle E. Craine, "The Muskingum Watershed Conservancy District: A Study of Local Control," *Law and Contemporary Problems,* XXII, No. 3 (1957), 378–404; Roscoe C. Martin, "The Tennessee Valley Authority: A Study of Federal Control," *ibid.*, 351–77; Wesley C. Calef, *Private Grazing and Public Lands: Studies of the Local Management of the Taylor Grazing Act* (Chicago: University of Chicago Press, 1960); M. E. Marts, "Regional vs. Local Level: Objectives and Social Accounting of the Columbia Basin Project," *Papers and Proceedings,* First Western Meeting (1961), Regional Science Association, unpublished; Mason Gaffney, "Diseconomies Inherent in Western Water Laws: A California Case Study," *Water and Range Resources and Economic Development of the West,* Report No. 9, Conf. Proceedings of the Western Agricultural Economics Research Council (1961), pp. 55–82; Ian Burton, *Types of Agricultural Occupance of Flood Plains in the United States,* Dept. of Geog. Research Paper No. 75 (Chicago: Dept. of Geography, University of Chicago, 1962), see esp. pp. 42–143; Richard A. Cooley, *Politics and Conservation: The Decline of the Alaska Salmon* (New York: Harper & Row, 1963); Winston W. Crouch and Robert N. Giordana, "The Example of Dairy Valley," *A Place to Live,* The Yearbook of Agriculture 1963 (Washington: Government Printing Office, 1963); James Hudson, *Irrigation Water Use in the Utah Valley, Utah,* Dept. of Geog. Research Paper No. 79 (Chicago: Dept. of Geography, University of Chicago, 1963).

[5] A series of case studies of parallel interest but emphasizing political, legal, and administrative aspects of resource management is found in the Inter-University Case Program, *Cases in Public Administration and Policy Formation* (University, Ala.: University of Alabama Press). Examples of these studies dealing with resources are Arthur A. Maass, *The Kings River Project,* CPAC Case Study (rev. 1950); Russell P. Andrews, *Wilderness Sanctuary,* ICP Case Study No. 13 (rev. ed., 1954); Thomas H. Eliot, *Reorganizing the Massachusetts Department of Conservation, ibid.*, No. 14 (1953); Donald E. Pearson, *The Whittier Narrows Dam, ibid.*, No. 17 (1953); Roscoe C. Martin, *From Forest to Front Page, ibid.*, No. 34 (1956); Owen Stratton and Phillip Sirotkin, *The Echo Park Controversy, ibid.*, No. 46 (1959); Irving K. Fox and Isabel Picken, *The Upstream-Downstream Controversy in the Arkansas-White-Red Basins Survey, ibid.*, No. 55 (1960); Phillip O. Foss, *The Grazing Fee Dilemma, ibid.*, No. 57 (1960); John DeGrove, *The Florida Flood Control District, ibid.*, No. 58 (1960); Edith T. Carper, *Lobbying and the Natural Gas Bill, ibid.*, No. 72 (1962).

HENRY GANNETT

THE FORESTS OF THE UNITED STATES

The woodland and forests may be considered from two points of view, (*a*) as a source of lumber supply, and (*b*) as a physical factor with effects upon climate, erosion, and the flow of streams.

As a source of lumber supply the forest is, to all intents and purposes, an agricultural crop differing from most other agricultural products in the fact that it requires a long time to reach maturity—generations—while other crops require only months or, at most, a few years. The forests of the United States consist in part of what is commonly called original growth—which means simply that the forest is composed in the main of old trees which have, by sufferance of fire and the ax, been permitted to reach or exceed maturity—and in part of young growth of various ages, covering regions which have been either wholly or partially cleared by fire or the ax. The former areas bear a mature crop, the latter a crop in process of growth; thus the forest is constantly restoring itself in all those regions where the rainfall is sufficient to encourage tree growth; and in time, if not interfered with, these regions will furnish a supply of lumber as large, and presumably of the same quality, as that available when settlement first invaded them. Hence, the timber supply of the country is, in a sense, a continuous one. Timber is constantly growing to supply that which is used, and in this respect it differs from our supplies of iron ore, coal, and other minerals. These, when exhausted, will never be replaced.

The study of the forests of this country has been carried on almost entirely upon the botanical side. Our forests have been studied thoroughly and exhaustively by botanists, but the geographic and economic sides of the question have received very little attention, except for purely commercial or utilitarian purposes. Even such an elementary fact as the extent of woodland in this country we know only in a broad, general way, except for certain limited areas which have been mapped in connection with topographic surveys. Of the amount of standing timber available for use we know almost nothing. In view of the agitation for the protection of our forests which has been going on for at least a generation, and which has reached such intensity that it has become with many persons almost a religion, it is strange that there should be practically no knowledge to serve as a basis for such a cult.

In the following pages I propose to set forth the best estimate which, so far as I can see, it is possible to make at present of the woodland in this country, with its distribution by states. The sources of information will be given in such a way as to show their degree of reliability. I shall follow this with a summary of the little information we have regarding the quantity of timber, including all estimates with which I am acquainted that appear to be worth republishing; and as certain of these estimates concern the same area and the same species of timber and differ greatly

• Henry Gannett (1846–1914) was a geographer, and at one time served as Chief of the Forest Division, U.S. Geological Survey.

Reprinted from U.S. Geological Survey, *19th Annual Report,* Part 5 (1888), pp. 1–3.

from one another, I wish to say at the outset that the conflicting estimates are not published for the purpose of criticism, but simply to show that the best of available estimates do not agree and must be accepted with reservations.

We know in a broad way that the eastern part of the country, extending from the Atlantic coast to the prairies, is naturally a forested region, owing to the fact that rainfall is sufficient to encourage the growth of trees. Throughout this region the only areas not forested at present are those which have been cleared by man, and most of these are under some form of cultivation. Wherever the land is left waste, forests reproduce themselves. Upon the prairies and the plains and in the Rocky Mountain region trees grow wherever the climate will permit—i.e., wherever the rainfall is sufficient for their needs, and as rainfall is greater upon the mountains than upon the plains and in the valleys, timber is commonly found upon the mountains. One the other hand, on the northwest coast, where the rainfall is ample, and in some cases excessive, the country is heavily forested.

Wooded Areas, by States

The wooded area of the country—the area upon which the timber crop is growing—is a subject of interest and importance, whatever may be the stage of growth of the timber upon it.

Concerning the areas upon which timber is at present growing, we are in position to make certain definite statements, although we know the entire area only approximately. Over large parts of the country the topographic maps prepared by the Geological Survey show the extent of woodland with a high degree of accuracy. The Hayden, Wheeler, and Powell surveys of the western states and territories mapped the woodlands over other large areas. The Northern Transcontinental Survey, carried on by the Northern Pacific Railroad Company, and the Northern Pacific Railroad Company itself have mapped considerable areas in the State of Washington. California, through its forestry commission, has similarly mapped the forested areas in the northern part of the state. From these sources the timbered areas of Massachusetts, Rhode Island, Connecticut, New Jersey, Kansas, Colorado, Utah, and parts of other states have been depicted in detail.

In most of the Eastern States, which are naturally forested, a close approximation to the wooded area has been obtained from the figures of the Tenth and later censuses. These give the total land area, the area included in farms, and, of the area included in farms, the woodland. The item of woodland given in these statistics does not include waste or brush land, but only that properly classified as woodland. It is assumed that the area not in farms is, in these states, composed of woodland, an assumption which is for most of these states substantially correct, and for those states where it is not true, allowance has been made for the area naturally devoid of timber. In the states of the prairie, plains, and Cordilleran regions, for which this assumption is incorrect, other means of obtaining the timbered areas have been used. . . .

J. W. MILLIMAN

WELFARE, ECONOMICS, AND RESOURCE DEVELOPMENT

I shall present a few of the conclusions and highlights of a recent water-supply study of which I am a co-author, along with Jack Hirshleifer and James C. DeHaven.[1]

Before turning to the book, however, let me make two general points. First, it seems to me that the major problems of natural-resource use and development are to be found not in the realm of theoretical niceties—granted that economic theory and social-welfare analysis are pretty crude tools—but rather in the operational or applied field. I suspect that our gross mistakes and blunders stem from our inability and unwillingness to apply more of the elementary principle of economic analysis to natural-resource decisions, particularly at the public level. There is nothing mystical about natural-resource capital. It should be subject to the same rules and analysis that apply to all economic goods.

Second, despite the abuse of benefit-cost analysis in public water projects, it is clear that the level and stringency of analysis—crude as it is—greatly exceeds that accorded to many other types of public investment. Conservation of *urban* resources and lands will probably be one of the major problem areas to be faced in the next century. Indeed, the amount of urban investment to be made in the next two decades will undoubtedly dwarf the total amounts spent on water resources in the last hundred years. But I have yet to see an urban-renewal project which has been subject to a critical and searching benefit-cost analysis. In other words, there are presently no clear-cut standards for judging the proper amount, kind, scope, and direction of public investment in the urban sphere. It is my belief that the benefit-cost framework can be modified and reworked so that it may be used with other kinds of public investment. And public urban facilities and city planning are certainly logical candidates for the rigors of such analysis. What we need is a "Green Book" for city planning.[2]

Allocation and Pricing Policies in Water Use

The analysis in the water supply book was divided into two major phases: (1) an examination of the allocation of *existing* supplies; and (2) a study of the alternatives for developing *new* supplies. For each phase we first set forth the basic economic criteria and then examined current prac-

• Jerome W. Milliman is Professor of Business Administration, Indiana University, Bloomington.

Reprinted from H. L. Amoss and R. K. McNickle (eds.), *Land and Water: Planning for Economic Growth,* Western Resources Conference Papers, 1961 (Boulder: University of Colorado Press, 1962), pp. 183–90, with permission of the author and the publisher.

[1] Jack Hirshleifer, James C. DeHaven, and Jerome W. Milliman, *Water Supply: Economics, Technology, and Policy,* A Rand Corp. study (Chicago: University of Chicago Press, 1960). Many of the comments here are taken from chap. 12, "Some Controversial Conclusions and Their Implications."

[2] U.S., Inter-Agency Committee on Water Resources, Report by Subcommittee on Evaluation Standards, *Proposed Practices for Economic Analysis of River Basin Projects* (rev. ed.; Washington: Government Printing Office, 1958). This report is commonly called the "Green Book."

tices to see how these actual practices measured up to our theoretical standards. In this connection, we undertook two major case studies: the New York City "water crisis" and the proposals for carrying water to southern California.

Perhaps our most surprising finding was that water supplies are often grossly misallocated among uses and between uses. Discriminating and subsidized pricing patterns and defective systems of water rights are responsible for this waste. It is these misallocations and other defects of administration, rather than lack of water, which lead to the frequent claims of "shortage" and eventual rebuilding of water supplies.

In Los Angeles, as in many other cities, large users are charged prices less than the marginal cost of processing and delivering extra water to them. As a consequence, industries which are large water-users have no incentive to install recirculating devices which would permit a large reduction in the amount of water used. This is wasteful because more highly valued resources are used to supply the extra water used at these low prices than would be needed to build water-conserving devices.

Contrary to popular opinion, industry does not have a fixed "requirement" for water. Economic demands must consider costs and prices. The degree of substitution of other inputs for water will reflect changing economic feasibility. Time and time again we studied projections for the future use of water based purely upon crude extrapolations of present consumption patterns, with no consideration of economic substitutibility. In economic jargon, this amounts to the false assumption that the demand for water is perfectly inelastic.

A current example is to be seen in a recent report of the U.S. Senate Select Committee on National Water Resources, a report now being widely quoted as *the* authoritative study on the prospective demand for and supply of water in the United States in 1980 and 2000. Although the report was prepared by an economist, these projections of demand and supply were developed without reference to such basic factors as prices, costs, alternative uses of water, interregional shifts, and most of the factors affecting the elasticities of demand and supply.[3]

In contrast, we found that the demand for water has a good deal of price elasticity, particularly in such major areas of water use as irrigation and industrial cooling. I am certain that increases in water prices over the next 25 years will greatly increase the demand elasticity in all uses.

New York City presents another example of the way in which an improper pricing policy encourages wasteful use of water. In that city only about 25 per cent of water users are metered. By and large, only the larger commercial and industrial users are metered. Hence, 75 per cent of the water users pay a flat rate, and the cost to them of using extra water is zero. This means that they have no incentive to economize on its use, to fix leaks, or even to turn off faucets. The result is that New York has a high per capita domestic water use. The city is completing construction of the costly new Cannonsville project to increase its supplies, despite the fact shown by competent studies that the repair of serious leaks in the city mains and extension of metering could add as much to the city's water supply as the Cannonsville project at a small fraction of its cost.

In arid regions, irrigation agriculture typically pays very low prices for water and uses large quantities. In the state of California 90 per cent of total water use is for irrigation. The irrigator in Imperial Valley pays $2 per acre-foot for Colorado River water, while Los Angeles and other cities are paying over $25 per acre-foot,

[3] Nathaniel Wollman, *A Preliminary Report on the Supply of and Demand for Water in the United States as Estimated for 1980 and 2000,* U.S., Senate Select Committee on National Water Resources, Comm. Print No. 32, 86th Cong., 2d Sess., 1960, pp. v, 2. These limitations are explicitly recognized by Wollman (pp. 31–34, 76) but not by most persons citing the study.

wholesale, to the Metropolitan Water District for imported Colorado River water. Retail prices go upward from $80 an acre-foot after distribution costs are added.

In presenting the advantages of *voluntary* transfers of water among uses and users and even between regions, we have been accused of wishing to dry up irrigation agriculture in the West. This is a completely unwarranted accusation. In California's Imperial Valley, for example, irrigators are using their two-dollar water to grow large amounts of low-valued crops. Suppose that only 25 per cent of their water rights—or about 1 million acre feet—were purchased for transfer to urban use in southern California. The irrigators would almost certainly remain in business. They could reduce the application to the initial crops, shift to crops demanding less moisture, or cut back the irrigation of low-valued crops (alfalfa, pasture, hay and grains, and field crops). Alternatively, they could eliminate some of the waste from seepage and evaporation, which often reaches 50 per cent of the amount delivered. It is our strong belief that the irrigators could make more profits from selling their valuable water rights than from growing low-valued crops.[4] The 25 per cent amount, furthermore, is a large amount by urban standards; the 1 million acre-feet involved is equal to about two-thirds of all the urban water used in the south central area of California!

Over-Investment in Water Supply

Undoubtedly, the most controversial substantive conclusion of the book, justified by a great variety of evidence from our survey of federal and municipal experience in water-supply decisions, is that in the United States *major water investments are typically undertaken prematurely and on an over-ambitious scale.* Consequently, at any one time there is over-investment in water supply.

Over-investment for any particular area is indicated when facilities stand idle or else are put to makeshift uses, either to avoid the appearance of idleness or to minimize the losses due to past mistakes. Uneconomic over-investment may be also indicated by relatively low return earned on capital invested in water supply. Here the water is actually being put to use, but the price charged is so low that the revenue to the water enterprise is small in relation to cost. There is over-investment because the same capital investment could have been put to work producing goods and commodities valued more highly on the margin by consumers; consumers' marginal values in use for water are low in comparison with what could have been obtained if the dollars had been spent elsewhere. Specifically, our two major area studies revealed the highly premature nature of the decision to build the Cannonsville Project in the one case and the proposal for construction of the Feather River Project in the other. Or, looking at return to capital, we found that, for the public water-supply systems in general, this is of the order of 2 per cent—an astonishingly low figure.

The reasons for the prevalence of over-investment in water supply are complex and interrelated. To a great extent they are outside the sphere of economic analysis, and so we only speculate about them. One possible explanation is that those responsible for the construction of "engineering wonders" become romantic figures, heroes not only to their own age but to later generations—and heroes whether their great projects were wise or unwise, timely or premature. In contrast, individuals credited only with sound stewardship of the resources of society are scarcely known in their own day and certainly never appear in history books. "The gravy train runs in the same direction as the glory trail." Political scientists have pointed out

[4] At $10 per acre-foot, the sale of 1 million acre-feet per year would bring $10 million net. In the latest year for which data are available (1954), the market value of *all* crops in Imperial County was $109 million, a gross figure from which all the costs of production must be subtracted. See Hirshleifer, DeHaven, and Milliman, *op. cit.*, p. 331.

the attractiveness to bureaucrats and politicians of the power inherent in being able to influence the award of contracts valued in the millions or hundreds of millions of dollars, the enhancement of real estate values on nearby lands, the creation of an enormous variety of business opportunities, and so on.

Perhaps the most important of these reasons for over-investment might be simple oversight; that, when the total of water use begins to approach system capacity, administrators simply do not think of attempting to make better use of existing supplies as an alternative to initiating new construction. The possibility of adjusting prices does not often occur to those responsible, even though studies have shown that demand is responsive to prices and the wide divergence of price levels and price structures in American cities suggests that a schedule currently in effect in a particular city is not necessarily the only one possible, or even the best available one in the circumstances. Peak-load pricing should be used to a much greater extent in water-supply systems. Introduction of a *peak-season* price (in the summer normally) will not require any special metering and seems clearly indicated as an alternative to expensive new construction when it is only the peak-season loads that press on system capacity.

BIAS OF PROJECT ANALYSIS

Another major class of error leading to other investment in water supply is the systematic bias toward excessive construction inherent in conventional techniques of project analysis. An obvious error consists of excessive counting of secondary benefits. Also interesting is the history of over-optimism in estimate of project benefits and costs. Most important of all is the failure to evaluate the future benefits and costs at realistic rates of discount. Commonly, interest rates used for discounting purposes are based upon the borrowing rate of the agency concerned. Consequently, little or no allowance is made for the risks involved in the *particular* project in question.

We have argued that the risks involved in public water projects are about as large as those faced by publicly regulated utility companies. These companies usually require an 8 to 10 per cent rate of return before taxes in order to allow for risk of failure. Consequently, if one wishes to maintain neutrality on the margin between public and private enterprises, public agencies should restrict themselves to a comparable yield.

The adoption of such a strict standard would make uneconomic a large part of the investment programs of the major federal agencies in the field. It should be stressed, however, that the same conclusion can be arrived at *without* use of an 8 to 10 per cent discount rate. If cost and benefit estimates are correctly estimated, making *full* allowance for risk and for over-optimism, we would advocate use of a long-term riskless rate of 4 per cent. I wish to emphasize that none of this denies the existence or possibility of social benefits accruing to the community and nation from a proposed project. Certainly social benefits should be counted in making efficiency calculations. But there is no necessary reason for benefits, just because they are social, to be discounted at an artificially low rate of interest. Social benefits should be subject to the same rate of discount that applies to other benefits and to other comparable projects.

The most sophisticated of the arguments for the adoption of inefficient water projects is the claim that the subsidy to water users involved is justified by a region's need for "development," or "balanced development." Water is conceived as possessing special properties for stimulating growth. But such a subsidy may cause the development to occur in a manner ill-suited to the natural advantages of the region. In particular, in an arid region where water is costly to provide, making water artificially cheap to users will encourage them to be wasteful. A likely and unfortunate result is the development of water-using industries poorly adapted to the region. If the taxes to support the project are borne within the region, economic activities that are justified will, of necessity, be required to support the subsidized users. Of course, if the subsidy is borne from outside the region, the area will be benefited. Even here the benefit will not be as great as if more productive projects were chosen.

The sheer irony of water subsidies, designed to help out poor and small water users, is that they often fail to do what they are intended to do. Time and time again, the real value of subsidized water is quickly capitalized in higher land values. This means that users gain only insofar as they are large landowners. "Cheap water" is counterbalanced by expensive land. The gainers are those who own land at the time the subsidy is approved. Land prices soon jump upward. This is a type of windfall gain. All later comers face high land prices.[5]

DEFECTS IN LAW

Much of the present misuse of water can be traced to imperfections in water law and its administration. Although the establishment of clear property rights to water does pose difficulties, we believe that the law of prior appropriation as developed in some western states has most of the elements required to make a workable system. This type of water law needs to be strengthened primarily in its provisions for the transfer of rights. Under the system we propose, the courts would function as they do for other real property, to adjudicate disputes as to the ownership and extent of the property right and to hear pleas relating to breach of contract in transfers or from parties who consider themselves injured by the actions of the owners of the water rights. The judicial system would be freed of its present inappropriate administrative-economic function of issuing and revising rights to use water based upon fuzzy criteria as "reasonable" or "beneficial" use.

Even the humid regions have begun to recognize the inadequacy of their doctrines of water law. We believe, however, that they are taking the wrong direction in modifying present laws, to judge from the drafts of "model" state water codes and from recent state water laws. The tendency is to set up machinery so that the allocation of water between uses and users can take place only through grants or permits issued by central administrative commissions or by cumbersome court procedures. In these circumstances, the fabric of water rights is weakened by becoming dependent upon the changing wills of the commission or courts. We believe that this line of development wil lead to serious misallocation of water between alternative uses, and it will tend to reduce local, regional, and private initiative in the development of water resources.

INVESTMENT IN WATER IN RELATION TO OTHER PUBLIC PROJECTS

In closing, I wish to stress that our study attempted to show that increased application of economic principles will produce greater efficiency in water supply *in relation to, and in competition with, all the other desires of the community as based upon values established by the community.*

Many of the conclusions we reach are at variance with the present practices governing both the use of existing water supplies and the development of new supplies. Also, they indicate that certain "reforms" now taking place may make matters worse. In other words, our study constitutes a plea for a major change in the current thought and practice on water-supply problems.

[5] I have analyzed this matter in greater detail elsewhere. See J. W. Milliman, "Land Values as Measures of Primary Irrigation Benefits," *Journal of Farm Economics,* LXI (May, 1959), 234–43; and "Land Values—a Further Comment," *ibid.*, LXII (February, 1960), 178–79. Excellent work by Edward F. Renshaw is cited in both papers.

GEORGE MACINKO

THE COLUMBIA BASIN PROJECT: EXPECTATIONS, REALIZATIONS, IMPLICATIONS

The Columbia Basin Project, construction of which was begun in the early 1930's, was designed to be the nation's largest single irrigation project and its prime example of planned land use. In 1939 the Commissioner of Reclamation initiated a 4-year program that was to become known as the "Columbia Basin Joint Investigations."[1] These investigations were truly joint endeavors, since federal, state, and private agencies assisted the Bureau of Reclamation in its attempt to provide a sound plan for the settlement and development of the project area. Planning consultant for the Bureau and director of the joint investigations was Harlan H. Barrows, then chairman of the Department of Geography at the University of Chicago.

Little more than a decade has elapsed since water was first brought to project lands, and already serious difficulties have been encountered. Development is virtually at a standstill, with less than half of the

• George Macinko is Assistant Professor of Geography at the University of Delaware.

Reprinted from *Geographical Review*, LIII, No. 2 (1963), 185–99, with permission of the author and the editor. (Copyright © 1963 by the American Geographical Society of New York.)

[1] Twenty-eight problems were set up for study by participants drawn from many federal, state, and private agencies. The results of the investigations were published by the Bureau of Reclamation between 1941 and 1946 as a series of twenty-eight reports. In addition, the scope and general plan of the investigations were printed separately in booklet form: U.S., Dept. of Interior, Bur. of Reclamation, "Character and Scope, Columbia Basin Joint Investigations" (Washington: Government Printing Office, 1941).

planned acreage under cultivation; and future growth is uncertain.

Despite the best efforts of planners, unforeseen problems arise. In this project the problems are many and diverse. Any of them—for example, the provision of adequate drainage facilities at a reasonable cost, the size of farms, crop emphasis, or repayment of construction costs, to mention but a few—would be worthy of extended discussion. However, at a time when irrigation agriculture is undergoing ever-closer Congressional scrutiny, an overview of the Columbia Basin Project may indicate what future developments are to be expected in the field of reclamation.

The project area is in the northwestern part of the Columbia Plateau. At the headworks of the project is Grand Coulee Dam key structure of the irrigation delivery system. Sixty miles to the south, within the "Big Bend" of the Columbia River, lies the northern edge of the reclamation area proper. This is sagebrush country, largely flat plateaus and rolling hills, in the rain shadow of the Cascades. The project area slopes gently to the southwest. Annual precipitation ranges from about 6 inches in the southwest to 10 inches in the northeastern uplands; most of the area receives between 6 and 8 inches. Evaporation rates are high, and potential evaporation exceeds precipitation in every month of the year.

Shortly after the close of the Civil War a land-use system based on open-range livestock grazing was begun by white men.

In the late 1880's scanty water supplies, winter cattle losses, and the success of wheat growers along the more humid eastern margin of the project area resulted in a decline in grazing activities. Wheat farming and settlement soon pushed westward into an area of low rainfall and light sandy soils, and between 1900 and 1910 wheat was grown throughout most of the project area. The extensive clearing of natural vegetation and the destruction of soil-binding properties caused by cultivation, in conjunction with low precipitation, led to widespread and severe wind erosion. By 1911 problems of weed control, wind erosion, and decreasing wheat yields had demonstrated that much of the project area was unsuited to grain production; wheat farming began a long decline, reaching its lowest ebb in 1934. By this time sagebrush and cheatgrass had invaded more than one-third of the lands that had been in wheat before 1911.

Failures in dry farming stimulated interest in irrigation. Irrigation agriculture never occupied large amounts of project land, and none of the early schemes were unqualified successes. Basic to all failures was the fact that water users could not receive enough money returns from crops to pay the cost of irrigation facilities. It soon became apparent that federal aid would be needed to irrigate any large part of the project area.

Project Size

Construction of Grand Coulee Dam, begun in 1934 when efforts to grow wheat were floundering, ushered in the land-use period that was marked by the unfolding of the Columbia Basin Project plan simultaneously with the gradual reestablishment of wheat growing in the eastern part of the project area. The project area comprises 2.5 million acres, of which about 1 million were classified as irrigable under the original land-classification survey. It is extremely unlikely that all the 1 million acres will ever be irrigated. Shortly after contracts were drawn up in 1945 between the Bureau of Reclamation and the project irrigation districts some 300,000 acres,[2] about 30 per cent of the irrigable acreage, were voluntarily withdrawn from project development. Most of the withdrawn lands belonged to wheat farmers in the eastern part of the project, where rainfall and soils favor dry farming. Here annual precipitation in excess of 8 inches and light-brown loessal soils with fair moisture-retention capability permitted three technological developments, put into effect after initial project planning had taken place, to revolutionize wheat farming. The tractor replaced the horse, and because of its greater efficiency it reduced the period of soil disturbance considerably and permitted better timing of farm operations: plowing, weeding, and cultivating could be accomplished in days rather than weeks, and thus soil could be worked under optimum moisture conditions. Rod weeders replaced harrows, and by cutting weed roots well below the surface they reduced soil pulverization at the surface and thereby improved the bedding quality of the top layer of soil. Disk plows kept stubble on the surface instead of burying it in the fashion of the moldboard plow.

The net effect of these innovations was an increase in soil moisture and a decrease in wind erosion, which made wheat growing under dry-land methods profitable. By 1948, the first year of project operation, wheat farming had been reestablished over most of the eastern third of the project area. This fact was the cause of the first of the major setbacks to the orderly implementation of the project irrigation plan—the withdrawal of 300,000 acres of the best project lands.

It is probable that the farmers who withdrew land in the late 1940's would have been eager to join in project development in the early and middle 1930's, when wheat farming in their area was a marginal

[2] O. L. Brough, Jr., *et al.*, *Columbia Basin Project: Relative Land Productivity and Income*, Washington Agric. Exper. Stations Bull. 570 (1956), pp. 1–2.

operation at best. The fact that almost all the withdrawn land could be dry-farmed profitably at the time of withdrawal but had been a poor risk in the 1930's implies that there should be some method to cut down the time lag between planning and implementation. This point will be discussed more fully in the section on farm size. The only alternative to a reduction in time lag would be greater accuracy in the prediction of future conditions so that plans could meet such conditions.

Project Costs

Ever-increasing costs of the irrigation construction program have resulted in further reductions of irrigated acreage. The situation is made more serious by the fact that the prices received by the irrigation farmer for his products have not kept pace —they remain at the old rather than at the new, inflated, level.

In October of 1945 the three irrigation districts constituting the Columbia Basin Project negotiated repayment contracts with the Bureau of Reclamation. These contracts called for $280,782,180 to cover the construction cost of works directly assigned to irrigation, of which water users were to repay $87,465,000.[3] This sum was derived by multiplying the net irrigable project acreage (1,029,000)[4] by $85. The decision that farmers could repay part of the cost of irrigation construction at the rate of $85 per irrigable acre seems to have been made by the Bureau more or less arbitrarily.[5] Nevertheless, water users were obligated to pay an average of $85 per irrigable acre, this sum to be paid by means of annual installments over a 40-year period following a 10-year developmental grace period.

It soon became evident that this amount would be far too little to cover costs of the entire irrigation construction program. By the summer of 1959 plans were made to bring construction to a virtual halt in 1963, and to stop it completely in 1968, at which time less than half of the million irrigable acres would be receiving water. To stave off this eventuality, the Bureau of Reclamation attempted to "renegotiate" repayment contracts that would obligate farmers to repay at the rate of $125 per acre instead of $85.[6]

3 Columbia Basin Project Repayment Contracts with the Quincy Columbia Basin Irrigation District, East Columbia Basin Irrigation District, South Columbia Basin Irrigation District (U.S., Bur. of Reclamation, n.d.), pp. 14, 16.

4 The 1945 contracts called for an irrigable acreage of 1,029,000 even though it was evident that much of this acreage was not or would not be available for irrigation. It was planned to make substitutions for the lands withdrawn from development by private owners, largely wheat farmers in the eastern part of the project area, so that the million-acre goal could be achieved.

5 For example, a 1953 report of the Bureau of Reclamation states: "The Commissioner of Reclamation in the findings of the feasibility of the Columbia Basin Project, tentatively determined that 'the water users will be able to pay at the average rate of $85 per acre for the net irrigable acreage of the project on the terms available under the Reclamation project act of 1939, subject to a possible reduction later if circumstances warrant' " (see U.S., Bur. of Reclamation, "Report of the Working Committee to the Advisory Committee on Allocation of Irrigation Construction Costs, Columbia Basin Project" [Ephrata, Wash., 1953], p. 53). The "feasibility" findings, refer to "Report by the Bureau of Reclamation, Department of the Interior," *Columbia River and Minor Tributaries,* House Doc. No. 103 (2 vols.), I, 73d Cong., 1st Sess., 1933, 479–537. Examination of this latter report reveals that the figure of $85 is mentioned only on p. 484, in Conclusion No. 4, here quoted in full: "The surplus from power revenues is estimated to be sufficient to repay within 40 years about 50 per cent of the cost of the irrigation development for the entire acreage of 1,200,000 acres proposed for the project, or an average of over $85 per acre. The balance of the irrigation investment must be repaid by the lands or from other sources." No analysis is given to back up the inferred conclusion that the land (water users) could in fact repay $85 per acre, and thus repay the 50 per cent of irrigation costs not met by power receipts.

6 U.S., Bur. of Reclamation, Amendatory Contract between the United States of America and the ——— Columbia Basin Irrigation District (Ephrata, Wash., 1959), mimeographed, pp. 12–13. This proposed amendatory contract was rejected by East Columbia Basin District farmers on July 28, 1959. See the *Tri-City Herald* (Kennewick, Wash.), July 29, 1959.

To understand the renegotiation problem, one must view it in historical perspective. In 1933, when the project was in its infancy, it was believed that surplus power revenues would repay 50 per cent of the cost of irrigation development and that project farmers would be able to repay the bulk of the remainder.[7] But by 1944, one year before the project was reauthorized and repayment contracts were negotiated, payments by water users would have offset only 28 per cent of irrigation construction costs,[8] and by 1959, at the height of renegotiation proceedings, water users would have paid for little more than 11 per cent of these costs.[9] In view of the long-term rise in the construction-cost index and its probable continuance into the future, it appears that water user repayments are not likely to exceed 10 per cent of the final costs of constructing irrigation works, regardless of the outcome of renegotiation proceedings.

Several factors have made project costs greatly exceed expectations as set forth in official pronouncements. Depreciation in the value of the dollar is an obvious factor. It seems that if one plans to build tomorrow, the only safeguard against inflation is to complete the job yesterday. This truism, obvious to all home builders, does not receive adequate recognition in federal cost accounting as applied to irrigation projects. Here it appears that standard practice is to base estimates of future costs on present conditions, and then to apply these estimates as though they would still be valid two or even three decades in the future.

A review of the economic history of the Columbia Basin Project suggests that in order to avoid inflationary costs some means must be found to push a project along at a rapid pace after authorization has been secured. Certainly all projects should be held suspect in which the construction program extends over several decades, with costs computed before the beginning of construction and based on the concept of a fixed value for the dollar.

But depreciation in the value of the dollar was not the sole cause of rising costs of the Columbia Basin construction program. Drainage costs proved to be more than had been expected. The original repayment contracts of 1945 set a limit of $8,176,000 for construction of drainage works for the million-acre project.[10] By the summer of 1959 it was estimated that an additional $25,400,000 would be needed to provide adequate drainage even for the greatly reduced construction program, which provided for a project of only 455,000 acres.[11] All drainage costs above the $8 million ceiling set by the original contracts would revert to an annual assessment against water users. As these costs promised to be high, drainage became the issue on which Bureau of Reclamation renegotiation efforts were concentrated. Farmers were informed that unless contracts based on a repayment rate of $125 per acre replaced those of 1945 based on a rate of $85 per acre the Bureau would have no alternative but to carry out a program of annual assessments for drainage which would result in a greater total cost to the farmer than the new contracts would.[12] Thus drainage had importance not only as a problem in its own right but also as the bargaining point for renegotiation proceedings.

[7] *Columbia River and Minor Tributaries, op. cit.*

[8] Calculated from data presented in U.S., Bur. of Reclamation, "Columbia Basin Project, Washington: Definite Plan Report," I (Ephrata, Wash., 1953), 21.

[9] Calculated from data presented in "Columbia Basin Project Repayment Contract Review," 86th Cong., 2d Sess., 1960, p. 96.

[10] Columbia Basin Repayment Contracts [footnote 3 above], pp. 6–11.

[11] The New Repayment Contract for the Columbia Basin Project: An Analysis Prepared by the East Columbia Basin, Quincy Columbia Basin, and South Columbia Basin Irrigation District (Columbia Basin Commission, 1959), p. 6.

[12] *Ibid.*, pp. 5–10.

Project planners were fully aware of the fact that when 40 to 60 inches of water is applied annually by irrigation to an area that ordinarily receives 6 to 10 inches of precipitation, supplemental drainage facilities will be required. However, recognition of the inevitability of a drainage problem did not provide light on where, when, and how much drainage construction would be needed. Any attempt to determine this would have required detailed, and therefore costly, drainage studies of project lands. Exhaustive studies were rejected on economic grounds, and in their absence the Bureau of Reclamation proceeded to construct drainage facilities designed to meet the most serious of the potential needs indicated by preliminary studies.

From the beginning of drainage construction reclamation officials conceded that they could not predict exactly when the irrigation-induced water table would make the construction functional, but they were confident that, given full project development, all drainage construction would be functional and would be located most advantageously. Certain project developments tend to support the Bureau of Reclamation assertion.[13] However, the fact that much of the construction carried out under the original $8 million drainage allotment was non-operational during early years at the same time that wet lands were developing elsewhere has occasioned strong disapproval of drainage activities. Water users pointed to the simultaneous existence of "dry" drainage ditches and hundreds of acres of land ruined by locally rising water tables to support their contention that not only were drainage funds being used unintelligently but they were being deliberately misused in order to expend the $8 million allocated for drainage and thus to provide the Bureau of Reclamation with a stronger stand on renegotiation.[14]

Although drainage construction may be entirely justified by future events, much damage has already been done. Because of the existence of drainage ditches that were dry at least in part, farmers were convinced that the drainage program was based on guesswork. The revision of the estimate of costs from $8.2 million to $44.5 million for the entire million-acre project[15] strengthened this viewpoint and the unwillingness of the Bureau of Reclamation to guarantee that the revised estimate would cover costs of all drainage required crystallized the issue.[16]

The implication here is that if budgets must provide for such unknown factors as drainage requirements, enough money should be set aside to take care of eventualities. This might, however, increase the costs of irrigation programs, which already encounter stiff opposition on economic grounds, to the point of impracticability. The alternative, assessing farmers annually for construction as needed, is undesirable because the amount and timing of future assessments must remain unknown—not a situation designed to generate farmer enthusiasm.

Farm Size

Farm units in the Columbia Basin Project were laid out on the basis of their ex-

13 For a more detailed discussion of the point that the Bur. of Reclamation drainage program may yet prove sound see the author's "Types and Problems of Land Use in the Columbia Basin Project Area, Washington" (unpublished Ph.D. dissertation, Department of Geography, University of Michigan, 1961), pp. 112–23.

14 See *Columbia Basin News* (Pasco, Wash.), Mar. 30, 1960. A large majority of the farmers interviewed by the author in the summers of 1958 and 1959 also believed the drainage program was characterized by wastefulness.

15 The New Repayment Contract . . . , *op. cit.*, p. 7.

16 Based on notes taken by the author during a series of meetings between project farmers and Bur. of Reclamation officials in June and early July of 1959. Bureau officials stated that they were confident the $44 million would be adequate to cover drainage costs, but they could not guarantee this. One estimate of the cost of drainage construction was as high as $175 million. See *Columbia Basin News* (Pasco, Wash.), March 30, 1960.

pected productivity. Size ranged from 40 acres for farms established on the best-quality lands to 160 acres for those on the poorest lands. The average was slightly less than 80 acres.

It soon became apparent that in a changing agricultural economy marked by a growing emphasis on farm mechanization some of the smaller units were uneconomic. Farm-equipment requirements were virtually the same for large and small farms, and on the smaller farms valuable equipment remained idle much of the time. Farmers argued that they needed to work more acres in order to make their investments in machinery pay off. Excessively small farms encouraged wholesale leasing, which worked against good farm practice, and owners of small farms experienced great difficulty in arranging for adequate financing of their farm operations. Furthermore, the vast social changes that had taken place since the 1930's had made the test of a farm's economic acceptability much more rigorous. The modern farmer, unlike his counterpart of the 1930's, is not content to operate his farm for a modest return, especially during its development stage. By the 1950's the dream of the farmer, like that of most of his countrymen, included a new car, deepfreeze, television, and other amenities.

As a result, farm ownership limits were revised upward; a family can now own 320 acres. This has led to serious complications. There is general agreement that the larger farms are more economic and therefore tend to increase the repayment ability of farmers. This is an obvious asset in view of the rise in project construction costs. However, because the farmer's repayment obligation now stands at only 11 per cent of the cost of bringing water to the land, an 80-acre farm receives in effect a subsidy of about $55,000, whereas a 320-acre farm receives $220,000. This is an enormous unearned increment to accrue to one individual and is difficult to justify in view of the historic reclamation goal of maximizing the number of farm settlement opportunities.

It is generally conceded that irrigation development benefits persons other than the water users. The service-station operator, the merchant, and others in the development area all benefit to a varying extent. Considering the poor performance recorded under past and present repayment schemes, some method must be devised to bring these beneficiaries into the repayment picture; for subsidies such as those in the Columbia Basin Project will meet increasing hostility in the future as more demands are placed on the nation's fast-dwindling water resources.

Crop Emphasis

The Columbia Basin Project was to be a model of planned land use. But despite detailed planning, actual land use has differed in several ways from that expected. In the first decade, 1949–58, hay occupied less than half the acreage expected,[17] pasture less than one-seventh; dry beans alone exceeded, by more than one-third, the expectation for all field crops. Ten crops accounted for 90 per cent of all acreage irrigated (Fig. 1); four crops—dry beans, alfalfa hay, wheat, and potatoes—accounted for two-thirds.

A number of reasons might be advanced for the differences between expected and actual land use. All planning estimates were based on conditions that were expected to prevail when the project was in a stage of mature development. To take into account the factor of maturity, six blocks, representative of both the better and the poorer project lands, were selected by the writer for further study. All had been irrigated for 5 years or longer.

Crop emphasis in these mature lands (Fig. 2) differed but little from that in

17 Data on crop expectations were taken from U.S., Dept. of Interior, Bur. of Reclamation, "Types of Farming: Columbia Basin Joint Investigations Problem 2" (Washington: GPO, 1945), p. xiv.

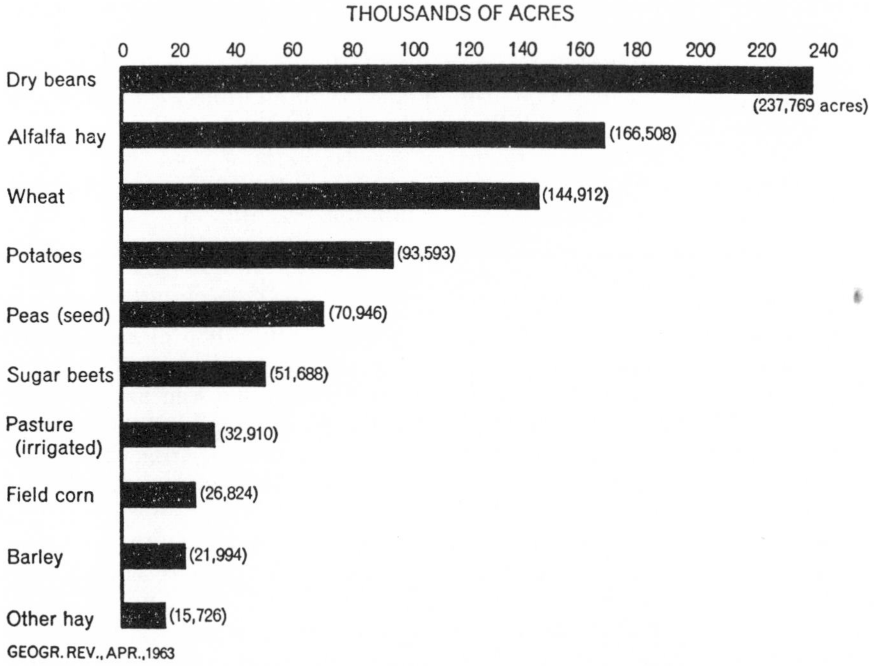

FIG. 1.—Cumulative acreage for ten leading crops, 1949–58

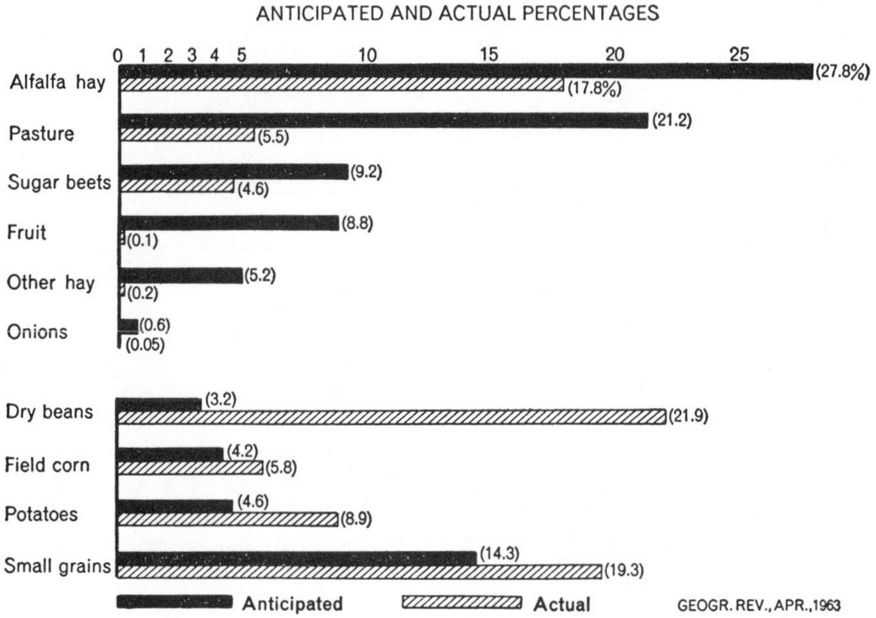

FIG. 2.—Crop acreages at mature development

the entire project.[18] Hay and pasture taken together were far below expectation; dry beans alone exceeded expectations for all field crops. In spite of the fact that hay and pasture crops in the project were intended to support a widespread dairy industry, it is evident that project farmers have so far emphasized low-value field and grain crops (the lower group in Fig. 2) instead of the higher-value fruit, truck, and livestock-support crops (the upper group).

Differences between actual and expected crop emphasis should lessen as time passes. Field investigations conducted in the project area during the summers of 1958 and 1959 indicate that the land use envisioned by the planners may yet materialize, but it will do so far later than was expected and for different reasons. Cropping patterns in planning reports all appear to be based on the assumption that farmers would grow those crops which the plant and soil scientists indicated were best suited to their lands. For a number of reasons, the most important of which are economic, this assumption was unwarranted. Few of the original settlers had sufficient capital to undertake livestock operations initially, especially on the scale that would have been required if the expected hay and pasture acreage was to be achieved. Most of the early farmers were underfinanced, and of necessity they grew cash crops. Declining yields, increasing weed, disease, and labor problems, and low prices on row crops have forced farmers to move in the direction of livestock-forage operations. Many could not afford to make this transition, and much land was abused by farmers who had to stay in the cash (row)–crop stage longer than had been expected. Land use in the Columbia Basin Project emphasizes the futility of expecting farmers to follow what is judged to be "scientifically" the best land-use practice if they are unable to finance this practice.

Some Effects of Project Development

A mere enumeration of the problems of irrigation development in the Columbia Basin Project could lead to the conclusion that the project has been a complete failure. This is not so. Irrigation has given rise to profound changes within the project area. Population doubled during the first decade of development. The area has experienced a complete economic revival.[19] Hundreds of businesses have been established, millions of dollars have been invested, and thousands of families have moved in. The increase in the dollar volume of business was more than twice as great as that in any other economic area of the state. Increases in revenue from retail sales taxes, the state's most important source of revenue, were three times greater than the state average. Similar increases in business or occupation taxes, property taxes, railroad freight shipments, industrial workers employed, and industrial wages paid confirm that irrigation development has greatly stimulated economic activity in the project area by changing its economy from one based on marginal dryland farming and grazing to one of diversified irrigation agriculture with a greatly broadened industrial base. Whether these gains are sufficient to warrant the massive subsidy required to develop irrigation agriculture is a topic requiring much more thought than has hitherto been given to it.

Recreational and esthetic benefits can

[18] Data on crop production of mature lands were taken from O. L. Brough, Jr., and A. L. Walker, *Crop and Livestock Production Possibilities,* Columbia Basin Project, Washington, Washington Agric. Exper. Stations Circular 239 (rev. 1958), pp. 8–13. Brough and Walker present data on crop acreages expected in 1965 for all lands receiving water by 1963. Since some of these lands would have been under irrigation development for as little as two years, it seems reasonable to assume that the lands referred to in the text, all of which had been irrigated for at least five years, would qualify for "mature" status.

[19] All data on the economic impact of irrigation development have been summarized from U.S., Bur. of Reclamation, "Progress Report on Irrigation Accomplishments, Columbia Basin Project, Washington" (1958), mimeographed.

also be traced to irrigation development. The project area now ranks as one of the foremost small-game, waterfowl, and fishing areas of the state. Lakes exist where only rocky canyons had been before irrigation development—lakes where trout growth exceeds anything known previously in the state.

Prospects for the Future

Irrigation has been a major factor in the development of the economy of the West. However, in the Columbia Basin Project the cost of irrigation construction has increased to the extent that without the aid of Grand Coulee power receipts the project would have suffered economic bankruptcy long ago. Therefore, what of the future?

Future irrigation development will be costly—more costly than that of the past, which is already receiving major subsidies. Heretofore this has not been cause for serious alarm. However, water is becoming increasingly scarce, especially in the western states, where rainfall is light and irrigation is prevalent. More and more one hears the argument[20] that western states, by according priority to irrigation, preclude the development of industries requiring large quantities of water, and thus tend to keep the areas predominantly agricultural despite the fact that industrial uses of water yield far higher economic returns than irrigation.

Thus a tendency appears to be growing[21] to view water not primarily in terms of its role in promoting maximum occupancy of land by people but, rather, in terms of its optimum use, whether this is industrial or agricultural. This optimum use probably will be determined more and more by economic measures.

For these reasons greater flexibility in programming, closer attunement to the state of the national economy, reduction in lag time, and new economic justifications will be required if reclamation developments are to thrive in the face of competing demands on the nation's water resources.

[20] Otto Eckstein, *Water-Resource Development, the Economics of Project Evaluation,* Harvard Economic Studies, CIV (Cambridge: Harvard University Press, 1958), p. 219.

[21] P. H. McGauhey, and Harry Erlich, *Economic Evaluation of Water, Part 1: A Search for Criteria,* Univ. of California Water Resources Center Contributions No. 13 (1956), p. 211.

> Mr. Gilbert . . . has reached the conclusion that a continuous flow of one cubic foot of water per second, i.e., a *second-foot* of water, will, in most of the lands of Utah, serve about 100 acres for the general average of crops cultivated . . . but to secure that amount of service from the water, very careful and economic methods of irrigation must be practiced. At present, there are few instances where such economic methods are used. In general, there is a great wastage, due to badly constructed canals, from which the water either percolates away or breaks away from time to time; due, also, to too rapid flow, and also to an excessive use of the water, as there is a tendency among the farmers to irrigate too frequently and too copiously, errors corrected only by long experience.
>
> J. W. Powell, *Report on the Lands of the Arid Region of the United States* (Washington: GPO, 1879), pp. 83–84.

GORDON R. CLAPP

AN APPROACH TO THE DEVELOPMENT OF A REGION

Introduction

To begin with, I shall present a somewhat general picture of the work, the purposes, and the results of the Tennessee Valley Authority, now in its twenty-first year. It is only fair to state at the outset that what I say will reflect a firm "belief in the wisdom and feasibility" of the TVA Act—a phrase contained in the oath of office of the Authority's directors.

The phrase "wisdom and feasibility," required by law as one of the tests of fitness for members of the board of directors, at once suggests that TVA is a special kind of agency with an assignment in fields where controversy is not unknown. It was a controversial subject before it was established. Controversy has beaten upon it throughout its history. And in some quarters TVA is a controversial subject today, perhaps more so than when it began. Some who opposed it did not believe it could succeed. They were against it in theory. "But why worry," they said, "it won't last long; it can't work." Some of today's opposition can be traced to a belated recognition that here was a feasible idea, indeed. So now we hear a revival of the view that it should not have been started in the first place.

But I do not intend here to debate the wisdom or feasibility of TVA. It is an existing American institution. The emulation of its approach to the development of natural resources in other parts of the world, of which there are many examples, testifies to its efficacy where the reality of resource problems is more compelling than abstract doctrine. World interest is evidence of its high export value. Some of the country's leaders who promote it as a source of exemplary suggestion for "other people" also use it as an example of questionable unorthodoxy in our domestic scene. A Valley Authority on the sacred Jordan River as a useful device for international cooperation is espoused by the same government officials who refer to its prototype at home as "creeping socialism"; an asp in the bosom at home, a dove of peace abroad.

Many of the 10,000 visitors from all over the world who have come to study the TVA development go home with a stimulating idea for which the United States gets widespread thanks. But our visitors are usually puzzled when they find it singularly alone in a country with so many great river valleys in need of attention. And once, when I attempted to explain why, our visitor smiled and told me how an Arabian monarch, intent on installing a telephone system in his desert palace against the opposition of the custodians of ancient tradition, invoked an ingenious ruse. The first trial of the Western innovation successfully relayed the message, "Allah be praised." No invention of the devil could possibly have subscribed to those words. The sacred doctrine was preserved and pragmatic values incorporated therein.

While the Tennessee Valley Authority has not been emulated in *form* within this

• Gordon R. Clapp (1905–63) was an administrator, well-known for his work with TVA and work in private resource development.

Reprinted from *The TVA: An Approach to the Development of a Region* (Chicago: University of Chicago Press, 1955), pp. 1–20, with the permission of Mrs. Gordon R. Clapp.

country, the domestic value of its substance has been widely recognized. Careful students of river-valley development and of federal-state relations see abundant evidence of the steady borrowing from its lessons within this country. The comment of our Arabian friend provides a ready explanation as to why the water carried from the well of the TVA experience to nourish other river valleys is put in new bottles bearing different labels to avoid identification of the source. Perhaps there is a place in our culture for what one might call a process of "semantic immunization" to make it easier for tender and brittle minds to assimilate and use knowledge distilled from real experience.

Perhaps the subtlety of a sometimes baffling and contradictory argument which greets TVA on all sides helps to explain why its very vigorous existence seems to engender controversy. One of its unprofound friends once remarked, "I wish something could be done so that the Valley program wouldn't stir up a row every time it is on the agenda in Congress." There is a way to do this.

The formula can be very simply stated: TVA will cease to become controversial when it fails to pursue vigorously the purposes for which it was established; when it ceases to be deeply devoted to the public interest; when it gives up its persistent effort to excel in its performance of the tasks assigned to it. Should these changes occur, and the pressures and actions to bring these changes have been unremitting since it was created, its essence as an idea and as a useful instrument of public service will have disappeared. TVA is controversial because it is consequential; let it become insignificant to the public interest, an agency of no particular account, and people will stop arguing about it.

Some of the controversy springs from deep-seated, genuine convictions about desirable and necessary limitations upon the tendency for governmental functions to push further and further into the area of decision more properly reserved to individual citizens, to communities, and to the states. I respect and share this concern. . . .

Much of the controversy, however, is fed by resort to myth, to noisy repetition of doctrine alleged to describe the American economic system against which the TVA idea is superficially assessed. With credit to its anonymous source this couplet serves me well:

> T'aint ignorance that does the damage;
> It's knowing so much that isn't so.

For example, TVA is viewed by some as an opponent of private enterprise. Yet in the last 20 years few regions of the country have witnessed a more rapid increase in the growth and expansion of private business than has taken place in the Tennessee Valley.

Others describe the Valley Authority as a heavy-handed extension of the powers of the federal government into the affairs of the states. The governors and agencies of the seven Valley states testify to the contrary. One frequently hears that federal funds, through this regional agency, have discouraged the development of state programs in agriculture, forestry, and water control. But, in truth, there has been a greater rate of increase in state funds applied to resource development programs in the Tennessee Valley than in the remainder of the country.

The Tennessee Valley, some allege, is a favored area, receiving larger federal aid than other regions. This is not true. A large proportion of the money provided for TVA has, in fact, gone to other parts of the country. Of the $1.4 billion it has used to buy equipment and materials, more than half, $866 million, was spent outside the Tennessee Valley states.

Figures on federal employment of civilians, grants-in-aid, military contracts, and personal income from *all* federal sources show that the Tennessee Valley is not a favored region.[1] For example, federal civil-

[1] Based on a comparative analysis of the Additional Reports of the Joint Committee on Reduction of Nonessential Federal Expenditures, *Federal*

ian employment in the Tennessee Valley in proportion to population is lower than in the Missouri Valley states, about equal to that in New England, and lower than in California, New York, and Illinois.

Why, then, should these myths about TVA persist?

There are undoubtedly many explanations, but I believe one of the major reasons springs from its very nature. It is a new approach to the conservation and development of the natural resources of a region by a federal agency for regional development, located in the area of its assignment. It is a government corporation, commissioned to seek a blend of federal, state, and local concerns, with responsibility defined in fairly specific terms. It is held to a strict accounting for results, yet it is without authority to prescribe and enforce a plan.

The subject matter of its work includes a good cross-section of the controversial issues inherent in the development of resources anywhere in the United States. The very nature of the problems or subjects it touches has, throughout our history, been subject to controversy—about the necessity or desirability of the objective, about the methods by which the result should be obtained, and about who should get the benefits. Who should get the benefits—there's the rub. This is true for most administrative assignments whether in the domain of private or public activity. But controversy can be especially sharp when the subject matter is land, water, forests, minerals, chemical fertilizers, and electric energy. For in these fields, as President Franklin D. Roosevelt pointed out in April, 1933, in his message to Congress requesting legislation to establish TVA, what is proposed "touches and gives life to all forms of human concerns."

As the federal Executive Branch is organized, the problems of resource development traditionally are divided among a large family of departments, bureaus, and offices. Each one has a part of the resource development assignment; each one has a special clientele whose interests are directly related to only a part of the whole. The stage is thus set for each bureau to keep peace with its own clientele. Conflicting interests, strong and real in the region where the resources exist, are not resolved locally; they come together for solution in the nation's capital, sometimes obscured or grossly distorted by lack of reliable information about the facts. One might almost say that these features of our federal organization encourage the convergence of special-interest groups on the capital and at times greatly increase the means by which they can enforce their will.

Precision of fit between problem and proposal, a difficult task at best, is made more difficult under these circumstances. The heavy mortality of factual analyses and professional judgments in the process of long-distance sifting and screening is tragic. Compromise on top of a whole series of compromises follows. The result is a policy and program frequently wide of the mark.

A regional agency has to face these conflicting interests within the region. TVA, having a wide variety of basic responsibilities relating to land, water, forests, and electric power, must do its best to resolve these conflicts within the region and present an integrated justification for its actions and suggestions—or fail.

That TVA has succeeded more than it has failed is perhaps the main reason why it continues to be controversial. Its continued existence as a regional agency, able and willing to act and to mobilize the active support and understanding of a large majority of people of the region, is a challenge to the administrative methods and the

---

Grants-in-Aid to States, Senate Doc. No. 101, 82d Cong., 2d Sess., 1952, Table 4; *Federal Civilian Employment, 1950,* Comm. Print, 82d Cong., 1st Sess., 1950; and income estimates derived from U.S. Dept. of Commerce data and other sources; prime contracts as reported by the Munitions Board; and employment estimates based on reports of the Bureau of Labor Statistics and Civil Service Commission.

jurisdictions of established national bureaucracies.

That it continues to be controversial is testimony also to the tenacity of public interest in the problems and promise of our natural resources. In this sense TVA is a stimulant to public discussion, a laboratory for experiment, a demonstration of the hazardous but fruitful relationship between management and politics where the lines of responsibility in each field are kept discernibly clear—clear enough to permit the public to know who did what and whom to hold accountable for what happened.

Some Historical Background

The work of TVA began in 1933. In May of that year the United States Congress enacted, and President Franklin D. Roosevelt signed, the Tennessee Valley Authority Act. This act created a government corporation which, in the words of the chairman of the House committee in charge of this legislation, was "charged with the duty of constantly *studying the whole situation* presented by Tennessee River Valley, and the adjoining territory, with the view of encouraging and guiding in the orderly and *balanced development* of the diverse and rich *resources* of that section."[2]

This new approach of balanced or unified development of natural resources has a long history.[3] In the fast-moving world of today the background of events tends to become blurred in the public mind. In the 20 years in which TVA has been operating, a whole new generation has grown up; it can have no direct recollection of the 15-year controversy prior to 1933 over the disposition of the Muscle Shoals properties of World War I out of which came the germ of the Valley Authority idea. It is a generation unfamiliar with the then-famous offer by Henry Ford to buy the Muscle Shoals nitrate plants and lease Wilson Dam—one of the many proposals carefully analyzed in a history of the Muscle Shoals issue written by Judson King, a still valiant champion of conservation.[4] Today's generation is unfamiliar with the long debates which led Congress to choose from a welter of legislative proposals on the subject—138 in all—and, twice before 1933, to pass legislation providing for government operation of the Muscle Shoals properties and the development of the Tennessee River Basin. Both bills were vetoed. President Coolidge used the pocket veto to kill a Muscle Shoals bill passed by a Republican Congress; clearly he was against it, but for reasons unstated. President Hoover's veto message was not ambiguous.

Two generations have grown up since the turn of the century, when such conservationists as Gifford Pinchot, an American forester trained in Europe, and W J McGee, a geologist and hydrologist, joined with President Theodore Roosevelt in initiating the "Conservation Movement." They gave voice to the idea that "a river is essentially a unit from its source to the sea" and ought to be developed for "all of the uses of the waters and benefits to be derived from their control."[5]

Thus the concepts which found their way into the TVA Act written in 1933 had their beginnings many years before. That Franklin D. Roosevelt of New York was in the White House in 1933, George Norris of Nebraska was in the Senate, and the country was prostrate with unemployment had almost everything to do with its creation at that time. But the ideas and policies

[2] *Muscle Shoals,* House Rept. 48, 73d Cong., 1st Sess., 1933, pp. 10–11. (Italics mine).

[3] See "The Historical Roots of TVA," *Annual Report of the Tennessee Valley Authority, 1953* (1953), pp. 51–52.

[4] "From July 1921 to May 1933 there were no less than 138 bills introduced in Congress affecting the disposition of Muscle Shoals. Many of these embodied the proposals of private power or chemical companies or other industrialists; the others were general leasing bills or proposals for outright public operation," Judson King, *The Legislative History of Muscle Shoals* (Knoxville: TVA, 1936), III, 127.

[5] *Report of the National Conservation Commission . . . ,* Sen. Doc. No. 676, 60th Cong., 2d Sess., 1909, I, pp. 45, 47.

written into the Act evolved from the reflective observations, studies, and experience of the scientists and the informed concern of laymen who initiated the conservation movement.

In historical perspective it is clear that none of the responsibilities assigned to the Valley Authority was new to the federal government. For decades the federal government had been carrying on projects for the development and use of water power, for navigation, and for control of floods; it had established laboratories for the improvement of minerals processing, for use of forest resources, and for the improvement and testing of fertilizers. Nor was TVA endowed with any new governmental powers.

The TVA Act and Its Purposes

What was new was the administrative device. The Act created, according to President Roosevelt, "a corporation clothed with the power of government but possessed of the flexibility and initiative of a private enterprise."[6]

A summary of its far-reaching purposes is found in Section 23 of the Act:

> for the especial purpose of bringing about in said Tennessee drainage basin and adjoining territory . . . (1) the maximum amount of flood control; (2) the maximum development . . . for navigation purposes; (3) the maximum generation of electric power consistent with flood control and navigation; (4) the proper use of marginal lands; (5) the proper method of reforestation . . . and (6) the economic and social well-being of the people living in said river basin.[7]

To this list should be added the extremely important responsibility: "to provide for the national defense."

The assignment was a big one, with great and complex responsibilities—quite enough for any one organization. But one should not regard the assignment as larger or more inclusive than it actually is. There are some, of course, who attempt to do so; thence comes the attempt to stigmatize the Authority as a "superstate" or to invest it with imaginary powers as an economic dictator for an entire region.

TVA's responsibility in the Valley region —an area about one and a half times the size of New England—is confined largely to the development of resources and their use. And development of resources is but one part—a fundamental part, to be sure— of comprehensive development. By contrast, a program for economic development might include many activities which are outside the scope of its task and responsibilities; for example, responsibility for mone yand banking policies, tax and fiscal matters, tariffs, social welfare programs, public investments in roads, schools, and hospitals, transportation rates and policies, agricultural affairs, immigration and emigration, and many other governmental activities which will vary with the contingencies of particular times and places.

TVA does not even have exclusive responsibility within the Valley region in the field of resource development. It has not supplanted, but rather has supplemented, the activities of other federal, state, and local agencies, which continue to exercise virtually all their traditional responsibilities. Its special function is to see the resource base in its entirety, to view the interrelationship among the various resources, and to guide and encourage development in the light of that insight.

. . . In cooperating with agencies of the states and the federal government . . . [TVA makes] it clear that it invites use of their specialized skills, facilities, and organization. In agriculture, for example, its expenditures since 1933 have totaled perhaps one-tenth of all federal funds used in the Valley by all agencies for agricultural development activities of one kind or another. Many more illustrations could be cited. For one other example, its dams have provided opportunities for the United States Fish and Wildlife Service and state con-

6 *Muscle Shoals Development,* House Doc. No. 15, 73d Cong., 1st Sess., 1933, p. 1.

7 Act of May 18, 1933, Sec. 23 (48 Stat. 69).

servation agencies to establish bird and game refuges along the shore lines of the new lakes.

There is another myth about TVA which is very easy for well-informed people to believe. That is the notion that it was set up as a special concession to a single, small region and that this region has reaped the benefits while the taxpayers of the rest of the nation bear the expense. This view asserts that the Valley Authority was set up in the Tennessee Valley region because it was a depressed area, needing special aid on the part of the federal government.

True, the area was in bad straits—and so was the rest of the country. But TVA was established for more than regional or local benefit. Federal funds were invested in this area, just as other activities of the federal government are carried on in other limited regions, for the national benefit. Although it operates largely in a specific region, it is, in fact, a national enterprise "for the general social and economic welfare of the Nation," as President Roosevelt stated in his message to Congress.[8] Moreover, some of its responsibilities extend outside the region. It helps to control floods on the lower Ohio and Mississippi. Its program of fertilizer research experimental production, and demonstration, while small in amount of expenditure, is national in scope. It contributes to the national defense through munitions research and production and the generation of great quantities of power for the production of chemicals, aluminum, and titanium and for the atomic-energy program. Atomic-energy plants are its largest customers. By 1955 at least one-half of TVA's power production—the largest power system in the world—will go to the atomic-energy facilities of the United States government.

In 1933 the entire country was in the throes of a depression. This may have struck with greater force in the Tennessee Valley and the Southeast generally because of the return of many of its people from northern industrial centers where their jobs had disappeared. But this was not the main reason for choosing the Tennessee Valley for the experiment in a new approach to resource development.

With a growing national interest in conservation measures, and with idle World War I facilities at Muscle Shoals as a starting point, the Tennessee River Basin presented an unusual opportunity to rebuild a whole river and its watershed. The notion that this region was especially favored by the federal government is nourished most by those who would persuade other regions to adopt "anything but a TVA" on the hypothetical ground that only poor regions need so drastic a remedy. And few self-respecting regions will admit to that description!

The development of other streams and other regions has gone forward, not in response to pleas of help from destitute people. Federal dams have been built on the Columbia River in the Pacific Northwest, giant dams and reservoirs dot the vast Missouri Valley, and more are being built. In the Ohio Valley multipurpose works for flood control and other purposes continue to be added. The Colorado is in part harnessed by the great Hoover Dam, the tallest in the world.

In all these regions, as in the Tennessee Valley, huge federal expenditures are being made. If that is favoritism, let us recognize it as favoritism for the strength and welfare of the American people.

TVA as a Method of Integration and Decentralization

The role of TVA in the Tennessee Valley is twofold. It has undertaken and carried out the program of physical construction and operation to put the river to work—a task of the federal government too great and too broad in scope to be accomplished by private organizations or by state or local agencies of government. In addition, it has provided the unifying influence, the sense of cohesion and direction, essential to a comprehensive program for conservation and development. By stimulating the inter-

[8] *Muscle Shoals Development, op. cit.*, p. 1.

est of state and local agencies close to the people, it has opened new avenues for joint action, strengthening rather than weakening state and local initiative. A brief description of TVA as an organization and its methods of work will make this clear.

In form it is a government corporation endowed with some of the flexibility of a private corporation. It is headed by a board of three directors appointed by the President and confirmed by the United States Senate. The President designates one of the three directors as chairman of the board. A general manager, appointed by the board, heads the staff, comprising civil, electrical, and chemical engineers; biologists; experts in public health, forestry, agriculture, political science, and economics; managers; and so on. At the peak of World War II, when TVA was building twelve dams at once to expand power supply for aluminum and atomic energy, its forces grew to more than 40,000 men and women. Today, in 1954, it employs about 22,000 people, about half of them in construction—for we still build to keep power supply in pace with the growth of the region and the requirements of national defense.

TVA is dependent upon Congress for annual appropriations required to finance activities of public benefit; these are traditional functions of the federal government, but they do not produce revenues for the Authority. Among these non-revenue–producing activities, most of them carried on in cooperation with more than a hundred state and local agencies, are flood control, navigation and research, experiments and demonstrations helpful to soil-fertility conservation, agricultural and industrial development, and the fuller use of all the resources of the Valley.

As the sole source of electricity for an entire region, and to assure the taxpayers a fair return on their investment, TVA is authorized by law to use its receipts from the sale of power in the conduct of its power business. This wise provision, customary in business and corporate practice, helps to make it possible to satisfy the expanding energy requirements of the area and to serve new needs and new customers promptly. But, like all other utilities, net earnings alone, particularly in a period of rapid expansion, do not provide enough capital to build new power plants. As a utility obtains capital by selling stock and borrowing money, so TVA goes to Congress to seek more capital for power expansion. All the money appropriated to it for power facilities is repayable to the government; the Authority is already paying back this money well ahead of schedule.

TVA is fully accountable to the President and to Congress for what it does and the way it performs its work. This accountability is achieved by full and complete audits of its financial records; by hearings each year before the Bureau of the Budget, acting for the President, and by hearings before the appropriations committees of Congress; by review and examination of all its activities before congressional committees; and by periodic reports to Congress, the President, and the public. TVA is subject to an even more penetrating scrutiny and accountability through its day-by-day work with the people and the agencies of the state and local governments in the Valley. . . .

Natural resources do not conform to man-made boundaries. The watershed of the Tennessee River includes parts of seven states. The fact that much of the developmental action must come from the separate state governments or institutions in several states has not proved an insurmountable obstacle; on the contrary, this circumstance is a fortunate invitation to joint planning and consultation.

The full development of a region for the benefit of human living depends as much upon the administrative or managerial resources of the region as it does upon the human and physical resources. The creation of the Authority established a new administrative resource in the Tennessee Valley to help the states to work together. The job in this respect is to see to it that the facts about the wise use of our resources of water, soils, minerals, and factors of climate are discovered and made available to become a part of the everyday voluntary decisions of people. . . .

Two Major Resource Problems of the Tennessee Valley

There was need for much joint counsel and planning with the people of the Valley when the Authority began its work. The full development of the natural resources of the region in the national interest faced two fundamental handicaps which pervaded the physical setting, depressed the economy, and restricted the freedom of the people.

For more than a century the Tennessee River had been identified as a stream of great undeveloped and wasted power, a potential inland waterway, but a destroyer of life and property as it ran in flood year after year. American capital, private and public, passed it by and chose instead to invest in other regions. Those who urged the enactment of the TVA Act apparently believed that, if the Tennessee River were conquered and its water power harnessed, the river would help transform the economic life of the region and increase the productive capacity of the nation. Nothing less than the resources of the United States government could cope with this task.

The second handicap which plagued the region was closely related to, if not part and parcel of, the wasted river. The Tennessee Valley has more rainfall than any other region in the country except the Pacific Northwest. Because of its temperate climate, it has a longer growing season than most other large areas of the country. It has abundant rainfall and a growing season in more effective combination than any other region of comparable size in the country, without exception. But these priceless natural assets of moderate sunshine and abundant rain had been used too little. Sunshine, soil, water, and human beings were not working together.

The agriculture of the region emphasized cultivation of row crops, principally corn and cotton. There are many reasons why this was done; one was the lack of soil minerals, especially phosphate, required to nourish a grass and animal agriculture. Reliance upon corn and cotton left the land idle and uncovered during what could have been a winter growing season, the period of the heavy rains. Wasted rain and wasted sunshine were serious losses in themselves. In addition, year by year, the fertility of the soil and the soil itself washed away. And the wealth of the soil captured in cotton seed, for example, was largely exported from the region never to return to the lands of the Valley.

Under these conditions a low level of productivity prevailed throughout the region. Few raw materials were produced for industry's use, and most of these were carried through only the simpler types of processing. This arrangement brought small return to the people of the Valley. In 1929, before the depression, the per capita income of the Tennessee Valley was only 44 per cent of the national average. Wasted water, wasted soil, and wasted sunshine depressed economic opportunity at home, and men and women were forced to migrate from the Tennesse Valley to work in the factories of other regions.

These, in brief, are some of the problems which helped to define TVA's assignment. The problems of the Tennessee Valley marked this region as a good place to apply modern engineering theories to a whole river and combine that development with the inseparable problem of conservation on the land.[9]

TVA and the River

The Tennessee River has its principal headwaters in the Appalachian Mountains

[9] For a brief but authoritative analysis of the evolution of law, engineering, and national policy in conservation of water resources see J. L. Fly, "The Role of the Federal Government in the Conservation and Utilization of Water Resources," *University of Pennsylvania Law Review,* LXXXVI (January, 1938), 274–94.

of Virginia and North Carolina. Ranked by volume of stream flow, it is the fifth largest river system in the United States. The Mississippi, Columbia, and Ohio outrank it; the muddy flow of the Missouri barely exceeds the Tennessee. The main stem of the river forms at Knoxville, Tennessee, where two of its major tributaries join—the Holston River from southwestern Virginia and the French Broad from western North Carolina. Its course goes southwest through eastern Tennessee, gathering the flow of important tributaries: the Clinch carrying water from southwestern Virginia, the Little Tennessee from North Carolina, and the Hiwassee and Ocoee rivers, whose headwaters are in North Carolina and Georgia.

Thus grown, the Tennessee flows into the northern part of Alabama. Here it turns north and west, crosses that state, and swings north through western Tennessee and Kentucky. Some 630 miles from Knoxville it joins the Ohio River to flow on into the Mississippi River at Cairo, Illinois. The stream flow of the Tennessee accounts for some 25 per cent of the Ohio's discharge into the Mississippi. The watershed of the Tennessee River is about 40,000 square miles.

This is the river that once wasted its great power in destruction of land, property, and human life. Today, the Tennessee River is the most completely controlled major river system in the United States. The integrated development of the Tennessee River and its tributaries has provided flood control, navigation facilities, and power at less cost than could have been achieved by single-purpose developments.

The present TVA system of dams and reservoirs provides nearly 12,000,000 acre-feet of storage for flood control at the beginning of the flood season each year. In the 17 years since Norris Dam was placed in operation, the reservoir system has prevented approximately $45 million of flood damage at one city alone, Chattanooga, Tennessee. On the lower Ohio and Mississippi rivers, this system can reduce flood crests by 2.5–3 feet, depending on the origin of the flood. This provides protection to 6,000,000 acres of rich bottom land outside the Tennessee Valley and will lessen the frequency of flooding on another 4,000,000 acres. When you hear about the several hundred thousands of acres TVA has permanently flooded in the Tennessee Valley to provide the reservoirs behind its dams, think of these millions of acres protected outside the region.

A 630-mile navigation channel has been created on which new traffic records are being set regularly. In the past year the new channel carried more than a billion ton-miles of freight. This was an increase of more than thirtyfold compared with river traffic before TVA began to improve the river. Formerly, the major traffic consisted of sand and gravel dredged from the river bed and hauled short distances and of forest products moved by barge. Now the modernized river—a chain of lakes joined together by single-lift locks—carries products of higher value, such as coal, oil, grain, and steel, and for longer distances, frequently between the Valley and the Middle West. In addition to the substantial annual savings in transportation costs afforded by the new waterway, now amounting to some $10 million a year, it proved itself to be a valuable asset in supplementing railroad facilities during the last war.

The same dams which control flood waters and provide a channel for navigation also produce hydroelectricity. TVA's electric-power system now generates twenty-three times as much electricity as the area produced in 1933—over 35,000,000,000 kilowatt-hours of energy annually for one and one-third million consumers over a territory of 80,000 square miles. The electricity sold from the same system of dams brings the government a return which has averaged more than 4 per cent annually on the investment in power facilities. The return on the investment, after depreciation and payments in lieu of taxes to states and counties, certifies a financial performance well beyond the original objective of a self-liquidating power system prescribed in the basic Act.

There is much more to the story than the earning record of TVA's power system. The power operations of TVA and the one hundred and fifty municipal and rural electric cooperative partners that distribute its electricity have stimulated neighboring private utilities in many ways. . . .

Electricity in greater abundance on the farms and in the homes and factories of the Tennessee Valley has helped to spark a great economic change. Per capita income, as one index of that change, is now 61 per cent of the national average, compared with 44 per cent in the boom year of 1929. Higher incomes in the Tennessee Valley have contributed to the economic life of the nation. For example, that part of the nation's total of individual federal income taxes which comes from the seven Valley states has steadily increased. In 1933 individual federal income taxes from the seven states were 3.4 per cent of the total of such taxes in the nation. In 1952 they were 6.2 per cent of the national total. Thus the states of which the Tennessee Valley region is a part are sharing more of the common burden of the costs of government.

TVA and the People on the Land

The fundamental handicap in the use of the region's soils, its abundant rainfall, and its life-giving sunshine is also slowly being corrected in a far-reaching program of education and experiment. TVA's chemical plants at Muscle Shoals, built during World War I, have been modernized. They contributed heavily to the requirements of the United States and its allies for munitions and other war needs during World War II. These plants are now used, as they were before the war, to develop and produce new and improved fertilizers, mainly high-analysis phosphates and nitrates. The fertilizer materials produced are significant, not for the volume produced, but for the way they are used. . . .

It may be enough now to point out that, as electricity and machines have moved into the rural areas and as grass, pastures, and livestock have substituted more of the sun's energies for human backbreaking toil, the land has released a new surplus of human energy. Hundreds of thousands of people within the Valley have found new employment opportunities in the towns and cities. The number of people employed in non-farm activities has almost doubled in the Tennessee Valley and in TVA's power service area since the prosperity year of 1929. From 1929 to 1954 the net gain in manufacturing plants has numbered more than two thousand, representing a rate of increase considerably greater than the rate of increase for the nation as a whole during the same period. These new enterprises are additions to the productive resources of the region and the nation. Less than a dozen, and all of these small, have moved from other areas of the country to the Tennessee Valley; the remainder are newly created additions to the nation's productive capacity.

This, in brief, is the summary of physical and economic change in the Tennessee Valley since TVA began its work. The task of full development of the region is not finished; it is only well begun.

We view the full development of the Tennessee Valley as something more than mobilization of economic assets for the achievement of greater material rewards. The Tennessee Valley's greatest asset is its people—people who generally prefer to live there because they like its hills and valleys, its mountains and forests, its prevailing sense of community, and the depth of the region's cultural roots and traditions. Characterize this as sentiment, and you miss the point. Because, when men and women find productive and satisfying work and exercise their initiative freely where they *prefer* to live, the results reach far beyond the dollar value of their labor. Under these circumstances people gain a new birth of freedom, and the world gains new wealth in goods, ideas, and human self-respect.

ERNEST M. GOULD, JR.

FIFTY YEARS OF MANAGEMENT AT THE HARVARD FOREST

Introduction

When forestry was first talked about seriously in the United States, about 1880, this country was a small nation of approximately 50 million people, with an economy geared to animal power and steam engines. By the turn of the century the population had increased fifty percent, and the economy was about to expand on a new power base of internal combustion engines and electricity. At the same time foresters were caught up in the forefront of a new liberal political movement. During the last fifty years the population has again doubled; and the economy now stands at the beginning of a new era based on atomic energy. Also during this time forestry has gradually gotten out of the salons and into the woods, so that foresters must increasingly produce results that carry conviction, rather than convince owners by what Fernow[1] called "propaganda."

Because forest resources have been in the thick of this turmoil of change, their uses have been continually redefined. As new demands for wood, water, grazing, and recreation have daily become more important, "multiple use" is no longer simply an academic theory but is an insistent management problem. While most of the old uses for wood continue, many have lost their importance; and wholly new products have become prominent. During the last fifty years, while the population doubled and the gross national product tripled, the amount of lumber used has remained remarkably constant. Total industrial wood consumption rose only 15 per cent between 1900 and 1952.[2] However, less conventional uses based on wood fiber have grown by leaps and bounds. The next 50 years are likely to produce even greater changes in the form of wood products and in the other demands made upon our forest resources.

Early in this century the original ideas of forestry provided a rational argument for the use of this resource that was enthusiastically promoted by many prominent people. These ideas helped prevent the complete disposal of the public domain and led to the setting up of the National Forests. But the basic concept of management which came from these ideas made little headway with forest industries, which were then essentially migratory. Today the wood-using industries have settled down, and many have hired foresters to procure their wood and help manage their forest lands. The U.S. Forest Service has exchanged its role of custodian of forest lands for one that involves active forest use and development; and even private owners of woodlots are becoming interested in improved practices. In this setting of continuous change in demands and objectives, as well as in the forest resource itself, the

• Ernest M. Gould, Jr., is Lecturer on Economics, Harvard Forest, Harvard University.

Reprinted from Harvard Forest Bulletin No. 29 (1960), with permission of the author and the director of Harvard Forest.

[1] Dr. B. E. Fernow, Chief, Div. of Forestry, U.S., Dept. of Agriculture, 1886 to 1898.

[2] U.S., Forest Service, *Timber Resources for America's Future,* Forest Resource Rept. No. 14 (Washington, 1958).

need is increasingly felt for new and better guidelines. Consequently, over the years the ideas of "management intensity," "input-output," "operating unit analysis," and, most recently, "investment opportunity," have been discussed in an attempt to devise methods of analysis that will help managers to make better decisions about the use of their forest and other resources in a dynamic and changing situation.

Here and there a few people are beginning to give thoughtful consideration to the role that management must be prepared to play in forestry. Traditionally, forest management has been largely concerned with the "application of business methods and technical forestry principles to the operation of a forest property."[3] Recently there has been some interest in such new fields as administrative management; but so far the emphasis is primarily on organization, efficiency, and evaluation. Experience at the Harvard Forest suggests that all these activities are carried out under very uncertain conditions, and that the success of resource development is greatly affected by the capacity of managers to cope with risk and uncertainty in their planning process. Although imperfect knowledge about the course of future events is not unique to forestry, the long production period needed for forest crops makes the problem of uncertainty so central to forest management decisions that it is of necessity receiving more serious consideration as the population pressure on resources leaves less and less room for trial and error methods.

A test of the early ideas about forest management was started at the Harvard Forest 50 years ago, and the history of this half-century of progress clearly shows the need for basing management programs on a continuing appraisal of biological and economic probabilities. The inherent uncertainties of forest production favor a management concept that provides enough program flexibility to take advantage of the promising new opportunities suggested by accumulating information and experience, and one that at the same time provides a hedge against an unfavorable turn of events.

In order to understand the basis of forestry at Harvard, it is necessary to look back to 1903, when the subject was first taught. Although the whole field was new to the United States, a definite set of objectives had already been developed in Europe. These ideas were imported almost intact and summarized by Gifford Pinchot when he said, ". . . a forest may yield its best return in protection, in wood, grass, or other forest products, in money, or in interest on the capital it represents. But whichever of these ways of using the forest may be chosen in any given case, the fundamental idea in forestry is that of perpetuation by wise use; that is, of making the forest yield the best service possible at the present in such a way that its usefulness in the future will not be diminished, but rather increased."[4]

From this and other contemporary statements, it is clear that the forest was thought of as a renewable natural resource, which, if properly handled, could produce a wide variety of values. Although this concept was the root of the idea that was later developed into "multiple-use," in 1905 there was little concern about whether or not all objectives could be achieved simultaneously. Management plans were generally made for some single dominant purpose, with the more or less tacit assumption that the other values would follow.

Thus Pinchot said, "A forest well managed under the methods of practical forestry will yield a return in one of the ways just mentioned. There are, however, four things a forest must have before it can be in condition to render the best service

[3] Society of American Foresters, Comm. on Forestry Terminology, *Forest Terminology* (Washington: The Society of American Foresters, 1950).

[4] Gifford Pinchot, *A Primer of Forestry. Part II. Practical Forestry,* U.S., Department of Agriculture, Bur. of Forestry Bull. No. 24 (Washington, 1905).

. . . protection from fire, overgrazing, and theft; strong and abundant reproduction; growing space enough for every tree; and finally, a regular supply of trees ready to cut." This last point he elaborated at considerable length, ". . . the amount of wood taken from a healthy forest and the amount grown by it should be as nearly equal as possible. If more grows than is cut, then the forest will be filled with overmature, decaying trees; but if more wood is cut than is grown, then the supply of ripe trees will be exhausted, and the value of the forest will decline."[5]

The concept of perpetuating the values of a forest by wise use was translated into a plan of action that focused attention almost exclusively on the production of timber by sustained yield. Parallel ideas were applied to grazing; but no body of management theory of comparable elegance was developed for the production of water and recreation. This timber management theory, that has been the continuing core of forestry practice, is biologically oriented, and apparently assumes that maximizing physical production over the years will automatically yield the largest income stream and the highest rate of interest on invested capital.

Fernow had considerable doubt about this assumption which he spelled out when discussing the fact that German forestry was returning three to four per cent on invested capital. "If, then, in a country with dense population, where in many places every twig can be marketed, with settled conditions of market, with no virgin woods which could be cheaply exploited and come into advantageous competition with the costlier material produced by managed properties, with cost of labor low and prices of wood comparatively high—if under such conditions the returns for the expenditure of money, skill, intellect in the production of wood crops is not more promising, it would seem hopeless to develop the argument of profitableness in a country where all these conditions are the reverse, and a business man considers a six per cent investment not sufficient inducement."[6]

He obviously believed that current economic, social, and forest conditions in the United States would not justify sustained yield management, and he proposed a simpler set of guidelines for owners and for government policy. "Before, however, we may apply the finer methods of forestry management as practiced abroad, it will be well enough to begin with common-sense management, which consists in avoiding unnecessary waste, in protecting against fire, in keeping out cattle where young growth is to be fostered, and in not preventing by malpractice the natural reproduction."[7]

Despite Fernow's early dissenting voice, the ideas epitomized by Gifford Pinchot's writings soon dominated the thinking of foresters in the United States. However, no experience was available in this country to document the results of sustained yield over time, or to show the difficulties likely to appear in putting such a program into effect. Thus the problems that would have to be solved by forest managers were largely undefined, and this fact, plus the lack of experience data, was a considerable handicap in demonstrating the worth of forest management principles.

Harvard Forest Case History

Therefore, in 1907, when a wooded tract in Petersham, Massachusetts, was offered to Harvard for forestry purposes, it seemed not only an ideal aid for teaching, but also afforded an excellent opportunity to put forest management into practice on a commercial scale. An added inducement to try out sustained yield was the fact that no

[5] *Ibid.*

[6] B. E. Fernow, *Report upon the Forestry Investigations of the U.S. Dept. of Agriculture, 1877–98,* House Doc. No. 181, 55th Cong., 3d Sess., 1899, p. 21.

[7] Fernow, *What Is Forestry?* U.S., Dept. of Agric., Forestry Div. Bull. No. 5 (1891), p. 15.

money came with the land, and the University had stipulated that the Harvard Forest must be self-supporting. The growing stock, therefore, was viewed as an endowment fund that could be made to produce income every year. Thus the Harvard Forest was started with three general purposes in mind: to demonstrate forest practices that could serve local landowners and show the value of sustained yield; as a field laboratory for student training; and as a research station to extend the scientific knowledge of forestry.

A roster of the Forest's students is ample evidence of the success of the teaching program, and a long list of bulletins, papers, and articles has been published that attests to its value as a research station. Most of these documents, however, describe research stimulated by the detailed biological problems encountered in managing the woods. Relatively little has been published about the other problems and opportunities faced by the Forest's managers, or about the over-all results of the sustained yield program.

THE FOREST SITUATION

The forested area in 1907 included about 1,600 acres, a figure that was gradually increased to 2,200 acres by planting and acquisition. The original stands contained a little under 12 million board feet of merchantable sawtimber, 90 per cent of it being old field white pine less than 70 years old. In addition, there were nearly 12,000 cords of wood in smaller trees. Thus the initial stocking per acre averaged 7,300 board feet of timber plus 7.5 cords of wood. Sawtimber growth on the whole property was estimated at 225 M.b.f. per year.

The left-hand bars of Figures 1 and 2 show how the stands were distributed by cover- and age-classes. Nearly half the area supported hardwood, but mostly of cordwood size. The sawtimber was concentrated mainly on the 39 per cent of the area classed as softwood. Only a small part of the area, 12 per cent, had very young stands, a little over a third of the land had sawtimber, while about half the area had pole-sized stands. The other bars show how these proportions changed over fifty years of management.

THE MARKET SITUATION

In 1907 the Millers River Valley, just 5 miles north of the Forest, was the center of the country's wooden box industry. In addition, cooperage, toy, and match factories were very active, and helped create a steady demand for white pine at stumpage prices that had for some time stabilized between $6 and $8 per M.b.f. A ready market and an abundant growing stock made the production of white pine sawlogs the logical base for the first management plans at the Forest. However, within a few years, local plants were buying hardwood logs of good quality at comparable prices, so other species were worked into the program.

By 1921 R. T. Fisher, Director of the Forest, was able to state that, "There are now no species and practically no size either of hardwood or softwood which cannot be marketed either at a profit or at least without loss. . . . The result of such a varied and convenient market has been that the greatest difficulty in handling forest crops is largely eliminated, namely, the presence of species that cannot be sold."[8]

In addition, there were many portable mill operators and woods workers in the area cutting and sawing pine logs. For the first few years the Forest had its own woods crew and sold logs delivered at a centrally located mill site on the property. Later a mill was hired, and finally one was purchased, so that logs were sawed and sold as lumber on-the-sticks or delivered at nearby plants. As it was cheaper during the depression to hire a mill than to own one, the Forest disposed of its mill. After the hurricane of 1938, logs were sold until another mill was acquired in 1949.

[8] R. T. Fisher, *The Management of the Harvard Forest,* Harvard Forest Bull. No. 1 (1921).

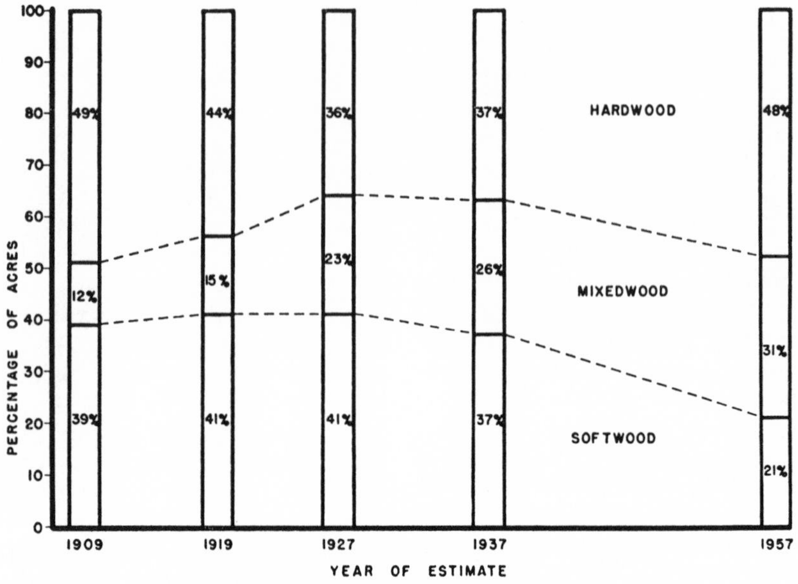

FIG. 1.—Percentage distribution of acreage by cover classes

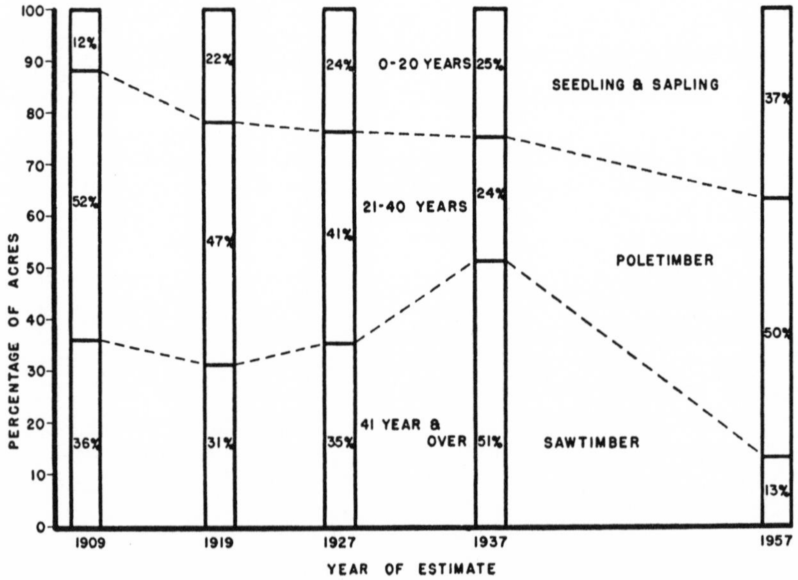

FIG. 2.—Percentage distribution of acreage by age or size classes

The Management Program Followed

A moderately well-balanced growing stock, stable markets for saw-logs, the need for a continuing income, and the desire for documented experience all made sustained yield an attractive management program. A rotation of 60 years for pine and 80 years for hardwood seemed most suitable, and a cutting budget equal to growth was set up. Operations were geared to stay within the allowable cut, at least during 5- to 10-year periods, and a record system was started to measure the development of the growing stock and to keep track of the amounts cut, the costs, and the cash returns.

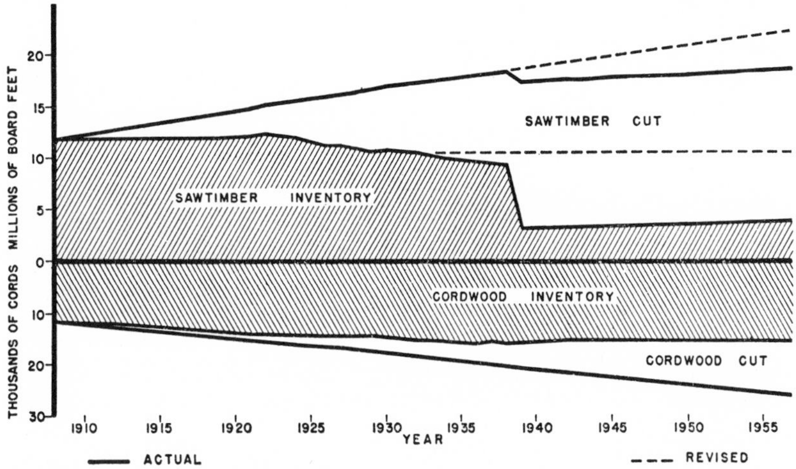

FIG. 3.—Management program followed at the Harvard Forest. Wood inventory plus cumulated cut. Estimates of yearly inventories are based on the measured cumulation of products cut plus a 2 per cent growth allowance, and on periodic timber cruises.

VOLUME DEVELOPMENT

Figure 3 shows how the sawtimber and cordwood inventory changed over time and how the cut of wood accumulated. During the first 14-year period, from 1908 to 1922, the annual cut varied from 50 to 350 M.b.f. but averaged 195 M.b.f. plus 85 cords of wood, well within the allowable cut. That this harvest was approximately equal to sawtimber growth is shown by the fact that the inventory estimate held almost steady at about 12 million board feet. At the same time the cordwood inventory increased by about 2,500 cords. During the next 16 years, from 1922 to 1938, annual operations averaged 420 M.b.f. plus 190 cords. This total was apparently a bit more than the growth of the larger trees because estimated sawlog inventory declined about 3 million feet, although a gain of about 1,500 cords of small wood was realized. This reduction in sawtimber stock was largely unintentional, and apparently resulted partly from the fact that the periodic cruises gave an over-optimistic view of growth, and partly from an attempt to maintain income in a period of falling prices. The amount of "over-cutting" would have shown up fairly soon and could have been corrected; but before this could happen the hurricane of 1938 blew down over 6 million feet of the remaining sawtimber.

The hurricane of 1938 which struck the northeastern United States on September 21st, devastated thousands of acres of land in New England and took several hundred lives. No storm of such magnitude had been known in this part of the country since 1815. Practically every owner of woodland was affected. In order to keep the market for logs and lumber from being completely demoralized, the Federal Government set up an agency, the Northeastern Timber Salvage Administration, to buy logs, saw as many as possible immediately, and store the remainder in various ponds until they could be released without glutting the market. When World War II broke out in Europe the following year, the demand for wood began to increase rapidly, and all the hurricane lumber was sold within a few years.

Salvage on the Harvard Forest was prompt; but, even so, an estimated million feet of lumber were lost in splintered trees and in logs that did not meet grade specifications. Most of the salvage logs were sold to the Northeastern Timber Salvage Administration. The small stumpage realized was more than used in cleaning up the woods and in reducing fire hazard.

The enormous loss of merchantable timber from the hurricane made necessary a drastic revision of the cutting program. The yearly cut during the last 18 years has averaged 23 M.b.f. plus 330 cords of wood. Because the sawtimber cut has been less than the annual growth, the inventory has increased by about 45 M.b.f. per year until it is now nearly 4 million board feet. At the same time the cordwood inventory has been maintained at a fairly constant level of about 15,000 cords. During this period, the first operations completed the hurricane salvage. Then a shift was made to partial harvest and improvement cuttings in the remaining older stands, and greater emphasis was placed on improvement cuttings in the cordwood areas.

Since 1908, a great deal has been learned about the silvicultural problems involved in managing pine and hardwoods. Hardwood competition from advance growth and seedlings was so vigorous on the moist upland till sites that repeated cutting back to release pine seedlings proved too expensive. Although a satisfactory catch of pine seedlings followed harvest cuts in good seed years, the attempt to keep weeding costs within reasonable bounds proved that the work was usually "too little and too late," with the result that most of the old field pine land on better sites was taken over by what finally became promising stands of transition hardwoods. In contrast, it proved easy and inexpensive to reproduce conifers on outwash sands and gravels. Between these two extremes was a large area of intermediate sites where hardwoods grew poorly and conifers might be helped to take over part of the land with fairly simple management practices.[9] The use of sprays to control hardwoods developed too late to help reproduce any pine stands at the Forest; but this new technique does promise lower cost and more effective control over poor hardwoods in the young, post-hurricane stands.

This natural shift toward hardwood in the new stands would eventually have made necessary a fairly drastic revision of the sustained yield program even without the hurricane. The pine growing stock would have gradually dwindled, and the slower growth of hardwoods on a longer rotation would have called for a downward revision of allowable cut. This adjustment would probably not have been needed for another decade or so, but after the hurricane attention perforce shifted toward hardwood management.

On balance, it seems that the sustained yield management program was successful in maintaining three-quarters of the growing sawtimber intact for thirty years. Improved control mechanisms might have made performance even better, but any gain would probably have been wiped out

[9] R. J. Lutz and A. C. Cline, *Results of the First Thirty Years of Experience in Silviculture in the Harvard Forest, 1908–38. Part I. The Conversion of Stands of Old Field Origin by Various Methods of Cutting and Subsequent Cultural Treatments,* Harvard Forest Bull. No. 23 (1947); also *Part II. Natural Reproduction Methods in White Pine-Hemlock Stands on Light, Sandy Soils,* Harvard Forest Bull. No. 27 (1956). J. C. Goodlett, *The Development of Site Concepts of the Harvard Forest and Their Impact upon Management Policy,* Harvard Forest Bull. No. 28 (1960).

in the hurricane. It is now apparent that a great risk was being run by carrying such a large volume of pine sawtimber. In 1938 most pine in the 20–40-year age-class and all of that which was older was windthrown, except in a few places on the Forest sheltered from the full impact of the storm. The same degree of loss did not occur in hardwood stands until they reached 60 to 80 years of age.[10] Observations to date indicate that although hurricane storms hit New England at least once a decade, the widespread devastation of 1938 comes only about once every 100 to 150 years.[11] These facts give a rough measure of the uncertainty due to wind devastation that managers must weigh in devising forestry programs, and suggest steps that will tend to prevent undue loss.

It is interesting to speculate about what might have happened if the older stands had escaped substantial damage from the hurricanes of 1938, 1944, and 1954, the November gale of 1950, and the tornado of 1954. If in the early 1930's "overcutting" had also been recognized and the yearly cut reduced to about 200 M.b.f., it is reasonable to suppose that the pine sawtimber could have been maintained at about 11 million board feet. The total cut for the 50-year period would now equal about 12 million feet rather than the 15 million board feet actually harvested. Thus by sacrificing about 3 million feet of timber sold (much of it for a low salvage value), the Forest would now have almost 7 million more board feet of standing timber that could be cut during the next few decades and replaced by hardwood and mixedwood stands. The probable inventory of sawtimber and the accumulation of harvest is shown by the dashed line on Figure 3.

In all probability the seedling, sapling, and poletimber stands would be of about the same caliber as those on hand today, judging from what we have learned about pine-hardwood succession and the cost of hardwood control. Thus the major physical gains in the last five decades would have been a more even flow of timber products and an increase of over one-half in net sawtimber production. Present and future sawlog harvest could also be larger and more regular than is now possible. As we now know, however, in this region the chance of hurricane devastation to susceptible pine stands get greater every year that they are held after 20 to 40 years of age. This fact suggests that a management program which shortens rotations as much as possible in exposed areas, and develops the largest trees in sheltered areas would be a wise move to maximize the production of usable wood. Thus where the chance of catastrophic physical loss is appreciable, a program aimed at producing the largest amount of usable wood may require relaxing allowable cut principles. Although the risk of physical loss that managers must anticipate will vary from region to region, it is present in some form everywhere.

INCOME

As Pinchot pointed out, volume produced is only one of the several objectives to be met by forest management. The flow of income over time and the accumulation of returns are also important to most owners. In fact, to the degree that market prices reflect the need of society for products, income is one way of weighing the usefulness the economy has realized from the management of a forest resource. The dollar returns, before taxes, shown in Figure 4 indicate how successful the Harvard Forest management program has been in meeting this objective.

The curve of the accumulated value of the yearly harvests in Figure 4 parallels that of the quantity cut during the early years when prices were relatively stable. The higher prices and larger cuts after the

[10] W. Rowlands, "Damage to Even-aged Stands in Petersham, Massachusetts, by the 1938 Hurricane as Influenced by Stand Condition" (unpublished Harvard Forest thesis, 1941).

[11] C. F. Brooks, *Hurricanes into New England: Meteorology of the Storm of September 21, 1938,* Smithsonian Inst. Annual Report, 1939 (Washington, 1940), pp. 241–51.

war steepen the curve until it levels off in spite of increased cutting when prices drop toward the depression lows. Since the hurricane, cut and returns have been very small, and the total for the fifty years now stands at nearly $118,000, or an average of $2,400 per year, equal to about $1.10 per acre per year. Of course most of this amount accumulated during the pre-hurricane years when returns averaged $3,600 per year, or $1.60 per acre per year.

It is interesting to note that the income flow likely to have been generated from a completely successful program of sustained yield without hurricane loss would have been very little different from that actually realized. The dashed line on Figure 4 shows the probable accumulation of income, assuming the same prices as those which prevailed. Returns would have accumulated more slowly after the early '30's because of reduced cutting, but would have speeded up by the mid-'40's, and would have been somewhat greater than the amount actually realized since 1949. Today the total accumulated income would be about $132,000, or about 12 per cent more than the actual. This return would be equal to about $2,600 per year, or $1.20 per acre per year, before taxes.

These average figures and the scale of the graph do not bring out the fact that the flow of income over the years has been quite erratic. Differences in returns, from a high of $23 per M.b.f. in 1923 to a low of nothing in 1940, have made income vary much more than annual cut. In operating the Forest, this fluctuation has made it hard to anticipate each year's income. If constant returns had been the objective, greater flexibility in the amount cut would have been a helpful, even if not a complete, solution.

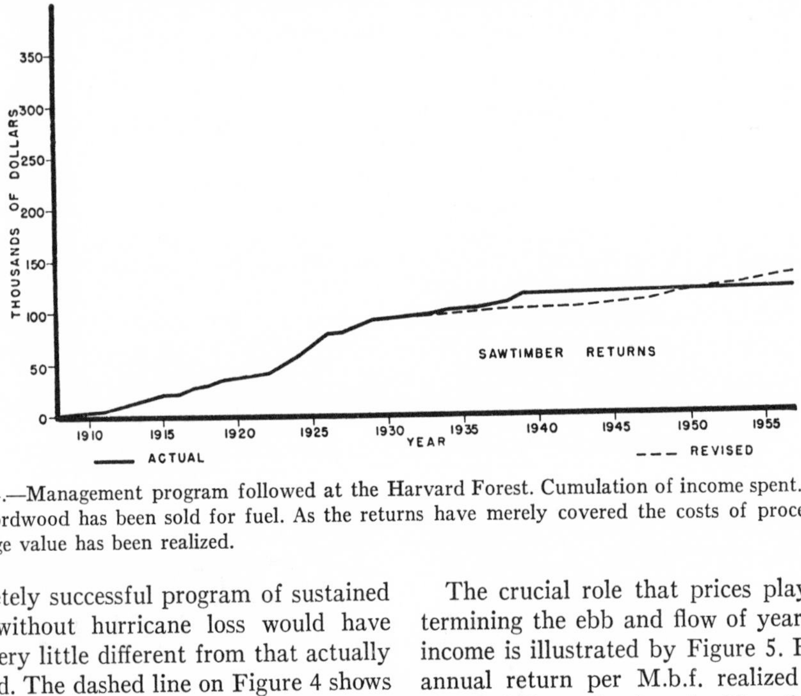

FIG. 4.—Management program followed at the Harvard Forest. Cumulation of income spent. Over the years cordwood has been sold for fuel. As the returns have merely covered the costs of processing, no stumpage value has been realized.

The crucial role that prices play in determining the ebb and flow of year-to-year income is illustrated by Figure 5. Here the annual return per M.b.f. realized by the Harvard Forest is plotted with estimates of the regional average average stumpage prices for white pine.[12] The Forest figures are the return per M.b.f. actually realized after paying all operating costs and before taxes. These returns thus contain not only normal stumpage but also any profit that

[12] H. B. Steer, *Stumpage Prices of Privately Owned Timber in the United States,* U.S., Dept. of Agric. Tech. Bulletin No. 626 (1938), and yearly supplements through 1945. New Hampshire, Cooperative Extension Service, *Forest Market Reports* (1946–57).

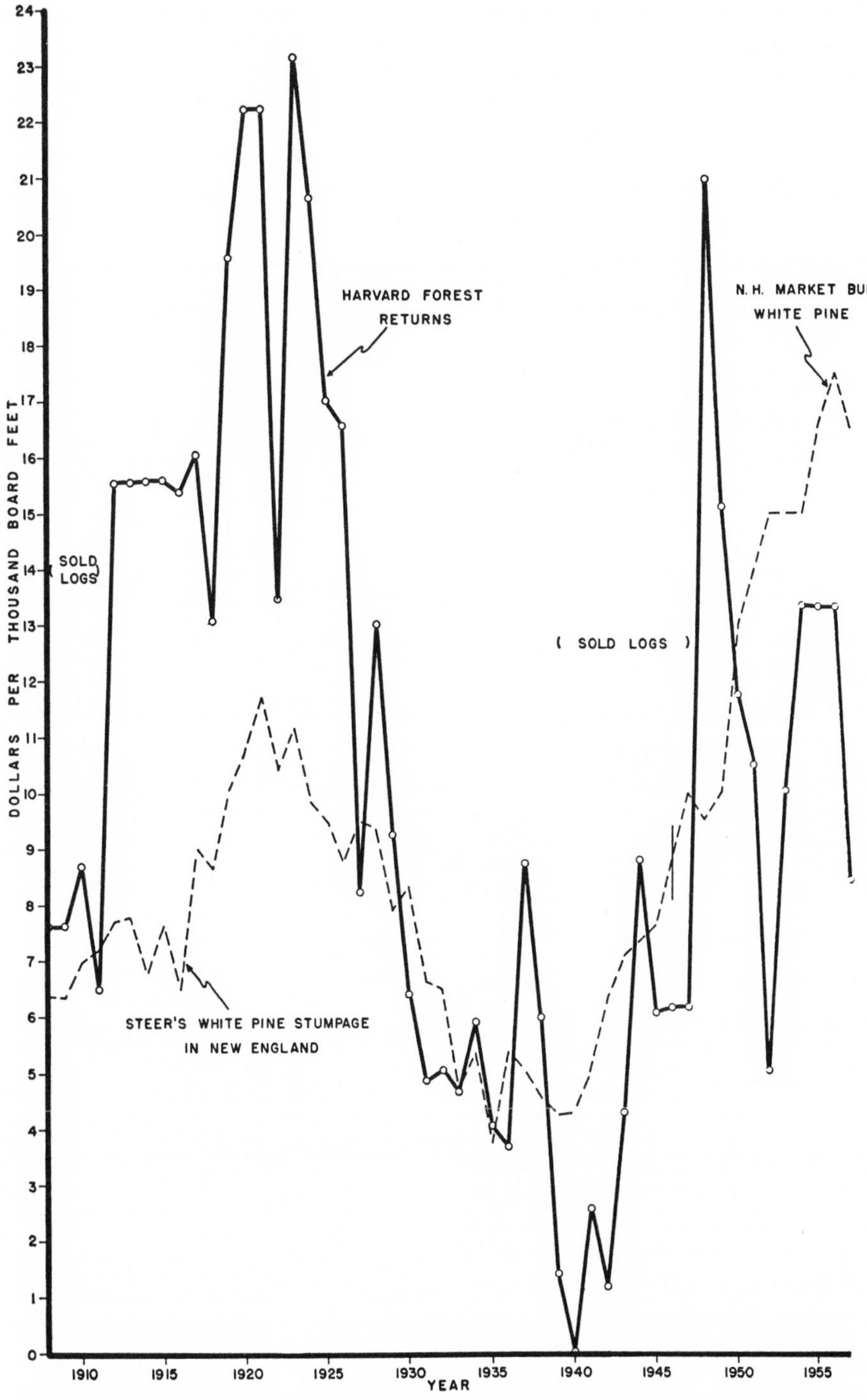

FIG. 5.—Annual Harvard Forest stumpage returns compared to regional estimates of stumpage prices

might have been made from the operation of the mill. The Forest's figures were generally greater than Steer's prices prior to the depression, and less than regional price estimates thereafter. The larger returns are due to the milling margin, a prosperous local wood-using industry, good cutting chances, and efficient operations. The later lower-than-average returns largely reflect the deteriorated condition of local industry and the higher costs of operating the scattered, low density stands left after the hurricane.

the return from a single year's operation. It might also be suggested that regional average prices could better be used to figure capital value; this would insulate it from the vagaries of local markets. Nevertheless, local shifts in value being so close to home are likely to have a greater impact on a landowner than a regional average that masks this variation. However capital values are related to market values, the same broad outline of variation is likely to appear as that shown in Figure 6.

It is apparent that capital values held

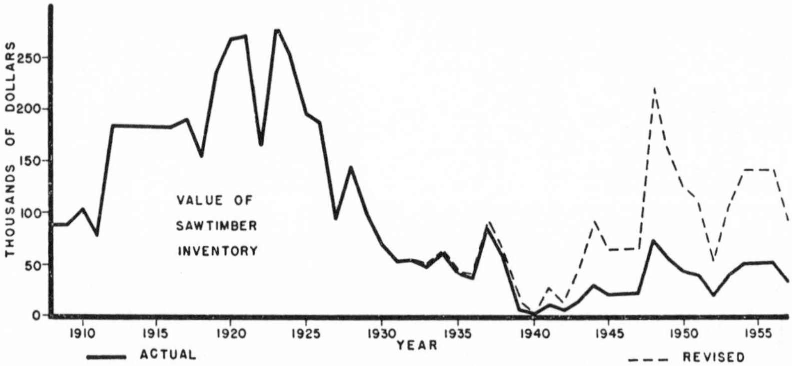

FIG. 6.—Management program followed at the Harvard Forest. Capital values. The first increase in capital value between 1911 and 1912 is more apparent than real, merely reflecting the fact that the Forest made less money selling logs during its first few years of operation than it did after 1911 when it hired a mill and sold lumber. The average market value of pine stumpage from 1908 to 1917 was fairly steady. In fact, this is the longest period of comparative stability in the whole half-century.

CAPITAL VALUE

Variation in the stumpage return from sawtimber also has had a marked effect on the capital value of the forest inventory, another of the objectives of management mentioned by Pinchot. Many owners are interested in the capital appreciation or depreciation of their forest resources, and the probable course of this development may have considerable impact on their management decisions. In Figure 6 the capital value of the sawtimber inventory each year has been estimated by multiplying the sawtimber volume by the return per M.b.f. realized during the current operating season. It can be argued with some validity that the unit value realized by selling the entire inventory would be different from

fairly steady in the early years, only to increase greatly during the period of high prices starting with the first World War and ending about 1924. Thereafter capital depreciation occurred at a much more rapid rate than inventory volumes justified, until after the hurricane. Since then, values have been erratic but have generally tended upward. Anyone carefully considering capital value would be much impressed by the fact that during the brief span of 2 years, between 1918 and 1920, the sawtimber volume was stable; but its value increased by more than $110,000, a rise of over 70 per cent. Conversely, in the 4-year period from 1923 to 1927 the sawtimber volume lost better than two-thirds of its value, over $180,000, due mostly to price changes.

The general outline of changes in the capital value of the sawtimber inventory is estimated to be about the same even if sustained yield had been more successful and blowdown had been avoided. The dashed line on Figure 6 shows that the trend is unchanged except that the variation since the hurricane is greater, and closely follows shifts in prices. If the sawtimber inventory were about 11 M.b.f. today, logging chances would be better than those we now have; and a more realistic estimate of capital value might be based on regional average stumpage prices. This would place the present capital value between 150 and 200 thousand dollars, about where it was in the early years of lumber sales. Of course with this larger inventory on hand, there would be a better chance to take advantage of any new speculative gains that might come from another large boost in prices. This opportunity for gain must be weighed against the chances of catastrophic loss, however, and in this case we now know the Harvard Forest gambled earlier and lost.

DISCUSSION

We can now judge how well three of the main objectives of forest management mentioned by Pinchot were met by the 50-year test carried on at the Harvard Forest. The primary control mechanism used to regulate cutting was the rate of wood production, especially in sawlog sizes. Although the managers were partially successful for a time, elements beyond their control devastated two-thirds of the sawtimber. Had this catastrophe not happened, however, net production of logs cut and grown might have been increased by as much as one-half. However, so far as long-run potential is concerned, the new stands would probably be about the same as the present ones. Therefore it may well be that the next 50 years will eliminate most of any volume difference that might have been developed in the first 50 years.

If we were starting over again, it seems likely that a careful assessment of stands by risk categories and a cutting program designed to reduce the area of highest risk types might have produced more usable wood. Whether or not this program could also be based on the concept of "allowable cut" would depend largely on the capacity and willingness of the manager to bear the necessary risk and his subjective balancing of possible losses and gains.

At the Harvest Forest a fairly even annual cut has not produced an even flow of income; in fact, income has been most erratic because of changing values that have been largely beyond the control of the managers. It seems unlikely that income could have been kept at a constant amount each year with any reasonable juggling of annual harvests, especially when prices took their long slide into the depression. It also seems that because of the reduced cutting required, a more successful sustained yield program without blowdown would have accumulated only about 12 per cent more income than was actually realized. Thus income differences in the programs seem even less than the estimated difference in the volume that might have been produced during the last half century.

Capital values have also been closely related to changing prices, and it seems physically impossible for any inventory control program to have smoothed out the vast variation that has occurred in the last 50 years. No program of growing trees could have increased their value fast enough to have offset the major drops in prices that occurred in over half the years.

During the last 50 years at the Harvard Forest the objectives of volume production, income flow, and capital appreciation could not have been equally well satisfied by any single management program, especially one controlled exclusively by biological growth rates. Value changes and the probability of physical and market losses or gains should have been considered in addition to the likely efficiency of capital in alternative uses. If these principles had been used to guide the management of the Harvard Forest, a number of alternatives were available. Two of these possibilities will be discussed to illustrate the range of considerations that managers might have taken into account.

A Partially Diversified Capital Management Program

In light of the alternative investment opportunities open to the Harvard Forest, it is interesting to see what another management program might have done to reduce the risks of physical and market loss and to take advantage of what might be called speculative gains. The fact that funds could have been safely invested with the University at any time and could have earned a minimum of 4 per cent shows one way of diversifying the Forest's "white pine endowment." To the degree that the sawtimber inventory could be converted to cash and reinvested with the University, the risk of forest production losses could be reduced; and if this conversion was timed properly to capture the values created by high prices, these speculative gains could have been made premanently productive. Of course the chances for growth and further speculative gain would have been corespondingly reduced for a time, and this fact suggests that some compromise between complete conversion and sustained yield management might have been desirable. If the allowable cut requirement of sustained yield had been given less attention and value and uncertainty given more consideration, then stumpage price changes and opportunity costs could have helped guide harvesting.

One simple and feasible alternative to strict sustained yield might have been a program that recognized the temporary nature of war-time prices and the transitional character of the old field white pine stands. Operations could have been unchanged during the 1908 to 1917 period of stable prices, but cutting could have been stepped up later to take advantage of the speculative gains resulting from high prices. Thus the managers would have helped to satisfy society's need for timber, reflected in these increased values, by cutting about half the sawtimber. Six million board feet could have been cut between 1918 and 1923, and later harvests reduced to about 100 M.b.f. a year when prices dropped. A little more than $118,000 would have been available over current spending as an investment fund, which at 4 per cent would have made a steady return of about $4,700 a year, in addition to any returns from later cutting.

Figures 7, 8, and 9 show what would have happened to the growing stock inventory, cumulative cut, income, and yearly capital values under this plan. Hurricane blowdown would have been less than half that actually experienced because of the smaller acreage of high-risk stands; and the post-hurricane sawtimber inventory would be practically the same as that actually realized. The major difference would appear in the younger stands where, instead of 700 acres dating from 1938, about half would be older, dating from the cuts of 1918–23. Thus there now would be less of a waiting period for these stands to produce usable products. In addition, more improvement cutting could have been done in the cordwood stands in order to keep the woods crew busy after 1923. Judging from what has been learned about the management of old field white pine stands at the Harvard Forest, this program would have resulted in new stands equally as productive as those now growing. The land could have been kept in valuable forest cover, so that long-run production would be little affected, In the short run of 50 years, the sawtimber cut would be only about 2 million feet less than that actually realized. The future flow of wood products would probably be smoother than that actually achieved because the "lumpiness" caused by 700 acres of 1938 blowdown would be reduced.

Income, of course, would have been more constant, and the total amount accumulated would now be over twice that actually realized, because the market losses of the depression years and the value and vol-

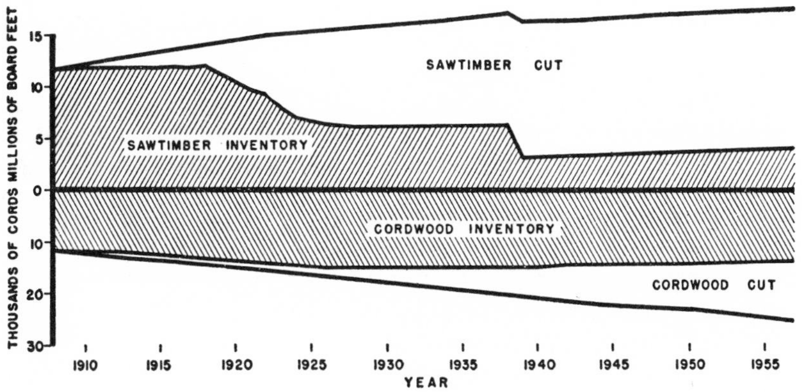

FIG. 7.—Cutting accelerated to remove half the sawtimber at high prices. Wood inventory plus cumulated cut.

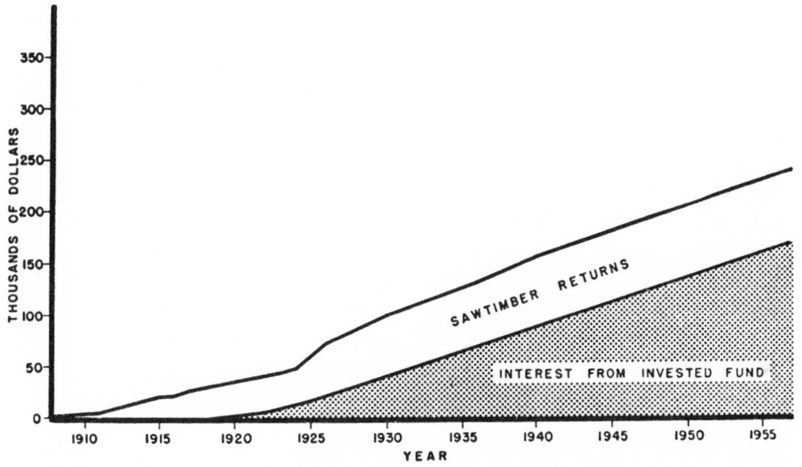

FIG. 8.—Cutting accelerated to remove half the sawtimber at high prices. Cumulation of income spent

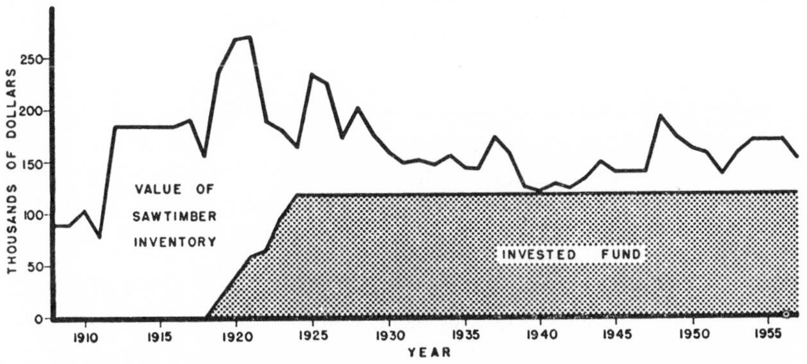

FIG. 9.—Cutting accelerated to remove half the sawtimber at high prices. Capital values

ume losses of the hurricane would have been greatly reduced. In addition, part of the speculative gains of the war years would have added a steady 4 per cent earning to income. While the returns spent now total about $118,000, this alternative plan would have produced about $239,000, or a yearly average of $4,800, equal to nearly $2.20 per acre each year.

Total capital value, consisting of the invested fund plus the value of the sawtimber inventory, would also have been consistently greater than that realized after 1925; now, it would be over four and one-half times greater. The invested fund would have put a floor under capital fluctuations that would have greatly increased its average value over the years. Thus, this method of diversifying the Forest's "investment portfolio" would have provided a safer and more conservative program than the management actually followed, or, for that matter, than the estimated results of sustained yield without blowdown loss.

A program very much like this one could have been developed from the ideas expressed by Austin Cary in 1908. In a letter to A. C. Cline in 1934 he said, ". . . Cut of the early years was right about 200 M.b.f. That was small for the tract, but suited the circumstances perhaps, and Fisher's caution in the early years certainly served him. At one point I certainly should have done different than he did, and I put the idea before him. Scattered through the older stands was a lot of overborne and dead stuff that couldn't last till he could get around to it the way he was going. I thought it good business and good forestry both to salvage that material through prompt cutting." If the idea of expanding operations during periods of high prices and contracting them when prices were down is added to Cary's concept of physical risk reduction and a recognition of the marginal efficiency of capital in other uses, new management guidelines might have been set up. However, this procedure would have required a reappraisal of such concepts as "allowable cut" and "regulation" as basic objectives of forest resource management.

If the managers of the Forest had either been blessed with perfect foresight or had been more impressed by the risks and uncertainty of long-run forest production, they might have devised an even more cautious and conservative management program.

Reinvestment of the Entire Growing Stock Capital

Practically the whole sawtimber inventory, about 12 M.b.f., could have been cut during the high prices of World War I, and the surplus return over current spending added to endowment. Under such a program, operations since 1924 would have been geared to a small sawlog cut of about 10 M.b.f. a year plus greater cutting in the cordwood-sized stands. The new stands reproduced would now be 34 to 39 years old, and it is likely that they would have about the same long-term potential as those now growing. In fact, with more income to spend each year on stand improvement, the Forest might be in better shape for future production than it now is. It is unlikely that a planned "unbalanced growing stock" would be any harder to deal with than the accidental one created by the hurricane. Figures 10, 11, and 12 show how this program would have affected inventory, cut, income, and capital value.

Income under this program would have been at an even higher constant level than that produced by the half-cut plan. Total income would now be nearly $388,000, or better than three and one-quarter times that actually realized. Average income over the entire period would be $7,800 a year, equal to a bit over $3.50 per acre per year. Actually, yearly income since 1924, when the reinvestment was completed, would never have been less than $10,000, and would continue at this level as long as the University's investment program remains as efficient as it has been in the past.

The capital fund created by this program would have been about $249,000,

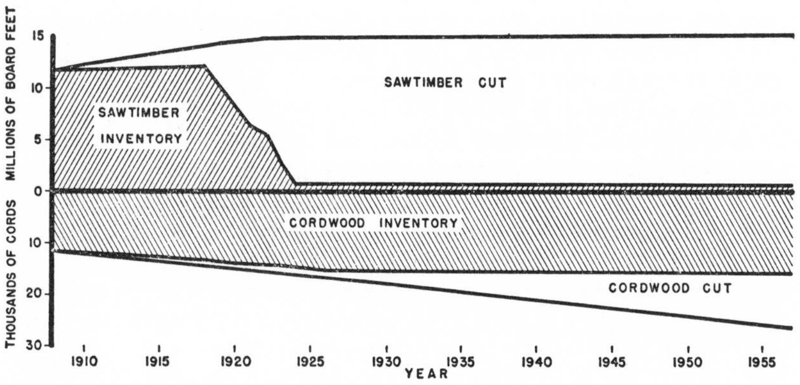

FIG. 10.—Cutting accelerated to remove almost all sawtimber at high prices. Wood inventory plus cumulated cut.

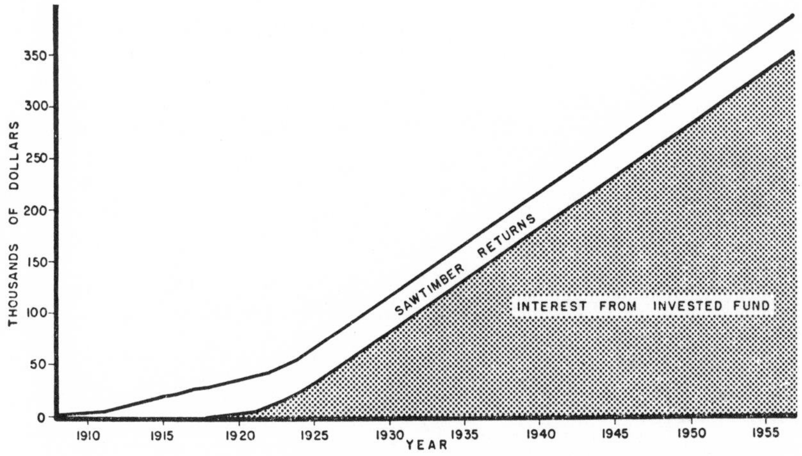

FIG. 11.—Cutting accelerated to remove almost all sawtimber at high prices. Cumulation of income spent.

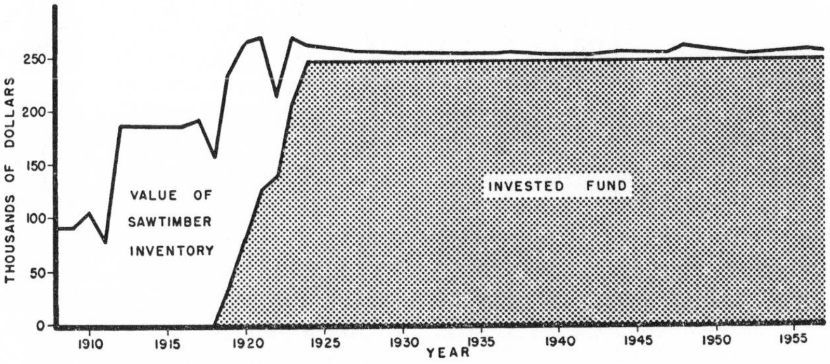

FIG. 12.—Cutting accelerated to remove almost all sawtimber at high prices. Capital values

making a yearly interest return of about $10,000. This program would have captured most of the peak value of the sawtimber inventory and would have placed a very high floor under capital fluctuations. During the next half-century sawtimber values would be recreated and would add considerably to the amount that would already be about seven and a half times greater than that actually realized.

Summary and Discussion

Table 1 summarizes the volume and value data for the several plans of management discussed so far.

than even successful sustained yield without blowdown. It seems clear that, contrary to expectations, the realities of the situation have been such that sustained yield management could not have automatically maximized wood production, income, and capital accumulation over time.

In order to satisfy these three objectives of management equally well, efficient production control and the reduction or elimination of catastrophic losses must be assumed, together with stable demand and prices, and low opportunity costs. In the last 50 years these assumptions have not been realistic. In fact this case history

TABLE 1

Results of 50 Years of Management of the Harvard Forest Sawtimber Stands
Estimated Volume and Value from Alternative Programs

Management Program	Volume—M.B.F.[a]				Value—Thousands $[b]			
	Start Vol.	Cut Vol.	End Vol.	Net ST Growth	Capital Value Start	Returns Spent	Capital Value End	Net Gain
All Capital in Forest:								
H. F. Experience with Sustained Yield	12	15	4	7	$90	$120	$ 30	$ 60
Complete Sustained Yield without Wind Loss	12	12	11	11	$90	$130	$ 90	$130
Diversified Capital:								
Plan I, Cut ½ at Peak Prices	12	13	4	5	$90	$240	$150	$300
Plan II, Cut Almost All at Peak Prices	12	15	1	4	$90	$390	$250	$550

[a] Rounded to the nearest million board feet. Unsalvaged hurricane losses are not included with the volume cut.
[b] Rounded to the nearest $10,000.

To recapitulate briefly, the above table indicates that although successful sustained yield management without blowdown might have produced over half again as much sawtimber and about three times more capital value in 1957, it would have brought in only about 12 per cent more income. However, there were other programs that could have been used to divert capital into more efficient uses that would have greatly increased and smoothed out the flow of income and the accumulation of capital value. During the last 50 years the net financial gain of management would thereby have been 130 to 320 per cent greater

highlights the overwhelming importance that imperfect biological, physical, and economic knowledge (and the resultant uncertainty) has for a manager laying plans for the future use and development of a forest.

At the Harvard Forest this uncertainty has taken several forms:

1. The manipulation of the timber inventory has not been entirely satisfactory. In addition, the response of the forest to management has not been predictable in detail. Reproduction has generally been adequate; but control of its composition during the establishment stage has been costly and uncertain. Better recognition of

site effects on reproduction and new techniques to eliminate poor trees are helping reduce this area of uncertainty; but the conditions under which the possible gains are enough to justify the added costs are not entirely clear.

2. The second dimension of uncertainty illustrated by this case history is the effect of natural loss on returns. The most important damage in Petersham has been caused by storm winds, although insect and disease losses have occurred. Fire loss has been very low, but is a much more important factor in some other places.

3. The local demand for primary forest products has changed remarkably during the last half century. Box-quality pine has lost most of its market as the box and cooperage plants have closed one after another in the face of competition from paper and plastic containers. The toy plants have retrenched, and the match factories have ceased altogether. Better quality pine is still in demand as well as high-grade hardwood logs, and new markets for low-grade wood for fiber seem likely to develop if the necessary plant investment is made. However, the local stumpage market is still largely a matter of "horse-trading," and fails to meet practically every test of the classical competitive market model. These facts, added to the actual changes in utilization that have taken place and may materialize in the future, make the shape of demand in the decades ahead seem uncertain indeed.

4. During its half century of operation, the Harvard Forest has experienced wider fluctuations in stumpage returns than average regional prices would indicate; but this statement is probably true for any specific forest property. In Harvard's experience price fluctuations have been more the rule than the exception. Increases or decreases of more than 10 per cent have occurred in 36 out of the 50 years. Six times prices have doubled or better in successive years, and four times they have fallen by one-half or more.

5. Finally, the returns earned by capital invested in growing trees at the Harvard Forest have not been as great as those earned by endowment funds managed by the University. Thus the 50-year experiment in sustained yield has cost the Forest nearly $500,000 of additional financial gain that it could have realized had a different management program been followed during the last half-century. This opportunity cost may take different forms in other operating units, but it is practically always present; and more often than not it may be the most important cost of forest management.

The 50 years' experience recorded in this case history have shown that the forest in Petersham is indeed a renewable natural resource that has produced, and will continue to produce, a variety of values. Thus the core premise of forestry, agreed upon from the beginning by both Fernow and Pinchot, seems sound. However, the perpetuation of values by "wise use" has been so narrowly interpreted in the past that many opportunities for financial gain have been lost without any clear benefit to forest production in the long run. The facts of the case suggest that the Forest's managers had much more silvicultural latitude for varying their management program than they originally supposed. Their capacity to adjust cutting schedules and methods is most important in view of the tremendous impact that catastrophic events have had on growth and on the flow of forest values during the last five decades.

Perhaps the most important highlight of Harvard's experience is the fact that events have turned out so differently from those on which plans were based 50 years ago. The demand and price of forest products has varied greatly, silvicultural control has been less effective than anticipated, and natural catastrophes have upset the best laid plans. These forces seem likely to continue, making our knowledge of future events so imperfect that flexibility to meet uncertainty and risk should be a central consideration of any theory devised to guide the prudent management of forest resources. To be most useful, production concepts should release the imaginations of foresters to analyze the full range of possibilities and project bands of probable results. Such activities will not eliminate the final subjective evaluation of risk that must be made by financially responsible management, but they will define and reduce the areas of uncertainty as much as possible in the light of existing knowledge.[13] Finally, the Harvard Forest case history suggests that both natural and social scientists have a great deal to contribute to the job of perfecting new and more realistic forest management concepts.

[13] Glenn L. Johnson, "Relevant Theories, Concepts and Research Techniques," *Proceedings of Research Conference on Risk and Uncertainty in Agriculture,* North Dakota Agric. Exper. Sta. Bull. No. 400 (1953).

. . . cut forests from necessity, but why destroy them? Russian forests are cracking under the axe, millions of trees are perishing, homes of beasts and birds are devastated, rivers are becoming shallow and drying up, wonderful landscapes are vanishing without a trace. . . . Man is endowed with reason and creative power in order to multiply that which has been given to him, but up to now he hasn't created, but destroyed.

Dr. Astrov in *Uncle Vanya,* Act I.

A. Chekhov, *Collected Works* (Moscow: State Publishing House of Fiction, 1962), Vol. 3, pp. 464–65. Trans. by Lydia Burton.

M. E. MARTS and W. R. D. SEWELL

THE CONFLICT BETWEEN FISH AND POWER RESOURCES IN THE PACIFIC NORTHWEST

The assumed incompatibility of two major resources—fish and power—constitutes one of the major obstacles to the development of the water resources of the Pacific Northwest of the U.S. and threatens to become a problem of even greater magnitude in British Columbia.[1] Traditionally the problem has been regarded as a choice between two mutually exclusive uses of the waters of certain streams in the region. These streams currently support large runs of migratory fish which provide the basis for one of the most important industries in the Pacific Northwest. These streams also represent important hydroelectric power resources. The conflict arises because hydroelectric power dams are barriers to fish migration, and, claim the fisheries agencies, constructed in sufficient numbers, would lead to the extinction of the fish runs.

Viewed as a choice between two mutually exclusive alternatives, the fish–power problem tends to lose perspective and hinders the development of solutions to the problem. In the broader context of river basin development, fish maintenance is but one of several possible uses of the waters of the basin. Reservation of these waters for fish migration alone may preclude the development of other desirable and complementary water uses, such as power generation, irrigation, and navigation. Actually, fish and power are not mutually exclusive uses in all circumstances, and some dams have been of benefit to fish maintenance.

The result of the fish–power conflict has been continued delays in developing the water resources of the Pacific Northwest. With fisheries agencies and power agencies firmly entrenched in opposite camps, prospects of the early development of mutually acceptable solutions to the problem are small. But failure to find a solution to the problem in the near future will present the Pacific Northwest with a choice between two alternative courses of action, both of them unsatisfactory.

On the one hand, the region may be forced to turn to more expensive means of generating power and so lose an important natural competitive advantage it has over the rest of the nation. On the other hand, pressure for the development of hydropower and other water uses may become so great that such development may proceed without a satisfactory solution to the fish maintenance problem.

The purpose of the present paper is to point out some of the broader implications

• Marion E. Marts is Vice-Provost, University of Washington; W. R. D. Sewell is Assistant Professor of Geography, University of Chicago.

Reprinted from *Annals of the Association of American Geographers,* L, No. 1 (March, 1960), 42–50, with permission of the authors and the editor.

[1] For discussions of possible effects of power dam construction on the Fraser River salmon runs, see E. S. Pretious, L. R. Kersey, and G. P. Contractor, *Fish Production and Power Development on the Fraser River* (Vancouver: B.C. Research Council, 1957); Fraser River Board, *Preliminary Report on Flood Control and Hydro-electric Power in the Fraser River Basin* (Victoria, B.C., 1958), pp. 141–52.

of the fish–power problem and to suggest some neglected aspects which merit consideration by policy makers.

Origins of the Problem

In the space of less than a century the Pacific Northwest has been transformed from an outpost of Western civilization to a region which enjoys one of the highest standards of living in the world. In this evolution, the development of both the fishery resources and the hydropower resources of the region has played a vital role, and it was only recently that the two came into conflict.

Fishing has always been a basic activity in the Pacific Northwest.[2] Today, the fishing industry employs as many as 100,000 persons during seasonal peaks and yields an average annual gross income to fishermen of approximately $30,000,000.[3] The fishing industry ranks fourth among the basic extractive industries of the region.[4] Salmon fishing accounts for more than half the value of the region's fishing industry, and the Columbia River has traditionally been the major single source of salmon.

Survival of the salmon fishing industry, however, is threatened by a number of factors of which the encroachment of civilization is perhaps the most potent. The Columbia River provides a good illustration of this encroachment. The various developments which have accompanied the expansion of population in the region—such as industrialization, irrigation, and hydropower generation—have all had serious effects on the maintenance of the Columbia's fishery resources.

From a record Columbia River salmon catch of 43,000,000 pounds (895,800 cases) in 1883, yields fell to an all-time low of 119,057 cases in 1954.[5] Although there has been some improvement in runs since that date, production is far below that in record years (Fig. 1). There are fears that yields will fall even further if more dams are constructed on salmon streams in the Pacific Northwest.

The Growing Desire for Power

The economy of the Pacific Northwest is still in a relatively pioneer stage of development, with major emphasis on extractive and primary processing rather than on secondary manufacturing and service industries. As a consequence, the region has experienced violent fluctuations in activity, and efforts have been made toward developing a more stable and diversified economic structure. The provision of an adequate energy supply has been regarded as a fundamental prerequisite in achieving this end.

The hydroelectric power potential of the region, including Columbia River tributaries in Montana, is estimated by the Bonneville Power Administration at 36 million kilowatts, which is about one-third of the total hydropower potential of the

2 Joseph A. Craig and Robert L. Hacker, *The History and Development of the Fisheries of the Columbia River,* U.S., Dept. of the Interior, Bur. of Fisheries Bulletin 32 (Washington, 1940), p. 212.

3 Source: Washington State Dept. of Fisheries and Oregon State Fish Commission. Estimation of "normal" employment in fishing and fish processing is difficult because of the highly seasonal nature of the industry, the high proportion of part-time self-employment, the uncertainty of reporting procedures, the exclusion of employment in sports fisheries, and the integration of Washington with Alaskan and high seas fisheries. The above figures would be much lower if expressed as annual-full-time-equivalent employment. Thus, using data from the Washington State Employment Security Dept. and the Oregon Dept. of Employment, average monthly employment estimates have been derived as follows: fishing, 2,007; canning and curing seafood, 3,077; and packaging fresh or frozen fish, 917 employees. These figures are the averages of employment as reported in 12 weeks, one week in each month, for Washington and Oregon during 1958. The figures represent persons covered by unemployment insurance; as such, they include some but not all self-employed persons.

4 After forestry, agriculture, and tourism.

5 *Pacific Fisherman Yearbook,* January, 1959. The Columbia River salmon pack represents approximately 70 per cent of the total Columbia River salmon caught commercially. For example, in 1958, canned salmon amounted to 6,552,384 pounds, compared with a frozen salmon pack of 2,990,115 pounds.

United States. Over 7 million kilowatts have been developed so far and projects with an additional 6 million kilowatts are under construction. How much of the remaining 23 million kilowatts will be harnessed depends on a number of factors, foremost among which are construction costs, the availability of alternative sources of energy, public policy with respect to resource development, and the resolution of various conflicts of interest.

At present, hydropower is the cheapest means of producing electrical energy in the Pacific Northwest and it appears that it will remain the principal source for some time to come. Power produced from hydro sources is being sold by the Bonneville Power Administration at wholesale rates of two to three mills per kilowatt-hour. Power produced from alternative sources, such as coal, oil, natural gas, or uranium, would cost significantly more. The region possesses reserves of fossil fuels but costs of exploitation are high and supplies are im-

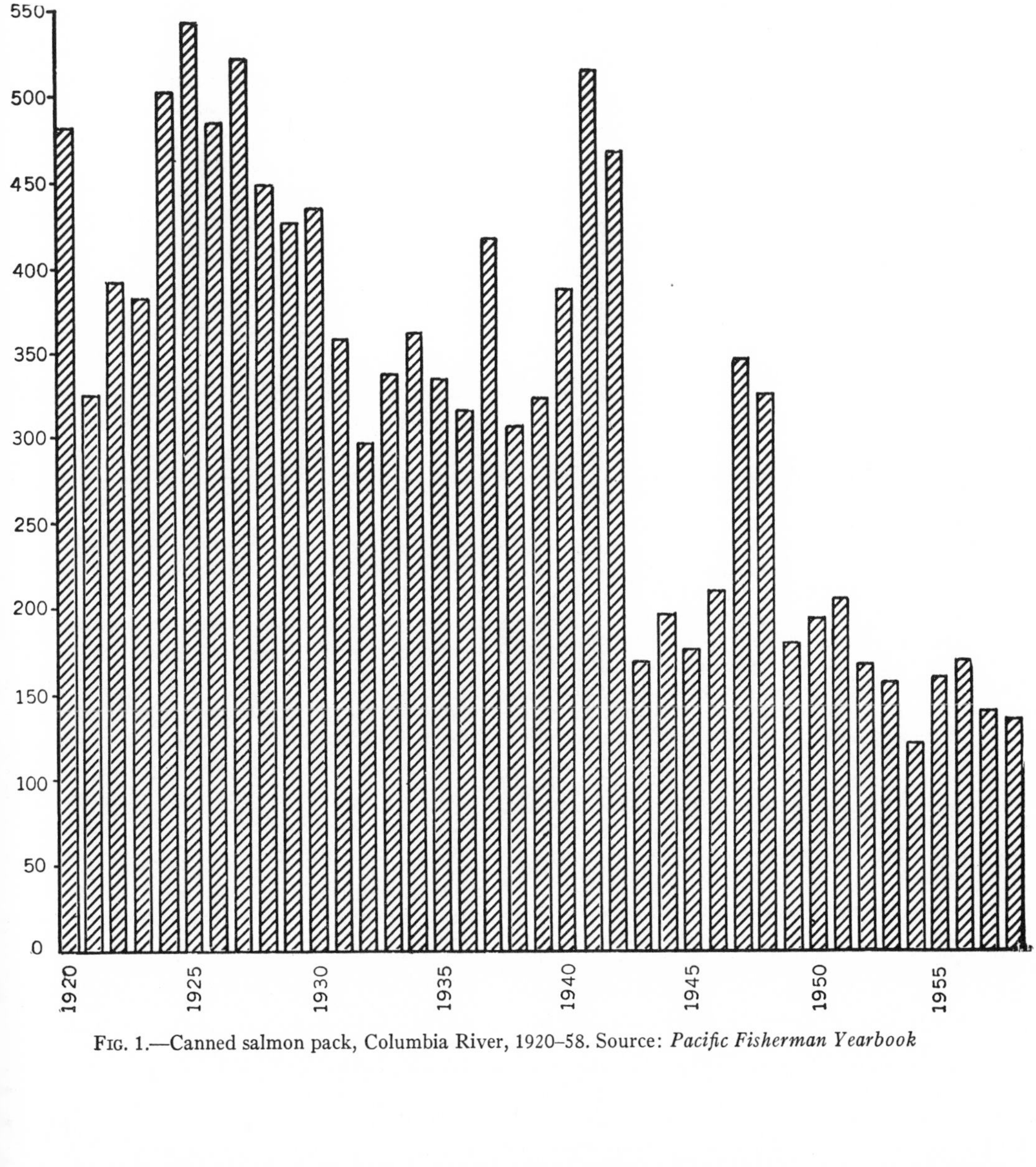

FIG. 1.—Canned salmon pack, Columbia River, 1920–58. Source: *Pacific Fisherman Yearbook*

ported from elsewhere. Costs of imported fuels, however, are not low enough to enable thermal power to compete with hydropower. Despite the tremendous advances that have been made in nuclear power technology, it seems unlikely that this means of generation will assume a truly dominant role in the Pacific Northwest for many years to come.[6]

Despite the cost advantages of hydropower in the Pacific Northwest, however, development of some of the most favorable sites is stalled, especially by problems of fish maintenance. On the basis of updated estimates of the Pacific Northwest Governors' Power Policy Committee, 22 projects with a total capacity of 5,000,000 kilowatts are being held up by fisheries problems.[7]

If the Pacific Northwest is to take maximum advantage of its water resources, earnest efforts must be made to find a solution to the fish–power conflict. It is pertinent at this point to examine what measures have been carried out so far, to comment on their effectiveness, and to suggest additional measures which might be undertaken.

[6] Most estimates of probable costs of nuclear power are in the nature of speculations. Generally they represent goals toward which nuclear power engineers must strive rather than costs based on actual experience. Many of them are based on assumptions regarding technical advances which have yet to be made. For discussions of the problem of estimating nuclear power costs, see D. P. Herron and A. Puishes, "The Prospects for Economic Atomic Power," paper presented to the ASME Semi-Annual Meeting, San Francisco, June 9–13, 1957; H. W. Nelson and W. R. Keagy, Jr., "The Economic Background for the Competitive Development of Nuclear Power," paper presented at the Second Nuclear Engineering and Science Conference, Philadelphia, March 11–14, 1957; and John Davis, *Canadian Energy Prospects,* Royal Commission on Canada's Economic Prospects (Ottawa, 1957).

[7] Pacific Northwest Governors' Power Policy Committee, *Status Report on the Relation of Fish and Wildlife Problems to New Hydro Power Development* (Portland, Ore., November 4, 1954), p. 5.

Efforts toward Fishery Rehabilitation and Development

The serious effects of encroaching civilization on resources in general were recognized by conservationists and others in the late nineteenth century, and various policies have been put into effect since that time to promote better utilization of our forests and farmlands. But it was not until the era of large dam construction on the Columbia River that really positive measures for rehabilitation and development of the fishery resource were initiated.[8] Through the programs of research and development, which have been carried out since the 1930's, it has been possible to gain a clearer understanding of the problem and to implement programs designed to increase, rather than merely rehabilitate, the fisheries.

Measures intended to offset losses due to hydro dam construction and to increase the Columbia River fishery may be grouped conveniently as follows: (1) fish-passage facilities, (2) fishing regulations, (3) sanctuary stream programs, and (4) research programs.

Fish-passage facilities have been installed at all main-stem dams downstream from Chief Joseph Dam in an effort to avoid or minimize fish losses at these dams. Although fish ladders may permit the safe passage of large numbers of fish, losses of both upstream and downstream migrants occur. The success of fish-passage facilities, therefore, is not yet assured. They are, moreover, very expensive and not considered technically feasible at high dams (such as Grand Coulee or the proposed Nez Perce dams). As of now they should be regarded as experimental expedients designed to prevent complete elimination of fish runs and applicable only at dams of low or moderate height. Combined with

[8] For a description of programs for rehabilitation and development, see U.S., Columbia Basin Inter-Agency Committee, Fisheries Steering Committee, *The Fisheries and the Multiple-Purpose Development of the Columbia River* (Portland, Ore., January, 1955).

other measures, however, the passage facilities may be instrumental in the restoration of the Columbia River fishery.

Recognition of the serious depletions in fish runs due to overfishing resulted in the enactment of laws restricting the use of various types of fishing gear, and confining fishing to certain seasons and certain areas. Because of the international nature of the problem, treaties with other nations have also been drawn up. The International Pacific Salmon Fisheries Commission was established in 1937 by the United States and Canada and the Pacific Marine Fisheries Commission in 1947 to provide for international regulation.

While regulation has probably done much to prevent further decline of the fishery, much more positive measures are required to rehabilitate it to former levels. At the same time, provision has to be made to compensate for additional losses that are likely to result from further dam construction on the main stem of the Columbia River.

A promising compromise was developed by the U.S. Corps of Engineers and the U.S. Fish and Wildlife Service in the Lower Columbia River Fisheries Development Program, which was begun in 1949. These agencies considered that if the comprehensive plan for the Columbia River were fully implemented, the salmon spawning grounds of the upper part of the Columbia Basin would be lost. They decided that the best alternative would be to depend mainly on the tributaries of the lower river and upon artificial propagation for the development of the salmon and steelhead runs of the Columbia River.[9] The program has two aspects: (1) enhancement of habitat and access conditions and development of means to supplement natural propagation; (2) protection of fish runs through setting aside streams as sanctuaries or fish preserves.

To date, the enhancement aspect has been largely implemented. Most of the stream clearing work to improve habitat has been completed, several fishways have been constructed, eight new or rebuilt hatcheries placed in operation,[10] and fish farming programs initiated. To implement the sanctuary concept the state legislatures of Washington and Oregon enacted fish refuge laws forbidding the construction of high dams on the lower Columbia Basin tributaries. Conflicting legal authority and jurisdictions, however, threaten the sanctuary concept. Specifically, the U.S. Federal Power Commission has licensed high power dams on the Cowlitz and Deschutes rivers, both recognized as sanctuary tributaries by the states and by the U.S. Fish and Wildlife Service.

Much of the hope in rehabilitating the fisheries can be attributed to the research programs undertaken by various international, federal, state, and private agencies and by the universities.[11] These programs have involved the expenditure of several millions of dollars. The Columbia River Fisheries Engineering Investigation and Research Program of the Corps of Engineers, for example, is estimated to cost between 2 and 3 million dollars.[12] The research is being undertaken to discover be-

9 U.S., Dept. of the Army, Corps of Engineers, *Review Report on the Columbia River and Tributaries, Northwestern United States,* House Doc. 531, 81st Cong., 2d Sess., 1952, Appendix P, p. 2919. All tributaries of the Columbia River below McNary Dam are included in the sanctuary stream program.

10 About twenty hatcheries are now operating in the Columbia River basin.

11 For a description of various research programs being undertaken, see H. A. Preston and Lewis E. Rydell, "The Co-existence of Fish and Dams," *Transactions of the American Society of Civil Engineers,* Journal of the Power Div. (October, 1957).

12 U.S., Dept. of the Interior, Fish and Wildlife Service, *Statement in Response to the Request, November 20, 1953, of Senator Styles Bridges on the Abundance, Distribution, and Value of the Columbia River Fish Runs, the Effects of Dams on These Runs, and Certain Other Related Information* (Portland, Ore., 1953), p. 34.

havior of salmon under natural and man-made conditions. From the results of the research it is hoped that it will be possible not only to compensate for losses which result from the encroachment of civilization but also to make unaffected areas more productive than they are at present.

Difficulties in Resolving the Fish–Power Conflict

The various programs which have been initiated to rehabilitate the salmon fishery of the Columbia River appear to be meeting with some success, and results of research programs indicate possibilities by which the fishing may be increased to levels several times those achieved today. Despite the large expenditures on research and the indications of success of many of the programs of rehabilitation, however, the conflict of fish and power seems to be far from a mutually acceptable solution, and as time goes on the likelihood of reaching a compromise seems to diminish. Foremost among the factors which tend to perpetuate the problem are: (1) the historic importance of the fishing industry in the Pacific Northwest, (2) inappropriate comparisons of values of fish and power, (3) increasing costs of fish preservation, and (4) the time required to study the biological aspects of the problem.

In view of the historic importance of fishing, and particularly salmon fishing, in the Pacific Northwest, it is understandable that the fisheries agencies are unwilling to sanction schemes which threaten to deplete the resource. They claim that once a run has been damaged, it may be impossible to rehabilitate it. As a consequence, even though results of research may suggest attractive means of compensating for fish losses, fisheries agencies may continue to oppose hydropower projects.

Another factor which tends to aggravate the fish–power problem is the attempt by the fisheries and power agencies to compare the monetary values of fish and power. Generally, little resort to economic analysis is made in such comparisons and many of them are based on highly unrealistic assumptions and grossly inflated figures. For example, the fisheries agencies have sometimes assumed that the installation of one dam will mean economic ruin to the fishing industry. Thus evaluations often compare the value of the power from the one dam with the value of the product of the entire fishing industry. In reality, of course, only part of the fishery would be affected. On the other hand, evaluations made by the power agencies seldom take into account long-run values of the fishery or the effect of the present investment in boats, gear, and other capital equipment.[13]

The net result of this type of comparison is to keep the fisheries agencies and the power agencies far apart and to preclude the possibility of compromise. Much more objective analyses of the values of fish and power involved at proposed hydro projects must be developed. Only then can the economic aspects of the problem be properly

[13] For an objective estimation of the income from and capitalized value of Washington fisheries, see James A. Crutchfield, "Economic Value of Washington Commercial Fisheries, 1955," *Pacific Northwest Business* (July 1957), pp. 5–15. Crutchfield's estimates are for the state of Washington, and so do not contribute directly to comparisons of the economic returns of fish and power on the Columbia River. A careful estimation of relative values is beyond the scope of this paper, and is difficult because of various uncertainties, including the intangible values of fish caught by sports fishermen. A rough comparison of gross income, however, may be developed. A U.S. Fish and Wildlife Service estimate prepared for Sen. Styles Bridges in 1953 (*op. cit.*, p. 6) places the value of Columbia River salmon and steelhead at $17,012,000 per year, based on average annual catch data for 1938–42 (catches in recent years have been much lower). By way of comparison, the Bonneville Power Administration's revenue from sale of power in 1953 was $38,442,000 (and in 1959 was nearly $67,000,000). This comparison does not constitute an economic evaluation, however, and must be used with great caution. For instance, it does not evaluate all effects that should be considered in making decisions, the values are gross rather than net, and the measurements are not at the same points in the chain from production to consumption.

evaluated and weighed *with other considerations* in the decision-making.

The importance of developing better evaluation techniques is emphasized by the increasing concern that has been expressed regarding the mounting costs of fish preservation in the Pacific Northwest. It has been estimated that over $127 million has been invested in facilities to protect Columbia River salmon since Rock Island Dam was constructed in 1933.[14] While expenditures at dams constructed to date have been large, such expenditures at dams constructed in the future may be even greater. For example, the Bonneville fish facilities cost about $7 million, whereas those at the Dalles Dam cost $18 million and those at McNary Dam cost over $27 million. The question has been raised as to whether these expenditures are justified.

It is not generally realized that as development in the basin proceeds, investment in fish facilities yields diminishing returns. As further dams are added, costs of preservation increase, but the number of fish preserved diminishes (although the value of the individual surviving fish may increase). This effect takes place because, even with the most efficient facilities so far devised, losses of migrants occur at each dam. Thus these losses tend to be cumulative both on the upstream and the downstream migrations, so that, if sufficient dams are added, the whole run may be eliminated.[15] Eventually a stage is reached where the cost of preserving the fish exceeds the value of the fish preserved. Further investment in fish facilities beyond this point cannot be justified on economic grounds.[16]

Unfortunately, very little attention has been paid to economic analysis in decisions relating to expenditures on fish maintenance programs. The decisions have been based mainly on the technical feasibility of the facilities rather than on their economic feasibility. The result has been to obscure the problem of diminishing returns of such investments and to divert attention from consideration of alternative schemes of fish preservation, such as relocation of fisheries, transport systems other than fish ladders, and fish preserves. In addition, no consideration appears to have been given to alternative employment of the labor and resources now employed in this segment of the fishing industry.

A fourth factor which tends to perpetuate the fish–power conflict and which inhibits a solution to the problem is the manner in which the time element affects the two groups of interests involved. The fisheries agencies have been interested primarily in the biological aspects of the problem, and their studies have concentrated mainly on the behavior and biology of the fish, as well as on the effects of dams on fish runs and on means of getting fish over dams. Because of the complexity of the problems, such studies involve great detail and are carried out at a wide variety of locations. Although these studies are essential to good solutions, they are very time-consuming and the general result is to push the resolution of the conflict even further into the future.

Meanwhile the power agencies, conscious of the problem of meeting rapidly growing power demands, are becoming increasingly impatient of time required for biological studies. Faced with an inflation-

[14] The $127 million includes costs of installing fishways, hatcheries, and conducting experiments designed to maintain the runs. See Bob Woods, "Kilowatts and Salmon," reprinted series of articles in the *Wenatchee Daily World* (Wenatchee, Washington, February 27–March 10, 1958), p. 1.

[15] The problem of fish losses is very complex and is related not only to the physical problem facing the fish in passing the dam, but also to changes in environment both upstream and downstream from each dam. These environmental changes involve such items as water temperature, predation, currents, siltation, etc. See, for example, C. H. Clay and P. A. Larkin, "Artificial Propagation is NOT the Answer," *B.C. Professional Engineer* (March, 1959), pp. 20–23.

[16] M. E. Marts and W. R. D. Sewell, "The Application of Benefit-Cost Analysis to Fish Preservation Expenditures: A Neglected Aspect of River Basin Investment Decisions," *Land Economics* (February, 1959), p. 48.

ary construction cost spiral, these agencies realize that prospects of taking maximum advantage of certain undeveloped cheap power sites in the Pacific Northwest are fading. They are also conscious of the real costs involved in adopting more expensive means of generation and truncating hydropower development, with the consequent inhibition of industrial and commercial growth. The power agencies are anxious to proceed with construction of high dams at sites such as Mayfield on the Cowlitz River and Nez Perce or Mountain Sheep on the Snake River, even though the fish–power problems involved at these sites are among the most intractable in the Pacific Northwest.

Neglected Alternatives

In addition to the approaches already discussed—namely, fishing regulation and sanctuary stream programs—there are a number of other at least theoretical possibilities for compensation which merit consideration. These include the development of runs on non-power streams, the development of alternative fisheries, and the provision of alternative occupations for fishermen. Although such alternatives would be expensive, they should not be rejected a priori. It has been noted that very large expenditures are planned for fish ladders without assurance of success. Careful investigation might or might not indicate that such sums could more effectively be invested in alternative schemes.[17]

Construction of certain hydropower projects may make it impossible to maintain fish runs in some parts of the basin. In some circumstances it may be possible to compensate for losses by relocation of runs and artificial propagation. The Grand Coulee Fish Maintenance Program, which was based on this approach, has achieved a measure of success. There may be attractive opportunities for such schemes, not only in the Pacific Northwest, but also along the British Columbia coast and in Alaska. Such possibilities, of course, are limited by the size and the nature of the run to be relocated.[18] While a program may achieve considerable success in one area, it may be a complete failure elsewhere. What is important, however, is that all possibilities be considered and thoroughly investigated.

It is possible that more intensive development of the Alaska fisheries might offset some of the losses which are expected to result from the installation of dams on the Columbia and Snake rivers. Currently the Alaska salmon pack is about 20 times the size of the Columbia pack, 3,347,446 cases versus 161,731 cases (Table 1). The U.S. Fish and Wildlife Service believes that "Intelligent management of resources, based on scientific knowledge, would increase the annual production in Alaska by at least 50 million pounds (1,041,000 cases)."[19] This represents a 31 per cent increase over the 1948–55 average annual canned salmon pack of Alaska. Development in Alaska seems particularly attractive since conflicts with other resource developments such as agriculture, forestry, and hydroelectric power, are minimal and there is an abundance of suitable streams for spawning throughout the area.

No mass migration of fishermen and their families would be necessitated by the development of fisheries in Alaska. Much of the Alaska fishery is now carried on by fishermen from Oregon and Washington who go north each summer to fish for

[17] Implicit in this discussion of alternatives is the assumption that compensation for damage to fishery resources will be made and that the problem is to find the most efficient means of compensation. The justification for compensation involves social and philosophical as well as economic considerations and is beyond the scope of this paper. The feasibility of significant compensation is suggested, as indicated, by the large investments now being made in fish-passage facilities.

[18] Clay and Larkin, *op. cit.*, discuss the magnitude of the problem of compensating for losses which might result from power developments on the Fraser River in British Columbia.

[19] U.S., Dept. of the Interior, Fish and Wildlife Service, *Fishery Resources of the United States* (Washington, 1945).

TABLE 1

CANNED SALMON PACK—COLUMBIA RIVER, ALASKA, UNITED STATES, AND BRITISH COLUMBIA, 1920–58[a]

(In Cases of 48 Pounds)

Year	Columbia River	Alaska	United States	British Columbia
1920	481,545	4,395,509	5,101,705	1,187,616
1	323,241	2,604,973	3,622,612	603,548
2	392,174	4,501,355	5,231,675	1,290,326
3	380,925	5,063,340	6,411,757	1,341,677
4	500,872	5,305,923	6,245,320	1,745,313
5	540,452	4,450,898	6,034,321	1,720,622
6	479,723	6,652,882	7,491,684	2,065,198
7	519,809	3,566,072	5,053,472	1,360,449
8	446,646	6,070,110	6,902,447	2,035,637
9	422,117	5,370,242	6,983,556	1,400,750
1930	429,505	4,988,987	6,044,093	2,221,783
1	353,699	5,432,535	6,780,492	685,104
2	296,191	5,260,488	5,914,853	1,081,031
3	336,711	5,226,698	6,360,742	1,265,072
4	362,721	7,470,586	8,361,990	1,582,926
5	332,739	5,155,826	6,037,454	1,529,022
6	316,445	8,454,948	8,983,217	1,881,026
7	416,830	6,654,038	7,526,197	1,509,175
8	307,990	6,791,544	7,274,209	1,707,830
9	322,472	5,293,211	5,971,527	1,539,070
1940	386,999	5,028,378	5,548,908	1,467,227
1	513,712	6,906,503	7,779,654	2,248,870
2	464,401	5,089,109	5,852,515	1,811,560
3	167,660	5,396,509	5,676,391	1,258,221
4	196,762	4,877,796	5,119,079	1,097,557
5	175,670	4,341,120	4,910,580	1,739,311
6	209,471	3,971,109	4,563,115	1,348,138
7	347,306	4,302,466	5,612,664	1,533,478
8	324,242	4,010,612	5,826,426	1,308,137
9	178,122	4,391,051	5,524,916	1,436,464
1950	192,990	3,272,643	4,274,462	1,482,560
1	203,123	3,484,464	4,645,570	1,956,397
2	167,616	3,574,128	4,455,022	1,293,435
3	153,199	2,925,570	3,910,646	1,825,267
4	119,057	3,207,154	4,163,147	1,742,736
5	161,557	2,457,969	3,361,885	1,406,100
6	167,121	2,950,354	3,432,658	1,118,279
7	138,016	2,441,894	3,184,897	1,449,120
8	136,508	2,948,371	3,706,636	1,908,056
Average, 1948–58	161,731	3,347,446	4,065,937	1,558,556

[a] Source: *Pacific Fisherman Yearbook*, January, 1959.

salmon in Alaskan waters. Part of this migration is a regular annual migration, and part of it is governed by fishing prospects in the Pacific Northwest as compared with those in Alaska. The development of fish runs in Alaska would probably not be opposed by a large number of Washington and Oregon fishermen. There might be substantial opposition, however, from fishermen who do not take part in the Alaska migration, and by fish handlers and processors who are dependent mainly on Columbia River salmon, and whose investment is immobile and specific to the Columbia River fishery.

In addition to a geographical re-orientation of production, it is possible that research may reveal or develop species and varieties of fish which are able to adapt themselves to the new conditions in the basin. Experiments in selective breeding and hybridization being conducted at the University of Washington indicate that it is possible to develop races of fish which are not only larger and stronger than present races but are also able to reproduce within a shorter cycle. In addition, the possibilities of fish farming techniques merit much more attention than they have been given to date.[20]

A further possibility of compensating fishermen for the loss of salmon runs would be to develop alternative occupations in fishing communities, perhaps by subsidizing other industries. The salmon fishing industry has experienced wide fluctuations in the price of its product in the past and in the volume of its catch. In consequence, there has been much economic instability in fishing communities depending on fishing for the main source of their income. The development of alternative occupations in such communities would serve the double purpose of helping to diversify the economy and to compensate for losses of income which result from depletions of the fish runs. A scheme based on the approach of the Development Area program in Great Britain merits consideration in this connection. Through lower taxes, provision of capital funds on attractive terms, and other amenities, the British government made formerly depressed areas attractive as locations for new industries. Typically, the industries which took advantage of the program were foot-loose industries, employing unskilled and semiskilled labor.[21] The problem of unskilled labor was overcome to some extent by vocational training schemes.

Another avenue of compensating for the social effects of depletion of salmon runs lies in the possibility of developing the markets for non-anadromous fishery resources. The traditional specialization on salmon in the Pacific Northwest has obscured the potential importance of other available species, such as herring, cod, sole, and flounder. Although these have not been prized so highly by the market as salmon, they do represent potentials for partially offsetting sources of income.[22]

Conclusions

Much of the basis for the long-standing difficulty in finding acceptable solutions to the fish and power problem has been the concern of protagonists that the opposite camp was claiming special treatment on the basis of special, subjective values. This has led to viewing the problem as a forced choice between mutually incompatible uses of the water resource and inhibition of the consideration of alternative solutions or methods of compensation.

[20] For a discussion of possibilities of artificial propagation and fish farming see Milo Moore, *Salmon Fisheries of the North Pacific Ocean*, Washington State Dept. of Fisheries (April, 1959).

[21] For a discussion of the Development Area program see S. R. Dennison, *The Location of Industry and the Depressed Areas* (New York: Oxford University Press, 1939), and G. R. Allen, "The Growth of Industry on Trading Estates, 1920–39," *Oxford Economic Papers*, III, No. 3 (1951).

[22] The herring, for example, is an important food fish in Europe but in northwest North America is taken primarily for production of meal and oil.

In the broad context of river basin development, fish maintenance is one of the several possible uses of the waters of a basin. Many of these uses may be complementary or at least compatible. In the case of fish, compatibility with other uses may be more difficult, and perhaps impossible to achieve at given sites or within given reaches of a river. But given sound planning, compatibility within the broad framework of comprehensive river basin and regional development may well be possible.

Sound planning in river basin development presupposes careful and objective evaluations of the costs and benefits of alternative developments; application of optimization criteria in which economic values are important but are not the only values to be considered; and a willingness to consider alternatives before fixing on a course of action. The failure to consider these factors has been the major reason for the prolonged conflict. Until such considerations are developed into policy and then implemented, optimum use of Pacific Northwest rivers cannot be achieved.

MELVIN G. BLASE and JOHN F. TIMMONS

SOIL EROSION CONTROL—PROBLEMS AND PROGRESS

Several objectives guided the analysis on which this article is based: (1) To learn how much progress farm operators were making in reducing erosion and in moving their own erosion control goals toward the public goal of reducing annual soil losses to 5 tons per acre; (2) to identify the obstacles preventing adoption of erosion control practices and to measure changes in obstacles over time; and (3) in view of the obstacles found, to examine present and proposed programs to reduce erosion.

THE LAND-USE LABORATORY

Research findings reported here are the result of investigations initiated in 1947 as a cooperative project of the Iowa Agricultural and Home Economics Experiment Station and the Farm Economics Research Division of the United States Department of Agriculture. This series of investigations has been termed "The Land-Use Laboratory" of western Iowa, since periodically, studies are made into the processes of erosion control in the area composing the laboratory.

The laboratory is located in the Ida-Monona Soil Association in western Iowa.[1]

• Melvin G. Blase is Assistant Professor of Economics at Iowa State University; John F. Timmons is Professor of Economics at Iowa State University.

Reprinted from *Journal of Soil and Water Conservation*, XVI, No. 4 (1961), 157–62, with permission of the authors and the editor. (Copyright 1961 by the Soil Conservation Society of America, Inc.)

[1] L. K. Fisher and J. F. Timmons, *Progress and Problems in the Iowa Soil Conservation Districts Program*, Res. Bull. 466 (Ames: Iowa Agric. and Home Ec. Expt. Sta., 1959).

Approximately 5 per cent of the land in the State is in this area. Ida and Monona soils constitute more than half the land in the Ida-Monona Soil Association. Both soils were formed from calcareous loess on hilly topography. The thickness of the loess ranges from a maximum of about 120 feet

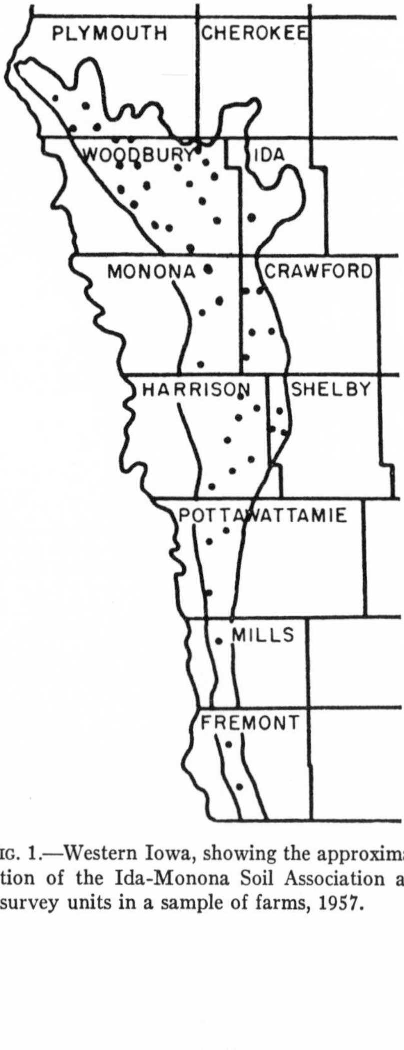

FIG. 1.—Western Iowa, showing the approximate location of the Ida-Monona Soil Association and the survey units in a sample of farms, 1957.

near the river valley, which is thought to be its source, to a thin loessial mantle in north central Missouri.

Ida and Monona soils are susceptible to erosion and drought. Measures that reduce runoff aid in minimizing both of these hazards. Without these practices, erosion proceeds rapidly through gullying, which, once started, is difficult to control. Partly as a result of erosion, fertility problems are more acute in this association than in most others in Iowa.[2]

The modal erosion classes for Monona silt loam and Ida silt loam are 2 (moderate) and 3 (severe), respectively. The dominant slope group for Monona silt loam is 5 to 13 per cent; the largest acreage of Ida silt loam occurs on slopes from 9 to 17 per cent. Although the modal use-capability class for Ida and Monona soils is 3 (suitable for cultivation with complex or intensive practices), substantial acreages of Ida, Monona, and terrace position Monona are in classes less suitable for cultivation.

The agricultural economy of this area is predominantly feed-livestock production. This type of farming is based on intensive use of land for production of intertilled crops and this leads to high levels of soil erosion.

Initial Study—1949

The initial study in the Land-Use Laboratory of western Iowa was made in 1949 by John C. Frey.[3] He estimated the average annual soil loss on a sample of 144 farms in the Ida-Monona area in 1949 as 21.1 tons per acre. Eighty-nine per cent of the farmers had not reduced their soil losses to the annual rate of 5 tons per acre, which is the goal used by public action agencies in the area. Also, 79 per cent of the farmers had erosion control objectives that would allow soil losses of more than 5 tons per acre. If these farmers had adopted the erosion control practices they believed to be necessary, soil losses would have averaged 16.4 tons per acre per year.[4]

Frey found four major obstacles that appeared to retard farmers in reaching desired erosion control objectives: (1) the change required in farm enterprises (primarily to more livestock) on 40 per cent of the farms; (2) current rental arrangements and lack of landlord's cooperation on 34 per cent of the farms; (3) mortgage indebtedness and annual fixed cash outlays for operating and living expenses on 30 per cent of the farms; and (4) short expectancy of tenure on 19 per cent of the farms.[5]

Second Study—1952

The second study in this series was made by R. Burnell Held.[6] In 1952, he interviewed the operators of the same farms that Frey used in 1949. Soil losses on the sample farms in the Ida-Monona soil area were estimated to have decreased 1.6 tons per acre between 1949 and 1952, but the average soil loss was still 19.5 tons per acre. As a group, the operators had not reached the goals of erosion control they had indicated in 1949; nor did they set goals in 1952 that were more ambitious than those set earlier. If they had used the practices they named as needed on their farms,

[2] R. W. Simonson, F. F. Riecken, and G. D. Smith, *Understanding Iowa Soils* (Dubuque: Wm. C. Brown Co., 1952), pp. 58–62.

[3] John C. Frey, *Some Obstacles to Soil Erosion Control in Western Iowa,* Res. Bull. 391 (Ames: Iowa Agric. and Home Ec. Expt. Sta., 1952), p. 945.

[4] Soil losses were computed using the system of factors designed by Browning which takes into account and weight various physical factors that affect erosion. These are soil type, crop management, vegetative cover (as expressed in terms of rotations), use or non-use of contouring, terracing, strip cropping and listing, degree of slope, length of slope, extent of previous erosion and a constant term. The weight given each factor was based on experimental data for the particular condition found. The product of the factors represents the estimate of the amount of soil lost from an acre in one year with normal weather. Iowa State University of Science and Technology, Dept. of Agronomy, *Browning's Erosion Factors* (rev.; Ames: Iowa State University, 1957).

[5] Frey, *op. cit.*

[6] R. B. Held and J. F. Timmons, *Soil Erosion Control in Process in Western Iowa,* Res. Bull. 460 (Ames: Iowa Agric. and Home Ec. Expt. Sta., 1958).

the results would have been soil loss rates averaging 16.7 tons per acre.

Although the average soil loss changed little, there were noteworthy increases and decreases on individual farms. Of particular interest were the 36 farms on which the rates of loss were high in 1949 but on which, by 1952, the losses were lowered by 5 tons or more. Other farms showed increases in the rate of loss that were just as striking.

Held diagnosed the major causes for failure to reduce soil losses as uncertainty of tenure, lack of adequate finances, reluctance to assume risk, and lack of confidence in the recommended practices. The major causes of success in reducing soil losses from 1949 to 1952 appeared to have been increased appreciation of the seriousness of soil losses, increased security of tenure, and increased appreciation that shifts to more grass on the steeper slopes and to more forage-consuming livestock were conducive to erosion control and profitable farming over the long pull.

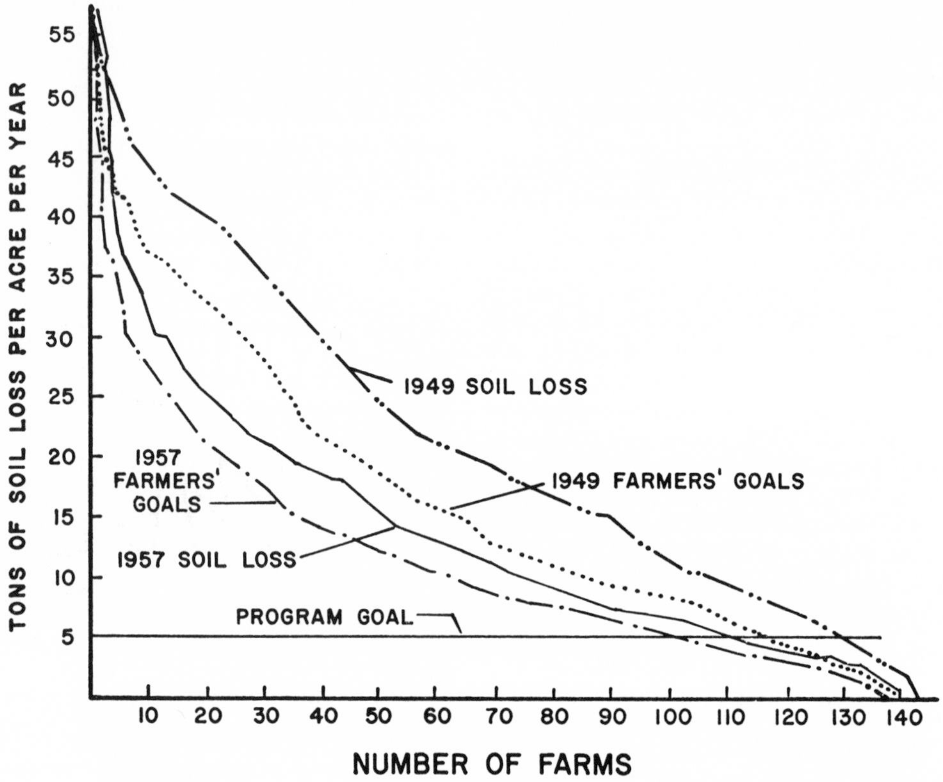

FIG. 2.—Erosion losses on 138 farms in western Iowa, arrayed according to decreasing soil loss in tons per acre shown in terms of observed soil losses, farmers' goals of erosion control, and program objectives, 1949 and 1957.

THIRD STUDY—1957

The third study in the series was made by the senior author of this article in 1957 to provide data comparable with the previous studies. Once more, operators of the same sample of farms were interviewed. In addition to obtaining farmers' reactions to erosion control plans, information was obtained about their use of land and characteristics of their farms. The non-operating landowners of farms in the sample were interviewed also.

Many changes occurred on the sample

farms between 1949 and 1957. Consolidation and division decreased the number of farms by 6, to 138 in 1957. Only 77 of the farms had the same operators in 1957 as in 1949. Fourteen operators had moved onto their farms between 1949 and 1952. The remaining 47 farmers had begun operation of their farms after 1952.

In 1957, the average soil loss estimated for the sample farms was 14.1 tons per acre. Had farmers attained their goals of erosion control, the loss would have averaged only 11.7 tons. Thus, both the observed soil losses and soil loss rates given as farmers' goals decreased substantially between 1949 and 1957. A comparison of the observed soil losses and the farmers' goals in 1957 and 1949 is shown in Figure 2.

The reduction in soil losses resulted from increased use of erosion control practices and from changes in land use. Table 1 shows the proportion of farms on which specific erosion control practices were used in 1949, 1952, and 1957. The greatest percentage changes during the period were in extent of terracing and construction of grass waterways. Figure 3 presents the proportion of land in the sample in various uses in 1949, 1952, 1957, and the proportion for various uses in two plans of use recommended by the Soil Conservation Service in 1957—a mechanical practice plan and a high forage rotation plan. There was a consistent decrease in proportion of land in row crops from 1949 to 1957.

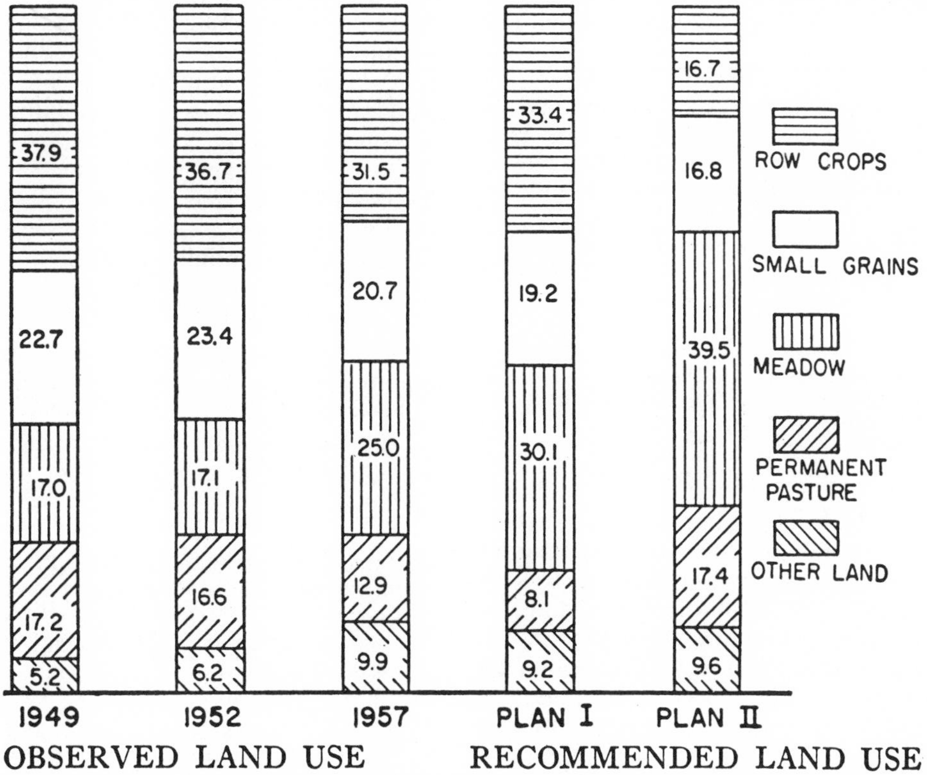

FIG. 3.—Percentage of total land in a sample of western Iowa farms in various uses, actual 1949, 1952, 1957, and use recommended by the Soil Conservation Service in 1957—Plan I (mechanical practice plan) and Plan II (high forage rotation plan).

EROSION CONTROL OBSTACLES—1957

In the course of interviews during each of the three surveys, each operator of the sample farms was shown two erosion-control plans for his farm prepared for this study by the Soil Conservation Service—a mechanical practices plan and a high forage rotation plan. Between 1952 and 1957, the erosion control practices considered by soil conservationists as needed to achieve the 5 tons per acre soil-loss goal changed. Results of agronomic research at Iowa State University and other midwest experiment stations had shown that some practices were more effective and others less effective than was formerly believed. Table 2 shows that the percentage of all land in the sample recommended for row crops in the mechanical practice plan increased from 21.6 in 1949–51 to 33.4 in 1957. There was a corresponding increase in the percentage of small grains recommended and a decrease in the meadow and pasture recommended in the mechanical practice plans. There was little difference in recommended land use in the high forage rotation plans.

TABLE 1

PROPORTION OF FARMS ON WHICH EROSION CONTROL PRACTICES WERE USED ON AT LEAST ONE FIELD, 1949, 1952, AND 1957

PRACTICE	PERCENTAGE OF FARMS ON WHICH PRACTICE WAS USED ON AT LEAST ONE FIELD		
	1949	1952	1957
Grass waterways....	33	46	72
Contouring.........	51	65	62
Commercial fertilizer.	42	60	47
Terracing...........	15	27	40

During each interview, the mechanical practice plan and the high forage rotation plan were described in detail. The farm operator was then asked if there were obstacles that would prevent the adoption of practices recommended in either plan. In 1957, sixteen obstacles were mentioned by the operators as factors that would prevent adoption of at least one erosion control practice. Table 3 shows the number of farmers who named specific obstacles to particular practices and the total number of farms on which each obstacle was mentioned.

The relationships between the obstacles named and soil losses in 1957 were examined by means of multiple variable linear regression. Results of this procedure indicated four main obstacles to reduction of soil losses: (1) need for immediate income, (2) failure to see the need for a recommended practice, (3) custom and inertia, and (4) field and road layout. These obstacles and others were examined in detail to determine the reasons for their existence, and to find possible remedies.

NEED FOR IMMEDIATE INCOME

Need for immediate income constituted an obstacle for two basic reasons. One was the large out-of-pocket expense involved in adopting some erosion control practices. The other was the opportunity cost; that is, the income that operators believed they would have had to forego if they had adopted the recommended erosion control practices.

TABLE 2

PROPORTION OF ACREAGE (PER CENT) RECOMMENDED IN 1949–52 AND 1957 BY THE SOIL CONSERVATION SERVICE FOR WESTERN IOWA FARMS, BY TYPES OF CROPS UNDER TWO KINDS OF PLANS

LAND USE	MECHANICAL PRACTICE PLAN		HIGH FORAGE ROTATION PLAN	
	1949–52	1957	1949–52	1957
Row crop......	21.6	33.4	14.6	16.7
Small grain.....	15.9	19.2	15.5	16.8
Meadow........	37.7	30.1	41.6	39.5
Permanent pasture.........	15.3	8.1	14.7	17.4
Other..........	9.5	9.2	13.6	9.6

In Table 4, farm operators are grouped according to the percentage change in gross returns they anticipated 1, 5, and 10 years after the adoption of Plan I, the mechanical practice plan. Farm operators were not optimistic about increasing their gross returns as a result of this plan. There was evidence of a substantial lack of knowledge about the change that erosion control practices could be expected to make in their gross farm incomes.

Farm operators were more pessimistic about the effects on their gross farm income of Plan II, the high forage rotation plan (Table 5), than about those from Plan I. However, the number of operators expecting a decrease in their gross income, or no change, tended to decrease with time after the practices were adopted.

Farm operators in the sample had little knowledge of projected costs of adopting soil erosion practices. In the course of the interview, each farm operator was asked to estimate the costs of erosion control practices in the mechanical practice plan. A majority of the operators had no idea of the expected costs. Of those who estimated the cost, three-fourths overestimated it relative to a budgeted cost based on data obtained from Soil Conservation Service personnel in the area.[7]

Another indication of operators' expectations of the profitability of control practices was that they rated erosion control practices relatively low as either a first or second investment preference. Self-rationing of capital prevented most operators who needed to borrow funds for erosion control practices from doing so. The uncertainty of income from these practices was the reason most frequently mentioned for unwillingness to borrow.

Many owner-operators thought investments in erosion control practices would

TABLE 3

NUMBER OF FARM OPERATORS WHO REPORTED OBSTACLES TO INDIVIDUAL EROSION CONTROL PRACTICES AND NUMBER OF FARMS ON WHICH EACH OBSTACLE WAS REPORTED ON 138 WESTERN IOWA FARMS IN 1957

Obstacle	Number of Operators Who Reported Obstacles to Specified Practices								Number of Farms on Which Obstacle Was Reported
	Contouring	Terracing	Waterways	Fertilizer	Structures	Contour Fencing	Rotation I	Rotation II	
Amount or kind of recommended practice	3	39	3	8	0	3	59	38	90
Need for immediate income	0	9	7	25	6	1	9	47	70
Insufficient roughage consuming livestock	0	0	0	0	0	1	15	49	51
Failure to see the need for recommended practice	12	31	9	16	1	18	0	0	47
Custom and inertia	6	14	3	10	0	1	18	10	33
Rental arrangement and lack of landowner's cooperation	2	16	4	6	2	1	4	10	25
Field and road layout	10	5	0	0	0	13	2	2	22
Lack of adequate machinery and power	5	10	0	0	0	0	1	3	17
Short expectancy of tenure	3	5	3	10	3	5	3	3	12
Lack of cooperation of neighboring farmers	0	1	10	0	1	0	0	0	12
Terrace design	0	10	0	0	0	0	0	0	10
Small size of farm	0	1	0	0	0	0	3	9	10
Lack of adequate labor supply	0	1	0	0	0	3	1	3	8
Risk and uncertainty	0	1	0	3	0	0	0	5	8
Lack of adequate buildings	0	0	0	0	0	0	0	4	4
Inability to shift erosion loss	1	0	0	0	0	0	0	0	1

[7] The cost estimate excluded that part of the costs which would be covered by incentive payments from the Agricultural Conservation Program if the operator were a cooperator.

not increase the value of their farms. This belief was confirmed by analysis by multiple linear regression of the relationships between changes in land values and changes in soil loss from 1949 to 1957. For a subsample of farms, the regression coefficient indicated that changes in erosion did not explain statistically significant amount of change in land values.

TABLE 4

NUMBER OF OPERATORS WHO ESTIMATED SPECIFIED PERCENTAGE CHANGES IN GROSS RETURNS TO THEIR FARMS FROM THE ADOPTION OF PLAN I, 138 SAMPLE FARMS IN WESTERN IOWA, 1957

PERCENTAGE CHANGE IN GROSS RETURNS	NUMBER OF OPERATORS ESTIMATING SPECIFIED PERCENTAGE CHANGE IN INCOME AFTER		
	1 Year	5 Years	10 Years
Minus or none	71	32	28
1 to 33 per cent increase	28	59	54
34 to 66 per cent increase	4	10	16
67 per cent increase and over	0	2	4
No estimate given	35	35	36

FAILURE TO SEE THE NEED FOR A PRACTICE—CUSTOM AND INERTIA

Because of the similarity of the obstacles of failure to see the need for an erosion control practice and of custom and inertia, the two were combined as one obstacle. Operators' responses to this obstacle were not as explicit as they were to others. They included such statements as: contouring not needed, terraces too difficult to farm, waterways and commercial fertilizer not needed, and contour fencing not wanted. Some operators said they just did not want to change their established methods of farming.

FIELD AND ROAD LAYOUT

Because of the difficulties of farming rectangular fields on the contour, the importance of field and road layout as an obstacle seemed to increase with recommendations for more contouring and terracing in the area. Many farm operators said they would adopt terraces if they could be laid out in parallel fashion.

OTHER OBSTACLES

Several other obstacles, although not statistically significant, were important because they were interrelated with obstacles that were significant. To the question of whether amount or kind of a recommended practice was an obstacle, typical responses included objection to the number of terraces, too much corn or corn several years in succession in rotations in the mechanical practice plans, or lack of enough corn in the high forage rotation plans. Reasons given for such responses were that: (1) the operator did not share the public goal of reducing soil loss to 5 tons an acre, (2) he would have approved an intermediate erosion control plan rather than either of the extreme plans presented to him, or (3) more erosion practices were recommended in his plan than he thought were necessary to reduce erosion to the 5-ton goal. Evidence indicated that, in many instances, the latter judgment was correct.

TABLE 5

NUMBER OF OPERATORS WHO ESTIMATED SPECIFIED PERCENTAGE CHANGES IN GROSS RETURNS TO THEIR FARMS FROM THE ADOPTION OF PLAN II, 138 SAMPLE FARMS IN WESTERN IOWA, 1957

PERCENTAGE CHANGE IN GROSS RETURNS	NUMBER OF OPERATORS ESTIMATING SPECIFIED PERCENTAGE CHANGE IN INCOME AFTER		
	1 Year	5 Years	10 Years
Minus or none	82	66	63
1 to 33 per cent increase	15	31	30
34 to 66 per cent increase	3	3	6
67 per cent increase and over	1	1	1
No estimate given	37	37	38

Two other important obstacles were lack

of sufficient roughage-consuming livestock, and rental arrangement combined with lack of landowner's cooperation. The former obstacle was closely related to the need for immediate income, and often included dislike for the kinds of livestock necessary to utilize the forage produced in the erosion control plans. The landowner's failure to cooperate resulted either from his need for immediate income, his lack of interest in the farm, or his expectancy of owning the farm for a short time.

Characteristics of Farm Operators and Their Farms

In addition to the obstacles mentioned by the operators, relationships between characteristics of their business and soil erosion were analyzed. It was found that soil losses were significantly lower on farms on which the operators participated in soil conservation districts and higher where they did not participate. Also, soil erosion was lower on farms on which the operators recognized the seriousness of the erosion problem. More soil was conserved on farms on which the operator worked at some nonfarm job, thus relieving the pressure for immediate income. Soil losses were higher on farms with large natural erosion hazards than on those without this problem. Finally, soil losses were significantly lower on farms on which the operators were willing and able to borrow funds to install erosion control practices.

Obstacles of Non-operating Landowners

The earlier inquiries by Frey and Held indicated that the lack of landowners' cooperation was an obstacle preventing the adoption of erosion control practices on some tenant-operated farms. In reality, obstacles named by tenants and by non-operating landowners function simultaneously to prevent the adoption of erosion control practices. Therefore, non-operating landowners (owners of tenant-operated farms) in the sample were interviewed in 1957. The procedure for obtaining and analyzing the data was similar to that used for the farm operators.

The obstacles given by non-operating landowners were similar to those mentioned by the farm operators. The most frequently occurring obstacles were (1) amount or kind of recommended practice, (2) need for immediate income, (3) failure to see the need for a recommended practice, and (4) insufficient roughage-consuming livestock. The second and fourth obstacles (closely related to soil loss in a statistical sense) were most frequently given.

Characteristics of Tenant-operated Farms and Landlords

The regression of several characteristics on soil loss explained a significant amount of variation in soil losses on tenant-operated farms. The independent variables with statistically significant regression coefficients were (1) acres of additional land owned, (2) expectancy of continued ownership of the farm, (3) need of owner to borrow funds for erosion practices, and (4) operator's need for immediate income. These characteristics were considered to be the most closely related to soil losses through, or in addition to, owners' and operators' obstacles.

Landlords who were certain of owning the farm 1 year after date of interview had lower soil losses. Soil losses tended to be lower on farms owned by individuals who had additional farms. They tended to be high on farms whose owners needed to borrow funds to install erosion control practices and whose tenants named as an obstacle the need for immediate income.

Possible Remedies

As a result of this series of studies, we suggest several possible approaches for overcoming obtacles to erosion control. Three alternative courses of action—education, additional research, and direct public action—were considered in developing these suggestions.

EDUCATION AND RESEARCH

Additional education about the seriousness of the erosion problem, directed particularly toward nonoperating landowners, is needed to overcome custom, inertia and failure to see the need for erosion control practices. To increase farm operators' and landlords' knowledge of the profitability of erosion control practices, a more broadly directed educational program should stress the costs and returns associated with these practices. With a better basis for appraisal of the profitability of conservation practices, fewer farmers might have been concerned about reduction in immediate income. In addition, the importance of this obstacle would be lessened by dissemination of information concerning the advantages and methods of including the costs of erosion control practices in long-term loans.

Educational programs directed particularly toward owners and operators of tenant-operated farms should emphasize the profitability of livestock, crop-livestock share leases, and methods of incorporating compensation clauses in leases.

Information is needed about methods, appraisal and purchasing arrangements for transfer of small tracts of land that could be farmed on the contour more easily by neighboring farmers than by present owners. Also, educational activities constitute a prerequisite for revision of real estate tax rates to correspond with land capability.

Expanded Extension Service and soil conservation district programs could facilitate these educational efforts. Farm operators indicated that one of the most acceptable methods of receiving such information was through neighboring farmers who are community leaders.

EXTENDED FARM PLANNING AND RESEARCH NEEDS

The objections to the choice and amount of a recommended practice indicated that additional effort should be made to make erosion control plans more acceptable to farmers. This could be done by making them more comprehensive—economic as well as physical considerations are essential. The need for revision of plans for the sample farms and the desire of many operators to adopt practices slowly over a long period of time showed that farm plans need to be flexible and dynamic.

The accuracy, completeness, and low cost of budgeting with electronic computers recommend it as a possible method of enlarging the amount of soil erosion control farm planning. A successful computational service for farm planning might require personnel in action agencies to work with farm operators in obtaining the necessary data and interpreting the results. If required data were made available, the capacity of electronic computers to handle large volumes of data would make possible the revision of farm plans as the need arose.

FURTHER RESEARCH NEEDS

Further research analysis is needed to develop an estimate of future land use by areas in the United States to serve as a guide in determining the total amount of soil erosion control needed, as well as the particular practices that would be consistent with the economic advantage of each area. The growth of surpluses and the need for immediate income indicate that this information is needed by public agencies and individual farmers as a focal point in making long-range plans.

Federal agricultural programs such as price supports and the soil bank also need to be analyzed with respect to their expected effects over time on erosion control.

Before educational programs that relate to the profitability of erosion control practices can proceed far, additional and better information about costs and returns of erosion control practices will be needed.

The obstacles of field and road layout suggested that further research is necessary to determine methods of modifying some erosion control practices. Farm operators frequently stated that terraces would be acceptable if they were laid out in parallel fashion. Research concerning the physical possibility and economic feasibility of parallel terracing and cut-and-fill terraces may provide information for educational programs that will help to overcome this obstacle. An inquiry into the economics of land-forming practices, currently in process, will provide some insight into this problem.

Emphasis is needed on the effects of erosion control practices on land prices. Findings of this series of studies about obstacles to erosion control in western Iowa indicate that obstacles change over time. Consequently, continuing analysis of problems and development of remedies for the obstacles will be needed in the future.

OTHER PUBLIC ACTION

Additional research, particularly that concerned with estimating costs and returns of erosion control practices, may reveal that individual landowner's interest in erosion control falls short of public interests to such an extent as to warrant an increase in or revision of incentive payments for some eroson control practices. Incentive payments seem justified only for those practices which are in the public interest but are not profitable to individual farmers. For instance, incentive payments appear to be justified as part of the remedy for the obstacle of field and road layout. In 1957, the Crawford County Agricultural Conservation Program made incentive payments for changing fences to conform to the contour. Facilitation of erosion control and the inadequacy of economic incentives for individuals to undertake the practice justified this use of federal funds.

The Conservation Reserve Program facilitated continuous forage production on many farms between 1957 and the program's termination in 1960. A more permanent shift in the use of land might be obtained through land use easements. Under a land use easement program, landowners would have the opportunity to sell to the federal government their rights to produce specified crops. In areas with great erosion hazards like those in the Ida-Monona Soil Association the government might purchase the rights to produce all except forage crops. Such a program would facilitate both control of soil erosion and control of production of surplus crops.

We abuse land because we regard it as a commodity belonging to us. When we see land as a community to which we belong, we may begin to use it with love and respect.

ALDO LEOPOLD, *A Sand County Almanac* (New York: Oxford University Press, 1949).

L. SCHUYLER FONAROFF

CONSERVATION AND STOCK REDUCTION ON THE NAVAJO TRIBAL RANGE

The Navajo country in northeastern Arizona, 92 per cent of which is desert and steppe, is an area in delicate physical balance. As in many other semiarid areas of the world, a few tenths of an inch of precipitation can vastly change the appearance of the land. Within this setting are placed an enormous livestock load and a dense Indian population. The repercussions of such a situation are generally destructive both to the land and to the people. This paper analyzes the livestock-reduction program instituted by the government in the 1930's as a conservation measure, with reference to some of the human problems incurred.

The Soil-Erosion Menace

The Navajo Reservation does not give the impression of a land of abundance. The arroyos that dissect a large part of the Colorado Plateau, to depths as great as 50–100 feet, have reduced much of the range to a critically low level of forage production, and in many places to barrenness.

Despite the fact that the Navajo tribal range showed definite signs of overgrazing as early as 1893, it was not until the late 1920's that any specific plan of attack was formulated to head off what had come to be recognized as impending disaster. By this time the range was being denuded at an appalling rate, and the sedimentation along the Colorado River watershed, as revealed by the Boulder Dam engineering survey, suddenly received nationwide attention. The situation was no longer a local Indian matter but had become a problem in the effort to conserve natural resources on a national scale. Until then, administration of the Navajo Reservation had been more or less routine or casual, performed with a paternalistic laissez-faire attitude.

By 1928 the tribal range was stocked with not quite 2 million sheep units.[1] The physical destruction of the land had reached the critical point, and some definite effort had to be made before physical and economic deterioration overcame the people. Soil erosion was progressing at such a rapid rate that even the Navajo goat, accustomed to sparse range, had to move continually to higher hillsides. Unless something was done, and soon, all but the tribe were convinced that within a few decades the Navajo range would resemble the Painted Desert.

The vigorous nationwide conservation movement of the early decades of the twentieth century was inadequately organized, and on the reservation its leadership was almost nonexistent. The public quickly lapsed into relative indifference, and the warnings of Malthus, Muir, Pinchot, and others were soon forgotten. In contrast with the Roosevelt and Coolidge-Hoover administrations, which had championed re-

• L. Schuyler Fonaroff is Assistant Professor of Geography at San Fernando Valley State College.

Reprinted from *Geographical Review,* LIII, No. 2 (1963), 200–23, with permission of the author and the editor.

[1] Reservation range carrying capacities are stated in "sheep units": five sheep equal one horse; four sheep equal one cow; one sheep equals one goat.

spectively forest conservation and petroleum conservation, the New Deal program was focused on soil conservation, and the Boulder Dam emergency survey dramatized the Navajo Reservation sedimentation menace, which, it was asserted, would shorten the life of the dam. To head off this situation, the ultimate objectives of the reservation survey were ambitiously oriented toward (1) checking destructive erosion and conserving the water supply; (2) regulating the use of forest and range cover with a view to restoring the climax type vegetation in each environment; (3) promoting the best practicable use of agriculture, forestry, and other phases of land management and, in cooperation with the Indian Service, integrating land use with the other arts, occupations, and problems of the Navajo people . . . ; (4) furnishing to the Indians, so far as consistent with the program, profitable employment and useful training in land management.[2]

This type of pressure helped revitalize the fight against range depletion and eventual economic collapse. Hugh Bennett and, later, Fairfield Osborn, William Vogt, and others preached conservation, and the movement caught on with farmers, legislators, and the public at large.

By 1930 the Navajo were spilling over into neighboring off-reservation communities in four states. Population increase, diminishing land use instead of land enlargement, and lower per capita income appeared as specters on the Navajo horizon. The number of livestock owned was greater than at any other period since 1900,[3] but the Navajo was no longer able to wander indiscriminately across the desert with his flocks.

In 1930, William H. Zeh, an Indian Service forester, submitted to a Senate subcommittee a general report on the grazing situation among the Navajo in Arizona and New Mexico.[4] Zeh was concerned with such subjects as water development, proper stocking rates, improved grazing control, and educational programs. Recognizing the seriousness of the situation, he proposed two types of remedial measures: those which would provide results in a comparatively short time (water development, rodent control, and so on), and those which would not show rapid results but were nevertheless of great importance (for example, education in proper livestock handling techniques).

In 1933 the Soil Erosion Service was organized through the recommendations of the Soil Conservation Advisory Committee. A committee of specialists was formed to examine the Navajo range problems, which eventually would be administered cooperatively by the Departments of the Interior and Agriculture. What was obviously needed was a complete program of conservation, oriented, as Ciriacy-Wantrup[5] would put it, toward a "redistribution of use . . . in the direction of the future." The Navajo range has always been natively used in the "direction of the present."

The chairmanship of the committee was given to H. H. Bennett. His committee reported, in part:[6]

> This committee finds that . . . the greater part of the land has undergone exceedingly serious erosion . . . it is perfectly obvious that the present rate of unrestrained soil washing cannot be permitted to proceed much further. This land of the Navajos, which as with all people, is the life-blood of those who live on it, is threatened. If something is not done to stop the losses a great deal of suffering is in store for the people of the Reservation,

[2] Reservation records, Navaho Service.

[3] George A. Boyce and E. R. Fryer, *Dineh and Government in Kaibeto District* (Washington: U.S., Dept. of Interior, 1939), p. 1.

[4] William H. Zeh, "General Report Covering the Grazing Situation on the Navaho Indian Reservation," in *Survey of Conditions of the Indians in the United States: Hearings before Subcommittee of Senate Comm. on Indian Affairs,* 71st Cong., pt. 18 (1932), pp. 9121–32.

[5] S. V. Ciriacy-Wantrup, *Resource Conservation: Economics and Policies* (Berkeley and Los Angeles: University of California Press, 1952), p. 51.

[6] H. H. Bennett, Statement Presented to Navajo Tribal Council Meeting, June 7, 1933, Fort Wingate, Arizona (Tribal Council Records).

suffering that cannot be withstood. . . . Being convinced that the very life of the Navajo Nation is at stake because of this evil, the Committee recommends that there be started without further delay, and before it is too late, the development of sound plans for controlling the widespread wastage now stealing the substance of the land . . . it is the belief of the Committee that an Erosion Control Station should be set up and conducted by experienced men with the help of the Navajo people themselves for the purposes of meeting this challenge of a rapidly wasting country.

The drought of the early thirties complicated the problem and brought the reservation to the brink of catastrophe. The Soil Erosion specialists prepared "A Unified Program for the Navajo Indian Reservation," which in essence was a recommendation to reduce the some 1 million sheep units on the reservation by about 50 per cent. The Navajo themselves, ironically, were only dimly aware that something was wrong. Life on the reservation continued to flow smoothly; enlarging arroyos, shorter grass, and the greater intensity of use to which the land was being subjected were merely incidental matters. These Indians do not hold to our own cause-and-effect relationship for range depletion.[7] Many Indians believe that the rains come from God to make the grass grow, and the Navajo were inclined to trust that nature would in time readjust the ecological balance.

Boyce and Fryer[8] assessed the plight of the tribe during the thirties and enumerated the important questions to which the government sought solutions:

In terms of their resources, could the Navajos long anticipate being self-supporting? On what plane of living? To what extent might increased efficiency raise the economic level? In what ways were cultural practices of the Navajos affecting adjoining white lands and economy and vice versa? What adjustments were necessary to maintain a balanced set of socioeconomic relationships both internally and externally? To what extent might necessary adjustments involve a major change in the cultural patterns?

Demonstration Areas

The Bennett report was presented to the Tribal Council on June 8, 1933. The Council reacted by permitting the establishment of an Erosion Control Station at Mexican Springs. At the Council meeting of November 1, 1933, the Commissioner of Indian Affairs, John Collier, spoke of the large expenditure of federal funds, amounting to $1,250,000, that was earmarked for this demonstration area for the next two years. It was estimated that at least $800,000 would go to the Navajo in wages.

The stated purpose of the demonstration-area program was "to serve as a proving ground to the Indians and ourselves; that by proper range and stock management, the income from livestock will be materially increased as a result of their adjustment to the carrying capacity of the range."[9] A total of 129,143 acres, with a yearlong carrying capacity of 4,456 sheep units, was set aside in seven demonstration areas. A report that summarized the outcome of the program stated that it was reasonable to expect Indian stockmen to get results comparable with those of commercial (non-Indian) operators, and that the Navajo rangelands were potentially equal to any others in the Southwest. All that was needed was proper stocking, proper animal husbandry, and improved stock, and "if the demonstration area results can be taken as criterion, the total income from the rangelands, grazed on a sustained yield basis, will actually increase."[10]

The Indians, however, were not receptive to the idea of adopting techniques that the government used successfully on the demonstration areas. For one thing, it is difficult to make a Navajo think in the

7 Boyce and Fryer, *op. cit.*

8 *Ibid.*

9 "Navajo Indian Problem" (New York: Phelps-Stokes Fund, 1939), pp. 32 ff.

10 *Ibid.*

future, particularly beyond one year.[11] If a demonstration cannot be completed within a relatively short period, the results hold little meaning for most Navajo. But the conservationists and range ecologists of the Navajo Service could not produce results within a short period; their results of necessity came from long-range plans. Moreover, demonstration-area techniques were based on a premise of cause and effect: if the carrying capacity was adhered to and recommended grazing techniques were practiced, better stock and better land would result. The Navajo, however, did not believe overstocking and overgrazing caused erosion and range depletion. Their concept of cause and effect was what the philosopher Ladd terms "temporally remote"; that is, *current* situations are not the result of something that is presently occurring but, rather, of something that has already occurred.[12] Gullies were believed to have existed for several generations and were the result of some disharmony between man and nature. Removing excess stock, introducing new range plants, or herding flocks in another fashion would have no influence on the face of the land.

The tribal members were convinced easily enough of the benefits from wage work. But to the surprise of the Service, they insisted on an *increase* in livestock. It was not at all clear to the Navajo that wage work could be depended on to furnish a living; in their estimation, herding was more dependable. "Each sheep," they said, "has many within." Most of the Navajo had never earned wages before and believed a large flock would be insurance in emergency.

The dissension that followed the government's proposal must have come as an unbelievable shock to the Indian Service, which did not realize to what extent the Navajo were dependent on their livestock.

The October and November sessions of 1933 were also significant. At the Tuba City meeting of the Council, Commissioner Collier inaugurated the New Deal program for the Navajo. This comprehensive plan for economic rehabilitation and resource conservation included the first definite proposal for stock reduction. This stock "adjustment" (the preferred but seldom-used term) was to consist of a reduction by 100,000 head of sheep.

At this time the average Navajo herding family was estimated to own about 150 sheep, 60 goats, and 10 horses, and reduction would push it to bare subsistence. At first an across-the-board reduction was recommended to reduce all herds, regardless of size, to a stated number. This was quickly recognized as harmful; large owners needed only to cull their herds, but small owners would often be forced to reduce productive stock. Clearly seeing the inevitable consequences, the Indian Service decided to institute the reduction program on a "sliding scale," with the large owners bearing the major part of the burden and the smaller owners reducing little or no livestick. As it turned out, the large owners balked and merely culled their herds of unproductive stock. Needless to say, the program was a failure.

The Indian Reorganization Act

This was apparently the beginning of a new feeling of antagonism toward the federal government. To judge by what was to

[11] Walter Dyk (recorder), *Son of Old Man Hat: A Navaho Autobiography* (New York: Harcourt Brace & Co., 1938). Left Handed [Navaho Indian]: "About the year, my folks would say 'This year,' or 'Next year,' but I couldn't discover what they meant. I used to wonder what it meant, when they said, 'A year,' or 'Two years,' and sometimes, 'Many years.' I wondered what a year was, and where it was. I used to think, It must be around here. But I couldn't see it. I always thought that a year must have arms and legs and a head. It must have a body like an animal. I used to wish that I could see it when it comes around again. But I never saw the year. . . . I used to wish to see a month. I was wondering what it looked like. . . . I thought it was something that moved or walked about," p. 43.

[12] John Ladd, *Structure of a Moral Code: A Philosophical Analysis of Ethical Discourses Applied to the Ethics of the Navaho Indians* (Cambridge: Harvard University Press, 1957), p. 20.

follow, for both parties the honeymoon was definitely over. As Kluckhohn and Leighton[13] observed: "Without adequate preparation along the lines of emotional reorientation and education, the government has tried to alter the whole technological basis of Navaho society in a few years time."

When the Navajo were released from federal imprisonment in 1868 and returned to their homeland, the government issued 15,000 head of sheep to them and encouraged the accumulation of livestock. The reduction program therefore came as a grave reversal, and one that they could not comprehend. The ensuing distrust and misunderstanding were to prevent any successful adjustment on the part of the tribe, or even a mutual understanding of the problem. So strong was the feeling of the Navajo against stock adjustment that it acted as a block against their examining the ramifications of the New Deal proposals. These proposals culminated in the Indian Reorganization Act of 1934 (Wheeler-Howard Act).

The Indian Reorganization Act (IRA) was planned to terminate the General Allotment Act of 1887 (Dawes Act), the primary objective of which had been to change the cultural habits of the Indians. Under this act each adult was to be allotted a parcel of land for his own, on which he would learn to earn a living as a farmer. Intertribal differences were overlooked, and the fact that many Indians were neither agricultural-minded nor living on land suitable for farming was also ignored. Indian life was considered barbaric, and the task was to transform Indian traits "into industry . . . and Christianity."[14]

> Interesting as are many of the ancient customs of the North American Indians . . . , and picturesque as the savage life may seem to be in the pages of the romantic writers, all who study the Indian problem at first hand and note the effect upon the morals of Indian people of the recent revival of praise for their old customs . . . realize the bad effect upon the Indian people of this attempt to make them face backwards and step out of the line of education and progress. We trust that the necessary and most interesting work of ethnologists may be so conducted as not to emphasize these reactionary tendencies. Only education and the teaching of Christian morals can fit these native-born Americans for American citizenship.[15]

Under the General Allotment Act, by 1933 the Indians had lost to white men 90 million acres of land and the *use* of additional acres.[16] The privilege of selling land was taken advantage of by many Indians who were either frustrated by not knowing how to use their allotted plots or uninterested in learning to pursue an agricultural livelihood.

The IRA was intended to help orient the Indian to white ideas while still preserving his native customs. Certain changes were to be effected in Indian society, other changes were to be controlled. The creators of the act were aware that there were differences between Indian societies. They recognized the need to preserve and encourage native social controls and values upon which to improvise change. They further recognized that the continuity and security both of the group and of the individual had to be preserved for stability to exist, that "change" in itself was not enough, and that for constructive change there must be a transition period within which initiative and interest must be developed.

Each tribe was given the prerogative to accept or reject the act. A series of regional meetings was held to explain the plan to the tribes, a phase in Indian-government relations that Collier termed "bilateral,

[13] Clyde Kluckhohn and Dorothea C. Leighton, *The Navaho* (Cambridge: Harvard University Press, 1946), p. 35.

[14] *Ann. Rept. Commissioner of Indian Affairs for the Year 1887* (Washington, 1887), p. vi.

[15] *Ann. Rept. Board of Indian Commissioners for . . . 1903* (Washington, 1904), p. 19.

[16] John Collier, *The Indians of the Americas* (New York: W. W. Norton, 1947), p. 227.

mutually consenting, contractual."[17] Two-thirds of the Indians in the country accepted the IRA. The Navajo did not. Their fear of herd reduction was always present, and Section Six of the act directed the Secretary of the Interior to restrict the number of livestock grazed on Indian range units to the estimated carrying capacity of the range, to protect ranges against overgrazing, to prevent soil erosion, and to insure full utilization of range units.[18]

Coupled with the fear of reduction were opposition to the newly established central agency at Window Rock and distrust of promises made by Collier regarding wage work and irrigated-land extension, and of the school programs. Too many speakers from Washington and too many meetings caused confusion. There was a lack of confidence in the Commissioner of Indian Affairs and a feeling that he was putting something over on them.[19] And there was undoubtedly a basic lack of understanding concerning the IRA.[20]

The misunderstandings and the pressure for a prompt vote made impossible the deliberation that was customary and important to the Navajo and influenced them toward rejection. But despite their rejection of the IRA, the Navajo do benefit from certain of its provisions, though many Navajo are still bitter about "having IRA benefits when we never voted for them."

Post-IRA Events and Consequences

Collier's reaction to their rejection was considered intolerant by the Navajo. They were informed that the administration had no intention of altering its policies regarding reduction. Termination of the General Allotment Act brought with it termination of land allotments. The Navajo were given self-rule through Tribal Council government, credit programs, and other developments similar to those in tribes voting to accept the IRA.[21]

During the Tribal Council meeting at Crown Point, April 9–11, 1934, a resolution was passed in which the Navajo did agree to sell 150,000 goats, the means of the sale to be worked out in Washington. The Council also agreed to sell 50,000 sheep, to castrate all billy goats, and to sell 80 per cent of the following year's lamb crop.[22]

17 William Zimmerman, Jr., "The Role of the Bureau of Indian Affairs since 1933," *Annals of the American Academy of Political and Social Sciences,* CCXI (1957), 32. Collier's successors have been oblivious to "consent," and the Commissioner in 1956 stated that ". . . consent is 'insidious' and too costly," *ibid.* Zimmerman, who was Asst. Commissioner from 1933 to 1950, observed that "one of the basic disagreements between Indians and administrators [is] the difference between letting the Indians make decisions and having the bureaucrats, no matter how sympathetic they may be, decide what is best for the Indians," *ibid.*, p. 33.

18 Collier, "Analysis of Wheeler-Howard Act" (manuscript, n.d.), pp. 2–3.

19 "Wheeler-Howard Act," *Indian Truth,* XII (1935), 6.

20 L. Schuyler Fonaroff, "Navajo Attitudes and the Indian Reorganization Act: A New Document," *Plateau,* XXXIV (1961–62), 97–100.

21 The strong friction between the tribe and the government led to the loss of the following provisions incorporated in the IRA: continuance of existing periods of trust on Indian lands, and of restrictions on alienation; authorization to the Secretary of the Interior to restore to tribal ownership surplus lands for sale; sale or other transfer of restricted Indian lands or shares in assets forbidden except to the tribe concerned or to heirs of its members; authorization to the Secretary of the Interior to purchase or otherwise acquire water rights; establishment of tribal charters of incorporation; establishment of a revolving credit fund for economic development and educational allotment; preference in employment for qualified Indians in the Indian Service; permission for legal counsel for each tribe (William H. Kelly, *Indians of the Southwest: A Survey of Indian Tribes and Indian Administration in Arizona,* First Ann. Report, Bur. of Ethnic Research [Tucson: University of Arizona, 1953], pp. 106–107). However, the Navaho-Hopi Rehabilitation Act, passed in 1950, authorized adoption of a tribal constitution and bylaws and provided further benefits similar to those of the IRA, including economic and educational rehabilitation.

22 According to range ecologists, grazing goats and sheep together usually results in poor manage-

Sheep and goat sales were reluctantly made; and the other agreements were unsuccessful. Very few billy goats were castrated. An immediate review of the castration problem pointed up the fact that the destruction of the Navajo goat could disastrously unbalance the native economy. To many Navajo, goats were probably the sole source of milk. Goat meat, along with mutton, is still a preferred native food today, and goat's milk is drunk by both adults and children. The Indian Service compromised. They proposed a sectionalized castration program in concurrence with efforts to develop a milk-goat strain for Indian use, to be accomplished through maintenance of milk-strain bucks for breeding at various government centers.

The lamb sale was a complete failure. The tribe's excuse was lack of a market. To combat the almost nonexistent commercial outlet, the Service proposed to establish a federal fund sufficient to acquire the unsalable lamb surplus. It was predicted that $1.50 a head would move the estimated surplus of 250,000 sheep and goats in 1935, and the estimated 150,000 surplus stock in 1936.

By the end of 1934, the lack of rapport between agency and Indian was summarized as follows:[23]

> There is still the problem of convincing the mass of the Navajo that stock reduction is in their interest, that the weight of the reduction will fall on the larger owners, and that those deprived of subsistence will be given opportunity to earn a living until such time when the revegetated range can carry large flocks again. Field workers were advised to try to make the Navajo understand that they are not doing the government a favor by reducing their stock, but rather themselves. . . .

Furthermore, the Navajo were obsessed by their basic practice of accumulating wealth in the form of livestock. Just because an animal had no value on the market owing to poor weight or general condition did not mean that it was a cull. They were appalled by one method of reduction that called for field men to shoot thousands of goats, which were then left to die in heaps in Navajo Canyon. It was estimated that on one occasion 3,500 animals were shot.[24] Hundreds of goats and sheep were slaughtered before the eyes of their owners, the carcasses left to decay where they fell. To the Navajo, this was a barbaric and inexcusable waste; the fact that the animals were in excess had no meaning to them.

The government proposed three programs to assist in the transition period: (1) a minimum two-year work-relief program to provide wages to make up for reduced stock income; (2) direct relief for unemployable ex-sheepmen (the relief program also made use of inferior stock as meat for the destitute); and (3) a purchase fund large enough to acquire the excess sheep not disposed of commercially, the funds to be used for relief.

In the purchasing program the government faced a problem. Many Navajo lambs, as a result of deteriorated range, were underweight and were classed as unmarketable. The buyers would take the cream of the crop, and the rest were thrust back on the reservation. The Collier administration therefore began attempts to appropriate reimbursable tribal funds to bring lambs to the minimum sales weight. For old or poor stock, Senate funds were appropriated to establish a small packing plant to manufacture dogfood. A cannery

ment for both sheep and range. Goats tend more than sheep to rely on browse and are at home in country that abounds in live oak, oceanothus, cat's-claw, and the like. Little of this kind of browse is found on the reservation (Robert V. Boyle, *Range Management and Policy Statement,* Soil Conservation Service, Navaho Proj. [Washington: U.S., Dept. of Agriculture, 1935], p. 6), and the pine, juniper, and piñon stands suffer when range is overstocked and forage is meager.

[23] General staff meeting, Comm. on Reduction, Washington, Nov. 6, 1934.

[24] U.S., Congress, *Survey of Conditions of the Indians of the United States,* Senate Doc. Y4, 2-2, pt. 34, 75th Cong., 1st Sess., 1937, pp. 17, 988.

was constructed at Many Farms at considerable expense, but it closed after a short period because of the unwillingness of the Navajo to supply cull stock.

There was in addition an adverse sociological effect. The small owner was more prone to sell his stock than the large owner. The small owner was in want, and it was he who had the most stock taken away. The dipping records do not show this trend; rather, they indicate a widely scattered small ownership, which may have been the result of the large owners' distributing their stock to family members. Those who had few sheep soon had none. Those who had many sheep continued to acquire more. The range problem remained unchanged.

The reduction program did not aim to deprive the Navajo of a livestock livelihood. The plan was to change the composition of the flock and to provide a more diversified means of making a living. The Secretary of the Interior and the Indian Service were acting on the assumption that it would be desirable from the Navajo point of view to diversify; they seemed unaware that for the Navajo this meant a venture into the unknown. Even though the potential for increased individual productivity was implicit in the livestock adjustment program, many Navajo viewed the change with fear. They could not be convinced that wage work and other income sources could afford them the intangible benefits that livestock management offered—security of property and freedom of mobility.

The Sliding-Scale Approach

To the Indian Service the sliding-scale approach to reduction appeared to be just; the burden was to be placed where it would be most easily borne. The larger stockmen, however, sensing the situation, outmaneuvered the government, and the problem of reducing the large herds remained unsolved. Small stockmen saw the results of resisting the government and realized that the large operators, now antigovernment in sentiment and actions, were much better off. The smaller owners were forced into submission. They even at times, from ignorance, confusion, and fear, sold below their required quotas. Government records show instances where families owning only twelve head of sheep were forced to reduce to seven.[25]

Many Navajo recalled the promise of work if they reduced their flocks. Small stockmen, on occasion, sold sheep and goats for $1–2 a head. Some were still unable to get work, others received jobs that lasted less than two months. Acting Administrator William Zeh assessed the situation briefly thus:[26] "It is necessary . . . to keep in mind the fact that to date the Navajo tribe as a whole (1) is not sold on the idea of stock reduction, (2) is not sold on the idea of day schools, (3) is not . . . sold on the Indian Reorganization Act, and (4) is not sold on the Soil Erosion Service and its programs."

It was now obvious that the prime objectives of the Collier program, "human adjustment and land rehabilitation," were not being achieved according to schedule. However, of the two there seemed to be much greater progress in land rehabilitation. Land-management plans were outlined by the Soil Erosion Service; they included floodwater spreading, irrigation, erosion control, and farm development. The 11,000 acres of irrigated land (1935) were to be increased to 37,750. Forestry policies were formulated to conserve timber resources by strict cutting regulations, establishment of community forests and sawmills, management of logging, restriction of livestock in areas recently cut over, protection from overcutting and fire, introduction of game that would not damage the land, and training of Indians to handle conservation of the forest and range. Extension work was proposed to "improve the economic status of the Indian people by furnishing them with the kind of information, advice

[25] *Ibid.*, pp. 17, 449.

[26] Memorandum to John Collier, Jan. 26, 1935.

and constructive help which will enable them, through their own efforts, to conserve and develop their resources and thereby secure more adequate food supply, better homes and a higher standard of living."[27]

Nevertheless, stock adjustment became the prime concern of the Soil Erosion Service and the backbone of its attempts to decelerate erosion and revitalize the range. By 1935 sheep reduction to a little less than half a million head was the next step in the Navajo program. The burden was once again planned for the areas where it could be borne, and once again the program was administered by the sliding-scale method. The plan called for establishment of a base grazing preference or an ownership right for each livestock owner (individual or family) based on average dipping records for mature animals for the 5-year period 1929–34.[28] The dipping records were grossly inaccurate, but this fact was not to be a deterrent to the program. Commissioner Collier tried to explain before a Senate subcommittee the disparity between the dipping records, which showed ownership increase, and concurrent reduction of livestock numbers. He quoted a Navajo stockowner who "reduced" his herd from 1,400 to 200:

> I distributed as follows: 300 head of sheep to my boy . . . 200 sheep to my daughter . . . 300 head of sheep to another daughter; and 330 to another daughter that became of age also. I have distributed my sheep to my family. During the reduction I sold 40 head voluntarily, but the snow took many, in the year 1933, 100 head of sheep. So, the snow helped to reduce my herd down to the 200. I have at the present time 200 head of sheep.[29]

By this time the administrators were beginning to realize that ideally problems should be solved at the local level. Ryan's statement to Collier called for "a grazing reconnaissance and range management plan for the entire reservation . . . to be completed as rapidly as possible in order that beginning with 1936, the reduction program can be based upon local conditions and ownership."[30] However, at that time, drastic reduction had been occurring throughout the reservation since 1933.

Rapid action to stem the tide of silt was once again declared the program's prime objective, lest the reservation be washed into the Colorado River. The 1935 grazing problem was stated in sharp terms by Robert Marshall, the grazing and forestry director, to Collier. Marshall asserted that the prevailing program was a "wishful and prayerful attempt to improve the situation." He also stated that if silting continued:

> 1. The Navajo Reservation will be wrecked for centuries.
>
> 2. Most of the 50,000 Navajos will become in effect landless and will have to depend for a livelihood on a government dole.
>
> 3. Mead Lake will be silted and the Boulder Dam project damaged to the extent of many million dollars more than it would cost to buy up the entire . . . excess Navajo sheep units, even if you paid five times their market value.
>
> 4. All your enemies will howl like hell and Congress will make a nasty investigation of why you permitted the Navajos to destroy their own civilization.
>
> Unless you meet the hard necessity of taking drastic action, all of our conservation talk is merely hypocritical chatter, and the Navajo Reservation will be ruined.[31]

The constant emphasis on the immediacy of action was not unlike that in most "emergency" conservation movements of the preceding decades. There is little wonder that the tribe was confused. Aside from the frontal assault on the reduction prob-

27 Dr. Ryan's memorandum to John Collier, Apr. 18, 1935.

28 The base-preference number was the number of sheep units each owner could have, provided the carrying capacity was equally divided among them.

29 Statement presented by John Collier before Senate Comm. (ms., n.d., in Navaho File, National Archives, Washington).

30 Ryan, *op. cit.*

31 Robert Marshall, Memorandum to J. Collier, May 22, 1936 (Navaho File, National Archives).

lem, of the sanity of which the Navajo were never convinced, there seemed to be endless confusion about the general procedures and intentions of the Service. As Kluckhohn and Hackenberg[32] have noted:

> Mr. Collier insisted that the Indian Service should learn in a systematic and orderly way something about the ways of life of the various tribes that were being administered. This was done, and given the inevitable limitations of time and money, it was reasonably well done. But what was not done was a study of the other tribe, the tribe of the bureaucracy which is a very special subculture: The United States Indian Service.
>
> And a great deal of what Mr. Collier and his associates planned in a sophisticated way in Washington was not put into effect because insufficient attention was paid to the habitual ways of thinking and reacting of the group out in the field. It was not that Indian Service field representatives were irresponsible, or insincere, or unintelligent, by and large. It was simply that their own subculture screened both the instructions they got from Washington and their appraisal of the local situation.

Also, a distinct lack of unification existed between Indian Service personnel and workers in the miscellaneous survey programs being conducted by other departments. It was not until 1938 that the responsibilities of soil-erosion protection, until then handled by both the Department of the Interior and the Department of Agriculture, were taken over by the Navajo Service.

Land-Management Districts

In 1936, as the result of a suggestion by Collier, a new—or at least a narrower—approach to the range problem called for the division of the reservation into eighteen land-management districts. The Service was instructed to assemble facts and to reorganize planning data in order to delimit the districts geographically. These districts materialized in 1937.

At the time it was felt that the administrators could deal with the varying problems and interests more adequately on this smaller scale. However, the program was the same for all districts: reduction of stock to the carrying capacity of the district, establishment of more water developments to cope with cropping hazards, erosion control, protection of timber, and correction of land misuse. There were two subtle variations. One was that the new reduction technique was diametrically opposed to the old, at least in theory. The new strategy was essentially political, based on organization of a popular movement within each district and the creation of "genuine localized function mechanisms." What was actually intended was to force the minority of large stockowners to reduce herd size by placing them between popular opinion and government pressure. If need be, court injunctions could be invoked, and compulsion could be resorted to without inviting rebellion.

In order to cope successfully with other aspects of management, conservationists formulated a program requiring the assistance of natural and social scientists. A member of the project staff was put in charge of each land-use survey group as field coordinator. At the completion of the first district survey an integrated report was to be made, which was supposed to cross disciplinary lines. Actually, however, neither the field men nor their chiefs had a broad enough background to write such a report, and the closest the survey came to this objective was the preparation of individual reports, which eventually were stacked one upon the other.

The land-management districts were conceived as "natural units of land (drainages or sections thereof) in which all natural resources of the land appear in proper perspective in management and are allotted their proper role with respect to present and future human needs from the stand-

[32] Clyde Kluckhohn and Robert Hackenberg, "Social Science Principles and the Indian Reorganization Act," *Indian Affairs and the Indian Reorganization Act: The Twenty Year Record,* ed. William H. Kelly (Tucson: Bur. of Ethnic Research, University of Arizona, 1954), p. 31.

point of use."[33] In other words, each district was supposed to be balanced and as close to an ideal unit as possible in its economic, political, educational, social, physiographic, and botanical aspects. District supervisors were chosen from the ranks of the Indian Service and the Soil Conservation Service. They assumed their posts after a *two-week* training session at Mexican Springs, during which they received instruction in the land-use sciences and administration; their duties included stock reduction, operation and maintenance of irrigation projects and reservoirs, farm management, forest management, management of reimbursable accounts, organization of district councils, organization of cooperatives, relief, and collection of information or certain surveys.

The concept of the land-management district was valid. The maximum limits of flock size were based on stock counts in the 1937 livestock census.[34] The practical geographical boundaries, however, resulting in carrying capacities that ranged from less than 100 sheep units to more than 300, drew resentment from the Navajo. It was incomprehensible to Navajo herders that they no longer were able to roam the range but were confined within their own district. The owners who were understocked were issued stock permits, and until 1942, when these became negotiable, they could not build up their herds to the carrying capacity of the range.

By now, confusion was widespread. Few if any Navajo grasped the significance of "districts," "base preferences," "maximum limit," "sheep units," and the like. But the surveys continued.

After continual failure to get the tribe to reduce the stock voluntarily, the government attempted to try violations in the federal courts. By mid-1938 Indian opposition had become so strong that the government waited for a court order before taking any other steps. In 1939 the Indian Service picked three western Navajo leaders to face court action for infraction of the general grazing regulations. The government won. The general reservation attitude changed from opposition to a desire for cooperation—under threat of arrest. That summer, 16,000 horses were removed from the range.[35] However, the newly elected Tribal Council, which was definitely antigovernment, was relied on to increase the authorized stocking capacity of the range. Compliance was only partial, and tension mounted rapidly; by 1941 the government was considering the possibility of calling in troops to head off what appeared to be a gradual progression from the "talking stage to the shooting stage."

The decade 1930–40 illustrates the basic problems of the sheep industry, which with little improvement still exist today. Some experts have asserted that erosion has been checked and that the range has started to revegetate. This may be true in some areas. However, in 1960 every range manager, district supervisor, land-management officer, or other reservation official interviewed by the writer stated that the range was in "bad shape," and the general condition is considered to be growing worse each year, and has been doing so since the 1930's.

According to official Indian Service records stock units on the reservation were reduced by an approximate 30 per cent between 1932 and 1936.[36] The livestock-adjustment report in 1942 stated that "the Navajo ranges are yet in a very critical condition."[37] The unpleasant fact remained that if the vast majority of Navajo families were permitted to run only subsistence-size herds, the reservation would be ruined,

33 Planning and Policy Records, 1930–1940 (National Archives).

34 Permissible flock size was determined by dividing the carrying capacity by the number of owners.

35 Solon T. Kimball, "The Crisis in Colonial Administration," *Applied Anthropology*, V, No. 2 (1946), 8–16.

36 See, for example, *Navaho Yearbook 1959* (Window Rock: Navaho Agency), p. 383.

37 Bur. of Land Management, U.S., Indian Service, *Livestock Adjustment Report, 1942* (Window Rock: Navaho Agency), mimeographed.

and no substitute source of income was yet in sight.

Pledges by various districts to remove excess stock were freely given—and freely broken. Range regulations were continually being revised, and unrelenting pressure for reduction was felt by every Navajo. The Navajo were powerless to fight the government and also what they considered the government's "artificial offspring," the Tribal Council. Tension increased, and when a Navajo gets scared, he does nothing. He did nothing; he did not reduce his herd, and he was now definitely convinced he had to keep away from government men, since he suffered after each contact.

Some Positive and Negative Effects

There are, however, some positive aspects to the problem. Through the early and middle 1940's the newly established Fort Wingate Sheep Breeding Laboratory impressively increased the income value of the sheep, most noticeably within the demonstration areas, where the wool clip rose from a fleece of less than 4 pounds to about an 8-pound fleece.[38] Unfortunately, not more than fifty Navajo a year take advantage of the laboratory.[39] Non-demonstration-area animals did not show the same increase, though some improvement was noted.

To some extent by inbreeding (and possibly through a "modified natural selective process"), fleece weight has increased since 1882. Riordan recorded a 1.5-pound fleece in 1882–84, Kneale a 2.5-pound fleece in 1923, and Assistant Superintendent Cooper a 4-pound fleece in 1931; by 1948 fleece weight was estimated at 6.5 pounds.[40] After about 400 years the old-type Navajo sheep had become hardy and well adapted to the rugged reservation environment. The ewes were prolific and long-lived and possessed a highly developed maternal instinct. They were excellent milk producers and raised a high percentage of lambs. Their deficiencies were a lack of desirable mutton and a light fleece that was a mixture of wool, hair, kemp, and medullated fibers. Although suitable for the weaving of rugs, this wool had low commercial value.

The early practice of breeding the native ewes with purebred rams improved the sheep. But there was an accompanying loss of certain qualities—adaptability, longevity, fecundity, and maternalism. Furthermore, the wool, though of higher market value, tended to be unsatisfactory for hand weaving.[41] Since the mid-1930's, the Sheep Breeding Laboratory has been experimenting to perfect a breed that would combine the hardiness of the old-type Navajo sheep with a wool-type animal and meet the requirements both of the native weaver and of the outside market.

The wool from unimproved sheep was initially the reason for the wide reputation of the Navajo rug. Weaving was one of the principal means of income from the sheep industry. During the early 1930's about 750,000 pounds of wool, about one-fourth of the reservation's annual production, were used in rugs and blankets woven by the women. In recent years, however, weaving income has taken a downward trend. Perhaps, when the educational and off-the-reservation employment programs attain maximum acceleration, weaving will be another lost art. It is almost certain never to regain the economic importance it once had in the family income.

By 1947 fifteen of the eighteen districts were at the carrying capacity. The reservation average, however, showed overstocking by some 100,000 sheep units. Despite stock reduction, the total wool production, largely improved through laboratory techniques, yielded about the same amount, since each sheep averaged a more than 50 per cent increase in wool weight. The mo-

[38] Kluckhohn and Leighton, *op. cit.*, p. 40.

[39] Personal communication from Stanley Smith, laboratory director, 1960.

[40] Letter from J. M. Stewart to John Collier, March 12, 1948.

[41] James O. Grandstaff, "Comparison of Corriedale X Navajo and Romney X Navajo Crosses," *Journal of Animal Science,* VII (1948–49), 455.

hair production likewise remained stable but more than doubled in value.

By and large, reservation averages show considerable improvement in all income categories. However, one must keep in mind the general characteristics of income distribution. The wealthy Navajo has benefited greatly as compared with the average sheep herder, who still lives on little more than a subsistence-size herd. In 1948 the government reported that a breeding herd equivalent to 250 sheep units was necessary to support the average Navajo family and to bring in a net income of $750 a year. Surveys undertaken at that time revealed that fewer than 200 families had more than 250 sheep units.[42] However, in the past decade wage work has become the largest single income source; at present, only 9 per cent of the total tribal income is derived from livestock. Although the livestock distribution by families is unknown, all agree that more than 50 per cent of the tribe are vitally concerned. The tribal population, growing at a fantastic rate, probably numbers close to 95,000, and most stock-raising families are not too far from bare subsistence.

Native Grazing Techniques

Despite rapid range deterioration, the native herding techniques have not changed since the Navajo were released from Bosque Redondo, more than 90 years ago. Supervision of the flocks is primarily in the hands of the children except during seasons of exceptional activity (for example, shearing or dipping). Early in the morning the flocks are led from the corral to graze the range; they remain grazing during the hottest part of the day, and in the evening they are returned to the hogan for bedding.

This so-called hogan grazing is an exceedingly destructive practice, and one that the Indian Service has not been able to alter by education or by other means. The range is subjected to excessive cropping and is severely trampled twice a day. The only recourse is gradually to enlarge the area covered in the daily cycle. A recommended solution was to have several groups band their flocks together and follow a migratory route that would take weeks to cover. However, Commissioner Collier[43] believed that a vacancy in nearby range would be claimed by other bands under the "ownership-while-in-use" property concept. This may be only a partial explanation. The Navajo are distinctly individualistic; moreover, they distrust strangers. A practical Navajo remarked that if he banded his flocks with others, as the Indian Service suggested, whenever a sheep was stolen, "It would be my sheep," or whenever a coyote killed a sheep, "It would be my sheep." The Navajo seldom feels at ease away from his family or clan surroundings, and strangers—and strange places—are always regarded as possible sources of trouble. Also, some potentially good grazing and farm lands are not fully used because it is said they harbor ghosts.[44]

According to agronomists,[45] the two big hazards in grazing are too early grazing (in the spring, when the ground is soft and the forage is not sufficiently grown to withstand cropping) and poor distribution. One of the best methods of handling sheep is by the "open" or "blanket" system. The sheep are allowed to graze at will during the day, scattering as widely as they please within reasonable limits, never congregating in large masses if this can be averted. In the evening, instead of being driven en masse to a corral, they are permitted to bed down in small scattered groups. Thirty per cent

[42] J. A. Krug, *The Navajo: A Long-Range Program for Navajo Rehabilitation* (Washington: U.S., Dept. of Agriculture, 1948), p. 14.

[43] M. and J. Collier, "Navaho Farmer," *Farm Quarterly,* III, No. 3 (1948), 17–24 and 103–6.

[44] It was suggested that part of one canyon be fenced off to contain ghosts. A barbed-wire fence was erected, making the remainder of the valley safe for use. The writer was not able to determine just what constituted a "ghostproof" fence; however, one or two lengths of barbed wire seemed sufficient.

[45] See, for example, W. C. Barnes, "The Problem of Systems of Grazing," *Journal of the American Society of Agronomy,* XVI, No. 3 (1924), 202–5.

more sheep can be grazed on a range with this method, and predators become less of a menace because of the changing bedding grounds. However, this proposal is complicated by the Navajo fear of the night. The Navajo believe only witches and ghosts feel safe wandering outdoors during the night.

The agronomist's grazing pattern would perhaps be ideal to help maintain the land, but for various reasons the destructive Indian grazing methods continue.

TABLE 1

PERCENTAGES OF SHEEP UNITS YEARLONG VERSUS STATED CARRYING CAPACITY, 1943

District	Carrying Capacity	1937	1942	1944	1946	1948	1950	1952	1954	1956	1958
1....	34,221	139	109	83	66	73	76	79	92	91	95
2....	20,506	127	112	84	67	73	81	88	95	134	125
3....	47,288	108	104	89	76	72	74	72	96	82	80
4....	23,372	153	173	170	125	123	141	152	173	167	180
5....	26,351	110	101	87	83	72	73	67	72	74	81
7....	49,727	103	81	91	81	78	77	75	82	87	87
8....	29,978	118	114	102	74	77	89	81	101	115	126
9....	21,018	122	176	161	105	106	124	109	127	160	194
10....	33,717	115	105	98	85	80	88	82	96	96	104
11....	17,261	112	88	96	82	77	80	72	84	93	99
12....	52,385	122	141	130	98	95	101	90	98	106	111
13....	16,703	130	114	97	81	85	72	59	60	65	74
14....	25,321	149	161	154	128	117	121	115	147	126	124
15 (on)[a]	7,171	145	164	110	119	88	99	86	87	97	74
17....	74,895	....	93	97	84	82	83	74	78	85	84
18....	33,008	....	91	103	89	83	85	91	80	82	82

These figures are a composite of yearly reports issued by the Bureau of Land Management, U.S., Indian Service (Window Rock: Navaho Agency, mimeographed). District 6 (Hopi) is excluded.

[a] District 15 is partly on the reservation and partly off. District 16 is heavily populated by Navajo but is not on the reservation proper, and consequently is not under the "normal" jurisdiction of the Bureau of Indian Affairs.

THE DISTRICT STOCKING PATTERN

Table 1 shows stocking, 1937–58, by districts. Seven districts were overstocked in 1958, with District 4, one of the "longhair"[46] districts, and District 9 veering off by themselves as they had done throughout the reduction era. They never did come down to carrying capacity. By 1944–45, at the end of the reduction period, the reservation itself had come down to carrying capacity—on an average. In other words, if the livestock had been evenly spread over the reservation, each district would have been at carrying capacity. However, since there is no unused usable range because of peculiarities in the land-use ownership rights, even stock redistribution is impossible. A Navajo stockowner establishes his right to "ownership" of a section of range by grazing his flock there. As long as he is using the range, other families will not normally infringe on his right, even though the section could carry many more sheep units. If his range is not in use, anyone may claim "ownership" by stocking it. This ownership-while-in-use peculiarity of the Navajo property concept was never broken by the Indian Service. It has contributed considerably toward stalemating the scarce-land problem. Since pastoralism is frequently associated with more "traditional" values, districts such as District 4 balked at the reduction idea and were least able to comprehend what the Indian Service referred to as the "rational thing to do." In many areas where agriculture or seasonal wages might have produced more income

46 The term "longhair" refers to the more primitive Navajo male who traditionally does not cut his hair. District 4 is a backward area with the highest longhair population of all the districts.

most people still felt that sheep raising, even though they did not practice it, was the traditional or "preferred" way to earn a living. The economic value of sheep might be changing, but the social value still remained, particularly among the older people.

In most districts the end of the reduction program was marked by a progressive stock increase in following years. The carrying capacity established in each district was never changed in spite of the fact that the range was continually downgrading, and reducing the carrying capacity as it deteriorated. Needless to say, the original carrying capacities, established during the late thirties and early forties, were in themselves an inaccurate and unreliable gauge of the potentials. Efforts are being made today to re-evaluate the situation, but the original carrying capacities remain unchanged.

First of all, how may we, as a nation, plan better for our outdoor recreation needs? . . . A closely related problem is: how can we estimate with more confidence the future demands for outdoor recreation, so that we shall neither neglect to provide what is needed nor make unnecessarily large expenditures? . . .

Secondly, *how* can we best finance the expected greater costs for outdoor recreation in the future? . . .

Thirdly, what are the most appropriate relations between governments, federal, state and local, in the matter of providing outdoor recreation? . . .

Fourthly, how can we best reserve needed outdoor recreation areas at the most appropriate time? . . .

Lastly, how may we best raise the quality of the outdoor recreation experience for the average user? . . .

These policy issues are primarily economic, social, governmental, not technological, nor concerning resource availability. Some of the latter kinds of problems do indeed exist, but in our judgement they are not the critical ones. These human problems partly grow out of the changing volume and nature of outdoor recreation demand; they also arise in part because they have had little attention in the past. Such issues, when they have arisen, have tended to be debated on an emotional and preconceptual basis; social science research has generally not been brought to bear upon their solution. It could be [that] this may be the real challenge for young people entering this field today.

Marion Clawson, *Land and Water for Recreation* (Chicago: Rand McNally, 1963), pp. 142–44.

ROBERT C. LUCAS

WILDERNESS PERCEPTION AND USE: THE EXAMPLE OF THE BOUNDARY WATERS CANOE AREA

Wilderness as a Resource

For centuries North American wilderness was viewed only as land to be developed—cleared and farmed, mined, or logged. The wilderness was a challenge. If the challenge was met, material benefits could be drawn from the former wilderness. Now, however, many people in the United States and Canada see wilderness as a resource in its own right. These people oppose conventional development of the remaining wilderness and argue that such areas have greater utility in their wilderness state. Groups such as the Sierra Club, the Wilderness Society, and the Quetico Foundation present this argument forcefully and seek to influence resource management in the direction of wilderness preservation.

Changing ideas provided the impetus for the re-evaluation of wilderness, and economic conditions made the shift possible. The late eighteenth and nineteenth centuries constituted a period of major reinterpretation of the resources of scenic wildlands. Before that time, Americans seldom wrote of nature or scenery with aesthetic appreciation.[1] For example, William Bradford described the New England wilderness as hideous and desolate.[2] European ideas, particularly Romanticism and a growing scientific interest in nature, influenced American writers such as Bryant, Emerson, Thoreau, Irving, and Muir, and they along with painters began to portray scenery as an object of beauty.[3]

Besides the new attitude toward the natural scene, the almost complete conquest of the wilderness gave a certain scarcity value to the remnant.[4] The status of the frontier movement, as a national epic, encouraged keeping some wilderness as a symbol of the frontier and as a setting for re-experiencing its challenge.[5] Finally, the general mastery of the more productive portion of the original wilderness reduced the incentive to develop the remainder. The agricultural frontier, in fact, has retreated as production of agricultural crops has risen, although mining, logging, and highways continue to spread.

The Wilderness Resource

"Wilderness" is difficult to define precisely.[6] The Wilderness Bill states: "A wil-

• Robert C. Lucas is Economic Geographer and Project Leader of Forest Recreation Research, Lake States Forest Experiment Station, USDA, Forest Service, St. Paul, Minnesota.

Reprinted from the *Natural Resources Journal*, III, No. 3 (1964), 394–411, with the permission of the author and the editor.

1 Hans Huth, *Nature and the American* (Berkeley & Los Angeles: University of California Press, 1957), pp. 2–9.

2 Roderick W. Nash, "The American Wilderness in Historical Perspective," *Forest History*, VI, No. 4 (1963), 3.

3 Huth, *op. cit.*, pp. 10–53.

4 Aldo Leopold, *A Sand County Almanac, and Sketches Here and There* (New York: Oxford University Press, 1949), pp. 188–94.

5 Nash, *op. cit.*, pp. 10–11. For an interesting criticism of this view see David Lowenthal, "Not Every Prospect Pleases—What Is Our Criterion for Scenic Beauty?" *Landscape*, XII, No. 2 (1962–63), 19–23.

6 Wildland Research Center, University of California, *Wilderness and Recreation—A Report on Resources, Values, and Problems*, Outdoor Recrea-

derness, in contrast with those areas where man and his own works dominate the landscape, is hereby recognized as an area where the earth and its community of life are untrammeled by man, where man himself is a visitor who does not remain."[7]

The most easily defined wilderness is that area officially established by law or administrative declaration. The largest acreage of such established wilderness is located in the National Forests of the United States. In 1961 this consisted of eighty-three areas and over 14 million acres, which is about eight per cent of the National Forest System.[8] This acreage has been stable since the late 1930's.[9] The areas are roadless and closed to timber cutting. Other uses, such as grazing or water impoundments, are more restricted than on other National Forest areas.

The National Park Service in the United States has no specific wilderness areas. All land under its jurisdiction which is located away from roads or other developments is considered wilderness and is closed to logging, grazing, and usually to hunting.[10] The National Park Service recently classified sixty-six of its areas as scenic-scientific parks and monuments, in contrast to more purely historical sites.[11] These sixty-six locations included over 22 million acres. About 7 million acres were considered wilderness in the study conducted by the Wildland Research Center under a strict definition[12] (a definition that excluded 2 million acres of established National Forest Wilderness). Like the National Forest Wilderness, National Park Wilderness appears to be holding its own in acreage.

A few state areas are established as wilderness. The largest is the Adirondack Forest Preserve in New York; however, it includes a good deal of intermixed private land.[13]

Informal or unreserved wilderness is also important but more difficult to define or measure. The Wildland Research Center considered that almost 9 million acres of unreserved land met wilderness standards, compared with over 19 million acres of established wilderness.[14] This area is probably declining because of lack of formal designation, and because it often surrounds established areas and thus is more accessible.

These wilderness areas have two main attributes. First, they are closed to recreationists using mechanized transportation including jeeps, motor scooters, airplanes (with a few exceptions), and motorboats (with more exceptions). Second, ecological conditions are relatively undisturbed although probably quite different from pre-white entry characteristics because of fire protection, exotic plants, diseases, animals, and recreation use, to name but a few influences.[15]

There is, however, another type of area, semi-wilderness, which provides a refuge from mechanized recreation but permits some logging and other uses. Established semi-wilderness is rare. The Boundary Waters Canoe Area of the Superior National Forest in northeastern Minnesota is the

tion Resources Review Commission Study Report No. 3 (Washington: Government Printing Office, 1962), pp. 16–26.

7 There have been a series of wilderness bills. S.174, 87th Cong., 1st Sess., 1961, is quoted here.

8 U.S., Dept. of Agriculture, Forest Service, *Wilderness* (Washington: GPO, 1961), p. 5.

9 *Idem, The National Forest System and Outdoor Recreation,* prepared for the Outdoor Recreation Resources Review Commission (Washington: GPO, 1960), p. 52.

10 Wildland Research Center, *op. cit.*, p. 4.

11 U.S., Dept of Interior, National Park Service, *The National Park Wilderness* (n.d.), p. 17.

12 Wildland Research Center, *op. cit.*, pp. 40, 50–51.

13 Roger C. Thompson, "Politics in the Wilderness: New York's Adirondack Forest Preserve," *Forest History,* VI, No. 4 (1963), 14.

14 Wildland Research Center, *op. cit.*, p. 50.

15 For a full discussion of the problem of defining and attaining "primitive America," see the Leopold Committee Report to the Secretary of the Interior, "Wildlife Management in the National Parks," reprinted in *American Forests,* LXIX, No. 4 (1963), 32–35, 61–63.

only example found in the United States. Its name prior to 1958, the Superior Roadless Area, suggested its character as a refuge for rugged recreation, but it was inaccurate because temporary logging roads, closed to the public, do exist there. Canada has several semi-wilderness areas. Both the Quetico and Algonquin Provincial Parks in Ontario are managed in this way. The Boundary Waters Canoe Area, which is the focus of this article, adjoins Quetico Provincial Park to the north; the two combined (often also including some of the surrounding land) are called the Quetico-Superior Area. These two semi-wilderness areas cover about 2 million acres (Fig. 1).

This rarity of established semi-wilderness is surprising. Robert Marshall, who contributed greatly to the development of the National Forest Wilderness Areas and founded the Wilderness Society, called for semi-wilderness in 1933.[16] The Outdoor Recreation Resources Review Commission,[17] the Wildland Research Center,[18] and a recent recreational planning monograph[19] have repeated Marshall's plea. Informal semi-wilderness is probably shrinking fast. As recreation booms, improved public roads, public recreational facilities, resorts, and especially summer homes are spreading into many unreserved semi-wild areas.

Resource Use

A wilderness area serves a number of uses. It can be a setting for education and research, a protected watershed, and, simply by existing, a source of psychological satisfaction as a symbol in some natural philosophy. The main use, however, is for high-quality recreation, frequently with inspirational overtones. The Forest Service estimates there were 757,000 visits to established wilderness-type areas in 1961, out of a total of 102 million visits to the National Forests.[20] In 1960, 1,100,000 visits were estimated for National Park wilderness[21] compared to 65 million for the entire National Park System, omitting the National Capital Parks.[22] The Boundary Waters Canoe Area tallied 217,000 visits in 1961,[23] which is a very substantial proportion of all wilderness visits.[24]

Use has generally been increasing somewhat faster for wilderness areas than for conventional recreation areas.[25] Visits to the Boundary Waters Canoe Area rose twelve per cent a year from 1946 to 1960 (before a change in estimation procedures sharply increased use figures); this is close to the national figure for wilderness visits. A tenfold increase in wilderness man-days has been projected for the year 2000, and an eightfold growth for the Boundary Waters Canoe Area.[26] This compares to a threefold increase projected to the same year for all outdoor recreation, and a fourfold projected expansion in general camping.[27]

16 Robert Marshall, "The Forest for Recreation," *A National Plan for American Forestry* (the "Copeland Report"), Sen. Doc. No. 12, 73d Cong., 1st Sess., 1933, pp. 473–76.

17 Outdoor Recreation Resources Review Commission, *Outdoor Recreation for America* (Washington: GPO, 1962), p. 71.

18 Wildland Research Center, *op. cit.*, pp. 11, 303.

19 Arthur H. Carhart, *Planning for America's Wildlands* (National Audubon Society, National Parks Assn., The Wilderness Society, and Wildlife Management Institute, 1961).

20 U.S., Dept. of Agriculture, Forest Service, *Report of the Chief of the Forest Service, 1961* (Washington: GPO, 1962), p. 40.

21 Wildland Research Center, *op. cit.*, pp. 119–21.

22 U.S., Dept. of Interior, National Park Service, *Public Use: National Parks and Related Areas, December, 1960* (Washington, n.d.), Table 2*a* (unpaged).

23 U.S., Dept. of Agriculture, Forest Service, *Report of the Chief . . . , op. cit.*, p. 40.

24 The Forest Service's definition of a "visit" requires counting a person every time he enters the reporting area. Thus, a person camping or staying at a resort just outside a wilderness area and entering it every day for a week would technically produce seven visits.

25 Wildland Research Center, *op. cit.*, p. 124.

26 *Ibid.*, p. 236.

27 Outdoor Recreation Resources Review Commission, *op. cit.*, p. 46.

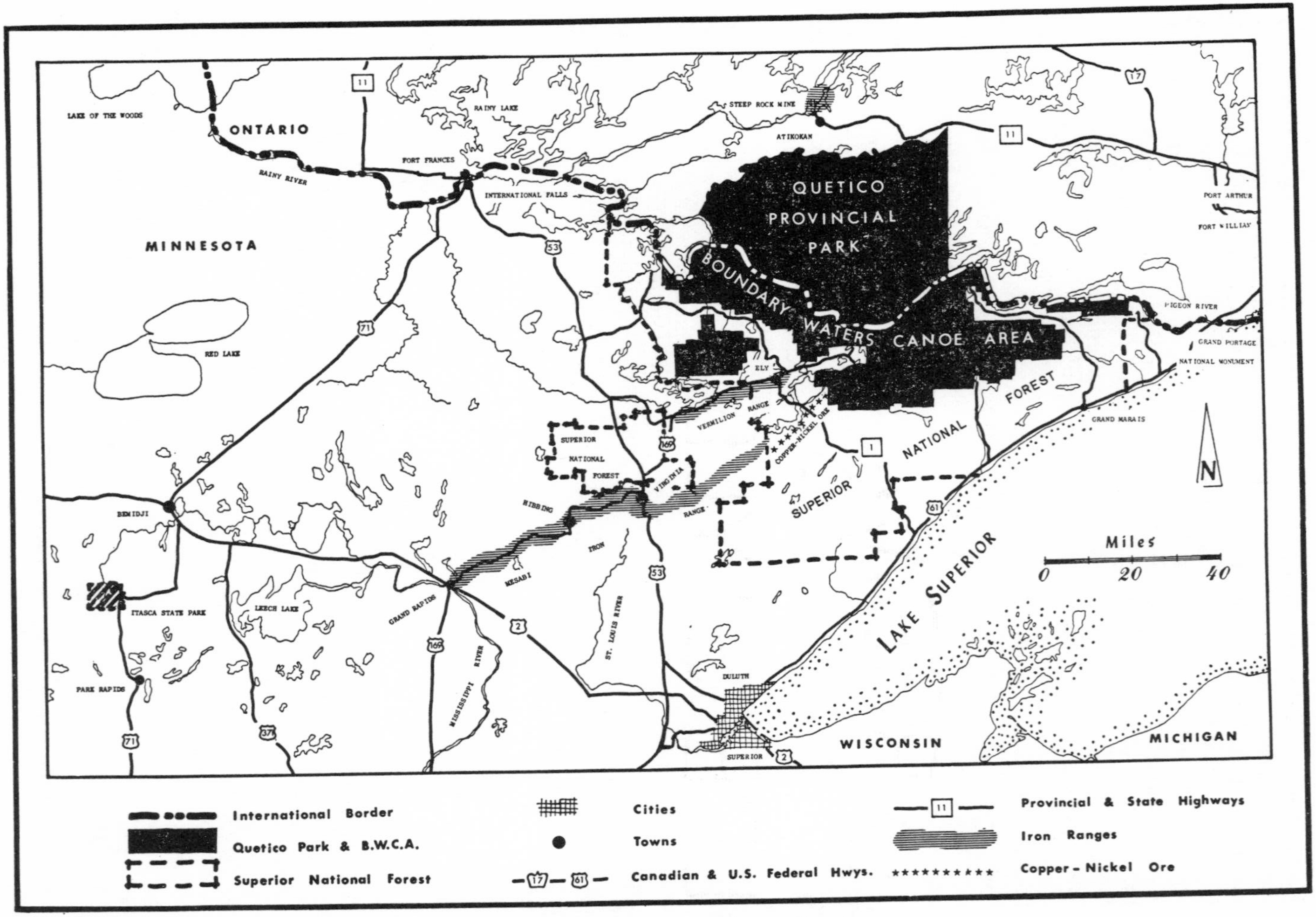

FIG. 1.—The regional setting of the Quetico-Superior area

Perception of the Wilderness Resource in the Boundary Waters Canoe Area

For both public agencies and the visitors, three elements of environmental perception in the Boundary Waters Canoe Area will be considered: (1) the importance of the wilderness qualities relative to other potential uses, (2) the area considered to be wilderness, and (3) the essential characteristics of the wilderness—particularly the types of uses accepted.

The recreational visitors to the Canoe Area were studied in 1960 and 1961. A random sample distributed with equal probability over the entire area during the summer season was interviewed.[28] Almost 300 groups were questioned, and data were recorded on a formal questionnaire. A major part of the data collected dealt with wilderness resource perception.

The resource managers include the staff of the Superior National Forest, Regional and National Forest Service Officers, and to a limited extent state and county officials. Although this group was not studied directly, the development of the policy of management for the area was studied. Based on this information and considerable informal contact with the National Forest staff, some inferences about resource managers' perception were drawn and are presented here.

The Resource Managers' Perception

The Superior National Forest was established in 1909 (the same year as Quetico Park). The area was viewed as conventional forest land, in need of roads and development, although there had been some earlier proposals for an international park.[29] After World War I an extensive road system was proposed, but a different picture of the resources of the area and its potential was presented by a young landscape architect in 1921. Arthur Carhart, employed by the Forest Service regional office, visited the area and stressed the value of the now unique forested land and undeveloped lakes and streams in a plan prospectus.[30] Basically he proposed the semi-wilderness management now practiced, combining logging with "the presentation of natural scenic beauties" along the waterways, and the exclusion of auto recreation.

The ideas in the Carhart proposal were taken up by private groups and gradually adopted by the Forest Service. The importance of the wilderness aspects of the area grew in the managers' view from minimal, or even negative, to dominance.

The area considered to be wilderness by the Forest Service has generally corresponded closely to the changing official boundary (Fig. 1). This official area grew until 1939, contracted slightly in 1946, and has been stable since then. The map shown in Figure 1 is in front of the National Forest staff almost daily, and the boundary strongly affects their daily plans and activities.

The resource managers' view of appropriate uses in the Canoe Country has also changed. The decision to exclude public roads was made, unmade, and remade by the Forest Service and the Secretary of Agriculture in the 1920's. After 1926, the decision was firm.

28 The probability of a party of a given type, e.g., resort guests, falling in the sample was equal everywhere. The probabilities were not equal between types—e.g., between campers and canoeists—because of necessary differences in the way of contacting the different types. For example, each access point was sampled on six randomly chosen days, two weekend days for one hour each day, and four weekdays for 1¼ hours each day, and every returning party was interviewed during these times. Each campground was visited on one randomly selected weekend day and two weekdays, and one-half of the occupied campsites were randomly chosen for interviews.

29 For a more complete history of the management policies, see Robert C. Lucas, "The Quetico-Superior Area: Recreational Use in Relation to Capacity" (unpublished Ph.D. thesis, University of Minnesota, 1962), pp. 70–111.

30 Arthur H. Carhart, *Preliminary Prospectus: An Outline Plan for the Recreational Development of the Superior National Forest* (n.d.).

Water impoundments were proposed on a large scale in 1925, weighed at the international level, and rejected in 1934. The International Joint Commission announced:

The boundary waters referred to in the Reference . . . are of matchless scenic beauty and of inestimable value from the recreational and tourist viewpoints. The Commission fully sympathizes with the objects and desires of the State of Minnesota and the Quetico-Superior Council . . . that nothing should be done that might mar the beauty or disturb the wildlife of this last great wilderness of the United States.[31]

The Commission did state that under different conditions in the future some carefully controlled dams might be considered, but approval by each country would be a prerequisite. This appears to have been a meaningless concession to the development interests, because the Shipstead-Nolan Act prohibited water level alterations in the Minnesota portion of the Quetico-Superior.[32] The area covered by this Act included almost all of the Canoe Area, plus a considerable amount of land outside the Area.

Another provision of the Shipstead-Nolan Act withdrew federally owned land from private entry (except for agriculture, which was virtually nonexistent), recognizing that more cabins and resorts were inappropriate in a wilderness environment.[33]

A third provision of this 1930 law was specific protection of forests for 400 feet from the shores of navigable lakes and streams.[34] The Forest Service has also applied these restrictions to the small part of the Boundary Waters Canoe Area outside the area defined by the Shipstead-Nolan Act, supporting the statement that the map boundary defines "the wilderness" for the resource managers. In 1941 the Service established a zone closed to *all* logging covering the northern third of the area, and in 1948 the Service prohibited logging in a even wider waterfront strips where topography would expose cutting to canoeists or boaters.[35]

Air traffic to cabins and resorts and for fishing trips mounted after World War II, and after a prolonged and sharp controversy, airplanes (except for administration) were banned below 4,000 feet above sea level by order of President Truman in 1949.[36] The courts upheld the order.[37]

In 1948 about 14 per cent of the Boundary Waters Canoe Area was privately owned, and about forty-five resorts and one hundred cabins were located in the supposed wilderness.[38] The incongruity of this situation was recognized early. In 1926 it was decided that in the future no leases for resort or summer home sites would be granted on at least 1,000 square miles of National Forest land containing the best of the lakes and waterways.[39] The means to eliminate developments were limited, however, until 1948 when the Thye-Blatnik Act[40] was passed. This law authorized ac-

31 International Joint Commission on the Rainy Lake Reference, *Final Report* (Ottawa: J. O. Patenaude, 1934), p. 48.

32 46 Stat. 1021 (1930), 16 U.S.C. section 577*b* (1958).

33 46 Stat. 1021 (1930), 16 U.S.C. section 577*a* (1958).

34 46 Stat. 1020–21 (1930), 16 U.S.C. section 577*a* (1958).

35 Superior National Forest, *Plan of Management: Superior Roadless Areas* (1948), pp. 11–12, 14.

36 Executive Order No. 10092, Federal Register, XIV (1949), 7637, 7681.

37 For a full discussion of the President's decision to issue this order and the subsequent cases, see Russell P. Andrews, *Wilderness Sanctuary,* Inter-University Case Prog. No. 13 (rev. ed.; University: University of Alabama Press, 1954).

38 From the files of the Superior National Forest, Duluth, Minn.

39 William M. Jardine, *The Policy of the Department of Agriculture in Relation to Road Building and Recreational Use of the Superior National Forest, Minnesota* (Washington: processed September 17, 1926), pp. 1–2. Actually, the most popular section of the present Boundary Waters Canoe Area—northeast of Ely—was not a part of the National Forest until later.

40 62 Stat. 568 (1948), as amended, 16 U.S.C. sections 577*c–h* (1958).

quisition of developed property and appropriated money for purchases. The funds for acquisition have been increased several times and now total $4,500,000. Only a few private properties now remain, and within the past year the federal government has resorted to condemnation, which will probably result in completing acquisition soon.

Motorboats in a wilderness canoe country have also been recognized by the managers of the resource as being inconsistent. The Forest Service has moved cautiously on this problem, perhaps because of the large number of boaters using the area but also because of uncertainty as to the extent of their legal jurisdiction over navigation, which is generally within Minnesota's authority.[41] The policy is that motorboats "will be prohibited except where well established."[42] No map of prohibited areas has ever been issued, so the restriction is toothless. Motorboats are being restricted somewhat, however, starting in 1963, under the Secretary of Agriculture's regulation number T-15, which prohibits leaving unattended trailers, boats, and other equipment on National Forest land. In the Boundary Waters Canoe Area this will stop the storage of boats over portages on many interior lakes and reduce the amount and area of boat use.

Quetico Provincial Park has generally similar policies, except that a lack of private land has eliminated the acquisition problem, and a small local population and an abundance of informal wilderness have reduced the controversy over the air ban and other restrictions in the park.

In summary, the resource managers have increased their evaluation of the relative importance of the wilderness qualities of the Canoe Country. The area considered wilderness was first vague, then was defined, gradually grew, and has been stable for 25 years. The standards of how a wilderness should be used if it is to be a wilderness have been defined more sharply, restricting more and more commodity and recreational uses other than canoeing in an undeveloped setting. These changes in evaluation were largely a reflection of national trends in thinking within forestry, the United States Forest Service, and the conservation organizations, some of whom took a particular interest in the Quetico-Superior. All of the administrators' attention so far has been on eliminating *inappropriate* uses; no policy prevents *excessive* use of a resource which has solitude and relatively unmodified physical conditions as major components, although the managers are aware of this problem and concerned about it.

THE RECREATIONISTS' PERCEPTION

The visitors to the Canoe Country in 1960 differed markedly in their view of the resource, both among themselves and with the resource managers. They differed on all three counts: importance of wilderness, area of wilderness, and essential qualities of wilderness.[43] There was order, however, in the variation related to the type of recreational activity being pursued.

Wilderness was a major attraction for canoeists, important for roadside campers, but secondary for all other visitor types. Table 1 presents responses to the question: "Does this area have some characteristics that caused you to come here rather than some other vacation region in the United States or Canada? If yes, what characteristics?" ("This area" was defined for the respondents and included the Boundary Waters Canoe Area and its immediate periphery.)

It is interesting to note that the two classes of canoeists differed markedly in their view of the area's distinctive attractions. The paddlers viewed the area as a wilderness in which to travel and camp. The canoeists using outboard motors saw the area as a place to enjoy wilderness fishing. Similarly, the boat campers differed from the car campers. Previous research

[41] Wildland Research Center, *op. cit.*, p. 314.

[42] Superior National Forest, *op. cit.*, p. 15.

[43] For a general discussion of the internal, subjective definition of "wilderness," see Carhart, *Planning for America's Wildlands, op. cit.*, pp. 34–42.

has contrasted the wilderness images of canoeists and campers, grouping these quite different subtypes of canoeists, and perhaps campers as well (the definition of a camper is unclear).[44]

The area considered wilderness was estimated by asking each sample group, "Do you feel that you are in 'the wilderness' now? Where did the members of your group feel 'the wilderness' began?" "Wilderness" was not defined. Each group's route was also obtained and mapped. This made it possible to classify each lake or section of road visited by the group as wilderness or not-wilderness, in their terms. The aggregation of these classifications produced wilderness-perception maps for each user type, with isolines indicating the proportion of visitors considering that place as wilderness. Figure 2 shows this map for paddling canoeists. This was the most demanding group (and produced the most complex map). The paddlers' wilderness is smaller than the officially defined area, even if the 10 per cent isoline is taken as the limit. Only one significant area, directly north of the town of Ely, was outside the official boundaries but inside the paddlers' wilderness. It should be pointed out that the location of the official boundary was not well known among the public.

A summary map was drawn (Fig. 3) from the series of maps for each user type, taking only the 50 per cent isoline from each. All the groups except canoeists were quite similar in their areal perception of the wilderness. Whether people slept in beds in a resort, camped by their cars, often in a trailer, or bedded down on the ground on a rocky islet reached by a cruiser, they all entered their wilderness at about the same places. What all of these groups had in common was the use of boats rather than canoes. All of these boating groups saw the wilderness as much larger than the established area. The three separate official areas fused into one large wilderness. The 90 per cent isolines were also

TABLE 1

PER CENT OF PARTIES CITING CERTAIN QUALITIES AS A BASIS FOR CHOICE OF THE AREA (SUMMER, 1960)

Type of Recreationist (and Number)	Attractive Qualities Cited				
	None, Vague, Tautological	Wilderness[a]	Fishing	Scenery	Facilities
Canoeists......... (85)	6	71	29	28	6
Paddlers........ (64)	6	73	16	28	8
Motorized...... (21)	5	62	67	24	0
Day-use.......... (9)	33	33	33	11	0
Auto campers..... (83)	8	51	30	31	13
Boat campers..... (23)	17	35	48	26	13
Resort guests..... (57)	12	39	42	42	9
Private cabin users. (21)	38	10	14	33	0
Total............(278)	12	49	33	32	9

[a] The six major types of recreationists (ignoring the subdivision of canoeists) differed significantly in the frequency of mention of wilderness attributes at the .005 level when tested by chi-square. The other qualities were not tested.

Note: All responses, sometimes three or four per party, were tabulated; therefore, the totals exceed 100 per cent.

[44] Marvin Taves, William Hathaway, and Gordon Bultena, *Canoe Country Vacationeers,* University of Minnesota Agric. Exper. Station Misc. Report 39 (St. Paul, 1960); Bultena and Taves, "Changing Wilderness Images and Forestry Policy," *J. of Forestry,* LIX, No. 3 (1961), 167–71.

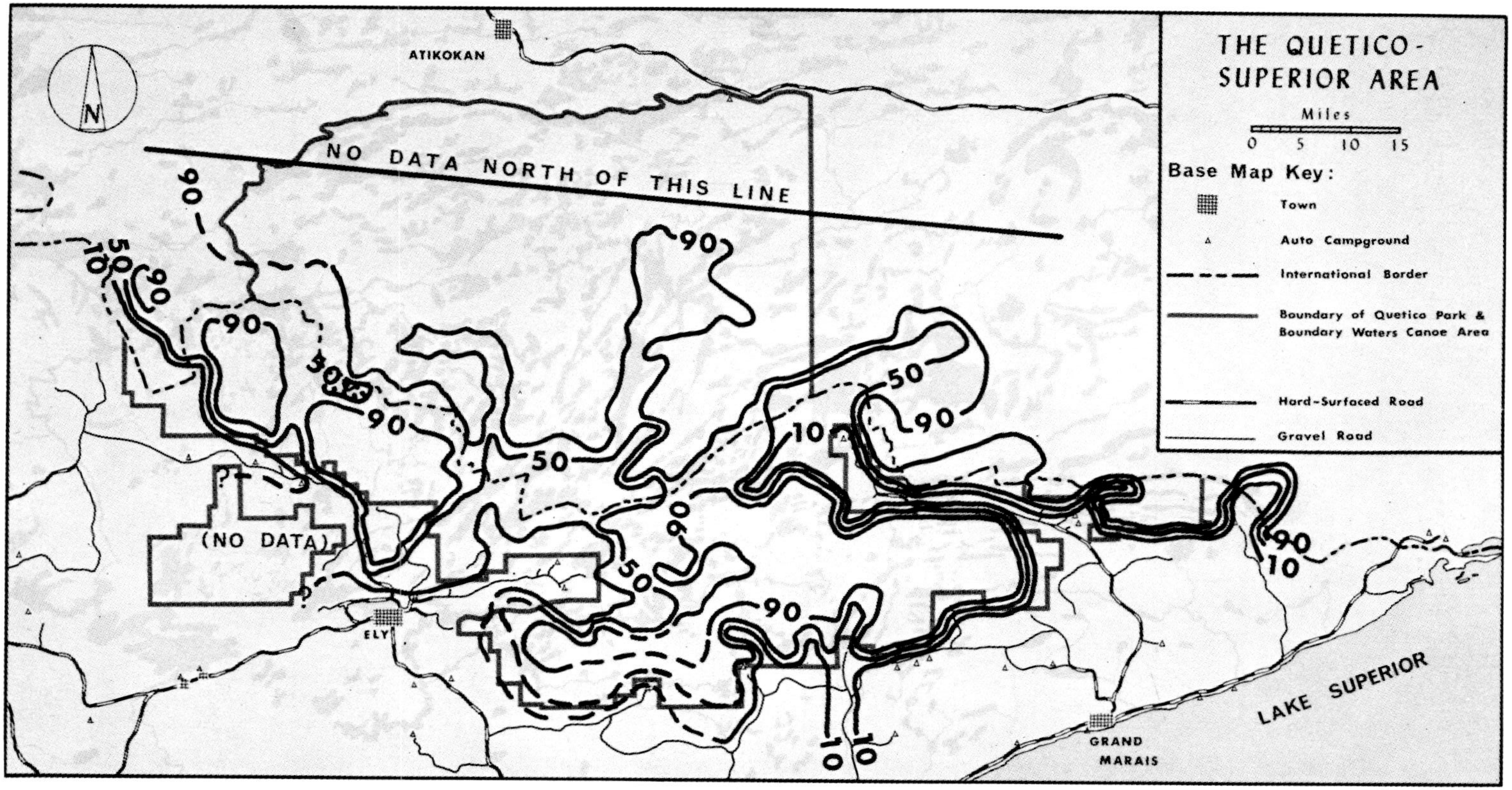

FIG. 2.—The area considered "wilderness" by the paddling canoeists. The isoline values are the per cent of parties visiting each area which described that area as being "in the wilderness." The broken portions of the isolines indicate that data were lacking and subjective estimates were made. The map is based on 1960 data.

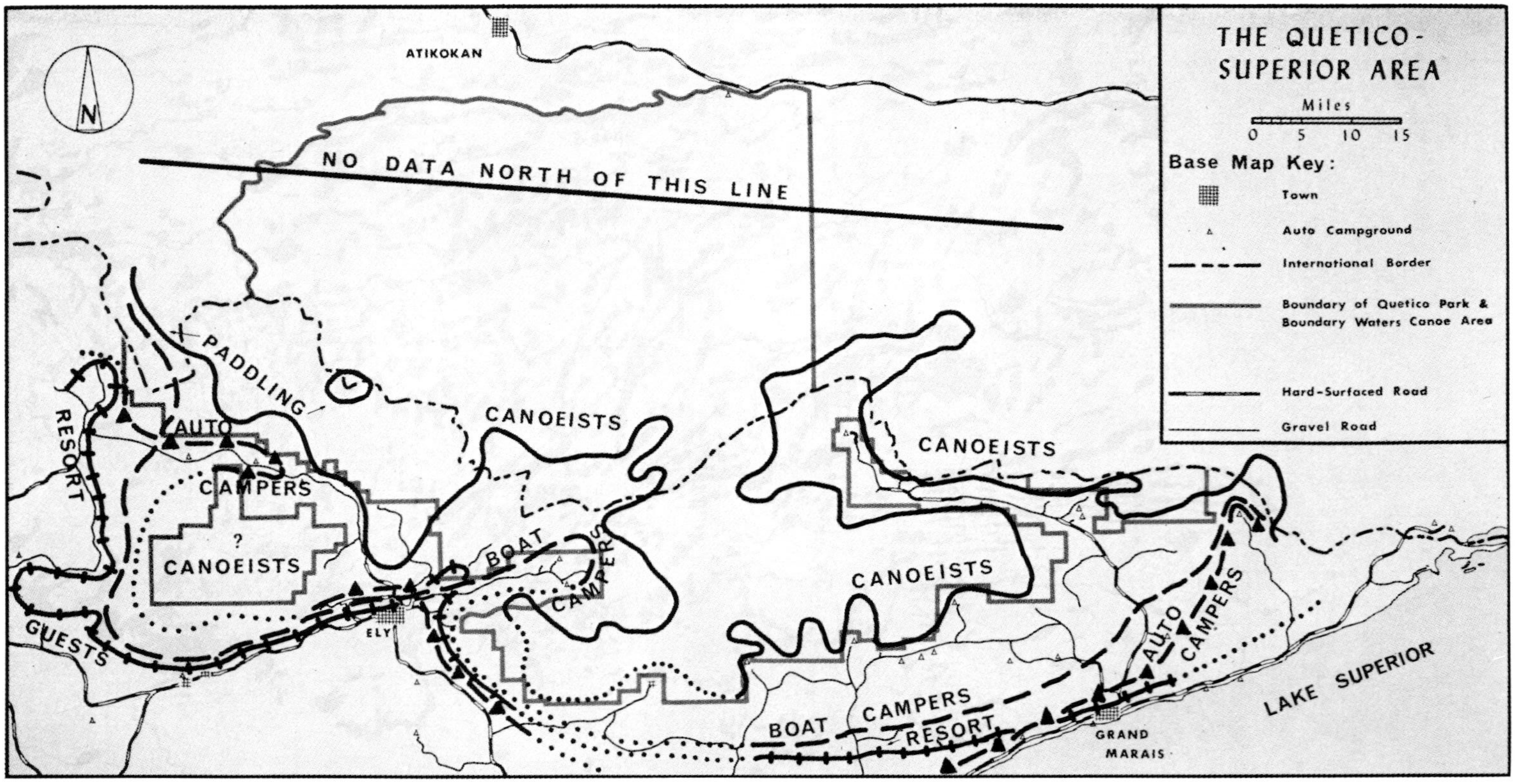

Fig. 3.—The areas considered "wilderness" by at least 50 per cent of the visitors in each of the four major user types. The area in the interior—that is, away from the areas and generally to the north of the line for each user type—was rated as "wilderness" by 50–100 per cent of the visitors of that type reaching the area. The dotted portions of the lines indicate data were lacking and subjective estimates have been made, based on 1960 data.

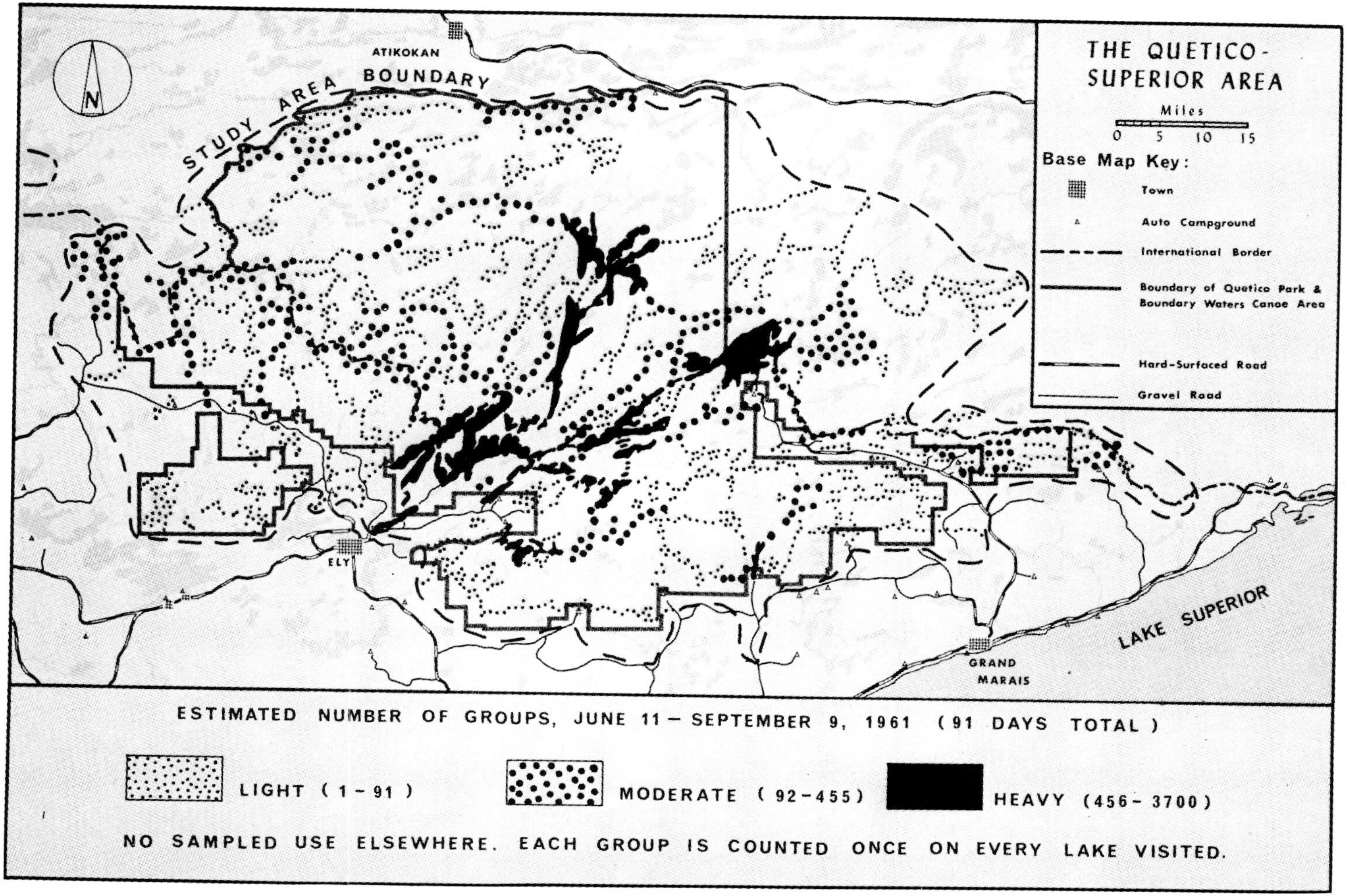

THE QUETICO-SUPERIOR AREA
Miles
0 5 10 15
Base Map Key:
Town
Auto Campground
International Border
Boundary of Quetico Park & Boundary Waters Canoe Area
Hard-Surfaced Road
Gravel Road
ATIKOKAN
STUDY AREA BOUNDARY
N
ELY
GRAND MARAIS
LAKE SUPERIOR
ESTIMATED NUMBER OF GROUPS, JUNE 11 – SEPTEMBER 9, 1961 (91 DAYS TOTAL)
LIGHT (1 – 91)
MODERATE (92–455)
HEAVY (456–3700)
NO SAMPLED USE ELSEWHERE. EACH GROUP IS COUNTED ONCE ON EVERY LAKE VISITED.

FIG. 4.—The distribution of canoe use

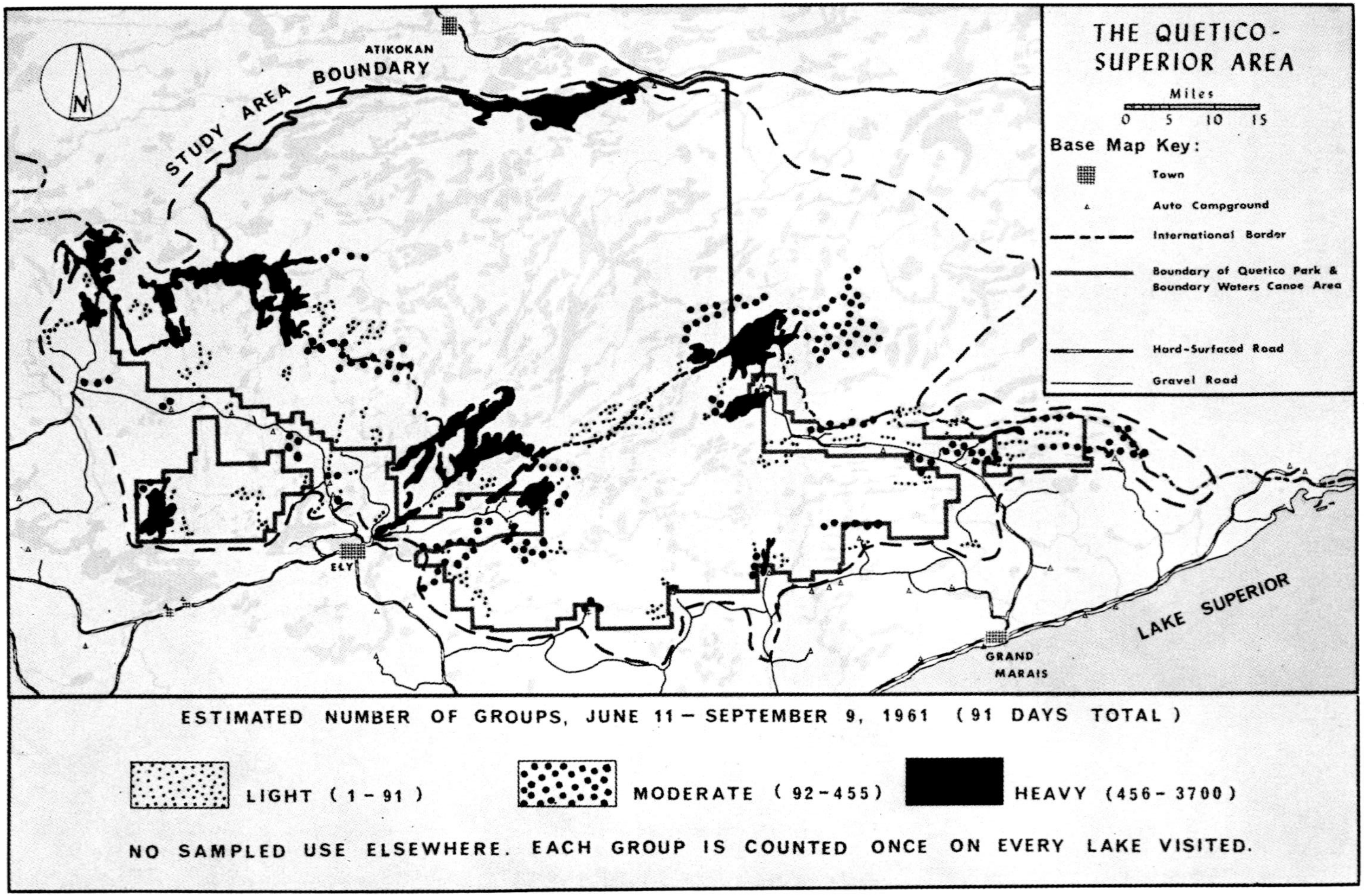

FIG. 5.—The distribution of motorboat use

very similar for these boating classes, and approached the official boundary fairly closely.

The motor canoeist sample was too small for a satisfactory map, but the data suggest that such a map would be intermediate between the paddling canoeists and the motorboaters.

The views of the essential characteristics of these differing wildernesses can be inferred in part from the maps, and were also directly investigated in the interviews. Again, the type of water transportation seems to account for a large part of the variation.

The paddlers' map shows that roads are almost never in "the wilderness." The effect of buildings was not directly tested, and since buildings and motorboats go together the two effects cannot be completely separated in interpreting the maps.

However, recreational use seems to affect the paddling canoeists' wildnerness perception importantly. Heavily used areas were much less often considered wilderness. Moose Lake, located east of Ely and the most heavily used point, was considered non-wilderness by all twenty-three paddling canoeists groups that were sampled there. Total seasonal visitors for each location were estimated and the places were ranked accordingly. The locations were also ranked on the basis of the per cent of the paddling groups classing each location as wilderness. The Spearman rank correlation coefficient for the visitor and the wilderness ratings was —.42. This correlation seems fairly strong when it is considered that season-visitor totals are only a rough index of the number of other visitors observed by the sample parties on a given lake, particularly because of the variation in lake size. The absence of buildings where use was heavy did not raise the level of perceived wilderness.

The type of use encountered seemed even more important to paddlers. Comparable levels of use produced a higher level of perceived wilderness where boats were absent (about three times as high, generally). This antipathy for boats was also brought out in questions about the groups' reaction to meeting other types of groups. Of the paddling canoeists 61 per cent disliked meeting motorboats, 37 per cent were neutral, and only 2 per cent (one party) enjoyed meeting other boats. In contrast, only one group disliked meeting fellow paddlers.

Remoteness, surprisingly, did not have an identifiable relation to the paddlers' wilderness. Where use was comparable, lakes near access points were perceived as wilderness as often as those four or five portages away. This finding needs further substantiation, but it may have interesting implications for a policy establishing more small wild areas.

Logging appeared much less incompatible with wilderness recreation than crowding and conflicting types of recreation.[45] The area northeast of Ely was not generally considered wilderness by canoeists. This area is in the no-cut zone, but it is heavily used by canoeists and boaters. Lightly used, boat-free areas in the west and south-central portions of the Boundary Waters Canoe Area were being logged, but they were considered wilderness by almost all of the sample parties there. These samples were small, of course, because of light use.

The hypothesis that use was light because people were avoiding the logging areas cannot be definitely rejected at this point, but it appears unlikely. Only 30 per cent of the sample even knew logging was permitted. This compares to 28 per cent of the Wildland Research Center's smaller sample.[46] Only 8 per cent of the canoeist sample reported noticing any signs of logging, and only half of these objected to what they observed. Low local relief and lack of travel off water routes appear to make the restricted timber harvest policy

[45] See Lucas, *Visitor Reaction to Timber Harvesting in the Boundary Waters Canoe Area,* USDA Forest Service Research Note LS-2, Lake States Forest Exper. Station (St. Paul, 1963).

[46] Wildland Research Center, *op. cit.*, p. 153.

quite effective. However, public opinion appears strongly opposed to the idea of logging. The Wildland Research Center found 75 per cent of their sample (91 per cent of the sample were canoeists) opposed to timber cutting.[47]

The motorboaters were not as demanding in wilderness standards as canoeists. Roads were accepted in their wilderness. Over half of the groups in each boating type entered their wilderness after passing the last town on the forest roads. Some of these roads are asphalt-paved, but they are relatively free of signs and buildings. Lakes with buildings were still considered wilderness by almost all motorboaters.

Motorboaters tolerated recreational use at high levels. Even on the most heavily used wilderness lake—Moose Lake east of Ely—58 per cent were in their wilderness and 79 per cent of the boaters reported they were not bothered by crowding at all. Only 7 per cent were "bothered quite a bit" by crowding. In contrast, at the same location, only 45 per cent of the paddling canoeists made no complaints about crowding, 29 per cent were "bothered quite a bit," and none considered Moose Lake to be wilderness.

The visitors using powerboats did not distinguish between the types of recreationists encountered. Boats and canoes were perceived essentially as one class, except that somewhat more motorboaters reported enjoying meeting paddlers, apparently as a touch of local color. Only 3 per cent of the boaters disliked meeting other boaters or motor canoeists. None objected to paddlers. Neutrality toward boats and motor canoes marked 73 per cent of the sample, and 55 per cent were neutral toward paddlers. One-fourth enjoyed meeting boats or canoes with motors, and 45 per cent enjoyed meeting the purists doing it the hard way—the paddlers.

Logging was observed by a slightly higher proportion of boaters than canoeists. This is probably because the question included a broader area than the Boundary Waters Canoe Area, and these groups tended to see and report logging trucks and other activities associated with logging outside the established area more often than canoeists. Of the boaters, 21 per cent observed logging but only 8 per cent were bothered by what they saw.

Resource perception has been differentiated on the basis of the type of recreation, particularly the type of transportation used. This, in effect, says that the choice of a boat or canoe reflects a cluster of present values and ideas. The stability of this relation over time is unknown; the effect of future technology is unforeseeable. The clusters of values are also unlikely to remain constant. Many questions remain to be answered—and some yet to be asked—about the development and meaning of outdoor recreational resources and the wilderness.[48]

Resource Use as Influenced by Perception

Three rather different perceptions of the wilderness resource of the border lakes held by three groups (managers, canoeists, and boaters) have been presented in this article. To what extent do these perceptions influence the use of the resource by these three groups?

RESOURCE MANAGERS

Much of the influence of the land managers' views of the resource was reflected in the policies developed, and this has already been discussed. However, there are a few other indications of the effect of their resource perception. The examples which come to mind all hinge on the perception of the boundary of the wilderness. I have suggested that the Forest Service thinks of the line on the map as the boundary. Indeed, the law requires them to do so in

[47] *Ibid.*, p. 159.

[48] See William Burch and Marvin J. Taves, "Changing Functions of Recreation in Human Society," *Outdoor Recreation in the Upper Great Lakes Area,* USDA Forest Service, Lake States Forest Exper. Station Paper No. 89 (St. Paul, 1961), pp. 8-16.

many ways, such as road building, logging, and private airplane travel. One result of this view is that the Forest Service has favored improving access roads to make it easier and pleasanter for people to reach the wilderness, which the Forest Service has assumed is the attraction and has considered to begin at the official boundary. But to many visitors these roads are located in their "wilderness": only 38 per cent of the sample groups thought that "straightening and blacktopping more roads" was "a good idea."

The same resource image may have contributed to the location of many boat accesses and campgrounds at the ends of the roads, as close to the wilderness as possible, while some large, attractive lakes outside the official wilderness area have no developments.

In a few cases in the past, this view of the resource may have contributed to decisions to bring access roads directly to lakes partially within the Boundary Waters, building past other lakes which are on canoe routes to the peripheral lakes, and thus reducing the effective size of the roadless area. This may have had some role in the construction of the last section of the Gunflint Trail many years ago, or of the road to the shores of Brule Lake after World War II. There seems to have been some reappraisal on this point, and plans to extend a road and make access easier on the Moose River have been set aside.

RECREATIONISTS

The canoeists used almost all of the area, penetrating to the core (Fig. 4).[49] This was most true of the paddling canoeists and appears consistent with the high value they place on the wilderness attraction, their perception of a small wilderness located in the core, and their objection to crowding at a low level of use.

However, canoeists were heavily concentrated at one access point. Over half used Moose Lake, although there were more than fifty other possible starting points, at least twenty of them seemingly very attractive. This is not consistent with the objection to crowding. The basis for the popularity of Moose Lake appeared to be its location deep within the interior (the road to the lake is surrounded by the Boundary Waters Canoe Area) and its closeness to the main, central entry to Canada's Quetico Park. These aspects of the situation are all evident on the map, but new visitors learn of the heavy use only after the choice of route is made. Knowledge of alternative locations may be limited, but this was not studied.

Another element in the wilderness perception of many people apparently affects the distribution of use. This is the lure of the North and Canada. Thus, the separate portion of the Boundary Waters Canoe Area south of the road running north and west from Ely was almost unused.

The motor canoeists did not go as far as the paddlers. In most cases they apparently went just far enough to find their wilderness fishing.

The motorboaters, on the other hand, were concentrated around the periphery and on several large international border lakes with truck or tramway portages leading to them (Fig. 5). Most of the core was unused. The attraction of the North was weak. This is consistent with boaters' greater interest in fishing and scenery than wilderness, their large wilderness, and their lack of concern with crowding.

CONCLUSION

All resources are defined by human perception. This has been said more often than used as an organizing concept in research. The importance of resource perception is particularly obvious for recreational, scenic, and amenity resources because of

[49] The maps of use distribution are based upon estimates developed in a field survey in 1961 involving traffic counts, sample interviews, and business records. The procedures and details of estimates for all types of users are included in Lucas, *The Recreational Use of the Quetico-Superior Area,* USDA Forest Service Research Paper LS-8, Lake States Forest Exper. Station (St. Paul, 1964), and in the thesis by Lucas cited above.

the internal, personal, and subjective way such resources are used. Within the general class of amenity resources, the perception of wilderness resources is even more obviously necessary to understanding or action because of the prominence of the subjective aspect.

Despite the complete subjectivity of wilderness and the variation in its perception, neither the social scientist nor the land manager need throw up his hands in bewilderment. Empirical research in one wilderness-type area, the Boundary Waters Canoe Area, suggests that considerable order can be imposed even upon subjects as elusive as solitude and beauty.

This order in perception of the wilderness resource has implications for the management of the resource. The implications all suggest a more flexible concept of "the wilderness" by the resource managers, both in area and in content. There are two main wildernesses—the paddling canoeists' and the motorboaters'—with a smaller group of motor canoeists defining an intermediate wilderness. None corresponds closely to the official wilderness.

The differences between these wildernesses may provide a key to increasing the capacity of the area in order to provide high-quality recreation. The highest priority use by established policy is wilderness canoeing. The canoeists' wilderness is easily destroyed by heavy use, especially boat use. The boaters value wilderness much less highly and fishing more highly, accept heavy use, and are usually in their wilderness before they reach the areas used by the canoeists, or the canoeists' wilderness. It would seem that the canoeists' satisfaction could be raised, or kept high as visitors increase, without reducing the motorboaters' satisfaction by concentrating new access points, campgrounds, and resort or cabin site leases, and managing the fishing intensively in the band of forests and lakes away from the Boundary Waters Canoe Area but inside the wilderness for most boaters.[50]

The study also implies that a decision must be made between limiting the numbers using a wilderness and letting the wilderness as defined by the visitors vanish from overuse. This disappearance has already taken place in part of the Canoe Country for the more sensitive types of users, and use trends suggest that the wilderness will retreat farther in the future for all types of visitors if use is unlimited.

The same zoning approach might have value in western mountain wilderness-type areas. The paddling purist may have his counterpart in the "backpacker." The jeep or motorscooter may play the motorboat's role.

The wilderness perception framework for research may be useful in developing the semi-wilderness concept and applying it to different settings. Despite the apparent objection to the idea of semi-wilderness in the abstract in the Canoe Country, pragmatically the system seems quite successful. There may be critical points in all competing uses which correspond to breakpoints in wilderness perception by certain classes of recreationists. Empirical research within this theoretical system may identify these thresholds. Perhaps some wilderness should have pre-Columbian ecological conditions restored insofar as possible and use limited to a few backpackers, while other "wilderness" may only need to be a place where a family can pitch a tent by their car isolated from trailers, portable electric generators, and transistor radios. If research on wilderness perception can identify segments within this range which are characteristic of certain types of recreationists, it should be possible to increase both the amount and quality of wilderness recreation. Greater diversity in wilderness management will probably increase the complexity of administration, but growing use and changing perceptions may make more flexibility essential in the future. Guidelines will be needed.

50 This conclusion agrees with the suggested system of concentric zones of progressively less primitive character surrounding strict wilderness cores in Carhart, *Planning for America's Wildlands*, *op. cit.*

GILBERT F. WHITE

CONTRIBUTIONS OF GEOGRAPHICAL ANALYSIS TO RIVER BASIN DEVELOPMENT

This is an effort to outline against the background of one experimental area the contributions which geographical analysis is making or might be expected to make to the strategy of river basin development. It begins in the Lower Mekong but then expands its view to other basins where geographers have taken a hand.

The international experiment in river development in the Lower Mekong is unique not only in being the first attempt under United Nations auspices to bring several nations together in managing the waters of a large basin before contending claims arise, but also in seeking to relate the full array of scientific knowledge and method of planning before major construction begins. Cambodia, Laos, Thailand, and Viet Nam have been interested since 1957 in putting together whatever data and analytical techniques would enable them to move ahead with building and operating an integrated system of river regulation works in the shortest time at reasonable cost.

As a consultant during 1961–62 to the Coordinating Committee of the four countries, I shared with three colleagues the task of reviewing the current cooperative investigations[1] and of recommending whatever further social, economic, and administrative studies and arrangements would then seem appropriate.[2] At the time this required examination of what geographers as well as other workers in social science could contribute to the undertaking. Since completing the formal report I have given further thought to the problem, and now use the Lower Mekong as a point of departure for appraising ways in which geographical analysis may advance the wise planning of river development. By river development I mean the control and use of water for multiple human purposes in river basins as a whole or in major sub-basins, a concept that has been stated by the United Nations Panel on Integrated River Development[3] and most recently in papers at the United Nations Conference on Science and Technology.[4] In reviewing geographical work in basins where comprehensive river management is in progress I may well have overlooked some important analysis, and I must present this as a first effort to draw together the evidence. I am unin-

• Gilbert F. White is Professor of Geography, University of Chicago.

Paper read before the Royal Geographical Society, March 18, 1963. Reprinted from the *Geographical Journal,* CXXIX (1963), 412–36, with the permission of the author and the editor.

1 The review was supported by the Ford Foundation.

2 G. F. White, Egbert de Vries, Harold B. Dunkerley, and John V. Krutilla, *Economic and Social Aspects of Lower Mekong Development,* a Report to the Committee for Coordination of Investigations of the Lower Mekong Basin (Bangkok), reprinted with revisions (Chicago, 1962).

3 U.N., Dept. Econ. and Soc. Affairs, *Integrated River Basin Development,* Report by a panel of experts (New York: UN, 1958).

4 Eugene W. Weber and Maynard M. Hufschmidt, "River Basin Planning in the United States," *Natural Resources, I. Energy, Water, and River Basin Development,* U.S. Papers prepared for the United Nations Conf. on the Application of Science and Technology for the Benefit of the Less Developed Areas (Washington: Government Printing Office [1963]), pp. 299–312.

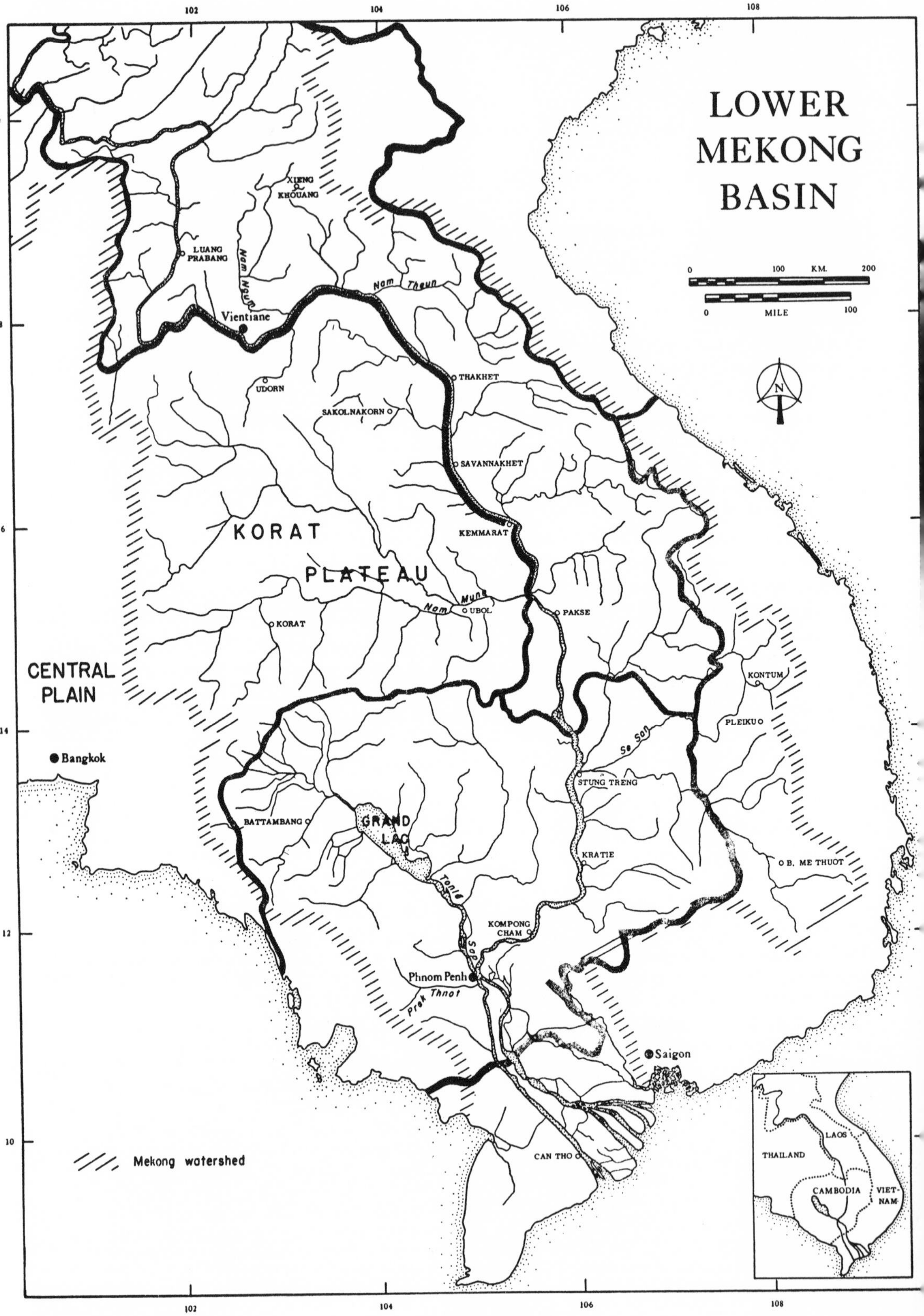
LOWER MEKONG BASIN
0 100 KM. 200
0 MILE 100
N
XIENG KHOUANG
LUANG PRABANG
Nam Ngum
Vientiane
Nam Theun
THAKHET
UDORN
SAKOLNAKORN
SAVANNAKHET
KEMMARAT
KORAT
PLATEAU
Nam Mune
UBOL
PAKSE
KORAT
CENTRAL PLAIN
KONTUM
PLEIKU
Se San
Bangkok
STUNG TRENG
BATTAMBANG
GRAND LAC
KRATIE
B. ME THUOT
Tonle Sap
KOMPONG CHAM
Phnom Penh
Prek Thnot
Saigon
CAN THO
Mekong watershed
THAILAND
LAOS
CAMBODIA
VIET-NAM
102
104
106
108
20
18
16
14
12
10

FIG. 1

formed on recent progress reported in the People's Republic of China.[5]

It is a temptation to devote this full paper to a description of the continuing challenge and the modest but promising achievement of the Lower Mekong experiment, but I refrain for two reasons. First, the more detailed description can be found in reports which shortly will be made public.[6] But more important to geography, the problems and lessons of the Lower Mekong can be used to suggest in concrete fashion the opportunities—realized and unrealized—for geographical analysis wherever man seeks to manage water resources on an integrated basis. He now is engaged in giant transformations of landscape by such development, and he has begun to see physical as well as economic limits to the amount of management he can accomplish. The strategies and plans devised in the next few decades are likely, unless there is some radical shift in technology of water control, to set patterns for resource use for much longer periods to follow. The supplies of water are finite, the opportunities for management are large but limited, and as each new reservoir or channel improvement is constructed the choice is narrowed. Unfortunately, in some countries a large dam, like a nuclear reactor, is a status symbol to be sought with little regard to its relative efficiency in advancing the national welfare.

The Lower Mekong in 1962 provides an especially suitable case with which to begin an appraisal, in that it starts from scratch and draws upon numerous disciplines. From the Mekong, I shall go farther afield in place and time to point out, within a general model of decision making in river development, the accomplishments of geographical analysis to date and some problems that remain unsolved.

[5] Stanislaw Leszczycki, "The Development of Geography in the People's Republic of China," *Geography,* CCXIX (1963), 145–47.

[6] C. H. Schaaf and R. H. Fifield, *The Lower Mekong* (New York: Van Nostrand Searchlight Series, 1963); G. F. White, "The Lower Mekong Plan," *Scientific American,* CCVII (1963), 49–59.

Water in the Lower Mekong

In some respects the drainage basin of the Mekong below the Lao-Burma-Chinese border where its gorge cuts deep through the rugged Yunnan Plateau is an admirable demonstration of problems of integrated river development. It embraces an area of about 600,000 square kilometers in which more than twenty-two million people produce a relatively low national product (£23–35 per capita) from field, forest, and associated pursuits. Wet-season rice is the principal product: upland rice in the burned clearings of shifting agriculture where population densities generally are below 13 per square kilometer; and paddy in the valleys of the plateaus and in the broader alluvial plains that stretch from below the Sambor Falls and around the Great Lake (Tonlé Sap) to the fretted lower margins of the Delta. In parts of the Delta intense cultivation is practiced and population widely exceeds 300 per square kilometer. Navigation and drainage are vital to the commercial life of the alluvial valley and Delta, but water management outside the individual paddy fields now plays a minor role in the economy. It is nevertheless one of the promising means of supporting economic growth.

If over the next 25 years the food and fiber production is to meet demands of a population growing at 3 per cent per year, and at the same time is to maintain foreign exchange balances and support a modest increase in individual income, there must be strong expansion in agricultural and energy production linked with industrialization. The river has the water and gradient to generate tremendous amounts of electrical energy and to supply irrigation for dry season cultivation of diversified crops and for opening up new lands. Flood control and low-water control would be essential in many sections to improvement of crop production by irrigation and drainage. Channel improvements could promote cheap water transport along the main stem. The volumes of water, the hydraulic heads, the availability of some lands that could be settled, and the readiness of governments to join in cooperative studies combine to favor a comprehensive approach to river regulation.

On the other hand, there is a sobering shortage of data, trained personnel, and capital with which to undertake whatever program of management might seem wise. These conditions, together with the urgent need to stabilize political organization in Asia, make it important for the four countries to use every available man-hour or bit of currency as efficiently as practicable in moving toward national goals of human welfare. The political situation is precarious at best. In 1957 there was not one long-term accurate measurement of discharge of the river, and basic population estimates for some areas of the basin varied as much as 40 per cent. Yet the pressure of events, opportunities, and human vision of them has led to a broad attack upon the problem of designing the right works to serve social aims.

Cooperative Investigations

Financial and material aid has been contributed by fourteen other countries, eleven international agencies, and several foundations. The spread of studies now under way or completed is indicated by the array in Table 1. These have been organized under the Coordinating Committee of the four countries working with staff and sponsorship of the United Nations Economic and Social Commission for Asia and the Far East.

Maps are, of course, essential to engineering studies and, while the entire lower basin probably will be covered by topographic sheets at a scale of 1:50,000 by 1965, there was immediate need for leveling to establish basic controls and for large-scale maps of promising dam sites and reservoir areas. Geological investigation of dam sites and of possible resources of bauxite and other minerals suitable for commercial exploitation is under way. Engineering studies on a reconnaissance scale of basins and on an intensive scale for three main-stem projects and seven tributary projects include hydrology and soil studies along with customary design work. At four tributary project sites, designs are also being drawn for pilot farms. A skeleton network of hydrologic observations has been established. Hydrographic survey is closely linked with a program of navigation improvement in the lowermost reaches of the stream. The complexities of water movement and quality in the lower alluvial channels are being explored by studies of silt and of fish life in the Great Lake area and by construction of a mathematical model of the Delta.

The extent and detail of these investigations are much greater than specified by Table 1, but the main lines of work are there evident. Basic topographic, hydrologic, and geologic surveys are providing data for preliminary engineering designs, and accompanying studies are looking to special questions of water, silt, and fish behavior and of raw materials which may arise as planning moves further. A remarkable degree of cooperation among national and international agencies has been achieved so far. A Japanese engineering team while working on Cambodian terrain may use Canadian maps, Australian geological studies, French soil maps, and American hydrological observations.

Recommended Investigations

Our mission recommended that in addition to these studies the four countries take further steps in the social, economic, and administrative field with a view to assuring optimum returns from the first projects selected. In view of the limited resources and time it seems important to begin "about right" with building and other action that promises substantial net gains. Eleven separate actions were suggested, as summarized in Table 2, in addition to the studies already in progress. Our report was released by the four countries in January 1963, and some of the suggested work already has been initiated.

In general, the recommended studies are

intended to obtain information on resources and resource use which would provide a base for a large number of more detailed investigations over a long period, and to initiate the more urgent of these. In very practical terms it could be argued that final design and construction of any river project on the Lower Mekong could proceed without such investigations. This is correct, but it also seems certain that to move ahead without them would incur heavy cost in the form of projects which failed to achieve their anticipated social gains. The hazard of building concrete and steel structures that meet technical requirements and fall short in their promotion of a stable life in the basin is great. In the present state of our knowledge, it is easier to design a safe irrigation dam than to design an effective scheme for agricultural settlement below the dam and it is less difficult to predict the financial cost of a new channel than to anticipate its physical and social consequences in adjoining lands and downstream.

The recommendations omit desirable studies which did not seem certain to yield practical returns or which would employ methods not yet shown to be fruitful. For example, it had been proposed to make a

TABLE 1

SUMMARY OF INVESTIGATIONS IN PROGRESS OR COMPLETED

Description	Agency	Estimated Cost (Thousands of U.S. Dollars)
Mapping—Aerial photography	Canada	1,365
Topography	Philippines	235
Leveling	Canada, U.S.A.	[a]
Hydrographic survey—Navigation	New Zealand	183
	United Kingdom	364
	Special Fund	[a]
Hydrologic measurements	U.S.A.	2,200
	W.M.O.	45
Dam site explorations	Australia	409
Soil surveys	France	[a]
Minerals prospection	France	750
	Special Fund	[a]
Fisheries and sedimentation	France	[a]
Major projects: Engineering		
Pa Mong	U.S.A.	2,500
Sambor	Japan	[a]
Tonlé Sap	India	282
Tributaries		
Engineering reconnaissance	Japan	652
7 projects—Engineering	Japan	[a]
	Special Fund	2,719
	Israel	75
	Pakistan	[b]
Agricultural pilot projects—4	Special Fund, FAO	[a]
Public health study	WMO	5
Delta model	UNESCO	17
Shifting agriculture and forestry	FAO	186
Manpower study	ILO	12
Economic and social	Ford Foundation	[b]
Flood warning system	France	[a]
Power market surveys	France	[a]
	Special Fund	[a]
	Resources for Future	[b]

[a] Cost included under other item for same agency.

[b] Detailed cost estimate not available.

comprehensive anthropological–archaeological survey,[7] but this approach had not been demonstrated to be essential to sound planning at this stage. The more refined or experimental work can come later.

Four of the recommended studies would, it is expected, call for large participation by geographers. The synthesis of existing data would be organized around preparation of a basin atlas and accompanying statistical summaries. In the inventory of land use and land-use capability there would be need for geographical talent in classifying uses and in recognizing natural land types. The assessment of measures for achieving agricultural improvement should go very deep into the conditions in which, upon the basis of experience both within the basin and in comparable areas, the desired flow of benefits from water management in the face of hazards of drought and flood may be assured.[8] Economists, anthro-

[7] W. G. Solheim and R. A. Hackenberg, "The Importance of Anthropological Research to the Mekong River Project," *France-Asie,* CLXIX (1961), 2459–74.

[8] E. de Vries, ***Land, Water, and Rice in the Mekong,*** Report of International Institute for Land Reclamation and Improvement (Wageningen, 1962), pp. 5–19.

TABLE 2

SUMMARY OF ADDITIONAL STUDIES RECOMMENDED FOR THE LOWER MEKONG[a]

Problem	Method of Work	Approximate Cost (Thousands of U.S. Dollars)
1. Synthesis of available data on resources, resource use, and social characteristics affecting land development	Basin atlas	180
2. Inventory of land use and land-use capability (in two steps)	Aerial photo interpretation, field observations and map compilation	2,500–6,500
3. Assessment of measures for achieving agricultural improvement	Study by interdisciplinary agricultural team, followed by seminar	135
4. Comprehensive analysis of power market potential:		
a. Domestic markets for residential, commercial and normal industrial-loads	Country surveys	120–60
b. Transport-oriented electro-process industries producing for area and intra-regional markets	Regional market study	150–450
c. Power-oriented electro-process industries producing for inter-regional or world market	World market appraisal	80
5. Flood forecasting and flood damage reduction	Analysis of present and possible adjustments to flood hazard	45
6. Cooperative examination of methods of estimating economic feasibility	Joint review in field and in office by study groups	100
7. Scale and scope of ultimate Mekong system	Simulated systems analysis	225
8. Critical problems of economic and social analysis within basin, such as estimating benefits, fiscal policy, power marketing policy, domestic investment and foreign exchange	Research and short-term training of committee and national agencies staff	500
9. Regional problems and prospects, such as markets for agricultural products, national income accounts and economic projections, and levels of living	Cooperative study under international agencies	....
10. Exploration of practical administrative arrangement for international construction and operation	Consultant and subcommittee	100
11. Comprehensive rural demonstration project of 3,000–5,000 hectares under water management	Unified regional administration	2,500

[a] The mission also recommended measures to strengthen committee staff and to experiment with forest plantings.

pologists, administrators, and geographers should join in this. Given a program for making hydrologic forecasts of floods, geographical studies of types of adjustment to flood hazard would be essential to developing methods of flood-loss reduction.

In addition, geographers might well play a part in other lines of investigation, such as in the demonstration project and in the examination of certain of the regional problems. There is much on the physical side not covered by these recommendations that should command their attention and that may be highly important in shaping the basin program. These possible contributions will be apparent as we review the broad process of planning for river development.

Strategies of River Development

Implicit in these recommendations is the belief that there is a strategy or alternative set of strategies for water management that will better serve the welfare aims of the four Lower Mekong countries than others. The kinds of strategies which they might adopt and the ways in which they might make their selection are highly diverse, as the record of efforts at integrated river development around the world reveals most colorfully. To state the possibilities systematically, let us set up a general model of the elements that enter into decision making in water management, and then indicate how these may vary.

Let us assume that the groups or individuals which decide how funds, physical resources, and personnel will be allocated for river development—that is, the people who allocate money to build a dam or who set power rates or who rearrange holdings in irrigated land—act always from imperfect knowledge and reach their decisions by processes that are partly explicit and conscious, and partly unconscious, being influenced by inarticulate attitudes. Their knowledge is bound to be imperfect notwithstanding our increasing understanding of the niceties of human and physical processes. Considerations such as prestige, power, and preference will affect decisions that might be formulated as basically economic. Let us also assume that at any given time these people can state roughly the aims which they have in mind in considering an alteration in water regimen and that they are capable of some modification in plans when they become aware of the possible consequences.

With these assumptions we can identify at least six chief aspects of decision making, the last of which modifies each of the other five. One is the range of choice of resource use which is considered possible: the number and character of ways of using water and associated land and minerals. A second is the estimation of the resources available in terms of assets and liabilities for specified uses. A third is the technology which it is expected will be both available and applied in using the resource. Fourth is the expected economic efficiency of the resource use in operating units such as farms or industrial plants. Fifth is the spatial linkage between resource use in one place and in adjacent or functionally related places. And finally, there are the social guides which society uses directly or inadvertently to affect the conditions of choice.

To be concrete, in the Lower Mekong the responsible Committee is having to decide as it goes along: (1) what uses of water it will consider in its planning; (2) what resources of water, land, and minerals are available; (3) the kind of technology it expects may be applied in developing them; (4) how the economic costs and returns to individual farmers and industries will be computed; (5) what linkages between resource use in one place and other places in the region will be taken into account; and (6) what social incentives and restraints will be applied to water and land use. The criteria for choice in each case permit a wide set of answers. Many economists pursue the optimum solution which maximizes the net returns. A cautious farmer may seek the strategy which minimizes the maximum losses possible if uncertainties of weather or man turn for the worst. A politician may seek to stabilize a situation of community tension or to redistribute income to benefit distressed areas. A biologist may favor the arrangement which would generate the least physical disturbances over the long run or that would maintain maximum diversity. A social reformer may prefer that which would generate the greatest social change in a desired direction over the short run.

Depending upon the assumptions that are made and the criteria which are applied, quite different strategies will emerge. There is no correct plan for all circumstances. Rather, there are at least as many best plans as there are sets of aims, assumptions, and criteria, and there may well be several different but equally satisfactory solutions for a given set. To assert this is to challenge much of the engineering practice by which one plan is recommended for a given basin. A single plan customarily means that the engineers have tacitly defined most of the aims, assumptions, and criteria which underlie the planning. Rarely does the client specify them. Oftentimes they are accepted without challenge and without recognition that with slightly different definitions the resulting recommendations would diverge widely.

Thus, a decision to store and divert water for irrigation in the Korat Plateau involves a judgment that irrigation warrants consideration in meeting agricultural needs, an estimate that soil and water resources are adequate to such use, an assumption as to the kind and conditions of technology to be used in applying water and handling the crops, an estimate of the probable streams of social benefits and costs which would flow from the investment, an estimate in both physical and social terms of the spatial linkages of that use with resource use in other areas, and a program of legal, credit, and educational arrangements to guide the new development.

One of my colleagues cautions that this is the wrong place to present a decision-making scheme; the British, he argues, do not make decisions, they get into situations and get out of them without deciding anything or by stretching out the process in a series of minor adjustments. Indeed, I have it on presently high political authority that there is not inconsiderable segment that "couldn't say yes and couldn't say no." But finally, even in the coldest weather, some decision is made, although it may be so ambiguous as to assume, for example, that never again will there be a winter as severe as 1963.

The Range of Choice

If the people who plan river development were all-knowing and wise, their design studies always would canvass the whole range of uses and use combinations which experience in the basin or in similar areas suggests as being productive. This was substantially the case in the Lower Mekong where the examination of navigation, power, irrigation, flood control and related purposes came against the background of an ECAFE inquiry into river development throughout its region as well as other regions. The cooperative studies in the region led to a series of descriptive appraisals of water management experience,[9] and to a manual of river-planning procedure.[10] U.S., Bureau of Reclamation reconnaissance in the Mekong had applied a view that had grown up in an arid temperate environment.[11] The Wheeler Mission in its membership had brought to bear the perspective of engineering experience from Canada, France, India, and Japan in addition to the United States.[12]

9 Economic Commission for Asia and the Far East, *Development of Water Resources in the Lower Mekong Basin,* Flood Control Ser. 12 (Bangkok: ECAFE, 1957).

10 *Idem, Multiple-Purpose River Basin Development, Part I: Manual of River Basin Planning,* Flood Control Ser. 7 (Bangkok: ECAFE, 1955).

11 U.S., International Cooperation Administration, *Report of Bureau of Reclamation Reconnaissance of Lower Mekong* (Washington: ICA, 1956).

12 Economic Commission for Asia and the Far East, *Programme of Studies and Investigations for Comprehensive Development, Lower Mekong Basin* (Bangkok: ECAFE, 1958).

Yet, the record of multipurpose river development in many parts of the world is unhappily ornamented by instances where less than the full range of possible uses of water management was considered, often with serious social consequences. The omissions can be traced to several causes. One is the simple limitation of administrative authority of a government agency, as in the Tennessee Valley Authority where the enabling legislation specifically and for constitutional reasons named navigation, flood control, and, as an auxiliary, hydroelectric power as the major purposes, and made no mention of recreation, industrial water use, and irrigation.[13] These uses did receive attention in the area thereafter, with recreational water use the first to be the subject of intensive analysis from TVA staff. A second is the restriction of aims to those offering monetary returns or bearing a presumably direct relationship to national income flows, as in the Kariba Development on the Zambezi or the Volta Scheme in Ghana, where vendible benefits from hydroelectric power were dominant considerations. In some cases private power interests have opposed public development of competitive water-control works. More difficult are the constraints that stem from cultural blunders such as the assumption that unlike places are alike. Many of the single-purpose and ineffective efforts at water development have come from people who set out to implant the methods of another culture in inhospitable social soil.

The geographer may help correct this myopia by two types of studies. In his efforts to find homologues among the immensely diversified patterns of the Earth's surface he can identify situations which are similar to the basin under study. Thus, the arid homoclimates of Meigs,[14] and the mapping of indexes of economic development,[15] offer valuable grounds for comparing environmental complexes from place to place and for asking whether or not all the kinds of water management practised in similar places will be assessed in the basin under study. Elementary questions as to the role irrigation might be expected to play in an area such as the Korat Plateau with sandy soils and a seasonal water deficit, or as to areas comparable in national product and electric energy consumption *per capita,* then may be raised with profit.

The more searching regional and historical studies also provide information on systems of water management which have been tried and abandoned or still are practiced in a basin. Any consideration of the opportunities for water management in the Lower Mekong must be in the debt of scholars such as Gourou, Peltzer, Pendleton, and Robequain for their thoughtful investigations of sectors of that area.[16] It also is helpful to have brief outlines of regional patterns such as that by Johnson.[17] Regional geographical studies are not necessarily useful beyond giving a very broad background for the more detailed studies required for basic planning; they may be so general as to lack meaning, they may sacrifice analysis to description, or they may address themselves to questions which, however interesting for other pur-

13 C. Herman Pritchett, *The Tennessee Valley Authority, A Study in Public Administration* (Chapel Hill: University of North Carolina, 1943).

14 Peveril Meigs, *World Distribution of Arid and Semi-arid Homoclimates,* Reviews of research on arid-zone hydrology (Paris: UNESCO, 1952).

15 Norton Ginsburg, *An Atlas of Economic Development* (Chicago: University of Chicago Press, 1960).

16 P. Gourou, *La Terre et l'homme en extrême-orient* (Paris: A. Colin, 1940); *idem, L'Utilisation du sol en Indochine Française,* Publications du centre d'études de politique étrangère (Paris: Hartmann, 1940); R. L. Pendleton, *Thailand, Aspects of Landscape and Life* (New York: American Geographical Society, 1962); K. J. Pelzer, *Pioneer Settlement in the Asiatic Tropics,* American Geographical Society Spec. Pub. 29 (New York, 1945); C. Robequain, *The Economic Development of French Indo-China,* transl. by I. A. Ward (London: Oxford University Press, 1944).

17 B. L. C. Johnson, *Lower Mekong River Basin,* An outline of its salient geographical features (Food and Agriculture Organization of the United Nations, 1958), mimeographed.

poses, are useless for this purpose. Samples of those appearing to have had some direct relevance to later river development decisions are ones of Central Africa and the Missouri.[18]

Probably the most influential analysis thus far made by a geographer of the ways in which water management might affect an area was that by Barrows of problems raised by the decision to build the Grand Coulee Dam and associated works for power, irrigation, and flood control on the upper Columbia River.[19] His definition of the impacts to be examined not only outlined a framework for comprehensive investigation of the implications of water control for the Columbia Basin, but thereby established an approach and yielded findings that were applied elsewhere in investigations by participating agencies. Barrows set twenty-eight problems for attack and organized teams of researchers from a wide assortment of disciplines to try to solve them. A similar scheme then was carried into the Central Valley of California but with less success and with less participation by geographers.

This same form of analysis was employed in the appraisal of water problems in ten major river basins in the United States in 1950, an interdepartmental and interdisciplinary effort which was directed by a geographer (Ackerman) and claimed the aid of geographers in various government bureaus.[20] From the work of that group and the discussion it provoked new criteria for the evaluation of water projects were drawn up for federal agencies by the Bureau of the Budget, and subsequent investigations and plans thereby were affected.

It may well be that in some countries such as the United Kingdom the principal contribution made by geographers to river development planning is in their participation in the local planning surveys that provide a broad base for various types of development schemes. Without sharing directly in the water studies, they may help prepare local resource and resource-use inventories that then are used by others to set aims and criteria. In the Soviet Union and in Poland, geographical studies are important for economic regionalization and also figure in later stages of planning.[21] In the Union of South Africa geographers are taking a significant part in studies made by the Natural Resources Development Council to assist regional development associations in planning new programs and to aid in selecting national schemes. Thus, Fair and Moolman headed NRDC teams looking into broad opportunities in the Orange and Pongola basins before detailed plans were prepared. More precise examination of conditions and opportunities for resource use in the interior delta of the Niger was undertaken in 1957 by a group of geographers under the leadership of Gourou with support by the Services de l'Hydraulique de l'Afrique occidentale française et due Soudan.[22] It will be interesting to see how much of their findings are reflected in the report on development of the Niger now being completed by a United Nations team.

18 Frank Debenham, *Report on the Water Resources of the Bechuanaland Protectorate, Northern Rhodesia, The Nyasaland Protectorate, Tanganyika Territory, Kenya, and the Uganda Protectorate,* Colon. Res. Publ. No. 2 (1948); E. A. Ackerman, "Report on Missouri Basin," U.S., Commission on Organization of Executive Branch, *Organization and Policy in the Field of Natural Resources* (Washington: GPO, 1949).

19 U.S., Bureau of Reclamation, *Columbia Basin Joint Investigations: Character and Scope* (Washington: GPO, 1941).

20 U.S., President's Water Resources Policy Commission, *Ten Rivers in America's Future* (Washington: GPO, 1950).

21 I. V. Komar, "Problems of Zonification for the Development of National Economy," U.N., Conf. on Science and Technology (Geneva, 1963), unpublished.

22 P. Gourou, "Étude du Monde Tropical (géographie physique et humaine)," *L'Annuaire du collège de France* (1961–62), 237–45; J. Tricart, *L'Épiderme de la Terre* (Paris: Masson, 1962), pp. 116–20.

Resource Estimates

Few basins begin their planning with as little data on the basic resources of water, land, and minerals as did the Lower Mekong, for there the stream-flow records are extremely sparse, the meteorological data are spotty, cover and soil surveys are chiefly reconnaissance, and mineral surveys are scattered and incomplete. Preliminary estimates of these resources are necessary to the early planning. Without at least hazy notions of how much water, soil, and mineral there is to use, the main lines of study cannot be laid out, and once under way more detailed and precise estimates become essential for detailed project planning. To a large extent both detailed and reconnaissance estimates must be the work of specialists who command the niceties of hydrology or pedology or geology, but there are at least two points at which geographical analysis may advance the estimating efforts.

In the absence of detailed surveys which may require decades for completion there is urgent need for generalized knowledge of distributions of major resources. Geographers long have been interested in description of hydrologic phenomena, and Pardé's work on flood and mean stream discharge is a prominent example.[23] The problem is to obtain results which are directly relevant to engineering or social design. Water-balance analysis, as developed by Thornthwaite and his associates[24] and by Lvovich and other Soviet workers,[25] offers a means of showing water deficit, water surplus, and potential evapotranspiration over large areas by interpolating from temperature and precipitation records. They also give insight into problems of the hydrologic cycle not revealed readily by stream-flow and precipitation measurements. The Soviet geographers have carried this type of study into detailed area appraisals and a number of them have been active in the Hydrometeorological Institute under Davitiya.[26] Such estimates are likely to be less exact than those based upon adequate stream discharge records, but may be more effective than stream flow from short-term and sporadic observations, and they have had value in computing amounts of water available and the amounts required for plant growth in dry areas. Polish geographers have pressed hydrographic mapping of both surface and ground waters assiduously, and now are moving ahead with comprehensive mapping of these characteristics for the entire nation and with detailed discussions of sheets on a scale of 1:50,000.[27] Considerable attention is given to associations among terrain and hydrologic characteristics.

Similar generalization as to soil and natural land types over wide areas at low cost in short periods of time are much more complex, but some promising ventures have been made in that direction. In Australia the CSIRO has pioneered with field classification of "land systems," using geogra-

[23] M. Pardé, "Sur les Coefficients et Déficits d'Écoulement des Très Grandes Crues," *Ann. Inst. Polytech. Grenoble,* Vol. III (1954).

[24] C. W. Thornthwaite and J. R. Mather, *The Water Balance,* Publications in Climatology, VIII (1955).

[25] M. I. Lvovich, "The Water Balance of the Land," *Materiali k III Syezdu Geogr. Obsch. S.S.S.R.* (1959); "On the Complex Utilization and Protection of Water Resources," *Izvestia Geogr.*, II (1961), 37–45; Lvovich, S. V. Bass, A. M. Grin, N. N. Dreier, and E. I. Kupriyanova, "Water Balance of the U.S.S.R. and Prospects of Its Remaking," *ibid.*, VI (1961), 36–46.

[26] J. K. Efremov, "Nature Conservation Law in R.S.F.S.R. and Tasks of the Soviet Geographers," *Izvestia Geogr. Obshchestva,* XCIII (1961), 193–98; K. P. Voskresenski, *Norma I Izmenchivost Godovogo Stoka Rek S.S.S.R.* (Leningrad, 1962); V. L. Vilenkin, "Geographer's Activities on the Realization of Nature Conservation Law," *Izvestia Geogr. Obshchestva,* XCIX (1962), 319–20.

[27] S. Leszczycki, "The Application of Geography in Poland," *Geographical Journal,* CXXVI (1960), 420; M. Klimaszewski, "The Detailed Hydrographical Map of Poland," *Przeglad Geogrogiczny,* 28 suppl. (1956), 4147; Krystyna Wit and Z. Ziemonska, *Hydrografia tatr Zachodnich,* Zaklad Geomorfologii i Hydrografii Gor i Wyzyn w Krakowie (1960), Polska Akademia Nauk.

phers in cooperation with botanists, geologists, and pedologists.[28] Tricart is developing methods of hydrologic mapping at a scale of 1:50,000 in France. He also has experimented with morphometric observations which would permit estimates of stream regimen, and could be carried out with geomorphological studies for soils and geological purposes.[29] Some of the more sophisticated land classifications for land settlement purposes have been made by Dutch workers.[30]

Identification of areas subject to flood and of the different degrees and types of flood hazard is fundamental to any scheme for reduction of flood losses as well as in proper siting of structures in valleys. The flood perimeter sometimes can be drawn from hydrologic or historical evidence, but where this is inadequate a satisfactory classification may be achieved from geomorphological evidence using aerial photo interpretation, as Tada and Ohya have demonstrated in several Japanese flood plains.[31] Their procedures were in fact applied in a portion of the Lower Mekong by the Japanese reconnaissance team studying tributary drainage basins. Studies of flood siting are reported by the Strasbourg center.[32]

Large-scale classifications of land capability are, of course, essential to proper design of land reclamation, and these commonly are made by soil scientists and agricultural engineers. Geographers have been interested in broader inventories and particularly in land use inventory. In the early days of the Tennessee Valley Authority a combined classification of land use and land-use capacity was launched by a geographic group under Hudson and proved useful in setting severance lines for acquisition of lands to be inundated by reservoirs as well as in dealing with some other land planning problems,[33] but the work was discontinued by TVA and has not been copied on a large scale except in Puerto Rico. There, the entire island was covered by a land classification program during 1949–51, and direct applications were subsequently made in advising on the economic feasibility of a proposed irrigation project, and in suggesting the adjustments in crop and land tenure patterns which would be required to assure sustained productivity in new irrigation lands in the Lajas Valley of the semi-arid southwest.[34] An explanation of why such geographical appraisals have not been emulated elsewhere must include personal administrative prejudice, but also must embrace the argument that unless they apply criteria and classes directly relevant to technical and economic decisions they are fruitless for river planning purposes.

The same problem applies to the land use inventory alone, which sometimes is advanced as a rough measure of land-use capability and which now is being practiced over wide areas.[35] Here, as with some other types of analysis to be noted later, there is doubt as to whether it is designers who have failed to see the utility of land

[28] Commonwealth Scientific and Industrial Research Organization, *Lands of the Alice Springs Area, Northern Territory, 1956–57,* Land Research Ser. 6 (Melbourne, Australia, 1962).

[29] Tricart, *op. cit.*, pp. 49–52.

[30] J. P. Bakker, "Dutch Applied Geomorphological Research," *Revue de Geomorphologie Dynamique,* X (1959), 67–84.

[31] Fumio Tada and Masahiko Ohya, "The Flood-Type and the Classification of the Topography," *Proceedings of the I.G.U. Regular Conference in Japan, 1957* (Tokyo, 1959), 192–96; Japan Resources Council, *Reconnaissance Topographical Survey on Areas Subject to Flood* (Tokyo, 1957).

[32] Tricart, *op. cit.*, pp. 70–72.

[33] Donald Hudson, "Methods Employed by Geographers in Regional Surveys," *Economic Geography,* XII (1936), 98–104.

[34] David Gomez Montoya and Hector H. Berrios, "Uses Made of the Data Obtained in the Rural Land Classification Programme," *Symposium on the Geography of Puerto Rico,* ed. Clarence F. Jones and Rafael Pico (Rio Piedras: University of Puerto Rico Press, 1955), pp. 473–86.

[35] International Geographical Union, *Report of the Commission on Inventory of World Land Use* (New York, 1956); *idem,* Commission on a World Land Use Survey, *I.G.U. Newsletter,* IX (Zurich, 1960), 38–46.

use inventory or geographers who have failed to produce findings that are clearly responsive to planning needs. In a few areas the fault may rest with narrowly conceived schemes which are little concerned with the consequences. There can be no doubt that accurate inventory is basic for wise design of river development. Yet it has not demonstrated its value so persuasively that it automatically figures in new investigations. The test always should be whether or not the resource appraisal employs classes that have concrete meaning for aspects of the decision process. In recommending a combined land use and land-use capability survey for the Lower Mekong we recognized the danger that it might be so executed as to yield solely a soggy, sterile mass of data. Only by relating it closely to questions of technical and social judgment, and by assuring that results are in a form usable by decision makers, could such a survey promise to be genuinely helpful.

There is, however, another aspect of resource estimation that is fundamental. This is the problem of the contrast between the perception of environment by scientists and by individual farmers, merchants, officials, or others who make practical decisions in managing resources of land and water. We know, for example, that the owner of property in a flood-plain may see the flood hazard in quite different perspective than does a hydrologist who has analysed the historical and stream flow records for the same area.[36] Unless a farmer perceives a flood or drought hazard in dimensions similar to those of the scientist he cannot be expected to share fully the scientist's judgment as to ways of coping with it. Likewise, the estimate of available water may differ from one part of a basin to another, as in the Jordan Valley where from the same evidence radically different views are shared among responsible government officials. Although this difference between the two images may affect the whole design of a river development program, there have been few precise studies of the way in which it changes over area or of the limits that it places upon decisions.

Technology of Water Management

Any assessment of possible management of water must assume some level of technology to be applied in the storage, collection, transport, use, and disposal of water. It would be comforting to expect that every new storage reservoir on the Lower Mekong would employ the most advanced hydraulic and mechanical design, and that every farmer once supplied with irrigation water would practice the methods of cultivation and water application best suited on scientific grounds to optimum physical efficiency. But we know that everywhere there is a gap between knowledge and application and that realistic planning must allow for these differences and for their eradication. This requires recognition of the gap in particular places and of reasons for it. In the Lower Mekong it would be important to understand the farmers' present techniques of water management sufficiently well to be able to predict with a bit of confidence how these might change if water supply, land drainage, flood crests, or other factors were to be altered. It is possible that the diffusion models of Hagerstrand and others would be helpful in such analysis.[37]

Ackerman and his associate Löf have given us the most searching examination of water technology and its geographical implications.[38] They show the rough technical limits to the various technologies of water collection, storage, transport and disposal, and indicate conditions affecting their present or future use. Keller in his studies of

36 Robert W. Kates, *Hazard and Choice Perception in Flood Plain Management,* Dept. of Geog. Research Paper No. 78 (Chicago: Dept. of Geog., Univ. of Chicago, 1962).

37 T. Hagerstrand, *The Propagation of Innovation Waves,* Lund Studies in Geography, B, IV (Lund, Sweden: Royal Univ. of Lund, 1952).

38 E. A. Ackerman and George Löf, *Technology in American Water Development* (Baltimore: Johns Hopkins Press, 1959).

water in Germany, and particularly in the Ruhr-Westphalian area, has shown the extent to which sophisticated technology can be brought to bear upon industrial production in perhaps the most intense fashion yet recorded.[39] From their work and the studies of Sporck and others it is apparent that great increases in industrial use could be achieved with only very modest increases in supply, and that much of the fear of exhaustion of supplies in manufacturing concentrations may be exaggerated.[40]

Although there have been few incisive examinations of agricultural water technology,[41] it is to be hoped that more searching studies will be made by geographers, for the gap is especially wide and fluctuating in that sector of use. Any new ventures in irrigation and flood control will be sharpened by explanation of the way in which technology differs over area. In one well established irrigated valley the physical efficiencies differ by a factor of two or three from district to district or from farmer to farmer within the same district.[42] There is widespread need for studies of precisely how and why technologies of water use and disposal vary in space and time.

Economic Efficiency

For any combination of resources and technology it is possible to recognize optimum and limiting uses of water under given social aims, so that, for example, the limit of economic justification for a new hydroelectric and flood control installation on the Mekong's main stem, or for a small irrigation and power project on one of its tributaries, can be appraised. The determination of economic efficiency involves an estimate of future streams of benefits and costs for a desired time horizon at a suitable interest rate, and may be performed as an aid in selecting projects, in choosing among alternative designs for projects or systems so as to find the optimum one, or in deciding upon repayment, financial and administrative arrangements. Such an analysis is primarily economic in nature, and has been greatly refined in recent years,[43] but to be effective requires geographic contributions beyond the special considerations of spatial linkages to which attention will be given later. Private managers will be concerned with internal economies, while public agencies may also look to external economies and diseconomies. If land is irrigated, what will be the subsequent flow of benefits to the farmers and to merchants or farmers in other areas? If it is protected from occasional floods, what will be the resulting readjustments in land use and vulnerability to flood loss? If a reservoir is constructed for recreational use, to what extent will it draw visitors to its shores? If a waterway is improved, how will it affect the movement and composition of freight traffic in the area?

Geographers have thrown light on some of these questions. Without presuming to offer the full economic answer they have given insights that might otherwise have been omitted. New ventures in irrigation in South Asia and, indeed, in any tropical land, are indebted to Farmer for a careful analysis of the effects of colonization plans

39 Reiner Keller, *Gewässer und Wasserhaushalt des Festlandes* (Berlin: Haude & Spenersche, 1961), pp. 465–75.

40 J. A. Sporck, "L'Eau et la Géographie de la Localisation de l'Industrie," *Travaux Cercle Géographie Liège* (1956), p. 98; J. B. Graham and M. F. Burrill (eds.), *Water for Industry* (Washington: American Assoc. for the Advancement of Science, 1956); G. F. White, "Industrial Water Use," *Geographical Review,* L (1960), 412–30.

41 John D. Eyre, "Water Controls in a Japanese Irrigation System," *Geographical Review,* XLV (1955), 197–216; P. Gourou, *Le Tonkin* (Paris, 1931).

42 James Hudson, *Irrigation Water Use in the Utah Valley, Utah,* Dept. of Geog. Research Paper No. 79 (Chicago: Dept. of Geog., Univ. of Chicago, 1963).

43 Arthur Maass, Maynard M. Hufschmidt, Robert Dorfman, Harold A. Thomas, Jr., Stephen A. Marglin, Gordon Maskew Fair, and others, *Design of Water-Resource Systems* (Cambridge: Harvard University Press, 1962).

in the irrigated arid section of Ceylon.[44] His examination of the outcomes of these projects together with the reports of the Gal Oya Authority goes a long way toward building understanding of the economic impacts—both gains and losses—which would figure in a full social accounting of such an enterprise.

One of the more controversial questions concerning economic feasibility of irrigation projects is the degree to which benefits, from increased production of land are passed on to indirect beneficiaries such as merchants in nearby towns. Marts made a pioneer investigation of this problem in the Boise Valley of Idaho which is subject to challenge on its definition of benefits, but which provides a basis from which more refined work may proceed.[45]

Because only a little is known of the spatial variations in the demand and supply functions of water, it is important to press ahead with research which would elucidate them. Recent studies of flood-plain occupance in the United States have suggested some of the limits and form of these functions so far as flood loss reduction is concerned, and have revealed, for example, the types of changes in land use which may be expected to follow various forms and degrees of flood protection on urban lands and on agricultural lands.[46] In Canada several geographers have investigated land use in flood-plains as a basis for appraisal of proposed flood loss reduction in local projects and on the Fraser River scheme.[47] Marts and Sewell have shown the character of certain benefits and costs from wildlife conservation in water projects.[48] Sewell has collaborated with economists in a general guide to benefit-cost analysis.[49] The geographers working on the Meramec Valley study in Missouri have suggested a relationship between distance of residence and use of reservoir frontage that should be of value in estimating demand for and benefits from new reservoir construction.[50] There also seems to be interest among some Soviet geographers in benefit-cost analysis.[51]

A more popular form of estimate of economic impacts has been the prediction of changes in traffic movement which will result from completion of a new link in a waterway system. The construction of the St. Lawrence Seaway provoked a rash of predictions by geographers as well as others as to economic effects.[52] These used rela-

44 B. H. Farmer, *Pioneer Colonization in Ceylon, A Study in Asian Agrarian Problems* (London: Oxford University Press, 1957).

45 M. E. Marts, "Use of Indirect Benefit Analysis in Establishing Repayment Responsibility for Irrigation Projects," *Economic Geography,* XXXII (1956), 95–114.

46 Ian Burton, *Types of Agricultural Occupance of Flood Plains in the United States,* Dept. of Geog. Research Paper No. 75 (Chicago: Dept. of Geog., Univ. of Chicago, 1962); G. F. White, W. C. Calef, J. W. Hudson, H. M. Mayer, J. R. Sheaffer, and D. J. Volk, *Changes in Urban Occupance of Flood Plains in the United States,* Dept. of Geog. Research Paper No. 57 (Chicago: Dept. of Geog., Univ. of Chicago, 1958).

47 L-E. Hamelin, "Sainte-Marie de Beauce: Études d'Urbanisme," *Revue Canadienne d'Urbanisme,* V (1955), 93–97; *idem,* "La Géographie Physique Appliquée au Canada: Deux Exemples Québecois," *Cahiers de Géogr. Québec,* V (1959), 19–22.

48 M. E. Marts and W. R. D. Sewell, "The Nez Perce Dam and the Value of a Fishery," *Land Economics,* XXXVII (1961), 257–60.

49 W. R. D. Sewell, J. Davis, A. D. Scott, and D. W. Ross, *Guide to Benefit-Cost Analysis* (Ottawa: Queen's Printer, 1962).

50 Edward L. Ullman, Ronald R. Boyce, and Donald J. Volk, *The Meramec Basin: Water and Economic Development* (St. Louis: Meramec Basin Research Proj., Washington Univ., 1962).

51 G. L. Magakyan, "The Mingechaur Multi-Purpose Water Management Project," *Soviet Geography,* II (1961), 43–50.

52 Harold M. Mayer, *The Port of Chicago and the St. Lawrence Seaway* (Chicago: University of Chicago Press, 1957); Pierre Camu, "Effects of the St. Lawrence Seaway Project on the Port of Montreal," *Actualité Économie,* XXVIII (1953), 619–37. (Trans. from Geogr. Branch, Canadian Dept. of Mines and Tech. Surveys); Joseph A. Russell, Jerome D. Fellmann, and Howard G. Roepke, *The*

tively simple projections of trends then current and deserve greater refinement if the methods are to become widely useful in appraisal of new projects. A geographer (Olson) took part in a more elaborate estimate of effects of the Seaway upon shipping movement, allocating the expected traffic among competing ports.[53]

Economic efficiency in all aspects of water management has received attention from geographers in numerous investigations in the Soviet Union. A recent review of their widespread activity in the field of natural resources emphasizes the importance of identifying "territorial resource complexes" and of making economic appraisal of resources singly and in association.[54]

Spatial Linkages

If estimates of economic impacts, including internal and external economies and diseconomies, were to be sufficiently precise and comprehensive to describe all of the effects which might be anticipated from a water management project, there would be no need to look beyond those results for other impacts which would link the project with resource use elsewhere. But this never is the case; it is patently not so where the resource manager judges economic efficiency by strictly monetary criteria, as in the case of a farmer repaying the cost of his irrigation water by the returns from his own land or of a government recouping in cash revenue the full cost of a new dam yielding both vendible and non-vendible benefits; and even where a public agency sets out to give a complete social accounting of a project there are some effects that cannot yet be expressed effectively in terms of benefit-cost analysis or that show themselves in ways that affect spatial distributions without altering the total streams of benefits and costs. The nature of such spatial linkages may be indicated best by describing some that have received the attention of geographers.

Physical geographers have begun to explore the shift in hydrologic and sediment regimen resulting from the battery of measures man has designed to manage water. Tricart and his associates in applied geomorphology have examined the basic processes which would be involved in changing river flow and bed where the discharge is altered by up-stream works, where silt load is modified, or where the current is deflected by engineering works.[55] They have shown its practicality in a few reaches of French streams, in the Senegal Delta, on the middle Niger River and in Brazil.[56] Wolman in the United States has canvassed some of the down-stream effects of reservoir construction upon channel characteristics. He has observed degradation in reaches where silt loads have been reduced, and diminished channel capacity and increased water loss from vegetation where stream discharges have been diminished by storage.[57] Swedish students of fluvial morphology have given extensive attention to the effects of river control

St. Lawrence Seaway, Its Impact, by 1965, upon Industry of Metropolitan Chicago and Illinois Waterway-Associated Areas (2 vols.; Springfield: State of Illinois, 1959).

53 U.S., Congress, *Great Lakes Harbor Study—Interim Report on Milwaukee Harbor,* House Doc. 134, 87th Cong., 1st Sess., 1961. Method is described in unpublished Appendix A.

54 D. L. Armand, I. P. Gerasimov, K. A. Salishtchev, and Yu. G. Saushkin, "The Role of Geographers in the Study, Mapping, Economic Appraisal, Utilization, Conservation, and Renewal of the Natural Resources of the U.S.S.R.," *Soviet Geography,* I (1960), 3–10.

55 Tricart, *op. cit.*

56 J. Tricart, "Enquête sur les Organismes Faisant des Recherches de Géomorphologie Appliquée," *Revue de Géomorphologie Dynamique,* X (1959), 85–96; C. Lecarpenter and P. Perrin, "L'Amènagement du Bas-Chassezac," *Revue de Géomorphologie Dynamique,* XII (1961), 120–29.

57 M. Gordon Wolman, "Downstream Effect of Dams on Alluvial Channels," paper in press (1963); [also in press is a paper on "Two Problems Involving River Channel Changes and Background Observations"].

works.[58] As systems of reservoir take shape and as water uses increase, these intricate relationships within river basins will become of increasing importance.

Even more difficult to discern and of great significance in the long run are the biological relationships which, when disturbed by water management, may have profound impacts upon the resource base and the quality of human life. These seem to have received only passing attention from geographers.

The external economies and diseconomies of certain social changes and the extent of such effects also have been examined in a few areas. Beyer's study of the disorganization of a grazing industry by an irrigation project designed to stabilize that industry is one such case.[59] Marts's work on indirect benefits from irrigation already has been mentioned. A comprehensive research effort dealing with both social and physical phenomena in a basin of modest size was undertaken in the Hunter Valley of New South Wales in 1957 and has launched studies on regional income, water resources and land resources and has made flood-plain information studies. Although the group has not yet tackled detailed engineering planning its experience may suggest applications elsewhere.[60] Their geographers have been active in the inventory of land use following World Land Use Survey standards, and have carried on research on the evolution and prospects of both agricultural and urban land-use patterns in the area in a fashion paralleling some of the work in South Africa. Indian geographers are taking part in an exploratory "Diagnostic survey of the Damodar Valley," which follows construction of major river regulation works.[61]

In general, any research which increases power to predict the spatial consequences of an alteration in one of the basic circulatory systems adds to the capacity of river development planners to carry out their work. Essentially, water management alters the circulation of water, silt and biota with a view to changing the circulation of goods, people, ideas and income. Were we to understand these interlocking circulatory patterns and processes sufficiently to forecast how changing one changes the areal dispersion of the others the geographer's task would be well done. But we lack this command and, while research on the nature of both hydrologic and transportation networks continues, only a beginning has been made.[62] Awaiting more fundamental gains, we must be content with crude judgments of the type of the St. Lawrence predictions as to how the patterns of traffic movement, land use and settlement as well as the behavior of water and sediment flows will be modified.

Social Guides

All aspects of decision making affecting river development are shaped and modified by the character of constraint or encouragement which society gives through its institutions of custom, attitude, education, and organization. These vary in place and time and, as we have seen in the choice of water uses or the level of technology adopted, may have a profound influence

58 Lennart Arnborg, *The Lower Angermanälven*, Pub. Geogr. Inst. Uppsala, Phys. Geogr. I and II (1958–59).

59 Jacquelyn Beyer, *Integration of Grazing and Crop Agriculture: Resources Management Problems in the Uncompahgre Valley Irrigation Project*, Dept. of Geog. Research Paper No. 52 (Chicago: Dept. of Geog., Univ. of Chicago, 1957).

60 Hunter Valley Research Foundation, *River Basin Research* (Newcastle, N.S.W., 1962).

61 S. P. Chatterjee, Presidential Address, *Geographical Review of India,* XXIV (1962), 1–6.

62 A. E. Schiedegger, *Theoretical Geomorphology* (Göttingen: Springer Verlag, 1961); William L. Garrison, Brian J. L. Berry, Duane F. Marble, John D. Nystuen, and Richard L. Morrill, *Studies of Highway Development and Geographic Change* (Seattle: University of Washington Press, 1959), pp. 5–35; B. J. L. Berry, "Recent Studies Concerning the Role of Transportation in the Space Economy," *Annals of the Association of American Geographers,* XLIX (1959), 328–42.

upon the final program of work. To the extent that geographers discover the effect of particular social arrangements upon distributions of resource use they strengthen the ground upon which effective measures for resource management can be erected. For the record is all too clear that the full benefits of irrigation investment cannot be realized without sensitive use of complementary measures such as transport, credit and education. In the Lower Mekong the comprehensive appraisal of experience with agricultural improvement efforts must accompany engineering construction if bitter disappointment is to be avoided. We have seen enough of river development to know also that flood control or flood forecasting may reduce flood losses little unless other complementary measures are taken; that generating large blocks of electric power may fall short of stimulating new manufacturing of desired types unless accompanied by suitable pricing, distribution, and tax policies; and that a program to provide new water supplies may actually expand rather than reduce water shortage unless paired with suitable price and use policies.

General appraisals such as those of the Gezira,[63] Helmand,[64] and smaller Northern Rhodesian schemes[65] help identify some of the problems of social guidance, but the more detailed investigations of how resource management responds to different constraints and inducements are especially useful. Broad regional studies are of little value unless they come to grips with predicting the results of institutional changes. Thus, the Farmer study in Ceylon, and several studies of response to flood hazard information in flood-plains[66] yield rudimentary grounds for designing new social measures. We must envisage a major expansion of this kind of analysis, in association with anthropologists, economists, and political scientists, if genuinely effective development programs are to be realized.

It is encouraging to learn that Church recently has completed under the auspices of the Economic Commission for Africa a reconnaissance appraisal of experience with selected irrigation projects in Africa.[67] The large multi-purpose schemes are only beginning to receive support on that continent, and assessment of this character may yield some valuable lessons early in the game. There are interesting prospects for international cooperation with United Nations support in the Niger and Senegal basins.

An extension, perhaps, of the regional approach is the very broad interest which some geographers have shown in public policy affecting water management at the national level. Drawing upon wider studies and upon experience in particular areas, they have stimulated or joined in appraisals of the role of government agencies and of the policies which should be pursued to maintain water resources or to use them more widely. Among such activities have been those of Balchin in the United Kingdom,[68] Awad in Egypt,[69] the Soviet geographers in both landscape and hydrometeorological investigations and in national eco-

63 William A. Hance, "Gezira: An Example in Development," *Geographical Review,* XLIV (1954), 253–70.

64 Aloys A. Michel, *The Kabul, Kunduz, and Helmand Valleys and the National Economy of Afghanistan* (Washington: National Research Council, 1959).

65 George Kay, *Agricultural Change in the Luitikila Basin Development Area,* Hum. Probs. in Brit. Centr. Africa No. 31 (1962).

66 Kates, *op. cit.*; Wolf Roder, "Attitude and Knowledge of the Topeka Flood Plain," *Papers on Flood Problems,* Dept. of Geog. Research Paper No. 70, ed. G. F. White (Chicago: Dept. of Geog., Univ. of Chicago, 1961), 62–83; Ian Burton, "Invasion and Escape on the Little Calumet," *ibid.,* 84–92.

67 R. J. H. Church, *Problems of Large-Scale Irrigation Projects in Africa,* Agric. Economics Bull. for Africa No. 4 (Addis Ababa: Economic Commission for Africa, 1963).

68 W. G. V. Balchin, "A Water Use Survey," *Geographical Journal,* CXXIV (1958), 476–82.

69 Hassan Awad, "L'Eau et la Géographie Humaine dans la Zone Aride," *Bulletin of the Society of Geographers, Egypt,* XXXI (1958), 195–208.

nomic planning,[70] Pleva in the Ontario conservation district program,[71] and the Americans who at various stages have taken part in the work of the Mississippi Valley Committee, the National Resources Planning Board, the President's Water Resources Policy Commission, the two Hoover Commissions and the Senate Select Committee on National Water Resources.[72] Individual geographers have, of course, taken larger responsibility for planning studies that embrace other disciplines, but their chief assets in these situations seem to have been administrative skill linked with a breadth of view that enables them to work with a wide range of problems.

This paper has outlined elements in the process of decision in setting basin plans and has noted ways in which geographers take part in them. It would be misleading, however, to think of major programs of study looking to river basin design as ever being largely geographic. If my description of the decision-making process is credible the preparation of plans will draw heavily upon engineering, economics, hydrology, geology, agronomy, anthropology, and other fields. The geographer may be expected to collaborate with and gain from workers in those disciplines.

That river basin development can proceed without benefit of any analysis of the types described is apparent from the record in a number of countries. Responsible engineers and financing officers often ignore it or consider that their horseback judgments are sufficient. But they do so at the peril of efficacy of resulting works. Shortage of time or money, inadequate personnel and lack of awareness of the consequences are among the reasons it is absent from the planning efforts. The Lower Mekong countries may defer land classification because they regard other needs as more pressing, or they may avoid appraisal of water management systems because they fear the findings would retard the construction of symbolic concrete dams. While such considerations are bound to influence public allocations of survey funds, it is likely that to the degree governments are anxious to optimize their returns on water resource investment they will support analysis along the lines suggested.

Here a further qualification should be stated. Commitment to such work does not necessarily involve geographers, for much of it is in borderline fields: hydrologists are involved in water balance study, soil scientists and foresters in land classification, economists in estimating external economies and so forth. Although geographers have done useful work which suggests that they have a certain competence and may expand their service in those directions, there is no assurance that they will handle the work in future. I am not interested in staking out professional claims in this domain of science. What does seem important is to recognize intellectual problems which call for solution, and which because of their relation to spatial distributions and human adjustment to differences in physical environment are of interest to geographers.

What are the types of geographical analysis which seem especially pertinent to river development and currently promising for advancement? Beyond atlas compilation of background data, the range of choice for methods of river management can be defined more accurately by studies of homologues and by regional and histori-

70 S. L. Vendrov and G. P. Kalinin, "Surface-Water Resources of the U.S.S.R.: Their Utilization and Study," *Soviet Geography,* I (1960), 35–50.

71 Edward G. Pleva, "Multiple Purpose Land and Water Districts in Ontario," *Comparisons in Resource Management,* ed. H. Jarrett (Baltimore: Johns Hopkins Press for Resources for the Future, Inc., 1961), pp. 189–207.

72 U.S., Senate Select Committee on National Water Resources, *Water Requirements for Pollution Abatement,* Comm. Print No. 29, 86th Cong., 2d Sess., 1960; E. A. Ackerman, "Questions for Designers of Future Water Policy," *Journal of Farm Economics,* XXXVIII (1956), 971–80; see also Ackerman's *The Impact of New Techniques on Integrated Multiple-Purpose Water Development,* U.S., Senate Select Comm. on National Water Resources, Comm. Print. No. 31, 86th Cong., 2d Sess., 1960.

cal studies of water management. Resource estimates can be improved by refining the mapping of water balance, hydrologic characteristics of terrain, and land use, and by examining the nature and distribution of human perception of resources. The application of new technology can be strengthened by discovery and partial explanation of variations in patterns of water use and disposal. Benefit-cost analysis can be sharpened by finding normalities in the spatial variations of water use control and demand. The effects of water management upon the stream system and upon movements of human activities within and outside the basin can be identified more clearly. Possible responses of land and water management practice to changes in social guides in different environments can be estimated from critical regional studies. In these and other ways geographical analysis can aid in so deepening our understanding of the flows of water, silt, people and goods and of their setting that as each is altered by human initiative we may recognize a bit more precisely the likely consequences to the interconnected systems.

Every change in landscape or resource use on a large scale disturbs a complex set of relationships. To do so is not necessarily to do wrong by upsetting a "natural equilibrium"; the existing situation may in effect be out of equilibrium as in the case of shifting cultivation in the Lower Mekong plateaus; or a new more productive relationship may be established, as where permanent irrigation rice culture replaces hazardous wet-season cropping. The decision to change may, however, go far wide of the intended goal of lasting human betterment if the strategy of development is built upon narrow and distorted models of these relationships. Nothing less than a systems analysis of the whole complex of natural and social processes at work will yield in the long run a sound basis for decision, and it is toward this that we should move.

CHAPTER 6

RESOURCES AND ECONOMIC DEVELOPMENT

During the period of decolonization and cold war which started in 1945, there has been a considerable growth of interest in the economic development of the underdeveloped parts of the world. Although it is not possible to do justice to the large volume of literature that has grown up on this subject,[1] this volume would be incomplete without some mention of the role of resources in in economic development.

That there is no simple relationship between resources and economic growth is clear. The large untapped resources of Africa, India and China, Brazil and Canada suggest that not all countries with a high resource endowment are highly developed. Similarly, examples like Switzerland and Japan suggest that a high level of development is possible on the basis of apparently meager natural resources.

On the other hand, the United States is both rich in resources and highly developed. Western Europe is highly developed and continues to make rapid progress, although its once-rich stock of resources is now somewhat depleted and it relies to an increasing extent on the import of natural resource commodities. The complex web of differing trends and levels of economic development has been described and mapped by Ginsburg.[2]

When we attempt to measure the role of resources in economic development, we come up against complex problems of data and their interpretation which Schultz describes. Accepting these data more or less at face value, however, Schultz concludes that natural resources are a declining factor in production costs and that natural resources are a greater part of the economy of poorer countries than of richer ones. Even so, there is little evidence to suggest that the growth possibilities of poorer countries are restricted by their natural re-

[1] Some measure of the extent of this literature may be obtained from Arthur Hazlewood (comp.), *The Economics of Under-developed Areas* (London: Oxford University Press, 1959), 2d ed., an annotated reading list of books, articles, and official publications issued prior to May, 1958 and including 1,027 items. See also Saul M. Katz and Frank McGowan, *A Selected List of United States Readings on Development* (Washington: Government Printing Office, 1963). This contains an annotated list of 1,195 items. *Economic Development and Cultural Change* is a stimulating journal devoted solely to this field. Some interesting essays are in Norton Ginsburg (ed.), *Essays on Geography and Economic Development,* Dept. of Geog. Research Paper No. 62 (Chicago: Dept. of Geog., University of Chicago, 1960).

[2] Norton Ginsburg, *Atlas of Economic Development* (Chicago: University of Chicago Press, 1960).

source endowments. Ginsburg also argues the case for a diminishing róle of resources as countries attain higher levels of development, although a more conventional view has laid great stress on the importance of resource endowment,[3] in keeping with the "classical" views of Malthus and Ricardo. Ginsburg refers to Spoehr's paper (see Chapter 2) in pointing out the difficulties in defining a "natural resource endowment." If we side-step this complex question, however, we are free to ask, with White, what the special problems are of underdeveloped countries with respect to natural resources. Many studies of resource endowment have been made in poorer countries since the end of World War II, and these are continuing at an accelerating rate.[4] Many studies have also been made of specific resource commodities.[5]

Quite a different aspect of the problem of natural resources and economic development is the role of resources in the regional development of single countries. The major industrial cities of northern England grew up on coalfields at a time when that resource was of major importance.[6] Exhaustion of the better seams plus changed technology has robbed these cities of part of their *raison d'être*. Population is now moving away from them, back to the South and East, leaving behind depressed industrial cities with many slums and an intolerable burden to support.[7] Similar trends have occurred in North America from Nova Scotia to Kentucky.[8] The varying significance of regional resources is illustrated by Perloff and Wingo by reference to the economic history of the United States. Not only does the resource endowment of places differ, but it changes in significance over time. Moreover, it is the less tangible "amenity" resources that assume increasingly greater significance.

[3] For an elementary discussion of this point, see chap. 2 of Richard T. Gill, *Economic Development: Past and Present,* Foundations of Modern Economics Series (Englewood Cliffs: Prentice-Hall, Inc., 1963). More comprehensive treatment of the general problem of economic growth and of the role of natural resources may be found in the following:

Colin Clark, *Conditions of Economic Progress* (3d ed.; London: Macmillan, 1957).

Benjamin Higgins, *Economic Development* (New York: Norton, 1959).

W. W. Rostow, *The Stages of Economic Growth* (London: Cambridge University Press, 1960).

J. A. Schumpeter, *The Theory of Economic Development* (Cambridge: Harvard University Press, 1934). Originally pub. in German, 1911.

E. E. Hagen, *On the Theory of Social Change: How Economic Growth Begins* (Homewood, Ill.: Dorsey Press, 1962).

Karl Polanyi, *The Great Transformation* (New York: Farrar & Rinehart, 1944).

[4] An extensive listing of these studies may be found in Jaleel Ahmad, *Natural Resources in Low Income Countries: An Analytical Survey of Socio-economic Research* (Pittsburgh: University of Pittsburgh Press, 1960). Other commodity reviews may be found in O. T. Mouzon, *International Resources and National Policy* (New York: Harper & Bros., 1959).

[5] See, for example, the cases quoted in Marion Clawson (ed.), *Natural Resources and International Development* (Baltimore: Johns Hopkins Press for Resources for the Future, Inc., 1964).

[6] John H. Clapham, *An Economic History of Modern Britain* (Cambridge: Cambridge University Press, 1926–38); Thomas S. Ashton, *The Industrial Revolution, 1760–1830* (London: Oxford University Press, 1948).

[7] Michael Chisholm, "Must We All Live in Southeast England?" *Geography,* XLIX (1964), 1–14.

[8] Mary Jean Bowman and W. Warren Haynes, *Resources and People in East Kentucky: Problems and Potentials of a Lagging Economy* (Baltimore: Johns Hopkins Press, 1963).

THEODORE W. SCHULTZ

CONNECTIONS BETWEEN NATURAL RESOURCES AND ECONOMIC GROWTH

My topic is burdened by a heavy intellectual tradition based on a widely held belief that economic progress is severely subjected to diminishing returns of labor and capital against land. The belief persists despite much evidence to the contrary. Clearly the role of land in economic growth is no longer nearly as important as it appeared to Ricardo and his contemporaries. Yet, it is not easy to free ourselves from old ideas, especially when such ideas have become entrenched behind strong doctrines.

My purpose is simply to clear the deck of these ideas so we can see the more relevant connections between natural resources and economic growth. I propose to examine three closely related questions: What is the value of natural resources as a factor in production? Are the economic growth possibilities of a country, especially so if it is poor, substantially restricted by its endowment of natural resources? Are we confronted in the case of the services of natural resources by a rising supply price?

Before turning to these questions, I do want to pay my respects to the rich intellectual history about natural resources; there is no dearth of literature. I have already alluded to the well-known concern of the older economists about land as a limitational factor in economic growth. There are also well-developed treatments of particular natural resources in mining, fishing, forestry, and agriculture and of urban uses of land. Then, too, location and transport have received much careful thought. There are now some good estimates of land as a stock of wealth and also as a factor of production. In this respect we enter an old and well-maintained vineyard and our task might be viewed as simply one of gathering the fruit of these intellectual efforts.

But my purpose cannot be achieved by merely building on received knowledge. It does not, as things now stand, place natural resources in their proper economic perspective, because all too little account has been taken of the rise in substitutes, the rise in the quantity and value of other resources, and the dynamic properties of modern economic growth in developing substitutes for ever more classes of natural resources. One's conception of economic growth is not unimportant in this regard. We do well to restrict it to increases in national income that can be identified and measured. Much, however, depends on the sources of these increases in national income. If it were only the result of additions to the stock of conventional reproducible non-human wealth and to the number of persons in the labor force, it would be simple. But, we know that this conception leaves most of the increases in national income unexplained. I propose to think of economic growth as a particular type of dynamic disequilibrium, during which the economy is absorbing various subsets of superior resources. They are superior re-

• T. W. Schultz is Charles L. Hutchinson Distinguished Service Professor, Department of Economics, University of Chicago.

Reprinted from J. J. Spengler (ed.), *Natural Resources and Economic Growth,* Conference Papers (Washington: Resources for the Future, Inc., 1961), pp. 1–9, with the permission of the author.

sources in a special sense, namely, they provide investment opportunities with relatively high rates of return; and these relatively high rates of return imply inequalities in the way resources are allocated and a lagged process in bringing these rates of return into equality; moreover, this dynamic disequilibrium will persist to the extent that additional superior resources are developed and absorbed.

1. What is the value of natural resources as a factor of production? There are presently two very different views and treatments of this measure of the economic importance of these resources. One attributes a dominating role to natural resources as is the case in the classical dynamics,[1] and the other attributes to them no role whatsoever; e.g., there is no land in the Harrod models.[2] Harrod said, "I propose to discard the law of diminishing returns from land as a primary determinant in a progressive economy. . . . I discard it only because in our particular context it appears that its influence may be quantitatively unimportant."[3]

I leave it to others to decide whether these magnificant growth models are tools or toys. What is clear, however, is that both of them are based on a grand, country-wide, macroconception of a particular economy at a given period in its history. The particular economy under consideration was England in Ricardo's day and the United Kingdom at the present time, respectively. The underlying circumstances were indeed very different, as I have attempted to show in another paper, "The Declining Economic Importance of Agricultural Land."[4]

Neither of these contrary views has any general validity. Whether we measure natural resources as a *stock* of wealth or as *flow* of productive services rendered by them, we are in the domain of estimates. For the United States we have Goldsmith's estimates which indicate that between 1910 and 1955 the proportion of national wealth represented by "all land" fell from 36 to 17 per cent and agricultural land dropped from 20 to 5 per cent of national wealth.[5]

When we measure the flow of productive services, we would expect natural resources to represent an even smaller fraction of all productive services than they are of the total stock of non-human wealth. The "Paley Report"[6] provides a clue, if we assume that there has been a fairly stable linkage between the flow of raw materials produced and the stock of natural resources on which this flow has been dependent. The value of all raw materials consumed in the United States declined, relative to gross national product, from about 23 to 13 per cent, between 1904–13 and 1944–50. For agriculture, the income attributed to farm land, excluding capital structures that have been added to such land in the United States, fell from 3.2 to .6 of 1 per cent of net national product between 1910–14 and 1955–57.[7]

There are, so it seems to me, two general relationships between natural resources as these are traditionally defined and all resources that have strong empirical support (both of these relationships are ex-

1 William J. Baumol, *Economic Dynamics* (New York: The Macmillan Co., 1951), chap. 2.

2 R. F. Harrod, "An Essay in Dynamic Theory," *Economic Journal* (March, 1939). See also, *Towards a Dynamic Economics* (London: Macmillan and Co., 1948).

3 *Ibid.*, p. 20.

4 T. W. Schultz, *Economic Journal* (December, 1951). Also, *The Economic Organization of Agriculture* (New York: McGraw-Hill Book Co., 1953), chap. 8.

5 Raymond W. Goldsmith and Associates, *A Study of Saving in the United States,* III, Special Studies (Princeton: Princeton University Press, 1956), Table W-I; and Goldsmith's estimates appearing in the *Thirty-seventh Annual Report of the National Bureau of Economic Research* (New York, May, 1957).

6 The President's Materials Policy Commission, *Resources for Freedom* (Washington, June, 1952).

7 T. W. Schultz, "Land in Economic Growth," *Modern Land Policy,* ed. H. G. Halcrow (Urbana: University of Illinois Press, 1959).

pressed in terms of the *flows* of the productive services of these resources and not in terms of *stocks* of wealth):

1. When we compare countries as of a particular date, we observe that the proportion of natural resources to all resources employed to produce the income is greater in poor countries than it is in rich countries. (I would venture that the upper limit in the proportion of natural resources to all resources in poor countries is in the neighborhood of 20 to 25 per cent and the lower limit in rich countries is about 5 per cent.)

2. When a country achieves economic growth that increases its per capita income over time, natural resources become a decreasing proportion of all resources that are employed to produce the income. (It would appear that during recent decades the rate at which this particular proportion has declined has been large.)

2. How large a contribution can natural resources make to the economic growth of poor countries? The answer to this question turns basically on the growth possibilities of poor countries. Here, too, we are confronted presently by two contradictory assessments.

There is a widely held belief among economists that primary production—mining and especially agriculture—is essentially a burden on the economic growth of poor countries. Poor countries are overcommitted to agriculture. Land is, as a rule, used intensively, and the supply of land is virtually fixed. The marginal returns to labor in agriculture are at or near zero. These conditions are thought to be such that additional effort to increase the production of primary products can add little or nothing to the national product. On the other hand, large gains are to be had from a comparable effort and investment to produce industrial products. Furthermore, according to this view, backwardness is an intrinsic complement of the land-using sectors, notably in the case of agriculture; and, in addition, to add to its economic woes, in producing primary products a country is particularly vulnerable to the economic instability of rich countries. For these several reasons it is held that the natural resources sectors, especially agriculture, are less rewarding than are the sectors that contribute to industrialization on which the economic growth of poor countries, so it is presumed, is basically dependent.

The other assessment of the economic growth possibilities of poor countries holds that the endowment of natural resources in such countries, including farm lands, is a relatively important asset and that differences in stocks of these resources among poor countries are a major variable in determining the growth possibilities of such countries.

This issue is plagued by confusion and by a lack of firm evidence. A part of the confusion arises from a difference in the weight that is given to natural resources. As already noted, they are as a rule more important relative to all resources in poor than in rich countries. Most of the confusion, however, originates from a failure to distinguish between the rate of return to be had from additional reproducible capital of *the existing forms* and the rate of return that can be realized from *new and better forms* of reproducible capital.

There is first the fact that the technical properties of these two forms of reproducible capital are different, and there is the further fact that the economic attributes are also different inasmuch as the marginal rate of return from additional resources of the existing forms is low relative to the rate of return from investments in the new forms of resources. Once this distinction is made between these two forms of reproducible capital, the critical question is whether the new forms of capital are unique in that they have technical specifications that make it impossible to use any of them in primary production.

I have no doubt whatsoever that these new and better forms of reproducible capital are not restricted to industry. Many of them are applicable to agriculture and to other sectors heavily dependent upon natural resources. If the choice were only one of adding another irrigation well, a ditch, a bullock, or a few more primitive tools and pieces of equipment of the type that are being employed in a poor country, the prospects of winning a relatively high rate of return from such additions to the stock of capital would be dim indeed. But this is not the choice, whether it be in agriculture or industry. The choice that can be made and that carries with it the prospect of larger rewards entails new and better forms of reproducible capital both in agriculture and industry.

It has long been an accepted tenet of economic thought that the rates of return on additional capital in poor countries are relatively large. According to this tenet, these returns are large because poor countries have a relatively small supply of reproducible capital to use with their labor and land. The view that these earnings are relatively high has gained support from the vast movements of capital historically out of particular Western countries into many a poor country. These large transfers were in response, so it is held, to the differences between the *low rates* that had come to prevail in some of the comparatively rich countries and the *high rates* that characterized the production possibilities awaiting such capital in poor countries. What has not been made explicit in this assessment is the fact that for the most part these capital transfers were not employed simply to multiply the then existing forms of reproducible capital; instead new forms of capital were introduced into these poor countries as a consequence of these transfers.

3. I want to comment on still another proposition about natural resources. It is widely held to be true that the supply price of the productive services of natural resources must rise relative to the prices of the services of the reproducible factors as a consequence of economic growth. We have been taught that this is inevitable as the stock of reproducible capital increases along with the growth in population and production. Lower transport costs and improvements in the arts of production could temporarily hold the rise in the supply price of productive services of natural resources in check but that was the best that could be hoped for. Ultimately, however, diminishing returns of labor and capital against land would always prevail. This economic dictum is clearly at variance with our estimates; it is time that we relegated this dictum to our stock of folklore.

But the image of a fixed supply of natural resources and a rising supply price of the products of these resources, persists. Let me quote from another paper.[8]

> Yet no less an economist than Colin Clark, no longer ago than 1941, in his book, *The Economics of 1960,* came to the conclusion that the world was in for a dramatic rise in the relative price of primary products. Clark did not come to this conclusion by indulging in some easy, intuitive guesses, nor did he rely on a simple projection of past trends. He drew upon his vast stock of data; he proceeded to put them into his "analytical model" with its strong bent for diminishing returns against land and ground out the following conclusion for 1960: ". . . the terms of trade for primary produce will improve by as much as 90 per cent from the average of 1925–34."[9] To speak of so violent a rise in the relative price of primary products as an "improvement" is a neat twist. . . . But what are the facts as we reach 1960? Clark missed the price target altogether; his shot went off into space in the wrong direction. What went wrong? Did he assume too large a rise in population? On the contrary, the upsurge in population has been much greater than he assumed it would be. Has there been much less industrialization than he anticipated? Again, the answer is in the negative. Clark simply assumed a lot of secular diminishing returns against land and this assumption turned out to be invalid.

A plausible approach is to treat raw (crude) materials as if they were produced

[8] *Ibid.*

[9] Colin Clark, *The Economics of 1960* (London: Macmillan & Co., 1943), p. 52. A reprint of the 1st ed.; the "introduction" is dated May 15, 1941.

under constant supply price conditions. This is the basic assumption that has made the Paley Report useful. It is a rough approximation to what has been happening, and the projections of the consumption of raw materials in the United States (to about 1975) based on this assumption have been doing quite well thus far.

I am aware, however, that there may be many a slip between the prices of the services of natural resources and the prices of raw materials. Unfortunately, there are all too few estimates of the prices of the services (rents) of natural resources; the studies that have come to my attention stop with raw materials. This led me to undertake some estimates of the changes in the prices of the services of farm land in the United States.[10]

Although my estimates are subject to a number of qualifications, they strongly indicate that the price of the service of farm land declined substantially between 1910–14 and 1956 relative to farm product prices and even more so relative to the prices of all inputs used in farming.[11] In interpreting these estimates it should be borne in mind that farm product prices receded about 15 per cent, both relative to the prices of all commodities at wholesale and relative to prices of all consumer items at retail, between 1910–14 and 1956.

Land as an input in farming is cheaper now than it was just prior to World War I. This decline in the supply price of the services of farm land in the United States is not a freak event. It did not occur from a contraction of agriculture, because farm output rose about 80 per cent between these two dates. Nor is it a consequence of large increases in the amount of such land. On the contrary, crop land harvested actually declined slightly, from 330 million (average for 1910–14) to 326 million acres (1956). I shall not enter at this juncture upon an explanation of this decline in the relative price of the services of farm land. Suffice it merely to note that the proposition that price of the services of natural resources must rise relative to the services of reproducible capital over time as a conse-

TABLE 1

U.S. FARM OUTPUT AND INPUT PRICES, 1910–14 AND 1956

Item	Increases between 1910–14 and 1956 1910–14 = 100	Increases Relative to the Prices of Farm Products 235 = 100
1. Prices received by farmers for farm products	235	100
2. Prices of classes of farm inputs		
(1) Farm wage rates	543	231
(2) Building and fencing materials	374	159
(3) Farm machinery	329	140
(4) Farm supplies	279	119
(5) Fertilizer	150	64
(6) Farm land[a]		
a. Price per acre of farm land	158	67
b. Price per constant unit of farm land	181	77
c. Rent per constant unit of farm land	166	71

(Table based on Table II in "Land in Economic Growth," *Modern Land Policy.*)

[a] In each of these three estimates I have attempted to exclude the reproducible capital structures that have been added to farm land. Also see Ross Parish, *Trends in the Use of Summer Fallow in Saskatchewan: An Economic Interpretation* (unpublished Ph.D. dissertation, University of Chicago, 1959), for estimates that show the price of the services of farm land in Saskatchewan as having decreased substantially relative to the price of wheat and relative to other major farm inputs.

[10] Schultz, "Land in Economic Growth," *op. cit.*

[11] Of the major classes of farm inputs only the price of fertilizer did not rise relative to the price of the services of farm land.

quence of economic growth is demonstrably false.

Let me now turn to a more general view of the connections between natural resources and economic growth. Up to this point my purpose has been to show that natural resources at factor costs have been declining in value relative to aggregate value of all resources and that the supply price of the services of these resources has not been rising relative to the supply price of other major classes of resources. Implied in this treatment is the inference that the marginal contribution of natural resources over time has not been increasing. Then, too, although natural resources are mainly an integral part of so-called backward sectors of the economy of most poor countries, it does not follow that the production possibilities of these countries are such that their natural resources act as a burden on their economic growth.

The connections between natural resources and reproducible non-human capital and the labor force are being altered substantially over time by economic growth. The type of economic growth that we have been experiencing represents a form of dynamic disequilibrium brought about by the introduction of new and superior resources. These resources, among other things, have been at many points in the economy effective substitutes for one or more classes of natural resources. To see the process broadly it will be necessary to use a comprehensive concept of capital, a concept that includes both non-human and human wealth, in order to take into account additions to stock of capabilities of a labor force that are useful in economic endeavor, capabilities that can be had by investments in man.[12]

We are accustomed to thinking of new and better machines as a substitute for labor. Surely, in agriculture they have become an important substitute for farm land as well as for labor. Johnson's study of grain yields attributes a third of the increase in the yield of corn since 1880 to farm mechanization. Improved seeds have also become a major substitute for farm land, and they appear to have contributed as much to increasing yields as has mechanization.[13] The economic effects of hybrid seed corn are noteworthy in this connection.[14]

Then, too, new forms of capital have entered into the production of fertilizer; these seem to have reduced substantially the real price of fertilizer, so that it has become a strong force not only in holding but in reducing the price of the services of farm land because of substitution. Not least of all have been the improvements in the capabilities of man (in this case of farmers and others in the farm labor force). Some of these new capabilities have also acted as substitutes for farm land.

The long established practice of treating these new and better resources as an *ad hoc* variable under the label of "technological advances," is a convenient way of covering up ignorance. Moreover, it is inconsistent with the economic logic of the properties of a production function. To assert that a production function (say, in farming) has improved, or has been shifted to the right, because of an advance in technology, can only mean that at least one new resource (input) has been introduced in production, because a production function can only be derived from the properties of the resources that are employed in that production. If a production function has changed, it always means that at least one additional resource with different

[12] See T. W. Schultz, "Investment in Man: An Economist's View," *Social Service Review* (June, 1959).

[13] D. Gale Johnson and Robert Gustafson, *Grain Yields and the American Food Supply: An Analysis of Yield Changes and Possibilities* (Chicago: University of Chicago Press, 1962), 146 pp. [Ed. note: Original reference is to 1959 manuscript copy of this paper.]

[14] See the studies of hybrid corn by Zvi Griliches, among others, "Research Costs and Social Returns: Hybrid Corn with Comparisons," *Journal of Political Economy*, Vol. LXVI (August, 1958).

technical properties has been introduced in production. The analytical task, therefore, consists of developing concepts and of building models that will permit us to identify and measure the resource that provides the new technical properties and not to treat all or part of the unexplained residual by simply calling it "an advance in technology."

Lastly, the persistent and impressive economic growth that we observe in not a few countries and that we want to understand does not fit into into the pattern of traditional thought. It does not fit because not all of the history of economic growth has been an exercise in stationary long-run equilibrium based on land, labor, and capital as these have been traditionally conceived. Diminishing returns, as labor and capital have been increased against a given stock of natural resources (land), is not the only game that history has been playing. In the history we want to understand, the game has been altered as a consequence of a couple more aces having somehow gotten into the deck. New and better production functions have entered from somewhere. The capabilities of labor have been improved, and the line of demarcation between capital and labor has become very blurred by investments in man. And so has the line between capital and natural resources as new, useful knowledge has entered.

I shall attempt to deny that the ratio of the income originating in Sector A [for example, natural resources] to national income is a valid measure of "importance" in the context of economic development. What the ratio measures is the importance of Sector A as a source of national income at a given time. It asserts a fact. What I wish to deny is that this fact carries around with it any implication about the process of economic development. In the context of economic development I claim that the fact is irrelevant.

J. H. Dales, from a comment on the paper by T. W. Schultz ("Connections between Natural Resources and Economic Growth") in J. J. Spengler (ed.), *Natural Resources and Economic Growth,* Conf. Papers (Washington: Resources for the Future, Inc., 1961), p. 16.

NORTON GINSBURG

NATURAL RESOURCES AND ECONOMIC DEVELOPMENT

The preoccupation of economists and other social scientists with the phenomenon of economic development, especially in the so-called underdeveloped countries and increasingly since the end of World War II, has resulted in a spate of literature concerning the developmental process.[1] This literature displays an extraordinary diversity of interpretations and hypotheses regarding economic growth, suggesting the deep-seated uncertainty about its character and the causal factors which together may account for it. Increasingly, moreover, recourse has been made to economic history for data with which to study and forecast the course of economic growth in both developed and underdeveloped countries.

The contributions of geographers to consideration of these problems, however, have been few. This is all the more surprising since one of the major factors entering into the course of economic development—natural resources—is of particular concern to them. Furthermore, the areal differentiation of economic conditions and prospects has long been at the heart of economic geography.

This paper presents some reflections on the role natural resources play in the course of economic growth, especially in the lesser developed regions of the world. The basic questions it asks are: How important are natural resources in the course of economic development, and what relationships do they bear to other factors which enter into the developmental complex? No attempt is made to provide a complete conceptual framework within which geographic research on development problems can be pursued more meaningfully, but the conclusions may help prepare the foundations for such a structure.

• Norton Ginsburg is Professor of Geography, University of Chicago.

This paper was prepared originally for the Institute for Economic Development at Vanderbilt University in July, 1956. Reprinted from *Annals of the Association of American Geographers,* XLVII, No. 3 (September, 1957), 197–212, with the permission of the author and the editor.

The Measurement of Development

The terms "developed" and "underdeveloped" have by no means been defined

[1] Among the publications of particular interest are: N. S. Buchanan and H. S. Ellis, *Approaches to Economic Development* (New York: Twentieth Century Fund, 1955); S. H. Frankel, *The Economic Impact on Under-Developed Societies* (Oxford: Basil Blackwell, 1953); B. F. Hoselitz (ed.), *The Progress of Underdeveloped Areas* (Chicago: University of Chicago Press, 1952;) S. Kuznets, W. E. Moore, and J. J. Spengler (eds.), *Economic Growth: Brazil, India, and Japan* (Durham: Duke University Press, 1955); W. Arthur Lewis, *The Theory of Economic Growth* (London: George Allen and Unwin, Ltd., 1955); W. W. Rostow, *The Process of Economic Growth* (New York: W. W. Norton, 1952); Jacob Viner, *International Trade and Economic Development* (Glencoe: The Free Press, 1952), and certain issues of the *Annals* of the American Academy of Political and Social Science, especially that of May 1956, "Agrarian Societies in Transition." In 1951, the journal *Economic Development and Cultural Change* was founded at the University of Chicago to provide an outlet for research papers dealing with problems of economic development. In addition, there have been a number of . . . studies concerned with food, population, and economic growth. . . . Of special interest among these are Richard L. Meier's *Science and Economic Development* (New York: John Wiley and Son, 1956) and the PEP report, *World Population and Resources* (London: George Allen and Unwin, Ltd., September 1955).

precisely. If we adopt the broad interpretation of "development" as meaning the maximization of all available resources (in the economist's sense, whether "natural" in origin or not), then no country can be termed developed, since none can demonstrate completely efficient use of all its assets. The United States, the U.S.S.R., and the Western European countries, as well as Afghanistan, all may be considered "underdeveloped" in this sense.

Commonly, therefore, the terms are defined on a comparative basis. The criterion most commonly employed is that of *per capita national product,* that is, the value per person in a given country or region of all goods and services produced in one year by its total population. National product (or income)[2] per capita provides an index to the state of an economy and to the position it occupies along the continuum between development and underdevelopment. In this connection, it is important to point out that these two terms refer specifically to economics. They in no sense represent value judgments concerning the non-economic achievements of any society.

Per capita national product clearly is a better indicator of economic conditions than gross national product, which ignores the essential relationships of population to national economies, and tends toward bias in favor of countries with large populations, whatever their demographic characteristics.[3] For example, in 1955, India was estimated to have a gross national product of 27.4 billion dollar-equivalents (slightly more than Canada), which ranked it seventh among the nations of the world. In terms of national product per capita, however, India ranked next to China among the major nations, near the lowest levels of the scale; the figure assigned it ($72) was only about 3 per cent that for the United States. Per capita national product, therefore, is an index to individual levels of living, and these in turn are assumed to reflect the state of economic well-being.

It also is an index particularly applicable to the measurement of *rate* of economic growth and the degree to which economic production is keeping ahead of or following behind population growth. A country's economy may be expanding rapidly, as reflected in a growing gross national product. On the other hand, individual incomes and levels of living may decline if population is increasing more rapidly than gross national product. This point is of crucial importance in the cases of the densely populated, underdeveloped regions, such as India or China, where the rate of economic growth must exceed the rate of population increase by a considerable margin if economic difficulties are to be resolved and economic growth is to become self-generating. In other words, the individual worker under such circumstances must be able to "save" (or have put aside in his stead) enough capital to enlarge the productive facilities of the country sufficiently, after his own wants are satisfied, to permit expansion of the means of production at an accelerating rate.[4]

[2] Frederic Benham, in his *The National Income of Malaya, 1947–49* (Singapore: Government Printing Office, 1951), pp. 3–6, provides a succinct explanation of the terms "national product" and "national income." He points out that the two aggregates are the same, except where payments are made abroad (in either direction) for reasons other than the provision of goods and services (remittances to China from Malaya would be an example). Such payments normally are small relative to the total aggregates. More important, production data normally are more abundant than consumption data, thus encouraging the use of national product as an economic indicator. In the case of Benham's study, despite its title, the data employed are production rather than income data.

[3] Mr. Leo Silberman points out that a measure defined in terms of per capita *adult* population would be an even better indicator since it would reflect real productivity and not discriminate against countries with high birth rates and/or large numbers of persons below 15 years of age. The logical extension of this reasoning would be an index based upon product per member of the labor force, but both of these tend to hide the significance of large families in given societies.

[4] Hoselitz *et al.* estimate that "an economy can break out of the vicious circle of poverty and underdevelopment only if it succeeds in allocating a minimum of 15 per cent of its gross national product for capital investment." *Op. cit.*, p. 6.

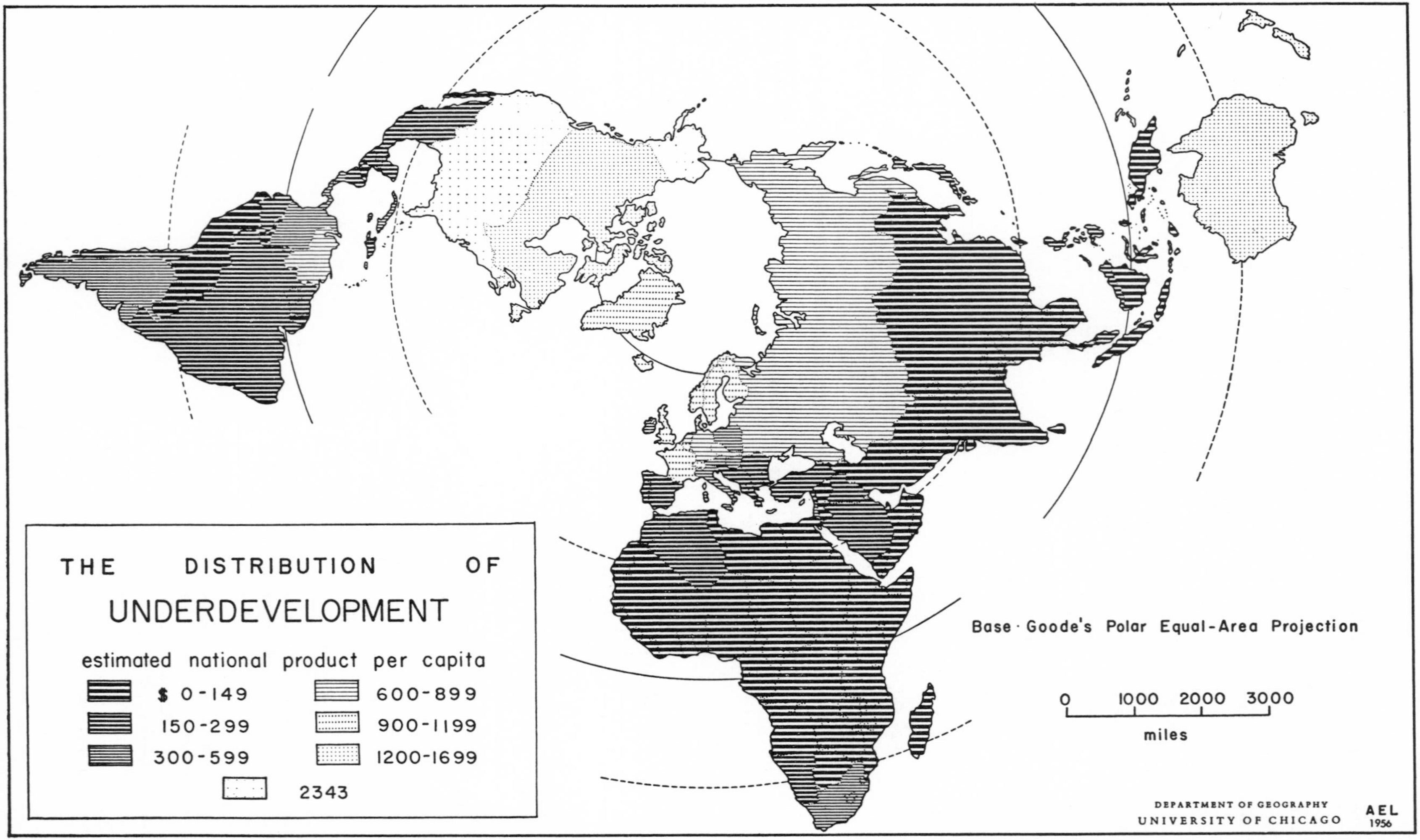
THE DISTRIBUTION OF
UNDERDEVELOPMENT
estimated national product per capita
$ 0-149
150-299
300-599
600-899
900-1199
1200-1699
2343
Base · Goode's Polar Equal-Area Projection
0 1000 2000 3000
miles
DEPARTMENT OF GEOGRAPHY
UNIVERSITY OF CHICAGO
AEL
1956

FIG. 1

The range of development among countries, as measured in these terms, is enormous. In 1955, for example, the United States is reported to have had a per capita national product of $2,343; Sweden, $1,165; the United Kingdom, $998; the U.S.S.R., $682; Italy, $442; Colombia, $330; Japan, $240; Mexico, $187; Egypt, $133; Thailand, $100; the Central African Federation, $61; and China (exclusive of Taiwan), $56.

These estimates of per capita national product have been mapped on Figure 1.[5] If we assume quite arbitrarily that a per capita product under $300 defines "underdevelopment," then we find that the underdeveloped peoples dominate the world, not only in area, but also in numbers. Almost all of Asian Asia, all of Africa except the Union of South Africa, and most of Latin America fall into the underdeveloped category. Included are some 1,780 million people, roughly 68 per cent of the world's population.[6]

[5] These data are derived from the Office of Statistics and Reports, the International Cooperation Administration, and appear as Appendix I in the report by Hoselitz *et al.*, *op cit.*, pp. 81–82. Since data for a few areas were not available, as for Outer Mongolia, North Korea, Southwest Africa, Bechuanaland, Madagascar, North Vietnam, French Guiana, and certain of the Eastern European communist countries, estimates have been made from trade and other data of the value of national product. The crudeness of these estimates does not, however, alter substantially the world pattern of development and underdevelopment.

[6] The distribution of "underdevelopment," or what might be called "economic problemness," presents a fascinating prospect for geographical analysis. Observe the association of the underdeveloped countries for the most part with the lower latitudes; their concentration north of the thirtieth parallel in the Americas and the fortieth parallel in Eurasia; the splendid isolation of Australasia; the fact that, apart from Europe, it is the former "vacant" lands of the New and Australasian worlds which have become most developed economically; the colossal concentration of "underdevelopment" as opposed to the nearly as imposing localization of "development"; and the contrast between the two, the "West" on the one hand and the rest of the world on the other.

Problems of Comparing Resources with Product

The preceding discussion is designed to introduce the problem of evaluating the importance of the natural resources factor in the developmental process. If we assume that per capita product is a sound indicator of stages of economic development, then what is required is an analysis of the relationship between the natural resource endowment and per capita product or income in different countries or regions. Unfortunately, for a number of reasons this seemingly practical approach is fraught with difficulties, and indeed may be misleading or impossible.

In the first place, the very concept of national product (or income) per capita is elusive, and its measurement is extremely difficult. The data supplied by International Cooperation Administration are in U.S. dollar-equivalents, converted from local currencies at the official exchange rates. However, the greater purchasing power of the dollar in certain countries may markedly alter the indicated rank-ordering along the continuum between development and underdevelopment. Differences between the real and official value of the dollar also may explain in part the enormous discrepancy in product value between the United States and Canada on the one hand, and certain of the western European countries on the other.

Furthermore, and this may be far more significant, the data assume value systems in non-Western societies which are similar to those in the West and place high monetary value on the same sorts of goods and services.[7] In addition, the data for the lesser developed regions vastly understate the importance of goods and services about which we know little, but which may be of

[7] Frankel, *op. cit.*, pp. 31 ff. In his discussion, Frankel points out the hidden assumption underlying many universally applied indices to national production and income, such as Colin Clark's, that societal differences "would not affect the purposes for which [an individual] desires or spends income."

great importance to the natives of those regions. This understatement, together with the value-system objection, is exemplified in the case of Pakistan, for example, where the per capita product is estimated at 56 U.S. dollar-equivalents annually. If we assume that the consumption requirements of the Pakistani in any direct way resemble those of Americans, then we also would have to assume that there would have to be many fewer Pakistanis than there now are, since most of them would be dead or dying of starvation and exposure. The actual per capita production in Pakistan, therefore, must, on the one hand, be far greater than it appears to be and, on the other, be of quite a different character than that of the West in order to explain the continued existence of the Pakistanis themselves.

Finally, data concerning national income and production are of the very roughest order for many countries of the world. Indeed, it is only the countries of the West for which reasonably accurate national production and income data are available. The very data upon which the indicator to develop is so often based, therefore, are in themselves highly suspect.[8] Indeed, the degree to which data concerning economic phenomena are available provides almost as useful an indicator to economic development, or lack of it, as the indicator itself.[9]

In spite of these objections, per capita national product provides a rough and useful indicator, probably the best single indicator, of the stage a country has attained on the economic developmental scale.[10] If for the moment we accept it in this light, why cannot we proceed directly to relate natural resources to it? The objections are two. First, as Kuznets makes clear, "comparison requires reduction to a common denominator." In the case of economic development there is an index—per capita capital national product. What comparable index can be used to measure resources? One conceivable measure would be the extent of their utilization per capita and the nature of their exploitation. But utilization is in turn a covariant of the same economic processes for which per capita income is an index. It would be meaningless to compare one aspect of a process with another aspect that varies virtually identically with it. What we probably would be saying is a simple truism: that more highly developed regions (as defined in terms of high per capita production) exploit their natural resource endowments more effectively per capita (or per capita member of the labor force) than those less highly developed. Thus, the "common denominator" of which Kuznets speaks would become the very relationship we are trying to measure. The difficulty, of course, lies in the lack of a suitable alternative index to intensity of natural resource utilization, which can be compared directly with per capita indexes to economic development.

Second, any development of indexes to the utilization of natural resources presumes a substantial knowledge of the resource base itself, but attainment of this knowledge is circumscribed rigidly by the relative paucity of resource inventory data on a world-wide basis. Such inventories represent one of the primary needs for developmental planning in the lesser re-

8 The complexities inherent in estimating national products and incomes in underdeveloped areas are described in Benham, *op. cit.*, especially pp. 3–22.

9 As H. P. Minsky points out, however, available data often may reflect regulation by government. If the United States were to become committed to a policy of free trade, for example, the quantity and quality of the data about U.S. trade might well deteriorate.

10 One alternative is direct measures of levels of living, but creation of such measures presents enormous difficulties and drawbacks. For a discussion of these problems, see *Definition and Measurement of Standards of Living,* Report of a Conference of U.S. Experts Convened 30–31 January, 1 February, 1953, Presented to the Secretary-General of the U.N. (Chicago: Public Administration Clearing House, 1953), mimeographed; and *Report on International Definitions and Measurement of Standards and Levels of Living* (New York: United Nations, 1954, E/CN. 3/179 and E/CN. 5/299).

gions.[11] Even if such inventories were in existence, however, the problem would remain of developing an index comparable to that for economic development itself. It would mean developing common denominators for such varied resources as hydroelectric energy, soils, drainage, growing season, etc. Since these vary in significance from society to society, from place to place, and from time to time, the development of such indexes may prove insurmountably difficult.

This does not mean that we can afford to neglect natural resources in considering the economic realities or potentialities of a given country, despite the example of Switzerland which is called on interminably to illustrate the essential insignificance of the resource endowment to the development of a given region. The fact that orchids technically can be grown in greenhouses in Antarctica does not mean that hothouse agriculture is going to play a significant role in the development of that continent, although under presently unforeseeable circumstances, it might. At our present stage of knowledge, comparisons simply cannot be made between indexes to natural resources and per capita indexes to attained or potential economic growth, since the former do not yet exist and the latter need to be further refined. All that can be attempted, perhaps, are relatively imprecise and qualitative evaluations of the relations between natural resources available at any one time to any one region and the various other elements which together bear upon the course of economic development. Such evaluations, however, demand some explanation of these several elements and their interrelations.

11 Food and Agriculture Organization, *Land Utilization in the Tropical Areas of Asia and the Far East,* Development Paper No. 17 (January 1952), 10 pp. This booklet presents an outline of the need for resources inventories to precede agricultural and general developmental planning. See also F. L. Keller, "Resources Inventory—A Basic Step in Economic Development," *Economic Geography* (January, 1953), pp. 39–47.

Major Factors in Economic Development

The classical economists spoke of at least three major factors of production—land, labor, and capital. To these may be added at least two other determinants of economic development—technology and cultural configurations. These factors and determinants will be examined briefly in their reverse order, a reordering which may suggest, but does not define, their significance in the developmental process.

By *cultural configurations* is meant that system of social organization, combined with constellations of values, goals, or objectives, which all societies possess in different combinations. These social systems vary among societies, sometimes only to a modest degree, often sharply.[12] Without resorting to Parsonian terminology, it is clear that some societies are oriented toward goals which emphasize individual initiative and the production of goods and services beyond basic needs. In such a society wants tend to be unlimited, and the entrepreneur becomes a symbol of the means through which these wants may be satisfied and in turn expanded. In other societies, in contrast, material wants may be prescribed within a relatively inelastic cultural configuration to which the entrepreneurial spirit is alien.[13] These model conceptions are, of course, not wholly realistic, but they

12 For a provocative taxonomy of social organizations and the values associated with them, see Talcott Parsons, *The Social System* (Glencoe: The Free Press, 1951). A brief summary of Parsons' system is given in Kuznets, Moore, and Spengler, *op. cit.*, pp. 379–84.

13 The contrasts in attitudes toward natural resources, as between these two types of societies, are discussed by Alexander Spoehr in his chapter, "Cultural Differences in the Interpretation of Natural Resources," *Man's Role in Changing the Face of the Earth,* ed. W. L. Thomas, Jr. (Chicago: University of Chicago Press, 1956), pp. 93–101. [Ed. note: Spoehr's paper is reprinted in this volume]. In many non-Western societies man is regarded as part of a total "natural" environment over which he has little control. The Western conception is of a universe of animate and inanimate forces which can be "made to serve man's needs and wants."

serve to suggest that in some societies rapid or accelerated economic growth is actively demanded, whereas in others it may not be sought. If a presently underdeveloped country (as measured in terms of very low per capita product) is to develop rapidly, it must have a "will" to develop.[14] That "will" must be possible within the context of its value system, or its value system must be changed, since it lies at the center of institutional barriers to both economic and cultural change. The relations of these observations to natural resource use are direct and clear. Use implies *consciousness* of need and the *will* to invest in the effort required to exploit a given resource.[15] Without them, resource development will not take place, except by outsiders.

Awareness of need, moreover, implies both a knowledge of the uses to which given resources can be put and an understanding of the ways by which those resources can be made available to meet those needs. This knowledge and understanding may be subsumed under the heading of *technology*. All societies, of course, possess a technology, and some of these have made possible the production of surpluses which have introduced economic flexibility into the social system, but historically these technologies have differed conspicuously among themselves. What is meant here, moreover, is a more specifically Western technology, that combination of scientific knowledge and practical engineering which goes by the name "know-how" in the propaganda of American assistance agencies.

Perhaps the most significant aspect of this Western technology is its mobility.[16] All *literate* peoples can *in time* acquire it. Furthermore, it is cheap and rather easily available.[17] Its transfer, however, often may be slow, unless imported in the persons of foreign advisers. These can in turn direct the exploitation of natural resources in ways which probably were not possible by means of indigenous technologies and in directions of use which might not even have been contemplated before.

The fluidity of technology has long acted, in fact, somewhat to the advantage of countries of lesser degrees of development in that they may be able to incorporate into their industrial establishments the latest technical improvements and thereby make these establishments more efficient than the older plants in the already developed countries. It is not unlikely, all other things being equal, that the three new steel plants being constructed in India

[14] The idea of a collective "will" must be used with caution; otherwise it may de-emphasize unwisely the innumerable independent judgments and decisions within the framework of a given social system which result in economic and social change. See Frankel, *op. cit.*, pp. 74–75.

[15] In a personal communication, Edwin Munger points out that "not only must [a] society be conscious of the need and have the will to invest, but that investment often demands a rearrangement of the value system to provide incentive and reward for the handful of entrepreneurs who spark the change. Somehow, a climate for creativity must be created. I mean creativity [as] observation *plus* action. Westerman has suggested [for example] that the wheel . . . was invented repeatedly in West Africa, but that jealousy combined with the grip of the secret poison societies would wipe out the advance."

[16] Mobility may be characteristic also of non-Western technologies, but some of the latter are not recorded in written form, which fundamentally restricts their circulation.

[17] I am not suggesting that the transfer of technology is easy, cheap, or quick to pre-literate peoples, nor in cases where literacy rates are low. It is, of course, true that you can lead a man to a book, but you cannot make him read it, if (a) he cannot read or (b) it is in a foreign language he does not understand, even though he may wish to know what is in it. Illiteracy characterizes many of the underdeveloped regions, and the costs of its elimination are high, but the degree to which illiteracy needs to be overcome before accelerated economic growth is possible is a highly controversial question. I am assuming here that the transfer of technology can take place, initially at least, among a relatively small number of persons, both donors and receivers. In many instances the problem is less one of literacy in absolute terms than of translation facilities and the adaptability of a language to new expressions. Chinese and Japanese are examples of languages into which translations often have been difficult.

under British, Russian, and German supervision, respectively, will be among the more efficient in the world, although the differences in organization and tooling among them may in the long run be a national disadvantage rather than advantage. In this connection it also is conceivable that a lesser developed country can practice economies of scale by sizable "crash" programs of development in narrow sectors of its economy, whether they be agricultural or industrial, given suitable availability of other factors of production, especially capital.

If imported skills and services can be purchased relatively inexpensively with the third element of the five—*capital*—other needs for economic growth usually cannot be purchased so cheaply, and large capital accumulations are agreed generally to be necessary if economic development is to be rapid. The accumulation of capital is one of the major difficulties of the lesser developed countries, since many of them are characterized by value systems which place a low premium on saving and a high premium on the allocation of such surpluses as are available to ends that are capital-disseminating rather than accumulating. All, by definition, are characterized by low per capita incomes, which probably mean small surpluses to begin with.

Capital can be acquired and accumulated, however, in several ways—at least in the short run by (1) importation in the form of loans or grants, as in the case of many recipients of aid from the United States or the Colombo Plan countries, for example; (2) the squeezing of living standards to or even below the subsistence level, as was the case in the Soviet Union and may be the case in China; or (3) the rapid creation of surpluses through the application of rapidly acquired technology to given resource endowments.

The third method can take place on one of two levels, either (*a*) through the improvement of traditional methods of production, as in the case of agriculture and sericulture in immediately post-Meiji Japan or (*b*) through the introduction of new technologies directed toward the exploitation of hitherto unused resources, the production of which then can be exported.[18] Here, the examples of Saudi Arabia, Kuwait, Iraq, and Venezuela, and the exploitation of their petroleum resources provide striking examples, as do the mining of gold and diamonds in South Africa. *The role of natural resources in these situations is that of an agent for rapid capital formation,* which may be directed toward ends not directly related to resource utilization, such as improvements in public health and the spread of literacy.

Variations in the quality of public sanitation and medical care or education in turn substantially modify the character of our fourth major factor, *labor*. It is a truism that in order to economically develop, there must be people to develop economically, and their effectiveness as a labor force will vary almost directly with their numbers, health, skills, and discipline. In relatively "new" areas of pioneer settlement, where ratios of people to developable resources are low, every addition to the labor force means a major increment in regional product. This is particularly important when the additions to the labor force are skilled, rather than unskilled. As Hoselitz, Minsky, and others have noted, the rapid economic expansion of the United States from the middle of the nineteenth century on was in no small part due to the massive imports of "capital" in the form of some of Europe's most skilled workmen, although this form of capital does not appear in capital import figures.[19] The re-

[18] New crops may be included under the term "new technologies." In this sense the cultivation of cacao in the Gold Coast by native cultivators for export is a good example. Even more striking is the role of coffee production among the Chagga of Tanganyika on the slopes of Kilimanjaro. See E. S. Munger, "African Coffee on Kilimanjaro: A Chagga *Kihamba*," *Economic Geography* (April, 1952), pp. 181–85.

[19] The author's father exemplifies the case. By the time he migrated to the United States, he had completed his general education and acquired most

cipient country in such cases also is spared the costs of supporting and training the technician until such time as he is able to contribute to the economy; these costs are borne by the "exporting" country.

However, labor not only produces, it consumes; and in many of the great lesser developed regions the effectiveness of the labor force as a means for increasing productivity is hampered by its very numbers and the very high ratio of population to exploited resources. The stagnation which may be associated with these conditions is exaggerated by the wastage of human energy and the discouragement of ambition by seasonal underemployment, ill health, malnutrition, and a combination of ignorance and poor technology. The vicious circle of stagnation can be broken, it is true, but only by the introduction of new technologies which substantially alter the relations of labor to the natural resources it exploits, at costs of varying dimensions and at the initiative of foreign or indigenous elites which represent a discontinuity with traditional cultural configurations.

It is clear that the course of economic growth is singularly complex and the factors which enter into it are mutually interdependent. It is not correct to say, as some cultural anthropologists might, that indigenous cultural configurations alone determine the nature of economic growth; nor can one support the geographical determinist, if such there be, who would maintain that the nature of the physical environment (or the resource base) directs the course of economic progress. All elements move together, often disjointedly and arhythmically like a man on crutches, but, in sum, in one direction.

Natural Resources: The Fifth Element in Economic Development

If these intimate interrelationships can thus be demonstrated, and if each of these elements in economic growth varies with each of the others, then our fifth variable, *natural resources,* becomes a concept as elusive and dynamic as any of the other four. To the geographer, natural resources in their broadest sense include all the freely given material phenomena of nature within the zone of men's activities, at present a zone extending about 12 miles above the surface of the earth and about 4 miles below it, plus the additional nonmaterial quality of situation or location. The association of these elements of land, air, sea, and situation in a single area commonly is identified as its "resource base" or "resource endowment."

This definition is misleading, however, in that it assumes a complete knowledge of the ways in which the physical environment may be utilized. This knowledge is in no sense complete, and, in the words of Zimmermann, much of the environment is in fact composed of "neutral stuff" awaiting awareness of its possibilities and the development of technologies which can exploit it effectively.[20] The dimensions of these understandings and the abilities to exploit the resource base, however defined, vary with cultures, with time, and with space. It is necessary, therefore, to distinguish between resource potentialities and a resource endowment both available and understood.

In East Asia, for example, there tends to be a seemingly remarkable neglect of upland areas, that is, of those areas either not suitable for paddy cultivation or convenient for the production of dry crops, even under topographic, climatic, and edaphic conditions which are matched by many productive agricultural areas elsewhere in the world.[21] In large part this condition reflects technologies which are unable to cope with the conditions that exist

of the technical training which permitted him to earn a livelihood as a skilled tool and die maker almost immediately upon his arrival in this country.

20 E. W. Zimmermann, *World Resources and Industries* (rev. ed.; New York: Harper and Brothers, 1951), p. 8.

21 See the two volumes, *The Development of Upland Areas in the Far East* (New York: Institute of Pacific Relations, 1948).

in the upland areas or which are at least better suited to the physical conditions characteristic of the lowlands. The result is a system of agricultural production geared to the better lands which produce more per unit area at the cost of staggering labor outputs and which, at the expense of seasonal underemployment, suffer labor shortages at the key periods of planting and harvesting.

In the time dimension, resource variations are illustrated by the Great Plains, the rich grassland soils of which were almost entirely neglected by the Plains Indians and which now are one of the great granaries of the world. Another example is the fertile prairies of central Illinois, which at first were neglected by the white settlers from southern Indiana, Kentucky, and Tennessee, who first settled in the more familiar narrow, wooded fluvial lowlands which infrequently scar the smooth prairie surface.[22] Variations in time also may reflect simply the exhaustion of a given resource; witness the ghost mining towns of Colorado or the abandoned farms of western Oklahoma, where the fertile topsoil was partly removed by wind erosion, and drought completed the destruction of what might have been productive grazing lands under careful range management.

Existing resources may remain in the potential category also because of inaccessibility. Inaccessibility may reflect a technical inability to withdraw a material from its matrix of associated elements, as until recently in the case of titanium, one of the new wonder metals. Or it may reflect a simple lack of external economies, as in the case of some 10 per cent of Japan's forest reserves which remain unexploited because of a lack of transportation facilities.

This point leads to another caveat regarding the above definition of natural resources. If a given resource is not accessible, it cannot be described as "freely given," since it cannot be exploited without investment of "capital" in one of its several forms. The qualification may be extended to almost all resources, since they must be acted upon in order to become useful to men. It follows that many resources, as they come into use, are no more "natural" than they are "cultural." Is a long-fertilized, irrigated, and cultivated soil or a planted stand of Japanese cedar "natural"? Only to a degree, of course. We can conceive, therefore, of a classification of resources based upon their degree of "naturalness" in which classification would take place perhaps according to the amount of capital required to make them available.

Two other characteristics of resources remain to be noted. The first is their substitutability, the second their complementarity.

Changes in technology mean changes in resource uses and in a sense competition among resources for given uses. The substitution of certain plastics, some based upon coal, for metals provides one illustration. At one time the tin can was made of tin plate, that is, sheet steel dipped into molten tin; at a later stage electrolytic tin plating permitted major savings in tin through much thinner tin coatings over the steel; now many so-called tin cans are coated with a fine film of tin only on the outside and are lined with plastic on the inside. In addition, glass containers compete with the tin can as a means for packaging foodstuffs. Substitutability has its geographic aspects as well. A given resource in one area that cannot bear the costs of distant transport may be substituted for in another by a more abundant resource. For example, Philippine mahogany or *lauan* and other tropical hardwoods replace genuine mahogany in parts of Asia; and in many Asian countries the ubiquitous bamboo provides an inexpensive scaffolding nearly as efficient and far less costly than the timber, aluminum, or steel scaffoldings used in the middle-latitude West.

Finally, resources tend to complement each other, to be linked in a chain of utilization patterns and of productive processes

22 Each of the above examples illustrates cultural differentiation of resources as well. See Spoehr, *op. cit.*

in which the production of one demands or effects the production or availability of others. The mining and use of iron ore in steel manufacturing demand limestone and coal; the strip-mining of coal destroys valuable farm land in southern Illinois or southeastern Kansas; the clean-cutting of timber in forested areas in Japan is reflected in the silting of reservoirs downstream; and the development of hydroelectric installations in the Columbia River has accelerated the diminution of the salmon fisheries off the coasts of Oregon and Washington. Not only may resources be linked into a complex of productive processes, but also, as Colby has suggested,[23] the development of facilities for the exploitation of any one resource may make possible the utilization of an entirely unrelated resource. He cites the example of branches of the Southern Pacific Railway from Ogden, Utah, to San Francisco, which were constructed to provide access to the gold, silver, and copper ores of Nevada, but which then made possible the development of a profitable grazing industry centering in oasis-like settlements along the lower flanks of the mountain ranges crossed or paralleled by them.

It is a characteristic of the more highly developed and industrialized economies that they can take into account and integrate complementary resources into systems of production. *In this sense, they are less specialized, less fragmented, and more flexible in terms of resource use than the lesser developed economies in which extreme specialization of resource utilization tends to be practiced* partly because of less highly developed and therefore less flexible technologies. Even the Chinese, advanced as they were a millennium and more ago in the control of water, cleansed the silted channels of their irrigation systems simply by dredging or flushing out the silt periodically; integrated watershed control of water supplies, though known, was not practiced. In effect, the use-possibilities among resources are fewer than in the more highly developed economies.

[23] In a memorandum to the author.

ECONOMIC DEVELOPMENT IN RELATION TO NATURAL RESOURCES

The nature of resource utilization in any society depends upon, and in turn reflects upon, the nature of the economic development that is taking place within it. This development varies, however, with the size and nature of the unit under examination. The question may be phrased: "The economic development of what?" As Kuznets points out, we ordinarily would not seriously discuss the resource development problems of an Andorra or a Monaco.[24] Nevertheless, problems of economic variability arise for minute areas.

For example, Singapore, a British Crown Colony, is well on its way to independence within the Commonwealth. As a politically autonomous unit, Singapore, an island only 26 miles from east to west and 14 miles from south to north, is endowed with a minimum of significant natural resources. It consists of one great metropolis rapidly expanding its urbanized area, surrounded by wasteland and intensively cultivated Chinese market gardens and fishing villages which supply it with only a minute fraction of its food requirements. Its major natural resource, one most difficult to measure quantitatively, is its situation astride the chief maritime gateway between the Indian Ocean and the South China Sea. This situation, combined with certain qualities of British institutions in the area, such as political stability, a sound currency, and an elaborate system of shipping and banking services, plus the entrepreneurial enterprise of its largely Chinese population, make a viable economic future conceivable, much as in the commercial city-states of the Hanseatic League. Even though politically autonomous, Singapore as a great regional commercial center and entrepôt will be economically dependent on political and economic conditions wholly beyond its control. The point here is the relative irrelevance of natural resources other than situation as a positive factor in the economic development of such a city-

[24] Kuznets, Moore, and Spengler, *op. cit.*, pp. 4 ff.

state. In a negative sense, however, the absence of a resource endowment and a virtually complete dependence upon the outside world for subsistence is a crucial factor in determining Singapore's ability to survive world economic depressions and political transformations over which it has no control.

On the other hand, one can point to a tiny state, such as the Sheikhdom of Kuwait, only 1,930 square miles in size and mostly unproductive desert, which is riding the crest of a rising national income almost entirely from petroleum production alone. Here the significance of a single natural resource is overwhelming.

Nevertheless, under normal circumstances, it is reasonable to postulate that the larger and more varied the resource base of a given state, the more opportunities it will have, *ceteris paribus*, for rapid economic development. All of the major industrialized countries have, or have had, relatively large and diversified resource endowments, and the United States is perhaps the most striking example. But even the United States is far from self-sufficient in natural resources, and lesser political units are even less so.

This being the case, would it not be more productive in the long run to consider the economic development of some supranational unit, such as the British Commonwealth, or Western Europe, or the Latin Americas?[25] The prewar Japanese Empire was such a unit and was self-contained to a surprising degree, a degree hidden in part by the fact that Japan's prewar trade statistics did not include her most important trade orientations, those toward her dependencies—Korea, Taiwan, Karafuto, and later Manchuria.

Consideration of such supranational units of economic organization is beyond the scope of this paper, but one major point emerges from a consideration of them, that is, the distinction between the actual possession of a resource endowment *in situ* and *accessibility* to resources which may be under the control of foreign states. Trade and transportation are the devices by which inequalities among nations in resource endowments may be minimized; but they can be minimized only at a cost. Every country dependent upon foreign areas for certain of its raw materials must be able to pay for them and for such services as transportation, banking services, and insurance which are necessary in order to make them available.

How can these payments be made? For those countries which already are highly industrialized, capital may be obtained from the production of processed and manufactured materials and services which may be exported in partial payment for needed raw-material imports. In the lesser developed countries, however, this option is unlikely to exist. Payment for imported foodstuffs and raw materials, as well as the manufactured goods which make domestic resource exploitation in part possible, depends in part on the availability of products, usually raw materials, suitable for export. In this context, mineral resources, food surpluses, and forest products tend to play an inordinately important role, at least for short periods of time.[26]

In addition, the exploitation of certain resources and the availability of their products for export often require considerable investment in external services of which transportation may be the most important. Indeed, accessibility means transportation. In the highly developed regions, internal transportation systems have long since been developed and external communications facilities in the form of national merchant marines also may

[25] The productivity referred to here is solely economic. Integration may be practiced on a large scale for non-economic reasons. An example proposed by Munger is that of Portugal and her overseas dependencies for which integration is practiced only "by rigidly controlled departures from the world price system. . . . The values to the Portuguese are political not economic." From a communication to the author.

[26] The export of labor and remittances from nationals abroad are other sources of income, e.g., remittances to China and Lebanon from nationals overseas, or miners from Mozambique employed in the mines of South Africa.

have been created. In the lesser developed regions, however, these types of services often do not exist.[27] As a result, known resources may remain unexploitable, costs of imports will remain high, and raw-material exports may be disadvantaged on the world market. Grants and loans from foreign sources provide another source of capital, but grants tend to be few, and loans must be repaid. The importance of loans should not be minimized, but ultimate development depends upon a country's own savings, internally organized, unless it is to become integrated fully into a larger economy as a constant recipient of foreign aid.

Problems of this kind indicate the need for rational planning whereby economic development can be guided. Unfortunately, planning often reflects the erroneous assumption that economic development in lesser developed countries must follow the patterns of development which took place in the new developed regions, and that resources and the nature of their utilization are fixed. However, even in comparing the patterns of economic growth in the already developed and industrialized countries, significant differences in the developmental process are apparent. The relatively gradual economic growth characteristic of Great Britain has not been duplicated since. As Gerschenkron points out, early British industrialization took place without the large-scale participation of banking interests or government[28] and was financed primarily by an accumulation of wealth derived from trade with a great empire and to a degree with the remainder of the world as well. In Germany, France, Italy, the U.S.S.R., and Japan, among others, rapid economic growth took place under the leadership either of giant banking interests or of the state.

[27] In reality, the dimensions of these facilities vary markedly from country to country. In India, for example, the railway system developed by the British may be regarded as a "freely given, nonnatural" resource inherited from its colonial past by a free India.

[28] Hoselitz (ed.), *The Progress of Underdeveloped Areas, op. cit.*, pp. 13–14.

It is apparent that the nature of economic growth will vary within each unit under consideration and with the time at which accelerated economic growth begins. Indeed, the rates of growth that are either possible or desirable also will vary notably with place and time and with the five major determinants of economic development previously discussed. The reordering of comparative advantages in resource endowments as a result of new technologies, trade barriers, or intervening resource discoveries of necessity changes the possibilities and potentialities of resource use and planning.

Recent changes in power technology provide a useful illustration. According to Hartshorne, not one of the major industrial nations is or was without access to major sources of energy, particularly the mineral fuels. Britain acted as the coal mine of the world for a period of time, and it is worth pointing out as well that at the time it entered upon its period of modern economic development, Britain was unusually well endowed with other resources, such as iron ore, tin, and certain lesser minerals, and even timber with which to construct a merchant marine. Germany, France, and Russia also were well endowed with energy resources. Other countries, such as Italy, short of energy resources *in situ,* were able, albeit at a cost, to obtain mineral fuels from outside their boundaries, or they developed hydroelectric potentials to an exceptional degree. That the availability of energy raw materials has not induced economic development, however, is illustrated by the numerous underdeveloped areas well endowed with such resources—India is one example; China another.

More important, perhaps, is the future availability to the underdeveloped countries of energy from atomic reactors. At present this energy is not cheap, especially in the small units which are likely to be better suited to the needs of most of the lesser developed countries. However, such energy will become available, if not now, then within the next several decades. This does not mean that the development of more traditional energy resources should be delayed; quite the contrary, since these may remain less costly, given accessibility and high quality, for a long period of time. It does suggest two important considerations, however: (1) that planning for energy and other natural resource development in the "have" countries must be kept flexible and constantly subject to review, and (2) that the "have-not" countries possess possibilities for economic growth based upon ample supplies of energy that previously were unthinkable.

CASE STUDIES

Many of these various aspects of economic development and of the role of natural resources particularly—the variations that result from differences in the nature of the resource base, from differences in economic and political structure, and from differences in the state of the world economy at given times—may be illustrated by the comparative histories of Japan, Taiwan, Malaya, and, to a degree, China and India.

JAPAN

Japan's modern economic development began late and with a marked socioeconomic discontinuity after the fall of the Shogunate and the restoration of the Emperor in 1867.[29] At that time, Japan was a country living right up to its then known and developed resource endowment and emerging from a 200-year period of virtual isolation. Japan's resource endowment, then and now, is relatively niggardly. Arable land accounts for considerably less than 20 per cent of the total land area, as compared with 40 per cent in France, and the actual area under cultivation at present is not more than 15 per cent of the whole. Soils are of indifferent fertility; growing seasons are long enough in most of the country to permit double-cropping, except in the highlands and in Hokkaido in the north, but they are not long enough to permit the double-cropping of paddy. Forest resources were then relatively abundant, though they now supply about 75 per cent of Japan's wood needs only at the cost of their gradual diminution. Mineral resources are abundant in variety, but few are of great commercial significance, and coal, low quality though it may be, is the single most important mineral resource. Hydroelectric potential, however, is relatively high for a country of its size, about 148,000 square miles, the size of Montana, and the Japanese have developed the larger part of it already.

At the time of the Meiji Restoration, moreover, the press of a population of about 35 millions on these resources under then prevailing technologies was high, and population had remained virtually unchanged for a number of years. Nevertheless, Japan was able to develop economically with enormous rapidity. How was this accomplished?

One thing is certain. The initial stages of the developmental process were financed primarily internally. Foreign loans and capital investment were very small, if strategic. Accumulation of domestic supplies of capital was made possible by the extraordinarily rapid development of the natural resource base and rapid increases in productivity from it. Until after the Sino-Japanese war, Japan's chief source of revenue was raw silk. Quite small investments in sericulture, especially in standardizing the quality of silk output and in increasing silk-reeling capacities, resulted in Japan's displacement of China as the world's prime supplier of raw silk and in the rapid expansion (resulting partly from greater purchasing power in Western Europe and the United States) of the world silk market. At the same time, similarly small investments in agriculture through the provision of improved seed varieties, irrigation facilities, better transportation for marketing of

[29] For a detailed description see W. W. Lockwood, *The Economic Development of Japan* (Princeton: Princeton University Press, 1954) and his chapter in Kuznets, Moore, and Spengler (eds.), *op. cit.*, pp. 129–78. See also Edwin P. Reubens' chapter in *ibid.*, pp. 179–228.

agricultural products, and more fertilizers, resulted in agricultural surpluses, the profits of which were siphoned from the countryside by the government through improved tax mechanisms (forced saving), making possible the more massive participation of the state in providing external economies, in investing in alternative productive sectors of the economy, in restricting consumption in the rural areas, and in permitting the rapid growth of large urban complexes with their supplies of labor for modern industrial enterprises. It is even true that the Japanese cotton-textile industry was based originally on Japan-grown cotton, which was in adequate supply until the eighties when a sufficiently modern industry had been developed to require large imports of cotton from abroad. It was the textile industry, first silk and then cotton, that permitted rapid economic growth in Japan. It is safe to say also that the application of easily available improved technologies to the then Japanese resource base so increased its potential as to create surpluses for internal consumption and export. These then permitted the initiation by Japan of a program of heavy-industry development, later financed in part by foreign loans and capital as well as by an expanding export trade.

These assertions may be controversial, especially in light of the substantial inadequacy of Japan's resource base to support the present Japanese economy, but they should be regarded as partial justification for the previous description of natural resources as a means of capital formation and for the admonition that resource planning is a continuing process that varies with the needs and objectives of a given country and the changes in world resource equilibria.

TAIWAN

The developmental history of Taiwan has taken place under different circumstances and with different results. Taiwan is a relatively small island about one-fourth the size of Illinois, with an indigenous Chinese population of about 8 millions. Under the Japanese, both gross national product and per capita product rose rapidly. These increases in production also may be said to have been internally financed by more efficient utilization of the island's natural resources, especially agricultural resources.[30] Although only about a fourth of the island is topographically suitable for agriculture, soils are relatively fertile in that fourth, water supplies are relatively abundant, and the growing season permits double-cropping of paddy all over the island, except in the highest highlands. The Japanese invested sizable sums in Taiwan, but at the earliest stages these were designed more to promote political and military stability than not; at a later time, the evidence suggests that investment was far smaller than the value of the surpluses that continued to be produced from Formosan soil. Despite a rising population, agricultural production under the guidance of Japanese technical advisers backed by political authority forged ahead of population increases and permitted the export to Japan of three-quarters of a million tons of rice and a million tons of sugar each year. Some additional development took place in the mining of coal, but especially in the development of hydroelectric resources, which in turn made possible the establishment of aluminum and ferrometallic processing plants. Consumers' goods, such as textiles, continued to be almost entirely imported.

At the close of the war Taiwan was separated from Japan. It possessed a highly developed agrarian economy which specialized in food crops, was commercially rather than subsistence oriented, and possessed sizable surpluses with which to finance more diversified economic development. Had all other factors remained constant, it is reasonably certain that these surpluses, based upon further improvements in the utilization of agricultural resources, would

[30] For a more detailed examination of this problem see N. S. Ginsburg, *Economic Resources and Development of Formosa* (New York: Institute of Pacific Relations, 1953), mimeographed.

have permitted the establishment of a viable economy, either as a region of China or as an independent political unit. The great advantage was what we might call a "time cushion" in the form of surpluses for export by means of which economic planning could have been financed and implemented despite the other limitations of the resource endowment.

Unfortunately, all other things never are equal, and Taiwan's population was swelled by 2,500,000 refugees and troops from China proper, who consume many of the agricultural surpluses and demand capital expenditures on the part of the two governments on the island, which further hamper economic growth. At the same time, the withdrawal of the Japanese agricultural technicians, believed to have numbered up to 20,000 and the diminution of political stability resulted in substantial declines in production which were not overcome until about 1952.

Taiwan still possesses a "time cushion," but its dimensions are much smaller than they were. Economic growth is taking place, and at a rapid rate, but in part by means of major grants-in-aid, which do not require repayment, from the United States. The island's economy is still primarily agrarian, although the reasonable limits of the development of the resource base with given technologies are beginning to be reached, and the significance of other factors is beginning to dominate the scene.

MALAYA

The third and quite different example also concerns what might be termed a "colonial" economy, that of Malaya, due for independence in 1957.[31] Unlike the relationship between Japan and Taiwan, that between Britain and Malaya never was so intimate, on either economic or political grounds. Malaya's economy, apart from the commercial functions of Singapore, is clearly dual, and was so from the earliest period of British hegemony. One major sector is Malay, indigenous, primarily agricultural and subsistence, based upon the cultivation of paddy by Malay villagers in restricted areas and secondarily upon Malay fishing activities. The second major sector is basically foreign in that it is managed and manned by non-Malay labor and financed by non-Malay capital, is commercial, and is export-oriented. It in turn is divided into two basic subsectors—one, the production of rubber; the other, the mining of tin. Each of these major sectors displays a notable direct reliance upon the existing resource base of the country. But unlike Taiwan, where there is a time cushion based upon surpluses of foodstuffs, the time cushion in Malaya is of quite a different sort, as is the role of the resource endowment in future development.

Malaya does not feed itself. Indeed, it imports more than half of its food supply. The predominantly food-producing Malay community, 49 per cent of the total population, produces enough food only for itself and until very recently existed in relative isolation from the other communities in Malaya. Rubber and tin production have been primarily the result of foreign enterprise and labor—British, Chinese, and Indian. If Malaya were self-sufficient in foodstuffs *and* had the surpluses of tin and rubber for export, there would be an abundance of capital for internal development and for the provision of the increasing social services that are being demanded of the government. These considerations are apart from the huge drains on the Federation budget of the anti-communist campaigns.

Actually, there is capital available from the rubber and tin industries, and Malaya has been the Commonwealth's prime dollar earner, but the need for food imports to meet normal consumer needs means a much more gradual pace of economic development. This pace must vary also with the fluctuating prices for rubber and tin on the

[31] A detailed handbook covering Malaya by N. S. Ginsburg and C. F. Roberts, Jr., was published . . . under the auspices of the American Ethnological Society. [Ed. Note: Pub. as *Malaya* (Seattle: University of Washington Press, 1958)].

world market and the dependence of the colonial export economy upon forces beyond its control. This does not mean that Malaya's resource endowment is poor. Actually, its potentials are poorly understood as yet, and superficially the country is prosperous as compared with most lesser developed regions. But the *nature* of the resource planning and development problem is distinctly different from that in Taiwan where food supplies from domestic agriculture are adequate. In Malaya, a sudden and marked drop in both tin and rubber prices would be disastrous, and levels of living would fall in proportion, with concomitant political unrest. In short, the circumstances surrounding the utilization of the natural resource base are markedly different and require differing measures both of analysis and of policy implementation.

CHINA AND INDIA

On quite a different scale China and India possess still other developmental problems relative to their resource endowments.

Each of these countries is characterized by largely agrarian societies, with strong subsistence qualities, and by heavy pressures of population upon known and available resources. There are in effect no food surpluses; indeed there often are deficits. Both are following roughly similar courses of economic growth, though implemented in markedly different ways. Agricultural resources are being developed by the application of technological devices, more so in India it is true than in China, but the need may be greater there. Heavy industry is receiving the greater part of the emphasis in their developmental planning, although lighter industries in both countries have had a rather lengthy history of growth. Both have abundant supplies of energy in the form of coal, China more than India; both have reasonably large non-fuel mineral resources.

They differ substantially in the ways in which economic measures are implemented, as is to be expected when one, India, is essentially democratic, and the other, China, is totalitarian. Their greatest similarity, however, lies in the inflexibility imposed upon their developmental planning and policies by the necessity for increased agricultural production, not as a means for capital accumulation, but simply to prevent starvation, maintain a healthier labor force, and discourage rural (and therefore national) unrest. Both illustrate the degree to which high man-land ratios act as a deterrent to accelerated economic development.

Conclusions

From these preliminary statements concerning the role of natural resources in economic growth follow a few relatively simple generalizations:

(1) The possession of a sizable and diversified natural resource endowment is a major advantage to any country embarking upon a period of rapid economic growth. Diversification may be less important than the dimensions of one or more resources, if their reserves are large enough and long-run demand is steady and strong.

(2) Resources need not be situated within the confines of the country undergoing development, but they must be accessible. Accessibility implies transportation, and transportation in part implies imports, both of which demand accumulations of capital with which to obtain materials from extra-national or discontinuous resource endowments.

(3) One of the major means for capital accumulation is an abundance of easily exploitable natural resources (Saudi Arabia, South Africa, Venezuela).

(4) In no sense, however, are natural resources responsible for development and economic growth; they possess no deterministic power. However, "they possess latent utility and are part of an over-all regional capability."[32]

(5) They also may set limits upon the approaches to natural resource planning

[32] C. C. Colby.

and development. If a given raw material necessary for some phase of industrialization is not located *in situ* and is unavailable due to tariff barriers or high transportation costs, modification of that phase is likely. Or, if rapid rises in agricultural, forest, or mineral production are possible, they may strongly influence the system of priorities and scale of operations which will characterize a total developmental effort or history.

(6) Even if abundant, natural resources will not determine the *kinds of uses* to which they will be put. Their availability in agriculture particularly, however, may influence critically the shift from agricultural to non-agricultural employments.

(7) The significance and functions of natural resources in economic development will differ markedly with the stages in the developmental process. Under normal circumstances the role of the resource endowment is most important in the earlier stages of economic development, when it acts as a means for capital accumulation and an accelerator for economic growth if abundant, and as a depressant upon that growth if niggardly.

(8) Similarly, the significance of indigenous resources is much less to the highly developed countries with their discontinuous world hinterlands and larger supplies of capital, skilled labor, technology, and entrepreneurial experience, than to the relatively lesser developed regions frequently characterized by scarcities of all these factors.

(9) Any comprehensive program for economic development demands the development of a sophisticated inventory of resource endowments, an appraisal of present systems of resource utilization, an analysis of cultural and physical obstacles to resource development, and an estimate of resource potentials, taking into account conflicting uses and demands for given resources and the probable role of technological change over periods of time.

GILBERT F. WHITE

THE SPECIAL PROBLEMS OF THE UNDERDEVELOPED COUNTRIES WITH RESPECT TO NATURAL RESOURCES

In recent years we have witnessed a spectacular upsurge in interest focused on the non-industrialized areas of the world. These areas comprise most of the land surface and contain more than two-thirds of the world's population. Although there are wide differences in climate, terrain, and cultural heritage, from the standpoint of problems in economic development, they have some similarities. The development problem of such emerging countries is basically one of providing a decent level of living to people many of whom have lived continuously in grinding poverty and ill health. Within the framework of a productive system that depends heavily on primitive techniques and subsistence agriculture, labor is almost always relatively abundant and skills and capital equipment are relatively scarce. The low-income countries operate typically as one-sided, non-diversified economies specializing in production of food and raw materials and are thus generally in a position of comparative dependence upon the world economy as they develop commercial production.

Social factors reinforce the chain of relationships which lead to the ever-widening gap between the level of living of such countries and those of the more developed world. The huge economic gaps in the world today are of relatively recent origin. The United States and Europe attained their present high standards of living through a process of rapid economic development. The regions of Asia, Africa, Latin America, and Eastern and Southern Europe, which did not share in this development, have simply been left behind. Their per capita incomes today have remained relatively static, as compared with their situation hundreds of years ago. Although both types of countries are growing, their growth is at different rates, so that the absolute gap is widening. A distinction must be made between the countries that have already begun to move and those that have not, for the gap is closing between the richer countries and those that are growing industrially. Japan and Italy have already established a capital and institutional base for rapid change.

The industrial countries of the North Atlantic, without exception, although in varying degrees, are importers of raw materials from non-industrialized countries (Fig. 1). Exploration, development, and marketing of these raw materials are usually in the hands of large, international companies headquartered in the industrial nations. The producing countries, however, are becoming increasingly concerned with the means by which exploration for resources within their boundaries is conducted and the conditions under which discovered resources are developed and marketed. Under present conditions, this situation contains the seeds of future conflict.

Economic growth for the less-developed areas is a process of social transformation.

• Gilbert F. White is Professor of Geography, University of Chicago.

Reprinted from G. F. White, *Social and Economic Aspects of Natural Resources,* A Report to the Committee on Natural Resources (Washington: NAS–NRC, 1962), pp. 28–33, with the permission of the author.

Although there are limitations to the substitutions consistent with a given level of development, there are many alternative combinations of factors that can encourage growth or prevent it. Methods used in the already industrialized countries to stimulate further economic growth are rarely transferable "as is" to the emerging nations, primarily because a developed economy is characterized by a technical and cultural complex quite different from those of less-developed economies. Western methods utilize elaborate facilities and a tremendous amount of productive equipment per worker—the result of over 150 years of accumulation. They are deliberately devised for a system of scarce labor and abundant equipment, while the opposite prevails in the low-income countries. These have little capital per worker and the amount of equipment they can add per year, even with generous aid from other nations, is small by Western standards. Moreover, developed countries possess a largely literate and educated labor force which, because of the very nature of its mechanized civilization, has an understanding of the function and care of machinery.

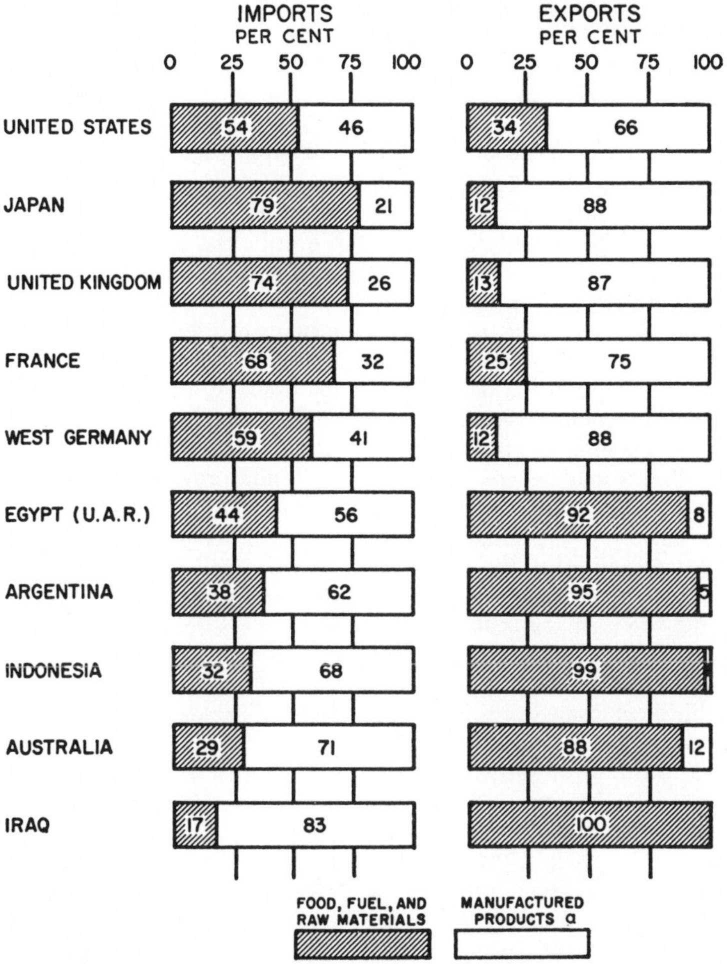

a Includes many semiprocessed goods.
Source: U.N., *Yearbook of International Trade Statistics, 1959* (New York: 1960).

FIG. 1.—International trade patterns, 1959

Every Western industry depends for its efficiency upon other industries and upon the ready availability of materials, components, and tools. It depends also on auxiliary enterprises that provide technical, financial, and managerial services, on a complex system of communication and transportation, and on an intricate system of business practices. Even where low-income countries could use Western methods in their original form it is often not efficient to do so.

In short, economic progress for an already industrialized country is, on the whole, a question of continuation of processes already begun, operating within an institutional framework already adapted through time to technological, economic, and social progress, which does not require as great an upheaval and readjustment to continue on the road of development. The less-developed countries must apply for themselves new economic and other structures and relationships to fit their conditions and needs.

At the heart of such endeavors lies creativity. Conventional economic theory has little to contribute to the question of how growth begins. Perhaps this is because the seeds of growth are multidimensional and may include social and motivational factors and changes that stimulate creativity. In this regard the achievement motivation of people in a society may be significant. Studies have indicated that the extent to which people care about doing a good job may determine how fast the economic machine operates. Thus, a society is not apt to enter upon continuing technological progress until some change occurs in its social structure. Dependence on tradition, custom, and a hierarchy of authority is not conducive to creativity or initiative. In some instances, economic change may be spearheaded by some group within the elite of the society that develops antipathy to old values—perhaps as a result of loss of its traditional status—and acquires new ones. If the availability of technological knowledge and the conditions of resources, markets, and capital are even moderately favorable so that economic progress seems a fairly satisfactory solution, then the unrest caused by such a group and their desire to regain their traditional status by economic power may be sufficient to germinate the beginning of deeper changes in the direction of economic development.

Transition requires a tremendous investment in health, education, and capital equipment from societies which are so poor that more than 80 per cent of the family income goes for food alone while the people remain malnourished. This problem of essential investment is tremendously complicated by the speed of population growth which may outstrip savings and increases in productivity.

In the emerging countries, government is limited in what it can do by lack of experience, trained people, and organization, and must try to attract additional personnel. Nevertheless, it plays a crucial, if not the leading role, in technological transition. Methods of direct and indirect governmental intervention are numerous. Governmental activity in education and research, for example, can do much to prepare and equip a country for technological and economic development through strengthening skills and providing means of technological adaptation.

The development of every country has been distinctive in consequence of the nature and quantity of its resource endowment. Resources set certain limits to what may be accomplished at a given time, with the state of technology, capital, and other factors. The unequal distribution of natural resources with respect to area and population is well known, although the resource quantities of the world have not yet been adequately determined. Because of the inequality of resource distribution, the prospects for economic growth and development are better in some parts of the world than in others. Nevertheless, the suggestion that the less-developed countries are poorly endowed with natural resources and that this is the principal cause of their poverty would be a vast oversimplification.

Natural resources commonly are seen as contributing to economic growth by providing materials, foreign exchange, and an attraction for capital. However, the precise role of natural resources in the growth of an economy is still not clear; only a few general comments can be made here. To begin with, the inherent qualities and attributes of a resource are in themselves not sufficient to enable them to participate in production or to be of value in that regard. Other factors must be considered, among them the accessibility of the resource, the existence of complementary resources, and the availability of markets for the resulting product. Resource endowment may limit productivity, income, savings, and internal development in an emerging country with limited external trade. Here it may be possible to develop trade relationships among the emerging countries, particularly where resource complementarities exist. Through its effect on per capita income, resource endowment may in turn influence levels of skill, education, and other attributes of the population. Even when the limitations imposed by an area's resources have been ameliorated, there may still remain cultural aftereffects of previous resource endowment. Old adjustments may become new barriers. Moreover, the character of a country's resources may determine the nature of its possible technological progress. Resource availability may increase an area's capacity to export raw materials in exchange for imports necessary to economic development, and to attract investment capital, thus changing the saving rate necessary to achieve a specific rate of growth. Among the emerging countries, there generally is a greater proportion of natural resources to all resources utilized in income production.

At the same time, there has been an observable trend in industrialized areas toward independence of economic activities away from a specifically localized resource base. Increased ability to substitute synthetics for natural materials, and to supplement missing resources by international or interregional trade or through appropriately directed technological change, have contributed to this trend. The amount of natural-resource input is declining relative to total output. Emerging nations customarily do not need to invest the same amounts of resources that we did in our development. To build a steel industry at the present time would take much less steel than was necessary in the past. A problem for the low-income countries is to move toward diversified economies despite backwardness of labor force and dependence upon marketing of raw materials.

There exist large reserves of resources still undiscovered, undeveloped, and unused in the emerging countries. The barriers to development are many, and significant changes in the technological, social, economic, and political structures of these areas may be necessary before they will be utilized. Such developments might prove beneficial not only to the countries themselves, but to the strengthening of the resource base of the world. It is unfortunate that figures are not presently available to indicate quantitatively the effect that such developments might have on resource availability. It is essential that efforts be made to inventory these untapped resources and to determine their significance in relation to the developing economies of the emerging nations.

The outlook for resource development in these areas spans a great range of possibilities. At one extreme, the low-income countries may reach the year 2000 with doubled population, continued high birth rates and a low level of per capita consumption that keeps them on the verge of calamity. Rapid population growth might well offset gains in efficiency of resource management. At the other extreme, it is possible that through progress in birth control and the beginning of technological transition, these countries will approach self-sustaining modernization despite increased population. The latter extreme might place much heavier immediate demands upon resources for industrialization, but it also would advance the time when the full impact of science and technology might be brought to bear upon the meeting of mounting human needs. World-trade operations making best use of the comparative advantage of each country will be involved and will depend to a large extent upon each country having access to world resources in addition to its own.

The individual condition is tragic. But that is no excuse for not doing our best with the social condition.

To think otherwise, to take refuge in facile despair, has been the characteristic intellectual treachery of our day. It is shoddy. We have to face the individual condition. . . .

Most people in Asia still haven't enough to eat—but they have a bit more than before. Most people in Asia are still dying before their time (on the average, Indians live less than half as long as Englishmen)—but they are living longer than before.

Is that Progress? This is not a subject to be superior or refined or ingenious about, and the answer is—of course it is.

Through luck we got in first with the scientific-industrial revolution; as a result, our lives became, on the average, healthier, longer, more comfortable to an extent that had never been imagined; it doesn't become us to tell our Chinese and Indian friends that that kind of progress is not worth having.

They are in search of what Leicester and Des Moines take for granted, food, extra years of life, modest comforts.

When they have got these things, they are willing to put up with a dash of American disappointment. And their determination to get these things is likely in the next 30 years to prove the strongest social force on earth.

Will they get them? . . . There is no technical reason why not. If [so], the level of moral kindness will go up in parallel.

Sir Charles Snow, *The Two Cultures and the Scientific Revolution* (New York: Cambridge University Press, 1959).

HARVEY S. PERLOFF and LOWDON WINGO, JR.

NATURAL RESOURCE ENDOWMENT AND REGIONAL ECONOMIC GROWTH

We are concerned in this paper with the relationship between the natural resources within the various parts, or regions, of a country and what might be called the geography of national economic expansion.

The development of the economy of the United States provides a case study of resources in space interacting with the other elements of economic growth that is especially illuminating: (1) it covers an extended spectrum of growth from early agricultural beginnings to status as an advanced, industrial-and-service-oriented economy, thus affording an opportunity to examine the role of resources in different stages of national economic growth, (2) it covers a wide variety of regional resources and growth situations, providing a rich set of variations on the interactions of the national economy with its geographic components, and (3) it can be examined with the help of a wealth of historical information and statistical data. Specifically, Resources for the Future has concluded a 3-year study of the regional characteristics of the growth of the U.S. economy. The results of this effort have been made available in a book entitled *Regions, Resources, and Economic Growth.*[1] This paper draws heavily on the research that went into this book and on the conclusions that emerge from it. Given this storehouse of materials, we have been tempted into speculation on the broad relationships involved in the resources-growth problem.

• Harvey S. Perloff and Lowdon Wingo, Jr. are both staff members of Resources for the Future, Inc.

Reprinted from a paper presented at the Conference on Natural Resources and Economic Growth, University of Michigan, April 1960. Published as RFF Reprint No. 24 (Washington: Resources for the Future, Inc., 1960), 25 pp., with the permission of the authors and the editor.

Resources and Growth in a Broad Historical Framework

One of the insights emerging from an examination of the history of American economic development is the difficulty of defining "resource endowment" in any long-run, substantive sense. In the short run, endowment is simply the inventory of those natural materials that are required in some degree by the national economy responding to internal consumption demands and to its position in international trade. As the

[1] Harvey S. Perloff, Edgar S. Dunn, Jr., Eric E. Lampard, and Richard F. Muth, *Regions, Resources, and Economic Growth* (Baltimore: The Johns Hopkins Press, 1960).

The discussion of growth here will be limited to changes in what we refer to as the *volume* of economic activities (e.g., increases in population, employment, value added, and the like), acknowledging that this is but one facet of economic growth. Growth as defined by changes in *welfare* (changes in per capita income, for example) is discussed in pt. V of *Regions, Resources, and Economic Growth;* changes in state per capita are analyzed in some detail by Simon Kuznets in "Industrial Distribution of Income and Labor Force by States, 1919–21 to 1955," pt. III of "Quantitative Aspects of the Economic Growth of Nations," *Economic Development and Cultural Change,* Vol. VI (July, 1958).

We assume that the broad features of regional economic expansion in the United States are familiar to our readers, and so we have presented no figures to describe them here. Those interested in such detail are referred to chaps. 2 and 3 of *Regions, Resources, and Economic Growth.*

requirements of the economy change, the composition of the inventory shifts, and in this sense "resource endowment" is a changing concept closely associated with the dynamics of economic growth. In short, the answer to what constitutes "resource endowment" is rooted in the determinants of final demand—consumer preferences and income distribution, as well as foreign trade—on the one hand, and in the current organization and technology of production on the other. As these variables change, so will the content of resource endowment. And, clearly then, as the composition of resource endowment changes, there will tend to be substantial changes in the relative advantage among regions supplying material inputs (and services) for the national economy.

The impact of these shifts can be sketched in with broad strokes by identifying stage by stage what have been the "nattural resources that count" in the national economy. This requires us to tell again a familiar story, but with a special focus.

THE EARLY AGRICULTURAL PERIOD

From its colonial origins the American economy developed as a producer of resource inputs into the rapidly expanding European economy. To serve such a function the endowment which counted in early America was arable land with its environmental complements of climate and water, and this, with access to the growing European market for agricultural staples, set up the conditions for regional growth in early America. It was quite logical, hence, that the regional economies developed a certain archetype: a good deepwater port as the nucleus of an agricultural hinterland well adapted for the production of a staple commodity in demand on the world market.

The growth potential of these nucleated regions depended heavily on the extent and "richness" of the hinterland accessible to port. Since good agricultural land was almost a free resource while labor and capital were dear, the expansion of production was effected by bringing more land into production and so extending the limits of the hinterland. Much of early American history is dominated by the great rivalries for control of hinterland that emerged between New York and Boston, Philadelphia and Baltimore, Charleston and Savannah. This expansion of the hinterlands took place through social overhead investment in transportation facilities beginning with the Massachusetts road system in the seventeenth century,[2] later producing the Erie Canal, and finally motivating the half-century of railroad construction stretching from the Baltimore and Ohio's first crude line reaching out to the rich wheatlands in Maryland and Pennsylvania to the driving of the golden spike at Promontory Point, Utah.[3] The force of the outward push for land is suggested by the fact that population west of the Alleghenies, which was estimated by the 1790 Census at 109,000, by 1840 had become almost 6.5 million, with more than 87 per cent of the labor force involved in agriculture.

Even though the data on this period are not very satisfactory, we can draw these general conclusions: (1) the *regional* endowment that made for growth was "good" land advantageously situated with respect to the market centers; (2) the distribution of economic activity in the period before 1840 was essentially a function of the expanding, nucleated, agricultural regions reaching into the economic vacuum of an unsettled continent to bring ever greater areas of land under cultivation; and (3) this resource-dominated expansion of the economy set the stage for the next important development by establishing a geography of markets, transport, and labor force to condition the nature of succeeding growth.

[2] The importance of hinterland in the growth of the early centers is vividly described by Carl Bridenbaugh, *Cities in the Wilderness* (New York: Ronald Press, 1938).

[3] A detailed treatment can be found in Paul H. Cootner, "Transportation Innovation and Economic Development: The Case of the U.S. Steam Railroads" (unpublished Ph.D. thesis, MIT, 1953).

THE MINERALS-DOMINANT ECONOMY

Somewhere around 1840–50 the next important resource stage began—as a result of the emerging minerals-dominant economy. The rapid growth of the railroads and the expansion of processing industries resulted in new input requirements: a new set of resources became important and a new set of locational forces came into play. The first part of this period was dominated by the growing demand for iron and steel and by the rapid elaboration of their production technology.[4] At this point it was the geographical juxtaposition of coal, iron ore, and the market which afforded the great impetus for growth. The importance of minerals, unlike agricultural land, was not alone in their direct contribution to regional growth so much as it was in the nature of their linkages with succeeding stages of production. It was not so much the mining of coal and iron that was important for growth, as the making of iron and steel products, which could not be separated from the sources of its mineral inputs. The early concentration of steel making in western Pennsylvania was a result of these relationships, for this area was not only well endowed with deposits of iron ore and coal but was central to a concentrated market stretching from Boston and New York westward. As the center of gravity of the market shifted west and as Mesabi ores replaced depleted local ores, the iron and steel industry also shifted westward along the southern shores of the Great Lakes.

With the increase in the demand for nonferrous metals, the depletion of accessible ore deposits in the East and the penetration of the West by the railroad net, a new role in regional growth was played by mineral resources endowment. In the Mountain region stretching from the Canadian border to the Southwest states, the mining of metal ores was the lead factor in economic development: in 1870 when mineral extractions involved the employment of 1.5 per cent of the labor force nationally, in the Mountain states it accounted for no less than 26.54 per cent, after which it declined until in 1950 the proportion was 3.44 per cent, still twice as much as the national average. Except for primary processing of ores, however, this resource base did not induce the location of any substantial amount of linked activity in the Mountain states. With most of the weight loss taking place during concentration and smelting, the distribution of the market governed the location of succeeding stages of metals fabrication, and the major markets were concentrated in the Northeast.

The extent to which changes in both demand and supply conditions influenced regional resources activities is suggested by the data in Table 1, showing figures for interregional production shifts for pig iron, copper, and lead. Several points are worth noting: (1) the period of great growth in the output of these mineral products (1870–1910) corresponds with the most extensive interregional shifts in their production; (2) truly huge shifts in lead and copper production took place from the Great Lakes region to the Mountain states (and to a lesser extent to the Southwest and Far West) during this period; and (3) there has been a steady shift in pig iron production throughout the entire period 1870–1950 from the Middle Atlantic states to the Great Lakes and, to a lesser extent, the Southeast. These data underline the highly selective regional effects resulting from the growth of a mineral-based economy.

Some notion of the extent of changes in national requirements of material resources is provided by a measure of the changes in the composition of the value of purchases in constant dollars within the broad mineral categories over the period 1870–1950. (This measure is the same as that employed in Table 1; namely, the end of period total which would have to be redistributed among classes to recreate the beginning of period percentage distribu-

[4] In 1880, some 70 per cent of steel output went into rails. Cootner, *op. cit.*, chap. 5, pp. 13–14.

tion.) Thus, within the mineral fuels the total shift over the period was equivalent to 57 per cent away from bituminous and anthracite coals and toward petroleum and natural gas fuels, that is, toward materials which would hardly have been considered as resources ten years before this period. Among the metals during the same period the total shift was almost 34 per cent, away from iron, lead, and tin and in the direction of the light metals and ferro-alloys—one-fourth of this shift has been in the direction of metals for which the economy of 1870 had little or no use, such as aluminum, manganese, nickel, and molybdenum. Finally, among the non-metals (and here the availability of data limits us to the period 1910 to 1950) the internal composition in this shorter period shifted by 31 per cent, away from stone and toward other construction materials, as well as toward basic chemical materials. Something more than one-fourth of the shift was to materials which would not have been considered as resources in 1870.[5]

[5] Calculated from the data in a forthcoming RFF study by Neal Potter and Francis T. Christy, Jr., "U.S. Natural Resource Statistics, 1870 to 1955" (Preliminary Draft, with revisions to 11/1/59), Tables McT-22-24, 33, and 35. [Ed. note—Published as *Trends in Natural Resource Commodities: Statistics of Prices, Output, Consumption, Foreign Trade, and Employment in the United States, 1870–1957* (Baltimore: Johns Hopkins Press for Resources for the Future, Inc., 1962)].

TABLE 1

PERCENTAGE CHANGE IN REGIONAL DISTRIBUTION OF U.S. PRODUCTION OF PIG IRON, COPPER, AND LEAD, 1870–1910 AND 1910–50

Region[b]	Pig Iron Percentage Shift[a]		Copper Percentage Shift[a]		Lead Percentage Shift[a]	
	1870–1910	1910–50	1870–1910[c]	1910–50[d]	1870–1910[c]	1910–50
New England	− 1.62	− .06	− 6.90	0	− .41	0
Middle Atlantic	−15.98	−15.65	− 1.44	− .08	− 1.02	+ .34
Great Lakes	+11.13	+ 7.37	−62.36	−17.72	−58.89	− .45
Southeast	+ 4.90	+ 5.80	− 6.39	− 1.57	− 3.89	+ .75
Plains	0	0	0	+ .33	+ 7.09	− 7.89
Southwest	0	0	+27.73	+23.77	+ 1.63	+10.30
Mountain	0	0	+39.49	− 2.28	+54.61	−10.17
Far West	+ 1.57	+ 2.54	+ 9.86	− 4.03	+ .88	+ 7.12
Total Shift	17.60	15.71	77.08	24.10	64.21	18.51
Growth of output	1,538%	115%	2,727%	67.8%	1,983%	11.7%

[a] The end-of-period percentage of total national production *less* the beginning-of-period percentage. Thus, with respect to pig iron in the period 1870–1910, New England percentage share of national production was 1.62 per cent less in 1910 than it was in 1870. The figure for Total Shift (sum of the absolute value of the shifts × ½), then, represents the percentage of total national production which would have to be redistributed in order to recreate the beginning-of-period percentage distribution by regions.

[b] The states composing the regions are as follows: *New England*—Maine, New Hampshire, Vermont, Massachusetts, Rhode Island, Connecticut. *Middle Atlantic*—New York, New Jersey, Pennsylvania, Delaware, Maryland, District of Columbia. *Great Lakes*—Ohio, Indiana, Illinois, Michigan, Wisconsin. *Southeast*—Virginia, West Virginia, Kentucky, Tennessee, North Carolina, South Carolina, Georgia, Florida, Alabama, Mississippi, Arkansas, Louisiana. *Plains*—Minnesota, Iowa, Missouri, North Dakota, South Dakota, Nebraska, Kansas. *Southwest*—Oklahoma, Texas, Arizona, New Mexico. *Mountain*—Montana, Idaho, Wyoming, Utah, Colorado. *Far West*—Washington, Oregon, California, Nevada.

[c] The 1870–1910 shift figures for lead and copper should be viewed with caution. The 1870 figures upon which the shifts are based represent the regional composition of the *current dollar value* of domestic mine production (the only data which were available), while all later figures used express domestic mine production in *short tons*. Since we are dealing with regional composition, the resulting shift figures would be seriously compromised if there were substantial price differentials at the mine head among the major producing regions in 1870. For the purposes of the discussion following, it is assumed that such price differentials would exert at worst a modest influence on the 1870–1910 shift figures.

[d] Excludes unallocated production in Pennsylvania, Tennessee, and Vermont of 1.59 per cent.

Sources for Table 1: Shift figures computed from Perloff, Dunn, Lampard, and Muth, *Regions, Resources, and Economic Growth* (Baltimore: The Johns Hopkins Press, 1960), T. 75, p. 205; T. 76, p. 208; T. 77, p. 210. Growth of output computed from the long-term series in a forthcoming RFF study by Neal Potter and Francis T. Christy, Jr., "U.S. Natural Resource Statistics, 1870 to 1955" (Preliminary Draft, with revisions to 11/1/59 [Pub. as *Trends in Natural Resource Commodities* . . . ; see footnote 5]), Lead, Table MT-14; Copper, Table MT-12; Pig Iron, Table MT-28.

An especially important instance of the regional effects of changes in national requirements is provided by the case of petroleum and natural gas in the Southwest in recent decades. Here the effect resulted not only from a powerful, direct mining leverage (as was noted in the case of the Mountain region), but also from the availability of a cheap, convenient fuel which altered substantially the region's relative advantages for certain classes of industry. The happy coincidence of these mineral fuels with rich deposits of salt and sulfur provided a resource base for a rapidly expanding chemical industry. Thus, petroleum and gas extraction and refining, responding to a huge and growing national demand, served to change the economic conditions of production throughout the entire Southwest.

Summarizing the broad sweeps of the period of very rapid growth from about the middle of the nineteenth century, we note that during the first half of this period (to the end of the nineteenth century) there were two great overlapping resource effects conditioning the subnational distribution of economic activity: (1) geographically the more widespread effect was that of agriculture continuing to spread out over the arable lands—as in the early period of economic development, but pulling with it an increasing component of processing and servicing activities; and (2) the developmentally dominant effects emerged from the growth of the minerals economy, shifting rapidly among regions, triggering, intensifying, or transforming the nature of regional growth patterns.

The second part of this modern period—that is, the first half of the twentieth century—has been largely characterized by an elaboration and "deepening" of the subnational economy building upon the geographic pattern of activities brought about by the great interregional resource shifts of the nineteenth century. Resource activities declined in relative importance in the national economy throughout the period, but their real importance lay in the role they had played historically in defining the economic basis for the succeeding stages of regional growth—in the movements of population and industry among the regions. In a very real sense the classical resource effects were playing themselves out, as the service sector moved into a dominant position and as technological and other changes (such as price changes which made recapture of waste products economical) brought about a long-range reduction in the proportion of raw materials to total output,[6] thus weakening the linkages of economic activities to their resource inputs. The power of the "market magnet" loomed as the dominant locational force operating in the economy.

THE "SERVICES" ERA AND "AMENITY RESOURCES"

By mid-century, moreover, an additional resource effect was beginning to influence the distribution of economic activity among the regions. To understand the importance of this effect requires us to move away from a definition of resource endowment which sees resources exclusively as tangible materials upon which technology works in the production of goods, and toward one which sees natural resources as including other features of the natural environment which have consequences for economic decisions. Natural resources, then, need not *enter* directly into the processes of production, but only *influence* directly the location of markets as well as of production.

[6] The Potter-Christy data indicate that between 1870 and 1955, when real GNP expanded sixteen times, the output of the resources industries expanded only 5.5 times. In terms of output (in 1954 prices), the extractive industries dropped over this period from $\frac{1}{3}$ of GNP to 12 per cent. The greatest declines were in the products of forestry, fishing, and agriculture. Output in mining rose as a percentage of GNP until the 1920's and since has shown a moderate decline relative to GNP. Kindleberger finds a similar trend in the declining relative use of raw materials in Europe. Charles P. Kindleberger, *The Terms of Trade: A European Case Study* (Cambridge and New York: Technology Press and Wiley, 1956), chap. 8, pp. 176–212.

This broader definition embraces a group of physical environmental conditions which we will refer to as the "amenity resources" —that special juxtaposition of climate, land, coastline, and water offering conditions of living which exert a strong pull on migrants from less happily situated parts of the nation.

This amenity-resource effect derives from the interplay of a number of developments within the national economy and society. First, there is the growing importance of the nonjob-oriented, as well as the job-seeking, migrant. Some 8 per cent of the U.S. population is over 65 years of age, and the proportion of this age group in the total is growing. Approximately two-thirds of these persons are not working and many enjoy some form of paid retirement. Since most consumption items can be acquired with only minor interregional differences, many of these persons will seek out the more intangible resource services, such as climate and coast, that do have substantial interregional variations.

Another important development is the growth in the number and significance of industries whose ties to resource inputs and national market centers are relatively weak. These are the so-called foot-loose industries which are distinguished from other industries in the fact that they have an unusually broad spectrum of locational alternatives available. Such an industry may be labor-oriented in terms of requiring unskilled or semi-skilled labor, such as the apparel industries, or in terms of a highly technical labor requirement, such as the research and development industries. It may be climate-oriented, as in the case of the aircraft industries. Or it may be an industry whose unit transportation costs are negligible in terms of the value of the product, such as instrument and optical goods producers. All of these have in common an array of locational possibilities which permits them to settle in amenity-rich areas without doing violence to the economics of their activities. The growth of the transportation equipment industry (mainly aircraft) in California is an excellent example. During the period 1939–54 California realized some 35 per cent of the national shift in employment in the industry, and this accounted for a very large share of California's total increase in manufacturing employment.

Finally, there is the effect of a rising per capita income throughout the nation. Given the high elasticity of demand for travel and recreation, rising incomes have meant an increasing export market for regional amenity resources in the form of tourist services to vacationers.

Even before mid-century the great shift in population was in the direction of states that had advantages in these amenity resources: Florida, the Southwest, and the Pacific Coast states. During the 1940–50 Census period, this great arc of states stretching from Florida on the southeastern rim to Washington on the northwestern rim[7] (which contained 16 per cent of the national population in 1940) absorbed some 40 per cent of the total increment of national population growth.[8] The movement in the direction of the amenity resources is strong, and even though we are not certain how much of the movement to specific regions can be attributed directly to this resource influence and how much to other factors, given a highly mobile population with rising incomes and retirement payments, it seems fairly certain that the

[7] Florida, Texas, New Mexico, Arizona, California, Oregon, Washington.

[8] In the case of Florida, between 1940 and 1950 the native white population of the state increased by 54 per cent, adding an increment of 707,300 to the 1940 population of 1,304,000. Of this increment the increase in Florida-born residents accounted for 210,000, while the increase of residents born in other states accounted for 497,300, some 251,600 of which were born in states north of the Ohio River. New York alone accounted for 30 per cent of these. Everett S. Lee, Ann R. Miller, Carol P. Brainard, and Richard A. Easterlin, *Population Redistribution and Economic Growth, United States, 1870–1950* (Philadelphia: The American Philosophical Society, 1957), Table P-3, p. 257.

direct influence of the amenity resource will increase rather than diminish.

And so, in the broad perspective of history, the changing content of resource endowment has had a succession of effects in the interregional distribution of economic activity. As "new" resources moved to the forefront of the national economy, new advantages for economic growth were created for those regions well endowed. This much seems certain: in terms of the distribution of national economic activity over the landscape, resource endowment has mattered a great deal.

Resources and the Mechanics of Regional Growth

Regional growth typically has been promoted by the ability of a region to produce goods or services demanded by the national economy and to export them at a competitive advantage with respect to other regions. We have already referred to three such cases touching upon resources—the leverage of minerals in the growth of the Mountain states, of petroleum and natural gas in the growth of the Southwest, and of amenity resources in the growth of Florida. The role of timber in the development of the Pacific Northwest and the role of agricultural commodities in the development of the Plains states are equally instructive. This ability to export induces a flow of income into the region which, through the familiar multiplier effect, tends to expand the internal markets of the region for both national and region-serving goods and services. The extent of the multiplier effect is related to certain "internal" features that characterize the economic and social structure of the region. Regions tend to differ substantially in the degree of development that becomes associated with the growth of the export industries and in what happens to the income that flows in from the export sales.

Some of these internal features are related to the nature of the export industries and particularly to the localized industrial linkages, and services attaching to the export sector are also important here. Thus, for example, it has been noted by historians that the shipment of *heavy* export products from a region has influenced the development of substantial transportation facilities and services within the region. The quantity and type of labor required by the export industries and relative levels of wages paid have, of course, an obvious relationship to the "internal" development of a region. Another important feature is the income distribution that tends to be associated with a given type of regional export product. Douglass North has pointed to the differential effect on regional development in the nineteenth century of the plantation system in the Southeast for the production of cotton and tobacco—with its highly unequal distribution of income, as compared to the independent-farmer production system of the Midwest—with its broad income base and its growing markets for local goods and services.

"Internal" regional development takes the form both of internal structural changes (such as an increase in the proportion of the labor force employed in manufacturing and service industries) and an expansion of the local market for all sorts of goods and services. As the regional market expands and region-serving activities proliferate conditions may develop for self-reinforcing and self-sustaining regional growth, and new internal factors may become important in determining the rates of regional growth, such as external economies associated with social overhead capital and the agglomeration of industries, and internal economies of scale. At any rate, the occurrence of rapid self-sustaining growth involves a shift in the relative importance of growth factors—away from the dominance of the export sector and in the direction of the internal organization of production—which makes it possible for the region to play a more elaborate role in the national economy. This highly simplified exposition of the regional growth process needs to be hedged with many reservations, but it brings to the fore the context within which the effects of resource endowment play out their role.

The "export" and "internal" determinants of regional economic expansion can be brought together in the concept of *cumulative advantage*. But any advantage which a region may have *vis-à-vis* other regions is, of course, always relative. This is so whether the focus is in terms of input and market advantages in the production of a single product or the products of a single industry, or whether the focus is in terms of cumulative advantages for over-all economic growth.

The conditions making for relative advantage can be of many sorts. Given our focus on the role of natural resource in growth, it is suggestive to view relative advantage as resource-based and nonresource-based. As already noted, resource-based advantages have afforded the conventional route to regional economic growth in the United States. In terms of their consequences for regional economic expansion, resources can be described as "good" or "bad" depending on their capacity to provide a vigorous economic linkage with the national economy and to extend the internal markets of the region. A good resource for a region can be identified, first, by its ability to support an extensive stream of nationally-wanted production. Here attention is focused on the characteristics of the national demand curve for the resource and the relationship of the region's supply conditions to those of the other regions: these must afford a substantial promise that production of the resource in the region will expand. In short, the demand for the resource must be derived from final and intermediate demand sectors of the national economy exhibiting a high income-elasticity of demand. Secondly, production of the resource must be characterized by extensive locationally-associated forward and backward linkages. And, finally, the resource must be characterized by a high regional multiplier—that is, a substantial proportion of the returns from the export sector must find its way into active demand for regionally produced goods and services.

Thus, a region's resource endowment is "good" to the extent that it is composed of resource products which rate high by these criteria. A "poor" resource endowment is one whose potential for inducing growth is, accordingly, not very high. In general, the importance of resource endowment in regional growth derives from its ability to alter the region's over-all cumulative advantage position. This will vary among regions and among resource components, and especially will it vary over time as shifts in the composition of rapid and slow growth sectors of the national economy change the bill of inputs.

Most agricultural products rate low on this "growth" scale. The agricultural sector in recent decades has expanded at about the rate of population growth[9] and its products have had an income-elasticity of much less than one.[10]

Thus, taken in aggregate, agriculture will rarely make much of a contribution to the cumulative growth advantages of a region, except in the case of a region whose relative advantage for the production of agricultural products is improving relative to the rest of the nation, as in the Plains states for the period 1870–1910.[11] How-

9 The index of per capita agricultural production has changed as follows: 1870 at 86.33; 1910 at 100.00; 1950 at 100.05.

Source: Agricultural production data from Potter and Christy, *op. cit.*, Series AT-28; Population data from *Historical Statistics of the United States, 1789–1945*, Series B-2, and *1950 Census of Population.*

10 Income-elasticity of demand for food has been estimated at 0.2 to 0.3; Harlow W. Halvorson, "Long Range Domestic Demand Prospects for Food and Fiber," *Journal of Farm Economics*, XXXVI (1953), 760.

11 The index of the share of the Plains states in the value of the national agricultural product is 1870 at 41.48; 1910 at 100.00; 1950 at 91.07.

Source: Perloff, Dunn, Lampard, Muth, *op. cit.*, T. 38, p. 138, and T. 100, p. 249: "Regional Distribution of Value of Resources Extracted, by Major Resource Industry, 1870, 1890, 1910, 1930, and 1950."

ever, to focus our inquiry at the "1-digit" level is to conceal by aggregation the considerable variation among agricultural products at the three- and four-digit level. Some agricultural products in some specific instances can make significant contributions to regional economic growth. Thus, where cotton and cattle would rate low across the board as growth-generating items, the ability of California to engage in capital-intensive cotton production, and of Florida to exploit new breeds of cattle on the basis of excellent feed conditions, make these comparatively "good" resource products for these states. In other cases, there are agricultural specialties whose patterns of consumption have suggested a relatively high income-elasticity of demand—such as fruits, nuts, and horticultural specialties—so that they tend to contribute to the economic growth of those areas which are suited to their production.

The minerals sector has expanded much more rapidly than agriculture as a whole and regional endowment in mineral resources has always been looked upon as a positive asset for regional growth. As in the case of agriculture, there are great variations among the various mineral categories as to their contribution to regional growth. In addition, there are two characteristics of minerals that deserve special attention: first, minerals are nonrenewable resources, so that the depletion phenomenon becomes important in assessing the relative advantage conveyed by them; second, there is a high degree of substitutability among mineral products, so that the advantage of an endowment involving bituminous coal, for example, may become ephemeral as petroleum products become utilized as a substitute fuel. The impact of substitution cannot always be easily identified; it would be difficult to say, for example, how much production of steel, copper, lead, and zinc have been displayed by the growing production of aluminum. In general the big mineral-using manufacturing industries, and, particularly, the metals-using industries, have been among the most rapidly growing sectors of the economy. Also, at the level of final demand, the products of these industries have a high income-elasticity of demand. Equally important, they are the terminal products of an intricately linked production sequence.

The role of petroleum and natural gas deserves a special comment. Throughout the first half of the twentieth century their production has continued to increase at a tremendous rate: over the period 1910 to 1950 the increase in output was almost elevenfold, and during this same period almost half of the total interregional shift in mining activities was accounted for by the oil-rich states of Texas, Oklahoma, and Louisiana. During the more recent period of 1939 to 1954, while employment in mining as a whole declined by 8.84 per cent, employment in this sector increased by 92.4 per cent. In terms of national levels of consumption, petroleum and natural gas have clearly been "good" resources. In terms of their multiplier effects and their linkages these resources do not rate so high. Production and refining of petroleum products is one of the most capital intensive activities in the economy so that a considerable proportion of the returns to these activities is in the form of returns to capital, which is largely imported. At the same time, while petroleum extraction and the manufacture of petroleum products are tightly linked together, the more general backward and forward linkages are relatively limited—for example, almost 80 per cent of petroleum products were destined for final demand in 1947, while absorbing only 13.1 per cent of the total inputs from other manufacturing activities. The answer to the question of how good an endowment petroleum and natural gas are is also affected by the nature of the regional supplies. These mineral fuels are strongly conditioned by the discovery-depletion cycle, so that areas narrowly specialized in the production of these mineral fuels may well find these products to have substantial disadvantages for growth if the depletion of reserves takes place at a greater rate than the augmentation of reserves by new discovery.

The fairly limited, direct, localized linkage with other economic activities is not only a characteristic of petroleum and natural gas, but of other minerals as well. For regional economic growth, the linkage between resources and other economic activities is not only a matter of *product-linkage* and value added (since the value may be added elsewhere geographically), but is even more a question of *locational linkage* —the extent to which other activities cluster in the same general area as the resources. There is some evidence to suggest that these types of "geographic" linkages are fairly limited, and that they are becoming even more so. In this category are data showing the rank correlation of employment in manufacturing with population and resources employment, by states, some of which are presented in Table 2, using data for 1954.

TABLE 2

RANK CORRELATIONS OF SELECTED RESOURCE-USING MANUFACTURING GROUPS WITH RESOURCE EMPLOYMENT AND POPULATION, BY STATES, 1954

Correlated Sectors	Coefficient
Employment in First-Stage Resource-using Manufacturers with Resource Employment	.677
Employment in Second-Stage Resource-using Manufacturers with Resource Employment	.583
Population with Resource Employment	.666
Employment in First-Stage Resource-using Manufacturers with Population	.915
Employment in Second-Stage Resource-using Manufacturers with Population	.935

Note: These groups were based upon input-output relationships. The industries classified as first-stage resource users were those sectors in the 200-industry BLS table that received more than 10 per cent of their inputs (by value) from the resource sectors. The second-stage resource users received little directly from the resource sectors but received more than 10 per cent of their inputs from the first-stage resource users. These two groups combined accounted for slightly less than half of the total manufacturing employment. The 10 per cent dividing line was an arbitrary choice, but was based on what seemed to be in both cases a logical division in terms of the nature of the basic productive processess involved.

Source: Perloff, Dunn, Lampard, Muth, *op. cit.*, T. 148, p. 394.

The proliferation of stages in the manufacturing processes has permitted the increasing separation of resource processing stages from later stages. Since the processing stages are generally the primary weight-losing points in the production process, remaining stages become increasingly freed from their resource bases to seek more strategic market locations. This is reflected in the different correlations for the first-stage and second-stage resource-using manufacturing groups with relation to resources employment and to population.

Employment even in the first-stage resource-using manufacturing industries has a high degree of geographic association with population, but a relatively limited association with resource employment (roughly equal to that between resource employment and population). The second-stage resource users show a higher degree of association with population and a lesser degree with resource employment. The major part of manufacturing (those not included in the two classes shown) is even further removed from resource association. For all stages of manufacturing, taken in broad categories, closeness to markets (intermediate and final) tends to be the dominant locational factor.

This underlines the point made earlier: while export of resource products provides the basis for regional economic development, extensive and continued growth can be expected to take place only in those regions which achieve sizable regional (internal) markets. Here the notion of *cumulative* advantage is useful. Rapid advances are possible as a region reaches "threshold" size for the internal production of a wide variety of goods and services. This type of regional development is greatly enhanced where the building up of social overhead proceeds rapidly—especially in the development of an extensive internal transportation network—and where particular attention is paid to the human resources and to the conditions for living. The latter, as noted earlier, is in no small part helped by the natural conditions of the area.

Where resource and nonresource advantages come together are to be found the best conditions for a high level of economic development.

Resources in the Relationship of the Regional and National Economies: Heartland and Hinterland

In the development of the U.S. economy the role of cumulative advantage is most clearly seen in the growth of the Middle Atlantic region and, later, of the Great Lakes region. Here are regions which have enjoyed unequaled access to national market. Each was endowed with unusually good agricultural resources from the beginning, and the emergence of the minerals-dominant economy found each with excellent access to vast deposits of iron ore and coal. With these resource and market advantages, they developed into the most significant feature of regional economic growth on the American scene—the emergence of an industrial heartland coincident with the center of the national market.[12]

The emergence of the industrial heartland set the basic conditions for regional growth throughout the nation—it was the lever for the successive development of the newer peripheral regions: as its input requirements expanded, it reached out into the outlying areas for its resources, stimulating their growth differentially in accordance with its resource demands and the endowment of the regions. The rapid growth of the U.S. economy was accompanied (and to some extent achieved) by this process of industrial nucleation.

A major consequence of the process of expansion and regional differentiation has been the *specialization* of regional roles in the national economy, and the nature of this specialization has influenced the content and direction of regional growth. In following this process of growth, we see the working out of the general principles touched upon in the previous two sections.

Using a three-sector classification of economic activity and eight multistate regions (as in Table 1) for the period 1870–1950, we can use a simple index of specialization[13] to describe the dynamics of regional specialization in the national economy during this period. This is plotted for two of the three major industrial sectors—resource activities and manufacturing—in Figure 1 (100 = national average). The data serve to highlight the nucleation process. In the three regions which have coalesced into the industrial heartland—New England, Middle Atlantic, and Great Lakes—strong manufacturing specialization has characterized the entire period; however, during this 80-year period there has been a relative decline in manufacturing specialization (i.e., as compared to the nation as a whole) in the eastern end (New England and Middle Atlantic) and a continuing increase in the western (Great Lakes) end as (1) the center of gravity of the national market shifted toward the west, and (2) the superior resource endowment of the western end helped tip the scales in its favor.[14] The great outlying regions (with the exception of the Far West) have maintained or increased their relative specialization in resource activities over the whole period, while in the heartland resource activities in relative terms have continuously declined, suggesting the progressive reaching out of the heartland into the hinterland areas for its resource inputs.[15] These data

[12] New England, which is also part of the Manufacturing Belt, can be considered a lesser-endowed, junior partner in the industrial heartland.

[13] $I = 100 \times \dfrac{\text{per cent of region's labor force in given sector}}{\text{per cent of nation's labor force in given sector}}.$

[14] It is worth noting that the industrial "heartland" itself is not a static geographic area, but an area whose size and extent (and even role) shift with significant changes in the national economy.

[15] As in so many other indexes, the Far West (especially California) emerges as a unique case which, at least since the end of the nineteenth century, has followed neither heartland nor hinterland patterns, but which can be described in terms of a subnucleation in the national economy, or, if one prefers, as a second nucleation. The develop-

highlight the significance of the heartland-hinterland construct in the development of the national economy, and its persistence and stability in the face of dramatic structural changes during this period. The nature of this process has a number of important implications for regional growth.

In the hinterland regions the working out of comparative advantage can result in a narrow and intensive specialization in a single resource subsector, in effect tying the future of the region to the vicissitudes of national demand for the products of that subsector. This will set at least ultimate limits to the region's growth rates: shifts in national demand patterns, the emergence of substitutes, depletion, technological advances, or the relative shifting of regional advantage may at any time choke off

ment of California thus suggests some interesting questions—for example, about the possibilities of "second-growth" (or new-conditions) nucleations, as well as the possibilities of a gradual spreading out of nucleation-type or high-level development in advanced stages of national economic growth. Even under the latter circumstance, the heartland-hinterland concept retains valuable explanatory power in analyzing regional development over time.

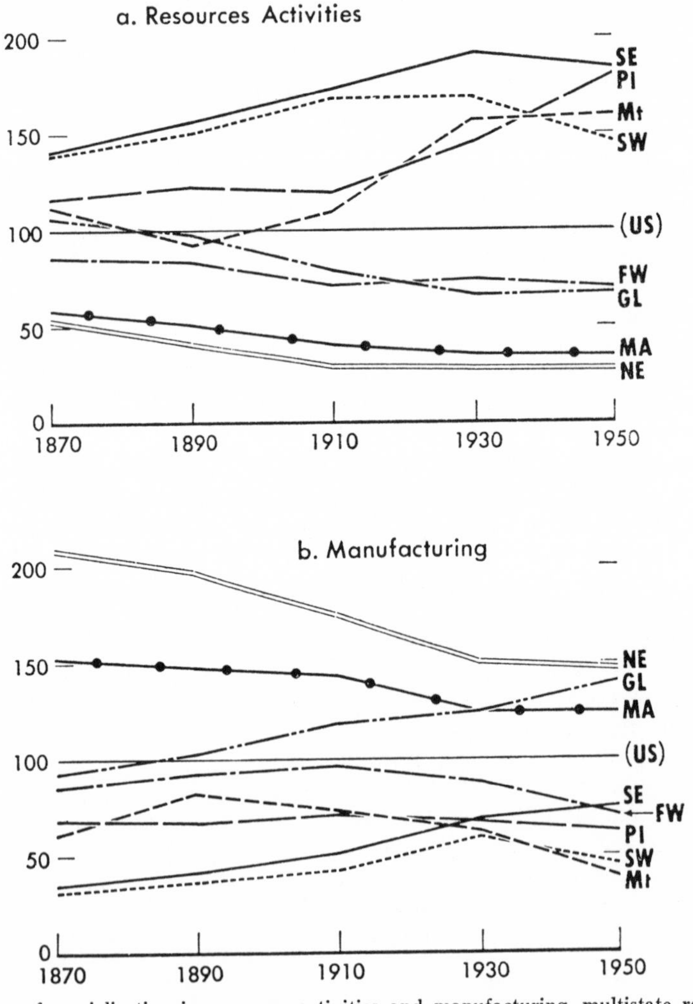

FIG. 1.—Indexes of specialization in resources activities and manufacturing, multistate regions, 1870, 1890, 1910, 1930, and 1950 (U.S. = 100).

growth and leave behind enclaves of unemployed resources and economic stagnation. At its extreme, the Western experience of "boom-town to ghost-town" is a dramatic illustration, but almost as severe has been the history of the tobacco and cotton producing areas in the South. These consequences are not confined to single-product specialization. Broader, sector-wide regional specializations may produce similar problems where the degree of specialization is great and where the products in the aggregate have a low income-elasticity of demand. Typical of this kind of problem is the experience of the Plains states which has been increasing specialization in agriculture since 1910, at the same time that their relative contribution to total national value of agricultural products has been declining.[16]

On the other hand a broad and diverse resource specialization involving products in growing demand may provide a continuing impetus to regional expansion, especially where there is some complementarity among the resource activities. The Southwest illustrates the advantage of such a condition. Here a flourishing chemical industry has emerged based on rich endowments of petroleum, natural gas, sulfur, and salt—this is doubly fortunate, considering the high rate of growth of chemicals industries in the national economy.[17]

In short the economic expansion of the hinterlands is closely associated with their resource endowments and the manner in which their endowments contribute to the evolution of favorable patterns of specialization or substantial levels of cumulative advantage.

[16] See footnote 12.

[17] Annual growth rates of the following chemical end-products groups are suggestive:

	Period	Average Annual Growth
1. Synthetic fibers (not including rayon and acetate)	1940–54	36.1%
2. Synthetic organic plasticizers	1936–54	16.8%
3. Synthetic plastics and resins	1940–54	16.6%
4. Fixed nitrogen in fertilizers	1939–55	13.4%

Source: Harold J. Barnett and Frederick T. Moore, "Long Range Growth of Chemical Industries," *Chemical and Engineering News* (April 7, 1958), 81.

When we look at the manufacturing sector, some important regional facets also emerge. Thus, the economic expansion of the hinterlands is accompanied by a certain amount of induced manufacturing growth. This falls into two general classes: (1) Industries devoted to the processing of regional resource products loom large. If we classify all manufacturing into first-stage resource users, or "processing" industries, and later-stage, or "fabricating" industries, and plot by State Economic Areas which class of industry is dominant, we find that the processing industries dominate throughout the resource hinterlands, while the fabricating industries dominate in the industrial heartland. Thus, the process of industrialization not only defines the resource role of the hinterlands, but also sorts out the kinds of manufacturing activities between the heartland and the hinterland. (2) Less distinct is the role of region-serving industries in the regional growth process. These are generally market-oriented industries, producing products for regional final demand: As regions grow, their expanding markets offer increasing opportunities for economies of scale, so that one dimension of regional growth is a kind of "filling-in" generated by emerging regional market possibilities. This kind of growth frequently takes place at the expense of imports from other regions, so that one characteristic of regional growth may be a decline in the relative advantage of other regions from which imports have flowed in the past.

A general idea of this total effect is provided by a measure of the "differential shift" in manufacturing employment, as shown in Figure 2. This measures the extent to which the growth of employment in the major (2-digit) manufacturing industries within each of the states of continental United States has exceeded or fallen below "expected" growth; that is, the average national growth for each of the industry categories during a given period (here, over the period from 1939 to 1954). These "within-industry" shifts are netted out for each state, and each state total is shown as a percentage either of all the above-average growth states taken together (i.e., a percentage of the "upward shift") or of all the below-average growth states taken together (a percentage of the "downward shift"), depending on which category the state falls into. Thus, for example, Texas had 11.4 per cent of the total gain—or greater than expected increases—of all the states that experienced above-average growth in employment for all the two-digit manufacturing industries taken together.

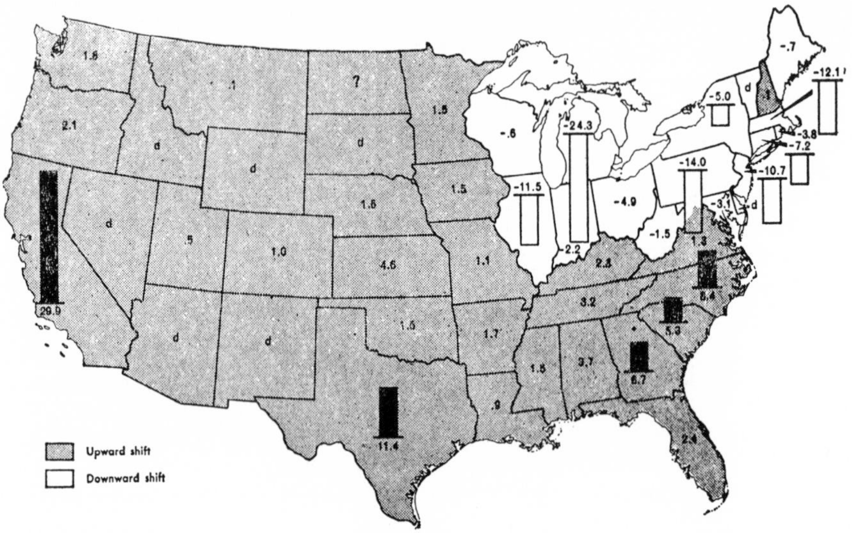

FIG. 2.—Total differential net shift in all manufacturing employment, 1939–54. (Disclosure problems made it difficult to measure this dimension accurately for those states marked "d"; the direction of shift was ascertainable, however, in all states but North Dakota. The per cent figures are rough indications of dimension only.)

At the same time, however, the rapid-growth (often the new) manufacturing industries have continued to find their most favorable location to be in the industrial heartland. This is shown by the "proportionality shift" in manufacturing employment—a measure of the relative change in manufacturing employment among the states due to their industrial *composition*[18] (see Figure 3). The significant role in regional economic growth of industrial composition can be highlighted by noting the very wide range of industrial employment growth rates during the same period, 1939–54 (Table 3). The regions which have contained or attracted the machinery, metals, and chemical industries have, of course, gained volume-wise through the unusually rapid growth of these industries. It would seem that these industries find that the massive markets, economies of agglomeration, and the extensive social overhead investment of the Manufacturing Belt provide them with the economic environment most conducive to their growth and prosperity.

As highlighted by a comparison of Figures 2 and 3, the industrial heartland tends to grow in a different way than do

18 Even if manufacturing employment in each industry had grown at the national average for the industry within each state, some states would have had a greater than average increase in total manufacturing employment because of a "favorable" industrial composition; that is, a high proportion of "rapid growth" industries. That is what is measured in the "proportionality" or composition effect, shown in Figure 3. For a more detailed description of these measures, see Perloff, Dunn, Lampard, and Muth, *op. cit.*, chap. 5.

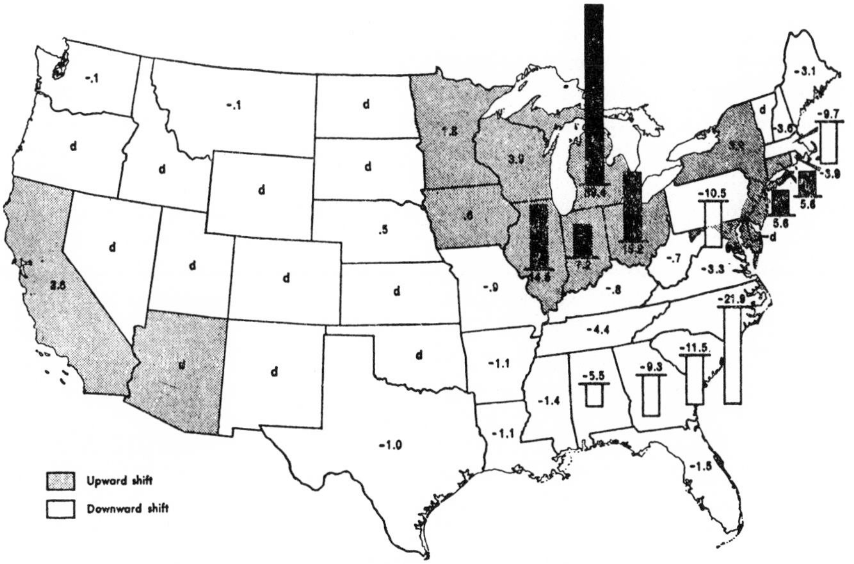

FIG. 3.—Total proportionality net shift in all manufacturing employment, 1939–54. (Disclosure problems made it difficult to measure this dimension accurately for those states marked "d"; the direction of shift was ascertainable, however. The per cent figures should be taken as rough indications of dimension only.)

TABLE 3

PERCENTAGE CHANGE IN MANUFACTURING PRODUCTION WORKER EMPLOYMENT FOR 2-DIGIT MANUFACTURING SECTORS, 1939–54

S.I.C. Code	Industry Sector	Per Cent Change	Employment in the Industry as: Per Cent of Total 1939 Employment	Employment in the Industry as: Per Cent of Total 1954 Employment
36	Electrical machinery	+191.39	3.2	5.8
37	Transportation equipment	+143.70	7.0	10.7
38	Instruments and rel. prod.	+130.48	1.1	1.6
39	Miscellaneous mfg.	+129.91	3.1	4.5
35	Machinery (except elect.)	+118.50	6.9	9.5
34	Fabricated metal prod.	+ 82.04	5.8	6.6
28	Chemical and allied prod.	+ 81.84	3.5	4.1
30	Rubber prod.	+ 62.53	1.5	1.6
26	Paper and allied prod.	+ 61.24	3.5	3.5
	TOTAL MANUFACTURING EMPL.	+ 58.46	100.0	100.0
32	Stone, clay, and glass prod.	+ 54.26	3.4	3.3
27	Printing and publishing	+ 54.04	4.2	4.0
29	Petroleum and coal prod.	+ 52.11	1.4	1.3
25	Furniture and fixt.	+ 51.36	2.4	2.3
23	Apparel and rel. prod.	+ 42.10	9.6	8.7
20	Food and kindred prod.	+ 41.90	10.3	9.2
33	Primary metal industries	+ 39.57	8.6	7.6
24	Lumber and prod.	+ 21.47	5.4	4.6
31	Leather and leather prod.	− 1.84	4.2	2.6
22	Textile mill prod.	− 12.41	13.8	7.7
21	Tobacco manufactures	− 19.78	1.1	0.6

Source: Perloff, Dunn, Lampard, Muth, *op. cit.*, Table 147, p. 391.

the hinterland areas. The industrial heartland serves not only as the focal point of the national market taken as a whole, but also as the industrial seedbed of the economy. The newer products tend to be started here, nourished along, and as they find wide acceptance and volume grows, often the manufacturers find that they can supply the outlying markets more economically by producing on a decentralized basis. There are cases, of course, where the reverse is true and experimentation begins away from the center, but these have been relatively limited in number. In broad terms, the hinterland areas have grown mainly by the "filling-in" process referred to above, a threshold-by-threshold upward movement as resource exports expand and as the regional markets grow in size.

Focusing, then, on the specialized role of the regions in the national economy we get a picture in broad strokes of the spatial dimensions of the national economy. Central to it is the great heartland nucleation of industry and the national market, the focus of the large-scale, nation-serving industry, the seedbed of new industries responding to the dynamic structure of national final demand, and the center of high levels of per capita income.[19] Radiating out across the national landscape are the resource-dominant, regional hinterlands specializing in the production of resource and intermediate inputs for which the heartland reaches out to satisfy the input requirements of its great manufacturing plant. Here in the hinterlands, resource endowment is a critical determinant of the particular cumulative advantage of the region, and hence of its growth potential. This heartland-hinterland relationship seems to be the basic morphology of the subnational economy; through it we can better understand the role of resource endowment in regional growth.

Summary

In summary, the U.S. experience suggests the following set of propositions. "Resource endowment" is continuously redefined by changes in national final and intermediate demand, production technology, and economic organization. The relative economic growth of a region is directly related to its relative advantages in the production of goods and services for the national market; these may result from resource endowment on the one hand, or from a favorable degree of access to the national markets on the other—more generally, from a combination of the two. These advantages are normally conditioned by other elements, such as the quality of the labor supply and relative labor costs. The working out of cumulative advantage is exhibited in the specialized role that a region plays in the national economy, and this specialized role can best be described in terms of the heartland-hinterland relationships.

19 While a discussion of the welfare aspects of regional growth is beyond the scope of this paper, it is worth noting at least briefly that among the more dramatic features of the evolving heartland-hinterland relationship has been its consequences for levels of per capita income. If we divide the nation into two parts—the heartland (including the Far West as a subnucleation) and the resource hinterland—and take the per capita personal income in the former as an index of 100, the comparable index for all the hinterland regions taken together is 58 for 1920 and 69 in 1950. Thus, although the per capita income differences have tended to narrow with the process of hinterland development, the advantage in welfare terms for the industrial heartland is still tremendous. As several studies have shown, the structural origin of the income differences is associated with the agricultural-nonagricultural dichotomy, so it is not surprising that we find such significant income dominance by the nuclear regions. This is, of course, not a hard and fast relationship. That a high degree of manufacturing specialization in industries with a relatively low income-elasticity of demand not only can dampen regional growth rates but depress a region's relative welfare levels has been indicated by the New England experience. At the same time, it is possible for resource regions to enjoy comparatively high per capita incomes, as the Mountain states have proven by turning up periodically with per capita incomes exceeding the national average. The important conclusion, however, is that so long as income differentials are associated with industrial structure, and structure is regionally determined by this ongoing process of nucleation, there are likely to continue to be interregional differences in welfare levels.

CHAPTER 7

SCIENTIFIC AND TECHNOLOGICAL CHANGE

Technology has been described as an "inexhaustible resource."[1] It is certainly true that the rapid technological advances of recent decades mean that we are much better equipped to wrest a livelihood from our environment than any previous generation of mankind. But it is not technology that is inexhaustible—rather it is man's ingenuity and inventiveness. A leading question here is whether the present rate of technological advance can be maintained or even stepped up to cope with future gargantuan needs for food, energy, and materials. This is one of the major challenges of man's future.[2] For those who would be quick to answer in the affirmative, there are some encouraging signs. One is that there are more trained and qualified scientists at work now than all the scientists who have previously lived and worked during man's tenure of the earth. If amount of effort is any guide, the prospects for continued rapid technological advance, barring any major catastrophe, look good.

The preceding chapters on the role of resources in economic development[3] and the managerial experience suggest a distinctive role for technology in resource management. Landsberg poses well the dilemma facing resource projectionists in dealing with the great uncertainties of technological change.

In view of the vital significance of technological advance, and in view of our lack of knowledge of the nature and process of technological change, it is perhaps surprising that no more than a little inquiry has gone into this subject.[4] Indeed, it is only from the days of World War II that the notion of managing the direction of scientific development has taken hold. Increasing

1 Thomas B. Nolan, "The Inexhaustible Resource of Technology," *Perspectives on Conservation*, ed. H. Jarrett (Baltimore: Johns Hopkins Press for Resources for the Future, Inc., 1958), pp. 49–66.

2 Harrison Brown, *The Challenge of Man's Future* (New York: Viking Press, 1954).

3 U.N., *United Nations Conference on the Application of Science and Technology for the Benefit of the Less Developed Areas: February, 1963, Geneva* (8 vols.; New York: U.N., 1964).

4 This is rapidly changing. One measure of the increase in studies dealing with technological advance is the annual survey of the National Science Foundation, published as *Current Projects in Economic and Social Implications of Science and Technology* (Washington: Government Printing Office, 1959–64). Beginning with 96 reported projects of research in 1959, the 1963 volume contains 356 entries. An introduction to two major sectors of this growing research field may be obtained by reference to the Universities–National Bureau Committee for Economic Research, *The Rate and Direction of Inventive Activity: Economic and Social Factors* (Princeton: Princeton University Press, 1962), and to the bibliographic section of Herbert Lionberger's *Adoption of New Ideas and Practices* (Ames: Iowa State University Press, 1960).

acceptance of this notion has been accompanied by an expanded power over our own destiny. The Manhattan Project to develop the atomic bomb showed what could be done by intensive research concentrated in a particular direction. Similar efforts are now under way, directed toward such diverse goals as the exploration of space and the desalinization of sea water.[5]

In its broadest sense scientific and technological change is associated with the knowledge industry and the selection from Machlup's study of *The Production and Distribution of Knowledge in the United States* introduces new terminology and ways of thinking about knowledge. This is a crucial point. Too often technology has been associated solely with highly tangible things, mechanical devices, or artifacts. Only recently have such intangibles as good ideas been accorded a place in the market as both producer and consumer goods.

Knowledge once produced must be disseminated, and the rate and direction of diffusion of innovations may be as crucial in resource planning as the development of the innovations themselves. Two selections, dealing with both industry and agriculture, are included as representatives of a new and actively growing research sector.

Finally, Ackerman and White highlight in specific ways the direction and opportunity for the research and development of new technologies in both the physical and human aspects of resource management.[6]

[5] See the Annual Reports of the U.S., Dept. of Interior, Office of Saline Water, *Saline Water Conversion Report* (Washington: Government Printing Office, various dates). See also Dept. of Interior, Office of Saline Water Report to the Sen. Select Comm. on National Water Resources, *Saline Water Conversion,* Comm. Print No. 26, 86th Cong., 1st Sess., 1959.

[6] See also E. A. Ackerman and G. O. Löf, *Technology in American Water Development* (Baltimore: Johns Hopkins Press for Resources for the Future, Inc., 1959).

FRITZ MACHLUP

PRODUCTION AND DISTRIBUTION OF KNOWLEDGE IN THE UNITED STATES

Every branch of learning takes a good many things for granted. If these things *have* to be explained, "Let George do it." George is always someone in another discipline. Hence, the analysis of the production and distribution of knowledge falls into George's field.

George has always been a popular fellow. People were inclined to rely upon him even if they did not know whether he really existed. In recent years, however, Georges have actually appeared on the scene in increasing numbers. Many of them are called "interdisciplinary research workers."

The Economist as a Student of Knowledge Production

Anything that goes under the name of "production and distribution" sounds as if it clearly fell into the economist's domain. An analysis of "knowledge," on the other hand, seems to be the philosopher's task, though some aspects of it are claimed by the sociologist. But if one speaks of the "communication of knowledge in the United States," the specialist in education may feel that this is in his bailiwick; also the mathematician or operations researcher specializing in communication theory and information systems may prick up his ears. In fact, some of the knowledge to be discussed here is technological, and thus the engineer may properly be interested. When I tried out the title of this study on representatives of various disciplines, many were rather surprised that an economist would find himself qualified to undertake this kind of research. Of course, they did not really know what kind of research I was planning under that intriguing title.

Knowledge as a Datum in Economic Analysis

Knowledge has always played a part in economic analysis, or at least certain kinds of knowledge have. There has always been the basic assumption that sellers and buyers have *knowledge of the markets,* that is, of their selling and buying opportunities. The theories of supply and demand, of competition and monopoly, of relative prices, interdependence, and all the rest, all have been based on the assumption that sellers know the highest prices at which they can sell and buyers know the lowest prices at which they can buy. In addition, it has always been assumed that producers have *knowledge of the technology of the time,* that is, of their production opportunities. In other words, the assumption has been that they know the lowest cost at which they can produce. The usual supposition has been that all producers in an industry are familiar with the "state of the technical arts."

This does not mean that economic theorists have regarded technological knowl-

• Fritz Machlup is Professor of Economics, Princeton University.

Reprinted from F. Machlup, *The Production and Distribution of Knowledge in the United States* (Princeton: Princeton University Press, 1963), pp. 3–10, with permission of the author and the publisher.

edge as unchanging. But to most economists and for most problems of economics the state of knowledge and its distribution in society are among the data assumed as given. There is nothing wrong with this. When an economist analyzes the effects of new taxes, of changes in interest rates or wage rates, it would be unreasonable for him *not* to assume a given state of technology. And even when he analyzes problems of growth and development, he will often find it expedient to assume either a given state of the arts or a given rate of progress, whatever this may mean.

An increasing number of economists these days concern themselves with the prospective growth of the economy during the next 20 or 30 years. Needless to say, they cannot take the state of technical knowledge as given and constant. On the other hand, they do not want to burden their models with more stuff than is absolutely necessary for their task and, therefore, they choose to assume a given rate of advance of productivity, to project the past rate of advance into the future. In other words, the progress of technical knowledge is made an exogenous variable, or a simple trend function, a function of time.

Incidentally, the same practice prevails concerning other important variables in growth economics—for example, population and labor force. There was a time when economists regarded the explanation of population growth as their business. Later they got out of this job and assigned it to George—this time a specialist, the demographer. Only very exceptional economists today concern themselves with the economic determination of population changes, and would include population as a dependent variable in their growth model. The choice between taking a variable as exogenous or making it an endogenous one, a variable determined by the system of functions, is a matter of relevance and convenience. No economist, for example, would refuse to recognize the explanation of capital formation as a part of his job. He constructs elaborate models in which investment functions and saving functions, together with several other equations, are supposed to serve this task. Yet, there are problems—for example, projections of national income figures into the future—for which a rate of accumulation will expediently be assumed as given, and the underlying functions be left aside.

Now, the growth of technical knowledge, and the growth of productivity that may result from it, are certainly important factors in the analysis of economic growth and other economic problems. But with one very minor exception—namely, the theory of patent protection—the stock of knowledge and especially the state of technology have customarily been treated as exogenous variables or as trend functions in economic models. Yet we have implicitly recognized that the stock of knowledge can be increased by special efforts; that the allocation of resources to education and to research and development is an important economic variable which can significantly alter the rate of increase of knowledge, both basic and applied. During the last few years economic statisticians have given a good deal of attention to the appropriations made by society for the creation and communication of knowledge. The economics of education and the economics of research and development are new areas of specialization which are now developing, partly with the generous aid of research foundations.

KNOWLEDGE AS A PRODUCT, A FUNCTION OF RESOURCE ALLOCATION

The "promotion" of knowledge from the rank of an exogenous independent variable to that of an endogenous variable dependent on input, on the allocation of resources, is an important step. Not that this idea is a novel one. Adam Smith in 1776 wrote that "man educated at the expense of much labor and time . . . may be compared to one of those expensive machines,"[1]

[1] Adam Smith, *An Inquiry into the Nature and Causes of the Wealth of Nations,* I (New York: Everyman's Library, 1910), 88–89.

and the notion of the "capital concept applied to man"[2] has never completely disappeared from the economic treatises. It was especially emphasized by writers, such as Friedrich List, who gave much prominence to the development of the productive powers of man. In connection with several policy issues the differences between the private and social benefits from such investment in knowledge were discussed with great intensity—for example, in the arguments for infant-industry protection. But never before our time was the interest of economic writers so closely concentrated upon the analysis of economic growth and development, and thus it is not surprising that there is now such a burst of activity in studying the productivity of investment in knowledge.

The focus of these studies is upon education, basic research, and applied technical research and development, thus, upon the production of such types of knowledge as may be regarded as an investment in the sense that it will pay off in the future through increased productivity. A few economists aim their analytical weapons at a somewhat different target: market research. Recognizing that the assumption of full knowledge of selling and buying opportunities cannot be maintained for all problems, and that increased effort in market research may lower the costs and raise the revenues of the firm, economists have started to analyze the marginal efficiency of investment in market research. All these kinds of knowledge have in common that they are instrumental in increasing the efficiency of the economy.

There are, however, several other types of knowledge, besides those designed to pay off in the future; there are, for example, types of knowledge that give immediate pleasure to the recipients, and society is allocating ample resources to the dissemination of such knowledge. While it would, of course, be possible to confine a study of the production and distribution of knowledge to types of knowledge that are expected to yield a future return in terms of increased productivity, such a limitation would not satisfy a transcendent intellectual curiosity. Moreover, whether an investigator's interests be wide or narrow, he could not study "productive" knowledge without paying considerable attention to "unproductive" knowledge because ever so often they are joint products. What is taught at school, printed in books, magazines and newspapers, broadcast over the radio, or produced on television is knowledge of many sorts; and to study one is to analyze all.

An even further expansion of the scope of the study seems promising. As an economy develops and as society becomes more complex, efficient organization of production, trade, and government seems to require an increasing degree of division of labor between knowledge production and physical production. A quite remarkable increase in the division of labor between pure "brain work" and largely physical performance has occurred in all sectors of our economic and social organization. This increase can be observed in the growing role, measured in terms of manpower, of the government of most political bodies as well as of the management of business firms; it can also be observed in the ratios of "non-productive" to "productive" labor in many industries. The so-called non-productive workers are those who shuffle papers and give signals, who see to it that others "know" what to do. To include this sort of "knowledge production" may look strange to most readers at first blush but will become more understandable and look more sensible at later stages of the discussion. Thus, besides the researchers, designers, and planners, quite naturally, the executives, the secretaries, and all the "transmitters" of knowledge in the economy will eventually come into the focus of our analysis of the production and distribution of knowledge.

If society devotes considerable amounts

[2] R. J. Walsh, "Capital Concept Applied to Man," *Quarterly Journal of Economics,* XLIX (1935), 255 ff.

of its resources to any particular activity, economists will want to look into this allocation and get an idea of the magnitude of the activity, its major breakdown, and its relation to other activities.

Terminological Proposals

The economist undertaking this study will have to prepare himself for it by developing a conceptual framework for an analysis for which he does not find ready-made tools. He will have to use terms that have established meanings in other fields of discourse, and may not find these meanings suitable for his task. At this point, however, we propose a time-saving terminological agreement.

PRODUCTION AND DISTRIBUTION

So far in this introduction we have always referred to pairs of economic activities, such as "production and distribution," "acquisition and transmission," "creation and communication" of knowledge. We can save words and drop the twin phrase as soon as we realize that we may designate as "knowledge" anything that is known by somebody, and as "production of knowledge" any activity by which someone learns of something *he* has not known before even if others have.

In this sense, disclosure, dissemination, transmission, and communication become parts of a wider concept of "production of knowledge." Of course, we shall then have to distinguish a special kind of "socially new knowledge"—that which no one has had before—but since we shall have much more to say about the production of old knowledge in new minds—"subjectively new knowledge," if you like—the proposal will on balance save words.

Thus, if I tell you something that you have not known, or only vaguely known, or had forgotten, I am producing knowledge, although I must have had this knowledge, and probably several others have too. In other words, "producing" knowledge will mean not only discovering, inventing, designing, and planning but also disseminating and communicating.

KNOWLEDGE AND INFORMATION

By the same token, I propose that we get rid of the duplication "knowledge and information." There are those who insist on distinguishing "information" from "knowledge," for example, by having "information" refer to the act or process by which knowledge (or a signal, a message) is transmitted. But even if the word is not used for the act of communicating but for the contents of the communication, one may want "information" to refer to disconnected events or facts, and "knowledge" to an interrelated system (though others want to confer upon "systematic" or "ordered" knowledge the nobler title, "science"). One author, for example, proposes to contrast "knowledge," or "contextual knowledge," which "illuminates the basic causal structure of some field of operations," with "information," which "provides current data on the variables in that field."[3] The specialist in "information theory" uses the word, as he frankly admits, in a "rather strange way," in "a special sense which . . . must not be confused at all with meaning." To him, "information is a measure of your freedom of choice when you select a message. . . . Thus greater freedom of choice, greater uncertainty and greater information all go hand in hand."[4] This concept serves a significant purpose in an important field, but it is not what is commonly meant by "information." Perhaps the fact that the special use of the word is becoming increasingly current should make it more desirable to use,

[3] The same author, however, decides later to treat both as "information," yet he continues to oscillate between talking about "bits of knowledge" and "bits of information." Anthony Downs, *An Economic Theory of Democracy* (New York: Harper, 1957), pp. 81, 208, 215, 219.

[4] Warren Weaver, "The Mathematics of Information," in *Automatic Control* (New York: Simon & Schuster for *Scientific American,* 1955), pp. 100, 104.

whenever possible, the word "knowledge" for the ordinary meaning of "information." *Webster's Dictionary* defines "information" as "knowledge communicated by others or obtained by personal study and investigation," or alternatively as "knowledge of a special event, situation, or the like." Hence, in these ordinary uses of the word, all information is knowledge. We may occasionally refer to certain kinds of knowledge as "information," but we shall avoid the redundant phrase "knowledge *and* information."

The Task before Us

Perhaps another word or two about the desirability of this undertaking: an economist's investigating the production of knowledge.

The production of knowledge is an economic activity, an industry, if you like. Economists have analyzed agriculture, mining, iron, and steel production, the paper industry, transportation, retailing, the production of all sorts of goods and services but they have neglected to analyze the production of knowledge. This is surprising because there are a good many reasons why an economic analysis of the production of knowledge seems to be particularly interesting and promising of new insights. Some of the reasons refer to observed facts, others to probable relations to economically significant developments, still others to novel hypotheses that call for investigation.

Some of the Reasons for Our Curiosity

1. It is a fact that increasing shares of the nation's budget have been allocated to the production of knowledge.

2. It can also be shown that a large portion of the nation's expenditures on knowledge has been financed by government, so that much of the production of knowledge depends on governmental appropriations.

3. One may strongly support the judgment that the production of knowledge yields social benefits in excess of the private benefits accruing to the recipients of knowledge.

4. It is probable that the production of certain kinds of knowledge is limited by inelasticities in the supply of qualified labor, which raises questions of policy, especially concerning the allocation of public funds.

5. The facts that the production of knowledge of several types is paid for by others than the users of the knowledge, and that these types of knowledge have no market prices, raise questions of their valuation for national-income accounting as well as for welfare-economic considerations.

6. The production of one type of knowledge—namely, technology—results in continuing changes in the conditions of production of many goods and services.

7. One may advance the hypothesis that new technological knowledge tends to result in shifts of demand from physical labor to "brain workers."

8. There is evidence of a change in the composition of the labor force employed in the United States, in particular of an increase in the share of "knowledge-producing" labor in total employment.

9. There is ground for suspicion that some branches of the production of knowledge are quite inefficient, although it is difficult to ascertain input-output ratios and to make valid comparisons, especially since the very wastefulness is held to be productive of psychic incomes and social benefits.

10. It has been suggested that some of the growth in the production of knowledge may be an instance of "Parkinson's Law," which implies that administrators tend to create more work for more administrators.

11. There is probably more validity in the hypothesis that the increase in the ratio of knowledge-producing labor to physical labor is strongly associated with the increase in productivity and thus with the rate of economic growth.

These points indicate some of the reasons why it may be said that an economic analysis of the production of knowledge is not only justified but overdue.

EDWARD A. ACKERMAN

THE GENERAL RELATION OF TECHNOLOGIC CHANGE TO EFFICIENCY IN WATER DEVELOPMENT AND WATER MANAGEMENT

A basic public objective in water development [during the forty years 1960–2000] will be improvement of the efficiency of water supply. It therefore becomes desirable to define efficiency.

Very simply defined, efficiency is the relation between the amount of input and the amount of resulting useful output. The larger the useful output per unit of input, the more efficient the process.

In water development and management, illustrative actions directed toward improvement of efficiency would be measures which reduce waste of water, design of dams which reduces storage costs per acre-foot, and measures of management which increase complementarity among competing uses. It must be noted that considerations of efficiency are always related to some predetermined objective or objectives. In water development and management this might be an increase in gross national product, an increase in regional income, an increase in income for a particular producing group, additions to outdoor amenities, or still other changes. Definition of these objectives is beyond the province of this report. Instead, it is the purpose of the report to examine the means which may be made available by technologic advance for increasing efficiency of water supply *whatever specific objectives are chosen by the Congress*. However, these objectives must ultimately be defined and understood if improvements in efficiency are to be meaningful.

It is essential to understand that regional and local water shortages of varying degrees of seriousness can appear and may be forecast for the future of the United States. However, the multiplicity and versatility of modern techniques of planning, development, and operation are so great that if they are properly applied in time, crises may be avoided and all requirements may be at least adequately and probably well served.

Techniques with Potentials for Effecting Integrated Multiple-Purpose Development

As new demands arise in the future, they may for a time and everywhere be met by extensions of existing practice, particularly as existing practice of integrated multiple-purpose development is applied. It is even likely to serve indefinitely for some few areas without modification. In addition, there are certain windfall events which may be depended upon to improve the efficiency of future development which remain unseen and unsusceptible to evaluation until they appear. A notable example of this in the recent past was the perfection of high-capacity earthmoving equipment. On the other hand, these windfalls cannot be depended upon to solve the huge problems of

• Edward A. Ackerman is Executive Officer of the Carnegie Institution of Washington, D.C.

Abridged from U.S., Senate, Select Committee on National Water Resources, *The Impact of New Techniques on Integrated Multiple-Purpose Water Development,* Comm. Print No. 31, 86th Cong., 2d Sess., 1960, pp. 13–32, with permission of the author.

matching supply and demand which can be foreseen in the years ahead. A methodical evaluation of technical possibilities therefore may assist in meeting public responsibilities. These possibilities may be sought in: (*a*) improved planning, design, construction, and operation of systems of integrated multiple-purpose works; (*b*) exploration for, discovery, and exploitation of new supplies; (*c*) conservational and other measures for reducing requirements; and (*d*) treatment of waters having substandard quality. Thus conscious steps toward efficiency are to be sought both in an improvement of the techniques of integrated multiple-purpose development themselves and in supplementing them with other measures.

A summary is presented in Table 1 of certain aspects of new technology related to future efficient water resource development thought to be of interest to the select committee in its policy study. Brief notation is made in the table of the estimated earliest state of first practical application of a technique, the water development purposes most affected by the technique, the geographic regions most affected, the added water supply, water savings, or other economies, the present status of research or use of the technique, and suggested strategic immediate action concerning it. Although the minimal essential information for policy consideration in this field is contained in Table 1, some further elaboration and emphasis are appropriate. The succeeding discussion will follow the headings given in the table in order.

PLANNING DESIGN, CONSTRUCTION, AND OPERATION OF SYSTEMS OF MULTIPLE-PURPOSE WORKS

Among the many spectacular technical developments of the last 20 years there has been a quiet one with relatively little news appeal. Nonetheless it has been revolutionary, and yearly it is becoming more pervasive. This is the application of methods of rigorous formal analysis based upon mathematical thought to planning, design, and operational problems which have interdependent variables.

Integrated multiple-purpose development is basically a problem in the efficient organization of interdependent units within a system. Hence those tools which have been proven as applicable to organizational efficiency are certain to be applied to this field in the future. They may generally be grouped as the techniques of "operations analysis" or "systems analysis."

The application of these techniques will be particularly important as the need for interbasin systems arises more frequently in the future.

Operations analysis has been greatly aided by the development of mechanical systems of computation represented in the large analog and digital computers. Linear programing is perhaps the most familiar among these methods, having been widely applied to problems of defense organization during the last war and now to a great variety of industrial planning and operational activities. Others are probability analysis, and more recently, game theory. It is virtually certain that some of them can be applied with resulting gains in efficiency to integrated multiple-purpose development in the future, from the small watershed to the large river basin. These methods promise to be of great assistance in achieving future design of systems of water control facilities, or, for that matter, a lone multiple-purpose work. They also may be applied to the evaluation of other techniques in combination with integrated multiple-purpose development.

It must be stressed that operations-research methods can aid in setting objectives, but they in no way eliminate the need for public policy decisions on objectives. There is no need for the Congress or other public bodies to fear any arrogation of policymaking function by technical planners through the future application of these methods. Indeed they are best applied to problems in which an objective has been clearly set prior to the analysis.

The field for their application may come

TABLE 1

SOME TECHNIQUES RELATED TO FUTURE EFFICIENCY OF U.S. WATER RESOURCE DEVELOPMENT

	Estimated Earliest Date of 1st Practical Application	Water Development Purposes Affected	Geographic Regions Most Affected	Added Water Supply, Savings, or Other Economies	Present Status	Strategic Immediate Action
Planning, design, construction, and operation of systems of multiple-purpose works:						
Systems analysis, linear programing, etc., applied to basins	1961–64	All	Any watershed or river basin	Substantial investment savings and contributions to operating efficiency possible	Simple systems have been explored experimentally	Application to actual planning on small- and medium-sized watersheds
Consumption models, applied geography	1962–64	All	All	Timely preparation for meeting requirements	1 water analysis made, techniques most applied to transportation	Employment and income maximizing studies by State or basin Study of navigation
Prognostic hydrology	Some in 1960	All	All	Reduce risk of overbuilding, substantial savings in planning production if cyclic moisture fluctuation understood	Some research and experiment	Considerably expanded fundamental research
Materials economizing design of hydraulic and accessory structures	Previous to 1960	Some	All	Not presently evaluable	European and American prototypes of materials economy are in existence	Consulting technical review of designing practices
Use of nuclear explosives and other unorthodox engineering approaches to underground storage, and other earth and rock movement	Not presently evaluable	Irrigation, industrial, domestic water supply, pollution control, navigation	Western states	Not presently evaluable	Atomic Energy Commission has experimented with underground explosion, other experiments in planning stage	Further nuclear experiment under AEC direction Further study of geology of underground storage
Water pipeline and other movement techniques	Previous to 1960	All consumptive uses	West	Facilitates inter-basin movement	Available	
Exploration for, discovery and exploitation of, new supplies:						
Weather modification	Some previous to 1960	All	Western states	Annual addition of 15,000,000 acre-feet to supply	Much empirical experiment. Recent expansion of research	Added fundamental research Pilot experiment in entire river basin Economic study
Geophysical and other exploration of unknown aquifers	Previous to 1960	Irrigation, industrial, and domestic water supply	Western states	Billions of acre-feet of ground water available on "mined" basis	Methods available	Field study
Appraisal of ground water movement	Previous to 1960	Irrigation, industrial, domestic water supply, and pollution control	All	Not evaluable	Method needs further development	Further laboratory, experiment, and field study
Lifting ground water to surface	Not evaluable	Withdrawal uses in localities dependent on ground water	Western states; Atlantic and Gulf Coastal Plain	Goal: lifting water economically beyond 1,000-foot depths	Private companies have development programs	Public support of promising engineering experiment Study of local energy costs
Measures for conservation and reduction of demand:						
Recycling	Previous to 1960	Industrial water supply	All	Probably 200,000,000 acre-feet of withdrawal annually, thus saving investment costs on storage, against which treatment costs to be charged	A variety of techniques are known	Study of comparative economies of storage and recycling needed

TABLE 1—*Continued*

	Estimated Earliest Date of 1st Practical Application	Water Development Purposes Affected	Geographic Regions Most Affected	Added Water Supply, Savings, or Other Economies	Present Status	Strategic Immediate Action
Water-conserving agronomy	Previous to 1960	Irrigation	Western states 1960–80; 1980–2000, also southeastern states	Not presently evaluable because of large variation of local agronomic environments	A variety of techniques are available, but few methodically related to water supply problems	Technical evaluation of water-conserving aspects of agronomy to direct further research Experiment with known techniques as a part of watershed and basin management
Forest and range management for water yield	1965?	Irrigation, industrial, and domestic water supply	Western states	Not presently evaluable	Experiment under way	Continued experiment and economic evaluation
Evaporation suppression	1963?	All	Western states	Goal: water saving of 10,000,000 acre-feet	Experiment under way	Continued experiment
Planned location of demand by publicly controlled land use	1960	All	All	Substantial reduction in public investment costs theoretically possible	Techniques known, local acceptance growing	Study of the economics of planned land use related to water development
Treatment and use of waters having substandard quality:						
Treatment of organic wastes producing a biological oxygen demand	Previous to 1960	Domestic and industrial water supply; recreation; fish and wildlife	All	Can avoid very large, and economically inestimable losses from pollution	Techniques known, but local hesitance about capital expenditure can create many future problems	Further experiment with reduction of treatment costs and use of reclaimed water Study of means of accelerating provision for treatment
Treatment of chemical wastes	Previous to 1960	All withdrawal uses; recreation; fish and wildlife	Manufactural localities; some in suburban residential localities	Can avoid very large, and economically inestimable losses from pollution	Some unsolved technical problems, as in detergent use	Further research and development of practical treatment processes Establish minimum standards of effluent quality Study of means for monitoring water quality
Decontamination and disposal of radioactive wastes	1960	All except navigation	All	Not evaluable	1960 risk of contamination small	Continued study of control and preparation for an economy with wider use of nuclear materials
Desalting sea and brackish waters	Some in 1960	Domestic and industrial supply; possibly irrigation at an undetermined future date	Great Plains, Great Basin, Tex., Calif.	Depends on success with cost reduction; potentially large added supply	All present operating processes high cost; varied experiment under way	Expansion of fundamental research; continuation of pilot plant program Study of needs for desalted water
Sediment control	Some previous to 1960	Domestic and industrial water supply; recreation; fish and wildlife	All; of most immediate interest in West and southeast	Large economic savings; esthetic values	Widely used processes in municipal water supplies	Continued erosion control Research and experiment directed toward large-scale low-cost elimination in water
Use priorities corresponding to water quality	Some previous to 1960	All withdrawal uses	Northeastern-midwestern urban area; western states	Substantial in water-scarce districts, but at some economic cost	Salt waters and sewage effluent already used in some localities for manufacturing, electricity generation, and agricultural use	Methodical study of quality tolerance of water uses Further experiment with means for using mineralized water

at any level, depending upon the objective chosen. The following may illustrate the possible application of these methods to system design.

Suppose that the Congress decides that in the future development of a given U.S. river basin a principal objective is to be the provision of full employment for the labor force of the State or States within the given river basin by the year 1980 (or any other chosen year). One qualifying restraint is that employment should be so provided that existing income levels will be equaled or exceeded at the future date. Appreciation of the value of such an objective is entirely possible at some time in the not-distant future. As population grows, the connection betwen resource use and employment in most regions is certain to demand attention. For water the question might typically be: what is the "mix" of irrigation, industrial use, water recreational facilities, and other use which will allow the attainment of the objective posed? One answer could be provided through an arbitrary decision made from existing knowledge about man-days of employment provided by an acre-foot of water used in agriculture, differing types of manufacturing, and other use. Such an answer is in the nature of an intelligent guess.

Although they have been little tried thus far, formal analytical methods can give a more precise and dependable answer than the arbitrary decision. Assuming the social objective of full employment stated above, operations-analysis techniques can assist by increasing the precision of planning and design, and by guiding system operations toward high output after facilities have been built. Planning might begin with consumption model study, in which the employment effects of several different "mixes" of water use would be tested. One of the "mixes" presumably would show a combination of employment effects approaching those which had been set in the congressional objective. This model, with its estimate of quantities of water needed for the several purposes to attain the objectives, would be the basis for the physical planning of required future water development. Similar methods can be applied in the determination of land-use effects of water development through the methods of applied geography. No study of water projects along this latter line has yet been undertaken, although the methods have been applied to similar cases of highway development.

At this point, the traditional method of the past would be one of applying engineering experience and hydrologic data in a set of cut-and-try designs, arrived at by hand calculation. Engineering experience will guarantee the design of a good system of facilities, but the laboriousness of hand calculations places a definite limitation on the number of alternatives which can be examined in the design. The probability that the best system will have been arrived at is low.

One operations-analysis approach to the same problem of physical design would simulate streamflow or other hydrologic characteristics on a high-speed digital computer. A great many alternatives then can be examined among the possible variants of physical design. Such a method much increases the likelihood that a "'best" system will be arrived at. In this case it would be a system which would provide the proper balance of regulation and other facilities to supply water in the amounts indicated at least cost. Another operations analysis technique which may be used toward the same end is that of the mathematical model, as in quasi-linear programing.

The use of consumption models already has been experimented with in the State of New Mexico, with some interesting results.[1]

[1] *Report of the New Mexico Project Committee on the Income and Product Results of Alternative Water Uses.* The committee was composed of representatives of the University of New Mexico and various State of New Mexico agencies. [Ed. note: See Nathaniel Wollman, *The Value of Water in Alternative Uses* (Albuquerque: University of New Mexico Press, 1962).]

Experiment with simulation techniques has been undertaken by the Corps of Engineers in their recent 308 study of the Columbia, by the International Boundary and Water Commission on the Rio Grande, and by the Harvard Program of Research in Water Resources Development. The use of mathematical models is now under study by the Harvard program.

Operations-analysis techniques also should be able to increase the precision of system operations. Here again, the simulation technique and the mathematical model can be used. The first has been applied in electric-power system analyses by the Tennessee Valley Authority, the Bonneville Power Administration, and by private electric utilities. The Corps of Engineers has experimented with the use of a linear programing model for operating the reservoirs of its Missouri River Basin system.

The attractiveness of operations-analysis techniques for future system design and operation in water devlopment can best be understood through the key role of the high-speed computer. Both the civil engineer and the economist are freed from the restraints of routine computations. The number of alternatives which they can examine is multiplied many times, each of the alternatives may be examined more precisely, and the engineers especially can devote more time to imaginative planning.

Some of the possibilities of operations analysis have been described in a Rand Corporation study.[2] Probably the most intensive experiment with the application of these methods has been in the Harvard University Program of Research in Water Resources Development, where they have been applied to a hypothetical river system. The simulation method also has been used as part of an interesting analysis by Resources for the Future, Inc., of sequence and timing in project planning on the Columbia River.[3] When perfected, the application of these more precise tools of analysis can do much to avoid the confusion and costs which may have attended the simple addition of fragmentary economics and good engineering in the past.

PROGNOSTIC HYDROLOGY

The design of every water resource facility to a certain extent is dependent upon hydrologic projections or forecasts. It is also apparent that many water management operations may be influenced, some vitally, by the accuracy of projections of water receipts and runoff within a basin. Projections are particularly important for the design and operation of systems of water regulation and flood control facilities. For all but a few planning purposes, hydrologic projections for design and operation now are made largely on the historical records of streamflow. These projections are not adequate and experiment toward their improvement is very much in order.

Like over-all weather forecasting, hydrologic forecasting may be divided into the short-range and the long-range aspects, although the parallel to weather forecasting is not exact. Short-range forecasts[4] have been given considerable attention, and to some extent are a part of management in most systems of water storage and release. However, long-range projections or forecasting have been less fully studied and potentially can be of great value in both design and operation. . . .

It is here suggested that an important new set of techniques may be described under what we shall term prognostic hydrol-

[2] Roland N. McKean, *Efficiency in Government through Systems Analysis—with Emphasis on Water Resources Development,* a Rand Corp. Research Study (New York: John Wiley & Sons, 1958).

[3] John V. Krutilla, *Sequence and Timing in River Basin Development with a Special Application to Canadian–United States Columbia River Basin Planning* (Washington: Resources for the Future, Inc., 1960), pp. 21–26, 32–35.

[4] Short-range forecasts here are interpreted to mean anything from diurnal to seasonal range; long-range, on the other hand, is concerned with the fluctuations in maximums-minimums and means of annual water receipts and runoff.

ogy. These include (1) the application of heretofore unused statistical techniques to the actual hydrologic record, so as to improve interpretations of that record, or projections, and (2) the development of new bases for prediction. Among the applications of statistical techniques, experiment with synthetic hydrology,[5] probability analysis,[6] and other analytical tools already have produced promising results. However, it must be stressed that some of the most important advances in this area will depend upon fundamental research in dynamic meteorology and in knowledge of the fluctuations of radiation receipts and their physics on the earth's surface. Hence, it is from new bases of prediction that the most influential long-range results are to be expected.

One well-known student of the sun has testified that the study of solar changes and their correlation with the general circulation of the earth's atmosphere shows promising clues toward explaining rainfall fluctuation in western United States.[7] Other scientists are more hesitant about predicting results, but all agree that study of the earth's incoming and outgoing energy is vital to attack upon the most basic questions of hydrometeorology. It is important, therefore, that the unity of widely varying research activities must be kept in mind as part of a subject having a single and potentially most influential objective. These may extend from observation of solar magnetic fields to the electrical attributes of a raindrop, and mathematical models of the general atmospheric circulation.

NEW TECHNIQUES OF PHYSICAL DESIGN AND CONSTRUCTION

There is no doubt that developments favoring still further economies in the costs of storage and other water system facilities will be achieved in the future. These may come either through (*a*) new concepts of structural design, or (*b*) new and more efficient applications of energy, labor, and materials to engineering problems. The first is illustrated by recent innovations in European hydraulic structures where competitive designing has resulted in some daring concepts which achieved substantial economies of materials over traditional designs.[8] The particular subject of materials economy, as well as the economies to be achieved from standardization of components, has not yet received the attention in American hydraulic designing practice that it might. Some opportunity in this direction thus lies open for the future.

New applications of energy and materials already have had a profound influence on the construction of water control systems, particularly in the introduction and perfection of heavy earthmoving equipment, improved concrete mixing equipment, and long-distance conveyor belt haulage of construction materials.

[5] Synthetic hydrology generates streamflow data by application of statistical techniques. For example, mean monthly flows of record may be serially correlated so as to derive a systematic base. Appropriate random components may be applied to the base to generate synthetic monthly flows, which may provide the construction planner with a more useful projection of hydrology than an actual historical series.

[6] See Luna B. Leopold, *Probability Analysis Applied to a Water-Supply Problem,* U.S. Geol. Survey Circular 410 (Washington: Government Printing Office, 1959), and Walter B. Langbein, *Water Yield and Reservoir Storage in the United States, ibid.*, Circular 409. Leopold notes that there is a difference between a forecast and probability analysis. The latter uses an actual record as an indication only of the probability of events occurring in the future, not as an exact forecast. In the absence of a basis for a true forecast, like synthetic hydrology, it can facilitate the construction of a much better prognosis of hydrologic events than a simple projection of past records.

[7] Walter O. Roberts, "Recurring Droughts—A National Problem," testimony before U.S., Senate, Select Comm. on National Water Resources, Denver, Colo., Nov. 20, 1959.

[8] The 1959 failure of the Malpasset Dam in southern France, however, has reinforced a conservative hesitation to adopt such design techniques, even though the cause of the failure was officially ascribed to unusual weathering of anchoring rock formation.

The next potential or revolutionary techniques of this class would appear to be related to the use of nuclear explosives. Knowledge of radiation effects and their control at present is incomplete so that no firm forecast of the future use of nuclear explosives can be made. However, their theoretical potentialities for large-scale earth and rock movements at very low cost are so great that long-range planning for water policy must contemplate them. The possibility of considerably altered engineering approaches to problems of storage, particularly underground storage, should certainly be entertained in policy planning.

Exploration for, Discovery, and Exploitation of New Supplies

It is obvious that a first line of approach to the problem of meeting water requirements will always be the exploitation of a new supply, where it is obtainable, rather than the application of restrictions in use or compromises on water quality. Where possible, in the future, these new sources will be sought in the traditional surface supplies. However, it is already apparent that new types of source would be welcome even now in large sections of the country and they may be essential in still larger areas during future years. Such sources may be sought either in the atmosphere or underground. The sea also may reasonably be considered a new source, but it is considered here in the later paragraphs on the waters of substandard quality.

The art of weather modification is still so near its beginning that the full extent of its future impact upon water supply techniques is not presently evaluable. Enough is known, however, to enter weather modification as a source of water in the western states of at least modest potential. On the basis of the conclusions of the Advisory Committee on Weather Control it would seem reasonable to plan on the eventual addition of approximately 15 milion acre-feet annually to western water supplies from this source (Table 2). This would not be a major factor in the design or operation of systems of multiple-purpose works in the region.[9] The final answers on weather modification, however, are in the future—perhaps many years in the future—after the completion of a great deal of painstaking fundamental research. The more revolutionary impacts of weather modification on water supply still retain enough probability to warrant not only careful attention in research but also continuous monitoring in water development planning. Runoff from weather modification promises the cheapest additional water to be obtained in the future.

An early need in determining final policy is an exploratory study of the economics of weather modification to assist decisions on the amount and kind of effort which publicly should be placed in this field.

The other major source of new supply will be the aquifers which lie beneath the surface. In the past we have been handicapped by the limited means which we have had for discovering aquifers and appraising their productiveness. Some change in the situation has come from the development of sensitive geophysical instruments and means of interpreting the water content of underground structures.[10] The perfection of these means and their application in a large-scale program of exploration in the western states must be counted upon as one of the technical events of the future.

The extent to which these supplies are exploited, particularly below the present critical level for water lifting of about 1,000 feet, will depend upon three things: (*a*) the public attitude of the affected states or regions toward ground water withdrawal which exceeds aquifer recharge, (*b*) the mechanical efficiency of lifting devices and the costs of energy which these devices must depend upon, and (*c*) the costs of locating and appraising aquifers, and drilling wells to them. All three aspects—appraisal, improvement of lifting devices, and energy

[9] See E. A. Ackerman and G. O. G. Löf, *Technology in American Water Development* (Baltimore: Johns Hopkins Press, 1959), pp. 377–78.

[10] *Ibid.*, pp. 384–406.

costs for ground water exploitation—appropriately should enter public policy consideration insofar as it is mindful of the future of the West. Important eastern aquifers, like those of the Atlantic and Gulf coastal plains, should not be forgotten in the appraisal.

The possibility that full knowledge of the extent and the movement of underground waters may weaken our attachments to watersheds and river basins as units for development must be entertained. The water development of the future will be able to consider the integration of surface and ground waters in management plans as well as the integration of related watersheds. As techniques of underground storage are improved, such integration increasingly will become important. Thus in the West particularly we may look forward to the day when water management may be integrated in varying degrees on a "three-dimensional" basis, including atmospheric and underground sources as well as the surface waters under one plan of supply.[11] It has been noted that the present ratio between surface and underground sources of water withdrawn in the United States is about 4 to 1. The forecast has been made that this ratio will change to something between 2 to 1 and 1 to 1 for a country like the United States sometime during the next 20 to 50 years.[12] Although ground water supplies as compared to sur-

TABLE 2

ESTIMATE OF POTENTIAL PRECIPITATION INCREASES BY ARTIFICIAL CLOUD SEEDING IN WESTERN STATES

State	Total Area (acres)	Annual Precipitation (inches)	Estimated Part of Annual Precipitation from Orographic Clouds (per cent)	Estimated Possible Maximum Increase in Precipitation by Artificial Seeding		Estimated Possible Maximum Increase in Runoff by Artificial Seeding[a]	
				Inches	Thousand Acre-Feet	Inches	Thousand Acre-Feet
Arizona	72,901,760	12.5	20	0.3	2,300	0.02	100
California	101,563,520	20.9	50	1.0	8,500	.4	3,400
Colorado	66,724,480	16.5	40	.7	3,900	.2	1,100
Idaho	53,476,480	17.2	60	1.0	4,500	.5	2,200
Montana	94,168,320	14.8	30	.4	3,100	.1	800
Nevada	70,745,600	8.6	20	.2	1,200	.02	100
New Mexico	77,866,240	14.3	20	.3	1,900	.02	100
Oregon	62,067,840	27.8	40	1.1	5,700	.6	3,100
Utah	54,346,624	13.2	30	.4	1,800	.05	200
Washington	43,642,880	32.0	50	1.6	5,700	1.0	3,600
Wyoming	62,664,960	14.6	30	.4	2,100	.1	500
Total	760,168,704	....	....	....	40,700	....	15,200
Total 5 Pacific Coast and Rocky Mountain States[b]	....	....	....	....	....	....	13,400
Percentage in 5 States	....	....	....	....	....	....	88

[a] Computed by use of natural ratio of runoff to precipitation.
[b] Washington, Oregon, California, Idaho, and Colorado.
Source: Ackerman and Löf (see footnote 9), Table 30, p. 375.

[11] Integrated management of ground and surface waters already is practiced in parts of the West, as in the Roswell Basins of New Mexico.

[12] Alfred Loehnberg, "Water and Economic Development," *Impact of Science on Society,* IX (1958), 23–44.

face supplies have the disadvantages of higher costs, service to a limited number of purposes, and frequently higher dissolved solids content, they also have some outstanding advantages. These include their wide dispersal within a region, lack of evaporation loss, lower temperatures, lesser fluctuation, and natural protection against radioactive contamination or other military action.[13] Recognition of these characteristics along with more methodical application of the techniques of discovery and appraisal in the future is likely to become a familiar part of water management which goes beyond integrated multiple-purpose river basin management.

Measures for Conservation and Reduction of Demand

In situations where new supplies fail to meet requirements or where additions of physically available supply are impractically expensive, water management can turn from the engineering of supply to the engineering of demand. The old British maxim "a penny saved is a penny got" has a parallel in water development, for the drops of water saved certainly are drops available.

A variety of measures is available and is likely to be considered a part of future water management which might be classified as means of engineering water demand. One simple and effective means of conservation which awaits adoption in many localities is metering. Other pertinent techniques are recycling, water-conserving agronomy, forest and range management for water yield, evaporation suppression, and planned location of demand through controlled land use.

There are three aspects to the possible reduction of demand for water or water services: the reduction of requirements for withdrawal of water; the reduction of consumptive depletion or disappearance; and the reduction of demand for non-consumptive water development purposes, like flood control. For the first, by far the most important technique of the future is likely to be recycling, or the intraplant reuse of water for manufacturing purposes.

RECYCLING

Every indication of trend suggests that manufacturing use will be the most rapidly growing of the requirements for water withdrawal in the future, and recycling already has been proven a potent means of reducing requirements in the face of local or regional water scarcities. In the future it can be a most influential means of regulating withdrawal requirements where there are scarcities of supply, or where thermal pollution is considered a harmful condition. Recycling can reduce fresh-water requirements to a small fraction of normal once-through use. It has been estimated that a severalfold increase in the Nation's industrial output is possible at little or no increase in its total fresh-water demand, mainly because of recycling.[14] It should be noted, however, that the techniques of recycling are not likely to effect much reduction in consumptive depletion or water disappearance; their effects are limited principally to the withdrawal requirements. The principal cause of water disappearance during industrial use is evaporation to transfer to the atmosphere heat absorbed by cooling water in steam-electric plant condensers and manufactural processes. The amount of water evaporating may be expected to be approximately the same whether recycling is used or "once-through" water is released to streams or other natural water bodies.

VEGETATIONAL MANAGEMENT FOR WATER YIELD

The techniques most likely to alter favorably water disappearance or consumptive depletion are those concerned with vegetation. The reduction of water requirements through forest and range management practices and through water conserving agronomy does not have the

[13] *Ibid.*, p. 35.

[14] Ackerman and Löf, *op. cit.*, p. 441.

same potentiality for reducing withdrawal requirement as recycling, but it appears to be the direction in which to look for any major change in water disappearance. Already the reduction of water wastage through phreatophyte control has illustrated some of the possibilities.[15] Experiments which are being conducted now in Arizona may give some more conclusive answers as to the water releasing capacities of forest and range management directed toward water yield. Some of the most difficult questions surrounding these techniques are those of economic evaluation of comparative benefits from different types of management (i.e., forest- or range-intensive management or water-intensive management). Water conserving agronomy also would seem to have possibilities. Much already is known about the adaptation of crops to restraints on water consumption. However, the theoretical potentialities that accompany plant physiology and plant genetics research alone make water conserving agronomy worthy of inclusion in water management now.[16] In addition, there are already proven techniques of water budgeting in irrigation practice which deserve wider consideration than they have had. Finally, the further study of soil moisture, vegetation relations, and the connection of ground-water manipulation with them holds promise of increasing water yield through vegetative management.

EVAPORATION SUPPRESSION

Because of the amount of water which can be evaporated from any open surface during the summer season in western United States, evaporation suppression recently has become an enticing subject for investigation. The immediate goal is the development of economical methods capable of saving the 10-million-plus acre-feet of water estimated to be evaporated annually from reservoir surfaces in western United States.[17] Under certain conditions, as for treated water in municipal supply systems, physical coverage of storage facilities is economically justified to prevent evaporation. In other cases advantageous location of reservoirs so that there is a low ratio of exposed surface to volume may reduce evaporation loss considerably. The most favorable location, of course, is underground storage, and evaporation suppression certainly is one reason for attention to underground storage in the future. However, storage with extensive exposed surfaces almost inevitably will continue to be a part of stream regulation. Because physical coverage of such surfaces is prohibitively expensive, recent investigation has concentrated on the monomolecular chemical films which have shown promising results on small reservoirs.

The importance of evaporation control studies extends much beyond the im-

15 Phreatophytes are water-loving plants like the salt cedar which grow on the edge of water courses or on reservoir borders. A Department of the Interior *Report on Phreatophytes* is contained in U.S., Senate, Select Comm. on National Water Resources, *Evapo-Transpiration Reduction,* Comm. Print No. 21, 86th Cong., 2d Sess., 1960.

16 See the following references for treatment of vegetation-water yield relations: Edward A. Colman, *Vegetation and Watershed Management: An Appraisal of Vegetation Management in Relation to Water Supply, Flood Control, and Soil Erosion* (New York: The Ronald Press, 1953), esp. pp. 129–42; Leon Lassen, Howard W. Lull, and Bernard Frank, *Some Fundamental Plant-Soil-Water Relations in Watershed Management,* U.S., Dept. Agric. Circular No. 910 (Washington: GPO, 1952); Paul R. Nixon, *Water Yield Predictions Based on Watershed Characteristics,* Iowa Agric. Exper. Station Journal Paper No. J-2969 (Ames, 1956); for an interim report on the Arizona program see Arizona Watershed Program, *Recovering Rainfall* (Tucson, 1956).

17 See E. D. Eaton, "Control of Evaporation Losses," memorandum of the chairman to members of the U.S. Senate Comm. on Interior and Insular Affairs, April 14, 1958 (Washington: GPO); also Ackerman and Löf, *op. cit.*, pp. 451–57. Estimates vary over a wide range and basic data are meager. The Bureau of Reclamation estimates that 2,000,000 acre-feet annually might be saved by 1980 in the western states by monolayer use. U.S., Dept. of Interior, Bur. of Reclamation, *Measures for Minimizing Water Storage and Conveyance Losses in the 17 Western States* (Denver, 1959), p. 7.

mediate goal, attempting to save a substantial part of the conjectured 10-million acre-feet now lost. In his study of water yield and reservoir storage, Langbein has suggested that there are definite practical limits to the use of storage for regulation of any given streamflow.[18] Evaporation loss from reservoir surfaces is one of the factors, particularly in western United States, diminishing the effects of storage upon regulation for all surface storage increments beyond a certain regulation-flow ratio.[19] Successful suppression of evaporation could alter the basic relation between storage and flow determined by Langbein, and therefore the completeness of regulation that would be economically feasible for a given stream. The less evaporation from storage is, other things being equal, the longer the period of flow which can be regulated. Where significant flow fluctuations occur over a number of years, as in western United States and other arid and semiarid environments, this has substantial practical significance. For example, if reservoir evaporation on Colorado River storage systems of the sizes described by Langbein were reduced by 50 per cent, the reservoir capacity at which maximum regulation is reached is 78-million acre-feet rather than 52-million acre-feet, as under estimated natural evaporation. Where added storage becomes feasible, all flow and consumptive uses benefit. Hydroelectric generation is increased in proportion to the added volume of water available; and irrigation, industrial, and municipal use gains similarly.[20]

[18] Langbein, *op. cit.*

[19] *Ibid.*, p. 4.

[20] The effects of evaporation suppression upon storage and regulation also might be interpreted from another point of view. Thus, Louis Koenig has noted that the amount of regulation provided under existing evaporation conditions could be given by a much smaller reservoir capacity, and smaller capital expenditure, assuming a 50 per cent reduction in evaporation. For example, a 50 per cent reduction on 1959 Colorado reservoirs would increase annual regulation by 400,000 acre-feet (Louis Koenig, informal report to Walter B. Langbein, undated).

An interesting special application of evaporation suppression techniques could occur where moderately saline lakes exist. If the evaporation-inflow ratio were reduced, water of these lakes might become usable.

To realize such possibilities, however, fundamental research and continued experiment may be necessary for a long period. Present evaporation suppression methods, while promising for small water bodies, do not appear to have the capacity for general application needed for major effect upon feasible storage-flow ratio in river basin development. The value of subsurface water storage, where physically possible, should be considered in this connection.

LOCATION OF DEMAND BY PLANNING LAND USE

Each of the techniques discussed in this section in some way has touched upon a process which we might call the engineering of demand. Thus, recycling is designed to increase the units of output in a manufacturing plant for the unit of water withdrawn or consumed. Water-conserving agronomy may seek to maximize the financial returns to the farmer per unit of water used through selection of crop plants, carefully determined means of application, and other measures. Forest and range management for water yield should seek to maximize the economic return from the water that falls within a given watershed by management which takes account of municipal, industrial, and irrigational uses of water. Evaporation suppression is directed toward a reduction of the water consumed in the operation of facilities for flow regulation. A final and potentially powerful measure is the planning of land use in such a manner that location of demand for water facilities will be compatible with efficient development.

There is nothing unprecedented or novel in the idea of planned land use. Perhaps its most familiar form is urban area zoning, but zoning of rural land use also has occurred, as among the non-agricultural counties of the lake States during the 1930's.[21] These zoning regulations, in effect, were public decisions upon the location of demand for public services in sparsely settled, low-income areas. Generally, many important decisions of this kind usually have been initiated from private sources as in the location of a residential subdivision in a metropolitan area. Zoning or other measures toward forming and enforcing a public decision about land use have been used relatively little in water development. The relatively few cases of application have concerned principally flood control; indeed, it is for the function of flood-damage prevention that the first really vital need for publicly controlled land use is being felt in water development.

Gilbert White has aptly summarized the situation which has caused the Nation to commence recognizing planned land use as an important adjunct technique in water development. He has stated

> . . . although there have been remarkable engineering achievements over the period of 22 years since the first national flood-control act passed, flood damage has continued to mount. . . . The occupance of flood plains has continued to spread. . . . It is a hard fact that the traditional approach to flood control through engineering works alone has not achieved the reduction in the annual bill the Nation is paying in flood losses. Major reductions had been anticipated 22 years ago when engineering efforts were launched outside of the lower Mississippi and Sacramento valleys. It is a losing battle in some areas, and it is one which cannot be won simply by redoubling the investment in dams, levees, and channel improvements. . . .
>
> Moreover, there are areas where no engineering works can be justified. In many such areas, as well as along some streams where reservoirs have been constructed, there is continued construction of new buildings within the reach of floods. It is not enough to say, "No further work warranted."[22]

These facts and others have stimulated some careful examination of the possibilities of planning land use for flood-damage prevention within the last few years. Metropolitan or urban agencies in a number of cases have developed urban renewal plans with reduced flood-damage potentials.[23] Federal agencies like the Tennessee Valley Authority, the Corps of Engineers, and the U.S. Geological Survey have commenced studies to provide technical information, like flood-hazard estimates, which later can assist the development and application of this technique.[24] States like the Commonwealth of Pennsylvania and the State of Tennessee also have undertaken some preparatory work.

Although care will have to be taken in the application of public-land-use control for flood-damage prevention so as not to foreclose upon high value occupance where it is warranted, the field for application of these techniques in flood-damage prevention is so wide and their contribution to efficiency in water development of such high potential that they appear certain to be a part of future public planning.

The outlook which has been opened in flood-damage prevention raises questions as to the potential application of planned land use to other aspects of demand for water facilities. It is obvious that planning

21 Erling Day Solberg, *Rural Zoning in the United States,* U.S., Dept. of Agric. Information Bull. 59 (Washington: GPO, 1952).

22 Gilbert F. White, "Action Program for the States: A New Attack on Flood Losses," *State Government* (Spring, 1959), reprint, pp. 1–2. See also White *et al., Changes in Urban Occupance of Flood Plains in the United States,* Dept. of Geog. Research Paper No. 57 (Chicago: Dept. of Geog., University of Chicago, 1958).

23 White, "Action Program for the States: A New Attack on Flood Losses," *op. cit.*, p. 2.

24 U.S., Senate, Committee on Public Works, *A Program for Reducing the National Flood Damage Potential,* Memorandum of the Chairman to members of the Comm., 86th Cong., 1st Sess., 1959; and U.S., Senate, Select Comm. on National Water Resources, *Flood Problems and Management in the Tennessee River Basin,* Comm. Print No. 16, 86th Cong., 1st Sess., 1959. See also U.S., Geological Survey, *Hydrologic Investigations Atlas,* e.g., "Floods at Topeka, Kans.," HA-14 (Washington, 1959).

practices which determine the location and density of urban settlement also can influence the location of requirements for domestic water supply and for investment in facilities developing that supply. An interesting and virtually unexplored area in thought about these techniques concerns industrial location. Although many other factors in addition to water availability must be considered in the location of new manufacturing plants, it is obvious that future water demands, and therefore demands for publicly financed water facilities, will be influenced by decisions on industrial location. The extent and degree to which the public should share in these decisions may demand future attention; accordingly, preparatory examination of the possibilities would seem a prudent part of policy. The sort of problem which will have to be considered is clearly indicated by the statement of a prominent Colorado scientist to the select committee:

> . . . we should take cognizance that population growth is now very great in regions where the peril of severe drought is highest. This implies, particularly, that it is only sound judgment to deflect away from drought-prone areas those industrial developments that use large amounts of water.[25]

This question in the future will be of particular importance where pressures for interbasin diversions exist or can be foreseen. Examination of planned land use as a measure for introducing efficiency of development within a given basin also has potentialities and needs study.

Treatment and Use of Waters Having Substandard Quality

A drought may be created or it may exist because of the presence of unusable waters no less than by the physical absence of water. This is a fact upon which poignant testimony was provided by many early settlers in western United States who found water supplies with too high a salt content for domestic, irrigation, or livestock use. It is a fact which also may be attested to by many more recent well-drillers in sections of the Great Plains running from the Canadian border to that of Mexico. Moreover, it is a type of drought to which no part of the country is immune, not even humid areas. As the density of settlement in the country has increased and industrial growth proceeded, we have turned many naturally usable supplies of water into an unusable state by pollution and contamination. This may come through disposal of bacterial and other untreated organic wastes, disposal of inorganic chemical wastes, increasing stream sediment loads, and through salt water encroachment in mined aquifers. A potentially powerful and potentially pervasive new pollutant also must now be contemplated. This is pollution by radioactive wastes. The possibility that man-made "drought" may occur within localities or regions of the future United States must be entertained as the density of settlement increases and as our capacities for polluting or contaminating water also increase. It can affect all withdrawal uses and recreation.

However, the droughts created by man's contamination or by the substandard quality of naturally occurring waters are less harsh over the long term than the droughts created by lack of precipitation. There are within our means methods for avoiding contamination, reclaiming polluted and other substandard waters, and adjusting use to a variety of quality requirements.

Today nearly all water supplied by municipalities, much of that withdrawn for industrial use, and even some irrigation waters are treated before use. A number of practices have been developed to improve the quality of water. It can be mechanically processed by filtration, aeration, or sedimentation, and it can be treated chemically in many ways. Today practical means exist to remove calcium and magnesium salts present in water as bicarbonates, chlorides, sulfates, or nitrates, iron compounds, sodium compounds, and other inorganic materials which may be present in water solu-

[25] Roberts, "Recurring Droughts . . . ," *op. cit.*, transcript, p. 14.

tion. Nearly all undesirable microorganisms which can live in water can also be destroyed and means exist for the elimination or neutralization of most wastes which can be waterborne. As is now well known, even sea water can be desalted and the product made available for consumptive uses which can support high costs.

Means thus already have been recognized and applied to the treatment of waters with substandard quality. However, there are three problems which they present for future policy and future management: (1) lowering the cost of treatment; in some cases the objective must be lowering to levels considerably below the known most economical means of the present; (2) the development of methods of coping with new pollutants of innovational nature; (3) recognition that these techniques are effective tools for increasing the availability of water and can be a part of comprehensive management.

THE QUESTION OF ECONOMICAL MEANS OF TREATMENT

As already suggested, there is a great variety of water treatment processes already applied to the remedy of undesirable water conditions of different kinds. Some are applied on a very wide scale, like the treatment of organic wastes. Nonetheless, they all fall short of the truly effective contribution to water availability which may be considered desirable. For example, processes for treating organic wastes (like ordinary sewage) are familiar and relatively simple. Yet there are many communities whose citizens believe that their financial resources would be or are severely taxed by treating organic wastes so as to eliminate contamination of water by those wastes. One answer has been to supply federal or state aid for such communities. While this is entirely commendable from a social point of view, it is at the same time an indication that technology still has opportunity to contribute toward a lasting answer to the problem of treating organic wastes. Such an opportunity lies before technology until the time that any community can treat its wastes without encountering financial difficulties in so doing.

Although the treatment of chemical wastes from industry has advanced enormously in the last 20 years, the problem of costs still appears to be present. Few states or districts which are now attempting to attract new industries tolerate the release of untreated wastes into their waters. However, the problem is still a significant one in many older industrial areas where treatment costs may seem prohibitive to a reluctant management or on a marginal operation.

Perhaps the most striking area of water quality improvement where costs are critical is in desalting sea water and brackish water. The accelerated experiment now underway in federally supported programs essentially is a search for cost reduction. A number of interesting and ingenious methods of desalting now are under investigation by the Department of the Interior Office of Saline Water and its contractors.[26] As yet, however, no truly low-cost process is in sight. Costs in the range of 50 cents per thousand gallons ($165 per acre-foot) are contemplated although not yet achieved.[27] If desalted water at 50 cents per thousand gallons becomes available, important effects on local water supply in critical areas are readily apparent. Such water comes within the cost range estimated for some important interbasin diversion projects. For example, a proposed project for bringing additional water to the Nevada Desert from the Columbia River, as-

[26] See U.S., Department of the Interior, Office of Saline Water Report to the Senate Select Committee on National Water Resources, *Saline Water Conversion,* Comm. Print No. 26, 86th Cong., 1st Sess., 1959.

[27] See Ackerman and Löf, *op. cit.*, pp. 348–49; U.S., Atomic Energy Commission, Report to the Senate Select Committee on National Water Resources, *Application and Effects of Nuclear Energy,* Comm. Print No. 27, 86th Cong., 2d Sess., 1960.

suming that this were politically feasible, has been estimated to involve total costs of about 40 cents per thousand gallons.[28]

Although it is clear that demineralized water at these costs could not be used for irrigation purposes, it presently shows promise of being competitive for industrial and domestic uses in some areas. Although only a few American coastal cities have immediate need for additional water supply, a number of water-scarce inland municipalities are either within feasible pumping distance of sea water or accessible to saline ground water supplies. Coastal sections of California and Texas seem especially interesting in this connection. So do many parts of the Great Plains underlain by saline water-bearing aquifers (Table 3). It must be stressed, however, that any widespread application of desalinization processes will depend on the reduction of

[28] K. C. D. Hickman, "The Water Conversion Problem," *Industrial and Engineering Chemistry*, XLVIII (1956), 7A–20A, ref. on 18A. This calculation includes amortization of investment and estimated electricity costs for pumping about 5 mills per kilowatt hour.

TABLE 3

REGIONS OF POTENTIAL DEMAND FOR DEMINERALIZED SEA WATER FOR IRRIGATION

Region	Feasible Pumping Elevation for Demineralized Sea Water (feet)	Ultimate Deficiency in Local Supply (annual acre-feet)	Estimated Potential Market for Converted Sea Water (annual acre-feet)
CALIFORNIA			
Central Valley	...	...	[a]
San Francisco Bay	[b]	1,330,000 to 2,400,000	1,000,000 to 2,000,000
Sacramento Delta	[b]	...	3,000,000
Santa Cruz County	500	13,000	5,000
Pajaro River Basin	...	[c]	...
Salinas River Basin	500	[c]	...
San Luis Obispo	500	180,000	150,000
Santa Maria River Basin	500	80,000	80,000
Santa Ynez River Basin	500	80,000	60,000
Santa Barbara County	300	70,000	70,000
Ventura River Basin	200	5,000	5,000
Santa Clara River Basin	500	190,000	150,000
Antelope Valley and Mohave District	...	[d]	...
Los Angeles metropolitan area	2,000	2,100,000	2,100,000
San Juan Creek area	1,000	140,000	135,000
Santa Margarita River Basin	1,000 }	1,116,000	{ 160,000
San Diego metropolitan area	1,000 }		{ 728,000
Salton Sea—Colorado District	...	[d]	3,500,000
Owens River area	...	[d]	...
TEXAS			
Eastern and central Texas gulf coast	...	...	...
Guadaloupe–Rio Grande	500	2,860,000	2,860,000
Lower Rio Grande	500	1,650,000	1,650,000

[a] Undetermined.

[b] Converted sea water would be usable at lower elevations. Maximum elevation not determined.

[c] Currently planned fresh-water developments adequate for anticipated future demand.

[d] Ultimate deficiency undetermined.

Source: U.S., Dept. of Interior, Bur. of Reclamation, "Potential Use of Converted Sea Water for Irrigation in Parts of California & Texas," *Saline Water Conservation Program Research and Development Report No. 3* (Washington, 1954); and Ackerman and Löf, *op. cit.*, Table 29, p. 345.

total costs of operation to levels not yet achieved, even though such costs are likely to be attained. The critical part of the desalting program thus still centers on cost reduction. Economical reduction of the sodium content of western irrigation water is a special challenge for the future. Every degree of sodium ion reduction in presently employed irrigation waters can reduce water demands for leaching, lessen drainage problems, decrease salt additions to soil, increase crop productivity, and decrease the cost of irrigated farm output in such circumstances. The stakes connected with the desalting program thus are high.

Another field which deserves cultivation but which has not had either the popular appeal or the legislative attention given to desalination concerns the techniques of sediment control. In the economy of this day they have a very wide significance. Reduction or elimination of sediment content has aesthetic, public health, and economic effects which certainly must be considered more heavily in future planning of development. To some development purposes, like domestic, industrial, and municipal water supply, and recreation, sediment control or elimination is absolutely essential. For others like navigation, or power production, it is an economic asset. To meet desirable standards of water quality in the future it is obvious that the cheapest means of sediment control is that of erosion control. It is assumed that their value now so widely recognized will be continued to be applied as needed. However, there are limits to the practical extent of applying measures of erosion control for sediment reduction. One need only consider many local situations in semiarid and arid western United States to understand this. While natural deposition ultimately takes care of the problem there are situations in which this too is costly or impractical. There is certainly a field for study of possibilities of cost reduction in reducing or eliminating the sediment content of water supplies.

PROBLEMS PRESENTED BY NEW TYPES OF WASTES

The many benefits conferred by the application of modern chemistry, and, now, modern physics, upon our means of agricultural and industrial production and upon our domestic pursuits are often accompanied by problems of public safety or convenience. Every existing pollution problem from industrial sources is witness to this fact. These problems may be expected to continue their emergence in the future. One of them, the risk of contamination from the use of radioactive materials, is so spectacular that public interest has stimulated a large and apparently entirely adequate program for developing radioactive waste disposal techniques.[29] However, problems are appearing from less spectacular sources which also deserve methodical attention.

Our increasing realization that many modern chemicals may have subtle but nonetheless harmful physiological effects underlines the need of keeping the chemical waste contamination of water prominently in review. For example, there are no satisfactory means for removing detergents from domestic water supplies, and the use of insecticides and weed killers can produce detectable residues in some water supplies. While we may assume that the effects of these residues are physiologically harmless, recent history in the United States is studded with the discovery of danger in substances hitherto carelessly assumed to be safe. The problem of chemical waste removal therefore may be considered a dynamic one in which public responsibilities are not to be discharged alone by attention to the spectacular or by waiting for the appearance of crises.

29 The program of the Atomic Energy Commission and the projects of its contractors. This is not intended to suggest that satisfactory and tested solutions to the problems of disposal which can be foreseen now exist. However, there is an existing establishment with apparent competence for developing such solutions.

RECOGNITION OF TREATMENT TECHNIQUES AS A PART OF WATER DEVELOPMENT

There is certainly some appreciation of the potentiality of treatment techniques in water development and active interest expressed from a variety of sources within the country. Although the federal government has shown leadership in some important fields, as in radioactive waste disposal, desalting, and some aspects of organic waste treatment, there is still a degree of reliance on technical leadership at a more local level. This seems to be the case for at least some important problems of chemical waste treatment and some of organic waste treatment. Moreover, the federal programs and the existing programs at state and local levels have an isolated individual orientation. They are not yet considered as related to each other or as a part of a whole set of techniques, including multiple-purpose development, whose joint consideration can greatly increase the efficiency and rate of progress in national development. Improved means of weighing the adequacy of current research, development, and application would seem a very natural result from a more comprehensive review.

USE PRIORITIES CORRESPONDING TO WATER QUALITY

Water uses have differing degrees of tolerance to specific water qualities. Some industrial uses, for example, require very nearly pure or salt-free and sediment-free water. On the other hand, irrigation water may have a high turbidity and a salt content as high as 3,500 ppm and still remain useful in some special situations.

Where treating water of substandard quality is temporarily or permanently impossible, it is therefore apparent that the cause of efficiency in water use may be served by "pairing" of tolerant uses and low quality supplies. This long has been practiced in agriculture, where salt-tolerant crops and salt-tolerant animals like sheep have been employed to make use of water supplies with relatively high salt content. For many years certain coastal industrial plants also have used sea water, principally for cooling purposes. Until recently such use has been deterred by the corrosive action of sea water on metal surfaces and the fouling of heat-transfer equipment by precipitated salts and marine organisms. However, improvement in corrosion-resistant alloys in recent years has led to a lessening of corrosion problems in sea water use, making the employment of sea water cooling much more feasible than it has been. As a result, clean sea water now is a generally cheaper and more satisfactory coolant than the contaminated fresh water requiring considerable pretreatment.[30] Besides cooling, sea or other salt waters have other industrial uses, such as flushing or washing operations, sluicing ash, movement of logs and wood chips in pulp mills, laundering and other functions. While decisions on the pairing of use and quality of supply should be and will be made on an economic basis, it is evident that this tool for achieving some efficiencies in water use now is practical enough to be entertained as an alternative to treatment or other means of providing an adequate supply under some local conditions.

[30] Ackerman and Löf, *op. cit.*, p. 351.

TECHNOLOGICAL ADVANCE AND RESOURCE PROJECTIONS

The article that follows is based upon notes that Hans H. Landsberg, the senior author of Resources in America's Future,[1] *has used in informal talks on the subject.*

It is as certain as anything in this world that advances in technology will improve methods of extracting and using natural resources and resource products, and that these changes will have profound effects on both supplies and requirements. But in what manner, and when, and how much? No one can say with any assurance. In looking ahead, the choice is between building conclusions on very slender evidence and ignoring a basic element in the future resources picture.

The authors of *Resources in America's Future* encountered this dilemma at every turn of their projection making. An account of how they coped with it sheds light not only on the study itself but also on the extent to which technology has come to pervade the outlook for natural resources.

Technological change already has played a major role in resources adequacy. Characteristically this has taken the form of increased efficiency—getting more service or performance out of each unit of resources—and of widening the choice among resources. The pound of coal that was burned up in the course of generating 1.0 kilowatt-hour of electricity twenty years ago would produce over 1.5 kwh today. At the 1960 rate of 700 billion kwh generated thermally, the savings in fuel consumption due only to this 20-year progress in efficiency is the equivalent of some 165 million tons of coal (about the same, incidentally, as all fuels burned for power generation as recently as the year 1950). Best practice in the production of aluminum today can bring forth a pound of metal with an electric power expenditure of as little as 6.5 kwh, compared with 9 or 10 kwh not so long ago. Data are hard to come by, but if we assume current industry-wide power consumption to be about 2 kwh per pound below the experience of the early forties, then, in terms of a 2-million-ton output, the annual savings from this improvement amount to 8 billion kwh of electricity—only slightly less than the annual consumption of Connecticut or Iowa.

Similar calculations in other resource fields yield similarly striking illustrations. Had corn yields been at the level of the forties, it would have taken nearly 100 million acres to produce the crop grown in 1962 on 57 million acres. Analogous comparisons for other crops would lead one to estimate the total amount of cropland "saved" through yield increases in the past two decades at perhaps 200 million acres. The whole agricultural picture in the United States would be radically different from what it is today, if no yields had changed since 1940–45.

The need to allow for technical change in considering future resource adequacy is

• Hans H. Landsberg is a staff member of Resources for the Future, Inc.

Reprinted from the *1963 Annual Report,* Resources for the Future, Inc. (Washington), pp. 13–21, with the permission of the editor.

[1] Hans H. Landsberg, Leonard L. Fischman, and Joseph L. Fisher, *Resources in America's Future: Patterns of Requirements and Availabilities, 1960–2000* (Baltimore: Johns Hopkins Press for Resources for the Future, Inc., 1963).

clear enough, but the statistical methods for putting this conviction to work are rough at best and must be grossly applied. Yet, it seems preferable to be vulnerable in the magnitude of the allowance made than to attempt no correction at all for future technological change. One may not hit the bull's-eye but one is less likely to miss the target altogether.

The examples cited—more power per pound of fuel burned, more aluminum per kilowatt-hour of electricity consumed, and more crops per acre planted—are deceptively persuasive. Few would argue against projecting into the future some continuation of these experiences (though one could get quite a good argument when it comes to filling in the blanks). The principal reason for this likely consensus is the nature of these particular technological changes.

For our purposes we can distinguish between (1) technological advances that, while emerging from new scientific insights, lead to improvements, modifications, and extensions of known and previously applied techniques and procedures; and (2) innovations that perform traditional functions in radically new ways or perform radically new services.

The suggested division is often cloudy. But in dealing with the likely effect of changing technology on future adequacy of natural resources, the distinction is important enough to justify even rough approximations. For, given the element of systematic probing and advance that is the hallmark of the scientific age, one may without undue trepidation assume that a large variety of recent and continuing trends in technology—in its widest sense—belong to the first grouping.

This kind of assumption is made throughout the study for crop yields, fertilizer applications, or efficiency of livestock production per animal; increasing use of electric power, but declining use of energy from all sources per unit of industrial output; continuing abandonment of coal use in space heating; increasing efficiency of conversion of heat to energy in conventional power generation; utilization of a larger portion of each tree felled and greater flexibility in choice of species in lumbering operations; a continuing trend toward alloyed metals combined with a decided preference for the lighter metals; further reductions of the share of materials in the value of much durable equipment, both in the consumer field and in industrial equipment; or further substitutions of man-made materials for natural substances, be they fibers, rubbers, films, drying oils, cleansing agents, and so forth.

Projected changes in the factors enumerated—and many others—are represented by changes in specific coefficients, that is, in the relationships of one statistical series to another. True, one cannot divine and describe the precise nature or engineering characteristics of the underlying newly available technique, but this need not prevent him from making use of the generalized assumption.

It is important to distinguish here between the appropriateness of making this kind of provision for technical change in the projection and the chances of "being right." To illustrate, one might in the early twenties have felt every justification for assuming that locomotives would burn coal with increased efficiency—for taking account, that is, of probable improvement in the performance of the traditional function of the steam engine. But it is likely that one would have missed entirely the radical turn from the coal-fired to diesel engines with all its consequences for both the coal and the oil industry. To allow generally for improvement was clearly legitimate, but as it happened history took a different, unforeseeable turn in the specifics. Similarly, the continuing flow of improvements from which steam-electric plants have profited is essentially an instance of doing the same thing better, though this has come about only through great scientific progress. Without significant advances in both solid state physics and thermodynamics and without advances in knowledge of water purification, it is hard to imagine a modern generating plant operating, as it now does, at temperatures of 1,200° F. and pressures up to 5,000 psi.

Yet, while basic research has played an undeniably strong part in the instances cited, the net outcome is nothing revolutionary. As far as resource demand is concerned, it consists simply of using a smaller and smaller quantity of fuel to produce a given amount of electric energy in a traditional process. This is the kind of situation that lends itself to projection, even though one must remain vague as to the exact paths that science and engineering will take toward the anticipated goal. For example, it has been assumed in the RFF projections that by the end of the century only 625 pounds of coal will have to be burned in electric utility plants to generate 1,000 kwh of electric power—down nearly 30 per cent from the 1960 level. While it may be taken for granted that this will not hit the nail on the head, it is even more certain that what may seem an arbitrary choice is preferable to assuming no change. Indeed, the effect of a "no change" assumption is staggering. Assuming coal, gas, and oil to be burned in the proportions estimated in the RFF projections but at 1960 steam plant efficiencies the additional fuel demand in the year 2000 would be nearly 1,500 billion cubic feet of gas, plus 50 million barrels of oil, plus some 190 million tons of coal. The hypothetical increments in that year would be equal to about three-fourths the gas, over 90 per cent of the coal and almost one-half the fuel oil now consumed annually in electric power generation.

It is difficult to find any single factor that exerts an influence upon resources demand comparable to that of technological change. Therefore, the difficulties often leading to inability to allow for it, constitute perhaps the most serious weakness in any appraisal of resource adequacy.

Where this deficiency is most marked is in innovations that represent radical departures in ways of doing things, and in the emergence of altogether new types of products and services. For example, conversion of fractions of petroleum or natural gas to synthetic substances which possess combinations of qualities not present in any resources found in nature may lead to replacement of traditional products or open the way to the creation of new services. Other examples are the invention of the vacuum tube, which led to radio and television and therewith to entirely novel categories of services and human wants, and nuclear fission, which provides not only a wholly new source of energy, but as yet only partially explored ways of manipulating traditional materials through irradiation.

At the far end of this spectrum are those innovations that represent the most radical departures from established paths. For example, a "quantum jump" in genetics might permit a major degree of control over the conformation and characteristics of livestock or enable the agriculturist to extend to all major crops and to trees as well the advantages that he has reaped from the development of hybrid corn; a decisive advance in weather control could eliminate much of the chance factor in the raising of crops; a breakthrough in desalinization methods could make fresh water available to coastal areas and their hinterlands at such cost as to permit not only industrial but also agricultural operations; and the taming of the thermonuclear fusion process could provide a cheap source of energy without radioactive waste products and one that would be available into the indefinite future. These and many others are the types of development that one can think about, talk about, and list, but whose consequences cannot conscientiously be used in statistics. Yet they carry a far greater potential for upsetting projections of future resource adequacy—and in more ways—than do most factors that can be more easily expressed quantitatively and are therefore more frequently allowed for.

Let us trace just a few of these all too probable upsets. The immediate consequences of an innovation in the field to which it directly applies—be it power generation, metal refining, wood processing, or whatever—will be compounded by chain reactions in areas of living and segments of the economy that at first glance seem far removed. This is to some extent true for all innovations. The astounding increases in agricultural productivity have their counterpart in the greater input of resources into fertilizers, pesticides, and other branches of the chemical industry, the machinery industry, and others.

Although quantification remains tentative, one hopes to "catch" these sequels in a projection that utilizes historical trends, since the various time series involved are most likely to have moved in sympathy with one another. In our study, for example, a corn yield of 100 bushels per acre is projected for the year 2000, compared with a current national average yield of under 60 bushels. While greater use of existing knowledge will contribute to this rising curve, additional fertilizer, irrigation, pesticides, improved seed preparation, perhaps new machinery, and new departures not yet thought of will be other potent factors. Yet, to put down explicitly even the approximate combination of these factors that will produce something like a 100-bushel yield forty years hence is impossible. Instead, the added investment and production that must occur in the segments of the economy that deliver inputs to agriculture are for the most part derived independently of the development of yields. Since the upward sweep that is assumed to characterize the crop yield curve would similarly be assumed for the input factors, both would be rooted in past behavior, thus providing at least an indirect connection by way of a common history.

Emergence of a new process presents far greater difficulties. As noted earlier, it is reasonable to assume that the amount of electric energy required to produce one ton of aluminum will continue to decline. But just *how* this might happen can be quite important. By improved arrangement of the process, in other words by combining previously employed material, equipment, and labor more efficiently? By increases in size of the operation? By an increase in

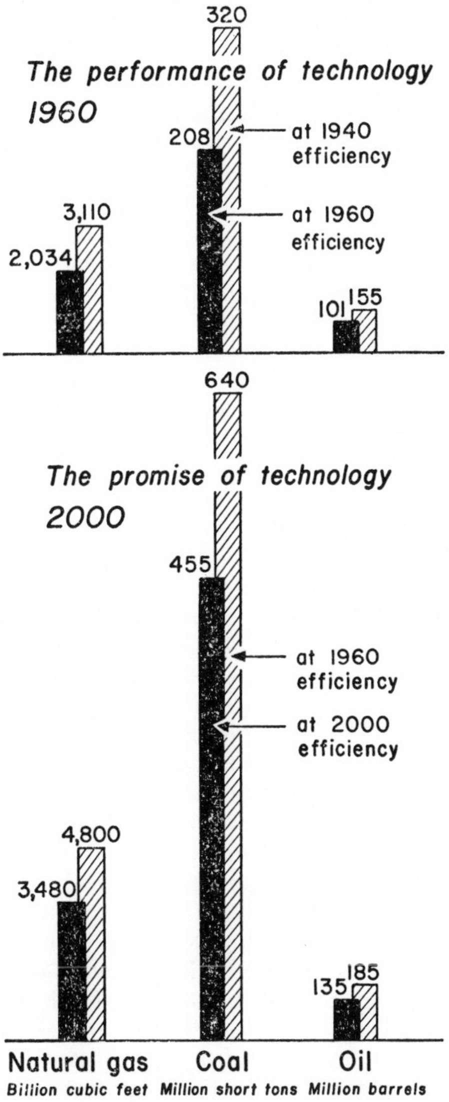

FIG. 1.—Comparison of projections to the year 2000 illustrates the influence of technology on expected fuel consumption in the generation of electricity. Looking at the record since 1940 it is apparent that the amount of fuel consumed would have been very different had 1940 technology remained unchanged until 1960. Thus the forty-year projections reflect continuing improvement and the probability of innovation.

the quantity of any of the ingredients used? Or by an altogether different process?

The implications for natural resources will differ. For example, a recently announced improvement based upon a different kind of electrode is an instance in which natural resource adequacy may be affected, for the electric cathodes used may contain titanium, zirconium, and possibly other substances. These would represent a demand neither involved in the conventional process nor automatically bracketed into the demand projections for these metals, since the past record in such an instance can be no guide. There is the additional quirk here that, if this improvement were to become a standard feature in aluminum refining, the added consumption of electric power in titanium production, for example, would act as a partial offset to the increased energy efficiency (and therefore reduced power consumption) in aluminum production.

The projection in *Resources in America's Future* provides only for the most obvious of the likely developments; that is, a continuing drop in power used per pound produced—possibly a conservative extrapolation because the level of 7.75 kwh per pound of aluminum assumed for the year 2000, is probably even now being bettered in some modern refineries. Power consumption for the group of minor nonferrous metals that includes titanium appears only as an aggregate projected to triple between 1960 and 2000, and not specifically derived from possible future technologic changes such as the new electrode mentioned above. One may console oneself with the thought that the amounts involved in any particular instance are small but, of course, the sum of many small errors may, over a 40-year period, add up to an impressive total.

An instance where not only the magnitude but even the area of secondary impact is difficult to identify is the production of isotopes, a by-product of nuclear fission. Their use in metallurgical quality control, and therefore in the development of improved or perhaps new materials needed in modern engineering, as a new tool in mineral exploration and therefore in the widening of resource availability, and as a tracer element in the biological sciences—to name only three areas of application—may have consequences for both the demand and supply of natural resources that are far removed from the more easily traced energy aspect of nuclear fission and that altogether escape quantitative appraisal.

No such uncertainty attends the basic characteristics of another major novelty in the energy field, the fuel cell. It has been successfully used to power a tractor and is likely to play a prominent part in providing power (and, as a by-product, water) on space flights. The basic principle of the fuel cell is simple: continual feeding of a fuel and an oxidant (in a pure form the mixture would be hydrogen and oxygen) to electrodes separated by a suitable electrolyte in a battery-like device causes an electric current to flow between the two gases when connected to a load. The great advantage of the fuel cell is direct conversion into energy and consequent high efficiency.

Development of a commercially feasible process is not so simple. The device in which this reaction is produced should be small, inexpensive, and in need of as little external heat as possible. Also, a cheap source of hydrogen is required. Coal, oil, and gas producers are all engaged in perfecting a fuel cell in which their particular hydrocarbon will be that source. If some or all of them succeed, the principal effect would be a change in the efficiency with which traditional fuels are converted into electric energy. This change may be drastic enough to considerably lengthen the life span of U.S. fuel reserves, but with one exception it is unlikely to create altogether new situations over a span of several decades. The exception—which, incidentally, would improve rather than worsen over-all adequacy of energy resources—would be a fuel cell based principally on coal and engineered to propel surface vehicles. However, the tenacity with which the internal combustion engine has dominated the engine field, despite the existence of turbines, free-piston, multifuel, and other types of engines, suggests that such a development would cast a long shadow ahead, thus permitting ample time for a second look and for adjustments.

A field in which technological change makes demand projections hazardous even for five, let alone forty years ahead, is that of chemical products; and, indeed, the very definition of that term is becoming increasingly difficult. The projections in the RFF study are probably the least realistic in terms of product identification and yet, because of the continuing revolution in the materials field, perhaps not too far off the mark. When the consumption of propylene for synthetics production is projected to spurt from 150 million pounds in 1960 to 12 billion pounds in the year 2000, or synthetic moldings and extrusions from 1.8 to 25.6 billion pounds during the same forty years, the shapes and uses of the end products, vague even now, must become more so. The specific chemical and physical forms into which the hydrocarbons will be combined at various times must be left out of the picture. What remains is a steep path of expanded application of known broad groupings, augmented by discovery and development of new ones. The recent announcement of a commercially feasible process of making a synthetic substitute for shoe uppers is a case in point. This is a field in which the natural product had pretty much held its own. RFF's study, completed before this announcement, had assumed that synthetics would make further inroads on leather shoes; consequently a declining ratio of leather to shoes produced had been projected. The emergence of the new product thus merely puts meat on the bare statistical bones of this particular projection, which was made, one might say, "on principle."

But this is likely to be an exceptional case manageable mainly because we are dealing with a specific product, identifiable in numbers, use, etc. Generally, as the molecule or the atom becomes the basic building block of the materials that modern society requires for both its perishable and durable paraphernalia, the possibilities of substitution widen to such an extent that only dealing in large aggregates provides a safeguard, albeit a modest one. At the same time, because the advances of the scientific age are systematic, cumulative, and proceed from understanding to understanding, it is feasible for the curious to peer ahead without having to go entirely by hunch or instinct. This removes some but not all of the discomfort associated with the making of projections, but its soothing action is offset—especially when one comes to products nearer the consumer end than the resource end—by the concurrent multiplication of substitution possibilities.

At the same time, however, that the increasing opportunities for substitution diminish confidence in the calculated future consumption of any specifically identified material, the decreased dependence on the form in which materials are encountered in nature widens the horizon. One may consider adequacy in terms of meeting the demand not for a specific resource product or service but for the rather broad groups that we have termed "requirements for living." If steel won't do, aluminum may; if aluminum won't do, magnesium may; and if no metal will do, petrochemicals may be the thing. To feed the nation's blast furnaces, domestic high-grade iron ore has been followed by imported high-grade iron ore, only to be increasingly supplemented by domestic low-grade ore, without a significant effect upon the cost of steel. Any future transition from high-grade bauxite to high-alumina clay apparently would have similarly small effects upon cost of aluminum. The cost implications of these and many other shifts in raw materials become less disconcerting as technology comes nearer to reaching what Harold Barnett and Chandler Morse call a "plateau of constant quality"; that is, availability of a resource at practically constant cost for very large quantities. Extreme examples of this are extraction of oxygen from the air and of magnesium from sea water.

Both growing substitution opportunities and widening resource availability have been brought about largely by the achievements of the scientific age: understanding instead of ingenuity, systematic investigation instead of the lucky accident. In these contrasting pairs, Barnett and Morse epitomize the difference between the scientific age and the mechanical age that preceded it. As they point out in their recent RFF study, *Scarcity and Growth,*[2] "the heritage of knowledge, equipment, and economic institutions that the industrial nations are able to transmit to future generations is sufficient to overcome the potentially adverse effects of continual and unavoidable shift to natural resources with properties which, on the basis of past technologies and products, would have been economically inferior." This, as we have seen, is apt to be matched by increasing versatility, flexibility, and adaptability on the demand side. These features suggest that any allowance for technological advance that one is able to build into adequacy projections is likely to be on the conservative side; they also suggest that without strongly continuing technological advance our society would quickly run up against inconvenient and perhaps critical material limitations.

[2] (Baltimore: Johns Hopkins Press for Resources for the Future, Inc., 1963).

GWYN E. JONES

THE DIFFUSION OF AGRICULTURAL INNOVATIONS

Introduction

The diffusion and adoption of new and improved farming practices have provided a major area of research conducted by rural sociologists during the postwar years. A fairly rapid international spread of this kind of research has occurred, although the majority of the studies have been carried out in the U.S.A. Two major syntheses of this research have now been published.[1] The studies by rural sociologists have also been acknowledged as a stimulus for research by other social scientists—some by agricultural economists into the economic mechanism underlying the spread of an agricultural innovation, and a growing number of projects by sociologists and psychologists into the adoption of a variety of innovations, from the acceptance of new drugs by medical practitioners to the adoption of various new household gadgets by urban housewives.

Some Definitions

An *innovation* may be defined as "any thought, behavior, or thing that is new because it is qualitatively different from existing forms. Strictly speaking, every innovation is an idea, or a constellation of ideas; but some innovations by their nature must remain mental organizations only, whereas others may be given overt and tangible expression."[2] Thus, although agricultural innovations are often considered as including only new husbandry practices, new management techniques, such as gross margin analysis or grassland recording, are equally appropriate examples. Moreover, improved practices may also be regarded as innovations insofar as they are modified in form, or have new functions, or are of wider or more restricted applicability compared with their forerunners. An innovation may not be a recent invention, but the form in which it is perceived or in which it is made available is new to farmers of the present generation. The fate of an innovation, however, is as important as its invention. Unless it is widely adopted it will fail to make any effective social or economic impact.

The two terms "diffusion" and "adoption" are intimately interrelated but have come to signify somewhat different concepts. *Diffusion* embraces the spread of new practices and ideas in both a social and a geographical sense. Social diffusion refers to the spread of an innovation from its originating sources (in the case of new farm practices usually agricultural scientists) among a group of potential users. This may be termed the micro aspect of diffusion. Geographical diffusion refers to the changing distribution of an innovation

• Gwyn E. Jones is Lecturer in Agricultural Economics, University of Nottingham.

Paper read to the Agricultural Economics Society, December, 1962, and reprinted from the *Journal of Agricultural Economics,* XV, No. 3 (June, 1963), 387–405, with permission of the author and the Agricultural Economics Society.

[1] Herbert F. Lionberger, *Adoption of New Ideas and Practices* (Ames: Iowa State University Press, 1960); Everett M. Rogers, *Diffusion of Innovations* (New York: The Free Press, 1962).

[2] H. G. Barnett, *Innovation: The Basis of Cultural Change* (New York: McGraw-Hill Book Co., 1953), p. 7.

as it spreads from one or more areas where its use has become more general at an earlier time than in surrounding areas. This represents the macro aspect of diffusion. The passage of time is implicit in both concepts, although the rate of diffusion may vary for different innovations. Thus, diffusion also implies a time lag between early and late accepters of an innovation, and between the early and late attainment of a particular level of acceptance by area. Communication between individuals and between groups forms a basic element in the diffusion process, since diffusion is concerned with the collective response to an innovation.

The diffusion of an agricultural innovation thus refers to its interpersonal spread among farmers. *Adoption* is the act of accepting an innovation, normally an individual reaction. It is the final stage of a mental process[3] by which the "unit" of adoption (usually, but not always, an individual) passes from first becoming aware of an innovation, or becoming conscious of the need for a particular practice, to finally accepting it as part of his normal activities. An appreciation of the adoption process adds depth to an understanding of diffusion.

The Curve and Process of Diffusion

The recent spate of rural sociological studies on the adoption and diffusion of agricultural innovations has derived considerable stimulus from earlier and contemporary studies by economists, historians, geographers, and particularly by anthropologists and early sociologists. Numerous anthropological investigations among primitive and peasant communities have demonstrated the influence exerted by the diffusion of particular traits and artifacts of an innovative character on social change within such communities. During the interwar years several early sociologists, in the anthropological tradition, developed the thesis that the diffusion of a cultural trait follows a curve over time which, expressed cumulatively, approximates an S-shaped growth curve.[4]

This thesis has been considerably strengthened by recent studies into the diffusion of farming innovations. It is still a matter of dispute whether the resultant curves are closer approximations to a cumulatively expressed normal distribution or to a more or less symmetrical logistic curve.[5] An S-shaped curve re-plotted in terms of increments for constant time units produces a "bell-shaped" curve, which may or may not be symmetrical. Several empirical studies, however, have shown a high degree of symmetry and close approximation to normality in the curves of annual adoption increments for particular innovations.

The acceptance of a normal curve as a conceptual model for the diffusion of an innovation within a farming group is convenient since it allows further deductions. If we use the year of adoption as the variable, the two parameters of the distribution (the mean year of adoption and the standard deviation of the distribution) can be used to divide the normal curve into time categories (the sigma units) and thus to classify the adopters. Rogers[6] has suggested

[3] The model of the adoption process which has been developed by rural sociologists in the Middle West of the U.S.A. and has become widely known consists of five consecutive stages whose nomenclature is largely self-explanatory, viz., awareness, interest, evaluation, trial, and adoption. For the reasoning in favor of this model rather than some alternatives, see Rogers, *op. cit.*, pp. 95–98.

[4] For example: Stuart F. Chapin, *Cultural Change* (New York: Century Co., 1928), pp. 203–14, and H. E. Pemberton, "The Curve of Cultural Diffusion Rate," *American Sociological Review,* I (1936), 547–56.

[5] Zvi Griliches, "Hybrid Corn: An Exploration in the Economics of Technological Change," *Econometrica,* XXV (1957), 501–22; Rogers, "Categorizing the Adopters of Agricultural Practices," *Rural Sociology,* XXIII (1958), 345–54; and "Profitability versus Interaction: Another False Dichotomy," *Rural Sociology,* XXVII (1962), 327–38. Contributors include Zvi Griliches, Everett M. Rogers, A. Eugene Havens, and Jarvis M. Babcock.

[6] Rogers, "Categorizing the Adopters . . . ," *op. cit.*

a division of this distribution into five categories (Fig. 1), and the nomenclature which he used has now been widely accepted by rural sociologists. Any individual's position (U_i) for the adoption of a particular innovation in this time scale is determined from:

$$U_i = \frac{X_i - \bar{X}}{\sigma_{\bar{x}}},$$

where X_i is an individual's actual date of adoption; $\bar{X}$ is the mean adoption date in the complete diffusion of the innovation; and $\sigma_{\bar{x}}$ is the standard deviation of adoption dates among the population of adopters.

This provides a measure of an individual's position in relation to other members within the distribution. If it is accepted that the normal curve ideally describes the diffusion of several innovations, although the total time involved in the diffusion of each may be very different, then an individual's earliness or lateness in his general adoption behavior may be determined, since his scores (U_i) for particular innovations are additive and free from the original measure of time units. Thus, Rogers' method may be used to classify an individual farmer as an "innovator," "early adopter," etc.[7]

In a comparable fashion, the adoption of a farming innovation over an entire country may be expected to approximate a normal S-shaped curve. However, it would be unlikely that all the different regions, counties, or smaller areas within that country would adopt a particular new practice at the same pace as the country as a whole. A time lag may be expected between the most progressive and the least progressive areas. Thus, assuming that the innovation is equally available in all parts of the country simultaneously, and that the last farmers, in all areas, to whom the innovation is applicable do not adopt it until the same time, diffusion curves approximating those in Figure 2 may be hypothesized.

However, the assumptions that an innovation is equally available in all areas simultaneously and that the stage of complete diffusion in all areas also occurs at a single specific time may not be tenable.

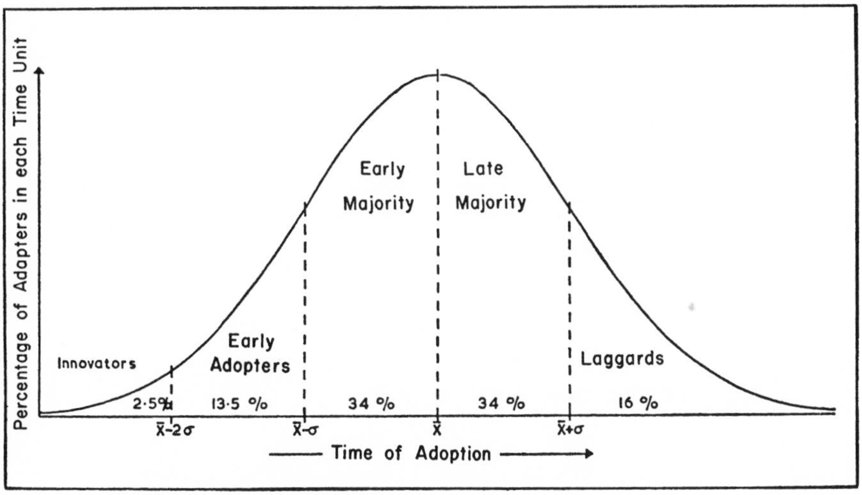

FIG. 1.—Classification of adopters on the basis of relative time of adoption of innovations (after Rogers).

[7] The method requires some modification if the total number of innovations applicable to all farmers in a population being investigated is not equal or if new farmers enter the population after the diffusion process has commenced.

In practice, the interarea lag in achieving a particular level of adoption may be equal at all times, or greatest at one or more points during the diffusion period, or completely variable. The ideal situation (Fig. 2), however, serves as a useful hypothesis and as a conceptual framework for investigating the geographical diffusion of an innovation. Further, the scale developed for distinguishing between the relative earliness or lateness of adoption by individuals within groups of farmers may be used to rank areas within a region.

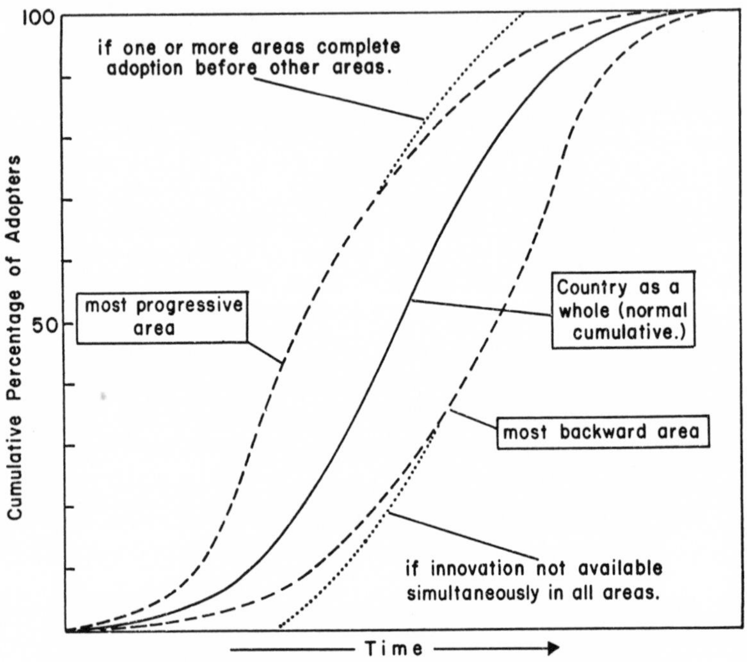

Fig. 2.—The national diffusion curve and possible regional variations

The process which determines the speed at which various innovations, agricultural or otherwise, are adopted within a group, or become diffused over a country, is partly influenced by national forces. Some of these may stimulate or inhibit the spread of an innovation because they influence the climate of opinion toward the technical progress. For example, an agricultural policy may operate so as to stimulate a reduction in unit costs in farm production and thereby the adoption of cost-reducing innovations, or a fiscal policy may encourage or discourage investment in new equipment. Again, the availability of innovations to potential users obviously affects their rate of diffusion. If an innovation is in any way prevented from being made generally available, for example by legal patents (which are rare among new agricultural techniques), or is "rationed" (e.g. tractors during World War II), or lacks sales outlets in particular parts of a country, the diffusion period is prolonged.

Rural sociologists, however, have not been primarily concerned with these wider factors, but rather have concentrated on those which are overtly present at the level of the individual adopter. Three broad groups of factors are involved at this level: the characteristics of the innovations; the media of communication; and the personal and sociological characteristics of the potential users.

THE CHARACTERISTICS OF INNOVATIONS

The character of a new idea or practice is an important determinant of the rate at which both its adoption and diffusion proceed. Basically, the characteristics of an innovation are of an economic or a technical kind, but these may be closely interwoven.

The *economic* characteristics of a farming innovation include its initial cost, its operating and maintenance costs, the rate at which an investment in it is recovered, and its net effect on farm income. It might be hypothesized that the higher the initial cost, or the higher the operating and maintenance costs, or the slower the rate of return on the capital outlay, then the slower will be the rate of diffusion of a particular new farm practice. However, these hypotheses require empirical investigation in a variety of situations. A recent study covering fifty-nine innovations available to Pennsylvania dairy farmers[8] has shown that the association between the diffusion rate and the three economic aspects mentioned was in each case in the opposite direction to that hypothesized. Further research is required into these relationships, but the Pennsylvania study clearly casts doubts upon any claim that these economic factors occupy a pre-eminent position as the determinants of an innovation's diffusion. It also lends support to Wilkening's view which, while acknowledging the importance of economic factors, asserts that "if economic considerations were the only basis of acceptance, improved practices would be adopted as rapidly as their economic advantage were demonstrated."[9]

However, where an innovation is being considered which is designed to replace an existing technique that involved a relatively high capital investment, there are weighty economic arguments why an individual entrepreneur should delay its adoption even after its commercial advantage has been demonstrated. Joan Robinson, writing in this context, points out that "the speed at which new methods are diffused throughout the economy depends partly upon the physical life of capital goods,"[10] an aspect which has been recently explored by Salter.[11]

Briefly, Salter's thesis states that at any given time best practices (in productivity terms) are not fully adopted since this would involve the scrapping of existing equipment which has only partly paid for itself and is in any event not worn out or obsolete. Thus, whereas an entrepreneur may be aware of better practices than those he is currently using, he cannot, for economic reasons, yet adopt them. By the time he is economically justified in replacing his existing equipment further innovations will inevitably have appeared so that he will probably adopt the best practice of that time, only to fall once more below the technological potential in the succeeding period. This reasoning is undoubtedly operative in the diffusion of capital-requiring innovations in agriculture.

The *technical* attributes of innovations also bear on the speed at which they become diffused. Among these characteristics are the complexity, divisibility, and conspicuousness of innovations and their compatibility with existing practices.

The *complexity* of an innovation may be expected to affect the rate at which it will be diffused. This attribute covers not only the mechanical and operational complexity of innovations but also the economic characteristics and consequences of adoption,

[8] Frederick C. Fliegel and Joseph E. Kivlin, "Farm Practice Attributes and Adoption Rates," *Social Forces*, XL (1962), 364–70.

[9] Eugene A. Wilkening, *Acceptance of Improved Practices in Three Coastal Plain Counties*, North Carolina Agric. Exper. Station, Tech. Bull. No. 98 (May, 1952), p. 5; and Wilkening, "The Process of Acceptance of Technological Innovations in Rural Society," *Rural Sociology: An Analysis of Contemporary Rural Life*, ed. Alvin L. Bertrand (New York: McGraw-Hill Book Co., 1958).

[10] Joan Robinson, *The Accumulation of Capital* (London: Macmillan Co., 1956), p. 85.

[11] W. E. G. Salter, *Productivity and Technical Change*, Monograph No. 6, University of Cambridge, Department of Applied Economics (1960).

the ease with which their best use may be achieved, and, in the case of a management technique, its mental complexity. The more complex the practice the slower its diffusion may be expected to proceed. This was one of the most significant relationships demonstrated in the previously cited Pennsylvania study.[12]

Complexity thus embraces the ease by which an innovation can be described, demonstrated, and be understood. This becomes especially apparent when the description and demonstration have to be conducted at a "local" level[13] to secure the widespread use of a new practice among specific groups of farmers, particularly among late adopters.

The *divisibility* of a practice determines the extent to which an innovation can be tried by a farmer before he adopts it fully. Whereas this is clearly possible with new or improved seed varieties, fertilizers, etc., most items of new machinery and equipment require a farmer to adopt them completely at one time, possibly following an evaluation based on their use by other farmers. The feasibility of a personal trial reduces the uncertainty attached to the final decision to adopt or reject a new practice. Despite the addition of a trial stage in the adoption process, this may, nevertheless, accelerate rather than retard the diffusion of an innovation.

The *conspicuousness* of a practice, that is its general attractiveness and visibility, is largely a technical attribute. A highly conspicuous innovation may offer prestige to its adopter among his neighbors or other attachment groups. It may also accelerate an innovation's diffusion among farmers who notice it. A combine harvester and its operational capacity, for example, are apparent to any passer-by; a grain drier, its method of working and efficiency, or a farmer's accounts and the techniques he uses to make them assist his farm management and planning, are concealed from neighbors' view.

Finally, the *compatibility* of an innovation with existing techniques is partly a technical and partly a cultural attribute. If a new practice is relatively easy to assimilate into the existing range of practices which a farmer uses, its adoption and diffusion may be expected to be more rapid than otherwise. Some innovations are functionally related to other techniques and are thus more likely to be acquired if the related practices have been previously adopted. For instance, investigations have shown that the adoption of bulk milk tanks is closely associated with the prior adoption of pipeline milking or milking parlors, or both.[14] Similarly, if an innovation is recognized by a farmer as a natural extension of his prior experience a quicker adoption may be anticipated. A lack of congruence with pre-existing practices and experience may lead to a slow rate of diffusion even if the innovation is in all other respects ideally suited to a particular environment. Thus, for example, Brandner and Straus[15] have shown how hybrid sorghum seed was adopted much faster in an area of Kansas where its use was not recommended but which was accustomed to using hybrid corn than in a traditional sorghum-growing area of the State.

THE MEDIA OF COMMUNICATION

The pace at which an innovation is diffused is also a function of the existence of appropriate media of communication[16] which inform potential users of its avail-

[12] Fliegel and Kivlin, *op. cit.*

[13] Cf. Edgar Thomas, "The Conflict between Change and Stability in Agriculture," *Journal of Agricultural Economics,* XI (1954–56), 296.

[14] Gwyn E. Jones, *Bulk Milk Handling: An Investigation into the Adoption of a New Dairy Technique in Lindsey,* University of Nottingham, Department of Agricultural Economics, F. R. No. 146 (April, 1962).

[15] Lowell Brandner and Murray A. Straus, "Congruence versus Profitability in the Diffusion of Hybrid Sorghum," *Rural Sociology,* XXIV (1959), 381–83.

[16] Cf. M. L. M. Reeves, "The Dissemination of Technical and Economic Information in Farm Advisory Work," *Journal of Agricultural Economics,* XI (1954–56), 383–96.

ability and characteristics, and which advocate its acceptance. Mace has claimed that "in large measure the resistance to change lies in the resistance to communication—the refusal, the disinclination, the incapacity, or the simple failure to receive a message."[17] Clearly, information and advice required by farmers during the adoption and diffusion of farming innovations must at least be comprehensible and originate from an acceptable source.

The media of communication vary in their usefulness and importance at various points during both the adoption and diffusion processes. During the individual adoption process the relative importance of the available sources of information and advice changes.[18] In the initial awareness and interest stages the mass media (radio, T.V., and the press) are normally the main sources, which are followed by neighbors and farming acquaintances, agricultural advisory services, and merchants, dealers, and salesmen. At later stages the mass media become the least important sources, while neighbors and friends normally predominate. Personal experience is usually decisive in the continued use of an innovation (i.e. the transfer from the trial to the adoption stages); this may also be important at the evaluation stage.

The extent to which a particular source of information is used varies not only for the individual at different stages in the adoption process, but also varies between individuals at different positions in the diffusion process.[19] For example, during the awareness and information seeking stages, innovators and early adopters (Fig. 1) are likely to make greater use of specialist journals and of the more scientific literature produced by government agencies and commercial firms, than are the laggards. Innovators are also likely to have greater contact with professional agricultural advisory officers, although the role of the advisers during such contacts may be largely one of providing an objective second opinion on new ideas derived from elsewhere. Innovators invariably travel widely and acquire information on new practices, and consequently have a dispersed circle of farming acquaintances (usually also innovators) on whose knowledge and experience they can draw.[20]

By contrast, the later adopters of an agricultural innovation rely heavily on their farming acquaintances (particularly neighboring or local farmers) for information and advice. Within farming communities certain farmers are often looked upon as leaders in particular enterprises and neighbors seek their advice.[21] Such leaders may not be innovators, distinguished by behavior abnormal to their group, but rather they will usually personify the ideal norms of the group.[22] If they are relatively early adopters of farming innovations they will thus usually perform a special function of disseminating information on new practices among later adopters.[23] Agricultural merchants, dealers, and salesmen are also important information sources among later adopters, while agricultural advisers, when used, perform the role in which they are normally envisaged—that of providing information.

This is in line with two interconnected

[17] C. A. Mace, "Resistance to Change," *Occupational Psychology,* XXVII (1953), 27; and *Advancement of Science, London,* X (1953), 53–54.

[18] Lionberger, *op. cit.*, and *Adopters of New Farm Ideas: Characteristics and Communications Behaviour,* Central Regional Extension Pub. No. 13 (October, 1961), p. 7.

[19] Rogers, *Characteristics of Agricultural Innovators and Other Adopter Categories,* Ohio Agric. Exper. Sta., Research Bulletin 882 (May, 1961).

[20] Cf. A. W. Ashby, "The Farmer in Business," *Journal of the Proceedings of the Agricultural Economics Society,* X (1952–54), 93.

[21] David Sheppard, *A Survey among Grassland Farmers* (London: Social Survey, Central Office of Information, 1960), SS274; Lionberger and C. M. Coughenour, *Social Structure and Diffusion of Farm Information,* Missouri Agric. Exper. Sta., Research Bulletin 631 (April, 1958).

[22] George C. Homans, *The Human Group* (London: Routledge & Kegan Paul, Ltd., 1951), p. 141.

[23] Lionberger, *Adoption of New Ideas . . . , op. cit.*

theories regarding the operation of communications media which may be applied to the dissemination of information on farming innovations. First, as increasing numbers of farmers adopt a particular practice, interaction between them and those who have not so far adopted it has a cumulative effect in spreading that innovation.[24] This tends to give rise to the S-shaped diffusion curve over time, since the initial, increasingly rapid rate of diffusion loses its impetus as the proportion of potential adopters nears its maximum. Secondly, modern communication theory has established the importance of distinguishing at least two stages in the flow of information from its originating sources to an entire community.[25]

This theory maintains that the original sources of information (e.g. scientific institutions and their publications) are influential only among particular opinion leaders and change agents. These, rather than the original sources, become, in turn, the immediate source of the information for the remainder of a community. Currently, this concept is being extended to investigations into the existence of a multistep flow. The process probably contains numerous steps as the information "trickles down," usually in an increasingly simplified and more relevant form, from the originating sources to the laggards.

By extension, geographical diffusion is influenced by the ease with which information on a farming innovation "trickles across" a country. Frequently in this age innovations originate abroad, but international mass media, shows and demonstrations, and foreign travel bring it to the attention of the innovators. Within some countries the mass media, which American studies have shown to be important information sources for the early adopters, may be wanting, or the necessary sponsors and agents of change (professional advisers, salesmen, or leaders amenable to change) may be lacking. In Britain this is certainly not the case, but the geographical remoteness of certain areas and their isolation, in both a geographical and a social sense, does appear to be one factor retarding the adoption of certain innovations.

THE PERSONAL AND SOCIOLOGICAL CHARACTERISTICS OF ADOPTERS

The predominant emphasis in a large number of the studies of innovation adoption has been to identify statistically significant relationships between certain personal and sociological characteristics of adopters and their relative earliness in adoption, or the degree to which they have adopted innovations which are applicable to their system of farming.

On a personal and situational level, the main factors which have been considered in relation to the adoption of farming innovations are the farm size and income of the adopter, his age, education, socioeconomic status, and social origin. Almost invariably the earliness and degree of adoption are positively related to farm size and income. Similarly, the higher the educational attainment and socioeconomic status[26] of a farmer the earlier and greater does his adoption of new farming practices tend to be. The results of studies of the relationship between farmers' age and their adoption behavior are more conflicting, although elderly farmers, as might be expected, are less prone to change their methods and practices.

A farmer's social origin, broadly whether

[24] James Coleman, Elihu Katz, and Herbert Menzel, "The Diffusion of an Innovation," *Sociometry,* XX (1957), 253–70; Havens and Rogers, "Adoption of Hybrid Corn: Profitability and the Interaction Effect," *Rural Sociology,* XXVI (1961), 409–14.

[25] Elihu Katz and Paul F. Lazarsfeld, *Personal Influence: The Part Played by People in the Flow of Mass Communications* (Glencoe: The Free Press, 1955); Katz, "The Two-Step Flow of Communications: An Up-to-Date Report on an Hypothesis," *Public Opinion Quarterly,* XXI (1957), 61–78.

[26] Socioeconomic status is normally measured by a weighted index comprised of scores for certain attainments and amenities enjoyed by an individual. See W. H. Sewell, "A Short Form of the Farm Family Socio-Economic Status Score," *Rural Sociology,* VIII (1943), 161–70.

he was brought up on a farm, in a rural or in an urban area, may be regarded as one facet of a more comprehensive factor, namely the degree to which an individual displays modern urban traits in his activities. Much sociological theory has been based on the identification and acceptance of a continuum on which communities and (in recent studies) small groups and individuals may be classified. This continuum has been variously defined and termed, according to its poles, as *Gemeinschaft–Gesellschaft*, rural–urban, or localite–cosmopolite.[27] In terms of innovation adoption the more cosmopolitan the personality and sociological traits of a farmer or a group of farmers, the greater tends to be the propensity to accept new agricultural practices. This result is invariably obtained whether adoption behavior is related to a composite measure of an adopter's "urban" characteristics, or whether individual aspects of such a measure (e.g. urban origin, urban experience, or participation in urban activities) are used in the relationship.

The association between such characteristics and early or high adoption of farming innovations may not, however, be direct. Rather, the cosmopolitan traits may influence the groups and communications media with which the individual farmer comes into contact. If, on the other hand, a farmer's social participation is largely confined to local activities and institutions, it is unlikely that his propensity to change his farming practices will be very high. However, in an intergroup comparison (e.g. a comparison between adjacent neighborhoods) differences in the average adoption time or level may exist. This situation arises from the different personal characteristics of group members, their degree of interaction with one another, and their extra-local orientation.

Some Examples

The preceding section of this paper has been mainly based on foreign research. Relatively few empirical studies have been pursued in this country to test the broad hypothesis that, on the micro level of a group of farmers, the adoption and diffusion of agricultural innovations (in terms of the level or time of adoption) are related to farmers' characteristics which are more or less independent of each other.[28] Similarly, although some suitable data are available, little work has been undertaken on the macro level, that of the geographical diffusion of farming innovations.

In a study of fifty-five farmers in a group of four mid-Cardiganshire parishes it was found that a highly significant relationship existed between the level of adoption of a number of innovations and farmers' total gross income, socioeconomic status, the use of information and advisory sources, the farm social type,[29] farming type, and farm acreage. However, the factors were closely interrelated to each other, suggesting that insofar as these characteristics affect farmers' adoption behavior they act as a trait complex. It may be reasonably assumed that some of these characteristics can only be related to the others in one direction (e.g. farm size may influence a farmer's use of information and advisory sources: an influence in the opposite direction cannot be envisaged). In this manner, three of the interrelated factors (namely, total gross income, socioeconomic status, and the use of information and advisory sources) can be distinguished as a primary

27 Bruno Benvenuti, *Farming in Cultural Change* (Assen: Van Gorcum & Co., N.V., 1962), pp. 37–73; Havens, "Measuring the Localite-Cosmopolite Dimension," paper read to the Rural Sociological Society Conference, August, 1960; F. E. Emery, O. A. Oeser, and Joan Tully, *Information, Decision, and Action: A Study of the Psychological Determinants of Changes in Farming Techniques* (Melbourne: Melbourne University Press, 1958), pp. 10–11, 17–54.

28 Sheppard, *op. cit.*, and Jones, *Factors Affecting the Adoption of New Farm Practices, with Particular Reference to Central Wales and the East Midlands of England* (unpublished B.Litt. thesis, University of Oxford, 1960).

29 The types distinguished were full-time operator, part-time operator, and elderly partially retired operator.

complex associated with farmers' level of new farm practice adoption.

In this mid-Cardiganshire investigation two further sociological characteristics were closely related to the level of new practice adoption. First, a significant difference existed between one neighborhood, which displayed a distinctly low level of adoption, and the five other neighborhoods delineated in the area. This low adoption area was comparatively isolated by physical features from the other neighborhoods and lacked a central focus for local activities. Significantly, it was characterized by an extremely low level of average gross income and by a high proportion of part-time and elderly farmers. Secondly, the majority of farmers in all six neighborhoods tended to concentrate their social participation in local activities, the degree of such participation being remarkably even among the entire population. The relatively few farmers who also participated in activities outside their immediate locality were also notable for the significantly greater number of new and improved farming practices they were using compared with their neighbors.

Farmers who have adopted a substantial proportion of innovations applicable to their system of farming have probably done so relatively sooner than low adopters. The more backward farmers, in terms of their technology, tend to accumulate a backlog of unadopted practices but they will usually acquire these before more recently introduced techniques. Thus, it may be postulated that relatively high adopters of farming innovations at any given time will also tend to be early adopters and, conversely, that low adopters will be late adopters. This relationship was demonstrated in a survey of the adoption of twenty-one new and improved farming practices among fifty-two mixed type farmers in the East Midlands.[30]

Among the East Midlands farmers early adopters were predominantly farmers of under 45 years of age who had received a relatively high standard of education (beyond the School Certificate or Ordinary G.C.E. level [U.S. equivalent is high school diploma]) and whose total turnover for 5 years averaged £12,000 and over per annum. Early adopters also tended (although the relationships did not achieve statistical significance) to be of urban origin, to participate to a greater extent than late adopters in social activities (particularly in extra-local activities), and to use more of the available information sources as an aid to making decisions on whether or not to adopt farming innovations. It is significant that the early adopters relied to a greater extent than late adopters on personal reasoning, past experience, and observation together with information acquired from advisory services and reading material. In particular, the early adopters gained their first information of new practices from mass media and the N.A.A.S. [National Agricultural Advisory Service, a branch of the Ministry of Agriculture, Fisheries and Food, established in 1946 to provide free advice to farmers in England and Wales]. The late adopters, on the other hand, received most information from neighbors and farming acquaintances, their first knowledge about an innovation being largely derived from the earlier adopters and from commercial sources. To some extent, the late adopters are maintained in this position due to their reliance on these sources of information and advice.

A similar picture is obtained from a study of the adoption of a particular innovation. For example, the first ten milk producers in Lindsey to adopt bulk milk tanks

30 "Early" and "late" adopters have been distinguished as the first and last 27 per cent of adopters. This provides 14 early and 14 late adopters for comparison, compared with only 8 in each category if Rogers' 16 per cent "innovators–early adopters" and 16 per cent "laggards" classification were used. The statistical basis for using 27 per cent as a dividing point is given in T. L. Kelly, "The Selection of Upper and Lower Groups for the Validation of Test Items," *Journal of Educational Psychology,* XXX (1939), 17–24; Jones, "The Differential Characteristics of Early and Late Adopters of Farming Innovations," *University of Nottingham, School of Agriculture Report,* 1960, pp. 75–80.

had a relatively high educational attainment, included an unexpectedly high proportion of producers of non-farm origin, mostly operated relatively large farms and dairy herds, and had manifested their predisposition toward adopting new practices by the large number of other dairying innovations they were using.[31]

In this investigation the use of formal information sources[32] was unrelated to the adoption of a bulk milk tank since the adopters were unaware of most of the available sources. In the event, they maintained a certain degree of contact with each other and pooled their information, one milk producer in particular having close contact with six of the others. However, only one of the first ten adopters of a bulk tank was generally recognized as a leader in dairy farming by the remainder of medium- and large-sized milk producers in the area who could be regarded as potential users of this innovation. Thus, although the first adopters might be expected to act as exemplars and information sources for later adopters of bulk tanks, the fact that they were not recognized as leaders could retard the diffusion process.[33] This is in keeping with the stepped-flow theory of communication, but it may indicate that the step between the innovators and the next group of adopters is one of the most difficult for information to "descend." This could be particularly true for an innovation concealed from public view as in the case of a bulk milk tank.

The macro diffusion of farming innovations has been a neglected area of research compared with the micro aspects. In this country, national data for certain innovations allow this type of research to be undertaken, particularly since the data are often available for countries or smaller areas. Much information is available in the agricultural machinery censuses, which have the advantage of a complete enumeration or, since 1956, of being based on a one-third sample. The diffusion of particular items of machinery and equipment can be easily derived from such data (Fig. 3).

The census data have certain disadvantages,[34] although some of these may be overcome by the use of complementary information from other sources. First, an item is often not enumerated in the census until it is in fairly common use. This precludes any discussion of its early diffusion. For example, self-propelled combines were not separately enumerated until 1959, by which time there were nearly 29,000 in use in England and Wales and they were rapidly replacing tractor-drawn models. Secondly, the form of the question in the census may periodically be changed, so that estimation is necessary to complete a series. In 1956 and 1958, for example, milking machines were enumerated in terms of milking units rather than by installations as in other years. Thirdly, a $33\frac{1}{3}$ per cent sample may give rise to sampling error, which may be serious at the level of a county or smaller area.

Finally, the number of particular items of machinery in use is an extremely crude measure of the extent to which they have been adopted. To be fully relevant in the context of diffusion it is necessary to know what *proportion of potential users* has adopted a particular technique at various times. Thus, whereas the number of mechanical sugar beet harvesters in Great Britain has increased from under 200 in 1946 to nearly 10,000 in 1960, this is of less significance than the British Sugar Corporation's data that the proportion of the sugar beet acreage mechanically harvested had risen from 1 per cent to 63 per cent in the same period. Even this is not synonymous with the proportion of sugar beet growers who are using mechanical

[31] Jones, *Bulk Milk Handling . . . , op. cit.*

[32] I.e., sources whose major function is to inform or advise, e.g., mass media and advisory agencies or personnel.

[33] Rogers, *Diffusion of Innovations, op. cit.*

[34] David Sheppard, "Rate of Adoption of New Techniques," *National Agricultural Advisory Service Quarterly Review,* XIV, No. 60 (Summer, 1963), 166–70.

harvesters, which is the most appropriate information in terms of the innovation's diffusion. Similarly, the proportion of milk producers using milking machines at various times, or the proportion of T.T. (tuberculin tested) milk in the total sales off farms (which is almost equivalent to the proportion of T.T. milk producers), is a more relevant indication of the diffusion of the particular practices than merely an enumeration of the numbers of milking machines or the quantity of T.T. milk (Fig. 4).

Apart from studying the rate of diffusion of a farming innovation in these national percentage terms, it is also relevant to enquire into its spread over a country. County data, although not entirely satisfactory, allow such analyses of the diffusion of certain innovations. Ecological studies of this kind are fundamentally different from the sociological type of enquiry, although areal data of physical, agricultural, economic, or social phenomena may be used as correlates to the time and level of adoption in various parts of a country. Hardly any studies of this nature have been undertaken,[35] but a few examples may be given to expand some of the hypotheses.

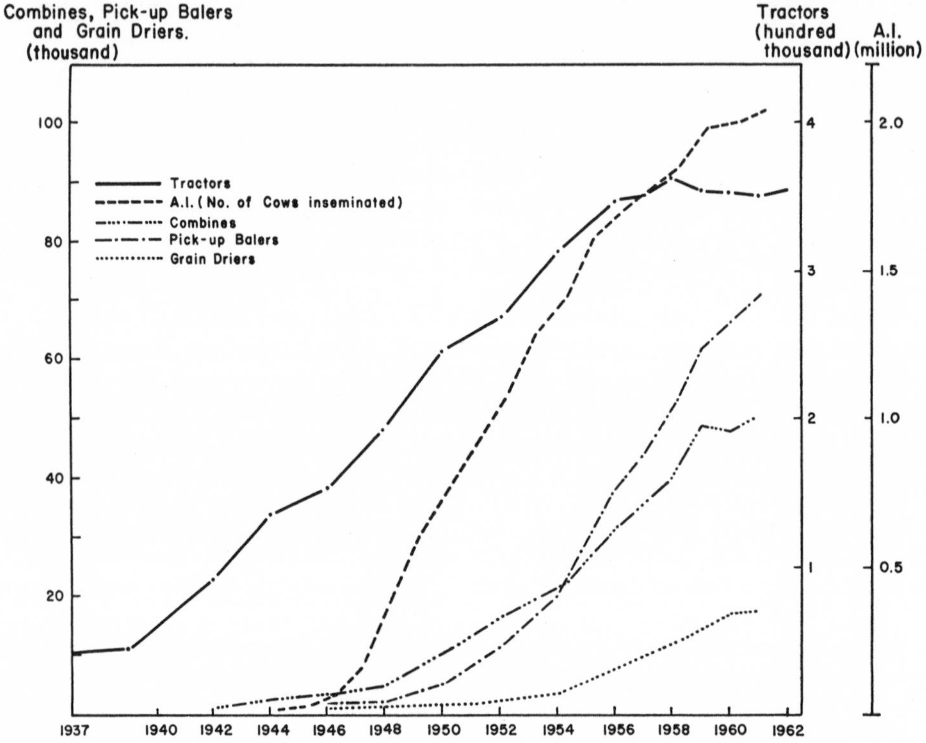

FIG. 3.—The growth in numbers of five agricultural innovations in England and Wales. (A.I. = artificial insemination.)

Combines were first used in this country in 1928, but a rapid increase in their numbers and their widespread acceptance has occurred only during the past 20 years. Currently, there are over 50,000 combines in England and Wales, or approximately 8 combines for every 1,000 acres of cereals. The degree of diffusion which this represents cannot be accurately ascertained

[35] Torsten Hägerstrand, *The Propagation of Innovation Waves,* Series B (Human Geography), Lund Series in Geography, B, IV (Lund, Sweden: Royal Univ. of Lund, 1952), 20 pp. and map.

since the published census data do not disclose the number of cereal growers or the number who own more than 1 combine. However, 1 combine per 1,000 acres of cereals must clearly indicate a relatively early stage in the diffusion process. This was achieved in Gloucestershire and Wiltshire in 1946, but it was 10 years later before every county in England and Wales attained a similar density of combines. A map depicting the first census year in which each county reached a density of 1 combine per 1,000 acres of cereals (Fig. 5*A*) tends to support the hypothesis that if any area attains a lead in the early adoption of an innovation then the diffusion of the innovation will spread, in a wavelike fashion, from that area. This geographical diffusion, however, may not occur at an even rate in all directions since the numerous factors which encourage or inhibit adoption are unlikely to be equally distributed in all areas. For example, most of Eastern England, mainly characterized by a high proportion of large farms and an arable emphasis, had 1 combine per 1,000 acres of cereals 4 to 6 years earlier than might be expected on the simple hypothesis of an even rate of spread from the Gloucestershire-Wiltshire "center." One method by which this may be induced is to construct time isolines from the "center" (1 combine per 1,000 acres of cereals in 1946) to all coasts (1 combine per 1,000 acres of cereals by 1956) (cf. Figs. 5*A* and 5*B*).

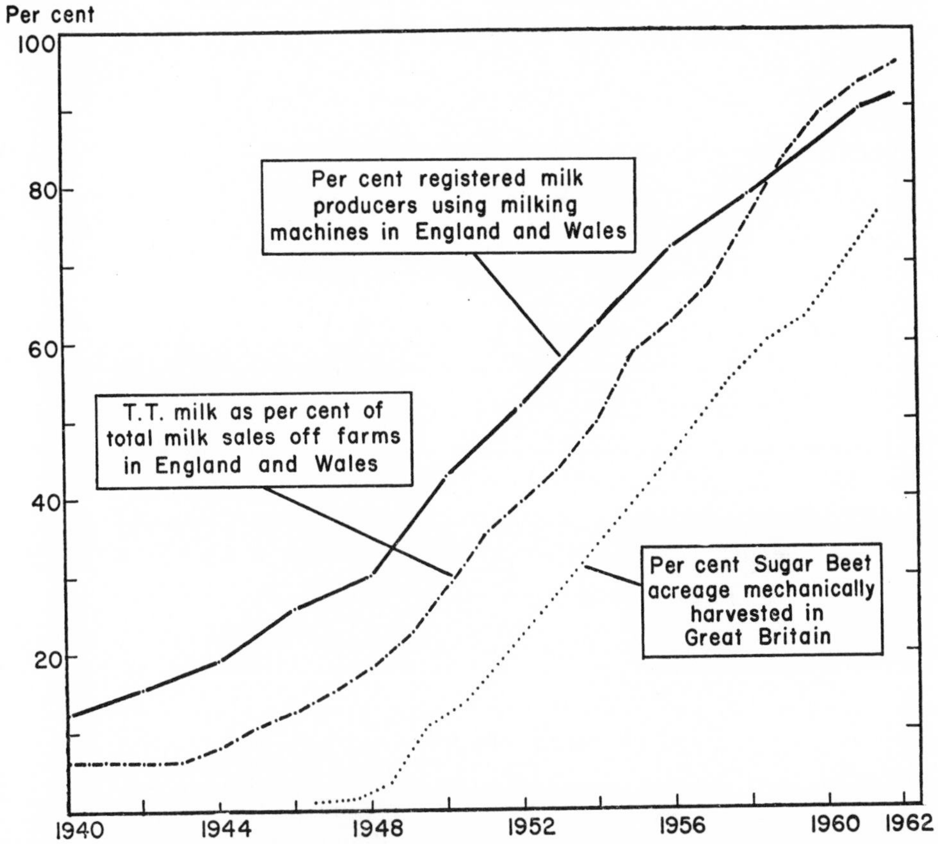

FIG. 4.—The diffusion curves of milking machines and T.T. milk production in England and Wales, and of mechanical sugar beet harvesting in Great Britain.

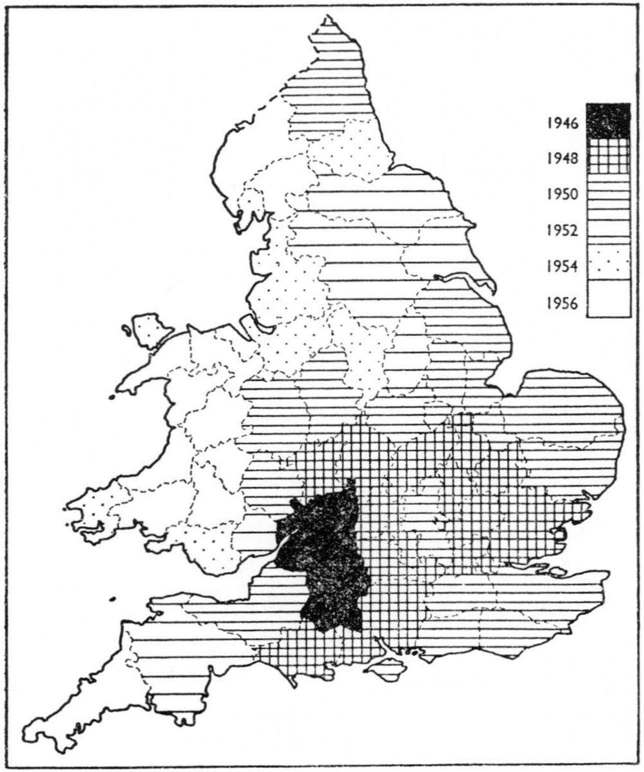

FIG. 5*A*.—Year by which each county had achieved 1 combine per 1,000 acres of cereals (based on *Agricultural Statistics*).

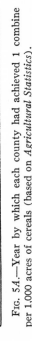

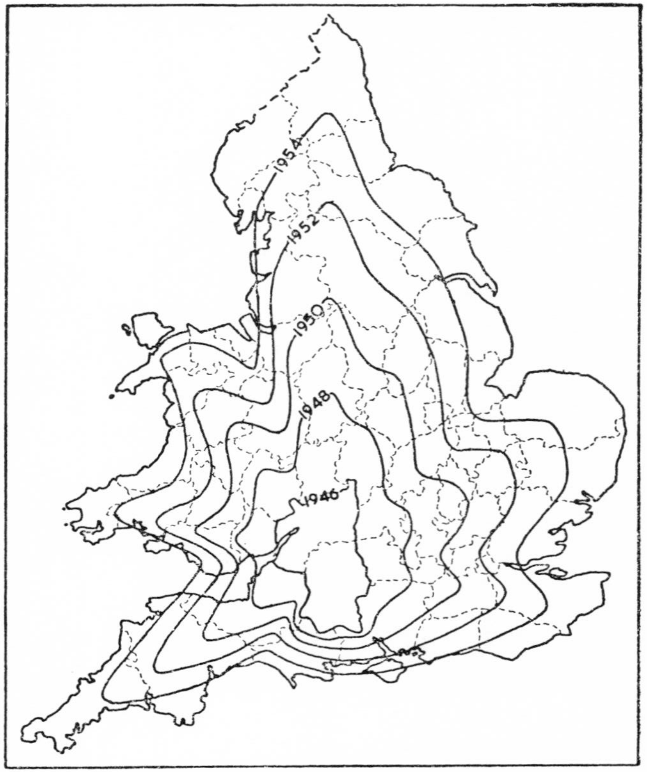

FIG. 5*B*.—Time isolines for 1 combine per 1,000 acres of cereals, assuming an even rate of spread from Gloucestershire–Wiltshire to all coasts.

Another suggested hypothesis was that whereas the cumulative national diffusion of an innovation may be described by a normal **S**-shaped curve, the most progressive and least progressive areas would be located on either side of this curve (Fig. 2). Some evidence to support this is available in data on the diffusion of T.T. milk production in England and Wales.[36]

June, 1962, it accounted for over 95 per cent of all milk sold off farms in England and Wales.

Figure 6 reproduces the national growth of T.T. milk as a proportion of total milk *sales* off farms, together with the curves for the most and least progressive M.M.B. regions in this respect in each year; these approximate closely to the diffusion curves

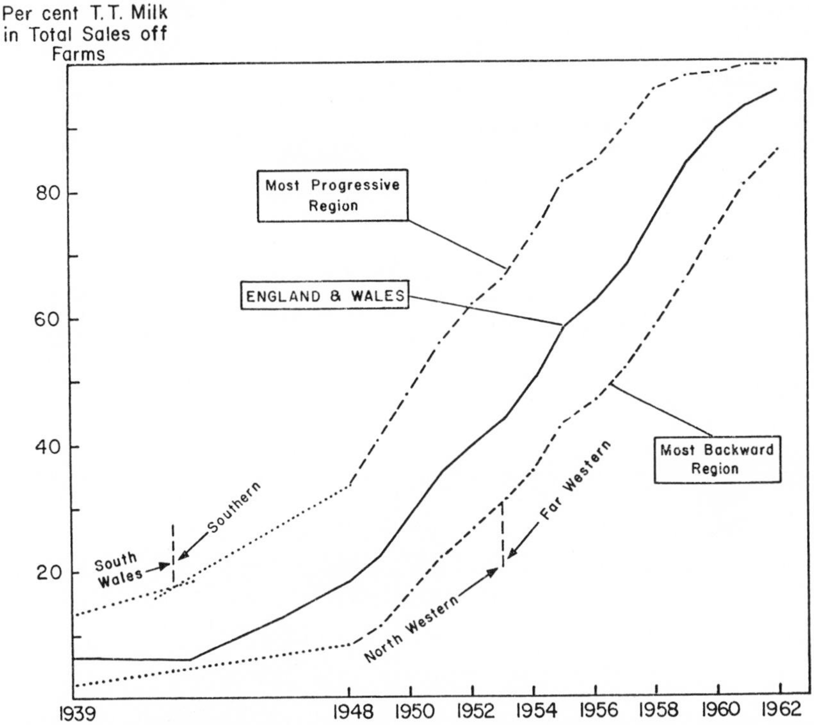

FIG. 6.—The diffusion of T.T. milk production in England and Wales showing extreme regional variations (based on M.M.B. regional data).

The antecedents of the T.T. milk designation date back to the first World War, but a designation akin to the current definition dates from 1936. By 1938–39 about 6 per cent of all milk sold off farms in England and Wales was of T.T. standard. Since then, under the stimuli of a price premium and schemes to attest the national herd as free from tuberculosis, the production of T.T. milk has increased and by

[36] Based on data kindly provided by the Milk Marketing Board.

which would represent the proportion of milk *producers* selling T.T. milk. Complete regional and county data are not available prior to 1948, but most of the diffusion process has occurred since that time. The interregional time lag in adoption tends to be greatest at between 50 per cent and 60 per cent T.T. milk, with the exception of the last stage of the process where the lag appears to increase (no region so far produces 100 per cent T.T. milk, although four counties have attained this ideal). A

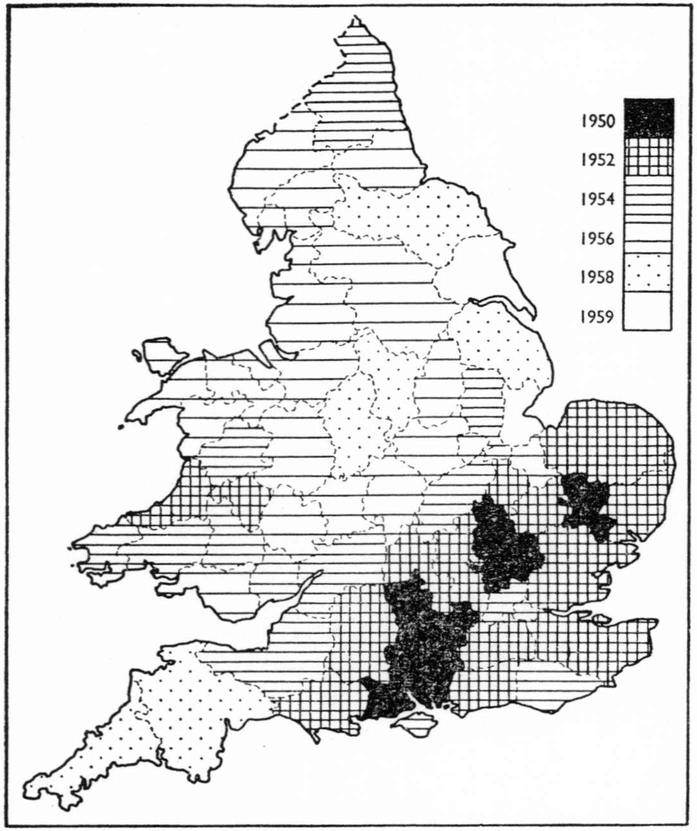

FIG. 7A.—Year by which each county had achieved 50 per cent T.T. milk production (based on M.M.B. data).

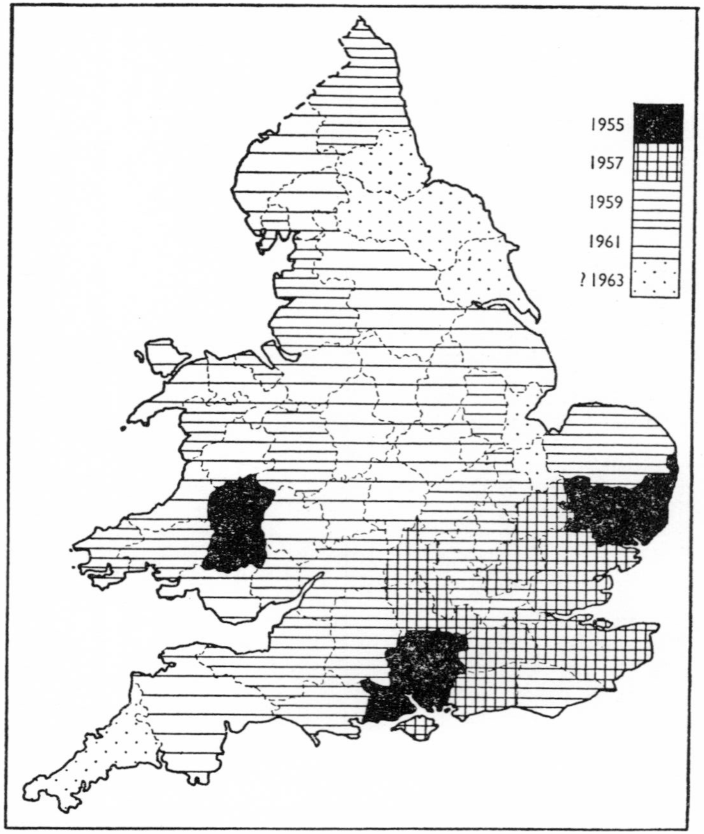

FIG. 7B.—Year by which each county had achieved 84 per cent T.T. milk production (based on M.M.B. data).

similar situation may also have been true in the early stage of diffusion, although the production of T.T. milk could have been adopted by all producers in all parts of the country in 1936.

The T.T. milk data may also be used cartographically to show the county pattern of diffusion, particularly for the second half of the diffusion process (Fig. 7*A* and Fig. 7*B*). Whereas the time lag between the most and least advanced *regions* in achieving 50 per cent T.T. milk in their total milk sales was about 6.5 years, the lag between the earliest and last *counties* was 11 years; at the 84 per cent T.T. milk stage the interregional lag is about 5.5 years compared with 10 years at a county level.[37]

This further suggests, as might be expected from statistical theory, that the smaller the areas being considered the wider the variation about the national mean.

It may also be observed that the time taken for the national production of T.T. milk to become diffused from 50 per cent to 84 per cent of total milk sales is 5 years, but individual counties vary from 2 to 8 years in completing this section of the diffusion process. On a map, the varying county rates of progress appear randomly distributed, which suggests that, at least in the latter half of the diffusion process, particular counties do not necessarily maintain a previous *rate* of adoption. Even so, the Home Counties, most of East Anglia, parts of the West Country, and parts of Wales retain their leading *position* in the geographical diffusion of the innovation as a result of their relatively early attainment of a 50 per cent level of T.T. milk production. The frequency of the county time-periods involved in moving from 50 per cent to 84 per cent T.T. milk is symmetrical and heavily concentrated around the 5-year mean, which, although it may be fortuitous, suggests that additional investigation may reveal further patterns in the geographical diffusion process.

37 Assuming that the three counties below 84 per cent T.T. milk in June, 1962, will achieve this level in 1963.

Conclusion

It is now widely recognized that the adoption and diffusion of new ideas, and of the techniques and practices which arise from them, are of cardinal importance in the process of economic growth and social change. "It is not enough that knowledge should grow; it should also be diffused, and applied in practice."[38] Whereas sociological research into the adoption and diffusion of innovations has so far concentrated on demonstrating the processes involved, the development of increasingly refined methods of analysis may provide a basis for predicting the rate, pattern, and consequences of technological change.

A few exploratory studies in this area have attempted prediction using sociometric or multiple correlation techniques. A reasonable degree of success may be achieved in predicting the adoption pattern within a group of farmers, on the basis of their previous behavior; prediction over several groups may be more difficult. Nationally, the pace of an innovation's diffusion may be forecast fairly accurately, given a knowledge of its characteristics and the early response to it, although the regional variations in its diffusion may be more difficult to predict. International comparisons of an innovation's fate are considerably more difficult since the cultural differences involved introduce numerable variables which are unique to particular countries. Very few cross-cultural studies in adoption and diffusion research, which are essential preliminaries to international comparisons, have so far been undertaken. The consequences of technological change are even more elusive since most of an innovation's direct and side repercussions, particularly those of a sociological nature, can rarely be foreseen.[39]

38 W. Arthur Lewis, *The Theory of Economic Growth* (London: George Allen & Unwin, Ltd., 1955), pp. 177 and 191.

39 *Ibid.* and Rogers, *Diffusion of Innovations, op. cit.*

Just as the nature of adoption and diffusion research is interdisciplinary, so its findings are of relevance in a variety of fields. Among the major "users" of the results of investigations by rural sociologists into the adoption and diffusion of farming innovations may be included agricultural economists, advisory agencies, and their officers, and commercial organizations marketing agricultural requirements In the past the interest of agricultural economists in farming changes and adjustments has too often ignored the non-economic aspects of agriculture. The "human factor" has frequently been mentioned but rarely included as a variable in empirical studies. A major problem facing all advisory officers and salesmen is to narrow the time lag between the appearance of farming innovations and their adoption and widespread use. In this context a knowledge of the factors and processes involved—those personal and sociological characteristics of their farming clientele which inhibit or stimulate change, the function of the various media of communication at various points in the adoption process, and the nature of the diffusion process—is of crucial importance. It should also be recognized that technological change, especially if its pace is accelerating, is usually accompanied by social tension and conflict as old customs, traditions, and values have to be cast aside. The adoption and diffusion of appropriate social organizations and individual patterns of behavior are essential complements to technological progress. In the final resort the conservative attitude among farmers toward organizational and behavioral change is, to quote Mr. Tristam Beresford, "the chief reason why our agricultural revolution has not gone further and faster than it has."[40]

[40] J. T. Beresford, "Thoughts on the Agricultural Revolution," *National Provincial Bank Rev.*, XLVIII (November, 1959), p. 4.

DIFFUSION OF TECHNOLOGICAL CHANGE

Once a technological innovation has been introduced by a firm, how long does it take other firms in the industry to adopt the innovation? What factors determine the speed with which these firms imitate the innovator? The importance of these and related questions has long been recognized in discussions of technological change. It is unfortunate that so few attempts have been made to answer them and that we know so little about the mechanisms governing the rate at which new techniques are adopted by industry.

To help answer these and related questions, an intensive study of the acceptance process has been carried out by Edwin Mansfield, Associate Professor of Economics at Carnegie Institute of Technology, in partial fulfillment of a contract with the Office of Special Studies, National Science Foundation.[1] This paper comprises a non-technical summary of some of the findings.

The purpose of this study is twofold: (1) to determine how rapidly the diffusion process was effected for a small group of important innovations; and (2) to construct and test theories that will explain differences in the rates of diffusion. Data were collected concerning the rates at which major firms adopted the innovations. The same data were used to test the theories and to determine the effects of various factors on the rates of diffusion.

Rates of Diffusion

Twelve important innovations in four major industries were selected for study. The four industries (bituminous coal industry, iron and steel industry, brewing industry, and railroad industry) were chosen because representative firms were accessible for purposes of consultation and data collection in the Pittsburgh area. Only firms exceeding a predetermined size were included in the study due to the difficulty of obtaining adequate data from small firms, many of which had not been able to utilize the innovations when they were first introduced. Descriptions of the four major industries will be found in the *Technical Notes* at the end of this bulletin, together with sources of Mansfield's data. Necessary information was obtained in part from published materials, in part directly from the firms.

Innovations were chosen on the basis of their outstanding importance and the availability of data regarding their diffusion throughout the four major industries. Essentially the same firms were included for one innovation as for another, so the data are quite comparable in this respect. The twelve innovations included in the study

Originally published by the National Science Foundation, Washington, D.C., in *Reviews of Data on Research and Development,* No. 31 (October, 1961).

[1] Mr. Mansfield accepts full responsibility for the statements and conclusions contained herein, which do not necessarily represent those of the National Science Foundation. See also Edwin Mansfield, "Technical Change and the Rate of Imitation," *Econometrica,* XXIX (October, 1961), 741–66. Other studies of the acceptance process by Mansfield are "The Speed of Response of Firms to New Techniques," *Quarterly Journal of Economics* (May, 1963) and "Intrafirm Rates of Diffusion of an Innovation," *Review of Economics and Statistics* (November, 1963).

were: shuttle car, trackless mobile loader, and continuous mining machine (in the bituminous coal industry); by-product coke oven, continuous wide-strip mill, and continuous annealing (in the iron and steel industry); pallet-loading machine, tin container, and high-speed bottle filler (in the brewing industry); and diesel locomotive, centralized traffic control, and car retarders (in the railroad industry).

All twelve innovations, with the exception of the tin container, were types of heavy equipment whose use resulted in substantial reductions in production costs.[2] The earliest, the by-product coke oven, was introduced before 1900; the most recent, the high-speed bottle filler, was introduced well after the end of World War II. In all cases, the bulk of the development work was carried out by equipment manufacturers rather than by the firms themselves, and the diffusion process was not impeded by patent restrictions.

Mansfield plots the proportion of major firms adopting each innovation (in per cent) against time (in years) to measure the rate of diffusion. Results are shown in Chart 1. The earliest date shown for each innovation is the year in which a firm first introduced the innovation, regardless of the scale on which it did so. Some objections to this procedure will be removed when it is considered that the innovations had to be introduced on a fairly large scale to be effective at all.[3]

Chart 1 indicates that the diffusion of a new technique is a fairly slow process. Measured from the date of first commercial application, it took 20 years or more for all the major firms to install centralized traffic control, car retarders, by-product coke ovens, and the continuous annealing process. In only three instances—the pallet-loading machine, the tin container, and the continuous mining machine—was the time period 10 years or less.

Chart 1 also shows that there are very marked differences among the rates of diffusion. For example, almost 15 years elapsed before 50 per cent of the major pig-iron producers had adopted the by-product coke oven. On the other hand, half the major coal producers were using the continuous mining machine within 3 years of its introduction into the industry.

Principal Factors Influencing Rates of Diffusion

What factors explain the fact that one innovation spreads relatively quickly, whereas another in the same industry takes so long to become generally used? Mansfield formulates a theory to explain this fact, basing it on the following four hypotheses. Each of these hypotheses involves a factor that might reasonably be expected to enhance the probability that a non-user of an innovation, in any particular year, will have become a user by the following year. Obviously any factor that enhances this probability also increases the rate of diffusion. These hypotheses are:

As the number of firms in an industry adopting an innovation increases, the probability of its adoption by a non-user increases.[4]—As experience and information regarding an innovation accumulate, the element of risk associated with its introduction grows less. Competitive pressures mount, and "bandwagon" effects occur. In cases where the profitability of an innovation is difficult to assess, the mere fact that

[2] Actually, continuous annealing was often no cheaper than previous processes, but it was required to meet customer requirements.

[3] The only alternative would have been to use the date when a firm first produced a specific percentage of its output with the new technique. In most cases such data had not been published and could not be obtained from the firms. Note that we are interested here only in the rate of diffusion among firms, not in the over-all rate at which a new technique replaced an older one. "Intrafirm Rates of Diffusion . . . ," *op. cit.*, deals with the latter phase.

[4] This is not necessarily true for innovations such as an entirely new product line, whose profitability may decrease with imitation. Mansfield is concerned here, however, only with innovations in processes and techniques, and there is no evidence to show that the profitability of any of the twelve innovations decreased with widespread use.

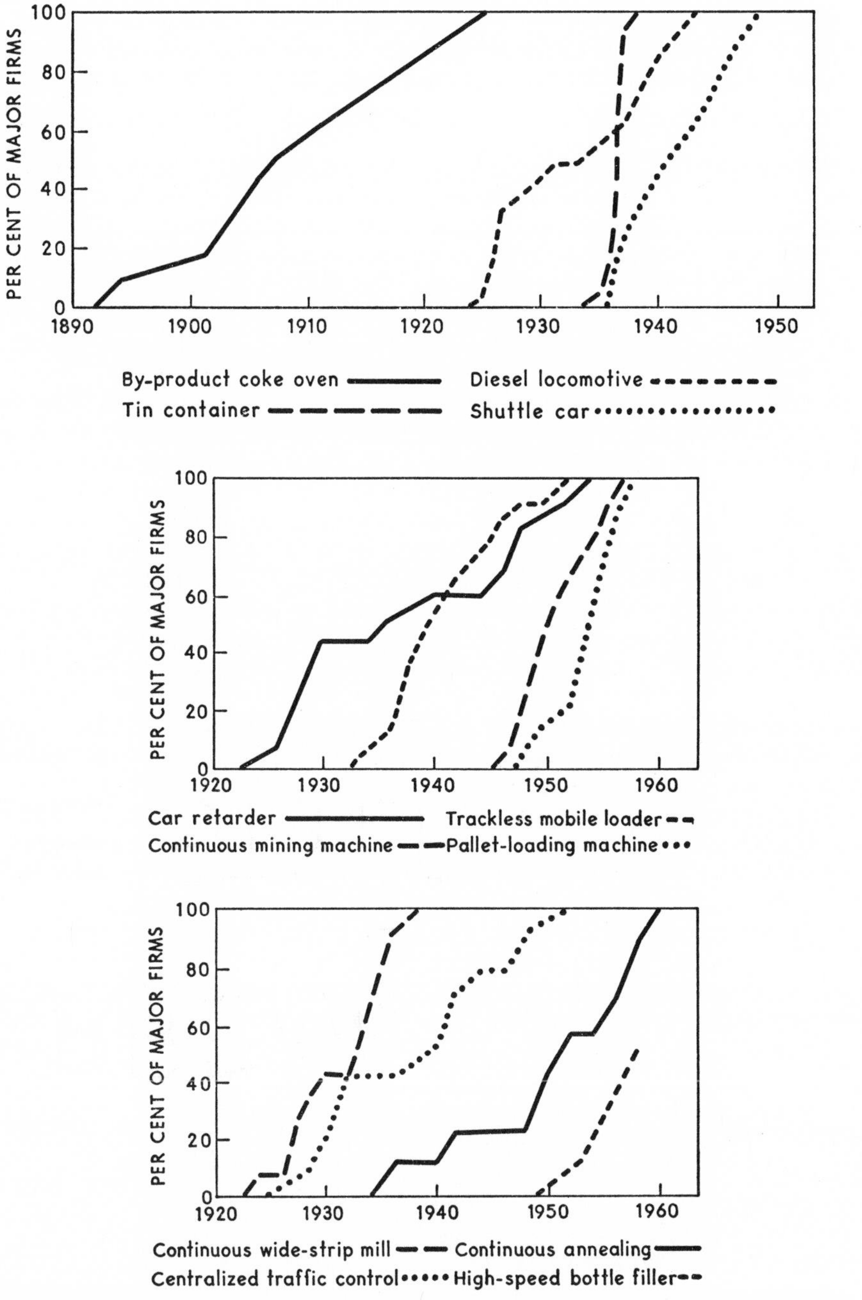

CHART 1.—Introduction of twelve technological innovations in four major industries, 1890–1958[a]

[a] Based on data for 2-year periods, with the exception of the by-product coke oven (6-year periods) and tin container (6-month periods). Zero is arbitrarily set at 2 years prior to date of initial data used in the charts.

Source: See *Technical Notes* at the end of this paper.

a large proportion of a firm's competitors has adopted the innovation may prompt the firm to consider its adoption all the more seriously. Both the interviews with executives in the four major industries[5] and the data presented in Chart 1 indicate that this is the case.

The expected profitability of an innovation influences the probability of its adoption.—The more profitable the investment in an innovation promises to be, relative to other available investments, the greater will be the probability that a firm's estimate of its potential profitability will compensate for the risks involved in its installation. In other words, it will seem to be worthwhile to install the new technique as soon as possible, rather than to wait for further proof of its profitability. Both the interviews and the few other studies that have been made regarding rates of diffusion[6] suggest that this is so.

For equally profitable innovations, the probability of adoption tends to be smaller for innovations requiring relatively large investments.—It is to be expected that firms will be more cautious before committing themselves to large, expensive projects and that they will have more difficulty in financing such projects. This is often an important factor, according to the interviews.

The probability of adoption of an innovation is dependent on the industry in which the innovation is introduced. For equally profitable innovations requiring the same investment, the rate of adoption in one industry might be higher than in another because (*a*) firms in that industry are more inclined to experiment and take risks, (*b*) the industry's markets are more keenly competitive, and (*c*) the industry is healthier financially. Observation suggests that such differences between one industry and another may have a significant effect on rates of diffusion.

If these hypotheses are correct, and if some subsidiary assumptions hold, Mansfield shows that β, a particular measure of the rate of diffusion, will be linearly related to the profitability of the innovation and the size of the investment required (the intercept of the linear equation differing among industries). The rather complicated theoretical argument underlying this and the conditions under which it holds must be omitted here because of its highly mathematical nature.[7]

Rather than define β explicitly, we provide in Chart 2 the values of β corresponding to various intervals between the time when a few firms (20 per cent of those considered) had introduced the innovation and the time when most firms (80 per cent) had done so. This chart indicates the rate of diffusion implied by any particular value of β. (Actually, the chart shows the theoretical relationships between β and this time interval, assuming that the model holds. An examination of the data for the twelve innovations shows that this relationship holds in fact as well as in theory.)

To test the theory and to see how it can be used in explaining the observed differences among the rates of diffusion, Mansfield computed the values of β for the twelve innovations and determined if they were in fact linearly related to the variables discussed above. The results seem to indicate that they were. Chart 3 compares the actual values of β for the twelve innovations with those computed from the formula

$$\beta = \begin{Bmatrix} -.57 \\ -.50 \\ -.29 \\ -.59 \end{Bmatrix} + .53P - .033S,$$

in which the figures in the brackets pertain to the bituminous coal industry, the iron and steel industry, the brewing industry,

[5] Information on the interviews carried out by Mansfield, including the positions of the officials interviewed, is given in *Technical Notes*.

[6] E.g., Z. Griliches, "Hybrid Corn: An Exploration in the Economics of Technological Change," *Econometrica,* XXV (October, 1957), 501–22.

[7] See Mansfield, "Technical Change and the Rate of Imitation," *op. cit.*, for the mathematical argument.

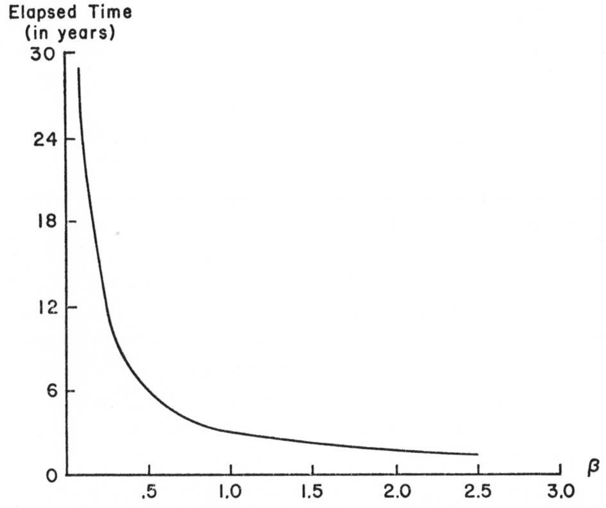

CHART 2.—Relationship between β[a] and the number of years elapsed from the time 20 per cent of major firms had introduced the innovation to the time when 80 per cent had done so.

a A particular measure of the rates of diffusion (see text).

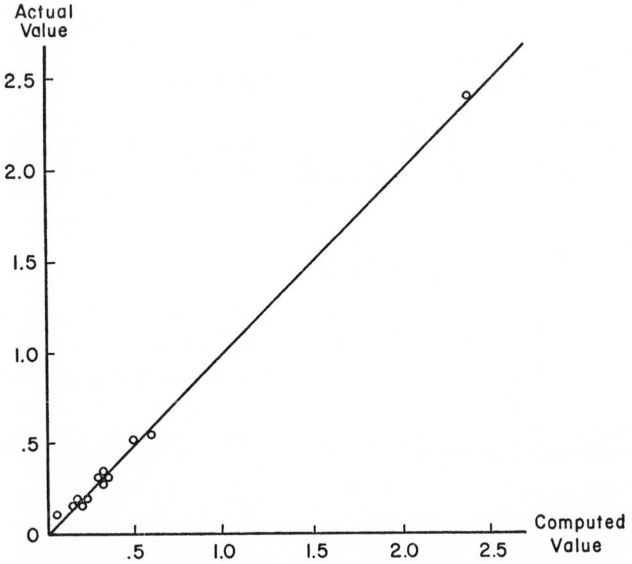

CHART 3.—Comparison of actual and computed[a] values of β for twelve innovations

a Computed from the equation given in the text. Difference in values is measured by the vertical distance from the circle to the line; the line represents perfect correspondence.

and the railroad industry, respectively. P is a measure of the relative profitability of an innovation, and S is a measure of the size of the investment.[8]

It appears that this theory explains almost all the observed variation in the rates of diffusion. As shown in Chart 3, the theoretical relationship between β, on the one hand, and P and S, on the other, seems to hold very well. Moreover, although there are too few data to warrant any conclusive statement, the interindustry differences seem roughly consistent with the hypothesis that rates of diffusion are higher in the more competitive industries.

Other Factors Influencing Rates of Diffusion

There are additional factors that may have an important influence on rates of diffusion, and their inclusion in this analysis may help to explain variations in the adoption rate of innovations. It is also possible that the effects of the factors already considered may be due in part to these additional factors. Mansfield investigates the possible influence of three other factors on the probability that a non-user of an innovation will have become a user within a reasonable period of time. These are as follows:

If an innovation displaces very durable equipment, the probability of its adoption is lessened.—Even if rational economic calculations indicate that replacement is profitable, a firm may be reluctant to scrap equipment that is not fully written off and is capable of serving for many years to come.[9] When this factor is included in the analysis, there is some apparent tendency for rates of diffusion to be lower in cases where an innovation required the replacement of very durable equipment. However, the effect is *not* statistically significant.[10]

The probability of adoption will be higher in firms that are expanding at a relatively rapid rate.—Once a firm is convinced of the superiority of an innovation, it will be introduced in new plants built to accommodate the growth of the market. If there is little or no expansion in a firm, installation of an innovation often must wait until the firm is ready to replace existing equipment. When this factor is considered in the analysis, there is an apparent tendency for the rate of diffusion to be higher in industries whose output is increasing at a very rapid rate, but the effect is *not* statistically significant.

All other factors being equal, the probability of the adoption of an innovation increases with time.—This hypothesis (i.e., the later the date of introduction, the higher the rate of diffusion) has been advanced by economists on numerous occasions. Presumably the reasons for such a trend would be the development of improved communication channels, more sophisticated methods for determining the time at which equipment should be replaced, and more favorable attitudes toward technological change. If the date at which an innovation is introduced in an industry is included as another variable in the analysis, results indicate that, while there is some tendency for rates of diffusion to increase as the date increases, the effect is *not* statistically significant.

Consideration of these three additional factors in the analysis does not lead to a significantly better explanation, in the statistical sense, of observed differences in β. They can be expected to have some effect on the rates of diffusion, however, and the apparent effects are in the expected direction. But data on more innovations will be required before one can be reasonably sure

[8] P = average payout period to justify investments (during the relevant period) divided by average payout period for investment in the innovation divided by average total assets (from *Moody's*) for the relevant period. The figures in the formula are least-square estimates.

[9] Durability is based on the number of years a piece of equipment was in use before replacement (prior to the appearance of the innovation in the industry).

[10] If the probability is greater than 1 in 20 that an observed effect is due to chance, the factor is considered not statistically significant.

of the quantitative effect of these factors. Moreover, there was no evidence that the observed effects of the four factors considered in the previous section were due, in any statistically significant sense, to the operation of the three factors considered here.

Limitations

In evaluating these results, the limitation of the data, methods, and scope of the investigation must be taken into account. Before concluding, Mansfield points out the following limitations:

First, there is the matter of scope. Although the scope of this investigation far exceeds that of the few studies previously conducted, it nonetheless is limited to twelve innovations in four industries. While the four industries vary in regard to such respects as market structure, size of firm, and type of customer, they can hardly be viewed as a cross section of American industry. None is a relatively young industry with a rapidly changing technology. Furthermore, the innovations considered are all important innovations, requiring fairly large investments, and their diffusion was not impeded by patents.[11] Minor improvements requiring small outlays were not included. To check and extend these results, similar studies should be carried out for other industries and other types of innovations.

Second, the data were not always as precise as could be desired. For example, it was necessary to obtain much of the data regarding the profitability of an innovation from questionnaires and interviews. Although the information was checked against information obtained from suppliers of equipment, trade journals, etc., the estimates are fairly rough. Estimates of the minimum rate of return required to justify investments are in the same category.

Third, the data measure rates of diffusion among large firms only. As already noted, only firms exceeding a predetermined size were included. Moreover, the rate of diffusion considered was the rate of diffusion among firms, not the rate at which a new technique displaces an old one or the rate at which investment in a new technique increases. These related topics are taken up in other parts of Mansfield's over-all study, but they could not be dealt with here.

Fourth, various factors not considered undoubtedly exerted an influence on the rates of diffusion. For example, changes over a period of time in the profitability of introducing the innovation, due to improvements, the business cycle, etc., are not included.[12] Sales and promotional efforts by producers of the equipment and the perceived risks assumed by firms in introducing the innovations are likewise excluded. Although no way was found to measure these variables, further research may help to solve this problem and to disclose the effects of these and other factors on rates of diffusion.

Conclusions

With these limitations in mind, Mansfield draws four principal conclusions from this study:

1. The diffusion of a new technique is often a fairly slow process. With a few exceptions, it took 10 years or more for all the major firms in an industry to introduce the innovations.

2. The rate of diffusion tends to be higher for more profitable innovations and for those requiring relatively small investments. The rate of diffusion also differs among industries.

3. The theory based on the four hypotheses listed above accounts for almost all observed variations among rates of diffusion.

4. There is an apparent tendency for the

[11] The tin container may be regarded as a somewhat different type of innovation from the others. If it is excluded from the analysis, however, the results are much the same.

[12] Mansfield also finds that the phase of the business cycle, during which an innovation was first introduced, has no statistically significant effect on its rate of diffusion.

rate of diffusion to be higher when the innovation does not replace very durable equipment, when an industry's output is growing rapidly, and when the date of an innovation's introduction into an industry is taken into consideration (i.e., the later the date, the higher the rate of diffusion). None of these apparent tendencies, however, was found to produce a statistically significant effect.

Technical Notes

BITUMINOUS COAL INDUSTRY

Practically all firms producing over 4 million tons of coal in 1956 (according to the *Keystone Coal Buyers Manual*) were included. A few firms that did strip mining predominantly were excluded in the case of the continuous mining machine, and a few had to be excluded in the case of the shuttle car and trackless mobile loader because they would not provide the necessary data. About 16 firms were included in each case.

The date when each firm first introduced these types of equipment was usually obtained from questionnaires filled out by the firms but, in the case of the continuous mining machine, data for two firms that did not reply were derived from the *Keystone Coal Buyers Manual.*

The payout periods for each type of equipment and those required for investments, as well as data regarding the size of the investment required and the durability of old equipment, were obtained from the questionnaires and interviews. The interviews were with two vice presidents of coal firms, several executives of firms manufacturing the equipment, employees of the Bureau of Mines, and representatives of an independent coal research organization. The data on growth of output were annual growth rates for bituminous coal production during 1934–51 (trackless mobile loaders), 1937–51 (shuttle car), and 1947–56 (continuous mining machine).

IRON AND STEEL INDUSTRY

For the continuous wide-strip mill, all firms having more than 140,000 tons of sheet capacity in 1926 were included; for the by-product coke oven, all firms with over 200,000 tons of pig iron capacity in 1901 were included; and for continuous annealing of tin plate, the nine major producers of tin plate in 1935 were included. A few of these firms merged or went out of business before installing the strip mill and coke oven, and there was no choice but to exclude them. About twelve firms were included for each innovation.

The date when each firm first installed a continuous wide-strip mill was taken from *The Modern Strip Mill* (Association of Iron and Steel Engineers, 1941). Similar data for the coke oven were obtained from various editions of the *Directory of Iron and Steel Works* of the American Iron and Steel Institute and issues of the *Iron Trade Review* and *Iron Age.* The date when each firm installed continuous annealing lines was obtained from correspondence with the firms.

The estimates of the payout periods, the size of the investment required, and the durability of replaced equipment came from correspondence with the firms and from interviews. The interviews were with major officials of three steel firms, the president and research manager of a firm that builds strip mills, officials of a firm that builds coke ovens, and representatives of a relevant engineering association and of a trade journal. The data on growth of output were annual industry growth rates and were for sheets during 1926–37 (strip mill), pig iron during 1900–25 (coke oven), and tin plate during 1939–56 (continuous annealing).

BREWING INDUSTRY

An attempt was made to include all breweries with more than $1 million in assets in 1934 (according to the *Thomas Register*), but several would not provide the necessary data, and it could not be obtained elsewhere. About twenty firms were included.

The date when a firm first installed each type of equipment was usually taken from a questionnaire, but in a few cases it was provided by manufacturers of the equipment or obtained from articles in the *Brewers' Journal.*

The payout periods for each innovation and those required for investments, as well as the size of the necessary investment and the durability of equipment that was replaced, were obtained from the questionnaires and interviews. The interviews were with a number of officials in two breweries and sales executives of two can companies. The data on growth of output were annual growth rates for American beer production during 1935–37 (tin containers), 1948–57 (pallet loading machine), and 1951–57 (high-speed bottle filler).

RAILROAD INDUSTRY

For centralized traffic control, all Class I line-haul roads with over 5 billion freight-ton miles in 1925 were included. For the diesel locomotives and car retarders, essentially the same firms were included. (The Norfolk and Western, a rather special case, was replaced by the New Haven and Lehigh Valley in the case of the diesel locomotive. Some important switching roads were substituted in the case of car retarders, an innovation in switching techniques.) An entire system is treated here as one firm; about twenty-five such firms were included in each case.

The date when a firm first installed centralized traffic control was usually derived from a questionnaire filled out by the firm. For those that did not reply, estimates by K. Healy, "Regularization of Capital Investment in Railroads," *Regularization of Business Investment* (Princeton, 1954), were used. The date when each firm first installed diesel locomotives was determined from various editions of the Interstate Commerce Commission's *Statistics of Railways*. The date when each firm first installed car retarders was taken from various issues of *Railway Age*.

For centralized traffic control and car retarders, some of the payout periods were estimates published in the *Signal Section, Proceedings of Association of American Railroads*, and the rest were obtained from questionnaires filled out by the firms. All estimates of the payout period for the diesel locomotive and the payout period required for investment were obtained from questionnaires. Information regarding the size of the investment required and the durability of old equipment was obtained primarily from interviews with eight officials of six railroads (ranging from president to chief engineer) and three officials of a signal manufacturing firm and a locomotive manufacturing firm. The data on growth of output were annual growth rates for total freight-ton miles during 1925–41 (diesel locomotive) and 1925–54 (centralized traffic control and car retarders).

It is true, that what is settled by custom, though it be not good, yet, at least, it is fit; and those things which have long gone together, are, as it were, confederate within themselves; whereas new things piece not so well; but, though they help by their utility, yet they trouble by their inconformity; besides, they are like strangers, more admired and less favored.

Francis Bacon, "Of Innovations," *The Essays* (9th ed.; Boston: Little Brown and Co., 1876), p. 138.

GILBERT F. WHITE

NEEDED RESEARCH

It is desirable to know for any resource the present and potential quantity available and the significant factors regarding its use, the state of technical knowledge, and the possibility of substitutions. Any such estimates, no matter how routine the physical analysis, require a series of estimates as to the social conditions in which resources may be produced and used. Often these assumptions go unstated and unchallenged. The natural scientist may assume cost and demand conditions that need not apply, and the social scientist may ignore technical solutions that are theoretically possible but not perfected. In the interest of wise policy-making, it is important to feed back to the natural scientists facts regarding the probable effects upon society of alternative means of approach and for natural scientists in turn to specify the limits and conditions of different uses.

An example will illustrate the point. An increasing problem in years to come will be the provision of an adequate and inexpensive source of protein in the human diet. One promising solution might be harvesting the sea, thus making use of the rich proteins of fish and other marine life. This might become economically feasible, but, attractive as it sounds, unless it is known how societies would react to such a solution and what the institutional and other impacts of this would be, any attempt along this line would be greatly handicapped, even to the point of waste and uselessness. Human preferences and habit may block certain actions or indicate need for technical modifications in processing or transport. If the social sciences are not presently advanced enough to predict such impacts and reactions, then at least they should be able to suggest relevant research to obtain that knowledge.

Thus, natural-resources studies must be recognized as having many interdependencies, requiring coordination between basic and applied research, between research, policy formulation, and action, and, in the final analysis, between resource development and the over-all welfare of society. Research on discovery, use, and development of resources encounters numerous obstacles created by the wide variety of specialists studying resource problems and in the institutional frameworks within which resource analyses are undertaken, as well as in differences in the analyses and value considerations applied to such problems. Much of the needed social science involves complex analysis within a multi-disciplinary framework in the absence of institutional structures conducive to such work.

Unless close and constant collaboration between the natural and social sciences, theoretical and applied, prevails, it is unlikely that research, dealing with the interrelations of man and society with the equally intricate systems operating in nature, so vitally needed, can be accomplished. In a broad sense, any research that deepens understanding of man and his activities has potential value for wise resource manage-

• Gilbert F. White is Professor of Geography, University of Chicago.

Reprinted from G. F. White, *Social and Economic Aspects of Natural Resources,* A Report to the Comm. on Natural Resources (Washington: NAS–NRC, 1962), pp. 34–49, with the permission of the author.

ment. Any advance in the theory of economic growth or of acculturation or political organization is a gain for resource management. A decision as to a new public policy or the introduction of a new technology for resource exploitation may draw heavily on knowledge of human preferences, response to risk, community organization, and legal and political mechanisms. In a more strict sense, resource management rests upon the understanding of several aspects of the processes of resource use and upon the kind of analysis that is made. Research is needed both to illuminate these processes and to improve methods of making choices.

Strengthened research efforts are urgently needed in several directions. These are presented in segmented fashion here only for convenience. A large degree of interdependence exists among them, and the order of presentation does not imply order of priority.

Human Aspects of Technological Change

In the face of increasing stress upon technology in solving resource needs, it must be recognized that there are major gaps in knowledge as to how technology is diffused in a society and as to the ways in which technical advances interact with other sectors of human life. Why is it that some innovations, such as hybrid corn, spread rapidly and widely while some others are very slow in finding acceptance? What conditions foster or block technological change? What dislocations are caused by adopting new resource-use techniques, and how can these be shaped to serve society's welfare?

Studies leading to more accurate projection and measurement of the economic implications of technological change are needed in each field of resource use. Work along these lines would facilitate the inclusion of such variables in economic models used for planning and development. The results will never be definitive (the larger the realm of technology, the less predictable is the future), but they can help point out the major certainties and uncertainties. This effort would involve research into the interdependencies among industry, trade, technology, and social phenomena, tending to create the forces of development in an attempt to determine what the coefficients of linkage are. It is possible that input-output tables could be developed for use in assessing the significance of resources and projecting the opportunities for development. Research on technological change affecting land use is an example. Depending upon its character, technological development may increase or decrease the demand for land as such, and it also may increase or decrease the effective supply of land.

Increased attention should be given to the factors that stimulate, motivate, and guide technological development; to the predictability of its path and its responsiveness to economic motivation; and to exploration of the variety of social settings in which technological development has occurred. This would throw light on the means of communicating technical knowledge and the conditions necessary for successful transference of known techniques. A particularly interesting question is the relation of personal aspirations of achievement to the economic productivity of a society.

Changing demand for land and changing technology of land use alike point to heroic and widespread adjustments in land use in the United States. Human considerations offer major obstacles to making adjustments in use. Farmers wish to stay in farming; workers in exhausted mining areas are reluctant to move. The factors that account for their reactions must be understood in seeking sound, humane solutions.

Assessing Efficiency of Resource Use

The means of estimating the economic efficiency of different methods of resource use still are far from satisfactory, yet it is necessary to make frequent judgments as to which programs or policies will best serve national ends. Heavy emphasis should be given to the development of techniques of economic evaluation and their application to the natural-resource field. For example, it is important to find more accurate ways of measuring the value of water in irrigation or industry, the value of land for recreation, or of wetlands for wildlife preservation. Likewise, better means should be devised to measure the full social costs of a given resource use.

Associated with this kind of research are problems of determining the exact effect of a reduced rate of population increase on economic growth and resource use, the realistic regional groupings over the world for maintaining comparative advantages and yielding growth essential for sustaining the level of hope to maintain a stable society, and the different paths that economic growth can follow.

Methods of benefit-cost analysis probably are more precise in the planning of river basin development than in any other area of resource use, but they are still very rough. They would gain from refinement so as to take account of aims that do not lend themselves to simple market pricing and to deal more realistically with the social costs of alternative investments. The cheapest investment is not always the best, nor is the one yielding the largest returns necessarily the most efficient use of available capital. Detailed methods of measuring efficiency deserve study in other fields.

In both energy and mineral production, findings on the demand and supply side should be compared to determine at what costs future energy requirements can be met, and through what pattern of dependence on the different energy commodities and on foreign and domestic sources. As a companion effort, it is necessary to develop strategic indicators of future directions, as indicated by current trends. A substantial research effort to define appropriate cost indicators and to indicate feasible methods of current data collection is called for.

Application of principles such as those of re-cycling and re-use of resources may result in a major increase in the efficiency of resource use. Many policy problems that involve the efficiency with which a system is functioning, as in production of minerals, should be analyzed by methods entirely different from those appropriate to the study of trends in demand and cost. Study is needed in order to deal intelligently with proposals for restriction of use (or perhaps for preventing so-called inferior uses, as some designate the burning of natural gas for raising steam in thermal power plants) that may be made in the future. The usefulness of such efforts is not only for the policy-maker, although some policy problems do require this information, but also for the investor.

The whole process by which economic activities locate in particular places requires examination. Geographic analysis suggests that there is some order to the clustering in certain patterns of cities and to the localization of industrial production. As this is recognized, it gives a clue to planning viable new schemes for resource development.

Over the business cycle, the demand and the price for many products fluctuate considerably. Such changes are not uniform among different countries, however, and result in changes in foreign-trade patterns. One problem that requires more or less continuous attention is a factual one: for which commodities are domestic costs rising more rapidly than elsewhere and what are the differences? A second range of problems involves the low-income countries that are specializing in mineral production. We need to know more about the effects of fluctuations in the demand for mineral products and in their prices on the investment programs of these countries, and we need to know how these effects themselves vary under different methods of adjusting to fluctuations in the demands and prices of mineral products.

Impacts of Resource Management

Closely related to assessment of resource use is understanding of the full impacts of programs for resource management. Typically, we have been more ready as a nation to give detailed attention to planning a new project than to finding out what happened after it was completed. Thus, we still do not have adequate measures of the consequences to the nation as well as the value of investment in water and land improvement in the Tennessee Valley. These consequences are difficult to trace and do not show on any ordinary balance sheet, but means can be found to trace them.

This information is invaluable in planning new resource-management programs for particular areas. It may be especially significant where a change in resource use may trigger widespread transformations in a local economy, or where it is expected to do so.

Within our own country, changes in the cost of producing mineral, forest, and agricultural products become evident in the decline of certain producing areas and in the rise of others. Problems associated with the decline of a producing area are serious, and we know very little about the best ways of handling them. We need to study these problems for at least two reasons. First, it is possible that an unjust share of the social costs of contracting production is being borne by a few people who, for whatever the reason, are unable to escape the unfortunate consequences. Second, the existence of low production and stranded population has important effects on the nation's trade and foreign policy.

These problems are not the same in different parts of the country for the same resource products. We need clearer ideas of these differences and of the seriousness of the problem in each of the different regions of the country and in each of the industries involved. In this context, the effectiveness of governmental measures to improve the lot of depressed areas should be evaluated. Is the problem of declining mineral production in some areas any different from the more general problem of depressed areas? If such differences are present, are different measures called for or not? Which measures offer lasting improvement and which are merely palliatives?

Decision-making in Its Institutional Setting

It has become almost commonplace to ascribe the low efficiency of some resource uses or the failure to adopt new technologies to the intransigeance of people or their institutions. The obstinacy of farmers, the inflexibility of water law, the narrow interests of legislators, and the selfishness of exploiting business firms are some of the frequent and easy explanations for the very complex process by which decisions as to resource management are made at many levels in our society. The true explanations are much less simple and are often difficult to discern. The whole process of decision-making as it goes on in the market place and in government agencies deserves much more searching examination, and this must be done with an eye to the practical guides which public attitudes, laws, and political organization give to particular actions in handling resources.

We recognize general ways in which land tenure may limit a farmer's acceptance of new production techniques, or in which water law doctrine may impede greater efficiency in water use, or in which tax policies may influence mineral exploration; but we know little of the precise influence of such institutions on management decisions. Public prejudices may block a new water-supply scheme, but we are ignorant as to how the attitude has been formed and what events might alter it.

Most decisions about natural resources must be made in the face of uncertainty as to aspects of supply and demand, and yet there has been almost no searching study of how people deal with uncertainty.

New investigations should range over different levels of decisions and different kinds of social institutions, but they would center on understanding how the final choices are arrived at.

Studies concerning the decision-making process should include coordination of needed research in the fundamental, perhaps highly specialized, fields and their application. For example, certain aspects of physiological psychology, the border areas among communication theory, information theory, biological nerve networks, and semantics should be studied along with geographic, economic, and political characteristics.

Studies in this field should also cover effects of different types of administrative organizations in setting goals and promoting growth. On a broader scale they should canvass procedures for effective international collaboration in resource development, taking into consideration the obligations and unique capacities of the multilateral agencies, advanced donor nations, and the emerging countries.

Research on both urban and rural land institutions seems to fall into two general categories: examination and appraisal of existing institutions, and invention or proposal of new ones. Research may properly be directed to an examination and appraisal of all kinds of land institutions such as tenure, taxation, and community organization. For what purposes were they created? How do they operate and what are their effects? What changes in economic values do they create, and who gains and who loses by their application? These and many related questions could appropriately be asked concerning the wide range of institutions affecting land use of all kinds. The actual operation of the various institutions in specific resource situations should be appraised as far as possible. But the conditions of the future will demand either new land institutions or material modification of present ones. Research into different situations can suggest some of the attributes of desirable new institutions, including attributes that are likely to receive public acceptance.

A large variety of public programs now affects land use, and a still larger variety of programs of probably greater effect seems likely for the future. Research programs could well be directed toward appraisal of present public programs affecting land and could help to guide new policy. Policy research is perhaps even more delicate than institutional research, yet it is equally or more important. As in the case of research on land institutions, research on public programs affecting land might fall into two major categories: examination and appraisal of present programs and policy, and model building for new policy and programs.

Numerous other instances might be cited in which studies of institutions and policies would advance resource management. For example, despite the many years devoted to the matter by the U.S. Federal Power Commission, there is not yet a satisfactory formula for regulating field prices of natural gas. At issue in the FPC determinations, and requiring research, is the problem of how to achieve a formula which (*a*) is administratively feasible; (*b*) will treat fairly the equity considerations of all parties involved; and (*c*) will not inhibit investment in the future exploration and development of natural-gas resources.

In the petroleum industry, a program of mandatory import quotas has been in effect for several years, but the policy situation is far from being stable. The difficulty that requires research is the conflict between (*a*) obtaining "energy" raw materials at the lowest cost; and (*b*) the national security aspects of relying on low-cost foreign sources of supply which may be unreliable. The difficulty is further complicated by the social problems of the depressed coal mining areas and the social costs involved in permitting the continued decline of mining in these areas. How can conflicting policy objectives be reconciled? What are the characteristics of an optimum policy solution with due regard to the objectives sought and the costs incurred in achieving these objectives?

The minerals industries in the United States enjoy special tax treatment, primarily with respect to the percentage depletion allowance, but also in regard to other aspects of taxation. These tax provisions are under constant attack in various quarters and are vigorously defended by the industries. Study is needed on (*a*) the underlying justification for the special tax provision; (*b*) the effects they produce on investment, price, and profitability in the industries concerned; (*c*) the costs to the government of these provisions; and (*d*) alternative ways of achieving the effects that preferential tax treatment is supposed to achieve. Study is also needed on (*a*) the merits and effects of inter-commodity differences in tax treatment, and (*b*) international differences in the tax treatment of minerals.

The production of oil and gas is subject to severe controls in many states. These regulations are justified as a means of preventing the waste of oil and gas resources. They are, on the other hand, attacked as a legalized means for controlling production and, thereby, price. Objective research is needed on the exact features of the present state systems for oil and gas control to estimate the benefits yielded by the different control systems and the resulting extra costs of producing crude oil.

One of the means of adjustment of gradually rising costs of mineral products is searching for and utilizing so-called hidden mineral deposits. From the social sciences standpoint we may question the efficacy of existing institutions, notably mining law, in encouraging the search for and exploitation of such deposits even when it becomes easier to find and utilize them from a physical point of view. It is not too early to begin thinking intensively about the possibilities of altering institutional arrangements in such a way as to improve the effectiveness of this process.

With respect to the reliance of low-income countries on natural-resources production there is great need to explore the question of what terms for exploitation of mineral resources are desirable. Research is needed to reveal for both producer and consumer countries the extent to which they are bound together by conditions of economic interdependence from which both sides stand to benefit. Research is also needed on the specific financial, legal, and institutional arrangements that govern the present pattern of investment and trade and on alternatives to the present arrangements in order to find new approaches that will minimize conflict through improved accommodation of different national interests. This would mean, of course, taking into account the possibility of subsequent changes in the expectations initially held by one or both countries concerning the richness of the resource reserve.

Methods of fashioning cooperation among timber producers and federal agencies are undergoing rapid change and deserve careful appraisal.

Supply and Demand Projections

Substantial progress has been made in the decade following the pioneer work of the Paley Commission in disciplined, systematic projections of demand and supply for basic resources and derived products and services. A variety of new statistical and other techniques has been developed with special encouragement from Resources for the Future. Key factors are the march of technology, discovery of new sources of supply, and perfection of substitutes as these may affect the prospects for demand and supply. Long-range projections of this sort should be consistent with the over-all capacity of the economy and increasingly have become a useful tool in the planning of sectors of the economy in private industry as well as government. When done comprehensively over the span of resources they integrate the approaches and findings of different disciplines. This is a complex and tricky operation and deserves improvement.

The time is at hand when government should shoulder the responsibility for making a basic set of systematic resource projections and for regularly revising and improving them. If done properly, this would require continuing inquiry into the effects of new technology and economic conditions and into ways of sharpening the resulting estimates. The more this is done, the more desirable it is to state and present for public examination all of the assumptions and judgments that enter into the calculations, thus promoting public recognition of the variables in the future outlook. In many instances, it will be desirable to present the findings in ranges rather than single estimates. In any event, government projections should be subject to running appraisal by non-government agencies that are free to challenge assumptions and implications.

Perhaps one of the more important corollaries in this effort is delineation of basic data collection necessary for effective resource planning and development. What proportion of the national budget of an advanced nation should properly be devoted to data collection? With respect to the emerging areas of the world, another field requiring investigation is exploration of possible shortcuts in data collection and provision of means to develop such methods fully. Population censuses in areas marked by much land surface and few settlements provide examples of the kinds of problems that demography must solve. Such critical appraisal of data collection would also be of great help in finding and assigning degrees of priority to future research.

Energy deserves high priority. Policy decisions are continually being made on the basis of inadequate information or loose estimates. A joint research effort is warranted to develop new methods, including statistical approaches, for making supply estimates; for improving quantitative estimates of reserves and resources; and for estimating the costs at which these reserves and resources could be made available.

Systems Analysis of Resource Industries

A more comprehensive and difficult task that is closely related to preparing supply and demand estimates is analysis of the full set of technical and social factors affecting the use of resources in a major sector of the economy. The difficulty lies in encompassing a sufficient amount of realistic detail while at the same time providing a sufficiently comprehensive analysis of the industry, its inputs, and its products. Methods of analysis have come into existence in recent years that promise to produce the desired understanding of the way in which resource requirements develop and grow. Borrowing from the disciplines of mathematics, physical sciences, economics, and social sciences, and capitalizing on the development of the modern computer, they have produced greatly improved understanding in a variety of fields as diverse as military tactics, retailing, automobile traffic systems, mining, and inventory management. Such methods, generally referred to as systems analysis, have now reached a sufficiently advanced point to justify some hope that they could be used to define and measure the critical places in the whole intricate system by which resources contribute to meeting human needs. If these were to be applied with discretion, they could serve to give the nation a balanced understanding of the resources outlook and to isolate the lines of research or policy changes which promise the greatest returns to the nation.

This approach may be illustrated by some examples in water use, beef production, and coal production.

Water supply and management: an example of systems research needs in renewable resources.—When increasing numbers of people must rely on a largely unchanging resource base, such as water, they must strive for the most effective use of the resource they have. There is great need for techniques that will allow simultaneous evaluation of a large number of combinations of alternative uses, operating procedures, and structures for the development and management of water resources in a specific area. Such techniques have the capacity to use much greater amounts of technical and economical information on the several uses of water resoures than are presently available. Thus, research should be undertaken simultaneously on the technological relationships such as the application of different quantities of water to different crops or to different industrial products and on the prices, costs, and benefits of the many purposes of water-resource development. Among other studies, this would require additional research on projections, national and regional, of water needs, and on the basic demographic and economic components of these needs.

As example of systems research needs in renewable resources: cattle enterprise.—Cattle and calves produced for meat comprise the largest farm enterprise. They return about $6 billion gross income, of which about $4 billion is value added over feed cost. They consume one-third of the total feed used. They use about 600 million acres of pasture and range. They consume feed grains and harvested forage from about 50 million acres of crop land. Thus about one-third of the land surface of the United States is used for production of cattle and calves.

We have no surplus of cattle and calves; indeed we import about a billion pounds of beef, including the live equivalent, each year. It is estimated that we will need a 45 per cent increase in production of cattle and calves to meet the requirement for our increased population by 1980.

Since beef cattle are the major users of our publicly owned range lands, compatibility of increased production from this source with the multiple use of these resources for timber, water, recreation, and wildlife habitat poses one major problem of national concern as well as of acute individual concern to about 30,000 cattle ranchers and their communities.

Shift from cultivated crops to grass for beef production may require only about one-quarter as many farm people per acre used as does crop production. Value of land so shifted may be affected as will be the trading communities in the area.

Beef-cattle feeding is moving into mass production units involving thousands of animals each. These feed lots tend to provide a continuous flow of cattle of uniform quality specified by mass distributors. That quality involves possible genetic modifications as well as feeding management which may be required to meet consumer preference for tender, lean beef.

Beef is a prestige meat, and its consumption tends to vary with expendable income. The people of the United States generally prefer beef to lamb. Why? May this preference change? Similar considerations apply to leather, which has been competing with plastics, but the use of which fluctuates greatly with technological and sociological developments.

The difficulties in evaluating the cattle enterprise are further compounded by the fluctuation and uncertainties of the dairy industry. The trend toward reduced consumption of animal fats in favor of vegetable oils, with consequent search for substitute uses of dairy products (for instance, increased emphasis on protein content or diversion of fat to industrial uses), may serve as an example of the instability of the system, which will affect and reciprocally be affected by socioeconomic developments, including controls of farm prices and marketing. Increased tendencies to raise the efficiency of beef production by localization and concentration will meet with limitations inherent in biologic systems, which militate against excessive crowding because of hazards of epidemics, reduced growth and reproduction rates, and the like.

In summary, aggregate analysis of the beef industry should include research on costs, benefits, soil, climate, markets, organization and integration of the enterprise, institutions and laws, population shifts, technology, human factors, capital, credit, agronomy, husbandry, diseases and pests, physiology, and their interactions. The complexity of those interactions is suggested by Figure 1.

Similar studies are needed for all major commodity groups in the renewable-resources field as well as for the aggregate of them. The renewable resources of food, fiber, and forest products in turn should be subjected to aggregative analysis. The major problem of assuring our capacity to meet future needs calls for canvass of geographic shifts, shifts among commodity groups, and transfers of people and capital within, from, and into agriculture. It involves the interrelationship of farm and forest enterprises with associated nonfarm enterprises, and with enterprises serving farm and forest or processing and distributing farm and forest products.

Coal production: an example of systems research needs in the non-renewable resources.—Study of the economic structure of the mining, smelting, and refining industries should have early priority. Ordinarily, studies of economic structure in the mining industries have been made from a national

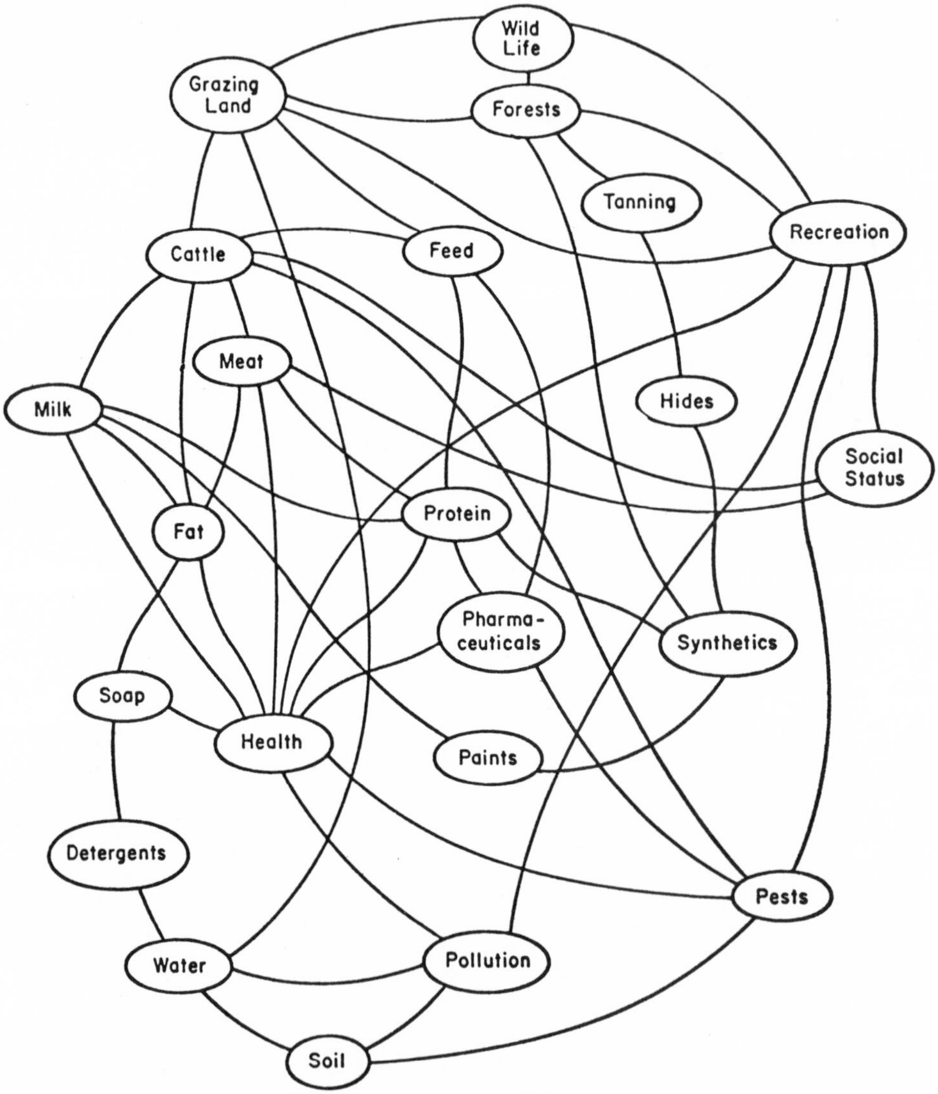

FIG. 1.—Illustration of the interrelationship existing among the renewable resources in the beef industry

point of view or been confined to a single nation simply because data are more easily available for the nation in which the study is made than for the world as a whole. A discerning systems analysis of the coal industry would seek to relate possible effects of new organization and technology in coal mining upon world energy supply situations on the one hand and upon the welfare of United States communities on the other. It might well reveal promising lines for physical research looking to different production methods and uses.

Investigations of this character should be pressed at an early time and continued so that periodic examinations of the natural-resources situation could be made public. The probable effects of political developments reflected in cutting down overseas sources of supply or in changing market situations or in altered productivity of emerging countries, would need to be considered along with a canvass of domestic implications. In the course of such analysis, it is likely that important new research needs would be identified and that new strategies of resource development would emerge.

CHAPTER 8

THE CHOICE OF ALTERNATIVES

Flood control, navigation, and electric power were the three water-related purposes for which Congress established the Tennessee Valley Authority in 1933.[1] Almost 30 years later, in initiating a major river basin study,[2] eleven functions were recognized, plus "such other . . . purposes not herein enumerated."[3] This growth from three to "eleven-plus" of the types of benefits from river basin development is symptomatic of two trends in our society. One is the increase in "needs" generated by a growing and increasingly affluent population. The second is the potential to meet these needs provided by rapid technological advance in control over the environment, substitution and complementarity of resources, and the development of greater economies of scale.

On both counts, the range of choice open to decision-makers at all levels is widening rapidly. Both the problems and the opportunities are multiplying. There has always been a need for choice in resource use, but the choice has never been as wide and as complex as it is now. There is need for new knowledge, for a new calculus to guide our choice, or for new choice mechanisms that can weigh the relative importance of problems and employ the full range of solutions offered by an impressive technology.

The types of choices that need to be made are reviewed by a committee of the National Academy of Sciences–National Research Council. These include the choice of objectives, the choice of use and scale of development, and the sharing of benefits and costs. In a broad sense, there is need to express a fundamental time preference for a present or future orientation, and in the particular this takes the form of choice of interest rate.

The need to express time preference may be universal. The Soviet Union does not formally recognize the need or place of an interest rate in a socialist society. Yet in facing the real choice between hydro and thermal power, Khrushchev expresses in anecdotal style, the need for discounting future benefits to present value.

1 Electric power, the most significant present function of TVA, was actually placed subordinate to navigation and flood control. 49 Stat. 1076 (1935).

2 U.S. Study Commission–Southeast River Basins.

3 72 Stat. 1090 (1958). The U.S. Study Commission–Southeast River Basins was established under P.L. 850, 85th Cong., 2d Sess., Aug. 28, 1958.

Hubert Marshall explores the requirements of a choice process suitable for rational decision-making but finds it frustrated by the realities of the political process. If the present mechanisms are not adequate, what might be done? Marshall advocates the strengthening of the executive. Others have concerned themselves either with improving existing practice or devising new practices. The rapid development of benefit-cost analysis is an effort of this type and Sewell and his colleagues provide an elementary statement.[4] A more sophisticated relative, by the marriage of engineering and economics, is the application of systems analysis to comprehensive river basin development.[5] A report on recent work is found in the selection by Hufschmidt.

In perspective, resource management problems may be seen to have three components. The first component reflects those aspects that might be ameliorated by the application of improved technology or the development of new technology. Improvements in nuclear reactors or the desalinization process are of this type.[6] The second component reflects aspects of problems amenable to organizational or institutional solution because they stem from inadequacies of human organization. The development of efficient transfers of water rights from agriculture to industry in the West would be such a development.[7] The third component is the most difficult, for these are problems that arise from general conflicts in values and often require mutually exclusive choices. The

[4] The best-known statement of the technique of benefit-cost analysis in the United States is the U.S., Inter-Agency Committee on Water Resources Report, *Proposed Practices for Economic Analysis of River Basin Projects* (Washington: Government Printing Office, 1958), otherwise known as the "Green Book." See also The President's Water Resources Council, *Policies, Standards, and Procedures in the Formulation, Evaluation, and Review of Plans for Use and Development of Water and Related Land Resources,* Sen. Doc. No. 97, 87th Cong., 2d Sess., 1962. See also Maynard M. Hufschmidt (Chairman), John Krutilla, Julius Margolis, Stephen Marglin, *Standards and Criteria for Formulating and Evaluating Federal Water Resources Developments,* Report of Panel of Consultants to the Bureau of the Budget (Washington, 1961).

Studies of the role of benefit-cost analysis will be found in R. N. McKean, *Efficiency in Government through Systems Analysis,* a Rand Corp. Research Study (New York: John Wiley & Sons, 1958); John V. Krutilla and Otto Eckstein, *Multiple Purpose River Development* (Baltimore: Johns Hopkins Press for Resources for the Future, Inc., 1958); Eckstein, *Water-Resource Development,* The Economics of Project Evaluation (Cambridge: Harvard University Press, 1958); Ian Burton, "Investment Choices in Public Resource Development," *The Prospect of Change,* ed. A. Rotstein (Toronto: McGraw-Hill, 1965).

[5] Edward A. Ackerman ("Where Is a Research Frontier," *Annals of the Association of American Geographers,* LIII [1963], 429–40) calls for the wide application of systems analysis to geographic research, and Gilbert F. White (chap. 7) makes a similar plea for research in resource management. The work of the Harvard Water Program reported on in Arthur Maass *et al., Design of Water-Resource Systems* (Cambridge: Harvard University Press, 1962) and in the contribution by Hufschmidt is an outstanding example of this approach in the resource field. For a review of the variety of applications of systems theory to scholarly research, see the yearbooks, commencing with 1956, of the Society for General Systems Research, *General Systems* (Vols. I–VII, Ann Arbor, Michigan).

[6] National Academy of Sciences–National Research Council, Comm. on Natural Resources, *Natural Resources: A Summary Report to the President of the United States,* Pub. 1000 (Washington: NAS–NRC, 1962).

[7] Nathaniel Wollman, *The Value of Water in Alternative Uses* (Albuquerque: University of New Mexico Press, 1962).

continued flooding of the canyons of the Colorado represents one such problem; the storage of water behind a high dam bars forever the scenic enjoyment of the canyons.[8]

Choices are not always mutually exclusive. More often several choices can be made, and the problem becomes one of their relative weighting. Storage for flood control, irrigation, power, and recreation can all be provided by the same dam. But how to decide the proportions for each? Here the selection of objectives necessarily reflects values. Economic efficiency or optimizing is one well-established and highly regarded objective in our society. But any normative objective suffers in translation from theory to practice. Caulfield succinctly points out some of the more serious of these problems. Ciriacy-Wantrup suggests another criterion—the safe minimum standard of conservation that prevents economic irreversibility of resource depletion.

The Ciriacy-Wantrup selection sounds reminiscent of the conservationist views expressed in Part II. This direction is confirmed by the final major selection, provided by Barnett and Morse. In suggesting that our values or criteria for choice should show a concern for the quality of life, they bring back the wheel, full circle, to the Conservation Ethic.

Having examined the Malthusian and Ricardian constructs of scarcity and found them wanting in the light of present experience, Barnett and Morse, nevertheless, share the ethical motivations of many earlier students of resource problems. If they would seek to liberate us from the constraining hypothesis of natural resource scarcity, it is not for blissful enjoyment of a utopian world, free from want. Rather, it is to focus our attention on the effort "to counteract adverse qualitative change (of nature) and take advantage of opportunities to improve the quality of life." In this broadest sense, choice in resource management should involve a love for man, a respect for nature, and a great deal of knowledge.

8 Anthony W. Smith, "A Possession of All Mankind," *National Parks Magazine,* XXXVIII (April, 1964), 2.

NAS–NRC

PROBLEMS IN ACHIEVING SOIL AND WATER CONSERVATION

Many conditions obstruct and compromise the development of measures to achieve soil and water conservation. Research and education are needed to understand and ameliorate these conditions. In this [paper], an attempt is made to identify major problems which are hampering soil and water conservation efforts. Oriented in these problems, research may be undertaken to provide an improved understanding of the problems and to develop alternative means of overcoming them.

Initial problems in soil and water conservation result from confusion as to the nature and meaning of conservation. What are the nation's needs from our resources? What is the role of conservation in satisfying these needs? Are resource conservation programs confused by mixed objectives? What about different viewpoints held by various groups and in different sections of the country? Are these viewpoints reconcilable? What are the conflicts between major land and water uses? What about conflicts in choice of particular practices? Are uncertainties as to consequences of particular physial and biological reactions holding up remedial action? What about scale of development? Should we have large or small dams? What are the basic conflicts between present and future uses of, and investments in, resources? How important is the interest rate? Are adequate steps being taken to protect the public interest in projects with substantial public investments? How should benefits and costs of conservation developments be shared (1) between public and private interests, (2) between individuals, (3) between private individuals and groups, and (4) between units of government?

These are the kinds of questions that pose serious problems in proceeding with conservation of our natural resources. Answers to these questions await research and the use of research through education, legislation, and other means.

Confusion regarding conservation objectives occurs for several reasons. Differences in the concept of the meaning of conservation, lack of appreciation or knowledge of the long-term national needs, confused objectives in programs, and differing viewpoints from various segments of society all contribute to this confusion. In many instances, physical data upon which sound conservation objectives may be planned and developed are incomplete or totally lacking.

A definition of conservation by which research and public policy may be oriented . . . [is needed]. [We propose that] production practices [be] defined as causing changes in output at a particular level of resource productivity. Conservation . . . [may be] defined in terms of increasing potential productivity either through preventing or decreasing irreversible declines in productivity or through investments to further increase productivity. Important in the application of this concept is the nature of the resources under consideration. Flow

Reprinted from National Academy of Science–National Research Council, *Principles of Resource Conservation Policy,* Pub. No. 885 (Washington: NAS–NRC, 1961), pp. 25–42.

resources differ from fund resources. Storable and renewable features of flow and fund resouces condition the application of the implementing principles of this concept.

Frequently, the effects of the two methods—production practices and conservation investments—overlap in terms of accomplishment. Whether conservation investments are economical at a particular time and place may be determined, in part, by applying [known or accepted] principles. . . . The difficulties of applying . . . principles are outlined [below] . . . along with possible remedies.

The concept of conservation presented here is dynamic in the sense that it maintains a freedom of choice in the use of our natural resources. It helps prevent use that causes irreversible changes, as when intensive cropping of sloping soils without water-control practices causes [major] gullies. The economic problem is to so direct our public and private conservation efforts that the maximum results socially desired may be achieved.

Because this concept is complex, it is not surprising that different segments of the general public disagree about the meaning of conservation. Some want to "lock up" resources and prevent economic use. Preservation of natural or wilderness conditions in certain areas appeals to many large groups. Others favor unlimited development of resources without considering present and future needs or alternative costs.

The Congress and state legislative bodies in various laws have given many broad definitions of conservation. Resource conservation is usually considered to be a protection and promotion of "the general welfare." Much of the apparent confusion in national objectives arises from these differences in the concept of conservation.

In a dynamic concept of conservation, long-run national needs and long-run production potentials are important factors that have a changing relationship over time. These long-run needs and potentials are vague, hard to foresee, and subject to considerable controversy. If the country is to have a sound conservation policy, it must have the best possible estimates of trends in population growth, economic activity, food preferences, technological change, yields, imports and exports, and all the various competing uses for land and water resources.

Population growth is a major factor in determining total requirements for agricultural resources. Population projections vary widely, depending on assumptions used in the calculations. One projection for the year 2010 ranges from a low of 300 million to a high of 440 million, with a median projection of 370 million. The past trend and the medium population projections are shown in Table 1. If the population should more than double in the next 50 years, as indicated in the medium projection, the nation could expect similar increases in the requirements for food and fiber. While population growth is the most important factor in estimating future requirements, others enter into the determinaton, such as the composition of diets and the development of substitutes and synthetics.

TABLE 1

POPULATION, SPECIFIED YEARS, 1929–58, AND PROJECTIONS FOR SPECIFIED YEARS 1965–2010

Year	Population (millions)
Actual:	
1929	122
1950	152
1955	165
1956	168
1957	171
1958	174
1959	177
1960	180
Projections:	
1965	195
1975	230
1980	248
2010	370

Source: U.S., Department of Commerce. Projections developed by U.S., Department of Commerce, Office of Business Economics.

Change in technology is one of the chief

factors affecting the productivity of our land and water resources. It is also one of the most difficult factors to evaluate and to estimate for the future. Changes in technology affect the production, marketing, and utilization of agricultural products.

TABLE 2

LAND UTILIZATION, 1950, AND PROJECTED UTILIZATION FOR 2010

Item	1950 (million acres)	2010 (million acres)
Cropland used		
Chiefly for crops.........	409	415
Rotation pasture (periodically used for cultivated crops)................	69	160
Total cropland..........	478	575
Pasture and grazing land[a]....	951	795
Special uses[b]...............	105	190
Miscellaneous other land[c]....	370	340[d]
Total................	1,904	1,900[e]

Source: *A 50-Year Look Ahead at U.S. Agriculture* (Washington: U.S., Dept. Agr., 1959).

[a] Includes forest and woodland grazed. Excludes cropland used only for pasture. From 1950 to 1954, it is estimated that about 50 per cent, or 300 to 320 million acres, of the forest and woodland areas were used to some extent for grazing.

[b] Special uses include urban and town areas, highway and railroad rights-of-way, airports, parks, wildlife refuges, national defense areas, flood control areas, farmsteads, and farm lanes. In 1953, 26 million acres of forest and woodland were reserved for parks and other special uses. By 2010, it is calculated that these reservations will increase to 40 million acres.

[c] Other land includes forest and woodland not grazed, marshes, bare rock areas, sand dunes, deserts, and miscellaneous unaccounted for areas. In 1953, the total forest and woodland acreage was estimated to be 648 million acres, including 26 million acres in reserved areas, such as parks, wildlife refuges, and other special use areas. Net reductions in forest by 2010 through clearing for cropland, pasture, and special uses are calculated at 30 million acres, with additional reservations for special uses at 14 million acres, thus leaving a total forest and woodland acreage of about 478 million acres, exclusive of 40 million acres reserved for special uses.

[d] Not a projected requirement.

[e] The decrease of 4 million acres from 1950 to 2010 represents an estimate of a decrease in the land area from flooding caused by the building of additional reservoirs.

Marked technological changes in any of these steps in the economic process can change the use and productivity of land and water resources. In terms of future needs, technological development can be substituted for land development.

Exports and imports and other international matters are factors in appraising future requirements. Increased imports can reduce land and water requirements, while increased exports and international commitments can add materially to requirements and drains on our natural resources.

Non-agricultural uses of land and water will become increasingly important as population increases. Not only do the total requirements for urban, industrial, transportation, and recreation increase as our population increases, but the per capita water uses will also increase as the economy becomes more industrialized. Non-agricultural land uses as projected for the future are shown in Table 2.

Uncertainties of the future regarding population growth, national security in time of possible war, and other possible international crises suggest that the nation's resources need to become sufficiently productive to meet such unpredictable contingencies.

It is not surprising that there are many different interpretations of these factors, and, consequently, different attitudes toward long-run conservation policy. Long-run trends probably are not reflected in today's market place economy and individual firms cannot be expected to assume the risk involved in taking them into account. Krutilla and Eckstein have pointed out, "When we accept an interest rate determined by the preferences of the present generation—as we do in our quantitative model—we implicitly accept the time preference of the present generation of decision-makers. Children and unborn generations have no vote in the market place."[1] It is the responsibility of the general public through its federal, state, and other levels of government, and through private and quasi-public groups to plan for the future of society. Governments find it difficult to invest in basic research, conservation, and development for the future while struggling with pressing problems of the present. But today's future becomes tomorrow's present,

[1] John V. Krutilla and Otto Eckstein, *Multiple Purpose River Development* (Baltimore: Johns Hopkins Press for Resources for the Future, Inc., 1958).

and today's research is essential in solving tomorrow's problems.

Mixed Objectives in Programs

Government programs often have multiple purposes and sometimes are justified on the basis of the most popular of these purposes. Conservation benefits may be incidental to programs for price support or income distribution, or there may be conflicts among the various purposes. In many cases, nothing would be gained from either the public or individual viewpoint by separating conservation from other programs.

When programs are applied to farms they may complement each other. For example, an income-increasing program may enable a farmer to adopt the needed conservation practices that would not otherwise be possible. Assistance in shifting to livestock production may enable a farmer to make use of the grass needed to achieve soil conservation.

Perhaps the greatest cause of confusion is the different viewpoints in different sectors of the economy. Individual landowners, local groups, states, regions, and national groups approach problems differently. This is partly due to economic reasons arising from differences in the incidence of benefits and costs as between different groups.

Evaluation principles are based on a general public viewpoint which is supposed to represent a summarization of all other viewpoints. . . . But there is a question as to whether an evaluation procedure for the national public also fits the individual or various local groups. One test of this is to consider international problems. People from different countries place different values on the same things. As we consider the long-run aspects of conservation of natural resources, these non-market values become of prime importance. Thus, we might visualize evaluation from the individual viewpoint, the national viewpoint, the United Nations viewpoint, and all modifications in between.

The items to be included in the evaluation would vary, and in many instances the non-market values placed on these items would also vary with the different viewpoints. In fact, markets may operate within institutional barriers that result in different market prices for the same commodity in different localities, states, or countries. These differences in value concepts account for many of the differences between interest groups in our economy. These differences are further complicated by different time preferences between various parts of society.

Conflicts between Major Land and Water Uses

There are many situations in which conflicts arise between competing land and water uses. Some conflicts have their origin in the confusion of objectives and confusion of wants. Some also grow out of conflicts of interest between persons or groups who have rather clear ideas as to what they want, but whose wants and objectives disagree. There is a limited area of land and a limited volume of water in the United States. Nationally, we are not seriously short of either at present, but locally and a particular times competition for land and water may be intense. An increase in population, larger per capita incomes, and other factors also increase the demand for land and water. When such a rising demand confronts a fixed area of land and a fixed volume of water, conflict is inevitable.

In such situations, there is a general underemphasis on the importance of nonagricultural users of land and water. The history of the United States partly explains this, since agriculture used to be the source of income and the way of life for a majority of our people. In the Census of Agriculture more and better data are available on agricultural use of land and water than on other uses. Land-Grant Colleges and Universities with their research and extension programs, the U.S. Department of Agriculture, farm organizations, and other agencies bring a number and variety of professional opinions to bear upon agricultural land and water use.

The current concern over conversion of land from rural to urban uses is an example of this underemphasis upon non-agricultural uses. The United States has become an urban nation. Sixty-four per cent of the people live in cities and towns. Sixty-eight per cent of all jobs are in urban areas, and 74 per cent of all tangible wealth is physically located there. Most or all the net gain in population in the future and most of the net investment of capital will take place within towns and cities. The area of all towns and cities is now less than 1 per cent of the total area, but the area may double in the next 30 years or so.[2] Growth of cities creates new problems of land and water use and conservation. Paving of streets and parking lots and construction of other large impervious surfaces are creating an "asphalt desert" with serious implications for water conservation and control. Disposal of urban wastes creates serious pollution problems, and the wholesale reworking of the land surface is creating serious erosion problems. Many of these urban created problems fall on agriculture. But the whole problem has often been approached as though the city were anti-agricultural, and to be treated as such.

A somewhat similar set of conflicts arises from uses of land for recreation. The extent of specialized recreation has increased greatly in the past. More people, higher per capita incomes, more leisure, and greater mobility of population will mean a greatly increased demand in the future for outdoor recreation areas. This will create a demand for more land and water for this purpose. Parks and other specialized outdoor recreation areas often foster conservation in the narrow sense of the preservation of full plant cover and the absence of soil erosion, but they also conflict with agriculture, forestry, mining, range, and other uses.

Reclamation of arid land by irrigation is another example of conflict for use of scarce water resources and of the overemphasis upon agriculture as a resource user. In the West, there is a strong emotional and political drive to "develop" water supplies. Next to urban and domestic use of water, irrigation is usually in a preferred position in Western water law. Federal irrigation has been supported by subsidies of various kinds, yet the value of recent developments can be questioned. If subsidized expansion of agricultural output were needed—and there is little evidence that it is needed now or likely to be in the immediate future—there is still no evidence that irrigation of arid lands is the most efficient means of stimulating agricultural output. However, the drive to develop local areas and regions remains strong.

Much confusion has been brought to agricultural resource conservation because it has been used as a screen for farm income support. It appears that "conservation" payments to farmers have been used as a means of increasing their incomes. Participating farmers have been required to "earn" these payments by following various farm practices, but it is frequently charged that some of the practices required were those which farmers would have found profitable to follow in any case. Many of the practices have worked more toward increasing agricultural output than toward establishing bona fide conservation. In recent years, these programs have had a larger component of conservation than they originally contained. Effort has been made to base the program and the payment schedule more nearly upon the actual conservation needs of an area.

Side by side with these "payment" programs and often confused with them in the public mind have been the "technical" assistance programs to farmers and ranchers in evaluating the conservation needs of their land and in selecting and laying out conservation and land-use practices. Tech-

[2] However, only 20 per cent of the land area is cultivated, and cities frequently expand into cultivated land. If the urban expansion were entirely on cropland, the reduction in cropland would be 5 per cent rather than 1 per cent.

nical assistance programs may also result in adoption of practices that work more toward increasing output than toward conservation. These programs work primarily through local soil conservation districts established in counties, watersheds, or other small governmental units.

Thus "conservation" has been a key word in the titles of payment and support programs as well as technical assistance programs. This has been a major factor in creating confusion in the minds of farmers and of the general public as to the meaning, content, and purpose of "conservation."

Another factor leading to conflict between land and water uses has been the attempt, in most public and private programs, to solve the problems of land and water use within the boundaries of existing farms. The size and boundaries of farms often constitute obstacles to conservation systems. To the farmer and his family, they often have a fixity that seems permanent. If land and water conservation problems must be solved within the boundaries of an existing farm, measures may be adopted that would be undesirable if more land and water resources were available to the farmer or if several farms were planned at once. Public agencies find it easier at any time to work with farmers and farms as they find them. But this may contribute to a division of land and water resources into small and artificial units. Inadequate resources of families are likely to impede the working out of sound general programs—sound even from the long-run view of the farmers involved. Current highway and urban development tend to intensify these problems of size and shape of farms.

Conflicts in Practices and Uncertainties of Physical Changes and Biological Reactions

Basic to the present discussion is the concept that decisions concerning resource use should be influenced by three principal factors: (1) a well-defined and well-understood objective, goal, or benefit which is sought, (2) a scheme for comparing and judging various alternative courses of action, or put another way, a theory of relationships, and (3) possession of facts, knowledge, and data of sufficient scope and accuracy to allow for testing of the theory or framework of comparative analysis. . . .

Inadequacy of information has handicapped those attempting to solve conflicts in soil and water conservation programs. There also may be as yet undiscovered but harmful effects of apparently beneficial practices.

An example of unknown or unforeseen results of some practices is the effect of water storage on evapo-transpiration and the consequent effect on downstream water yield. Farm ponds or stock-water ponds have been widely recommended by farm planners for improving grazing distribution (better forage utilization), for gully control, sediment retention, and, in some instances, for recreation. At least, for purposes of stock water, small reservoirs built without gates and with a minimum of spillway have been both popular and successful. Unfortunately, little sound data are available to fully determine the net effect of such a system of impounding structures on the total downstream water yield from a basin.

One area, the Cheyenne Basin in Wyoming, where good data on number of stock ponds are available, contains several thousand impounding structures, averaging one pond per square mile. Studies of evaporations and seepage losses from sample reservoirs estimate that these reservoirs might reduce the potential supply to the downstream channel by as much as 30 per cent. There are insufficient data, however, to permit a positive statement as to what the channel loss of this water would have been had it been permitted to enter the channel directly. Thus, there is no definite information as to the net effect of the reservoir system upon total yield at the mouth of the basin. This study exemplifies the need for more comprehensive research concerning the effects of watershed treatment on water yield of a river basin.

In areas where channel losses may be very high, such as in Arizona or New Mexico, the net effect of storage structures might be to hold water that otherwise would be lost by seepage and evaporation in the channel.

In considering such examples, one must consider the on-site use of the stored water; i.e., is it in the common interest for the water to be used at the storage site rather than along the channel or at the basin mouth?

Small impounding structures to trap sediment and inhibit gully growth have been used for decades in the United States. Other than small dams with vegetated spillways, probably the most widely used engineering measure for sediment control in the semiarid West is the water spreader. A spreader is usually comprised of a series of en-echelon low dikes oriented on contour across a valley. Water passes around and between the dikes at non-eroding velocities and infiltrates into the valley alluvium rather than running over the surface to a stream.

In the first decade of soil conservation activity, a wide assortment of different kinds of small structures was built to control gullies. These included wirebound rock sausages, check dams of stone, wood or brush, brush spreaders, gully-head drops, earthen dams, and others. After all this effort, current evidence reveals that many of the earlier structures have failed and that vegetation has not taken over the temporarily stabilized channel. In some instances, though the immediate cause of structure failure becomes obvious, the basic trends, directions, and rates of gully changes leading to failures were obscure or unknown. The signal lack of progress in gully control and gully healing argues strongly for more study of both the mechanics of erosion and gully development and the effect of various treatment measures on erosion under different field conditions. It must also be recognized that in many instances there is sufficient knowledge of how to control the gully, but the related land has such a low productivity that the cost of treatment is prohibitive under a conventional cost-benefit analysis.

To reiterate, the evaluation of alternative plans for resource development or conservation depends in large part on sufficient knowledge of the physical or biological effects of the alternatives. The few examples mentioned merely indicate that in many circumstances, the effects of various practices cannot be forecast. Even when observed, the effects can be only partially understood.

Problems in sound land and water use also arise from a different but closely related source, e.g., conflicting results of various nominally accepted practices. For example, various watershed treatments designed primarily for erosion control also have a resultant effect on downstream water yield. Increased vegetative cover on an area tends to decrease erosion. A correlative effect is that increased density of cover usually increases infiltration. However, the additional water infiltrated may be consumed under many conditions by evapotranspiration and consequently less water would be supplied to the channel downstream.

So many are the combinations of plant association, vegetal density, soil type, precipitation, surface slope, and other pertinent factors that it is not possible to estimate, except crudely, the quantitative effect of any change in culture or management practice on water yield downstream. But it is generally true that vegetation manipulations that tend to reduce soil movement tend to decrease water yield downstream. A practice desirable for saving soil may reduce stream flow and a conflict of purposes is created. Data on these effects are meager.

As another example, building roads into large tracts of forest is often necessary for fire control. But the roads themselves encourage a larger recreational use of the same land and thus tend to enhance the probability of fire.

The example of fire control in forest land

brings out another conflict with possible detrimental effects. Elimination of fire is thought to encourage the excessive growth of brush and understory, which competes with the original vegetation and is usually less valuable. For example, fire control in Western parkland and in the Texas grasslands is considered to be partly responsible for the encroachment of useless brush species on areas formerly grass covered. Experiments in controlled burning have demonstrated that fire can be successfully utilized for establishing, controlling, and improving the balance of shrubs and trees in certain types of woodlands.

Conflicts in Scale of Development

An excellent example of a public controversy that was essentially a matter of scale of development involved the Hells Canyon power development. One proposal was for a single high dam to be built by the federal government. Another proposal was for three relatively low dams to be built by a private power company. The controversy was generally discussed as a public versus private power fight, but this missed the major issue. The three low dams would provide a total of less than 800,000 kilowatts of generating capacity at the dam. This total could be developed in stages. The dams would also make possible some additional power production at downstream sites because of stream regulation.

In contrast, the single large dam would provide 900,000 kilowatts at the site (plus a large amount possible at downstream sites). However, this total would necessarily be largely in a single unit if the costs of the dam were to be met by early power development. The private power company has a present system capacity of less than 400,000 kilowatts. Thus, even one of the three lower dams would represent a major addition to this company. The company does not have the financial capacity to build the one large dam nor can its trade territory absorb the power.

The two methods of developing the site also have implications for downstream projects. If publicly developed, the value of additional power made possible by better stream flow regulation could be captured by additional generators at present federal dams. If privately developed, under present legal arrangements, the private power company could not be compensated for the values it would create by stream regulation. Thus, what appeared popularly as a public versus private power fight had important meaning as a scale of development issue. Of course, other issues may be involved. The big dam might flood scenic areas highly regarded by recreation groups. Intangibles in the form of scenic values and displacement of people may constitute offsetting factors to economies of scale measured in terms of kilowatt output.

Another aspect of the reservoir problem is that evaporation losses from reservoir surfaces depend on the ratio of exposed water surface area to total storage volume for any set of climatic conditions. As a given amount of storage is subdivided into successively larger numbers of small reservoirs, the evaporation loss increases. The scale of development, then, influences evaporation losses. Because the flood control effect decreases rapidly with distance downstream from the dam, more or less complete flood damage prevention requires both small upstream and large downstream dams. Full development of both types will reduce flood damage but will increase water loss by evaporation.

Some conflicts in land and water use are, or can be, resolved in the private market place. This is done by buying and selling or renting of land. The fact that these conflicts can be resolved does not necessarily mean that the resulting action is in the public interest. The transfer of land from agricultural to urban use is decided by purchase and subdivision of the land, yet there is evidence that in many situations this process is wasteful. All markets operate under institutional limitations imposed by government, for example, the right to make and enforce contracts. When agricultural land is subdivided for urban use, the decisions made are based upon the transportation and other services provided by one unit of government or another, by zoning and subdivision restrictions, or by credit and other aids.

The institutional framework may or may not be well-designed to meet the public interest. If not, the remedy may lie in amendment of the institutional framework rather than in criticism of the operations of the market. But some conflicts in land and water use are settled in legislative halls and administrative offices, with little or no reference to market place decisions. The area of land and water reserved for recreation and the capital invested in it, for instance, is determined primarily by a political rather than by an economic process. Most water-development projects today are publicly financed and carried out, and the process of decision-making for them is largely political with only modest consideration given to economic forces.

Present versus Future Conflicts

A major difference in social and individual viewpoints on conservation arises from differences in time preference. As pointed out earlier, this is not the only difference but it is an important one. As one author puts it, "Society, which is expected to exist in perpetuity, should have a different standard of values as between the present and the future from that of the individual, whose appraisal of the future is governed by his own short span of life, and perhaps for a shadowy allowance for a generation or two of his descendants."[3]

This difference is reflected in the interest rate and in other ways not related to the interest rate. Individuals usually discount future returns according to the amount of capital they can borrow or by alternative rates of return on investments. However, society may establish values that are not reflected in the economic negotiations of individual firms as measured by market prices.

Society may also exploit resources for defense or war without regard for their market values or for future needs.

To the extent that public decisions in resource conservation are guided by economic analysis, the interest rate selected is of considerable importance.

Some programs use two rates—a private rate and a lower public rate. Others use a public rate for all calculations. Some use a low public rate for costs and compare this with private costs at a high private rate.

The question arises as to whether the interest rate should be used to express the public concern with some phases of resource conservation. For example, should the prevention of irreversible damage be favored over other conservation activities such as development for future use? Should gully control in good farming areas be favored over irrigation projects that will not be needed for many years?

One way of answering these questions is to vary the public interest rate according to criteria measuring the irreversibility of the use. Thus, a low rate might be used to reflect the public interest in preventing gullies, erosion, permanent pollution of water supplies, or loss of irreplaceable species of plants or animals. The purpose would be to maintain as much freedom of choice as possible in future management of land and water resources. If society used such an interest rate, it should include a calculation of a comparison with an interest rate derived by opportunity cost.[4] Such an opportunity cost rate might be around 6 per cent, as suggested by Krutilla and Eckstein. If the public rate were 2 per cent for preventing gullies, the difference of 4 per cent would be a public cost of maintaining this resource for future use.

Failure To Protect Public Interest

Governments may influence the conservation of land and water by use of several basic powers. These are taxation, spending, regulation, and ownership. The spending

[3] Eric Englund, "What Price Conservation," *Land Policy Review,* Vol. III, No. 2 (1940).

[4] Opportunity cost refers to the return that would have been realized had the funds been used otherwise.

power has been used primarily to support research, education, technical assistance, cost-sharing for conservation practices, leasing programs, and direct governmental activities. Regulation has been used only in limited cases for conservation objectives. Taxation has considerable impact on conservation of resources but this is usually incidental to other effects, and it is as likely to be detrimental as it is to enhance conservation. Government ownership is used when it is desired to give resources special protection and management and when multiple uses and long periods of time are involved.

A combination of these powers may be found in many programs. In addition, there is usually a mixture of conservation objectives with other purposes. But there are many programs in which conservation is a major objective. The estimated expenditures in 1959 for programs with conservation objectives are shown in Table 3. Expenditures for programs with conservation

TABLE 3

FEDERAL EXPENDITURES FOR PROGRAMS WITH CONSERVATION OBJECTIVES, 1959

Item	Conservation Objective			
	Budget (millions)	Major	One of Several	Minor
Farm Price Stabilization:				
Price support, surplus disposal, acreage reduction and control	$ 5,386			×
Financing Farm Ownership:				
Farm Credit Administration and Credit Agencies of USDA	251			×
Farm Conservation and Watershed Management:				
Watershed protection and flood prevention, SCS and ACPS conservation activities including Soil Bank and Great Plains Program	514	×		
Research and Other Agricultural Services:				
ARS, FAS, AMS, FCS, and Extension Service	299		×	
Development of Water and Related Land Resources:				
Corps of Engineers, Bureau of Reclamation, Federal Power Programs, management and development of public lands	1,209	×		
Conservation and Development of Forest Resources:				
USDA and USDI, Forest Protection, Management and Administration	194	×		
Conservation and Development of Mineral Resources:				
Mineral exploration, development and conservation of minerals	78	×		
Conservation of Fish and Wildlife Resources:				
International and state fish and game management	69	×		
Recreational Use of Natural Resources:				
Outdoor recreation resources, Review Commission, and National Park Service	97		×	
General Resource Surveys:				
Surveys, investigations, research, and administration	61		×	
Civilian Weather Service:				
Weather Bureau	49			×
Total, Conservation the major objective		$2,064		
Total, Conservation one of several objectives			$457	
Total, Conservation a minor objective				$5,686
Total, U.S. budget	$80,871			

Source: *The Budget of the United States Government for the Fiscal Year Ending June 30, 1960*, Special Analysis L (Washington: U.S. Govt. Print. Off.), pp. 1013–1014.

as a major objective totaled $2,064 million and for those with conservation as one of several objectives totaled $457 million. In contrast, programs with incidental or minor conservation objectives totaled $5,686 million. About 2.5 per cent of the total federal budget was spent on programs with major conservation objectives and another 0.5 per cent on those with conservation as one of several objectives. If expenditures for conservation could be classified according to the definition of conservation used in this report, they would represent a very small per cent of the federal budget.

Comparable data are not available for state-financed activities, but costs would be only a fraction of federal conservation expenditures. While the amount of federal expenditure for conservation is not large when compared with other expenditures, there is an almost complete reliance on federal spending to protect the public interest in conservation of our land and water resources.

Most of the states have authorized soil conservation districts to enact land-use regulations to support conservation and to protect investment of public funds in conservation measures. But in only two states has even limited use been made of this authority. Technical and financial assistance has not been made conditional on local land-use regulations to complement, protect, and maintain conservation measures.

In many states, authority exists that would enable local units of government to use rural zoning to protect the public interest in conservation of resource use. Again, very little use has been made of this authority.

In the Southern Plains, land-use regulations have been used to some extent to prevent and control soil blowing. This action apparently came about because of the critical local problems caused by soil blowing and not because of a plan for a long-run solution to the problem. In the same way, local action for weed control districts and fire protection is more acceptable to local people. Apparently, people will favor limited regulation of their property for direct, tangible local benefits but will not favor land-use regulations for less tangible and deferred conservation benefits.

In those states that follow the appropriation doctrine in allocating water there is usually a provision that water diverted must be put to a beneficial use. This is intended to limit individual water users to reasonable amounts in order to prevent waste and to insure widespread and maximum benefits from water use. In those states following the riparian doctrine there is a concept of reasonable use which is intended to protect other riparian users. As with land use, these concepts are most likely to be enforced when the rights of other local users are directly affected.

Measures to prevent pollution of water and air have not been enacted at the local level when the damages occur to property remote from the source of pollution.

While local interest groups are slow to enact regulations on the use of their land and water resources, they do not hesitate to exert pressure for federal aid for local projects. The incidence of costs and benefits in terms of geographic areas and purposes greatly influences the position taken by interest groups in relation to various lines of public action.

Many more examples could be cited to indicate that a serious problem exists in designing, adopting, and carrying out measures for protecting the public interest in conservation. At present, the nation relies almost exclusively on federal spending without commensurate use of other means available at federal, state, or local levels. Often the federal spending does not achieve long lasting results because landowners have little or no obligation to continue conservation programs. Such obligation and intention as some owners have may be cancelled out by the frequent turnover in landownership.

Sharing Benefits and Costs

Economic evaluation of conservation and improvement measures from a public viewpoint has been concerned with the relationship of benefits and costs with little attention to the incidence of either. The problems of cost-sharing, however, center attention on the distribution of incidence of conservation benefits and costs. Economic efficiency in attainment of public goals is the controlling consideration in evaluation of conservation and improvement, while in cost-sharing the emphasis is on equitable arrangements for distribution of costs in relation to benefits.

Cost-sharing problems arise out of several situations: (1) benefits accrue to different firms or groups in proportions that differ from those in which the costs are shared; (2) benefits accrue over different time periods than costs; (3) secondary and direct benefits and associated and direct costs are variously distributed; and (4) benefits and costs may be hard to identify.

In addition to the problems of allocating costs between purposes and between users or interests are many problems of collections and financing. Often organizational arrangements do not fit the needs either in geographical terms, interest groups, or ability to operate over long periods of time.

Many cost-sharing problems arise from differences among federal laws and between federal and state laws. There has been little progress in achieving uniformity between programs for comparable activities.

The report of the Missouri Basin Survey Commission illustrates the wide differences in actual division of costs between different purposes. Expenditures for some purposes are borne entirely by the federal government, others by non-federal sources. There seems little relation between the incidence of these costs and the incidence of benefits. For example, multipurpose flood control cost is borne entirely by the federal government while multipurpose power cost is borne largely by non-federal sources. Examples of cost-sharing distribution are shown in Table 4.

Changes are needed in federal law and in administrative procedure to bring about more uniformity in allocation of costs among purposes and among project users. Such changes would need to be accompanied by adjustments in state and local institutions in order to relate cost-sharing to the incidence of benefits.

TABLE 4

DIVISION OF COSTS BETWEEN THE FEDERAL GOVERNMENT AND NON-FEDERAL SOURCES FOR DIFFERENT PURPOSES, MISSOURI BASIN[a]

Item	Total Cost of Construction and Operation, Maintenance, and Replacement Borne by:	
	Federal Government (per cent)	Non-federal Sources (per cent)
Municipal and industrial water	0	100
Power	16	84
Agriculture:		
Conservation measures	16	84
Watercourse stabilizing measures	38	62
Irrigation	70	30
Flood control:		
Single purpose units	83	17
Multiple purpose units	100	0
Total flood control	95	5
Recreation	100	0
Fish and wildlife	100	0
Navigation	100	0
Main stem erosion control	100	0
All purposes	58	42

Source: Missouri Basin Survey Commission Report, *Missouri: Land and Water* (Washington: GPO, 1953), p. 105, Table 1.

[a] This study, which was based on data gathered from several agencies, compared the costs borne by the federal government and non-federal sources. Non-federal sources included state and local governments and private individuals. Total cost including construction, operation, and maintenance and replacement was calculated at 2.5 per cent for a 100-year period.

NIKITA KHRUSHCHEV

WHAT IS MORE ADVANTAGEOUS?

Our country has achieved such a high level in the development of our economy, science, and technology that we can embark on and implement in the next 15 to 20 years the task set by the great Lenin: total electrification. This is a great and noble task. It is understandable that all the questions regarding the solution of this task must be well thought out from every angle. To do this, a commission must be set up in which experienced specialists must take part. It is essential to integrate the development of power engineering with the long-term plan for the 15-year development of the national economy which is being worked out by the Gosplan. This plan will really be a program for the building of communism.

Now I would like to make a few observations on this question: Which is the more expedient, to build hydroelectric power stations or thermal power stations? To put the question of which is better, comrades, is the same as arguing which is the best way to eat bread: with or without butter. In my opinion, it would be silly to argue. If there is no butter and little bread, then it is good without butter, but if there are stacks of bread and butter, then it is good with butter. Or let us take another comparison. Let us say that you wrapped up a hydroelectric power station in one bag and a thermal power station in another one for me, the chairman of the Council of Ministers, and said: "There you are, Comrade Khrushchev, take your pick, the hydroelectric or the thermal power station." The cost per kilowatt-hour from the hydroelectric power station is, let us say, half a kopek or a kopek, and from the thermal power station, let us say, five kopeks. I think, comrades, with such a proposal, each of us would give preference to the hydroelectric power station.

I would say: "I choose the station which produces a kilowatt-hour for half a kopek and shelve the thermal station." But that is true when I can choose the one or the other. Yet when you say: "We will give you a cheap hydropower station, Comrade Khrushchev. It will produce a kilowatt-hour of power 6 or ten times more cheaply. But you will get it 5 years later than its thermal counterpart." Then I must do something.

Even a fool can understand that the power produced by a hydroelectric station is cheaper. But the question is what is more advantageous if one takes account of the time it will take to get the power. Will it be advantageous to build the station which will yield power 5 years later? That is worth thinking about, because we can lose 5 years in our competition with capitalist countries.

• Nikita Khrushchev was Premier of the Soviet Union until October, 1964.

From text of a speech by Mr. Khrushchev delivered November 28, 1959, to the All-Union Conference of Power Industry Construction entitled, "The Implementation of Lenin's Ideas on Electrification Is a Sure Road to the Victory of Communism." Reprinted in *Relative Power Resource Development in U.S.S.R. and U.S.A.*, Committee Print No. 2, 86th Cong., 2d Sess., 1960, p. 183.

HUBERT MARSHALL

RATIONAL CHOICE IN WATER RESOURCES PLANNING

Recently we have heard a great deal about the affluence of our society. It is argued that we are too preoccupied with increasing the production of goods and services and that we are starving the public as against the private sector of the economy.[1] Yet whatever conclusions one reaches about the import and consequences of our affluence, the fact remains that now, as always, governmental budgetary decisions are made within a system of constraints. Resources do remain scarce, they must be allocated between the public and private sectors of the economy, and within government they must be used in such a way as to maximize human satisfactions. Perhaps an affluent society can tolerate considerable slippage, but it cannot ignore the question of efficiency.

Given the need for a wise allocation of resources, it follows that rational choice is essential.[2] By rational choice nothing more is meant than behavior that is realistically adapted to its ends. Thus, a decision is rational if the alternative chosen is an appropriate means for reaching a desired end or maximizing a desired value. However one phrases it, the task of rational decision involves (1) the identification of the value or values to be maximized, (2) the listing of alternative courses of action, (3) the determination of the consequences that follow from each of the alternatives, and (4) the comparative evaluation of these sets of consequences in terms of the value or values to be maximized.

This definition of rational choice inevitably raises the question of knowledge. Shall we call a behavior "rational" when it is in error, that is, when the goals sought are not obtained, only because the information on which the choice is based is faulty? When the mental processes of the decision-maker are rational but his knowledge is inadequate or in error, the decision may be called "subjectively rational." A decision is subjectively rational, then, if it maximizes attainment relative to the *actual* knowledge of the subject.

On the other hand, a decision is "objectively rational" if *in fact* it is the correct behavior for maximizing given values in a given situation. In this case, as in the former one, the logical processes are sound, and in addition the knowledge available is sufficiently accurate to permit the correct choice among alternatives. In this discussion, the term "rational decision-making" is used in the sense of objective rationality, and attention will be focused not on the logical processes involved but on the adequacy of the knowledge available to decision-makers. Objective rationality, to be sure, can never be fully achieved because knowledge is never complete. But it remains the goal and the purpose of this inquiry to determine how closely we ap-

• Hubert Marshall is Associate Professor of Political Science, Stanford University.

Reprinted from *Water Resources and Economic Development of the West,* Report No. 8, Conference Proceedings of the Western Agricultural Economics Research Council (Berkeley: WAERC, 1960), pp. 1–18, with permission of the author and the publisher.

[1] John Galbraith, *The Affluent Society* (Boston: Houghton Mifflin Co., 1958).

[2] For an extended discussion of rational choice in administration situations see Herbert A. Simon, *Administrative Behavior* (New York: The Macmillan Co., 1951), pp. 45–78.

proximate it in the non-engineering aspects of federal water resources planning.

This approach to the problem of the wise allocation of resources makes possible a value-free analysis. That is, one may evaluate the effectiveness of the decision-making process without committing oneself to economic efficiency as a goal, or to some pattern of income redistribution implicit in objectives such as Western development. To be sure, Congress in the Flood Control Act of 1936 presumably committed itself to the goal of national economic efficiency when it provided that:

> the Federal Government should improve or participate in the improvement of navigable waters or their tributaries, including the watersheds thereof, for flood-control purposes if the benefits to whomsoever they may accrue are in excess of the estimated costs. . . .[3]

But whether or not one accepts national economic efficiency as the paramount goal in water resources development, rational decision-making requires objective economic evaluation from a national point of view, for only in this way can decision-makers be appraised of the losses to economic efficiency entailed in the decision to embrace any other goal. We conclude, then, that full knowledge, upon which rational choice depends, requires reliable and objective economic evaluation, the consideration of alternative means of achieving project goals, and the assessment of the costs and gains to goals other than national economic efficiency.

Adequacy of the Decision-Maker's Knowledge

Generally speaking, decision-makers have been accurately informed regarding the physical adequacy of structures and the likelihood of their accomplishing specified physical tasks. To be sure, the Corps of Engineers was wrong in the claims it made during the mid-1920's for the system of flood protection levees on the lower Mississippi River. But since that time it would be hard to support the proposition that Congress and the President have been freuently misinformed regarding the adequacy of engineering structures. Our problems, rather, lie in the field of economic evaluation and in the failure of the construction agencies to consider alternative means of achieving project goals.

Reliability of Estimates of Direct Benefits

In light of the many accusations that have been directed over the years at rivers and harbors bills, it is surprising that no Congressional committee or central staff agency of the Federal Government, such as the Bureau of the Budget, has ever investigated the soundness of the field estimates of the benefits which find their way into benefit-cost ratios. Such an investigation, however, was undertaken by the second Hoover Commission's Task Force on Water Resources and Power.

The Task Force investigation, conducted by Professor Fred A. Clarenbach, was directed principally to securing an answer to the question: "Are the estimates of agricultural flood damage and of land enhancement from flood reduction [made by the Corps of Engineers and the Soil Conservation Service] reasonable and dependable?"[4] The inquiry involved an examination of the work sheets of the two agencies and interviews with agricultural economists, independent appraisers, bankers, farmers, and others who were intimately acquainted with the productivity and value of agricultural land in a small number of basins in Kansas, Oklahoma, and Texas on which the agencies had recently completed economic evaluations.

One area investigated comprised 10,430 acres of cultivated land along the Verdigris River, valued by the Corps at $94 per acre —a figure confirmed by Clarenbach. The

[3] 49 Stat. 1570 (1952), 33 U.S.C. § 701*a*.

[4] Fred A. Clarenbach, "Reliability of Estimates of Agricultural Damages from Floods" in U.S., Commission on Organization of the Executive Branch of the Government, *Water Resources and Power,* III, 1278.

Corps claimed many benefits arising from construction of a dam to protect this area, the most easily verified being direct crop damages and other direct damages to agriculture (including supplies, stock, equipment, land, and improvements) which the Corps claimed would be averted if floods were checked by construction of the dam. Corps data, based on 1949 prices, indicated that in flood-free years the net earning power per acre of cultivated land was $8.28. For the same area, the Corps estimated average annual crop damages due to floods at $6.87 per cultivated acre. Other estimated annual (non-crop) losses to agriculture came to $0.97 per cultivated acre, making a total average annual loss of $7.84 per acre. If the Corps figures are accurate, these flood losses leave a residual net return to cultivated land of only $0.44 per acre. At a capitalization rate of 5 per cent, this annual return would justify a land value of only $9 per acre. Nevertheless, actual land values, as noted, were approximately $94 per acre. The most reasonable explanation for the evident inconsistency in the Corps' appraisal results would seem to be that direct flood damages were significantly overestimated.

In his investigation of Soil Conservation Service projects, Clarenbach found an even greater inflation of direct benefits. In one of these projects, he found that the *net* residual return to *flood-free* bottom land averaged less than the average annual direct flood damages to crops and pasture claimed by the SCS. What the SCS was saying was that the farmers in this area annually lose more from flood damages than their land can produce even in a flood-free year! This is simply not believable.

Another field check of the validity of the estimates of benefits accruing from a federal water development project was made when the Missouri Basin Survey Commission investigated the Corps of Engineers' navigation program for the Missouri River. The Commission's report, published in 1953, gives no hint of the methodology used in checking the Corps' estimates. But where the Corps of Engineers claimed $11,795,000 annually as benefits from erosion control along the Missouri, the Commission estimated these benefits at $964,000.[5] The Corps estimated annual savings due to the navigation project at $6,699,000, while the Commission estimated them at $2,050,000. For erosion control, the Corps' estimates were twelve times larger than those of the Commission; for navigation, the Corps' estimates were more than three times those of the Commission. For the navigation project as a whole, the Corps calculated a benefit-cost ratio of 1.9 to 1; the Commission arrived at a ratio of 0.8 to 1. Hence, it is clear why Clarenbach refers to the economic evaluations now conducted by the agencies as a "considerable accumulation of absurdities,"[6] why the Jones Subcommittee holds that benefit-cost analysis serves "only an expedient self-deception,"[7] and why Wantrup says that "benefit-cost analysis can be and has been distorted and abused."[8]

Obviously economic evaluation is not an exact science, and reasonable men may differ on the assumptions and estimates that find their way into benefit-cost ratios. But differences of the magnitudes cited here are not dictated by the inexactitude of engineering and economic science. The result, of course, is to misinform high-level decision-makers in both the executive and legislative branches and the public at large.

AN APPROPRIATE INTEREST RATE

The use of an appropriate interest rate in economic evaluation is, of course, cru-

[5] U.S., Missouri Basin Survey Commission, *Missouri: Land and Water* (Washington: Government Printing Office, 1953), p. 122.

[6] Clarenbach, *op. cit.*, p. 1298.

[7] U.S., Congress, House, Committee on Public Works, *Economic Evaluation of Federal Water Resource Development Projects,* Committee Print No. 24, 82d Cong., 2d Sess. (Washington: GPO, 1952), p. 51.

[8] S. V. Ciriacy-Wantrup, "Benefit-Cost Analysis and Public Resource Development," *Journal of Farm Economics,* XXXVII, No. 4 (1955), 676.

cial. A rate that is too low may result in the waste of resources on a project yielding less satisfaction to the community than would alternative uses. An excessively high interest rate, on the other hand, may leave water resources undeveloped as compared with other aspects of the nation's economy. In the past, federal construction agencies have used an interest rate approximating the cost of borrowing to the government.

Krutilla and Eckstein challenge this practice, holding that the true social cost of federal financing is not the rate at which individuals voluntarily lend to the government, but rather the interest rate that reflects the value of money to those from whom the necessary taxes are collected.[9] In their view, when government imposes taxes in order to finance public investment, it levies a compulsory loan or forced saving on the community, which releases resources for the public undertaking. The taxes inevitably lead to a reduction of consumption by households, to a decline in investment, or both. The social cost of the capital raised from foregone investment is clear: it is equal to the foregone rate of return on private investment. On the consumption side, Krutilla and Eckstein argue that individuals borrow at rates ranging from 12 per cent on automobile loans down to 5 per cent (in the year in which they made their analysis) for home mortgages, and that these interest rates reflect the value of consumption to these individuals. Taxation reduces consumption and hence the cost of this part of federal financing is equal to the interest rates that individuals face in borrowing. Without going into the elaborate analysis made by Krutilla and Eckstein, suffice it to say that they arrive at a social cost of federal financing of about 5.5 per cent, a figure considerably in excess of the rate of interest currently used in economic evaluation.

Krutilla and Eckstein thus define social cost in terms of the opportunities foregone in the private sector of the economy, either because of curtailed investment or of curtailed consumption. Defining social cost in this way is surely open to criticism because it attaches greater weight to consumer sovereignty, to the private judgments of individuals, than it does to the collective wisdom of the community. It may lead to inadequate amounts of saving and investment for society as a whole. But these are value-laden arguments and of no concern here. What is pertinent is that the economists neither of the construction agencies, nor of the Bureau of the Budget, nor of the staffs of Congressional committees have seen fit to raise this matter for the explicit consideration of decision-makers. The matter is not beyond the comprehension of intelligent laymen, and it is an important issue of policy. To fail to call it to the attention of decision-makers is to make rational choice impossible.

CONSIDERATION OF RELEVANT ALTERNATIVES

Surely one of the requirements of objective rationality is that decision-makers have the opportunity to consider alternative proposals that may better accomplish specified goals or may accomplish them at less real cost. Unfortunately, the jurisdictional jealousies of the several construction agencies make the dispassionate consideration of alternatives all but impossible. A few examples will illustrate the point.

On January 11, 1960, the Chief of Army Engineers recommended the construction of flood control and hydroelectric power projects on the Columbia River, estimated to cost well in excess of $1 billion.[10] Although the Columbia loops for a considerable distance into Canada, all of the projects recommended by the Chief of Engineers were located in the United States. John Krutilla, who has spent a considerable period of time in the Northwest checking the Corps' estimates of benefits and costs and checking with Canadian authori-

[9] John V. Krutilla and Otto Eckstein, *Multiple Purpose River Development* (Baltimore: Johns Hopkins Press for Resources for the Future, Inc., 1958), pp. 78–130.

[10] *New York Times,* January 12, 1960, p. 17.

ties on a number of sites along the Columbia in Canadian territory, agrees with the Corps that projects providing approximately 195 million-acre feet of additional usable storage are needed on the Columbia main stem.[11] But he feels that the most economic sites are located in Canada. The water storage in Canada would, of course, greatly increase flood protection and power output in the United States. A joint international commission, consisting of representatives of Canada and the United States, exists for the cooperative development of the Columbia; but the Corps prefers to ignore development alternatives in Canada.

Other agencies are no more anxious than the Corps to have agency objectives met by activities performed by others outside the agency's areal jurisdiction. Thus the Bureau of Reclamation argues that there is no justification for comparing the relative merits of a proposed federal irrigation development with some other reclamation possibility, such as draining a swamp.[12] In any event, our moral must again be the same. Congress in its wisdom may wish to locate dams in the United States rather than in Canada, or to irrigate arid land in the West rather than drain swamp land in the Southeast; but objective rationality requires that the cost of doing these things be made explicit—and they cannot be made explicit if the alternatives are not investigated.

Finally, a recent study by Gilbert White underlines the urgent necessity for considering alternatives.[13] No doubt most Americans who give the matter any thought have been under the impression that the Corps of Engineers' flood-control program has resulted in some net progress in protecting the nation from floods. In the 20 years following 1936, some $4 billion was spent on this program. Yet if White's data are correct, "mean annual flood losses increased over the period of record and at a rate that has not declined notably since 1936."[14] Even when one discounts the rise in damage resulting from increases in the price level and from a rise in the frequency of disastrous storms, the record is one of rising damage. Apparently the Corps' failure to reduce the nation's flood hazard arises from the continuing invasion of flood plains by industry, commercial enterprises, and residential housing. In one sense, the Corps has become one of ahe nation's major real estate developers; even as engineering plans are announced to provide an incremental degree of protection, developers invade the flood plain and begin raising new structures that require an even greater degree of protection.

It *may* be true that construction costs on sloping ground are so greatly in excess of those on the flood plain that economic efficiency dictates a national system of flood protection, perhaps even involving outlays in excess of those currently being made. But it is conceivable, also, that the costs of public flood protection are in excess of the *extra* cost involved in locating structures outside the flood plain or in making private adjustments to reduce flood losses, in which case economic efficiency would dictate a flood warning system or flood plain zoning, or both. But over the years the Corps has shown no interest in these alternatives.

There is much evidence to show that the President and Congress, generally speaking, are not as uninformed on other issues of public policy as they are on water resources development. On a host of issues —tariff and labor policies are examples—

[11] John V. Krutilla, *Sequence and Timing in River Basin Development* (Washington: Resources for the Future, Inc., 1960), 35 pp.

[12] "Comments and Recommendations for Revision of Bureau of the Budget Circular No. A-47," a memorandum attached to a letter from Ralph A. Tudor, Acting Secretary of the Interior, to Joseph M. Dodge, Director, Bureau of the Budget, January 14, 1954.

[13] Gilbert F. White *et al.*, *Changes in Urban Occupance of Flood Plains in the United States*, Dept. of Geog. Research Paper No. 57 (Chicago: Dept. of Geog., University of Chicago, 1958), 235 pp.

[14] *Ibid.*, p. 3.

well-organized interest groups make certain that decision-makers hear arguments on both sides. On foreign and fiscal policy issues the tradition has developed in recent years for Congressional committees to seek out testimony from disinterested university experts. Indeed, recent Congressional inquiries on economic growth and the adequacy of our decision-making apparatus for foreign and military policy have actually assumed a scholarly cast. The government may act wisely or unwisely on these issues, but it tends to be informed.

No doubt Congress could become as well informed on water resources issues as on other great issues of public policy if it wished to. Surely there is nothing in the nature of the issues to make water resources more difficult to understand than monetary policy. But there is much evidence that Congress prefers to remain uninformed, to leave serious issues of water policy unexplored. Here a variety of circumstances, mainly in the form of institutional arrangements, conspire to aid those who favor water projects and make it difficult for their opponents to secure the necessary information or to mobilize for effective opposition. The result, of course, is inadequate exploration of water issues, false information, little awareness of alternatives, and hence a lack of that knowledge which is essential to rational choice.

We turn now to an examination of some of the institutional arrangements that make rational decision all but impossible in the water development field.

The Balance of Interests

John Adams once wrote: "The nation which will not adopt an equilibrium of power must adopt a despotism. There is no other alternative."[15] This was the prevailing doctrine of our constitutional period, and its hold on our minds continues undiminished today. We conceive government to be an automatic machine, regulated by the balancing of competing interests. This image of politics, of course, is closely related to the official image of the economy; in both an equilibrium is achieved by the pulling and hauling of many interests, no one of which is powerful enough to dominate the scene. In politics the fragmentation of power necessary to achieve the balance is secured by the division of authority between legislative, executive, and judicial branches, by federalism which divides power geographically, and by seeing to it that no part of the economy—business, labor, or agriculture—has sufficient power to dominate the government. With power thus divided, liberty prevails.

The essential concept behind the theory of balance is that action cannot take place until something approaching a consensus has been reached. No transitory majority will have the sustained strength necessary to control the several private interests and sectors of government whose assent is necessary before a proposal becomes policy. In the present century, many writers have dwelt on an additional advantage of balance: its contribution to rational choice. The role of political parties in this respect has long been recognized. Issues are raised, arguments are put forth, the opposition's contentions are analyzed and criticized, fallacious arguments are exposed, fact-finding is encouraged, and in the end the nation is better prepared to reach a rational choice. We now recognize that interest groups, including the three branches of government, participate in the process and contribute perhaps more than the parties themselves. So much has this idea appealed to political scientists and so powerful do the groups seem in actual case studies of decision-making that group studies of one kind or another have all but dominated postwar scholarship in the field of politics.

The contribution of group conflict to rational choice seems very real, indeed. The Farm Bureau and National Farmers Union dissect each other's proposals. The unions and the National Association of Manufacturers debate the right to work. The United

[15] *Discourses on Davila* (Boston: Russell and Cutler, 1805), p. 92.

Steelworkers and the steel industry provide data in support of their positions. Organized small business, importers, exporters, independent retailers, the chain stores, the National Association for the Advancement of Colored People and a thousand other organizations and interests contribute to the process. No one believes that this great debate is carried on solely for our edification, nor need one believe that the information presented is unbiased. But there is considerable evidence that the public is at least partially enlightened by the process of mutual criticism, and Congressmen report that they gain much information and insight available in no other way.

But where in the field of water resources is there evidence of countervailing power? Where are the organized groups supported by effective staff research who stand ready to criticize, point out and defend alternatives, or argue for no program at all? Opposition exists, to be sure, to public power and river navigation programs. But even here the opposition is based largely on principle, since the construction agencies provide no opportunity for scrutiny of the manner in which benefit-cost ratios are calculated. One may oppose public power on principle, but there is little chance to criticize water projects on a strictly economic basis. As Senator Douglas once lamented, "Any member who tries to buck the system is only confronted with an impossible amount of work in trying to ascertain the relative merits of a given project."

Thus we have the comparatively unusual situation in which the absence of countervailing power places great power in the hands of the executive agencies and Congressmen who, as we shall see, have so much to gain by serving local interests. Nor does the balancing power of the President have much effect. In his first 6 years and 8 months in office, President Eisenhower vetoed 145 acts of Congress, and his veto in each case was amazingly sustained. His 146th veto was of a public works appropriation bill, and this veto was overridden with almost no debate.[16] No President will lightly challenge Congress on a water resources measure.

Moreover, presidents have had difficulty in developing independent information on water projects. When the National Resources Planning Board was abolished by Congress, the President was forbidden to transfer its duties in checking water projects to any other executive agency.[17] Thus we face a situation in which the absence of countervailing power outside the government and the weakness of executive authority make it difficult for anyone outside the construction agencies to form an independent appraisal of the merits of individual projects.

The Representative's Role

Why is it that Congress evidences so little desire for the information that would make objective rationality possible? Perhaps a good way to begin is with Burke's famous Speech to the Electors of Bristol (1774). Parliament, he said:

> is not a *congress* of ambassadors from different and hostile interests; which interests each must maintain, as an agent and advocate, against other agents and advocates; but parliament is a *deliberative* assembly of *one* nation, with *one* interest, that of the whole; where, not local purposes, not local prejudices ought to guide but the general good, resulting from the general reason of the whole.[18]

In this statement Burke was speaking of two analytically separable roles that the legislator may play. The first, which we can call his style of representation, deals with the *how* of his representation. Does he come to the legislative body as an ambassador, carrying instructions from the represented that dictate his every move? Or does he come empowered to use his own judgment in a deliberative assembly?

16 *New York Herald Tribune* (Paris edition), September 11, 1959, p. 1.

17 57 Stat. 170 (1943).

18 *The Works of Edmund Burke,* II (Boston: C. C. Little & J. Brown, 1839), pp. 12–13.

These are respectively the roles of Delegate and Trustee.

The second analytically separable role, which we can call his focus, deals with *whom* or *what* he represents. Does he come to serve the interests of his district, or the general good of the entire nation?

Recently Professor Eulau and a group of associates published the results of a series of interviews with state legislators which are of interest in this connection.[19] Asking state legislators what they conceived their roles to be, he found that Trustees outnumbered Delegates in the ratio of about 4 to 1. This is not surprising in view of the ethically higher role of the Trustee. But the large number of Trustees was attributable to another factor as well: many citizens lack the information to give intelligent instructions; the representative is unable to discover what his clientele wants; preferences remain unexpressed; or interest groups are so nearly equal in power that the representative perforce must use his own judgment.

Turning to the *focus* of representation, he found that district-oriented representatives outnumbered state-oriented representatives in the ratio of 2 to 1. Interestingly enough a great many Trustees were district-oriented; but no Delegate was state-oriented.

While Professor Eulau was not concerned with public works legislation, it is possible to surmise the impact of such legislation on the role orientation of the representative. As indicated, all of Eulau's Delegates were district-oriented, and it takes no great imagination to figure out how such a representative, in Congress, would vote on public works legislation. His Trustees were about equally divided between district-orientation and statewide-orientation. But many of his Trustees had a statewide-orientation only because they had no instructions from constituents, because legislative matters were so complex that constituents could not make up their own minds, or because important interest groups were aproximately balanced in power. But a public works bill gives the Trustee no such freedom. The issue here is clear. Increased local economic activity and other advantages flow directly from the construction of veterans hospitals, military installations, flood control, or irrigation works, while the tax burden is distributed throughout the nation and is largely masked in the public mind by taxation for defense and other items that loom large in the annual budget. While the taxes are largely masked, the project is conspicuous. Finally, organized local interests will not divide on a public works bill and cancel each other's effective power. The district will be united, and the Trustee of statewide-orientation will on this issue, of necessity become a Delegate. And, of course, all Delegates are district-oriented. Only the representative who plays the Trustee role out of ethical conviction will use his own judgment on a matter of this sort; and of course he, like Burke, may pay for it by retirement from office.

The legislator's need to play the role of Delegate on matters of direct concern to his constituents is insured by the nature of the American party system. A realistic examination of Congress reveals that its members, vis-à-vis the national parties, constitute separate islands of power. Each member is in fact responsible not through his party but directly to his constituency. He is nominated by securing a modest number of signatures on a petition and winning a primary election in which he raises his own campaign funds. Having won the primary, he enters the general election under the banner of his party no matter how widely his views diverge from those of the party leadership or how much independence he will show in Congress if elected. In the general election, he must again raise campaign funds with little or no assistance from the party's national committee or Congressional campaign commit-

[19] Heinz Eulau *et al.*, "The Role of the Representative: Some Empirical Observations on the Theory of Edmund Burke," *American Political Science Review,* LIII, No. 3 (1959), 742–56.

tees. The general election won, he enters Congress beholden to no one but the electorate of his constituency and the local interests which financed his campaign or otherwise delivered the vote. No national party organ or leadership group in the Congress commands his allegiance or has the power to control his vote. No mechanism exists to compel or even to direct his attention to the national interest. Power is fragmented, party cohesion is minimal, and party responsibility all but nonexistent. Indeed, no single group speaks continuously for the party or can claim to represent it; our parties in fact are an odd confederation of state and local parties onto which have been grafted such weak or transient institutions as the national party committee and the quadrennial convention. Hence it is that political scientists characterize American parties variously as weak, decentralized, or irresponsible. But however the parties may be characterized, the result is a Congress from which the emerging legislation represents not a coherent party view of the national interest but a summation of the parochial views of constituency interests.

Whatever the defects of our party arrangements, there is much to suggest that they mirror rather accurately the diversity of our national economic and social structure, our sectional differences, and the federal nature of our governmental system. This being the case it seems likely that reforms will be slow in coming. Nevertheless, the literature of political science is filled with speculation on how our party system might be modified in order to make the parties more effective instruments of our national purposes and needs.

Many of the reforms suggested would affect minor institutional arrangements and, except in concert, would not likely have any dramatic impact on the parochial outlook of Senators and Representatives. Short of adoption of the British parliamentary system (which is no longer seriously proposed), reforms which seem adequate to the task are national party control of the nominating process and of campaign finance. In Great Britain candidates are nominated by local party associations, but before the candidate's name is placed on the ballot he must be approved by the central organ of the party. In this way the candidate's loyalty is insured and he is made subject to party discipline in the House of Commons. A similar arrangement here might require the candidate to secure approval of the party national committee before he entered the party primary. Without doubt such a reform would weaken the primary system by restricting the range of choice available to the voter, but the primary is already under some attack and the fact must be faced that one cannot have simultaneously the advantages of party centralization and unmitigated local control.

The second reform—national party control of campaign finance—could come in several forms. In its more extreme form, Congress might simply require that all campaign contributions for Senate and House contests be sent to the national committees of the respective parties to be reallocated by them at their discretion to the parties' candidates throughout the country. Such a reform would have a revolutionary effect on American politics, releasing the congressman from bondage to local interests by placing him under heavy obligation to the central organ of his party. True, neither the congressman nor his national committee could ignore his constituency interests since the voters could always turn to the opposition party, but the shift in power relationships would be substantial. A more moderate step in the same direction might be achieved by the provision of federal appropriations to the national committees to be used at their discretion (with strict accounting) in supporting Congressional campaigns or by offering federal income tax credits to those who contribute to the *national committees*. Either plan would again greatly strengthen the national party organization and in some degree compel the congressman to balance national interests and needs against those of local interests.

Even to state reforms of this sort is to indicate the unlikelihood of their adoption. Social change comes slowly, and the American people must evidence considerably more awareness of the weaknesses of their party system before change will be supported. In the meantime, the decline of sectionalism, the nationalization of many political issues such as welfare, housing, and education, and the growing importance of foreign policy may slowly wreak changes in our party structure. In the meantime we must look elsewhere for the means of introducing more rationality into the decision-making process.

Organizational Loyalty

To the constituency orientation of the legislature and the absence of countervailing power in militating against rational decision, we must add the phenomenon of organizational loyalty. It is a commonplace in the study of the natural history of organizations to note that members of a group tend to identify with that group. Usually in business and government organization, the values of the group are initially imposed on the individual through the exercise of authority; but in time the values become internalized and are incorporated into the psychology of the individual. He acquires a loyalty to the organization that automatically guarantees that his decisions will be consistent with the values and goals of the group. Indeed, one may say that through the internalization of organization values, the participant in an organization in time acquires an organization personality distinct from his personality as an individual.

This loyalty to the organization has two analytically distinct facets: it may involve an attachment to the service goals of the organization, that is, the goals the organization was created to serve; or it may involve an attachment to the organization itself, to its survival and growth, and hence to the power, prestige, income, and status of its members. Both forms of loyalty exist in all organizations and at least in some degree in all their members; but it is no great task to identify organizations or even individuals in whom one form of loyalty predominates over the other. Examples of the commitment to substantive objectives are seen in the Trotskyite Movement, the Prohibitionist Party, and in a number of minor religious sects which have preferred to remain "pure" at the expense of organizational growth. Yet in far more numerous instances—our major political parties are examples—one finds individuals behaving as though the organization's welfare was the primary goal to be served.[20] This, rather than the conflict of service goals, is the principal cause of the interbureau competition and wrangling which characterize so much of organizational life.

Viewed in one fashion, there is little conflict between service goals and organization welfare in the water resources field. The larger the agency and its program, the more it is likely to accomplish. On the other hand, if efficiency is an aspect of service goals (as clearly required by the Flood Control Act of 1936), the conflict is real indeed, and we are forced to conclude from our examination of agency behavior that the organizations have in part become ends in themselves. As we have seen, benefit-cost ratios are unreliable, and alternative means of achieving agency goals remain unexplored if they conflict with organiza-

[20] For the development of this idea as applied to the business firm see Robert A. Gordon, *Business Leadership in the Large Corporation* (Washington: The Brookings Institution, 1945). On page 306 he says: "Power thus secured increases with the size of the firm. Here lies an important explanation of the tendency of many large firms to become larger, even if sometimes the profitability of such expansion is open to serious question. The working of the power urge in this respect is reinforced by the tendency of businessmen to identify themselves with their enterprises. Expansion is desired for the enhancement of personal power and also because of the satisfaction of being associated with a powerful organization."

tional welfare. What we have here is administrative behavior conditioned heavily by loyalty to the organization. It has the desirable effect of imbuing agency personnel with enthusiasm and commitment; but its cost is opportunistic behavior at the expense of the public purpose the agency was created to serve.

The Road Ahead

It has been argued in the preceding sections of this paper that objective rationality in the making of water decisions in the Federal Government is hampered by (1) the near absence of countervailing pressures, (2) the constituency rather than national orientation of Congress, and (3) the commitment to bureaucratic ends which are an inevitable accompaniment of organizational life. It has been argued further that little can be accomplished by way of reform through the conscious manipulation of institutions to create countervailing presures or to alter the constituency orientation of congressmen, although the gradual nationalization of life in the United States may ultimately strengthen our central party organizations to the point where local concerns are to an increasing degree subordinated to the national interest. In this final section, attention will be focused on two developments which, if they occur, could do much to undercut organizational loyalty and mitigate its undesirable effects. The first deals with the professional identifications and loyalties of economists in the government service; the second concerns possible shifts in the location of decision-making authority in the national government.

PROFESSIONALIZATION

In the preceding section we saw how loyalty to the organization limits the perspective of the employee, making it possible for him to reach decisions essentially opportunistic in nature without a sense of personal conflict. Barnard[21] and Simon[22] have developed the concept of the "zone of acceptance" within which the employee will permit the organization to guide his behavior. The breadth of the zone depends, of course, upon a variety of factors including salary, status, opportunity for promotion, and psychological identification both with the organization and its goals. The greater these inducements, the greater the zone of acceptance. But there are limits to the zone of acceptance beyond which the individual will not behave organizationally. At this point competing values and identifications assert themselves, the individual resists authority, and the existing equilibrium within the organization is disturbed. In the adjustments which follow, the organization may alter its demands upon the individual, adjusting to his values, or the individual may withdraw from the organization.

An important competing identification which may limit the zone of acceptance is the employee's commitment to the professional standards that are relevant to his activities. To the extent that they exist, the employee will desire to adhere to the standards of craftsmanship and technical knowledge pertinent to his profession, and in doing so he may be motivated by the powerful compulsion of professional group opinion. To ignore this compulsion may entail the loss of professional status or self-respect, or both. One corrective, then, for the abuse of economic analysis or the unwillingness to consider project alternatives which are not organizationally desired is to so strengthen the professional identification of agency economists and engineers that efforts to impose organizational values at the expense of professional standards will fall outside the individual's zone of acceptance. Obviously much will depend upon the strength of the employee's professional commitment; and this in turn will depend upon (1) the degree of professional con-

[21] Chester I. Barnard, *The Functions of the Executive* (Cambridge: Harvard University Press, 1938), pp. 167–70. Barnard uses the term "zone of indifference."

[22] Simon, *op. cit.*, pp. 131–33, 204.

sensus regarding technical standards, and (2) the success of the profession in communicating this consensus to practitioners as well as generalist decision-makers.[23]

If this line of reasoning is correct, the obvious need in strengthening objective rationality in the water field is to counterbalance organizational loyalty with professional loyalty. Progress, of course, has been made in reaching professional agreement on principles of economic evaluation. Publication of the Green Book[24] was a milestone in the development of professional standards, and in the brief decade since its appearance there has been a greater contribution to theory and more exposure of agency malpractice than in any comparable period. While this outpouring of comment is not indicative of complete consensus on matters of theory, still it is certain to have great influence in strengthening the professional identification of agency economists. If the current attention to project evaluation continues, as now seems certain, there can be little question but that it will have an influence on agency practice.

But the slow osmotic process by which a developing professional consensus penetrates agency practice may take needlessly long. Since economic analysis is relevant to human affairs only as it becomes a basis for social action, it becomes an obligation of the profession to do what it can to see that agency practices keep pace with developing theory. But on what matters could economists, operating through professional associations, agree in sufficient degree to justify making statements on acceptable theory and practice? Given the economists' commitment to efficiency and the optimization of social welfare, there should be no difficulty in insisting upon (1) the full development of relevant information, (2) the full consideration of alternative means of achieving project goals, (3) objectivity and reliability in the estimation of benefits and costs, and (4) the planning of projects subject to the criterion of efficiency except where clearly stated goals involving income distribution or extra-market values dictate the contrary. Perhaps, also, agreement could be reached on more specific matters such as the appropriateness of counting secondary benefits during periods of full employment and a defensible interest rate and period of analysis. A variety of other matters suggest themselves upon a few moments' reflection.

Precedent for professional society activity of this sort exists, of course, in a number of fields. Some professional associations in the natural sciences prescribe specifications for materials, and some have adopted resolutions on matters which affect them but range far from their fields of professional competence. The cost accountants have been active in urging their preferred systems on the Internal Revenue Service, and the American Statistical Association has played an important role in advising several government agencies on appropriate professional practice.[25]

More relevantly, perhaps, in 1949 the Engineers Joint Council, representing 5 national engineering societies,[26] appointed a National Water Policy Panel and charged it with developing an official position on water policy for the engineering profession. When President Truman appointed the President's Water Resources Policy Commission in 1950, the Engineers Joint Council authorized its National Water Policy

23 For two case studies illustrating the conflict for economists between organizational and professional loyalty, see "Indonesian Assignment" in Harold Stein (ed.), *Public Administration and Policy Development* (New York: Harcourt, Brace & Co., 1952), pp. 53–61; and Corinne Silverman, *The President's Economic Advisers* (University: University of Alabama Press, 1959).

24 Federal Inter-Agency River Basin Comm., Subcommittee on Benefits and Costs, *Proposed Practices for Economic Analysis of River Basin Projects* (Washington: GPO, 1950).

25 See, for example, "The Attack on the Cost of Living Index" in Stein, *op. cit.*, pp. 773–853.

26 American Society of Civil Engineers, American Society of Mining and Metallurgical Engineers, The American Society of Mechanical Engineers, American Institute of Electrical Engineers, and American Institute of Chemical Engineers.

Panel to cooperate with the new commission and "to present to it, on behalf of Engineers Joint Council, specific proposals for a desirable revision of National Water Policy."[27] The Panel went about its work with the assistance of 10 committees composed of some 78 experts representing mainly the engineering profession, but geology, agricultural economics, and wildlife as well. Some months later the Panel submitted its report to the President's commission and subsequently published it for general distribution under the title *Principles of a Sound National Water Policy.*

Whatever one thinks of the generally conservative cast of the Engineers Joint Council recommendations, the fact remains that 5 engineering associations played a responsible role in formulating and seeking adoption of what they conceived to be appropriate standards for the planning and operation of federal water development projects. In their endorsement of value-impregnated policies, the engineers went far beyond the suggestions made in the paragraphs above and perhaps in doing so undermined the effectiveness of their presentation. Whatever one thinks of the substance of the Engineers Joint Council recommendations, it can hardly be denied that professional agreement on the few relatively value-free matters listed above would be hard for the agencies and Congress to ignore.

STRENGTHENING THE EXECUTIVE OFFICE OF THE PRESIDENT

We have seen in the sections above that the institutionalized individual develops a personal interest in organizational success and so identifies with organizational goals that in making decisions he takes into account only a limited set of values. As Simon put it, "it is unsound to entrust to the administrator responsible for a function the responsibility for weighing the importance of that function against the importance of other functions."[28] Clearly the only person who can approach competently the task of weighing the relative importance of two functions is one who is responsible for both or for neither. Thus no agency is psychologically free to balance objectively its financial needs against the financial needs of other agencies—and hence the universally recognized need for a centrally located budget agency that is free of the biases certain to afflict an operating agency. More specifically, and in terms of water development programs, final authority in the executive branch over program and budget must be located in the Executive Office of the President where (1) there is no vested interest in organizational survival or growth and (2) the need for water development can be weighted objectively against the need for all other federal programs with some degree of freedom from the localized constituency pressures found in Congress.

Yet in practice the expenditure of billions of dollars for water projects is being justified by economic evaluations that receive *no* review whatsoever, despite the evidence of bias in their calculation. The importance of the benefit-cost ratio in securing Congressional authorizations cannot be overestimated. Projects with unfavorable ratios are never authorized by Congress, and those with favorable ratios generally receive favorable consideration unless—as

[27] National Water Policy Panel of Engineers Joint Council, *Principles of a Sound National Water Policy* (New York: The Author, 1951), p. 5. The Panel was quite certain of the propriety of making recommendations to the government, holding that "many members of the engineering profession are technically skilled in the field of water projects, and—in the aggregate—professional engineers represent the group which has the primary knowledge and economic perspective in the field of water resources. Moreover, they are by no means without sociological instinct and experience. It is natural, therefore, that the organized engineering profession should be extremely sensitive to any matter of confusion, waste, or conflicting policy in this field, and that others should turn to that profession for assistance in the analysis of our water problem as a whole and for recommendations for the creation of a comprehensive national water policy to govern future operation." *Ibid.*, p. 1.

[28] Simon, *op. cit.*, p. 215.

rarely happens—local interests are opposed. It is simply a fact that, given our commitment to the symbols of the market economy and the concept of investment and return, a favorable benefit-cost ratio has a soporific effect upon Congress and the public which all but transfers final authority over decision-making to the construction agencies. No American willingly passes up an opportunity to secure a return greater than his investment.

Given the importance of the benefit-cost ratio in the decision-making process, one would think that the Bureau of the Budget would check on the reliability of agency estimates of direct benefits and costs and would prohibit the very considerable dependence upon secondary benefits that has developed in the Bureau of Reclamation. But Congress prohibited the Bureau of the Budget from assuming the functions of the defunct National Resources Planning Board, and in the ensuing years the Bureau has not found the means or the Presidential support for checking on the methods by which benefit-cost ratios are developed. It is an interesting sidelight indeed on our attitudes toward government that neither the President nor Congress will permit the expenditure of money by an executive agency without a preaudit and postaudit of the integrity and legality of the expenditure; yet President and Congress permit themselves to remain wholly at the mercy of the economic calculations of agencies with an obvious interest in the outcome.

But, it may be argued, the Budget Bureau controls the appropriations requests sent to Congress, and the President can veto either authorization or appropriations bills. Yet these are slender reeds upon which to lean. First, the President himself is at the mercy of the economic evaluations of the agencies, and hence may have little objective basis for opposing authorizations or appropriations. Second, Congress often increases water resources appropriations over the President's requests.[29] And third, Congress shows no hesitation in overriding Presidential vetoes of authorization and appropriation bills. Hence, the crucial nature of the benefit-cost analysis. Congress will pit its judgment against the President's on matters of authorization or appropriation so long as it can argue that the return will exceed the investment. But given the symbolic importance of the investment-return concept, Congress will not lightly challenge the President over projects with unfavorable ratios. Hence the benefit-cost ratio, which has been a powerful instrument in the hands of the construction agencies, can be turned into a powerful instrument for objective rationality if only the President can control its use and insist upon its reliability.

Over the years, many proposals have been made to reorganize federal water agencies in order to improve the quality of decision-making. The most frequent proposal has been to consolidate the Corps of Engineers with the Bureau of Reclamation and place the unified agency in the Department of the Interior or a new Department of Natural Resources (or Conservation). Others would blanket part or all of the nation with valley authorities.[30] Either proposal would constitute an advance toward true multiple-purpose planning since all of the present agencies emphasize one or at

[29] This is easily done in the case of the Corps of Engineers since the Corps publishes annually in November or December (a month before the President's budget is released) "a detailed statement of the amount that can be profitably expended in the next succeeding fiscal year for new work on all projects." This estimate may be several times the size of the President's budget request and hence it is an easy matter for the Congress to appropriate more than the President desires. See Arthur Maass, *Muddy Waters: The Army Engineers and the Nation's Rivers* (Cambridge: Harvard University Press, 1951), pp. 57–58. Further, the Corps shows no hesitation in sending to Congress authorization requests not in accord with the President's program.

[30] For a brief account of early reorganization proposals see Maass, *ibid.*, pp. 61–68; and for an account of more recent proposals and an incisive discussion of the dilemmas of organizational theory see James W. Fesler, "National Water Resources Administration," *Law and Contemporary Problems*, XXII, No. 3 (1957), 444–71.

most to functions at the expense of others, and either would probably in some degree promote the consideration of relevant alternatives since interagency competition would be reduced. But neither proposal would eliminate organizational loyalty nor promote the full consideration of alternatives, especially where the latter might lead to flood plain zoning, or a flood warning system, or otherwise obviate the need for construction. Moreover, for all its desirability, Congress seems unwilling to approve the wholesale reorganization of executive agencies barring the accidental concurrence of an extremely influential President and a catastrophic flood. We may get one or the other in the near future, but statistically our chances of getting them simultaneously are not great.

This leads us to return to the need for strengthening the Executive Office of the President in its control over the several water development agencies. The advantage of this approach is that it can be accomplished gradually and without the fanfare certain to attend any effort at wholesale reorganization. Through the gradual strengthening of the Bureau of the Budget and the concomitant imposition of regulations governing the calculation of benefit-cost ratios, Presidential control would be increased. Field checks on the reliability of the estimates of benefits and costs could be instituted, and the construction agencies could be forced to consider alternative means of achieving project goals. A determined President could insist upon a loyal Chief of Engineers, he could forbid the Corps to transmit to Congress reports not in accord with his program, and he could impound appropriations in excess of his budget requests. No President will lightly embark on such a program. After all, if he opposes subsidy he will find it in larger amounts and more conspicuously visible in the agricultural price support program and in the Post Office. And given the amounts of money involved, a President may elect to trade water resources projects for Congressional support of his major foreign and domestic policies. But this is only to recognize the normal difficulties that lie in the path of any governmental change. Given a determined President, the advantage of strengthening the Executive Office lies in the fact that it cannot so readily be thwarted by Congress. In this reform and in the development and expression of professional consensus on economic evaluation lies the major hope for objective rationality in the making of water resource decisions.

W. R. D. SEWELL, JOHN DAVIS, A. D. SCOTT, and D. W. ROSS

A GUIDE TO BENEFIT-COST ANALYSIS

INTRODUCTION

Benefit-cost analysis can provide a logical framework for the evaluation of one or more courses of action. It is also a comprehensive method for dealing with a number of factors, some of which may be highly conjectural in nature. Numerous authorities, both in industry and government circles, have found it to be an excellent tool for the evaluation of alternative projects or programs, their ultimate purpose being the selection of the one which would be the most suitable under a wide range of circumstances.

The main aim of economic policy should be to maximize human welfare. Obviously the principal factors of production—land, labor, and capital—can be combined in various ways. Our real objective, however, should be to assemble them in such a manner as to produce the greatest possible benefit for a given cost. Productivity can be increased in the process. Also, the rest of the economy will benefit as these are the prerequisites to a maximum rate of economic growth.

Probably the greatest challenge which the modern decision-maker faces is the increasing complexity of the society in which he lives. His horizon is constantly expanding. Increased incomes are creating fresh demands, while technology, in turn, is providing mankind with new ways in which these demands may be satisfied. Greater mechanization frequently means that the latest projects become even more capital intensive. Being more durable, they often create benefits which will continue over a longer time. Meanwhile, developments on the transportation front are reducing the penalty of distance. Not only do these developments give the consumer a wider range of choice, but individual projects may affect people in widely separated areas. From this it must be apparent that no technique for the selection of the most efficient course of action can be satisfactory unless it takes into account longer term, interregional or demand-related values.

Those who make analyses as a basis for decision-making inevitably face certain difficulties. In the first place, they must make a series of judgments or estimates whose validity can only be tested by the passage of time. Besides the hazards of forecasting, there is also the question of measurement. Certain benefits, though recognized in a general way, are not normally measured in dollars and cents. The same applies to costs. To the extent that benefit-cost analysis is able to take these intangible factors into account, it represents an improvement over older and more limited methods of analysis which are more strictly technical and financial in character.

Various methods of project evaluation

• W. R. D. Sewell, Assistant Professor of Geography, University of Chicago, was formerly with the Water Resources Branch, Dept. of Northern Affairs and National Resources, Canada; A. D. Scott is Professor of Economics, University of British Columbia; John Davis is a Member of Parliament, Ottawa; and D. W. Ross is Secretary, Advisory Committee on Water Use Policy, Ottawa.

Reprinted from *Resources for Tomorrow—A Guide to Benefit-Cost Analysis* (Ottawa: Queen's Printer, 1962), pp. 1–13, with permission of W. R. D. Sewell and the publisher.

have been employed in the past.[1] The majority, however, have suffered from a common fault: they have been too limited in scope. Generally, they have not provided a sufficient framework upon which the various benefits and costs involved could be set out in their true perspective.

A more complete evaluation would require that each project be examined in detail before it is judged against its alternatives. Economies of scale would have to be studied. Different project sequences should also be established and whole programs ranked against each other, using different assumptions as to rates of market growth, price trends, interest levels, and so on.

Each of the professions has an important contribution to make. The engineers are in a position to establish the technical feasibility of any scheme or combination of proposals. Those who are more familiar with financial and accounting matters can help to translate streams of costs and benefits to their "present value." Still others, with a training in the social sciences, can help to trace secondary and intangible effects into related areas of the economy. The task of integrating ideas has always been a problem. Benefit-cost analysis, however, provides us with a comprehensive method whereby the right questions may be asked and answers produced in such a way as to provide the *means* for more intelligent decision-making.

Sight must not be lost of the fact that benefit-cost analysis, as a device for mobilizing information, is capable of considerable improvement. Definitions must be sharpened up and misconceptions in certain areas must be removed. Nor should the reader be misled by the appearance of mathematical precision. We are trying to think more logically and consistently. But most of the numbers which we employ are little more than estimates. Despite the problems of application, due in part to lack of data and the need to forecast, however, benefit-cost analysis provides the most useful framework for the evaluation of projects and programs of resource development.[2]

Approach to Project Evaluation

Benefit-cost analysis may be used for three broad purposes:

(1) To assess the economic characteristics of a particular project;

(2) To determine which of a number of projects designed to serve a given purpose results in the largest ratio of benefits to costs; and

(3) To determine which of a number of projects designed to serve different purposes confers the largest net benefit on the economy as a whole.

So far benefit-cost analyses have been undertaken mainly for the first purpose and only to a limited extent for the selection of the most economically desirable project among alternatives. If, for technical reasons, only one project can be undertaken to achieve a given objective, the study must necessarily be limited to a test of

[1] Benefit-cost analysis techniques have been developed in the U.S., Europe, and elsewhere. U.S., Inter-Agency Committee on Water Resources Report, *Proposed Practices for Economic Analysis of River Basin Projects* (Washington: Government Printing Office, 1958), popularly known as "The Green Book," surveys current U.S. federal agencies' practices in this field. Examples of the use of benefit-cost analysis in Canada include: Royal Commission on South Saskatchewan River Project, *Report on the South Saskatchewan River Project* (Ottawa: Queen's Printer, 1952), and Royal Commission (Manitoba) on Flood Cost-Benefit, *Report of the Royal Commission on Flood Cost-Benefit* (Winnipeg, 1958).

[2] Possibilities of using benefit-cost analysis in a number of fields have been examined by R. N. McKean in *Efficiency in Government through Systems Analysis,* a Rand Corp. Research Study (New York: John Wiley & Sons, 1958), where he suggests that benefit-cost analysis techniques might be used in the evaluation of the performance of government departments; and by John Davis in *The Economics of Nuclear Power in Canada,* a brief presented to the Special Committee on Research, House of Commons, Ottawa, June 1, 1961, in which the benefits and costs of nuclear power research are examined.

economic feasibility (i.e., to decide whether the benefit-cost ratio is greater than 1). But in other instances, where more than one project or program may be undertaken to serve a given purpose, benefit-cost analysis must be extended to a comparison of the benefit-cost ratios of each of the projects in turn.

It is also possible to compare the benefit-cost ratios or projects or programs with quite different objectives, the purpose being to decide which confers the largest net benefit on the economy as a whole. These undertakings might be for different purposes such as the development of irrigation or the preservation of wildlife. Or, they might be located in widely different parts of the country. In any case it is necessary, as far as possible, to reduce the estimates of results and expenditures to monetary terms. Despite difficulties of measurement and the existence of widely different economic circumstances, this type of analysis organizes information in such a way that the final decision can be made in the context of prevailing social and political circumstances.

Essentially benefit-cost analysis attempts to do, more methodically, what people are doing every day when they make decisions about the future. A businessman, for example, is always searching for the most profitable alternative. A similar challenge, leading to the maximization of benefits, presents itself to government officials and agencies. The objective should always be to select the most economic alternative.

When assessing the merits of alternative proposals, the decision-maker must ask himself a number of questions:

(a) Which projects are feasible from a technical point of view?

(b) Which projects can also be defended on economic grounds? (I.e., will the benefits which they produce exceed the costs involved?)

(c) Which, among these alternatives, is the most economic project, taking into account different basic assumptions as to market growth, interest rates, wage levels, and so on? (Which has the highest benefit-cost ratio?)

Another question which the analyst may have to bear in mind relates to financial feasibility. For a project to be financially feasible, the revenues must exceed the expenditures involved. Some proposals, though technically feasible and economically desirable, may be unable for some reason to attract funds necessary for their completion. In such instances they must be dropped from consideration for the time being.

In order to answer these various questions a great deal of information is required. Data describing the components of each alternative project and various project sequences must be examined in order to give a clear idea of which over-all plan or program will be the most economic: The amount of effort involved in the analysis itself can, on the other hand, be tailored to suit the manpower, time and budgets available for this type of research. In the interest of efficiency those responsible for this work should consider limitations of a technical nature first. Economic and financial considerations may then be introduced.

Before a benefit-cost analysis can get underway, the various alternative technical possibilities must be identified. In any situation there are controlling factors which limit the range of choice. These factors may be physical, legal, or economic. For example in the case of a hydro power project, the topography often limits the range of choice. In some cases, legal rights may prohibit some developments. Having identified the various technical possibilities in this way, a number of questions relating to their benefits and costs may be asked. Clearly, unless the project or program can be shown to be technically possible, there is no point in launching an extensive economic analysis.

The next step is to determine the economic characteristics of the alternative projects or programs. It must be borne in mind that economic analysis, even at this stage, should go beyond a mere examination of project revenues and expenditures. Feasibility, in the economic sense, calls for a weighing of the relevant benefits and costs. Various side effects may have to be included—effects which are neither technical nor strictly financial in character. Measures which would help to stabilize prices, attract new industries, and generate more purchasing power, or employ idle workers, are all cases in point. By recognizing their existence, benefit-cost analysis helps us to gain a clearer understanding of the relative importance of various factors, some of which are bound to influence the decision-making process in any case.

If it can be shown that the total benefits of a given project or program exceed its total costs, it may be said to have passed the minimum test of economic feasibility. If this is the only possible way in which the designated need can be served, then this particular project or program will also be the most economic solution in sight. However, alternatives are often available to provide given benefits and must be assessed accordingly. Only that project or program with the highest benefit-cost ratio among these various alternatives is the most economically desirable. Benefit-cost analysis provides a mechanism for ranking these several projects or programs in their true order of economic merit.

The real test of optimum use is found in the answer to the question—"Could these resources be used more efficiently elsewhere by another firm or public agency, and in the satisfaction of an alternative need?" Society, in other words, is searching for a course of action which maximizes benefits relative to costs. A variety of needs may, of course, be met by projects or programs of widely different dimensions. The mere fact that one alternative offers more net benefits than another is insufficient proof of its economic desirability. It is possible to increase the amount of net benefits by spending more money on a given project. However, there may be more profitable ways of spending that money. The proper criterion, therefore, must be expressed in relative terms. The benefit-cost ratios which can be used to describe different alternatives, therefore, provide us with a much better test of which is the most economic thing to do.

It is true that the most economically desirable project or program may not always be financially self-sufficient, and, therefore, not of interest to private firms or to some local government agencies. Larger provincial or national organizations could undertake them and cover the costs because of their greater powers of taxation. Flood control projects and improvements in navigation facilities have sometimes been provided on this basis. Care must be taken, however, to make sure that estimates of nonreimbursable values are not exaggerated and that planning is not unduly biased in this way.

Enthusiasm for a particular project may sometimes obscure the fact that other alternatives exist. Such enthusiasm may lead to the claim that a given proposal is desirable simply because its benefits exceed its costs. Sometimes the mere size of the net benefits is also taken as a valid measure of economic desirability. Yet it should be apparent from what has already been said that the mere existence of net benefits is not enough. Even a large excess of benefits over costs falls short of being a final proof. Each alternative which is open to selection will have differing degrees of feasibility. To qualify they must be, first of all, technically feasible. The funds must also be available for construction and operation. But no one of the projects could be undertaken with confidence until it has been ranked against its competitors and its benefit-cost ratio has been shown to be greater than that of relevant alternatives.

Definition of Terms

The same words often mean different things to different people. This is particularly true of the terms commonly employed in benefit-cost analysis. In order to avoid confusion, it is therefore appropriate at this stage to define, quite specifically, what is meant by certain terms which are used repeatedly throughout [this paper].

PROJECT

The word project refers to a particular method of achieving a particular purpose. To the extent that it is altered in scale, site or purpose, it becomes a different identifiable project. A given entity, or project, may serve one or several purposes. It is, nevertheless, an undertaking whose benefits and costs are identifiable, and whose feasibility can be determined in technical terms.

PROGRAM

A program of development may contain one or more projects. In a program involving several projects, each of the component projects must be separately analyzed and shown to have a benefit-cost ratio which is greater than 1.

PURPOSE

The word purpose is used to describe the goods and/or services which a given project or program is capable of producing. More than one purpose may, of course, be served. A water resource development project or program may, for example, produce benefits in the form of generation of electric power, navigation, flood control, irrigation, recreation and pollution abatement. It would, in this instance, qualify as a multipurpose project or program. Its primary effects usually constitute the principal reasons for going ahead with undertakings of this kind, although other significant advantages may exist. One of the principal objectives of benefit-cost analysis is to take these related secondary and indirect effects into account.

BENEFITS

Benefits are defined as advantageous effects. They represent real values resulting from any action which brings about increases in the output of useful goods and services. Benefits are akin to the total *output,* while costs resemble the total *input* of goods and services, which are involved in the development and operation of a given project or program.

Primary or direct benefits consist of the gains which accrue to those people who make use of the goods and services which can be provided by a given project or program. Theoretically, the real value of these primary or direct benefits is the maximum amount of money which the consumers are willing to pay for them.[3] Obviously there is an upper limit to these benefits, as the community will not pay more for these advantageous effects than it would have to pay in order to obtain these same goods and services from the most efficient alternative source of supply.

The primary or direct benefits of a hydropower project, for instance, are represented by the market value of the electricity produced by the project. This can be established by multiplying the volume of energy delivered to consumers by the price the consumers would be willing to pay if the most economic alternative source were to provide the power. On the other hand, the primary or direct benefit from an irrigation project may be determined by computing the *increase* in agricultural income which is directly attributable to the existence of the project.

Secondary or indirect benefits stem indirectly from, or are induced by, the project or program in question. If, as a result of the provision of irrigation water, a sugar beet factory is set up to process the sugar beets from the irrigation project, the net income of the sugar beet factory should be counted as a secondary benefit of the project. Although it is not the primary purpose of the project, the existence of this new industry should properly be credited to it.

A note of caution should be sounded here. Every care should be taken to show that these secondary effects do in fact constitute a genuine increase in the net income

[3] There are some goods and services such as meteorological forecasts, provision of lighthouses, and so on, that are considered collectively, whose costs are not paid for directly by the users per se.

of the community. They must not merely constitute a transfer of production from one place to another. Clearly, if the analysis is national in scope the location of a secondary industry in one area as opposed to another does not result in a national gain equal to that industry's value of production. On the other hand, if the viewpoint of the analysis is confined to a certain area and an industry is induced to build its plant in this particular region—e.g. as a result of the irrigation project mentioned above—its net output may be regarded as a secondary benefit.

Intangible benefits differ from other benefits to the extent that they are services not usually bought or sold at a price or at a fee, nor can their value be derived indirectly from the price of secondary products produced by using these services. They may, however, be measurable in monetary terms by procedures which involve attributing a value to them. It should be noted that there are direct and indirect intangible effects (see Fig. 1).

A distinction should be made between "intangible" (not priced in a market) and "unmeasurable" (not capable of quantification in monetary terms). For example, scenic amenities, prevention of loss of life, and the preservation of selected tracts of land in their natural state may be desired on aesthetic or philosophical grounds. Yet because quantification is difficult, they cannot be readily incorporated into analyses. Instead, we may be reduced to thinking of them simply as preponderantly positive or negative factors. Thus, the analyst is forced to regard the benefit-cost ratios of tangibles—shown in Figure 1—which he develops from financial and other data as being either on the high or the low side, to be modified by the value of intangibles.

COSTS

Primary or direct costs consist of the goods and services which must be surrendered in order to construct and operate a given project or program. Not only do they include all of the monetary expenditures, but provision must also be made for economic losses whether compensated or not. Interest during construction should be taken into account, as should promotional expenses, engineering and supervision, acquisition of land and the relocation of existing facilities . . . [other factors involved include the cost of financing and the problem of tax allowances].

Associated costs are those costs which are incurred by the primary beneficiaries of a given project or program and which must be made in order to realize the full value of the benefits.

There are two schools of thought about how associated costs should be treated in the analysis, and both schools have their adherents among analysts. One school subtracts associated costs from primary benefit (see Fig. 1). Usually the projects involved have irrigation as a main purpose, and the associated costs in this case are the *private* associated costs incurred by farmers in preparing to use irrigation water provided by a *public* authority. The aim of the analyst in this instance is to isolate private from public costs involved in the project.

The other school of thought is not interested in the division between public and private outlays. They argue that all benefits should be confronted by total costs, by whomsoever they are incurred.

Since it is possible to affect the magnitude of the benefit-cost ratio by subtracting the associated costs from the numerator rather than adding them to the denominator, the analyst must ensure that whatever procedure is used for analyzing one project, the *same* procedure must be used for all projects analyzed and compared. It is recommended that since the division of associated costs must always have an arbitrary element in it, it is advisable to put all costs together in the denominator. The division of expenses can then be dealt with in the financial analysis.

Secondary or indirect costs comprise those costs involved in the production of secondary benefits. For example, in the case of the sugar beet factory cited earlier,

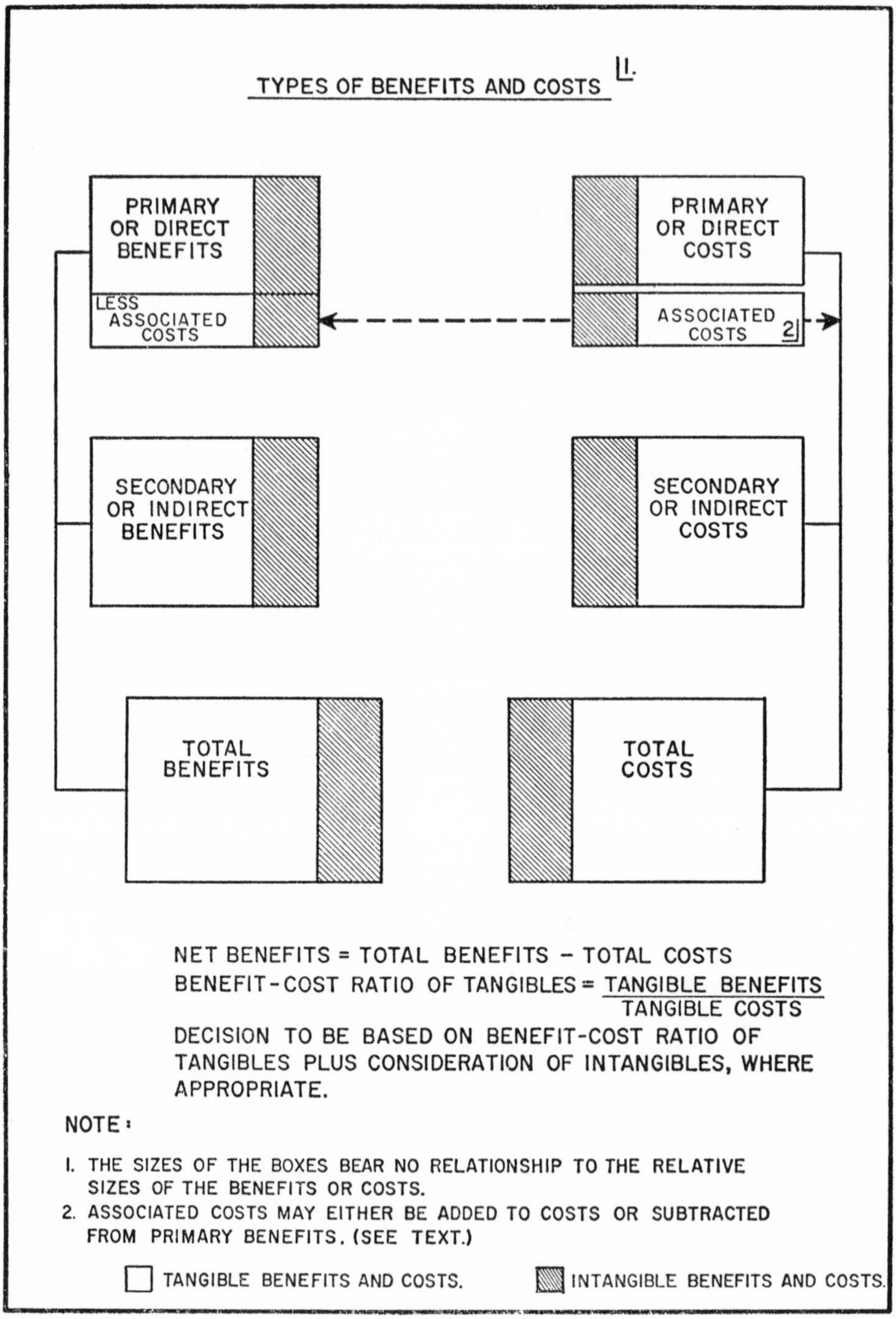
TYPES OF BENEFITS AND COSTS 1
PRIMARY OR DIRECT BENEFITS
LESS ASSOCIATED COSTS
PRIMARY OR DIRECT COSTS
ASSOCIATED COSTS 2
SECONDARY OR INDIRECT BENEFITS
SECONDARY OR INDIRECT COSTS
TOTAL BENEFITS
TOTAL COSTS
NET BENEFITS = TOTAL BENEFITS − TOTAL COSTS
BENEFIT-COST RATIO OF TANGIBLES = TANGIBLE BENEFITS / TANGIBLE COSTS
DECISION TO BE BASED ON BENEFIT-COST RATIO OF TANGIBLES PLUS CONSIDERATION OF INTANGIBLES, WHERE APPROPRIATE.
NOTE:
1. THE SIZES OF THE BOXES BEAR NO RELATIONSHIP TO THE RELATIVE SIZES OF THE BENEFITS OR COSTS.
2. ASSOCIATED COSTS MAY EITHER BE ADDED TO COSTS OR SUBTRACTED FROM PRIMARY BENEFITS. (SEE TEXT.)
TANGIBLE BENEFITS AND COSTS.
INTANGIBLE BENEFITS AND COSTS.

FIG. 1

whose establishment resulted from the development of an irrigation project, its income constitutes a secondary benefit of the project. The costs involved in the production of sugar at the factory are secondary costs of the project.

Intangible costs, like intangible benefits, are those values which are not usually priced in the market. One example might be the loss of a sports fishery as a result of the construction of a dam or other works which interfere with the flow of a river. . . .

An attempt should be made to attach monetary values to such effects as far as possible. Where unmeasurable costs—such as the loss of scenic values or other aesthetic values—are involved, a qualitative statement should be prepared, and considered together with the benefit-cost ratio in the decision-making. Treated in this way they can, at times, tip the balance away from one alternative and result in the selection of another.

Historical or sunk costs consist of sacrifices of goods and services which have been incurred in the past.[4] To this extent they represent a sacrifice which is over and done with. Although they have a bearing on future development, their amount cannot possibly weigh in favor of one future course of action as opposed to another. Historical or sunk costs, therefore, must be excluded from benefit-cost analysis. Benefits resulting entirely from historical expenditures must similarly be excluded from the analysis. In both private and public decision-making, bygones must be bygones. We are starting with a clean slate and our purpose is to decide which future course of action is most appropriate. An example may clarify this point. An agency may be concerned about the deterioration of an irrigation canal. Should it be supplied with a concrete lining or should a steel lining be employed? Certainly the costs and the benefits associated with each of these alternatives should be considered carefully before a decision is made either way. But no one, surely, would argue that the original cost of the canal should also be brought into the calculations.

In the case of a hydro power system, a decision may have to be made as to whether to add further storage capacity. Clearly none of the costs previously incurred has relevance to this decision. It is only the incremental or new additional costs that should be counted.

Joint costs are those expenditures of goods and services which cannot be identified with a single specific purpose. They must, in other words, be shared among several purposes. Joint costs must be distinguished from separable costs, as the latter can be fully attributed to particular purposes. In a multi-purpose water project which provides both hydroelectric power and flood control benefits, expenditures on the dam might constitute a joint cost; whereas the cost of the turbines and generators might be fully allocated to that of the production of electricity, and expenditures associated with the erection and operation of flood gates allocated to flood control. The latter two cost categories are obviously separable costs. They can be identified with a given use; something which is not possible in the case of joint costs.[5]

In conclusion, reference might be made to the comparison of benefits and costs. Not only must the benefit and the cost data used in the case of each project or program be mutually comparable, but equal emphasis must be given to both sides of the comparison. As a result of human enthusiasm, there is sometimes a tendency to overstate certain benefits and to ignore certain costs. This is true particularly of intangible benefits, as there are sometimes credited to the benefit side of the ledger without making a comparable provision for

[4] For discussions of treatment of historical costs see J. H. Dales, *Supplement "A" to the Brief on Flood Control Measures of the Upper Thames Watershed: Benefit-Cost Analysis* (London, Ont.: Upper Thames River Conservation Authority, 1957); and McKean, *op. cit.*, p. 43.

[5] The allocation of joint costs cannot be a matter for economic analysis. Allocation for financial purposes may, however, be necessary. . . .

intangible costs. Or, even more likely, the sum total of all types of economic benefit may be weighed against certain limited costs which are clearly identifiable and strictly financial in nature. Perhaps the best rule to follow is that of making certain that for each benefit claimed, a related cost is entered into the calculations. In this way, a natural tendency toward project or program "promotion" may be overcome.

Principles of Benefit-Cost Analysis

Benefit-cost analysis is based on the following principles:

(a) The goods or services produced by a project or a program have value only to the extent that there is, or will be, a demand for them;

(b) A project or program, in order to qualify as the best alternative for development, must be the most economic means, whether public or private, for supplying the goods or services for which it is designed. The cost of proceeding with the next best alternative, meanwhile, establishes an upper limit to the value of the labor, materials, and other resources which may be employed in its construction and operation;

(c) The first-added, or most economic, alternative should be that project or program which exhibits the highest benefit-cost ratio. It should be remembered, however, that the selection of a given project or program for development usually changes the economic circumstances against which the remaining projects must be evaluated. It is, therefore, necessary to undertake further analyses after the decision to adopt a given project in a program has been made; and

(d) In order to determine the scale on which the first-added project should be built, it is still necessary to maximize its economic effectiveness. The point at which its benefit-cost ratio is a maximum is rarely the point at which the project can make its greatest economic contribution. This can only be determined by reference to its next best alternative. In order to optimize the first-added project, its scale must be increased to the point where its benefit-cost ratio is above, but only just above, that of its next best alternative. For instance, a benefit-cost analysis may show that Projects A, B, and C have ratios of 6:1, 5:1, and 4:1, respectively. The scale of Project A may be increased so long as its benefit-cost ratio does not fall below that of Project B.

Terms of Measurement

The products of any activity which can satisfy human wants are referred to in [this paper] as "goods and services." To the greatest extent possible, the value of goods and services should be expressed in monetary terms, determined through the medium of the market place. Some goods and services demanded by the public, however, are not bought and sold in the market place. These items are sometimes referred to as "intangibles." In many cases it is possible to attach a monetary value to them. . . .

Evaluation of Benefits and Costs

When goods and services are allocated to a given purpose, the effect is obviously to preclude their use for any other purpose. This is the same thing as saying that the economic cost of utilizing a given supply of goods and services for a particular purpose is equivalent to the benefits foregone, i.e. the value which would have been realized had they been employed in their best alternative use. In circumstances where the resources of labor and materials are fully employed, it may be assumed that the value of the goods and services in question is reflected in the volumes consumed and the market prices paid for them. Alternative applications would presumably have used these amounts and paid the same prices for them. Hence, these are the values which represent the true economic cost of goods and services diverted from other uses and employed in a given project or program.

VIEWPOINT FOR ECONOMIC ANALYSIS

The viewpoint from which project and program effects are evaluated is of fundamental importance to the economic analysis.[6] The viewpoint of an individual assessing the positive and negative effects of a given course of action upon his own immediate interests may well be different from that of the community as a whole. Similarly, the outlook of a small group of individuals organized either as a private firm or as a municipal undertaking could differ from that of a provincial authority or of a federal agency. Projects which are national in scope necessarily involve a more comprehensive approach to the evaluation of benefits and costs, since at this level a greater number of alternatives frequently present themselves.

Appropriate allowances must, of course, be made for all transfers, cancellations and offsetting influences. This warning becomes progressively more important as the viewpoint of those responsible for the analysis is expanded to cover neighboring areas and related sectors of the economy. It also turns out that, as the viewpoint adopted in the analysis broadens, some of the secondary effects tend to cancel each other out. In other words, secondary considerations tend to be of lesser importance and the results of the analysis rest more directly on an assessment of primary benefits and costs as the scope of the exercise is increased.

Provincial authorities may, however, include in their analyses effects, some of which can be properly ignored by the federal authorities. Because of these legitimate differences, it is important that the secondary benefits and costs be clearly identified so that negotiations in respect of these differences can proceed in an intelligent manner.

[6] The problem of selecting an appropriate viewpoint is discussed in R. S. Hammond's *Benefit-Cost Analysis and Water Pollution Control* (Stanford: Food Research Inst., Stanford University, 1960), pp. 27–29.

It is apparent, from what has already been said, that the results of benefit-cost analysis may differ according to the viewpoint adopted by the corporation, agency or department carrying out these studies. Whether the viewpoint is local, provincial, regional or national, public or private, however, it should be clearly stated in the analysis. In this way comparisons can be made and negotiations conducted in objective terms.

PROJECT AND PROGRAM FORMULATION

The following principles and procedures, while they are frequently described in terms of single projects, are also applicable to identifiable segments of projects and to entire programs which consist of a number of projects.

The analysis from beginning to end, is essentially a matter of weighing alternatives. Each transportation route, each power site, and each recreational area is considered for possible development. The most promising site or location is then selected by a process of elimination, the one exhibiting the highest ratio of benefits to costs coming out on top. This site or location must then be examined by itself with a view to optimizing its scale.

The first step in a detailed benefit-cost analysis is the estimation of demand for goods and services which can be met by developing the project or program in question. This initial estimate may have to be revised at a subsequent stage:

(1) If substantial reductions in cost are in prospect; or

(2) If higher costs are indicated, thus altering the prices (and so the volumes) of the goods and services demanded. Revisions of this kind may have to be made several times depending upon the number of stages through which the analysis is carried.

Usually the analyst is presented, at the outset, with a specific proposal. A project may have been selected, on the basis of preliminary investigations. Certain technical and financial data are available and, from this, benefits and costs can be calculated in a preliminary way. Conclusions can also be drawn as to:

(a) The extent to which these benefits and costs vary with the size or scale of the project;

(b) The benefits and costs involved in including or leaving out selected projects from a given program;

(c) The benefits and costs involved in including or excluding certain purposes from a multi-purpose project or program.

The optimum scale for a given development occurs at the point where its net benefits are at a maximum. This is the point at which the benefits added by the last increment of scale have fallen to the point where they are just equal to the costs involved in adding this same increment. These increments cannot, of course, be less than the smallest physical additions of plant and equipment that are practical. The same considerations apply when selecting a sequence of projects to form a program.

Expressed in graphic terms (see Fig. 2) three points are significant in the selection of the most economic scale of development of a project or program. The first (Point X) is the scale at which the ratio of benefits to costs is the greatest. The second (Point Y) is the scale at which the benefits exceed the costs by a maximum amount. The third (Point Z) is the scale at which the benefits attributable to the project or program are equal to the costs involved.

If the scale of project development were established at Point X, the rate of benefit accrual per unit of cost would be at a maximum. This is not to say, however, that the full economic potential of the project would be realized at this point. The latter condition is, in fact, realized at Point Y where the net benefits are at a maximum.

At Point Y, the cost of adding another increment to the scale of development is equal to the benefits added as a result of taking this step. Total benefits also exceed total costs by a maximum amount. Beyond Point Y, incremental expenditures exceed the benefits added. These additional steps, therefore, cannot be justified in economic terms.

At each intermediate point between Point Y and Point Z the over-all ratio of benefits to cost is still greater than 1. However, the benefits added with each increase in the scale of the development are less than the costs involved in this expansion. Clearly, increases in scale in this zone of negative net benefits are economically unsound.

The extent to which it is possible to move toward Point Y is, of course, limited by the benefit-cost ratio of the next best alternative. Optimization, under these circumstances, rarely leads to a maximization of net benefits. It should, nevertheless, ensure that the benefits attributed to the first-added project or program are as large as they can be without, at the same time, reducing its benefit-cost ratio to a level below that attainable by its next added alternative.

CRITERIA FOR COMPARING PROJECTS

Economic comparisons may be made by:

A comparison of net benefits.—By comparing the excess of benefits over costs for several projects we discover which will produce the greatest net benefits. This surplus does not, however, take into account the absolute level of costs involved in realizing these values. Two projects with equal surpluses of benefits over costs, following this reasoning, would appear to be equally desirable even though the cost of one were several times that of the other. It follows that the net benefit method of comparison is useful *only* in circumstances where the projects or programs are similar in character and in their scale of development.

For example, if a Project A costs $1,000,000 and produces an excess of benefits over costs of another $1,000,000 and Project B also produces $1,000,000 in net benefits but costs ten times as much as Project A, then B obviously does not merit equal status with A as a resource development opportunity.

A comparison of the rates of return on

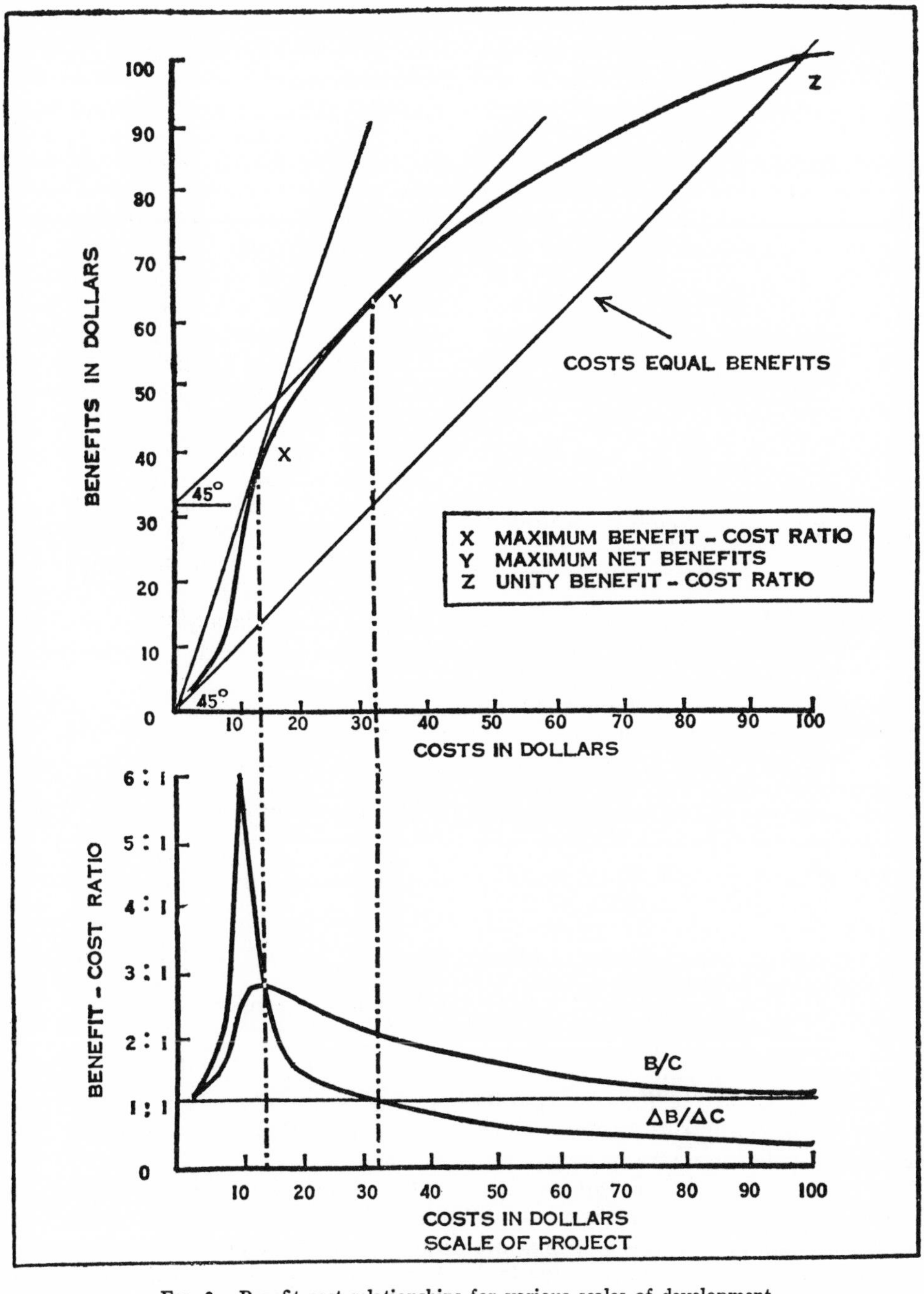

FIG. 2.—Benefit-cost relationships for various scales of development

investment.—The relative profitability of different types of investment can be determined by computing the percentage relationship between annual *net* benefit and the capital invested in the project or program. This method can be useful in the case of alternatives which are capital intensive. However, where they differ in capital intensity and where production, maintenance, and other operating costs are more important, this criterion is a less useful guide for ranking alternatives. The use of this method should, therefore, be confined to the preliminary evaluation of capital intensive projects and programs.

TABLE 1

COMPARISON OF NET BENEFITS

Benefits and Costs	Project A ($)	Project B ($)
Total Costs.......	1,000,000	10,000,000
Total Benefits....	2,000,000	11,000,000
Net Benefit...	1,000,000	1,000,000
Benefit-Cost Ratio	2.0	1.1

For projects with high operating costs in relation to total costs, the ratio of net benefits to investment can be helpful in project selection. In the following example both projects require a total outlay of $11,000,000 and produce benefits of $15,000,000. On the basis of net benefits and benefit-cost ratios they are also identical. If the net benefits of the two projects are compared with their total capital investment, however, Project B has a definite advantage over Project A.

A comparison on the basis of benefit-cost ratios.—Benefit-cost ratios, when uniformly applied, are the principal criteria for selecting economic alternatives. They must be used whenever it is necessary to rank projects or programs and to select one of them for the next stage of development. But having served this purpose, they give way to an optimization procedure which permits the maximization of net benefits.

Clearly, the benefit-cost ratio is a measure of *relative* and not *absolute* merit. It is used, primarily, in comparing projects and programs, one with another. Yet the most economic use of a given resource rarely occurs at that scale of development where the benefit-cost ratio is at a maximum. Usually there is something to be gained by maximizing the net benefits attributable to a given development.

In Figure 2, for instance, the maximum benefit-cost ratio is achieved with an expenditure of $14, whereas net benefits are maximized with an expenditure of $32.

Most analyses make use of benefit-cost ratios. But only in the simplest case, that where only one project is available to serve a given need, does a maximization of net benefits serve as the overriding criterion of economic usefulness. In all other instances, where alternatives exist, the project with the maximum benefit-cost ratio is chosen. Its scale may then be adjusted in such ways as to ensure that its net benefits are increased to the point where its benefit-cost ratio is not below that of the next alternative.

TABLE 2

RATES OF RETURN ON INVESTMENT

Benefits and Costs	Project A ($)	Project B ($)
Capital Investment.....	10,000,000	1,000,000
Lifetime Operating Costs	1,000,000	10,000,000
Total Lifetime Costs....	11,000,000	11,000,000
Total Lifetime Benefits..	15,000,000	15,000,000
Net Lifetime Benefits...	4,000,000	4,000,000
Benefit-Cost Ratio.....	1.4	1.4
Net Benefit-Investment Ratio..............	0.4	4.0

The analysis is repeated to determine which, among the remaining alternatives, should become the next added project. Again the choice is made on the basis of benefit-cost ratios and, again, the project with the higher ratio is optimized in relation to its next best alternative.

Assuming there is still a requirement for

the goods and services which can be produced by the remaining projects, they are reviewed yet another time—and so it goes. Finally, using benefit-cost ratios for purposes of selection, combined with net benefit maximization, the analyst arrives at a schedule or program of projects which is capable of producing the largest excess of benefits over costs.

Project sequence and interdependence.—The *sequence* in which resource development projects are constructed should be examined carefully, as the initial stages of a program usually produce the greatest benefits. For example, the unit value of the first storage reservoir added to an existing hydroelectric power system is often higher than the unit value of additional storages of comparable size built later in the same program. In other words, the prior selection of a given project can greatly improve its economic feasibility. Conversely, the economic feasibility of the remaining projects may be diminished—some of them to the point where they are forever eliminated as reasonable possibilities for development. It follows that a thorough examination of different sequences should be an integral part of any analysis which endeavors to rank projects in their order of economic merit.

The interdependence of projects must also be taken into account. This is true particularly where the construction of one project may change the benefits attributed to the others, even where they form an integral part of a larger scheme of development. Storage dams and downstream run-of-river dams are examples of interdependent projects. These projects or purposes are interdependent when the economic feasibility of one depends, to a significant extent, on the construction of another.

To achieve a better and fuller life it seems to me necessary that we look beyond the temple idol of monetary evaluation. We must think beyond the prayer sticks of the voluminous reports which ostensibly determine whether a project is justifiable.

It would seem to me less esoteric and far more honest to decide that certain elements are necessary for better and fuller lives without dreaming up ways to put meaningless dollar values on them; then to weigh the other elements having monetary value by uniform and objective procedures, so that alternative uses of the resource can be compared, and choices among the alternatives made on sound monetary grounds.

We who call ourselves conservationists must be the first to identify land-use and resource-development measures which are financially sound investments, quite justified without a conservation label. We would then fortify our position and consolidate our ranks when there was need to maintain or protect some esthetic value, some piece of scenery, some wood lot full of ladyslippers, some stretch of white water or of wilderness, which could never be justified on strictly economic grounds. It will require a self-restraint which can come only with the development of a conservation attitude for us to fly the conservation banner only on those things whose value lies not in our pocketbook but only in our heart.

LUNA B. LEOPOLD, *The Conservation Attitude,* Part C, Geological Survey Circular 414, Conservation and Water Management (Washington, 1960), p. 19.

MAYNARD M. HUFSCHMIDT

THE METHODOLOGY OF WATER-RESOURCE SYSTEM DESIGN

Ever since the report of the Inland Waterways Commission in 1908, comprehensive planning of water resources on a river-system basis has been part of our natural resources policy. Indeed, many comprehensive plans have been prepared and much of our water-resource development has been based on such plans. In recent years, however, the methodology of water-resource planning or, as used in this paper, water-resource system design, has been under systematic and critical study for the purpose of determining how new techniques of analysis—engineering, economic and political—can be used in the planning process.[1] A major research program in this field has been under way at Harvard University since 1956, and the following discussion of methodology of water-resource system design is based largely on the research findings of the Harvard Water Program.[2]

• Maynard M. Hufschmidt is Director, Harvard Water Program, Harvard University.

[1] A summary of current status of water-resource system design in the United States is contained in Eugene W. Weber and M. M. Hufschmidt, "River Basin Planning in the United States," *Science, Technology and Development; U.S. Papers Prepared for the U.N. Conference on the Application of Science and Technology for the Benefit of Less Developed Areas. I, Natural Resources* (Washington: Government Printing Office, 1963), pp. 299 ff. Broad surveys of historical development of water-resource planning are given in Gilbert F. White, "A Perspective of River Basin Development," *Law and Contemporary Problems,* XXII, No. 3 (1957), 157; and Theodore M. Schad, "Perspective on National Water Resources Planning," *Proceedings of the American Society Civil Engineers, Hydraulics,* LXXXVIII, HY4 (1962), 17.

Nature of the Design Problem

DECISION-MAKING AND DESIGN

Water-resource system design, in common with other types of public planning, is a technique of decision-making—specifically, public investment decision-making. The decisions of system design relate in good part to the allocation of scarce resources among competing claims; to this extent, system design is an economic problem, to which one can apply the theoretical apparatus of production and allocation economics. In order to choose among alternative courses of action, an objective or set of objectives must be specified and developed as a guide to the optimal design—the one that best meets the objective or set of objectives. Expressed more formally, the decision problem of system design is to maximize the value of an objective function, subject to limitations imposed from outside the system and to the production function imposed by nature and the state of technology.

SYSTEMS NATURE OF DESIGN

An important characteristic of water-resource development is the peculiar nature of its production function. There are very close relationships among individual

[2] Results of research under the Program through 1961 are contained in A. A. Maass, M. M. Hufschmidt, R. Dorfman, S. A. Marglin, H. A. Thomas, Jr., and G. M. Fair, *Design of Water-Resource Systems* (Cambridge: Harvard University Press, 1962). See also M. M. Hufschmidt, "Water Resource System Design," *Water and Sewage Works,* CX (May, 1963), 195.

development units (dams, canals, power plants) and among the various purposes of development (water-supply, irrigation, electric power). These interrelationships, which may be economic and social as well as physical, are typically so strong as to require that design be accomplished on a systems basis with the river basin often (but not always) taken as the relevant system. In fact, the general move toward comprehensive water-resource planning is founded on a recognition that these close system relationships require unified treatment in the process of design.

These production-function characteristics allow designers to make use of the principles, insights, and techniques of that branch of operations research known as systems analysis. Insights on the nature and boundaries of systems and details of the theory and application of mathematical models (linear, quasi-linear, and dynamic programming models) and simulation techniques will all prove useful in water-resource system design. In fact, the important concepts of linkages and feedback derived from systems analysis can serve as powerful analytical tools for determining the geographic and functional boundaries of water-resource systems—that is, for making decisions on the areas and kinds of resource uses which must be included within the system, and those which can be treated as independent entities.

INVESTMENT NATURE OF DESIGN

Another important characteristic of water-resource design is the important role of investment decisions. Typically, a water-resources design includes a program for capital investment for the use and control of water, often accompanied by a schedule for installation of works over an extended period of years. Two important considerations flow from this attribute of the design problem: (1) Because investment implies that resources (which involve costs) must be dedicated in lumps at the outset, or at discrete points in time in the future, while returns from investment in the form of goods and services (which generate benefits) are obtained as a flow over an extended period of time, designers require a discount rate to bring costs and benefits to a common dimension in time. The value of the discount rate plays a crucial role in investment decisions; the basic factors which are involved in its determination, e.g., rate of economic growth, are policy decisions which must be made at the highest level of government; and (2) the nature of investment dictates that, while we *must* incur some investment costs before we can expect any returns, we are far from certain of receiving the returns in the quantity and according to the schedule as originally estimated, especially during the later years of investment life. Because changes in technology and economic demands intervene, this uncertainty will be present even if we know for certain the physical output that can be obtained in future years from our investment—and, in water-resource developments, we cannot even be sure of obtaining the estimated physical output. Our inability to predict accurately the demand for, and hence the benefits from, physical outputs adds a major element of uncertainty to the design problem, that, along with technologic uncertainty, contributes greatly to the complexity of analysis.[3]

THE FOUR STEPS OF DESIGN

Given that water-resource design involves application of decision-making techniques to investment problems in a systems context, it follows that a workable methodology for design must be capable of dealing effectively with all of these attributes. The methodology presented here has been devised to this end; it contains four related steps: (1) specifying the *objectives* of design; (2) translating these

[3] A caution is required here lest water-resource design be cast entirely in an investment mold. There are important water-management and land-use control techniques that involve little or no initial investment. Flood plain zoning and improved operation of existing water management systems are important examples.

objectives into *design criteria;* (3) using the criteria to formulate specific designs of development and management for water-resource systems that fulfill the objectives to the highest degree; and (4) evaluating the consequences of the designs that have been developed. The discussion which follows is organized according to these four steps.

THE OBJECTIVES OF DESIGN

By objective of design we do *not* mean instrumental goals such as providing a certain quantity of water supply or hydroelectric energy or designing for a particular level of flood protection. Our concern is with fundamental national goals that relate to human welfare—objectives such as increases in national income (economic efficiency); redistribution of income to classes, groups, or regions; economic growth; maintenance of a satisfactory level of employment; and maintenance and enhancement of cultural, historical, and aesthetic values.[4]

Several propositions follow from the statement of objectives in this form.

1. The fundamental nature of these economic and social objectives requires that, whatever the type or level of government involved, the objectives of design be specified by the highest policy-making unit or units of government. For example, in a constitutional-democratic system of government as in the United States, objectives would be set at the national level by the President and the Congress in the legislative process—at the State level, by the Governor and the Legislature.[5]

2. These objectives are not necessarily, or even typically, complementary or consistent with each other. They usually will be in conflict, at least to some degree. In general, it will therefore not be possible to design a water-resource system which will fulfill each of a number of objectives to the highest degree. In order to maximize the value of one objective—say, economic efficiency—it will usually be necessary to sacrifice some increment of value of another objective—say, regional income redistribution. The conflicting nature of objectives is an important cause of many difficulties and controversies that arise in water-resources planning.[6]

3. The value assigned to the contribution of a design to meeting an objective is usually called a *benefit.* It follows, therefore, that the term benefit, when used in this context, has meaning only in terms of an objective. We can properly speak of "economic efficiency benefits," or "income redistribution benefits," of a design; in contrast, it is not enough merely to speak of the "benefits" of a design, without identifying the underlying objective or objectives.[7]

This multiplicity of objectives creates problems in the process of design. In formal terms, our design task is to maximize the value of an *objective function.* If only one objective is relevant, the formal statement of the problem is straightforward (although solutions of the design problem may be quite difficult). But if more than one objective must be considered, the statement turns out to be more complicated.

For the single objective of economic efficiency, the objective function whose value is to be maximized can be stated in mathematical terms as follows:

$$\sum_{t=1}^{T} \frac{E_t(y_t) - M_t(x_t)}{(1+r)^t} - K(x),$$

[4] For discussion of public policy goals in relation to social welfare, see J. Rothenberg, *The Measurement of Social Welfare* (Englewood Cliffs: Prentice-Hall, 1961), and the literature cited therein.

[5] A broad framework for the political process involved in setting objectives is given in A. Maass, "System Design and the Political Process," *Design of Water-Resource Systems, op. cit.*, chap. 15.

[6] The running conflict between various groups and public agencies on the proper development of the Potomac River Basin stems primarily from disagreement over fundamental objectives. See U.S., Army, Corps of Engineers, *Potomac River Basin Report,* U.S. Army Engineer Baltimore District, III (Feb., 1963), processed.

[7] For a detailed discussion of the objectives of design within the context of welfare economics, see Stephen A. Marglin, "Objectives of Water-Resource Development: A General Statement," *Design of Water-Resource Systems, op. cit.*, chap. 2.

where $E_t(y_t)$ = gross efficiency benefits in the tth year for the output (y) of the system in that year;

$M_t(x_t)$ = operation, maintenance, and replacement (OMR) costs in year t for the constructed system (x);

$K(x)$ = capital costs for the constructed system (x);

r = discount rate;

T = length, in years, of the economic time horizon.

The summation yields the present value of the stream of gross benefits less OMR costs for a period of T years, discounted at interest rate r. Subtraction of undiscounted capital costs (assumed to be incurred in year 1) yields the present value of net efficiency benefits, which is the quantity to be maximized.

Where two objectives—say, economic efficiency and income redistribution—are involved, the objective function can be presented in the following three alternative forms:[8]

1. Maximize economic efficiency benefits subject to the constraint that at least a specified level of income redistribution benefits be attained over the life of the system.

2. Maximize income-redistribution benefits, subject to the constraint that at least a specified level of efficiency benefits be attained.

3. Maximize a weighted sum of efficiency and income-redistribution benefits.

From this brief introduction to the concept and form of the objective function, it should be evident that a clear and unambiguous statement of objectives to be served is a first requisite to the design task. But those who must formulate the designs that maximize the value of the objective function, that is, the field level planners, need additional guides in the form of detailed specifications or, as we shall call them, design criteria.

THE DESIGN CRITERIA

In presenting alternative statements of objective function, we have introduced implicitly the notion of design criteria. There follows a listing of the more important criteria required for a typical field-level design:

1. The objective function, which itself is an important design criterion, defining the mix of objectives, their relative weights, and their form: i.e., as values to be maximized or as constraints to be fulfilled.

2. The discount rate, r, which serves to place all cost and benefit streams on a common basis in time.

3. A weighting factor, to be applied to capital and/or OMR costs, which reflects the existence of a budgetary constraint on capital and/or OMR funds.

4. A weighting factor, to be applied to capital and OMR costs, to reflect the "opportunity cost" of funds, i.e., the returns elsewhere in the economy per dollar of funds that would be foregone should these funds be used for the development under study.

5. A weighting factor, to be applied to capital and/or OMR costs, to reflect divergencies between real costs and money costs, which arise under conditions of less than full employment.

6. Instructions on how to construct gross-benefit functions for each major purpose of water-resource development—domestic and industrial water supply, irrigation, hydropower, flood-damage alleviation, pollution-control, recreation, navigation, preservation and enhancement of fish, wildlife, scenic, cultural, and historic resources.

7. Instructions on how to handle uncertainty, including (a) uncertainty situations whose outcomes can be defined by a probability distribution—for example, uncertainty arising from the hydrology of a system—and (b) uncertainty situations where probabilistic statements on outcomes cannot be

[8] For a more detailed treatment, including a formal mathematical statement, discussion of the close relationship among the three forms of objective function, and the role of the Lagrangean multiplier, see *Design of Water-Resource Systems, op. cit.*, pp. 70–84.

made—for example, uncertainty arising from technological change or changes in economic conditions.

8. Definition of the geographical area and functional scope of the field-level design problem.

9. Constraints arising from political and institutional factors such as (a) international relations, (b) federal-state relations, and (c) inter-state relations, involving (in the United States) agreements by interstate compact or judgments by the U.S. Supreme Court.

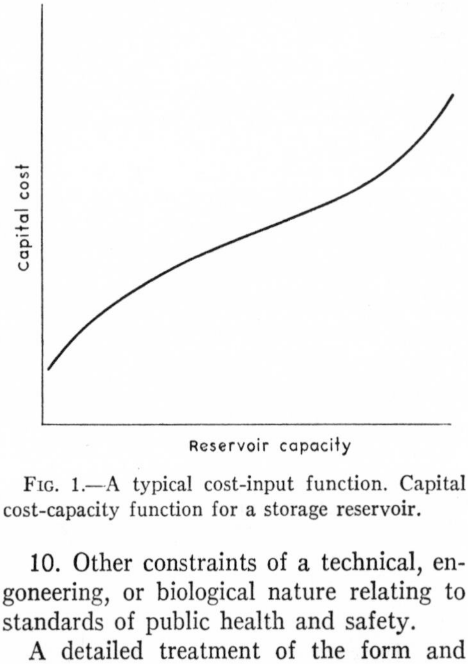

FIG. 1.—A typical cost-input function. Capital cost-capacity function for a storage reservoir.

10. Other constraints of a technical, engoneering, or biological nature relating to standards of public health and safety.

A detailed treatment of the form and content of design criteria is beyond the scope of this article, but it should be clear that the policy content of the criteria is high. As with the objective function, planning at field level cannot be accomplished effectively unless the design criteria to be applied are clearly set forth by higher level policy-makers.

SYSTEM DESIGN AT FIELD LEVEL

With the objective function and major design criteria specified, the field-level planner seeks to prepare the design which maximizes the value of the objective function subject to the constraints and the general rules set by the design criteria. Expressed another way, he strives within the constraints to maximize net benefits—gross benefits minus costs—where benefits are defined in terms of the objectives.[9]

The study of field-level planning can best be approached by describing three important relationships or functions. These are (1) the *cost-input* function, (2) the *benefit-output* function, and (3) the *output-input* function, also known as the technological or production function.[10] In essence, the process of system design is the derivation of these fundamental relationships and their application to the system under study. A thorough grasp of these functions and their relation one to another and to the objective function is thus essential to an understanding of the problem of system design.

The cost-input function is perhaps the most straightforward and easily understood. It expresses the response of cost—capital or OMR—to resource inputs. These resource inputs can be expressed as a vector of the quantities of all the goods and services required to build a structure, say a dam. If we assume that for any given structure size, the most economical design is known, we can regard the cost of this most economical design as summarizing and measuring the entire resource cost of a structure of given size. The relationship between structure size and cost can then be simply portrayed as in Figure 1, where

[9] To express the design task in this way is to rule out other approaches such as "satisficing," under which the planner seeks an acceptable design, defined as one that meets certain minimum standards or goals. See H. A. Simon, *Models of Man* (New York: John Wiley & Sons, 1957), Sec. IV, and *idem*, "Theories of Decision-Making in Economics and Behavioral Science," *American Economic Review*, XLIX (1959), 253.

[10] A more detailed (and more sophisticated) discussion of these functions and their relation to optimal design is contained in Robert Dorfman, "Basic Economic and Technologic Concepts: A General Statement," *Design of Water-Resource Systems, op. cit.*, chap. 3. The material presented here is largely adapted from chap. 3.

capital cost only is considered and where dam size is expressed in terms of units of storage capacity of the reservoir created by the dam. Similar cost-input functions both for capital and OMR costs can be developed for all of the system structures under study through use of standard techniques of cost estimating and engineering design.

The benefit-output function depicts the relation of gross benefits to output of goods and services from the system. The output of a water-resource system is typically a vector which may take on complex characteristics that depend both upon the nature of the system and on the purpose being served. For example, a "water supply" output can be defined as an assured quantity of annual supply, of acceptable quality, available at a specific location (perhaps at the dam site) according to a specified schedule during the year. Analogous definitions can be developed for hydropower and irrigation, and modified versions can be constructed for flood-damage alleviation and recreation. When so defined, and under certain restrictive assumptions as to hydrology, we can depict a benefit-output function for water supply from a reservoir as in Figure 2.[11]

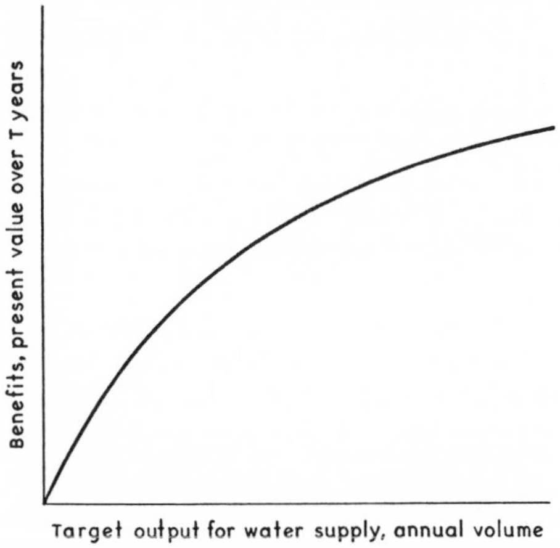

FIG. 2.—A typical benefit-output function. Benefits (in present value terms) as a function of annual target output over economic life of the system.

The output-input or production function expresses the relationships between resource inputs to the system and the outputs of goods and services that result.[12] Figure 3 shows a production function for a storage reservoir with a single output—water supply (assumed to have the temporal, spatial, and quality characteristics described above). Any point, such as *A*, in the region below the curve is inefficient, because it is possible, by moving vertically to point *B* on the function, to obtain a greater output on water supply without increasing reservoir size. Conversely, points (such as *C*) above the curve are technologically infeasible; that is, attainable outputs from the reservoir cannot exceed the values described by the curve.

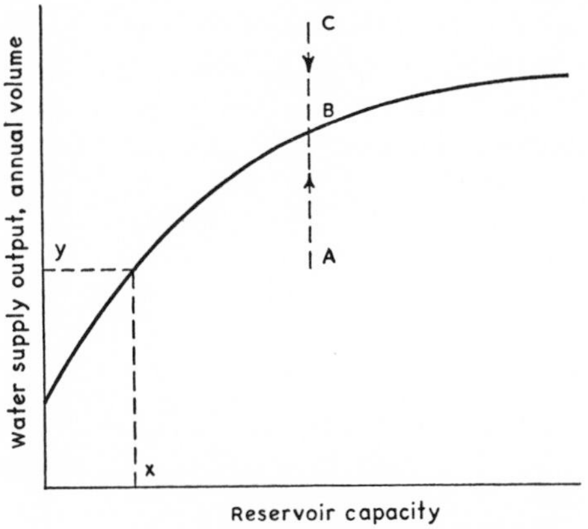

FIG. 3.—A typical production function. Water supply output, as a function of reservoir capacity.

At this point it is convenient to combine

[11] Benefits are in terms of present value of a stream of equal annual benefits, over the economic life of the system. The discount operator is $1/(1+r)^t$ where r is the discount rate and t the index of the year. The benefit function is shown with a decreasing slope to reflect one common case—the economic situation of decreasing unit price with increase in quantity of output.

[12] In formal terms, it is the locus of all technologically feasible inputs and outputs such that the output vector cannot be exceeded without increasing some input and, conversely, the input vector cannot be decreased without decreasing some output.

the cost-input and production functions into a cost-output function, as in Curve *C* in Figure 4 which represents a combination of the curves in Figures 1 and 3. In order to represent all three functions on a single graph, we transfer the benefit-output function in Figure 2 to Figure 4, labeling it Curve *B*.

FORMAL CONDITIONS FOR OPTIMAL DESIGN

With the information shown on Figures 3 and 4 for this simple, single-reservoir, single-output case, it is possible to determine (1) the optimal level of output (from

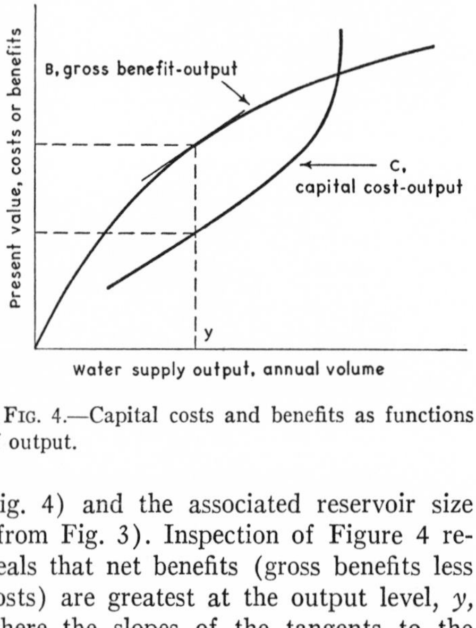

FIG. 4.—Capital costs and benefits as functions of output.

Fig. 4) and the associated reservoir size (from Fig. 3). Inspection of Figure 4 reveals that net benefits (gross benefits less costs) are greatest at the output level, *y*, where the slopes of the tangents to the benefit and cost curves are equal. For, at this point the marginal cost (MC) of a unit of output just equals its marginal benefit (MB). At outputs in excess of this, marginal cost increases and marginal benefits decrease; additional units of output are thus not worth their cost. Furthermore, at levels of output immediately below the optimal level, marginal cost is less than marginal benefit and it therefore pays to increase output to the point where MC = MB. By inspection of Figure 3, the reservoir capacity *x* required to produce the optimal level of output, *y*, can be determined.

The formal condition MC = MB is sufficient to determine optimality of the single-reservoir, single-purpose case. Where more than one purpose (output vector) or more than one reservoir (input vector) is involved, however, other conditions must be met. For the multiunit, multipurpose case these are[13]

(1) $MC_i/MC_h = MRS_{hi}$, which means that, at any fixed level of output, the rate at which one input *h* can be substituted for another input *i* (for example, 2 units of *h* for 1 unit of *i*) must equal the ratio of the cost of a unit of *i* to the cost of a unit of *h* (that is, where one unit of *i* costs $2 and one unit of *h* costs $1, the ratio is 2/1). As economists put it, the ratio of the marginal costs of any two resource inputs (*i* and *h*) must equal the marginal rate at which the second (*h*) input can be substituted for the first (*i*) to achieve a fixed level of output.

(2) $MB_j/MB_k = MRT_{kj}$, which means that the rate at which an output *k* is sacrificed to obtain a second output *j* (for example, 2 units of *k* must be sacrificed to obtain 1 unit of *j*) must equal the ratio of the benefits obtained from a unit of *j* to the benefits obtained from a unit of *k* (that is, where 1 unit of *j* has a value of $2, and 1 unit of *k*, a value of $1, the ratio is 2/1). Or, put another way, the ratio of the marginal benefit of any two outputs (*j* and *k*)

[13] These relationships can be derived by straightforward application of the theory of maximization of the differential calculus. They are therefore subject to the limitations of that theory. Three important limitations are (1) the formal conditions listed above are necessary but not sufficient conditions for a maximum; (2) even when sufficient conditions for a maximum are met, the methods of the calculus guarantee only that a local maximum has been achieved; and (3) if the permissible range of variation of the input and output variables is limited, it is possible for a maximum to appear at a point that does not even meet the "necessary" conditions for a maximum. For a more detailed discussion, see Dorfman, "Basic Economic and Technologic Concepts: A General Statement," *op. cit.*, chap. 3.

must equal the marginal rate at which the second output (k) is sacrificed to obtain the first (j), when the levels of all inputs are fixed.

THE PROCESS OF FIELD-LEVEL DESIGN

With the objective function defined, design criteria specified, and formal conditions for optimization outlined, we now turn to the application of the theoretical apparatus to design problems at field level. Only a summary treatment is given here. For details, the reader should consult cited references.

Again, it is convenient to organize the discussion in terms of the four fundamental relationships: the cost-input, benefit-output, production, and objective functions. The task of system design at field level is to assemble and analyze basic physical and economic data relating to these functions, and, with these data at hand, to apply analytical techniques to determine the physical and economic behavior of alternative system designs, continuing the process until the optimal design is identified.

The field-level design process contains the following major elements of work:

1. Collection and analysis of basic data on resource supply, involving studies of climate, soil, topography, geology and hydrology.
2. Collection and analysis of basic data on present and projected demands for resources, including studies of population, economic activity, and economic demand schedules for water-derived goods and services.
3. Assembly of an inventory of development and management alternatives, including possible dams, reservoirs, irrigation developments, power schemes, flood-damage alleviation measures, and the like.
4. Preliminary screening of alternatives in a systems context, to identify high-quality measures for further, more detailed analysis.
5. Detailed analysis of systems of alternative development measures—structural and non-structural—leading to identification of the optimal design, or a set of alternative optimal designs, each appropriate to an alternative objective function.

Work elements (1) and (3) supply data essential to definition of the input-cost and production functions, and element (2) performs a similar purpose for the output-benefit functions. Element (4) represents the initial use of these functions in concert to screen out alternatives that are grossly inferior. At this stage, data on the cost-input, benefit-output, and production functions are based on only rough estimates, although analysis would be carried on within a systems context, if only in simplified form. In element (5), however, full-scale, detailed systems analysis is applied, with refined cost and benefit data and with detailed elaboration of system relationships, in the search for the optimal design.

Much work in water-resource planning is concerned with assembly and analysis of physical and economic data, classified under (1)–(3) above. While this work is essential to proper performance of systems analysis and optimization as in elements (4) and (5), we forego any discussion here in order to introduce certain techniques of systems analysis which have been the subject of research by the Harvard Water Program. These techniques fall into two broad classes: mathematical models and simulation. Each class relies heavily for its utility as a design tool on the high-speed computer. Because use of mathematical models usually requires that design problems be simplified drastically, this technique is more appropriate for the preliminary screening stage of analysis [element (4), above], than for the final design stage [element (5)]. Conversely, simulation works most effectively at this final stage where the number of relevant alternatives is relatively few and where there is need to study performance of systems in considerable detail.

SIMULATION[14]

While simulation has long been in use as an analytical technique, its extensive use on large systems today stems from the availability of the large computer whose high speed and great data-storage capacity allow rapid manipulation of vast amounts of data. The most general meaning of the term simulation is to reproduce the behavior of a system in all relevant detail without actually attaining reality. Alternatively, simulation is defined as the elemental representation of the operation in time of some real physical system.

Systems analysts have turned to simulation because it is often the only way effectively to deal with large and complex systems that defy analytical solution (in the sense of formal solution of a mathematical problem). Because most problems of water-resource system design take on this characteristic, simulation appears to be particularly appropriate for their solution.

Simulating a water-resource system on a computer involves representing all of the inherent characteristics and probable responses of the system to control by a model that is largely arithmetic and algebraic in nature but which also includes some non-mathematical logical processes. For a typical design, variables consist of reservoirs, power plants, recreation facilities, irrigation works, target outputs for water supply, energy, irrigation, and specified allocations of reservoir capacity for active, dead, flood, and recreation storage. By target output, we mean a specified set of output quantities (e.g., volumes of water or energy) which are to be provided, if possible, by operation of the system.

Hydrology is typically provided in mean monthly flows, except for flood-control analyses, where flow data are provided for very short periods, such as 3, 6, or 12 hours. These flows are routed through the system for an extended period of years (which may be as long as 500 or 1,000 years) according to a specified operating procedure, and the magnitudes of the physical outputs actually realized and resulting gross and net benefits are determined. If desired, systems can be analyzed in dynamic terms, that is, capital investment in system units need not be made at the outset but can be scheduled over a number of years, and levels of target outputs can be changed over time.

Preparing the information on the system for computer use is a major task. First, basic physical and economic data, including hydrologic data, must be assembled and arranged in a form easily handled by the computer. This may involve data for many cost-input and benefit-output functions, parameters, and constants relating to internal configuration of the system and the statistical characteristics of the hydrologic record. Next an operating procedure is formulated to serve as the fundamental control for the simulation. Finally, the instructions for handling the data and operating the system are coded for use on the computer. This usually turns out to be a time-consuming and tedious task, especially if the system is at all complicated.

A simulation program typically starts with a monthly operating procedure having monthly inflows, releases, constraint levels, and target outputs; when a flood month is encountered, program control shifts to a flood-routing procedure based upon a shorter time interval—3-hr, 6-hr, or 12-hr. At the conclusion of flood routing, program control returns to the monthly operating procedure which then proceeds to deal with the next month.

Results of the simulation are stated in economic terms, through use of the cost and benefit functions to evaluate capital and OMR costs, benefits from target outputs, and monetary losses and gains arising from deficits and surpluses in outputs. Economic results are converted to present values of net benefits by applying the discount rate.

[14] For a detailed discussion of simulation as a technique of analysis for water-resource system design, see M. M. Hufschmidt and M. B. Fiering, *Simulation Techniques for Design of Water-Resource Systems* (to be published).

An example of a moderately large simulation program is that for the Lehigh River, a tributary of the Delaware River in Pennsylvania, which was coded for the IBM 7094 computer at Harvard.[15]

As shown in Figure 5, the Lehigh system consists of six storage sites; each can be used to provide (1) regulated flows for water supply or water quality improvement at a use point (Bethlehem), (2) recreation services at the reservoir sites, (3) storage for flood-damage prevention, and (4) storage and head for hydroelectric energy. A diversion channel can be provided from the Lehigh River at a point below reservoirs 1 and 2 to reservoir 3 so that flows in the Lehigh can be diverted and stored, if desired, in reservoir 3, which thereby functions as an off-channel storage unit.

Reservoirs 3 through 6 are each associated with but a single hydropower plant. But, as shown in Figure 5, reservoirs 1 and 2 can have more than one (although only one for each design).

As arranged for simulation, the Lehigh system contains forty-two major design variables. Sixteen variables deal with physical facility components—sizes of the six reservoirs, nine power plants, and the diversion works from the Lehigh River to reservoir 3. At most, only five reservoirs and five power plants can have positive values in any one design. Twenty-four variables relate to allocation of reservoir capacity; in a sense they are parameters or basic decision elements of the operating procedure. These allocations are to dead, flood-control, and recreation storages. For each system design there is but a single value for dead storage capacity associated with each reservoir; but the flood-storage and recreation allocations for each reservoir are twelve-element vectors, one element for each month of the year.

Finally, there are two output design variables—for water supply and electric energy. These appear as twelve-element vectors, with target volumes of water and energy to be provided.

The Lehigh simulation model is dynamic, in that investments in reservoirs, power plants, and recreational facilities can be scheduled over time to meet changing levels and patterns of demands for system outputs. The model can accommodate up to ten changes in investment and

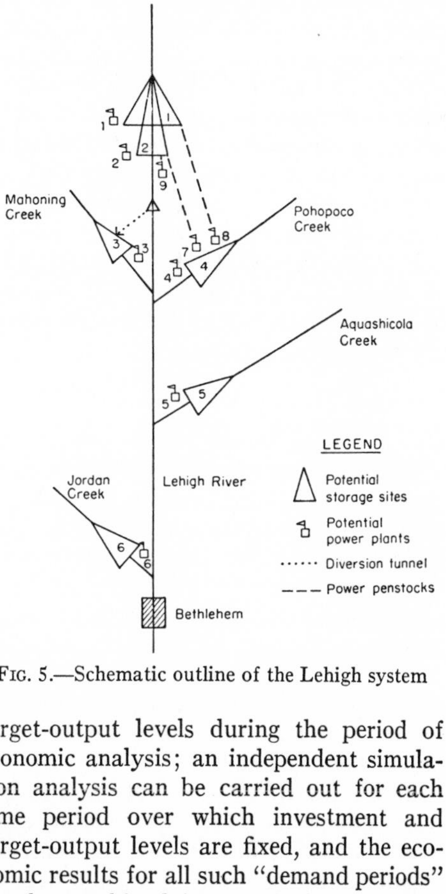

FIG. 5.—Schematic outline of the Lehigh system

target-output levels during the period of economic analysis; an independent simulation analysis can be carried out for each time period over which investment and target-output levels are fixed, and the economic results for all such "demand periods" can be combined into a single payoff for the entire period of economic analysis. The dynamic dimension has the effect of adding ten time-associated design variables to the model, thus giving a problem with fifty-two major design variables.

The model contains the usual capital and OMR cost functions for resource inputs, long-run benefit functions for target out-

[15] A detailed description of this program is given in Hufschmidt and Fiering, *Simulation Techniques for Design of Water-Resource Systems, op. cit.*

puts for water supply, energy, and recreation, and flood-damage–discharge functions. Functions which relate losses in economic value to output deficits (failures to meet the specified target outputs) are provided for water supply, energy, and recreation outputs. Economic payoffs in terms of net benefits for each demand period and for the entire period of economic analysis are provided for any specified discount rate. Information is provided on both the mean and standard deviation of annual benefits for water supply, energy, and recreation, and annual flood losses with and without the system.

In the simulation, either the historical trace of monthly and flood hydrology or synthetic traces (generated internally as part of the program) can be used. Simulation can be carried out for as many years as desired; the simulation period need not be identical in length to the demand period or the period of economic analysis.

LIMITATIONS OF SIMULATION AND THEIR SOLUTION

There are three important limitations to simulation as applied to water-resource systems. First, simulation alone does not give optimal answers to design problems. A single simulation run, with a unique set of values for the design variables, provides an estimate of system performance, including information on benefits and costs, for this unique design. However, it gives little information to guide the analyst to the selection of better designs. Yet, even a relatively simple water-resource system, with but a few design variables, can have an enormous number of unique designs; thus, the search for the optimal design is a difficult task. In effect, it involves exploration of an n-dimensional net-benefit response surface, in which the results, in net benefits, of any single simulation with a unique set of the design variables constitutes a single point on this surface.

A second limitation derives from the relatively short length of historical streamflow records. They are run through the computer in the order of their occurrence—in the case of the Lehigh, over the 37-year period of record. Yet the brevity of historic records operates to provide a very limited representation of the possible configuration of flows. Estimates of system performance obtained from simulations using but the single historic trace of hydrology are an inadequate representation of possible performance as they tell nothing about performance under other, equally likely, hydrologic configurations.

The third limitation results from the unfortunate fact that optimal operating procedures cannot readily be devised for simulation programs of the type described here. At the very least, therefore, operating procedures ought to be extremely flexible. Yet the necessity to be specific about operating rules in constructing a simulation program impairs flexibility. Although we should like to treat operating procedure as a free variable along with other design variables, our ability to do so without a substantial and time-consuming rewrite of the program is limited by the very nature of the simulation program.

SAMPLING[16]

A partial solution to the first limitation is the use along with simulation of sampling methods for the efficient selection of combinations of design variables to be tested by simulation. The only practical means of finding the optimal combination of the n design variables is to use some method of sampling the variables, and thereby to explore the net benefit response surface.

Sampling can be systematic or random. In systematic sampling the magnitudes of the variables are selected in accordance with some ordering principle; in random sampling, purely by chance from an appropriate population. Among systematic sampling methods are the uniform-grid or factorial, single-factor, marginal-analysis, and steepest ascent. An effective sampling strategy consists of a combination of ran-

16 For a discussion of sampling as applied to water-resource system design, see M. M. Hufschmidt, "Analysis by Simulation: Examination of Response Surface," *Design of Water-Resource Systems, op. cit.*, chap. 10.

dom and systematic methods. Typically, analysis would start with large samples—random or systematic—covering the broad domain of the response surface. Regions of high net benefits would then be explored systematically by the methods of steepest ascent and marginal analysis until there was no further gain in net benefits.

With a well-designed sampling strategy, it is possible to identify approximately optimal designs in a few hundred trial simulations at most. Sampling, therefore, has proved to be a powerful means for reducing to manageable proportions the task of examining a wide range of possible designs by computer simulation.

SYNTHETIC STREAMFLOW SEQUENCES[17]

The limitation of water-resource simulation analysis to historic streamflow sequences has been effectively breached by the development of statistical models for generating synthetic streamflow sequences of any desired length. Various models of operational hydrology for synthesizing monthly flows have been developed and validated; the most elaborate current model is based on multivariate statistical analysis of historic flows at a number of gauging stations throughout the river basin. This analysis produces synthetic flow data which, in effect, are samples from the same parent distributions as the original hydrologic observations and are indistinguishable from the observed flows by common tests of statistical significance.

In contrast to these models for synthesizing monthly flows, models for synthesizing flood hydrographs are in early stages of development. Experiments on synthesizing the flood hydrology of the Clearwater (Idaho), Meramec (Missouri), and Lehigh (Pennsylvania) basins have indicated that no single model is equally applicable to all. A reasonably good representation of flood peaks and hydrographs has been achieved for the Lehigh basin with a model that uses correlation of flood peaks and durations to monthly flows. But, limitation on flood data and complexity of the problems involved indicate that flood hydrograph models will probably not attain the generality possible for monthly flow models.

OPERATING POLICIES[18]

Conceptually, there is associated with each system design an optimal operating policy. The derivation of this policy is likely to be impracticable, however, with existing techniques of simulation analysis because only a few of the relatively large number of possible policies can feasibly be tested when change in operating policy requires a substantial recoding of the simulation program. If, however, the essential parameters of an operating policy—such as upper and lower constraints on reservoir storage and the sequence in which releases are made from reservoirs to meet various target outputs—can be varied along with other system inputs, many alternative policies can be tested without recoding the simulation, and an optimal policy can be approximated. In constructing the Lehigh simulation program, the approach involves specifying as input data the relevant parameters of a generalized operating policy such as constraint levels for flood control and recreation storage. This gain in flexibility is accompanied, however, by greater complexity in coding the simulation program.

From this discussion of simulation, it should be obvious that the complexity and difficulty of constructing and coding simu-

[17] The details of theory and application of operational hydrology are contained in H. A. Thomas, Jr., and M. B. Fiering, "Mathematical Synthesis of Streamflow Sequences for the Analysis of River Basins by Simulation," *Design of Water-Resource Systems, op. cit.*, chap. 12; Fiering, "Queuing Theory and Simulation in Reservoir Design," *Transactions of the American Society of Civil Engineers,* CXXVII, Part 1 (1962), 1114; *idem,* "Multivariate Technique for Synthetic Hydrology," *Hydrology Division, Proceedings of the American Society of Civil Engineers,* XC, HY5 (September, 1964), 43, and *Simulation Techniques for Design of Water-Resource Systems, op. cit.*

[18] For details on operating policy problems, see B. T. Bower, M. M. Hufschmidt, and W. W. Reedy, "Operating Procedures: Their Role in the Design of Water-Resource Systems by Simulation Analyses," *Design of Water-Resource Systems, op. cit.*, chap. 11.

lation programs for water-resource systems increase rapidly with the number of development alternatives. Experience with coding a simulation program for the Delaware Basin indicates that systems of up to forty-five development alternatives can be handled with present-generation computers.

But simulation of systems with several hundred alternatives is impracticable with present equipment and techniques. Therefore, some method of preliminary screening is necessary in water-resource planning to reduce the number of development alternatives to a level where simulation can be applied effectively.

MATHEMATICAL MODELS[19]

One possibility is to use simplified mathematical models for this purpose. The successful application of optimizing techniques such as linear, non-linear, and dynamic programming to the solution of many problems of resource allocation has led to attempts to apply the methods to problems of water-resource system design. These attempts have yielded only modest results thus far.[20] Two major difficulties arise: (1) The simplifications that are required to apply the model to the design problem are often so drastic as to limit the usefulness of the solution; and (2) even with drastic simplification of the problem, present computer capacities place limits on the number of design variables and constraints that can be handled feasibly. The power of mathematical models in finding optimal solutions is so great, however, that it is worthwhile to explore the limits of applicability of the models to water-resource design problems.

EVALUATING CONSEQUENCES OF DESIGNS

In the fourth and final step of the idealized methodology, water-resource system designs, prepared in the field on the basis of objectives and design criteria provided by central-office policy makers, are submitted (in the United States) to the President and Congress for review of and action on the proposed plans. At this stage, the consequences of applying the objectives and design criteria to actual situations become known to policy makers. These consequences cannot always be anticipated at the time objectives and criteria are established, and thus the consequences may or may not be to the liking of policy makers. Based upon review of completed designs, policy makers may wish to revise some of the objectives and design criteria to accord with new facts and situations. With this last step of the design process, the circle is closed and the process of system design at field level begins anew, this time with new statements of objectives and criteria.

CONCLUSION

Finally, we point out the dynamic nature of planning methods for application of water-resource systems. The full impact of new techniques of systems analysis and operations research and dramatic changes in computer technology are only beginning to be understood by planners and designers. Thus, changes in practice may assume forms in detail somewhat different than those discussed in this paper, but we can be sure that major changes will be along the general lines presented here.

19 For detailed discussion of various mathematical model approaches, see H. A. Thomas, Jr., and P. Watermeyer, "Mathematical Models: A Stochastic Sequential Approach," chap. 14, and R. Dorfman, "Mathematical Models: The Multistructure Approach," chap. 13, *Design of Water-Resource Systems, op. cit.*; P. Watermeyer and H. A. Thomas, Jr., "Queuing Theory and Reservoir Design," *Proceedings of a Harvard Symposium on Digital Computers and Their Application* (Cambridge: Harvard University Press, 1962); and H. A. Thomas, Jr., and R. Burden, *Operations Research in Water Quality Management* (Cambridge: Harvard Water Resources Group, Division of Engineering and Applied Physics, Harvard University, 1963). See also Warren A. Hall and David T. Howell, "The Optimization of Single-Purpose Reservoir Design with the Application of Dynamic Programming to Synthetic Hydrology Samples," *Journal of Hydrology,* I (1963), 355, and the references cited therein.

20 Research has been undertaken on two types of linear and non-linear programming models which differ in their method of handling the random component of streamflow.

HENRY P. CAULFIELD, JR.

WELFARE, ECONOMICS, AND RESOURCES DEVELOPMENT

The words which have been used to specify this discussion—*welfare, economics,* and *resource development*—no doubt evoke in each of our minds different images of fact, different structures of thought, different senses of value, and different notions as to the relation of the content of each of these words to that of the others. Nevertheless, as teachers, researchers, and professional public servants devoting our varied skills to the field of natural resources, I am sure that we must have a high degree of common awareness of the significance for us of each of these words and of the interrelationship of their meanings. This discussion, I take it, is to see what common ground actually exists and also what real differences we have.

I propose to make my initial contribution to the discussion by answering three questions:

What are the images of fact, structures of thought, and senses of value that each of these words evokes in the minds of persons intellectually concerned with natural resources?

What are the general relationships which must or should obtain between the content evoked by these words?

What should we do, as intellectuals, to try to perfect social welfare?

• Henry P. Caulfield, Jr., is Director of the Resources Program Staff, Office of the Secretary, Department of the Interior, Washington, D.C.

Reprinted from H. L. Amoss and R. K. McNickle (eds), *Land and Water: Planning for Economic Growth,* Western Resources Conference Papers, 1961 (Boulder: University of Colorado Press, 1962), pp. 171–76, with permission of the author and the publisher.

THE SIGNIFICANCE OF OUR TERMS

RESOURCE DEVELOPMENT

By reference to "resource development," rather than to "natural resources" or "nature," this part of our subject—as I see it —is already loaded. The concept, the relevant content of which really needs exploration first, is "natural resources" or, as it would have been said in the nineteenth century and before, "Nature," with a capital N.

Nature, as a "unity" and a substitute for the orthodox Judeo-Christian deity; man in a state of nature as naturally good (as in the thought of Rousseau); and communion with nature as a source of moral renewal—all of these ideas have long been held valid by an educated élite and others in our society, at least since the impact of Emerson and Thoreau in the middle of the last century. They are still so held today. Nature untouched is thus considered, on grounds of a natural theology, to be a fundamental social value. Nature as a source of esthetic and exhilarating pleasure is a parallel value in terms of its operational impact.

These values have been traditionally viewed by Americans as non-utilitarian or, as we might say here, anti-developmental. Gifford Pinchot had no use for them. His celebrated difference with John Muir in the Hetch Hetchy controversy of 1913 relating to Yosemite National Park turned, at least in intellectual terms, on the differences between the two men with respect to these values. The Echo Park controversy is one of many recent reminders of their reality and political potency. Our current professional effort to measure these values is another reminder.

Ecology is another prevalent mode of thought relating to natural resources of which account must be taken. For ecology, nature is naturally in a state of dynamic balance. Disturbance of this balance beyond critical limits produces, in many instances, irreversible changes. Such changes, in the view of many persons imbued with ecological truths, are bound to be bad. Ecology thus leads to strong resistance to use of nature, except in such a way as will not destroy its balance. Ecology also leads to strong efforts to overcome, at whatever cost, the depredations of man. High social value is placed upon maintaining nature's balance because such balance is a good in itself and because the existence of future generations depends upon it.

The last major intellectual opposition to development of natural resources is concerned directly with their "running out." In the crudest form of this opposition, projected physical requirements are related to known reserves of currently usable quality, and the doom of future generations is predicted. This type of thought has brought forth the neo-Malthusian vs. faith-in-technological-advance issue of our time.

Underlying the concern with this issue is the value that the current generation places upon its moral responsibility to future generations for resource supplies. The Judeo-Christian belief that man is but the steward of God in the use of God's earth and that each generation must account for its use of the earth's resources is the moral factor involved here. This social value, which calls for denial in the present so as to honor responsibilities to generations yet unborn, of course, runs counter to the time preference assumed by economists to be involved in individual valuation of goods and services.

Proposals for resource development—in the context of these social-value considerations, the realities of the physical interrelatedness of things in nature, and the state of scientific or engineering knowledge—become involved in one of two factual situations or a combination of both:

—complementarity in the use of resources, where two or more uses can be made of the same resource more cheaply than if each use were based on a separate resource; and
—conflict in the use of resources, where real choices among social and individual values have to be made—one value cannot be obtained in whole or in part if the other is.

ECONOMICS

The foregoing summary, in matter-of-fact terms, of the problem of *values* in the use of resources clearly invites discussion of the role of economics in the solution of the problem. For economics, in its normative form, thinks of itself as pre-eminently qualified to solve value problems. For some economists, no doubt, the whole concern with resource use should be viewed as subsumed within economic thought. If this line of thought is followed, resource-use problems fall within the special competence of economists for final analysis leading to inevitable conclusions before which all should bow.

That economic thought as a normative scheme for the determination of human welfare, that competitive private enterprise which economic thought idealizes, and that economic analysis as a professional practice can and do make substantial contributions to efficient solution of value problems of a free society (including value problems in resource use), I do not doubt. But this paper is not the occasion to justify these beliefs. What is important to bring out here, rather, are the major difficulties of normative economic thought generally, and some of the difficulties in the application of this thought to resource problems. These difficulties, as I see it, underlie many decisions that society has actually made to arbitrate value problems in the field of resource use—indeed, in much of economic life—through the political market places rather than the economic market places of our times. . . .

1. In many instances, the creation of

resource values involves costs, but the values created cannot effectively be internalized by firms and marketed only to those who are willing to pay an appropriate fee. Instead, once created, they are available to all; for example, smog-free air. Thus, if these values are to be created, they must be created by public enterprise and covered by taxes.

2. In many instances, resource use involves costs external to development firms involving compensation to others, or extra costs to the firm to prevent external costs, but this is so only when the public policy intervenes and compels the firm to bear such costs. Costs borne by firms for abatement of pollution are an example.

3. In some instances, the time preference expressed through available interest rates in the private sector does not coincide with the social time preference expressed in the political market place. The public role in soil conservation is a response, I believe, to this difference.

4. Logical necessity, in the conclusions of most normative economic thought, is predicated upon the assumption of "perfect competition." Problems of monopoly are thus put to one side. However, the public does not ignore problems of monopoly and it does care about the over-all structure of the economy, despite its protests that interference will breed inefficiency. The 160-acre limitation in reclamation law is an interference that reflects a social value.

5. Logical necessity, in the conclusions reached within most normative economic thought, rests on the assumption that income and wealth distribution prior to a given economic action are in some sense "proper" and, in any case, will not be different after the action has occurred. The public historically has not accepted this assumption. The most obvious examples of public concern with the distribution of income and wealth are estate and inheritance taxes and the progressive income tax. With regard to natural resources, the public concern with "give-away" of natural resources, except to homesteaders and mineral prospectors, is a clear example.

6. Normative economic thought in which efficiency is being maximized is a static scheme of thought which is indifferent to space; regional inequalities in economic development are what they should be, and need not be a concern of public policy. The special concern and action of the federal government with the economic growth of the West is a clear indication that something more than the "invisible hand" was needed, or at least the public has clearly thought so.

Admission of these difficulties does not mean (for me at least) abandonment of economic thought in the solution of problems of value. The field cannot be left to a combination of the natural sciences and political action. Rather, as has been said by others . . . a synthesis of the thought and skills of economists and natural scientists should present society with technically feaible choices for action, reflecting all relevant differences in social valuation.

WELFARE

Welfare, in any sense meaningful to society as a whole, is clearly not just the sum of the net values obtained by individuals in the economic market place, where each individual makes his own, presumably unique, subjective valuation, which is reflected objectively in prices and costs. The political market place is the forum where collective values—common, majority, minority, regional, and other group values—are expressed and realized through the political process. Viability of any society, to say nothing of anyone's concept of the "good society," depends upon the realization of welfare through both markets!

Thrusts toward Creation of Resources Policy

In the American political market place over the past 150 years, as I have attempted elsewhere to summarize the history of natural resources policy, there have been what I have called "policy thrusts." These have been substantial policy drives trying to realize different objectives at the same time. Three such thrusts have been identified, and all detailed objectives in policy history have been taken to be subsumed under one or the other of these three:[1]

Development thrust, which clearly has been the strongest of the three, expresses the desire for economic development—collective and individual. Both the public reluctance to fetter private enterprise either by direct regulation or by public competition in exploitation of the public domain, and also the public enthusiasm since the Civil War to develop water resources through the federal government are clear expressions of this thrust—even though, in a sense, they are somewhat contradictory. The western regional orientation of this thrust as it realized itself in positive public policies is of particular importance to note.

Progressive thrust expresses the popular response to the emergence of "trusts," large organizations generally, "monopoly profit," and the apparent maldistribution of income to farmers and laborers in comparison to those who are profiting most from industrial development. The progressive income tax is the most obvious policy expression of this thrust. But the antitrust laws, public-utility regulation, public and cooperative power, and federal policies for lease, rather than sale, of public lands containing oil and gas are other important examples. The spirit of Henry George, if not the letter of his views, has animated much public policy concerning natural resources.

Conservation thrust expresses most potently the reaction by an educated élite, initially located in the East, to natural-resource "exploitation" generally. I have already alluded to the specific contents of this thought in my discussion of natural resources. In summary, despoliation of wilderness and natural beauty is deplored because of the importance of man's communion with nature as a means of moral regeneration. Also, the "exploitation" manifest in private disregard of long-run costs to society believed evident in the findings of ecologists is a segment of this thrust. And lastly, concern for the long-range adequacy of the natural resources available to man, the fear of a running-out of resources, has animated the conservation thrust.

These then—the development, progressive, and conservation thrusts—have been historically, and in large part still are today, the forces in the political market place which are at work forging natural-resources policy. As individuals, our total welfare derives from the subjective valuations we make and realize through the political market place, from those we make and realize through economic markets, and from those values we create within ourselves without direct benefit of either market.

If, intellectually, we would contribute to the achievement of welfare—as regards natural resources or more broadly—we must do more than pursue natural science and technology. We must do more than pursue the social sciences and achieve an interdisciplinary operational synthesis with the natural sciences. We must engage in social criticism, grounded in knowledge of past and present realities projected into the future, with a view to arriving at specific value judgments, derivative of social thought and values, including ethical postulates, that each of us takes to be valid.[2]

[1] See Henry P. Caulfield, Jr., "The Living Past in Federal Power Policy," *Resources for the Future Annual Report 1959* (Washington: RFF), pp. 24–33. This article summarizes the author's perspective on natural resource policy history.

[2] See, as an effort in this regard, Irving K. Fox and Henry P. Caulfield, Jr., "Getting the Most out of Water Resources," *State Government,* XXXIV (Spring, 1961), 104–11.

S. V. CIRIACY-WANTRUP

A SAFE MINIMUM STANDARD AS AN OBJECTIVE OF CONSERVATION POLICY

THE SOCIAL RISK OF IRREVERSIBILITY

When the objectives of conservation decisions in private economics [are] discussed, an important influence of uncertainty [can be] noted: in striving for the economic optimum, planning agents are frequently confronted with choices between possible losses of various magnitudes and probabilities. Generally, the possibility of larger but less probable losses can be avoided only by accepting the possibility of smaller but more probable ones. . . . As a special case (but an important one), planning agents are interested in avoiding the possibility of the losses which . . . we call "immoderately" large, those contingencies which would entail bankruptcy—threaten the continuity of the utilization plan.

A similar situation prevails in social economics. Governments also are confronted with choices between possible losses of various magnitudes and probabilities. The possibility of immoderate losses—contingencies which threaten the continuity of a social group—is even more important for government decisions than for private ones. One such contingency in the field of conservation is the economic irreversibility of depletion in that important class of flow resources which is characterized by a critical zone. This class contains soil, water, plants, and animals. Why does irreversibility in the depletion of these resources carry the possibility of an immoderate social loss?

From a certain degree onward—for example, if more and more acres of land or species of plants and animals are affected—irreversibility in the depletion of critical-zone resources limits opportunities of adaptation and narrows the potential development of a society. Both the biological and the social sciences have come to the conclusion that such a limiting and narrowing force directs development toward specialization rather than diversification. Such a direction has been held responsible for retarded and abortive growth—in the sense of growth toward a dead end—stagnation, and death of species and civilizations. Examples for such results in the field of genetics have been pointed out by Dobzhansky[1] and his co-workers. In the field of social studies this theme has been emphasized by Toynbee, Kroeber, and others.[2]

. . . Economic irreversibility of depletion is uncertain, since it depends, at a given time and place, on "presently foreseeable conditions" in technology, wants, and social institutions. These conditions are in constant change. There is an additional uncertainty in the present context—namely, whether such irreversibility will actually

• S. V. Ciriacy-Wantrup is Professor of Agricultural Economics, University of California, Berkeley.

Reprinted from S. V. Ciriacy-Wantrup, *Resource Conservation* (Berkeley: University of California Press, 1963), pp. 251–68, with permission of the author and the publisher.

[1] Theodosius G. Dobzhansky, *Genetics and the Origin of Species* (2d ed., rev.; New York: Columbia University Press, 1941).

[2] Arnold J. Toynbee, *A Study of History* (6 vols.; London: Oxford University Press, 1935–39); Alfred J. Kroeber, *Configuration of Culture Growth* (Berkeley and Los Angeles: University of California Press, 1944).

lead to immoderate social losses. In other words, we are not considering reliable relations of cause and effect but a contingency to be guarded against: there is no certainty that depletion will actually prove economically irreversible in the future—although this outcome may seem probable under presently foreseeable conditions. Furthermore, there is no certainty that economic irreversibility—if and when it actually does occur—will be a necessary or sufficient condition or "cause" for the stagnation or disintegration of a social group; this outcome may well have a rather small probability (although, according to some serious students, it has actually occurred in the past).

A decision to avoid the social risk of irreversibility is not dependent on whether or not the losses which threaten are immoderate. As we know, avoiding the possibility of immoderate losses is merely a special case of making choices between the possibility of larger but less probable losses and that of smaller but more probable ones. If the more probable losses are small in relation to the less probable ones which may be avoided by accepting the former, the economic choice between the two alternatives would not be difficult. What, then, are these smaller but more probable losses?

The Safe Minimum Standard of Conservation

They are connected with maintaining what we . . . call a "safe minimum standard of conservation." In the resource class under consideration, a safe minimum standard of conservation is achieved by avoiding the critical zone—that is, those physical conditions, brought about by human action, which would make it uneconomical to halt and reverse depletion. A safe minimum standard of conservation involves losses if its maintenance necessitates costs (either use foregone or positive efforts) and if the contingency guarded against should not actually occur—that is, if depletion should not prove economically irreversible. These losses are similar to the costs of flexibility in private economics. The similarity is more than formal: as implied above, a safe minimum standard of conservation is essentially an increase of flexibility in the continuing development of a society.

. . . Critical-zone resources are the most important ones from the standpoint of the economic and social problems created by depletion. Conservation policy is mainly concerned with this class. Thus, a safe minimum standard is of great significance for conservation policy, although it applies only to one particular class of resources.

The critical zone may be defined in terms of a certain flow rate and of some corresponding use rate. In this sense, the safe minimum standard is a "state of conservation." . . . However, actual maintenance of any particular use rate is not the primary objective of a safe minimum standard but merely a by-product. The primary objective is to maintain the economic possibility of halting and reversing a decrease of flow and use.

Let us ask, then, how large—absolutely and relatively—are the costs of maintaining the safe minimum standard of conservation?

Costs of Maintaining a Safe Minimum Standard

The costs of maintaining a safe minimum standard are absolutely small if proper action is taken in time and if the proper tools of conservation policy are employed. . . . At this point, we will proceed to discuss the costs of maintaining a safe minimum standard of conservation under the assumption that these two conditions are realized.

In *some* practical situations, maintenance of a safe minimum standard necessitates that use is foregone. Use rates in the neighborhood of the critical zone are small and, in the alternative case—that is, if a safe minimum standard were not maintained—could continue over only a small number of intervals. It is well to remember that the safe minimum standard of conservation is more modest than a theoretical social optimum. Frequently, such a standard corresponds to a state of conservation which is considerably lower than even the private optimum. Many private enterprises, frequently the majority, may be operating above the safe minimum standard, on the basis either of economic calculation or of habit patterns.

In *many* practical situations, maintenance of a safe minimum standard does not involve any use foregone; rather, it involves a change in the technical ways (not the quantities) of utilization. Such changes may be brought about by the tools of conservation policy. These changes may or may not necessitate costs in the sense of positive efforts (inputs) by individual planning agents or by the public or by both. Sometimes a change of social institutions without any inputs is sufficient. Sometimes the costs are only public—for example, if education or a temporary subsidy is the most economical tool of conservation policy. If private costs are increased—for example, as a consequence of regulation by governments or public districts—only a few enterprises may be affected, because, as emphasized above, the minimum standard of conservation is a rather modest objective even in terms of the private optimum.

With proper timing and choice of tools (the two conditions mentioned above), costs of maintaining the safe minimum standard are not only small in absolute amount, but very small relative to the loss which is being guarded against, a decrease of flexibility in the continuing development of a society. Costs of maintaining the safe minimum standard of conservation are also very small as compared with generally accepted expenditures of a social group for safeguarding its continuity in other fields. Such fields are, for example, public health and safety and national defense. In these fields, likewise, a safe minimum standard is frequently adopted as an objective of public policy. The reason is the same as in the field of conservation: it is impractical to determine the social optimum in the state of public health and safety or national defense because of uncertainty and because of the difficulties of valuating social revenues and costs. On the other hand, it is practical to set up standards which would avoid serious losses—threats to social continuity—in cases of epidemics, internal disorder, and foreign military involvements.

Whether costs of maintaining a safe minimum standard of conservation are small absolutely and very small relatively is a question of fact. It is necessary, therefore, to spell out in more detail the safe minimum standard for the various flow resources which are characterized by a critical zone in their depletion. We will attempt to do this in two stages: First, we will try to get a clearer idea of the physical conditions—brought about by human action—which are involved in the economic irreversibility of depletion for important flow resources. Secondly, we will try to define—for the practical purpose of conservation policy—a safe minimum standard applicable to these physical conditions.

The Critical Zone

The physical conditions which characterize the critical zone are comparatively simple for individual species of animal and plant life: with the destruction of the breeding stock or, frequently, its natural habitat,[3] flow becomes economically (and technologically) irreversible.

Depletion of ground water becomes economically irreversible through compaction and certain forms of pollution. The former may occur as a consequence of sustained overdraft; the latter may occur through changes in the salt balance and direct salt-water intrusion, also made possible by overdraft, or if the protection by impervious strata separating a usable aquifer from a chemically unusable one is destroyed through improper drilling and other activities.

[3] Frequently a breeding stock cannot be maintained in botanical or zoological gardens—sometimes the cheapest way—if highly complex biological relations are involved. In such cases, appropriate reserves must be established and protected.

Soil depletion may become economically irreversible if a protective plant cover is destroyed by cultivation, improper degree or timing of grazing, and repeated burning in areas where topography, climate, or soil render precarious any existing balance between erosive forces (water, wind) and the stabilizing force of plant cover. Erosion, even if it becomes irreversible, is somewhere offset by deposition. Sometimes, deposition by floods is an economic gain—for example, if fertile silts are deposited or if movement and deposition of coarse materials are necessary for maintaining infiltration areas to replenish ground water. More often, however, such deposition—in rivers, reservoirs, harbors, on cultivated flood plains—is an additional social loss rather than a gain. Furthermore, acceleration of the processes of erosion and deposition may make another important resource, surface water flow, unusable for many purposes (drinking, bathing, fishing, and some industrial uses).

In the depletion of cultivated agricultural soil—in contrast to the soil under forests and permanent grasses—erosion may become economically irreversible at a rather early stage if it proceeds in the form of gullies. Gullies quickly make farming operations uneconomical.

In the depletion of forests and range, another physical condition—besides soil erosion—must be considered in connection with economic irreversibility. Forests and grasslands are plant (species) associations of often great complexity and sensitivity with respect to influences which upset the ecological balance. Repeated burning and improper degree or timing of grazing may upset this balance to such an extent that the valuable species are replaced entirely by other less valuable ones. Such a degeneration of plant associations has occurred, for example, on some cutover forest areas in the northern Great Lakes states, in the arid grasslands in the intermountain region, and in some mountain meadows of California. In such cases there may be a good plant cover and no serious soil erosion. Still, serious depletion has occurred which may be economically irreversible.

Depletion of recreational resources may become economically irreversible if the specific recreational uses depend on keeping an area "unspoiled." Spoilation may be caused by improper construction of access roads, permanent structures (hotels, dams), cutting of selected groves of trees (especially species which require a long time to reach impressive recreational value, such as redwoods and sequoias), man-made erosion (overgrazing of mountain meadows), and other effects of use.

Practical Definition of a Safe Minimum Standard

The great variety and complexity of physical conditions which characterize the critical zone in the depletion of the various flow resources make it generally impractical to define a safe minimum standard for each resource simply in terms of a single flow rate which is to be maintained. It is more practical to define a safe minimum standard in terms of conservation practices designed to avoid the critical zone. Such a definition may be in terms of conditions to be maintained—that is, in terms of the results of a number of unspecified conservation practices (definition in terms of results), or in terms of the performance of specific conservation practices (definition in terms of performance). A few illustrations may be helpful.

Definition in terms of results prevails in the following cases: In soil conservation, a safe minimum standard may be defined as the avoidance of gullies or as a maximum rate of erosion (in cubic feet per acre or acre-feet per square mile per year). In forest conservation, a safe minimum standard may be defined as a maximum rate of burn (in per cent of total area per year) or as maintenance of a given plant association; through the study of plant indicators modern ecology has made it practical to define a plant association and to check its maintenance periodically. In the conservation of grazing lands, a safe minimum standard may be defined in terms of a certain minimum amount of plant material (in tons per acre per year) left aboveground after the grazing season or, as in forest conservation, in terms of maintenance of a certain plant association. In the conservation of a plant or animal species, a safe minimum standard may be defined in terms of maintaining a certain breeding stock or in terms of protecting a certain area of natural habitat. In the conservation of water resources, a maximum degree of pollution (in terms of total or specific solids, bacterial count, oxygen conditions, and so on) may be used for defining a safe minimum standard.

If we now turn to definitions in terms of performance of specific conservation practices, we may first of all remember that mere limitation of use may be an important conservation practice. Frequently, therefore, a safe minimum standard may be defined simply in terms of a maximum use rate—"safe yield" (in acre-feet per year for a certain aquifer) in ground-water conservation, maximum rate of stocking (in animal-unit-months per acre per year) in the conservation of grazing lands, maximum annual harvest in hunting and fishing, maximum admission of people to avoid overcrowding of recreational facilities.

However, limitation of use is only one among many conservation practices. Particularly in agriculture and forestry, a maximum use rate is not very practical because use consists of a highly complex composite of products. These maximum use rates would have to be defined in terms of some common denominator (calories, digestible nutrients, dry matter, tons weighted by value, and the like) of various products. Other conservation practices—contour cultivation, mulching, strip cropping, terracing, leaving of a minimum number of seed trees, removal of slash and many others—are usually more practical. Definition in terms of conservation practices other than a maximum use rate may be employed even in fields where the latter is practical—rotation of pastures in grazing, proper capping and perforation of wells in ground-water pumping, specific processes in the treatment of polluted surface waters, prohibition of certain methods in taking game and fish.

All these practices are merely examples. Others may be better suited to particular practical situations.

Advantages and Disadvantages

The main advantages of defining a safe minimum standard in terms of conservation practices are great adaptability to local conditions, easy understanding by resource users, and fairly economical administration by governmental agencies charged with the execution of conservation policy.

The main disadvantage is that the suitability of conservation practices for avoiding the critical zone in resource depletion must be established first. This takes time and a considerable amount of observation and analysis. For establishing such suitability, it is not sufficient to show that a given conservation practice or combination of practices is technologically effective in avoiding the critical zone. It must also be shown that no other practice or combination of practices accomplishes the same result more economically. Adoption of a safe minimum standard as an objective of conservation policy does not mean that economic calculation can be neglected: a safe minimum standard of conservation should be realized with minimum total social costs.

The administrative advantages of defining a safe minimum standard in terms of conservation practices will probably lead to the employment of this method not only in agriculture and forestry, where it appears to be the only practical one, but also in cases—such as wildlife and range conservation—where a definition would be feasible which is more directly related to the maintenance of minimum flow rates. This trend in itself is not objectionable provided the relations between conservation practices and maintenance of a minimum flow rate are carefully analyzed, not only in their technological but also their economic aspects.

A Safe Minimum Standard and Private Enterprise

For many flow resources in many regions of the world, at various historical periods, the state of conservation established by individual resource users has fulfilled the requirements of a safe minimum standard without any influence from conservation policy. Such a state of conservation may be established on the basis of either economic calculations or habit patterns or both.

In northern and central Europe, at the present time, most agricultural soils, forests, and grasslands are managed by private individuals on the basis of economic calculations with an optimum state of conservation far higher than the safe minimum standard. Possibly the same would be true for the management of water and recreational and wildlife resources if their conservation were left to private economic calculations. In these resources, however, the problem of allocation of social revenues and costs seemed so important that the people have not taken the risk of leaving the maintenance of a safe minimum standard entirely at the mercy of private economic calculations.

In some parts of the world, habit patterns rather than private economic calculations or public policy have established a state of conservation above the safe minimum standard. . . . In such cases a state of conservation which would be established on the basis of private economic calculation might be lower than the state of conservation which exists on the basis of habit patterns—possibly even lower than the safe minimum standard. Where that is true, a conservation policy which relies on educating resource users to employ a more calculative attitude and more refined systems of accounting would defeat its own purpose.

In the United States, by far the largest portion of agricultural, forest, and grazing lands are managed by private individuals with a state of conservation at or above the safe minimum standard. Mostly this is due to economic calculation; but habit patterns, traditional standards of good husbandry, are by no means irrelevant even in a country where economic calculativeness is generally held in great social esteem. Adoption of a safe minimum standard as an objective of conservation policy therefore does not interfere with the practices of the great majority of private resource users. For the rest, a safe minimum standard would involve a minimum of restrictions both in geographic extent and degree. This limitation with respect to interference with private initiative and control may be regarded as a distinct advantage of adopting a safe minimum standard as compared with the adoption of any higher state of conservation, whether based on some notion of a social optimum, preëxisting conditions, or the status quo. Whether or not this particular advantage is accepted as such, constitutes, of course, a value judgment on other than economic grounds.

The Safe Minimum Standard as an Economic Base Level

The statement just made—that by far the largest portion of agricultural, forest, and grazing lands in the United States is managed by private individuals with a state of conservation at or above the safe minimum standard—does not necessarily conflict with the surveys of several government agencies and many individual writers. Such surveys suggest that most soils, forests, and grasslands of the United States are still being seriously depleted and, in many individual cases, could be utilized with greater private profit if conservation practices were applied.

Adoption of a safe minimum standard does not mean that public conservation policy should not be concerned with these conditions of depletion and insufficient information. A safe minimum standard of conservation should be generally adopted as a social objective and should actually be realized under all conditions as a kind of economic base level in conservation policy. . . . The economic rationale for adopting a safe minimum standard defined in physical terms is allowance for uncertainty; actual realization of a safe minimum standard is subject to the economic requirement of minimum total social costs.

After a safe minimum standard is assured, conservation policy should explore whether and how the social optimum in the state of conservation could be more closely approximated in [a] step-by-step fashion. . . . Thus, from a safe minimum standard of conservation as the base level, the economic advisability of further conservation practices may be calculated by comparing additional total social revenues and costs.

Safe Minimum Standard and Resource Relations

The safe minimum standard of conservation as an objective of public policy applies to the resources of one particular class (Class II, 2, *b*).[4] It may be asked what is the effect upon the economic rationale of such a standard if relations between these resources and others in different classes are involved? Such relations [may be] classified as complementarity, competitiveness, or neutrality in supply and in demand.

The economic rationale of a safe minimum standard is based on the proposition that the costs of maintaining it are small in relation to the possible losses which irreversibility of depletion might entail. Complementarity in supply or in demand or in both means that the costs of maintaining the safe minimum standard are decreased or the losses of irreversibility are increased or both, as compared with that situation which would prevail if relations between resources could be neglected in the analysis (neutrality). Thus, complementarity between resources strengthens the argument for maintaining a safe minimum standard; for this reason we need not discuss the problem of complementarity further. The opposite—that is, a weakening of the argument for a safe minimum standard—would seem the consequence of competitiveness; this problem, therefore, must be explored further. First we may take up competitiveness in demand and then competitiveness in supply.

Competitiveness in Demand

If critical-zone resources were competitive in demand with (could be replaced by) other flow resources (those without a critical zone) or with abundant stock resources, then the possible losses which irreversibility might entail could not be very great. That such competitiveness in demand prevails is implied in some speculations concerning the world's future food supply.

It has been asserted that industrial photosynthesis will become feasible on a large scale (either based on lower organisms—unicellular algae—highly efficient in photosynthesis, or on synthetically produced chlorophyll), and that the resulting carbohydrates will be transformed into proteins and fats through certain yeasts already

[4] [Ed. note—Ciriacy-Wantrup's classification of resources is as follows:]

- I. Nonrenewable or Stock Resources
  1. Stock not significantly affected by natural deterioration: metal ores *in situ;* coal; stones; clays.
  2. Stock significantly affected by natural deterioration: refined metals subject to oxidation; oil and gas in cases of seepage and blowoff; plant nutrients subject to leaching; radioactive substances in process of nuclear disintegration; surface water reservoirs subject to evaporation.
- II. Renewable or Flow Resources
  1. Flow not significantly affected by human action: solar and other cosmic radiation; tides; winds.
  2. Flow significantly affected by human action.
     - *a*) Reversibility of a decrease in flow not characterized by a critical zone: precipitation; special locations that form the basis of site value; services from a species of durable producer or consumer goods.
     - *b*) Reversibility of a decrease in flow characterized by a critical zone: animal and plant species; scenic resources; storage capacity of groundwater basins.

available and by other techniques under experimentation.

Let us assume that these transformations will become actual fact, that the products will contain not only calories and proteins but all the necessary nutrients, and that they will be no less digestible to man and no more expensive than the products now derived from plants and animals. Even under these heroic assumptions, the resources under consideration here—plants, animals, soil, clear stream flow—would still remain vital: Man does not live by bread alone. The present degree of synthetic living—small as it is compared with the degree just assumed—has already set in motion strong counteracting tendencies in human needs. These needs in some form or other drive man "back to nature." They can be expected to increase greatly if plants, animals, and soil should ever be replaced by the laboratory and the factory as sources of calories, proteins, and other components of human nutrition.

In that case, these critical-zone resources would still remain unique to satisfy the demand for recreation (in the true etymological meaning of the word), for aesthetic enjoyment, for exercising all those physical, mental, and emotional capacities of man not needed any more for obtaining his daily bread but still necessary for his happiness, and necessary for his culture, as we can think of it, to survive. Culture in all its forms has developed in close interaction with plants, animals, soil, and clear stream flow. In different words, the demand for these resources is not based solely on their use in nutrition. In other, even more important, uses, competitiveness in demand with resources in other classes does not exist.

Competitiveness in Supply

Let us now turn to competitiveness in supply. If relations between resources are competitive in supply, the question arises whether maintaining the safe minimum standard in one resource might not make it economically impossible to utilize the related one. Such an outcome would defeat the social objective of a safe minimum standard, namely to avoid a narrowing and specialization in the resource base of a society . . . —for example, the competition of agricultural production with coal production in the strip coal mines in several eastern states and the competition of grazing with placer gold mining in many alluvial valleys of California.

Competitiveness—like complementarity and neutrality—depends on the numerical values of use rates. As has been emphasized, the safe minimum standard is a very modest one in this respect. The safe minimum standard does not require that use is maintained uninterruptedly, but that use may be resumed at some future date. An uninterrupted (small) use is merely a frequent byproduct of maintaining the safe minimum standard. Thus, a safe minimum standard in one resource is usually compatible with the utilization of a resource which is competitive in supply, although any higher state of conservation would not be compatible. Let us consider a practical illustration:

A safe minimum standard in soil conservation does not require that after strip or placer mining the land must be restored to such a condition that the previous use could be resumed at the same level immediately.[5] If such a requirement did exist, mining would become uneconomical privately as well as socially.

The requirement of a safe minimum standard is more modest: the land must be restored to such an extent that under presently foreseeable economic conditions resumption of the previous use at some level at some future date is not impossible. In practice, this means the requirement that spoil piles are releveled and also revege-

[5] It may be noted that the present value of net revenues from utilizing the stock resource (coal, gold) is invariably much greater than the market value (price) of an acre of land on the basis of its use in agriculture, forestry, or grazing. However, this relationship of values, in itself, does not make a safe minimum standard of soil conservation irrelevant as a *social* objective.

tated (revegetation need not necessarily involve the previously existing species and need not necessarily be done by artificial means). The natural processes of soil formation will do the rest—provided that spoil piles do not contain toxic substances that make impossible all types of plant growth; the latter situation is comparatively rare.

In some states, such a minimum standard of soil conservation is imposed on strip-mining companies by law. One state—West Virginia—goes further: it requires that soil removed from coal beds (the overburden) be replaced. More will be said about the actual implementation of a safe minimum standard when soil-conservation legislation is discussed.

Conservation Policy if the Critical Zone Has Been Passed

The question may be raised what conservation policy should do in those cases in which the critical zone has already been passed. For example, in large sections of the loess areas of China and in some smaller sections of the Piedmont area in the southeastern United States, gullying has made it uneconomical to restore farmlands to their previous uses for cultivated crops.

On practically all of these lands the critical zone for other, "lower" uses—for example, grazing, forestry, production of game—has not yet been reached. Conservation policy should be concerned with establishing a safe minimum standard for these uses but not *necessarily*—as a base level in the terminology used above—with restoring such a standard for the previous use (cultivated crops). This course is implied in the definition of irreversibility. Such a definition, as we know, is in economic and not in physical terms. If the critical zone has been passed for a certain use, the horse has been stolen, and no effort should be wasted in safeguarding it.

Safe Minimum Standard and Natural Changes of Flow

Finally, to avoid any misunderstanding, it may be well to repeat that the critical zone and, accordingly, the safe minimum standard as an objective of conservation policy, apply to changes of flow brought about by human action. It has already been emphasized that flow, in the absence of human action, need not be constant or infinite. Many natural[6] changes of flow of critical-zone resources exist and, in some cases, the rate of such changes is fairly well known. Such natural changes are connected, for example, with geologic erosion by water and wind, climatic changes, changes of ocean currents, volcanic activity, mutation of genes, and many others. It is perfectly possible that such natural changes decrease a flow irreversibly. There is no implication in our use of the concept "minimum standard of conservation" that avoidance of such an irreversibility is necessarily an objective of conservation policy.

On the other hand, the limitation of the concept just reëmphasized does not mean that natural changes of flow could not (technologically) or should not (economically) be affected by human counteraction or, more specifically, are not the concern of conservation policy. It is desirable to investigate carefully how far changes of flow are due to natural and how far to human causes. Such a differentiation may be relevant for selecting the proper tools for an attack both in the field of technology and policy. However, even if human action is not involved as a cause, this *in itself* does not mean that nothing could or should be done about it. Whether and what counteraction is to be taken is a problem of economics not essentially different from determining the optimum state of conservation in those cases in which a decrease of flow is caused by human action. The difference is that in the former case a safe minimum standard as a base level for conservation policy does not necessarily have an economic rationale—because the costs of maintaining it may be excessive—whereas in the latter case such a rationale exists.

[6] The term "natural" is used in this study in connection with changes that take place without human action or influence.

A few examples may serve to illustrate the foregoing statement.

In many arid areas of the world, wind has had and still has major effects upon the soil formation and movement and plant growth (for example, in the dust bowl of the High Plains, the southern San Joaquin Valley in California, and the southeastern Ukraine of Soviet Russia). Whether and how far man, through grazing and plowing, has accelerated natural rates of wind erosion of these dust soils is still a controversial point. Regardless of the outcome of this controversy, it is relevant for public policy to ask whether it is economical to influence the effects of wind upon soil movement, soil moisture, and directly upon plants. The experience with shelter belts and several other conservation practices gives an affirmative answer to this question —at least for some areas.

In flood and stream control, likewise, conservation policy deals largely with natural phenomena. Here, also, a controversy rages how far the latter have been aggravated by man—for example through clear cutting and repeated burning of forests. There is some indication that these and other man-made changes of watersheds are more important for reducing the quality of runoff (increased load of gravel and debris, increased water temperature, lowered oxygen content, and so on), than for increasing flood peaks. Still, it may be economical to modify both natural and man-made conditions of a watershed—through reservoirs, channel rectification, fire protection, land-use practices, and so on.

Although it is obvious, it may not be entirely amiss to mention that, in order to decide whether or not it is economical to modify natural phenomena, their beneficial effects must be as fully considered as their damages. Geologic erosion by wind or water and floods frequently have such beneficial effects.

Safe Minimum Standard as a Constraint on Economic Optimizing

The safe minimum standard . . . is defined in *physical* terms: as a flow rate, as specified physical conditions necessary for maintaining such a rate through unspecified conservation practices, or in terms of performance of specified practices. In this sense, the safe minimum standard may be regarded as a technological constraint in economic optimizing. This interpretation is helpful for increasing understanding and encouraging closer cooperation between technologists and economists. Such understanding and cooperation is essential in many areas of conservation policy—for example, in the conservation of fisheries, upland game, soils, and forests.[7]

Economic analysis, however, is deeply involved in identifying technological constraints conceptually, and in specifying them operationally. In essence the safe minimum standard is a partial solution for applying economic optimizing operationally under conditions of great uncertainty. Strictly speaking, therefore, the safe minimum standard belongs to the "objective function" rather than to the constraints in economic optimizing. In this respect the safe minimum standard is more akin to an institutional than to a technological constraint.

[7] For further discussion of this point see Food and Agriculture Organization of the United Nations, *Economic Effects of Fishery Regulation,* Report of an FAO Experts' Meeting held at Ottawa, Canada, June, 1961 (Rome: FAO, 1962).

HAROLD J. BARNETT and CHANDLER MORSE

NATURAL RESOURCES AND THE QUALITY OF LIFE

Modern societies have evolved economic institutions and procedures which respond to signals of cost and demand by introducing resource-saving or cost-reducing innovations and substitutions. The prospect, therefore, is that economic welfare, as measured by indexes of output per unit of input, will continue to increase. But what of the other aspects of welfare? If, along with the achievement of increasing returns, the distribution of income becomes inequitable; or market processes become more imperfect in their allocation of benefits and costs; or the quality of the available product mix changes unfavorably; or there is a net reduction in the intangible satisfactions derived from the appearance of the environment; or in any other way the social framework becomes less desirable—if any or all of these types of changes should occur there might be a consensus that total welfare had not increased along with economic welfare, that the quality of life had, in some significant respect, been impaired.

This type of question has occurred to many of those who have seriously considered natural resource questions. John Stuart Mill looked forward to population stabilization from concern over what would happen to the quality of life "with every rood of land brought into cultivation, which is capable of growing food for human beings . . . and scarcely a place left where a wild shrub or flower could grow without being eradicated as a weed in the name of improved agriculture." A number of conservationists, both in the original Movement and today, have argued strongly for control of natural resource use in order, on the basis of their value standards, to prevent damage to the quality of life from the process of economic growth. The leaders of the Conservation Movement believed that monopoly and industrialism, with consequent neglect of the public interest and impairment of the values of rural life, were related to man's efforts to exploit the natural resource environment. One need not subscribe to these earlier views to recognize that the contest between man and nature, especially man's efforts to overcome nature's limitations, may have many undesirable consequences if conscious and timely efforts are not made to avoid them. Increasingly, for these and other reasons, contemporary social scientists have been calling attention ot the possibility of conflict between the materialistic aspects of continuing economic growth and the achievement of a high quality of life.[1]

• Harold J. Barnett is Chairman of the Department of Economics, Washington University; Chandler Morse is Professor of Economics, Cornell University.

Reprinted from H. J. Barnett and C. M. Morse, *Scarcity and Growth: The Economics of Natural Resource Availability* (Baltimore: The Johns Hopkins Press for Resources for the Future, Inc., 1963), chap. 12, pp. 252–66, with permission of Harold J. Barnett and the publisher.

[1] By way of illustration, we quote two such observations, one by an American political scientist, the other by a British economist. (1) "Welfare: faring well, well-being. How well are we going to fare in the new society without poverty and hunger? In many ways, pretty badly. In many ways, our standard of living, our well-being, is very likely going to be much worse than that of our grandparents. . . . Utopia may be a pretty frustrating, irritating, inconvenient, unpleasant, disagreeable place, a place of ill-fare rather than welfare." Robert A. Dahl, "The Role of Govern-

Modern societies may be less able to counteract adverse qualitative change, or take advantage of opportunities to improve the quality of life, than they are to circumvent increases in the economic scarcity of natural resources. Political and other social decision-making processes are available, but their operations are more cumbersome and less assured than technical and market processes. The problems of qualitative evaluation are more difficult, especially where they require joint evaluation of consequences for large numbers of people; they are a social rather than a private value problem. Cases of this kind arise with particular frequency as a result of the impact on natural resources of economic growth, depletion, population expansion, and technological change.

We identify several such cases of impact which have emerged during the past generation: urban agglomeration; waste disposal and pollution; changes in income distribution, particularly in relation to distressed areas; water supply; land use; international relations with underdeveloped nations. These illustrate the need for social analysis and decisions, beyond simple acceptance of the results produced by the operation of existing economic and other institutions.

---

ment in Individual and Social Welfare," an unpublished manuscript (New Haven, 1956). (2) "While accepting, therefore, 'an expansion of the area of choice' as synonymous with an increase of welfare for the individual, and as an unexceptionable norm of policy, it requires an alarming degree of complacency to believe that a rising standard of living as commonly understood is the certain instrument of an expanding horizon of opportunities. Obviously the growth of material prosperity, and its dispersion among the populace, entails—by definition, we might say—more goods, and new kinds of goods, among the mass of the people. But it is scarcely less obvious today that the concomitant subtopiaisation of society involves a continual erosion of opportunities, at least for a sensitive minority." E. J. Mishan, "A Survey of Welfare Economics, 1939–59," *Economic Journal,* LXX (1960), 255–56.

Social Problems Related to Natural Resources

Urbanization has been a striking feature of economic growth in the United States and other major countries, including those just beginning the process of industrialization. To a large extent, this results from the economies of scale and the consequently higher productivity that is characteristic of urban agglomerations. Stated otherwise, agglomeration is one of the conditions which has resulted from, and contributed to, man's efforts to reduce costs and increase income. But it is also one that is coming under increasing question for its possible negative effects on the quality of life. As cities grow, there are the accompanying phenomena of urban sprawl, traffic congestion, blighted areas, and pollution of water supplies and atmosphere. Even increased mental tension, juvenile delinquency, and crime have been among the alleged consequences of agglomeration. Such effects, to the extent that they occur, imply a need for analysis and possibly for decision-making procedures beyond those now available.

Consider, in particular, the earthy and undramatic problems of waste disposal in urban centers and of pollution in general. These clearly require policy decisions at the societal level. But it was not always so. Families in sparsely settled regions were once free to dispose of their waste on the basis of self-interest; they did not adversely affect the environment of others. The habit so formed persisted when cities came into being. Progressive cities then proscribed use of the streets as sewers, and substituted direct discharge into rivers, lakes, and oceans. In terms of local interest this is reasonable—sewage treatment is expensive. But it is becoming anachronistic for large communities to determine their methods of disposal independently. The problem has been greatly augmented by the growth of industrialization. The wastes of modern industry have reached huge volume. In terms of individual interest, industrial firms—paper mills, chemical plants, refineries, and so on—find economy in downstream disposal of untreated waste and heat, but this reduces and often destroys the value of the streams for individual use, recreation, and other purposes. In terms of their interest, it is equally reasonable for great metropolitan centers to claim pre-emptive rights to regional waters for waste disposal, as when Chicago reduces water levels in the Great Lakes to flush its sewage down the Mississippi River.

The problem in industrial societies has been extended beyond discharge of wastes into water. The atmosphere has increasingly become a waste trap. Multiple deaths have been caused (as at Donora, Pennsylvania); and whole communities have been subjected to distress, and possibly damage to health (as in Los Angeles), or seriously inconvenienced (as in Pittsburgh and London). Four of the world's leading nations have found it necessary, each according to its own calculus of benefits and costs, to increase world-wide radioactive fallout.

Less dramatically—and less urgently in relation to health—land, too, is despoiled by waste and debris. Most striking are the lands denuded of plant and animal life by noxious smelter gases and the like. Lesser forms of disfigurement, the unplanned by-product of efforts by firms and individuals to minimize costs, include the mountains of mine tailings, the urban dumps and scrap piles, and the vacant lots and highway margins strewn with bottles, cans, and other rubbish, which our value standards and institutions have thus far condoned.

True, the problem of waste disposal, once a problem solely for individual decision, is coming to be recognized as a problem requiring the application of social decision processes, but only slowly. There is a lag in social cognizance and a reluctance to assume new responsibilities. The consequences of continuing practices are not widely appreciated; or they are not deemed sufficiently disadvantageous to warrant action; or the institutional arrangements required for effective evaluation and decision do not exist. Often, as in the case of radioactive fallout, all three reasons operate simultaneously.

Social problems concerning water have been created by growth. Most advanced societies are faced with such problems. Some are related to pollution. Others are those of providing adequate supplies at reasonable cost and allocating supplies among competing claimants. Owing to lack of data, water was not included in our investigation of the cost of extractive output in the United States, but it is reasonably certain that the costs have increased and may increase further.

Water, of course, is a resource for which, in many uses, there is no available substitute. But it is also a resource which, until now, has been virtually a free good, and has been used with corresponding lavishness in modern societies. Already the provision of water at a nominal charge is ceasing to be appropriate in the arid American Southwest, where rapid population growth, due largely to immigration, has begun to strain available water supplies. In the course of time, provision of water at nominal charges could also become impractical in more humid regions.

There is a possibility, of course, that private and public research on desalinization and other methods of augmenting water supplies will rob the problem of some of its importance and urgency. But it is also likely that important changes will have to be made in institutional arrangements concerning water, and perhaps in value standards. One possibility is adoption of the price system as a device for rationing the use of water whenever its increased availability is subject to increasing cost. Another possibility is to change value standards concerning the use of water—to foster and develop a resource-saving ethic so far as water is concerned.

Land use, in our society, is often regarded as solely the owner's business. There is a degree of social decision-making, but the extent of planning for the use of land is extremely variable among the larger urban areas, is frequently absent in the smaller ones, and is virtually nonexistent elsewhere. It is legitimate to ask whether the present system is producing the kind of physical environment we want for ourselves and our children; and, if it is not, whether we want to pay the price, in dollars and restrictions, for better surroundings.

This question is often treated as if the only standards of value involved were entirely individual—matters of personal preference for urban parks and tree-lined avenues versus bare and narrow streets; for the outdoors versus the bustle of city life; for hunting and fishing versus non-predatory modes of recreation; for the preservation of nature in the wild versus the creation of man-made harmonies or discordances. Regarded from the individual point of view it is true that these are matters of personal predilection. But the fact is that our preferences were largely built into us by the preceding generation, and that individuals as such have very limited opportunity to shape their environments. This suggests that the maintenance of a wide variety of alternative choices has social value, is likely to provide a larger number of people, in both the present and future, with environments permitting a more satisfactory quality of life than more restricted choice would do. It may often be difficult to obtain consensus on how to amend the environment in a particular case, especially if the decision caters to local and perhaps transitory interests, but there should be a possibility of substantial agreement on such general and durable goals as provision of widely accessible recreational opportunities, elimination of obsolete and ugly structures, preservation of the unusual, and so on. The chances of consensus should be further increased by knowledge of the effects of environmental conditions on physical and mental health.

The problem of the availability of recreational areas, which is likely to become more acute as the work week shortens and vacations lengthen, can surely be approached more deliberately and objectively than has been our custom. Similarly, the strand of conservationist thought which is concerned with parks, wildlife, and preservation of the natural biological environment generally reflects recognition that such resources have a unique and irreplaceable contribution to make to the quality of modern life. If society deems specific characteristics of the environment worth preserving, they must be saved from irreversible destruction. We say "irreversible" because, even though later generations could restore what earlier had been destroyed, often this could be done only with lavish outlays of time, trouble, and economic inputs. The future can reconstruct selected aspects of the past, and sometimes may do so at quite reasonable cost, but frequently the cost will be very high indeed.

The major problem of social interest in land use concerns the procedures for balancing benefits and costs. In many situations, institutional obstacles prevent this question from being faced. There are few adequate mechanisms for reaching community decisions concerning the physical environment, for matching the intangible benefits of a quiet and pleasing outlook to the tangible costs of acquiring it. Part of the problem is lack of a value consensus, for unless there is wide agreement that provision of pleasant surroundings, and replacement of monotony with variety, are good for everybody, the allocation of costs on an acceptable basis is difficult. Given better knowledge of consequences, however, and availability of enough alternative environments, existence of personal idiosyncrasy in matters of taste can be wholly consistent with the development of a new value consensus concerning the aesthetics and other non-economic features of land use—a consensus conducive to an improved quality of life.

Natural resources, because of their high specificity and immobility, exert a particularly important influence on the geographic distribution of income, a circumstance stressed by the leaders of the Conservation Movement (who acquired some of their views from Henry George). In a Ricardian world, the influence would be predictable: a concentration of income in the owners of agricultural land. In a modern world of technological change, owners or developers of other types of resources sometimes benefit—often, as in the case of Oklahoma and Texas oil fields, or real estate in a rapidly expanding metropolis, to an extreme degree. But sometimes they suffer serious losses, as in the case of Pennsylvania anthracite. More important, it is not only the owners and developers of natural resources that gain or lose but entire communities and regions. Prosperity has accrued to broad sections of the Gulf States as the result of petroleum and other mineral reserves, but much of West Virginia is a distressed area. The cutting of forests has created and then stranded many communities. Agriculture provides numerous examples of regional distress resulting from the impact of growth. Social decision-making with respect to agriculture has been extensive. The dust bowl of the 1930's, for example, led to adoption of the federal Soil Conservation Program. But solutions have sometimes brought forth new problems. Partly in consequence of publicly initiated and financed research and extension services, increases in productivity since the 1930's have exceeded the growth of demand for agricultural staples. Thus, growth and technological change, in a variety of combinations and circumstances, have created substantial shifts of income distribution, have been responsible for the creation of distressed areas, and have led to social decisions in the form of government interventions in markets, income distribution, and research.

The modern natural resource problem in these cases, it appears, is not diminishing returns, but social adjustment to a variety of adverse indirect effects of technological change and economic growth.

International arrangements concerning the use of natural resources, or for dealing with the consequences of such use, present a number of increasingly important and difficult problems. Radioactive fallout, already mentioned, may cease in time to constitute a menace, but the development of large numbers of atomic power plants will raise problems of the disposal of dangerous wastes. Radical climatological control, already envisioned by meteorologists, holds great potential for improving social welfare. It also poses serious problems of social control. If used by particular nations for their individual benefit, the damage to other nations could be substantial. In extreme form, used as a weapon, the manipulation of ice caps could match the destructive potential of nuclear war. The use of man-made space satellites for weather prediction, and especially for the establishment of world-wide communications channels, is another area that transcends the interests of particular nations. The exploration of the moon and space have potential implications that are not parochial.

There is also a set of less dramatic international problems centering around world trade and investment in extractive products in less developed countries. One is the division of nations into two groups—the industrial countries, and the less industrialized, mainly raw material producing countries. During the past generation or two, technological advances and economic policies in the industrial countries may have worked against the interests of the less industrialized countries more often than in their favor. Synthetic fibers, rubbers, resins, detergents, dyestuffs, nitrates, and other chemicals have adversely affected the producers of natural products in underdeveloped areas. Increased agricultural productivity in the industrial countries, coupled with policies designed to protect their producers from adverse price effects, have disturbed world markets, again to the disadvantage of low-income nations. The protection of other domestic producers—as in U.S. petroleum and other minerals—has also denied low-cost producers in the raw materials countries ready access to industrial markets.

The prospect is possibly for further shifts, due to research, investment, and market dominance, which would favor the industrial countries. The case of iron ore is instructive. Technological research is making the abundant North American taconites competitive with traditional ores; and this could adversely affect the Latin American and African countries which expected to advance toward industrialization by transforming exhaustible natural assets into valuable man-made wealth. In this case perhaps, and probably in others, the tendency of technological advance to make natural resources more homogeneous reduces the actual or potential value of high-quality natural resources that once were essential for industry. Since the unexploited reserves of rich mineral resources are located mainly in the less industrialized countries, these countries are harmed, not helped, by such technological developments. It is possible that, on a broad criterion of social welfare, and probably also in the long-run interests of the industrial countries themselves, this problem requires social analysis and action.

Population growth is the most pervasive, persistent, and pressing of all the influences affecting quality of life in the poorer countries, mainly because its high rate retards the rate of growth of per capita income. The problem is not one of increasing natural resource scarcity and consequent diminishing returns, but of ability to achieve and maintain a desired rate of economic growth. In the well-to-do nations, population growth presents no immediate threat to welfare, and if or when it does it will be manifest as deterioration in the quality of life due to overcrowding, not as an inadequate rate of growth of material welfare. In the poorer nations, now urgently seeking economic growth and development, the difficulty is primarily a severe shortage of capital per head, which is needed to exploit technological advance. At current rates of population increase, they cannot achieve the rate of capital formation, and the accompanying measure of technological progress, which are required for the rate of economic growth to which they newly aspire. Coale and Hoover, for example, have estimated that in India the growth of per capita output could be more than doubled in the next two generations from the single influence of a 50 per cent reduction in fertility rates and its effect on population numbers, age distribution, and capital formation.[2] To achieve such a goal is painful and difficult, no less for being the consequence of institutional and technical conditions, than if it were the result of an inexorable law of increasing resource scarcity. To the extent, therefore, that scientific and social assistance is wanted by the underdeveloped nations which already have family planning programs, or subsequently establish them, they should be able to obtain it. Indeed, it is a valid question whether the industrial nations, and such international agencies as the World Health Organization and United Nations Educational, Scientific, and Cultural Organization, should not help to initiate a basic and long-term program of study and research designed to make responsible planning of family size effective and acceptable. Such investigations, designed primarily to help the poorer countries meet their current pressing problems, would have the further advantage of helping the world society to consider how to limit its population when and if this should become a recognized social problem.

Reasons for Emergence of These Social Problems

The problems we have just identified, and others like them, have arisen because favorable technological changes, and the growth of output and population which they have made possible, have brought about certain unfavorable changes in other parameters of our existence. Undesirable conditions have been created which it would be very costly for individuals and private enterprises to correct, or which ex-

[2] A. J. Coale and E. M. Hoover, *Population Growth and Economic Development in Low-Income Countries* (Princeton: Princeton University Press, 1958).

ceed their capacity to act. Such conditions, therefore, constitute social problems which, if not solved, deteriorate the quality of life.

The rate at which social problems arise, and their complexity, have increased with technological progress. Scientific advance, so rapid over the past century and a half, has increasingly become the strategic determinant of the influence of natural resources on the trend of social welfare over time. In advanced countries, it has freed man of the need to be concerned about diminishing returns but it has brought new problems in its wake.

The innovations that have increased productivity have vastly multiplied the alternatives among which, as producers and consumers, we are compelled to choose. Choice itself has thus become a problem, and therefore the mechanisms by which choices are made. The increasing division of labor that characterizes technological progress persistently increases economic and social interdependence, so that the number of persons affected by any given decision expands steadily. Economies of scale, also, are a notable feature of modern industrial societies. The resulting concentrations of productive capital in huge enterprises, and of people in urban areas, lend a special importance to many decisions with respect to natural resources. The method and extent to which some resources are developed and produced are determined in a relatively few corporate and governmental offices; and the mere fact of population density creates the increasingly difficult problems of waste disposal and pollution. Government increasingly has had to accept responsibility to mediate conflicts between interdependent interests, or to exercise its authority to solve problems that arise. But the procedures by which government evaluates alternatives and reaches decisions often lead to actions that are ill-conceived, poorly analyzed, insufficiently considered, and irrationally decided.

The capacity of scientific progress to create new problems for society, it appears, has outrun the capacity of social progress to solve them. Because of the lag of social innovation, it is possible to be concerned with whether man has learned how to avoid something comparable to diminishing returns in the quality of life, a point on which Mill was optimistic. The dynamic, accelerative character of technological change seems to suggest that expansion in the number of social and individual choices available to us is an endlessly cumulative prospect. But our calculus of decision-making and our social value standards are not much changed from Mill's day. And, unlike Mill, we do not look forward to a stationary state, with endless time to contemplate and devise a steady, costless improvement in the quality of life. There is, therefore, a question of whether requisite changes in our mechanisms of choice will keep pace with the dynamic development of the scope of choice. The classical economists saw the process of growth as subject to limitations, and we agree. But they saw the limitations as residing in nature, and we see them as residing more in man. The consequential problems may be old but their form and urgency are new.

Need for Improved Social Evaluation and Decision-making Procedures

Great social progress, it is true, has occurred without collective concern over society's direction. A market system tends to generate changes in sociotechnical parameters, to modify its own conditions of operation, to produce a stream of innovations which help to provide escape from diminishing returns. If we are prepared either to forego making judgments concerning the total welfare value of market-generated decisions which change the conditions that determine how we work and live, or to adopt the postulate that such decisions always promote total welfare, the question of subjecting them to independent evaluation does not arise. If we are not prepared to take either of these steps, there is need to look beyond the "automatic" processes by which changes in sociotechnical conditions are brought about, and to consider whether in some respects social decisions beyond the market place—in addition to those already institutionalized—are necessary to prevent deterioration in the quality of life. We believe that there is need to look beyond the automatic processes, and to do so in a manner, and to a degree, somewhat different from current practice. The question is whether, if market decisions were supplemented, perhaps guided, to a greater extent than at present, by social decisions reached on the basis of social value judgments and analyses, this might not forestall some of the adverse effects on the parameters that determine the quality of life—effects which often accompany technological advance. In social benefit-cost analysis, so-called, an attempt is made to estimate corrections to be applied to market results, and to recommend social action. This technique, however, treats only external economies and diseconomies, and only a part of these. A broader approach is needed. In particular, account especially needs to be taken of adverse parametric change, and methods for preventing or ameliorating the change need to be devised.

Adherents of the doctrine of consumer sovereignty may object that, although man has the power to make social decisions broader than those of the usual social benefit-cost analysis, he has not the right to do so.[3] This is a value judgment. It implies the shape of welfare, generation to generation, will be better under absolute consumer sovereignty, with its limited horizons, its given sociotechnical parameters, and its individual-oriented decision processes, than if analysis and action are extended to include changes in sociotechnical parameters within their scope. Of course, the effectiveness of market mechanisms in permitting individuals to attain their chosen positions, or close approximations thereto, should not be lightly interfered with. This is our major means in a free society to achieve allocative efficiency within any given parametric framework. What we are saying is that we also regard the quality of the framework, and especially its rate and direction of change, as important. By its very all-embracing nature moreover, the framework is a matter of political and social, as well as economic, concern to each individual, and thus a matter for societal decision. Standards of social value, in addition to private value, must be applied.

Society, it must be recognized, is not only a competitive but also a cooperative enterprise. Although ultimate ends are, in considerable measure, individual, cooperation is one of the ways of attaining individually valued ends more efficiently than in its absence. But it is quite impossible to maintain effective cooperation if each of the cooperators is concerned solely with his personal ends.[4] The means for their attainment involve other cooperators—some very close to him, as in family or business firm, some so remote as to belong to a different nation and culture. Since no individual or subgroup can possibly control all the conditions to which he or it is subject, the consequences of action must be, and are, evaluated to some degree in terms of their

[3] We say "may object" because the fundamental issue—evaluation of the parameters of choice—has been neglected. It is difficult to build a theory of welfare optimization if the parameters of choice are themselves among the items to be chosen. But if they are taken as given one must be a historical determinist to maintain that they are the best attainable at any given point in time.

[4] Chester Barnard, in his classic monograph on the theory of administration, puts the matter this way: "Cooperation compels changes in the motives of individuals which otherwise would not take place. So far as these changes are in a direction favorable to the cooperative system they are resources to it. So far as they are in a direction unfavorable to cooperation, they are detriments to it or limitations of it." *The Functions of the Executive* (Cambridge: Harvard University Press, 1938), p. 40.

value for others. Otherwise the system of cooperation would break down, and all would lose.

Thus social value judgments have as their reference point what is good for mankind in general.[5] This does not require us to make subjective, interpersonal comparisons, to decide what is good for others in their individual capacities. Rather, it requires us to find out, objectively, what promotes the biological, psychic, and social health of the human animal—to determine the appropriate parameters for the fruitful exercise of freedom. Value judgments viewed collectively, the value consensus of a society, are the distillation of experience of what has been good for mankind. And, like all experience, this is capable of penetration and interpretation by the methods of science.[6] There is nothing odd in the familiar notion that the conditions of biological and psychic health are subject to empirical investigation, or that the assignment of a high social valuation to the attainment of such conditions is desirable. Modern societies promote such values where they do not exist. Much of what we do through the agencies of government and private association is based on the assumption that values are not wholly relative and ephemeral—that there are absolute, or at least long-enduring, needs and wants for which provision ought to be assured.

The problem with respect to much of the social framework is more difficult, however, than for health. The ill effects of agglomeration, for example, and the benefits of an environment with less ugliness and noise, are perhaps observed only by a minority. Water shortages and smog-laden air make an impression when they actually occur, but as mere potentialities they excite little serious concern. Distressed areas are often regarded as unavoidable features of a private enterprise society. The acts of one's own sovereign state are usually but liitle questioned, regardless of the unintentioned bad consequences they sometimes have for others. Population growth as a social problem is avoided in legislative halls. Yet the more extensive, pervasive, and persistent adverse consequences of the ways in which we handle natural resources are capable of analysis and, presumably, of prevention by acceptable means. To recognize the possibilities is the first step. Our skill at analysis and social innovation will then determine how well we shall succeed.

In short, one may accept the desirability of increasing the opportunities for individual choice (itself a value judgment), while maintaining that a series of social judgments is necessary to define the limits of individual freedom in accordance with the criterion of what is good for mankind in general, or for society as a cooperative enterprise; and recognizing as a corollary of this proposition the implicit involvement of social value questions whenever there is the possibility of change in the conditions that define what can be done.

The difficulty, of course, is that, of all social processes, the most mysterious and

[5] That is, value standards are not wholly relative. Many, as G. C. Homans has observed, have universal or near universal validity. Thus, he writes, "Social assumptions [value premises] stand because a large number of people accept them and for no other reason. . . . Some may be unconscious assumptions *of all human behavior*. In their emphasis on cultural relativity, the anthropologists have almost—not quite—forgotten that *there may be some premises held by all mankind*." *The Human Group* (New York: Harcourt, Brace, 1950), p. 128. Italics added.

[6] Compare Emery Castle in "Criteria and Planning for Optimum Use," a paper given at the 1961 Annual Meeting of the American Association for the Advancement of Science: "The resolution of value conflicts will result from the 'hammering' out of policies which will differ only incrementally from those we now have. In this process empirical information will be of use; by their nature it is possible to achieve agreement on empirical propositions. . . . The acceptance of any given set of values represents an assumption with respect to the desirability of those values. It may well be that if the consequences of a given set of values were clearly understood they would no longer be accepted by the society."

the least subject to guidance are those by which value standards are formed and changed. But the formation and modification of a social value consensus are obviously legitimate and crucial objects of concern. We think it would be desirable to act on the assumption that it is, in fact, possible to apply a more objective methodology to our value problems than we have been accustomed to believe. Man's relations to nature, we could well remember, were once regarded as governed by uncontrollable natural forces. Science, indeed, had just crossed the threshold to objectivity when the classical economists wrote; and this is why they held its potential in such low esteem. We may hope that we may be on the threshold of a similar transition to greater objectivity with respect to man's relations to man, which in our time has become crucial for handling man's relationship to the natural environment.

AUTHOR INDEX

SUBJECT INDEX